D1447699

J/XVIII.4.61ᵃ

Nigeria

The British Documents on
the End of Empire Project
gratefully acknowledges
the generous assistance of
the Leverhulme Trust.

The Project has
been undertaken
under the auspices
of the British Academy.

BRITISH DOCUMENTS ON THE END OF EMPIRE

General Editor S R Ashton
Project Chairman A N Porter

Series B Volume 7

Nigeria

Editor
MARTIN LYNN

Part I
MANAGING POLITICAL REFORM
1943–1953

Published for the Institute of Commonwealth Studies
in the University of London

London: The Stationery Office

First published 2001

© The Stationery Office 2001

Introduction © Martin Lynn, 2001

Documents from the Public Record Office © Crown copyright

ISBN 0 11 290597 8

British Library Cataloguing in Publication Data
A CIP catalogue record for this book is available from the British Library

If you wish to receive future volumes from the British Documents on the End of Empire project, please write to The Stationery Office, Standing Order Department, PO Box 29, St Crispins, Duke Street, NORWICH NR3 1GN, or telephone on 0870 600 5522, quoting classification reference numbers 04 03 017 and 04 03 018

Published by The Stationery Office and available from:

The Stationery Office
(mail, telephone and fax orders only)
PO Box 29, Norwich NR3 1GN
Telephone orders/general enquiries 0870 600 5522
Fax orders 0870 600 5533

www.thestationeryoffice.com

The Stationery Office Bookshops
123 Kingsway, London WC2B 6PQ
020 7242 6393 Fax 020 7242 6394
68–69 Bull Street, Birmingham B4 6AD
0121 236 9696   Fax 0121 236 9699
33 Wine Street, Bristol BS1 2BQ
0117 926 4306 Fax 0117 929 4515
9–21 Princess Street, Manchester M60 8AS
0161 834 7201 Fax 0161 833 0634
16 Arthur Street, Belfast BT1 4GD
028 9023 8451 Fax 028 9023 5401
The Stationery Office Oriel Bookshop
18–19 High Street, Cardiff CF1 2BZ
029 2039 5548 Fax 029 2038 4347
71 Lothian Road, Edinburgh EH3 9AZ
0870 606 5566 Fax 0870 606 5588

The Stationery Office's Accredited Agents
(see Yellow Pages)

and through good booksellers

Printed in the United Kingdom by The Stationery Office, London

TJ3227 08/01 C4

Contents

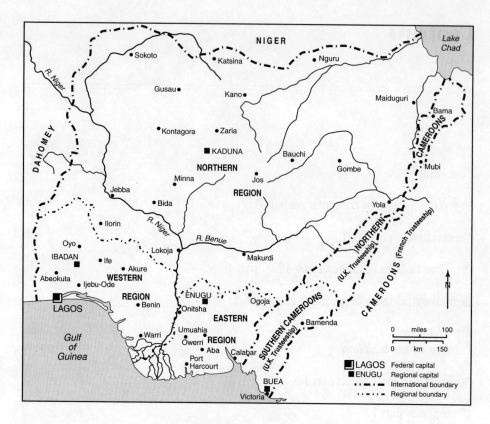

Nigeria *circa* 1955

Foreword

The main purpose of the British Documents on the End of Empire Project (BDEEP) is to publish documents from British official archives on the ending of colonial and associated rule and on the context in which this took place. In 1945, aside from the countries of present-day India, Pakistan, Bangladesh and Burma, Britain had over fifty formal dependencies; by the end of 1965 the total had been almost halved and by 1985 only a handful remained. The ending of Britain's position in these formal dependencies was paralleled by changes in relations with states in an informal empire. The end of empire in the period at least since 1945 involved a change also in the empire as something that was more than the sum of its parts and as such formed an integral part of Britain's domestic affairs and international relations. In publishing official British documents on the end of empire this project is, to a degree, the successor to the two earlier series of published documents concerning the end of British rule in India and Burma which were edited by Professors Mansergh and Tinker respectively. The successful completion of *The transfer of power* and *The struggle for independence*,[1] both of which were based on British records, emphasised the need for similar published collections of documents important to the history of the final stages of Britain's association with other dependencies in Africa, the Middle East, the Caribbean, South-East Asia and the Pacific. These documents are crucial research tools for scholars both from sovereign independent states which emerged from colonial rule as well as those from Britain itself. BDEEP is also set in the much wider context of the efforts made by successive British governments to locate Britain's position in an international order. Here the empire, both in its formal and informal senses, is viewed as an instrument of the domestic, foreign and defence policy of successive British governments. The project is therefore concerned with the ending of colonial rule in individual territories as seen from the British side at one level, and the broader political, economic and strategic considerations involved in that at another.

Despite the similarities, however, BDEEP differs in significant ways from its predecessors in terms both of presentation and content. The project is of greater magnitude than that undertaken by Professor Mansergh for India. Four major differences can be identified. First, the ending of colonial rule within a dependent empire took place over a much longer period of time, extending into the final years of the twentieth century while having its roots in the Second World War and before. Secondly, the empire consisted of a large number of territories, varying in area, population, wealth and in many other ways, each with its own individual problems but often with their futures linked to those of neighbouring

[1] Nicholas Mansergh *et al*, eds, *Constitutional relations between Britain and India: the transfer of power 1942–47*, 12 vols, (London, 1970–1983); Hugh Tinker, ed, *Constitutional relations between Britain and Burma: the struggle for independence 1944–1948*, 2 vols, (London, 1983–1984).

territories and the growing complexity surrounding the colonial empire. Thirdly, while for India the documentary record for certain matters of high policy could be encapsulated within a relatively straightforward 'country' study, in the case of the colonial empire the documentary record is more diffuse because of the plethora of territories and their scattered location. Finally, the documents relating to the ending of colonial rule are not conveniently located within one leading department of state but rather are to be found in several of them. As the purpose of the project is to publish documents relating to the end of empire from the extensive range and quantity of official British records, private collections and other categories of non-official material are not regarded as principal documentary sources. In BDEEP, selections from non-official material will be used only in exceptional cases to fill gaps where they exist in the available official record.

In recognition of these differences and also of the fact that the end of empire involves consideration of a range of issues which operated at a much wider level than that normally associated with the ending of colonial rule in a single country, BDEEP is structured in two main series along with a third support series. Series A represents the general volumes in which, for successive British governments, documents relating to the empire as a whole are be published. Series B represents the country or territory volumes and provides territorial studies of how, from a British government perspective, former colonies and dependencies achieved their independence and countries which were part of an informal empire regained their autonomy. In addition to the two main documentary series, a third series—series C—has been published in the form of handbooks to the records of the former colonial empire which are deposited at the Public Record Office (PRO). Series C consists of two volumes which form an integral part of BDEEP and also serve as PRO guides to the records. Together they enable scholars and others wishing to follow the record of the ending of colonial rule and empire to pursue their inquiries beyond the published record provided by the general studies in series A and the country studies in series B. Volume one of the handbooks, a revised and updated version of *The records of the Colonial and Dominions Offices* by R B Pugh which was first published in 1964, is entitled *Records of the Colonial Office, Dominions Office, Commonwealth Relations Office and Commonwealth Office* (1995*)*. It covers over two hundred years of activity down to 1968 when the Commonwealth Office merged with the Foreign Office to form the Foreign and Commonwealth Office. Volume two, entitled *Records of the Cabinet, Foreign Office, Treasury and other records* (1998), focuses more specifically on twentieth-century departmental records and also includes references to the records of inter-departmental committees, commissions of inquiry and international organisations. The two volumes were prepared under the direction and supervision of Dr Anne Thurston, at the time honorary research fellow at the Institute of Commonwealth Studies in the University of London, and now executive director of the International Records Management Trust.

In the two main series the research is organised in stages. Stage one, covering the years 1925–1957, is now complete and consists of three general volumes and five country volumes, collectively published in twenty-one individual parts. In series A there are volumes on *Imperial policy and colonial practice 1925—1945* in two parts (1996), *The Labour government and the end of empire 1945–1951* in four parts (1992), and *The Conservative government and the end of empire*

1951–1957 in three parts (1994). In series B there are volumes on *Ghana* in two parts (1992), *Sri Lanka* in two parts (1997), *Malaya* in three parts (1995), *Egypt and the defence of the Middle East* in three parts (1998) and the *Sudan* in two parts (1998). Starting in 1999, the project began publishing volumes in a second stage which covers the period 1957–1964. Here there are five volumes, a general volume on the *Conservative government and the end of empire 1957–1964* in two parts (2000), and country volumes on the *West Indies* in one part (1999), *Nigeria* in two parts (2001), *Kenya* and *Malaysia*.

The criteria which have been used in selecting documents for inclusion in individual volumes are explained in the introductions written by the specialist editors. These introductions are more substantial and contextual than those in previous series. Each volume also lists the PRO sources which have been searched. However, it may be helpful to outline the more general guiding principles which have been employed. BDEEP editors pursue several lines of inquiry. There is first the end of empire in a broad high policy sense in which the empire is viewed in terms of Britain's position as a world power and of the inter-relationship between what derives from this position and developments within the colonial dependencies. Here Britain's relations with the dependencies of the empire are set in the wider defence, economic and foreign policy contexts of Britain's relations with the United States, with Europe, and with the Commonwealth and United Nations. Secondly, there is investigation into colonial policy in its strict sense. Here the emphasis is on those areas which were specifically - but not exclusively - the concern of the leading department. In the period before the administrative amalgamations of the 1960s,[2] the leading department of the British government for most of the dependencies was the Colonial Office; for a minority it was either the Dominions Office and its successor, the Commonwealth Relations Office, or the Foreign Office. Colonial policy included questions of economic and social development, questions of governmental institutions and constitutional structures, and administrative questions concerning the future of the civil and public services and of the defence forces in a period of transition from European to indigenous control. Finally there is inquiry into the development of political and social forces within colonies, the response to these and the transfer of governmental authority and of legal sovereignty from Britain to its colonial dependencies as these processes were understood and interpreted by the British government. Here it should be emphasised that the purpose of BDEEP is not to document the history of colony politics or nationalist movements in any particular territory. Given the purpose of the project and the nature of much of the source material, the place of colony politics in BDEEP is conditioned by the extent to which an awareness of local political situations played an overt part in influencing major policy decisions made in Britain.

Although in varying degrees and from different perspectives, elements of these various lines of inquiry appear in both the general and the country series. The aim in both is to concentrate on the British record by selecting documents which illustrate those policy issues which were deemed important by ministers and offi-

---

[2] The Colonial Office merged with the Commonwealth Relations Office in 1966 to form the Commonwealth Office. The Commonwealth Office merged with the Foreign Office in 1968 to form the Foreign and Commonwealth Office.

cials at the time. General volumes do not normally treat in any detail of matters which will be fully documented in the country volumes but some especially significant documents do appear in both series. The process of selection involves an inevitable degree of sifting and subtraction. Issues which in retrospect appear to be of lesser significance or to be ephemeral have been omitted. The main example concerns the extensive quantity of material devoted to appointments and terms of service—salaries, gradings, allowances, pension rights and compensation—within the colonial and related services. It is equally important to stress certain negative aspects of the official documentary record. Officials in London were sometimes not in a position to address potentially significant issues because the information was not available. Much in this respect depended on the extent of the documentation sent to London by the different colonial administrations. Once the stage of internal self-government had been reached, or where there was a dyarchy, the flow of detailed local information to London began to diminish.

Selection policy has been influenced by one further factor, namely access to the records at the PRO. Unlike the India and Burma series and the current Foreign and Commonwealth Office series of Documents on British Policy Overseas (DBPO), BDEEP is not an official project. In practice this means that while editors have privileged access (in the form of research facilities and requisitioning procedures) to the records at the PRO, they do not have unrestricted access. For files which at the time a volume is in preparation are either subject to extended closures beyond the statutory thirty years or retained in the originating department under section 3(4) of the Public Records Act of 1958, editors are subject to the same restrictions as all other researchers. Apart from cases where files or series of files are withheld, official weeding processes now tend to remove sentences or paragraphs from public view, rather than the whole document; such omissions are indicated in footnotes. To date access has not impeded the research undertaken by the project to any significant degree, and the project has been successful in securing the release of a number of hitherto withheld documents from the Historical Section of the Cabinet Office and the Records Department of the Foreign and Commonwealth Office.

A thematic arrangement of the documents has been adopted for the general volumes in series A. The country volumes in series B follow a chronological arrangement; in this respect they adopt the same approach as was used in the India and Burma series. For each volume in both series A and B a summary list of the documents included is provided. The headings to BDEEP documents, which have been editorially standardised, present the essential information. Together with the sequence number, the file reference (in the form of the PRO call-up number and any internal pagination or numeration) and the date of the document appear on the first line.[3] The second and subsequent lines record the subject of the document, the type of document (letter, memorandum, telegram etc), the originator (person or persons, committee, department) and the recipient (if any). A subject entry in a heading in single quotation marks denotes the title of a document as it appears in the original. An entry in square brackets denotes a sub-

---

[3] The PRO call-up number precedes the comma in the references cited. In the case of documents from FO 371, the major Foreign Office political class, the internal numeration refers to the jacket number of the file.

ject indicator composed by the editor. This latter device has been employed in cases where no title is given in the original or where the original title is too unwieldy to reproduce in its entirety. Security classifications and, in the case of telegrams, times of despatch and receipt, have generally been omitted. In the headings to documents and the contents lists, ministers are identified by the name of the office-holder, not the title of the office (ie, Mr Macleod, not secretary of state for the colonies).[4] In the same contexts, officials are identified by their initials and surname. In a general volumes, ambassadors, governors, high commissioners and other embassy or high commission staff are cited in the form Sir H Foot (Cyprus). Footnotes to documents appearing below the rule are editorial; those above the rule, or where no rule is printed, are part of the original document. Each volume provides an initial summary list of which principal offices were held by whom, and a separate series of biographical notes (at the end) for major figures who appear in the documents. Other figures are identified in editorial footnotes on the occasion of first appearance. Link-notes, written by the volume editor and indented in square brackets between the heading and the beginning of a document, are often used to explain the context of a document. Technical detail or extraneous material has been extracted from a number of documents. In such cases omission dots have been inserted in the text and the document is identified in the heading as an extract. Occasional omission dots have also been used to excise purely mechanical chain-of-command executive instructions and some redundant internal referencing has been removed, though much of it remains in place, for the benefit of researchers. No substantive material relating to policy-making has been excised from the documents. In general the aim has been to reproduce documents in their entirety but where available space is a major constraint on editors, a consideration which applies particularly in the case of general volumes, where the documentation is voluminous, this is not always possible, and some purely factual information may be omitted. It must also be emphasised in this context that the BDEEP volumes do not remove the necessity for researchers to study the original records themselves. The footnote reference 'not printed' is used only in cases where a specified enclosure or an annex to a document has not been included. Unless a specific cross-reference or note of explanation is provided, however, it can be assumed that other documents referred to in the text of the documents included have not been reproduced. Obvious typing errors in the original are in the main silently corrected, but abbreviations and contractions stand. Each volume has a list of abbreviations together with a consolidated index, and country volumes include a chronology of principal events.

One radical innovation, compared with previous Foreign Office or India and Burma series, is that BDEEP reproduces many more minutes by ministers and officials.

Crown copyright material is used by permission of the Public Record Office under licence from the Controller of Her Majesty's Stationery Office. All references and dates are given in the form recommended in PRO guidelines.

*   *   *   *

---

[4] This is an editorial convention, following DBPO practice. Very few memoranda issued in their name were actually written by ministers themselves, but normally drafted by officials.

Formally launched in 1987, BDEEP has been based since its inception at the Institute of Commonwealth Studies. The work of the project is supervised by a Project Committee chaired by Professor Andrew Porter, Rhodes professor of imperial history in the University of London. Professor Porter succeeded Professor Anthony Low, formerly Smuts professor of the history of the Commonwealth in the University of Cambridge, who retired in November 1994. Professor Michael Crowder became the first general editor while holding a visiting professorship in the University of London and a part-time position at Amherst College, Massachusetts. Following his untimely death in 1988, Professor Crowder was replaced as general editor by Professor David Murray, pro vice-chancellor and professor of government at the Open University, who played a critical role in establishing a secure financial base for the project and in negotiating contracts with the volume editors and the publisher. His invaluable advice and expertise in dealing with the early manuscripts are acknowledged with particular gratitude. Mrs Anita Burdett was appointed as project secretary and research assistant. She was succeeded in September 1989 by Dr Stephen Ashton who previously worked with Professors Mansergh and Tinker during the final stages of the India and Burma series. Dr Ashton replaced Professor Murray as project director and general editor in 1993.

The project benefited from an initial pump-priming grant from the British Academy. Thanks are due to the secretary and Board of the Academy for this grant and for the decision of the British Academy to adopt BDEEP as one of its major projects. The Academy made a further award in 1996 which enabled the project to employ a research assistant on a fixed term contract. The Managers of the Smuts Memorial Fund in the University of Cambridge are also to be acknowledged. They made possible the workshop from which the project developed and they have since provided a further grant for work on two of the stage two volumes. The principal funding for the project in stages one and two has been provided by the Leverhulme Trust and the volumes are a tribute to the support provided by the Trustees. A major debt of gratitude is owed to the Trustees. In addition to their generous grants to cover the major costs of both stages, the Trustees agreed to a subsequent request to extend the duration of the first grant, and also provided a supplementary grant which enabled the project to secure Dr Ashton's appointment. It is thanks largely to the Leverhulme Trust that BDEEP has developed into one of the country's most successful historical research projects.

Members of the Project Committee, who meet annually at the Institute of Commonwealth Studies, have provided valuable advice and much needed encouragement. Professor Low, the first chairman of the Committee, made a singular contribution, initiating the first exploratory meeting at Cambridge in 1985 and presiding over subsequent developments in his customary constructive but unobtrusive manner. Professor Porter continues in a similar vein and his leadership and experience are much appreciated by the general editor. The director and the staff of the Institute of Commonwealth Studies have provided administrative support and the congenial surroundings within which the general editor works. The editors of volumes in both stages one have benefited considerably from the researches undertaken by Dr Anne Thurston and her assistants which resulted in the publication of the two handbooks. Although BDEEP is not an official project, the general editor wishes to acknowledge the support and co-operation received from the Historical Section of the Cabinet Office and the Records Department of the Foreign and Commonwealth Office. He wishes also to record his appreciation of the spirit of friendly co-operation received from the editors of DBPO. Dr Ronald Hyam, editor in stage one of the general volume on the post-war Labour government and co-editor of the stage two volume on the Conservative government, played an important role in the compilation of the house-style adopted by BDEEP and his contribution is acknowledged with gratitude. Thanks also are due to The Stationery Office for assuming publishing responsibility and for their expert advice on matters of design and production. Last, but by no means least, the contribution of the chief executive and keeper of the records and the staff, both curatorial and administrative, at the PRO must be emphasised. Without the facilities and privileges afforded to BDEEP editors at the PRO, the project would not be viable.

S R Ashton
Institute of Commonwealth Studies
October 2000

Nigeria

Schedule of Contents: Parts I–II

Abbreviations: Parts I–II

ACB	African Continental Bank
ADO	Assistant District Officer
AG	Action Group
AMOO	Assistant Medical Officers
ANTUF	All-Nigeria Trade Union Federation
Ass sec	Assistant secretary
AVOO	Assistant Veterinary Officers
BAT	British and American Tobacco
BBC	British Broadcasting Corporation
BDEEP	British Documents on the End of Empire Project
BDPP	Benin Delta People's Party
BOT	Board of Trade
CAMDEV	Cameroons Development Corporation
CAST	College of Arts, Science and Technology
CCTA	Commission for Technical Co-operation in Africa
CBE	Commander of the Order of the British Empire
CDC	Colonial/Commonwealth Development Corporation
CDFC	Commonwealth Development Finance Company
CD&W	Colonial Development and Welfare (Act)
CENTO	Central Treaty Organisation
CID	Criminal Investigation Department
CIGS	Chief of Imperial General Staff
CMS	Church Missionary Society
CO	Colonial Office
Col	Colonial
COLA	Cost of Living Allowance
Con	Conservative (Party)
COR	Calabar-Ogoja-Rivers
COS	Chiefs of Staff

CP	Communist Party
CPP	Convention People's Party
cr	created
CRO	Commonwealth Relations Office
CS	Chief Secretary
CSD	Chief Secretary's Department
Dept	Department
DMS	Director of Medical Services
DO	District Officer/Dominions Office
DOO	District Officers
DPNC	Democratic Party of Nigeria and the Cameroons
ECA	Economic Commission for Africa (UN)
ECN	Electricity Corporation of Nigeria
EP	Eastern provinces
EPC	Economic Policy Committee (Cabinet)
ERDC	Eastern Region Development Corporation
ERPDB	Eastern Regional Production Development Board
Exco	Executive Council
FBI	Federation of British Industries
F(C)O	Foreign (and Commonwealth) Office
FAO	Food and Agriculture Organisation (UN)
FAMA	Foundation for Mutual Assistance in Africa (South of Sahara)
GC	Gold Coast
GCE	General Certificate of Education
GOC	General officer commanding
Gov	Governor
Gov-gen	Governor-general
HE	His Excellency
HMG	His/Her Majesty's government
HMOCS	Her Majesty's Overseas Civil Service
HMPSSFA	Her Majesty's Principal Secretary of State for Foreign Affairs
H of C	House of Commons
H of C Debates	*House of Commons Debates (Hansard)*
HOGM	(Commonwealth) Heads of Government meeting

IBRD	International Bank for Reconstruction and Development (World Bank)
ICA	International Co-operation Administration (USA)
ICFTU	International Confederation of Free Trade Unions
ICS	Indian Civil Service
IDC	Imperial Defence College
IGP	Inspector-general of police
IRD	International Relations Department (CO)
IS	Internal Security
ITP	Ilorin Talaka Parapo
IUC	Inter-University Council
JIC	Joint Intelligence Committee
JSC	Joint Select Committee
KBE	Knight Commander of the Order of the British Empire
KC	King's Counsel
KCMG	Knight Commander of the Order of St Michael and St George
KNC	Kamerun National Congress
KNDP	Kamerun National Democratic Party
KPP	Kamerun People's Party
Kt	Knight bachelor
Lab	Labour (Party)
Leg Co	Legislative Council
L-G	Lieutenant-Governor
MBPP	Middle Belt Peoples Party
MOD	Ministry of Defence
MOF	Ministry of Food
MOO	Medical officers
MP	Member of parliament
MZL	Middle Zone League
NA	Native authority/Native administration
NATO	North Atlantic Treaty Organisation
NBC(S)	Nigerian Broadcasting Corporation (Service)
NCNC	National Council of Nigeria and the Cameroons
NCO	Non-Commissioned Officer

NEC	National Emergency Committee/National Economic Council
NEPU	Northern Elements Progressive Union
NIP	National Independence Party
NKDP	Northern Kamerun Democratic Party
NNDP	Nigerian National Democratic Party
NNFL	Nigerian National Federation of Labour
NP	Northern provinces
NPC	Northern People's Congress
NPF	Nigeria Police Force
NYM	Nigerian Youth Movement
OAG (N)	Officer administering the government (of Nigeria)
OIC	Order-in-Council
OHMS	On His/Her Majesty's Service
OKP	One Kamerun Party
OPEX	United Nations Technical Assistance Programme
P and T	Posts and Telegraphs Department
PC	Privy Council
PIN	Political Intelligence Notes
PRO	Public Record Office/Public Relations Officer
PSC	Public Service Commission
PQ	Parliamentary Question
PWD	Public Works Department
QC	Queen's Counsel
RAF	Royal Air Force
RASC	Royal Army Service Corps
RDA	Rassemblement Démocratique Africain
Regs	Regulations
REME	Royal Electrical and Mechanical Engineers
RN	Royal Navy
RNC	Royal Naval College
RWAFF	Royal West African Frontier Force
S & P	Secret and Personal
SEATO	South-East Asia Treaty Organisation
Sec	Secretary

SG	Self-government
S of S	Secretary of state
T	Treasury
Tel	Telegram
TUC	Trades Union Congress
UAC	United Africa Company
UDC	Urban District Council
UK	United Kingdom
UMBC	United Middle Belt Congress
UNIP	United National Independence Party
UN(O)	United Nations (Organisation)
UNP	United National Party
UPC	*Union des Populations du Cameroun*
USA	United States of America
USSR	Union of Soviet Socialist Republics
VCIGS	Vice Chief of Imperial General Staff
VOO	Veterinary Officers
WAASC	West African Army Service Corps
WAC	West Africa Conference/Council
WAD	West Africa Department
WAEME	West African Electrical and Mechanical Engineers
WASU	West African Students Union
WFTU	World Federation of Trades Unions
WIDF	Womens' International Democratic Federation
WRPDB	Western Region Production Development Board

Principal Holders of Offices 1943–1953: Part I

UNITED KINGDOM

1. *Ministers*[1]

(a) *Wartime coalition (10 May 1940–23 May 1945) and Conservative caretaker government (23 May–26 July 1945)*

Prime minister	Mr W L S Churchill (10 May 1940)
Secretary of state for the colonies	Mr O F G Stanley (24 Nov 1942)
Parliamentary under-secretary of state for the colonies	Duke of Devonshire (1 Jan 1943)
Secretary of state for dominion affairs	Mr C R Attlee (19 Feb 1942) Viscount Cranborne (24 Sept 1943)

(b) *Labour governments (26 July 1945–26 Oct 1951)*

Prime minister	Mr C R Attlee (26 July 1945)
Secretary of state for the colonies	Mr G H Hall (3 Aug 1945) Mr A Creech Jones (4 Oct 1946) Mr J Griffiths (28 Feb 1950)
Minister of state for the colonies	Earl of Listowel (4 Jan 1948) Mr J Dugdale (28 Feb 1950)
Parliamentary under-secretary of state for the colonies	Mr A Creech Jones (4 Aug 1945) Mr I B Thomas (4 Oct 1946) Mr D R Rees-Williams (7 Oct 1947) Mr T F Cook (2 Mar 1950)
Secretary of state for dominion affairs (from 1947, Commonwealth relations)	Viscount Addison (3 Aug 1945) Mr P J Noel-Baker (7 Oct 1947) Mr P C Gordon-Walker (28 Feb 1950)

---

[1] Details to 15 July 1953, the concluding date for Part I.

(c) *Conservative government (from 26 Oct 1951)*

Prime minister	Mr W S Churchill (26 Oct 1951)
Secretary of state for the colonies	Mr O Lyttelton (27 Oct 1951)
Minister of state for the colonies	Mr A T Lennox-Boyd (2 Nov 1951) Mr H L D'A Hopkinson (7 May 1952)
Parliamentary under-secretary of state for the colonies	Earl of Munster (5 Nov 1951)
Secretary of state for Commonwealth relations	Lord Ismay (28 Oct 1951) Marquess of Salisbury (24 Mar 1952)

2. *Civil servants*

(a) *Secretary to the Cabinet*   Sir Norman Brook (1947–1962)

(b) *Colonial Office*

(i) Permanent under-secretary   Sir George Gater (1942–1947)
       of state   Sir Thomas Lloyd (1947–1956)

(ii) Deputy under-secretary   Sir William Battershill (1942–1945)
        of state   Sir Arthur Dawe (1945–1947)
                                                         Sir Sydney Caine (1947–1948) ⎤ joint
                                                         Sir Charles Jeffries (1947–1956) ⎦
                                                         Sir Hilton Poynton (1948–1959) ⎦ joint

(iii) Assistant under-secretary   A J Dawe (1938–1943)
        of state, responsible   G H Creasy (1943–1946)
        for the West Africa   G F Seel (1946)
        Department and, from 1947,   T I K Lloyd (1946–1947)
        the Africa Division   A B Cohen (1947–1951)
                                                         W L Gorell Barnes (1952–1954)

(iv) Assistant secretary,   O G R Williams (1938–1946)
        head of the West Africa   K E Robinson (1946–1947)
        Department   L H Gorsuch (1947–1951)
                                                         T B Williamson (1952–1958)

(c) *Commonwealth Relations Office*

(i) Permanent under-secretary   Sir Percivale Liesching (1949–1955)
       of state

(ii) Deputy under-secretary
    of state

(Sir) Saville Garner (1953–1956)

(iii) Assistant under-secretary
    of state

R R Sedgwick (1949—1954)

NIGERIA

1. *Governors*

Sir A F Richards (18 Dec 1943)
Sir J Macpherson (14 Apr 1948)

2. *Chief commissioners*
(from 1951 lieutenant-
governors of regions)

Eastern Provinces

(Sir) F Carr (1943–1948)
Cmdr (Sir) J G Pyke-Nott (1948–1952)
(Sir) C Pleass (1952–1956)

Northern Provinces

(Sir) J Patterson (1943–1947)
Capt (Sir) E Thompstone (1947–1951)
Sir B Sharwood-Smith (1952–1957)

Western Provinces

(Sir) G Whiteley (1939–1946)
Capt (Sir) T Hoskyns-Abrahall (1946–
    1951)
Sir H Marshall (1951–1954)

3. *Commissioner of the Cameroons*

E J Gibbons (1949–1956)

4. *Chief secretary*

C C Woolley (1938–1941)
A W G H Grantham (1941–1944)
G F T Colby (acting, 1945)
G Beresford Stooke (1945–1947)
H M Foot (1947–1951)
    vacant
A E T Benson (1951–1954)

5. *Executive Council (1946–1951)*

Governor

Chief secretary

Chief commissioner, Eastern Provinces

Chief commissioner, Northern Provinces

Chief commissioner, Western Provinces

Attorney-general   G L Howe (1946–1950)

Financial secretary   S Phillipson (1945–1948)
                                          A W L Savage (1948–1949)
                                          E Himsworth (1949–1952)

Director of medical services   Dr J W P Harkness (–1946)
                                          Dr G B Walker (1946–1951)

Director of education   R A McL Davidson (1944–1951)

Appointed members: Sir Adeyemo Alakija
                                          G H Avezathe
                                          Alhaji Usuman Nagogo, Emir of Katsina
                                          Sir Hubert E Walker
                                          Maj-gen C R A Swynnerton
                                          E A Carr
                                          Dr F A Ibiam
                                          G I Obaseki
                                          (Sir) K A Abayomi
                                          Maj-gen C B Fairbanks

4.   *Council of ministers 1952*

Minister of works   Malam Abubakar Tafawa Balewa

Minister of social services   Shettima Kashim

Minister of natural resources   Alhaji Muhammadu Ribadu

Minister without portfolio   Alhaji Usuman Nagogo, Emir of Katsina

Minister of lands, survey and   Okoi Arikpo
   development

Minister of mines and power   Eni Njoku

Minister of commerce and industry   A C Nwapa

Minister without portfolio   Dr E M L Endeley

Minister without portfolio   Sir Adesoji Aderemi, Ooni of Ife

Minister of communications   Chief Arthur Prest

Minister of transport	Chief Bode Thomas
Minister of labour	Chief S L Akintola

Members ex-officio:

The governor

The chief secretary

The lieutenant-governors of the
three regions

The attorney-general	A McKisack (1951–1956)
The financial secretary	E Himsworth (1949–1952) A R W Robertson (1953–1956)

Chronological Table of Principal Events: Parts I–II

1943

Dec	Sir Arthur Richards assumes office as gov of Nigeria

1944

Aug	Foundation of NCNC
Dec	Richards's constitutional proposals forwarded to CO

1945

Mar	Richards's proposals submitted to the Legislative Council
Mar	Four 'obnoxious' ordinances passed
June	General strike
July	General election in Britain; Labour victory
July	Banning of *West African Pilot* and *Daily Comet*
July	Alleged assassination plot against Azikiwe
Aug	George Hall appointed S of S for colonies
Dec	Ten-year plan of development presented to the Legislative Council

1946

Jan	Visit to Nigeria by Hall
Feb	Inauguration of the Zikist movement
Feb	Sir Sydney Phillipson appointed to review financial and administrative procedures for local government
Apr	Ten-year plan of development commences
Apr	Tudor Davies report on the cost of living completed
Oct	Arthur Creech Jones appointed S of S for colonies
Dec	UNO General Assembly approves trusteeship agreement for the Cameroons
Dec	Harragin Commission Report on salaries completed

1947

Jan	Richards constitution comes into effect
Jan	Inaugural sessions of regional Houses
Feb	Bristol Hotel incident
Mar	Richards's statement to the Legislative Council on racial discrimination
Aug	NCNC delegation meets Creech Jones
Sept	Legislative Council approves establishment of Nigerian Cocoa Marketing Board

Nov   African governors conference in London
Nov   Sir John Macpherson appointed gov

1948

Jan   University College, Ibadan opens
Feb   Accra riots in the Gold Coast
Apr   Macpherson assumes office as gov
Apr   Kaduna Meeting of NCNC and declaration of the Freedom Charter
May   Appointment of the Foot Commission on Nigerianisation
June   Inauguration of *Egbe Omo Oduduwa* in Nigeria
June   Inauguration of Yoruba Federal Union
June   Watson Report on Accra riots published
Aug   Foot report on Nigerianisation completed
Aug   Decision to revise constitution announced to the Legislative Council
Aug   Education Ordinance
Oct   Report of select committee of Eastern House of Assembly on local government
Nov   Arrest of Anthony Enahoro and Osita Agwuna for sedition
Dec   Inauguration of Ibo State Union

1949

Feb   Trial of Zikist leaders
Mar   Commencement of local and regional consultations on the proposed new constitution
Apr   Establishment of marketing boards for groundnuts, cotton and oil palm produce
Apr   Gibbons Report on local government
Oct   Coussey Report on constitutional change in the Gold Coast published
Nov   Enugu shootings
Nov   Formation of the NEC
Nov   Appointment of the Fitzgerald Commission
Nov   UNO Trusteeship Council visiting mission to the Cameroons
Dec   Formal establishment of the NPC

1950

Jan   Ibadan constitutional conference
Jan   Formation of the MZL
Feb   Assassination attempt on Sir Hugh Foot
Feb   General election in Britain; Labour retains power
Feb   James Griffiths appointed S of S for colonies
Mar   Inaugural meeting of the Action Group
Mar   Opening of Nigeria Office, London
Apr   Zikists banned
May   Eastern Region Local Government ordinance receives royal assent
June   Fitzgerald Report on the Enugu shootings published
Aug   NEPU established

Dec   Maddocks and Pott Report on local government in Northern Nigeria
            completed

1951

Jan   Opening of Nigeria Liaison Office, Washington
Feb   Nkrumah appointed leader of government business in the Gold Coast
Mar   Hicks-Phillipson Report on revenue allocation
Apr   Formal launch of the Action Group
June   Macpherson constitution approved by S of S
June   Nigeria (Constitution) Order in Council 1951, laid before parliament
Oct   General election in Britain; Conservative victory
Oct   Oliver Lyttelton appointed S of S for colonies
July   Commencement of elections to regional Houses of Assembly
Nov   Macpherson constitution comes into effect
Dec   Completion of elections to regional Houses of Assembly

1952

Jan   Council of Ministers inaugurated
Mar   House of Representatives formally opened
Mar   Nkrumah appointed prime minister in the Gold Coast
Apr   Establishment of the Phillipson-Adebo Commission on the
            Nigerianisation of the civil service
May   Visit of Lyttelton to Nigeria
Oct   Declaration of a state of emergency in Kenya (Mau Mau)
Nov   UNO visiting mission to the Cameroons
Dec   Expulsion of NCNC central ministers at the Jos Conference
Dec   Establishment of the UNIP
Dec   'Non-fraternization' policy adopted by AG

1953

Jan   'Sit-tight' crisis commences in Eastern Region
Feb   Formation of NIP
Feb   Western Region local government law receives royal assent
Mar   Enahoro motion for self-government in 1956
Apr   Macpherson and gov Arden-Clarke visit the CO for joint discussions
Apr   West African Forces conference, Lagos
May   Kano Riots
May   Northern House of Assembly 'Eight-point motion'
June   Dissolution of Eastern House of Assembly
June   Coronation day riot in Lagos
July   Commencement of the London constitutional conference
July   Formation of the MBPP
Sept   IBRD (World Bank) mission to Nigeria
Dec   Eastern Region elections; NCNC victory
Dec   Chick Report on revenue allocation completed

1954

Jan	Lagos resumed conference
Jan	Declaration on the public service by Nigerian political leaders
Feb	Phillipson-Adebo Report on Nigerianisation published
July	Alan Lennox-Boyd appointed S of S for colonies
Aug	1954 Constitution Order-in-Council receives royal assent
Sept	Report of IBRD (World Bank) on Nigeria completed
Sept	Oyo riots; Alaafin leaves Oyo
Oct	Lyttelton constitution comes into effect
Oct	Ban on communists holding Nigerian government posts
Oct	Awolowo, Azikiwe and the Sardauna appointed regional premiers
Oct	HMOCS established
Oct	Southern Cameroons becomes a semi-autonomous region with its own House of Assembly
Nov	Commencement of elections to the House of Representatives

1955

Jan	Lennox-Boyd visits Nigeria
Apr	Approval of the interim development plan
Apr	Sir Anthony Eden becomes prime minister
May	General election in Britain; Conservative victory
May	UPC revolt in French Cameroons
June	Report of the Gorsuch Commission on salaries completed
June	Sir James Robertson assumes office as gov-gen
June	Western House of Assembly motion for a Mid-West Region
June	Lloyd report on the Oyo riots published
June	UMBC formed
Sept	Eastern Region government appoints Ikpeazu Commission into bribery and corruption
Oct	Robertson and regional govs visit London to brief S of S on Nigerian affairs
Nov	Azikiwe interview with the S of S
Nov	UNO visiting mission to the Cameroons
Dec	Nicholson report on Ibadan District Council
Dec	Western House of Assembly motion for regional self-government in 1956

1956

Jan	Preparatory conference in Lagos
Jan-Feb	Royal Tour of Nigeria
Mar	Awolowo visit to the S of S concerning regional self-government
May	Effiong Eyo submits motion in Eastern House on ACB affair
May	Elections to the Western House of Assembly; AG victory
July	Replacement of West Africa Command by Nigeria Command
July	Inquiry into ACB affair announced in parliament
July	Eastern Region 'summit conference' on the constitutional conference
Aug	Appointment of Sir S Foster-Sutton to lead inquiry into ACB affair
Nov	Elections to Northern House of Assembly; NPC victory

1957

Jan	Foster-Sutton report into ACB affair published
Jan	Harold Macmillan becomes prime minister
Feb	Hudson Report on local government in Northern Nigeria published
Mar	Independence for the Gold Coast as Ghana
Mar	Elections to Eastern Region House of Assembly; NCNC victory
Mar	Elections to Southern Cameroons House of Assembly; KNC victory
Mar	S L Akintola motion for independence in 1959
Apr	Eastern House of Assembly motion for regional self-government
May	Commencement of London constitutional conference
Aug	Self-government for the Eastern and Western Regions
Aug	Abubakar Tafawa Balewa appointed prime minister
Nov	Commencement of Willink Commission hearings on minorities

1958

Jan	School fee riots in Eastern Nigeria
Feb	'Ad hoc conference' in Lagos
Mar	Merthyr Commission report on constituencies completed
Mar	Death of Adegoke Adelabu; rioting in the Western Region
Apr	Nigerian Defence Council established
Apr	Southern Cameroons gains full regional status
May	Appointment of Dr Endeley as premier of the Southern Cameroons
June	Raisman Commission Report on revenue allocation
Aug	Northern House of Assembly motion for regional self-government in 1959
Aug	Willink Commission report on minorities published
Aug	Motion in House of Representatives for self-government in April 1960
Aug	Formation of Democratic Party of Nigeria and Cameroons
Sept	Commencement of London constitutional conference
Oct	Special List B established
Dec	UNO visiting mission to Cameroons

1959

Jan	Nkrumah visit to Nigeria
Jan	Southern Cameroons elections; KNDP victory; John Foncha appointed premier
Mar	Regional self-government for the Northern Region
May	Lennox-Boyd visit to Nigeria
July	Central Bank of Nigeria formally opened
July	Commonwealth Assistance Loan to Nigeria agreed
Aug	Minister of State, Lord Perth, visits Nigeria
Sept	Report of the Mbanefo Commission on salaries
Oct	Cameroons becomes a direct responsibility of Britain
Oct	General election in Britain; Conservative victory
Oct	Iain Macleod appointed S of S for colonies
Nov	Plebiscite in Northern Cameroons
Dec	Dag Hamarskjold visit to Nigeria and Cameroons

Dec   Okpara becomes Eastern premier; Akintola becomes Western premier
Dec   Federal elections; NPC-NCNC form a government under Tafawa Balewa
        as prime minister

1960

Jan   Republic of Cameroun gets independence from France
Jan   House of Representatives resolution for independence in Oct 1960
Jan   Macmillan visit to Nigeria
Feb   French atomic tests in the Sahara
Mar   Sharpeville shootings in South Africa
May   London conference
May   Commonwealth HOGM in London
June   Israeli loan controversy
July   Lagos conference
July   Nigerian independence act passes Parliament
July   Sir Adesoji Aderemi sworn in as first Nigerian governor of the Western
        Region
Aug   House of Assembly elections in the Western Region; AG victory
Oct   Independence
Nov   Departure of Robertson; Azikiwe becomes gov-gen

1961

Feb   Plebiscites in Northern and Southern Cameroons
Oct   End of British trusteeship in the Cameroons

Introduction

'This is the biggest colonial exercise ever', noted Alan Lennox-Boyd, secretary of state for the colonies, in April 1957, of the move towards Nigerian independence (document 392). With a population of some 31 million in the early 1950s, Nigeria was, following the independence of India and Pakistan, Britain's largest dependency. One in three of the inhabitants of the British empire in this period lived in Nigeria; each of the Nigerian regions created in 1951 had a population larger than any other British overseas possession, with the exception of Tanganyika. The political importance of Nigeria for Britain's standing in the world in the 1950s was considerable; as the largest state in tropical Africa Nigeria's potential leadership role clearly would be central to Britain's relations with the continent once independence had been achieved. Yet the potential for disaster in Nigeria was also immense, given the threats of secession that were voiced by different groups in these years and given the ethnic tensions that later were to explode so tragically in 1966. The importance of the Anglo-Nigerian relationship in this period and of the handling of the process of political withdrawal that reached its culmination on 1 October 1960 can hardly be gainsaid therefore.

Selection of documents
The documents in this collection have been selected to illustrate this process of British political withdrawal from Nigeria. As outlined in the general editor's foreword, the intention is to publish documents that illustrate those policy issues relating to this process that were deemed important by British ministers and officials at the time. The aim is thereby to illuminate the nature and timing of the British decision to grant independence to Nigeria. As set by the project, the focus is on the policy concerns of the British government; it should be stressed that these concerns often differed from those of officials in Lagos, let alone in Enugu, Ibadan or Kaduna, the capitals of the Nigerian regions, and certainly would have been sharply divergent from those of the leaders of Nigeria's political parties. That is not to imply that these other concerns were irrelevant to this process, but it is to suggest that policy-making in London needs to take its place in the story if that story is fully to be understood. It must be stressed that, for reasons of space, the emphasis in this collection is primarily political; economic, legal or military affairs have been included where they had an impact on the politics of decolonisation, but documents on these subjects have not been chosen for their own intrinsic importance. To do them justice would have required several further parts. Equally, in accordance with the practice of the project, there has been a bias in the selection against documents—such as command papers—that were published at the time and are otherwise available; overwhelmingly the emphasis of selection has been on unpublished documents.

The collection begins in 1943. No single date of course, can be identified as the definitive start of the process of decolonisation for Nigeria. Good cases could be made for 1939, the year of governor Bernard Bourdillon's 'political memorandum'; 1944, with the formation of the NCNC; or for 1945, with the ending of World War II and the publication of governor Arthur Richards's proposals for constitutional reform. Certainly World War II marked a turning point in Britain's relationship with her Nigerian colony, as it did for most of Britain's possessions.[1] Although proposals for major constitutional change had been discussed during the 1930s—most seriously by Bourdillon—the pace of discussion and the seriousness of the changes being proposed increased strikingly during the war years. 1943 has been chosen as the start for this collection because it was the moment the various ideas about post-war constitutional arrangements began to coalesce, as seen in the meetings held in the Colonial Office during that year to discuss Nigeria (1). The appointment at the end of 1943 of Richards as governor, with a mandate to introduce constitutional change, emphasises this further. It was to be his proposals for the constitution, arising out of these CO meetings, that were to give impetus to the post-war debate about Nigeria's future, a debate that in effect, was to continue for the next decade and a half. The aim of this selection of documents is therefore to trace the evolution of British government policy towards Nigeria from the CO meetings in 1943 through to independence in October 1960. The selection is broken into two parts, with July 1953 marking the break; this date, it should be said, was picked purely for editorial convenience in order to arrive at two parts of roughly equal size.

The process of political change in Nigeria was affected by the position of the Cameroons.[2] The Cameroons had been divided between Britain and France following its capture from Germany in 1916, and then held as a mandate of the League of Nations. Following World War II the Cameroons were administered as trust territories of the United Nations, with a trusteeship agreement settled in December 1946. Thereafter, the CO was aware that British administration in the territory—which was administered in two separate parts, Northern and Southern Cameroons—would be subject to periodic inspections by the UNO and that major policy decisions relating to it would ultimately have to be acceptable to the Trusteeship Council (92).

The Cameroons raised important questions for the selection of documents for this volume, firstly as to whether the territory should be included at all in a work primarily designed to examine British policy towards Nigeria and secondly as to whether any such selection should end in October 1960, given that British administration in the Cameroons continued until 1961. It was decided that the Cameroons should indeed be included, not least because the Northern Cameroons voted to join its neighbour in 1961, and because until 1960 both parts of the territory were in fact administered as part of Nigeria; the Southern Cameroons was administered as part of the Eastern Region until becoming a semi-autonomous region in 1954 and gaining full regional status in 1958, while the Northern Cameroons was governed as part of the Northern Region. None the less, the focus of selection has remained firmly on policy towards Nigeria as a whole; material included on the Cameroons has been chosen, with only minor exceptions, to illustrate the policy concerns of the Nigerian decolonisation process more generally rather than anything specific to the territory itself; as with other issues a further part would have been necessary to do full justice to the Cameroons in these years. An appendix at the end of part II has been used to cover the period between Nigerian independence in October 1960 and October 1961 when Britain relinquished the administration of the Cameroons.

As determined by the project, the documents used in this selection are chosen from those held in the Public Record Office, Kew. In short, the documents are derived from the government departments in London that dealt with Nigerian affairs. The main files consulted were those of the Colonial Office; from the start of this period documents relating to Nigeria were held in the CO 583 series, while some relating to intelligence and political matters were filed in CO 537; from 1951 CO 554 was the series used for Nigerian material. These three series provide the backbone of the selection in the present volume. In addition material in other CO series relating to economics, defence, social and educational matters, as well as the Council of Ministers, was consulted. Nigeria documents were also examined in the Dominions Office (from 1947, Commonwealth Relations Office) files and in the Foreign Office, Treasury and Ministry of Defence series, all of which departments had an input into the policy-making process for Nigeria. Finally, the papers of the Cabinet (including Cabinet committees) and the Prime Minister's Office relating to Nigeria were also surveyed.

Material generated within Nigeria itself is necessarily limited in this collection, given the considerations outlined above. To the extent that material was forwarded to London from Nigeria, its presence can be traced in the documents contained herein. Clearly however, much was not forwarded and the unfolding story seen from London remains just that, the view seen from London. Fully to understand Nigerian politics in this period, the growth of Nigerian nationalism and the role of Nigerian individuals and organisations in the decolonisation story, requires the use of these PRO documents alongside study of the files held in the National Archives of Nigeria.

The main problem in dealing with the documents available for this project is the sheer quantity of the files. Well over 1,000 files were read in the course of the research for this volume. Of course a good deal of the documentation can safely be ignored: material relating to personnel matters, technical detail and such like. Yet the volume of material that still remained forced difficult choices to be made; it bears repeating that what determined the selection was the degree to which it illustrated the policy debates being undertaken by ministers and officials in London. However, despite the volume of material in the PRO, there are important gaps in the record. Not always was an issue covered in the files, whether through having been 'destroyed by statute' or for other reasons. CO material on the 1948 Foot Commission on Nigerianisation for example, has not been located and appears to have been 'destroyed by statute'. Equally, some material relating to security and intelligence matters or which might be sensitive for other reasons, has been 'retained by department'. Appeals by the project to the FCO for the release of such documents were, it should be recorded, treated sympathetically in many cases, in particular relating to the Kano Riots of 1953 and the African Continental Bank affair of 1956–1957.[3]

None the less, some areas of policy remain closed to the researcher. It is difficult to assess precisely how extensive this is. The problem with files 'retained by department' is that while the file number may be listed in the series list in the Public Record Office, the subject of the file is not and it is therefore impossible, ultimately, to tell exactly what has been withheld. Several files apparently relating to mid-1950s Nigeria, to the 1957 London conference and to the Southern Cameroons in the period 1958–61 (when a significant terrorist campaign was waged in its francophone neighbour) are apparently so retained. Equally, material relating to intelligence and security matters more generally appears to be missing from the available documentation; some of this material can be traced in other files where individual letters might be copied for cross-referencing purposes and a rough picture of the type of material held in the retained files can be guessed at. While it is impossible fully to assess the extent of such material, it is believed that whatever these closed files might contain, they will not alter substantially the picture drawn by the selection in this volume.

The files available in the Public Record Office are coloured by two factors: firstly the nature of the political process that generated them and secondly the policy-making structure of the government department that considered them. The changing context of the political process to which these files relate clearly had an important impact on the material they contain. Over time it is noticeable that the material reaching London from Nigeria becomes much less detailed as far as Nigerian domestic developments are concerned; instead the business in the Colonial Office moves towards consideration of major policy issues, such as the date of independence, or the degree of financial aid to be negotiated with Nigeria, or alternatively the technical minutiae of the requisite Orders-in-Council; the several constitutional conferences held in London and Lagos during the 1950s become the major time-consuming concern of officials. This does not mean that the amount of paper on Nigeria circulating in London declined or that the importance of the issues being considered in the CO diminished—on the contrary—but it does indicate that the focus moved over time from administration to constitutional structures. Material from the local government level—never copious in London anyway—dries up completely. This occurred at different dates for the different regions, depending on the speed of local government reform; it is clear for the Eastern Region from an early date but for the North much later. This had, of course, important consequences for the amount of intelligence available for the CO.

Similarly, as the process of granting self-government to the regions—1957 for the East and West, 1959 for the North—gets underway it is noticeable how the amount of material being sent from regional governors shrinks significantly, except that which related to the changing constitutional arrangements. By 1960 even the material arriving from the governor-general in Lagos himself is of relatively limited import; indeed concern began to be expressed in London from as early as 1954 as to the degree to which the Colonial Office was being kept fully informed of developments within the colony (274). This process prompted the CO to encourage governors to produce regular, more discursive despatches—sometimes termed 'chatty' despatches—reviewing political events in their region or, in the case of the governor-general, the federation as a whole; a number have been included in this selection (353, 539). These provide an excellent window into events in their respective constituencies, but are no substitute, for the historian, for coverage of the struggles for political power which were now increasingly occurring among Nigerian politicians and within the Nigerian government.

The progressive concession of political power to Nigerian leaders raised important issues for the administration about the handling of sensitive or politically delicate material. This was seen most obviously following the creation of the Council of Ministers in 1952. It was decided to restrict the circulation of some material sent to

Nigeria to the governor and his staff alone and not to draw attention to this; the discovery by ministers in late 1952 that material relating to their own policy concerns was passing directly between the governor and the Colonial Office caused a major upset (169).[4] Although this upset was resolved, in practice from 1952 something almost akin to two secretariats were operating in Lagos—one for ministers and one for the governor—with some material being restricted in its circulation between the two.

Policy and policy-making
The policy-making structure of the government department in London that processed this material also colours what is included in this volume. Within the Colonial Office it was the West African Department, under the responsibility of an assistant secretary, which was at the centre of the handling of Nigerian business in this period. In 1954 this department was divided into two, West African 'A' and West African 'B', with the former, under an assistant secretary, responsible for Nigeria. The assistant secretaries responsible for Nigerian business reported, before 1947, to an assistant under-secretary responsible for West Africa; in that year all the African departments were brought under one Africa Division under an assistant under-secretary with specific responsibility for African affairs. In 1955 this organisation was changed again and the division split into two, with an assistant under-secretary appointed for West African affairs and another for Central and East Africa. This remained the situation—with St Helena, Ascension and Tristan da Cunha being added to West African responsibilities in 1957—until independence. The way an incoming document was handled on its way up this official hierarchy can be seen clearly in document 301 concerning the Eastern Region crisis of 1955.

The official who played the critical role in formulating Nigerian policy throughout this period was the assistant under-secretary responsible for African or West African affairs. These figures—Arthur Dawe, Gerald Creasy, G F Seel, Andrew Cohen, William Gorell Barnes and Christopher Eastwood who held this post between 1943 and 1961—assessed the incoming documentation and made the critical recommendations. Only rarely were their recommendations ignored. Below the assistant under-secretary, the assistant secretaries responsible for Nigeria—between 1943 and 1961 O G R Williams, Kenneth Robinson, Leslie Gorsuch, Tom Williamson and Aaron Emanuel—were of considerable influence; their position was one where they were able to couch policy options in ways that greatly influenced later decision-making. Certainly these assistant secretaries were the most knowledgeable within the Colonial Office about Nigeria—a knowledge reinforced by the several visits the holders of this post made to Nigeria in these years—and their grasp of the processes and personalities involved in these events is certainly impressive to the later reader. Only rarely did the principal, who staffed what might be termed the 'Nigerian desk' and who was the first official to deal with material arriving from Lagos, play an important role but towards the end of our period Maurice Smith (principal, CO, 1955–1959) was clearly taking an increasing and unusually active part. Although there were within the CO specialist departments relating to law, economics, defence and social welfare, which often were involved in Nigerian business, only occasionally can they be seen—the development of the ten-year plan of 1945 would be an example—making the running in policy-making.

The permanent under-secretary of state was not involved in routine Nigerian business but did play a more active role than might be imagined in the events of these years. For the early part of this period, Sir Thomas Lloyd (permanent under-secretary between 1947 and 1956) was the official involved. His interventions can be seen most notably when constitutional conferences were approaching and briefing papers had to be agreed. His involvement in the various problems thrown up by the Eastern Region during the mid-1950s is certainly marked; he can also be seen as especially active in constitutional issues such as the question of creating more regions in 1955, the implementation of the Chick Report on financial allocation also in 1955 and the regionalisation of the police in 1956. Interestingly, his successor, Sir John Macpherson, fresh from his term as governor, and who brought to the post a degree of knowledge of Nigeria that few predecessors would have had, appears to have played a less interventionist role than Lloyd. This might reflect awareness of the stresses and strains of the gubernatorial post and the difficulties caused by untimely intervention from London, or more pressing concerns elsewhere in the empire.

Ministerial involvement in Nigerian business was limited but critical in a number of instances. Initially there were two Colonial Office ministers—the secretary of state and the parliamentary under-secretary of state—but from 1948 a minister of state was added to this. Oliver Lyttelton (secretary of state, 1951–1954) and Alan Lennox-Boyd (1954–1959) were central to the Nigerian story. Both these two were 'hands-on' secretaries of state as far as Nigeria was concerned and played critical roles at a number of vital moments. This can be seen not least, in Lyttelton's breaking of the log-jam over self-government at the London conference of 1953 and Lennox-Boyd's resolution of the date of independence dispute at that of 1958 (235, 464). Lyttelton also appears to have been decisive in the decision in early 1953 to review the 'Macpherson' constitution (190, 191). Lennox-Boyd is notable too for his close cultivation of relationships with Nigerian leaders and his visits to Nigeria in 1955 and 1959.

The link from principal to secretary of state was the spine along which information flowed and policy-making occurred in the CO, as far as Nigeria was concerned. However, the CO was not isolated from the rest of Whitehall and policy-making involved other departments and other influences. Outside the CO the government department most involved in Nigerian business, at least for the latter part of this period, was the Commonwealth Relations Office. As the transfer of power approached, the CRO became more directly involved in Nigerian affairs. In particular the CRO was involved over Nigeria's future external affairs and a CRO official, Stanley Fingland, was appointed to the Lagos secretariat from 1958 as adviser concerning this. The relationship between the CRO and the CO was by no means a smooth one, and from an early date the CRO began to express concern at the way the CO was rapidly pushing on for independence before Nigeria, in the CRO's view, was ready, thus threatening to leave the CRO—it believed—to pick up the pieces.[5] The dispute in 1957 between the two departments over the date of independence had to be resolved by the lord chancellor's intervention (404). Even thereafter the question of Nigerian membership of the Commonwealth, not least because of South Africa's earlier concerns over Ghana's membership, and the issue of financial aid after independence, both involved the CRO in the policy-making process for Nigeria.

The Foreign Office was only tangentially involved in the Nigerian story. Certainly consideration of constitutional change in Nigeria was not restricted to Anglo-Nigerian relations, nor was the Nigerian case not seen in a wider context. American and French involvement can be seen on a number of occasions in this story. The USA as the major world power after 1945, had ambitions and concerns of her own towards Africa, ambitions and concerns that the Colonial Office was all too aware of but by no means always in sympathy with. At least as far as Nigeria is concerned, CO views of USA policy were not necessarily positive ones, as seen in the concerns raised over US provision of financial aid and US business ambitions in the region (477). Equally, the CO, though never as worried as the French about militant Islam, monitored French policy in other parts of West Africa while also observing developments in North Africa, particularly, though by no means only, at the time of the Suez crisis.[6] Intelligence material was clearly shared with the French authorities in West Africa.[7]

The Ministry of Defence was not involved in the process of granting independence for Nigeria until a very late date. The Chiefs of Staff Committee did become involved in the mid-1950s over the issue of control of the Nigerian forces and the issue of secondment of officers, but it was only when the proposed Anglo-Nigerian defence pact came to be discussed in the late 1950s that the Ministry of Defence began to play a significant role. None the less the Ministry of Defence allowed itself to be guided by CO views on the feasibility of the pact, illustrating both the paramountcy of the CO in this process and the relatively limited importance of Nigeria in broader UK defence concerns. The Treasury was occasionally called on by the Colonial Office, primarily of course, when financial inputs were required as in the funding of Special List B in 1958 or for the negotiations concerning financial aid for Nigeria after independence (421, 510). Although Treasury refusal to provide finance for the Southern Cameroons was critical in influencing policy on a number of occasions towards the territory, and financial constraints more generally affected policy to Nigeria in the late 1950s, it would be an exaggeration to suggest that Treasury influence greatly altered the thrust of the CO's approach to the territory.

For the key decisions concerning Nigeria, particularly over the date of independence, reference to the Cabinet was involved. This was important not just to obtain broader government approval for policy, but also to resolve differences between departments, as between the Colonial Office and the CRO over the date of independence, mentioned above. Reference to the Cabinet was necessary for any major change in constitutional arrangements, as occurred with the Macpherson proposals in 1950, and on the 1953 decision to revise the constitution; the threatened collapse of the 1953 talks in August over the position of Lagos, again resulted in reference to the Cabinet (105, 202, 234). As time went on Nigerian business reached the Cabinet more often. The decision on the date of Nigerian independence led to reference to the Cabinet three times between July and October 1958; reference was again made in May 1959 as part of a review of African policy generally and finally in early 1960 to approve the grant of independence (507). None the less there is no evidence of Cabinet discussion changing the broad parameters of CO policy towards Nigeria; policy remained something formulated in the CO and approved in Downing Street.

Cabinet committees of course, often considered issues before they reached the Cabinet itself. The committees dealing with Nigerian business were somewhat transient and ad hoc in their existence however.[8] The 1940s, and particularly the war years, saw several committees covering West African issues, colonial affairs and colonial development. This efflorescence of committees was only repeated in the mid-to-late 1950s, when a Colonial Policy Committee was established in 1955 and an

Africa Committee (of officials) in 1957; the Committee on Commonwealth Economic Development (established 1957) also considered Nigerian business. Again however, the function of these committees was less to formulate policy than to sort out the critical issues to be considered at Cabinet and confirm policy directions already decided on elsewhere. The only critical moment, when a committee had a decisive role, came with the debate in the Colonial Policy Committee in 1957 over the date of Nigerian independence.

The prime minister was rarely involved in Nigerian affairs in this period, though he was regularly kept informed on key issues. Clement Attlee was consulted over the handling of the Fitzgerald Report on the Enugu shootings in 1950 while Lyttelton kept Winston Churchill informed on the progress of the Lagos conference in early 1954 (262). Much of course, depended on the personality of the prime minister. Churchill and Anthony Eden gave little attention to Nigerian matters in this period, but Harold Macmillan, as a former CO minister, was much more involved, as can be seen not least in his visit to Nigeria in 1960. He was involved in the discussions over the date of independence in 1958, again over the Southern Cameroons in 1959, on the issue of aid to Nigeria after independence, and above all on the negotiations concerning the defence pact in 1960 (444, 471, 502).

Behind all these departments and offices sat parliament. Criticism of colonial policy in the Commons was to be avoided at all costs and it is clear, especially in the early years covered by this volume, that the CO and its officials were acutely concerned about the possible reaction of parliament to policy decisions. Parliament was regularly used for the announcement of important policy decisions and the placing of parliamentary questions by MPs interested in colonial affairs such as Reginald Sorensen or Fenner Brockway, prompted quick action by the CO. Debates on issues like the Fitzgerald Report on the Enugu shootings in May 1950 were a major concern for officials. None the less the fact was that colonial affairs generally and Nigerian affairs more particularly, were only of limited interest to public or parliament in this period. The discussion of Richards's constitutional proposals in November 1945 took place in an almost empty House. While Lyttelton spoke to the Commons following the Kano riots and on the decision to revise the constitution in 1953, Lennox-Boyd on the Eastern crisis of 1955, and Iain Macleod, secretary of state for the colonies, 1959–1961, on the independence bill in 1960, none of these announcements was followed by a major debate.

Outside bodies like the Fabian Colonial Bureau and the League of Coloured Peoples attempted to lobby the Colonial Office, but their influence was severely circumscribed. Businesses like the United Africa Company or Shell also attempted to make their voice heard within the corridors of the Colonial Office. James Griffiths, secretary of state for the colonies, 1950–1951, met representatives of British firms operating in Nigeria in 1950 who wished to express their concern over Macpherson's constitutional proposals, but while these firms received a sympathetic hearing they had no more influence over the final decision—which in this instance ignored their demands—than organisations like the Fabian Colonial Bureau did (114, 143). Business influence over constitutional policy in Nigeria was limited.

It was impossible to isolate Nigeria from events in the rest of West Africa; through the story of Nigerian decolonisation runs a sharp awareness of the pace of change on the Gold Coast, and to a lesser extent, French West Africa. At a number of moments in the Nigerian story, developments in the Gold Coast were to have a critical impact.

The report of the Watson Commission in 1948 and the granting of ministerial responsibility with the appointment of Nkrumah as prime minister in 1952, were the two major instances of this; as officials in Nigeria complained, these events acted as stimuli for more urgent demands from Nigerian leaders (44, 49, 152, 153). Thereafter concern about Nkrumah's regional ambitions coloured British policy-making towards Nigeria, with repeated references in the late 1950s to the need for Nigeria to provide a counter-weight to the more radical vision of Africa's future emanating from Accra (474, 475, 504). Developments in French West Africa were of less concern but were not ignored, particularly given the close ethnic and religious ties between much of the population of Northern Nigeria and its immediate neighbours, and given the close relationship of the Southern Cameroons with its neighbour to the east. The latter clearly became a major concern following the UPC revolt in French Cameroons in 1955.

In Nigeria, policy-making took place in the Secretariat in Lagos. This meant, in essence, the governor (from 1954, the governor-general) and his staff, of which the most important for this purpose was the chief secretary. Richards and Macpherson clearly played critical roles in the evolution of the constitutions that popularly came to bear their names; in their terms of office constitution-making was still something determined between officials in Lagos and London. However James Robertson, governor-general 1955–60, arrived in Nigeria once the discretion over constitutional decisions had moved to the various conferences involving Nigerian leaders and the secretary of state, and his role as governor was correspondingly reduced, at least as far as the direction of major political change in Nigeria was concerned; there is no 'Robertson' constitution to match the 'Richards' and 'Macpherson' versions. None the less his input into events was not negligible, as seen in his choice of prime minister in 1957 and 1959 and in the relationship between himself and Tafawa Balewa that ensued (410, 497). This does not compare with the renowned Arden-Clarke/Nkrumah relationship in the Gold Coast, but Robertson's sympathy with and respect for, Tafawa Balewa is palpable in the files of these years. A chief secretary like Hugh Foot (1947–1951), who clearly had views very close to those of Macpherson—not to mention Cohen in London—could play a very influential role in policy-making. Foot was not only active in prompting Nigerianisation but also in pushing the ideas for constitutional change that emerged in the late 1940s.[9] His speech to the Legislative Council on constitutional change in March 1949 clearly holds a major place in the Nigerian story (65); later chief secretaries like A E T Benson or Hugo Marshall played a much more circumscribed role as political power moved to the Council of Ministers.

At the outbreak of World War II Nigeria was still administered under arrangements that derived from the 1922 constitution.[10] This, the so-called 'Clifford' constitution after the governor responsible for its introduction, administered Nigeria through a Legislative Council of 46; of the 19 unofficial members, three were elected by a restricted electorate of adult males in Lagos and one for Calabar.[11] The Legislative Council's remit applied only to the colony of Lagos and the protectorate of Southern Nigeria; legislation for Northern Nigeria continued to be issued by proclamation by the lieutenant-governor as it had been since before the unification of 1914. The two parts of Nigeria were administered after amalgamation through separate lieutenant-governors (from the mid-1930s termed chief commissioners) for the North and South based at Kaduna and Enugu; in 1939 the South was split in two, separate chief commissioners were appointed for the western and eastern provinces and a new secretariat built at Ibadan.

Underlying the separate administration of the North and South were deep divisions that had ethnic, religious and historical origins. Obafemi Awolowo, the leader of the AG, in 1947 referred to Nigeria as 'a mere geographical expression' and these divisions were the warp across which the weft of events was woven in these years.[12] Much of the North was Muslim, the major ethnic groups were the Hausa-Fulani and the Kanuri, and much of the area had been subjected to the rule of the Sokoto caliphate during the nineteenth century. The so-called 'middle belt' of the area by contrast, was neither Muslim nor Hausa-Fulani-Kanuri and parts of it had fought fiercely in the nineteenth century to maintain their independence from caliphate rule. Moreover, the centralised authority that characterised the societies of the Sokoto caliphate and Bornu was lacking for many of the peoples of the Middle Belt. In the South the Yoruba were the major ethnic group west of the Niger, though as with the North, it is important not to assume a monolithic identity for the region; parts of this area did not conform to the cultural or political hegemony of the dominant ethnic group. These areas, which came to make up the Mid-West Region after independence, lay to the east and south-east of the Yoruba heartland and were the predominantly Edo and Itsekiri areas of Benin and the western Delta. To the east of the Niger, the Igbo were demographically the major group, though once again areas of Efik/Ibibio and Ijo speakers—to the east and south—challenged the numerical dominance of the majority.[13] Igbo political structures, characterised by the dispersal of authority and by segmentary systems, contrasted sharply with the more centralised authorities typical of the Yoruba and Edo.

Nigeria was administered through 24 provinces (plus Lagos), each under a resident, with the provinces, between 1939 and 1951, arranged together into three groups for the east, north and west. Local administration was characterised, in theory at least, by varying degrees of adherence to the principle of indirect rule. Although indirect rule was a protean phenomenon which varied greatly according to local circumstances and financial exigency, in its idealised form it involved administration through the existing ruling authorities of a given society, structured into a Native Authority system overseen by the guiding hand of residents, district officers and ADOs.[14] Underpinning this, at least in the Nigerian case, was the assumption that the true representatives of the numerous ethnic groups in Nigeria were their existing authorities, and that the real identity of Nigerians lay in their different ethnic origins. Underlying this in turn, was the idea that the existing authorities represented the 'natural' system of political administration and that the western-educated Nigerian of the cities represented an anomalous, detribalised African. Within this indirect rule structure, rulers were given considerable leeway concerning the administration of their area and most exploited this; one consequence of the NA system in many areas was a considerable reinforcement in the power and authority of existing rulers.

From 1951 Nigeria was a federation of three regions, with, after 1953, Lagos removed from the West as a separate capital territory. In Enugu, Ibadan and Kaduna, and to a lesser extent Buea, secretariats also operated under the regional chief commissioners (from 1951, lieutenant-governors and from 1954, governors); there were deputy governors for the East and West from 1955 and for the North from 1958. As self-government progressed these posts became less significant in terms of political discretion, though for major decisions, Robertson still called the governors to meet in Lagos in conclave. Much depended on circumstances and on personality, and Bryan Sharwood-Smith (lieutenant-governor and governor of the Northern Region, 1951–1957), played a much more significant political role, and for much longer, than his counterparts elsewhere in the federation, not least because of the pivotal position of the North in these years.

Below the level of the provinces and the regions lay the realm of local government. Local politics is beyond the remit of this volume, except in so far as local government reform raised issues of policy. Following the Creech Jones despatch of 25 February 1947 moves began to reform local government in Nigeria; beginning with the East in 1950 and following with the West in 1953.[15] Reform of local government in the Northern Region remained a major political issue throughout the period covered by this volume, generating much concern not only among the existing northern rulers, but also among the leaders of the opposition parties in the region and Nigerian leaders from the South who both saw the power of the NA system in the north as underpinning the dominance of the NPC and British rule in Nigeria more generally. Local government reform—and the power and influence of NA rulers—was thus the backdrop against which the more dramatic story of constitutions, riots and conferences was played out. Here the residents, district officers and ADOs remained the governor's (and London's) eyes and ears and their information made up the substance of the Joint Intelligence reports that were forwarded to the CO. The key struggles at the lower levels of politics in these years involved the control of appointments to the chiefly thrones and councils of local government and much more research remains to be undertaken of this story.

*   *   *   *

The period of managed reform, 1943–1953
Even before the outbreak of World War II, figures within the Nigerian administration recognised the need to revise the 1922 constitutional arrangements. One problem that had to be addressed during the 1930s was the evident need to reform the system of indirect rule. What prompted this were the numerous allegations of abuse that characterised its operations in many areas. This was at least partly because, in its idealised form, it failed to reflect the complexities of Nigerian social structures. Such a system might possibly have made sense for the highly developed states of the Hausa-Fulani emirates of Northern Nigeria or the Yoruba chieftaincies of the West but it most certainly did not for other areas like the more politically dispersed societies of Eastern Nigeria, as was seen in the political unrest there in the late 1920s.[16] Significant changes to administration in the East, with the so-called 'Warrant Chiefs' being replaced by councils of varying degrees of power and scale, occurred during the 1930s. Elsewhere, the extent of abuse in the Native Authority system, even in areas where the system might be argued to be more appropriate, such as in the North, was increasingly recognised by the CO and the Nigerian administration during the 1930s and 1940s. Indirect rule in the North, one official was to write, made the area the home of 'feudal graft and oppression').[17]

A second problem came at the level of central administration. Congruent with indirect rule was the idea that central administration would be a largely British preserve and that the western-educated Nigerians, being, it was assumed, unrepresentative of the bulk of the population, could be ignored in the political structures of the country. Implicit in the principle of indirect rule was the idea that if political change was to come it would be evolutionary rather than revolutionary in its progress and would begin from the bottom up; the western-educated Nigerian would continue to be largely ignored at the central level. Yet well before World War II it was clear that this assumption was in need of revision, not least because it failed to account for the growing numbers of western-educated Nigerians produced by social and economic change. The western-educated elite, still small in number but with a long history of trenchant criticism of British rule behind it, was being reinforced by a number of factors not least of which was the spread of educational opportunities both within and without Nigeria; many Nigerians, of whom Nnamdi Azikiwe was but the most prominent, returned during the 1930s and 1940s from study in British and American universities.[18] The pivotal role this elite would play in the future was recognised by Bourdillon:

> It would be a great mistake to over-rate either their influence or the extent of the interests which they represent. It would be a greater mistake still to under-rate them. But the crowning mistake of all is to under-rate the sincerity of their motives and to class them as mere mischief-makers. They have a great potential for mischief. They have also a great potential capacity for good. Which way they develop will depend to an enormous extent on the sympathy and understanding which they receive from us.[19]

The various Nigerian political organisations that emerged in the inter-war years attempted to articulate the political aspirations of these figures. Prominent among these was the Nigerian National Democratic Party of Herbert Macaulay, formed in the early 1920s, which won the Legislative Council elections for Lagos through most of the inter-war years, but which despite its name, remained little more than a Lagos-based organisation. In 1936 a further organisation, the Nigerian Youth Movement, emerged and, helped by a sustained press campaign articulated by Azikiwe—who since his return from the USA in the mid-1930s had been a prominent journalist and editor—successfully challenged the NNDP to win the 1938 Lagos Legislative Council and the Lagos town council elections; the particular significance of the NYM was that it was the first such organisation to attempt to appeal across the whole of Nigeria. Although it split between Samuel Akinsanya and Ernest Ikoli in the early 1940s (with ethnic tensions seemingly coming to the fore), its Nigerian Youth Charter of 1938 set out many of the key issues addressed by its successors and its activities paved the way for the formation of the NCNC in August 1944 under Macaulay as president and Azikiwe as secretary.

These developments reinforced the thinking of figures in the administration in the 1930s who believed that the constitution had to be revised to incorporate more fully the western-educated Nigerian. Their re-thinking of policy was also stimulated by broader changes in colonial attitudes. Lord Hailey's *African Survey*, published in 1938—and his subsequent *Report on Nigeria 1940–1942*—were pivotal to these changing attitudes, though Hailey's view of them was somewhat ambiguous; he wished both to reinvigorate indirect rule and to encourage the integration of the western-educated African into the wider political system.[20] Also important was the reconsideration of colonial social and economic policy that derived from the impact of the early 1930s depression and which culminated in the CD&W Act of 1940.[21] The unrest in the West Indies that led to the establishment of the Moyne commission of 1938–1939 reinforced this, as did—for West Africa more particularly—the cocoa hold-up on the Gold Coast in 1937 that produced the Nowell Commission.[22]

In the case of Nigeria, the period in office of both governor Cameron (1931–1935) and governor Bourdillon (1935–1943) saw proposals emerge to reconsider the way Nigeria was administered. Bourdillon in particular, was responsible for a number of attempts to spell out such ideas particularly during the 1939–1942 period. In his *Memorandum on the future political development of Nigeria* of September 1939, which reinforced his earlier memorandum urging increased spending on social and economic matters, he argued, like Hailey, that the critical need was to incorporate the western-educated Nigerian into the political structures of the administration, and went on to urge the need for increasing the pace of reform in order to give Nigerians greater responsibility for their own affairs.[23] He urged the need to increase the number of Nigerians in the public service, to increase the responsibilities of the existing NAs and to ensure that those Nigerians already on the Legislative Council should be encouraged to play a more active part in the formulation and discussion of legislation. He suggested too, that serious consideration should be given to appointing a Nigerian to the Executive Council.

Although this was a debate that had begun much earlier, the outbreak of war in 1939 was undoubtedly a significant moment in it. War gave Nigeria a new importance to her imperial ruler, not least as a source of raw materials and foodstuffs, but also in providing many thousands of troops (particularly for the fight against the Japanese in Burma), and in its broader strategic value for the campaign in North Africa. This importance was reflected in the creation of a resident minister for West Africa in 1942. The war effort required government intervention in a whole series of new activities. The significance of this, in that it showed how the government could take on new responsibilities and functions within the colony if it so wished, could not be gainsaid. War also led to major changes for colonies more broadly. The emergence of the USA with its anti-colonial feelings, and the publicity given to the ideas of self-determination expressed in article three of the 'Atlantic Charter' of August 1941, all were signs that the wider world was changing; the Atlantic Charter in particular had an important impact on Nigerian leaders like Azikiwe.

The war years saw a ferment of discussion within the CO about the future of Britain's West African colonies and particularly Nigeria. Initially the CO took a cautious position and emphasised Hailey's rejection of the idea of unofficial majorities in the legislative councils of the region. Yet there were powerful voices urging significant changes concerning the place of the western-educated African in the new structures that would be required after the war. In this a new generation of officials, of whom Andrew Cohen (assistant secretary from 1943, assistant under-secretary from 1947) was the most prominent, played a marked role. Pressures from colonial administrations reinforced the views of this new generation. The Gold Coast administration, and particularly governor Burns (who was also temporarily responsible for Nigeria during part of 1942), led the way in this with Burns in 1941 proposing the appointment of unofficials to the Gold Coast Executive Council and raising the issue of establishing an unofficial majority in the Legislative Council;

Bourdillon supported these proposals and when attention turned to Nigeria, the need for an unofficial majority in the legislative council was taken as read, at least by the CO.[24]

One sign of the changing priorities of colonial policy came with the invitation to eight West African journalists and editors—including Azikiwe—to visit Britain and more specifically the CO, in 1943. The symbolism of the visit was significant; the CO was recognising that the future lay with the western-educated elite. Azikiwe's memorandum, 'The Atlantic Charter and British West Africa', which demanded self-government fifteen years after the end of the war, and which he presented to the CO during his visit, was taken seriously as the policy of colonial reform gathered pace.[25] 'This memorandum', minuted Cohen, 'is of interest not so much because of the details of its contents, which are familiar, but for the aspirations which it represents. It illustrates the strong feelings on the West Coast that HMG should show their hand as to future policy, particularly in the sphere of constitutional development'.[26] Although its conclusions were formally rejected, many of its ideas found later expression in official policy.

In this process of rethinking, the CO was not assuming the immediate decolonisation of the African empire. On the contrary, the changes that officials were proposing were designed to preserve British rule not end it. Even Bourdillon believed that it would be at least 50 years before Nigeria was ready for such a move to be contemplated.[27] Nor was the acceptance of the ideas underlying this new emphasis of policy automatic or general. Many in the CO itself remained sceptical as did others in the colonial administration and particularly in the field. How to bring such figures along with the new policy objectives emanating from London was to be a perennial problem in these years.

As the tide of war turned evidence of the emerging new approach could be seen in Nigeria. In 1943 the first two Nigerians were appointed as members of the Executive Council and the first Nigerians were appointed to senior service posts within the administration.[28] Bourdillon's *Further memorandum on the future political development of Nigeria* of October 1942 urged the integration of the Northern provinces into the legislative council, the creation of regional councils and the abolition of the distinction between official and unofficial members by allowing official members to vote as they chose.[29] Similarly, work began on a Nigerian educational plan, prompted at least partly by pre-war proposals, approved by the West African governors, for a West African University; in 1943 the Asquith and Elliott Commissions to examine higher education in the colonies and in West Africa respectively, were established.[30] Work on a development plan for Nigeria was inaugurated in 1944, following the decision that the 1940 CD&W Act would be extended beyond 1951. The Nigerian administration submitted proposals in October 1944 for such a plan, and pointed out that the implementation of their proposals would require a sharp increase in personnel and—more significantly—in numbers of educated Nigerian staff.[31]

More specific ideas concerning post-war political structures in Nigeria began to be spelt out within the CO, commencing with the memorandum on 'Constitutional development in West Africa' produced in 1943 by O G R Williams, the head of the West African Department.[32] Williams's memorandum, which was initially designed as a briefing paper for Stanley's visit to West Africa in late 1943, attempted to build on Hailey's ideas. He endorsed Hailey's principle of the need to avoid rapid change but argued that it was important not to alienate the educated African and that this required spelling out in detail precisely what the government's ideas were. He proposed a five-stage plan of progressive reform for the West African colonies building from local government upwards. Only at stage four would an unofficial majority be conceded on the legislative councils and only at stage five—which would take 'a good many years'—would self-government become an issue.

Williams's memorandum was discussed at a meeting in the CO involving Stanley and Lord Hailey in July 1943.[33] Three months later, Alexander Grantham, chief secretary of Nigeria, gave the administration's response.[34] He broadly agreed with Williams on the need for change but stressed that self-government was 'very remote' and urged the government to make it clear to Nigerians that it would be 'many years' before West Africa was ready for it.

The significance of Williams's proposals can be exaggerated, but clearly the importance of his memorandum was that it enabled the broader debate about policy for West Africa to coalesce around specific proposals and a broad timetable. Also important in this process was the ill-health of Bourdillon during 1942 and 1943 which necessitated his departure in May and a consequent need to find a new governor for Nigeria. This provided a major stimulus for the CO to think through specific constitutional proposals for Nigeria and to articulate their future policy for the colony. The appointment of Sir Arthur Richards as governor in November 1943, marked this moment precisely.

What was emerging in the CO in these years was a policy of managing colonial reform in order to pre-empt the demand for self-government and draw the sting of a still relatively unarticulated nationalism. It was unfortunate therefore that the person the CO appointed as governor, while being the most experienced available, was from the start, not entirely in sympathy with the line emanating from Church House. On 19 November 1943, Richards met Stanley—fresh from his visit to West Africa—to discuss reform of the Nigerian constitution (2).[35] What was striking about this meeting, although it expressed broad approval for the idea of an unofficial majority in the Legislative Council, was Richards' apparent reluctance to entertain radical changes in case these upset the rulers of the North. From the start, a gulf appeared to be opening between Richards and the CO over the extent of reform to be proposed for Nigeria and, crucially, over the degree to which the North should determine the pace of constitutional change.[36] 'It would be wrong to go too fast', stated Richards (2).

When in July 1944 Richards's first draft of the constitution was ready it owed much to Hailey's and Bourdillon's ideas, as seen in the proposals to establish three regional councils and to bring the North under the Legislative Council's remit for the first time (3). Yet it also owed much to Lugard in continuing the pre-1914 boundary between North and South and in its failure to break up the North into more than one unit. Here lay the genesis of many later problems, for implicit in Richards's approach was an acceptance of the North as the dominant part of Nigeria. More generally, it represented little advance on the 1922 arrangements. Richards in fact proposed *official* majorities in the Legislative Council and in the regional councils—which in the latter case could only discuss policy and advise by resolution—and proposed the abolition of the four directly elected members representing Lagos and Calabar that had existed since the 1920s. Cohen was disappointed with the scheme in that the draft did not, in his view, mark any advance

on the status quo, particularly because it did not include an unofficial majority in the
Legislative Council (4). The educated African, he felt, would dismiss the proposals as
'reactionary' and he made it clear where his own sympathies lay. The tension
between what Cohen felt was necessary and what Richards was prepared to accept
meant that revision was necessary (5, 6). Indeed when Richards's revised proposals
were forwarded to the CO in December 1944—now including unofficial majorities in
the regional councils and the Legislative Council and the continuation of direct
elections for Lagos and Calabar—they required still further revision by Cohen, before
they could be laid before the Legislative Council on 5 March as sessional paper no 4
of 1945 (7).[37]

Even then the secretary of state in his official response of 4 December 1945 revised
the scheme further (21).[38] George Hall altered the numbers of officials and
unofficials in the Legislative Council and in the regional councils in order to reduce
their overall size and increase the unofficial majorities. In addition, Hall cut the
number of seats reserved for special interests (such as business and commerce) from
four to three and reduced the electoral qualification for adult males in Lagos and
Calabar from £100 income p.a. to £50.

The publication of Richards's constitutional proposals represented the keystone of
the CO's post-war policy for Nigeria, but they were only part of a much broader
course of political, economic and educational change for the colony being promoted
in the years after 1945. Other policy initiatives considered in the early to mid-1940s
bore fruit once the war ended. The revised ten-year plan for development and welfare
was presented to the Legislative Council at the end of 1945.[39] It proposed to spend
£55 million over the following ten years; £23 million of this would come from the
CD&W funds with the rest from Nigerian revenues or loans. Proposals for 'mass
education'—what might better be described as 'community development'—were
initiated, building on the renowned project at Udi (36). In 1946 the Elliott
Commission recommended the creation of three universities in West Africa; initially
the recommendation of the minority report that only one should be established, but
that this should be built in Nigeria at Ibadan, was taken up and the University College
of Ibadan began admitting students in 1948 (27).[40] A scheme for commodity
marketing boards, designed in part to protect producers from the vagaries of sharp
price changes on the world market, led to the inauguration of the Nigerian Cocoa
Marketing Board in 1947.[41] Proposals for Africanisation in the administration were
considered, though tempered by the belief held by some that this would lead to
increased corruption and inefficiency. Meanwhile the Bristol Hotel incident of early
1947 caused Richards to make a statement to the Legislative Council condemning
racial discrimination and stimulated the Nigerian government to issue a circular
against it (31, 32).[42] Other political structures were not ignored. Creech Jones's
renowned local government despatch of 1947 prompted consideration of local
government reform—soon underway for the eastern provinces—and implied a
greater role for western-educated Nigerians at the local government level (50).

For Richards the social, economic and educational measures of this new line were
a good deal more congenial than the modifications to the constitutional proposals
that the CO had obliged him to accept. The problem however was that far from being
welcomed by Nigerian leaders, Richards's constitutional proposals in particular, and
his approach more generally, were to come under considerable criticism from the
start, as they clearly fell short of the hopes that had emerged among some Nigerians

during the war. Part of Richards's problem was his unwillingness to take seriously the views of such western-educated Nigerians. This was reinforced by the wider situation within which he was having to operate. The severe social and economic dislocation in Nigeria following the ending of the war was not the most conducive context within which to launch major constitutional reforms. In particular the inflation that had characterised the war years had severely eroded the wages of public sector employees and lay behind the general strike that broke out in June 1945 (11).[43]

The general strike, which lasted over five weeks before the promise of a commission of inquiry into public sector pay levels brought about a return to work, while overblown as a symptom of nationalist unrest was to have significant consequences for the rest of Richards's governorship (17, 26).[44] Although not initiated in reaction to Richards's constitutional proposals, the strike was to have a major impact on their reception for it poisoned the governor's relations with Nigerian leaders, and confirmed him in his view of Azikiwe—as seen in the banning in June of Azikiwe's *West African Pilot* and *Daily Comet*—as an irresponsible and dangerous figure (18).[45]

Azikiwe grew in political stature during the strike. Although it was generated by economic factors in the articulation of which Azikiwe had had little part, his quick move to express support for the strikers and his use of his papers to publicise their grievances finally confirmed his emergence as a genuinely national leader. His allegations in July 1945 about a government-inspired plot to have him assassinated reinforced this (16). Significant was the extensive publicity Azikiwe achieved in the USA over the next twelve months concerning this alleged plot. The difficulty he posed for the administration can be seen in Richards's somewhat hysterical call for a Navy frigate to be sent to Lagos when, in November, talk of a further strike developed.[46]

The situation into which the Richards's proposals emerged in March 1945 was therefore not the most auspicious. In the event only one unofficial, Dr N Olusoga, opposed the scheme in the Legislative Council. More importantly however, the NCNC, established but seven months earlier, made clear from the start its view that Richards's proposals were not acceptable (8). It objected to the lack of consultation, to the fact that that the electoral principle was limited to Lagos and Calabar, and that special interests still retained representation in the Legislative Council. It complained that the unofficial majorities in the proposals were more apparent than real because the number of unofficials included chiefs who were government functionaries in all but name. In addition, the NCNC focused on the four so-called 'Obnoxious Ordinances' of March 1945—the minerals ordinance, the public lands acquisition ordinance, the crown lands (amendment) ordinance and the appointment and deposition of chiefs (amendment) ordinance—which although in reality doing little more than regularising the legal position in each instance, appeared to be increasing the government's powers over land and resources and over chiefly appointments.

The controversy concerning the constitutional proposals, like the simultaneous uproar concerning the general strike, was important in reinforcing the NCNC's posi-tion at the head of critics of British rule. Although the NYM still played an active part in these events, it was clearly the NCNC that was now the major organisation among such critics. Its decision to launch a fund-raising tour around Nigeria in 1946—in order to send a delegation to London to protest against Richards's scheme—further emphasised its nation-wide appeal, an appeal reinforced by the death of Macaulay during the tour and Azikiwe's subsequent assumption of the leadership of the organisation. The meeting of the NCNC delegation with the secretary of state in London in August 1947, and its presentation of a memorandum outlining its objections to the constitution, confirmed the organisation's newly achieved status (38).

Yet, significantly, not all Nigerian politicians accepted the NCNC's claims to speak for Nigeria. Abubakar Tafawa Balewa, a northern member of the Legislative Council, rejected an invitation to join the London delegation, and in the Council in March 1947 expressed his concerns at talk of independence before the North was ready; more ominously he referred to the North continuing its 'interrupted conquest to the sea'.[47] Equally, the *Daily Service*, hostile to Azikiwe's papers, repeated serious and unanswered allegations about the mismanagement of funds by the London delegation. Further evidence of the polarisation of Nigerian politics came with clashes between Igbo and Yoruba in Lagos in 1948 and the formal establishment in Nigeria in June of that year of the *Egbe Omo Oduduwa*, a Yoruba cultural organisation first set up in London in 1945 and in which Obafemi Awolowo was to be prominent; this was followed in late 1948 by the transformation of the Ibo Federal Union into the Ibo State Union with Azikiwe as president, with its aim to organise the Igbo people into a political unit (46, 52). In turn the rump NYM became an increasingly Yoruba-dominated body. Politics was polarising around ethnic identities. 'I am very much concerned about the growth of ill-feeling between the Yorubas and the Ibos', noted Macpherson, 'and I am inclined to think . . . that the Society [*Egbe Omo Oduduwa*] is mainly concerned with resistance to Zik and the Ibos rather than with a constructive programme. . . . It has certainly been very active in the past few months and in its resistance to the Ibos, if in little else, it can claim considerable early success'.[48] These divisions, undoubtedly reinforcing and reinforced by the polarities reflected in Richards's creation of regional councils, were significant pointers to the future and meant that the NCNC's period at the head of a united Nigerian opposition to the administration was brief. After launching its 'Freedom Charter' at its Kaduna convention in April 1948, the NCNC passed into a period of relative quiescence (45). When it re-asserted itself in 1951 it was as an increasingly Igbo-dominated body.

The 'Richards' constitution came into operation in January 1947. Within months its author had retired. Richards went reluctantly, feeling that the work he had begun was still unfinished but clearly the CO was determined on a change, for his attempts to obtain an extension of his term of office were firmly rebuffed.[49] His successor, Sir John Macpherson, was appointed in November 1947 and took up office in April 1948, accompanied by a new chief secretary, Hugh Foot, who was clearly convinced of the desirability of further constitutional advance.

The failure of the constitutional proposals was not entirely Richards's fault. The CO was being unrealistic in believing that Nigerian leaders would meekly accept whatever package was offered to them, particularly if such a package emerged from deliberations within the confines of Church House. Yet in retrospect, Richards had been an unfortunate appointment. Although Creech Jones tried to sweeten the pill by expressing his admiration for what the governor had achieved, it was clear that Richards had too little sympathy with the policies that had emerged in the CO during the war years to be fully at ease in such a critical post in Nigeria.[50] He had little time for the educated African, and little vision of what was needed in the situation facing Nigeria after 1945. His limited understanding of the problem could be seen at the November 1947 African Governors' conference in London, where, in taking the side of the NA chiefs against what he saw as the dangerous theorists of the CO, he stood firmly behind an older tradition of colonial thought. A peerage, as Lord Milverton of Lagos and Clifton, was his compensation, but even from the Lords he continued his criticisms of what he was to call 'the intellectual dreamers of Whitehall' (127).

Macpherson's appointment was therefore seen by the CO as an opportunity for a fresh start after the hiatus of the Richards years and a chance to regain the ground lost during 1945–1947. The situation facing Macpherson when he arrived in Nigeria was in fact a critical one. Two months earlier, in February 1948, serious rioting broke out in Accra. In themselves these riots meant little for Nigeria, but they were followed by the appointment of the Watson Commission to examine the background to the violence. The commission's report, when completed later that year, made a number of far-reaching recommendations, and in particular that the 1946 Gold Coast constitution should be radically reshaped to give a much greater role for Africans in the administration of the territory. With this went an emphasis on the need to speed up moves towards eventual self-government.[51] The report of the Coussey Committee at the end of 1949 further recommended the introduction of ministerial government with Africans responsible for government departments; by February 1951 Kwame Nkrumah had become leader of government business in the Gold Coast and the territory was moving towards self-government.

These, relatively rapid, developments in the Gold Coast had their impact on Nigeria, though the precise nature of that impact is difficult to assess without turning to counter-factual arguments. The administration certainly *feared* the knock-on effect of Gold Coast developments on Nigeria, but the expected uproar over the Watson Report for example, failed to materialise. None the less, the pace of change in the Gold Coast meant it was difficult if not impossible to delay change in Nigeria. It was too easy for Nigerian leaders to point to developments in their near-neighbour and argue for the application to Nigeria of similar measures.[52] Certainly Macpherson was concerned at what he saw as the pressures within Nigeria generated by the changes occurring in the Gold Coast. Although it was not until 1951 that he specifically complained to the CO of the way the pace of change in the former was undermining his more measured approach in Nigeria, his unease about Gold Coast developments was evident from an early date (49).

The chief problem facing the administration as Macpherson arrived in Nigeria was the development of a much more radical brand of nationalism and how to contain it. The period from 1948 through to 1950 saw the emergence to prominence of militant organisations like the Zikists, the perceived threat of Soviet infiltration, an attempt on the life of the chief secretary and widespread rioting following the Enugu shootings in November 1949. This unrest not only raised the possibility, admittedly faint, that the administration would loose control of the Nigerian situation, but threatened to undermine the whole thrust of CO strategy to Nigeria since the war.

The Zikist movement had emerged in late 1945 through the initiative of younger followers of Azikiwe and had been formally inaugurated early the following year. By 1948 its popular appeal, at least among younger and more radical elements, was growing. Although not linked directly with Azikiwe, who kept an ambiguous distance, its name reflected the movement's admiration of his work and reinforced his appeal among such figures. The Zikist movement,—estimated by the administration to have a membership of 800–900 at most—focused around an ill-defined philosophy of 'Zikism' and developed its own flag, symbols and songs.[53] However vague its ideology may have been, its programme was clear in its objective which was self-government. Its activities were characterised by increasingly strident demands for militant action against British rule that in time began to approach calls for a violent uprising. This was talk rather than action, but it was talk that the authorities refused to ignore. When a leading Zikist, Osita Agwuna, in a lecture given in October 1948 entitled 'A call for revolution' made a public call for a revolutionary struggle against British rule and appealed for 'positive action', he was arrested and, along with other Zikist leaders and the journalist Tony Enahoro, who chaired the lecture, tried and imprisoned for sedition (57).[54] The attempt by a Zikist in February 1950 to assassinate Foot was followed by a sharp clamp down on the movement and in April 1950 by its banning (100). Thereafter the Zikist movement became effectively moribund.

The actual threat posed by militant nationalism in Nigeria never became serious, but its potential in 1948 was, as far as the administration was concerned, significant. What gave this militant nationalism its potency was the broader international background against which these developments were occurring and wider fears of Soviet expansionism in these years. Concern was expressed, though no evidence ever found, of Azikiwe's links to the USSR.[55] The main fear of Soviet penetration in Nigeria in this period concerned finance (132). Soviet subsidies to Nigerian trade unions, it was believed, were considerable.[56] However, fears were also expressed concerning Marxist literature entering the country and strong objections voiced about Azikiwe's papers and their willingness to report sympathetically the Soviet side of arguments at the UNO. Although very few individual communists or fellow-travellers were ever identified in Nigeria, it was believed that Nigerian students overseas and Nigerian visitors to international conferences were being subverted and that firm action to prevent the growth of communism in the country was needed.[57]

In fact the degree of Soviet influence in the late 1940s and early 1950s in Nigeria was extremely circumscribed. There was no meaningful Soviet involvement in Nigerian politics in these years, as the FO report on communism in Africa in June 1951 was to confirm (115). Never the less the fear was very real, as were the actions taken by the administration to contain any potential Soviet threat. 1948 indeed saw a wide-ranging review of security measures within Nigeria, prompted by Creech Jones's circular of 5 August 1948 (53).[58] Not least, measures were considered to try to control bank accounts to prevent Soviet subsidies entering the country and there was talk of banning Nkrumah if he ever proposed visiting Nigeria.[59] In 1948 the CO created the post of police adviser to the secretary of state concerning security matters generally and the official visited West Africa in early 1949 to review policing and the intelligence-gathering apparatus. Furthermore, counter-measures to deal with Soviet influence in West Africa were agreed at a meeting in Accra of representatives of the territories in early 1951 and a broad swathe of measures to contain the putative Soviet threat were developed. Intelligence reports were drawn up, the post monitored, measures to influence broadcasting devised, communist literature entering the country seized, academic employees at Ibadan University College vetted and communists banned.

Such concern at unrest—real or imagined—characterised policy in the 1948–50 period and was central to Macpherson's decisions once he took up office. His approach was two-fold, to crush the unrest and to push on with constitutional advance. On the one hand firm measures were taken to contain possible threats, hence the actions he took against Agwuna and leading Zikists in late 1948 and the subsequent banning of the organisation. On the other, the decision was taken to pursue further constitutional reform. Soon after his arrival in Nigeria, the new governor called a meeting in Government House to discuss the constitution, the conclusion of which was that it should be scrapped and a new one drawn up.[60] On 17 August 1948 Macpherson announced this decision to the Legislative Council. The gloss was that the constitution had been such a success that Nigeria was ready for further changes, several years before the nine years originally contemplated, but little could disguise the fact that Richards's proposals had failed in their task of gaining the consent of Nigerian leaders. The only solution was a fresh start, as Macpherson realised. 'We couldn't put a ring fence around Nigeria', he wrote later about his deliberations in this period, 'we had to take the initiative and not wait to be overtaken by events' (153).

Macpherson's 'constitution mongering' was to be a long-drawn out affair lasting for a period of some three years from his statement to the Legislative Council in August 1948. The intention behind this lengthy process was to ensure that as wide an array of views as possible within Nigeria should be expressed, thus undermining one of the NCNC's main criticisms of Richards. But it was designed too, to allow the process to be channelled by the administration; Macpherson's aim in this, no less than Richards's had been, was to marginalise the NCNC by judicious but controlled reform. Macpherson set his face firmly against the NCNC demand for a constituent assembly; his aim was to call in the 'masses'—and not least the NA chiefs—as a counterweight to the educated 'classes' of the NCNC. He outlined to the CO in January 1949 the constitutional changes he hoped would result from this consultative process: greater regional autonomy, a decrease in the number of official members of the various regional houses and the Legislative Council, more scope for unofficials to act, and steps, albeit limited, towards an embryonic ministerial system as were occurring in the Gold Coast (61).

In the short term at least, Macpherson's strategy was effective. He proposed that the process of constitutional reform would begin in the Legislative Council—in itself a contrast with Richards's approach four years earlier—with the setting up of a select committee, 'that we might consider together what changes should be made' as he said (65). Thereafter the intention, outlined by Foot in his speech to the Legislative Council on 11 March 1949, was to establish village, divisional and provincial meetings throughout Nigeria where as broad as possible an array of opinion could be canvassed. Over the next few months such meetings were initiated, culminating in regional conferences for the East, North, West and Lagos which made recommendations to a Constitutional Drafting Committee, headed by Foot, which in turn drew up proposals to put to the General Conference held in Ibadan in January 1950 (87, 90).

The process of constitutional consultation was accompanied by other measures to increase the role of Nigerians in the administration. One of the most notable of these was the decision in May 1948 to establish a commission under Foot to look at the Nigerianisation of senior posts in the government service—a necessity given the new functions the colonial state was taking on in these years. The Foot Commission, which included Azikiwe among its members, recommended that 'no non-Nigerian should be recruited for any Government post except where no suitable and qualified Nigerian is available'.[61] In addition it recommended the establishment of public service boards to oversee appointments, and that a number of government scholarships over the following three years should be awarded for the training of Nigerians for the public service. Not least of the changes represented by the Foot commission was the new tone it evinced concerning the government's attitudes towards educated Nigerians; in 1948 some 208 Nigerians were employed in the senior service, by 1951 this had reached 597 (145).

Equally in education, 1948 saw a changing emphasis towards Nigerians that Macpherson was quick to encourage. The 1948 Education Ordinance, already in process, set up education boards, launched increased spending on education and gave NAs the right to levy education rates to pay for schools. This approach, coinciding with the measures for mass education and the opening of University College, Ibadan, earlier that year, showed the degree to which the pre-war hesitations over the relationship between the NA system and the educated Nigerian had been resolved; the long-term future of Nigeria lay with the latter.

This could be seen too in the reform of local government initiated by Creech Jones's despatch of 1947 and which proceeded apace under Macpherson. The aim was to attempt the democratisation of local government by progressively abandoning the old NA system where power lay almost exclusively with a chief and his council. The Eastern provinces—where 'chiefly' power had been progressively abandoned since 1929—were the first to initiate reforms, for in this region there was already considerable debate among officials about the need for change, as reflected in the 1949 Gibbons Report.[62] The appointment of a select committee of the Eastern House of Assembly in August 1948, initiated a process which culminated in the creation of a three-tier network of county, district and local councils in the Eastern Region Local Government Ordinance which received royal assent in 1950 (86). This structure was accompanied by the extension of the elective principle, the integration of the educated Nigerian into the NA system and the reduction of the functions of the DO vis-à-vis local government.

Reform in the East was followed, in 1949, by moves to initiate reform of local government in the West and the North. The West was first in this (159), with the Western Region Local Government Ordinance receiving royal assent in February 1953, and, as in the East, establishing both a three-tier system of divisional, dis- trict and local councils and the elective principle; it was followed shortly there- after by legislation to systematise succession to chieftaincies. The North was slower to proceed along this road, even though it was the critical region for local government reform, given the strength there of the NA system, and the determi- nation both of elements in the CO to urge its reform and of elements in the field service to protect the position of the ruling caste in the region. The Maddocks and Pott Report of 1950 surveyed the existing situation in the region, and was consid- ered by a select committee of the Northern Regional Council in mid-1951.[63] Then progress slowed. The CO considered that reform of the North was urgent, as indeed did the Lagos administration, but the fact that most of the members of the select committee belonged to the ruling caste in the North made radical reform unlikely, at least in the short term.[64] Only in 1952 were the first steps taken when the system of the sole NA in the North was abolished and replaced by the 'chief- in-council' (147).

By late 1949, much of the ground lost in the Richards era had been made up. However, Macpherson's policy was to come under serious strain with the Enugu shootings of 18 November 1949 (79, 80). The shootings at the Iva Valley mine near Enugu, which resulted from a bungled attempt by the police to remove explosives from a store during a miners' strike, led to 21 deaths and to widespread rioting across the Eastern provinces. This was a critical moment for the policy of managed reform and one that threatened to undo everything Macpherson had achieved since his arrival nineteen months earlier.

The rioting, encouraged in many areas by local Zikists, led to a three-week state of emergency (83). These weeks represented the one moment in the post-war Nigerian story when violence against British rule became relatively widespread. In themselves however the significance of these riots can be exaggerated; they were always containable and at no point did the security forces ever look like losing control. But much more important than the riots themselves were the political developments that followed them. The uproar that accompanied the shootings led to a rapprochement of the various political organisations in Nigeria—divided as they had been by ethnic tension in 1948—around the National Emergency Committee, with Dr Akinola Maja as president, and Mbonu Ojike as secretary, and with Azikiwe prominent among its backers. For the next twelve months or so, until its collapse in late 1950, the NEC threatened to provide the united opposition to the administration that had been lacking for most of the period since the Igbo-Yoruba tensions in Lagos in 1948 (111).

However, the combination of a security clamp-down on the rioters together with the appointment of the Fitzgerald Commission—which reported in June 1950—to look into the causes of the shootings, succeeded in buying the administration time.[65] The breathing space thus gained, allowed the constitutional consultations to proceed. The Ibadan General Conference met in January 1950 with fifty-three members, of whom all but three were Nigerian, and considered the recommendations proposed by the Constitutional Drafting Committee (90). The conference recommended increased regional autonomy, increased legislative powers for regional houses, a degree of ministerial responsibility and a commission to examine financial allocations between the centre and the regions: precisely the ideas that Macpherson had outlined to the CO at the start of this process. More radical suggestions by NCNC representatives were marginalised at Ibadan as were demands for the creation of several smaller regions.

From Macpherson's point of view the conference represented a triumph, not least coming so soon after the Enugu shootings. However the conference was also the moment when the issue of relations between North and South began to come into sharp focus and an issue that was to bedevil Nigerian politics throughout these years and after, moved firmly to centre stage. What was striking about the Ibadan conference was the sharpening of regional tensions over several issues including whether Lagos should be treated as part of the West or as a separate, quasi-federal territory, over the boundary between the North and the West, where large numbers of Muslim Yorubas in the North were separated from their compatriots in the West, and, above all, over the demand of the Northern delegates that the North should be given parity with the *combined* Eastern and Western Regions in the number of seats in the future central legislature or House of Representatives, and thus effectively be the dominant element in Nigeria (117). This latter demand was accompanied by the threat from two Northern delegates that the North would go its own way if their demand was not accepted: secession, as so often in these years, was the threat the North was prepared to use to get its way.[66] These issues were of such divisive import that the question of the composition of the central legislature had to be left unresolved in the conference recommendations.

Northern leaders looked on with unease at the changes that were being considered at Ibadan. Underlying this lay broader fears held by many in the North concerning the whole pace of change in Nigeria since the Northern provinces were brought under the remit of the Legislative Council after the war. For the Northern rulers, established in their NAs and with their authority reinforced under the indirect rule system, the pace of proposed reform seemed to threaten their power and thereby their whole political and social—and indeed religious—position. At root, their unease coalesced around the increased influence of educated southerners under the reforms proposed by the administration. For these Northerners, Nigerianisation meant 'southernisation', for the western-educated Nigerian of the urban areas of the south would be best placed to take advantage of the changes Britain was proposing; the offices being created by the constitutional proposals would, it was feared, go to southerners with their more developed education system. In the longer term the concern was that an independent Nigeria would be a Nigeria dominated by the South.

This was not entirely a universal response in the North. Indeed not only were there significant differences of emphasis between individual Northern leaders, but also between representatives of the larger and smaller emirates, and between the Hausa-Fulani emirates generally and Bornu. Significant too was the fact that the Middle Belt did not share the religious, ethnic or social identities of the majority and that organisations were beginning to emerge to stress its distinctive interests in these changes; in 1950 the Middle Zone League was established. Perhaps most important of these tensions however, was that which began to emerge between the radicals and populists on the one hand and those of a more conservative bent on the other.

During late 1948 the first significant political grouping to develop in the North, the *Jam'iyyar Mutanen Arewa*, or Northern Peoples' Congress, emerged; in December 1949 it held its first formal convention in Kano.[67] Initially intended as a largely cultural organisation for educated Northerners, the NPC soon took on a more overt political slant. The party split in August 1950 with the more radical elements, who were to be joined by Aminu Kano a few months later, breaking away to form the Northern Elements Progressive Union with its dedication to the emancipation of the *talakawa* (commoner class) of the North. Aminu Kano was thereafter to be the leading light of these more radical elements in the region. The split of 1950 left the NPC temporarily moribund, until it was revived as a straight-forward political party, but with clear links to the rulers of the NAs of the North, in October 1951. The revived NPC, in which its vice-president, the Sardauna of Sokoto, was the dominant influence, was thereafter to lead the way in opposing many of the more radical suggestions emanating from southern leaders.

For these Northern figures, parity of seats with the South in the proposed central House of Representatives was the essential first step to protect their interests in any new constitution. For Southerners however, such parity represented a Northern 'veto', and a potential block on their aspirations for self-government in the near future. There seemed little chance, either at Ibadan or thereafter, that these two positions could be reconciled. The deadlock meant considerable delay over the constitutional issue during 1950 in order to find a solution.

When the Ibadan recommendations were considered by the Legislative Council early in 1950 and then by the UK Cabinet in May, the question had to be left open (106). The delays however represented a form of brinkmanship by the North— including a threat to send a delegation to London to argue their case—which eventually worked.[68] When in September the Legislative Council debated the report of a select committee on the constitutional proposals, the issue of the representation of the North was resolved by agreement that it should indeed have half the seats in the proposed House of Representatives; the representatives from the East, worried at the implications of Northern intransigence for constitutional advance broadly and more specifically the dangers implied in Northern threats of secession, gave in. This was not without controversy, with the three elected Lagos members of the Council, including Azikiwe, continuing to object to the grant of parity to the North and urging the use of a bicameral legislature to safeguard Northern interests.

Northern intransigence over these constitutional changes suited British interests. Macpherson was pleased at the outcome and described it as 'extremely satisfactory' (117). The counter-balance to NCNC radicalism that the NPC represented was welcomed by many in the CO and the administration. Throughout this period there were figures, particularly in the Northern administration, who, if not directly encouraging Northern resistance to Southern demands, certainly did little to overcome it. There was a community of interest between the North and the administration more broadly. This went back a long way; British officials were undoubtedly concerned to protect Northern interests from the start of the constitutional changes that had begun in 1943.[69] Yet it would be wrong to infer from this a deliberate policy of 'divide and rule'. For one thing, Northern intransigence to Southern radicalism did not need British encouragement, and for another, Northern leaders made clear, on more than one occasion, their ability to challenge British interests when it suited them to do so. In any case, British interests were simple: the unity of Nigeria was central to CO aims. The greatest fear for the CO, right up to 1960, was the danger of secession and particularly, through by no means exclusively, secession by the North. Avoiding this required, the CO believed, the building in to the constitutional changes demanded by Southern leaders, safeguards for Northern interests. The acceptance of Northern parity in the House of Representatives in 1950 was by no means the last of these.

The other issue to cause problems following the Ibadan conference was that of the powers of ministers in the proposed constitution (123, 124). The select committee of the Legislative Council had proposed a central Council of Ministers, with ministers having the power to formulate policy and to direct executive action in conjunction with heads of department. Macpherson resisted the idea of ministerial responsibility in favour of what he termed a conciliar system with ministers' powers left deliberately vague in the hope that in time they could flexibly be adjusted. He was conscious of developments in the Gold Coast where considerable power was being conceded to ministers at this time, but felt that Nigeria was not ready for such advance. He was keen therefore that while ministers should propose policy, officials should be responsible for executing it, in *partnership* with ministers. He still saw officials—subject to the governor—as the dominant figures in this relationship, at least for the initial phase of the constitution's existence. For Nigerian leaders however, this was inadequate and ministerial responsibility in the fullest sense was essential if the constitutional changes were to have meaning.

Late in 1950 the CO expressed concern about the ill-definition of this minister-official relationship (123, 127). The CO view was that the vagueness meant in practice that it would not work for long, and that the precise degree to which ministers could direct officials had to be spelt out in advance: 'ministers should have no reason to believe that the Secretariat is the real power behind the throne or that the ministers are merely figureheads'.[70] Once again the CO was showing itself as being in advance of the views of the administration, for the CO was prepared to accept, if necessary, a much greater degree of ministerial responsibility than Macpherson.

The constitution was finally approved in mid-1951 and came into effect in November.[71] Popularly called the 'Macpherson constitution', it established a House of Representatives of 148, of which 6 seats were reserved for special interests and 6 for officials.[72] Of the remaining 136 seats, the North was to have 68, the remaining 68 being divided equally between the two southern regions; members would be elected by the regional Houses. The constitution also set up a Council of Ministers of six officials together with twelve unofficials as ministers but without a prime minister. At the heart of the constitution was the formalisation it gave to the regionalism that the 1947 constitution had initiated. Legislative powers were given to the regional Houses of Assembly (those in the North and West also having a second chamber in the form of a House of Chiefs) and the regional chief commissioners became lieutenant-governors; regional Executive Councils were also established. The principle that underlay British policy towards Nigeria right through to 1960—of reassurance to the North coupled with constitutional advances for the South—was clearly apparent.

In addition the constitution regularised the position of the Cameroons as part of Nigeria. The territory had been visited by a UNO mission in late 1949 which had issued a generally favourable report on the UK administration; more specifically it had approved the integration of the Northern Cameroons into the Northern Region and the administration of the Southern Cameroons as part of the Eastern Region (92, 96). The 1951 constitution reserved thirteen seats in the Eastern Region House of Assembly for the Southern Cameroons and seven in the House of Representatives; one seat in the Executive Council was also allocated to the territory.

Macpherson felt pleased with the outcome. He had achieved the general principles of the proposals that he had outlined to the CO in early 1949 and had done so despite the Enugu shootings and the ensuing unrest. For Macpherson at least, the constitution had regained the ground lost by Richards and had done so while sticking to the measured approach first articulated during the war by O G R Williams. While designed to evolve over time, the 1951 provisions were seen as an end in themselves rather than the start of a process leading to self-government in the foreseeable future; Macpherson spoke at this time of his view that independence was at least thirty years in the future.[73]

For the success of the new constitution, much depended on the outcome of the elections scheduled for late 1951. These were indirect elections, operating through an electoral college system on a taxpayer suffrage. In these elections the AG won 44 out of the 80 seats in the Western Region, (though many of the NCNC opposition defected to the AG thereafter), the NCNC 65 (soon increased to 72 by defections) in the Eastern Region and the NPC a majority in the North. The resulting regional Houses then chose members from their House for the House of Representatives and in practice a winner-takes-all approach by the majority party came into effect; only the two seats reserved for Lagos in the House of Representatives—to be chosen from the Western House of Assembly—and which had voted for the NCNC broke this pattern.

The problem indeed came with the five Lagos seats in the Western House of Assembly. These had been won by NCNC representatives, including Azikiwe. Azikiwe's determination was thereby to gain one of the two Lagos seats in the House of Representatives, and to ensure this he arranged for three of the NCNC representatives to refuse nomination in order to allow himself to have a clear run. At the last moment however two of the three, Adeleke Adedoyin and Ibiyinka Olorun-Nimbe, refused to honour the agreement and Azikiwe failed to be nominated.[74] The situation thus resulted that the leading figure of Nigerian nationalism since the war, and an easterner to boot, remained the leader of the opposition in the Western House of Assembly, circumstances that made the NCNC more determined than ever to break the 1951 constitution.

The constitutional crisis of 1953
In the event, the constitution that had taken nearly three years to devise was to last for a mere 15 months or so. At root was the fact that what had seemed appropriate to Nigeria in 1948 was no longer relevant to the situation when the constitution came into operation in late 1951. Although Macpherson believed he had given Nigeria 'a constitution that is in advance of its true capacity', circumstances had changed and few Nigerian leaders would have shared the governor's view (153). By May 1953 indeed, the constitution had effectively collapsed under the weight of its own weaknesses.

There were two problems with the constitution from the start. Firstly, although Macpherson had seen the constitution as something that could grow and develop over time as Nigerian leaders became more experienced in operating it, its provisions fell well short of what were, by 1951, Nigerian aspirations. This particularly concerned the powers of the Council of Ministers which first met at the start of 1952 with four members each from the AG, the NCNC and the NPC. The question concerned ministerial responsibility, the issue that Macpherson had left deliberately vague in drawing up the proposals. Very quickly the aspirations of ministers to run departments became apparent. This related in turn to the question of collective responsibility. Ministers were expected to be collectively responsible to the House of Representatives for policy decisions, yet did not have the power to instruct officials concerning the execution of those decisions. Further, the lack of a prime minister— in a Council of Ministers made up of three different parties—inevitably led to problems. Party political considerations generated increasing suspicion between ministers and led to deadlock.

This was related to a second problem. In its formalisation of regionalism the constitution gave great encouragement to ethnic tensions in Nigeria. Ethnic tensions long pre-dated 1951, but the constitution of that year fatally exacerbated this problem. This was because of the relationship between the central House of Representatives and the regional Houses of Assembly, and the provision that members of the former would be elected by members of the latter. The 'winner-takes-all' principle meant that power at the centre depended on power in the region and encouraged regional ethnic solidarity; in turn this stimulated appeals to ethnic minorities by rival parties in order to undermine that solidarity. Any chances of a genuinely national party appealing broadly across Nigeria were stymied by the constitution.

Such centrifugal forces were in turn related to the position of the North. For the North, despite their victory over the issue of parity of representation at the centre, the 1951 constitution did not offer sufficient safeguards. The degree of regional autonomy it offered was less than Northern leaders wished, given their concerns that concessions to Southern leaders at the central level would simply facilitate southern domination over the North in the future. The view of Northern leaders was that if further concessions at the centre were to be made then much greater regional autonomy was necessary. Thus the two problems with the constitution—lack of ministerial responsibility and ethnic tension—inter-related and, as will be seen, were to do so in a fatal way during 1952 and 1953.

With time, these problems might have been resolved. However, the problem was the pace of change in the Gold Coast. In early 1952 Nkrumah became prime minister and ministerial responsibility was conceded by governor Sir Charles Arden-Clarke.[75] When Macpherson heard of these proposals he flew to London for discussions in February (152). As Macpherson realised, these changes in the Gold Coast made it likely that Nigerian leaders would begin to push for similar concessions for themselves, well before the period he had envisaged. He was also as conscious as anyone of the likely impact of such concessions on Northern leaders. In a number of forthright letters to the CO in 1952 and 1953 Macpherson expressed both surprise at the pace of change in the Gold Coast and distress at the implications of this for what he was trying to achieve in Nigeria. These changes were, he said, 'catastrophic' for Nigeria and threatened 'to save the Gold Coast for the Empire' at the cost of the loss of Nigeria (152). Nigeria needed, he felt, a good run at the new constitution but the developments in the Gold Coast would prevent this.

Underlying Macpherson's concerns was his realisation that some Nigerian leaders were determined to show the constitution to be unworkable. As far as the two main southern parties were concerned, the 1951 constitution had strengthened their determination to push for self-government; self-government by 1956 became, during 1951, their rallying cry. In itself this showed how far the constitution had failed in its intention of regaining the initiative and buying time for the administration. What had been acceptable in 1948, clearly was not by 1951. 'Nationalism, once it is in the saddle, rides hard', noted Macpherson (153). Indeed during 1951 there were several signs that Nigerian leaders were attempting to regroup, following the splits and tensions of the 1948–1950 period. Behind this lay the impending elections under the new constitution, due in late 1951. In early 1951 following the demise of the NEC, Kingsley Mbadiwe and Ojike attempted to establish a Committee of National Rebirth, to bring unity to Nigeria's fractured political scene and in particular to bring supporters of the AG and the NCNC into a united front. Little came of their efforts, but in September of that year, at its Kano Convention, it was clear that the NCNC was re-grouping. Re-organisation of the party—prompted by the forthcoming elections—led to the establishment of committees for each region, a Central Working Committee to co-ordinate the party, and the creation of individual membership. The NCNC remained pledged to fighting for the unity of Nigeria and was the one party at this time genuinely attempting to operate across the whole country. It developed links with NEPU in the North and also targeted the West, in the hope of establishing a pan-southern power base. Its policy, in 1951 at least, was one that stressed the unity of the country and consequently the need for a powerful centre. It stressed too, the need for self-government and at Kano re-affirmed this as its central policy.

For the NCNC therefore, its failure to achieve a substantial presence in the West in the 1951 elections was a disappointment, for not only did it undermine its hopes of establishing a nation-wide appeal, but by showing the strength of regional loyalties it reinforced similar tendencies within the party. Moreover Azikiwe's failure to win a seat in the House of Representatives caused him major difficulties. Given the emerging divisions within the party between those who wished to operate the 1951 constitution in order to exploit whatever opportunities it provided and those who were determined to destroy it, Azikiwe's absence from the centre of power made it difficult for him to maintain party unity. It also made him determined to ensure the collapse of the constitution.

Opposition to the constitution was also articulated by the AG. In mid-1952 the AG ministers in the Council submitted a memorandum demanding increased ministerial responsibility similar to that which had been conceded in the Gold Coast (157, 158). The memorandum was a well thought-through demand for ministers to be allowed to instruct officials directly and the governor to be obliged to consult civil servants only through the relevant minister; further, it argued that the governor's reserved powers should be exercised only after consultation with the Council. The memorandum was debated in the Council of Ministers but both NPC and NCNC ministers stalled, arguing that while they were sympathetic to the AG proposals the time was not ripe for their implementation; the AG plan was defeated. Macpherson for his part, agreed, early in 1953, to accept the creation of four individual ministries but refused anything further.[76]

The real significance of the defeat of the AG proposals for ministerial responsibility however, lay in the NCNC leaders' reluctance to co-operate with the AG. The NCNC reaction, felt Macpherson, was partly based on simple dislike of the AG leaders, but was also a reflection of a desire to maintain the unity of Nigeria; changing the constitution at the behest of the AG would, felt the NCNC, simply open the flood-gates to AG demands for greater regionalisation. NCNC suspicions of the regionalist tendencies in the AG were acute. Macpherson, however, admitted the convenience of this reaction and his readiness to play on it. Nonetheless the AG's defeat undoubtedly poisoned relations with the governor in the short-term and contributed to the party's decision, at its Benin conference in late 1952, to adopt a policy of 'non-fraternisation' with Macpherson.[77]

Regional and ethnic tensions now took on an added importance. A number of issues emerged which generated considerable strain between the parties. One was the Ilorin boundary between the North and West (161). This in turn related to the position of Lagos (163). The NCNC—not least because of Azikiwe's experiences in the 1951 elections—wanted Lagos excised from the West, and submitted a motion accordingly in the House of Representatives; the NPC supported this, at least partly because of its leaders' fears of AG regionalist tendencies and the desire therefore to keep open the possibility of Lagos as a port for the North should the West secede. But the AG reacted to this by demanding that the Ilorin boundary be adjusted in the favour of the West as compensation.[78] The NCNC motion failed, being ruled out of order, but the episode showed the willingness of politicians to trade on ethnic and regional differences for party political gain.

Perhaps the critical factor in this heightening of regional and ethnic tensions during 1952 was the determination of parties to consolidate power in their 'home' region, given the need under the constitution to control a region in order to exercise influence at the centre. This gave encouragement to the need to eliminate rivals and to stress ethnic solidarity against other parties. The desire to eliminate potential rival regional sources of power could be seen in the Western Region local government bill, introduced in the Western House of Assembly in July 1952 which enhanced the power of the (AG) local government minister and downplayed that of the DO who became little more than a 'local government inspector'. Although Williamson at the CO was relatively sanguine about the implications of this, Macpherson expressed concern that the AG was using the bill to assert greater autonomy for the West (159). Similar political considerations could be seen in the politicisation of marketing board appointments by the AG in 1952 in the West, a process that prompted considerable concern in the CO (181).[79]

The consolidation of AG power in the West, together with Azikiwe's experiences in the Lagos elections, in turn had an impact on the NCNC. The problem throughout this period, as both Macpherson and the CO recognised, was Azikiwe's absence from the centre. This absence prompted Azikiwe to push for strict party discipline in the NCNC under his leadership, for he feared that this was threatened while he remained isolated in the West. This fear was reinforced by the emerging divisions over the constitution within the NCNC. In December 1952 at the Jos special convention of the NCNC, Azikiwe enforced the expulsion of three of the four Eastern ministers in the Council because of their refusal to accept party instructions for non co-operation with the administration (171).[80]

Azikiwe followed this, in January 1953, by insisting on the resignation of the nine NCNC ministers in the Eastern Region Executive Council (175). In doing this, Azikiwe was not only attempting to assert his own authority in the party while he remained outside the region but flexing his muscles vis-à-vis the Eastern lieutenant-governor. At the last moment however, six of the nine (soon to be dubbed the 'sit-tight ministers') led by Eyo Ita, the deputy national president of the NCNC, withdrew their resignations, precipitating a major crisis in the East. The six ministers joined in alliance with the existing UNP members in the House of Assembly to form the NIP, and were supported by the AG in this; ethnic tensions between Igbo and Efik can be seen as a factor in these developments. The six ministers were defeated on an NCNC motion of no confidence in the House of Assembly in April but as the CO, to its surprise, had come to realise, poor drafting of the relevant instruments meant that a regional House could not be dissolved without every regional House—and the House of Representatives too—being simultaneously so dissolved, something that could not at this stage be contemplated (157). This left a minority government in power in the East and prompted the NCNC to vote down every piece of government business; the 1953 budget had to be passed by use of the lieutenant-governor's reserve powers. In turn Macpherson talked of using emergency powers to keep the administration functioning. Only in June, when fresh instruments could be drafted, was the impasse resolved by the dissolution of the Eastern House. In the ensuing Eastern elections, the NCNC, this time with Azikiwe standing unopposed for Onitsha, was elected with a large majority. It was a victory for Azikiwe, but in a deeper sense a defeat, for he had now accepted the logic of the regionalist tendencies in the constitution—that political power derived from control of a region—against his earlier policy of emphasising the country-wide appeal of his party. Ethnic tendencies were now colouring all of Nigerian politics.

The 'sit-tight' crisis in the East coincided with an even more significant crisis at the centre in early 1953. This was the crisis prompted by the AG 'self-government in 1956' motion submitted to the House of Representatives (184). Underlying this was rivalry between the AG and the NCNC and the issue of which party would dominate the south. AG leaders were determined to push their own credentials as nationalist leaders and determined too, to take advantage both of Azikiwe's difficulties in the East and his absence from the House of Representatives. At its Benin conference in 1952 the AG had passed a motion calling for self-government by 1956 (the year the 1951 constitution was to be reviewed) and it was clear the party was determined to break the constitution in order to gain greater powers for regions and to press for speedier moves to self-government.[81] At least partly motivated also by a desire to pre-empt the possibility of a similar motion by the NCNC, Tony Enahoro, an AG member, moved a motion in the House of Representatives for self-government in 1956.[82] The AG's fear was that if the NCNC beat them to it, this would reinforce NCNC appeals to the West, and ultimately allow it to emerge as the dominant party in the South as the NPC was in the North; AG-NCNC rivalry over which was to be the dominant party in the south remains a constant motif in the Nigerian story. According to the Ooni of Ife, (the senior traditional ruler of the Yoruba), the AG 'were determined to destroy Azikiwe; if they failed to pursue this self-government motion with the utmost vigour it would mean death for the Action Group' (188). In the event the Enahoro motion neither destroyed Azikiwe nor gained self-government by 1956 but it certainly destroyed the Macpherson constitution.

Moreover, the motion had the other effect of exposing the weaknesses in the constitution concerning ministerial responsibility. The motion was considered in advance in the Council of Ministers (184). The divisions revealed there between the various parties meant no Council line could be agreed; given the lack of ministerial responsibility for the Council in the House, and given the fact that the Council was split with the four Western ministers in a minority, Macpherson insisted on members of the Council abstaining from speaking or voting on the motion in the House, a decision that caused deep unrest among the AG ministers and prompted the resignation of the Ooni, followed later by the other three AG members.[83] Tensions in the Council were clearly rising and the conciliar system Macpherson had placed such emphasis on was collapsing.

The Enahoro motion was a defining moment in the decolonisation process in Nigeria. Not only did it put self-government firmly on the agenda but it brought into focus the issue of ministerial responsibility and the position of the Council of Ministers. Perhaps most importantly however, it exacerbated Northern fears of Southern ambitions. In the ensuing debate on Enahoro's motion on 31 March, NPC leaders made clear their position (187). Their anxieties were that independence in 1956 would mean Southern dominance of the North, and their opposition to Enahoro's motion led to its failure, following a proposed amendment put forward by the Sardauna of Sokoto, to replace the words 'self-government by 1956' by 'as soon as practicable'.[84] For Northern leaders, conscious of their region's political, educational and economic backwardness compared to the south, self-government in 1956 would simply mean the replacement of British rule by domination by Southern politicians more versed in western ways. There were religious tensions in this too. In a heated debate, apparently slighting references to Shehu Usuman dan Fodio, leader of the nineteenth century *jihad* that had established the Sokoto caliphate (and great-grandfather of the Sardauna) caused uproar and led to the eventual adjournment of the House; Enahoro's motion was lost.

It was the wider consequence of the debate that was the real significance of this episode. Both on arriving and leaving the House, Northern representatives were jeered and heckled by the Lagos crowd; further abuse occurred from crowds during their rail journey home.[85] This treatment confirmed to Northern leaders the failure of Southern politicians to recognise Northern fears and their apparent determination to push for an independent Nigeria where the North would be a junior partner. This sharpened Northern determination to defend their interests thereafter. The attitude of Northern leaders after these events, was, it was noted, 'hard, cold, and implacable'. Remarks in the House by the Sardauna about 'the mistake of 1914' (when Nigeria had been unified) hardly helped (188, 190).

Events following Enahoro's motion further confirmed Northern leaders in their fears. A rapprochement between the AG and the NCNC announced in April 1953 appeared to threaten the isolation of the NPC while press attacks on Northern leaders as the allies of British imperialism heightened this. Separatist ideas began to be taken seriously by the Northern administration, with, somewhat to the CO's surprise, Sharwood-Smith, the lieutenant-governor, initiating a 'coloured lights' exercise to look at the various options open to the North, including the possibility of secession (189). Indeed on 22 May the Northern House of Assembly debated and approved (followed by the House of Chiefs) the so-called 'Eight-points motion' that called for separation from the South in all but the most limited spheres such as defence and foreign affairs; it meant the break-up of Nigeria in all but name (207).[86]

Meanwhile press comment in the South continued to attack the administration, with not-so-veiled references in the AG *Daily Service*, to 'Mau Mau or no Mau Mau?', referring to the violent rising recently begun in Kenya, and repeated by Akintola, the publisher of the paper, in the House, encouraging fears that were later heightened by the Coronation day riot in Lagos in June and AG threats of launching a civil disobedience campaign.[87] When Henry Hopkinson, minister of state for colonial affairs, visited Nigeria for the West African Armed Forces conference in April he met Northern leaders and found them 'deeply disturbed' and 'charged with emotion' over the Enahoro motion and determined to get a greater degree of autonomy from the rest of Nigeria. According to Tafawa Balewa, 'no good would come from co-operation with the South' (193). Western leaders meanwhile impressed on him the need for further constitutional advance, particularly over ministerial responsibility and the creation of an office of prime minister as in the Gold Coast.

Macpherson's constitution had been fatally undermined by this crisis. Officials in the CO began drafting ideas in late March—even before Enahoro's motion was debated—for a revised constitution giving greater powers to the regions and Macpherson was called to the CO to discuss the situation with Lyttelton in April. The CO was not entirely sympathetic concerning his handling of the Enahoro motion. Officials believed that he had put too much pressure on the AG in expecting them quietly to accept defeat over the motion and that his insistence on conciliar responsibility to prevent ministers speaking in the debate had not helped either; a more skilled operator would have prevented things coming to a head in the way they did. At meetings in the CO in April the concern was with the way out of the impasse, and particularly with addressing the danger of possible secession by the North (190, 191). It was clear, even before the 'Eight-points motion', that the cleavage between North and South was deepening and the CO fear was that Northern leaders would refuse to attend any future meetings of the House of Representatives, leading to the collapse of the government and the very real possibility of secession. Further, concerns were expressed at what might replace the NPC should the CO fail to act to stabilise the situation; 'NEPU must be taken seriously', warned Williamson, going on to point out how a similarly radical movement in the Gold Coast, Nkrumah's CPP, had been ignored until too late.[88]

At the April meetings and others that ensued in early May, Lyttleton made it clear the constitution would have to be 'radically recast' but that 'dilatory tactics' would need to be followed to prevent any immediate changes before the situation had settled (191, 198). Once it had, he proposed that a conference be held in London to consider the best procedure to take to revise the constitution. He suggested that there was a need for a much looser form of association at the centre, greater regional autonomy and clear assurances to the North that changes would not be made over their heads.

Lyttelton's proposals went to Cabinet and were approved on 13 May (202). Yet events on the ground were removing the initiative from the CO. A planned nation-wide tour by the AG to publicise the AG demand for self-government in 1956 led to proposals for a rally in Kano in May. The proposed rally sparked four days of rioting in the city. Exacerbated on the one hand by suspicions that the Kano NA—egged on by the Sardauna who had visited the city shortly before the riots—was encouraging the violence as revenge for the abuse received in Lagos, and on the other by the fact that the bulk of the police contingents involved in containing the violence were made up of Southerners, the riots became straight-forward ethnic clashes between Hausa and Igbo and left 36 dead and 241 injured.[89] The killings said much about the underlying tensions between stranger and indigene in the North.

The Kano riots did not destroy the Macpherson constitution—they came three days after the Cabinet on 13 May had approved Lyttelton's decision to revise it—but they did lead to a speedier implementation of that decision (201, 204). The riots also led Macpherson—reinforced by appeals from Hopkinson who was still in Nigeria—to demand an early announcement of Lyttelton's decision, contrary to the latter's wish to keep the decision quiet until the dust had settled.[90] On 21 May Lyttelton announced to the House of Commons that the constitution that had taken three years to set up, would have to be recast.

The move to managed decolonisation 1953–1958

Lyttelton's statement was designed to regain the initiative in a process that had been slipping out of CO hands. Yet in the short term the Nigerian reaction to it was any-thing but positive. Lyttelton proposed calling Nigerian leaders to London to consider what mechanism might best be used to consider possible changes to the constitution. Both Awolowo and Azikiwe—who had formed a pact after the defeat of the Enahoro motion—refused to attend on this basis; they would come to London only if the pur-pose was to hold substantive talks on substantive issues. The pace of change in Nigeria was such that by June the CO had conceded that this was inevitable; the talks in London would indeed be substantive and would focus on what changes were necessary to the constitution in the light of Nigeria's present circumstances.

In July delegates from the main parties in Nigeria met in London under Lyttelton's chairmanship to discuss the revision of the constitution (228). Even in itself, the holding of this conference was significant: the 1947 constitution had been drawn up by officials and that of 1951 by a tightly controlled process of consultations that had been shaped throughout by the administration. Now the CO was willing for the first time to pass control over constitutional change to a conference where Nigerian leaders would hold considerable sway and where there would be only limited guarantee of the outcome.

What this decision represented was the recognition that the CO policy that had characterised the late 1940s and early 1950s—of managed reform to pre-empt nationalist demands—had been overtaken by events. Self-government had long been admitted by the CO as the ultimate goal of policy in Nigeria, but it was now clear that that it would occur in the not too distant future. When Macpherson called Awolowo, Azikiwe and the Sardauna to a meeting at Government House in June to discuss their attendance at the conference, he stressed how things had changed and stated unequivocally that 'the clear political objective for Nigeria . . . by Her Majesty's Government . . . was self-government'.[91] A new CO strategy was emerging and this strategy was making explicit its acceptance that self-government in the near future was the goal. The precise date and nature of that self-government remained to be decided, but that it would occur in the near rather than the distant future was now no longer in doubt.

This was in no way a policy of scuttle. The CO recognised in the early 1950s that it still had room for manoeuvre in Nigeria and that 'dilatory tactics' could be used to effect. The CO, initially at least, had plenty of options to play with and was determined, following the decisions of April-May 1953, to spin out the move to independence for as long as possible. The gaining of time remained the key to CO policy after 1953, and remained so until the 1958 conference set a firm date for independence.

The long-term aim of both the CO and the administration throughout this period remained unchanged from earlier years. 'Our objective', wrote Macpherson in March 1953, 'is to keep united Nigeria in the Commonwealth of its own volition. This is good for Britain and good for Nigeria' (182).[92] However it was now recognised that two new emphases were necessary to achieve this end. One was to acknowledge that since self-government had become a much more immediate objective of policy, ministerial responsibility at the centre, and at the regional level too, would have to be conceded. The AG and NCNC pact ensured that, whatever the CO felt, this would be a major issue at the forthcoming talks.

The second emphasis in CO policy after 1953 was the stress on the need for greater regional autonomy if the unity of Nigeria was to be maintained. As Williamson wrote to Sharwood-Smith in April 1953, in a statement that firmly reflected his own position as a supporter of greater autonomy,

'We firmly believe that unity is in the best interests of all regions of Nigeria, but we recognise that the only solution for present difficulties and probably the only hope eventually of achieving and preserving that unity, lies in some modified and looser form of association at the Centre at this stage.'[93]

Not least, it was hoped, this looser association would deflate demands for immediate self-government.

These two issues—of ministerial responsibility and of greater regional autonomy—were to dominate CO thinking as it prepared for the July 1953 London conference. While the CO was willing to concede these, self-government in 1956 was to be resisted.[94] Yet clearly both AG and NCNC delegations at the conference would press for this, which raised a dilemma for the CO. The CO was determined not to lose the initiative in Nigeria through being forced into negatively resisting demands for self-government. Yet the gaining of time, no matter how little, was seen as essential if the other element of CO strategy after 1953 was to succeed, namely the need to reassure the North in order to maintain Nigerian unity.

The North loomed large in the CO's thinking in this period. However the CO attitude to the North remained equivocal. On the one hand the CO was determined to push for a greater pace of reform in the local government structure in the North, given the abuses that had characterised the NA system in the region. On the other, the CO was responsive to pressure from the administration in the North to respond to Northern fears of Southern domination. The CO clearly shared Northern scepticism about imminent self-government. Yet the CO was also alive to the demands of the AG and the NCNC for faster progress and was aware that some concession would be necessary if the conference was not to collapse in acrimony.

The CO believed that to maintain Nigerian unity it needed to reassure the North that its interests would be protected. Behind this lay several factors that coloured CO views of the North. For one thing there was a recognition that the North represented more than half the population of Nigeria and held half the seats in the House of Representatives; this was a powerful argument in favour of the North, though the counter argument, that the North was not monolithic and that the NA caste of chiefs and emirs in the NPC did not represent those Northerners in the Middle Belt or for that matter in the NEPU, was only rarely heard in the corridors of the CO. But there were other factors at work too. On a personal level, British officials undoubtedly found the NPC leadership more agreeable than the politicians from the South. There is a palpable sense of personal dislike in responses to Azikiwe in the CO files of this period coupled with an equally palpable sense of unease (coupled with respect) at how formidable an opponent Awolowo was. References to Northern leaders—particularly Tafawa Balewa—were characterised by much warmer feelings.[95]

The 1953 crisis, while pushing the CO towards a recognition that AG and NCNC demands for constitutional progress would have to be met, was followed by a CO determination to reassure Northern leaders concerning the future direction of British policy. This could be seen in Macpherson's insistence to Lyttelton in May 1953 that HMG 'should not leave Northern leaders in doubt about their determination to fulfil their obligations to the 17 million people of Northern Nigeria' (201). At a Cabinet meeting that month, Lyttelton stressed that the constitutional revision 'provided an opportunity of according a larger measure of autonomy to the 14 million Moslem inhabitants of the Northern provinces who were more favourably disposed to this country than the Southern Nigerians' (202). At a subsequent Cabinet he added that 'we cannot let the North down. They are more than half the population, more attached to the British and more trustful of the Colonial Service than the others too' (234). These attitudes, reinforced by the Kano Riots and by Sharwood-Smith's warnings of the dangers of further ethnic clashes in the North, meant that the CO, for all the desire of officials to push for reform of local government, pulled its punches in its dealings with the *ancien regime* in the North.

This however, merely reinforced Northern leaders in their determination to resist radical local government reform and rapid moves to self-government.

This was not simply a crude policy to ensure Britain's friends inherited the mantle of rule in independent Nigeria. That may well have been the outcome of the policy the CO followed, but the starting point was different. The unity of Nigeria was the key, as Macpherson had stressed in March. This was made explicit with Lyttelton's statement to the House of Commons in February 1954 that 'I cannot repeat too often that HMG firmly believe that it is in the interests of the peoples of Nigeria that the unity of the country be preserved'.[96] A united Nigeria would, it was expected, be a major player in African politics and thereby a vehicle, it was hoped, for maintaining British interests more broadly in an independent Africa. British policy, as it was accepted that self-government was approaching, was determined to create a Nigeria that would be a powerful force in Africa and this required a united Nigeria rather than a balkanised one. In this the Kano riots and the subsequent 'Eight-points motion' were pivotal, for they raised the spectre of secession, either before or after independence. The consequence of this was that the British were therefore keen to encourage Northern influence in Nigeria, not because this would delay independence, but because this was seen as a necessity if the secession of the North was to be avoided. The problem however, was that in placating the North's fears that self-government was imminent, the British were exacerbating Southern fears that it was not, and thereby making division of the country more likely. In turn, this encouraged the South to make greater demands for progress to independence, demands that thereby fuelled Northern fears that the South was out to obtain self-government before the North was ready.

These issues became apparent once the London conference began in July 1953. The CO was willing to concede Nigerian leaders' demands for greater regional autonomy; this had been agreed within the CO before the Nigerian delegates arrived and was seen as the essential minimum required to keep Nigeria together. It was agreed that Nigeria would become a formal federation with all residual powers allocated to the regions. Further, a commissioner, Sir Louis Chick, would be appointed to examine the financial implications of this and a follow-up conference in Lagos would consider the details. The demand for self-government in 1956, however, was less palatable to the CO and time was taken in advance to consider a formula that would satisfy both Northern concerns and Southern aspirations. Macpherson stressed that the demand had to be resisted come what may. He emphasised, as the conference started, that it must be made clear 'that HMG will not bring any pressure to bear on the North to accept any self-government in Nigeria . . . before the North wish it to'; in effect a Northern veto over Nigeria's independence (225). Yet the delegates from the Southern parties were determined for an explicit statement of British intentions to withdraw, if not in 1956 then certainly as soon as possible thereafter. The AG and NCNC pact held firm on this, even though the AG briefly walked out of the conference in protest at the decision of the secretary of state to excise Lagos from the Western Region as a Federal territory and over the issue of the re-appointment to the Council of Ministers of the four (western) ministers who had resigned in March. Bridging the North-South gap was going to be difficult, and to try to do so, Lyttelton made a statement promising that internal self-government would be granted to any region that demanded it in 1956, while standing firm against setting any date for self-government for Nigeria as a whole. In agreeing for the first time to make a commitment for regional self-government, Lyttelton was acknowledging that self-government more broadly was the objective of British policy, that there was a timetable for this, and that Nigeria was well down the road to it.

The 1953 London conference agreed the outlines of what popularly came to be known as the 'Lyttelton constitution'. Lyttelton agreed to the removal of *ex-officio* ministers in the regions (except in the North), full regional ministerial responsibility with regional premiers, elections to the House of Representatives (rather than appointment by the regional Houses of Assembly), and the calling of a further conference in 1956 to review the constitution. In addition, the possibility of the Southern Cameroons separating from the Eastern Region as a quasi-federal territory with its own Assembly, should the Eastern elections in late 1953 confirm this, was accepted. Shortly after the London conference ended, the CO also agreed to the principle of ministerial responsibility at the centre (239).

The resumed conference in Lagos in January 1954 considered the details of these decisions. Consideration was given to the financial, judicial and public service implications of regionalisation. The Chick Report, which stressed the principle of financial derivation (ie the regions that contributed the most would receive the most), was accepted and the public service divided into four (ie three regional services plus a federal service).[97] Perhaps most significantly the issue of secession was addressed. The AG had urged that such a right should be included in the constitution. The NCNC, in light of its sentiments for Nigerian unity, took a stand against this and was strongly supported by Lyttelton, a decision that confirmed the collapse of the AG-NCNC pact.[98]

The new constitution came into operation in October 1954, with the creation of regional governments under Awolowo, Azikiwe and the Sardauna as premiers and with each of the three main parties controlling a region. The results of the elections to the House of Representatives that followed in late 1954 were however, something of a surprise, both to Nigerian leaders and to the CO. The NPC as expected won the North, and the NCNC the East but what was not expected, was the NCNC victory in the West where the party capitalised on dissatisfaction with AG tax policies and separatist aspirations in the Benin and Delta areas; in addition local leaders of the NCNC like Adegoke Adelabu played skilfully on intra-Yoruba rivalries to win seats in areas like Ibadan and Oyo (276). The fact that the NCNC had won in two regions meant that while the NPC was the largest party in the House, the NCNC was entitled—since posts were allocated on a regional basis—to six ministerial posts, to the NPC's three and the AG's none, making the NCNC the dominant party of the government, a possibility that had apparently never occurred to the draftsmen of the CO.

This raised all sorts of difficulties for the CO. The alienation of the AG—who still formed the regional government in the West—was clearly dangerous, but more worrying for the CO was the triumph of the NCNC with its radical rhetoric and its commitment to reverse much of the regionalism of recent years. Not only would this undo many of the measures the CO saw as vital to hold Nigeria together, but there was the danger of the likely reaction to this by the conservatives of the NPC, particularly if the NCNC pressed for early self-government.

The CO feared that the NPC would react to the NCNC victory by, at the very least, boycotting the Council of Ministers and at worst, by moving towards an AG alliance.

The possibility of an AG-NPC axis—the two parties who had flirted with secessionist ideas—raised great concern. A clandestine meeting of the Sardauna with Awolowo and Akintola on November 20—monitored by Special Branch—appeared to raise such possibilities (276). In the House of Representatives Tafawa Balewa threatened such an alliance and to vote down all government business in response to NCNC domination of the ministerial council. For a moment the prospects for the new constitution, if not for the future of Nigeria, looked difficult and the constitution designed to move Nigeria on from the crisis of 1953 had plunged her back to the days of the 'Eight-points motion'. H R E Browne, the acting governor of the North, met NPC leaders and urged them to accept the election results (279). Lennox-Boyd, the new secretary of state, similarly urged officials to reassure the NPC leadership. He reaffirmed Lyttelton's statement that 'HMG would not let the North down . . . there would . . . be no question of HMG granting self-government at the Centre so long as the North wanted the Federal government to remain dependent'. He urged officials to counter any secessionist tendencies 'at this critical juncture' (277). Only in January 1955, two months after the elections, did Balewa inform Macpherson of the NPC's willingness to accept the results and co-operate in making the government work. A coalition government of six NCNC ministers and three from the NPC (plus one from Southern Cameroons) was set up. Yet this willingness to co-operate in government masked a deeper alarm within the NPC at the NCNC success; Sharwood-Smith noted the 'increasing tendency of many [Northern] ministers . . . to indulge in anti-Southern diatribes'.[99]

The 1954 elections gave major impetus to regional consolidation of party political power. The dilemma for the two Southern parties in particular was that the more they stressed ethnic solidarity in order to consolidate their power in a particular region, the less able they were to appeal more broadly across the federation as a whole, making them less able to challenge for national power. This dilemma in turn stimulated attempts by the parties to expand into regions other than their 'own' through the use of promises to break up the existing regions and create smaller regions for minorities, thereby reinforcing the ethnic characteristics of Nigerian politics. The CO was keen to avoid regional fragmentation, even though it was its own constitutional provisions that had generated these pressures. As a CO *Appreciation* in early 1955 noted, 'a main aim of UK policy for Nigeria in the immediate future is therefore to prevent further fragmentation of the territory and to preserve the unity of the Regions within the federation against possible moves to secede' (289). The origins of this problem went back before 1954 and had an earlier precedent with the excision of Lagos from the West. After the NCNC electoral victory in the West, fresh impetus was given to demands to create new regions out of existing ones. 1953 saw the emergence of the Benin Delta People's Party, encouraged by the NCNC, seeking to create a Mid-West Region out of the West. This was a non-Yoruba area, and supported the NCNC in the 1954 Federal elections. The AG tried to get round this threat by themselves sponsoring a motion in the House of Assembly in June 1955 to create a Mid-West, the aim being thereby to cut away NCNC-supporting areas from the West and guarantee an AG majority in the House. Concurrently, AG support encouraged demands for a COR (Calabar-Ogoja-Rivers) Region out of non-Igbo areas of the NCNC-dominated East.

Related to this was the separation of the Southern Cameroons from the Eastern Region in this period. As noted above, it had been agreed at the 1953 London conference that the Eastern Region elections at the end of that year would be treated in the Southern Cameroons as a referendum on secession from the region. The elections had been a victory for Dr Emmanuel Endeley's KNC, which won all the seats on a platform of separation, with the result that in late 1954 the Southern Cameroons became a quasi-federal territory with its own Assembly and Executive Council.[100]

The reverse of attempts to encourage fragmentation were moves to consolidate power within a region. This was particularly the case in the West. Throughout the years between its formation in 1951 and its victory in the 1956 elections in the West the critical factor for the AG was the NCNC threat in the region, a threat whose potency had been proved in 1954. Thus throughout this period the AG drove hard at consolidating its control of the West and in doing so articulated a particularly acute form of ethnic, more specifically Yoruba, nationalism. At times the AG flirted with secession, though in practice the AG accepted federalism as the future for Nigeria. It was a party of the economically and educationally-rising elites in Yorubaland, committed to business enterprise and capitalism, though with a strong welfarist wing, and elements in the CO saw the party as representing the more able administrators within Nigeria. Awolowo, the AG leader, was respected by the CO, though seen as 'intolerant of opposition' and deeply suspicious both of the British and Azikiwe; the leadership of the AG generally was described by Williamson in 1955 as 'able and hardworking'.[101] To the CO Awolowo was a formidable opponent whose legal training made him a difficult figure to finesse at the constitutional conferences of these years.

The AG responded to the NCNC threat to its position in the West in two ways. Firstly, it attempted to push for co-operation with the NPC during 1953 and again, following the breakdown of its pact with the NCNC, in 1954. The formation of the NCNC-NPC government in 1955 broke these moves. These were coupled with attempts to break into the East in 1954, through the use of the COR Region issue. Equally it attempted to push into the North, undertaking a major drive into the Middle Belt for the 1959 Federal elections, when it won 25 seats.

AG attempts to expand outside the West were always going to be of limited success. Its second approach was to consolidate its power within the West. In particular it determined on asserting its control over the NA chiefs in the region, given the influence these figures held both within local administration and over ordinary Yorubas. This was coupled with proposals to increase party influence over the Nigerian Police Force contingents in the region. Political Intelligence reports stressed the AG campaign on this issue: 'continuous pressure is being brought to bear to gain regional control of the forces of law and order', not least through building up the NA forces.[102] Complaints that most of the NPF forces in the region were Igbo, not Yoruba, were followed by moves during 1955 to demand the regionalisation of the NPF and to expand the NA police, moves that, admitted governor John Rankine, were causing some concern (285). As the local government reforms came into effect, the DO was progressively pushed to one side and the party began to assert its authority over the NA court system (278). Further, the removal of the NCNC-sympathising Alaafin of Oyo in 1954 had clear implications for other traditional rulers in the region; so too did the Nicholson Report on the administration of Ibadan in 1955 (271).[103] This was followed by continuing press attacks on expatriate civil servants and AG demands for political control over the Public Service Commission in order to control appointments to the public service.

This attempt to remove their opponents in the West came to fruition with the resignation of the Western NCNC leader Adegoke Adelabu as a federal minister in 1956, shortly followed by his death in a motor accident. This policy was interwoven with a stress on the party's nationalist credentials, as seen in the motion for self-government in the West, moved by Awolowo in the House of Assembly in December 1955. When House of Assembly elections were held in the West in May 1956, the AG won 48 seats to the NCNC's 32, reversing the NCNC's federal victory two years earlier.[104] The AG consolidation of power in the West had succeeded.

In the North too, these were years when the NPC consolidated its hold over the region. The prime issue was 'fragmentation', and whether the North would remain a monolith—under NPC control—and thereby able to dominate the central institutions of the federation as it had done since the acceptance of Northern parity in the House of Representatives in 1950, or whether the Middle Belt would be separated from the region. The Middle Zone League had, with various other organisations, merged into the United Middle Belt Congress by 1955, and the new party received much support from both the AG and the NCNC in its demands for the Middle Belt to be excised from the North. The two southern parties' aim to split the North in order to reduce its power in the House of Representatives was resisted by the CO. This resistance required however, as Sharwood-Smith argued forcefully, local government reform in the North, in order to devolve power to local communities and thereby to undermine support for a Middle Belt state.[105] Thus fresh impetus was given to demands for the reform of local government in the North, reform that the traditional rulers in the North continued to view with deep scepticism.

In early 1957 the Hudson Report on local government in the North appeared (384). It recommended the creation of an intermediate level of administration between the region and the NA at the local government level, through the establishment of provincial administrations, a proposal that owed much to Sharwood-Smith's earlier ideas.[106] These middle-tier administrations would include a provincial council that would have law-making and revenue raising powers; this would address, it was believed, the unrest of Middle Belt areas concerning their inclusion in the North and thereby avoid secessionist demands. However, the danger for the existing NAs was that the administrations envisaged by Hudson would take over powers currently held by the NAs with a corresponding reduction in the resources and offices available at that level. Although provincialisation was endorsed at the subsequent constitutional conference, once the threat of fragmentation of the North was removed with the decisions of the Willink Commission of 1957–1958 (see below), the Hudson scheme was progressively watered down. The bill for provincial councils passed by the Northern Assembly in 1959 owed little to Hudson's original proposals and the provincial councils it established were little more than advisory bodies.

It was in the Eastern Region that this process of regional consolidation after 1954 posed the greatest threat to the CO determination to maintain Nigerian unity. The East was of critical importance to the CO, because in its view, Azikiwe remained the most dangerous Nigerian leader. He was not to be trusted, felt the CO, and his policies represented a sharp challenge both to British interests in Nigeria and to the managed decolonisation process more specifically. He was 'an exceptionally skilful politician . . . but completely unprincipled and ruthless', noted Williamson.[107] While the

CO welcomed the fact that the NCNC was anti-communist, it feared the radical policies it pursued and was concerned at apparent NCNC attempts to politicise the public service. Not least, from the CO's point of view, the policies that Azikiwe introduced in the East raised the stakes more generally and forced other Nigerian leaders, especially Awolowo, to respond in turn—or see the AG hold on the West fall to the NCNC—while generating great fears among Northern leaders, with serious ramifications for the future unity of Nigeria.

In early 1955 the Assembly passed a budget that, by removing expatriation pay for several senior posts, effectively 'Nigerianised' the upper echelons of the Eastern public service; only by using his reserved powers could governor Clement Pleass reinstate the allowances. The impact on the morale of expatriate officers in the East, already concerned at the regionalisation of the public service, was significant, with CO fears that some sixty per cent of expatriate staff would resign by 1956, leading to, it believed, administrative breakdown (296). The clash over allowances in 1955 was only the start of a much deeper crisis in the Eastern Region that, despite the brief hiatus of the Royal Tour in early 1956, consumed CO energies for much of 1955–1957.

The significance of this crisis was that it was the last occasion upon which the CO seriously contemplated halting the progress to Nigerian self-government. The background lay both in the ambitions of Azikiwe, who was determined to assert the NCNC's nationalist credentials, and in the breakdown in relations between the governor and the regional government that went back to Pleass's support for the 'sit-tight' ministers in 1953, together with his use of his reserved powers to get that year's budget approved. Allegations of corruption against ministers during 1955 further poisoned relations, even without the new budget crisis of that year. Spending by the government on development projects—viewed as long overdue by the NCNC and its supporters—was seen as deliberately designed to spend reserves so compensation for expatriate staff when they retired would not be available (298). An NCNC-sponsored motion of no-confidence in the governor was tabled in the House in the middle of 1955 although deferred *sine die*. Thereafter Azikiwe simply continued government by ignoring Pleass's existence.

By May 1955 the 'Eastern Question' had become the major issue facing the CO in Nigeria. Officials began warning of 'chaos in the East' and talk began of the possible need to suspend the constitution in the region and to rescind the promise of regional self-government in 1956. Williamson wrote to Pleass suggesting that it might be best to allow the breakdown to happen sooner rather than later, so that it occurred while Britain was still responsible for the region and could thus suspend the promise of regional self-government and impose direct rule; 'we should like you to think this over very carefully' (294, 298).

Supported by Robertson (who replaced Macpherson as governor-general in June 1955), Pleass argued against suspension (301). He stressed that Azikiwe was too astute to allow chaos to occur before self-government and that if the CO chose to suspend the Eastern constitution it would simply allow the premier to pose as a martyr. Extensive debate in the CO continued and concluded that although there was no immediate case for suspending the constitution or the promise of regional self-government, contingency plans should be drawn up (307). In late July, Sir Thomas Lloyd wrote to Pleass outlining that Lennox-Boyd was 'prepared . . . to consider . . . the possibility of withdrawing or suspending the promise of Regional self-government in 1956 from the East', if Pleass and Robertson should so advise. There were wider considerations here, he argued, for a breakdown in the East 'would . . . bring serious discredit on British colonial policy as a whole' (308). In the meantime, Robertson and the three regional governors were called to the CO in October 1955 to discuss the crisis.

If a suspension was to occur, military preparations would be necessary. These began. One CO official stressed the need to involve British troops 'as a precaution and a stiffener.' Major-General G. H. Inglis, GOC Nigeria, reported on military planning in September (318). His view was that military force could indeed successfully crush any disorder but he stressed that the CO would have to consider the political fallout from using British troops in Eastern Nigeria. His warnings had a sobering effect and officials began to back-track. The refusal of Pleass to support suspension proved decisive and at the October meetings in the CO alternative ways forward were searched for.

However, if the promise of regional self-government could not be suspended there were few other possibilities open to the CO, as the October meetings with Robertson and the governors established. The decision was taken to call Azikiwe to the CO for what was called a private 'talking to' by Lennox-Boyd on 10 November (320). While the CO stressed it was not trying to slight him, none the less the message was clear. At the meeting Lennox-Boyd criticised Azikiwe's financial and economic policies, stated that the attacks on expatriate staff were unjustified, suggested that the Eastern government was heading for disaster and made pointed criticism of the party corruption and nepotism he saw in the region, before urging Azikiwe to mend his ways (332).

This headmasterly 'talking to' (to an elected minister of the Crown) is an astonishing episode but it is striking how, as a substitute for the suspension of the constitution and the introduction of British troops, it reflected the narrowing options left to the CO by 1955. However a way out of the impasse seemed to open as it became clear that the NCNC might do the CO's work for it. In early 1956 the African Continental Bank (ACB) affair blew up in the East and in the fallout from this it looked possible that Azikiwe would have to resign (355).

The origins of the affair lay in the appointment by the Eastern government in late 1955 of a commission of inquiry under a barrister, Chuba Ikpeazu, to examine allegations of corruption in public life (331). The commission soon became bogged down in claim and counter-claim, but its significance was that it opened up the issue of corruption in the East to wider debate. One of the figures most ferociously attacked both before the commission and in the Assembly was E O Eyo, government chief whip and chairman of the Eastern Region Development Corporation. Early the following year Eyo struck back.[108]

In April and May 1956 Eyo made public allegations that Azikiwe had abused his position as premier by arranging the transfer of £2 million from the Eastern Region Marketing Board to the Eastern Finance Corporation; the Corporation then invested a large part of this in the ACB by buying up a significant proportion of ACB shares. However the major shareholders in the ACB were Azikiwe and his family and the bank had been in financial difficulties and unable to meet its commitments under the 1952 Banking Ordinance, under which it required a certain proportion of its reserves to be liquid; in 1953 it had been refused a banking licence for this reason.

The CO had been aware of these developments long before Eyo made them public;

its belief was that the ACB was being geared up to finance an assault on the AG position in the West to consolidate the NCNC electoral victory of 1954 (317). Once again issues of regional consolidation were central to Nigerian political developments. The allegations were serious and given Azikiwe's refusal to respond to Lennox-Boyd's invitation to appoint an Eastern Region commission of inquiry, in July 1956 the secretary of state announced to the Commons the setting up of his own, eventually to be headed by Sir Stafford Foster-Sutton, to examine Eyo's claims.[109] In addition he announced that the proposed constitutional conference to examine regional self-government which was planned for 1956 would be delayed pending the outcome; regional self-government would thus be delayed too. Azikiwe struck back, attacking both Lennox-Boyd and the expatriate banking monopoly in Nigeria and pointing out how the transaction met NCNC policy to bypass the power of British banks in the region. This attack he repeated when the Foster-Sutton Report was published in January 1957 and criticised his conduct with regard to the ACB as falling short 'of the expectations of honest, reasonable people' and found him 'guilty of misconduct as a Minister' in failing to relinquish his financial interest in the ACB when public monies were injected into it.[110] He refused to resign as premier, attacked the report in turn as falling short 'of the expectations of honest, reasonable people' and in the subsequent election the people of the East made their sympathies clear, returning him and the NCNC to power with a large majority. Azikiwe's handling of the affair had shown not just how skilled an operator he was but also just how limited the CO's room for manoeuvre in Nigeria now had become.

Yet this did not mean that the CO had no options left, nor that the survival of Azikiwe meant the end of CO attempts to manage the process of political change in Nigeria. The CO was still determined, even after the Eastern crisis, to delay the date of independence as long as possible. This was not a blind rearguard action. Rather, the CO view was that the longer the decolonisation process could be spun out, the more likely it was that Nigerian unity could be preserved and equally, the more likely the links and structures could be put in place to ensure a Nigeria sympathetic to British interests once independence was achieved. The dilemma for the CO in this, however, was that the best way of ensuring Nigerian sympathies for British interests was by granting independence as quickly as possible.

The balancing act pursued by the CO in this period in order to maintain Nigerian unity, thus also required moves to reassure the East and West that their interests were being acknowledged and that self-government was not being delayed unduly. During the early months of 1957 these issues took on an increased importance, not least because of the pressures generated by the Gold Coast's gaining of independence on 6 March 1957. This made it clear that independence for Nigeria could not be far away and that the momentum of constitutional change had to be maintained if, at the very least, goodwill was to be preserved and political unrest avoided.

When Harold Macmillan arrived in Downing Street in January 1957 he called for a 'cost-benefit analysis' of colonial territories in the light of the granting of self-government.[111] The resulting 'Skeleton Plan' for Nigeria was completed in March and showed the influence of Sir John Macpherson, the new permanent under-secretary at the CO (386). While recognising the growing pressures for independence, it was full of forebodings at the rapid pace of constitutional change in the territory and the possibilities of administrative breakdown; it blamed—as Macpherson had done five years earlier—the Watson Commission which it was argued, had cost Britain 15–20 years in Nigeria. None the less when the Plan considered British interests in Nigeria, these were not seen as a barrier to independence. Britain's economic interests in the country were not under threat. 'It seems to me', noted Eastwood, 'that the economic effects of independence on the U.K. are likely to be pretty small'.[112] More important were Britain's strategic interests, and in particular the use of Port Harcourt harbour and Kano airport, and related over-flying rights, but these too did not represent a barrier to self-government.

Ghana's independence in March could hardly be ignored in Nigeria. It was the stimulus for a motion moved in the House of Representatives later that month by Samuel Akintola, the AG leader of the opposition, for independence for Nigeria in 1957 (subsequently amended to 1959). The Akintola motion—like the Enahoro motion four years earlier—was a surprise to the CO (388, 390). As officials realised, Nigerian leaders were attempting to force the CO into a corner. 'No more important papers have come forward about Nigeria since the crisis in the spring of 1953' noted Williamson on reports on the motion (390). More of a shock to the CO was the fact that the motion—in contrast to Enahoro's—was carried unanimously in the House with even Tafawa Balewa and the NPC representatives supporting it; the Sardauna claimed, somewhat disingenuously, to be equally surprised at this.[113]

The Akintola motion meant that the forthcoming May 1957 conference—delayed since 1956 because of the Eastern crisis—would have to address the issue of setting a date for independence. Robertson outlined the dilemma for the British government when he wrote of the choice 'either to give independence too soon and risk a complete breakdown of administration, or to hang on too long, risk ill-feeling and perhaps disturbance, and eventually to leave bitterness behind' (390). Articulating the CO reaction to Akintola's motion, Williamson argued that Nigeria still needed 'a generation or so' before it would be ready for independence, but that 1960 was probably the latest it could be put off to; 'it is not worthwhile risking the forfeiture of Nigeria's goodwill . . . for the sake of hanging on for . . . a further three or four years' (392). Lennox-Boyd was more sanguine and took the view that Britain could hold on for a little longer, arguing that 1959 as a date had to be resisted and that delaying tactics could succeed in putting it off (393). His view was reinforced by Sharwood-Smith who also believed that independence could be delayed to 1961, 'spanners to be provided by participants' (400).

The question came to the Cabinet Colonial Policy Committee in May in the run-up to the London conference (399, 402). Lennox-Boyd proposed making a statement at the conference to the effect that, if the various Nigerian governments were to agree to ask in 1959 for independence, the government would agree to consult with them over this, leaving the actual date undecided. Lord Home, the secretary of state for Commonwealth Relations, demurred on the grounds that other Commonwealth countries objected to the precipitate grant of independence to African territories and that 1959 was too early; he proposed a five year trial period for regional self-government after which (ie in 1962) independence could be reviewed by a commission. The lord chancellor, Viscount Kilmuir, was asked to resolve the differences. He drew up a declaration that stated that HMG would consider the Nigerian demand for a date for independence after the life of the present House of Representatives came to an end in 1959, but which left the exact date of independence open. This compromise was accepted, though reluctantly by the CRO (404). Yet events at the conference were to push the government much further than it had envisaged.

The May 1957 conference began with the submission of a memorandum from the three regional premiers, plus the leader of government business in the Southern Cameroons, asking for independence in 1959—a blank cheque, as Lennox-Boyd termed it, that he refused to sign. Lennox-Boyd stood behind the decision not to agree to a date until the present House of Representatives reached its term in 1959. 'It was received', noted Lennox-Boyd of his reply, 'in stony but not unfriendly silence' (407). After conferring with Home he elaborated that the government would sympathetically consider the request during 1960, should the House of Representatives to be elected in late 1959 agree a resolution asking for independence, but he refused to set a specific date.

Although no date was conceded at the conference, CO options were being narrowed down. This raised the issue of safeguards for the North (400). Tafawa Balewa had contacted Sharwood-Smith to express concern about this before the conference. As Sharwood-Smith recognised, the key was to avoid fragmentation of the North; an undivided North was one that would be the major player in an independent Nigeria. The government must therefore stand firm, in his view, against demands for a Middle Belt region. The decisions of the conference avoided this by establishing three commissions to deal with issues relating to federal-regional relations. One (which came to be led by Sir Jeremy Raisman) was to consider revenue allocation, another (under Lord Merthyr) the delimitation of the 320 constituencies it had been agreed the House would have, and a third (under Sir Henry Willink) to consider the position of minorities.

Other significant decisions were also taken at the conference. It was agreed—as per the undertakings made by Lyttelton in 1953—to grant regional self-government to the East and West in 1957 and consideration was given to self-government for the North in 1959. The Southern Cameroons would become a full region with its own premier. Given the moves to regional self-government, there was considerable debate over central-regional powers, particularly concerning control of the police, which it was agreed should remain in federal control. It was agreed too, to create an upper House or Senate at the centre, and, perhaps most significantly, to agree to establish the office of prime minister (409). In September, Tafawa Balewa was appointed as the leader of a national unity government involving members of all three main parties (410).

Tafawa Balewa was respected by the CO and clearly liked by Robertson. He was regarded as the most able administrator in the government and his appointment as prime minister was warmly welcomed by officials. The problem however was that his weight within the NPC was a good deal less than the CO would have wished. In particular the administration was aware that the key figure within the NPC remained the Sardauna, the premier of the Northern region. The CO was concerned at the Sardauna's attitude to Tafawa Balewa who was described by the former as 'my prime minister'; he 'will do what he is told' he said.[114] The Sardauna's ability to influence the government from afar was seen by some in the CO as malign. Williamson noted that the Sardauna was 'able' but that his 'intransigence' towards the South had dangerous implications for the future.[115]

Tafawa Balewa's popularity in the CO was because he was seen as moderate and the very opposite of a radical demagogue. Thus it was something of a shock for the CO when the issue of the date of independence resurfaced at Balewa's insistence during the early months of 1958. In May 1958 he made it clear that he hoped Nigeria could gain its independence on 2 April 1960, a prospect the CO did not welcome, not least because of the likely impact of this on other territories in Africa; 'all this worries us a good deal', wrote Macpherson (422, 427). Ralph Grey, the deputy governor-general, met Tafawa Balewa in June to try to persuade him to drop the date, but noted that 'the real power to determine the pace of events has in fact passed from us to the local people' (430). As the proposed constitutional conference which was to consider the reports of the three commissions, to be held in London in September 1958, drew nearer, the issue of the date of independence became more acute. Grey attempted to soft-pedal the issue with Nigerian leaders (430), but it was clearly going to be the critical issue at the conference. In August 1958 a motion in the House of Representatives moved by R A Fani-Kayode of the AG urged 2 April 1960 as the date of independence (436).

By end of August, Robertson wrote to the CO proposing acceptance at the forthcoming conference of a date sometime in 1960 (442).[116] Even the CRO had by now reluctantly come round to acceptance of this. By September Burke Trend, the deputy secretary of the Cabinet, 1956–1959, was writing to Macmillan that the government had no choice but to accept independence in 1960, and should take steps accordingly to ensure British interests were guaranteed (444). The date was considered at a Cabinet meeting in early September 1958, with Lennox-Boyd, in the face of further unease from the CRO about the CO handling of the transition to independence, expressing his determination not to be held to a specific date in 1960; but implicit in this was an acceptance that it would occur that year (437).

The London conference which began in September 1958 was the last of the three major constitutional conferences that characterised the Nigerian story. Its main purposes were to consider the reports of the commissions established in 1957 and to resolve the date of independence. The key commissions were those of Merthyr and Willink, both of which had implications for the proposed regional self-government for the North in 1959. The Merthyr Commission recommended that the North should have 174 out of 320 seats—slightly more than a majority—in the House of Representatives and this was approved (419). Willink recommended various safeguards for minorities including written guarantees for minority rights, but came down against the creation of new regions (441). This was not popular with all Nigerian leaders. The NPC welcomed Willink's recommendations, as did the NCNC and the CO itself. The AG however, opposed the Willink conclusions; the AG were determined, at the very least, to break the North into two and argued strongly for conference support for this.[117] In the event the Willink recommendations were approved, on the basis that the reform of local government in the North—provincialisation—as proposed by Hudson would proceed; further, CO insistence that the creation of any new regions would delay independence, persuaded the AG to drop its demands (456). At a Cabinet meeting held during the conference on 22 October 1958, agreement was finally reached that independence could be granted for autumn 1960 (461). Three days after the Cabinet, Lennox-Boyd addressed the conference and announced his agreement to a date of 1 October 1960.

Shaping independence 1958–1960
The agreement at the London conference over the date of independence meant that the final contentious issue at stake between the British government and Nigerian leaders had been settled. The remaining two years of British rule were taken up with

undramatic and largely technical negotiations over the terms and conditions under which Nigeria would gain independence. This was not of minor importance, however. CO—and increasingly now CRO—policy in these years was clear; it was determined to ensure that the Nigeria that gained its independence in October 1960 did so as a country firmly in the western camp. A CO memorandum in early 1959 outlined British objectives in the run-up to independence. These were:

'to make the best arrangements to secure U.K. interests in Nigeria after independence, these interests being primarily to help Nigeria to maintain a satisfactory unity under the system of Parliamentary Government that has been adopted, to preserve U.K. economic and financial interests and to gain maximum support for U.K. and general Western policies'.[118]

The years 1958–60 were therefore characterised by the efforts of the CO to achieve these ends through formalising the economic, technical, military and diplomatic links that were seen as central to these 'best arrangements'.

At the heart of this was the 'Special List B' scheme for expatriate officials that came into operation in October 1958. This scheme was the culmination of a lengthy period of consideration of the public service in Nigeria that went back to the late 1940s; to understand its significance one needs to consider both CO attitudes to the public service in Nigeria and the genesis of the 1958 proposals. The future of the Colonial Service in Nigeria was of overriding importance to the CO and was so for a number of reasons. There was a strong sense of responsibility within the CO towards British officials serving in Nigeria, many of whom had only recently begun their careers. Further, threats to their position generally, or to their pay and conditions specifically, appeared to raise the spectre of a mass exodus of staff with all that that would imply for British rule, not to mention the knock-on effect on other territories in the empire. Moreover, the CO believed that the continuation in Nigeria of large numbers of expatriate staff up to independence and after, would both ensure administrative stability in the immediate future and maintain British influence in the territory thereafter. Governor Rankine stressed to the CO the importance of avoiding an exodus:

'it is to our advantage . . . that Nigeria should be prosperous and stable, should become one of the pillars of the Commonwealth and not the equivalent of a third-rate South American republic, an easy victim for communism'.[119]

However, the employment of expatriate staff had come under repeated attack from Nigerian leaders, as being unduly expensive and an affront when many equally qualified Nigerians found it difficult to gain employment in the Colonial Service. From the Foot Commission onwards the presumption had been that expatriates would be employed only when a qualified Nigerian was not available, though to Nigerian leaders the progress of Nigerianisation seemed none the less slow. The attacks on expatriate staff by Nigerian leaders during these years raised serious concerns in the CO.[120] If British interests were to be protected in Nigeria and an exodus avoided, mechanisms to guarantee the conditions of expatriate staff—and their independence from party political control—needed to be put in place.

Such concerns stimulated Lyttelton to prompt Nigerian leaders to issue a statement at the Lagos conference in January 1954 stressing their recognition of the need to employ expatriate staff and their determination to respect public servants' political neutrality (260, 263). They led also to the appointment of the Gorsuch Commission in July 1954 to review the structure of the service in Nigeria following regionalisation, and pay and conditions more broadly, a review which led to significant increases in salary levels and allowances. Further, proposals were brought forward to set up a lump-sum compensation scheme, funded by Nigerian governments, for staff who chose to retire once regional self-government had begun, in the hope that such guarantees would avoid a precipitate departure of expatriate staff. The scheme was strongly criticised by Nigerian leaders who objected to having, as they saw it, to buy their freedom by paying-off expatriate staff. Perhaps the most significant move to address this problem came in June 1954 with the creation of Her Majesty's Overseas Civil Service. Under this scheme staff would transfer from local territorial control to HMOCS and be employed centrally by the secretary of state, thereby guaranteeing the officer's employment.[121]

Yet HMOCS was only a partial solution to the problems in Nigeria. Fears of an exodus from Nigeria, particularly from the East, were reinforced by the division of the civil service into four separate services following regionalisation in October 1954 and concerns about growing party political interference. The Eastern crisis of 1955 had a particularly damaging impact on expatriate morale, not least when the regional Assembly voted to abolish expatriate allowances for some posts. By 1956 Lennox-Boyd noted, 'I am continually receiving the most disquieting evidence of the appalling deterioration of morale in the oversea service, especially in Nigeria' and clearly further measures were necessary.[122] From this emerged the idea in 1956 of a 'Special List' for expatriate staff in territories like Nigeria whereby officers would receive guarantees of their pay and future employment. This scheme was approved at the 1957 conference, though it remained to be considered by the various governments of Nigeria.

Although these several measures did much to reassure expatriates and maintain both numbers and morale at least in the short term, in the longer term, as independence approached, expatriate staff continued to depart from Nigeria, and few applied for Special List status. It was these concerns that led the CO to send Sir John Martin, deputy permanent under-secretary of state, to Nigeria in early 1958 (418). Martin estimated that up to a quarter of all expatriate staff were on the point of leaving and warned of the danger of administrative breakdown. He proposed the establishment of a 'Special List B' to which expatriate staff could transfer and have their allowances guaranteed, with the British government guaranteeing the payment of the lump sum compensation which staff could take if choosing early retirement, or alternatively could 'freeze' if not. Lennox-Boyd echoed Martin's concerns. 'There is in the Colonial field no matter of greater urgency or importance' than the future of the Colonial Service, he stressed, 'the main problem is in Nigeria' (418). The scheme came into operation in October 1958 and did achieve what had been intended, namely avoiding a mass exodus of expatriate staff. In June 1960, there were 1,749 expatriates, of whom some 800 were on pensionable terms, still serving in the federal service in Nigeria, (with others employed in the regional services, particularly in the North), and the CO estimated that some 600 of these would stay on after October (542).

Retaining a cadre of British officers in Nigeria up to and beyond independence was a major aim of the CO after 1958. Financial and economic aid was another. Appeals from the Nigerian government for economic assistance in 1957 had caused great difficulties, given Britain's own economic problems in this period and officials were aware of the dangerous long-term implications of having to refuse such requests (413). During the early months of 1959 this issue again came under close scrutiny in the CO. There were international dimensions to this. American officials stressed to the British the need to settle financial terms with Nigeria well in advance of independence; American fears were that in the event of Britain failing to make adequate provision for Nigeria the USA would be called on to fill the gap (477). British concerns however, were the reverse, that if the USA stepped in, valuable influence in Nigeria would be lost to Washington. Negotiations in London in 1959, between Lord Perth, minister of state for colonial affairs, and Chief Okotie-Eboh, the Nigerian finance minister, took place against a background of CO unease at allegations of corruption concerning the latter (481). A further problem came from the Treasury's refusal to grant more than a £10 million Commonwealth Assistance loan to Nigeria, an offer that fell well below the £25 million Okotie-Eboh was looking for. Both the CO and the CRO attached great importance to increasing the Treasury's offer, the CRO stressing the need to keep 'Nigeria, as the biggest country in free Africa, on the side of the West' (483). Such was the importance of the issue that the CO, in order to persuade the Treasury to raise its offer to £12 million, proposed a £3 million Exchequer Loan, to bring the total assistance until 1962 up to £15 million, this sum being finally agreed at a meeting between Perth and Okotie-Eboh at the end of July 1959 (485).

Negotiations concerning financial aid were accompanied by consideration of a technical assistance scheme, to provide equipment, training and the supply of technical experts to serve in Nigeria after independence. This issue was coloured by concerns over USA involvement (540). Proposals concerning technical assistance were considered at meetings Lennox-Boyd held during his visit to Lagos in May 1959 and a draft proposal, worth nearly £1 million, agreed between officials of the two countries in May 1960.[123]

The most controversial of the issues the British government addressed in this period was that of defence. Consideration of Britain's defence interests in the light of Nigerian independence had occurred at length in the 'Skeleton Plan' in early 1957. This consideration was further stimulated by Nigeria's assumption of control over its defence forces in April 1958, the end of a process of devolving control over the Nigerian army going back to the West African Forces conference in 1953.[124] The Chiefs of Staff reviewed Britain's defence interests in Africa in 1958 and concluded that Britain required over-flying and staging rights in Nigeria, in order to reinforce British forces elsewhere in Africa and in the Indian Ocean; this, it was believed, would require the use of Kano airport and would necessitate the signing of some sort of defence agreement, an issue the CO took up thereafter (423). As the September 1958 London conference approached, Duncan Sandys, the minister of defence, proposed that such an agreement should allow Britain to retain an enclave in Nigeria after independence; this latter idea both the CO and Robertson balked at. None the less at a meeting between Lennox-Boyd and Sandys, it was agreed that an outline defence agreement would be presented to Nigerian leaders for approval during the conference—but before the date of independence should be agreed, in effect implying that agreement on the latter was conditional on the former. The meeting with Nigerian leaders took place on 24 October and an outline document was initialled by Tafawa Balewa, Awolowo, Azikiwe and the Sardauna—though the exact details were not published (463). The outline made no mention of an enclave such as Sandys had originally proposed but did allow Britain to lease land and facilities at Kano, gave over-flying and staging rights, plus the use of Lagos and Port Harcourt harbours, in the event of war; in return Britain would provide military training and assistance, including equipment.

Further impetus in drawing up a formal agreement came in January 1960 when Macmillan, during his tour of Africa made famous by his 'wind of change' speech in Cape Town, met Tafawa Balewa in Lagos (502). At a meeting on 12 January Tafawa Balewa raised broader concerns about the defence of Nigeria, given French withdrawal from Nigeria's neighbours, concerns that Macmillan forwarded to the Chiefs of Staff. In their subsequent report the COS identified the Cameroons as the most likely defence threat to Nigeria's future. This gave the British government the chance to subsume the original agreement within the broader needs of Nigerian defence. Once a detailed agreement had been drawn up in March 1960, Macmillan forwarded it to Tafawa Balewa for consideration (514).

However, the political climate had changed in Nigeria—not least because of French atomic tests in the Sahara—and it was now clear that a pact would be deeply unpopular. By April the CRO was advising of the benefits of delaying the signing of any such pact until after independence in order to avoid charges of having pressurised the Nigerian government to sign. In any case, Nigerian ministers rejected the idea of a lease while expressing their willingness to provide facilities for over-flying and naval use as required; at the May 1960 conference it was agreed that there would be no lease (523, 527). Instead there would be a pact that simply covered mutual co-operation and assistance, plus over-flying and staging rights; it was also agreed that the pact would be approved by the Nigerian Parliament *after* independence. In return, proposals for paying the training costs of Nigerian officers in Britain were drawn up and approved by the Treasury (533). In September the revised proposals were agreed by the Council of Ministers and the following month approved by the Nigerian parliament. In the event these efforts were in vain; such was the public opposition, articulated in particular by Awolowo, that in early 1962 the pact was abrogated.

A further area that the British government attempted to shape as Nigeria approached independence was its future foreign policy. Central to this was Nigeria's membership of the Commonwealth. This however raised the question of South Africa, which was increasingly alienated from a Commonwealth that was taking on, in the form of Malaya and Ghana, a growing Afro-Asian block. From late 1958 the possible South African reaction to Nigerian membership was giving cause for concern in the CO (466). The South African problem was inverted following the Sharpeville shootings in March 1960, which led to considerable protest in Nigeria and which, it was feared, would have a knock-on effect concerning Nigeria's foreign policy position more generally.

Behind this lay concerns that Nigeria might align herself with perceived Soviet interests in Africa after independence. The CO and the CRO lost no opportunity in these years to stress to Nigerian leaders how inimical to Nigeria's interests—as they saw it—Soviet ambitions were (480, 486). Early in 1959 a CRO memorandum on Nigerian foreign policy after independence was presented to Tafawa Balewa—in response to the latter's request—stressing the dangers of Soviet expansionism in Africa. This was followed in mid-1959 with a CRO memorandum to advise Nigerian staff in London about dealing with Soviet approaches. When early in 1960 Tafawa Balewa made a request to the British government for the supply of foreign policy intelligence after independence, this was quickly addressed; by July the CRO had arranged for the future high commissioner in Lagos to pass on relevant intelligence material (509).[125]

The hope was, noted the CRO, that Nigeria would be 'relatively moderate in international affairs and generally friendly to the West, in particular to the U.K.'.[126] None the less, by early 1960 Robertson was warning of a growing tide of neutralism in Nigeria (520). Tafawa Balewa caused alarm when he gave a major speech in August of that year stressing non-alignment as the key to Nigeria's future foreign policy. The CRO and CO were relatively sanguine however. The CRO took the view that 'Nigeria will take a formal anti-colonial stand. They cannot afford not to. Sir James Robertson [said] that he advised Sir Abubakar that he would do better in some of his public speeches to talk about Nigeria's imminent liberation from the Colonial "heel"'.[127] The CO too believed that such statements on neutralism did not threaten British interests and were necessary if Nigeria's stand was to have any credibility. E C Burr, a principal in the CO, recognised that

'if Nigeria is to retain influence among African states after independence it will have to behave like an African state and not like some Western appendage. This may from time to time result in their acting contrary to our interests but I think we will just have to accept that'.[128]

More specifically, the CO welcomed signs of Tafawa Balewa's growing suspicions of Ghana's ambitions. He rejected proposals for a West African Union put forward by Nkrumah in March 1959 and remained suspicious of Nkrumah's alleged ambitions to break up Nigeria (474).[129] The CO saw Nigeria as a useful counterweight to Ghana in West Africa, given the latters' radical rhetoric at the UNO.

Influencing the public service, aid, defence and foreign policy were all clearly important for the CO in the run-up to independence, but the critical issue concerned the political arena. None of these schemes would mean anything if the Nigerian government elected on the eve of independence was hostile to Britain. Precisely who would form the government that led Nigeria to independence was therefore the single, central concern for the CO in these years. As noted above, when the office of prime minister had been created in 1957, Tafawa Balewa had formed a national unity government composed of members of all three of the main parties. However two related developments began, in time, to threaten the unity of this government. One was the drawing away from the others by the AG, which had ambitions of its own to form a government, albeit in coalition with other parties. This required the AG to strengthen its influence in other regions in opposition to the NCNC and NPC. The other, related, development was a growing rapprochement between the NPC and the NCNC that became apparent during 1958 (433) and particularly following Azikiwe's meeting with the Sardauna in June. Underlying this were two further factors, the first of which was the NPC's concern that it would not win an outright majority in the House of Representatives' elections scheduled to be held at the end of 1959 which would elect the independence government. The second was the realisation within the NCNC of its weakening appeal outside the East and the challenge to Azikiwe's position as leader with the emergence of the NCNC Reform Committee in 1958 under K O Mbadiwe, federal minister of commerce and industry and former leader of the NCNC group in the House of Representatives. By late 1958 the Reform Committee had become the Democratic Party of Nigeria and the Cameroons under Mbadiwe, with an ostensible commitment to socialist-leaning policies.

Throughout these years the CO took the view that an NPC-led government for an independent Nigeria was in the best interests of Britain. At root, the concern was that if the NPC were excluded from government, this would prompt separatist tendencies; the meetings Northern leaders held with representatives from Chad in 1960 (531), although only an insurance in case of tension with the South after independence, showed that the secessionist option had not been dropped.[130] As the 1959 elections approached, the CO expressed the greatest unease about the possibility of an NCNC government led by Azikiwe, or even an NCNC place in a coalition. Eastwood commented, 'I am not sure all this augurs very well for Nigeria after independence', but recognised there was little the CO could do to prevent it if it occurred.[131] Clearly, given the electoral realities of Nigeria, the NCNC could only form a government in coalition, but the fear was that in any such a coalition, Azikiwe would become foreign minister, with all that would imply for Nigeria's position at the UNO or more generally. When this idea was mooted in mid-1958, Smith noted that 'this is most depressing' and his concerns were reiterated by others (433, 500).

The federal elections of December 1959 to determine who would rule Nigeria in the first few years of independence were therefore critical.[132] In the event the NPC did not gain an overall majority of seats, and, after negotiations, formed a coalition government with the NCNC under Tafawa Balewa as prime minister; the Democratic Party's challenge to Azikiwe came to nothing. Balewa's appointment was welcomed by the CO—'our very good friend' was how Macleod described him shortly after—as was the fact that Azikiwe was kept out of the Foreign Ministry; Robertson had briefed Balewa on this repeatedly (523). None the less Azikiwe received the largely ceremonial post of president of the Senate and it was clear that he would become governor-general after independence (499).

The results of the elections were as good as the CO could hope for. The creation of the new government was followed, as had been agreed at the 1958 conference, by a formal resolution in the new House in January 1960 asking for independence. This the British government accepted. There followed two further conferences, one in London in May and one in Lagos in July, to settle the technical and legal details of independence and the process moved rapidly to its conclusion on Lagos racecourse on 30 September–1 October in the presence of Princess Alexandria. At midnight, following the usual ceremonies and an exuberant mock battle display—an empire ending not with a whimper but a bang—the Union flag was lowered and Nigeria gained its independence.[133]

The lowering of the Union flag on 1 October was not however, the end of the story. There remained British administration in the Cameroons (471). As independence for Nigeria approached, serious issues concerning the future status of the Cameroons remained to be resolved, as the UNO Visiting Mission in late 1958 recognised. In 1958 the Southern Cameroons had gained full regional status within the federation; the Northern Cameroons remained an integral part of the Northern region. The North seemed willing to continue this but the situation in the Southern Cameroons was more complex. The KNC under Endeley, who had been appointed premier of the territory in 1958, supported continued integration with Nigeria as a separate region after independence. John Foncha, the leader of the KNDP, however, exploited local distrust of Nigerians and particularly the large numbers of Igbo merchants in the territory, and campaigned instead for union with the French Cameroons, which gained its independence as the Republic of Cameroun in January 1960. His campaign, it became clear, had considerable support.

For the CO the danger was the possibility of sentiment developing for the Southern Cameroons to go it alone as a separate state. Given its parlous economic viability, this raised the threat of British financial obligations continuing indefinitely into the future.[134] In any case a terrorist campaign in Cameroun in this period necessitated the continuing and costly presence of British troops along the border. Further, as Perth pointed out, if the South opted for independence this might have a knock-on effect on the Northern Cameroons; this possibility, he stated, would cause problems for Northern Nigeria and 'would really I think upset our relationship with Nigeria as a whole and for a long time to come, and that is something which we must at all costs avoid. The Southern Cameroons and its inhabitants are undoubtedly expendable in relation to this'.[135]

Continued association with Nigeria by both Northern and Southern Cameroons would have suited the CO best, with merger with Cameroun preferable to either separate independence or continued British rule. The result of the Southern elections at the start of 1959 that saw Endeley defeated by the KNDP on a platform opposing integration with Nigeria, thus caused concern for the CO when Foncha almost immediately started to blow cold on prospects for union with Cameroun. As was recognised by all however, the critical decisions would have to be made by the UNO. In March 1959 the UN decided on plebiscites in the two parts of the Cameroons concerning their future; in the North to be held in November 1959, and in the South before April 1960 (471). When the plebiscite in the Northern Cameroons was held in November, much to observers' surprise, the electorate, far from voting as expected for integration with Northern Nigeria, voted to delay a decision; this caused alarm in the CO. In the light of this outcome, the UNO decided to separate the Northern and Southern Cameroons from Nigeria in October 1960 and to undertake plebiscites in both parts before 31 March 1961. These plebiscites, held in February 1961, were unequivocal. The North voted for integration with Northern Nigeria while the South voted for union with Cameroun. On 1 June 1961, the Northern Cameroons joined Northern Nigeria. Four months later, on 1 October 1961, and a full year after withdrawal from Nigeria itself, the British withdrew from Southern Cameroons.

Political withdrawal from Nigeria and the Cameroons was of course but part of the story. Yet it was an important part. What is striking to the observer of this process is the emphasis both sides put on the symbols of political rule and the relatively restrained conflict between Britain and Nigeria that accompanied this. 'Our general relations with Nigeria have gone very amicably in recent years', noted Macleod with satisfaction once Nigeria gained its independence.[136] That, at least, was the view from London. The view from Lagos, as it would have been throughout these years, would have been different.

* * * *

Contrary to its image, academic research is rarely, if ever, a solitary effort and the present piece of work is no exception. In particular I owe an immense debt of gratitude to the BDEEP series general editor, Stephen Ashton, for his unfailing support and encouragement; without these, it hardly needs to be said, this volume would never have been completed. In addition, I am grateful to Shaun Milton, BDEEP research assistant for Kenya and Nigeria, who carried out basic background work on issues such as defence, the Commonwealth and the economy early in the undertaking. Thanks are also due to Richard Rathbone, editor of the Ghana volume in the BDEEP series, for his encouragement, particularly at the start of the process when the size of the task seemed, to me at least, overwhelming. I am also grateful to John Smith, who served in Nigeria, and who shared with me his extensive knowledge of this period and of the personalities involved in it. David Killingray and Tony Kirk-Greene helped out on a number of matters of factual detail, while Peter Blair generously shared his extensive knowledge of British politicians of the 1950s; I am grateful to all three. Maura Pringle provided her usual excellent cartographic input. The staff of the Public Record Office were a great help throughout; in particular Mandy Banton, to whom I owe immense thanks. Several libraries provided assistance above and beyond the call of duty; it may be invidious to pick out only a couple, but the service received from the library staff of the Institute of Commonwealth Studies, London and of Queen's University, Belfast deserves special praise. I am grateful too, to Queen's University for the study leave that helped complete this volume and to Janice Jardine, Heather Kinning, Catherine Reid and Gloria Rickard for their secretarial assistance. Ken Barnes, James Bourn, Anthony McClellan and Charles Swaisland answered detailed questions on their time in the Colonial Service; their help is gratefully acknowledged. A major debt of gratitude is also owed to Roger and Clare Goldby, Harriet and Peter Hall, Andrew and Linda Hutchinson, and Mary Johnston, who so readily, repeatedly and uncomplainingly provided the accommodation in London without which this volume simply could not have been completed. I am deeply grateful to them. Finally, I wish to record my thanks for the support and encouragement I received throughout this research from Mary and John Lynn.

M Lynn

Notes to Introduction

1 Strictly speaking only Lagos was a colony; Northern and Southern Nigeria were both protectorates.

2 Cameroons has been used in this volume as the spelling of the territory before independence; Cameroun is used to refer to the independent republic after 1960.

3 It should be added that not all files requested were released and that in some cases, individual documents within released files continued to be retained.

4 Williamson at times went to considerable lengths to ensure that Nigerian leaders were not aware the CO received copies of material relating to the Council of Ministers, CO 554/258 minute by Williamson, 27 July 1953.

5 DO 35/10457, minute by Allen, 23 July 1958. Similar tensions were apparent in the Gold Coast case, BDEEP series B, vol 1, R Rathbone, ed, *Ghana* (London, 1992) part II, 233.

6 Britain's apparent indifference to the possible growth of militant Islam was a French concern in this period; in contrast the CO believed the French administration was unduly unconcerned at the spread of communism, CO 554/744, no 10, brief for Anglo-French ministerial discussions, May 1953.

7 CO 537/4726, no 30, Harding to Gorsuch, 29 June 1949.

8   BDEEP series C, Anne Thurston, ed, *Sources for colonial studies in the Public Record Office, vol II, records of the Cabinet, Foreign Office, Treasury and other records* (London, 1998) pp 15–260.

9   Macpherson was ill during parts of this period and more responsibility was thus devolved onto Foot.

10   This is outlined in Joan Wheare, *The Nigerian Legislative Council* (London, 1950) pp 29–42.

11   There were also fiercely fought elections to the Lagos Town Council which was established in 1917.

12   Obafemi Awolowo, *Path to Nigerian freedom* (London, 1947) p 47.

13   Igbo is the current spelling, but during the period covered by this volume, Ibo was usually used.

14   The best guide to the ideas behind indirect rule remains Margery Perham, *Lugard: the years of authority 1898–1945* (London, 1960) pp 138–173.

15   BDEEP series A, vol 2, R Hyam, ed, *The Labour government and the end of empire 1945–1951* (London, 1992) part I, 44.

16   BDEEP Series A, vol 1, S R Ashton and S E Stockwell, ed, *Imperial policy and colonial practice, 1925–1945*, part I (London, 1996) 49.

17   CO 583/286/5, minute by Pedler, 29 Sept 1944.

18   N Azikiwe, *My odyssey: an autobiography* (London, 1970). Not to be forgotten in this process was the role of the West African Students Union in London as a meeting place where ideas concerning the future of West Africa circulated.

19   B Bourdillon, *Further Memorandum on the Future Political Development of Nigeria* (Lagos, 1942) p 8.

20   Lord Hailey, *An African survey* (London, 1938); Lord Hailey, *Native administration and political development in British tropical Africa, 1940–1942* (CO, 1944).

21   Ashton and Stockwell, part II, 100–103.

22   *Report of the Commission of Inquiry on the Marketing of West African Cocoa* (Cmd 5845, 1938).

23   B Bourdillon, *Despatch of 5 April 1939 on the Social and Economic Development of Nigeria* (Lagos, 1939); *Minute on Apportionment of Revenue and Duties as between the Central Government and Native Administrations* (Lagos, 1939); *Memorandum on the Future Political Development of Nigeria* (Lagos, 1939).

24   Rathbone, part I, 1–8.

25   CO 554/133/3, no 1, 'The Atlantic Charter and British West Africa'. Strictly speaking this memorandum was from the press delegation as a whole, though Azikiwe drew it up and not all the members were prepared to sign it.

26   CO 554/133/3, minute by A Cohen, 21 Sept 1943.

27   CO 583/261/30453, no 13, Bourdillon to Gater, 5 Sept 1943, enclosing 'Outline proposals for constitutional reforms in Nigeria'

28   Sir Adeyemo Alakija and Justice S B Rhodes were the first Nigerians appointed to the Executive Council, shortly followed by G H Avezathe and the Emir of Katsina.

29   Bourdillon *Further Memorandum*.

30   *Report of the Commission on Higher Education in the Colonies* (the Asquith commission) Cmd 6647, 1945; *Report of the Commission on Higher Education in West Africa* (the Elliott Commission) Cmd 6655, 1945.

31   CO 583/271/4, no 14, CO summary of Nigeria preliminary development plan, 20 Oct 1944.

32   Ashton and Stockwell, part II, 70.

33   *ibid*, part II, 71.

34   CO 554/132/20, no 13, Grantham to Dawe, 11 Oct 1943.

35   A further meeting with Richards was held on 22 Nov.

36   One of Richards's very earliest meetings following his arrival in Nigeria was with the Sultan of Sokoto, whom he clearly regarded as a critical figure for the acceptance of his plans.

37   The constitution was originally to be reviewed after nine years.

38   Published as Cmd 6599.

39   Sessional Paper no 24, of 1945.

40   K Mellanby, *The birth of Nigeria's university* (London, 1958).

41   'The primary producers are ... the very backbone of our social and economic structure', CO 852/509/15, no 21, 'Economic policy in the West African colonies', memorandum by Lord Swinton, 24 Feb 1943.

42   Hyam, part IV, 348.

43   Discontent concerning wartime inflation had led governor Bourdillon to award a cost of living allowance in July 1942.

44   The commission of inquiry under W Tudor Davies reported in 1946 and recommended a substantial increase in the cost of living allowance, *Enquiry into the Cost of Living and the Control of the Cost of Living in the Colony and Protectorate of Nigeria* Col No 204 (London, 1946).

45   Beresford Stooke, in a comment symptomatic of a widespread attitude in the administration at this time, compared Azikiwe to Hitler (see document 35).

46   CO 583/275/9, no 125, Richards to Hall, 21 Nov 1945.

47   T Clarke, *A right honourable gentleman: Abubakar from the Black Rock* (London, 1991) p 99.

48   CO 583/287/4, no 5, Macpherson to Creech Jones, 19 June 1948.

49   CO 967/117, Creech Jones to Richards, 22 Apr 1947.

50   'You ... have put through the most important constitutional development so far attempted in British Africa', CO 967/117, Creech Jones to Richards, 22 Apr 1947.

51   Rathbone, part I, 21–67. Concerns were expressed in London at the possibility of the Accra riots sparking off similar developments in Nigeria but such did not materialise.

52   'One striking feature that emerged ... was that [the AG] had devoted considerable time and study to the Gold Coast Constitution and were determined, as far as they were able to do so, to obtain as much power, and on the financial plane, as much money, as their opposite numbers in the Gold Coast', CO 554/290, no 8, Shankland to Benson, 28 Dec 1951.

53   CO 537/5801, no 4, Macpherson to Creech Jones,7 Feb 1950.

54   Enahoro was editor, and Agwuna assistant editor, of the *Daily Comet*. Agwuna's lecture was more a call for civil disobedience than violence.

55   CO 537/4630, no 6A, Macpherson to Creech Jones, 26 Sept 1949.

56   The belief of the administration was that Soviet finance was reaching trade unions in Nigeria from Prague and being lodged in Azikiwe's African Continental Bank, Lagos, CO 537/6782, no 3, Macpherson to Griffiths, 18 Jan 1951.

57   The administration's concern about possible Soviet influence in this period can be seen in the reaction to Azikwe's proposal to attend a conference in Prague in 1949, CO 537/4630, no 2, Macpherson to Creech Jones, 12 Aug 1949.

58   CO 537/2787, no 1, circular despatch by Creech Jones to all colonies, 5 Aug 1948.

59   CO 537/4626, no 1, Macpherson to Creech Jones, 17 Nov 1949.

60   H Foot, *A start in freedom* (London, 1964) pp 103–104.

61   *Report of the Commission appointed to make Recommendations about the Recruitment and Training of Nigerians for Senior Posts in the Government Service of Nigeria* (Lagos, 1948).

62   E J Gibbons, *African Local Government Reform: Kenya, Uganda and Eastern Nigeria* (Lagos, 1949)

63 K P Maddocks and D A Pott, *Report on Local Government in the Northern Provinces* (Kaduna, 1951).

64 CO 554/235, no 1, Macpherson to Williams, 6 Sept 1951.

65 *Report of the Commission of Enquiry into the Disorders in the Eastern Provinces of Nigeria, Nov 1949* Col No 256 (London, 1950).

66 The two Northern delegates concerned were the Emirs of Kano and Zaria. The population of the three regions had been determined by the 1952–1953 census as 17 million in the North, 8 million in the East and 6½ million in the West.

67 The NPC emerged out of several groupings that had been in existence in the north of Nigeria during and after the war. These included the Bauchi General Improvement Union established in 1943 by Sa'ad Zungur, later a member of the NCNC, and the Northern Elements Progressive Association established in Kano by Raji Abdallah, later a prominent figure in the Zikists.

68 CO 537/5786, no 26, Marshall to Griffiths, 10 May 1950.

69 This can be said to go back to Lugard, but one of the arch exponents of it was Sir Theodore Adams, chief commissioner of the Northern provinces, 1936–1943.

70 CO 583/306/5, no 10, Williamson to Macpherson, 3 Aug 1951.

71 The Nigeria (Constitution) Order-in-Council (1951).

72 Ezera makes the point that more correctly it should be termed the 'Foot' constitution, K Ezera, *Constitutional developments in Nigeria* (London, 1960) p 126.

73 J Smith, *Colonial cadet in Nigeria* (Durham, NC, 1968) p 6.

74 The two Lagos seats were eventually taken by Adedoyin and Olorun-Nimbe.

75 Rathbone, part I, 116.

76 These were ministries for transport, mines and power, commerce and industries and natural resources.

77 O. Awolowo, *Awo: the autobiography of chief Obafemi Awolowo* (London, 1960) p 239.

78 Macpherson ruled in Aug 1952 against any change in the Ilorin boundary, CO 554/679, no 9, Macpherson to Lyttelton, 26 Aug 1952.

79 CO 554/366, minute by Williamson, 10 Sept 1952.

80 The three ministers were O Arikpo, R A Njoku and A C Nwapa; the fourth Eastern minister, who did not resign, was Dr Endeley who represented the Southern Cameroons.

81 Awolowo, *Awo*, 238.

82 A Enahoro, *Fugitive offender: the story of a political prisoner* (London, 1965) pp 119–132.

83 The three ministers, in addition to the Ooni, were S L Akintola, Arthur Prest and Bode Thomas.

84 A Bello, *My Life* (London, 1962) pp 114–128.

85 Railway employees being largely southerners at this time.

86 Arguably these moves must have been encouraged by officials in Northern Nigeria. J N Paden, *Ahmadu Bello, Sardauna of Sokoto* (London, 1986) p 222 states that even as late as 1956 Sharwood-Smith was prepared to facilitate secession for the North.

87 'If constitutional methods fail to bring us self-government we reserve the right to adopt other methods … The Mau Mau, with all its terror, with all its horror, … may still be the way out of Nigeria's bondage', *Daily Service*, 16 Apr 1953; 'Nigeria is not without her own Mau Mau. Indeed when Nigeria's Mau Mau is let loose it may dwarf the activities of its Kenya counterpart', *Daily Service*, 21 Apr 1953.

88 CO 554/260, no 90, minute by Williamson, 5 May 1953.

89 *Report on the Kano Disturbances, 16–19 May 1953* (Kaduna, 1953).

90 CO 554/261, Hopkinson to Lyttelton, 16 May 1953.

91   CO 554/262, no 222, 'Note on a meeting held at Government house ... 19 June 1953', enclosure in Goble to Gorrell Barnes, 26 June 1953.

92   The consistency of British ambitions for Nigeria can be seen by comparing this with Creech Jones's statement in 1948 that ' politically, our long term aim must be to secure that when the African territories attain self-government they do so as part of the Western world', T 220/117, no 3, memorandum by Creech Jones, Jan 1949.

93   CO 554/236, no 46A, Williamson to Sharwood-Smith, 18 Apr 1953.

94   CO 554/261, no 163C, 'Notes on changes to be made in the present Nigerian constitution', memorandum by Huijsman, 22 May 1953.

95   Though such feelings did not extend to all Northern leaders, such as the Sardauna, CO 554/840, no 86, 'Basic brief on Nigeria for Sir James Robertson', 14 April 1955.

96   *H of C Debates*, vol 523, 10 Feb 1954, col 1183.

97   *Report of the Fiscal Commissioner on the Financial Effects of the Proposed New Constitutional Arrangements* (Cmd 9026, 1953.

98   The AG-NCNC pact had come under increasing strain towards the end of 1953 and had effectively already broken down .

99   CO 554/1161, no 1, Sharwood-Smith to Lennox-Boyd, 14 Feb 1955.

100   But not, as yet, a premier.

101   CO 554/840, no 86, 'Basic brief on Nigeria for Sir James Robertson', 14 Apr 1955. In contrast Sharwood-Smith saw Awolowo as 'an aspirant Nigerian Nkrumah', CO 554/1583, no 22E, Sharwood-Smith to Robertson, 30 Mar 1957.

102   CO 554/1030, no 11, Extract from Western Region PIN, Jan 1955.

103   E W J Nicholson, *Report of the Commission of Inquiry into the Administration of Ibadan District Council* (Abingdon, 1956).

104   These Assembly elections were called at Awolowo's request.

105   Hence his so-called 'Twelve Pillars Policy', CO 554/1078, no 11, Sharwood-Smith to Lennox-Boyd, 18 May 1955.

106   *Commission Appointed to Advise the Government on Devolution of Powers to Provinces: Report by the Commissioner Mr R S Hudson* (Kaduna, 1957); CO 554/1078, no 22, Sharwood-Smith to Eastwood, 23 Aug 1955.

107   CO 554/840, no 86, 'Basic brief on Nigeria for Sir James Robertson', 14 April 1955.

108   This story can be followed in *Report of the Tribunal Appointed to Inquire into Allegations Reflecting on the Official Conduct of the Premier of ... the Eastern Region of Nigeria* Cmnd 51 (London, 1957).

109   *H of C Debates*, vol 557, 24 July 1956, cols 215–221.

110   *Report of the Tribunal Appointed to Inquire into Allegations Reflecting on the Official Conduct of the Premier of ... the Eastern Region of Nigeria* p 42.

111   CO 554/1533, no 1, minute by Macmillan, 28 Jan 1957.

112   CO 554/1533, no 5, minute by Eastwood, 14 Mar 1953.

113   Sharwood-Smith claimed that two NPC leaders, Tafawa Balewa and Makama Bida, in response to the Akintola motion, stated to him their continuing belief that 'early Federal Self-Government on existing lines would mean the extinction of Northern aspirations', CO 554/1583, no 22E, Sharwood-Smith to Robertson, 30 March 1957.

114   CO 554/338, no 25, Niven to Williamson, 23 Sept 1953; CO 554/2129, no 119, Eastwood to Grey, 21 July 1958.

115   CO 554/840, no 86, 'Basic brief on Nigeria for Sir James Robertson', 14 Apr 1955.

116 Though it blamed the CO for this, 'the milk being spilt', DO 177/84, minute by Allen, 8 Aug 1958.

117 CO 554/1842, no 26, Mooring to Lennox-Boyd, 31 July 1958.

118 CO 554/1537, no 15, 'Future of the posts of the governor-general and regional governors and the deputies,' CO memo, 1959.

119 CO 554/1842, no 5, Rankine to Lennox-Boyd, 4 Jan 1958.

120 CO 554/604, minute by Williamson, 7 July 1953.

121 BDEEP series A, vol 3, D Goldsworthy, ed *The conservative government and the end of empire 1951–1957* (London, 1994) part II, 219–226.

122 *ibid*, part II, 237.

123 DO 35/8807, no 35B, 'Technical assistance: notes of a meeting held at the CRO on Tuesday 17 May 1960'.

124 Rathbone, part II, 129.

125 DO 35/10489, minute by Greenhill, 4 July 1960. Implicit in this was that the intelligence would involve Ghana.

126 DO 35/10488, minute by Belcher, 26 Feb 1960.

127 DO 35/10499, minute by Hunt, 1 July 1960.

128 CO 554/2479, minute by Burr, 4 May 1960.

129 Nigerian suspicions of Ghana, which had a long history, were greatly exacerbated by the Ghanaian expulsion of Nigerians in 1958.

130 CO 554/2391, no 4, Johnston to Eastwood, 14 July 1960. These meetings involved senior members of the NPC including the Sardauna.

131 CO 554/2129, no 119, Eastwood to Grey, 21 July 1958.

132 The party leaders threw themselves into these campaigns with gusto, Awolowo handing the Western premiership to Akintola and Azikiwe the Eastern to Okpara in late 1959.

133 'Sufficient thunderflashes were exploded to last the British Army of the Rhine for a year', DO 35/10428, no 102, Hunt to Sandys, 27 Oct 1960.

134 The Treasury expressed its concern that if the CO treated the Cameroons with 'your normal generosity' this would prompt demands for continued trusteeship status under the UK, CO 554/2337, no 5, Peck to Eastwood, 7 Jan 1960.

135 CO 554/2412, no 27, minute by Perth, 12 Oct 1960.

136 DO 35/10511, Macleod to Sandys, 3 Nov 1960.

Summary of Documents: Part I

Chapter 1
Constitutional change during the war and the post-war reforms,
June 1943–Apr 1948

Chapter 3
Regaining the initiative: Macpherson and the constitutional review, Dec 1949–Dec 1951

Chapter 4
Operating the new constitution: ministerial responsibilities and the politics of regionalism, Jan 1952–Mar 1953

Chapter 5
The self-government crisis and the decision to revise the constitution, Mar–July 1953

1 CO 583/261/30453, no 7   22 June 1943

[Constitutional revision]: CO note of a meeting with Sir B Bourdillon to discuss the future development of Nigeria

[Considerable discussion concerning the future constitutional development of the West African colonies occurred within the CO during the war years, and particularly during 1943. This debate was stimulated both by officials like Sir Bernard Bourdillon, governor of Nigeria, and Sir Alan Burns, governor of the Gold Coast, and by figures like Lord Hailey and Nnamdi Azikiwe, one of the members of the West African press delegation that was invited to visit Britain that year. As far as Nigeria was concerned, at the heart of this debate were the various memoranda produced immediately before and during the war by Bourdillon; the most important of these being his *Memorandum on the future political development of Nigeria* (Lagos, 1939) and *A further memorandum on the future political development of Nigeria* (Lagos, 1942). The retirement of Bourdillon and the consideration during 1943 of a replacement sharpened this discussion. A key document in focusing these ideas during this period was the memorandum on 'Constitutional development in West Africa' drawn up by O G R Williams in mid-1943 (CO 554/132/20, no 1; printed in BDEEP Series A, S R Ashton and S E Stockwell, ed, *Imperial policy and colonial practice, 1925–1945* part I, (London, 1996), 70), which drew on various sources to propose a broad outline for constitutional change in West Africa in the future. Coinciding with this, Bourdillon was called to a number of meetings at the CO to discuss the future of Nigeria, of which the one outlined in this document was the first. Present were the secretary of state, Oliver Stanley, and the parliamentary under-secretary of state, the Duke of Devonshire, as well as Sir George Gater, Sir Arthur Dawe, O G R Williams, A B Cohen and other officials. Following the meeting Bourdillon produced a further memorandum for CO consideration (CO 583/261/30453, no 13, 'Outline proposals for constitutional reforms in Nigeria', 5 Sept 1943).]

Sir Bernard Bourdillon began by outlining the present social and political background in Nigeria and contrasted conditions in the three main divisions of the Territory. In the Northern Provinces under the autocratic rule of the Emirs with a predominantly Moslem population, there was a strong tradition of implicit and unquestioning obedience which while making for ease in administration, tended to the suppression of true popular feeling. Signs were, however, beginning to appear of the emergence of educated opinion.

In the West well organised traditional administration was also to be found under able and intelligent chiefs, but here the conciliar system prevailed more strongly, and the Chiefs were bound by tradition to consult their established councils on all matters. Here public opinion was much more vocal; the grievances of the people were thus easier to ascertain and deal with and there was not the same danger of their taking deep root as in the North. In the West the Chiefs were admitting educated Africans to their Councils.

In the East political development had hardly advanced beyond the patriarchal stage, and the family council was the largest political unit. There was practically no tribal organisation and there thus existed a large number of very small units, a single comparatively small community having as a Native Authority an unwieldy council on which every family was represented. These Native Authorities were not sufficiently developed to enable them to undertake executive duties and there was in effect direct rule by the District Officer. An encouraging development in this area, however, was the rise of Youth Movements, e.g. the Ibibio Progressive Union, which, while having no official status, were generally accepted as representing the views of the advanced section of the community, and for the most part co-operated very harmoniously with the Native Authorities. Sir Bernard thought that the further development of Native

Authorities in this area might depend very much on youth movements such as this. The Government was trying to encourage the development of small executive committees on which the more intelligent and educated Africans might serve where the Native Authorities themselves were too large and unwieldy.

Having thus outlined the present diverse political conditions in Nigeria, Sir Bernard turned to the consideration some of the problems attending the future development of the Colony as a whole. It was of first importance to avoid the rise of antagonism between the old traditional authorities and the advanced opinion of the rising generation. At present the relations between the educated Africans and the Native Authorities are very satisfactory. The danger of a conflict was naturally greatest in the Northern Provinces, but he had observed within his own experience the beginnings of development in the freedom of speech there. Certainly there was much greater freedom of speech on the councils than seven years ago and in one case an Emir had actually invited an educated African, a schoolteacher, to attend a Council Meeting when the Governor was present and to give his views.

Sir Bernard then commented on the unsatisfactory character of the existing Legislative Council. There was no unofficial representation of the Northern Provinces and he believed that the Emirs' lack of concern at this state of affairs up to the present was due to a failure to appreciate that the Council in any way concerned itself with Northern affairs. He was afraid that this lack of interest might to some extent have been encouraged by Administrative Officers in the North.

Moreover the vast majority of the people of Nigeria, who were peasant producers, were not adequately represented on the Council. He did not believe that the country was ready for any form of numerical franchise, but suggested that representation might be through the Native Authorities, who did, he was convinced, genuinely represent the peasant. For this reason he had made a practice of consulting the Native Authorities concerned before appointing provincial members to the Legislative Council. Sir Bernard said that he proposed to formulate proposals for future constitutional development which he would submit to the Secretary of State.

Turning to economic questions, Sir Bernard pointed out that Nigeria was a predominantly agricultural country and could not hope to develop and maintain its financial position without the growth of secondary industries, e.g. the manufacture of produce containers. He was not, however, concerned merely with the development of new schemes; there was considerable leeway to be made up in the financing of existing services. Labour had in many cases long been underpaid and during the war he had been compelled to make concessions on this account, e.g. the grant of an increase in wages to railway workers in October 1941. He had suggested that assistance might be afforded to Nigeria in the form of an easing of her loan obligation.

A co-ordinated plan for the development of Nigeria was required and this should be drawn up not by an *ad hoc* body but by the ordinary machinery of the Government which was to administer it. The present Secretariat machinery in Lagos, with its bottleneck caused by the passage of all papers to the Governor through the Chief Secretary, was defective, and was not capable of dealing adequately with the plans which were already being submitted by the individual departments, such as the 10 year Education Plan. The Secretary of State emphasised the importance of Nigeria being ready with a comprehensive scheme of post-war development when the time came.

Turning aside briefly to the educational problem, Sir Bernard contrasted the comparative apathy which existed in the Northern Provinces with the great demand for secondary education in the South. He suggested that a rural type of secondary school might be evolved to meet the need of ensuring that the majority of the boys passing out of the schools would return to the land.

Speaking of the general feeling of the people towards the Government, Sir Bernard said that this was very good. Of such discontent as existed 99% was due to economic causes, e.g. differences in rates of pay between European and African appointments and better opportunities for European trading companies. The question of social barriers was not a live issue. The loyalty of the mass of the peasantry was unquestionable; they had a genuine desire to help in the war efforts, and in appreciating the extent of their financial contribution it was necessary to remember that only a very small proportion of the people had a money economy at all. He attributed the general spirit of contentment among the rural population to the policy of indirect rule, under which the people were governed through machinery with which they were thoroughly familiar and which they could understand. He emphasised, however, that when introducing changes in methods of native administration the criterion should not be whether the modification was in accordance with tradition but whether it was acceptable. Thus, when Native Authorities were introduced in the Colony, their constitution was left to the people themselves to devise. The occasional press attacks on the policy of indirect rule were not really directed at the system itself but at the alleged use of the Native Administration by the Central Government as a facade.

Replying to the Secretary of State, Sir Bernard said that there was no 'Nigerian' feeling, but this would grow in time. At present the only occasion on which such feeling could be said to take concrete shape was in the face of any suggestion of fusion between Nigeria and any other West African Colony, on which subject the people of Nigeria had strong feelings.

Sir Bernard then spoke of the tremendous field for the development of social welfare, and in particular mass campaigns against diseases such as yaws, leprosy, venereal disease etc. He instanced the achievements of the anti sleeping sickness work in Zaria. Very large sums of money will be needed and Sir Bernard was anxious that the scope of assistance available under the Colonial Development and Welfare Act should be defined. The Secretary of State pointed out the dilemma with which Nigeria was faced. The need for expanding the social services in Nigeria was well recognised here, but the amount which the United Kingdom taxpayer could be asked to contribute was naturally limited, and it would not be possible to undertake any appreciable extension of departmental activity unless the Government confined itself to the payment of salaries bearing some proportion to the economic position of the people as a whole. He instanced the difference between the standard of living of teachers and of the peasants among whom they worked. The cost of development must be kept down. Only a limited sum would be available for the whole Empire and this must be spread over as wide an area as possible. Sir Bernard suggested that the financing of the development of education might be assisted by the imposition of an education rate.

It was agreed that the various points raised by Sir Bernard should be discussed at a further meeting to be held on 2nd July and that an agenda should be circulated in advance.

2   CO 554/132/20, no 16   19 Nov 1943
[Constitutional revision]: CO record of a meeting with Sir A Richards to discuss Nigerian constitutional development

[Shortly after his appointment as governor in late 1943, Sir Arthur Richards attended two meetings in the CO, on 19 and 22 Nov, to discuss his views on future constitutional change for Nigeria. Present at the meeting on 19 Nov were Stanley and the Duke of Devonshire, as well as Sir George Gater and other officials including Williams and Cohen.]

The *Secretary of State* referred to the proposals put up by Sir Bernard Bourdillon for constitutional development in Nigeria and to the memoranda by Lord Hailey[1] and others on the same subject. These had been seen by Sir Arthur Richards and Colonel Stanley asked Sir Arthur for his views on them.

Sir Arthur Richards said that he had read the memoranda and felt that he could join in the general approval of the proposal to establish Regional Councils. He felt considerable doubt however whether it would be possible immediately to secure unofficial representation from the North on the Central Council, as Lord Hailey and Sir Bernard Bourdillon had suggested. He had not of course the advantage of knowing the country, but *prima facie* his impression was that the Emirs, with their intense loyalty to the Crown, would be suspicious of any proposal which would place them under a Central Council or subject them to criticism by Coast lawyers. A similar situation had arisen in Fiji, where the Chiefs had asked to withdraw from the Council rather than be forced to sit there and listen to Indian politicians violently criticising the actions of Government.

Sir Arthur Richards emphasised that at the present time our authority in the North was derived from the support given to the Government by the Emirs and he said that if we were to take any action which might give the Emirs the impression that their position was being impugned, they might well lose their confidence in the Governor.[2] If they were to be compelled to send representatives to the Central Council, their attitude might be one of disapproval and non-cooperation. Sir Arthur felt that it might be possible gradually to persuade the Emirs into acceptance of a Central Council, but he felt that it would be wrong to go too fast. He thought that it would be necessary for him to tour the Northern Provinces and in personal discussion with the Emirs to put to them the ideas underlying the proposal to establish a Central Council. He might then be able to secure their confidence and to endeavour to convince them that constitutional development on the general lines suggested was in the best interests of the Northern Provinces. This process might take time.

The *Secretary of State* said that he appreciated Sir Arthur's point of view, but he asked whether this would mean that no step forward could be made with regard to the Central Council. The difficulty would then be to hold the position in relation to the Lagos politicians. *Sir Arthur Richards* thought that it would not be essential for

---

[1] W Malcolm Hailey (1st Baron cr 1936); ICS 1895–1934; director, African Research Survey, 1935–1938; member, Permanent Mandates Commission of League of Nations, 1935–1939; head of Economic Mission to Belgian Congo, 1940–1941; chairman, Colonial Research Committee, 1943–1948.

[2] One of Richards's very earliest meetings, following his arrival in Nigeria, was with the Sultan of Sokoto.

the north and south to move forward at the same pace. He did not feel that it should take long for him to work out suggestions for the Eastern and Western Provinces, but he felt that the process must be a slower one in the north.

The *Secretary of State* said that it might be possible to set up a Central Council, leaving a gap for the Northern Territories to fill later when the time was appropriate. The Council could be given an unofficial majority and this would meet the local politicians to some extent. He said that when he was in the Northern Territories he was given to understand that Azikiwe's paper was fairly widely read and he was not sure that the position of the Emirs was quite so sound underneath as it appeared on top.

Sir Arthur Richards said that it might well be that their position was now not so powerful as it had been in the past and it might be well for him in talking privately to the Emirs to put it to them that their own position required consideration and that unless they progressed with the times, they might find their position precarious. He thought that if the Governor travelled and talked to the Emirs privately and secured their confidence they would accept such views from him. He had no doubt that the Governor could, by personal persuasion, obtain their immediate approval for proposals for constitutional reform, such approval would, if forced, probably not be sincere. It would require time, education and persuasive methods, to convince them of the need for progress.

The *Secretary of State* agreed. He was not at all in favour of the appointment of a commission to investigate this matter and felt sure that Sir Arthur Richards was right in thinking that the proper course was to discuss these matters with the Chiefs and others on the spot and then to frame his ideas on what the procedure for making progress should be. He added that he had gained the impression that there was considerable uncertainty among officials in the North as to the Emir's [sic] position.

Sir Arthur Richards said that Sir Theodore Adams[3] had confirmed this in his talks with him and had said that the North were full of vague fears as to the future.

The *Secretary of State* said that his impression was that some officials in the North had begun to feel that the Emirs were a ban to progress, but that the Emirs still enjoyed the full support of the peasant population.

Sir Arthur Richards said that our authority rested on the fact that the Emirs gave the Government their support. If one or two of the older Emirs were enlightened and progressive men, it might be possible to make an advance.

The *Secretary of State* said that unfortunately the older men were not enlightened or progressive. Some of the younger ones were. He said that it was essential to avoid giving the impression that the other regions were being held back because of the difficulty in making progress with regard to the North. Even if the representatives of these regions could be persuaded of the necessity for slower progress in the North, they would not accept this as a reason for delaying their own progress. Moreover, they might well accuse the Government of using the North in order to stall on the question of making progress in the other regions.

Sir Arthur Richards said that, as he had said, he saw no reason why there could not be different rates of progress for the North and the other regions.

---

[3] Chief commissioner, Northern provinces, 1936–1943.

The *Secretary of State* said that a start might be made with Regional Councils with a Central Council for the South, leaving a gap for the North to come in later on.

Sir Arthur Richards said that he thought that the Legislative Council should not be allowed to discuss matters concerned with the affairs of the Northern Provinces. He had the impression that the Legislative Council did not at present deal with Northern affairs.

Mr. Cohen said that this was the constitutional arrangement, but the Legislative Council did in fact, sometimes discuss the matters. Indeed, it was very difficult to avoid them, especially in connection with finance.

The *Secretary of State* referred to the question of granting an unofficial majority and said that Sir Bernard Bourdillon had rather brushed aside this proposal. This was the question about which unofficial opinion was most concerned in the Gold Coast, as it no doubt also was in Nigeria, and it would be most difficult to concede an unofficial majority in the Gold Coast without also doing so in Nigeria. He thought it very unlikely that, with the official vote at its disposal, Government would be outvoted on important questions. In any case the Governor would always be able to certify legislation and he did not himself feel that it would be more difficult for the Governor to do this than to enact legislation by means of an official majority in the face of unanimous opposition on the part of the unofficial members.

Sir Arthur Richards said that he agreed and would not himself object to an unofficial majority. He did, however, entirely disagree with Sir Bernard Bourdillon's view that officials should be allowed to vote as they chose. This would certainly result in chaos.

The *Secretary of State* said that it was desirable that Sir Arthur Richards should keep in close touch with Sir Alan Burns on these matters.[4] It would, he thought, be very difficult to allow the Gold Coast to go ahead in advance of the other West African Territories.

Sir Arthur Richards said that he felt that progress with the North would depend upon the amount of the Governor's influence on the Chiefs. If he could convince them that they were not being handed over to the South and assure them that their position would be adequately safeguarded, and if the pace were not forced, he did not see why the North should not eventually be brought in. He proposed when on tour to talk to the senior Administrative Officers and as many of the junior officers as possible to obtain their views. Once the Government's policy was settled he would make it clear to them what the aims were and he would also make it clear in matters of policy that it was their duty to accept what had been decided and act upon it, even though they might not themselves agree. It followed that the administrative organisation would have to be rather more closely knit than it was at present. He was not however, inclined to agree with Mr. Grantham that the Chief Commissioner should disappear.

Mr. Cohen raised the question of the presentation locally of Government's policy with regard to constitutional advance.

Sir George Gater said that this raised the question of the treatment of Lagos, since the Lagos politicians were likely to be the most vocal critics of any proposed reforms.

Sir Arthur Richards said that he was inclined to agree with Lord Hailey that Lagos

---

[4] Gov of the Gold Coast 1941–47; acting gov Nigeria 1942.

and its immediate surroundings should become a Municipality not subject to the Western Regional Council.

The *Secretary of State* said that Sir Alan Burns was prepared to accept something similar for Accra and Kumasi and that under his proposals they would direct representatives to Legislative Council. He thought this was wise.

Sir George Gater remarked that the development of local government bodies was not dealt with in Sir Bernard Bourdillon's proposals. He thought this a very important part of constitutional development and that it would require a closer examination than had been given to it up to date.

Sir Arthur Richards suggested that there should be an announcement sketching out Government's objectives and stating that progress would be according to the willingness and fitness of the people to advance and that the North would not be forced and further that every step would require the assent of the people concerned.

The *Secretary of State* said that this led him to a suggestion which he had been turning over in his mind that a White Paper should be published for the whole of West Africa setting out the objects, political, social and economic, which HMG had in mind for the four Territories.

Sir Arthur Richards said that he thought that this was an excellent idea. The White Paper could perhaps sketch out the general policy and it could be left to him to fill in the blanks.

The *Secretary of State* said that he thought that the idea should be worked the other way round. He thought that Sir Arthur Richards and Sir Alan Burns should discuss these important matters and put up their ideas to the Secretary of State who could then, in the light of those ideas, formulate a policy. A White Paper could then be produced.

Sir George Gater wondered whether Sir Alan Burns would in the meantime be able to hold the position in the Gold Coast.

The *Secretary of State* said that in his talks with Sir Alan it had been agreed that it would be necessary for him to discuss these matters with Sir Arthur Richards. He did not get the impression that the Gold Coast position was so urgent that it was likely to get out of hand before decisions could be taken in the light of these talks. The Secretary of State said that it was essential that the Gold Coast and Nigeria should keep in step.

Mr. Cohen referred to the position of the African unofficial members of the Executive Council. One of them was also a member of the Legislative Council and could attack in that Council measures which had been agreed upon previously by a majority in the Executive Council. It was agreed that the position was not entirely satisfactory and this was a matter which Sir Arthur Richards would look into after his arrival in Nigeria.

The *Secretary of State* then left the meeting.

The question of the substitution of election or selection of members of Councils for nomination by the Governor was discussed and *Sir Arthur Richards* said that he thought that if possible it was preferable for the method of selection or election to be defined in the constitution, since this would show that the members of Council concerned were really the representatives of the people and not nominees of the Government. . . .

3   CO 583/286/5, no 1   19 July 1944
[Richards's proposals]: despatch from Sir A Richards to Mr Stanley
setting out proposals for reform of the Nigerian constitution.
Annexures

I have the honour to address you on the subject of the political and constitutional
future of Nigeria. I shall endeavour to set forth my views with a brevity which is no
measure of the time and trouble taken to form them.

As you are aware, I studied a number of relevant documents in London last
November and I had the advantage of many discussions with officers of your staff[1]
Since assuming office in Nigeria I have read all the local memoranda with which the
enquiring student is afflicted and I have to confess to a resultant impression of
unreality and sterility. My predecessor[2] collected a vast number of written opinions
before formulating the proposals which you were unable to accept. During the very
extensive travelling which I have undertaken in the last six months I have kept the
subject constantly in mind and have, I hope, retained an objective outlook. The
background of the different races comprised within the area known as Nigeria and
the diversity of their customs, beliefs, habits and aspirations has been drawn by many
pens, the most notable and the latest being that of Lord Hailey.[3] The picture is
complete and relieves me of a difficult preliminary task in that I may now assume as
common property the knowledge released by so competent an observer. I have also
steeped myself in the writings and the thought of Lord Lugard, who has had no
successor in knowledge of the people and in grasp of the principles and practice of
colonial administration[4] He was confronted with the difficult setting of an artificial
unity which existed only on the map. His problem was to build a system which would
allow organic growth and make the unity superimposed from outside into a living
thing which might progress through varying stages of adolescence to adult
nationhood. If I may be permitted the observation, the special distinction of Lord
Lugard is that he never allowed principles to become divorced from practice and that
he never thought he had solved difficulties by evading them. He would have been the
last to launch the Ship of State on a maiden voyage of discovery through uncharted
seas in the sublime faith that the winds of chance would blow her at last into some
safe haven.

2.   I have made these preliminary remarks because I feel very strongly that
political progress must be planned deliberately and that while allowance must be
made for changes and any constitutional experiment must be flexible in its
provisions, there must be some framework of design. We cannot leave all the

---

[1] See 2.   [2] ie Sir Bernard Bourdillon
[3] *An African Survey* (London, 1938) and *Native administration and political development in British
tropical Africa, 1940–1942* (London, 1944).
[4] Frederick Lugard (1st Baron Lugard of Abinger cr 1928). KCMG, 1901; high commissioner and gov of
Northern Nigeria, 1900–1907; gov of Hong Kong, 1907–1912; high commissioner and gov of Northern
Nigeria, 1912–1914; gov of Southern Nigeria, 1912–1914; gov-gen of Nigeria, 1914–1919; privy
councillor, 1920; member, Permanent Mandates Commission of League of Nations, 1922–1936; died
1945.

difficulties to Time and Fate. As I see it, there is only one test to apply to new political
and constitutional proposals—will they work, and, if so, how? The main problem in
Nigeria to-day is how to create a political system which is itself a present advance and
contains the living possibility of further orderly advance—a system within which the
diverse elements may progress at varying speed, amicably and smoothly, towards a
more closely integrated economic, social and political unity, without sacrificing the
principles and ideals inherent in their divergent 'ways of life'. It is not possible to
retrace our steps and to break up Nigeria into three or four separate entities—like
Kenya, Tanganyika and Uganda—bound only by transport, customs and postal
unions for the common convenience.

It is not possible to impose upon unwilling peoples an immediate but artificial
political unity based on false analogies of the United Kingdom.

Nor is it possible to continue in face of pressure, external and internal, the present
system of Government which is full of inconsistencies and is intrinsically unsuited
for expansion on a Nigerian basis. A governing factor in my thoughts has been the
physical size of Nigeria—one third of British India or the size of France, Belgium and
the United Kingdom—with a population double that of the Dominion of Canada.[5] It
is a potential Empire in itself and I submit that planning should therefore be on an
Imperial scale, far different from the small scale planning which is adequate for a
Colony of the normal size. We have been urged to take some risks and I agree that we
should do so. To refuse to take risks is to admit political insolvency. In any case the
risk involved in bold planning by experienced colonial administrators is far less than
the risk of having plans thrust upon our inactivity by the enthusiastic amateur and
the political theorist buttressed by dangerously false analogies.

It is not the 'Westminster model' but the principles which lie behind it and make it
work that I have tried to apply. The 'model' is a facade of purely local and national
value and perishable; the principles are of universal application and imperishable.

3.   I now make the following proposals, for which I ask nothing better than the
searching scrutiny and the unsentimental analysis of your advisers. I recommend a
system of Government outlined in this form, which I will expand later.

(a) Legislative Council of Nigeria

(b) Northern	(c) Western	(d) Eastern	(e) Colony
Provinces	Provinces	Provinces	No
(2 Houses)	(1 House)	(1 House)	separate
House of Chiefs	House of	House of	council
and House of	Assembly	Assembly	
Assembly.			

The present system of Native Authorities and of indirect rule would continue
precisely as at present under the guidance of the Administrative Service. Initially, all
legislation would be dealt with by the Legislative Council of Nigeria, pending
consideration by a Committee of what legislative powers, if any, could be devolved
upon the three Regional Councils. But all Bills—other than those introduced under
Certificate of Urgency—before submission to Legislative Council to be laid on the

---

[5] In the 1952–1953 census Nigeria's population was calculated as slightly over 31 million.

table of the Regional Councils for general discussion if desired and for submission of advice by Resolution if any amendments were desired.

Regional Councils to meet once annually in January. Legislative Council to meet for Budget Session as at present in March, with possibility of other meetings during the year when and if desired.

The Governor to preside as at present over the Legislative Council of Nigeria and to be assisted by an Executive Council precisely as at present.

Finance Committee of Legislative Council to operate as at present with a small quorum to admit of absence of many members who could not regularly attend.

Finance

I propose to devolve upon Regional Councils a large measure of financial responsibility, each to have its own local Budget.

(a) At present Native Authorities exercise a growing amount of responsibility and are financed by being allowed to retain a percentage of direct local taxation. The power has been reserved to the Governor to increase or decrease such percentages for good reason. In order to simplify the system still further and to encourage Native Authorities to adopt progressive policies I have recently frozen their contribution to central revenue at the amounts paid in by them in the year 1943–1944. The remainder, and the whole of any increase due to increased taxation is to be retained by the Native Authorities. I propose to allot the whole of the amount fixed for contribution to the Central Government to the Regional Council.

(b) I propose further to supplement the funds of the Regional Councils by block grants from Central Revenue (i.e. indirect taxation receipts such as Customs and Excise), calculated on a pro rata basis which would not be difficult to devise, after the Central Government had retained the amount required for Central services and Central finance such as loan and reserve accounts. The salaries of all Government personnel employed in the area would be shown on the Regional Budget, only those offices and their staff who serve directly under the Central Government being borne on the Central Estimates.

Regional Councils

(a) Northern Provinces. I have rejected, initially at any rate, the suggestion to divide the Northern Provinces into two regions or to attach areas not predominantly Mohammedan to the West and East. I think it is desirable to keep the Northern Provinces heterogeneous and to avoid creation of a Mohammedan bloc—a Pakistan—looking to Cairo rather than to Lagos for guidance. This tendency is already visible.

The House of Chiefs, Northern Provinces

I propose that the Chief Commissioner should preside and that membership should be settled on the lines so successfully followed at present for the Chiefs Conference. The Regional Budget would be finally submitted to this House for approval. They would have the right to veto or amend items but not to insert new ones. Final approval of the Budget would be given by the Governor, who would possess an over-riding power to amend, delete or add to it, before authorising its submission to the Central Council as a block vote in the Central Budget, the itemized Budget forming an appendix to the Central Budget.

The House of Assembly, Northern Provinces
I suggest membership as follows, under the Presidency of the Senior Resident:—

Official
Senior Resident (President)
All other Residents (12) (including Secretary Northern Provinces)
Deputy Financial Secretary
Deputy Director of Education
Deputy Director of Agriculture
Deputy Director of Medical Services
Deputy Director of Public Works
Crown Counsel

Unofficial
Twelve Provincial Members to be nominated from Native Authorities
Six Members to be nominated by the Governor to secure representation of
   industry and commerce and of the Sabon Gari community and any other
   important aspects of life not otherwise unofficially represented

This would give an official majority of one (19–18) including the President, who
should have an original and a casting vote.
   Initially all members would have to be nominated by the Governor—for a period of
three years.
   Place of meeting—Kaduna. Once annually.
   The present two Annual Conferences, of Residents and of Chiefs, would disappear.
   Language for both Houses—Hausa.

Western Provinces

House of Assembly

President—The Chief Commissioner

Chiefs—3 Chiefs

Officials
Residents (7) *Note.* The Secretary Western Provinces to be raised to status of
   Resident
Deputy Financial Secretary
   „   Director of Education
   „   Director of Agriculture
   „   Director of Medical Services
   „   Director of Public Works
Crown Counsel

Unofficials
Six Provincial members nominated from Native Authorities
Four nominated by the Governor from prominent citizens representing industry,
   commerce or other important aspects of life not otherwise unofficially represented

The President to have an original and a casting vote.
   This would give an official majority of 14 to 13, reckoning the Chiefs as unofficial.

All nominations for three years. Initially by the Governor.
Place of Meeting—Ibadan. Once annually.
Powers and limitations as given to two Houses in Northern Provinces.
Present Annual Conferences of Residents and Chiefs to disappear.
Language—English.

Eastern Provinces (including Cameroons)

House of Assembly

President—The Chief Commissioner

Officials
Residents (6) *Note.* The Secretary Eastern Provinces to be raised to status of Resident
Deputy Financial Secretary
    „   Director of Education
    „   Director of Agriculture
    „   Director of Medical Services
    „   Director of Public Works
Crown Counsel

Unofficials
Seven Provincial members nominated from Native Authorities
Five nominated by the Governor from prominent citizens to represent industry,
commerce, or other important aspects of life not otherwise unofficially represented

The President to have an original and a casting vote. This would give an official
majority of 13–12.
Place of Meeting—Enugu.
Other conditions as in notes to Western Provinces.

The Colony
To continue directly under the Legislative Council of Nigeria, Lagos becoming a
Municipality with extensive powers and to comprise its present town limits divided
into urban and suburban areas. Population circa 210,000
    The rural areas of the Colony to remain as at present under a Commissioner and three
District Officers with Native Authorities functioning under them as at present.
Population circa 200,000. Departmental activities also to remain as at present organized.

Finance
The Colony Budget—a small matter excluding the Municipal area—to form part of
the Central Budget. The Lagos Municipal Budget to be an appendix to the Central
Budget like the Regional Budgets, only a block grant of such subsidy as may be
considered suitable being included in the body of the Central Budget.

The Legislative Council of Nigeria[6]

President—His Excellency the Governor

---

[6] Cohen noted in the margin against this passage 'Present Membership. Governor, 24 Officials, 21
Unofficials of whom 14 Africans.'

Chiefs
Four Emirs (nominated by Upper House Northern Provinces)
Two Chiefs from Western Provinces (nominated by the Governor)

Officials
Chief Secretary
Chief Commissioners (3)
One Senior Resident each from Northern, Western and Eastern Provinces (3)
Resident Cameroons
Attorney-General
Financial Secretary
Director of Medical Services
Director of Education
Director of Agriculture
Director of Public Works
Director of Marine
Comptroller of Customs & Excise
General Manager of the Railway
Commissioner of Police
Commissioner of Colony

Unofficials
4 members from Northern Provinces (to be nominated by House of Assembly
   Northern Provinces from their own body)
3 members from Western Provinces (to be nominated by House of Assembly
   Western Provinces from their own body)
4 members from Eastern Provinces (to be nominated by House of Assembly from
   their own body)
1 member from Cameroons (nominated by the Governor)
2 members from Lagos (to be nominated by Municipal Council)
1 member from Colony (to be nominated by Governor)
1 member to represent Banking
1   ,,   ,,   ,,   Shipping
1   ,,   ,,   ,,   Commerce

The Council would thus be composed, under the presidency of the Governor, of 6
Chiefs, 19 Officials and 18 Unofficials.
    The Governor to have a casting vote only.
    The whole range of Nigerian affairs would be open for debate in this Council,
especially on the second reading of the Budget.
    Budget Meeting to take place alternately in Lagos, Kaduna, Ibadan and Enugu. All
other meetings to be in Lagos.
    The Council would also legislate for all Nigeria, not excepting the Northern
Provinces as at present.
    In nominating two Chiefs from the Western Provinces the Governor would first
ascertain through the Chief Commissioner the wishes of the major Chiefs in the
matter. It is desirable to prevent these nominations from becoming the subject of
political intrigue or public contention.

General remarks

(a) I should propose that the New Constitution would be reviewed at the end of nine years, but in the intervening years—at the end of the third year and the sixth year—the possibility of substituting a form of nomination, by choice according to African custom instead of by the Governor, for membership of the Regional Councils, would be studied and where possible adopted. That policy to be declared.

(b) I have retained effective Government control in all Councils initially in order to give them stability and a chance of success.

(c) I think that holding the Budget Meeting once in four years in each of the Provincial Capitals would be of psychological value and would help to create the sense of Nigerian unity.

(d) The judicial system as recently revised would remain unchanged.

(e) The correlation of Native Authority salaries to those prevailing in Government Departments will facilitate the policy of increasing the trained staff and responsibilities of Native Authorities so as to avoid the existence of parallel and overlapping Government and Native Authority spheres of work.

(f) The House of Chiefs in the Northern Provinces will of course be able to originate motions if they so desire. The Houses of Assembly would naturally possess this right.

(g) I have not overlooked the idea of a Municipality for Port Harcourt. It is not yet ripe for that move but for this and other towns in the Eastern Provinces the objective will remain in view for action as occasion merits. The Municipal idea in the Northern Provinces and Western Provinces has not yet taken the public imagination and runs counter to established ideas.

Conclusion

(a) In conclusion I should like to emphasize that my chief difficulty in considering this difficult question has been how to bring the Northern Chiefs willingly into a scheme devised to develop into real Nigerian unity. It would be useless to pretend that any such unity at present exists or that clumsy attempts to achieve it would result in anything less than accentuated opposition. The verbiage of democracy neither impresses nor deceives the Northern Emir whose judgment of men and motives is more acute than is commonly supposed.

The type of Emir is slowly changing and the new ones tend to be English-speaking and educated. But we have to remember that their counsellors are not so advanced. They represent the forces of reactionary Conservatism and have to be cajoled along the road of progress. Progress is in the air and the pace can be accelerated, but too great haste or too great carelessness in dealing with ingrained sentiment and belief can only defeat its object. I have reason to believe that the Chiefs might accept the proposals which I am submitting to you, with the elaborate safeguards of their dignity and position.

The proposals also provide for the individualism and the craving of each to paddle his own canoe, which distinguishes the aspiring Eastern Provinces people.

Not the least merit is the opportunity given to let Lagos, its Press and its politicians, sink into their true Nigerian perspective.

Furthermore, I feel that the interest of the Administrative service will be stimulated by having regional councils with all the Residents free to take an active part in the financial dispositions of their own Provinces and in considering the legislation which affects them. Although Nigerian policy would be settled at a higher level the chance of public contribution to the making of such policy would be present in the debates of the regional council.

(b) It will be noticed that the proposals involve creation of regional deputies to the Heads of all the principal departments. In any case this step is long overdue. Excessive centralization of authority in Lagos has left the Chief Commissioners without authoritative guidance at their headquarters and has so overloaded the Head of Department himself that he cannot travel as he should and cannot give the leisured attention to planning which the country increasingly demands. It is lamentably true to say that most of the Emirs have never met the principal Heads of Departments and know neither them nor their names. The difference which might come from the courtesy of an occasional call and sympathetic discussion and explanation of policy and practice cannot be overstressed. Under my proposals the principal Heads of Departments, with three deputies in the Provinces and another at Headquarters would be able to travel and to think.

A Nigerian Establishment pool, from which the regions would be fed with officers, would be organized at Headquarters in Lagos and would present no practical difficulty in management.

(c) The Financial Secretary (Mr. Farquhar) has just proceeded on leave, while the Chief Commissioner Northern Provinces hopes to take leave in September. Both would be available for consultation if you think fit.

I venture also to offer the suggestion that Lord Lugard might be given the opportunity of comment on this Despatch.

(d) The draft in its original form was sent by me to each Chief Commissioner for his comments. Their replies are attached as Annexures I, II, III. I have also annexed a note on Municipal elections in Lagos. It will be seen that I have accepted the main criticisms of the Chief Commissioner Eastern Provinces and Chief Commissioner Western Provinces and have embodied the necessary amendments in my proposals.

I had originally planned two Houses for the Western Provinces as in the Northern Provinces, though I felt some misgivings about the suitability of a House of Chiefs. The experience, and the arguments of the Chief Commissioners based thereon, have convinced me that a one House system for the Western Provinces would be more appropriate and more acceptable to the people.

I have also accepted the Chief Commissioner Eastern Province's criticisms of specific sectional representation and have modified that part of the Regional proposals.

Two suggestions only I have been unable to accept—that of the Acting Chief Commissioner Western Provinces for a House of Assembly totalling 43, because it seems to me too cumbrous; and that of the Chief Commissioner Eastern Provinces that no reference should be made to a policy of ultimate substitution of choice according to African custom for nomination by the Governor, if it proves to be feasible, because I regard it as essential to indicate the probable line of future progress towards democratic control.

(e) It is worthy of note that my proposals in their final form have now the wholehearted support of the Chief Commissioner Northern Provinces, the Chief Commissioner Eastern Provinces, the Acting Chief Commissioner Western Provinces and the Acting Chief Secretary.

Annexure I to 3: Letter from—J Patterson (Northern Provinces) to Sir A Richards 14 July 1944

The idea of a bi-cameral organisation in the Northern Provinces has not previously been developed and it has been necessary for me to give some thought to the question whether it would achieve the objects which Your Excellency sets out in the draft despatch and in particular surmount the difficulty which is mentioned in the first paragraph under the heading 'Conclusion'. Just as it seemed important to ensure that in a single council, were it set up in the Northern Provinces, an unreal opposition should not be created, following western examples, for that 'opposition' could at the present stage be anti one thing only, namely anti-Emir, so it will be important, it would seem, to ensure that the two Houses now proposed shall not be contending but complementary organisations. I think that can be assured by carefully settling the details of the functions of each House and by a wise choice, which need not thereby be fettered, of the African members of the House of Assembly. It is the feature of the proposals on which, on first reading, I felt some misgiving. The powers of the two Houses in finance should be a decisive factor in maintaining a proper relationship between the two: but the House of Chiefs must not be allowed to degenerate into merely a Committee on finance, The mixed membership of the House of Assembly will probably promote a more vigorous political growth there and having started with the two Houses it would be difficult for them to coalesce at any future time without the Chiefs being regarded as on one side and the other members from the House of Assembly, on the other.

2.   There is, as Your Excellency has noted, a good deal of reactionary Conservatism among the older men, especially those Arabic scholars whom it is difficult to convince that modern education on western lines will not necessarily mean the eclipse of their learning and their religion. There are many Emirs whose way of thinking is far in advance of that of many of their counsellors; but even so I can not imagine that those men would choose to be 'represented' by anyone except their Emir. Similarly, though some young men express, while not always realising what it means to hold, advanced opinions on social and political matters, the respect and even affection on which I see everywhere for Emirs who show themselves to be sympathetic towards progressive ideas leaves no doubt that these young men's 'representation' too would be through their Emir. This idea is preserved in the nomination of four Emirs as members of Legislative Council.

3.   Your Excellency has mentioned certain characteristics of the Northern Provinces in the draft: there is one other which I think it is important to bear in mind. A very large section of the community in these provinces has not yet shown any signs of the awakening of its political consciousness. The organisation now proposed will cater for political thought so far as it has emerged and in the flexibility of the organisation will lie the safeguard against any section of the community, which at the moment may happen to be in a favoured position, being able to obtain a dominating place in public affairs. This flexibility should also ensure that political development will be directed by the people themselves and so be of lasting value. To bring the large mass of the population into the constitutional scheme it will be necessary, I feel, to foster more resolutely than has hitherto in general been possible the formal meetings of district and village councils as part of the Native Authorities and indirect rule which, Your Excellency mentions, will continue precisely as at

present. It is in these councils, I feel, that the habit of political thought will be inculcated that will make possible the wise choice of the African members of the House of Assembly: it can not effectively be administered like a dose of patent medicine through the mouth of the body politic.

4.   The problem that has to be solved in the Northern Provinces and the material that is provided for its solution can perhaps be described in the following way. No religion is more democratic than Islam, the religion of the majority of the people. It avoids all the difficulties created by the caste system of some Indian religions. There is therefore a natural sense of social democracy in the Emirates and it is growing as the numbers of educated youths increase. One of the principal tasks of administrators is to teach the people that political democracy is not a political system on a Whitehall or any other pattern but a way of life, a habit of thought, of thought for others. The proposals which are made in the draft for the political development of the Northern Provinces on lines familiar to the Chiefs and people should, I feel, do this.

5.   I consider that the proposals follow sufficiently closely the lines of political development so far as it has emerged to be acceptable to those whom they affect and, though they are an appreciable step forward from the present position, will be realistic to them. As I have indicated in the foregoing paragraphs the growth of the two Houses as complementary parts of the machine will need careful handling and as a corollary to the changes now to be made the development of political thought in the mass of the people should be quickened.

6.   The following observations occur to me on matters of detail:—

(i) Page 5 of the draft under heading 'Regional Councils'. (a) Northern Provinces. For 'certain pagan areas' read 'areas not predominantly Mohammedan': there are numbers of Christians in the areas in question.

(ii) Page 6 of the draft under heading 'The House of Assembly, N.P.' The Director of Veterinary Services, though no longer head of a 'Northern Provinces Department' will probably retain his headquarters in the Northern Provinces. The activities of the department will affect increasingly the domestic economy of a large number of people in these provinces and a less number in other parts of Nigeria. He should perhaps, therefore, have a seat in this House. Your Excellency may, however, be contemplating changes in the organisation of the department which would make this unnecessary. I do not think he should be admitted in place of any of the proposed official members, but I suggest a second Member for Commerce who would be an African to balance him.

(iii) Page 10 of the draft under heading 'General Remarks' (e). This is an important consideration and it is, I submit, a matter of urgency for Government to discontinue appointing to its staff African members of the executive in technical departments. Forestry Assistants, Veterinary Assistants and similar officials and even more so those in lower grades should be carried on the Native Authority estimates. Not only will this avoid the development of identical staffs along parallel lines but it will remove one factor which might give rise to an impression that in the new political organisation a distinction is to be made between 'Native Administration' and 'Government'. It is not always easy to convince Heads of Departments that the Native Authorities and their organisations are the instruments through which, on the advice of a Head of Department and under the supervision of his Officers, departmental activities are normally carried out.

Annexure II to 3: comments by H F M White[7]

While I am in complete agreement with the general scheme, I am not happy about the proposal that in the Western Provinces there should be a House of Chiefs apart from and superior to the House of Assembly. The proposal springs no doubt from an analogy between the Obas of the Western Provinces and the Emirs of the North and between the two Chiefs Conferences of the West and North. Regarding the first comparison I would quote the following passage from a memorandum written by Sir Gerald Whiteley[8] on Lord Hailey's Reports on Native Administration and African Political Development:—

> 'It is my opinion, shared I believe by many Western Province officers, that our administration, applying the Northern Emirate model to the Western Provinces, was responsible for giving the principal Obas an autocratic position which was foreign to Yoruba custom and constitution.
> Democratisation of the Native Authority is in my view in the Yoruba States not only not inconsistent with or opposed to their own customs, but to a certain extent is merely a return to the *status quo* before our advent. The process will have to be carried a good deal further than it went before, since the people have become and are becoming more educated and vocal, but it will be a natural process'

2.   The Western Provinces Chiefs Conference which was inaugurated as a 'Conference of Yoruba Chiefs' in 1937 has gradually been extended to include representatives from the Native Authority Councils in the Benin and Warri Provinces so that the complexion of the Conference has begun to change. It is moving from its beginning as a Conference of individual chiefs to a Conference of representatives of Native Authorities. But, even so, although the Conference is more representative than it was, it would have far to go before it became fully representative of the Western Provinces both in character and extent. I do not feel, therefore, that the proposed House of Chiefs would be qualified to exercise revising powers over the House of Assembly. Moreover, if it bears on the question, I feel that the House of Assembly would be a considerably more competent body than the House of Chiefs. My view is, then, that a House of Chiefs should have no greater powers than the House of Assembly.

3.   Another though perhaps minor point is the proposal that the President of the House of Assembly should be the Senior Resident. This means, in effect, that the President would be the most senior of the Residents in charge of Provinces at the time. It does not seem to me very suitable that the President of an Assembly which will deal with the affairs of the Western Provinces as a whole should be an officer whose normal activities are confined to the boundaries of only one Province. The obvious President, as it seems to me, is the Chief Commissioner, but it is not practicable, I take it, that he should be President of both Houses.

4.   Having regard to the above considerations—that the House of Chiefs should not be qualified to play the part of an Upper House, that it would not be satisfactory

---

[7] Acting chief commissioner, Western Provinces   [8] Chief commissioner, Western Provinces, 1939–1946.

to have two Houses of equal powers, and that the most suitable President of any Assembly would be the Chief Commissioner—I prefer that the Regional Council for the Western Provinces should consist of one House rather than two. I think that Sir Gerald Whiteley must have had such a plan in mind when he wrote in the memorandum from which I have already quoted:—

> 'The Regional Council should ultimately become completely representative and I agree that the best method of securing this object is to provide that it should be composed of a mixture of Native Authority and Unofficial Members, in addition to Official or Government Members'.

5.   The House of Assembly for the Western Provinces, like the proposed Legislative Council of Nigeria, would thus consist of Chiefs, or representatives of the Native Authorities, in addition to Officials and Unofficials. I hesitate to make definite recommendations as to the representation of Native Authorities in the House of Assembly but I would tentatively suggest 21, varying from 5 for the Oyo Province with its population of 1,340,000 to 2 for the Ijebu Province with its population of 306,000. The membership of the House of Assembly would then be:—

President	–	Chief Commissioner
Officials	–	12
N. A. representatives	–	21
Unofficials	–	10
		43

The total membership is the same as proposed for the Legislative Council.

6.   It is not out of place to mention that just as the Legislative Council will be largely based on the Regional Councils, so the Regional Councils in their turn must have some foundation and their basis must be Provincial Councils. Such Councils have already been envisaged by Sir Gerald Whiteley who has written:—

> 'The Provincial Councils would be composed of a fixed number of official members, say the Resident, Divisional Officers and Senior Departmental Officers in the Province; and of such number of Native Authorities and Unofficial Members chosen by Divisional Councils as would be decided by the Resident, the guiding principle being to secure as adequate a degree of representation as possible, from the qualitative as well as from the quantitative point of view. To begin with I think it would be desirable to leave this decision to the Resident. Later no doubt the Councils themselves would be able to work out the basis on which representation should be apportioned.
>
> Similarly Provincial Councils would choose representatives from among themselves to send to the Regional Council'.

I draw attention to the last sentence.

7.   The proposal that the Regional Council should, from the outset, have its own Budget is a bold one, but I support it. Financial responsibility will at once give the Council a sense of reality and although some of the members will be unable to grasp the details of finance, the majority will be able to deal with it and the others will learn.

8.   I am in agreement with all the other proposals contained in the Despatch.

Annexure III to 3: letter from F B Carr (Eastern Provinces) to Sir A Richards (3 July 1944)

I have considered carefully the draft despatch sent to me under cover of Your Excellency's demi-official letter of 25th June 1944. There is one point of importance with regard to the proposed House of Assembly in the Eastern Provinces on which I am not clear. Is it intended that the 'five provincial members' should be directly representative of the Native Authorities within the respective Provinces? I suggest that it is essential that they should be and, doubtless as Your Excellency is aware, this was advocated by my predecessor, Mr. G G Shute CMG.[9] I use the word 'essential' as it seems to me that for provincial representation one must draw from among those who have the true interests of the people at heart and who have some inherent right to be chosen as representatives, however small and limited that right may be at the moment. I also suggest that the number of provincial members be increased to seven. The Cameroons, Ogoja and Onitsha Provinces could well do with one member each, but there is a sharp cleavage between the Ibibios and Efiks in the Calabar Province, and the Ibos and Creek living peoples in the Owerri Province. (These extend into the Calabar Province, e.g. the Opobos, but one representative should suffice). I am aware of the danger of attempting to provide representation for all the diverse elements of the Eastern Provinces, but these I consider necessary.

2.　I suggest that it is unwise to designate sectional representation as, to my mind, this can but lead to clamour from other sections for representation and possible intra-sectional dispute. For instance, I cannot visualise the Church Missionary Society accepting representation by a Roman Catholic or vice-versa, and I can imagine clashes in commercial interests.

3.　I am doubtful as to the intention of 'extra numbers' but assume that the nominations would be of outstanding Africans such as might receive nomination to the present Legislative Council.

4.　I consider that the number of Residents should be increased to six. The Secretary is, at present, a Senior District Officer, but with the advent of Deputy Heads of Departments I am of opinion that he should be a Resident and a member of the House.

5.　Should the preceding paragraphs be accepted I suggest that the membership of the House of Assembly for the Eastern Provinces should read:—

Officials
　　President—the Chief Commissioner
　　All Residents (6)
　　Deputy　Financial Secretary　　　　　　E
　　　　"　　Director of Education　　　　　　"
　　　　"　　Director of Agriculture　　　　　"
　　　　"　　Director of Medical Services　　"
　　　　"　　Director of Public Works　　　　"
　　Crown Counsel

---

[9] Chief commissioner, Eastern Provinces, 1939–1943.

Unofficials
Seven Provincial members nominated from among Native Authorities
Five nominated members.

(Note: The number of five nominated members might be reduced to four if it be desired to retain the official majority at two).

6. I assume that the language for the House would be English, though it is not stated.

7. As to the proposed Legislative Council, I would ask whether the unofficial members to be nominated by the three Houses of Assembly are to be nominated from their own number, and suggest that this should be made clear one way or the other.

8. As to (a) of the 'General Remarks', I can see no possibility of 'substituting a form of nomination by choice according to African custom instead of by the Governor for membership of the Regional Councils' in the Eastern Provinces. I suggest, therefore, that no declaration of policy to consider such a possibility be made.

9. As to (f), would not the House of Assembly in the Eastern Provinces be able to originate motions if it so desires. I suggest that it should.

10. I should like to record my emphatic agreement, insofar as the Eastern Provinces are concerned, with the second paragraph on page 12 of the draft despatch, that the effect of the Regional Councils will be stimulating to the Administrative service, and would add that I consider that it will be stimulating to all.

11. On the proposals for the Northern Provinces I do not feel competent to comment, and I am hesitant to comment on those for the West. I have, however, had some experience in that group of Provinces, particularly the Ondo Province, and feel that I should record that I am apprehensive regarding the constitution of a House of Chiefs. The Chiefs of the West, no matter what the position is of those in the North, have not, I believe, autocratic powers being very closely linked with their Councils. Moreover, it has been the policy, for some time now, further to democratise the Native Authorities, and this is brought out clearly in the memorandum of 19th September, 1942, written by the Chief Commissioner Western Provinces on Lord Hailey's Reports on Native Administration and African Political Development. If I read the situation correctly I am unable to escape the conclusion that the establishment of a House of Chiefs would largely undo the work of democratisation which I am aware was demanded by the people of the Ondo Province, at least, and give to the Chiefs a position and power which is not theirs inherently and which would not readily be accorded to them by many of their subjects.

Annexure IV to 3 Note on municipal elections in Lagos
1. The actual number of people in Lagos entitled to vote can only be estimated— it is not less than 7,000 and not more than 10,000. Of these, those who took the trouble to register amount to only 1021. We can thus safely say that at the outside only 15% of those entitled to vote are on the register.

2. But not all on the register did vote, as the figures below will demonstrate:—

Wards	Total registered voters	Actual votes
A	129	Unopposed
B	130	ditto
C	325	191 (5 illiterates)
D	193	133 (5 „)
E	244	163 (1 „)
	1021	

Of the registered voters of C, D and E, which total 762, votes were recorded by 487. Lagos is of course largely illiterate—only 11 of them voted.

3. This is not a very good advertisement of democratic government via the franchise, especially when one considers that people should naturally be more interested in their representative on their own town council, with an African majority, than on the remoter Legislative Council, with its official majority.

4   CO 583/286/5, no 4   9 Aug 1944
[Richards's proposals]: memorandum by A B Cohen on Sir A Richards's proposals for reform of the Nigerian constitution

Sir Arthur Richards asks that his proposals should be submitted to searching scrutiny and unsentimental analysis.[1] His despatch only represents a broad outline and no doubt he wishes to know whether the Secretary of State is prepared to agree with the general principles of his recommendations before the details are filled in. But before the general principles can be accepted, their implications in practice require careful examination and for this purpose detailed scrutiny cannot be avoided at this stage. Before anything like a final view on the proposals can be formed a considerable degree of discussion and consultation will be required. Meanwhile the following comments call attention to what appear to me to be the more important points:—

(1) *Main features of proposals*
Sir Arthur Richards' general constitutional scheme is based, as he says, on Lord Hailey's factual analysis. It is also in accordance with Lord Hailey's general conclusions and does not differ in its principal features from the scheme worked out by Sir Bernard Bourdillon last year. It does, however, have the very great merit of filling in the more serious gaps in Sir Bernard Bourdillon's proposals. In the first place it provides a means, likely to be acceptable to the northern Emirs, of bringing the north straight away into the general constitutional scheme, so that the new Legislative Council will be able to legislate for the whole of Nigeria.[2] In the second place it gives the regional councils, or Houses of Assembly as they are to be called (with an additional House of Chiefs in the north), a concrete function to perform, the control of regional finance. In the third place it recognises the necessity of providing

---

[1] See 3.
[2] Despite the amalgamation of Northern and Southern Nigeria in 1914, the legislative council's remit had been restricted to the latter.

an administrative foundation, in the staffs of Chief Commissioners, for the regional legislative bodies which are to be established. On the other hand the scheme, while it provides the framework for future constitutional advance on a Nigerian basis, does not itself constitute any advance at all. In this respect it goes even less far than Sir Bernard Bourdillon's scheme, which was itself thought not to be sufficiently progressive. Sir Arthur Richards says that the main problem in Nigeria to-day is how to create a political system which is itself a present advance and contains the living possibility of further orderly advance. Sir Arthur Richards' scheme achieves the second objective, but not, I think, the first.

(2) *The Northern Provinces*
With the support of the Chief Commissioner, Sir Arthur Richards proposes a bicameral legislature for the north with a House of Assembly, of which the composition is described on page 4[3] of the despatch, and a House of Chiefs composed in the same way as the present Chiefs' Conference. This Conference consists at present of the thirteen first class Emirs and approximately thirteen representatives of the other Emirs and Chiefs sitting in rotation. It has two secretaries, one African and one European political officer, but no other European attends it, not even the Chief Commissioner. Sir Arthur Richards' House of Chiefs is to be presided over by the Chief Commissioner.

It will be remembered that when Sir Arthur was discussing Sir Bernard Bourdillon's proposal for a regional council for the north he expressed the view, after discussion with Lord Lugard, that the Emirs would not readily agree to such a council and ought not to be pressed to accept it.[4] This difficulty, as he says, gave him more trouble than the whole of the rest of his constitutional scheme. He has visited the north twice and it may safely be assumed, and indeed is implied on page 8[5] of his despatch, that a scheme on the lines which he proposes will be acceptable to the Emirs. One point which will require careful examination is the relation between the House of Chiefs and the House of Assembly. Presumably the House of Chiefs will meet immediately after the House of Assembly in January. Will the House of Chiefs consider all other resolutions passed by the House of Assembly as well as the regional budget?

(3) *Functions of Houses of Assembly*
Under Sir Bernard Bourdillon's proposals the regional councils were to have the functions in the legislative sphere of making recommendations on bills submitted

---

[3] Page 11 in the text as reproduced here.
[4] That the Northern Emirs were a problem for British policy was recognised by F J Pedler who commented in a minute written on 29 Sept 1944: 'In the Northern Provinces we have hitherto supported a conservative regime which is rapidly becoming reactionary. Though it is the home of the native authority policy, it is the place where that policy works worst ... while, in our dealings with the Emirs, we go to extreme lengths to avoid offending the susceptibilities of the Emirs and their immediate advisers, the Emirs rarely follow the same practice in the arrangements they made (sic) for governing their own people ... If the true state of affairs in Northern Nigeria were really known, I believe it would be more damaging to British Colonial prestige than any other situation in Africa. It is therefore most important that these reforms should be worked in such a manner that a platform will be given for educated elements in the North, who are not associated with the interests of the Emirates' (CO 583/286/5, no14A).
[5] Page 14 in the text as reproduced here.

to them by Government, of discussing Native Authority subordinate legislation designed for enactment throughout the region, and of putting forward private bills; in the deliberative sphere of discussing motions brought forward by the members; and in the financial sphere of considering and making comments on a skeleton budget for the whole of Nigeria showing the expenditure region by region. The regional councils were thus to have no powers either legislative or financial. Sir Arthur Richards' Houses of Assembly are to have approximately the same functions in relation to legislation at first, although a committee may decide that certain legislative powers should be devolved by the Legislative Council on them. No mention is made of private bills. The Houses of Assembly are also to have the same deliberative functions with regard to motions. In the sphere of finance, however, they are to have definite powers. They are to consider and pass the regional budgets, which will include all expenditure other than Native Authority expenditure in the region. The revenue of each region will consist of the whole of the Government's share of direct taxation not retained by the Native Authorities, together with a block grant from central revenue. After the regional budgets have been considered by the House of Assembly, and in the case of the north by the House of Chiefs, which, however, will only have the right of veto and not of initiation, they will be submitted to the Governor, who will have the over-riding power of addition, amendment or deletion. They will then be referred to the central council and will appear in the printed estimates in the form of appendices to the central budget. Apparently the Legislative Council will not consider the regional budgets in themselves and will only exercise control over them in so far as it has the right to vote or withhold the block grants from central revenue. One point which is not clear is the powers which Houses of Assembly will have with regard to revenue. Under the scheme the direct native tax will be a wholly regional tax, divided between the regional bodies and the native administrations. Will the Houses of Assembly have power to propose and decide upon alterations in this or any other form of regional taxation?

One point of procedure which will require consideration is the question whether the interval between January and March will give the Government time to consider the regional budgets and the comments of the regional councils on legislation and other matters before the Legislative Council sits in March. There is everything to be said for making the interval as short as possible, so that the period during which the Government is absorbed in legislative questions may not take up too large a part of the year.

(4)   *The effects of the scheme on the structure of administration*
One of the weaknesses of Sir Bernard Bourdillon's scheme was that it made no provision for any administrative foundation for the proposed regional legislative bodies. When questioned about this he said that he thought the establishment of such an administrative foundation unnecessary, as there could be no certainty that the regional councils would be a permanent feature of the constitution. But it was not clear how the regional councils could have any reality or any chance of developing into effective political instruments unless they were fitted into not only the constitution but also the administrative framework of the country. Sir Arthur Richards has evidently recognised this weakness. Under his scheme deputy directors of all the more important departments, including the financial department,

are to be established in each region. This will to some extent be a return to the old system under the Lieutenant-Governor regime, but it is a reform which, in my view, is absolutely necessary. Sir Arthur Richards himself describes it as a step which is long over due. Over-centralisation has proved a fundamental weakness in the administrative system of Nigeria. Even in much smaller Territories like Tanganyika the need for de-centralisation has been felt. How much more necessary is this in Nigeria, with its vast distances and its population of twenty-two millions. The evils of over-centralisation have been greatly accentuated by the unsuitable geographical position of Lagos. The Secretariat is out of touch with the country and is everywhere regarded as a dead weight on progress. Heads of departments have far too little time for travelling and become Lagos-minded. For all these reasons the de-centralisation which is envisaged is, in my view, a most welcome feature of the scheme. But it is not clear from the despatch how far this de-centralisation is to go. How great is the authority of the Chief Commissioner to be? Is the group of deputy heads of departments to be a sort of regional executive council for the Chief Commissioner? Or is each deputy to be under the orders of his director at headquarters as at present? In my view, if the scheme is to have any chance of working satisfactorily, it is essential that de-centralisation should be real and not merely nominal. At present if a Chief Commissioner and his senior departmental officers wish to put forward some proposal affecting policy there may have to be three or four separate references to Lagos. If regional government is to work, it is essential that this should stop. The Chief Commissioner and his departmental officers should speak as a single unit and should communicate with the Government through one channel, either from the Chief Commissioner to the Chief Secretary or from the departmental officer mainly concerned, speaking on behalf of the Chief Commissioner, to the head of his department in Lagos. Otherwise I cannot see how regional political development can become effective. The general tenor of Sir Arthur Richards' despatch suggests that these are also his views, but I think it important to find out whether this is in fact the case. If so, I am not sure that the departmental officers at the Chief Commissioner's headquarters should be described as 'deputies'. I would prefer to see some such title as 'regional directors'. Some Departments, such as the Railway, Posts and Telegraphs, Audit, etc., would have to remain centralised and these should be excluded from the regional budgets.

(5) Analysis of the proposed composition of the regional Houses of Assembly and and Legislative Council shows the following results:—

Houses of Assembly

	North	West	East
Officials	19	14	13
Chiefs	–	3	–
Native Authority members	12	6	7
Other Unofficial members	6	4	5
	37	27	25

The presidents of the Houses, who would have an original as well as a casting vote, are included in the above figures.

Legislative Council

	North	West	East	Colony	Central
Officials	2	2	3	1	11
Chiefs	4	2	–	–	–
Unofficials	4	3	5	3	3*
	10	7	8	4	14

*(These members would presumably be Europeans)

Thus, assuming that the three unofficial members nominated to represent banking, shipping and commerce come from the south, the Council would consist of ten members drawn from the north, twenty-two from the south and eleven Central Government officials all stationed in the south. It may be argued that the complexion of the Council is too southern, but at any rate it is a great improvement on the present Council and it is, I think, reasonable to assume that the interests of the northern members and of the unofficial members from the east and west representing the Chiefs and the Native Authorities would in fact very frequently be the same. In any case the solid official block would ensure that no purely sectional interest was allowed to prevail.

An analysis of the membership of the Legislative Council on a different basis gives nineteen officials, six Chiefs and eighteen unofficials (of whom two would be nominated by the Lagos Municipal Council with an African majority, eleven by regional Houses of Assembly with an official majority and five by the Governor direct). It will be noticed that, assuming that the three members nominated to represent banking, shipping and commerce were Europeans and that all the other unofficial members were Africans, there would be twenty-two Europeans and twenty-one Africans on the Council. The Governor, who would only have the casting vote, is not included in the above analysis.

(6)   *Probable attitude of educated Africans to the scheme*
What is likely to be the reception of the scheme among educated Africans? To take the Houses of Assembly first, they are to consist entirely of officials and of unofficials nominated direct by the Governor, mostly from Native Authorities. Native Authority representatives cannot be regarded as wholly unofficial. In the northern council only six out of the thirty-seven members would be wholly unofficial, in the western council only four out of twenty-seven and in the eastern council only five out of twenty-five. In the Legislative Council there would be an unofficial majority if the Chiefs can be regarded as unofficials, but I very much doubt whether it would be correct to regard them as such in Nigerian conditions. Of the eighteen unofficial members, five would be nominated direct by the Governor, eleven by the Houses of Assembly, which would themselves have official majorities, and only two, the Lagos members, could be regarded as democratically elected. Moreover direct election to the Legislative Council would be abolished. Lagos instead of having three elected members would have two members nominated by the Lagos Municipal Council. The Calabar elected member would apparently disappear.

It can, I think, safely be assumed that the scheme would be regarded as reactionary by educated African opinion. I do not want to exaggerate the importance of this opinion, which represents only a very small section of the community in Nigeria. But it is the only opinion which is vocal and it would no doubt influence opinion outside Nigeria both in this country and elsewhere. In any case the reactions of the politically conscious public in Nigeria would affect the working of the scheme and Sir Arthur Richards himself admits the necessity of introducing a system which is in itself an advance. Sir Arthur does not deal in his despatch with the probable reactions of public opinion, but he evidently does not regard the probable reactions of the educated African as likely to be sufficiently serious to prejudice the success of the scheme. Otherwise he would certainly have mentioned these reactions. Nevertheless I find it impossible to avoid feeling that the scheme would to some extent be prejudiced by the fact that it does nothing to mitigate the present complete bureaucratic control over politics in Nigeria. I think that we ought to consider the possibility of making this control less rigid while not sacrificing the substance of power. In effect Sir Arthur Richards' scheme means that there would be no political advancement for a period of nine years. In the present state of public opinion both in this country and West Africa can such a position be sustained?

(7)   *The possibility of an unofficial majority*
Sir Bernard Bourdillon's scheme envisaged the possibility of unofficial majorities in the Legislative and other Councils and the Governor was to be given reserve powers. But Sir Bernard did not attach importance to the question of unofficial majorities because he proposed to abolish the distinction between officials and unofficials by allowing officials to vote according to their own opinions. When he was informed that the Secretary of State could not accept this, he said that he was in favour of unofficial majorities. Sir Arthur Richards said the same during the discussions before he went out to Nigeria, but he has changed his opinion in the light of experience locally. On page 7[6] of the despatch Sir Arthur says that he has retained effective Government control in all councils initially in order to give them stability and a chance of success. But would not this effective control by Government be assumed without an official majority in the regional Houses of Assembly and also in the Legislative Council (if chiefs are regarded as being official)? In the Legislative Council itself there would be members representing the Lagos politicians, the educated Africans in the provinces and the Native Authorities all over the country as well as European representatives of various forms of commercial life. Is it likely that all these would vote together on any issue and would not the interests of some of them be closer to those of the Government than of each other? Provided that a solid Government block were retained, could not the numbers of unofficials safely be increased without endangering the control of Government? In the improbable event of solid unofficial opposition, it is most unlikely that the Government would wish to proceed with any measure unless it were absolutely vital to do so, thus justifying the use of the Governor's reserve powers. Similarly in the regional Houses of Assembly it would surely be safe to have an official minority, having regard to the fact that the majority of the unofficial members are to be representatives of the Native Authorities, which are themselves part of the Government. It is to be noted that the Acting Chief Commissioner of the Western Provinces recommends a House of

---

[6] Page 14 of the text as reproduced here.

Assembly in which there would only be thirteen officials, with twenty-one Native Authority representatives and ten unofficials. If an unofficial majority could be allowed, this could be achieved not by reducing the number of officials, but by increasing the number of unofficials proper. With the figures suggested for the Houses of Assembly there seems a danger that the more progressive elements will not be adequately represented, while the same may be true of the Legislative Council itself if any large proportion of the nominees of the Houses of Assembly are Native Authorities. In the Gold Coast Sir Alan Burns proposes that the central legislature should consist of six officials and probably fifteen unofficials, of whom, it is true, a number would be chiefs. At any rate the grant of an unofficial majority is the central feature of Sir Alan's scheme. Political development is less advanced in Nigeria, but can this essential difference be justified for the two Territories?

(8)   *Method of selecting unofficial members*

Except in a few cases the unofficial members of the Legislative Council are to be nominated by the Houses of Assembly and Lagos Municipal Council. The method of selection of unofficial members of Councils is therefore only important in the case of the Houses of Assembly. It will be remembered that Sir Bernard Bourdillon attached great importance to providing in the constitution for the substitution of some form of selection for nomination by the Governor. In practice he had arranged during his governorship, wherever possible, for members to be selected by those whom they represented. Sir Arthur Richards proposes that all the unofficial members should in the first instance be nominated by the Governor, but it is part of his scheme that it should be announced that after the first three years the possibility will be examined of substituting a form of nomination by choice according to African custom instead of by the Governor. What in fact does this mean? It will be seen that the Chief Commissioner of the Eastern Provinces does not think that it means anything in the conditions of the east. On the other hand the Acting Chief Commissioner of the Western Provinces attaches great importance to the selection by Provincial Councils of the provincial representatives in the regional councils. Clearly it would be both more satisfactory in practice and more democratic if nomination by the Governor could be dispensed with. Must we assume that it is quite impossible all over Nigeria for the representatives of Native Authorities in the regional Houses of Assembly to be nominated by the Native Authorities in each province? I can well imagine that this is quite impracticable in the Eastern Provinces, but is it equally impracticable in the Northern and Western Provinces? If such a system could be adopted in some parts of the Territory the Governor would have to retain the power of veto; otherwise unsatisfactory or exceedingly reactionary members might be appointed.

In the case of the other unofficial members the substitution of selection for nomination by the Governor would be more difficult. On the advice of the Chief Commissioner of the Eastern Provinces Sir Arthur Richards has abandoned specific sectional representation. Unless you have such sectional representation it is difficult to see how nomination by the Governor can be dispensed with.

It is interesting to note that both the Chief Commissioner of the Northern Provinces and the Acting Chief Commissioner of the Western Provinces stress the importance of developing deliberative bodies below the level of regional councils. The establishment and building up of such bodies is bound, I think, to play an exceedingly important part in the development of the country and to affect the pace at which political responsibility can progressively be granted to Africans.

(9)   Committees of the Houses of Assembly

The Houses of Assembly are to meet only once a year, so that a continuous association of their unofficial members with the government of the country will not be easy. Might it not be worth considering both as an educative and as a practical measure the creation of committees of the Houses of Assembly which would deal with such subjects as finance, development, education, etc? This is not an attempt to import the Ceylon constitution into Nigeria. The committees would be primarily consultative, but they would make it possible for the unofficial members of the Houses of Assembly to have much closer contact with the process of government at the centre of each region than could be acquired merely by attending an annual session of the House of Assembly itself.

(10)   Finance

Once the regional budget had been passed by the House of Assembly (and in the case of the north by the House of Chiefs), approved by the Governor and included as an appendix in the central budget passed by the Legislative Council, how would supplementary expenditure be dealt with? Would all proposals involving supplementary expenditure have to be considered by the central finance committee at Lagos? If they were, I doubt whether the financial scheme proposed would work. It seems clear that it would be necessary for the Chief Commissioners to have power to incur considerable supplementary expenditure on their own authority, and it might be desirable for all such expenditure above a certain limit to be referred to a regional finance committee meeting say once every three months. Only in the case of expenditure above a higher limit would reference to the central finance committee be necessary.

The relations of the Financial Secretary at Lagos with the Deputy Financial Secretaries in the regions would be a matter of some complication. It would seem desirable that the deputies should be given considerable latitude to frame their own financial proposals within the general policy of Government. It would be important to secure as great a degree of flexibility as possible in order that the division of the country's finances into three parts should not hold up the planning and execution of the post-war development programme. The financial side of the scheme will evidently require very careful working out.

(11)   The position of Lagos

Sir Arthur Richards proposes that the Lagos municipality should manage its own finances coming directly under the central legislature and that the rest of the Colony should also come direct under the central legislature and that it should be administered as at present by political officers and Native Authorities under the Commissioner of the Colony. This leaves the Colony, outside the municipality, subject to no regional political body, possibly rather an untidy arrangement. The alternative would seem to be Lord Hailey's suggestion that the Colony outside the Lagos municipality should be included in the Western Provinces. This point was mentioned to Sir Arthur Richards during his discussions here and it would be interesting to know the reasons why he has preferred the other alternative.

5   CO 583/286/5, no 17   30 Oct 1944

[Richards's proposals]: CO record of a meeting to discuss Sir A Richards's proposals for constitutional development in Nigeria

The Secretary of State said that the principle of decentralisation on a regional basis, contained in Sir Arthur Richards' proposals, appeared to him sound, but that, in the absence of fuller information as to the working of the proposed organisation, judgment on the details of the proposals would have to be reserved until after Sir Arthur Richards' arrival.

It was pointed out that the proposals as they stood would arouse considerable public criticism, since, so far from constituting an advance they were in fact retrograde to the extent that they involved the withdrawal from Lagos and Calabar of direct representation on the Central Legislature. *The Secretary of State* said that the introduction of the scheme would be difficult politically since it might be held to take away more than it gave, while it contained no important counter concession such as the grant of an unofficial majority. It was important that the new constitution should be acceptable to all parties in this country. Otherwise there would be a danger that it might be thrown over in the event of a change of Government in the United Kingdom. He did not himself see that, if all the unofficial members were to be nominated by the Governor, there would be any real danger in an unofficial majority in the Regional Councils.

Mr. Cohen explained that if the Emirs and Chiefs were included as unofficials, there would in fact be an unofficial majority on the Central Legislature, but that he was not sure whether in Nigeria the Emirs could be regarded entirely as unofficials. *The Secretary of State* thought that political opinion in this country would accept the proposed membership of the Central Legislative Council as constituting an unofficial majority. *Mr. Cohen* pointed out that the scheme provided for a European majority on the Legislative Council, with 19 officials and three unofficial members for commerce, banking and shipping who would presumably be Europeans as against 6 Emirs and Chiefs and 15 other African members.

The Secretary of State said that among the matters on which further explanation was required was the relationship between the House of Chiefs and the House of Assembly in the Northern Provinces. It would also be as well to ask Sir Arthur Richards to enlarge on the reasons for not creating a House of Chiefs in the Western Provinces similar to that in the North. It was explained that there was felt to be a danger of undoing the progressive development of the past ten years in these Provinces if a Council consisting entirely of Chiefs was set up.

The Secretary of State thought that the withdrawal of direct representation from Lagos and Calabar was a mistake. It must be accepted that Lagos was a cosmopolitan centre in a special position; and he could not see that there was any serious objection to retaining the vote in Calabar if this was strongly favoured by local sentiment.

As regards the time for the introduction of the proposals the *Secretary of State* said that it would be preferable for the introduction of the Nigeria proposals to be delayed until the New Year. *Mr. Creasy* said that Sir Arthur Richards had mentioned in a letter that his intention was to introduce his proposals to the Legislative Council next March.

Referring to the pledge given by Sir Bernard Bourdillon that the people of Nigeria would be given an opportunity of commenting upon any constitution proposals which he put forward, the *Secretary of State* said that the submission of the proposals to the Legislative Council could probably be held to meet this pledge, but that he had serious doubts about such a procedure. Sir Arthur Richards' views must be obtained on this. *The Secretary of State* thought that the introduction of the new Nigerian constitution would have to be treated in this country quite differently from that of the Gold Coast constitution. A white Paper would have to be prepared which would not merely explain the proposals themselves, but would set out in some detail, the historical and political background of Nigeria and in particular its natural division into three distinct areas.

Sir George Gater said that a point to be considered was whether the staff could be found to man the proposed regional administrations; since it seemed likely that decentralisation on a regional basis would involve an increase in the lower as well as the higher ranks of the administration.

Mr. Cohen said that it was not clear how the financial arrangements proposed would work in practice and there were a number of other matters which although points of detail would, he thought, have to be settled before the proposals could be finally approved. One matter which had been raised by the Commissioners of both the Northern and the Western Provinces was the question of the political organisation below the regional level and the need for the development of provincial councils from which the members of the regional councils would be elected and also of district councils.

Reference was made to the ultimate aim underlying the proposals and the view was a expressed that it would not be right to regard the proposed regional framework merely as a temporary phase in the development of Nigeria. *The Secretary of State* said that the scheme seemed to him to lead eventually to a federal system.

It was agreed that a meeting should be held with the Secretary of State as soon as possible after Sir Arthur Richards' arrival to enable the Governor to explain the general picture as he saw it. The details of the proposals could then be discussed with Sir Arthur at the departmental level and a final meeting with the Secretary of State should be held before Sir Arthur's departure.

6   CO 583/286/5, no 21   Nov 1944
[Richards's proposals]: memorandum by A B Cohen on points arising from discussions with Sir A Richards on constitutional development in Nigeria

As a result of the discussions between the Secretary of State and Sir Arthur Richards on the 2nd and 9th November, it was agreed that the following changes should be made in the proposals submitted by Sir Arthur in his secret despatch of the 19th July:—[1]

I *Legislative Council and Houses of Assembly*

(1) *African majority on the Legislative Council*
It was agreed that the membership of the new Legislative Council should be modified so as to provide for an African majority.

---

[1] See 3.

(2) *Unofficial majorities in the Houses of Assembly*
It was agreed that the membership of the Houses of Assembly should be modified so as to provide for unofficial majorities.

(3) *Direct election at Lagos and Calabar*
Sir Arthur Richards stated that he was most anxious to abolish direct election by means of the ballot box. He had therefore made no provision in his proposals regarding the Legislative Council for the retention of directly elected members from Lagos and Calabar. One of the main principles underlying his scheme was to provide a constitutional system more suitable to Nigeria than the Westminster model; but if direct election was retained even in one place only, it would act as a focus for demands for its extension elsewhere. The Secretary of State on the other hand pointed out that the withdrawal of direct election from places which had enjoyed it for a considerable time would be likely to be much criticised in certain quarters in this country and might lead to the scheme as a whole being unfavourably received as being reactionary. The Secretary of State informed Sir Arthur therefore that he was opposed to the abolition of direct election for Lagos, although he admitted that there was a stronger case for abolishing it in Calabar. He thought that the retention of a special arrangement for Lagos could be justified on the grounds of its cosmopolitan character.

It was agreed that, without disclosing the connection with a scheme of constitutional reform, Sir Arthur Richards should sound opinion in Lagos confidentially to discover what the probable reaction would be to the substitution for direct election to the Legislative Council of nomination by the Municipality (presumably by the unofficial members only) coupled with an extension of powers to the Municipality. Sir Arthur Richards, however, agreed that unless he was able, as a result of these soundings, to convince the Secretary of State of the necessity for abolishing direct election at Lagos, he would drop this proposal rather than prejudice the scheme as a whole. He also agreed that there should in any case be three instead of two members from Lagos itself in the Legislative Council.

As regards Calabar, it remains to be considered whether any special arrangement for its representation should be made if Sir Arthur Richards decides, after further consideration, to recommend the abolition of direct election to the Legislative Council. Possible alternatives would be to give the Calabar Town Council the right to nominate a member to the Eastern Provinces House of Assembly or to give the Town Council the right to nominate a member direct to the Legislative Council.

(4) *Method of appointment of representatives of Native Authorities to the Houses of Assembly*
It was agreed that it should be made clear in the Governor's despatch that the Native Authorities would themselves select their representatives in the Houses of Assembly, but that, in view of the experimental nature of the arrangements, the Governor would have to retain his right of veto at first. It should also be made clear that the possibility of withdrawing the Governor's right of veto would be considered after three and, if necessary, after six years. The nomination of other unofficial members of the Houses of Assembly and of the unofficial members of the Legislative Council, other than those nominated by the Houses of Assembly and the House of Chiefs in the north, would at first be direct by the Governor, but presumably this also would be subject to review after three and again, if necessary, after six years.

(5) *Method of nomination of representatives of Houses of Assembly on Legislative Council*
The members nominated by the Houses of Assembly to the Legislative Council would be nominated by means of a vote of the unofficial members only in each House of Assembly and only unofficials would be eligible for nomination.

(6) *Name for the House of Assembly and the Northern House of Chiefs*
The name 'Regional Councils' should not be used, in view of the danger of confusion with international bodies to be called Regional Councils. The three Houses of Assembly should simply be referred to as the 'Northern Provinces House of Assembly', etc. and if possible a suitable generic name should be found covering the three Houses of Assembly and the House of Chiefs in the north.

(7) *Meetings of Houses of Assembly and Northern House of Chiefs*
It should be made clear in the Governor's despatch that the Houses of Assembly and the Northern House of Chiefs would meet at least once a year. Once a year would probably be sufficient at first, but as the Councils developed meetings might take place twice a year.

(8) *Committees of Houses of Assembly*
Committees of the Houses of Assembly should be formed to keep the members in touch with administration and to give them practical experience of special subjects. In particular finance committees would be required, but there might also be committees to deal for example with development, education, etc.

II *Provincial Councils*
It was agreed that Sir Arthur Richards should examine the question of the development of Provincial Councils as a link between the Houses of Assembly and the Native Authorities and the possibility of using these in connection with the selection of Native Authority representatives in the Houses of Assembly. If possible, reference should be made in the scheme to the development of Provincial Councils and it might also be desirable to make reference to the development of district and village councils, particularly in the Northern Provinces, as suggested by the Chief Commissioner.

III *Financial Questions*
It was agreed that the financial arrangements under the scheme should be generally on the lines described in the attached note[2] and that these should be fairly fully explained in the Governor's despatch.

IV *Administrative Machinery*
It was agreed that the scheme would involve some adjustment of the relations between Chief Commissioners and the Central Government and between administrative and departmental officers in the Provinces. Sir Arthur Richards' general conception was that the Chief Commissioners, in consultation with the departmental Deputy Directors, should settle all local matters in the Regions, reference being made to Government on all questions of policy and to departmental Directors on technical

---

[2] Not printed, but see 7.

questions of policy. Deputy Directors at Chief Commissioners' headquarters would refer to their Directors, where necessary, on technical and departmental questions, but would be responsible to the Chief Commissioners on all local questions. It would appear to be desirable that this should be explained in the despatch.

V *Presentation and introduction of scheme*

(1) *Presentation of scheme*
It was agreed that the scheme should be made public during the next meeting of the Legislative Council in March, 1945. For this purpose a despatch should be prepared by Sir Arthur Richards setting out not only the details of the scheme, but also the background of Nigeria so as to explain why a scheme in this form was necessary. Sir Arthur Richards said that he would prepare a first draft of the despatch and would submit it in draft for the Secretary of State's consideration. When the time came for publication in March it would be published simultaneously in Nigeria by laying it on the table of the Legislative Council and in this country in the form of a White Paper under cover of a short note by the Secretary of State.

It was agreed that it would be desirable to make it clear in the despatch that Sir Arthur Richards had discussed the proposals with the Secretary of State, who had expressed himself as prepared to consider them favourably and had authorised him to lay them before the Legislative Council, but had not committed himself finally to their approval pending discussion of them in the Legislative Council.

After publication the scheme would be debated in the Legislative Council in Nigeria and it would probably be desirable to arrange, after this debate had taken place, for a debate on the proposals in the House of Commons before a final decision was taken on them; but this would have to be considered nearer the time.

It was also agreed that before the proposals were published they should be explained confidentially to certain persons in Nigeria. In the Northern Provinces the Chief Commissioner would first discuss them in detail with the Emirs and the Governor would then himself hold a special conference of the Emirs at which their assent to the proposals would be sought. In the Western Provinces the Governor would speak to the more important Chiefs. To cover the Eastern Provinces he would speak confidentially to the unofficial members of the Legislative Council.

(2) *Timing of introduction of scheme*
It was agreed that, assuming that as a result of the debates referred to above it was decided to give effect to the proposals, the aim should be to bring them into force about May, 1946, so as to enable preparations to start for the introduction of the first regional budgets in the Houses of Assembly in January, 1947, in respect of the year 1947/48.

7   CO 583/286/5, no 43   6 Dec 1944
[Constitutional revision]: despatch from Sir A Richards to Mr Stanley setting out revised proposals for Nigerian constitutional development. *Annexures*

[Following the discussions over Richards's proposals for constitutional change between the CO and the gov during 1944, a revised version of Richard's plans was drawn up and sent to Stanley on 6 Dec. This despatch, later to be further revised by the new secretary of

state, George Hall (see 21), was laid before the Legislative Council on 5 March 1945 as
Sessional Paper no 4 of 1945 and printed as Cmd 6599, *Proposals for the Revision of the
Constitution of Nigeria* (London, 1945)]

I have the honour to address you on the subject of the political and constitutional
future of Nigeria. I shall endeavour to set forth my conclusions and
recommendations with a brevity which is no measure of the time and trouble taken
to form them.

As you are aware, I studied a number of relevant documents in London during
November of last year and I had the advantage of many discussions with officers of
your staff. Since assuming office in Nigeria I have read all the local memoranda on
constitutional questions. During the very extensive travelling which I have
undertaken in the past twelve months, I have kept the subject constantly in mind and
have, I hope, retained an objective outlook. The background of the different races
comprised within the area known as Nigeria and the diversity of their languages,
customs, beliefs, habits and aspirations have been drawn by many pens, among the
most notable being that of Lord Hailey, whose writings have been the foundation for
my study of the subject. I also wish to record my indebtedness to my predecessor, Sir
Bernard Bourdillon; during his period of office he gave profound thought to the
problems of constitutional development and the conclusions which he formed have
been of the greatest assistance to me in framing my proposals. I have also steeped
myself in the writings and the thought of Lord Lugard, who has had no equal in
knowledge of the people and in grasp of the principles and practice of colonial
administration. He was confronted with the difficult setting of an artificial unity
which existed only on the map. His problem was to build a system which would allow
organic growth and make the unity originally superimposed from outside into a
living thing which might progress from varying stages of adolescence to adult
nationhood. If I may be permitted the observation, Lord Lugard never allowed
principles to become divorced from practice and he held always before him the ideal
of natural growth.

2.   I have made these preliminary remarks because I feel very strongly that
political progress must be planned deliberately and that, while allowance must be
made for changes and any constitutional experiment must be flexible in its
provisions, there must be some framework of design. We cannot leave all the
difficulties to Time and Fate. As I see it, the main test to apply to new political and
constitutional proposals is—will they work and, if so, how? The problem of Nigeria
today is how to create a political system which is itself a present advance and
contains the living possibility of further orderly advance—a system within which the
diverse elements may progress at varying speeds, amicably and smoothly, towards a
more closely integrated economic, social and political unity, without sacrificing the
principles and ideals inherent in their divergent ways of life. The present system of
Government in Nigeria has many inconsistencies and by its nature is unsuited for
expansion on a Nigerian basis. A governing factor in my thoughts has been the
physical size of Nigeria—one third of British India or the size of France, Belgium and
the United Kingdom put together—with a population double that of the Dominion of
Canada. Planning for such a country should, therefore, be on an Imperial scale, far
different from the small-scale planning which is adequate for a Colony of the normal
small size. We have been urged to take some risks and I agree that we should do so.
To refuse to take risks is to admit political insolvency. I have tried to avoid false

analogies. It is not the Westminster model but the principles which lie behind it and make it work that I have tried to apply, and in doing so I have retained the fundamental principle of real and practical training by progressive stages based on Native Institutions.

3.   In framing my proposals I have kept three objects before me; to promote the unity of Nigeria; to provide adequately within that unity for the diverse elements which make up the country; and to secure greater participation by Africans in the discussion of their own affairs. At present no unity exists, nor does the constitution encourage its growth. The Legislative Council does not legislate for the Northern Provinces, so that more than half the population is outside its range. Even in the Western and Eastern Provinces, which are within its sphere, the mass of the people are insufficiently represented. What is wanted is a constitutional framework covering the whole of Nigeria and a Legislative Council on which all sections of the community are given representation. But however widely representative it may be, a Central Legislature by itself is not enough. Nigeria falls naturally into three regions, the North, the West and the East, and the people of those regions differ widely in race, in customs, in outlook and in their traditional systems of government. This natural division of the country is reflected in the machinery of administration, the three sets of provinces being grouped together each under a Chief Commissioner; but this purely administrative arrangement, besides being incomplete in itself through the lack of an adequate regional organization at each Chief Commissioner's headquarters, has no counterpart in the constitutional sphere. Apart from Chiefs' Conferences, no bodies exist at which public affairs can be discussed on a less narrow plane than the purely local or one less wide than the Nigerian. Nor is there any constitutional link between the Legislative Council and the Native Authorities. What are needed are bodies where the affairs of each group of provinces can be discussed, bodies which on the one hand are linked by membership with the Native Authorities, and on the other hand can send delegates to speak for each region in the Central Legislature. And these bodies must be so constituted as to be acceptable to public opinion in the regions where they are established. Having set up such bodies and widened the scope of the Central Legislature, it would still remain to secure a greater voice in their affairs for the Africans themselves. At present officials are in the majority on the Legislative Council, but I feel that the time has come to create unofficial majorities.

4.   The recommendations which I put forward, with the support of all three Chief Commissioners, provide both for the widening of the scope and membership of the Legislative Council and for the establishment of regional Councils for the Northern, Western and Eastern Provinces. The Northern regional Council would consist of two chambers, the House of Chiefs and the House of Assembly, while in the West and East there would be a single chamber in each case, the House of Assembly. The new Legislative Council would legislate for the whole country including the Northern Provinces. The whole range of Nigerian affairs would be open for debate, especially on the second reading of the Budget. The Legislative Council would be so constituted as to have an unofficial and an African majority and, while direct election would be retained where it exists at present, the majority of the unofficial members would be selected from their own bodies by the Northern House of Chiefs and by the unofficial members of the Houses of Assembly. Thus the regional Councils would act as electoral colleges for the Legislative Council apart from their other functions. The

Houses of Assembly would themselves have unofficial majorities and the greater part of the unofficial members would be nominated by the Native Authorities in each province from their own numbers. In this way a chain of representation would be created from the Legislative Council to the people through the regional Councils and the Native Authorities, and it would be a type of representation which would be in accordance with custom, would fit in naturally with existing institutions, and would be readily intelligible to the people themselves.

5. I do not propose that there should be any change in the constitution of the Executive Council, the functions of which are purely advisory, and which has recently been enlarged by the addition of three unofficial members.

6. The system of native administration would continue its evolution precisely as at present and the progressive devolution of authority and responsibility to Native Authorities would proceed. But if the Native Authorities are to play their full part in the constitutional framework, they must be prepared continually to adapt themselves to modern conditions. The system of indirect rule cannot be static; it must keep pace with the development of the country and it must find a place for the more progressive and better educated men. Only in this way can the Native Authorities retain the confidence of the people as education spreads and only in this way can local administration be effectively carried on. Progress in this direction has, of course, been taking place for some time. In the Eastern Provinces the absence of any traditional political organization has made it possible to build up Native Authorities on democratic lines in the form of Councils on which all the individual family units within the larger tribal units have equal representation. These Councils include representatives of the political associations sponsored by the educated members of the community. In the Northern and Western Provinces also the traditional rulers have been encouraged to admit to their Councils representatives of progressive opinion. In the Western Provinces, in particular, only four of the Native Authorities consist of a Chief alone, the rest being 'Chief-in-Council' or 'Council' and the Councils include representatives of the educated element, who are often in effect chosen by the local political associations. This progressive modernization of the Native Authorities is an essential part of the policy which I put forward.

7. My proposals for constitutional development fit in well with the forthcoming reform of the judicial system, under which, instead of a Supreme Court for the Colony and a Protectorate Court for the rest of Nigeria, a single Supreme Court will be set up covering the whole country. The details of my proposals are set out in the paragraphs which follow.

Membership of House of Chiefs and Houses of Assembly

Northern Provinces House of Chiefs

8. I propose that the Chief Commissioner should preside and that the membership should be on the lines so successfully followed at present for the annual Chiefs' Conference. First-class Chiefs would sit as of right and other Chiefs would select a representative panel from among their own numbers, subject to the approval of the Governor acting on the advice of the Chief Commissioner. For the present Conference all First-class Chiefs (13) are invited. Second-class Chiefs are grouped Provincially and one from each group is invited, which results in annual attendance of about ten out of a total of twenty-nine Second-class Chiefs.

Houses of Assembly

9.   I propose the following membership:—

Northern Provinces
Official Members

Senior Resident (President).
All other Residents (12)—including Secretary, Northern Provinces.
Deputy Financial Secretary
Deputy Director of Education
Deputy Director of Agriculture
Deputy Director of Medical Services
Deputy Director of Public Works
Crown Counsel

$$= 19$$

Unofficial Members

Fourteen Provincial Members to be selected by Native Authorities from their members, other than major Chiefs.

Six Members to be nominated by the Governor to secure adequate representation of the Pagan community, smaller Native Authorities, the Sabon Gari community, industry and commerce or any other important aspects of life not otherwise represented among the unofficial members.

$$= 20$$

Western Provinces
PRESIDENT. The Chief Commissioner.

Official Members

Residents (7) (The Secretary, Western Provinces, being raised to status of Resident.)
Deputy Financial Secretary
Deputy Director of Education
Deputy Director of Agriculture
Deputy Director of Medical Services
Deputy Director of Public Works
Crown Counsel

$$= 14$$

Unofficial Members

Three Chiefs. (To be nominated by the Governor after consultation with Western Provinces Chiefs.)

Seven Provincial Members to be selected by Native Authorities from their members, other than major Chiefs.

Five Members to be nominated by the Governor from prominent citizens representing important aspects of life not otherwise represented among the unofficial members.

$$= 15$$

Eastern Provinces (including Cameroons)
  PRESIDENT. The Chief Commissioner.

Official Members
  Residents (6) (The Secretary, Eastern Provinces, being raised to status of
    Resident.)
  Deputy Financial Secretary
  Deputy Director of Education
  Deputy Director of Agriculture
  Deputy Director of Medical Services
  Deputy Director of Public Works
  Crown Counsel

                                            = 13

Unofficial Members
  Nine Provincial Members selected by Native Authorities from their members.
  Five Members to be nominated by the Governor from prominent citizens to
    represent important aspects of life not otherwise represented among the
    unofficial members.

                                            = 14

The President of each House would have an original and a casting vote, but there
would be an unofficial majority in each. All the unofficial members would be persons
of African descent domiciled in Nigeria. Nominations of unofficial members would be
for three years.

Functions of House of Chiefs and Houses of Assembly
  10. Although as stated below the regional Councils would not in the first
instance have any responsibility for the enactment of legislation, they would be
concerned with both legislation and finance in addition to their deliberative
functions. The Houses of Assembly would debate motions and resolutions whether
brought forward by the official or the unofficial members, although, in accordance
with the usual practice, the unofficial members would not be entitled to propose
money resolutions. The House of Chiefs in the Northern Provinces would equally
have the right to originate motions and resolutions other than money resolutions.
  11. In the first instance, I propose that the Legislative Council of Nigeria should
remain responsible for the actual passage of all legislation pending consideration by
a committee whether legislative powers, and if so what powers, should be devolved
on the regional Councils. Meanwhile all bills, other than purely formal bills or bills
introduced under certificates of urgency, would be laid on the table of the regional
Councils, before submission to the Legislative Council, for general discussion on the
lines of a second reading debate and for the submission of advice by resolution
should any amendments be desired.
  12. I propose to devolve upon the regional Councils a large measure of financial
responsibility. Each would have its own regional budget, on which would be borne
the cost of all Government services in the region, including the salaries of
Government personnel. The only exception would be the cost within the region of
services declared to be central services, such as the railway, posts and telegraphs,

income tax and audit which would continue to be carried on the Central Estimates as at present, together with the central organization of Government, the headquarters and central staff of all Departments and such charges as interest on public debt, pensions, etc. Regional revenue would consist in the first place of the share of the direct tax at present payable to the Central Government together with any receipts from fees, licences, etc., which might be allotted to the regional budgets, and in the second place of annual block grants from central revenue. The Houses of Assembly would debate the regional estimates in detail before passing them with such amendments as they desired to suggest. In the Northern Provinces the estimates would also be considered by the House of Chiefs, which would have the power to delete or amend items, but not to insert new ones. After passing the regional Councils the estimates would be submitted to the Governor, who would have the right to amend them if he thought this necessary in the public interest. When approved by the Governor they would appear in the central estimates as block votes, full details being given in the form of appendices. A statement is attached giving in greater detail my proposals for the financial procedure (Annexure I) of regional Councils and their relations with the Legislative Council on matters of finance.

13.   The arrangements which I propose for dealing with regional revenue and expenditure would in no way detract from the responsibility of Native Authorities for operating their own local services and financing them from their own revenues. These revenues are mainly derived from the share of the direct tax retained by the Native Authorities, a share which the Governor has power under the law to increase or decrease. In order to simplify the system and to encourage Native Authorities to adopt progressive policies, I have recently frozen their contribution to central revenue from the direct tax at the amounts paid in by them during the year 1943–44. The remainder, and the whole of any additional proceeds from any increase in the direct tax, is to be retained by the Native Authorities themselves. They will thus be in a position to play an increasing part in the development of their own areas and the recent correlation of Native Authority and Government salaries will make it easier for them to secure the trained staff which they need for this purpose and will also help to prevent overlapping between Government and Native Authority spheres of work.

14.   I have referred to the financial functions and responsibilities of Native Authorities because I regard their relations with the regional Councils as equally important as those of the regional Councils with the Central Legislature. Under my proposals the Native Authorities and the regional Councils would share the direct tax as a source of revenue and the presence of Native Authority representatives on the Houses of Assembly should ensure a proper co-ordination between regional and purely local expenditure.

Meetings of the House of Chiefs and Houses of Assembly

15.   The House of Chiefs and the Houses of Assembly would meet annually in January for their budget sessions. The place of meeting would be Kaduna for the Northern Provinces, Ibadan for the Western Provinces, and Enugu for the Eastern Provinces. The language would be Hausa in the North and English in the West and East. The present annual conferences of Residents and of Chiefs in the Northern and Western Provinces and of Residents in the Eastern Provinces would cease to take place. At first one annual meeting of the regional Councils would probably be sufficient, but the possibility of additional meetings would not be excluded and, in

order that the members of the Houses of Assembly might keep in touch with administration and obtain practical experience in special subjects, committees of the Houses would be formed to deal with such matters as education, development, etc., Finance Committees of the Houses of Assembly would also be established.

Membership of the Legislative Council
16. I recommend that the Legislative Council of Nigeria should have the following membership:—
PRESIDENT. His Excellency The Governor.

Official Members
Chief Secretary
Chief Commissioners (3)
One Senior Resident each from Northern Provinces, Western Provinces and
    Eastern Provinces (3)
Attorney-General
Financial Secretary
Development Secretary
Director of Education
Director of Agriculture
Director of Medical Services
Director of Public Works
Commissioner of Labour
Director of Marine
Comptroller of Customs and Excise
General Manager of the Railway
Commissioner of Police
Commissioner of the Colony

$$= 20$$

Unofficial Members
Four Emirs (to be nominated by the House of Chiefs, Northern Provinces).
Two Chiefs from Western Provinces (to be nominated by the Governor from the
    three Chiefs who are members of the House of Assembly).
Five Members from the Northern Provinces (to be nominated by the unofficial
    members of the House of Assembly, from their own body).
Four Members from the Western Provinces (to be nominated by the unofficial
    members of the House of Assembly from their own body).
Five Members from the Eastern Provinces (to be nominated by the unofficial
    members of the House of Assembly from their own body).
One Member for Calabar (to be elected from the township area as at present).
Three Members for Lagos (to be elected from the Municipal area as at present).
One Member for the Colony (to be nominated by the Governor after consultation
    with the Native Authorities).
One Member to represent Banking
    „   „   Shipping   ⎫ To be nominated
    „   „   Industry and Commerce   ⎬ by the Governor.
    „   „   Mining   ⎭
$$= 29$$

The Governor would have a casting vote only and the Council would thus have an unofficial majority of twenty-nine to twenty, and, on the assumption that the four members representing banking, shipping, industry and commerce, and mining would as at present be Europeans, an African majority of twenty-five to twenty-four. The Governor would be provided under the Constitution with the usual reserve powers to be exercised, if necessary, in the interests of public faith, public order and good government. Nominations of unofficial members would be for three years.

Functions of Legislative Council

17.　The Legislative Council's functions would be the same as at present, with the essential difference that it would legislate for the whole of Nigeria including the Northern Provinces. The Finance Committee of the Legislative Council would continue to operate as at present.

Meetings of the Legislative Council

18.　The Legislative Council would meet for the budget session as at present in March, with other meetings during the year as required. The Budget Session would be held in successive years at Lagos, Kaduna, Ibadan and Enugu to demonstrate the Nigerian character of the Council. All other meetings would take place at Lagos.

The Position of Lagos and the Colony

19.　Lagos itself, comprising its present town limits divided into urban and suburban areas with a population of about 210,000, would become a Municipality with extensive powers. The rural area of the Colony, with a population of about 200,000, would remain directly under the Legislative Council and would continue to be administered by a Commissioner, three District Officers and Native Authorities. Departmental activities in the Colony would remain as at present organized. The Colony budget, a small matter if the municipal area is excluded, would form part of the central estimates. The Lagos municipal budget would form an appendix to the central estimates like the regional budgets, only a block grant of such subsidy as might be considered suitable being included in the body of the central estimates.

20.　The Lagos municipal area would continue to elect three members to the Legislative Council and the Calabar township area would continue to elect one. The system of election by ballot is not, in my view, a suitable method in Nigerian conditions for securing the proper representation of the people, nor would it be understood by the mass of the population. I should therefore be opposed to any extension of election by ballot at present, but at the same time I do not propose any variation in the present electoral arrangements either at Lagos or at Calabar, although the small number of voters in proportion to those entitled to vote does not indicate any great attachment to this method of selecting members. A note on the qualifications required for entry on the electoral roll at Lagos and Calabar is attached (Annexure II).

21.　I have not overlooked the possibility of introducing municipal government in places other than Lagos, but I do not consider the time ripe for this development and indeed in the Northern and Western Provinces the municipal system has not yet taken the public imagination and runs counter to established ideas.

Administrative Machinery

22.   I regard it as essential to the success of the regional Councils that adequate administrative machinery should be established at each regional headquarters. The constitutional proposals involve the creation of regional Deputies to the Heads of all the principal Departments and it is my intention that the Chief Commissioners, in consultation with these Deputies, should settle all local matters in the regions, only referring to Government on questions of policy and to departmental Directors on major questions affecting their departments. Regional Deputies would refer to their Directors where necessary on technical and departmental questions, but would be responsible to Chief Commissioners on all local questions. The Chief Commissioner and the regional Deputies would in fact form what would amount to a regional executive council, responsible, under the Government, for the co-ordination of all activities in the region and for its general welfare and development.

23.   The appointment of regional Deputies is in any case long overdue. Excessive centralization of authority in Lagos has left the Chief Commissioners without authoritative guidance on technical questions at their headquarters and has so overloaded the Heads of Departments that they cannot travel as they should or give that full attention to major issues of policy which the interests of the country increasingly demand. It is impossible to overstress the difference which would be made to administration by the courtesy of an occasional call on officers in the field, if Heads of Departments had time to travel, and by sympathetic discussion and explanation of policy and practice with local Chiefs and Administrative Officers. Under my proposals the principal Heads of Departments, with three Deputies in the provinces and another at headquarters, would be able to travel and to think.

24.   I feel moreover that the interest of the Service would be stimulated by the establishment of regional Councils where all the Residents would be free to take an active part in the financial dispositions of their own Provinces and in the discussion of legislation affecting them. Although Nigerian policy would be settled at a higher level, the chance of public contribution to the making of such policy would always be present in the debates of the regional Councils.

25.   My chief difficulty in considering how best to promote Nigerian unity and political progress has been the patent diversity of outlook between the different parts of Nigeria. As I have already said, it would be useless to pretend that unity exists at present, nor would clumsy attempts to achieve it result in anything but opposition. The individualism and the craving to paddle their own canoes, which distinguishes the people of the Eastern Provinces, finds no counterpart in the disciplined and conservative north, where respect and affection for their Chiefs is a very real factor. Progress is in the air and the pace can be accelerated, but too great haste or too little regard for ingrained sentiment and belief can only defeat its own object. In the Northern Provinces a very large section of the community has up to now shown no signs of the awakening of its political consciousness in the modern sense. The constitutional system which I propose will provide an outlet for political thought so far as it has emerged, and the representative character of the Legislative and regional Councils will be a safeguard against the domination of public affairs by any section of the community which may happen temporarily to be in a favoured position. This representative character should also ensure that political development will be in accordance with the wishes of the people themselves and so be of lasting value. But if the mass of the population are to play an effective part in the constitutional scheme,

it will be necessary to foster more resolutely the formal meetings of village, district and, in some cases, Provincial Councils as part of the system of native administration. It is in these councils that the habit of political thought will be inculcated so as to make possible the wise choice of the provincial members of the Houses of Assembly. The encouragement of district and village councils will be particularly important in the Northern Provinces, where the main units of native administration are large, so that without these intermediate links there is a danger of the Native Authorities not being in close enough touch with the people themselves.

26. I propose that the new Constitution should remain in force for nine years and be reviewed at the end of that period; but that in the intervening years, at the end of the third and if necessary the sixth year, there should be a review of the system of direct nomination by the Governor for membership of the Houses of Assembly and of the Legislative Council, in those cases where I have proposed this form of selection in the first instance, with a view to substituting a form of nomination by choice of the people represented wherever this might be found to be practicable.

27. In conclusion I ask for your authority to make these proposals public by laying a copy of this despatch on the table of the Legislative Council at the forthcoming Budget Session and by inviting a discussion in the Council.

Annexure I to 3

It is proposed that the financial procedure of the regional Councils and their relations with the Legislative Council on matters of finance should be as follows:—

(a) *Accounting arrangements*
The system of accounting would remain exactly as at present and there would continue to be a single accounting organization for the whole of Nigeria and a single surplus and reserve. The regions would thus have no separate accounts and no separate surplus or reserve.

(b) *Regional estimates*
(i) *Expenditure.* The regional expenditure estimates presented to the House of Assembly would consist of a detailed statement, in the usual form, of all items of expenditure borne on the regional budgets. These would include all the main services functioning in the regions, *e.g.*, administration, medical, public works, agriculture, education, etc., but would exclude the cost within the region of services declared to be central services, such as the railway, posts and telegraphs, income tax and audit as well as such central expenditure as interest on public debt, pensions, etc.
(ii) *Revenue.* The revenue side of the regional budgets would show revenue divided into two heads:—
  (a) The revenue estimated to be derived from the regional Council's share of the direct tax (at present payable to the Central Government), plus any other revenue from fees, licences, etc., declared to be regional.
  (b) The block grant from central revenue.
(iii) *Functions of Houses of Assembly with regard to estimates.* The Houses of Assembly would consider the expenditure estimates presented to them and would

pass them with such amendments as they desired to suggest. In accordance with the ordinary practice, the unofficial members would not have power to propose increases on individual items or heads of the estimates, but only reductions or deletions. In the Northern Provinces the budget, after passing the House of Assembly, would be considered by the House of Chiefs, which would have the right to veto or amend any of the items, but not to insert new ones. After passing the regional Councils the estimates would be submitted to the Governor, who would have the right to amend them if he thought this necessary in the public interest. When approved by the Governor they would appear in the central estimates as block votes, full details being given in the form of appendices. The regional Councils would at first not be given power to appropriate expenditure and the appropriation of regional expenditure would be in the hands of the Legislative Council. If, however, as the result of the recommendations of the Committee referred to in paragraph 11 of the despatch, it should be decided to devolve any legislative powers on the regional Councils, it might also in due course be decided to devolve upon the Houses of Assembly the power of legally appropriating regional revenue.

(c) *Central estimates*

(i) *Expenditure.* All items of expenditure not included in the regional estimates would appear in the central estimates exactly as at present, while these estimates would include three block votes of expenditure covering the whole of the expenditure proposed for each region. The central Council would be discouraged from discussing the details of regional expenditure.

(ii) *Revenue.* The central estimates of revenue would remain exactly as at present.

(iii) *Future procedure.* Should the Houses of Assembly at a future date be given the legal power of appropriating regional expenditure, as suggested under (b)(*iii*) above, a further change in the form of the central estimates would become necessary. If the Houses of Assembly appropriated their own expenditure, it would follow that the Central Council would cease to appropriate the *whole* of the regional expenditure and would appropriate only the block votes made from central revenue to supplement regional revenue (*i.e.*, the difference between the total of regional revenue and the total of regional expenditure). Similarly the central revenue estimates would then exclude regional revenue, which would be shown on the regional estimates only.

(d) *Colonial Development and Welfare expenditure*

Colonial Development and Welfare expenditure would be shown in the central estimates divided up into central expenditure and expenditure in the three regions. The regional expenditure would also be shown, under a separate head, in the regional estimates, with a corresponding entry on the revenue side.

(e) *Supplementary expenditure*

Finance Committees of the Houses of Assembly would be set up to deal with supplementary expenditure. As wide as possible a devolution of power to the regions with regard to supplementary expenditure should be made. The exact arrangements would be a matter for consideration at a later stage, but as a general rule it should not be necessary to refer supplementary expenditure to the central Finance Committee unless an increase in the block vote for the region was involved.

Annexure II to 3

The qualifications for persons entitled to vote in Legislative Council elections are contained in the following Articles of the Nigeria (Legislative Council) Order in Council, 1922:—

Elected members
'VI. The Elected Members of the Council shall be elected as follows:—

(1) Three Members by persons duly qualified as electors as hereinafter provided, who are resident within the municipal area of Lagos.
(2) One Member by persons duly qualified as electors as hereinafter provided, who are resident within the municipal area of Calabar.'

Qualifications of electors
'XX. Every male person shall be entitled to be registered as an elector, and when registered to vote at the election of Elected Members of the Council who—

(1) is a British subject, or a native of the Protectorate of Nigeria;
(2) is of the age of twenty-one years or upwards;
(3) has been ordinarily resident for the twelve months immediately preceding the date of registration in the municipal area for which the election is being held; and
(4) was during the calendar year immediately preceding, in possession of a gross annual income, from all sources, of not less than one hundred pounds.'

Disqualification of electors
'XXI. No person shall be entitled to be registered as an elector, or when registered to vote at the election of Elected Members of Council who—

(1) has been sentenced by any competent Court in any part of His Majesty's dominions or in any territory under his protection, to death, penal servitude, or imprisonment for a term exceeding six months; and has not either suffered the punishment to which he was sentenced, or such other punishment as may by competent authority have been substituted therefore, or received a free pardon; or
(2) is, under any law in force in Nigeria, found or declared to be of unsound mind or adjudged to be a lunatic.'

8 CO 583/286/5, no 67   **26 March 1945**
[Constitutional revision]: inward telegram no 245 from Sir A Richards to Mr Stanley reporting the reaction of the NCNC to the constitutional proposals

[The publication of Richards's proposals for constitutional change in Mar 1945 prompted a storm of protest within Nigeria led by the NCNC. Partly this protest was generated by the limited nature of what was being proposed and partly by the fact that no consultation with Nigerian opinion had taken place during the drawing up of the provisions. Also important in the NCNC reaction were the four so-called 'obnoxious ordinances'— concerning mineral rights, public land acquisition, crown lands and the appointment and deposition of chiefs—presented during the same session of the Legislative Council; these ordinances, arriving at a time of considerable economic difficulty for ordinary Nigerians (see 11), were deeply unpopular and were used by the NCNC to generate widespread opposition to Richards' policies.]

I have been requested to forward following message to you.

Begins. Emergency meeting of National Council of Nigeria and the Cameroons Holden at Glover Memorial Hall, Lagos, Saturday 24th, 1945 resolved pray you advise His Majesty the King defer sanction of Sessional Paper No. 4 of 1945 entitled 'Political and Constitutional future of Nigeria' debated in Legislative Council Thursday 22nd March and following bills passed by budget session, Legislative Council viz Minerals Appointment and Deposition of Chiefs, Public Lands Acquisition, Crown Lands Ordinances pending receipt of views being respectfully submitted through Governor of Nigeria by National Council comprising 99 organisations representing over six million Nigerians. National Council prepared to send delegation to London to state native views. Herbert Macauley, President and Nnamdi Azikiwe, General Secretary. *Ends.*

9   CO 583/286/5, no 82   17 April 1945
[Constitutional revision]: letter from Mr Creech Jones to Mr Stanley outlining his views on the constitutional proposals

I undertook to send you my difficulties with the proposed Nigerian Constitution. I regard the proposals as a great step forward and I hope my criticisms will not seem to imply that I minimise their value and wisdom.

(a) Eligibility for the franchise is £100. This is far too high and gives comparatively few Africans the right to vote. (c.f. Gold Coast)

(b) The development of democratic municipal councils is not provided for. (I have urged for many years political advance in the townships towards municipalities. I recognise the difficulties at Ibaden [sic]. But Calabar, Port Harcourt and such places ought to move to proper municipal structure (¶21)[1]. I am a little apprehensive about the views of ¶20. I hope they are not conclusive.

(c) The African majority on the Legislative Council is likely to be only *one*. I think this errs on the side of over-caution and should be more generous. I do not appreciate the case for retaining in the Legislative Council such a formidable army of officials.

(d) It is proposed to give 4 seats on the Legislative Council to European interests, almost as good as the whole representation of the Eastern Provinces. Banking is to be as well represented as Calabar. I don't like this syndicalistic proclivity. Why exclude the Trade Unions, or other professions and services (e.g. Education). They are as important as some of those named.

(e) I notice that (¶6) 'progressive modernisation of the Native Authorities is an essential part of the Governor's policy', but in the Northern Provinces it is not clear what the constitutional relationship of the House of Chiefs would be with the House of Assembly, or what purpose it would serve. In any case, the chiefs in House of Chiefs would be divorced from their Councils, whereas actually the Chief has no existence apart from his Council. In the House of Assembly, the members go as representatives chosen by their Councils but this presumably is not the case

---

[1] Paragraph references refer to those in 7.

in the 'Upper House'. Apart from this it is imperative that the Native Authority Councils be democratised as quickly as possible. I welcome the sentiment of the second half ¶25.

(f) I am not sure that the relation of the Executive Council to the Legislative Council is at all satisfactory and there is no assurance that the situation will be adjusted. It is unfortunate when a Legislative Council, however representative, cannot start on the road of learning to participate in responsibility.

(g) It is unfortunate that it is to be specified that three members of the Assembly for the Western Provinces must be Chiefs. This has not been specified in other cases.

I hope the proposals will work out as the Governor would like them to—not a stiffening of the inflexible feudal element in the provincial and central authorities, but an elasticity which will permit of adjustment to changing conditions and needs, effective checks of public opinion and democratic safeguards, an increasing place for the educated and able men and women in government, and administration and an adaptability which eliminates the feudal character of indirect rule and find representative people (by democratic machinery) instead of hand picked chiefs and others who conform to 'official' needs.

10   CO 583/286/5, no 88   28 May 1945
[Constitutional revision]: letter (reply) from Mr Stanley to Mr Creech Jones outlining Richards's response

I have now had an opportunity or obtaining Sir Arthur Richards' views on the various points raised in your letter of the 17th of April[1] regarding the Nigerian Constitutional proposals. You have, I believe, already seen him during his present stay in London, but it occurs to me that you might like to discuss your points more fully with him. I am sure that he for his part would welcome a talk with you on them, and if you so wish I shall be glad to arrange a meeting.

It will, I think, be convenient if I comment on your points under the headings which you yourself followed in your letter.

(a) Sir Arthur Richards would be quite willing to consider reducing the franchise qualification to a level comparable with that which obtains in the Gold Coast. The Gold Coast system is, however, on a rather different basis in that the electorate for the Municipal Members of the Legislative Council there is the same as that for the Town Councils and the property qualification is the ownership of real property having an annual rateable value of not less than £6. It would, therefore, have to be considered whether a similar system should be adopted in the case of Nigeria, or whether it would be better to retain in Nigeria the present requirement of a stated annual income and simply to reduce its figure.

(b) I entirely agree that Municipal Government may develop in the future, but I think we have to recognise that it is not the only possible channel for the development of responsible local Government, and that even in areas which have

---

[1] See 9.

become urbanised the Native Authorities may still have an important part to play. The democratisation of existing institutions on the lines foreshadowed in paragraph 25 of the Governor's despatch is, I think, likely to prove more fruitful than an attempt to introduce ready-made democracy on a European model, and we must be careful to avoid the importation of alien ideas and methods against the wishes of all but a small section of the community. The Governor himself is satisfied that Nigeria is wholly unready and unequipped for the general introduction of municipal status at present, nor indeed does he consider that there is any widespread demand for such development. Where there is a demand for municipal status it is for the most part sponsored by a single political group and often, as in Port Harcourt, is accompanied by a determination not to pay for it. In fact, they want municipal status without rates—the worst possible training in responsibility.

(c) The Official members of the Legislative Council will not, of course, be mustered merely for the purpose of counter-balancing the Unofficials. It is essential that the Heads of the more important departments of Government should be present in the Council to explain and defend the Government's policies. However, the Governor will be prepared to consider the exclusion of some of the Official members and we will bear the point in mind.

(d) I think that it must be conceded that European commercial interests are in a special position. They have played a great part in the development of West Africa in the past, and undoubtedly have a big part to play in the future. I think that it is only reasonable, and indeed desirable, in present circumstances, that they should have a voice in the Council. That it will amount only to a voice is ensured by the fact that there will be an African and not merely an unofficial majority on the Council. The Trade Unions and the professions are not really in an analogous position, and in any case they have the ordinary channels of representation open to them. The Governor agrees, however, that some reduction in the European unofficial representation might be considered.

(e) The position of the House of Chiefs in the Northern Provinces would be roughly analogous to that of the House of Lords. I know that it is often claimed that there is no such thing as a 'sole Native Authority', but, so far as the Northern Provinces are concerned, I doubt whether this claim would bear examination. Indeed the people of the Hausa States would be very much surprised, I think, if you suggested to them that the powers of their Emirs were in any way limited by their Councils. I agree that we should not do anything to consolidate this feudal tradition but at the same time we cannot ignore that it still exists. It has always been the policy of the Administration to encourage the Emirs to act on the advice of their Councils in important matters and to admit to these Councils representatives of the more progressive elements of the community. But the process of democratisation, which is closely dependent on the spread of education, cannot safely be accelerated beyond a certain limit, and in the meantime we must provide for things as they are and not as we might wish them to be.

(f) I think that for the present we must leave the Governor complete freedom in the choice of his Unofficial Advisers in the Executive Council. Nigeria is not ready for a ministerial system, and it would be quite impossible to find the men capable of taking a broad enough view to see the country's interests as a whole. You will, however, see from paragraph 15 of the Governor's despatch that it is proposed to provide the Unofficial members of the House of Assembly with the opportunity of educating themselves in the problems of administration as members of Committees which are to be set up to deal with individual subjects such as education, development, etc.

(g) There are not sufficient Chiefs of 'major' standing in the Western Provinces to justify the creation of a special House of Chiefs as in the North, but it would be a great mistake on this account to omit them from the machine altogether. For this reason provision has been made for three out of the five to sit, in rotation, in the House of Assembly. Their own people, I am sure, would not have it otherwise. The only reason that similar provision has not been made in the Eastern Provinces is that there are no Chiefs there of comparable standing.

As regards the last paragraph of your letter, I have already referred, in connection with (e), to the steps being taken to break down the autocratic tradition in the North. I would only add here that the idea, popularised by the Southern intelligentsia, that a Chief is necessarily a 'Yes-Man' does not conform to the facts. It is interesting to note the tendency of African politicians in one breath to refer to these Chiefs as civil servants who can scarcely count as African at all, and in the next to claim that they are kings used to the exercise of independent authority. You will find a notable example of this in the speeches of the Unofficial Members of the Legislative Council in the debate on the constitutional proposals.

I take this opportunity of acknowledging the receipt of your letter of the 2nd of May, enclosing a copy of a telegram addressed to you by Mr. Azikiwe. I have already received a long memorandum on the constitutional proposals from the 'National Council of Nigeria and the Cameroons' and the views they put forward will receive due consideration before the proposals are finally approved. I must, however, admit to some doubts as to the truly representative character of this organisation, and I should certainly require more information about the bodies which, according to the telegram, adopted resolutions of no confidence in the African Unofficial Members of the Legislative Council, before I accepted their claim to represent the communities and 'constituencies' concerned. I notice the telegram states that the Member for the Ijebu Division was the only representative who opposed the adoption of the proposals. This Member did, in the course of the debate, ask that consideration of the proposals might be deferred for three months, but he did not actually vote against their adoption, which was approved without a division.

11 CO 583/275/9, no 15   22 June 1945

[General strike]: inward telegram no 554 from Sir G Whiteley to Sir G Creasy reporting the declaration of a general strike [Extract]

[The general strike by government employees that began in June 1945 was generated by the sharp rise in the cost of living during World War II; the cost of living allowance granted by Bourdillon in 1942 had been effectively eroded by 1945. The strike, which demanded a 50 per cent cost of living increase, was widely supported, particularly in Lagos, and generated considerable unease in the administration. Azikiwe's papers were quick to support the strikers, particularly once some trade union leaders repudiated the strike, and Azikiwe's popularity grew sharply during these weeks; his *Daily Comet* and *West African Pilot* were banned by the administration on 8 July for their coverage of these events (see 12). The strike ended in early Aug following the promise of the appointment of a commission of inquiry into employees' wages and the cost of living; the Tudor Davies commission reported in 1946 and recommended an increase in the cost of living allowance, backdated to 1945 (see 26).]

Regret to inform you that strike has been declared today. Union leaders had previously resigned and so far as I know no new leaders have yet been elected. Departments chiefly affected are Railway, Marine, Public Works, Printing and Lagos Municiple[Sic] Council, where all African Technical employees and labourers have ceased work. Partial strike in Postal Department confined mainly to Telegraph staff. Clerical staff in all department still at work. Emergency services are operating satisfactorily. Present food stocks in Lagos sufficient for twenty days. No signs as yet of civil disturbances. It is difficult at present to estimate duration of strike or solidarity of strikers. I will keep you informed. . . .

12   CO 583/275/9, no 44   9 July 1945
[General strike]: inward telegram no 608 from Sir G Whiteley to Mr Stanley on the politicisation of the strike

Your telegram No. 612.
   Strike.
   Position shows improvement and there are an increasing number of men returning to work. There is reason to hope that existing tendency will continue and increase, and that, once total number of returning strikers reaches a critical point, remainder will follow en bloc. In meantime, hard core of resistance remains in railway workshops.
   2.   It has become increasingly evident that the strike is now being used as a political weapon, and political party, sponsored by Azikiwe, has been encouraging the strike. This has been evident in his two papers 'The Pilot' and 'The Comet'. In paragraph 3 of my telegram No. 591 I alluded to this. Subsequent to the enactment of the regulations in question the two papers published a gross misrepresentation of a statement made by the Public Relations Officer, which was calculated to discredit the Trade Union Leaders. As a result of this, I have suspended the publication of both papers, which should have a salutory effect. I shall forward by the next bag all the documents connected with the suspension for your information.
   3.   As a means of bringing strike to an end, it is imperative to restore confidence in, and prestige of, union leaders who are making every effort to bring strikers back to work, and every endeavour is being made to this end.
   4.   Figures of strikers are necessarily approximate, since restricted telegraph service makes accuracy impossible. In general, however, proportion of strikers is high in Lagos and low or even negligible outside. Following numbers on strike:—

Railway	18,500 (decreasing rapidly)
P. and T.	927
Marine	2,700
P.W.D.	5,400
Lagos Town Council	2,900.

These figures include daily labour.
   5.   In regard to effect on export produce, this is, fortunately, slackest time of year and since ports are working normally, and as majority palm produce is evacuated by water, the only important hold-up is the movement of 50,000 tons grounduts from Northern Provinces.

6. In regard to emergency staff, Railway requires eight Railway Civil Engineers, eight Railway Inspectors of Works and eight track gangers. Suggest best means of obtaining them quickly is to borrow them from a Military Railway Company. These men are required owing to previous arrears of maintenance of permanent way due to shortage of staff. Arrears have been greatly accentuated by strike at a period of heavy rains and state of track now gives cause for considerable anxiety. Their services will be required for several months, irrespective of when strike ends, and it will not be possible to dispense with them until all permanent vacancies for such posts have been filled.

7.   P.W.D. require urgently

(a) Six Inspectors of Works (Waterworks), qualifications as in Staff Indent No. 331.
(b) Six Electrical Engineers and eight Mechanical Engineers, qualifications as in Staff Indents Nos. 302, 309, 320, 365.

Suggest J.O. Hall,[1] now on leave be consulted in regard to (b). Can these twenty men be borrowed from public undertakings in U.K. for period of six to twelve months, pending Crown Agents filling parmanent vacancies on indent. Suggest Northern Ireland as promising recruiting ground and possibility of obtaining ex R.N. Warrant and N.C.O. Engine-room Artificers.

8.   These men are most urgently required. Grateful you despatch by air.

---

[1] J O Hall, chief engineer, Nigeria.

13   CO 583/275/9   13 July 1945
[General strike]: minutes by N J B Sabine[1] on the handling of reporting on the general strike   [Extract]

[One of the consequences of the general strike was the growing political stature of Azikiwe and in consequence, his growing demonisation by the administration. His reporting of the strike, not least in the USA, caused problems for officials, a development exacerbated by the publicity generated by the alleged plot to assassinate him, see 16.]

Sir A. Dawe
Mr. O.G.R. Williams
We discussed this morning with Mr. Usill of the Ministry of Information and Mr. Grenfell Williams of the B.B.C. the present position as regards the handling of news about the Nigerian strike. . . .

We had discussed several times at the weekly Publicity Meetings the situation on the strike in Nigeria and had given the B.B.C. some guidance in writing, which had been supplied by the West African Department. The B.B.C.'s transmission on Sunday, to which reference is made in this telegram, was based on a Reuter message. . . . I think the B.B.C. News people were at fault in not referring this to us, and I have told Mr. Grenfell Williams so.

One of the main difficulties in this case is that the Reuter correspondent in Nigeria is Mr. Azikwe. The question was raised some time ago of pointing out to Reuters the

---

[1] Head of Information Dept, CO.

disadvantages of Mr. Azikwe as a correspondent, but it was decided to take no action for the time being. It would in any case have been delicate and possibly liable to misunderstanding to make an approach to Reuters which involved any reflection on anyone appointed as their correspondent.

I think, however, that the time has come when it would be of advantage for the Nigerian Government to issue an authoritative communique on the strike, including a factual account of the present position. I think that this communique should be prepared and issued in Nigeria. It is, however, more than possible that Mr. Azikwe will not feel inclined to transmit the text of this as a Reuter message and I would, therefore, propose that arrangements should be made for its simultaneous release here at a time to be agreed with the Nigerian Government. We could then ensure that copies were sent to the B.B.C. and the news agencies, including Reuters, who I am sure would carry the communique in full. My idea would be that it should be issued here under the description of a communique issued by the Nigerian Government. I submit a draft telegram to the O.A.G. accordingly.

In order not to confuse the issue, I think that the telegrams in which Mr. Azikwe expresses fears for his safety[2] should be dealt with separately and I have minuted on a separate sheet on this.

I also submit a draft reply to the personal telegram to me from Mr. Fletcher (marked A).[3]

---

[2] See 16.

[3] Sir A. Dawe minuted (13 July): 'I agree. The fact that Azikiwe is the Reuter's man at Lagos explains a lot.'

14   CO 583/275/9, no 72   13 July 1945
[General strike]: despatch from Sir G Whiteley to Mr Stanley outlining his views of the causes of the general strike

With reference to my telegram No. 608 of the 9th of July,[1] I have the honour to address you on the subject of the general strike of technical workers and labourers in Nigeria and to set out in some detail my views on the basic causes of this dispute and my recommendation as to the policy to be followed.

2. I am concerned in this despatch, in the first instance, to set out the views of myself and my advisers on the underlying causes of the present unrest. I should, I think, emphasise at the outset that the present strike is not an isolated incident and that when it is settled and the workers have returned to duty the general situation in Nigeria will remain basically unaltered. The strike is a manifestation of a number of tendencies which have been apparent since the earlier years of the war, and which have been strongly accentuated as a result of war conditions.

3. For some years before the war there had been what one might describe as a political atmosphere in Lagos. This had been, in normal conditions, a comparatively harmless and natural growth at a time when the majority of the population were progressing, albeit slowly, both economically and educationally. The outbreak of war found Nigeria, as it found all democratic countries in the world, unready for the

---

[1] See 12.

great changes which were inevitably necessary to deal with conditions imposed by the war and in the first few months the tempo altered little; in fact it was not until perhaps the later months of 1940 that any great changes became apparent. In these months arrangements were made to recruit what by West African standards was a very large army. At the same time substantial labour forces were required for service works. Consequently considerable numbers of men who were formerly simple peasants were taken out of their environment and to some extent detribalised in large towns. The Africans recruited into the Forces began to enjoy conditions of life of which previously they had no conception. They were clothed, cared for and fed on a scale which was entirely unprecedented in West Africa. At the same time considerable numbers of British and Allied soldiers were quartered in the larger centres of Nigeria, and particularly in Lagos, and the Africans began to realise that there were other sorts of 'white men' than those whom they had previously known. In particular there were private soldiers, able bodied seamen etc. of several nationalities who, themselves coming from comparatively lowly environments, fraternised quite freely with the local Africans, with the consequence that the Africans began to appreciate that there were in Europe and on the American continent large numbers of persons in much the same position as themselves. The African therefore began to revise his conception of Europeans as a race, and this in turn has evoked in the larger towns a fairly widespread consciousness of colour, and what might be termed a race inferiority complex.

4.   This brief recapitulation of the conditions which obtained in the years 1940–42 may appear irrelevant in a despatch dealing with labour unrest, but I submit it in the belief that it provides some background to the direction in which African thought and aspirations have been moving in the last few years.

5.   At the same time that this process was proceeding there was much talk of self-government and self-determination for Colonial peoples, and while the idea of self-government was attractive to the educated or semi-educated Africans and provided a fertile field for the political agitators to work in, they had and have no conception of what self-government really entails. In the more politically minded Africans of Lagos there is a considerable body of uninformed opinion which fondly believes that, if the Europeans were to leave Nigeria in a body, Africans could maintain the present standard of administration with little difficulty.

6.   It is also relevant to refer to the general economic conditions which have obtained during the war period. The year 1939 was a period of moderate slump and this slump continued without any major change until the end of 1941 when the loss of territory in the Far East necessitated a complete re-orientation of Nigeria's war effort; instead of being as it was up to that time a comparatively unimportant source of raw materials Nigeria suddenly became the most important source of oil seeds and tin in the Colonial Empire. There was consequently a great drive for increased production of these commodities and from the beginning of 1942 there has been a gradual increase in prices of all primary products. This outflow of money on produce coincided with, by Nigerian standards, a vast expenditure of funds by the Army, but concurrently the output of the manufacturing countries of the world became restricted and there was a considerable contraction in the imports of consumer goods. The result, which was inevitable, is that after nearly three years of these conditions there is marked inflation in Nigeria. This inflation has resulted in a considerable rise in food prices at a time when owing to the fact that very substantial

numbers of able bodied young men have been taken off the land there has been a contraction in the production of staple foodstuffs.

7. Another factor of which account must be taken is the unfortunate failure of Africans to understand that rights and privileges carry with them obligations, that promotion, for instance, carries with it the obligation to perform more efficient work and undertake greater responsibility and that an employee owes a certain duty to his employer. Freedom of the press in Nigeria appears to be interpreted as freedom to mislead the people and to abuse Government. This failure to appreciate responsibility makes it almost impossible to discuss questions with Africans in the light of the interests of the whole community and the responsibility of one individual to another and of one section to the remainder of the community.

8. In Nigeria, as in other tropical African dependencies, wage rates have been related more or less to the earning power of the peasant farmer and to the low standard of living in rural areas. Thus, while the minimum wage for a labourer in Government employment in Lagos has risen from 10d. a day before the war to 2/– a day in 1942 it must nevertheless be admitted that this minimum wage is too low, despite the fact that African employers of labour still pay as little as 1/3d. a day. The wage rates for the lower grade artisans, technicians and clerks might also be judged to be low by modern standards, and in relation to the cost of living, but on the other hand the output of the African in this class of employment is still distressingly low. At the present time, when in Lagos there is a shortage of food, a shortage of housing and a shortage of imported goods, it is clear that any attempts to improve wage levels now can have only an inflationary effect and could not have the result of improving real living conditions.

9. It is therefore against this background that the present labour unrest must be examined. There have been some comparatively minor labour troubles during the course of the last few years, and the settlement of these disputes in favour of the worker has given rise to an impression that the Government is readily swayed to give in to the demands of labour. In fact, there is a body of opinion locally which holds that in the war years the Government has shown weakness on many occasions. It would be improper for me to discuss the merits or demerits of this opinion and in this despatch I am chiefly concerned with the problem of the present. I should also mention the agitation for a cost of living allowance for African staff in 1941, and its culmination in the middle of 1942 in the award of allowances which were undoubtedly generous. In passing I should of course mention that this fact in itself materially increased inflation and has been an important factor in bringing about the present economic difficulties.

10. It has been evident during the past six months or more that there has been a growing demand among all sections of the salary earning community for increased wages. This demand crystallised in May last in the receipt of what might be fairly described as an ultimatum from the Technical Workers Union and was based on the argument that as the cost of living had materially increased since the cost of living award in 1942 there were grounds for increasing the cost of living allowance. In my reply, of which you have a copy, I attempted to give a reasoned appreciation of the economic conditions and of the effect on those conditions of increasing the cost of living allowance. I recognised freely that the cost of living had increased and I pledged myself to do everything that was possible to reduce the cost of living. You will appreciate that it is only possible to attack the cost of living in a comparatively

limited manner, but I think I can say with justice that I have taken every action in my power to reduce the cost of foodstuffs, and there is no question that in the last six weeks the cost of basic foodstuffs has been substantially reduced and supplies have been increased. In the negotiations which preceded the strike I was most impressed with the fact that the technical workers did not appear to be interested in the cost of living—they were interested only in increased wages, i.e. cost of living allowance, and it is my belief that had I been able at once to reduce the cost of living still more substantially they would still have persisted in their demands for what were in effect higher wages.

11. As you are aware, shortly before the ultimatum expired the Trade Union leaders decided to follow the machinery prescribed in the Defence Regulations for settling labour disputes, and I hoped that the risk of a general strike of technical workers had been averted. Unhappily the workers disregarded the lead given to them by their leaders and declared a strike on midnight of 21st June. This strike has persisted since that date and I have kept you informed of all the important subsequent developments. The strike has now been going on for three weeks and, although there has been during the past few days a tendency to return to work, I must record my disappointment that that tendency has not reached the proportions that I had hoped, and there is at the time of writing this despatch no reason to suppose that there is likely to be any general resumption of work in the immediate future. Consequently I feel the time has come to place the whole question before you for your consideration of my views as to the course which should be followed.

12. The maintenance of essential services has been most successful and the arrangements made before the strike have gone very smoothly. Although there has been a considerable measure of inconvenience both to the Government and to the public, there has been no failure of services such as to endanger either the health or the lives of the population in general. These services, however, cannot be maintained indefinitely on the present basis and if we are to make preparations for a long drawn out struggle it is essential that I should have assistance from outside in the shape of European personnel. I have already addressed you on this subject and stated my minimum requirements.

13. I feel, moreover, in present circumstances that there is very little more I can do in the way of positive action to end the strike. There appear, therefore, to be three possible lines of action. In the first place I could accede to the demands of the workers. Secondly, there is the possibility of meeting those demands in part, and thirdly there is the alternative of establishing skeleton services on a permanent basis and settling down to a long struggle with the workers which could be expected to end sooner or later by a general return to work owing to pressure of economic conditions.

14. I confess that the problem as it exists at the present time is somewhat baffling. I am satisfied that to accede to the demands of the workers, either in whole or in part, will not provide a solution. I am convinced that the political atmosphere which now exists in Lagos is such that if the demands of the workers were met either in whole or in part this would only be a palliative and the Government would be faced in the near future with a repetition of the existing unrest. In fact I believe that the mood of the people of Lagos in general is such that there are few lengths short of violence to which they would not go to secure greatly increased wages. With a population which is largely either uneducated or semi-educated, among which an

anti-European Press has had considerable licence, it is of no use to appeal to reason. It is, for example, fruitless to point out that if wages are increased the increase is paid by the taxpayer. There is an impression that the wages will be paid by 'Government' which apparently is regarded as some rather vague body which has unlimited supplies of cash under its control. I would mention in passing that the African Medical Officer of Health of the Lagos Town Council, a man of over 50 years of age and earning a salary of £1100 a year, could not be persuaded in conversation with the Commissioner of the Colony to see that if the demands of the workers of the Lagos Town Council were met a substantial increase of rates would be the inevitable consequence.

15.   I have reluctantly come to the conclusion that not only the technical workers but probably all employees of Government and the commercial firms are at the present time unwilling to listen to reason, and to accede to their demands would not only provide no solution to the problem in the long run but would only lay up further embarrassment for the Nigerian Government, since I believe it to be true that the population in general have the impression that if they pursue any objective with sufficient determination the Government will give in. I am therefore forced to the conclusion that the only course which can be adopted in present circumstances, and which has any hope of providing a permanent solution to these difficulties, is to establish the fact that the Government of Nigeria proposed to stand firm, and that this should be done by maintaining the attitude that there can be no negotiations until the men return to work, and by adhering to that decision. This may entail a long drawn out strike which will I am afraid bring in its train considerable bitterness and possibly even some measure of disturbance, and which will not, of course, remove the discontent, but I think it would be most unwise in present circumstances to recede from this position.

16.   It is of course impossible in a despatch to give you the full picture of the situation and all the various currents and cross currents which are involved, but I would suggest that if you require any further information in regard to the general background advantage should be taken of Mr. G. F. T. Colby's imminent departure on leave and that the matter should be discussed with him when he arrives in London on approximately the 17th of July next. He has been intimately concerned with this question, first in his capacity as acting Chief Secretary and latterly as the executive officer coordinating all action and information in regard to the strike.

15   CO 583/275/10/part 1, no 35   14 July 1945
[General strike]: letter from Mr Creech Jones to Mr Stanley giving his views of the causes of the general strike

I am disturbed by the telegrams coming to me from Nigeria on the subject of the strike and by the news and comments recorded here. There is much concern among Africans in London as well. I recognise the difficulties of the situation, as well as the responsibilities of government in such circumstances. I feel, however, that there is more to be said on the subject than is stated in your letter to me of July 3.

From your report, it would appear that the strikers have behaved irregularly, are carrying on an 'unofficial' strike and have prejudiced themselves by the repudiation of their leaders. All this I recognise but from the information to hand, it is fair to notice that these things arise from the strength of the men's feelings about their demands, the delays they have experienced in the handling of their case and the completely negative line taken by the Government.

From the information you supply, not until the strike was about to happen was a trade dispute declared and the prospect of conciliation and arbitration opened out. It looks as if by that time, the patience of the men was exhausted because the Government had already made it clear that they could concede nothing for the reasons you set out. To the men it undoubtedly seemed obvious that the Government wanted to postpone a decision, to play for time, and to let them stand by and watch their standard of living steadily deteriorate. As in many other disputes, so in this one—the psychological factors are important.

However much one may think that the final stage was bungled and that the men should have gone, after all, to conciliation and arbitration with their case, it seems ironic that in so many colonial disputes little happens until economic facts overtake governments and exasperated men take action and put themselves in the wrong.

In the present case, I have only limited information to work on but something might have been done earlier to have arrested a development of which the present unhappy situation is the outcome. It is impossible to expect harassed men to how to theoretical economic arguments about inflation and to persuade them that adjustments upwards only mean further deterioration. Nor can men be persuaded about their public duty and the responsibility of their labour when the concrete answer of government is a disquisition on economics. Britain went through that sort of thing in the years between the wars and by now we ought to know better. The men concerned know that their price-levels have risen and remain shaky; their needs are in short supply; rationing is inadequate and wage-earners are faring worse and worse—which is not so obvious to those with other sections of the public.

The men involved are without much tradition or experience in the practice of trade unionism. I imagine that the customary talk about 'agitators' and 'irresponsible leaders' will be heard in those circles which understand little about the industrial struggles of working class movements. When men are indignant I regret that they have too little respect for the niceties of procedure and correct action and as in this case too often they have too little experience to fall back on. Matters are made worse by imprisoning and deporting those singled out by authority.

Of course, the Government has to govern, maintain law and order, keep vital services running and has other grave responsibilities. Sooner or later, every section of the public learns that. I do not condone the irregular action of the men who must discover that their grievances are only likely to be dealt with when they return to work and that normal constitutional arrangements in regard to disputes must be followed if there is to be confidence, trade union progress and properly regulated standards. But Governments on behalf of society must themselves see that grievances don't fester and that proper means are employed for the attainment of justice. It is appalling how little has been done in the colonies to achieve proper wage regulation or to apply ordinances passed for the purpose.

In this dispute, the Government, however, is the employer. I am not clear whether it has a wage policy for those employed in public utilities and the civil service or what is the relation of such a policy to the wage problem and African standards of living generally. But as employers, the government is not blameless. I hope therefore, in spite of any waywardness on the part of the strikers, that no men will be victimized or their pension or other rights cancelled. Some concessions must be considered when work is resumed. I hope that the men who have been arrested for their part in the strike (I am not thinking of men guilty of violence &c.) can be released and that they will not be prosecuted or detained or deported. I learn, too, that several newspapers have been suppressed. I would like to be informed about this because only the most serious reasons can justify such action. Unofficial disputes are not unknown in this country (several are in progress as I write), and the war has receded some way from West Africa.

Another point disturbs me. Is the policy of the Government as set out in your letter, an adequate one for the difficulties that are arising? How is the circle to be broken? When and how are the standards to be put right or even their deterioration stopped? The problem in Nigeria is a common one in the colonies today; it has already produced trouble and disturbances elsewhere and unless the whole question is tackled there will be much discontent and many disturbances ahead of us. Nigeria is a depressed country; its living standards are deplorable; most of its people suffer from under-nourishment and underconsumption. I feel that your letter, if its arguments are to rest where they are, is little more than defeatism. I plead that we are not so bankrupt in experience and knowledge of economics that all we can say to the Nigerians: 'watch the value of your wages decrease—we will ration and peg prices if we can, but really there is little we can effectively do which will stop this unhappy drop in your living standards. Remember there has been and there still is a war. And all of us have to make sacrifices. Your country is poor and as yet we can't find the men and materials to improve things. We are destroying your co-operatives to help things along and we have tried forced labour in the mines. Big Business continues of right to do very well but for you our trustees we must let economic forces have their effects.'

16   CO 583/275/10/1, no 21   16 July 1945
[Azikiwe assassination allegations]: inward telegram no 636 from Sir G Whiteley to Mr Stanley reporting allegations of an assassination attempt on Dr Azilkiwe

[A major controversy in this period concerned Azikiwe's allegation in July 1945 that he was the target of an assassination plot; although never stated explicitly, implicit in the allegations was that British officials were in some way behind this. The alleged plot gained extensive publicity within Nigeria and in the USA. The allegations were telegraphed by Azikiwe to Stanley on 12 July 1945, 'Eye have reason to believe that my life is in danger stop in view of fact that almost all local high officials suspect me wrongly and unfairly to be at the bottom of the present general strike because am a journalist with strong views . . . It is obvious eye cannot rely much on official protection stop . . .' These allegations were said to be based on the interception of radio signals by a radio operator working for Azikiwe (CO 583/275/10/1, no 12). See 25.]

Your telegram No. 640.

No request for protection has been made to Police or to me by Azikiwe. My knowledge of his telegram of 11th July was from Censorship report on which I considered it inadvisable to take action. Now that you have given me official information of these telegrams, Chief Secretary has asked person named to see him this morning together with Commander of Police.

2.   His telegrams appear to be hysterical, but he is very astute and his object is probably to obtain sympathy and support from United Kingdom in his campaign, which ostensibly is to obtain better conditions for workers, but which is suspected to have ulterior motive of increasing his own political power. It is thought that he has been endeavouring to build for himself reputation as person whom Government is afraid to challenge and that temporary prohibition of publication of his newspapers is regarded by him as severe blow to his prestige (?which) he will spare no pains to restore.

3.   Nothing whatever is known of any plot to murder him nor has deportation even been thought of. He is, of course, native of Nigeria.

4.   Will report further after Chief Secretary's interview.

17   CO 583/275/9   18 July 1945
[General strike]: minute by Sir C Parkinson on ending the general strike

I understand that there is to be a meeting in the Secretary of State's room at 4.45 p.m. tomorrow, Thursday, to discuss the strike situation in Nigeria.

We have now received the despatch promised in (55).[1] I have no comments on the first nine paragraphs which give a general picture of the background against which the present troubles are to be viewed. I get the impression that Sir Gerald Whiteley has some sympathy with the school of thought which holds that the government has shown weakness in the past ie under the Bourdillon regime.

The alternatives with which the government is confronted are set out clearly in para. 13 of the despatch. Sir G. Whiteley reaches the conclusion that the only course is to maintain the attitude that there can be no negotiations until the men return to work, even if this results in a long drawn out strike. In the light of his comments, in paras. 10 and 14, on the attitude of the workers and the irrational and irresponsible character of local public opinion, I am sure that he is right and that any weakness now would only lead to further trouble in the future.

In a telegram received this morning Sir G. Whiteley seeks authority to issue a notice to the strikers warning them that if they do not return to work by the 1st August, they 'will not be able to rely on finding their posts still open to them' after that date. He admits that this will amount to a bluff, inasmuch as the Government could not hope to replace more than 10%, at the most, though the acting Governor considers that some response is to be hoped for.

The decision is a difficult one in view of the risk involved but if the Government is not to issue some such threat, the only alternatives would appear to be to let the strike drag on in the hope that the pressure of economic conditions will eventually bring the workers back. Sir G. Whiteley says that the Government cannot endure a strike on this scale indefinitely, though he does not specify what form the breakdown is likely to take. Para. 3 of the telegram suggests that there have already been casualties.[2]

---

[1] See 14.   [2] A train between Kano and Lagos was derailed during the strike, causing casualties.

The proposed notice does not say definitely that strikers who do not return by the 1st August will be regarded as having vacated their appointments, and it is presumably the intention to take them back after that date provided that it has not already been found possible to secure a replacement though it is not made clear on what terms they would be readmitted. It might be as well to leave this vague at this stage. In these circumstances I do not see that much harm would result from issuing the notice, even if it did not produce a general return; and it might act as a stimulus which would start the flow back. It would in any case appear desirable to make it clear that the Govt. proposes to stand firm. Personally I am in favour of allowing the notice to issue.

The despatch makes no reference to the suspension of the 'Pilot' and 'Comet', which is dealt with on 30647/3 below.

I am also circulating, separately, the subfile containing representations relating to the strike and the Azikiwe affair, which includes the letter from the National Council of Civil Liberties.[3]

---

[3] The National Council of Civil Liberties was one of the organisations contacted by Azikiwe concerning the assassination allegations.

18   CO 583/276/1/1, no 6   21 Aug 1945
[Azikiwe press]: inward savingram no 1741 from Sir G Whiteley to Mr Hall on Dr Azikiwe's newspapers. *Minute* by Sir C Parkinson

[The ban placed on the *West African Pilot* and *Daily Comet* at the start of the general strike was lifted in Aug. However a subsequent edition of the *Daily Comet* launched further attacks on British policy in Nigeria and led to the arrest and imprisonment of Anthony Enahoro, the paper's editor, for libel and sedition. He was released after six months.]

With reference to paragraph 3 of my telegram No. 739 in which I reported that the ban on the publication of the West African Pilot and Daily Comet had been lifted, I enclose herewith a copy of the first edition of the Daily Comet published after the raising of the ban and would particularly invite your attention to the marked paragraphs on page 3.[1] Reference to the record of the meeting of 7th July at Government House and to the preamble of the Order made by me on the 8th July (copies of which were forwarded under cover of Mr. Colby's demi-official letter to Mr. Creasy of the 10th July) show that it was admitted that no steps whatever were taken to communicate with the Public Relations Officer in order to ascertain the accuracy of the statements made by the reporter and that Mr. Azikiwe stated that reporters were instructed not to take notes at an interview so as not to waste the time of the person interviewed.

2.   The statement now published by the Daily Comet serves to illustrate the lengths to which Mr. Azikiwe's papers are prepared to go in fabricating and publishing deliberate falsehoods in order to attain their own ends. The Attorney-General advises me that the two paras, in question come within para. (a) of Regs. 3(1) of the Nigeria Defence (Press) Regulations No. 19 of 1945, but on this occasion,

---

[1] Not printed.

beyond drawing the attention of the Editor to this fact, I do not consider it advisable to take any action.

3.   I am, however, seriously concerned for the future. I fear that it is no exaggeration to say that Mr. Azikiwe and his friends are determined to foment disaffection and are prepared to be entirely unscrupulous in their attempts to achieve that aim. I would mention in passing that during the strike Mr. Azikiwe, who subscribes to Reuters News Service, went to length of publishing and circulating to other newspapers false reports, attributed to Reuters, of disaffection amongst West African troops overseas caused by ban on Pilot and Comet. The newspapers controlled by Mr. Azikiwe are the most influential in the territory and are widely read, particularly in Lagos and in the Eastern Provinces. Present conditions provide a fertile field for the agitator, and that field is liable to become even more fertile during and after demobilisation.

4.   Unless effective steps can be taken to check Mr. Azikiwe's activities in this direction I fear that the consequences will be serious. Mr. Azikiwe is, I think, sufficiently astute to avoid placing himself in the position of being successfully prosecuted for sedition, criminal libel or defamation, and while the establishment of an independent newspaper, conducted in accordance with the principles of sound journalism, would in the long run have a beneficial effect, it would naturally take some time for such a paper to acquire the reputation and circulation necessary to make it effective, and in the meanwhile a great deal of damage could be done.

5.   I have considered the question of incorporating in the Newspapers Ordinance (Cap. 149) the provisions of the Nigeria Defence (Press) Regs. No. 19 of 1945 amended in such a way as to provide for complaint being made to and the order being made by the Supreme Court. I appreciate that such legislation would evoke complaints of interference with freedom of press but on the other hand no properly conducted newspaper could suffer since no offence could be committed unless there were a misstatement or misrepresentation of fact calculated to have subversive effect.

6.   I have also considered question of withdrawing official recognition of newspapers concerned which derive not inconsiderable revenue from Government advertisements and notices. I should not, however, like to say that Mr. Azikiwe would not be capable of surmounting any consequent financial difficulties, and Government would by such action lose a considerable measure of publicity for its own announcements. Even so it is to my mind open to question whether Government should continue to use as a medium for official notices newspapers which are from time to time openly subversive.

7.   The question of policy raised in this saving telegram is of some importance and one on which I have not had an opportunity of ascertaining the Governor's views. You will no doubt wish to consult Sir Arthur Richards on this matter when he passes through London on his return from leave.

Minute on 18

One can sympathise with the Nigerian government in its difficulty but it is not easy to suggest a practical solution.

Azikiwe's conduct during the recent trouble has shown little evidence of any sense of responsibility and he appears to have acted with complete disregard for honesty or any kind of scruples. It cannot be denied however that his influence on such public opinion as exists in Nigeria is considerable and it is a question of policy whether the Government should declare open war upon him or should make some attempt to induce in him a more reasonable attitude. The Government may consider that such an attempt would be quite hopeless. It is no doubt true that the best way to combat misrepresentations is by publication of the true facts. But the Nigerian Government's difficulty is to ensure that such publication does in fact reach the public. As pointed out in paragraph 4 of the saving telegram it would take some time to establish an independent paper with the reputation and circulation necessary for the purposes of counter-propaganda; and in my opinion it would be very difficult indeed for a newspaper which was to any degree suspected of representing the Government's point of view to acquire such a reputation at all. The public is always readier to believe evil than good.

I feel some doubt about the suggestion in paragraph 5 that the provisions of present defence regulations for the control of the press should be incorporated permanently in the Newspapers Ordinance, even if the provisions were amended so as to provide for any restrictive orders to be made by the Supreme Court.[2] It would be very easy to raise a campaign of protest against such legislation and it would be equally difficult to defend the taking of powers which, so far as I am aware, have not found a permanent place on the statute book of any other territory. In any case I do not think that suppression is a real answer; and in practice it could probably only result in the consolidation of the opposition's influence.

As regards paragraph 6, I see no reason why the Government should [sic: not] refrain from publishing official announcements and notices in newspapers which are openly subversive, and I do not think that it could fairly be criticised for doing so. However I note that the Acting Governor doubts whether such action would achieve any practical advantage and in the circumstances I feel that it might merely serve to incite more bitter hostility.

Mr. Sabine and the Legal Adviser should see. Note for discussion with Sir Arthur Richards.

A.C.C.P.
29.8.45

---

[2] Sir H Duncan noted in the margin against this passage, 'It would not do at all'.

19 CO 583/277/4, no 2   23 Oct 1945
[NCNC]: inward telegram no 1045 from Sir A Richards to Mr Hall in reply to a request for information on the NCNC

[The NCNC had been established in Aug 1944 with Herbert Macaulay as president and Azikiwe as general secretary. It represented a coming together of the various organisations that had represented the political aspirations of western-educated Nigerians during the inter-war years; the NYM however, chose to remain aloof. In early 1945 the NCNC held its first constitutional convention, and its opposition to Richards's constitutional proposals in Mar launched it to prominence.]

Your telegram No. 972.

National Council of Nigeria.

The National Council has never informed the Government of its formation or supplied to the Government a copy of its constitution.

2. I can add little to the information given in my savingram No. 644 of 29th March on the subject of the composition of the Council, but should like to stress again that Tribal Unions[1] in Lagos, of which it is mainly composed, do not (repeat not) represent the views of the people of the areas from which they derive. They consist mainly of young men who migrate to Lagos to earn a living and who become to a greater or lesser extent detribalised. The Council can be said to represent the views of only a very small minority of the people and its political influence at present is negligible. Its main purpose is probably to spread propaganda.

3. The declared aims of the Council are to promote:—

(i) Political freedom
(ii) Economic security
(iii) Social equality
(iv) Religious toleration.

Included in these aims are self-Government for Nigeria, all land to be vested in the natives of Nigeria and abolition of all forms of discrimination and segregation.

4. I suggest that reply should include a statement that the National Council of Nigeria is not (repeat not) a representative body, but consists of a few Africans prominent in the political life of Lagos and a number of associations mainly composed of members of various tribes who are now living in Lagos and who are not in close touch with the views of the people in the areas from which they come. I should have no objection to announcement of the Council aims as set out in paragraph 3 of this telegram.

---

[1] The NCNC when initially formed was made up entirely of organisations such as trade unions, professional groups, literary societies and numerous tribal unions and improvement associations. These tribal unions and improvement associations, such as the Ibo Federal Union or the Ibibio Welfare Union, became increasingly prevalent in Lagos and other towns and cities in the inter-war years and were composed of members of a particular ethnic group, usually western-educated, who formed an association for mutual aid and for the benefit of their home areas.

20 CO 583/271/4, no 39   17 Nov 1945
'Nigerian development plans': CO note on the ten-year plan of development and welfare

This note gives—
   Firstly, a general summary of the position, and in amplification of this summary
   Secondly, a brief historical description of the way in which the present Nigerian proposals have evolved, and
   Thirdly, a statement of the present extent of the Secretary of State's commitments to the schemes included in the Nigerian Development Plans.

I. *General summary of present position*
The Colonial Office is committed to the broad outlines of Nigerian development programme. The commitment is contained in Mr. Creasy's letter to Mr. F.E.V. Smith[1] of 6th July (Flag A). The relevant passages in that letter are the following:—

---

[1] FEV Smith, principal assist sec (development), Nigeria, 1944–1945; development sec, 1945–1947.

'We are in general agreement with the main outlines of the revised plan, which provides for a total expenditure over the ten years ending March, 1956, of about £56 million, of which total it is proposed that sums of the order of £16 million should be found from Nigerian revenues, £17 million from the proceeds of public loans, and £23 million from grants and loans under the Colonial Development and Welfare Vote. . . .

'Subject to the comments of detail below, we agree with the general contents of the plan as now revised and the approximate allocation of funds made to the different services included in it. In accordance with the requirements of the Colonial Development and Welfare Act, it will be necessary to submit separately, for approval by the Secretary of State, applications in respect of those schemes already approved for shorter periods which it is desired to extend for the ten-year period covered by the new Act. When these applications are received, they must be subject to the usual criticism and consideration. It will also, of course, be necessary to submit separately schemes for all those services included in the plan for which schemes are not already in existence, except in the case of services which are to be financed without any assistance from the Colonial Development and Welfare Vote.'

It will be seen that the general effect of these passages is to approve the broad outline of the Nigerian development plan (see summary of this plan in Mr. F.E.V. Smith's letter to Mr. Creasy of 25th June—flag B), but that it was made plain that individual schemes within the plan must be subject to approval in the usual way.

The position regarding the individual schemes is set out in detail in the third section of this note.

It will be seen that certain schemes have been approved for varying periods up to 1950/51. The principal of these (i.e. those whose total cost exceeds £200,000) are Road, Rural and urban water supplies, Building programme, Technical education, Development officers, Electrical development, Tele-communications, Leprosy, Dredger for Lagos.

No Schemes have yet been approved beyond 1950/51.

We have been discussing with the Nigerian authorities first orally and then by correspondence, a number of other large schemes, the principal of which are for agriculture, veterinary services, forestry, medical and health services, education. These schemes have been framed in Nigeria to cover the ten year period up to 1955/56. We have also been discussing similarly schemes prepared in Nigeria for extensions of existing schemes, e.g. roads, up to the same date, 1955/56.

These discussions and correspondence have been on the basis that if the schemes could be reshaped in a manner considered acceptable here, they would be approved and in a telegram of 11th October (29 on file—Flag D) we said, 'The basic proposals for expansion of these services and the scale of assistance proposed over the ten year period covered by the colonial Development and Welfare Act are approved'.

2.   *Course of discussions*

Mr. F.E.V. Smith came to London in 1944, and discussed with the Department in some detail the Nigerian development proposals as they stood at that time. Proposals based upon these discussions were subsequently published in Nigeria as a Sessional Paper. When Mr. Smith again visited England in June and July of this year, he brought with him a sketch plan of development over ten years, showing the estimated Nigerian contribution from revenue and loans, and the proposed amounts for which C.D. & W. grants would be asked for under the new Act. These last were framed in the expectation that the total sum to be allotted to Nigeria would be about £23 million. This statement is flagged B. Mr. Smith saw the Medical, Agricultural and Forestry Advisers, and amended the three schemes for health, agriculture and forestry that he had brought with him in the light of these talks. He also discussed the broad scheme with the Department, and a record of the discussion is flagged E. The sketch plan was also sent to the Treasury, so that they had it before them when Nigerian loan proposals were under discussion.

Mr. Smith placed these figures on record under cover of a letter of 25th June to Mr. Creasy (flagged B), and in his reply of 6th July Mr. Creasy indicated (flagged A) general approval of the proposed allocation of the £23 million between all the various services covered by the general plan, subject to the qualifications mentioned in the letter.

Subsequently, in the telegram at 29, we told the Governor that the basic proposals for the expansion of agriculture, forestry, veterinary services, health and roads, and the scale of assistance proposed over the ten-year period, were approved, although we felt that modifications were required in the precise form in which the assistance should be applied, as between these services and year by year over the period. The telegram said further that this need not prevent the presentation to the Legislature of the general ten-year programme, and a statement of the scale of assistance intended towards these schemes. The statement might set out the ten-year programme in whatever detail the Governor thought necessary, and have appended to it details of schemes that had been finally approved.

3. *Statement of present commitments*

Before Mr. Smith's last visit, a number of grants had been approved. Since his return to Nigeria, further applications have been sent in, mostly for the ten year period 1946/7 to 1955/6. The following list shows all the large schemes so far approved. None of them has been approved for the years beyond the year 1950/1.

	£	
Dredger, Lagos	230,000	two years.
Leprosy control +	258,000	1944/5 to 1949/50
Roads	1,810,000	Up to 1950/1.
Rural water supplies	1,889,000	„ „
Urban water supplies	602,500	„ „
Telecommunications	230,000	1944/5 to 1948/9.
Electrical development	370,000	1944/5 to 1948/9.
Building programme	681,500	1944/5 to 1950/1.
Development officers	400,000	„ „
Technical education	401,000	1945/6 to 1950/1
Hausa newspaper	163,550	Up to 1948/9
Urban water supplies (Supplementary grant)	401,000	Up to 1950/1

+ Application for increase to £428, 880 for the same period since received, and awaiting Treasury agreement.

The total sum granted to Nigeria up to the present under the schemes listed above and miscellaneous smaller schemes, is £8,025,000. Certain other schemes have been approved by Mr. Creech Jones, but have not yet received Treasury approval, and are therefore not included in this total.

Nigeria have applied for further grants to enable a number of the above schemes to be continued for the five years 1951/2 to 1955/6. These outstanding applications are for:— roads, rural and urban water supplies, development officers, technical education, buildings (Nigeria have asked for the cancellation of the existing grant and its replacement by a revised grant for the full ten year period), and town planning and village improvement. As stated above, no grant for the second five years has yet been approved.

The following new applications were discussed by Mr. Smith when he was last in London, and most of them were gone over in detail with the Advisers concerned:— Agricultural (£1,597,630), veterinary Services (£200,470), Forestry (£482,805), Health (£3,494,048), and Education (£903,600). Each of these applications is for a grant for the full ten year period ending in 1955/6. The new draft telegram would commit us in principle to the sums mentioned for Agricultural, Veterinary, Forestry and Health Services, and to the framing of schemes along the lines proposed by the Governor in paragraph 3 of 36. It would contain no commitment on Education.

21   CO 583/286/5, no 99   4 Dec 1945
[Constitutional revision]: despatch no 397 from Mr Hall to Sir A Richards outlining his amendments to Richards's proposals

I have the honour to refer to your despatch of the 6th of December, 1944, in which you submitted your proposals for the political and constitutional development of Nigeria.[1]

2. These proposals have been given wide publicity as the result of their presentation to the Legislative Council of Nigeria in March as sessional paper No. 4 of 1945 and their simultaneous publication in this country as a White Paper (Cmd. 6599). They have been the subject of a special debate in the Legislative Council, the proceedings of which I have studied, and I have noted with satisfaction that at the conclusion as the debate a resolution was passed without a division signifying the Council's approval of the proposals and recommending them for adoption. More recently, the proposals have been debated in the House of Commons on the 19th of November, and I enclose a copy of the Hansard report.[2]

3. Apart from the consideration which these proposals have been given in Parliament and in Legislative Council, there has been full opportunity for organisations and individuals to make representations concerning them during the months which have elapsed since their publication. The various representations which have been received have all been carefully considered; and in certain particulars referred to below the original proposals have, in discussion with you, been modified to take account of the comments made. In other cases it has been considered impracticable or undesirable to give effect to the criticisms raised and,

---

[1] See 7.   [2] Not printed.

while I do not propose to attempt here to answer in detail all the criticisms and alternative suggestions which have been made, I think it desirable to explain why I have not felt able to accept the views on certain fundamental questions which have been put forward by certain sections of Nigerian opinion. But I would first observe that, even from this quarter, little criticism has been directed against the main framework of the proposed new constitution; and the creation of regional Councils in particular appears to be generally accepted. It is rather with the provisions for the selection of members to serve on the regional and central legislative bodies, and with the inclusion of Chiefs as members of these bodies, that dissatisfaction has been expressed.

4.   The demand that all unofficial members of both the regional and the central legislative bodies should be elected by ballot, and that for this purpose there should be universal adult suffrage, is common to several of the memoranda submitted from Nigeria. I will say at once that I share the view expressed in paragraph 20 of your despatch that this system would not be suitable, in the conditions obtaining in Nigeria today, for occuring the proper representation of the people, and that it would not be understood by the mass of the population. I believe that the proposed selection of members by the Authorities in accordance with local custom and tradition, combined with the progressive modernisation of the Native Authorities themselves which you have declared to be an essential part of your policy, will be much more likely to bear good fruit than an alien system transplanted from a very different political climate. Customs, of course, change under the influence of new ideas and it may well be that local methods of selection will in time assimilate themselves more closely to those which are followed in this country. But such developments must come as the spontaneous expression of the general will of the communities concerned, and there is no evidence that the desire for general election by ballot extends beyond certain limited sections and interests, confined for the most part to particular areas in the southern portion of Nigeria.

5.   Meanwhile the election by ballot to the Legislative Council of members to represent the municipality of Lagos and the township of Calabar is to continue, and you have agreed that the annual income qualification for the franchise should be reduced from £100 to £50. I shall be interested to observe the extent to which this concession stimulates interest in the local election.

6.   You have provided in the membership of the Houses of Assembly for the representation of special communities, minorities, and important aspects of life not otherwise represented. I agree that those members will have to be nominated by the Governor in the first instance but I note that you propose that at the end of the third year after the introduction of the new constitution there should be a review of the system of direct nomination, both in the Legislative Council and in the Houses of Assembly, with a view to substituting a form of nomination by choice of the people represented wherever this may be found to be practicable.

7.   In certain of the memoranda submitted to me, criticism has been directed against the fact that the proposals in your despatch provide for African majorities of only one both in the Houses of Assembly and in the Legislative Council. So far as the latter is concerned, this objection has already been met by your subsequent decision to exclude from the Legislative Council four of the official members originally proposed (viz. the Director of Marine, the Comptroller of Customs and Excise, the General Manager of the Railway and the Commissioner of Police) and one

European unofficial member (the Member for Banking). You have also explained with regard to the Members for Shipping, Industry and Commerce, and Mining, that, while you consider it desirable to have in the Legislative Council unofficial members capable of advising on the commercial and industrial needs of the territory, you see no reason why they should be appointed as representatives of specific interests, and it has accordingly been agreed that the three members referred to should be replaced by three members nominated, as in the case of certain of the unofficial members of the Houses of Assembly, 'to represent important aspects of life not otherwise represented amongst the unofficial members'; and that men best capable of giving the advice required, whether European or African, should be selected for this purpose.

8.   As regards the Houses of Assembly, you have explained that the number of Provincial Members proposed is provisional and that, if necessary in order to secure adequate representation of all communities, the number may be increased in the light of experience. It is proposed that, the constitutional instruments should be so drafted that it will be possible to make such increases at any time without waiting for the general review of the new constitution proposed for the ninth year after its introduction.

9.   I am unable to accept the view which has been expressed that the Houses of Assembly should comprise unofficial members only. It is obviously necessary at this stage of development that official members should be present to explain and define the Government's policy, and in any case, as there are to be unofficial majorities, there seem to be little substance in this objection.

10.   Criticism has also been directed against the inclusion of Chiefs in the legislative machinery and it has been represented that, because they have been described officially as 'an integnal part of the machinery of Government', they should, if included at all, take their seats as Official Members. It appears to me that there is some confusion of thought amongst those who have made this criticism, since the Chiefs are presented, in some cases in the same memorandum, as being on the one hand independent rulers whose traditional and customary authority is threatened by the new proposals; and on the other hand as civil servants who have no right to represent their people on the Councils of Government. I can see no reason why the Chiefs should not consider and advise on policy as well as assist in carrying it out. In fact, of course, they already do so, since the Government would not, I am sure, embark on any important measure without first consulting the Native Authorities; and I consider that this function should now be given constitutional recognition. You have assured me that there is no basis for the suggestion that the Chiefs are unwilling to express their own views or, where they consider it desirable, to take an independent line on Government proposals. For these reasons, and in view of the *de facto* authority which the Chiefs undoubtedly possess, I am unable to agree that they should not be admitted to the Councils of Government as representatives of their people or that the House of Chiefs in the Northern Provinces should have merely advisory and not legislative functions.

11.   The proposals have also been criticised on the ground that they provide no link between the legislative and the executive. As to this, you have informed me that you do not consider that Nigeria is yet ripe for anything in the nature of a ministerial system. I note, however, with satisfaction that it is proposed to give members of the Houses of Assembly opportunities of obtaining practical experience of administration

by the formation of committees to deal with particular subjects such as education, development, etc.

12.   I agree that it is necessary to provide the Governor with the usual reserve powers at the present stage, but these will be reviewed as part of the general review of the constitution to be held after nine years.

13.   I have noted your opinion that the time is also not yet ripe for further municipal development outside Lagos, and I would record my endorsement of the view which you expressed during discussions in London, that municipal status should not be granted unless the communities concerned are prepared to accept the financial responsibilities which go with it.

14.   After careful consideration of the proposals themselves, of the reception which they have been accorded both in Nigeria and in this country, and of the various criticisms which have been put forward, I have reached the conclusion that the proposals as now amended not only represent the most substantial immediate advance that can satisfactorily be made in the present state of development in Nigeria, but also provide a framework within which the development of responsible government can be expected to make further progress, given the goodwill and co-operation of the great mass of the people, which the reception of the proposals in Nigeria has led me to hope will be forthcoming. Furthermore, I believe that they give ample scope for the exercise of the talents of all public-spirited Nigerians who wish to serve their country and to hasten her progress along the road to self-government. The revised constitutional instruments to give effect to them are accordingly being prepared for presentation in due course for the approval of His Majesty the King.

15.   I agree that, the new Constitution should be generally reviewed at the end of the ninth year following its introduction. This would not, however, preclude the earlier introduction of particular modifications from time to time, where experience has shown these to be necessary or sufficient progress has been recorded to justify an immediate advance.

16.   You are at liberty to publish this despatch in Nigeria. I do not propose that it should be published in this country, but a copy will be placed in the Library of the House of Commons.

22   CO 583/294/1, no 1   4 Feb 1946
[Native administration]: despatch no 19 from Sir A Richards to Mr Hall on the need to review financial and administrative relations between central and local government. *Minutes* by J B Williams, S Caine, O G R Williams and Sir G Creasy

I have the honour to inform you that I propose, if you see no objection and if, as a result of the appointment of a substantive Deputy Financial Secretary, (a matter of great urgency now under your consideration), the staff position then permits, to relieve Mr. S. Phillipson[1] of his substantive duties as Financial Secretary to enable him to undertake, by direct consultation with the officers concerned throughout Nigeria, a comprehensive investigation into two problems of great importance

---

[1] Sydney Phillipson, financial secretary, 1945–1948, acting chief secretary, 1948.

which, in my opinion, call for early attention. These problems are (a) the financial and administrative procedure to be adopted under the new constitution and (b) the 'rationalization' of financial relations between the Nigerian Government and the Native Administrations.

2. It is hardly necessary to elaborate the proposition that it is necessary to embody in carefully considered instructions the financial and administrative procedure to be observed under the new constitutional arrangements and that this should be done before these arrangements come into effect. This is particularly true of financial procedure which will be fundamentally affected by the constitutional change. It will be no easy matter to define an orderly procedure by which the regional estimates will be prepared and approved in time to admit of their incorporation in the Nigerian Estimates. It will clearly be necessary to advise the Chief Commissioners very early in the financial year preceding that to which their Estimates will relate of the limits of revenue within which their Estimates of Expenditure must be confined and it will equally be necessary for the Chief Commissioners to present their Estimates to the Houses of Assembly at a date much earlier than the date on which the Nigerian Estimates are presented to the Legislative Council. There are also many problems of an administrative type relating to the channels of communication, delegation of powers, etc., which will require consideration. It is to these problems that Mr. Phillipson will address himself in consultation with the Chief Commissioners Heads of Departments and others.

3. The subject of financial relations between the Nigerian Government and the Native Administrations is generally recognized to be one of the most difficult and complex of Nigeria's problems. The matter was last handled at a high level by my predecessor, Sir Bernard Bourdillon, whose printed memorandum entitled 'Apportionment of Revenue and Duties as between the central Government and Native Administrations' constitutes an important statement on the subject. The subject is, of course, far wider than the mere question of the method of dividing the Direct Tax between the Nigerian Government and the Native Administrations. Financial relations are merely a reflection of the apportionment of responsibilities, which in turn is a reflection of the political organization of the country. Sir Bernard Bourdillon's memorandum indicates clearly and forcibly the essential elements of the problem and that memorandum would be an essential document of reference for anyone undertaking a comprehensive review. In general, however, it is a statement of principles rather than of their application and it may well be that in the light of the impending constitutional changes the principles will require reconsideration and it seems certain that their application should be more closely worked out. I recognize, as does Mr. Phillipson, how utterly unwise it would be to approach this considerable problem without full regard to its antecedents or with any desire to impose rigid uniformity of principles or methods clearly inapplicable to historical developments with many and varied manifestations.

Since it is quite clear that no settlement could be achieved by the exchange of correspondence or minutes, it seems to me advisable to detail an experienced officer to examine the problem in the light of its historical antecedents and in consultation with officers of the Administration and others qualified to advise with a view to making recommendations as to the policy and procedure which should determine the financial relations between the Nigerian Government and Native Administrations in the future.

4.   My proposal to detail Mr. Phillipson to go into these questions was put by me to the Chief Commissioners at a conference held in November last. The Chief Commissioners welcomed the proposals.

5.   It is my hope that Mr. Phillipson will be in a position to begin his investigations very shortly after the forthcoming budget meetings of the Legislative Council. It is impossible to say exactly how long will be required for the investigations and the issue of reports. It will be necessary for Mr. Phillipson to undertake extensive touring throughout Nigeria in order to meet officers and to acquaint himself with the working of present arrangements. Perhaps a period of four months might see the work completed but whether it will be possible to spare Mr. Phillipson for this special task for as long as that is uncertain. I have, therefore, directed that he should give priority of attention to the first problem.[2]

Minutes on 22

Mr. Caine

I think you will be interested to see the despatch from the Governor of Nigeria at No. 1 proposing that, on the filling of the present vacancy for a Deputy Financial Secretary, the Financial Secretary, Mr. Phillipson, should undertake an investigation estimated to last some four months of financial problems arising from the new Constitution and in particular the financial relations between the Nigerian Government and the Native Administrations.

It is perhaps, as Mr. Emanuel says, a little surprising that, even with a deputy appointed, the Governor should be able to release Mr. Phillipson from his duties for so long a period as four months to be spent in touring round Nigeria, but I do not think we are called upon to comment on that. I do, however, think that we should comment on a point of substance arising from the nature of the investigation which it is intended that Mr. Phillipson should undertake, since this raises a point which we have for some time felt to be very fundamental in the financial structure of Colonies, that point being the degree of real financial tenure which is enjoyed by the organs of local government in the Colonies, in most cases the Native Administrations.

At the present time there is undoubtedly a great deal of make-believe about the financial proceedings of native authorities. That is to say that while many of them go through the process of preparing budgets of revenue and expenditure, we know that in fact every item of revenue and expenditure is apt in many cases to be carefully scrutinised by the European officer in charge of the district and also that effective responsibility for the revenue even of the native authorities themselves is commonly apt to be much more in the hands of the Central Government than would appear from the formal position. This arises from the fact that the rates of tax imposed by the native authorities are usually either fixed by the Central Government or require the approval of the Central Government. In consequence the onus of defending their financial operations before the tax-paying community, in which surely lies a great deal of the educative value of representative government, is apt not in fact to rest with the Native Administration.

With these considerations in mind, I suggest that our reply to the Governor's

---

[2] See 42.

despatch should be rather fuller than is proposed in preceding minutes and that it should be to the following effect. The Secretary of State has learned with very great interest of the investigation on which the Governor proposes to employ Mr. Phillipson as soon as a Deputy Financial Secretary can take up his duties and that he entirely agrees with the Governor about the importance of framing the financial and administrative procedure under the new constitution on the right lines from the start and in particular on the importance of achieving satisfactory financial rela-

A tions between the Central Government and the Native Administrations. The despatch might then say that while the Secretary of State appreciates that it is not possible to attempt to determine satisfactory financial relations a priori and that the formulation of these must depend largely upon the results of the investigation on which Mr. Phillipson is to be employed, he would nevertheless be glad to learn whether the Governor has in his mind any general principles which he thinks should govern these matters. We might then say that the Secretary of State for his part is impressed with the importance of making the financial responsibilities of Native Administrations and other local authorities real and effective even though,

B in the case of many authorities, they can at present only be exercised within a limited sphere. In particular, he feels that it is of great educative value if the local authorities can be made increasingly responsible not only for the actual collection of local revenue, but also for fixing the rates of their own local taxation, since it is only by this means that the full onus of defending their own activities before the local community can be thrown upon the organs of representative local government.

We might conclude by saying that the Secretary of State would be glad to learn the Governor's views upon the considerations mentioned above, to be kept in general touch with the progress of Mr. Phillipson's investigations and to receive any material that will throw further light on the problems in issue even though the stage has not yet been reached when the Governor is in a position to put final proposals before the Secretary of State.

J.B.W.
21.2.46

I agree with Mr. J.B. Williams that this is an enquiry of very considerable potential importance, and that we might suggest certain general considerations to be borne in mind on the lines of his minute. I have always felt myself the high degree of make-believe in the financial independence of the average native authority. I suggest that we should bring out that the essential to aim at is a position in which the native authority has a clear responsibility for discharging certain specified functions, and, subject to the achieving of a certain minimum standard, can exercise its own discretion as to the amount of revenue it raises to be spent on those services.

S.C.
21.2.46

I think it is clear that Sir Arthur Richards Wishes to encourage a progressive spirit in the Native Administrations under the proposed new constitutional regime. This is shown by what he says in paragraph 13 of his despatch regarding the revision of the constitution, printed as CMD. 6599.[3] This paragraph runs as follows—

---

[3] See 7.

'13. The arrangements which I propose for dealing with regional revenue and expenditure would in no way detract from the responsibility of Native Authorities for operating their own local services and financing them from their own revenues. These revenues are mainly derived from the share of the direct tax retained by the Native Authorities, a share which the Governor has power under the law to increase or decrease. In order to simplify the system and to encourage Native Authorities to adopt progressive policies, I have recently frozen their contribution to central revenue from the direct tax at the amounts paid in by them during the year 1943–44. The remainder, and the whole of any additional proceeds from any increase in the direct tax, is to be retained by the Native Authorities themselves. They will thus be in a position to play an increasing part in the development of their own areas and the recent correlation of Native Authority and Government salaries will make it easier for them to secure the trained staff which they need for this purpose and will also help to prevent over-lapping between Government and Native Authority spheres of work'.

As will be seen, it is apparently intended that the Native Authorities should have power to increase the rate of direct taxation but not to decrease it. So long as the proceeds of the direct tax are to be used partly for Central Government purposes and partly to supply the main revenues of the Native Authorities, it would appear difficult, if not impossible, to leave Native Authorities entirely free to settle the rate at which they should be assessed.

Clearly, the policy of de-centralisation which will be embodied in the new constitution raises problems affecting financial relations between the Central Government and the Native Authorities far more fundamental than those discussed in Sir Bernard Bourdillon's minuts enclosed in (1) on 30421/39, which is referred to in paragraph 3 of the present despatch.

In any case it will be necessary for the functions of the Native Authorities to conform to the general pattern of the proposed new constitution in which emphasis is laid not on the Native Authorities but on the three Regional Councils, each comprising an area containing many Native Authorities.

In paragraph 12 of the Governor's despatch on the revision of the constitution, referred to above, he definitely states that he proposes to devolve on the Regional Councils (i.e. the three representative bodies to be created for Northern, Western and Eastern Nigeria), a large measure of financial responsibility. Each will have its own budget, on which will be borne the cost of all Government services (except services which are declared to be central services) in the Region, including the salaries of Government personnel. He goes on to say 'Regional revenue would consist in the first place of the share[4] of the direct tax at present payable to Central Government, together with any receipts from fees, licences, etc., which might be allotted to the Regional budgets, and in the second place of annual block grants from Central revenue'. The Regional Councils would debate the Regional estimates in detail before passing them with such amendments as they desire to suggest. When submitted to and approved by the Governor, they would appear in the Central estimates as block votes.

---

[4] O G R Williams added a marginal note here: 'i.e. what is shared amongst the various Native Authorities in the Regions'.

In the first place it is not proposed that the Regional Councils should be given power to appropriate expenditure and the appropriation of Regional expenditure will be in the hands of the Legislative Council. If, however, it is decided, as a result of the Committee which is to make recommendations on the subject, to devolve any legislative powers on the Regional Councils, it might also in due course be decided to devolve upon them the power of legally appropriating Regional revenue. When this change comes about presumably the question will also be considered of empowering the three Regional Councils to raise Regional revenue as well as to appropriate Regional expenditure.

The exact form of the budgets of the Native Authorities forming component parts of the three areas under the three Regional Councils will, of course, have to be worked out and this, I assume, is one of the matters which the Governor wishes Mr. Phillipson to deal with.

I think that it would only tend to confuse matters if we were to raise with the Governor at the present stage the question of the Native Authorities fixing the rates for their own local taxation. If it is thought desirable to do more than merely welcome the proposal contained in No. 1, I should very much prefer to confine it to that part of Mr. J.B. Williams' minute which I have marked in the margin.

O.G.R.W.
5.3.46

Mr. O.G.R. Williams's minute points out that there is a good deal of local background to the question of the revenue fixing powers of the native authorities and that in consequence of this, it is necessary to be careful what we say to the Governor if we are not to give the impression of ignoring the previous history. I felt, however, that to reduce our suggested comments to the Governor merely to the passage in my minute of 21st February marked by Mr. O.G.R. Williams, i.e., that marked A, would mean saying nothing very definite at all and while we must, as Mr. O.G.R. Williams says, be careful not to jump in and cause confusion, I think there can be no doubt that the general idea behind my minute of emphasising the desirability of making the financial responsibility of the local native authorities increasingly a reality is a point which deserves emphasising.

I have accordingly discussed with Mr. O.G.R. Williams and he has agreed to our including in our suggested reply to the Governor the additional sentence which I have marked B in my minute of 21st February. This puts the point in general terms, but does not drag in the vexed question (in view of the Nigerian history) of local native authorities fixing rates of tax. The essential reason for the particular difficulty of this question in Nigeria is, of course, the fact that by far the greater part of the native authorities' revenue is from the direct tax, the proceeds of which they share with the central government. This, of course, makes it a matter of greater difficulty and complexity to give the native authorities real responsibility for fixing the rates of tax than would be the case if, as in this country, the revenue raised by the local authorities was raised through taxes other than those by which the central government raises its revenue.

J.B.W.
6.3.46

I am still inclined to think that it is important, if we say anything at all other than an acknowledgment or welcome of the proposed investigation, that we should say something on the lines of my minute of 21st February. I am not much moved by the consideration that it has not hitherto been the practice or intention of the Nigerian Government to give native authorities any substantial discretion in the fixing of their own revenues. It is precisely because that has not been the policy that I feel that the matter should be reconsidered if the proposed investigation is really to get down to fundamentals. It seems to me most important to get over the basic idea that any governmental authority, if it is to be truly responsible for running a particular service, must also have the responsibility for finding the money to run it.

S.C.
13.3.46

... On the general question, I feel myself that Sir Arthur Richards is sufficiently a realist to need no reminding of the points to which Mr. Caine and Mr. J.B. Williams have drawn attention and, unless Mr. Caine feels strongly over it, I should much prefer to confine our reply to a short despatch welcoming the proposed investigation.

G.C.
20.3.46

23   CO 554/134/13   13 Feb 1946
[Higher education]: minute by M H Varvill[1] on the Elliot Report on higher education in West Africa   [Extract]

[This minute refers to the commission headed by Col Walter Elliott MP which was appointed in 1943 to look into the future of higher education in West Africa, and which reported in 1945. It included Creech Jones among its members. The majority report of the commission recommended the establishment of three Universities in West Africa, to be located in Sierra Leone, the Gold Coast and Nigeria. The minority report, which Creech Jones signed, recommended the creation of only one University, to be located in Nigeria; *Report of the Commission on Higher Education in West Africa* (Cmd 6655, 1945). See 27 and BDEEP series A, vol 2, R Hyam, ed, *The Labour government and the end of empire 1945–1951*, part IV, 361 and 362.]

... The position is that public opinion in both the Gold Coast and Sierra Leone has now come down strongly in favour of the Majority Report. Nigeria, as might be expected, has no objection to the Minority Report. In (d) of the W.A.C. conclusions the Governor, Nigeria, speaks of pseudo-nationalism as being a poor argument to set against the weighty facts which led to the Minority Report. Nascent nationalism is certainly a poor argument but I do not think that it should be lightly disregarded. A single University College, if it is decided to establish one, would perhaps be more likely to stimulate nationalism than to provide a broader outlook. By this, I do not mean that the products of the University would necessarily become more parochial in outlook, more aware of Gold Coast nationality than of their common West African origin. The numbers going to the single University College will be small and it is in the class who do *not* have the good fortune to reach the College that extreme nationalism is more likely to appear. I heard the Nigerian Leg. Co. debates in 1941 and 1942 when the Lagos Colleges had been taken over by the Military and a number of their pupils sent to Achimota.[2] The feeling at that time among members—who

---

[1] Colonial Service, Nigeria, from 1932; seconded to CO, 1943–1947.
[2] Achimota College in the Gold Coast.

might be relied upon to take a more impartial view than the local press—was certainly opposed to Nigeria sharing the excellent educational facilities of the Gold Coast: and I think that, wherever a single College may be placed, we shall probably find that this feeling grows rather than declines, however regrettable this may be. It is not difficult for the G.C. or S.L. educated class to point to Wales or Scotland with their Universities and to ask why they should be denied similar facilities—and, though this is easy to answer, it is not easy to persuade African opinion to accept our explanation, without some concession to local sentiment.

Action now rests squarely with the C.O. It will be necessary to decide on policy in the near future. . . .

24   CO 583/275/10/3, no 2   15 Feb 1946
[Azikiwe assassination allegations]: inward savingram no 348 from Sir A Richards to Mr Hall forwarding Dr Azikiwe's petition alleging an assassination plot. *Annex*
Minute by J E Miller[1]

My saving No. 328.

I forward a copy of a petition dated the 26th of July 1945 addressed to you by Mr. Azikiwe. According to Mr. Azikiwe the original of this petition was posted at Onitsha on the 26th of July under a covering letter addressed to the Chief Secretary to the Government. No such letter was received in the Chief Secretary's office and the present copy was forwarded under a covering letter dated the 4th of February 1946 which was received on the 12th of February.[2]

2.   In his petition Mr. Azikiwe puts before you the 'evidence' which led him to suppose that his life was in danger. This 'evidence' consists of 'Wireless Messages' which are said to have been intercepted by a wireless operator employed by the West African Pilot. These 'messages' are contained in Appendix II to the petition.

3.   Mr. Paul West, the wireless operator referred to, was formerly employed in the Posts and Telegraphs Department as a wireless operator. His employment ceased when he was sentenced to imprisonment for falsification of accounts and stealing, and on release he was engaged by Mr. Azikiwe.

4.   I have the following comments to make on these messages:—

(a) Local enquiries have failed to reveal any station WAPYEL.

(b) The messages are all said to have been received at the same time, namely 5.15 p.m. (G.M.T.) on Friday 13th July, 1945. Yet messages (2) and (4) would appear to be in reply to 'message' (1) and to have been sent at different times.

(c) The English used in the 'messages' does not suggest that they were written or spoken by a person having much knowledge of the English language. For example the word 'targeters' is, to say the least, unusual, and the phrase 'where all possibility assassination can take place in hall' is not one which would be likely to be used by a person normally speaking the English language.

(d) None of the 'messages' mentions the name of the person to be assassinated. Mr. Azikiwe's paranoiac tendencies may, of course, have led him to identify himself as one of the 'two most important persons'.

---

[1] Administrative officer, CO.   [2] See 16.

5.   The fact that Mr. Azikiwe, who is well educated and intelligent, expects you to accept these wireless messages, which are patently fictitious, as 'incontrovertible and conclusive evidence' (see your telegram No. 640 of the 15th July, 1945) can lead in my view to only one conclusion, namely that he is no longer sane. This conclusion is supported by Mr. Azikiwe's behaviour generally during the last eight or nine months.

6.   Although the circulation of Mr. Azikiwe's newspaper is believed to have declined recently, he still has a considerable influence over semi-educated and ignorant natives. That this influence should be wielded by an irresponsible lunatic is a matter which cannot be regarded with indifference. For this reason and for the further reason that the alleged plot on Mr. Azikiwe's life has received considerable publicity, I urge strongly that Mr. Azikiwe's petition and its enclosures should be published locally at once, and that your reply to the petition should be published in due course. I am sure that exposure by publication can do nothing but good, and should be grateful for telegraphic approval.

Annex to 24: Petition sent by Dr Azikiwe to Mr Hall, 26 July 1945

The humble petition of Nnamdi Azikiwe, Chairman, Zik's Press Limited, of 72 King George Avenue, Yaba Estate, Lagos, respectfully showeth:

1.   That G. Beresford Stooke, Esquire,[3] has informed me of your desire to peruse my evidence in respect of the plot to assassinate me, as alleged in my cablegram of July 14, 1945 to the Right Honourable Oliver Stanley. He has also requested me to furnish him with the evidence, vide Appendix I attached. The evidence is attached hereto as Appendix II and the two appendixes form part and parcel of this humble petition.

2.   That as will be observed, after perusing same, the plan to commit assassination is incorporated in a wireless message which was handed to me on Friday, July 13, 1945, at 5.45 p.m. or thereabouts, by Mr Collins Ulric Maximillian Gardner, Managing Editor of the *West African Pilot*, with the information that the wireless message was intercepted in Metre 51.5, at 5.15 p.m. or thereabouts, by Mr Paul West, and submitted to him for transmission to me for my information and necessary action. Mr. West is one of the Wireless Operators of the *West African Pilot*, a licensed station in accordance with the Laws of Nigeria.

3.   That the facts contained in the wireless message are very startling indeed, and being a British Protected Person, by birth, I am appealing through you to His Majesty's Britannic Government, to protect my life and my business interests from those who appear to be after my life and are bent on ruining my business, and to be more reasonable and sympathetic towards me and my business.

4.   That as indicated in my cablegram of Saturday, July 14, 1945, I desire to travel to the United Kingdom in order to place my case before His Majesty the King, through the Colonial Office, but in view of the portents in the wireless message, I am afraid that at present I do not feel secure in my person.

5.   That I submit that, if any British Protected Person, like me, cannot feel safe and secure in his person, even under the canopy of the Union Jack, then I fail to

---

[3] G Beresford Stooke, chief sec, Nigeria, 1945–1948; gov, Sierra Leone, 1948.

appreciate the necessity for the sacrifices in Men, Money, Man Power, and Material Resources which the Colony and Protectorate of Nigeria had contributed, and are contributing, to the war efforts of the British Empire and the United Nations.

6.   That I beg the liberty to say, in conclusion that, in proceeding to England, I desire to be accompanied by my Private Secretary, and I suggest that I be accepted in bona fide and be treated as a guest and friend of Great Britain, at my expense, if need be.

7.   That I very respectfully reiterate my appeal to you for the protection of my life and my business under the jurisdiction and protectorate of the British Government, as a Protecting State.

And your petitioner as in duty bound will ever pray etc.

Appendix I to Annex: Mr Beresford Stooke to Dr Azikiwe, 16 July 1945

I am so sorry to hear that you are not well to-day and trust that it is not serious.

The reason why I asked you to be good enough to come and see me this morning is that we have been told by the Secretary of State that he has received a telegram from you stating that your life is in danger and that you have incontrovertible and conclusive evidence of a definite plot to murder you. I at once communicated with the Commissioner of Police, to find that he knows nothing of this at all.

If you are unable to come and see me I would ask you to be so kind as to make the evidence you refer to available to me at the earliest possible moment in order that I may see that suitable steps are taken in the matter.

Appendix II to Annex: Wireless messages

1. Station: WAPYEL
2. Receiver: Paul West, Wireless Operator
3. Date: Friday, July 13, 1945
4. Metre: 51½
5. Time: 5.15 p.m. (GMT)

... xxx Reference ... air letter ... first item ... assassination of the two most important persons ... xxx already started on steps towards ... but proposed assassination will take place before ... xxx ... targeters are detailed watch cinema halls and dancing halls xxx arranging get round people beg 'A' give lecture where all possibility assassination can take place in hall xxx reward of hundred guineas to ... targeter who will get at him xxx if that proves futile they will watch by night to shoot into blue car xxx Strictly ... and till then.

(2)
... xxx air letter not received yet xxx suggest all messages come by code next time fear interception xxx Also suggest postpone assassination till ... but advise ... before then xxx

(3)
... xxx suggest ... demand ... before ... xxx shall give personal opinion on tragic move xxx

(4)

... xxx air letter unreceived yet xxx shall suggest ... immediately given and hold on bloody act yet unless ... xxx

(5)

... xxx am still of opinion assassination takes place between now and monday xxx just informed two of them were in a car this afternoon xxx ... was just late who was detailed to watch king george avenue xxx shall take your various advice then till ... xxx There shall ... but ... ready ... cold blood xxx ... no interception of message xxx ... all is safe

Minute on 24

Mr. O. G. R. Williams
On 12.7.45 (No. 12 on 30647/1A Part I), Mr. Azikiwe cabled to Col. Stanley 'I have reason to believe that my life is in danger ... cannot rely much on official protection. Could you do anything to preserve my life and my business'.

On 13.7.45 (No. 13) we asked the Governor Nigeria for background information on this.

On 14.7.45 (No. 19) Mr. Azikiwe cabled 'I implore you humbly for last time contact highest authorities, enable me escorted officially to London at my expense lay before His Majesty through Secretary of State incontrovertible and conclusive evidence definite plot to murder me. Please advise local Government protect my life otherwise this is last cablegram from me alive. Am still insisting my innocence and can prove it to the hilt. Believe me am willing leave Nigeria and go into exile since it obvious attempt being made make me scapegoat'.

On 16.7.45. (No. 21) Governor Nigeria reported no request for protection by Mr. Azikiwe and nothing known of plot to murder him.

At (22) Governor advised that Mr. Azikiwe regretted inability to meet Chief Secretary on plea of illness and Mr. Azikiwe was requested to place evidence of murder plot in hands of Chief Secretary at earliest possible moment.

On 17.7.45 (No. 30) the Governor advised no reply from Mr. Azikiwe.

On 18.7.45 at (39f) still no reply from Mr. Azikiwe and reminder sent to him by Governor.

On 23.8.45 at (95a) the Governor advised that Mr. Azikiwe left Lagos about the middle of July and went to Onitsha where he has remained ever since. The Governor added that according to a news item dated London 17th July and published in West African Pilot on 20.8.45. the story of a plot to murder Azikiwe was repeated and a local editorial note added 'Zik has since forwarded his evidence to the Government'. However, the Governor adds that no announcement or statement from Mr. Azikiwe has yet been received.

On 22.8.45 at (96) Dr. Harold Moody[4] forwarded a copy of a telegram from Mr. Azikiwe reading 'Thanks your seventeenth. Could not have presented myself personally on sixteenth vital date originally scheduled for my assassination. When

---

[4] Dr Harold Moody, a Jamaican doctor resident in London; founder (1931) and president of the League of Coloured Peoples.

invited state case was away hiding in jungle. Gardner Editor Pilot informed Chief Secretary I was out of town but was not believed apparently. Have just seen copies invitation by Chief Secretary and have written him enclosing my evidence and have asked him forward same plus appendices unabbreviated to Colonial Secretary. Am reasonably safe now but still vigilant.'

Nothing further is recorded on the files until arrival of Governor's savingram of 15.2.46 at (2) on 30647/1A/46 which covers Mr. Azikiwe's 'incontrovertible and conclusive evidence', which on examination of the papers would appear to be not a strictly accurate statement. With regard to this evidence the following points arise:—

(a) Wireless station Wapyel. Governor Nigeria states that he has been unable to trace this station. I have been in touch with Mr. Megson who has also failed to trace any such station. The prefix 'W' in the callsign is one of a series allotted to American stations; and if the first two letters 'WA' are regarded to mean West Africa, the prefix 'P' of the remaining callsign Pyel would then be one of a group allotted to Brazil. However, Mr. Megson is unable to trace either the callsign Wapyel or WA—Pyel, and states that if there were such a station it must be a pirate station.

(b) The peculiar style of English used throughout.

(c) The fact that the wireless operator obtained the most important parts of the message but failed to receive the less important sections.

(d) The use of the word 'unreceived' in message 4 at Appendix 2. This is purely 'telegraphese', not, repeat not, used in official circles.

(e) The fact that all these messages were received at the same time. (5.15 p.m. on 13.7.45)—which, incidentally is twenty-four hours later than Mr. Azikiwe's first cablegram to Col. Stanley that he had reason to believe his life was in danger.

(f) None of the messages mention the names of the 'two most important persons to be assassinated'.

With regard to No. 3 on this file—a further savingram from the Governor Nigeria on 19.2.46—the Governor encloses a copy of a document received by the Daily Service—a rival organ of the Zik Press. The original was typed on Crown Agents paper and enclosed in an O.H.M.S. envelope pasted over with plain paper.

The documents purport to contain copies of communications exchanged between the Chief Secretary and the three Chief Commissioners. The messages are fictitious, the Governor advises, but he forwarded them because passages in the first five messages correspond with passages in the messages said to have been intercepted by the West African Pilot wireless operator and quoted in Appendix 2 of No. 2. These messages fill the gaps left in the original messages.

Comments submitted are:—

(1) Apart from the fact that the Governor states that these messages are fictitious, that these messages were transmitted en clair in wartime is, of course, absurd.

(2) That this anonymous document should appear out of the blue five days after Mr. Azikiwe's forwarding of the evidence of the Chief Secretary is amazingly convenient.

(3) The even more peculiar English used by the Chief Secretary and the Chief Commissioners in the text of the messages.

(4) Again that all the messages should have been transmitted by one radio station at the same time when it is now most obvious that messages 2 and 3 are in answer to 1; and 4 is in answer to messages 2 and 3; whilst 5 is in answer to 1.

It is noticed that the Governor has not intimated what answer he would desire to be sent to Mr. Azikiwe, but he requests telegraphic approval to publish all Mr. Azikiwe's 'evidence'. As the discovery of the assassination plot caused such a furore throughout Nigeria, this approval to publish should be forwarded immediately?

? Approve attached draft telegram.

J.E.M.
26.2.46

25 CO 583/271/4/4, no 7　　　　　　　　　　　　　　　　23 Feb 1946
[Nigerian development plans]: despatch no 29 from Sir A Richards to Mr Hall on the Legislative Council approval of the ten-year plan of development and welfare　　　　　　　　　　　　　　　　　　　　[Extract]

... 8.　In accepting the Report of the Select Committee and the amended Plan[1] the Legislative Council passed the following resolution:—

'Be it resolved:

That this Council adopts the Report of the Select Committee appointed to consider the Ten-Year Plan of Development and Welfare for Nigeria set out in Sessional Paper No. 24 of 1945 and approves the Plan as amended by the Select Committee and recommends its acceptance as the general development policy of the Government of Nigeria for the next ten years, subject to periodic review of details in the light of experience and the inclusion of such additional schemes as may prove to be necessary as the result of unforseen circumstances.'[2]

In supporting the motion all of the Unofficial Members, in their speeches, referred to the desirability of this Plan being accepted and retained as the general development policy of the Government of Nigeria; an attitude with which I am in full support.

9.　Many Members also emphasized the necessity for a maximum of continuity, not only of policy but of personnel associated with the actual work. While it may not be possible, on account of the exigencies of the service, to ensure that the same officers will continue to deal with this development plan during the whole of the ten year period, I must endorse the view that a maximum of continuity of policy and staff, in order to ensure that the Plan is properly effected, is a most desirable thing and should be given careful consideration.

10.　It was evident throughout the debate, in which practically every Unofficial Member took part, that this Plan of Development and Welfare, together with the legislation connected with it, is regarded as being a thoroughly constructive piece of work and a clear indication of the desire both of His Majesty's Government, through

---

[1] See 20.

[2] Resolution passed on 7 Feb 1946. The ten-year plan was revised in 1951 and a new plan approved in 1955.

the generous allocation to Nigeria under the Colonial Development and Welfare Act, and of this Government to ensure that this country should be developed as rapidly as possible. Council was also very impressed with the statements which were made that the Development Plan would be used as a means of training Africans to accept further responsibility and to replace European officers in the course of time in a large portion of the services of the Dependency.

11.   In these circumstances, and in view of the fact that the majority of the component parts of the Plan have already been considered by your Advisers, I trust that you will not find any difficulty in giving your full approval of the Plan and to the desire of the Legislative Council expressed in the resolution set out above. . . .

26   CO 583/276/2/2, no 50   26 Apr 1946
[Cost of living]: outward telegram no 518 from Mr Hall to Sir A Richards on the Davies Report on the cost of living in Nigeria

Your telegram No. 553. Copy of Tudor Davies report is being sent to you by earliest practicable air mail.[1]

Following is brief summary of its specific recommendations.

(a) That cost of living allowances existing in July, 1945, shall be increased by 50 per cent. with effect from the various dates on which work was resumed after strike of 1945, until such time as the cost of living allowances can be absorbed in the reconstituted wages structure which will be put together by a team of statistical officers and a nutritionist working in collaboration with local committees as recommended elsewhere in the report.

(b) That above award of 50 per cent. shall apply not only to cost of living allowances paid to African employees earning £220 per annum or less, but also to separation or local allowances paid since October, 1944, to African employees whose salaries are over £220 per annum, except those receiving local allowances because they hold 'superior posts'.

(c) That although the future cost of living allowances payable under (a) will be payable together with future wages in the normal way, the retrospective cost of living allowances which are also payable under (a) shall be paid to African civil servants by being credited to them either in Post Office Savings accounts or in bank accounts, or in other ways, and shall be released to them in 12 equal sums over 12 months after payment begins.

(d) That this award shall remain in force until the new wages structure is set up by the team mentioned in (a) above, which should be effected within two years of the date of report.

(e) That family allowances shall not (repeat not) be granted to Nigerian workers on the same principle as separation allowances already granted to Europeans, but that the principle of separation allowances which already exists for certain African civil servants who are required by the nature of their duties to live away from their families and thus pay for two homes shall be extended.

---

[1] See 11. *Inquiry into the Cost of Living and the Control of the Cost of Living in the Colony and Protectorate of Nigeria. Part I, Report by W Tudor Davies, April 15, 1946. Part II, Despatch from the Secretary of State for the Colonies to the Governor of Nigeria, July 9, 1946* (Col. No. 204), 1946.

(f) That the same rates of cost of living allowances shall not (repeat not) be made payable to all workers throughout Nigeria.

(g) That Government's decision that while the period spent on strike should not count for pension it should count for purpose of continuity of service for pension was correct.

(h) That there shall be no payment from the Government to workers for the period of the strike, *ex gratia* or otherwise, it being the function of the Unions, not of the employer, to provide strike pay.

(i) That the claim made by the Federal Union of Native Administration Staffs for equal wages and cost of living allowances with the Government employees was not substantiated.

27   CO 554/134/13, no 26   6 July 1946
[Higher education]: despatch no 184 from Mr Hall to Sir A Richards on the Elliot Commission's Report on higher education in West Africa
[Extract]

In my despatch (1) No. 334 of 1st October, 1945, I had the honour to inform you of my preliminary opinion on the Reports of the Commission on Higher Education in West Africa. I have since given further consideration to the Reports and full consideration to the views which you have expressed to me in despatches and at the first meeting of the West African Council. I have also studied the considerable volume of advice and opinion which has been submitted to me from many sources, both official and unofficial. I have reached the following conclusions concerning action which should now be taken.

2.   Development of higher education facilities must form part of a balanced advance along the whole educational front, and I am gratified by the prominence that is being given to education in the development programmes which have already been submitted. In particular I wish to emphasize the importance which I attach to the expansion of secondary school facilities at the greatest speed consistent with the achievement and maintenance of high standards. The Elliot Report stressed the importance of this aspect of education both in regard to teaching and curriculum, if the new higher education institutions proposed are to receive a sufficient intake of students of suitable standard for university studies and if suitable personnel is to become available for the great constructive tasks which young persons will be required to perform in the services, economic activities and works necessary in the developing life of their country. The broadening of secondary school curricula with some regard to practical training and science is a feature of much importance to the needs of African development.

3.   I accept the advice of the Commission (pages 81–4 and 160) that there is urgent need to improve the training facilities for both secondary and primary school teachers, and commend to your special attention the recommendation that such training should be through special professional courses, clearly separated from attempts to make good the deficiencies of the general education of the students.

4.   I have given careful attention to the representations made to me as to the considerations which should guide me in reaching my conclusions on the central

problem of university development. I have been urged to give due weight to local political considerations as well as to those which are primarily educational and practical, and it has been suggested to me that a beginning in the founding of university colleges should now be made in two, if not three of the territories concerned or that arrangements should be made by certain of the existing colleges so, that the foundations of a federal university for West Africa may now be laid. I appreciate the contribution to African progress and educational advance made by Fourah Bay College[1] and Achimota College, and I cannot lightly disregard the hopes entertained as to the future of these foundations and the popular feeling for them engendered because of their long service. At the same time I am impressed by the arguments used in the Report of the Asquith Commission regarding university progress and am convinced that at this present stage it is most desirable that a unitary university college for West Africa should be established.[2] The arguments advanced by the minority commissioners in the Elliot Report seem to me to conform most nearly to the advice of the Asquith Commission and their case seems to me to be soundly conceived.[3] But I feel that my decision while respecting the considerations advanced by these commissioners must be such as to secure a wide measure of consent from the people of all the territories and to enjoy the co-operation and goodwill of local feeling in the tasks ahead.

5.   I am fully alive to the ultimate educational needs of a population of 27 million, but at this juncture, I must recognise that the facilities that can for some time to come be effectively used, can be adequately met by the provision of one university institution, and that insufficient students of the requisite standard for entrance to university studies are available or staff of sufficiently high degree of academical qualifications can be secured for more than one really good institution, i.e. a university college sufficiently comprehensive in its range of subjects in faculties of arts, science and medicine and adequately equipped for research. . . .

11.   For the development of university education in West Africa I propose that there should be established for West Africa a University College sited at Ibadan and that in the near future executive machinery should be set up to prepare and carry out the necessary plans. It is my intention to take the necessary steps for the creation of a Provisional Council of the University College of West Africa, which would be an autonomous body, legally competent to hold and spend funds, to make contracts of employment with staff, and to have such other powers as it will need for its task. Its membership would consist, in the first instance (since it would later need to include further academic members), of:—

The Chairman (nominated by the Crown).
The Principal-designate of the University College.
The Principal of Fourah Bay College.
   „   „   „ Achimota   „
   „   „   „ either the Higher College or the
                          Medical School, Yaba.

---

[1] In Sierra Leone.
[2] This commission, under Mr Justice Cyril Asquith, was appointed in 1943 to consider the principles which should guide the promotion of higher education and the development of universities in the colonies; *Report of the Commission on Higher Education in the Colonies*, Cmd 6647 (1945).   [3] See 23.

One person nominated by the Governor of Gambia.

,,   ,,   ,,   ,,   ,,   ,,   ,, Sierra Leone.

,,   ,,   ,,   ,,   ,,   ,,   ,, Gold Coast.

,,   ,,   ,,   ,,   ,,   ,,   ,, Nigeria.

One person elected by the African unofficial members of the Legislative Council and adopted by the full Legislative Council of Sierra Leone.

,,   ,,   ,,   ,,   ,,   Gold Coast.

,,   ,,   ,,   ,,   ,,   Nigeria.

Four representatives of the Inter-University Council for Higher Education in the Colonies (the membership would be reconsidered after the initial stage of bringing the University College into being).

The Council would have a full-time Secretary. In order to keep the Council in close touch with schools throughout West Africa, it is desirable that the four Directors of Education should attend its meetings; but to avoid overweighting the official element on the Council, I propose that they should not sit as members of the Council, but should attend as advisers.

12.   When a suitable candidate can be found, I propose to appoint a Principal-designate of the University College of West Africa, on the nomination of the Inter-University Council. Until the University College is able to strengthen the Council by adequate representation of the College staff, the Principal-designate would be ultimately responsible not to the Council but to me. He would however be required to act in accordance with the Provisional Council's decisions, over which I would reserve to myself during this interim period a power of review. It is my desire that at an early date these interim arrangements may be terminated, and that the College may become fully autonomous. I am proposing to make a scheme under the Colonial Development and Welfare Act for payments not exceeding £10,000 per annum for a period of three years to cover the salaries of the Principal-designate of the University College and of the Secretary, office expenditure, travelling expenses of members of the Provisional Council and similar expenditure.

13.   The Provisional Council, acting through the Principal-designate as its executive officer, would be requested to take appropriate steps (including the preparation of detailed financial estimates for submission to me for consideration by the Colonial University Grants Advisory Committee) towards achieving among other things, the following:—

(a) The selection and definition of the university site at Ibadan. Preliminary plans for the lay-out of the permanent buildings should be prepared and temporary accommodation at Ibadan should be acquired from the military authorities or other sources.

(b) An expert mission from the United Kingdom universities should visit West Africa to advise on plans for a permanent West African medical school at Ibadan, on the feasibility of the interim use of temporary accommodation (e.g. the military hospital if available), on the phasing of the transfer of the medical school from Yaba to Ibadan, and on the question whether the school should include provision from the start for dentistry training.

(c) Preliminary arrangements should be made with the Nigerian Government for transferring the responsibility for the direction of the higher training work now undertaken in the Schools of Agriculture and of Forestry at Ibadan, and (as recommended on page 111, paragraph 52 of the Elliot Report) of Animal Health at Vom, as far as possible, to the Principal-designate and Provisional Council. Schools for training at university level in these three subjects should be created or adapted from the present schools, designed to serve the whole of British West Africa, and developed to become integral parts of the University College.

(d) The staff for Ibadan should be steadily recruited and be sufficient in number and qualifications to provide teaching of full university standard, in both arts and science as the faculties are created. Adequate provision should be made in the temporary accommodation for laboratories, etc. for teaching and for research facilities for the staff. Students from all four territories should be admitted at post-intermediate level. It is essential from the start that a suitable entrance standard should be laid down.

(e) An Institute of Education, both for research and for professional training, on a West African basis, should be developed as an essential part of the University College at Ibadan. The scope of such Institute is set out on page 84 of the Report.

(f) A library of university standard should be built up at Ibadan.

(g) A scheme of scholarships on an inter-territorial basis should be established, including the co-ordination of existing scholarship resources.

(h) A Guild of Graduates should be formed, with branches in each territory, as recommended on page 162 of the Elliot Report. I appreciate that this can effectively be done only by the spontaneous action of the graduates concerned and that the College can do no more in this matter than issue an invitation. The Guild would later be represented on the Provisional Council.

(i) The research activities of the Institute of Arts, Industries and Social Science should be moved to Ibadan while the future of its other activities will be the subject of an enquiry as was decided at the meeting of the West African Council in January last.

14. I accept, and wish to see implemented at once, the recommendation of the Elliot Commission (pages 118–21) with regard to technical education, and I hope that technical and commercial institutes will be developed on the lines suggested in the report. I understand that in the case of Nigeria urgent consideration has already been given to technical education development and that steps are being taken already to transform the Higher College at Yaba into a Technical Institute, the change-over from academic to technical work to take place gradually and the Institute continuing the work started by Yaba Higher College until suitable arrangements have been made for the creation of the Territorial College and of the University College of West Africa. . . .[4]

---

[4] The University College at Ibadan opened for its first students in Jan 1948. In the event Sir Arthur Burns announced in March 1947 that work would begin on a University College for the Gold Coast.

28   CO 583/277/4, no 5   18 July 1946
[NCNC]: letter from Sir G Creasy to Sir G Gater on the activities of
the NCNC

When I was in Lagos I was shown a copy of Richards' Secret despatch of the 12th of July regarding the activities of the National Council of Nigeria and the Cameroons and the situation that may develop therefrom, and I discussed with Richards and Colby,[1] both separately and together, the possible steps that could be taken to meet it.

As you know, a mission from the National Council has recently toured the Northern Provinces to enlist support, both moral and financial, for the proposed delegation to England. The mission is now in the Eastern Provinces, which is of course the storm centre, and I understand that it will probably be back in Lagos towards the end of August after taking the Western Provinces on its way. The glowing accounts of the mission's progress that appear daily in the ZIK press are no doubt exaggerated, and I was told that the very considerable sums which are named in them as having been collected for the delegation's expenses are to a large extent promises rather than hard cash. But there is no doubt, I understand, that the delegation will come to London, especially as a few wealthy African merchants are said to be behind ZIK at present, no doubt entirely for their own ends.

It would be absurd for me to attempt to produce a first-hand appreciation of the position, but I am convinced in my own mind that it is potentially very serious, especially in the Eastern Provinces, and that there has been a definite deterioration since I was out earlier in the year. I enclose copies of the West African Pilot and the Comet for the last three days, every word in which I think I can claim to have read.[2] You will see from the accounts of the mission's meetings the extensive use that is made of the demobilised soldiers who are, at any rate in the Eastern Provinces, only too easy a field for ZIK propaganda: they have 'fought and bled' for Britain, a gross exaggeration, as the fighting man came largely from the North, and the E.P. man did not for the most part get beyond the Middle East; they were promised jobs (an absolute untruth) and this promise is not being kept; and so on. You will note also the constant use made of military metaphors: 'we must fight for Nigeria', 'we must strike for freedom', and so on. Articles on these lines appear now in the Nigerian press day after day. Richards is determined to take the offensive whenever possible and he has ordered that the editors, etc., should be prosecuted whenever there is any reasonable chance of conviction, while the Government's Nigerian Review has also been told to take an aggressive line in combating ZIK's propaganda. But ZIK is clever enough to keep within the law as it now is, and I am afraid he has ample opportunity to stir up and inflame racial bitterness without running any risk of conviction. The most casual observer cannot fail to see how these papers are read and studied everywhere in Lagos, and I feel that the Governor is fully justified in all that he has written about the cumulative effect of their anti-European and anti-Government contents.

It is comparatively easy to describe the position, and Richards has already done that at some length in his despatch of the 12th of July. It is extremely difficult,

[1] G F T Colby, administrative secretary, Nigeria, 1945–1948.   [2] Not printed.

however, to decide how it can be remedied. The spread of real education and the development of a steady and responsible public opinion are both long-term measures, and one of the most depressing features at present is the lack of moral courage on the part of those Africans, and there are many of them, who are essentially men of goodwill and who realise the harm that ZIK and his friends are doing, but who fail to raise their voices against him.

It will help in the immediate future if it is possible to ensure closer administration, especially in the Eastern Provinces, and this will be helped by the reinforcements to the Administrative Service that are now beginning to come out in some numbers: the spread of the Leopard murders in the Eastern Provinces is one result of under-administration.[3] It would be most valuable, however, if steps could be taken to ensure that the balance of the 100 cadets for whom Richards originally asked come out as soon as possible. If the projected Kemsley newspaper can be started soon, that too would be of some help: but I gather there is no early prospect of this. There remains the proposal which Richards has now made to the Secretary of State that an ordinance should be enacted on the lines of the Cyprus law. He realises the embarrassment that this may cause to the Government at home, but he is absolutely satisfied in his own mind that nothing else will do and that unless strong action is taken now trouble is bound to come, whether six months ahead, in a year's time, or later.

Richards also discussed with Colby and myself the question of the preparations that might be made now for the reception of the National Council's delegation in England. He has no doubt that ZIK and his fellow delegates will receive the reception they deserve at the Colonial Office, but he is concerned about the encouragement that may be given to them by elements at home who know nothing of the West African background and yet are only too ready to talk and write about self-government for Africa, as if its introduction was a matter of a few months or years, instead of decades. Richards will be thinking further about this and will, I was told, send a despatch to the Secretary of State with his suggestions. Amongst those made at our talk was one that papers such as the Times, the Economist, or the Manchester Guardian should be asked to publish articles giving an entirely objective and dispassionate account of the position out here as a corrective to the kind of picture that will be drawn by ZIK and so readily accepted by ignorant theorists.

Another suggestion which, I believe, Richards has already made is that a small party of Members of Parliament should visit Nigeria and study the position there for themselves. This would, I think, be excellent, if it could be arranged, and I know that such a mission would be most warmly welcomed by Richards and his senior advisers.

I come now to the security aspect. The G.O.C. was in Lagos ten days ago and I know that he was considerably disturbed by what he was told by Richards and very doubtful, I understand, as to his ability, with his present resources, to deal with any situation that may arise. But the position is now worse in that the G.O.C. has recently received a direct order from the War Office to reduce his present cadre of 3,900 British officers and N.C.Os. to 1,500 and to put the first cut of 1,000 in force by the 30th of September. He proposes to do this as much as possible at the expense of

---

[3] This is a reference to some 100 or so murders in Calabar province, 1945–1947, in which the bodies were mutilated as if they had been killed by leopards, and which were ascribed by the police at the time to the Idiong society.

the Gold Coast and Sierra Leone, but it cannot but have a very serious effect on the military resources available to maintain law and order in Nigeria, and Irwin[4] has told me that he will certainly put this to the War Office. Richards will also represent to the Secretary of State the additional risks that we *must* incur if this drastic reduction takes place, and he has promised to send me a copy of his telegram, so that I can keep Irwin fully informed.

I do not know how far we, that is, the Colonial Office, are committed on this, and I certainly have not been told anything about it from the Office, nor has anything been said to Burns or Richards. But I would urge most strongly that steps should be taken to hold the position until you have received and considered Richards' telegram and the War Office have had Irwin's appreciation. Irwin himself is due to leave Accra by air on the 7th of August for a two or three weeks' visit to the U.K. and I hope that you will be able to have a full discussion with him on the position.

You may, perhaps, think that in this letter I have gone somewhat outside my province, but I thought it right to let you know the impressions I brought back with me from Lagos.

---

[4] Lt-gen N M C Irwin, West Africa Command, 1946–1948

---

29 CO 583/277/4, no 7   9 Aug 1946
[NCNC]: despatch from Sir A Richards to Mr Hall on the plans of the NCNC to send a delegation to the UK. *Enclosure*   [Extract]

I have the honour to refer to my Secret Despatch of the 12th of July, 1946, in which I addressed you at some length in regard to the Nigerian Press and suggested that you should consider certain measures for dealing with a situation which was causing me considerable anxiety; in the same despatch I had occasion to allude to the activities of the National Council for Nigeria and the Cameroons, and I propose now to address you more fully on this subject.

2.   In paragraph 12 of my Despatch under reference I gave a brief account of the present activities of this body and made particular reference to the fact that a delegation of the Council is likely to visit the United Kingdom during the course of the next few months, and I feel that it is most advisable that I should ask you to consider in advance your attitude towards the members of the delegation when they arrive in the United Kingdom.

3.   In considering this matter, I make the basic assumption that, whether you will be willing to accord them an interview or not, you will not be able to accede to their demands for revision of the New Constitution of Nigeria, the Minerals Ordinance, the Public Lands Acquisition Ordinance and the Appointment and Deposition of Chiefs Ordinance.[1] As you are aware, these measures have received the detailed examination of myself and my advisers and have been introduced with your full approval. I find it difficult to submit advice at this stage whether or not you should consent to see the delegation, but I am assuming that it will be politic to do so.

---

[1] These ordinances, together with the Crown Lands Ordinance, were the so-called 'Obnoxious Ordinances' of 1945. See 8.

4.   You are aware, of course, that organizations and other groups exist in the United Kingdom who would be only too glad to accord them a measure of support and there is little doubt that the avowed objects of the delegation will receive sympathy and support in some sections of the British Press. It seems possible, however, that unless steps are taken to make the facts known, the delegation may enlist the support of a not inconsiderable body of well-meaning but ill-informed opinion, which is at present quite unaware of conditions as they really exist in Nigeria. Such developments might cause embarrassment to His Majesty's Government as there are perhaps certain elements in the House of Commons who would not be averse to seizing an opportunity to criticize Government's colonial policy.

5.   However that may be, there can be no doubt that any considerable measure of support for the delegation in the United Kingdom would considerably enhance the prestige of the National Council for Nigeria and the Cameroons in this country, a development which I am most anxious to avoid.

6.   I feel therefore that it is no more than prudent to consider now the measures which can be taken and to be ready with a working plan when the delegation arrives. I would suggest that as a first step the ground might be prepared by the Public Relations Officer at the Colonial Office and that he might give to the more reputable organs of the British Press some factual information about the Mission, a sketch of the individual members, and their history and, as a background some information with regard to the present stage of development in Nigeria and some facts in connection with the Ordinances which the delegation oppose and their reasons for so doing. With this object in view, I have had prepared a Memorandum on the National Council for Nigeria and the Cameroons and brief biographical notes on the principal figures in this organization.[2] It is important that the Press and the public should be left in no doubt as to what these people stand for, which is, of course, disruption of British rule in Nigeria, the achievement of their own selfish ends and the sacrifice of the vast majority of the population on the altar of their political and financial advancement. It is, I think, advisable that this question should be energetically and immediately tackled if a grossly misleading impression is not to be left upon the British public to the discredit of British colonial policy, and I feel that it would be of advantage if you felt able to make a direct approach to the Editors of 'The Times' and the 'Economist', in order to enlist their assistance in dealing with what may well become a most embarrassing situation.

7.   As there is little doubt that the delegation will be received by certain groups in the United Kingdom who are likely not only to be sympathetic to its views but to be uncritical of its aspirations it would, I think, be most salutary if it were possible to arrange for the delegation to meet bodies who would adopt a critical and questioning attitude. The myth of the National Council could be readily exploded by a few relevant questions, and with this object and, I must confess, in ignorance of what you regard as permissible in the circumstances, I suggest that it might be useful if a representative body of Members of Parliament could meet them in the presence of the Press, and if you could ensure that such Members were in possession of all the facts about the National Council. In these circumstances I feel convinced that there

---

[2] Biographical notes not printed.

would be nothing to fear from any wrong impressions being created in the House of Commons, and consequently the Colonial Office would be saved from considerable embarrassment.

Enclosure to 29: National Council of Nigeria and the Cameroons

... [A] few months after its formation the Council claimed to have a roster of Members which included the Trade Union Congress of Nigeria and the West African Union of Seamen, the National Democratic Party and the Union of Young Democrats, four literary societies, eleven professional associations, eleven social clubs and 69 Tribal Unions. At first sight this list appears impressive, but on examination by anyone with local knowledge it becomes far less so. To take first the Trade Union Congress of Nigeria. It is true that the majority of Trade Unions in Nigeria are affiliated to the T.U.C. but like all other Trade Union activities in Nigeria, the T.U.C. is entirely centered on Lagos, from which all its Executives are drawn, and the Executive is undemocratic and unrepresentative of the masses of the workers. If the Executive, which is drawn from a small semi-political clique, sees fit to give its support to any particular party in Lagos it will do so without consulting the member Unions and the men themselves will know nothing of it and will care less. The West African Union of Seamen has a membership of about 250.

To turn next to the two political parties. It will be appreciated that only in Lagos where Municipal and Legislative Council elections are held, do political parties, in the generally accepted sense, exist. The two parties mentioned are Lagos parties formed to fight Lagos elections and both of them were fostered by the promoters of the National Council.

For the purposes of this Memoranda the four literary societies, the eleven professional associations and the eleven social clubs may be considered together, for they all have this in common, they are purely local Lagos phenomena and can claim to be representative of nothing in particular.

However, to one unacquainted with local conditions the most solid backing of the National Council would appear to be the 69 Tribal Unions. It must be remembered that it is only since the advent of Government that the Nigerian has dared to leave his home and venture abroad. Prior to that it was only the very adventurous who ever willingly left the narrow confines of the place where he was born. Not unnaturally this has led to a strong sense of parochial patriotism which is symbolized by the way in which, when three or four men from some remote village come together in a strange town, they immediately band together to form a Union and give to the Union a high-sounding name such as the Ndoni Progressive Union.

Lagos is essentially a cosmopolitan town in the sense that it draws to it people from every corner of Nigeria, either in the course of their employment or in search of work. It is not surprising therefore to find in Lagos scores of these Progressive Unions, often consisting of only half a dozen members. Some of the members may be older men who have been away from their home town for years, but the majority will be younger men who have but recently arrived. The objects of these Unions are firstly social, secondly to look after their fellow-townsmen who happen to be in Lagos, and finally to promote the interests of the neighbourhood from which they come. It would be as wrong to suppose that these Unions are the voice of the areas from which they originated as it would be to suppose that the members of the Caledonian Club in Bnenos Aires expressed the unanimous opinion of Scotland. Incidentally only one of these Unions consisted of men from the Northern Provinces. This was the Tiv Progressive Union, a tribe which has little in common with the Hausa who forms the vast bulk of the population in the North.

At that time therefore it might have been true to say that the National Council expressed the views of a section of the population of Lagos, but it was patently untrue to claim, as the National Council did claim, that they represented 6,000,000 Nigerians. Even in Lagos it would be wrong to suppose that the National Council had all its own way. When Dr. Nimbe stood for Legislative Council in 1945 on the National Council ticket, he was opposed by another candidate who received one third of the total votes cast.

On its inception the avowed aims of the National Council were to oppose four Bills then about to come before Legislative Council. These Bills and the Council's comments on them are of interest. They were:—

(1) The Public Lands Acquisition (Amendment) Ordinance 1945.
(2) The Minerals Ordinance, 1945.
(3) The Appointment and Deposition of Chiefs (Amendment) Ordinance, 1945.
(4) The Royal West African Frontier Force (Nigeria Regiment) (Amendment) Ordinance, 1945.

The National Council alleged that the first of these Bills sought to transform public lands acquired by the British Government in Nigeria into Crown Lands; that the Minerals Ordinance contained a clause vesting in the British Crown, mineral rights in Nigeria; that the Appointment and Deposition of Chiefs Ordinance gave to the Governor the power to appoint and depose the people's natural rulers, and that the R.W.A.F.F. Ordinance sought to apply to Nigerian soldiers serving overseas regulations enacted under an Act of Parliament. Some of these allegations will be dealt with in greater detail later but it is worthy of note here that in each case the underlying suggestion was that the native was being deprived of his rights in the interests of the British.

It is impossible to think that men of the intelligence of Macaulay and Azikiwe really believed this, but it suited admirably the line of propaganda which they wished to put over to their gullible public.

The National Council, while not dropping its interest in these Bills, (except the R.W.A.F.F. Ordinance), next turned its attention to the new Constitutional proposals which had been published as a White Paper and which received the unanimous approval of the Legislative Council.

Their main contentions were that, in the Regional Houses, Government Officials should not be allowed to sit or vote but should only attend in the capacity of advisers, that Native Authority representatives should be regarded as 'Official Members', and that only members elected by popular ballot should be regarded as Unofficial Members and that they should be in the majority.

Their proposals for the Legislative Council envisaged 40 elected Unofficial Members and the proposed allocation of Members of it is of considerable interest. This was as follows:—

Lagos Municipal Area   5 members
Lagos (Rural Area)   2 members
Western Provinces   11 members
Eastern Provinces   11 members
Northern Provinces   11 members.

The 400,000 people in Lagos Colony would therefore return 7 Members, the 10 million in the Eastern and Western Provinces would return 22 Members, and the 11 million in the North, 11 Members. It is obvious how such a Constitution would play into the hands of the Lagos politicians, especially when it is remembered that such support as they have outside Lagos is almost entirely centred round the politically minded, semi-educated classes in the Eastern and Western Provinces.

During the next year the attitude or influence of the National Council did not materially change, but all the time the papers of the Zik Press whose policy is of course controlled by the National Council, was hammering away at its racial and anti-British propaganda, dispensing lies and half-truths to mislead a public which is barely literate and which is prepared to believe anything which it sees in print.

Early in its history the National Council planned to do a propaganda tour of the country. This was postponed owing to the strike of 1945, and for other reasons, and did not begin till the end of April, 1946, when Herbert Macaulay, Olorun-Nimbe and another agitator, Imoudu,[3] left Lagos for the North; they were joined by Azikiwe at Kaduna. They had planned a very extensive tour of the Northern, Eastern and Western Provinces, but when they had been away some ten days and had reached Kano, Herbert Macaulay slipped and sustained injuries. He was taken to the N.A. Hospital where an X-Ray revealed a broken thigh. Such an accident to a man of over 80 was of course very serious, but all facilities were available in the Hospital. In spite of this, Nimbe, who was the medical adviser to the delegation, refused to put him in Hospital but, because he thought it politically more expedient, brought him back to Lagos with the limb unset—a journey of 2½ days by train, which at the best of times can only be regarded as arduous. It is impossible to say whether Macaulay would have recovered had he been left at Kano; in the event he died 36 hours after arriving at Lagos, and his funeral was the occasion of much popular demonstration and much advertisement for the National Council.

After the funeral the delegation, now joined by Macaulay's ne'er-do-well son, Oged Macaulay, resumed their tour and in the past three months have visited most of the larger towns in the Northern and Eastern Provinces. Their avowed intention is to collect funds and the mandate of the people to send a delegation to England to protest against what they call the four 'obnoxious' Ordinances and the Richards Constitution. Their published target is £10,000, but why they should require so

---

[3] Herbert Samuel Heelas Macaulay, trained as a civil engineer; founder of the Nigerian National Democratic Party in the early 1920s, and of the *Lagos Daily News*; elected president of the NCNC in 1944. Dr Abubakar Ibiyinka Olorun-Nimbe, medical practitioner; member of the NCNC; elected to Lagos Town Council 1944 and to the Legislative Council 1945; elected mayor of Lagos 1950. Michael Ominus Imoudu, prominent in the formation of the Railway Workers' Union in 1932; elected vice-president of the African Civil Servants Technical Workers Union in 1941; detained under Defence Regulations 1943–45; member of NCNC; elected president of the Nigerian National Federation of Labour in 1949; president of the Nigerian Labour Congress in 1950; president of the All-Nigeria Trade Union Federation 1953; president of the Trade Union Congress of Nigeria, 1959.

considerable a sum to send a delegation to England—unless they believe that English politics are as corrupt as their own—has not been explained. Though their main plank has been the Ordinances and the Constitution they have missed no opportunity to ferment discontent, particularly among the demobilized soldiers of the Eastern Provinces, whom they encourage to believe that they are neglected by an ungrateful Government. Nor have they hesitated to spread rumours which they believe will be damaging to Government, as, for example, that Government has a large scheme for the settlement of 'Whites' on land seized from the native.

It is of importance to the delegation that when they visit England they should appear to have the backing of as much of the country as possible and with this end in view they have, wherever they have been, collected signatures in support of the delegation. There can be no doubt that they will collect an imposing list, but it is equally certain that the list will be as shallow as their original pretensions to represent 6,000,000 Nigerians. It must be remembered that they have confined themselves almost exclusively to the larger towns, in which there are always a number of literate, detribalized natives to whom their propaganda particularly appeals. The fact that certain of these men have signed their memorial is of course in no way an indication that the delegation has the support of even the majority of the town which the signatories purport to represent. To take the example of Zaria. Here, as elsewhere, they held a mass meeting which was attended by some 600 people, most of them Southerners. The chief sub-Editor of the 'Gaskiya ta fi Kwabo', the Government-sponsored Hausa newspaper, Mallam Makama, a native of Kano but a well-known man in Zaria, was sent to report the meeting. He was immediately invited to take a place with the delegation at the front of the meeting. After the usual speeches, an announcement was made that a Hausa was wanted to represent Zaria and append his name to the delegations' petition—as has been said very few Hausas and none of local importance were present. Mallam Makama was invited to sign for Zaria but he indignantly refused, saying that he was no one in Zaria and pointing out that in any case he, a Kano man, could not possibly claim to represent Zaria. Finally a Mallam who works for one of the European firms in Zaria signed for the town.

Needless to say, the Press has given the delegation the fullest publicity, and has made the usual extravagant claims. Again to take the example of Zaria, the press account states that about 15,000 men and women attended a mammoth meeting at which the Hausa community was fully represented and that without a dissentient voice the meeting authorized the delegation to represent them abroad. At Aba, which has a population of some 15,000, it was claimed that 85,000 people attended a meeting. At Calabar they claim 80,000; the total population not only of Calabar but of Calabar Division as well, scarcely passes this figure.

It would, however, be stupid and dangerous to pretend that the delegation has not won a considerable body of support for themselves; not among the peasants who form 95% of the total population, but among the educated, semi-educated and detribalized and unemployed populations of the larger towns. This class has been most influenced by the propaganda which has been so consistently handed out to them; propaganda deliberately designed to turn gratitude into envy, respect into hatred, trust into suspicion; to attribute to every act of Government the only motive which the propagandists understand—selfishness and lust for power. There is every reason to suppose that this propaganda is not entirely self-inspired, that the leaders of the movement are in close touch with Communist elements in various parts of the world from whom they receive inspiration and advice.

It may be worth considering how far the delegation's allegations are justified in fact. To take first the Public Lands Acquisition Ordinance. The National Council have attacked this Ordinance, or rather the amending Ordinance, on two grounds: first that it vests lands acquired for public purposes in the British Crown, and secondly that the ulterior motive behind the Ordinance is Government's intention to settle Europeans on the land.

It is, of course, essential that Government should have the power to acquire, if necessary compulsorily, land required for public purposes. Such a power has been given to the Government by various Ordinances, and the present Public Lands Acquisition Ordinance was passed in 1917. It defines the expression 'public purposes,' provides for payment of compensation on acquisition and for settlement of disputes with regard to compensation by the Courts. The 'Crown Lands Ordinance,' passed in 1918, defines Crown Lands, *inter alia*, as 'lands which have been or may hereafter be acquired by His Majesty for any public purpose or otherwise howsoever.' It follows therefore that, since 1918, lands acquired under the Public Lands Acquisition Ordinance have become Crown Lands, though the Public Lands Acquisition Ordinance was silent on this point. Some doubt had also arisen as to the position which would arise if land acquired for public purposes ceased to be wanted for that purpose. Under the Public Lands Acquisition Ordinance Government gets absolute title to land acquired under the Ordinance (other than land acquired for a term of years), all previous titles being extinguished. It is not possible therefore to hand back such lands to the previous owners. Moreover in many instances Government would have expended from public funds considerable sums on improvement, and it would not be equitable to the general public who had paid for improvements, to hand back these improvements to the previous owners who had already received compensation in full for their interest in the land prior to acquisition. The amending Ordinance of 1945, dealt with these points, and specifically provided that lands acquired under the Ordinance became Crown Lands, and that they remained Crown Lands notwithstanding that the purpose for which they had been acquired had ceased to exist. Up to June, 1945, the total area acquired by Government in the Colony, the area of which is 1,381 square miles, was 9 square miles, and in the Southern Provinces, the area of which is 89,515, 22 square miles. The Ordinance does not apply to the Northern Provinces. It is probable that more lands will have to be acquired in connection with the Development Programme, but the total area will still remain infinitesimal.

In the second place the Ordinance was amended to enable land to be acquired for/or in connection with, rural development or settlement. The object of this amendment was to create the machinery for re-settlement schemes for Nigerians, including ex-soldiers. It has never been the policy of this Government to encourage in any way European settlement. Outside the Colony a non-native cannot acquire freehold in land. With the approval of the Governor and the consent of the owners he can acquire a lease, but it is only in very exceptional circumstances that the Governor would approve a lease for agricultural purposes. There has been no change in Government policy, nor does the amendment of the Public Lands Acquisition Ordinance foreshadow any change in policy.

To turn next to the Minerals Ordinance. Here the line of attack is the same, namely that the Crown—the propagandist call it the British Crown where in practice the Crown in this sense means of course the Government of Nigeria—is taking to itself all rights in minerals which properly belong to the natives. As a matter of fact the Minerals Ordinance of 1945 made no change whatever in this respect. Section 3 of the Minerals Ordinance which was passed in 1916, and which is now replaced by the Minerals Ordinance, 1945, already vested in the Crown the entire property in and control of all minerals in, on or under any land in Nigeria. It is now a widely accepted view that mineral wealth should be vested in the State rather than in the person or persons who happen to own the surface rights. Adequate provision is made in the Ordinance for compensation for disturbance of surface rights but the minerals themselves remain the property of the State. The main alteration introduced by the 1945 Ordinance was that mining operators can now be required to restore the soil after mining operations have been completed, a measure which is plainly to the advantage of the surface owner.

The other Ordinance which has been violently attacked is the Appointment and Deposition of Chiefs Ordinance. Again the Ordinance is not a new one. The parent Ordinance is the Appointment and Deposition of Chiefs Ordinance, 1930. This Ordinance gave the Governor the power to approve the appointment of a Head Chief in the Protectorate or any Chief in the Colony who had been duly appointed in accordance with Native Law and Custom, and made the Governor the sole judge of whether such an appointment had been made in accordance with custom. It also gave the Governor the power to depose a Head Chief or Chief as the case might be if after enquiry he was satisfied that such deposition was required by Native Law and Custom or was necessary in the interests of peace, order and good government. The amending Ordinance of 1945 restricted the Governor's powers to a Chief who is a Native Authority or a member of a Native Authority but extended his powers to cover Chiefs, instead of only Head Chiefs, in the Protectorate. It further required the Governor to make due enquiry and consultation with the persons concerned in the selection before deciding a chieftaincy dispute or before deposing a Chief.

Chiefs and Head Chiefs form an important part, perhaps the most important part, of the machinery of native administration. In many parts of Nigeria chieftaincy is not hereditary and on a vacancy occurring there may be a large number of possible candidates. Before the advent of Government disputes were rapidly, though perhaps not permanently, settled, victory going to the strong, but in these more enlightened days when force majeure can no longer be used, disputes are apt to drag on interminably to the disruption of the administration and the disturbance of the neighbourhood. It is necessary to have machinery to settle such disputes, and individual enquiry followed by the Governor's decision has proved the most satisfactory. Similarly, in the old days a Chief who had outraged his subjects by mal-administration was given the choice of suicide, flight, or sudden death; he usually chose the former. These sanctions no longer exist and it is necessary to replace them with the sanction of the law.

These then are the laws which are being stigmatized as a wicked infringement of the natives' inalienable rights in the interests of the alien British Government.

To turn now to the new Constitution. As has been said, the National Council's main criticisms have been that representatives of Native Authorities should not be regarded as Unofficial Members and that the only Unofficial Members should be members elected by ballot who should have a majority in the Legislative Council.

The argument advanced on the first point is that native administrations form an integral part of the machinery of Government. This is true but it by no means follows that Native Authorities or their members are the mere mouthpieces of the administration. Anyone who has had any experience of dealing with Native Authorities knows well that they have very definite views of their own and are neither afraid to express them or to stick to them. Here again, the National Council is inconsistent; when it suits it it is fond of referring to the Chiefs as 'our natural rulers', and yet when it is suggested that certain of these natural rulers should represent their people on the Legislature, the Council denies their right to speak on behalf of their people. The real objection of the National Council to the representation of Native Authorities on the unofficial side of the House is that they know them to be a body of sober African opinion, with some experience of practical administration, who are far nearer than the politicians will ever be to the thoughts of the mass of the people and who therefore may be dangerous rivals to the politicians' own political aims.

But what of the alternative? The suggestion is seriously made that all Unofficial Members should be elected by ballot. This in a country where barely 5% of the population can read or write, where for generations the peasant has been far too concerned with the problem of existence to concern himself with anything but the most petty local affairs, where in large areas the natives, men and women, go unclothed, where cannibalism is still practised, where secret societies based on ju-ju can still indulge in mass murder, where the very leaders of organized labour invoke ju-ju to impart discipline; where the vast populations of the Moslem Emirates are only just emerging from the eastern feudalism of the Middle Ages. To attempt popular election in such circumstances would not be to introduce democracy but a sham disastrous alike to the true interests of the people and to the future of the country.

30   CO 554/152/1, no 4   Jan 1947
'The effect of Africanisation on the integrity of the Public Service': memorandum by the Nigerian government

1.   The West African Governments are firmly committed to a policy of Africanization of the Service. There can be no question of any change in this policy, but it is pertinent to consider the effects of this policy on the integrity of the public service.

2.   In considering this there are two aspects—financial integrity and loyalty to Government. The problem of financial integrity is a difficult and delicate one. It must be remembered that the African's background and outlook on public morality is very different from that which exists in present day Britain. Before the advent of Government he was accustomed to an administration and a judicial system which were based very largely on 'graft', and to the average African there was nothing unusual in having to pay for any services he might receive from a public servant or in the idea that those who judged his case should receive a 'gift' for their trouble.

3.   Although there are signs of an awakening of public opinion on this question of corruption, there can be no doubt that the average African believes that his fellow-

African, if put into a position of authority, will make the best of that position to further his own financial interests. Accusations, whether direct or implied, both against individual Africans and against some particular class of official, are of almost daily occurrence. On more than one occasion the local papers in Nigeria have drawn attention to the widespread corruption which, they allege, presently exists. Such accusations generally or specifically are extremely difficult to prove, but the fact that they are made *by* Africans *against* Africans is not without significance, particularly in view of the fact that, in spite of the present racial antagonism which has been engendered in Nigeria, accusations against Europeans on this score are extremely rare. It is pertinent to note that a prominent African has very recently been convicted of offering a bribe to an African Puisne Judge. Attempts to bribe European Judges are almost unknown. This attitude of mind towards his fellow-African is of importance, if only because it naturally follows that temptation is more likely to be put in the way of the African official than of the European.

4.   There is evidence, though it cannot be taken as conclusive, that corruption has increased during the war years as a result of the diminution of European supervision. Examples include the degree of corruption in the Produce Inspection Department which was revealed by a recent Commission of Enquiry; another Enquiry which showed that a number of African officers were trafficking in forged Motor Transport Warrants on a large scale; evidence of corruption in many Government hospitals where it is alleged that the African patient generally can receive no attention without payment; and recent indications that in the P.W.D. there is growing discontent among the daily paid workers with regard to their African 'bosses', whom they accuse of corrupt practices. A strike was recently staged at the Ijora Sawmill, based on the demand for the removal of certain members of the African supervisory staff on the grounds that their demands were becoming unbearable; a further instance is alleged corruption on the part of ticket collectors, booking clerks, etc., on the Nigerian Railway which is said to be costing the Railway Administration £300,000 per annum.

5.   To turn to the political aspect. It is a fundamental principle that the Civil Servant must subordinate his own political views to those of the Government which he serves. As a result of growing political consciousness in Nigeria there has of recent years been a notable falling off in the African Civil Servant's realisation of his responsibility in this respect, and instances multiply of African Civil Servants supporting subversive movements. It has also recently been found necessary in the interests of security to remove all Africans from the Secret Branch of the Nigerian Secretariat, and it becomes increasingly difficult to find Africans who can be trusted with regard to confidential matters.

6.   It appears therefore that the inevitable result of the policy to which we are committed will be a falling off in the general integrity of the public service and it is worth while considering whether this should be accepted as inevitable and if so to what extent.

7.   There is no ready solution to the general problem of corruption, and it is only public opinion which can deal with it in the long run. There is a deplorable lack of responsible public opinion in Nigeria and there are few Africans who have the moral courage to stand up and condemn the corrupt practices of their fellows. While it is quite evident in the present stage of development of Nigeria that progressive Africanization of the Service must result in a general lowering of standards, it is

nevertheless a fact that should that progressive lowering of standards become excessive there would inevitably have to be some slowing down in the rate of Africanization, and consideration might have to be given to replacing Africans in positions of trust by Europeans. There has been in recent years a constant and increasing clamour in the Press for an acceleration in the programme of Africanization. At the present time the rate of Africanization is controlled, almost exclusively, by the number of Africans with the necessary academic qualifications, little attention being paid to the character of the candidate. Present policy is directed to increase the number of potential candidates by the grant of Government scholarships, the establishment of Territorial Colleges and the opening of University Colleges. While this policy will widen the field of choice and accelerate the rate of Africanization, unless we are assured that the moral standards of the African will improve with his academic advancement—and unfortunately at the present time there is all too little evidence of this—the result will be only to lower the standards of the public service. In the future it will be necessary to insist not only on academic qualifications but on moral integrity and it becomes increasingly important to explain to the African public that academic achievement is not the only, or even the most important, qualification for the public service.

8. Consideration may therefore have to be given in due course to some public announcement which will explain somewhat bluntly the reasons why Africanization cannot proceed at a greater rate. It may be stated here that the writings of irresponsible sentimentalists in the United Kingdom have tended to give the African an inflated and wrong impression of his capacity and integrity, and it may well be that it would be in the interests of the African himself to make such an announcement.

31 CO 537/1917   22 Mar 1947
[Bristol Hotel incident]: minute by Sir T Lloyd reporting an interview with I G Cummings

[This minute concerns the visit to Nigeria by J L Keith, director of colonial scholars, and I G Cummings of the CO Welfare Department in Feb 1947. Accommodation for the two was reserved by the Nigerian government at the Bristol Hotel, Lagos. Following complaints by the hotel manager on their arrival that he should have been informed in advance that Cummings, who had a Sierra Leonian father and Yorkshire mother, 'was an African' and his statement that 'if he had known about Mr Cummings' race he would not have booked him', Keith and Cummings left the hotel without staying the night. The incident brought into sharp focus the issue of racial discrimination in hotels, clubs and bars in Nigeria and led to the formation of the United Front Committee of prominent members of the NYM and the NCNC, including Azikiwe. On 20 March 1947 Richards, who had initially been unmoved by the incident, made a statement to the Legislative Council that the government would not countenance discrimination based on race or colour; this was followed by the issuing of a circular outlining government policy (see 32).]

I had a talk of over an hour with Mr. Cummings yesterday. The first part of this was taken up with a most interesting account of his impressions of all four West African territories, particularly on the point of race relations. In that respect the Gold Coast is, of course, by far the best. Partly because that territory has a much higher proportion of educated Africans, partly because the Administration has shown goodwill by promoting Africans to quite senior appointments, but mainly through the personal influence and efforts of Sir Alan Burns and a few others who think with him, race relations in the Gold Coast are incomparably better than in any other territory Mr. Cummings knows.

In Sierra Leone matters have much improved in this respect since Mr. Cummings was last there in 1945. But present policy over higher education and over the Municipality are still strongly resented by many even of the better disposed Africans. In the Gambia Mr. Cummings thought that race relationships were reasonably good.

Mr. Cummings presents a quite different picture in Nigeria. He agrees that relationships are most embittered in and near Lagos but feels that a similar feeling is gradually pervading the whole country. He agrees that this is in part due to the influence of the Zik press but regards the attitude which a very large number of European officers take up towards Africans as contributing at least as much to present troubles. Several of the examples which he gave of that attitude are touched upon in the attached Reuters report (No. 13)[1] of Sir A. Richards' speech at the opening of the Nigerian Legislature. Sir A. Richards did not however, mention the European Club at Ikeja which so Mr. Cummings told me, will not admit Africans of whatever position even as visitors for a single meal. For example, Mr. Macarthy, when visiting Nigeria as a member of the West African Court of Appeal, is accommodated at Ikeja but not admitted to the Club and has to bring his own cook with him. Mr. Cummings mentioned this, together with the past exclusion of all Africans from the European Hospital at Lagos, as making for the embitterment of the more educated coloured people.

We spent the last half hour of our talk in discussing the Bristol Hotel incident. While Mr. Cummings naturally feels strongly over this, I am satisfied from my talk with him that he has no wish to be vindictive and would prefer not to cause embarrassment to the Secretary of State or the Nigerian Government. But he did represent strongly to me his view that the Greek proprietor of the hotel deserved to be expelled from Nigeria and that, if the Nigerian Government really wished to make it plain to the people of the country that they would not tolerate race discrimination, they ought to use powers which (as Mr. Cummings represents) they do possess to deport the proprietor without taking any preliminary legal proceedings against him. I said this would be a strong measure and told Mr. Cummings of the substance of the Governor's view in the telegram at No. 9. I also told him of the advice given to the Governor, and (as I understand it) upheld here, that as Mr. Cummings did not seek a remedy at law while in Nigeria, it would be difficult, in the absence of some conviction against the proprietor, to take punitive action. Mr. Cummings represents that the Nigerian Government could at least proceed against the proprietor for breach of contract in having at the instance of that Government reserved accommodation for Mr. Keith and Mr. Cummings on which reservation he later went back. This point should now be examined though I doubt whether there can be anything in it.

As the Governor has (see the third page of No. 13) now stated publicly that the future arrangements for the licensing of hotels and bars in Nigeria are to be based on the principle of no discrimination on account of race, I think that this unfortunate incident must be regarded as having served its purpose and that, subject to such further consideration as can be given to it in the light of the point raised in the preceding paragraph, no further action should be required in Nigeria.

---

[1] Not printed.

One point about which Mr. Cummings naturally feels badly is that not a single word of apology was ever spoken to him by the Governor, the Chief Secretary or the Administrative Secretary, all of whom were closely involved in this unhappy business. This point must be brought out in the reply which eventually goes to Sir A. Richards' letter at No. 12; I should like the Department to consider and to advise whether, as the Nigerian Government failed in what seems to me to be its elementary duty in this matter, Mr. Cummings should not have some letter of regret on this incident from the Secretary of State. I, of course, made my own views plain in the talk yesterday.

32   CO 554/152/1, no 22   April 1947
[Bristol Hotel incident]: letter from G Beresford Stooke to A B Cohen on the outcome of the Bristol Hotel incident.

Many thanks for your letter of the 6th March, 1947. May I congratulate you on your promotion to be Superintending Assistant Secretary—at least I assume that this is a promotion, and may I say, too, how pleased we were to find ourselves once again under your protecting wing.

We have been having rather a busy and exciting time lately. You will have heard all about the Bristol Hotel and the Colour bar. In many ways I think it is a very good thing that this happened. It has enabled us to clear the air very considerably, and I enclose for your information the notes of a meeting held between the Governor and a body known as the United Front Committee.[1] I think I can truthfully say that, with a few exceptions which I shall mention later, Africans on the whole are pleased and satisfied with the outcome. The Governor in his opening speech at Legislative Council took the further opportunity of making the attitude of the Government towards colour discrimination unmistakeably clear. The exceptions to which I refer are the politicians headed by Azikiwe who raised the question as a political issue and are disappointed that by the Governor's prompt action they have been deprived of what could have been a very formidable weapon.

Legislative Council has, I am thankful to say, gone extremely well in spite of the fact that Azikiwe and his two colleagues decided at the last moment to abstain from attending the Council. All the Unofficial Members present welcomed the new Constitution and most, if not all, of them appreciated the very real advance which has been made. They are taking their work as Members very seriously, so much so that proceedings in the Select Committee on the Estimates are taking rather longer than we thought they would.

The Provincial Members from the Northern Provinces were very outspoken about Azikiwe and the National Council for Nigeria and the Cameroons. They said quite plainly that they were capable of making their own representations and did not require the people from the South to do it for them. Their complete refusal to identify themselves in any way with the National Council for Nigeria and the Cameroons has, I am told, been a great disappointment to Azikiwe. The latter has, of course, made a great blunder in boycotting the Council, and has only succeeded in putting himself in an impossible position with regard to his proposed visit to

---

[1] Meeting held on 8 March 1947; notes not printed. The delegation included Azikiwe, Sir Adeyemo Alakija, Ernest Ikoli, H O Davies, Adeleke Adedoyin, Dr Olorun-Nimbe, J K Randle and Dr K A Abayomi.

London. Personally, I am very much inclined to doubt whether he will now continue with his plan to head a delegation to England, since the only possible outcome must be the further deflation of the National Council.

While one can never tell from day to day what these people are going to do next, they do not appear at the moment to have any very effective whip with which to beat the Government. The one which I am very much afraid they will have placed in their hands very soon concerns the question of palm oil prices, but as you have probably already seen all that we have said on that subject there is no point in repeating it. The only other question which is really worrying us at the moment is the shortage of trained Administrative staff with the result that in some parts of the country, at any rate, the Administration is rapidly losing touch with the people. Unfortunately, too, we have a number of Residents who should never have been promoted, and will I hope be retired under the new Harragin terms.[3] The position will right itself to a certain extent when the new Cadets have settled down, but it is the present situation which causes us some disquiet.

I might add that the air is still comparatively thick with threats of strikes—but that is a state of affairs to which we are now quite accustomed.

---

[2] A secretariat circular on 'Racial discrimination', issued to members of the Nigerian Service over Beresford Stooke's signature on 21 March, read:

'As a result of the recent incident at the Bristol Hotel, Lagos, His Excellency has given very careful consideration to various aspects of inter-racial contact in Nigeria with a view to eliminating all possible grounds for suspicion that it is the policy of Government in any way to countenance, let alone to encourage, colour discrimination in any shape or form.

2. For this purpose His Excellency met a deputation of the Island Club 'United Front Committee' and discussed with the members a number of questions which appear to have created among Africans the impression that Government condoned and was prepared to perpetuate such discrimination. In the course of the meeting His Excellency made a clear pronouncement of Government policy in this respect and, lest there should be any misapprehension in this matter, His Excellency has directed that a copy of the notes of the meeting and of this circular shall be sent to every European Government Officer.

3. It is apparent that there exists among Africans a considerable misunderstanding and that distinctions based on economic, social and cultural factors which apply between African and African are attributed to colour discrimination when made by Europeans. It will probably take time to dispel this mistaken idea and it can only be dispelled by continuous and conscious action by every European Officer.

4. I am therefore directed to invite attention to this reiteration of Government policy and to say that His Excellency, relies on every European Officer to co-operate in its fulfilment' (CO 554/152/1).

[3] The report of Sir Walter Harragin, chief justice of the Gold Coast, on the structure and remuneration of the civil service in the West African colonies, was completed in December 1946, *Report of the Commission on the Civil Services of British West Africa 1945–1946*, col. no. 209 (1947). It recommended, *inter alia*, wage increases for civil servants and the introduction of expatriation pay for expatriate staff, as well as a higher entry point for African technical staff; these recommendations were accepted by Creech Jones.

33 CO 583/296/6   2 & 3 June 1947

[Regional councils]: minutes by A Emanuel and K E Robinson on the regional councils established under the 1947 constitution

[The new constitution came into effect in January 1947. Under its provisions houses of assembly were set up for the Eastern, Western and Northern provinces, together with a house of chiefs for the Northern provinces. Concern was expressed within the CO both on how members were chosen and on the calibre of deliberations that ensued.]

On this file are the minutes of the meetings of the Northern House of Assembly on the 20th and 21st January and of the Northern House of Chiefs on 10th and 11th February.

2.   The meetings were not much more than inauguration ceremonies. At the first meeting of the Northern House of Assembly messages were read from the Governor and the O.A.G. and the Chief Commissioner of the Northern Provinces. Standing rules and orders were passed and an address made by the President of the House (Captain E.W. Thompstone, Senior Resident, Kano Province, who has since been promoted Chief Commissioner). At the second meeting the most important item was the selection of the Representatives of the House for the Legislative Council; 14 nominations were received out of which 5 were selected.

3.   There was apparently some debate in which most of the unofficial members took part but this was presumably of little interest since what was said was not recorded.

4.   Proceedings at the House of Chiefs were more or less in the same style but the minutes of the first meeting do record a reply to the message from the Governor by the Sultan of Sokoto.[1] The Sultan while welcoming the constitutional advance underlined the importance attaching to advice on the matters of religion.

5.   Mr. Robinson, Mr. Cohen and possibly higher authority may like to see these proceedings since they do after all mark the effective beginning of a new period of constitutional advance. They will also wish to see the similar proceedings of the Western and Eastern Houses of Assembly on /2 and /3, on which I have minuted separately.

6.   It is not of course possible to draw any conclusion from these first meetings, concerning the ability of the unofficial members of each House to represent effectively the views of the populations of their areas. For a guide to this we must await future meetings.

A.E.
2.6.47

I do not think the proceedings of the three Nigerian Regional Councils particularly impressive: though this was only the first meeting they have a formality which suggests to me I am afraid that there is little intention of making their proceedings a reality. Perhaps that is unduly cynical but I cannot help comparing these proceedings with those of the Northern Rhodesian African Representative Council, which you sent me recently: after all there is certainly no reason why at any rate the two Southern Councils in Nigeria should not be as good as the Northern Rhodesian one. It is of course too early to arrive at any definite conclusion on this point but I am sure that the line of policy is to insist on the maximum possible use being made of these Councils and for the Secretary of State to take every possible opportunity of satisfying himself that all important measures have been fully considered by them.

2.   I cannot help wondering whether the somewhat anodyne character of the proceedings may not reflect the rather mysterious process by which the members have been selected. I was not, as you were, concerned with the proceedings leading

---

[1] Sir Abubakar, KBE, Sultan of Sokoto, installed 1938.

up to the new Nigerian constitution but it has always seemed to me rather ominous that the constitution should provide that the unofficial membership of the Regional Councils should be composed in a manner of which we know nothing e.g. the Western House of Assembly is to consist inter alia of 'not less than 15 nor more than 19 unofficial members who shall be:— ...

(1) ...

(2) Such number of members not being less than 7 nor more than 11 (who shall be called provincial members) selected as hereinafter provided as the Governor may from time to time direct in writing.'

Similarly in the case of the provincial members of other regional councils in Nigeria. So far as I am aware we have never seen the Governor's directions in writing on this point and it appears to me to be one of major importance. It is perhaps worth remembering that in the Gold Coast, the 'electoral colleges' are themselves constituted independently of the Governor. The Joint Provincial Council (from which the Provincial members of the Legislative Council are elected) is itself constituted by the Gold Coast Legislative Council Order in Council and in fact consists of all paramount chiefs (or their duly accredited representatives) plus one member of the native authority for every area which does not include a State or part of a State, such member having been chosen by such native authority as there [sic] representative.

3.   It may well be that in the very different conditions of Nigeria it is unavoidable that these Regional Councils should have a somewhat artificial character: but I think we ought to know how in fact the provincial members of the Houses of Assembly are chosen. I think that we might well ask the Governor to provide us with this information.[2]

K.E.R.
3.6.47

---

[2] See 40 and 41.

34   CO 583/292/2, no 19   5 June 1947
[NCNC delegation]: despatch no 20 from Sir A Richards to Mr Creech Jones on the NCNC delegation to the CO

[During 1946 the NCNC undertook a tour of Nigeria to mobilise opposition to the new constitution and to raise funds for sending a delegation to London. The tour was a considerable success both in terms of the funds raised and the support gained, particularly when Herbert Macaulay, the doyen of Nigerian politics and the president of the NCNC, died during it. See 29. His funeral attracted massive crowds. The NCNC delegation visited London during 1947 and met Creech Jones on 13 Aug. See 38. However not all Nigerians accepted the delegation's claims to represent the whole of Nigeria and divisions began to appear among Nigerian leaders, most notably articulated by Abubakar Tafawa Balewa, a Northern member of the Legislative Council. This was soon to express itself in press allegations concerning the funds raised during the NCNC tour.]

I have the honour to refer to your Secret telegram No. 686 of the 10th May on the subject of the proposed visit to the United Kingdom of a delegation of the National Council of Nigeria and the Cameroons, and to inform you that it has now been officially announced that the persons who will comprise the delegation are Dr. Azikiwe, Dr. Olorun-Nimbe and Mr. Adedoyin[1] representing the Colony; Mrs. Ransome-Kuti[2] representing the Western Provinces; the Hon. Nyong Essien[3] representing the Eastern Provinces; Mallam Bukar Dipcherima[4] representing the Northern Provinces and Mr. P.M. Kale,[5] representing the Cameroons. Photographs of these persons are attached. Biographical notes on Azikiwe and Olorun-Nimbe were sent to you with my Secret Despatch of the 4th of August, 1946,[6] and I now enclose similar notes on the other members of the delegation (Enclosure A).[7]

2.   Dr. Nnamdi Azikiwe has already left Lagos, having sailed in S.S. 'Almanzora' on the 12th of May, with the intention of first visiting the United States and returning to the United Kingdom in time to meet the other members of the delegation when they arrive. These have provisionally booked passages in S.S. 'Elizabethville' which is due to leave Lagos on the 22nd of June.

3.   The history of the N.C.N.C., its place in Nigerian politics and the purpose of the proposed delegation were fully explained in the Note which formed an enclosure to my Secret Despatch of the 4th of August, 1946. The purpose of this despatch is to supplement that information with such additional material as may assist you in dealing with any matters the delegation may raise.

4.   When I wrote my previous despatch the N.C.N.C. delegates had not completed their tour and were about to enter the Western Provinces. There is no doubt that when they did so they found their reception disappointing. The principal Chiefs and their Councillors, together with other responsible men, either declined to receive them at all, or did so very coolly, and their attitude is perhaps summed up in a letter (Enclosure B) addressed by the Oni of Ife to the Senior Resident, Oyo Province. Several less important Chiefs who met them have since expressed annoyance that what amounted to no more than the traditional Yoruba hospitality, that would have been extended to any guest, should have been misrepresented in the reports issued by the delegation to the Press, as active support of the delegation's objects. True to their tactics, the delegates suited their approach to their audience. They adopted a reasonable and restrained attitude: they were not against the Government; the last thing they wanted was to see the Europeans leave Nigeria. Nevertheless, the attitude of the people generally was indifference and the only support they obtained was from teachers and some, though not all, of the younger generation of literates.

5.   Recent events have somewhat weakened the influence of the N.C.N.C. The three leaders of the movement, Azikiwe, Olorun-Nimbe and Adedoyin, made a grave

---

[1] Adeleke Adedoyin, magistrate and commissioner of Supreme Court; elected to Lagos Town Council and to Legislative Council, 1947; secretary of NCNC; elected to Western House of Assembly and to House of Representatives, 1951; joined the AG, speaker of Western House of Assembly, 1957.

[2] Mrs Olufunmilayo Ransome-Kuti, principal of CMS Girls School, Abeokuta; founder of the Egba Women's Union.

[3] Nyong Essien, clerk in the Nigerian civil service; leading member of the Ibibio Union; member of the Legislative Council and Eastern House of Assembly.

[4] Zana Bukar Dipcharima, teacher; member of the NCNC; joined the NPC in 1954; elected to House of Representatives, 1954; minister of state without portfolio, 1957; later minister of commerce and industry.

[5] Paul Monyonge Kale, headmaster of Salvation Army School, Lagos; president of Cameroons Youth League.

[6] See 29. 4 Aug should read 9 Aug.

[7] Enclosures not printed.

political blunder in failing to take their seats in Legislative Council and undoubtedly forfeited the confidence of a considerable number of people by their action. They committed a further blunder by falling out with the United Front Committee when that body achieved what was regarded as a great political success in connection with the 'Bristol Hotel incident'. The United Front Committee when originally formed consisted predominantly of Lagosians of moderate views and they did not take kindly to a suggestion put forward by Azikiwe that the Committee, of which Azikiwe was himself a member, should become merged in the N.C.N.C. An attack launched upon them by Zik's Press for 'failing to co-operate' completed the estrangement and resulted in an opposition group arising with the aim of breaking Azikiwe and the N.C.N.C. whose irresponsibility, they consider, can only spell ruin for the country. So far the United Front Committee has made no public pronouncement of its intentions but there is good reason to believe that a series of articles which have recently appeared in the 'Daily Service' and the 'Nigerian Daily Times' openly attacking the N.C.N.C. were inspired by this body. I enclose cuttings of these articles (Enclosure C) because there are indications that they reflect the growing distrust not only of the more moderate elements of Lagos but certain less irresponsible elements in other parts of Nigeria who were formerly disposed to support the N.C.N.C.

6. In the Northern Provinces, the N.C.N.C. and its doctrines have been flatly rejected, and the movement has achieved nothing beyond provoking extreme indignation at what is regarded as its impudent claim to be in a position to speak for the people of the North. The concern the Northern people feel in this matter is illustrated by a letter (Enclosure D) written by the Mallam the Hon. Abubakar Balewa[8] (Second Member for the Northern Provinces) to the Resident, Bauchi Province, and in the attached extracts (Enclosure E) from speeches made at the last meeting of Legislative Council by the Second and Fourth Members for the Northern Provinces. In presenting these unequivocal views the Members in question were undoubtedly speaking with the authentic voice of the North, and it will therefore be readily appreciated that extreme difficulty was experienced in finding any one at all in the Northern Provinces who was willing to join the delegation. This is further evidenced by the fact that after their unsuccessful efforts to entice Mallam Abubakar Balewa into the fold, the N.C.N.C. was reduced to accepting an obscure young man who has no standing in his own locality and who has never been heard of out of it.

7. Enthusiasm for the N.C.N.C. has undoubtedly waned with the subsidence of the excitement occasioned by their tour of Nigeria but it would be folly to assume from this, and from the critical attitude now being adopted by certain sections of the public, that the N.C.N.C. is a spent force. As long as Azikiwe lends it his support it will continue to command the backing of a large proportion of the literate and semi-literate elements, especially in the Eastern Provinces.

8. It is difficult to say what line the delegation will take when it arrives in the United Kingdom. When questioned their reply has invariably been that they have

---

[8] Abubakar Tafawa Balewa rejected the delegation's invitation to join it, 'with aims of which I do not agree. This invitation cannot be regarded as attempt to promote unity', enclosure D. In March 1947 he had spoken in the Legislative Council to repudiate the NCNC's leadership and, in the context of demands for early self-government, had referred with foreboding to the historic conflict between the north and the south of what was now Nigeria; once the British left, he said, the north would continue its interrupted march to the sea.

their plans and will reveal them when the time is appropriate. The only public announcement they have so far made is a 'Statement of National Policy' which Azikiwe published on the eve of his departure. It will be observed that this statement, (Enclosure F) contains nothing new beyond advocating a policy of non-co-operation, a policy which Azikiwe may well endeavour to carry into effect when he returns to Nigeria. The delegation's ostensible purpose is still to secure an alteration to the new Constitution and the repeal of the four 'obnoxious' ordinances, but it seems that their hope of being able to move you on any of these subjects has waned and it is probables that they will concentrate their energies upon contacting individuals and groups who they consider are likely to show sympathy to their cause. What their exact aims are is far from clear and it is doubtful whether the delegates have any clear idea themselves, beyond a desire to embarrass the Government.

9.   You are aware that the N.C.N.C.'s views on the Constitution are shaped by nobody but themselves but it is probable that this knowledge is not shared by many of the people and groups with which the delegates will seek to establish contact. In the hope that they may be of assistance in dispelling any erroneous impressions the delegates may create, I enclose further extracts (Enclosure G) from the speeches on the subject of the Constitution made by the African Unofficial Members of Legislative Council. I suggest that these alone furnish sufficient proof, if any be required, that the Constitution is not only acceptable to, but welcomed by, responsible Africans in all parts of Nigeria.

10.   I dealt with the so-called 'obnoxious' Ordinances in my Secret despatch of the 4th of August, 1946, but I desire to take the opportunity of correcting one small error. It was stated in the enclosure to that despatch that the fourth 'obnoxious' Ordinance is the Royal West African Frontier Force (Nigeria Regt) (Amendment) Ordinance, 1945, and the N.C.N.C. in fact stated when they commenced their campaign that this was the fourth Ordinance to which they took exception. They very soon dropped it, however, and substituted the Crown Lands (Amendment) Ordinance, 1945. This Ordinance merely enlarged the definition of Crown lands to include land acquired under the provisions of the Public Lands Acquisition Ordinance and was a corollary to section 3 of the Public Lands Acquisition (Amendment) Ordinance, 1945.

11.   With regard to the Appointment and Deposition of Chiefs Ordinance, during a recent tour of the Western Provinces, the Ibadan Divisional Council presented me with an address of welcome containing the following pertinent passage which more than speaks for itself:—

> 'One other matter that is worrying our minds is the alarming frequency with which chieftaincy disputes are being taken to the Magistrates' and High Courts, where, as it appears to us, native laws and customs are neither understood nor respected.
>
> When over a year ago Your Excellency's Government foresaw the evil and introduced an Ordinance presumably to save the situation and to preserve our time-honoured chieftaincy customs and usages criticisms came in torrents against Your Excellency and Your Government from those who knew little or nothing at all of our difficulties and the intricate customs upon which selection of chiefs rests, especially in the Yoruba land. We who are intimately connected and know our own customs in practice and not in theory, now

appreciate your vision and praise your wisdom in so far as that section of it which makes it impossible for chieftaincy disputes to go before British Law Courts is concerned. Our wish is that that Ordinance be made to cover all minor chieftaincies'.

12. It has been a characteristic of the N.C.N.C. to level abuse against Government Officers and particularly against the Administrative Service which is not surprising in view of the duty of Administrative Officers to give to the people entrusted to their care political advice which is seldom palatable to the N.C.N.C. It was particularly gratifying to me in the course of my tour to receive spontaneous assurances of the peoples' confidence in their Administrative Officers. In an address presented to me by the Ede District Council it was stated:—

'The Ibadan District in general and the Northern Districts in particular is always lucky in the type of Administrative Officers we have in our midst. We must therefore take this opportunity to pay tribute to their good work among us. They give us useful advices and guidance whenever we need them. In the hands of such men the destiny of the country is safe and sure'

Similar assurances were given me wherever I went, coupled invariably with the request that the number of Administrative Officers should be materially increased.

13. It is possible that the delegation will wish to raise the question of Lagos Town Planning proposals. Their arguments, if they do, are likely to be those that were advanced in the memorial which was forwarded with my confidential despatch No. 69 of the 31st of March, and I trust that that despatch and its enclosures will provide you with sufficient information to enable you to answer any representations on this subject that they may make.

14. The delegation expects to be away from Nigeria for a period of from three months to one year. That they have set such wide limits to the duration of their expedition is possibly due to the fact that they have mooted the possibility of visiting America, France and Russia. One of the objects of these visits, if they take place, will be to endeavour to establish business connections with West Africa but it is not improbable that a more important purpose will be to endeavour to obtain support for bringing their case before the United Nations Organisation. It is doubtful, however, whether the delegation's financial resources will permit them to embark on such extensive travels, though possibly Azikiwe himself may take the opportunity of going to Russia if he can get there. He is believed to be anxious to visit that country.

35 CO 583/292/2, no 21   10 June 1947
[NCNC delegation]: letter from G Beresford Stooke to A B Cohen describing the views of the Nigerian government on Dr Azikiwe's personality, his methods, his delegation and his financial support

The following comments on Dr. Nnamdi Azikiwe in particular, and the National Council for Nigeria and the Cameroons in general, may be of some interest to you in view of the proposed visit to England by a delegation of this body.

The first point to be made about Azikiwe is that he is an Ibo. An outstanding characteristic of the Ibos is that their tribal authority is unusually weak. A Yoruba commented to me the other day that the Ibo youth will speak to his local Chief, or indeed to his own father, in a manner which would not be tolerated for one moment amongst the Yoruba. The individualism and independence of the Ibo is very marked.

You will find when you meet him that Azikiwe himself is well spoken and, on the surface at any rate, very reasonable. He usually succeeds in impressing people with his sincerity of purpose and in persuading those who do not know him very well that he is sadly misunderstood. He will say that he is anxious to co-operate with the Government; that he is not at all anti-British, nor indeed, anti-European, but that he has been driven into his present position by an unsympathetic and hostile Government. That is where he can be so very dangerous. He is quite unscrupulous, and is always ready to say whatever he thinks will appeal to the audience of the moment. He has no regard whatever for the truth, and will make any statement or give any promise which will advance his cause with no more intention of keeping his promises than the late Mr. Hitler had. In fact, his methods in many ways remind one of Hitler, and have possibly been copied from him. However, the point is that he is able to impress people—particularly people who do not know very much about Nigeria.

In many ways he is clever. He has of course put us in a weak position by organising this delegation to England without giving us any intimation at all of what his real aims and objects are. We have no idea what he is going to ask for or what arguments he is going to put forward, and consequently it is very difficult for us to brief you satisfactorily. We can only guess the line that he is going to take and brief you on that.

It seems likely that he will object to the new Constitution on the grounds that it is not democratic, since Native Authorities are part of the Government of Nigeria, and that whatever we may say, their representatives will feel themselves bound to support Government. In this, of course, he hardly does justice to his own friend Nyong Essien. He may ask for universal franchise, but I think he will certainly demand an unofficial majority of Elected Members whatever the basis of franchise may be. On this point the remarks, at the last meeting of Legislative Council, of Chief Bowari Brown, himself from the Eastern Provinces, are of interest.[1]

It is important to note that Azikiwe has not succeeded in gaining the support of a single responsible and intelligent African. You will see from the biographical sketches of the other delegates that they can hardly be called a very impressive collection. The people of Lagos are getting so tired of Azikiwe that the United Front Committee led by Sir Adeyemo Alakija is now gaining considerable support.[2] It is also notable that the Lagos Chiefs, some of whom strongly supported Azikiwe a little time ago, have now withdrawn their support from the N.C.N.C.

---

[1] Chief Bowari Brown, the second member for the Eastern Provinces, referring to the issue of a 'substantial unofficial majority' in the Legislative Council, expressed his hope that the administration would 'give us a constitution equally as good as that of the Gold Coast, if not better', but urged patience on his colleagues. 'It is for us to be patient . . . and we shall eventually achieve our aim. It is not necessary I believe that there should be any employment of offensive or destructive weapons of any kind in endeavouring to achieve this aim. We certainly can do it peacefully, loyally and agreeably . . . I believe we shall not be denied self-government when it is time for us to get it—Rome was not built in a day . . . Let us therefore wait patiently, loyally and unitedly . . .' (CO 583/292/2, no 19, enclosure G, extracts from speeches of unofficial members of Legislative Council on new constitution).
[2] See 32.

It has been reported that the N.C.N.C. proposes to institute legal proceedings in England against the Nigerian Government for 'constituting an illegal Council' as they hold, apparently, that the presence of the Lagos Members in the Council is essential to its legal constitution. In this contention they appear to have been supported by some lawyers in London. We do not know the name of the firm but their telegraphic address is 'Rexworthys'. It seems that the only people who are likely to profit from this manoeuvre will be the lawyers themselves.

You may be interested to have a note of the finances of the N.C.N.C. If their accounts are anything like correct they have received over £13,000 in donations from the public. It is said that of this £13,000, some £5,000 is 'unaccounted for'. Of the money actually collected over £3,000 have already been spent. £1,120 appears under the vague heading of 'Allowances'. Postage has absorbed already the high figure of £254, and no less than £1,088 has been spent on transport. They expect that the costs of the delegation will be about £8,500 of which passages account for £1,400, board and lodging for the delegates £2,700, transport £1,000, Secretariat expenses £1,000, legal expenses £1,000, and propaganda £1,000 with £350 for outfits for the delegates. After Azikiwe left Lagos a meeting of the Executive Committee approved the payment to Dr. Nimbe of £1,000 down, plus monthly payments to cover the salaries of the staff at his Nursing Home during his absence in England. The account of the meeting states that Mr. Adedoyin presented a 'similar claim' which was also approved. These payments can be met either by reducing the expenses of the delegation at home, or by raising more funds, and it was decided to send the Assistant Secretary of the Council on a tour of Nigeria to raise more funds. He has, however, not yet left Lagos.

It is interesting to note that Azikiwe does not apply his democratic principles in the affairs of the National Council for Nigeria in that the selection of delegates to represent different parts of the country has been made, not by the subscribers, but arbitrarily by Azikiwe and his friends here in Lagos. In this he has had a little difficulty. His first selection, made as recently as last April, was as follows:—

Nnamdi Azikiwe
Dr. Olorun-Nimbe
Adeleke Adedoyin
Nyong Essien
Dr. Udo Udoma
Dipcherima of Bornu
Mallam Abubakar Balewa of Bauchi
    (2nd Northern Member of the
    Legislative Council)

and in addition:

Chief Oluwa
Chief Onikoyi, and
Chief Oniru

of Lagos, on the understanding that these last three paid all their own expenses. Mallam Abubakar Balewa replied to the invitation in the following terms: 'I will not join a delegation with the aims of which I do not agree'. Dr. Udo Udoma decided to join the United Front Committee instead.

Early in May the list of the chosen was:—

Azikiwe
Olorun-Nimbe
Adedoyin
Chief Shodipo of Abeokuta
Dipcherima of Bornu
Kale, from the Cameroons, and
Chief Amobi of Ogidi.[3]

By this time the Lagos Chiefs had ceased to take any further interest in the N.C.N.C. It is not clear whether or not Chief Shodipo of Abeokuta refused to go, or whether on reconsideration Azikiwe thought that Mrs. Ransom Kuti would be a better person. Chief Amobi of Ogidi was also dropped, and so we come to the final selection which has already been given to you.

Dipcherima recently visited Lagos and appears to have been so disappointed with the company in which he found himself that he returned to the North. He will not, we gather, join the deputation to London.

A report just received from Patterson says that the educated and progressive men in the Northern Provinces are so perturbed at the claim of Azikiwe and his friends to have authority to speak for the Northern Provinces that the proposal has been made that a delegation from the North should be sent to the U.K. for the sole purpose of denying this claim.

The people whom Azikiwe chiefly represents are the 'have-nots'—those members of the educated and semi-educated classes who are dissatisfied because their education has not given them the lucrative returns which they hoped for. If Azikiwe were to disappear from the stage tomorrow, his place would at once be taken by another. The movement is, in fact, a symptom of the stage of development through which Nigeria is now passing. A sound cure can be provided only by progressive economic and political development. The foundations for this development have been laid in the new Constitution and the Development Plan, but success will depend largely upon keeping economic and political development in step with each other. Azikiwe wants to push political development ahead of economic development. That would be fatal to both.

---

[3] See 34.

36   CO 583/292/3   12 Aug 1947
[NCNC delegation]: minute by K E Robinson on the NCNC memorandum for the meeting with Mr Creech Jones on 13 August

Secretary of State
The memorandum from the Delegation of the National Council of Nigeria and the Cameroons, which you are seeing tomorrow morning was only received in the Department this morning and in the time available it is obviously impossible to examine it in any detail.

2.   The Delegation divide their representations into the following groups:—

(a) Objections to the Richards' Constitution.

(b) Objections to the 'obnoxious' ordinances.

(c) Objections to certain laws or sections of laws which deny basic human rights.

(d) Complaints about alleged acts of maladministration.

(e) A protest against the Government of Nigeria and the Cameroons as if they are an exclusive Colonial possession of Great Britain. This is based on the alleged treaty obligations arising out of the protectorate status of most of Nigeria.

(f) Demands for immediate steps towards self-government for Nigeria and the Cameroons.

3.   As regards (a)–(e) separate notes are attached.[1]

4.   As regards (f), which is the nub of the whole memorandum, the Delegation ask that immediate steps be taken towards self-government for Nigeria and the Cameroons and that this should be done in three stages, namely,

(1) a period of 'at least 10 years' when an Anglo–Nigerian condominium will govern the country.

(2) a further period of 5 years during which the Anglo–Nigerian condominium will be replaced by a Nigerian interim government.

(3) at the end of these two periods a treaty should be concluded between Nigeria and presumably the United Kingdom under which Nigeria would become an independent self-governing Domination and an autonomous unit of the British Commonwealth. The proposed Condominium is not at all clearly explained but it is apparently intended that a central parliament should be established composed of equal numbers of members from each of the eight protectorates in [to] which it is proposed Nigeria should be divided and that the majority party in this parliament should provide the Cabinet composed of 15 Ministers together with the Prime Minister and three Secretaries of State (who seem reminiscent of the officers of state in the Donoughmore Constitution in Ceylon). Nothing is said about the Secretaries of State, however, in the Draft Constitution.

5.   Each of the Protectorates would have its own Governor and Lieutenant Governor and its own legislative council. Both the Central Legislature and the Protectorate Legislatures would be elected by universal adult suffrage.

6.   Quite apart from the details of these proposals, which are very confused, it is clearly premature to consider any such constitutional change in Nigeria at the present time. If you were going to be available in the United Kingdom in the immediate future you might wish merely to listen to anything the Delegation may have to say on this and other aspects of their proposals and then to appoint a time at which you would give them your reply. This, however, will not be practicable in view of your departure for the West Indies next week. Though, therefore, it will clearly be necessary for some of the new points of detail which they have now raised, especially under (c) and (d) to be referred to the Government of Nigeria and considered at more leisure, it is recommended that on the main issue of the immediate grant of self-government or a new constitution you should make it clear to the Delegation straight away that you cannot consider this at the present stage and that it is up to them to go back to Nigeria and make every effort to work the new Constitution and demonstrate their capacity for further advance. If you were merely to undertake to

---

[1] Not printed.

consider their views on this major issue it would not be possible for them to be given any final reply until after your return from the West Indies and there would be serious danger that in the meantime they would put it about that their proposals in this matter were being seriously considered by H.M.G. This would be most embarrassing to the Nigerian Government and would provide a useful excuse for the Delegation to remain in the United Kingdom.

7.   One general point which might also be made in this connection is that many of the points raised in their memorandum are matters which should be taken up, if they wish to do so, in the Nigerian Legislature and thrashed out there.

37   CO 859/136/5, no 4   20 Aug 1947
[Mass education]: despatch no 203 from Sir A Richards to Mr Creech Jones on the Nigerian government's programme for mass education

I have the honour to refer to your despatch No. 127 on the subject of Mass Education and to say that the Report on Mass Education in African Society (Col. 186) has been widely read in both official and unofficial circles in this country. Much has been written on the subject and a variety of opinions has been expressed. I will therefore in this despatch confine myself to informing you what has so far been achieved and the programme which I intend to follow in the future.

2.   The progress so far achieved has consisted of controlled experiments conducted in selected areas. At the present time and with our limitations in regard to resources I do not consider that the subject is suitable for a formal long-term plan and consider that it should be treated more empirically. My advisers are all agreed that the first essential for success is the active co-operation of the people. Efforts have therefore been concentrated on those areas where the people have shown the necessary energy and initiative to make a start under the guidance and with the assistance of Administrative and Education Officers.

3.   A report on these experiments was forwarded to your Education Adviser in December 1946 in response to your telegram 1645 of the 22nd of November, 1946. In addition an account of the territory's Mass Education work has been published in 'Overseas Education.' These publications have, I believe, evoked recognition that Nigeria is one of the areas in which a promising start has been made. My address to the Legislative Council in March 1945 and in March 1946 set out this Government's policy in regard to Mass Education. An expansion of the Welfare and Public Relations Departments is gradually taking place and they will assist with the social education side of this problem, while the Education Department will concern itself primarily with fundamental Adult Education.

4.   In regard to the future the Education Department will continue to concentrate its efforts on fundamental Adult Education which covers:—

(a) instruction in reading and writing and the vernacular;
(b) English for those who desire it;
(c) elementary arithmetic for farmers;
(d) organized discussions on matters of interest;
(e) instruction in matters which lend themselves to treatment by class room method, such as cooking and sewing for women;

(f) production of simple reading material in the vernacular and in English suitable for adults.

5.   I consider that a literacy campaign on these lines is essential. It is something in which all can play a part, either as teacher or pupil. Its success in a village can be a measure of the success [?extent] to which that village is likely to be prepared to discipline itself and undertake its own social education. Not counting Udi Division mass literacy campaigns are now progressing in nine homogeneous areas under the supervision of African Adult Education organizers, nine of whom are ex-soldiers. Each area has a population of about 80,000 and it has been selected after careful consideration. In deciding on the areas the factors advocated by the Advisory Committee were all considered, though in each case there was one factor which outweighed the others. It may be of interest to you to know the areas which have been selected and the reasons for their selection. They are as follows:—

Area	Principal Factor
Zuru	Contains large number of ex-soldiers.
Misau	A very progressive Emir whose people are readily adopting improved agricultural methods.
Abuja	A development area.
Southern Tiv	A development area.
Kankiya District	An area containing a large demonstration farm.
Ado-Ekiti District	The most educationally minded area in the Western Provinces.
Ilaro	An area in which an intensive campaign of children's education has recently started.
Ngwa area (Aba District)	A progressively minded people.
Eket Division	An area which spontaneously started a number of literacy classes.

6.   The work at Udi consists of nothing less than the reconstruction by voluntary work of the social and economic life of those villages that have accepted the scheme. The scheme has grown naturally out of the ordinary administrative work of the District Officer in the field, and although it is grafted on to, it is not a function of, the Native Administration. Nevertheless it was found that the work of Administrative Officers in the field since the introduction of Native Administration in the Eastern Provinces has prepared the ground for Mass Education in the fullest sense. By 1944 the people in Udi Division were demanding services within their villages which the Native Administrations, on account of their limited resources, could only supply at central points. The people became so enthusiastic that they expended thousands of man days of free labour on the construction of new roads, the erection of communally owned maternity units, subdispensaries, reading rooms, village halls, co-operative consumers' shops, etc. All the profits made by the shops have been expended on the erection of further buildings. In addition several sub-clans in the

Udi Division have been surveyed for leprosy, and a village for the segregation of infectious lepers has been erected by voluntary labour. This work of communal development was started before the Colonial 186 on Mass Education in African Society was received. On receipt of that paper experiments began with Mass Literacy, and it was found that the injection of a Mass Literacy campaign into the work of communal development gave the communities concerned greater self-confidence in their own ability to raise their standard of living. Thus, although Mass Literacy was not essential to the work of communal development and social education, and although some villages have made and are still making considerable progress without Mass Literacy, nevertheless it was found that where Mass Literacy was introduced it helped to accelerate the rate of progress.

7.   It is proposed that certain of the areas listed in paragraph 5 be selected for a Mass Education Campaign. In the first place it is probable that one village which has proved itself outstanding in the Literacy Campaign will be selected as a focus for the Mass Education Plan. If staff is available a Development Officer or an Assistant District Officer will be posted to this village to plan a mass education pro-gramme and supervise the continuance of the literacy campaign in the area. No for-mal plan will be laid down but it will be allowed to develop and emerge as the people desire, the object being that the plan should be related not so much to what we may consider to be good for the people, but more to the troubles and problems which are uppermost in their minds. The Development Officer will have available for discussion the specialists in the Province, i.e. Agricultural, Forestry and Medical officers and will come under the directing control of the District Officer. It is hoped that actual physical improvements by self-help will eventually result, and as the idea spreads to neighbouring villages they will start to copy in mutual rivalry the physical improvements in the pilot village. The Development Officer will be at hand to watch carefully for such movement so that he will be available for advice and guidance.

8.   The sum of £10,000 has been included in this year's estimates in order to provide for the necessary staff and teaching material. Adult Education Centres will be set up in selected areas and in order that they shall be closely linked with the development of the community, Native Authorities will be invited to take an interest in such Centres and where possible contribute towards their upkeep.

9.   I wish finally to refer to certain points made by the Advisory Committee in their Commentary on Colonial No. 186. In regard to paragraph 8 of the Commentary it is untrue to say as far as Nigeria is concerned that Adult Literacy is a field largely neglected. In fact the emphasis has been on Adult Literacy and progress has so far outstripped the work of the Public Relations and Welfare Departments which are both in early stages of development. In regard to paragraph 12 I can see no reason why there should be any conflict between the Mass Education and the Public Relations Authorities. As I have said above, I consider that the Education Department should be primarily concerned with fundamental education and the other Departments should concern themselves with the various aspects of social education.

10.   I am in general agreement with paragraph 8 of your despatch. A clearing house for the exchange of information will be most helpful in providing concrete advice by experts who know their ground, provided it does not merely concern itself with the collation of a mass of statistics.

38   CO 583/292/3, no 58   21 Aug 1947
[NCNC delegation]: CO record of a meeting held on 13 August 1947
with the NCNC delegation

The Secretary of State welcomed the delegation and thanked them for sending him
the memorandum. He said he was glad of the opportunity to hear the views of the
Delegation and invited them to speak on any points in the memorandum which the
Delegation desired particularly to bring to his attention.

Dr. Azikiwe thanked the Secretary of State and the Colonial Office for giving the
Delegation this opportunity for an exchange of views. He said that there was no need
for conflict; what was wanted was an adjustment of the present situation. The
Delegation had great confidence in the people and the Government of this country
and the Colonial Office. It was because they had this confidence that they left Nigeria
on their mission. The main problem at present was constitutional. It was desirable
that the people of Nigeria should have more representation in the conduct of their
own affairs. Other developments were also necessary in the social and economic
sphere but these were not possible without the people of the country having political
power. The Delegation had nothing against the officials of the colonial
administration, though they to some extent tended to ignore the literate and
educated elements in the country and to regard them as extremists if they put
forward political views. The policy of discrediting the educated elements was not,
however, a good one. They had a right to express themselves and felt that they should
be the spokesmen of their people more than anyone else.

Turning to the laws to which objection was raised in the memorandum, Dr.
Azikiwe said that the Delegation did not object in principle to the purpose of laws
permitting, for example, land to be acquired for public purposes. This was right and
proper. The Delegation objected, however, to those sections which gave arbitrary
powers to the Governor.

Dr. Azikiwe referred also to various grievances which should be removed, for
example, the employment of European women to the detriment of Nigerian ex-
service men; the breaking up of lawful processions as in the Idu Bridge incident
where there had been no provocation by the demonstrators; incidents elsewhere
involving arrests of people in procession; and the existence of deportation laws which
went against basic human rights. He referred also to a trade dispute at Ikoyi and to
the detention of a chief in the Ibibio division for six months without his having been
told of the nature of his offence. He objected to the use of taxpayers' money to
finance newspapers which were used to attack taxpayers. He also objected to the
discouragement of Africans in the Civil Service. In this connection, however, Dr.
Azikiwe expressed appreciation of the policy announced by the Governor of avoiding
racial discrimination in hospitals and schools, etc. There was no mention of the issue
of racial discrimination in the memorandum and Dr. Azikiwe instanced this as
showing that the Delegation had no intention of acting irresponsibly by making
accusations where these were not justified.

Dr. Azikiwe then referred to the relations between Great Britain and the
Protectorate as laid down in the many treaties. Under these treaties the native rulers
agreed to the abolition of sacrifices and of the slave trade and undertook to
encourage missionaries. On the other side, it was agreed that native law and customs

should be respected. In his view the treaties were not designed to give Great Britain exclusive internal jursidiction.

In these representations Dr. Azikiwe stated that the Delegation had a large measure of support throughout Nigeria. He did not claim that every Nigerian supported them, but generally speaking they were supported by all sections. There was full evidence of this, details of which could be provided in their tour of Nigeria in which they had raised the very large sum of £13,000, quite a notable achievement in view of the poverty of the country. This had been done despite the fact that in some cases officials had sought to besmirch their personal characters, and Dr. Azikiwe objected that even the Governor had seen fit to ask for enquiries to be made into their personal lives. Even embezzlement had been alleged by officials. Dr. Azikiwe emphasised, however, that the Delegation's action was purely constitutional and they were anxious to help evolve in Nigeria a constitution based upon a study of modern practices in, for example, Australia, Ceylon, New Zealand, the United States and Great Britain. He appreciated that the constitution which the Delegation had recommended was not necessarily perfect, but it was a genuine endeavour to harmonise modern democratic practice with the traditional African way of life, which was communal.

One of the aims of the proposed constitution was to enable a truly independent judiciary to be set up. Today the judiciary was not independent and the general impression he had was that persons not liked by the administration suffered in the courts. He suggested that there was scope for a commission of enquiry into the judiciary and also into the working of indirect rule.

Dr. Azikiwe drew attention to the fact that all parts of Nigeria, including the north, were represented on the Delegation. Moreover, many Emirs in the north had intimated to him in confidence that as servants of the Government they could not come into the open. Some Chiefs in the south similarly supporting the aims of the Delegation were also afraid to come into the open.

Lastly Dr. Azikiwe asserted that the powers given to the Governor over the Chiefs made the present constitution a mockery of democracy. He realised that there was a new approach to these problems in London but it would take a long time unless energetic steps were taken to bring about the changes which were desirable.

Mallam Dipcharima said that the position in the north needed particular scrutiny. The Emirs and most of their staffs were generally illiterate and there was no democracy of any kind. Administrative officers were content to leave things to the Emirs instead of ensuring that there was democracy. He emphasised the great poverty of the north and the limited provision of education and social services, and said that it was not right that the north should pay more in taxes than the south but yet receive out of the total revenue less than one-third. He also said that officials in their speeches had aimed at disuniting Nigeria and had given encouragement to one representative of the north who in Legislative Council had made a speech aimed at disuniting Nigeria. It was essential to improve the condition of life of peasants in the north and he felt that the N.C.N.C. provided the only way.

Mallam Dipcharima referred also to the United Nations Charter concerning which a pamphlet had been issued in April. He felt that the Nigerian people should have been consulted; as it was very few people in Nigeria knew anything about it. He also referred to the low prices received for crops owing to the distance from the sea, which was one of the reasons for the poverty in the north. He considered also that the administration in the north was getting further away from the masses and very little was being done to remove the marked difference between the north and the south.

Mr. Kale said that all people in the Cameroons were agreed that Great Britain should maintain its mandate or trusteeship. He thought it was wrong, however, that whereas under the old constitution the Cameroons were represented there was now no member of the Legislative Council representing the Cameroons. He also referred to the petition made in August 1946 by the Bakweri people against the alienation of Buea lands to which no reply had been received. The alienation of lands originally carried out by the Germans was not in accordance with tradition and the plantation system had led to great poverty for the people. He referred also to the Cameroons Development Corporation and said that it was looked upon as a commercial enterprise. This type of development and the absence of educational facilities, making it necessary for children from the Cameroons to go to Nigeria for secondary education, was placing a great strain on the people of Nigeria.

Mr. Adedoyin referred to the question of the independence of the judiciary and said that he spoke with the experience of a magistrate and knew that magistrates could not give decisions without being influenced by administrative officers. He also said that the native rulers were not pleased with the new constitution. In the western provinces there had been a conference of Obas who had at first objected but were induced in the end by Government coercion to accept. He also referred to the Ijebu Remo Treaty which established the district as a Protectorate. Despite this the territory was administered as if it were a Colony and the Government had broken the condition under which £100 per annum was payable to the Akarigbo.[1]

Mr. Adedoyin said that the Nigerian Youth Movement was not in agreement on all matters with the N.C.N.C. but they were in agreement with the N.C.N.C.'s criticisms of the constitution. He emphasised that under the constitution the nominated unofficial members would do what they were told by the Governor. In consequence the people had no say in the management of their affairs. He and Dr. Nimbe and Dr. Azikiwe had been elected as the people wished to show that they were really representative of them. They had been asked by those who elected them not to take their seats but to come to London on their mission.

He argued that the new constitution should have provided more representation by election. He pointed out that Lagos and Calabar had had elected members for many years and it could not be argued that there was no scope for elected members else-where. Literacy was not a necessary qualification for an electoral system and Nigeria was no worse off as regards literacy than India, where there was an electoral system. One good feature of the Richards constitution was, however, the regionalisation it afforded; this was generally applauded in Nigeria. Apart from this, however, the position of the Chiefs had been substantially weakened through the Constitution, the Deposition of Chiefs Ordinance and the Native Authority Ordinance, and he, as the son of the Akarigbo of Ijabu Remo, was personally interested to see that they were accorded their proper place in accordance with the Treaty.

Mrs. Ransome-Kuti said that the Delegation objected strongly to the appointment of *sole* native authorities which permitted the people to be oppressed. Many of these

---

[1] The Akarigbo was the ruler of Ijebu Remo.

Chiefs exercised autocratic powers. They were nonentities before their appointments and should have been mere figureheads. Now the people themselves had no say in the appointment of their Chiefs. Mrs. Ransome-Kuti added that the native authorities were not even able to use the funds raised by local taxes without the sanction of the Resident and instanced the fact that the people of Abeokuta had requested permission to use their reserves to start local industry but permission had not been given. As a result men were unemployed and more work had to be done by women. There was great poverty but this was due not to lack of materials but to the fact that the people had no voice in fixing the price of their produce, which was fixed by the combines and large firms. Mrs. Ransome-Kuti added that while there was no objection to income tax when properly assessed the authorities made arbitrary assessments based upon peoples' way of living.

Dr. Nimbe referred to the land question in Lagos and said that the recent measures introduced, including the Public Lands Acquisition Ordinance and the Town Planning Ordinance, were contrary to the Docemo Treaties of 1861. When the Town Planning Ordinance was introduced the Governor refused to allow the Lagos members, of whom he was one, to speak in the Legislative Council and consequently he had had to publish what he intended to say. Under the town planning scheme land was put on a leasehold basis. This was the equivalent of turning people into slaves and tenants and the fact that this was so could be seen from the experience of Port Harcourt, where people had to pay rent. A petition had been made to the Secretary of State but the petitioners had been informed that the Secretary of State was not prepared to intervene. They had asked to see copies of the Secretary of State's reply but so far they had not done so.

Dr. Nimbe said that in Africa there was no land without an owner. Since this was so it was difficult to understand how Government could introduce a Bill which provided that no compensation should be paid for unoccupied land acquired for public purposes. Dr. Nimbe also referred to the status of Nigeria as a Protectorate and said that it was laid down in the Treaty of 1862 that no ordinances would be passed which were not consistent with the Treaty.

Dr. Nimbe also objected to the Director of Medical Services having absolute discretion over private hospitals, and there were also other points he had to make on the medical services but he would appreciate the opportunity of discussing these with the Secretary of State's Medical Adviser.

Chief Nyong Essien said that the Chiefs Ordinance virtually made his people worse than slaves. He cited the deposition of the Obong of Calabar in 1926, and the arrest and detention without trial this year of Chief Ntuen Ibok, who was not even told why he was arrested. He said that Chief Ntuen Ibok had been honoured by the grant of a certificate of service. There should be confidence in such a man and such treatment as he was given placed a great strain on the loyalty of the people, which should be encouraged.

Chief Nyong Essien also said that in Opobo an increase of 1/- in taxation had been made for the specific purpose of providing for education, and on this basis it had been agreed by the people. After the money, amounting to £700, had been collected it was taken by Government into general revenue and no encouragement was given to education, in fact the district officers had prevented firms selling building materials for schools.

He also spoke of the importance of religion and said that Idiong was merely the legalised form of religion that was common throughout Africa. Yet priests in one area had been arrested, the shrines desecrated and the relics burnt on the suspicion that the religion was connected with the leopard murders. There was no proof of this and if Idiong led to leopard murders in one area then it should have led to murders in other areas. Idiong in fact had nothing to do with human bloodshed. The Government's action to attempt to destroy Idiong would destroy the people, who could not exist without religion.

He also asked that the local people should have control over the proceeds of the palm oil mill which had been set up, since at present the proceeds were simply going to general, revenue and did not benefit the local community.

Dr. Nimbe and *Mr. Kale* then instanced cases in which administrative officers acted arbitrarily, Dr. Nimbe reading a confidential letter of 1906 concerning an administrative officer in the Northern Provinces, and Mr. Kale citing the case of a Chief who he said had been imprisoned in July for failing to pay his respects to the Chief Commissioner. The Secretary of State invited Mr. Kale to send particulars of the case.

The Secretary of State said that the Delegation in their memorandum and in their speeches had covered a wide field and raised many questions, some of a major kind and some of a more particular local interest. It was impossible for him to deal with them all at the meeting, but he would arrange for them to be examined and would give the Delegation a considered reply in due course. It would, however, be necessary to refer some points to the Governor of Nigeria.

He appreciated the desire of the Delegation to state the problems as they saw them and to bring them home to those in London as matters of vital importance to them. He was, however, conscious of the inaccuracy of a number of statements made by the Delegation, no doubt not intentional but due to their not always having the full information in their possession. This impressed him with the vital importance of doing everything possible to ensure that the people of Nigeria had available to them all the essential facts.

The Secretary of State said that whatever had happened in the past—and no doubt mistakes had been made—it was of no avail to dwell on them now. We were responsible for the present and we had to adjust ourselves to a moving world. He would like to impress upon the Delegation that the Colonial Office earnestly desired the best interests of the colonial peoples. Neither he nor the officials of the Colonial Office, were anything but disinterested; there was no question of any personal advantage. He was anxious, too, that our administrations overseas should reflect the same spirit and he believed that the services overseas were manned by men who were only anxious to be of service to the peoples with whom they worked. No doubt individual lapses were inevitable, and where possible action would always be taken to correct this. Nevertheless, in general the aim of all concerned in the administrations was to devote all efforts to enabling Nigeria to become a nation.

He asked the Delegation not to imagine that he or the administrations objected to political criticism. It was fully realised that a healthy people must think and criticise. He did, however, ask that criticism should be constructive. There was certainly no desire on the part of Government to try and clamp down on criticism or on political movements. On the contrary it was a sign of healthy life and what we wanted was leaders of political movements to join with us in trying to find a solution to the very real problems which existed.

Nigeria was a vast complex state with a developing basic unity. The new constitution helped to provide a framework for that unity while allowing for the differences in regional conditions and the great variety of people. Nigeria was the largest colonial territory in the British Commonwealth and the Delegation had a great responsibility in trying to build up new political forces, and a great obligation to the people of the country. The Secretary of State said that he was fully conscious of deficiencies in the education, medical services and social services generally in Nigeria and was most anxious to do all that could be done to develop the resources of Nigeria so that a higher standard could be provided for all. This, however, could only be done by hard work on everyone's part. There were serious limitations of staff and other resources which inevitably slowed down progress. The Delegation should not believe that it was simply our aim to keep people in the British Empire against their will. It was our desire to press on so that people in the Colonial Empire could attain self government as soon as possible and also secure a good standard of living which alone made for happiness and stability. This was desirable even in the British people's own self interest.

As regards the Nigerian constitution, the Secretary of State emphasised that it was not to be regarded as something static and fixed for all time. There was no desire to hold the people back and this was shown, for example, in other territories such as Ceylon. The approach was the same in regard to Nigeria. The present Constitution could certainly be modified and amended in the light of experience but he made it clear that it was essential to give it a period of trial before it could be seen how it needed amendment. There could be no question of setting it aside and replacing it by something quite different which would not be suitable to Nigerian conditions. He wanted to leave them in no doubt about that and he urged them to work through it.

As regards the criticisms that had been made of the working of indirect rule, he reminded the Delegation that it was necessary to build upon the past. The present system had grown up from the past but the Colonial Office were giving their urgent attention to examining the whole problem, not only in Nigeria but elsewhere, of how best to facilitate development and growth and to achieve the machinery of a modern democracy and effective local government.

The Secretary of State referred also to accusations that excessive powers were given to the Governor and asked the Delegation to believe that there was no question of these powers being used arbitrarily. It was not to be expected that they would be used except where it was necessary for the benefit of the people, for example in seeing that the Chiefs discharged their responsibilities to their peoples.

On the question of African representation in working out development plans the Secretary of State referred to the fact that there was representation on the provincial Committees and informed the Delegation that he understood that possibly four Africans would serve on the Central Development Board.

As regards the allegations made against the judiciary, this was a serious charge and if the Delegation made such charges they should be prepared to substantiate them. He was of course prepared to consider any facts that might be put forward and he would certainly not tolerate abuses in the administration of justice in Nigeria.

As regards the accusation that the native rulers were instruments of Government, the Secretary of State asked the Delegation to believe that there was no desire to exercise undue influence over them. What was desired was their free and independent expression of opinion as representatives of the people.

As regards the Cameroons, he explained that the object of the Cameroons Development Corporation was to ensure development of the area under proper public control and that any profits arising from that development should not be used for private purposes but for the benefit of the people of the area as a whole.

As regards land in Lagos, he was surprised that arguments should be put forward in favour of freehold tenure, which was contrary to African conceptions. He would have expected the Delegation to be opposed to freehold.

In conclusion, the Secretary of State invited them to co-operate in trying to make the new constitution a success. He said that on the other points raised he would give a reply to the Delegation in due course after consulting with the Governor. He stressed that in the long run the degree of progress made must depend upon the efforts of the Nigerian people and he instanced the progress that had been achieved in the United Kingdom through voluntary effort. The Secretary of State said that the reply to the memorandum would take some time. They might of course have other business here, which was their affair, but he felt that there was no need, as far as the Colonial Office was concerned, for the Delegation to remain in this country pending the receipt of the reply.

39   CO 852/903/2   22 Sept 1947
[Marketing boards]: minute by J M Kisch[1] on the establishment of the Nigerian Cocoa Marketing Board   [Extract]

[The Nigerian Cocoa Marketing Board, which replaced the West African Produce Control Board established during the war, began operating in June 1947; the legislation setting it up was approved by the Legislative Council in Sept 1947. Marketing Boards for groundnuts, cotton and palm produce began operating in Apr 1949.]

The Nigerian Cocoa Marketing Board Ordinance at 74 has already been the subject of correspondence and discussion with Mr. F.E.V. Smith who is to be the Chairman. It is modelled on the Gold Coast Cocoa Marketing Board Ordinance at 48 from which however it differs in the matter of the constitution and method of appointment of members of the Board and in the establishment of an Advisory Committee (Sections 30–35).

Summarising these differences, the Gold Coast Board consists of 12 members, 4 including the Chairman being appointed by the Governor, 4 being nominated by the Governor on recommendation from African Councils, 2 being directly nominated by those Councils and 1 each being nominated by the manufacturers and the Gold Coast Chamber of Commerce. The Nigerian Board on the other hand consists of not less than 5 or more than 7 members of whom not less than 2 shall be Nigerians and all of whom will be appointed by the Governor who also appoints the Chairman. It will be an 'official' Board with a minority of Africans. In order to base the Board more broadly on the producers in whose interests it is to act, an Advisory Committee is to be established of not less than 9 members of whom not less than 5 shall be Nigerians, the 9 members to meet under a Chairman appointed by the Governor and are to include representatives of producers and commercial interests. All members are

[1] J M Kisch, formerly Board of Inland Revenue, CO principal from 1939.

appointed directly by the Governor. Section 20 directs the Board to seek the advice of the Advisory Committee on all matters in connection with the purchase and grading of Nigerian Cocoa and the development of the industry and in the use of its funds. If the Board fails to accept the advice offered it by the Committee, the Chairman shall report the matter to the Governor in Council giving the reason for such refusal.

It will be interesting to see how this arrangement works out. If there are frequent differences between the African Committee and the Board, an awkward position will result and the Governor in Council will continually become involved. We shall have to hope for the best. Perhaps eventually it will be possible to allow African Councils to nominate members for the Advisory Committee instead of all appointments being made by the Governor. . . .

40   CO 583/292/4, no 82   3 Oct 1947
[NCNC delegation]: despatch no 25 from Sir A Richards to Mr Creech Jones giving his views of the matters raised by the NCNC delegation
[Extract]

I have the honour to refer to your Secret Despatch No. 23 of the 21st of August on the subject of the memorandum submitted to you by the Delegation of the National Council for Nigeria and the Cameroons, and to offer my observations on the matters raised by the Delegation in that memorandum and at the interview which you accorded them.

2.   I concur in the answer you propose to give on the Constitutional issues and shall confine my observations to the allegation that the present Constitution is undemocratic. It has, of course, never been claimed that the Constitution is fully democratic in the sense that it provides a means whereby the sovereign will of the people may be carried into effect by their freely-elected representatives and it is obvious that no Colonial Constitution can ever be completely democratic in that sense until the stage is reached where it is possible to transfer full and complete powers of self-government. The Constitution purports to be no more than a step towards democracy but I consider that it may fairly be claimed for it that it represents the longest step towards that goal that the people of this country are at present capable of taking and that it provides the best means of ensuring that all sections of the people, in their differing stages of development, are represented by those best qualified to speak on their behalf. I can well understand that this view is not shared by those who are unable to appreciate that 'the people' means any but those who think the same way as themselves or that democracy is not synonymous with the ballot-box.

3.   In examining the extent to which the Constitution is democratic in the sense that the members of the House of Chiefs and the Unofficial Members of the Houses of Assembly and the Legislative Council are truly representative of those on whose behalf they purport to speak, it is necessary to distinguish between the Chiefs, the members nominated by the Governor to represent special interests and those who have been selected by popular choice.

4.   The criticism levelled against the Chiefs, that is to say, the Northern Emirs

and the three Chiefs from the Western Provinces, is that they are appointed by the Governor and are, therefore, virtually Government servants, that they are not free to speak their minds for fear of being relieved of their offices, that in any case they are an undemocratic anachronism and that for all these reasons they cannot be regarded as the true representatives of the people on whose behalf they purport to speak. These arguments are, of course, based on a complete disregard of the facts. The Governor does not appoint Chiefs, his powers in this connection being confined, under the Appointment and Deposition of Chiefs Ordinance, 1930 (No. 14 of 1930), to approving appointments made in accordance with native law and custom and to determining in cases of dispute, whether an appointment has, in fact, been made in accordance with native law and custom. It is true that under the same Ordinance the Governor may, if those concerned take no steps to appoint a Chief, appoint one himself but there is no record of it ever having been necessary for these powers to be exercised. That the Chiefs are not free to speak their minds is controverted by the sometimes startling frankness with which they express themselves and if proof were wanted that they are not anachronisms it is to be found in the respect and confidence reposed in them by the simple farmers who constitute the vast majority of their followers. With the awakening of political consciousness there is undoubtedly the danger of a cleavage between the Chiefs and the more progressive elements, but as I made clear in my Despatch of the 6th of December, 1944,[1] when setting out my proposals for constitutional reform, it is an essential part of the policy underlying the Constitution that the Native Authorities should be modernized by admitting to their councils representatives of progressive opinion.

5. The procedure for selecting the Provincial members of the Houses of Assembly necessarily varied according to local conditions and was in accordance with Directions, of which I enclose copies, which I issued in respect of the three Houses.[2] In those Provinces where the areas subject to the Native Authorities are extensive and the Native Authorities consequently few, it was sufficient for each of them to send representatives direct to the Provincial Meeting; in those Provinces where Native Authorities are small and numerous it was necessary to start at a lower level and to select at Divisional Meetings representatives to attend the Provincial Meetings. No procedure was prescribed whereby the Native Authorities and Divisional and Provincial Meetings should select their representatives, each of these units being left to transact their business in accordance with such procedure as, in the light of their custom, they considered appropriate. The extent to which this method can be deemed to be democratic depends, of course, on the extent to which the Native Authority councils or advisory councils, as the case may be, are democratic. So far as the Eastern Provinces are concerned, it is difficult to envisage a more democratic system for the Native Authorities are for the most part councils consisting of family or clan representatives who retain their position for only as long as they can command the support of those they represent. The same is true in considerable areas in both the Northern and Western Provinces but where the institutions are less democratic in character it is, as I explained above, a cardinal point of policy to force the pace as far as is compatible with safety to ensure that adequate representation is secured for the more progressive elements in the community.

---

[1] See 7.   [2] Not printed.

6.   It would be idle to contend that the selection of those members nominated by the Governor to represent interests otherwise unrepresented is truly democratic, but when no machinery exists whereby those interests may secure adequate representation for themselves it is, I conceive, more in the interests of democracy that they should be represented by nomination than that they should not be represented at all.

7.   Mr. Kale, in pleading that the Cameroons should be separately represented in the Legislative Council has apparently overlooked the fact that, under the terms of the Trusteeship Agreement, the Cameroons are administered as an integral part of Nigeria, that is to say, as far as the Cameroons Province is concerned, as an integral part of the Eastern Provinces. There is no more justification for according the Cameroons Province special representation in the Legislative Council than there is in respect of any other Province in Nigeria; moreover, such representation could not be in respect of the Cameroons Province alone but would also have to embrace that part of the Cameroons which is administered as part of the Northern Provinces, a course which in practice would be rendered impossible on account of the geographical, ethnological and administrative considerations which are involved. . . .

. . . 50.   One of the principal complaints of the Delegation is that the legislation of Nigeria places excessive powers in the hands of the Governor, and that this is undemocratic. It is true that the Governor or the Governor in Council is given powers to regulate many matters which in more advanced countries are controlled by boards or bodies of commissioners wholly or partly composed of private citizens but it has not in the past been possible to adopt this procedure extensively in Nigeria because there have been insufficient persons with the necessary qualifications to appoint to such boards. Only now is it becoming possible to make a wider use of this method of associating the people with public affairs and I think it is worthy of note, as indicating the development that is taking place in this direction, that of the twenty-one statutory boards and committees which have been set up to deal with public and quasi-public matters, twelve have been established in the last five years. As a further step in this direction I am at present considering proposals in connection with a new Education Ordinance and a new Agriculture Ordinance whereby the responsibility for operating these Ordinances will in a very large measure devolve upon Boards on which there will be unofficial majorities.

41   CO 583/297/1, no 5   2 Dec 1947
[Regional councils]: letter from H F Marshall to K E Robinson on the selection of unofficial members for the regional houses of assembly. *Enclosure*

I am sorry there has been such a long delay in replying to your demi-official letter to the Governor of the 12th of June, about the selection of Unofficial Members for Regional Houses. Copies of the directions issued by Lord Milverton regarding the procedure to be followed have, I see, already been sent to you under cover of our official Secret despatch No. 25 of the 3rd of October,[1] and these may have given you all the information you want.

---

[1] See 40.

2.   On the whole the selection of representatives passed off very smoothly indeed, and you may like to see the enclosed notes on the subject which I have received from the Regional Secretariats. There were, as you will observe, a number of teething troubles, but speaking generally, both the quality of the representatives and the degree of popular support which they enjoyed were fully up to expectations.

Enclosure to 41

The most outstanding event of 1946 was the coming into force of the new constitution and the preparations for the first meeting of the House of Assembly which was held just after the close of the year. At the direction of His Excellency Divisional and Provincial meetings were formed in order that the electoral chain could be forged by which the Provincial members could be elected to the House of Assembly. The Native Authorities of each Division selected from among their members such number of persons as the Chief Commissioner approved to constitute a Divisional meeting. The numbers of each Divisional meeting varied in accordance with the wishes of the Native Authorities from 12 in some cases to as many as 60 in others. Of their number the Divisional meetings again each selected from two to six persons, subject to the approval of the Chief Commissioner, as members of the Provincial meetings. And from these bodies in turn selections were made to attend the House of Assembly. The importance of literacy for the member of the House of Assembly, where the proceedings are in English, was strongly stressed but in other respects, with the one qualification that candidates must be members of a Native Authority, selection was left entirely to the Native Authorities themselves. In the existing fluid state of the Native Authorities of the Eastern Provinces some apprehension was felt as to whether or not the selections would be made without rancour but from the beginning no troubles were experienced. It must however be recorded that a hitch occurred in the Owerri Division through failure to realise the full implications of selection to the Divisional Meeting. In this Division selection was arranged by inviting the Federal Councils of the Division to choose representatives for the Divisional Meeting. Now the Federal Councils (Native Authorities) are composed of representatives of other Native Authorities subordinate to them and their membership is changed every six months. The invitation, therefore, made eligible for selection only those who were actual members of the Federal Councils at that time and debarred members of the compopent and subordinate Native Authorities. The choice was thus undoubtedly restricted and did not include many of those with the greater ability. The mistake was pointed out to the Federal Councils but they declined to reconsider their original selections and there were no means by which they could be compelled to do so. Discontent has since been overt and, regrettably, some loss of interest in the constitution has been occasioned but matters will be straightened out at the end of the first three-year period of election; it may even prove a useful lesson and tend to encourage greater stability which is so much to be desired. At Divisional and Provincial Meetings, though opportunity was taken to discuss matters of general interest at Divisional and Provincial levels respectively, during the actual election of members for the Provincial Meeting or House of Assembly the meetings were left to their own devices. There were no disputes and the most surprising unanimity was shown; judging from the general quality of the representatives who emerged successfully as members of the House of Assembly it can be said that considerable perspicacity was shown. The first meeting of the House proved highly successful: the members were dignified and made useful and interesting contributions, and the meeting augured well for the future.

42 CO 583/294/1, no 18   [Jan 1948]
'Summary of administrative and financial procedure under the new constitution': CO memorandum on the Phillipson Report

[Sydney Phillipson, financial secretary of Nigeria, 1945–1948, was commissioned in 1946 to review the implications of the Richards constitution for administrative and financial relations between central and local government, see 23. His report, *Administrative and Financial Procedure under the New Constitution: Financial Relations between the Government of Nigeria and the Native Administration* (Lagos, 1947) which influenced spending through to the 1950s, recommended the principle of derivation, that is that regions should receive funding proportionate to their contribution to central government revenue.]

I. *Administrative procedure*
The purposes of the new Constitution can be summarised as

Regionalization
Devolution
Representation of Native Administration.

The Administrative implications of the first two of these are clearly set out in paragraphs 2 to 4 of the Statement, and the Phillipson Report itself adds little to this account. In brief they are
    1.   the maximum devolution of executive functions from Heads of regionalized Departments to regional representatives.
    2.   that regional representatives should be responsible to Heads of Departments for strictly technical matters, but to the Chief Commissioner for the execution of approved policy within the Region, and for all local matters.
    3.   that the effect of this devolution should increase the authority of the Chief Commissioner through the association of a group of advisers who will constitute a kind of regional executive council.
    The Phillipson Report points out that these administrative developments to some extent preceded the constitutional changes and are already far advanced.

II. *Financial procedure*
The constitutional despatch embodying the original Richards proposals stressed the importance of the financial responsibility of the Regional Councils. The Report provides operative instructions designed to implement the Constitution in this respect.

1. *Limitations of regional responsibility*
Regional Councils will not possess any power of appropriating revenue for regional expenditure; all revenue available for regional purposes will be voted to the Regions by the Nigerian Legislative Council. Further devolution of financial responsibility is regarded as outside the terms of reference of the Report.

2. *Classification of services and works as Nigerian or regional.*
   (a) Regionalized Heads of Expenditure
   Accountancy
   Agriculture
   Co-operation
   Education
   Forestry
   Medical
   Police
   Provincial Administration
   Public Works
   Veterinary.
   (b) All other services and works will be classified as Nigerian, and provision will
also be made in the Estimates of Nigerian Expenditure for the following aspects of
the regionalized departments
   Nigerian H.Q. staff
   Research
   Institutions serving whole of Nigeria – e.g. Veterinary
   Training School
   Expenditure on Colony of Lagos
   (c) Regional Councils will be at liberty to *debate* matters connected with non-
regionalized departments.
   (d) C.D. and W. expenditure will be shown in the Nigerian Estimates divided into
Nigerian expenditure and expenditure in the three Regions. Regional expenditure
will also be shown under a separate Head in the Regional estimates with a
corresponding entry on the revenue side. This procedure is intended to ensure a
combination of Central Control of Development finance with Regional interest in
Development projects (the Regional Councils will of course have no power to
increase expenditure or to modify approved schemes).

3. *Revenues to be declared regional*
This falls under two heads
   (a) Revenue to be derived from Regional Councils' share of Direct Tax plus other
revenues to be declared regional – e.g.
   Licences
   Mining rents
   Court fees
   Earnings of Government Departments and
   Rent of Government property.
   (b) Block grant from central revenue.

4. *Basis of allocation to regions of available revenues not declared regional*
Owing to the conflict between the principle of derivation (and consequently of
financial responsibility) and that of even progress between Regions, this problem
presents some difficulty. The aim is declared to be 'to bring about a state of affairs in
which the contribution made by each Region to the non-declared revenues of Nigeria
is proportioned to the required scale of expenditure on regional purposes so that the
latter may correspond to the former', (this is far from being the case at present).

When that objective is reached 'any further available resources to be allocated according to the measure of the incidence per head of each regional population of the total true taxation . . . . Alternatively the available resources might be allocated with the express purpose of bringing on backward regions or parts of regions'. To achieve these aims the following recommendations are made:—

(a) *Procedure for 1948–9*

Allocation to be at least equal to present (i.e. 1947–8) Government expenditure on regional purposes plus a sum to cover unavoidable expansion plus a figure for Public Works moderately adjusted to give the Northern Provinces a share less disproportionate to its (greater) contribution to revenue.

(b) *Procedure after 1948–9*

(i) A Revenue Allocation Board to be set up, to meet annually and to submit recommendations regarding revenue allocation for the coming year with a view to achieving the objectives defined above within 5 years.

(ii) Sums to be notified to Regional Secretariats not later than 31 July each year within which the Estimates of Regional expenditure are to be formulated.

5. *Preparation of regional estimates*

(a) In order to review this provisional estimate in July it is necessary to provide for revision by Regional Councils in December and the Nigerian Legislative Council to set up:—

1 General and 3 Regional Committees on the Estimates
1 General and 3 Regional Committees on Finance

for subsequent revision. It is intended that Regional Councils shall brief their representatives on Leg. Co. with a list of priorities in case of an increase or decrease on the Estimates.

(b) Budget meetings of the Regional Councils are to be held not later than 20th December, giving the Regions 4 months to collect expenditure estimates.

6. *Preparation of estimates of Nigerian (i.e. 'central') expenditure and of estimates of Nigeria (i.e. including regional estimates)*

The responsibilities of the Nigerian Secretariat will include:—

(a) Compilation of Estimate of Revenue for Nigeria (as hitherto)

(b) Informing Chief Commissioners of the revenue allocation of the Regions. (4 above)

(c) Technical co-ordination of whole process of Estimates preparation.

(d) Preparation of Estimates of Nigerian (i.e. 'Central') expenditure.

(e) Composition of Estimates of Nigeria, which will henceforward include the following modifications

(i) They will be divided into 3 parts
    I. Nigerian
    II. Regional (consisting only of three one line Heads with the block vote in each case).
    III. Development and Welfare (divided into Nigerian and Regional).

(ii) Detailed Estimates of Regional expenditure and the statement of revenues will appear as appendices.

43 CO 583/292/5, no 8   10 Jan 1948

[NCNC delegation]: letter from S Phillipson to A Adedoyin[1] outlining the official response to the matters raised by the NCNC delegation

The Secretary of State has directed that the enclosed memorandum should be transmitted to you as his reply to the various detailed points contained in the memorandum which a Delegation of the National Council of Nigeria and the Cameroons presented to him on August 11th, 1947.[2]

2. The memorandum does not deal with the question of constitutional change which was dealt with at the Delegation's interview with the Secretary of State. The Secretary of State desires to state that he is always anxiously concerned about the growth of political life in the colonial territories and fostering a deepening sense and realisation of responsibility. He is therefore much preoccupied with furthering self-government and evolving free democratic institution for the better representation and government of the people. He wishes to record, however, that he does not accept the criticism that the present constitution and system of administration is static, unprogressive or undemocratic, having regard to present conditions in Nigeria. That constitution marks a substantial step forward in the degree to which the people of Nigeria can participate in the legislative machinery of the country. It is in no sense regarded by the Secretary of State as incapable of modification but in the Secretary of State's view, any modifications which are made should be such as are found necessary in the light of experience in the actual working of the constitution. It is in the Secretary of State's view essential as he stated at the interview with the Delegation that the present constitutional arrangements should be given a proper trial before it can be seen how they may need amendments: there can be no question, in his view, of setting the present constitution aside and replacing it by something which might prove to be unsuitable to Nigerian conditions.

3. One of the criticisms made by the Delegation concerns the role of the Nominated Unofficial Members whom the Delegation considers to be dependent on the will of the Governor and hence unable to fulfil their function of independent representation of the peoples of their areas. The Secretary of State considers that such a view clearly misrepresents the true position of the Members of the House of Chiefs and the Unofficial Members of the Houses of Assembly and of the Legislative Council. It is desirable to make it clear that the Governor does not appoint Chiefs, his powers in this connection being confined, under the Appointment and Deposition of Chiefs Ordinance 1930 (No. 14 of 1930) to approving appointments made in accordance with native law and custom and of determining in cases of dispute whether an appointment has in fact been made in accordance with native law and custom. It is true that under the same Ordinance the Governor may, if those concerned take no steps to appoint a Chief, appoint one himself, but there is no record that it has ever been necessary for these powers to be exercised.

4. So far as the ability of the Chiefs to speak their minds is concerned the reports of the proceedings of the Legislative Council alone are sufficient to show that they have no hesitation in doing so and that no attempt is made by Government to restrict in any way their freedom of speech. Indeed in every way possible the Government

---

[1] General secretary, NCNC.   [2] Not printed. See 36.

seems to encourage free discussion and independence of mind among the representatives of the people. A further disproof of the Delegation's assertions in this matter is found in the presence on the Delegation of one Nominated Unofficial Member.

5. The Secretary of State wishes to point out, moreover, that under the constitution the majority of the Unofficial Members of the Legislative Council are elected to that position by the Unofficial Members of the Houses of Assembly. The Provincial Members of the three Houses of Assembly are selected, in accordance with arrangements published in the Government Gazette on the 10th September, 1946, by Provincial Meetings, and where appropriate the members of these Provincial Meetings are selected by Divisional Meetings. These Provincial and Divisional Meetings are representative of the Native Authorities of the areas. The Secretary of State believes that indirect election of this kind is the best method under present conditions of securing the adequate representation of the great majority of the population of Nigeria and he understands that public men in Nigeria have expressed satisfaction at the manner in which the arrangements are working.

6. In conclusion the Secretary of State desires to stress that he fully appreciates that in a country such as Nigeria, which is, like many other parts of the world, undergoing a process of increasing development and change, there is a keen desire on the part of an ever larger number of its citizens to take part in the discussion and management of the affairs of the country. The Secretary of State, like the Nigeria Government itself, welcomes this tendency wholeheartedly, since progress in the improvement of the general conditions of life of the people must be greatly assisted by it. The Secretary of State and His Majesty's Government fully support the Nigerian Government in its present policy of seeking all possible ways and means of encouraging and facilitating the participation of the people in public affairs. It is recognized that, in co-operating in the tasks of development, improvement and general betterment, the representatives of the people will find it necessary to criticise the Government where they think that improvements can be made. Such criticism if made constructively and on the basis of study and understanding of the facts, is entirely welcome. Nigeria can, however, ill afford criticism for criticism's own sake or activities designed to obstruct and embarrass the Government, which can only have the effect of diverting the energies of Government and people away from the many constructive tasks which confront them. The Secretary of State hopes therefore that a policy of constructive co-operation with the Government in the many ways open to them will commend itself to the Delegation.

44 CO 583/292/5, no 23   24 Mar 1948
[Accra riots]: letter from G Beresford Stooke to Sir T Lloyd concerning the possible reaction in Nigeria to the Accra riots

Thank you so much for your letter of the 2nd of March about the Sub-Committee of the Select Committee on the Estimates. I shall certainly impress upon our witnesses the desirability of being perfectly frank and open with the Sub-Committee. There is, of course, nothing to hide and the more people in the U.K. know of the facts of the situation in the Colonies, the better it will be for us all.

We are still engaged with Legislative Council. The Select Committee on the Estimates has taken much longer than usual. There has been much discussion and a greatly increased demand for information but, even so, the Unofficial Members have not so far changed a single item.

Azikiwe has been sweetly reasonable throughout. This attitude is, however, reserved for the Legislative Council alone, and while he has been cooing like a dove in the Council Chamber his newspapers have, if anything, intensified their dangerous anti-European propaganda. It is, unfortunately, the newspapers which the public read, not Hansard.

I am not at present apprehensive about reactions in Nigeria to events in the Gold Coast, but we are fully prepared for any demonstration which may suddenly take place, and shall continue to keep 'on our toes'.[1] As you probably know, ever since the General Strike of 1945 we have had fairly elaborate plans drawn up to deal with general strikes and riots etc., and these plans are continually being revised and overhauled. Intelligence reports indicate a possibility that some attempt may be made to stir up trouble in Lagos over the Easter week-end, but, as I have said, we have our plans laid and between three and four hundred police will be standing by with motor transport and full anti-riot equipment. A force of that size, fully mobile and fully trained to deal with mobs, should be able to break up and disperse any unlawful assembly before it becomes dangerous. This, of course, is not a new organization. We had our amber warning three years ago, and have thus had plenty of time in which to organize security services.

You will be interested to learn that yesterday Azikiwe moved in Council "that this Honourable Assembly is entitled to know all the facts relating to the deputation of the National Council of Nigeria and the Cameroóns to the Colonial Office, and calls for all papers relating thereto'. This was strongly opposed from all sides of the Council on the grounds that the N.C.N.C. does not represent the people of Nigeria and had no authority to approach the Secretary of State. On the division, the voting was 38–4 against, the only persons who voted in favour being the N.C.N.C. delegates themselves – i.e. Azikiwe, Adedoyin, Nimbe, and Nyong Essien. This is a pretty clear demonstration of what responsible Africans think of Azikiwe and the N.C.N.C. It is a great pity that this irresponsible minority should control the popular press.

I hope to have the pleasure of seeing you in London next month when I shall be able to give you the latest news of Nigeria in greater detail.

---

[1] Serious riots broke out in Accra on 28 Feb 1948. BDEEP series B, vol 1, R Rathbone, ed, *Ghana*, part I, 21.

45   CO 583/292/5, no 28   28 April 1948
[NCNC Kaduna convention]: memorandum by J O Field[1] on the NCNC Convention in Kaduna and the Freedom Charter

The announcement that the N.C.N.C. proposed to hold a Convention, followed by a National Assembly, was made by Azikiwe shortly after his return from the United

---

[1] Secretariat, Lagos.

Kingdom. It was hailed as a masterly example of Azikiwe's statesmanship by all his supporters, but as a matter of fact it was not Azikiwe's idea at all.

After the Pan-Nigeria Delegation had had their (to them) unsatisfactory interview with the Secretary of State,[2] George Padmore[3] sent them a letter in which, after urging them not to lose heart, he gave them the following advice:—

> 'The first thing you should do on your return to Nigeria is to convene a popular rally at which you should give a full report about your mission to Britain. Similar meetings should be held in different parts of the country. . . .
>
> 'Following these mass meetings, the Executive Committee of the N.C.N.C. should convene a National Convention, to which should be invited not only delegates from the organizations affiliated to the N.C.N.C. but also from those bodies still outside the fold. The purpose of the Convention should be to ratify your draft constitution submitted to Creech Jones as the provisional Constitution of the Commonwealth of Nigeria and the Cameroons. . . .
>
> 'Having moved from the defensive to the offensive the N.C.N.C. will be able to pose to the entire country a positive alternative programme to the Richards Constitution on the one hand and the British Government's bureaucratic 10-year plan on the other. . . . In opening this new chapter, you must seize the initiative and you can only do this by forgetting the Richards Constitution and putting before the nation a Constitution which expresses the needs and aspirations of the people, and call upon them to make this their Charter of Freedom'.

This extract is quoted at length for it will be seen that Zik adhered very closely to this advice.

The Annual Convention met at Kaduna on the 5th–6th April. Forty-eight delegates attended representing thirty-seven of the one hundred and eighty odd bodies claimed by Zik to be affiliated to the N.C.N.C. Of these thirty-seven, twenty were bodies in the Eastern Provinces, seven were Northern Provinces branches of Southern Provinces (predominantly Ibo) organizations, four were Western Provinces bodies, one was a Northern Provinces body (the Tiv Progressive Union) and the remainder were miscellaneous organizations such as Zik's Athletic Club, the Kaduna Plot Owners' Union, and the Nigeria Legion. The Accra branch of the N.C.N.C. also sent a delegate. Of the forty-eight delegates, twenty-six were Ibos, ten Yoruba, three Ibibio, one Ijaw, one Uhrobo, one Bini, one native of the Cameroons and one Tiv. The tribes of the other four are unknown. It is noteworthy that the Northern Elements Progressive Union was not represented, nor apparently were any of the prominent Northern Zikists (such as Mallam Abdullah, President of the Zikist Movement)[4] present at the Convention, though they later attended the Assembly.

The most noteworthy absentees, however, were Adedoyin (General Secretary, N.C.N.C.) and Dr. Nimbe (Treasurer). The excuse they gave to their friends in Lagos

---

[2] See 38.

[3] George Padmore (Malcolm Nurse), Trinidadian political activist and writer, member of the Communist party of the USA; later personal adviser to Kwame Nkrumah.

[4] Habib Raji Abdallah, founder member of the Northern Elements Progressive Association, 1946; Zikist activist; president of the Zikist Movement, 1947; tried and imprisoned for sedition, 1948–1949; sentenced to two years gaol.

was that they had attended so many delegations and political gatherings of late that their practices were beginning to suffer, though it is well known that their real reason was that they are no longer on speaking terms with Zik. Dipcherima was also absent, though he sent a message to say that he still sympathised with the N.C.N.C. but had once given up his job for the cause and was not prepared to do it again unless they made it worth his while. P.M. Kale did not attend and gave no reason for his absence. In fact, the only members of the Pan-Nigeria Delegation who were present were Zik, Mrs. Ransome-Kuti (who came for one day) and Nyong Essien. For the rest, the delegates were nonentities.

The proceedings opened with a Presidential Address by Zik. After surveying in broad detail the aims and objects of the N.C.N.C. and the extent to which they have been achieved, he launched an attack on his enemies, who he classified as 'Negativists' and 'Nihilists' but for whose machinations even greater successes would have been achieved. The 'Negativists' are those who believe that the people of Nigeria are not yet ripe for self-government, i.e. the moderate politicians. The Nihilists are those who believe that 'nothing good can be done in this country unless it is done by them, therefore their task is to stultify the national will by obstructionist tactics'. (It is not clear to whom this refers, but it may be the Egbe Omo Oduduwa and the Nigerian Youth Movement, both of which have set themselves up in opposition to the N.C.N.C.) The 'Positivists', on the other hand, are all good men and true who support the N.C.N.C. Turning to the Delegation to the U.K., he described the Secretary of State's reply as an insult to the intelligence of the people of Nigeria and continued 'Mr. Arthur Creech Jones has told us bluntly that so far as the British Government is concerned, we are at liberty to do our worst'. He then went on to explain that the assistance of U.N.O. would be essential in the struggle for independence, adding:—

> 'I wish to make it clear that so far as I am concerned we must not expect national emancipation by relying on Great Britain to honour treaty obligations in the light of her own conscience. As a Colonial Power, he would be a simpleton who believes that Great Britain would grant us our independence without a struggle'.

Then followed an attack on the new Constitution, which his experience in Legislative Council had convinced him was but a device whereby the Government could 'divide and rule' and foster the evil of what he called Pakistanism. 'After attending the Budget Session of legislative Council', he said, 'I have come to the conclusion that it is embarrassing to co-operate in the working of the Richards Constitution', and he expressed the hope that the Convention would decide whether it was worth while continuing to co-operate. Then he turned to his own draft constitution which followed roughly his previous outline but with the significant difference that no longer was provision made for a transitional period or for the appointment of a Governor by the Colonial Office: instead power was to be vested directly in a President elected at an annual convention of the N.C.N.C. who would be assisted by cabinet ministers chosen by himself. All this, however, led up to the real point of his speech—a clear declaration of the intention to sever the British connection and to obtain independence, if need be by violence. This part of the speech is worth recording:—

> 'One distinguishing element between the N.C.N.C. and other organizations is our readiness to graduate from the "talking stage" to that of "positive action".

In years gone by I believed staunchly in Great Britain and in her ability to set us free without fuss. Even when I was in the United Kingdom with the N.C.N.C. delegation I had to debate within myself whether Great Britain will make self-government possible within the fifteen years I have been advocating since 1943. . . .

In reading through one of Barere's speeches during the French Revolution I ran across the following: "The tree of liberty grows only when watered by the blood of tyrants". In view of what has happened in the history of many countries, it saddens my heart to think of obtaining the independence of our country in this inhuman way.

In truth, my faith in Great Britain has waned and I am compelled to admit openly my belief that freedom for Nigeria and the Cameroons can no longer be expected to descend to us easily without tremendous sacrifice. . . . If we mean to liberate our country we must reckon with these realities and cease from living in a fool's paradise.

I have doubted the wisdom of these thoughts in the past, I have waited for one positive act on the part of those who govern to prove me wrong; and now I am free for I am no longer wishful in my thinking. . . .'

and he ended up with an exhortation to 'our youths, our wage-earners, our world war veterans, our patriots and our peasantry' to stand firm in the approaching struggle and see it through.

This is probably the most hypocritical speech Zik has ever made, for he sought to convince his public that he was driven against his will to claim complete independence and to obtain it, if necessary, by violence as a result of his disillusioning experiences on the Delegation and in Legislative Council. But he had these thoughts in his mind long ago. As early as 1943 he prepared a draft 'blueprint' which he set up in type but never published, in which he advocated an independent State outside the Commonwealth but in alliance with Britain, while he had already revealed that his mind was playing with the possibility of extreme measures in the 'Statement of National Policy' which he issued just before the Delegation left the shores of Nigeria.

The next item on the agenda was the presentation of the Secretary's report, but as the General Secretary had failed to attend to present it himself, some heated discussion ensued as to how the report was to be brought properly before the meeting. In the end Zik revealed that it hadn't been written by the General Secretary anyway, so Oged Macaulay signed it and read it out. It consisted of a resumé of the activities of the N.C.N.C. since its foundation in 1944 and contained nothing of note.

The Convention then got down to the real business of considering the various resolutions and motions that were brought before it. Most of these were of little importance and dealt with such minor and parochial matters as demands for increased educational facilities in Ogoja Province; support for Mrs. Ransome-Kuti in her crusade against the taxation of women in Abeokuta; the restoration of the Oba Falolu's stipend; and support for the claim of the people of Enugu Ngwo to a share of the profits of the Colliery.

More important resolutions were to the effect that 'whereas the N.C.N.C. is likely to be the party to take over the administration of the country in the event of Nigeria's freedom, any person elected president of the National Council by any National

Convention be allowed the discretion of electing his own cabinet ministers'. After an object on to the use of the word 'cabinet', because it savoured of foreign influence, had been hotly debated and over-ruled, the motion was carried nem. con. This was followed by a motion that 'this National Convention of the N.C.N.C. assume the right, claim the right, and exercise the right ... to continue defending Nigerian people's right by criticising Government and any legislation that might be passed in any Legislative Council meetings that shall be deemed incongenial to Nigerian peoples' freedom. ...' Following this came a resolution that 'the tenure of office of both the President and the cabinet ministers shall be extended to five years'. The motion was carried subject to an amendment that the period should be reduced to three years.

These resolutions are of interest because they form the basis of the 'shadow government', approval for the setting up of which it was one of Zik's principal objects to secure.

Then came a resolution condemning the manner in which the Nigerian representatives at the forthcoming African Conference had been selected and demanding that the three Lagos elected members and Nyong Essien should be included among the representatives.[5] One hot-head from the Cameroons suggested that the people should be called upon to refuse to pay tax unless these members were included. It was decided that this amendment had better be discussed in 'select committee', but the reporter of the 'Daily Times' had the temerity to report that it would be discussed in a 'secret committee', which indeed amounted to the same thing, with the result that he brought down the wrath of all the delegates upon his head and got himself excluded from further meetings for his pains. The real cause for the indignation however, seems not to have been the alleged mis-reporting, but because this little suggestion for 'positive action' leaked out. As Zik more than once remarked in the course of the proceedings, it is unwise to reveal one's plans to the enemy! The resolution as originally proposed was finally passed and it was agreed, in addition, to send a telegram of protest to the Secretary of State.

In the middle of the proceedings one of the delegates, whose mind was apparently still brooding on the first items on the agenda, suddenly jumped up with a proposal that a priority telegram should be sent to Adedoyin and Nimbe requesting them to report forthwith to the Convention by air, the cost, he obligingly added, to be borne by the Council. This proposal gave rise to considerable discussion in the course of which some rather uncomplimentary remarks were passed about the absentees, but in the end the motion was agreed to and the telegram was duly despatched. Nimbe ignored it. Adedoyin, however, sent a polite reply regretting that he was unable to comply because it was impossible to get an air passage. As a matter of fact, he never applied for one. It seems, however, that nobody thought it likely that Nimbe would comply with their request, for at the same time it was decided that if he did not produce the accounts for auditing within twenty-eight days, legal action would be

---

[5] This refers to the conference in Lancaster House, London, in Sept–Oct 1948 for representatives of each of the African territories. The Nigerian delegation was elected by the unofficial members of the legislative council; Azikiwe failed to be elected.

taken against him. It is difficult to believe that the N.C.N.C. executive would be so rash as to carry out this threat, for an examination of the accounts is unlikely to reflect any credit on any of them.

The rest of the Convention's time was taken up approving in principle the various matters to be brought before the National Assembly. Then they considered the report of the Commission of Inquiry into the conduct of Magnus Williams (see Political Summary No. 23) and decided that he should be expelled from the movement, and this having been done the Convention adjourned until next year. That evening they held a demonstration. A fair crowd followed them, most of them Ibos and the rest Hausa youngsters who were there to see the fun. Significantly, and to the chagrin of Zik, the not inconsiderable Yoruba population of Kaduna for the most part boycotted the demonstration. Led by a bodyguard of ten ex-servicemen and followed by a couple of brass bands with Zik perched somewhat nervously on a horse, the procession made its way through the town; but as a propaganda stunt it appears to have been a failure: most people – Hausas, Yorubas and Binis – thought it a presumptuous display and complained of the noise kicked up by Zik and his followers.

The National Assembly

After a day's rest, the delegates, considerably augmented, gathered again for the National Assembly. In accordance with George Padmore's advice, invitations had been issued to some three hundred organizations and individuals, many of them not connected with the N.C.N.C. Since the Assembly seems to have been open to anyone who cared to go in it is somewhat difficult to say exactly how many actually attended or to classify those who were present according to tribes, but an examination of the list of official delegates shows that there were fifty-two Ibos, thirteen Yorubas, Zik's five Northern lieutenants (Mallams Abdullah, Bida, Attah, Zungur, and Zukogi), four Ibibios, three Oras, two natives of the Cameroons, two Yagbas (Northern Provinces Yoruba), an Ijaw, an Uhrobo, a Bini, and a Tiv. Among the delegates were two women —a Miss Ogunrinka who represented the Youth Congress, Lagos, and a Mrs. Ekpo, an Ibibio who has recently begun to organize a Women's Party at Aba. All the delegates present were Zikists, with the single exception of Mr. J.V. Clinton, editor of the Calabar Eastern Mail, who went as an observer. Of the other non-N.C.N.C. organizations and individuals who were invited, most ignored the invitation and the rest declined it.

•The business of the first day was confined to speech-making, Zik starting the ball rolling with a Presidential Address. After remarking that the N.C.N.C. had been founded 'in order to hasten our march towards political freedom, economic security, social equality and religious toleration' he explained that the Assembly had been summoned so that the conduct of the N.C.N.C. could be placed 'in the crucible of public opinion'. In the past, he said, it had been difficult to determine what was the opinion of the country as a whole, but the convening of the National Assembly provided an opportunity for the question to be placed beyond doubt. He therefore proposed to lay his new constitution before them in the hope that, after examining it and amending it if necessary, they would adopt it as the nation's Charter of Freedom. The speech was brief and to the point and except, for one reference to the 'atrocious crime committed . . . by those who are determined to introduce 'Pakistanism' into 'this country', was moderate in tone.

This Address was followed by nine 'Goodwill Speeches' delivered by persons who purported to represent the nine 'protectorates' into which Zik's constitution divides the country, and a similar speech by Blankson on behalf of the Press. All the speeches consisted of strings of the usual Zikist catch phrases and none of them were in any way remarkable, except that of Jaja Wachuku,[6] who, no doubt to sustain his reputation as 'the silver-tongued orator of Iboland', let himself go without restraint in his threats and prognostications of violence and bloodshed.

The Assembly then got down to the business of considering the various motions that had been tabled. Like those before the Convention, many were merely the airing of local grievances and it was perhaps typical of the Assembly that for the most part they were unanimously adopted without discussion, though nobody present except the proposers could possibly have known anything about the merits of the case.

Considerable indignation, however, was shown during the discussion of a motion condemning the way the representatives to attend the African Conference had been selected, it being contended that only the Elected Members and Nyong Essien were qualified to speak on behalf of the people of Nigeria. The discussion ended in the action already taken by the Convention being ratified.

A motion that women should be exempted from taxation was carried but only after it had been amended by excluding women liable under the Income Tax Ordinance. The effect of this would be that European women would continue to pay tax while their African sisters would be exempt.

An interesting discussion centred round whether Zik should continue to sit in Legislative Council. The indications are that he hoped the Assembly would 'instruct' him to stay away in future, but the Assembly decided by a majority that he should continue to sit, because if he did not, they would have no watchdog to safeguard their interests in the Council.

The Assembly then turned to considering the future organization of the N.C.N.C. It is not easy to say what exactly was decided because it is difficult to determine when they were referring to the N.C.N.C. and when to their new Constitution, for it was their declared object to integrate the two, and thus prepare the way for the Federal State of Nigeria. The proposals, as they emerged, appear to be that in future the N.C.N.C. should be organized on the following basis:—

(a) A Federal Parliament (i.e. the Convention) which elects the Federal President and nine Regional Presidents. The Federal President to hold office for three years and to have power to select his own 'Cabinet Ministers'.

(b) Nine Regional Assemblies, presided over by the Regional Presidents who have power to appoint their own 'Regional Committees'. The Regional Assemblies appoint Provincial Presidents.

(c) Provincial Assemblies, presided over by the Provincial Presidents who have power to appoint their own Provincial Committees. The Provincial Assemblies elect Branch Presidents, who select their own Branch Committees, and, it appears, preside over the local branches of the N.C.N.C.

It is not clear how the members of the various Assemblies are to obtain their seats though presumably it is to be by some unspecified system of universal adult suffrage.

---

[6] Jaja Anucha Wachuku, elected to the Eastern House of Assembly, 1951 and to the House of Representatives, 1952; speaker of House of Representatives 1960.

This proposed re-organization was adopted, and the President was forthwith voted power to proceed with the formation of his 'cabinet'.

The next item of importance was the N.C.N.C.'s Education Plan. Very little information is available about this because it has never been made public, but its main provision is the raising of funds to found a University of Nigeria, to be run under the auspices of the N.C.N.C. for the purpose of training technicians and others, to take over all the senior Government posts and to staff the industries that are to be set up under the N.C.N.C.'s Industrial Scheme. Mr. Clinton, who rarely spoke, intervened to suggest that the N.C.N.C. could more profitably employ themselves by assisting the mass education campaign, but this unpalatable suggestion was ignored as was a suggestion that the N.C.N.C. should devote its attention to founding secondary schools before starting on a University. The University appealed to the majority and the plan was accordingly adopted.

Then came the Industrial Plan. There was a great deal of talk about Government's failure to establish local industries and much airy debate about what industries ought to be established. In the end it was decided to adopt the plan in principle and to leave the detailed planning to a committee, and the only concrete decision arrived at was that whatever else the plan might contain, it must make provision for the manufacture of gin.

The Assembly realized that the founding of a University and the establishment of industries would require money, so the next point considered was Finance. The Secretary announced that an appeal would shortly be made to the public to subscribe to a Twenty Million Shilling Fund. Mr. Jaja Wachuku thought this amount inadequate and increased it to Forty Million Shillings. Nobody explained how £2,000,000 was to be extracted from pockets which, according to the N.C.N.C., were long ago emptied and have since been kept empty, by the imperialist exploiters, but a gentleman from Aba wondered whether the public would take kindly to a further appeal when the N.C.N.C. was unable to account for what they had already got. The President explained that the action already taken by the Convention against Dr. Nimbe ought to restore public confidence and the launching of the fund was approved. It would perhaps be uncharitable to speculate whether there is any connection between these proposals and Zik's efforts to raise capital for his new Continental Bank.

At this stage an enthusiast arose to propose that

> 'In view of the fact that the N.C.N.C. has planned a series of positive action, be it resolved that this Assembly decides to instruct the N.C.N.C. Cabinet to appeal to India, Russia or America for alliance in case of belligerent attack'.

Zik rapidly intervened to explain that an open Assembly was not the place to discuss such things and the motion was promptly withdrawn. A number of minor motions were then debated and the Assembly adjourned for the day.

On the next day, the greater part of the morning session was taken up discussing the iniquities of the Daily Times reporter, who had further blotted his copy book by referring to the Convention and Assembly as an 'all Ibo affair'. The discussion ended with a decision to boycott the Daily Times for one month, but in the course of it the question arose of leakages of N.C.N.C. secrets. Nobody mentioned any names but S.A. George, the paid under-secretary, who everyone knows would cheerfully sell anything to anybody for a very small price, was so upset at the thought that his integrity might be open to doubt that he burst into tears.

The rest of the day was devoted to considering the proposed constitution. According to the 'Pilot'

> 'It was really dramatic to watch experts of both constitutional law and political science split hairs over a word or phrase for its technical, legal international and other implications Greek to the laymen'.

The result of the hair-splitting was to abandon the proposal to set up nine 'protectorates' on a geographical basis, and, instead, to carve the country up into a number of linguistic groups, each of which would form an autonomous state within the Commonwealth of Nigeria. They also abandoned the original proposal of a single chamber legislature and instead made provision for a House of Nationalities and a House of Representatives which together would form the Assembly of the Commonwealth. The revised Constitution has not yet been published, but as it apparently dispenses with the period of condominium which Zik originally proposed, it ought to differ radically from the suggested constitution which the Delegation presented to the Secretary of State, and it is not at all clear how it is to fit in with the previously adopted organization of the N.C.N.C. It is doubtful whether the delegates themselves know. When the revision had been completed, Nyong Essien suggested that before it was finally approved, the delegates should take it home with them to consult their 'constituents', but this suggestion was cried down as being quite unnecessary—an interesting side light on the N.C.N.C., seeing [as] one of their principal complaints about the Richards Constitution is that it was forced upon the country without the people at large being given an opportunity to say whether or not they liked it, and a typical example of the N.C.N.C.'s arrogant conviction that nobody but themselves are qualified to speak for the people of Nigeria. So Nyong Essien was overruled and the revised constitution was adopted as the 'Freedom Charter of Nigeria and the Cameroons' and the Cabinet of the N.C.N.C. was given a mandate to implement it.

The last item on the agenda for this day was the consideration of the report of a Committee which the N.C.N.C. set up to examine the question of conditional sales. Zik hoped to make considerable capital out of this but his teeth were drawn by Government having set up its own committee on which the chief complainants are well represented, with the result that this item fell very flat.

The proceedings on the last day opened with the ill-starred Daily Times reporter being again put on the carpet—this time for allegedly reporting that a resolution had been passed calling upon the people not to pay tax. As has already been observed, such a possibility had in fact been mentioned in the course of the discussions in the Convention, but no formal motion had been moved to this effect. After the possibilities of taking legal action against the reporter had been discussed and rejected, they finally decided to expel him again, which they did after passing another resolution that the Daily Times be boycotted.

From then on the proceedings became a kind of 'private members day', everyone trying to jump to his feet to propose some motion or another, most of which were adopted without discussion. Nyong Essien got himself into hot water by asking for £25 to cover his travelling expenses. Even the N.C.N.C. thought this was going a bit too far, for everyone knew that he had got free transport to Kaduna to attend Legislative Council, and that he had a warrant in his pocket to take him home again.

The final act was the expulsion of Nimbe and Adedoyin from the N.C.N.C. on account of their generally reprehensible conduct and in particular on account of their contempt of the Convention's summons to come to Kaduna and explain themselves. Nobody seems to have worried about the fact that the Assembly, not being the N.C.N.C., had presumably no power to expel anybody from that organization, nor were they troubled by the fact that membership of the N.C.N.C. is confined to organizations and that they had just defeated a motion that it should be thrown open to individuals. Perhaps it was as well they forgot it because had they remembered it they would have been put in the awkward position of having to expel the Democratic Party, which would have automatically resulted in expelling their worthy President as well!

There was no more business to transact, and after Zik had dismissed the delegates with a final address in which he expressed the hope 'that the sweat of our brows during this National Assembly will serve to water the trees of liberty which we have sown', the Assembly came to an end.

*   *   *

It is still too early to judge the full political results of Zik's latest manoeuvre, but as a political bombshell it has proved a rather pitiful misfire. His object in calling the Assembly was to strengthen his hand with a 'mandate' which would have the colour of having been given him by representatives of all shades of advanced political opinion and it is known that the fact that nobody of note showed any disposition to accept his invitation has caused him considerable mortification, which is in no way lessened by the manifest defection of Adedoyin and Nimbe. This was but an added rebuff to the many he has received of late. He held the Assembly in Kaduna in furtherance of his campaign to win over the North, and in that region he seems to have won a point or two, for he has undoubtedly quickened the interest of numbers of Northern young men, but against this he has lost heavily in the Yoruba country where his activities have only served to harden the opposition against him. It is difficult to say what the effect has been in the East, but as he has always drawn his main support from that area, his position there probably remains unchanged.

An interesting factor is Zik's apparent throwing of discretion to the winds and openly preaching a doctrine of violence. In the past, he has been circumspect enough to pay at least lip service to the necessity of proceeding in a constitutional manner. The change is probably due to the succession of blows which his pride has lately suffered—the failure of his delegation; the unexpected hostility which he experienced at Legislative Council, especially the slap in the face he received from the Unofficial members over the selection of representatives for the African Conference; the fact that Dr. Danquah[7] stole his thunder with the Gold Coast disturbance and finally the realization that for the first time in his life, he is faced by a considerable body of opposition among the politically-minded younger generation, which opposition is largely directed against him personally, and the most likely explanation of this new departure is that all these rebuffs have worked upon his unstable mind and forced him to indulge in this display of reckless oratory in order to re-instate himself in his own esteem. The principal factors militating against any deliberate resort to violence

---

[7] J B Danquah, founder member of United Gold Coast Convention, 1947; detained by colonial govt following Accra riots, Feb 1948.

are the trepidation with which he views any prospect of danger to his own skin and his well known lack of enthusiasm for landing himself in gaol. The principal cause for apprehension is that he will be carried away by the flood which he himself is in danger of setting loose.

Although, therefore, the possibilities of civil commotions certainly cannot be ignored, it is to be doubted whether these play any immediate part in Zik's plans of 'positive action'. His present intention seems to be to spend the next few years building up his organization, his aim being to secure his ends by creating a parallel administration which will slowly paralyze the Government by usurping its authority. It is for this purpose that he has set up his 'shadow government'—a political device not unknown elsewhere—and when he talks of the possibilities of bloodshed and violence he most likely has in mind what may possibly happen when, as it inevitably must, his rival organization comes into conflict with established authority.

A disturbing factor is the indication that Zik is becoming increasingly subject to outside influences. It has been shown that the idea of a National Assembly came from George Padmore, and anyone who has made a close study of Zik's writings and speeches cannot fail to observe in his recent utterances a note which is certainly not the authentic Zik. In the past he has been prepared to accept the support of Communist and other such organizations only in so far as they were likely to further his own decided ends. It would be to misjudge the situation to believe that Zik is, or ever has been, a communist, or that he is ever likely to be willing to further communism for its own sake, but the recent Convention and Assembly reveal disquieting indications that his moves are no longer inspired entirely from within and that he is now allowing himself to be pushed to some extent from without. And in that his prompters are clever, for they know that his egotism will blind him to the fact that he is being used as a pawn in the game of stirring up embarrassing situations wherever they can.

46   CO 583/287/4   21 May 1948
[Egbe Omo Oduduwa]: minute by F J Webber on the formation of the Egbe Omo Oduduwa

[The Yoruba cultural organisation, *Egbe Omo Oduduwa* (Society of the descendants of Oduduwa), was first formed in London in late 1945, and formally inaugurated in Nigeria at Ife in June 1948, with Obafemi Awolowo as general secretary, and Sir A Alakija as president. Initially a cultural body, it came to be seen as increasingly separatist and as articulating the political aspirations of Yoruba leaders against the NCNC.]

Mr. Gorsuch
I expect you have seen this interesting news item from the 'Times'.[1] It is obviously impossible to make a true assessment of its implications at this stage, but we ought to watch this kind of thing very carefully.

On narrow grounds the launching of this moderate movement may be beneficial to the extent that it discredits the N.C.N.C., and brings home the important fact that Zik is not the logical and recognised successor to the British Crown. But on broader

---

[1] Not printed.

grounds this news gives me cause for concern. In the first place I do not like the element of separatism which cuts across what I conceive to be our traditional policy of the unification of Nigeria: if this movement achieves any amount of success there may well be others, e.g. the Northern Provinces which I suspect are all too susceptible to this kind of development. In the second place this business of self-help when not inspired by Government is not a thing we should condone. Quite obviously they are taking a leaf out of the N.C.N.C. book who talk about their own development plans etc.

This attempt at independent executive action is bound to confuse public opinion in Nigeria, and impede the Government. It will be a stumbling block to our attempts to canalise public opinion in the accepted constitutional channels, and to provide government of the Nigerians for the benefit of Nigeria as a whole.

I do not propose that at this stage we should attempt to give any guidance but I feel that it would be useful if Mr. Cohen wrote to Sir John Macpherson as in draft attached.

47 CO 583/287/5, no 12A   30 May 1948
[Political development]: note by H M Foot on the Kaduna meeting of the Legislative Council

The Legislative Council met on the morning of the 23rd of March at Kaduna. This was the first time that the Council had met outside Lagos under the arrangement whereby the annual budget session of the Council is to take place in the Regional headquarters in rotation. Next year it will meet in Ibadan, in 1950 in Enugu and in 1951 in Lagos. There was at first some petty criticism mainly from the unofficial Lagos members and in the Lagos Press about the expense and inconvenience of meeting in Kaduna but special care had been taken to ensure that satisfactory transport and accommodation arrangements for unofficial members were made and although the Southern members suffered some discomfort from the dry winds of the North I think that before the meeting was over everyone was prepared to agree that the experiment had proved a success. The move to Kaduna at least brought home to those unofficial (and official) members who live in Lagos the necessity to keep in proper perspective the overwhelming claims of the great bulk of the people of Nigeria in relation to those of the comparatively tiny but vociferous minority in Lagos. The mere fact that the meeting took place four hundred miles from Lagos made it less likely that the tail would have much success in its persistent and energetic efforts to wag the dog.

The magnificent new building which is to be the home of the House of Chiefs and Northern House of Assembly is still under construction and was not therefore available for this meeting of the Legislative Council as had at one time been hoped. The Council therefore met in the Kaduna Trade Centre, which was perhaps rather bare (and hot in the afternoons) and provided for only about fifty members of the public in the visitors' gallery, but as a make-shift we could scarcely have hoped for a better debating hall. The seating arrangement was the same as that previously devised at Lagos, the Chief Commissioners and one Resident from each Region sitting with the unofficial members who were in four groups. Immediately on the President's left was the Northern block of nine Emirs and Mallams magnificent in their headdresses and flowing gowns: next to them on the left were the six Eastern members, most of them in European dress: opposite to the President sat the Westerners led by the Oni of Ife and Oba of Benin in their caps and robes with the four other Western members behind them: next, on the far right from the President were the Lagos and nominated members—a somewhat ill-assorted group headed by the Father of the House, the Rev. Ogunbiyi, sitting in front of Dr. Azikiwe (who startled the Council by an almost Churchillian weakness for varying head-gear, ranging from a headband with an Ibo feather to a Moslem tarboush). The other Lagos elected members, Dr. Nimbe and Mr. Adedoyin, were scarcely less colourful in comparison with their European neighbours, the nominated commercial members. Between this group and the chair (on the President's immediate right) sat the Attorney-General, Chief Secretary, Financial Secretary and the Heads of the principal Departments.

The proceedings of the Council were throughout orderly and, with only one or two lapses from Dr. Nimbe who insists on maintaining his reputation for being offensive to everyone, were good-humoured—though some doubts, anxieties and animosities, to which I shall presently refer, were moving below the surface.

Each day started, after prayers, with answers to questions, over three hundred of which (mainly asked by Dr. Azikiwe) had been put down just before or during the meeting. These questions were often well thought-out and searching and although the attempt to obtain all the information required threw a heavy strain on the officials concerned at a time when pressure of other work was exceptional, it is certainly satisfactory that members are now prepared to make full use of this means of obtaining official information and statements of policy. It is also to be welcomed that the practice of asking supplementary questions in the Council, which keeps the officials on their toes and enlivens the proceedings, is on the increase.

The first day of the meeting was mainly taken up with the President's address (of which copies were sent to the Colonial Office at the time) and the first reading of a number of comparatively minor Bills. It was not until the second day that the first skirmish took place over 'The European Officers' Pensions (Amendment) Bill'. On a vote the second reading of the Bill was, however, passed by thirty-three votes to eight (the eight being from Lagos and the East). Proposals for an annual grant-in-aid of £100,000 for five years to the new University College and for a contribution of £250,000 to the University College endowment fund were unanimously carried (after Mr. Adedoyin had attempted to attract attention to himself by proposing unsuccessfully that the contribution to the endowment fund should be doubled).

On the third day, having unanimously welcomed the Secretary of State's invitation to attend a Conference of African delegations later this year in London, the Council debated a motion put down by Dr. Azikiwe condemning 'any attempt to create ill-will among the various communities of this country'. The motion was supported from all parts of the Council and Dr. Azikiwe accepted with fairly good grace an amendment proposed by an Eastern member to substitute the word 'in' for 'of'. The Zik papers are of course the main instigators of ill-will against the white communities in Nigeria and the other unofficial members enjoyed putting him in the position of having to support the neat change proposed. Later in the morning a more important debate began on a motion put down by Eastern members seeking permission to introduce a Bill to enable the Courts to make maintenance orders for illegitimate children. The debate was important since it brought the East and the North into direct conflict.

The Northern members, backed by Moslem public opinion, were opposed to the Bill on religious grounds since under strict Moslem law the punishment for adultery is death and to provide by law for the maintenance of illegitimate children might in their opinion tend to condone a crime which they regard as unpardonable. After an interesting debate in which it became clear that the permission of the Council to introduce the proposed legislation would not be obtained the motion was withdrawn. Another interesting division of opinion occurred on a Motion proposed by a Western member for leave to introduce a Bill to exclude all matters relating to the selection, appointment and deposition of Chiefs from the jurisdiction of the Courts. This Motion was carried by a majority of seventeen to ten (the official members abstaining). All the Northern members voted for the motion together with four from the West, one from the East and one from the Colony, the opponents being five from the East, three from Lagos and two from the West (including, rather surprisingly, the Oba of Benin). The day finished with the debate on Dr. Azikiwe's motion for payment of salaries of £600 a year to unofficial members which was later defeated by 35 votes to 5 (the official view being that while there might be a case for payment of increased allowances to members the time had not yet come for payment of salaries).

For the next week following the Financial Secretary's statement on the budget made on the 6th of March what is usually called the budget debate proceeded. In fact most of the speeches made little or no reference to the budget. The widest latitude has in the past been allowed during the debate on the second reading of the Appropriation Bill for members to speak on almost any question they wish. Unofficial members feel moreover that they are under some obligation to speak in the debate and in fact all of them spoke on this occasion. It is of course valuable for members to have an oppor-tunity from time to time to discuss all aspects of Government policy but to listen over a period of a week to nearly thirty set speeches on end on the widest variety of uncon-nected subjects is a wearisome business (Dr. Azikiwe created a new record by speak-ing for about three and a half hours). The existing system is open to objection on other grounds. It is the practice for official members to wait until all the unofficial members have spoken before they intervene and then to reply to any points raised which con-cern their Departments or spheres of activity. This arrangement leaves the initiative to the unofficial members and tends to put the officials on the defensive. Too often after listening to days of criticism and complaint the official members are content with short statements in almost an apologetic manner on a series of unconnected points. The general impression is exactly the one which we are striving to avoid and if the Government is to take a bold initiative, outlining future policy, putting forward new proposals and seeking to win the enthusiastic support of the Council and the imagi-nation of the public some better system must be devised. A great deal of the detailed discussion of minor points should be left to the Select Committee, separate debates should be arranged on prinicpal questions of departmental policy and there is much to be said for restricting the budget debate to discussion of major financial matters, leaving questions of general policy to a debate on the Governor's opening address.

On the 13th of March the Council went into Select Committee on the Estimates, which is composed of the Financial Secretary and all unofficial members of the Council. It emerged ten days later very much the worse for wear. For that ten days it sat from early in the morning often till late at night questioning Heads of Departments, raising matters of major policy and also examining the most trifling points—covering in fact the whole range of Government activities. Dr. Azikiwe in particular, who was probably the only member who had taken real care to study in advance departmental reports and estimates, raised all sorts of questions often only remotely related to particular items in the estimates. His long cross-examination of Departmental Heads at first made many of the other members extremely restive. The Financial Secretary reports, however, that his lead resulted in the other members taking a much closer interest in a wide variety of subjects than has previously been the case and there is no doubt that the Select Committee has given to all members a most useful understanding of Government's achievements, problems and difficulties. The fact that the estimates and substantial increases in taxation were in the end approved without any important amendment is sufficient tribute to the tact and patience shown by the Financial Secretary and the confidence which he has won amongst all the members of the Council.

Throughout the sittings of the Select Committee there were two main issues in which all members were particularly interested and on which there was a wide measure of agreement. The members were first of all specially concerned about black market prices and conditional sales (the disorders which had just taken place in the Gold Coast[1] were no doubt very much in their minds). They were also most anxious that in all departments of Government there should be an acceleration of the training and recruitment of Nigerians for higher posts. The appointment shortly afterwards of Commissions of Enquiry on those two matters, on each of which there is a Nigerian majority, has since shown them that the Government has given full weight to their representations on these two important questions.

The Council resumed on the 24th of March and having passed the Appropriation Bill proceeded to dispose of outstanding official and unofficial motions. Dr. Azikiwe was granted formal permission to introduce a number of Bills but could obtain little support for a motion calling for papers about the visit of the N.C.N.C. delegation to the Colonial Office. He failed to explain what papers he wished to be published and the motion was lost by 38 votes to 4.

Meanwhile a Select Committee had been sitting on the selection of the delegation to represent Nigeria at the London Conference to be held in September next and on the 24th of March the recommendations of the Select Committee were unanimously adopted by the Council. A separate report on this Select Committee has been made and it is sufficient here to record that the decision of the unofficial members taken by secret ballot was the source of bitter disappointment to Dr. Azikiwe who received only three votes as against seventeen for the Member for Calabar who was the elected member selected to join the delegation.

Although they were not debated it should also be recorded that the Third Lagos Member (Mr. Adedoyin) put forward at the last moment the following two important constitutional motions:—

> 'That this Honourable House recommends that the Executive Council of Nigeria should include Members elected from the African Unofficial Members of the Legislative Council and that such Members assisted by Technical Experts should be responsible to the said Legislative Council for Government Policy in matters affecting Land, Agriculture, Education, Transport, Health and Social Services with a view to affording Nigerians opportunity of

---

[1] This refers to the Accra riots of Feb-March 1948.

participating in the management of their own affairs and thereby according them a measure of Political Responsibility in fulfilment of the oft declared British Colonial Policy of training the Colonies for Self-Government.'

'That this Honourable House approves of the unity of Nigeria by federation of the various regions which should become autonomous in due course, and that the whole country be developed towards self-government on this federal basis.'

Mr. Adedoyin agreed to postpone debate on both these motions until a subsequent meeting of the Council. They will no doubt be discussed at the next meeting which it is hoped to hold in August.

The main business of this meeting of the Council was of course to deal with the 1948/49 budget. This was done with thoroughness and with very little disagreement. The Bills taken to the Council were mainly uncontroversial and were passed without opposition. As for the legislative work accomplished the result can consequently be regarded as fully satisfactory. It was moreover a useful achievement to have secured the unanimous support of the Council for the statement of educational policy drawn up by the Director of Education and for the grants to the new University College.

In other ways the meeting can also be counted a success. The new constitution is still in its early stages and there is, I think, little doubt that many of the Northern members, and some from the West too, entered the Kaduna meeting with misgivings and anxieties.

The Northerners felt that there was some danger of being outvoted by the Southerners and being thus saddled with legislation contrary to Northern principles and susceptibilities. The Obas of the West were still a little uneasy at sitting with commoners. There were general doubts about what might result from the elected Lagos members taking their seats for the first time. My own impression was that by the time the meeting ended there was on all sides a realisation that effective work had been done and that the experiment of bringing representatives of all sections of the population into one legislative assembly had been well justified by results. Such animosities as had come to the surface during the debates—in particular the attacks on Dr. Azikiwe by the Second Northern member—were expressed in the best parliamentary manner. All members appeared to realise that the long hours of discussion—including particularly the gruelling work in Select Committee—had been well worthwhile. Even the elected Lagos members, in spite of the rebuff which they received in the selection of the London delegation, enjoyed the opportunities for unrestricted oratory, of which they took full advantage. Dr. Azikiwe in particular was at great pains to study his subjects and to adopt throughout a reasonable approach which did not fail to make some impression on the other members. I think that it can be said that the second meeting of the new Legislative Council has done much to consolidate the marked success which has already been achieved by the new Regional Houses.

There was another result of major importance which emerged from the meeting. It became clear as the debates proceeded that, while the experiment of bringing representatives of all the Regions together in the Legislative Council can and will lead to a growing appreciation of the needs of Nigeria as a whole, there is, on the other hand, a determination on the part of each Regional bloc to ensure that the internal interests of the Region it represents shall not be overriden by a majority opinion from outside. A strong tendency became apparent for each Region to express its wish to develop in its own way, and to allow the other Regions to pursue their own internal policies, unimpeded by outside interference. The Northern Emirs and Mallams want to be quite sure that the Moslem traditions of the North will not be disturbed, the Eastern members hope to see in their Region all sorts of reforms based on new ideas, the Western leaders wish to progress within the framework of the aristocratic system to which they are accustomed. The undoubted success which has been achieved by the united central legislature is accompanied by a new sense of Regional self-respect and a determination on the part of each Region not to allow unity at the centre to break down the strong and increasing determination of each Region to order its own internal affairs as it wishes. The trend of the debates in fact indicated that the thinking leaders of Nigeria are moving rapidly to the conception of a federal state. As the authority of the single bureaucratic government gives way to a more democratic system it becomes increasingly clear that a country of the size of Nigeria with its widely differing races must in future draw its strength not from power originating from the centre but from separate racial divisions, rooted in their own diverse traditions and developing in different ways, being at the same time prepared to send their representatives to meet together with mutual respect for the direction of those affairs which must be decided for the whole.

48   CO 583/287/4, no 4   3 June 1948
[Egbe Omo Oduduwa]: letter from H M Foot to L H Gorsuch on the formation of the Egbe Omo Oduduwa. *Enclosure*

Thank you for your letter No. 30453/3/48 of the 28th of May sending me a cutting from the 'Times' about the launching of 'a great Yoruba national movement'. You may now have seen our political summary for March–April on page 13 of which mention was made of the progress of the Egbe Omo Oduodwa which is the organisation to which the 'Times' report refers (I attach an extract from the summary).

It is true that the Egbe Omo Oduduwa has been rather more active lately and has been raising funds for scholarships. (Its leaders have up to now been at pains to explain that it is a non-political organisation). It has also, as the 'Times' says, arranged a rally at Ile-Ife to take place early this month. The correspondent who sent the report published in the 'Times' is however obviously a keen supporter of the Egbe and has allowed his party enthusiasm to run away with him. I do not myself think that we can look to the existing Yoruba leaders to start 'a great national movement' and I should feel rather more enthusiastic about their activities if there was more evidence that they have new and constructive ideas rather than merely a policy of opposition to Ibos and retention of their own influential positions.[1]

We shall send you a separate note about the Egbe in a week or two.

---

[1] Foot's concerns were echoed by Macpherson, 'While I warmly welcome increased social and political activity in the Western Provinces, I am very much concerned about the growth of ill-feeling between the Yorubas and the Ibos and I am inclined to think . . . that the Society is mainly concerned with resistance to Zik and the Ibos rather than with a constructive programme. It is, however, too early to say whether the Society will, in fact, make any useful contribution to progress among the Yorubas. It has certainly been very active in the past few months and in its resistance to the Ibos, if in little else, it can claim considerable success' (Macpherson to Creech Jones, 19 June 1948, CO 583/287/4, no 5)

Enclosure to 48

Other political moves

The Egbe Omo Oduduwa has continued to make slow, but undoubtedly steady progress. Numerous branches have been inaugurated throughout the Western Provinces, several among Yoruba communities in the North and one even at Abakaliki in the East. Although they continue to declare that their purpose is to unite all Yorubas and that their movement is not aimed against any other tribal group, the fact remains that their object is to combat the 'Ibo menace' and to break Azikiwe. They realise that the cause will be lost if Zik succeeds in his attempt to win over the North and so apprehensive were they of the possible effect of his activities in LegCo and at his Convention and Assembly, that they sent off Bode Thomas[2] and H.O.Davies[3] hot foot to the North to try to counteract his propaganda there. They did nothing very spectacular, though they are reported to have found warm support at the few public meetings they held. These, however, were attended for the most part by Yorubas and cannot be taken as any indication of the extent to which they were able to influence true Northerners, but it is reported that much of their time was taken up quietly visiting Northern men of influence, and that they were received with a considerable amount of sympathy. There is little prospect of the Egbe doing anything notable in the immediate future. They realise that they have no outstanding leader. and that, except for the 'Ibo menace', which they are not prepared to use openly, they have no plank in their platform which the N.C.N.C. have not already got in theirs. Their present policy, therefore, is to consolidate their organisation, to find a leader and start grooming him and to lie low until the Lagos Town Council and LegCo elections in 1950. They hope then to be able to come forward as a party with a programme based on whatever issues are the subject of public controversy at that time and make an all-out drive to capture all the vacant seats. It is idle to speculate on their chances of successfully carrying out their programme for, on past showing, the prospects of any Lagos political party adopting a programme and sticking to it for any length of time are exceedingly remote.

---

[2] Chief Bode Thomas, founding member and deputy leader of the AG; Federal minister of transport, 1952–1953.
[3] Hezekiah Oladipo Davies, teacher and barrister, founder and later chairman of NYM; president and secretary-general of WASU, legal adviser to *Egbe Omo Oduduwa*; QC 1958.

49   CO 583/287/5, no 2   28 June 1948
[Watson Commission]: letter from Sir J Macpherson to A B Cohen on the likely impact on Nigeria of the Watson Commission's Report

[The Commission of Inquiry under Aiken Watson was appointed following the Gold Coast riots of Feb–March 1948. Its report was published in June, *Report of the Commission of Enquiry into Disturbances in the Gold Coast, 1948*, col. No. 231 (see BDEEP series B, vol 1, R Rathbone, ed, *Ghana*, part I, 33, 34, 35, 36) and generated concern in the administration over the likely response in Nigeria. In the event the publication of the report did not cause the anticipated unrest elsewhere in West Africa.]

Many thanks for your secret and personal letter of the 12th of June with which you sent me a copy of the Gold Coast Commission's report. I am extremely glad to have to this so quickly. Gerald Creasy received his copy just as he was leaving the Gold Coast to visit us; he finished reading it while he was here and passed on to me the main findings and recommendations.

There will certainly be lively reactions in Nigeria to the report, and as you say, it is the proposals for constitutional advance that will arouse particular interest. My first thought is that it will be assumed here, as well as in the Gold Coast, that any constitutional advance that follows upon the proposals of the commission has been achieved as a direct result of disorder; this assumption will do great harm in leading colonial peoples to believe that advance is more certainly and more speedily achieved by violence than by constitutional means. Apart from the encouragement given to political extremists throughout West Africa the proposals in the report will cause serious misgivings amonst those in Nigeria (particularly in the North and West) who wish to see advance along different lines.

The timing of the report is very unfortunate for us in Nigeria. *So far* the new team has been given a very fair run by the extremist politicians and Zik told me the other day that, as far as the N.C.N.C. was concerned, this was the result of a considered decision, taken at the time of his Kaduna Convention, not to embarrass the new regime; hence their quiescence since my arrival. He added that he was being pressed by some of his more hot-headed supporters to take up the fight and admitted that his position was difficult. I expressed understanding of his dilemma! I think that there is some truth in what he said (although I discount the complimentary utterances that went with it) but principally I think he is puzzled and uncertain about his next course of action. The publication of the Gold Coast report may clarify his doubts and uncertainties.

On my month's tour of the country I moved too fast to get more than a superficial knowledge of how things were going, but even so I found much to be pleased about in the growing understanding and appreciation of the true purpose of the new Constitution. In some places the Native Authorities (up to Divisional level) said that they would not bother me with a lot of demands and problems, not merely because my visit was short and made for the purpose of getting to know folks, but because they already had their proper channel for the ventilation of these matters in the House of Assembly. And I met Provincial members of the Houses of Assembly (in the East and West) who had been having meetings with Provincial Committees at which matters of Regional or Provincial interest were discussed. Given time, and with flexibility on our part, the thing will work.

The press were gentle with me in regard to my 'defence' (really explanation) of the Constitution in speeches I had to make on tour, and at a Press Conference which I held immediately after my return I had to make it quite clear that I was putting no new interpretation on the Constitution; nothing that I had said was other than uppermost in the mind of its framer. I let it be understood that I wanted the Constitution to be given a fair and full trial, and that I had no intention of suggesting any major changes ahead of our timetable for review and modification. That was before I knew how high wide and handsome the Gold Coast Commission would be.

The recommendation of the Commission that will be most eagerly taken up is, of course, that relating to the Executive Council or Board of Ministers responsible to the Assembly. As you know, I am not satisfied with my Executive Council as now constituted; it is largely official and 'rubber stamp', and deals principally with death sentences and with draft legislation at a late stage in its preparation. Apart from the lack of unofficials the Chief Commissioners can seldom attend and I can get little or no advice from the Provinces. If Nigeria were a territory of normal size with a fairly homogeneous population I should probably already have been considering the conversion of Executive Council into a body for the formulation of policy. But the distances make it very difficult to contemplate frequent meetings (once or twice a week) of a truly representative body, though Zik would probably urge—following the Gold Coast Commission's proposal—that the members should be salaried full-time Ministers. (This would lend force to the objections to Emirs and Chiefs playing a full part on representative bodies). And even if we could get over the geographical hurdle the important consideration remains that we are trying to build up in the Regions so that, without destroying the unity of the whole, they can develop according to their own traditions and social patterns. We are in fact moving towards a federal system, by a gradual devolution from the centre.

To encourage this process of building up confidence in the Regions Hoskyns-Abrahall is beginning, with my full approval, to have informal committees—not statutory committees—in which the unofficial members of the Western House of Assembly are associated with Heads of Departments, or Regional Deputies, in considering various groups of activities. In the Eastern Provinces Carr is on very excellent terms with his unofficial members and freely discusses with them matters of policy which are not ripe for anything but confidential discussion. The members take great satisfaction in this and there has been no case of any breach of confidence. Thompstone too has informal meetings from time to time with members of the Northern House of Assembly and House of Chiefs to discuss general questions of policy. Here in Lagos I have just started a new arrangement whereby I can, without reducing the build-up in the regions, have friendly talks with the members of Finance Committee. To ensure that the work is not all carried out by the Lagos nucleus Savage brings in the up-country members on a roster, and we have now arranged that after the Committee has disposed of its formal business the members should meet with me in Government House for general discussion of matters affecting the country. We had our first of these meetings last week and I think the members appreciated the arrangement. These tender little shoots are likely to be shrivelled by the hot wind of clamour for spectacular constitutional advance.

It is not only the Executive Council proposals of the Commission that are unsuitable for Nigeria. The Commission proposes that the Regional Councils in the Gold Coast should be *local government* bodies, equivalent to County Councils, whereas in Nigeria our Regional Houses are part of our legislative organization, providing the basis for a federal system. This essential difference is not likely, however, to affect the attitude of the N.C.N.C. which will no doubt use the Gold Coast proposals as an additional argument for a system of ministerial responsibility at the centre.

I have referred earlier in this letter to the N.C.N.C's attitude towards the Emirs and Chiefs. The Commission made no immediate recommendation regarding the future position of the Gold Coast Chiefs but they gave a lot of space to the criticisms made by Africans with a modern political outlook, and they did not contemplate the retention of the Gold Coast Chiefs otherwise than 'in a form which is a pale reflection of the past'. This will upset our traditional elements and encourage the extremists; and the result will not be conducive to sound progress.

At a first reading I do not think that, apart from the Constitutional proposals, there is much in the report that will cause strong reaction in Nigeria. (We are engaged in action on Nigerianisation of the Senior Service[1] and on conditional sales. Our P.R.O. is good. And we have agreed to a swollen shoot rehabilitation subsidy which, though under criticism, is equal to the upper limit proposed by the Commission for the Gold Coast).

The real question is what action we should take as a result of the report. I shall not attempt in this letter to deal fully with that. The Chief Commissioners are coming to Lagos about the 9th of July and we shall consider the matter very carefully. Meantime I reject of course, any idea of adding new members to Executive Council in a hurry. We *may* have to alter our time-table for revision of the Constitution but even if that were decided I should be averse from making any statement of our intention in advance of publication of the Gold Coast report. Our next Legislative Council meeting will begin about the 17th of August and the question of appointing embryo ministers will in any case come up at that meeting (on a motion by Adedoyin —see my recent letter to you about a proposal to add Phillipson to Executive Council). We *might* avoid being put completely on the defensive by making a statement at the opening of the meeting. The N.C.N.C. will not have had much time to digest the report.

In any case I shall let you have my further thoughts after discussion with the Chief Commissioners, and you will no doubt keep me posted about the action proposed in the Gold Coast, following your discussions with Gerald Creasy, to whom I am sending a copy of this letter.

---

[1] The commission led by H M Foot, the chief secretary, was appointed in May 1948 to examine the recruitment and training of Nigerians for senior posts in the civil service. It reported in August 1948 and recommended that no non-Nigerian should be recruited for any government post except where no qualified Nigerian was available; that public service boards should be established to select staff, and that 385 scholarships should be established for training candidates over the subsequent three years, *Report of the Commission appointed to make Recommendations about the Recruitment and Training of Nigerians for Senior Posts in the Government Service of Nigeria* (Lagos, 1948).

50   CO 583/299/1, no 1A   29 June 1948
[Local government reform]: inward savingram no 990 from Sir J Macpherson to A B Cohen on local government reform in the Eastern Provinces

[Creech Jones's renowned despatch of 25 Feb 1947 on local government reform in the African territories (see BDEEP Series A, vol 1, R Hyam, ed, *The Labour government and the end of empire 1945–1951*, Part I, 44) was followed by a further despatch of 13 Jan 1948 (see BDEEP series B, vol 1, R Rathbone, ed, *Ghana*, part I, 20), urging an increase in the elective element at this level. In Nigeria it was the Eastern provinces that led the way in this process, with moves by the administration to initiate local government reform through the appointment of a select committee of the Eastern House of Assembly. The select committee reported on proposals for local government reform in Aug 1948. The importance of these local government reforms and the fact that the Eastern House drew them up, was stressed by Foot, 'We certainly appreciate how tremendously important it is that we should win and keep the initiative and I believe that in very many important directions we now have it' (CO 583/299/1, no 9, Foot to Cohen, 9 Sept 1948).]

Since you heard from Gibbons about the proposals for local Government reform in the Eastern Provinces he has written his report and I have fully discussed the whole question with Carr in Enugu. We think that some important modification of the proposals first put forward from the Eastern Provinces is necessary. In particular I am satisfied that it is essential that the new system when it is introduced should not replace subordinate Native Authorities but incorporate them. Carr and Gibbons now agree that the existing Native Authorities should not be scrapped as was first proposed but should be retained as authorities subordinate to the proposed new County Councils. The importance of having a small unit similar to Parish Councils in England needs no emphasis from me and it would, I am sure, be a great mistake to abandon the Authorities of this kind which we already have. Subject to that main modification I have already reached the conclusion that it is necessary to introduce local government reform in the Eastern Provinces on the general lines which Gibbons explained to you.

2.   You should also know that the other Chief Commissioners are disturbed by these proposals and feel that to introduce a new system in the East will prejudice the gradual process (which they are trying to accelerate) of making the Northern and Western Native Authorities more democratic. I am to discuss the whole question again with Chief Commissioners next month but while I have given full weight to the views of the North and the West I feel quite sure that progress in the East on the lines which the East wishes should not be held up.

3.   The Eastern House of Assembly is to meet towards the end of July, and I shall be most grateful if you will let me know soon if you agree that the Chief Commissioner should then make a public statement foreshadowing the reforms proposed. When ample time has been allowed for the Eastern House and the public to express their views legislation will be drafted and will of course be forwarded to the Colonial Office allowing ample time for detailed consideration before it is published here.

51   CO 583/286/5, no 102   13 July 1948
[Constitutional review]: inward telegram no 889 from Sir J Macpherson to Mr Creech Jones outlining his plans to review the constitution

[Macpherson arrived in Nigeria in April 1948. He faced a situation that, because of the ramifications of the Accra riots in the Gold Coast in Feb and Mar, was causing concern amongst officials (see 49). Shortly after his arrival the new governor began consultations within the administration about the need to review the constitution; this document concerns the outcome of these consultations. On 17 Aug 1948 Macpherson announced to the Legislative Council that the process of drawing up a new constitution would begin. See 65.]

I have now been able to hold a full discussion with the Chief Commissioners to review the progress made under the new Constitution and to consider what future course should be followed in the constitutional advance. We have taken into special account the repercussions likely to be caused in Nigeria by the publication of the report of the Gold Coast Commission at the end of this month.[1]

---

[1] Report of the Watson Commission, see 49.

2.   After only a few months in the country, I myself am not yet able to speak with full confidence on these matters, but during an extensive tour I have had good opportunity of hearing both official and unofficial opinion in many areas and from many different sources, and the proposals which I now wish to put forward are wholeheartedly supported by the three Chief Commissioners and my other advisers.

3.   There are two outstanding factors which have impressed me.

Firstly, the new Constitution in spite of early criticism and misunderstanding, has got away to a first rate start and has in fact been more widely appreciated and accepted than even those who created it could have hoped. Secondly, there has been remarkable move of opinion in all regions in favour of a policy of regional autonomy within a Federal State. The regions above all else (?gp omitted) to develop and advance in their own ways and they have been quick to realise that Regional Houses (although their functions are as yet purely advisory) provide the best medium for effective participation in the management of their own affairs, and at the same time the best safeguard for their regional interests and traditions. It must be added that although move towards regional autonomy mainly arises from a healthy urge towards a greater measure of self-Government, it has also been reinforced by a marked (? increase in) tribal ill-feeling.

4.   These developments would I believe have enabled me in any event to make proposals to you for constitutional changes to be introduced within the next few years, but I should have preferred to delay doing so for some little time to come. The forthcoming publication of Gold Coast Report and repercussions which will result here have, however, made it necessary for us to review the whole question of the course and pace to be followed in Nigeria as a matter of urgency.

5.   It must be emphasised that constitutional recommendations in the Gold Coast Report would be quite unsuitable for the very different circumstances of Nigeria. The first main difference is that Regional Councils proposed for the Gold Coast are Local Government Agencies, whereas in Nigeria the Regional Houses are legislative bodies. The second factor is that in Nigeria the association of representatives of the people with making of the policy and executive government must, I consider, be built up in regions before we can expect to create truly representative executive body at the centre. Such differences will be very well recognised by all responsible political opinion here, but we can be sure that those local extremists whose main aim is a quick transference of power to themselves will overlook them and shout for the same reforms here as those recommended for Gold Coast. That being so, I regard it as of the utmost importance for the Government to keep the initiative and take whatever action is possible to prevent an agitation which might do greatest harm to sound constitutional progress of the country.

6.   With these factors in mind I put forward this proposal for conservation[sic]. In my address to the Legislative Council when it assembles on 17th August I propose to make a statement on the following lines:—

(a) I have now had time to see something of the constitutions system in force in the Country and to appreciate rapid and sound progress which has already been made.

(b) I have come to the conclusion that we should review the timetable already proposed (that new Constitution should remain in force for 9 years, limit[ed] changes only being made at the end of 3 and 6 years-see paragraph 26 of Lord Milverton's despatch of 6th December, 1944)[2] and consider generally what changes should be made and whether they should be made earlier than at first suggested.

(c) I accordingly propose that if it is the wish of the Council and Country that earlier changes should be made, they should be introduced not at the end of 9 years but in the second 3 year period (we are halfway through the first at present).

(d) Before any change is made it is of the utmost importance to allow time for expression of public opinion and if Council agrees I propose, after a period has been allowed for preliminary public discussion, to set up a Select Committee composed of all unofficial members (and one or two officials) following budget session next year to review the whole position and make recommendations. *Ends.*

I do not expect such a course would kill extremists but it would, I believe, convince more responsible opinion in all parts of the Country that the Government is anxious to encourage constitutional advance in the way the people wish as fast as can reasonably be expected. At the same time, it would be plain to the more moderate political leaders who can speak for the bulk of the people and who would regard a hasty shifting of power at the centre in the present circumstances as a disaster, that no (? precipitated) [sic] change is intended.

7.   I have set out these important proposals in this brief form so that you may be aware of them while you have the Gold Coast Report under consideration. It will be most helpful if you can inform me as soon as possible whether you agree with general line which I propose to take. *Ends.*

---

[2] See 7.

52   CO 583/287/4, no 8   26 July 1948
[Yoruba-Igbo relations]: inward telegram no 952 from Sir J Macpherson to Mr Creech Jones reporting the deterioration in ethnic relations in Lagos

[A concern for the administration in mid-1948 was the increased tension between Yoruba and Igbo inhabitants of Lagos, following the emergence of the *Egbe Omo Oduduwa*. This tension was exacerbated by a press war between Azikiwe's *West African Pilot* and the *Daily Service*. The Yoruba Federal Union was established by supporters of the NCNC in June 1948 in Lagos, in response to the formation of the *Egbe Omo Oduduwa* and was followed in Dec by the formal launch at Aba of the Ibo State Union, with Azikiwe as president. Macpherson held secret meetings with both Azikiwe and Sir A Alakija to try to calm feelings in Lagos. This tension was one of the factors that underpinned the emergence of the AG.]

I think you should know that during the past few weeks there has been a serious determination in the inter-tribal relations between the Yorubas and the Ibos, especially in Lagos. There has been a press battle between the Zik papers and the Yoruba 'Daily Service', with a great deal of personal abuse and washing of dirty linen, and feelings are running so high that danger of a physical clash cannot entirely be discounted.

2.   This exacerbation of an (?underlying) hostility dates from the time when the Ibos reacted sharply to the formation of Egbe Omo Oduduwa by attempting to

inspire the creation in opposition thereto of a Yoruba Federal Union.[1] See note by Field transmitted with my confidential savingram No. 947 of 19th June. Situation was not helped by the action of Onyeama, fifth Legislative Council member for the Eastern Region, who, after being baited (?by omitted) Yoruba acquaintances in the Island Club, signed a statement to the effect that 'The Ibo domination of Nigeria is merely a matter of time'. Facsimile of this was published in the 'Daily Service'.

3.   There is little to choose between the parties in this unpleasantness, but on the whole the Daily Service has been more aggressive. It has been carrying on a vicious campaign with the declared object of driving Azikiwe out of Lagos and out of politics. Zik press has replied by personal attacks by Zik himself on Nimbe and Adedoyin, his erstwhile lieutenants, and on other Yoruba leaders. Zik on his part is, I think, seriously worried by the harm these attacks are undoubtedly doing to his position, and his papers have demanded that the Government should put a stop to 'unprovoked aggression'. His Yoruba enemies are confident that if the Government remains neutral they can achieve their purpose.

4.   At a press Club dinner in my honour on 14th July I took the opportunity to refer to these polemics. I said that I had no wish or intention to interfere with the freedom of the press or to discourage frank discussions about matters of public interest, but I gave serious warning of the danger that the present controversy might lead to deterioration of relations between Nigerian races, and I made it abundantly clear that the Government was unalterably opposed to any action that might have this effect and which would retard progress towards self-government.

5.   Full publicity was given to my remarks, but each side has, of course, claimed that they were addressed to the other, and although responsible opinion is becoming alarmed there has been no improvement in the press war indeed it has worsened. I have just received report, which I accept with reservation, but cannot ignore, that the Yorubas propose to provoke disorder at lecture to be delivered in Lagos on 24th July by Jaja Wachukwu, one of Zik's more hot-headed supporters who has attacked Yorubas in previous speeches. Yoruba leaders to whom I spoke on 23rd July deny that anything of the sort is contemplated, but the possibility of a clash which may spread on this or some subsequent occasion cannot be discounted.

6.   All possible precautions will be taken to check any breach of the peace and I shall report further if trouble occurs.

---

[1] See 46 and 48.

53   CO 537/2787, no 4   3 Sept 1948
[Intelligence apparatus]: letter from Sir J Macpherson to Mr Creech Jones on reviewing the security and intelligence apparatus in Nigeria

Thank you very much for your letter of the 20th of August about security forces and information services. We are preparing a full reply to the circular despatch of the 5th of August to which you refer but in the meantime I write to say that the questions which you raise have been the subject of the most careful review here in recent months. In my despatch No. 37 of the 15th of July and in the full Note attached to that despatch we explained the new intelligence organisation which is being created here. We have not only expanded and improved the Special Branch of the Police but have created a system whereby in each Region there will be both an Administrative officer and a Police officer giving their whole time to intelligence work and corresponding direct with the Central Intelligence Committee here in Lagos at which representatives of the Administration, Police and the Military meet every week, and more often when necessary, to collate and review the intelligence reports coming in. We have an excellent Administrative officer in the Secretariat giving his whole time to this work. This new system to which I attach the greatest importance has only recently been started and we still have to overcome certain difficulties arising from shortage of staff but when I saw the Chief Comissioners a week or two ago I told them that I considered it to be a matter of first importance to ensure that the new system gets into its full stride as quickly as possible and every one concerned is co-operating fully to achieve this.

We have at the same time been reviewing our Police strength while discussions have been proceeding about the strength of the military forces to be maintained in West Africa in the future. In Lagos itself, where trouble is most likely to originate, the Police are in good strength and very much on their toes in readiness to deal with any disorder which may occur. The numbers of Nigeria Police in the town centres elsewhere are, however, small and as you know in large areas of the country, particularly in the North, we rely principally on the Native Administration Police. We are considering a substantial addition to the numbers of the Nigeria Police in order to provide striking forces in different parts of the country available to deal immediately with any trouble which may arise.

It has been of the greatest assistance to us in the past week to have a full discussion with Rees-Williams on these matters.[1] He has illustrated to us by recent experience in other territories how vitally important these questions of security forces and intelligence services are and we shall certainly make quite sure that we follow up the steps already taken to ensure that our organisation is kept at the highest possible state of efficiency.

We warmly welcome the proposal to appoint a Police Adviser in the Colonial Office and look forward to co-operating with him in the ways which you propose.

---

[1] D R Rees-Williams, parliamentary under-secretary of state.

54 CO 583/287/4, no 20   4 Oct 1948
[Inter-tribal tension]: inward telegram no 1375 from Sir J Macpherson to Mr Creech Jones on the easing of Yoruba–Igbo tension in Lagos

My telegram No. 1186, Inter tribal tension and Your telegram No. 1106, Executive Council.

Although tension in Lagos has eased somewhat during September, the press still continues policy of mutual abuse of leaders and, as attacks on Azikiwe are regarded by the Ibos as attacks on the Ibo tribe while attacks on leaders of Egbe Omo Oduduwa are similarly regarded by the Yorubas, tribal feeling still, runs high and danger of a clash in Lagos is, by no means past.[1]

2.   In the meanwhile, these antagonisms have spread to parts of the Provinces and danger of repercussions in the Provinces (? leading omitted) to a clash in Lagos is now greater than before.

3.   A complicating factor is the changed attitude of the N.C.N.C. which has now openly declared its intention of attacking the Government which it claims to believe is secretly supporting the Egbe Omo Oduduwa in pursuance of a prearranged policy of 'Pakistanism'.

4.   As reported in my savingram No. 1280, Zik's press has been and still continues to run vigourous campaign for removal of Alakija[2] from Exco[3] and has hinted that Egbe Omo Oduaduwa receives its secret instructions from Government through Alakija who himself gets them in Exco.

5.   In these circumstances, announcement of Alakija's reappointment to Exco at present moment would almost certainly be taken by many as proof that Zik's interpretation of Government policy is correct and might encourage further animosity leading to possible tribal clash in Lagos with serious consequence in Provinces. I have, therefore, decided to postpone announcement and am holding consultation with my advisers including Chief Commissioners on 4th October. I will address you further in the light of conclusions then reached.

---

[1] See 52.
[2] Sir Adeyemo Alakija, KBE 1945; called to the Bar 1913; member of Legislative Council, 1933–1941; member of the Executive Council, 1943; founder of the *Daily Times*; president of *Egbe Omo Oduduwa*, 1948.
[3] ie the Executive Council.

55   CO 583/287/4, no 25   10 Oct 1948

[Inter-tribal tension]: inward savingram no 52340 (sic) from Sir J Macpherson to Mr Creech Jones on his attempts at a rapprochement within the Nigerian press

My telegram No. 1375, Inter-tribal tension. I am sorry that this further report has been delayed. After very full discussion with my advisers, including Chief Commissioners, I decided to try personal intervention and events have been moving rather fast.

2.   The danger is, of course, inter-tribal strife but in my telegram under reference I did not make sufficiently clear the perfection of the dilemma presented by the question of Executive Council membership. I referred to the obvious reactions of the National Council of Nigeria and the Cameroons to the reappointment of Alakija, but on the other hand, as you will realise a decision not to renew his appointment would be likely to impair confidence in the North and West. I had in mind a further statement by Government, part warning and part appeal to all men of good will, but any appeal coincident with action regarded as inimical to one side or the other would have been abortive.

3.   At the meeting with my advisers in Lagos on 1st October, including District Commander and Commissioner of Police, we discussed the whole situation in the

light of developments that had occurred during my two weeks absence from Lagos on tour ending on 30th September (see paras. 12–17 of Nigerian Political Summary No. 26). Everyone was in favour of my proposal to make a personal approach to both sides. I decided to call Chief Commissioners to Lagos for discussion on 4th October and in the meantime to invite Alakija and Azikiwe to meet me separately in the hope that I might be able to gauge their attitude towards a possible peace move. I saw Azikiwe that evening and Alakija on 2nd October.

4.   Azikiwe was very reasonable. I explained afresh Government's attitude to the dispute and the reasons why we had not so far intervened more vigorously. I made it quite clear that I was not at all disturbed by the fact that Government was being criticised but that I was seriously disturbed by reports from parts of the Provinces which indicated that the Lagos quarrels which were not understood up country were nevertheless likely to lead to inter-tribal strife with a consequent terrible set-back to the country. I said that I was considering a more direct approach and asked whether in his opinion anything could be done to prevent strife and whether there was any chance of Government effecting a rapprochment.

5.   Azikiwe thanked me for speaking so frankly to him and assured me that he and the responsible elements close to him had full confidence in the 'new regime'. He also had hot-heads in his party, however, and they wanted action. He agreed that nothing but harm could result from the present quarrels and made no attempt to suggest that the faults were all on one side. He thought that a further Government statement would be useful; it might point out that Government had been very tolerant but that licence was becoming licentiousness and that hereafter stern action would be taken against either side if it continued its incitement. He did not despair of good results from an attempt at a rapprochment.

6.   I put the same arguments to Alakija but additionally I explained frankly to him the difficulty presented by his reappointment to Executive Council while tempers on both sides are so hot. (He had been sounded by Savage[1] at my request during my absence on tour and agreed to his name going forward.) He was less willing to face realities than Azikiwe (and unlike Azikiwe he has disclosed what transpired at my private meeting with him) but he too thought that a statement might help, and equally he did not entirely reject the possibility of a peace move.

7.   On 4th October I discussed the situation very fully with the Chief Commissioners and my other advisers. All agreed that the danger of a flare-up in the Provinces had increased and felt that the time had come for a further declaration of Government's position, if only to give confidence to the honest decent citizens who still form the great majority of the population. The terms of a Government statement —copy attached—were agreed. No satisfactory solution was seen to the dilemma presented by the problem of Executive Council membership. With concurrence of all advisers I decided to try to see Alakija and Azikiwe together. I also decided to postpone a final decision about Executive Council pending consultation with the Unofficial members of the Regional Houses. (It may be wise to add someone temporarily from the Eastern Provinces and Carr agreed that the unofficials there would almost certainly not wish to see Azikiwe appointed). Alakija is not much admired even in Yorubaland but he has become an issue and it is unlikely that the Western Provinces would wish any other Yoruba to be substituted for him. If general

---

[1] A W L Savage, financial secretary, 1948–1949.

situation can be improved Executive Council membership might become a little easier.

8.   I saw Alakija and Azikiwe together on 6th October, Savage, Acting Chief Secretary, being present. The discussion was encouraging. After covering same ground as in separate talks (without reference to Executive Council) I produced copies of the proposed Government statement. Both expressed satisfaction with its terms. It was agreed that it should be published forthwith and it appeared in the Press on 8th October. They also agreed that it was worth while having an informal meeting with both sides representative of the Press—i.e. Zik Press and Daily Service—to see whether we could by agreement decide to change the tone of the press controversy so as to leave out of it anything likely to exacerbate inter-tribal relations.

9.   This meeting took place on 9th October and there were present:—

(a) Alakija, Maja (Chairman of Board of Directors of Daily Service) Rotimi Williams[2] and Bode Thomas (Members of Board);
(b) Azikiwe, Blankson (Zik Press) Ojike[3] (late Editor of the Pilot) and Coker (present Editor of the Pilot).

I enclose a copy of my opening statement.[4] The meeting lasted for two hours and although there were some vigorous exchanges there appeared to be at one stage a real hope that both sides would agree to cut out anything likely to create or intensify inter-tribal animosity. Unfortunately Ojike who is a real rabble-rouser was at times abusive and offensive. I believe that he wanted to wreck the proceedings and Azikiwe who was I believe seriously unhappy about this could not completely quell him. The discussion was primarily directed to the conduct of the press. We did not get as far as a mutual self-denying ordinance but both sides favoured action as follows in any future cases where press stories appear making allegations against Ibos or Yorubas. The matter should be investigated and thereafter the parties should be called together and the facts disclosed. If the story is proved to be without foundation the offending paper will publish a correction. I was prepared to agree to this without prejudice to immediate prosecution if this seemed to be warranted.

10.   It was left that nothing should be published about the meeting but that both sides should have consultations and report back on 15th October whether they were in favour of resuming discussion, probably with wider representation.

11.   It had occurred to me that reference in Government statement to possibility of introducing measures to control press might be embarrassing to you and that I should have consulted you before publication. I will say only:—

(i) time was pressing;
(ii) both sides agreed with the statement;
(iii) the statement refers to 'seeking' powers which means reference to Regional Houses and Legislative Council (if necessary at emergency meetings). To introduce press control otherwise would mean first declaring a state of emergency, and we hope that conditions will never justify this.

---

[2] Rotimi Alade Williams, barrister and leading member of the AG, attorney-general and minister of justice in the Western Regional government.
[3] M M Ojike, Eastern Region minister of finance, 1954.   [4] Not printed.

12.   Azikiwe is a very difficult person to assess. He wants power and I believe that he tried hard at March meeting of Legislative Council to work towards achieving this by constitutional route. He was then eliminated from delegation to London Conference as a result of most unwise ganging-up against him by traditional elements amongst unofficial members. Even after that he stayed his hand but at the urging of his wild men he might be tempted to throw caution to the winds and try to come to power through chaos. I believe that there is good in him and that the good part at least would genuinely like to cooperate with Government. He is knowledgable and useful as a member of Finance Committee. As regards the Yorubas, the Egbe Omo Oduduwa was, I believe, formed to wake the Yorubas from their lethargy; to create an enlightened ethnic group which could play its part in the new Constitution and resist being swamped by the more vigorous Ibos. This was very reasonable but unfortunately the creation of this body gave rise to controversy, in part because it challenged the position of the N.C.N.C., and in part because there are some irresponsible young hot-heads amongst the Yorubas in Lagos who thought that by vicious attacks in the 'Daily Service' they could drive Azikiwe out of Lagos and back to Iboland. If it came to a show-down my assessment is that the opponents of Azikiwe and the N.C.N.C. would 'go to bush' and Government would be left in direct conflict with the N.C.N.C. who could create all sorts of trouble throughout the country. Whatever one may think of Azikiwe he is a force to be reckoned with and I am determined not to drive him into violent opposition. Whether we can harness him to good use remains to be seen.

13.   Although I am not able to report real success I have at least brought the parties together for discussion and I have made Government's attitude quite clear. Even if the attempt fails we shall be in a stronger position when the lines are drawn for battle and we have to take such stern action as may be necessary.

56   CO 583/299/1, no 20   22 Oct 1948
[Local government reform]: CO record of the second meeting of the Colonial Local Government Advisory Panel   [Extract]

As requested by the Government of Nigeria, the Panel met to allow Sir Bernard Carr,[1] and Brigadier Gibbons[2] to consult it regarding proposals for the reorganisation of local government in the Eastern Region contained in 'The Report on Local Government Reform' and 'Report of a Select Committee of the Eastern Region House of Assembly set up to review the existing system of Local Government in the Eastern Provinces', (Circulated under cover of C.L.G.A.P. (48) 3).[3]

Sir Bernard Carr sketched the history of local administration in the Eastern Provinces. At first a policy of direct rule through 'Warrant Chiefs' was applied, but the Aba riot in 1929 discredited them. This was followed by an attempt to apply the principles of indirect rule on the Northern Provinces model, using, in the absence of

---

[1] Colonial Service, Nigeria, from 1919; chief commissioner, 1943.
[2] E J Gibbons, Colonial Service, Nigeria, from 1929; senior resident, 1947; author of *Administrative Reorganisation of the Colony Districts of Nigeria* (Sessional Paper No 9, 1939).
[3] See 50.

the institution of Chieftanship, mass collections of family heads gathered in unwieldy councils. In 1933 separate native treasuries were introduced and the councils assumed some degree of financial responsibility. The progressive literate Africans, however, continued to be excluded from the native authorities and formed 'Improvement Unions', often in opposition to them.

The proposed reorganisation of local government aimed to bring progressive Africans into the local authorities. To gain this end County Councils covering a population of the order of half a million, controlling an annual revenue of approximately £20,000, and consisting mainly of elected members would be set up. The existing Native Authority Councils, with some modification, would continue as authorities at a lower level, subordinate to the elected county councils. The lower councils would have no powers of their own, but County Councils would delegate work to them.

The Panel was uncertain as to the wisdom

(i) of placing too much power in the hands of the County Councils and leaving the subsidiary councils, which were closer to the people, without any powers, apart from those delegated by the County Councils;

(ii) of imposing so many duties on the Local Authorities and of such a kind that the Authorities could hardly discharge the otherwise than as agents of the Central Government.

English local government experience showed that County Councils were reluctant to delegate their powers to subordinate Councils. On the other hand it was pointed out that the wide powers at the disposal of County Councils would allow progressive Africans to stimulate and energise the local activities of the subsidiary Councils. The Panel felt that, although this may be necessary as a temporary measure, the ultimate structure should not be one in which the lower level authorities enjoyed only those powers which Country [sic] Councils were willing to delegate to them. Eventually the subsidiary councils should be granted a measure of independent authority in purely local matters and this aim should he kept constantly in mind. Otherwise the great majority of the people would not learn to govern themselves through local government, and power would be concentrated in the hands of the educated classes.

The Panel heartily endorsed the principle that in general urban and rural areas should be brought together in common local government [sic] had been made in separating rural from urban areas. In this way community of interests between town and country has been destroyed.

Regarding the proposed Local Government Board, the question was asked whether it would degenerate into a government department, or whether it would remain a really active and independent force representing local government and capable of standing up to the Central Government on behalf of the local authorities. It was explained that the aim was to place the regional direction of local government affairs in the hands of African literates by means of an unofficial African majority on the Board. The Board would control the unified local government service when established, co-ordinate bye-laws and rules made by various authorities and advise the Chief Commissioner, especially in relation to local government finance.

The Panel agreed in general that a unified local Government service was essential under present conditions, but some members felt that as a long term principle the idea was bad. The idea should be to make local government units employers of their own staffs, controlling and paying them.

There was some uncertainty as to whether a revenue of the order of £20,000 was sufficient to finance the activities of County Councils and it was suggested that the figure should be something nearer to £50,000 as a minimum.

The question was raised that if the membership of County Councils was restricted to 20 as proposed, it would be difficult to find enough members for the many Committees which would have to be set up, without overworking them.

The Panel was generally in favour of separating judicial from administrative functions and placing courts matters in the hands of the central government, rather than handing them over to local authorities.

The Governor of Nigeria had asked if one or two members of the Panel could visit the Colony to advise on the proposed reorganisation of local government in the Eastern Provinces and the new Municipal Authorities Bill. It was decided that until it was known more specifically on what points advice was needed, it would be impossible to decide which members, if any, should go.

57   CO 537/3557, no 6   Nov 1948

[Arrest of Zikist leaders]: despatch no 54 from Sir J Macpherson to Mr Creech Jones on the prosecution of leaders of the Zikist movement for sedition

[The Zikist movement that emerged in late 1945 and early 1946 put forward a radical critique of British rule in Nigeria, coupled with calls for militant action to gain independence. As its name suggests, its ideology was inspired by the ideas of Azikiwe, although he himself kept an ambivalent distance. Among its early leaders were Kola Balogun, M C K Ajuluchuku, Abiodun Abiola and Nduka Eze. In late 1948 it announced a positive action campaign against British rule, at the centre of which was the lecture by Osita Agwuna, 'A Call for Revolution' given in Lagos on 27 October. Three days later Agwuna and Anthony Enahoro, who had chaired the lecture, were arrested for sedition; this was followed by further arrests of Zikist leaders, including Raji Abdallah, Ralph Aniedobe and Fred Anyiam, in early Nov. They were tried in three separate trials during late 1948 and early 1949; one was acquitted while the remaining eight were found guilty of sedition and sentenced to fines and terms of imprisonment of up to two and a half years. See 66. The Zikist movement was banned by the government in Apr 1950.]

I have the honour to inform you that an honest difference of opinion has arisen between the Acting Attorney General (Mr. A. Ridehalgh) and myself on a matter of such importance that I feel it necessary to seek a ruling on it from you.

Briefly it arises from the considered opinion of Mr. Ridehalgh 'that the question of prosecuting in a case of sedition is one for decision by the Attorney General' and 'a matter within the exclusive province of the Attorney General' whereas I consider that where high political interests are involved the Governor, as being ultimately responsible for the maintenance of law and order, may intervene.

2. You will have learned from my secret Saving Telegram No. 1784 of the 10th November that it recently became necessary to institute proceedings against O.L. Agwuna,[1] Deputy Secretary General of the Zikist Movement, in connection with a speech he made in Lagos on the 27th October. The substance of this speech was reported to me on the following morning and I promptly agreed that a charge of

---

[1] Osita Agwuna, assistant editor of the *Daily Comet* and deputy president of the Zikist movement.

sedition should be laid. Later I learned that Tony Enahoro,[2] who had taken the chair at the meeting at which Agwuna had spoken, and two other persons who had taken part in the proceedings had also been charged. I was rather doubtful about the wisdom of instituting these further prosecutions in respect of a single speech but I was not aware of all the circumstances, and I thought it inappropriate that I should intervene.

3. It is necessary here to digress from the narrative and to give you my assessment of the present political situation. The Zikist Movement, of which the persons charged were all members, is composed of the more hotheaded followers of the National Council of Nigeria and the Cameroons and is a body which on many occasions has preached 'positive action'. How far the Zikist Movement takes its orders from the 'Cabinet' of the N.C.N.C. or from Dr. Azikiwe himself is largely a matter of conjecture. It is, however, known that certain members of the N.C.N.C. 'Cabinet' are much more inclined to violence than others, and there is some evidence to suggest that Dr. Azikiwe himself is not at present anxious to resort to violence. It has been reported, though the report may be inaccurate, that Dr. Azikiwe was aware of Agwuna's intention to deliver his speech but was strongly opposed to it and advised against it. Since I assumed office it has been a cardinal point of my policy not to drive Dr. Azikiwe into violent opposition, or to give him martyrdom. If Dr. Azikiwe decides that he can come to power only through violence and an attempt to create chaos I wish the decision to be clearly his. In that unfortunate event I should not hesitate to use the full rigour of the law against him, but as I have said I am most anxious that the decision to resort to violence, if it should be made, should come from Dr. Azikiwe himself and should not be induced by any precipitate or avoidable action of Government.

4. To revert now to the narrative. On the morning of the 4th November the Acting Attorney General informed the Chief Secretary that he had issued instructions for a search warrant to be obtained to search the premises of the 'West African Pilot' in connection with an article which had appeared on 27th October which purported to come from the Zikist Movement and was in fact a summary of parts of the lecture delivered by Agwuna later that day. The Chief Secretary immediately informed me of this development and at my request the Acting Attorney General agreed to postpone action until after I had had an opportunity to discuss the position with him and the Chief Secretary.

5. It will, I think, be fairest if I put the Acting Attorney General's views with regard to a possible charge against the 'West African Pilot' and its staff in his own words:—

'On 27th October I saw a copy of the West African Pilot, but, having interested myself in the objectional leading article on the new Court of Appeal I did not read further. The following day, after drafting a letter to the Editor about the leading article, I glanced through the rest of the paper and saw the article "Appeal to the People". I immediately formed the opinion that it was seditious, and I sought the opinion of Mr. Manyo-Plange, Senior C.C., which

---

[2] Anthony Eronsele Enahoro, journalist and editor; founding member of the AG; elected to Western House of Assembly and to House of Representatives in 1951; Western Region minister of home affairs, 1954; Western Region minister for mid-western affairs, 1957; AG spokesman on foreign affairs, 1959;

agreed with mine. At that time I had seen Mr. Finlay, Commissioner of Police, and had read a copy of the seditious speech which is now the subject of a criminal prosecution at my instance. I did not, however, connect the two at that stage.

'Having launched the proceedings in respect of the seditious speech. I turned my attention yesterday morning (4th November) to the seditious article (I had already come to the conclusion that proceedings should be taken in respect of it against Zik's Press Ltd., the printers and publishers, and one Coker, the Editor of the paper) and it was apparent that there was a connection between the "Appeal to the People" and the "Call for Revolution". I at once had an analysis made which shows that the former is a paraphrase of parts of the latter. I attach a copy of the analysis. I then decided that the proper procedure was to obtain a warrant to search the premises of Zik's Press Ltd., at 34 Commercial Avenue, Yaba, for seditious publications, and gave instructions to that end, reporting the action I proposed to Mr. Savage (Acting Chief Secretary). Later, I stayed action, at his request, until after the meeting at Government House, and I have since stayed police action until further instructions are given by me.

'My view of the whole matter being that there probably exists a treasonable or seditious conspiracy involving more persons than the four now charged, it is essential to search the premises at Yaba for evidence of that conspiracy, and also for further incriminating evidence in relation to the proposed prosecution in respect of the article. Incidentally, the occasion of the search would provide the opportunity to secure evidence as to who was the Editor of the Pilot on the 27th October. I should like to point out that a conspiracy to levy war against His Majesty is an offence punishable with death.'

6. At the discussion to which I have referred in my paragraph 4 above, which took place on the afternoon of the 4th November, I put before the Acting Attorney General my views with regard to the political situation and expressed the opinion that the search of the premises of the 'West African Pilot' at the present juncture might have most serious political consequences, and that it might well be the occasion which would finally decide Dr. Azikiwe to take his stand with those of his followers who were advocating violence. I need hardly point out that a campaign of violence led by Dr. Azikiwe would be likely to be far more serious than a similar campaign from which Dr. Azikiwe disassociated himself. In these circumstances I informed the Acting Attorney General that I had decided that the action which he proposed to take was undesirable but in order that it should be clear that I took full responsibility I asked him to submit his arguments on paper, when I would record my decision, (The Acting Attorney General later withdraw his instructions for the issue of a search warrant against the 'West African Pilot').

7. In accordance with the decision taken at the discussion the Acting Attorney General submitted his views. He contended that the assessment of a political situation was not a sufficient argument against the course of action he proposed to take as he considers it essential that

(i) the criminal law should be administered impartially;
(ii) the criminal law should be administered in its full rigour so as to demonstrate that it is no weak thing

(iii) the premises should be searched (under the authority of a search warrant) for incriminating evidence.

He then went on to examine the constitutional position of the Attorney General in relation to criminal prosecutions and again I think it will be fairest if I quote from his subsequent minute:—

'At this point, I refer to the constitutional position of the Attorney General. There can be no question that the institution and conduct of prosecutions in such criminal cases as come especially within his purview, is within his exclusive province: he is an officer of the executive, but in this sphere he acts in a judicial capacity *and should act without interference from the executive.* This principle was departed from in the famous case of the communist, Campbell, in 1924 when, after consideration in the Cabinet, the Attorney General (Sir Patrick Hastings, K.C., M.P.) gave instructions for the withdrawal of the prosecution, with the uproar and result we all know. It was, however, re-affirmed by Sir John (now Lord) Simon in the debate on the J. H. Thomas affair, and, I am glad to say, by the present Prime Minister and Mr. Chuter Ede as recently as last week in connection with the inquiry into the Board of Trades bribery allegations: see The Times 28th October, page 4, column 1 and 30th October, page 4, column 3. Dealing with the bearing of the inquiry on any criminal proceedings, Mr. Attlee said: "It may be that as a result of the inquiries now being conducted by the police under the direction of the Director of Public Prosecutions criminal proceedings are contemplated or may be fact be instituted. This is a matter within the exclusive province of the Attorney-General."

Mr. Chuter Ede, in reply to a question said: "I have no intention of being involved in a repetition of the Campbell case. It is not for me or for the Government to give any directions to the law officers of the Crown on the way in which they handle this case." Some authority is to be found for intervention by the executive in Berriedale Keith's Constitutional Law (7th Edn.) page 169, where he says:—

"It is clear that where high political interests are involved, the Cabinet may intervene, as responsible for the welfare of the realm though the action in the case in question (the Campbell case) was ill-advised, as may be seen from the resignation of the Ministry rather than face an investigation by a Select Committee."

This opinion is apparently based on the Campbell case, and I think that the better opinion is that the question of prosecuting in a case of sedition is one for decision by the Attorney-General. That, at all events, is my opinion, and, being one of principle, I am not prepared to depart from it.'

8. It clearly would not be right for me to question the legal advice given to me by my Acting Attorney General but you will, I think, agree that this matter raises a constitutional issue of the gravest importance. (Mr. Ridehalgh has asked that the enclosed note referring to certain provisions of the criminal code should be brought to your notice but in fact he had not drawn my attention to Section 65 (1) of the Criminal Code although its provisions do not alter the views expressed in this despatch).

I, as His Majesty's representative, am personally responsible for the order and good government of this territory and it appears to me in the highest degree undesirable that any officer serving under me should be in a position to take action which, in my opinion, may jeopardise the security of this territory. I fully appreciate how desirable it is that the law should take its course without fear or favour, but I submit that charges of sedition are essentially a political offence and that they must be viewed against the political background, and therefore that they should be instituted only with my consent.

You will be aware of the practice which existed in Palestine, India and other overseas territories where local conditions were or are not dissimilar to those obtaining in Nigeria. I know what the *practice* was in Palestine but not what the constitutional position is.

9.   I would add that this difference of opinion has in no way affected the friendly relations between the law officers and the executive and that Mr. Ridehalgh has agreed until such time as your decision is received to submit for my directions all cases in which he considers that action should be taken in connection with sedition.

10.   I should be grateful for an early reply.

58   CO 859/136/5, no 15   29 Nov 1948
[Mass education]: inward savingram no 1903 from Sir J Macpherson to Mr Creech Jones on the progress of adult education schemes in Nigeria

Your Savingram No. 1246 of 24th July, 1948.

Mass Education Movement.

The policy of this Government in regard to mass education was set out in paragraphs 4, 5 and 7 of Sir Arthur Richards' (now Lord Milverton's) despatch No. 203 of the 20th of August, 1947,[1] and the following observations thereon relate to the particular aspect of the problem raised in the supplementary question by Mr. Hughes.[2]

2.   As a result of the experience acquired in recent years it has been decided that assistance from the Adult Education vote can most usefully be given, firstly, by fostering in rural areas the creation of centres where instructors experienced in teaching adults are employed, and, secondly, by the production and distribution of low priced literature.

3.   In carrying out the policy laid down in the despatch under reference, it has not been the normal practice to pay instructors of adult classes. The organisations and agencies conducting such classes have, however, found that the most successful results are obtained through instructors who give regular service and that a small honorarium often achieves this end. In certain areas, therefore, the Education Department gives a small measure of financial assistance to those organisations and agencies that are served by competent instructors.

---

[1] See 37.   [2] H D Hughes, Labour MP for Wolverhampton West, 1945–1950.

4. In recent years a number of literacy campaigns have been attempted with voluntary instructors, and in almost every case these have proved to be short-lived. In some cases the volunteer instructers have desisted from their efforts, while in others the attendance at the classes have become increasingly irregular, very often because of dissatisfaction with the quality of the instruction given.

5. Broadly speaking, there are four types of adult instruction which have achieved a certain permanency and success. These are, firstly, adult classes, in both urban and rural areas, where fees are paid; secondly, classes of religious instruction (including literacy) where teachers are remunerated; thirdly, adult classes organised by certain Native Authorities in the Northern Provinces where instructors receive an honorarium of some five shillings a month: and, fourthly, village housecraft (and literacy) classes organised by societies whose local instructresses receive a small remuneration.

6. There are many variations in the detailed organisation of these experiments. These derive from the sociological requirements of the different Regions, but, broadly speaking, the Adult Education movement is proceeding along the following lines:—

(a) In most villages of the Northern Region there are no literates. To start adult education, therefore, Native Authorities have found it necessary to send out suitable men after they have received a short course of training. These men are housed and cared for by the villages concerned and receive a small remuneration of approximately five chillings a month, Block grants are made to Native Authorities for adult education campaigns organised on these lines since the instructors, with practice and experience, have achieved a fair degree of competence.

(b) In the Eastern and Western Regions, villages are encouraged to organise their own Adult Education Centres through Village Committees employing fairly competent instructors. Funds are collected by the Committee from various sources e.g. village contributions, public' subscriptions, the proceeds of concerts, pupils' fees (a penny or two pence per month), and in certain areas the Education Department gives financial assistance when satisfied that a reasonable standard of instruction has been achieved. The assistance, which is paid to the Committee's Chairman, is based on the enrolment and is approximately 5/- a month for 30 pupils. Village Committees normally use part of their funds to pay small honoraria to the instructore and so retain their regular service.

There is only one circumstance in which instructors are remunerated direct from the Education Vote. In a certain area where the women could not be approached except through female instructors, arrangements have been made whereby the latter each visit three or four villages weekly to hold afternoon classes in needlework and literacy. The villages give these instructresses some financial assistance, and, in view of the travelling and time involved, this is supplemented from the Education Vote on the same scale as for the Centres.

7. In conclusion, it must be remarked that the emphasis in this country has been placed initially on 'Mass Literacy' (in which the employment of competent instructors is regarded as essential to success) since it is considered that once literacy has been secured in any area there is a greater likelihood that mass—or social—education will eventually be achieved.

59   CO 537/3557, no 12   26 Dec 1948

[Arrests of Zikist leaders]: inward savingram no 2050 from Sir J Macpherson to Mr Creech Jones on possible reactions to the arrests of the Zikist leaders for sedition

My Top Secret Saving No. 1918. PROSECUTIONS FOR SEDITION.

There has been considerable talk in certain sections of the Zikist Movement of the action they propose to take in the event of any of the persons now charged with sedition being sentenced to terms of imprisonment. I enclose a copy of the instructions sent by the Headquarters of the Movement in Lagos to the branch at Enugu (and presumably to other branches throughout the country) which indicates the measures they have in mind.[1] Action on these lines was endorsed at a recent emergency meeting of the N.C.N.C. 'cabinet' to which delegates from the provinces were called.

2.   The prosecutions have not roused any widespread public feeling and the talk of violence is at present confined to a handful of reckless young Zikists who have a negligible personal following and is echoed only by similarly irresponsible young men in the provinces. Nevertheless they are creating a potentially dangerous situation which, if it got out of hand could seriously embarrass this Government. One of the greater dangers lies in the proposed campaign against the payment of tax for, in large areas of the country, the people are still far more willing to give credence to a doubtful rumour that tax need no longer be paid than they are to a categorical official statement that it must be. Such a campaign, however, could not become fully effective until the next tax paying season starts in about the middle of next year and a more proximate danger is that they will attempt to foment strikes among the workers.

3.   There is within the Zikist Movement a body of opinion which is opposed to these plans but the cardinal factor is the attitude which Dr. Azikiwe will adopt. He has been subjected to considerable pressure by the extremists in the N.C.N.C. 'Cabinet' but he has so far not committed himself and the impression he has given is that he is apprehensive of the lengths to which they are anxious to drag him but reluctant to lose their support by openly opposing them. He is clearly worried over the issue, as will be seen from the enclosed note of a conversation which he had a few days ago with the Acting Chief Secretary (Mr. A.W.L. Savage) when he stated, with apparent sincerity, that he was trying to bring himself to choose between throwing in his lot with the extremists and openly opposing them.

4.   If Azikiwe inclines to the right, the present loose talk may lead to small and isolated incidents, especially in Lagos and in parts of the Eastern Provinces, but it unlikely to lead to any widespread disorder, and the same is probably true if he continues to take the middle course. Should he swing to the left the possibility of serious industrial unrest, a successful anti-tax campaign and disorders resulting from a general flouting of authority will be very materially increased. At the moment the indications are that Azikiwe would prefer to incline to the right.

5.   As you will be aware from my Secret despatch No. 59 of the 8th of December, legislation conferring emergency powers on the executive has been drafted and is

---

[1] Enclosures not printed.

available to be brought into force immediately the situation warrants it, while other precautions of an administrative nature have been taken. I should, however, add that, while hitherto and especially during the period when the recent inter tribal tension was at its height the police have behaved admirably, in recent weeks the Commissioner of Police has felt some uneasiness over the effects of Zikist propaganda on Ibo policemen stationed in Lagos. The nature of the propaganda was explained in paragraph 33 of Nigeria Political Summary No. 27. It is reassuring that when a few days ago it was necessary to send police from Lagos to Shagamu in connection with the present agitation in that area they all, Ibos and others alike, went about their duties with their accustomed cheerfulness and efficiency and showed no signs of there having been any lowering of their morale. Nevertheless, this insidious propaganda may be expected to continue. The Commissioner of Police is, of course, taking all possible steps to counteract it.

60 CO 537/4727, no 1   Dec 1948
[Arrests of Zikist leaders]: Nigeria political summary   [Extract]

Political situation

1.   On the surface December has been a quiet month. There have been no more seditious speeches and no attempts to hold unauthorised meetings, while the sedition trials opened and continued in an atmosphere of public indifference and Christmas Eve, which had been fixed as the Zikist D-Day (see Possum No. 27, paragraph 7) passed off without incident, though this may have been due to the adjournment of the trials. Behind the scenes, however, the more extreme political groups have been active in making plans for future operations and trying to stem the tide of defections from their ranks by members who draw the line at violence. In the N.C.N.C. Cabinet in particular the rift between extremists and moderates has grown more and more marked and it is significant that the rift is also a tribal one, for it was the Yoruba members who were the first to take alarm. At the meeting during which the state of emergency was declared (see Possum No. 27), the Cabinet resolved on a policy of civil disobedience and non-co-operation with Government, but it was little more than a rump Cabinet that took the decision. Apart from Asikiwe himself there are now only a few men of any real standing left-amongst whom are Professor Eyo Ita[1] and Arthur Prest,[2] the Barrister—and both of these pleaded prior engagements: Prest adding in his telegram of apology that he hoped that any decisions reached would be constitutional. It is fairly clear that their other engagements were dictated by caution and that they have no intention of getting themselves involved in violence. E.D.A. Ojaleye, the Treasurer and the last of the moderates, resigned a few days after the meeting.

2.   The Zikist Movement has been particularly active, though scarcely united. Early in the month they set up two sub-committees, one for intelligence (one of the

[1] Eyo Ita, vice-president of the NCNC, 1948; member of Eastern House of Assembly, 1951; minister for natural resources and leader of government business, 1951; expelled from NCNC, 1953; founder of the NIP, 1953.
[2] Arthur Prest, policeman and barrister; member of NCNC, then joined AG; member of Western House of Assembly, 1951; member of House of Representatives, 1952; minister of communications, 1952–1954.

tasks allotted to it being to obtain secret information from the Nigerian Secretariat!) and the other the E.A. Committee whose functions were deemed to be of so secret a nature that it had been decided not to reveal them to members: it was, however, to form 'the spearhead of the attack when the movement puts its plan of positive action into effect.' On the 5th December an emergency conference was held in camera; it opened with a vigorous slanging match between members of the Central Executive: Abdullah, Eze, Aniedobe and Duke Dafe being particularly prominent in demanding apologies and counter apologies from each other for irregularities in procedure and the use of unparliamentary language. The Secretary's minutes then continue somewhat optimistically:—

> '*CORDIAL ATMOSPHERE*. Meanwhile there was a cordial atmosphere characteristic of Zikists practicalizing the "Spiritual Balance," a canon of the Zikist Philosophy, and the session began in earnest.'

The main decisions taken were to open a Defence Fund for Agwuna and the others on trial for sedition, to utilize labour movements for their political ends and to suspend action (on the plan outlined in the Zikist National Message?) until after the N.C.N.C. tour, the opening date for which has still to be fixed. Since then the Central Executive has sent out supplementary instructions to Provincial Branches: these do not appear to be uniform, the Northern Provinces being asked to provide martyrs on the Agwuna model and the Eastern to concentrate on the collection of rifles and ammunition which they are to obtain from the police and the military and which are to supplement the central armoury of sixteen rifles which are hidden in the house of 'a respected King who is also a Zikist.'

3.   The attitude of Azikiwe to this planning remains obscure, although the indications are that it is proving a source of considerable embarrassment to him. After his discussions with the Acting Chief Secretary (see postscript to Possum No. 27) he left Lagos to attend the Pan–Ibo Conference at which, he indicated, he expected a good deal of pressure to be exerted upon him by the more moderate Ibo elements to bring him to dissociate himself from the extremists, who, they consider, are dragging the Ibo name in the mud. He said that after the Conference he intended to take a rest and think things over quietly. He is expected back in Lagos at the end of January and he may declare himself one way or the other in the near future, but he has always been very careful not to commit himself in the past and has maintained his sometimes precarious seat on the fence with much adroitness: it would be more in keeping with his character to continue to do so to the last possible moment.

4.   The most interesting feature of the Pan–Ibo Conference was the foundation of the Ibo State Union with Azikiwe as the first State President. One of its stated aims is to support the N.C.N.C. 'Freedom Charter', but otherwise its organisation bears a somewhat embarrassing resemblance to that of the Egbe Omo Oduduwa—a fact which members of the latter have pointed out with relish. The list of office holders ranges from the entirely responsible Dr. Ibiam[3] through moderates like H.H. Kaine to vociferous Zikists such as Ojike and Wachukwu. A source usually considered reliable told the Governor in a private conversation that the meeting was organized by young men with University degrees but little wisdom. It is virtually certain that people like Dr. Ibiam were not consulted before publication of their names and

---

[3] Dr Francis Ibiam, medical practitioner; member of Legislative council, 1947; member of the Executive Council, 1949; gov of Eastern Nigeria, 1960–1966; president World Council of Churches, 1961.

source pointed out omission of names of influential moderates such as Egbuna and Mbanefo. It is understood that responsible Ibos have lectured the organizers and made it clear that if the Ibo State Union is to mean anything and is to have the support of prominent Ibos there must be a complete reorganization, in which the responsible elements must fully participate. The interest taken in the Pan–Ibo Conference was surprisingly small—the attendance never exceeded 1,000 in spite of the figure of 10,000 given in Zik's Press—and it is significant that a convention of Jehovah's Witnesses held simultaneously with, and adjacent to, the Conference attracted a larger 'gate.'

5.   An unsavoury development in the East has been the foundation of the 'National Church of Nigeria and the Cameroons.' at Aba, the service being a blasphemous travesty of that of the Church of England. At the first service, held on the 12th of December, nationalist hymns such as 'Alien Rule must go' were sung, the lesson was from a book called 'Renascent Africa' by a Zikist named Simbi Wellington, the sermon was on 'The God of Africa' and the service concluded with the Zikist National Anthem. Present information suggests that the local attitude is one of disgust and that this sort of think [sic], like Mbonu Ojike's anti-Catholic diatribes, is doing the Zikist Movement and the N.C.N.C. more harm than good.

The opposite camp too has not been idle. The N.Y.M. have pushed ahead with their preparations for the Representative Assembly and for the tour of Rita Hinden[4] and the Rev. Sorensen[5] who are now in this country. Zik's Press have lost no opportunity of ridiculing the whole affair at first taking the line that the two visitors are no more than imperialistic stooges sent to ensure that Nigeria is kept in slavery for a few years more. Here, however, they found themselves in a somewhat delicate position since the N.C.N.C. Delegation to London in 1947 made considerable use of the services of both—Sorensen for example was called in as peacemaker during a row between Dr. Azikiwe and Mrs. Kuti—and the opposition Press has naturally not been slow to point this out. The visit is proving an expensive one for the N.Y.M. who are bearing the whole cost and have already paid out nearly £400 on the air passages alone. They have the funds to meet this but it is estimated that a further £400 will be needed to cover the entire trip, and this they are having great difficulty in collecting. The leaders have worked out a series of preliminary recommendations for constitutional changes which will be considered at the Assembly, but they have been careful to insist that these recommendations are intended as a guide only and that every opportunity will be given to those attending to put forward their own proposals.

7.   Egbe Omo Oduduwa having started with a fanfare of trumpets has lost most of its first momentum. Their meetings are sparsely attended and missionary tours to whip up enthusiasm have fallen flat. During a recent tour of Ondo Province the missioners were told bluntly that the best thing they could do would be to affiliate Egbe to N.C.N.C. The younger generation, at any rate, of the Yorubas tend to look upon it with suspicion and in particular to question the motives of the leaders, whom they regard as more interested in preserving their old privileges than in promoting the welfare of the Yoruba race. . . .

---

[4] Rita Hinden, Fabian socialist and anti-colonial campaigner; secretary, Fabian Colonial Bureau, 1940–1950.
[5] Reginald Sorensen, Labour MP for Leyton West, 1929–1931 and 1935–1950; for Leyton, 1950–1964; cr Baron Sorensen 1964; government whip in the House of Lords, 1964–1968.

61   CO 537/4625, no 1   29 Jan 1949
[Constitutional review]: letter from Sir J Macpherson to A B Cohen
outlining proposals for constitutional reform. *Enclosure*

We have just completed a series of discussions here with Chief Commissioners on a
number of questions of policy, and first amongst these questions was the all-
important problem of constitutional reform.

It is hardly necessary to say that the discussion on the form which constitutional
changes might take and the procedure to be followed in formulating
recommendations for such changes was purely tentative and preliminary. As you
know we have been at pains to allow the maximum time for public discussion and we
want to arouse public interest in all parts of the country in the issues at stake. There
is therefore no question at all of a Government plan being framed and pressed upon
the country. Indeed the constitutional advance can obviously only succeed if it
carries the greatest common agreement after the fullest public discussion.

On the other hand there is a good deal of uncertainty, and some doubts and
misgivings, in the Service about the way things will go and we all thought that it
would be wise to clear our own minds as to the possibilities before we embark on the
confused currents and dangerous waters of constitutional review. The document
which I enclose is the result of the first discussion which we have had with Chief
Commissioners with this object in mind and I think that we have reached a very
satisfactory measure of agreement on the main line of advance which we would all
like to see. The document is to go no further than the Chief Commissioners
themselves but they are going to have informal talks with all their Administrative
staff, and their chief technical officers too, on the lines set out in the document. We
believe that by bringing our own people fully into discussion we shall enable them to
give some unofficial guidance to the public debate at all levels which we are anxious
to encourage. At the same time these discussions will, we hope, go a long way to allay
the misgivings of those officials in stations remote from head quarters who are
sometimes inclined to think that we are making quick changes as a result of pressure
from the talkative politicians of Lagos. We want to convince them that we are quite
genuine in our conviction that success already achieved under the present
constitution does in fact fully justify further substantial advance.

Although the document is, as I say, purely tentative and the suggestions which it
contains will no doubt be varied and modified in all sorts of ways as the stages of
discussion give us more experience of public opinion during the coming year, I shall
naturally be glad if you feel that you wish to comment at this stage on the main line
of advance which we have in mind.

Enclosure to No 61: Constitutional advance

The fundamental principle on which the present constitution is based is unity at the
Centre through strength in the Regions. That principle has not only won wide
support but has enabled the present constitutional experiment to succeed more fully
and more quickly than could have been hoped when it was inaugurated two years
ago.

For many reasons it is desirable that a constitutional advance should now be made, but the advance is not made as a result of political pressure: it is made because the solid achievements of the past two years render a further advance fully justified. That being so the basis of the further advance must be the same as that on which success has already been achieved—strength in the Regions.

The main purpose of the new advance should therefore be to give to the Regions a greater measure of autonomy under a federal system. (It is suggested that townships, other than Lagos which presents a special problem, should be represented in Regional Houses rather than have direct representation in the Legislative Council). The object should be mainly achieved by giving to Regional Houses legislative and financial powers in place of their present purely advisory functions. Experience over the past two years has made that major development both sound and necessary.

It is suggested that the time has also come to take one further step of great importance. In the existing constitution legislative and financial powers have been given to the Legislative Council acting with the advice of the Regional Houses. There is however no provision in the constitution for giving any share to members of the Regional Houses or Legislative Council in the responsibility for formation of policy. (It is true that there have been for some time past Nigerian members of the Central Executive Council but they were appointed individually to the Council and were not selected by or responsible to the Legislature). It is now suggested that in each Region there should be established a Chief Commissioner's Council composed partly of officials but with a majority of non-officials selected from their own number by the unofficial members of the Regional Houses. These Councils would have the task of formulating policy and directing executive action within the Regions. It will at once be realised that this would be a change of fundamental consequence and indeed could be regarded as the most important step yet taken in enabling Nigerians to take a leading part in the management of their own affairs. The sense of responsibility shown by members of the Regional Houses in the past justifies the confident hope that the success already achieved by the Regional Houses would be followed by the equal success of the new Chief Commissioners Councils.

At the centre it is suggested that a Governor's Council should be formed composed of officials, (including the Chief Commissioners), and non-officials selected from their own number by the unofficial members of the Legislative Council. It is for consideration whether the officials and unofficials on the Governor's Council should be in equal numbers or whether, as in the Chief Commissioners' Councils, the unofficials should be in a majority. The duties of the Governor's Council would be to meet from time to time (probably three or four times a year) to deal with questions of major policy affecting the whole of Nigeria. Another suggestion which has been made is that a Privy Council should be formed to take over some of the non-political duties now performed by the Executive Council (such as advising H.E. regarding the exercise of his prerogative in relation to death sentences and on questions affecting discipline in the Government Service).

It is suggested that we should go one step further. Already committees of the Regional Houses have been established to maintain contact with Government Departments. It is now suggested that in the Eastern and Western Regions (and possibly in the Northern Region too—though it is recognised that in the North there are special difficulties in this respect) an embryo Ministerial system might be introduced whereby certain unofficial members of the Chief Commissioners' Council would speak for a Department or group of Departments in the Chief Commissioners' Council and should be responsible for conducting legislative business affecting that Department or group of Departments in the Regional Houses. It would be made quite clear that in the first stage every decision on major policy including departmental policy would be taken not by the Minister but by the Chief Commissioners' Council. The Ministers would give their whole time to their official duties and would receive salaries.

It is not proposed that the unofficial members of the Governor's Council should be given any executive functions but it is for consideration whether they should each be made responsible for conducting legislative business affecting a Department or group of Departments in the Legislative Council (in which event they might be called Member of the Governor's Council for Education, Health, Communications, etc.).

Certain other proposals have been made regarding the legislature. It is suggested that in both the Regional Houses and the Legislature the number of official members should be decreased and the number of unofficial members increased and that a Speaker of the Legislative Council should be appointed instead of retaining the Governor as President.

The suggestions so far summarised do not touch on such important issues as the system of election or selection for the Regional Houses, the relationship of Native Administrations and local government bodies to the Legislature or the position of the Chiefs (as to the system of election or selection it is recognised that it will almost certainly be desirable to evolve some wider or different basis of representation for the future). In these matters it is likely that different solutions will be desirable in the different Regions and it is essential that each Region should be given the fullest opportunity to express its wishes as to the course to be followed.

There remains one other important matter to be decided. If the principal [sic] of Regional autonomy is accepted it is clearly necessary to make sure that the present Regional boundaries are the best. As to the Colony, it is suggested that at least the rural areas might be added to the Western Provinces. It will also probably be necessary to give constitutional recognition to the special status of the Cameroons as a Trusteeship territory. It is not proposed to make any change in respect of the parts of the Cameroons now administered as part of the Northern Provinces but it is suggested that the main area of the Cameroons (in the Eastern Provinces) should have direct representation both in the Eastern House of Assembly and the Legislative Council.

Those in outline are the proposals for the new system of Regional autonomy which have so far been considered. The proposals are based on three principles, firstly, that the advance made in the Regional Houses under the present constitution justifies the grant of further powers to those Houses, secondly that we should give to unofficial members of the Regional Houses an important part in the constructive work of framing policy and thirdly that the unity of Nigeria will not be jeopardised but in fact will be ensured by building on Regional strength.

Procedure to be followed in formulating recommendations for constitutional changes

1.   It is clearly desirable that the fullest discussion about constitutional changes should be encouraged at all levels.

2.   All discussion at this stage should be preliminary and attempts to formulate final recommendations at once should be discouraged.

3.   It is considered undesirable to form special committees at Divisional and Provincial levels to deal with constitutional matters: informal discussions with the widest possible representation are thought preferable.

4.   It is the present intention at the March meeting of Legislative Council to introduce a Government motion for the establishment of a select or special committee to make recommendations for constitutional changes. This committee would be composed of all unofficial members with the Chief Secretary, the Chief Commissioners, the Attorney-General, the Financial Secretary and the Commissioner of the Colony as official members. It is for consideration whether the committee should have the power to co-opt a fixed number of unofficials from outside the Council.

5.   Preliminary debates would take place on constitutional issues in the Regional Houses in July.

6.   Thereafter the Legislative Council committee would hear public evidence in Lagos and main centres in the Regions.

7.   A further debate would take place in the Regional Houses towards the end of the year.

8.   The Legislative Council committee would then meet to formulate its final recommendations.

9.   Government officials should refrain from making any public statement on constitutional issues but should be prepared to take part freely in informal discussions.

62   CO 537/4631, no 1   28 Feb 1949
[Political situation]: inward savingram no 435 from Sir J Macpherson to Mr Creech Jones warning of the possibilities of unrest in Nigeria. *Minute* by F J Webber

It is necessary to report on certain disquieting developments in the political situation.

2.   The hearing of the charges of sedition instituted towards the end of last year against a number of members and supporters of the so called Zikist Movement (which is probably the most extreme organisation of those affiliated to the N.C.N.C.) has proceeded and sentences have been imposed ranging from two years six months imprisonment to fines of £25. (See previous savingrams Nos. 1784 and 2050). It was at one time thought that the conviction of these extremists might be accompanied by disorder but while this has not been the case and while the legal action taken has certainly had some effect in maintaining public confidence in the Government amongst more moderate elements, the trials with the violent speeches made by some of the accused in Court have fomented increased anti-Government feeling amongst extreme nationalists. The attitude of the Zik Press, though it has recently avoided the sort of blatantly seditious material which led to the sedition trials, has not improved and the campaign of malicious lies and vicious attacks both on the Government and on rival political organisations (particularly the Nigerian Youth Movement) has continued unabated. Scarcely a day passes without the appearance in the Zik press of leading articles accompanied by cartoons suggesting that Nigeria is the miserable

victim of imperialist oppression and that a stream of 'white settlers' is arriving in the country (for which there is of course, as they well know, no foundation whatever in fact). The Press agitation is not so much an attack on specific acts or omissions of Government as an attempt to stir up feeling against the continued existence of 'Colonial status' by appealing to anti-European prejudice. Moreover, the Youth Movement whose leaders are much more reasonable and moderate have felt that they too must increase attacks on the Government in order to compete for popular support.

3.   The poisonous propaganda of the Press must have its effect and evidence from several sources indicates that in particular the Zikist Movement both in parts of the Eastern Provinces and in Lagos is becoming more bitter and more inclined to advocate violence and civil disobedience.

4.   It is difficult to estimate the strength of the Zikist Movement in relation to the N.C.N.C. Undoubtedly Azikiwe lost a great deal of ground, particularly with the Yorubas, during the tribal and personal controversies which took place in the Press last year, and responsible opinion in the Provinces (including the Eastern Provinces) is becoming increasingly critical of the Lagos politicians. But there is still strong support for Azikiwe and for the N.C.N.C. amongst the younger educated people particularly of the clerk type not only in Lagos and the Eastern Provinces but also to some extent in the Western Provinces and even amongst some of the educated Northerners. The Zikist Movement which was formed only a year or two ago apparently without Azikiwe's direct participation (the parallel with certain Jewish organisations in Palestine is interesting) has not a very large membership but it includes the most militant extremists. If a general situation of insecurity and unrest were created by an outbreak of strikes the more responsible elements might be terrorized and the extremists might make serious trouble.

5.   Against this background of increasing bitterness and pressure for more 'positive action' Azikiwe himself has found himself in a most difficult position. He apparently does not feel that the present time is one for violent opposition to the Government and he has been doing all he can to dissuade his followers from committing themselves to such a course. As a result there is a growing restlessness amongst the hotheads of the Zikist Movement. He has been pressed to give up his seat in the Legislative Council and his newspaper interests and devote his whole time and effort to extreme political activities. Zikist Movement documents have been obtained by the Police which talk of organising disorder, obtaining rifles by theft and even of assassinations whether Azikiwe approves or not. He is still standing against this increasing pressure and has persuaded his 'cabinet' to wait at least until the Legislative Council meeting has taken place at Ibadan next month. An N.C.N.C. Convention, to be followed by a countrywide N.C.N.C. tour has been arranged for April and it seems that he will have to reach a decision by then whether he is to follow the lead of his most extreme partisans (against his own better judgment) or whether he is prepared to resist them and so create a major split in his own party.

6.   There has been another disturbing development no less serious in its possible long term results. I have previously felt that the Nigeria Trade Union Movement gave many signs of developing on sound lines. Some of the leaders of the movement have gained valuable experience in Great Britain and many of them have shown common sense and responsibility and not a little courage in their handling of trade disputes. The movement cut across tribal affiliations and devoted itself more to the interests of

the workers than to nationalist politics. For some years past the T.U.C. had been affiliated to the N.C.N.C. but at a meeting in December last it was decided by a majority of 32 to 8 to sever that connection. The intention was, I understand, to start a new Labour Party with Trade Union support. This action has most unfortunately resulted in a few of the Trade Union leaders, particularly the Ibos amongst them and those who are fervent N.C.N.C. supporters, withdrawing from the T.U.C. and starting a campaign of abuse against the remaining majority of the Trade Union leaders. The main instigator of this defection is the paid secretary of the U.A.C. Union, called Eze,[1] who is, I gather, interested in Zikist politics and communism to the exclusion of almost everything else (see paragraphs 4 and 23 of Political Summary No. 27). He is a member of the N.C.N.C. cabinet and of the Zikist Movement Executive Committee. He is unbalanced and violent and quite unreasonable and is now engaged both in trying to set up a rival organisation to the T.U.C. and in preparing the ground for an attempt to call a strike of all U.A.C. employees as soon as possible. The new threat of industrial conflict is no doubt part of the Zikist Movement's plan to work up as much unrest as possible following the meeting of. Legislative Council next month. While the immediate threat is disturbing I am even more concerned at the prospect of the weakening of the whole Trade Union Movement which this split, carried out solely for reasons of political expediency, will probably cause.

7.   Another factor in the existing situation, though largely unconnected perhaps with those to which I have already referred, is the position in some parts of the Western Provinces about which I have recently submitted reports to you (my Secret Savingram No. 268 of the 7th February and my Secret Savingram No. 161 of the 24th January). There has been a number of minor disorders, first in Abeokuta and later in the Ijebu Province followed by more recent troubles in Owo[2] Province and agitation against the Oni of Ife in the Oyo Province. This unrest probably had its origin in local circumstances different in each case but the possibility of instigation from Lagos cannot be altogether discounted and the N.C.N.C. has been quick to support any dissatisfaction directed against the Native Authorities. It is particularly unfortunate that these potentially dangerous developments should be taking place in the Western Provinces at a time when the increased activities of the extremist elements in Lagos and the Eastern Provinces are causing concern.

8.   It should also be recorded that although the Press controversy in Lagos between Azikiwe and his enemies has been somewhat less virulent during the past few months the bitterness between the leaders of tribal groups has continued and discussions about constitutional advance may once again give rise to a flare-up of ill-feeling between leading Yorubas, Ibos and Hausas.

9.   All these disturbing factors indicate that a situation may soon arise when the danger of disorder will be considerably increased, possibly accompanied by strikes, extremist violence and agitation against Native Authorities as well as the Government.

10.   The purpose of this report is to give advance indication of those possibilities. I do not propose in this report to discuss in detail the measures to be taken in an

---

[1] ie Nduka Eze, trade union leader and political activist; secretary of the Amalgamated Union of UAC African Workers, 1946; general secretary of the NNFL, 1949, general secretary of the Nigerian Labour Congress, 1950; leading member of the Zikist movement.
[2] ie Ondo Province

endeavour to prevent such a deterioration of the position, except to say that I am convinced that the dangerous tendencies to which I have referred cannot be checked by repressive action alone. It has been my constant aim to try to win and keep the initiative by showing a readiness to make substantial advances in co-operation with all who are willing to put forward or discuss progressive and constructive proposals, and the increased dangers to which I have referred make it all the more necessary at the forthcoming meeting of the Legislative Council and thereafter to show our anxiety to press forward with projects already initiated for economic development, local government reform and constitutional advance.

Minute on 62

This important report contains most disquieting news. Government strategy is the traditional policy of winning the support and confidence of the 'moderates' and to try and prove that the extremists (who will denounce any forward move by the Government, whatever its merits) are sabotaging the political and economic future of Nigeria. But Government is sadly lacking in weapons to counteract a vicious press. I believe the press is the major factor: it must be in any semi-educated community. And I believe that if the situation deteriorates badly the press should be entirely muzzled. Any newspaper thrives on criticism however unjust and bitter it may be; but malicious distortion is quite another thing.

Para. 7 should be submitted to the Abeokuta and Ijebu pp. Note the references to Owo and Oyo.

? The S/S should thank the Governor for this report which he has read with some disquiet and while endorsing the aim at the end of 1[0] promise his full support to any stricter measures of control the Governor may deem it advisable to take in the interests of public security.

F.J.W.
5.3.49

63 CO 537/4625, no 5   4 Mar 1949
[Constitutional review]: letter (reply) from A B Cohen to Sir J Macpherson on the proposals for constitutional reform

With reference to your secret and personal letter of the 29th January[1] about the Nigerian constitution and my interim reply of the 10th February, I am now sending you herewith a copy of the notes I have written on the subject.[2] I do so with some trepidation, having only been in the country for five weeks, but the notes may be of some use to you as showing some of the points in which we are likely to be interested. Please treat the notes strictly for what they are worth and do not feel under any obligation to comment on them at this stage at any rate.

Since I wrote the notes I have received Foot's secret and personal letter of the 21st February, for which I am very grateful.

---

[1] See 61.   [2] Not printed.

I have shown both your letter and Foot's and their enclosures and my notes to the Secretary of State. Apart from what follows, he does not wish to make any comments at this stage either on the procedure for re-examining the constitution or on the substance of the tentative ideas set out in the memorandum enclosed with your letter of the 29th January. He was quite willing for my notes to be sent to you, but these are to be regarded as simply representing my views.

The only points which the Secretary of State wishes to make at this stage are as follows. He hopes that as little public currency as possible will be given to the term 'constituent assembly'. It is of course impossible to prevent the N.C.N.C. or others using this term if they wish to do so, and I imagine it is bound to appear frequently in the newspapers. The Secretary of State feels, however, and I am sure that you share this view, that it is important that the great bulk of the country with its moderate ideas should not get the impression that anything like a constituent assembly is to be established. Incidentally, when I was in Lagos Rotimi Williams and possibly one or two others talked to me about a constituent assembly and I always took the line that you could only have a constituent assembly if a country had reached the stage when it was in a position to settle its own future constitution without reference to some outside power or government. Rotimi Williams and the others I talked to seemed to accept this point. The Secretary of State of course realises that the committee which he agreed to in principle in his telegram No. 823 of the 20th July last year is in no sense a constituent assembly or anything like it. The point he wanted to make was that, in so far as it is possible to counter any suggestions from any quarter that the committee is to be a constituent assembly, this should be done.

The other point which the Secretary of State made was that in his understanding all that the committee was to embark on was a review of the various points in the existing constitution with a view to its improvement and development and not a complete re-writing of the constitution. He realises of course that it is always difficult to prevent people who want to do so from ranging over the whole field of constitutional reform, but he hopes that in the committee it will turn out to be possible to concentrate on practical methods of improving the working of the existing constitution and developing it. He is of course entirely happy about the discussion of all the points mentioned in the memorandum enclosed with your letter of the 29th January.[3]

---

[3] See 61.

64   CO 537/4731, no 11   16 Mar 1949
[Communism in West Africa]: memorandum by R E S Yeldham[1] summarising Soviet activity in Nigeria   [Extract]

... In Nigeria during the latter half of 1948 the Russian case at U.N.O. was fully reported in the Press, particularly by the Zik Press group of newspapers. Editorial comment followed two main lines: first, that the Russian demand for enquiry into the affairs of the Colonial powers is justified, and that resistance is inspired by the fact that Great Britain has so much to hide; and, second, that the Nigerian Government and the Colonial Office are using the Russian bogey as a justification for opposing nationalist agitation. The theoretical aspect of communism receives little attention.

---

[1] Principal, CO West African Dept.

Reference is made in the Nigerian report to *Mduka Eze*,[2] the Secretary of the U.A.C. Union, and a member of both the N.C.N.C. Cabinet and of the Zikist Movement Executive Committee. The fact that he is an ardent Communist has already been referred to in the West African Political Intelligence Summary No. 5 for March.

In Nigeria it is reported that there has been an increase in the import of Communist and pro-Russian pamphlets and books which command a ready sale among the young, educated classes. Steps are being taken, however, to counteract the influence of these publications as far as possible by increasing the import of anti-Communist literature from both British and United States' sources, and distributing them through the medium of reading rooms and similar institutions.

There is still no evidence of an organised Communist Party in Nigeria though it is known that two attemps have been made in the Provinces amongst some enthusiastic youths of the student type without any backing. Their efforts have come to nothing. There is no evidence that the inception of these two Communist groups was inspired from abroad. On the other hand some societies and individuals are known to be in contact with either Russia or the satellite countries. In July, 1948, the World Federation of Democratic Youth extended an invitation to *Koma Balogun*[3] of the Nigerian Youth Congress to attend the international Conference of Working Youth at Warsaw. He did not go. *Mrs. Kuti*, who has appeared once again in the political limelight, and is now the President of the Women's Union in Abeokuta, recently received a message of greeting from the women of Moscow. From a cutting which appeared in the 'Daily Worker' early in March this year it appears too that she has been corresponding with that paper, but on this occasion it is believed that it was purely in sympathy with the death of a U.K. editor of the 'Daily Worker.'

Although the Communist Party apparently does not accept Africans as full members the Nigerian report continues: 'we believe that Communists in Great Britain continue to make contact with Nigerian students arriving for courses in the U.K.' In summing up, this report concludes that 'although Communism appears to make little progress in Nigeria there is a disquieting increase in supplies of Communist literature, and extremist politicians are very ready to accept without question Russian propaganda when it is directed against British and American actions and policy'. . . .

---

[2] ie Nduka Eze.
[3] ie Kola Balogun, journalist and barrister, member of the NCNC; member of ie Western House of Assembly, 1953; member of House of Representatives, 1954; minister of research and information, 1956–1958; expelled from NCNC, 1958; high commissioner to Ghana, 1959.

65   CO 537/4635, no 6   24 Mar 1949
[Constitutional review]: despatch no 11 from Sir J Macpherson to Mr Creech Jones on the progress of the constitutional review. *Enclosures*: speech by H M Foot and report of the Select Committee of the Legislative Council
Minute by L H Gorsuch

I have the honour to report on the preparations for the review of the constitution of Nigeria following the announcement which I made with your approval in August last year.

2.   The announcement which I made in the course of a speech to the Legislative Council on the 17th of August, 1948, was as follows:—

'As Honourable Members are aware it was originally proposed that the new constitution should remain in force for nine years and should be reviewed at the end of that period, though limited changes might be made at the end of the third and sixth years. Nine years, as Lord Milverton said, is not a long time in the history of a country, and we are now little more than half way through the first period of three years. The progress already made however, has been, in my considered view, so rapid and so sound that I suggest that we might be justified in reviewing our timetable, and that we might consider together what changes should be made, and whether they should be made earlier than originally intended. I accordingly propose that if it is the wish of this Council and of the country that earlier changes should be made they should be introduced not at the end of nine years but in the second three-year period which will start at the beginning of 1950. Before any change is made it is of the utmost importance to allow adequate time for the expression of public opinion, and if the Council agrees I propose, after a period has been allowed for preliminary public discussion, to set up a Select Committee of this Council, following the Budget Session next year, to review the whole position and to make recommendations.'

3.   Since I made that announcement, which was well received in the Press and elsewhere, there has been an increasing amount of public discussion about constitutional questions and in particular about the methods to be adopted for the review of the constitution. The N.C.N.C. has published what it calls a Freedom Charter setting out proposals for an entirely new constitution under which a measure of autonomy would be granted to the linguistic or tribal groups within a federal constitution somewhat on the model of the United States of America. The Nigeria Youth Movement has not published its proposals but has had a series of discussions including a conference held in Lagos in January at which suggestions were put forward for a federal system based on the existing Regions, with certain important modifications in regional boundaries, and with ministerial responsibility at the centre. In most parts of the country outside Lagos these proposals have made little impression and general public opinion has not yet been formulated on most of the questions at issue. The prevailing feeling in the Provinces is, I think, anxiety lest important constitutional changes should be made without sufficient time being allowed to enable the public to understand what is proposed, together with distrust in many quarters of the intentions of members of the Lagos political groups which are suspected of merely seeking to secure a quick transfer of power to themselves.

4.   Public discussion has, however, been mainly concentrated at this early stage on the methods to be adopted for the constitutional review and spokesmen of both the N.C.N.C. and the N.Y.M. have urged that a 'constituent assembly' should be set up. Little or no attempt has however been made to indicate what is meant by a 'constituent assembly' and still less thinking has been devoted to the question of how such a body might be composed. Nearly all politicians and journalists are however agreed that the original suggestion that a Select Committee of Legislative Council should be formed to undertake the constitutional review is objectionable on the grounds that the Legislative Council as now constituted is not truly representative,

and during the past month or two there has been a number of indications that moderate as well as extreme opinion favoured an attempt being made to evolve some system of sounding public opinion on a wider basis.

5.   Though it is no doubt impossible to satisfy all opinion in this difficult matter—some of the extremists resent any proposal for consultation with anyone but themselves—I came to the conclusion that it would be unwise, in the face of a good deal of adverse public opinion, to proceed with the original suggestion that the constitutional review should be undertaken by a Select Committee of the Legislative Council. To do so would have certainly invited from the start the strongest opposition from the political parties who would have been able to gain fairly wide public support in a popular campaign directed against the Select Committee and the Legislative Council itself.

6.   I therefore decided that the best course would be to appoint a Select Committee of the Legislative Council not to review the constitution but to advise how the constitution should be reviewed. This proposal, which was welcomed in all sections of the Press, was accordingly put to the Council on the 12th of March and a Select Committee was accordingly set up to advise on the steps to be taken in the constitutional review. I attach a copy of the speech made by the Chief Secretary in moving the resolution.

7.   The Select Committee has now made its report, of which I enclose a copy, and the report has been unanimously accepted by the Council. I regard the fact that the report of the Select Committee was unanimous as most important and very much to the credit of the Committee (which included all unofficial members of the Council) and not least to the Chief Secretary who was Chairman. I also regard the proposals made by the Committee as sound and acceptable. It was important that the bodies to be set up should be based on the existing Legislative Council and Regional Houses but it was also most important, in my view, that other representative opinion should be brought in. It was also necessary, in order to allay fears that provincial and regional opinion would be disregarded, to ensure that discussion should be facilitated at all levels and not only at the centre. It was, I think, desirable (particularly in view of the composition of the committee set up to review the constitution in the Gold Coast)[1] for a general conference to be formed which would be predominantly Nigerian. It was also, I consider, essential to provide for consultation between officials and non-officials at some stage before final recommendations are prepared. All these objects have been included in the proposals of the Select Committee.

8.   I have little doubt that the report of the Select Committee will be attacked in the more extreme sections of the Press (in spite of the fact that Dr. Azikiwe who controls most of those sections of the Press was a member of the Select Committee) but I believe that it will be generally recognised as an honest attempt to arrive at a satisfactory procedure for ascertaining public opinion and that the proposed discussions at Provincial and Regional levels before discussion in the General Conference will be widely welcomed.

9.   It is now necessary for me to announce with the least possible delay whether I accept the recommendations of the Select Committee and I shall be most grateful if

---

[1] The Coussey Committee in the Gold Coast consisted entirely of Africans.

you will be good enough to inform me by telegram as soon as possible if you agree that I may do so.

Enclosure 1 to 65: Speech by H M Foot in the Legislative Council, 11 March 1949

Let me first of all emphasize the limitations of this discussion today and the limitations of the resolution which I am moving and the limitations of the functions of the Select Committee which we propose to set up.

We are not here today to try to find the answers to the constitutional questions which confront us—it would be obviously out of order to do so. Nor is the proposed Select Committee to concern itself with the answers to those questions. It is proposed that it should be set up with one simple purpose—to make recommendations to Your Excellency on the steps to be taken in the constitutional review. We are concerned for the moment, and so will the proposed Select Committee be concerned, not with the question of what constitutional changes should be recommended but merely with the question of how those recommendations should be prepared.

What in effect I am suggesting is merely this—that we should sit down together in Select Committee while we are here at Ibadan in order to advise Your Excellency on ways and means by which the constitutional review should proceed. I hope and believe that all Honourable Members will agree that it is wise and necessary to do so and that they will also agree that the test of those ways and means should be that set out in the motion—the test whether all sections of the population are given full opportunity to express their views on all the great issues involved.

We are in fact concerned today not with objects but with methods and I do not think that it is necessary to go into lengthy argument to justify the proposal to establish a Select Committee for the limited purpose which I have described.

Before the Council decides whether our proposal should be accepted I should however like to make brief reference to three matters which are very much in my mind and I believe in the minds of most of us at this time.

First let me say this. The task of working out constitutional reform for Nigeria is as complicated and difficult as any which has ever confronted any country. We have in Nigeria so many different peoples with different history and tradition and religion and outlook. We have the problems arising from the great distances which separate one area from another. We have the widely varying systems of local administration. We have so many different standards of education and ways of life. Let no one imagine that the problem of deciding on the best course of constitutional advance for a country such as this can be easily solved. It certainly cannot be solved by snap decisions and rhetorical resolutions and attractive catch phrases. We can only reach a sound solution by hard and honest thinking.

Let me try to emphasize what I mean by stating some of the principal questions which we have to answer. I shall certainly not try to answer these questions now—it would clearly be out of order to do so—and I do not pretend that the main questions which come to my mind are the only ones which we have to answer. I should however like to mention some of those questions to illustrate the point which I am making—that our task is to find answers to a whole series of complex questions each one of which demands the most careful examination.

What are the main questions which at once come to our minds? Let me endeavour to state a few of them.

Do we wish to see a fully centralised system with all legislative and executive power concentrated at the centre or do we wish to develop a federal system under which each different region of the country would exercise a measure of internal autonomy?

If we favour a federal system should we retain the existing regions or should we accept the existing regions with some modification of existing regional boundaries or should we form regions on some new basis such as the many linguistic groups which exist in Nigeria?

Should the regional legislatures be granted legislative and financial powers instead of being purely advisory as at present?

What changes should be made in the composition of the regional Legislative Houses and of the Legislative Council? Should the number of officials in each be reduced and the number of unofficials increased? Should the system of nominated members be retained?

Should there be a Council in each region to consider the policy to be followed in that region and to direct all executive action within the region and if so what should the composition and powers of those regional Councils be? Moreover, should the unofficial members of the regional Legislative Houses have the right to select from their own number members to sit on the regional Councils? If so, should each of the unofficial members who sit on the regional Councils be granted responsibilities in respect of the activities of a Department or group of Departments?

What should be the method of election to regional Houses? Should the existing system of selection through the Native Authorities be retained? Or should some new system of selection or election be worked out specifically for the regional Houses? If so, should election be by the direct system (each member being selected or elected by a single constituency) or by the indirect system of electoral colleges, and what should be the electoral qualification? Should each region be permitted to adopt a different electoral system?

What functions and powers should be reserved to the Central Legislative Council and Executive Council in order to achieve the overriding object of maintaining and strengthening the unity of Nigeria?

What should be the system of election to the Legislative Council? Should its unofficial members continue to be chosen by regional Houses or should some method of direct election to the Legislative Council be considered?

Should any towns be given the right of direct representation in Legislative Council (as Lagos and Calabar are now represented) or should they be represented in regional Houses?

What should be the powers and functions of the Central Executive Council? Should unofficial members of the Legislative Council have the right to select from their own number members to sit on the Central Council? If so, should each of the unofficial members who sit on the Central Council be granted responsibilities in respect of the activities of a Department or group of Departments?

What should be the future of the Colony in relation to any new legislative system? Should the Colony and the Western Provinces be treated as one unit for legislative and administrative purposes or should the rural part be added to the Western region? Or should the Colony be formed into a separate region?

Is some special constitutional arrangement necessary in regard to the Cameroons in view of the fact that it is a Trusteeship Territory?

Should all the changes decided upon be introduced at one time or should some be introduced progressively?

Should the system to be introduced in all these matters necessarily be the same in each region or should each region be given freedom to decide on certain modifications to suit its own peculiar circumstances and needs?

Your Excellency and the Council will note that I have made no attempt at all to answer any of those vital questions. It would be quite wrong to do so at this stage but the Council will, I believe, agree with me that it is useful for each one of us to think what the main questions are, not to hide them away but to bring them out into the fresh air of public discussion.

There have already been some views expressed about the kind of body which should make recommendations to Your Excellency on constitutional reform. We shall of course have to consider that matter as one of our chief tasks if the Select Committee which I have proposed is set up. But I should like to mention one reservation. We must certainly try to form the best body or bodies for this purpose which can be devised but it would be wrong in my view to imagine that everything will depend on the composition of whatever body is established. We must not put our faith in one body alone to the exclusion of other opinion. The solution to be found will and should depend not solely on some specially formed body but on the views and opinions of the people, expressed in many different ways. There is some inclination to believe that all that is necessary is to send a committee like Moses into the mountain and that all the people need to do is to watch and pray—pray that the committee will in due course return from the clouds with the perfect constitution to last for ever written on tablets of stone. No one can hand over his responsibility in this matter to others. Every Nigerian has a stake in his own country and it is for him by means of village meetings and Divisional meetings and Provincial meetings throughout the country and through the organisations of which he is a member to make his views known. Your Excellency has insisted that there should be the fullest opportunity for public consultation at every level. The Regional Houses in separate resolutions have already made it clear that they are of the same opinion. It is not only for the Government and Government officials and members of the Legislative Council and the Regional Houses and the Native Authorities and leaders of public opinion who have a responsibility in this matter. Every one in Nigeria has a responsibility. It is for us, on our part, to see that the people are consulted and it is for the people to see that their views are made known.

Finally may I say one word about our approach to the work of the proposed Select Committee. We well know that owing to the composition and history of the country we have many animosities and diverse interests in Nigeria. As Your Excellency has said, we have unfortunately had a good deal of evidence during the past year of how much harm those animosities can do. In the past there have no doubt been faults on all sides. On the part of the Government there have certainly been faults. On the other side, on the part of the public, there has, I believe, been one fault more than any other. There has, I believe, been a failure of Nigerians to co-operate with other Nigerians whether it be politically or commercially. As Your Excellency has emphasized to us a great nation cannot be built on the basis of individuals envious of others each seeking selfish and sectional interests. It must be based on free and constructive association to achieve common aims.

When Your Excellency made the announcement about constitutional advance last August that was the first step in a new era. We are to take the second step now. I claim, like Your Excellency, to be an optimist. I wonder if it is unduly optimistic to hope, as I do, that all of us concerned will enter on this new era with a new spirit? On the side of the Government we have had ample evidence of Your Excellency's readiness, indeed determination, to take the people into Your Excellency's confidence and give them great new opportunities and responsibilities. On the part of the people I hope that there can also be a new spirit of readiness to work one with another and to forget past antagonisms in the great task of building a sound constitution which can win and retain the widest possible public support.

Enclosure 2 to 65: Report of Select Committee (Chairman, H M Foot), 22 March 1949

I have the honour to submit the following unanimous report of the Select Committee appointed by Your Excellency on the 11th of March in accordance with the following resolution passed by the Legislative Council:—

> 'Be it resolved that a Select Committee of this House be set up to make recommendations to His Excellency the Governor regarding the steps to be taken for a review of the present constitution of Nigeria, with special reference to the methods to be adopted for ascertaining the views of all sections of the population on the issues involved.'

The Select Committee was composed of all the Honourable Unofficial Members of the Council together with their Honours the Chief Commissioners, the Honourable Attorney-General, the Honourable Financial Secretary, the Honourable the Acting Commissioner of the Colony and myself.

The Select Committee first of all agreed that in carrying out the constitutional review the widest public discussions should be encouraged and facilitated and ample time allowed at every stage of these discussions. With this in view the Select Committee recommends that the discussions should be concentrated at three levels—at the Provincial level, then at the Regional level and then at the Centre— and I set out below the functions and composition of the bodies which we accordingly recommend should be established.

Provincial conferences

Function. To give preliminary consideration to the question of constitutional advance after studying the views of village meetings and divisional meetings and of representative organisations in the Province: and to send a representative or representatives to a Regional Conference to state the views of the Province and to take part in discussions at the Regional level.

Composition. The object is to make the Provincial Conference as representative as possible of all sections of opinion in the Province. It is recognised that the methods of achieving that object must vary in different parts of the country. It will therefore be the duty of each Resident in co-operation with the member or members of the Regional Houses from that Province to consult all Native Authorities and other representative bodies in the Province and then to call a Provincial Conference as representative as possible, with due regard to the claims of minority groups.

Regional conference

Function. To give further consideration to the question of constitutional advance after studying the views of the Provincial Conferences. Each Regional Conference will send three representatives to be members of a small drafting committee and later send representatives in greater numbers to a General Conference.

Composition. Members of the Regional Houses together with an additional representative or representatives of each of the Provincial Conferences, the numbers of the additional representatives to be decided by the members of the Regional Houses.

Arrangements in regard to the Colony and Lagos

For purposes of preliminary consideration two conferences shall be called—the first representing the Colony and the second Lagos. The composition of the Colony conference shall be settled by the Commissioner of the Colony in co-operation with the Hon. Member for the Colony and after consultation with the Native Authorities and representative organisations in the Colony. The composition of the Lagos conference shall be settled by the Commissioner of the Colony in co-operation with the three elected Members for Lagos after consultation with the Town Council and representative organisations in Lagos. The two conferences will then meet in a joint Colony and Lagos conference for further discussion and will send representatives to the drafting committee and the General Conference.

Drafting committee

Function. To prepare a statement setting out draft recommendations for constitutional changes based on the views of the Regional and Colony and Lagos Conferences and to submit the statement for consideration to a General Conference.

Composition. Three representatives of each Regional Conference, one representative of the Colony Conference and one representative of the Lagos Conference, sitting with the Chief Secretary, Attorney-General and Financial Secretary, and such other official advisers as may be called in for consultation.

General conference

Function. To study the statement prepared by the Drafting Committee, to suggest any changes or amendments which it considers necessary and to submit its recommendations regarding constitutional advance for debate in the Regional Houses and the Legislative Council and then for submission to His Excellency the Governor and the Secretary of State for the Colonies.

Composition. All unofficial members of the Legislative Council together with additional representatives of the Regional Conferences and the Colony and Lagos Conference, providing that the additional representatives shall be drawn from the

Regions and the Colony and Lagos in the same proportions as those fixed in regard to the unofficial members of the Legislative Council. On this basis it is recommended that the full composition of the General Conference should be as follows:—

	Members
Northern Provinces	18
Western Provinces	12
Eastern Provinces (including two members from Calabar)	12
Lagos	6
Colony	2
Other existing nominated unofficial members of Legislative Council	3
Total	53

His Excellency the Governor shall be invited to appoint an independent Chairman (who shall have no vote). The Committee suggests that he should be a Law Officer and hopes that the Honourable the Attorney-General may be selected for this task.

The General Conference shall meet at a convenient centre to be later agreed upon by the Legislative Council, but shall not meet in the towns in which the Regional headquarters are situated or in Lagos.

Minute on 65

It will be recalled from (4) that at the Budget meeting this month the Legislative Council was to be invited to set up a Select Committee of the Council to make recommendations 'regarding the steps to be taken for a review of the present Constitution of Nigeria, with special reference to the methods to be adopted for ascertaining the views of all sections of the population on the issues involved'.

The despatch at (6) opposite reports that the Select Committee was set up, that it produced a unanimous report and that the report has been unanimously accepted by the Council.

The review of the Constitution which is proposed falls into four stages:—

(i) *At provincial level.* It is recognised that the composition of the Provincial Conferences may vary in different parts of the country. They will be set up after consultation between the Resident of each Province, in co-operation with the Member or Members of the Regional Houses from that Province, with the Native Authorities or other representative bodies. This will ensure consideration down to village and divisional level.

(ii) *At regional level.* (a) The Regional Conferences will consist of Members of the Regional Houses together with additional representatives from each of the Provincial Conferences as may be decided by the Members of the Regional Houses. (b)Special arrangements for the Colony and Lagos. For preliminary consideration there will be two Conferences—one for the Colony and one for Lagos. The composition of the

Colony Conference will be settled by the Commissioner of the Colony, in co-operation with the Member for the Colony, after consultation with the Native Authorities and representative organisations. The composition of the Lagos Conference will be settled by the Commissioner, in co-operation with the three elected Members for Lagos, after consultation with the Town Council and representative Lagos organisations. These two Conferences will later meet as a Joint Conference.

(iii) *Drafting Committee*. The object of this Committee is to prepare draft recommendations for constitutional changes based on the views emerging from the bodies at (i), (ii) (a) and (ii) (b) above, and to submit these recommendations to the General conference at (iv) below. The Drafting Committee will be representative: of each Regional Conference and of the Colony and Lagos Conferences, but it will also contain the Chief Secretary, the Attorney-General, the Financial Secretary and such other official advisers as may be called in for consultation.

(iv) *General Conference*. This Conference will study the statement prepared by the Drafting Committee, will suggest any changes or amendments which it thinks necessary and will submit its recommendations for debate in the Regional Houses and the Legislative Council. The final stage will be submission to the Governor and the Secretary of State. The General Conference will consist of all unofficial Members of the Legislative Council together with additional representatives of the Regional, Colony and Lagos Conferences. Representation of the latter three bodies will be in the same proportions as those fixed for unofficial membership of the Legislative Council. The Conference will number 53 in all. It will have an independent Chairman without a vote, and the Select Committee has expressed the hope that the Attorney-General may be the Chairman. It is provided that the Conference shall not meet in the towns in which the Regional Headquarters are situated or in Lagos.

Consideration of constitutional change is, therefore, bound to be a lengthy progress; but it will be none the worse for that, and the proposals seem to be eminently sound, as they are designed to give the widest possible representation, not only geographically, but to varying bodies of opinion, while, at the same time, preserving the right to participate fully at all stages both of the Regional Houses and of the Legislative Council. The insertion of the Drafting Committee at the third of the four stages seems to me well timed. The weight of official opinion and advice will be able to make itself felt at this stage without the imputation that the official element has steered the proceedings from the outset. The General Conference will also have the results of consultation at the previous stages put before it clearly and expertly. The provision that the General Conference shall go into retreat for its consultations is eminently sound. Finally, the questions posed by Mr. Foot in his speech, of which the text is attached to (6), present the Conferences at all levels squarely with the problems to which they will have to find the answer.

The Governor asks to be informed by telegram as early as possible whether the Secretary of State agrees to his announcing acceptance of the recommendations of the Select Committee. I can see nothing in these proposals to criticise. It may be assumed that the Conferences at provincial and regional levels will have the benefit of the advice of the financial and legal experts of Government if they choose to call it in. The General Conference will be predominantly Nigerian, and in this respect will resemble the Coussey Committee. The differences between procedure in the Gold Coast and Nigeria is that the Gold Coast has started with a Central Committee which will go down into the constituent regions of the Gold Coast during the course of its deliberations, whereas in Nigeria, owing to the much greater distances and differences in composition of the territory, a system of local consultation building up to eventual deliberation at the centre has been evolved.

The question at /P.Q.1 attached, which is for answer on Wednesday next, bears on this subject.[2] In drafting the answer I have assumed that the Secretary of State would wish to have rather more time for study of (6) herein before making any public statement.

L.H.G.
28.3.49

[2] Not Printed.

---

66 CO 537/4727, no 2   Mar 1949
[Political situation]: Nigeria political summary on developments since the sedition trials   [Extract]

1. *Political*

The sedition trials have come and gone, leaving six of the nine men who stood their trial serving prison sentences of varying lengths.[1] Agwuna, who was tried on two charges, fared worst, receiving one year on the first charge and two and a half years on the second; Abdullah[2] was given two years—the maximum for a first offence; Oged Macauley, Anyiam and Smartt Ebbi a year each and Tony Enahoro six months. Of the remaining three, Aniedobe and Duke Dafe were fined £25 each and J.J. Odufuwa, successfully pleading an alibi, was acquitted, although shortly afterwards, in his capacity of editor of the 'African Echo', he was fined £200 for a criminal libel on the acting Commissioner of Lands. Only three of the imprisoned 'martys' [sic] really matter; Abdallah is an effective orator with an attractive speaking voice and not lacking in courage and determination. The N.C.N.C. have always billed him as the man who speaks for the North and invariably refer to him as a Hausa, but in fact he is an Igbirrah and entered the Posts and Telegraphs under the name of Abdallahi Okene. (At one time he was married to the daughter of the Atta of Igbirrah but has since divorced her). He was a member of the radio monitoring service up to January 1948 when he was dismissed under G.O. 40(B) for making a violent anti-Government public speech. During his recent trial he took the opportunity to deliver a 90 minute harangue in which he repeated and underlined all the seditious opinions uttered in the speech for which he was being tried and, while no doubt this helped him to earn the maximum sentence, it has certainly increased his reputation and he has won a good deal of respect and admiration in nationalist circles for the way in which he has maintained his principles. Agwuna is a very much rougher diamond, but he too held firm—he refused throughout to make any defence, on the grounds that the Court had no jurisdiction over him—and has gained correspondingly in reputation with the extremists. At one time he held a very junior post in Posts and Telegraphs and later with the Air Ministry in Kano but he did not come to the fore until a few

---

[1] See 57.   [2] ie Raji Abdallah.

months ago when he became General Secretary of the Zikist Movement. He can hardly be described as fully literate but he has drive and directness of purpose and may well win more popular support when he emerges from prison. Tony Enahoro, in spite of his past record, is out of place in this galley; all our information suggests that he had no wish to be a martyr and did his best to avoid conviction, having had enough of prison after his last two sentences. The indications are that he is at heart a moderate and dislikes his fellow-prisoners, who are not his equals in ability and education, but his trouble is that he allows his impulses to run away with him and to land him in situations for which he has no relish. The other three are poor stuff, being looked down upon even by their own party. Oged Macauley [sic: Macaulay], the degenerate son of an attractive and able though unscrupulous father,[3] was drunk when he received sentence: Freddie Anyiam, who runs a pay-as-you-wear clothing service, is known as a cheerful rogue who specialises in doing other peoples dirty work. He was a member of the N.C.N.C. hierarchy for a brief period but was caught out in a 'fiddle' with the funds at the beginning of last year. Smartt Ebbi was an Army clerk during the 1939–45 War; though he is fond of referring to the way in which he fought for the Empire, he was at no time in contact with the enemy. After the war, he got a job with a firm of building contractors but was soon in the dock charged with extorting money from his fellow employees, and was sentenced to nine months imprisonment, since the completion of which he has earned a living as Assistant Editor of the 'African Echo'. The three last-named all pleaded 'not guilty' and did their best to avoid conviction—a course of action which has provoked adverse comment among the nationalists.

2.   There is not much doubt now that Azikiwe disapproved of the action of the seditionists, if only on the ground that it was premature. Perhaps the most important feature of the trials has been the use made of them by his own extreme left wing to attempt to force him to burn his boats and declare for violence. The 'African Echo', which now speaks for the extremists, has recently published articles openly criticising him for his inactivity, casting doubt on his personal courage and strongly hinting that if he is not prepared to make an issue of the imprisonment of the six 'heroes' and fight it out until their release is obtained then it is time for him to relinquish his leadership in favour of a more dynamic personality. But Azikiwe is a shrewd and experienced politician, adept at gauging the reaction of the public which, as a whole, does not appear to have been interested enough in the trials to justify his making a major issue of them. In the North and West they have created scarcely a ripple: in Lagos and in literate circles of the East they have been a topic of conversation but do not appear to have inspired any deep feelings. There have been indications in the Press that the extreme nationalists themselves are disappointed at the public indifference, but they have no intention of letting the issue die. On the contrary we have reliable information that they plan to demand the immediate release of all the imprisoned men, and to make the rejection of their demand the excuse for an attempt to start a campaign of civil disobedience and possibly of 'positive action'.

3.   The Zikist Movement has been very busy preparing the blue-print for this campaign and there has been much va-et-vient and interchange of letters between

---

[3] ie Herbert Macaulay.

Lagos and Enugu. Their chances of success depend on two factors—the attitude of Azikiwe and the support of the workers—and both of these must be regarded as doubtful at present. If the workers were solidly behind them the Zikists could probably dispense with Azikiwe altogether, since he is almost the only member of the N.C.N.C. Cabinet whose attitude is in question. Some, like Prest and Eyo Ita, have seen the red light and either resigned or retired out of harm's way, while the rest, including Imoudu and Emejulu are apparently working closely with Nduka Eze, now President General of the Zikist Movement in place of the imprisoned Abdullah.

4.   It is still difficult to assess how much of the Zikists' plans is based on reality and how much is hot air. They are talking—and writing—of plots to assassinate the Governor and other leading Government officials and there were sybilline references to April 1st and the shocks to come on that day, which was probably chosen because of the publicity it received in the Gold Coast as the deadline for freedom. But the ground has been cut from under the Zikists' feet by Kwame Nkrumah's explanation that actual violence on April 1st is not contemplated and the day passed with no incident. The potential threat, however, must not be underestimated: the Zikists have possibly a stock of hand grenades, probably a certain number of firearms, and certainly a considerable amount of .303 ammunition at their disposal. But, unless and until they can command the support of the mass of the workers, they will not be in a position to mount an offensive of more than local significance.

5.   It is perhaps upon the result of the competition for control of the workers, even more than on the constitutional issue, that the immediate future of Nigeria will turn. The latest developments are discussed in Paragraphs 10–13 but it should be noted here that the Nigerian Youth Movement have given somewhat tepid support to the T.U.C. and allotted them a certain amount of space in the 'Daily Service' for propaganda, not so much because of any inherent faith in that body as on the principle that any organisation opposed to the N.C.N.C. deserves encouragement. The career of N.Y.M.–Egbe has been a chequered one during 1949. The Representative Assembly (See Possum 28, paragraph 6) was a marked success— which seems to have surprised not only their enemies but the organisers themselves. The Rev. Sorensen and Miss Rita Hinden behaved circumspectly, always emphasising that Nigeria's problems must be dealt with by Nigerians and that they themselves held only a watching brief, the attendances were good and a lot of solid commonsense was talked. But almost immediately afterwards the N.Y.M. wearying of well-doing, decided that the only royal road to popularity—and votes at the 1950 Elections—was to join in the vilification of Government. This they did through the medium of the 'Daily Service' with a gusto not a whit lessened by their almost open admission that they did not believe in what they were saying and writing: indeed throughout February they might have said with the poet that they had seen and approved the better course but followed the worse.

6.   Their attack followed two main lines—the iniquity of Government in alienating their God-given land and discrimination in the Civil Service. Both were well-chosen—particularly the former, for the African is of course instinctively sensitive on the subject of land tenure and only too ready to assign the worst possible motives to any attempt to acquire land for public purposes even in the smallest parcels and for the most praiseworthy objects. A Mass Meeting held under N.Y.M. auspices on the 18th of February to protest against certain sections of the Land Acquisition Ordinance was very well attended. The leaders of N.Y.M. had intended to

stage a 'spontaneous' march on Government House, but news of this leaked out and on the advice of the Commissioner of Police Sir Adeyemo Alakija successfully appealed to the more responsible feelings of the gathering and a deputation to Government House was substituted. This was received by His Excellency a few days later and discussions are continuing. In this connection it is worthy of note that the sections of the law in dispute had been the subject of correspondence between Government and N.Y.M. for some months past and it is highly probable that N.Y.M. only decided to force the issue for reasons of political expediency. The series of articles by Magnus Williams on 'Spiritual Depression in the Civil Service' has had some effect in acerbating discontent in the ranks of the Junior Service, although the facts were twisted and distorted almost beyond recognition. The anti-Government campaign, however, has not been followed up with any vigour and of recent days the tone of the 'Service' has been distinctly more friendly.

7.   There has been a split in the ranks of N.Y.M. which began with the re-election of Dr. Maja as President in January: this post H.O. Davies had hoped to capture through the votes of his supporters who feel that Maja is now too old and that younger blood is needed. Davies is known to have felt considerable jealousy over Maja's re-appointment and in February he ran counter to the whole trend of N.Y.M. policy by accepting £1,000 from the faction opposed to the Oni of Ife to stir up trouble in Ifeland. Davies is now, quite naturally, looked upon as a traitor by some members of N.Y.M., particularly those who are also members of Egbe Omo Oduduwa which has always supported the cause of the Obas, and indeed, derives much of its strength from their adherence. In private conversation Davies has declared his intention of breaking the Egbe and on March 7th in the office of the Daily Service, a clash took place, during which blows were exchanged between himself and Bode Thomas over the wording of an article on the visit of the N.Y.M. and Egbe delegates to Ife . . . . Davies waited in the office until Thomas had left and then had the article re-set to his own liking, but to no purpose, as later in the evening M.A. Ogun, a supporter of Thomas came in, found out what had occurred and re-wrote the article to conform with Thomas's ideas, which no doubt came as an unpleasant shock to Davies next morning.

8.   The label N.Y.M.–Egbe has until now been used in these summaries to denote the two organisations which were so closely merged that they could safely be treated as one, but this tag has now outlived its usefulness, not only because of the split referred to above, but because the leaders of Egbe Omo Oduduwa have had second thoughts. Although such an object was carefully excluded from the prospectus, E.O.O. set out in the first place to play national politics but they have burned their fingers and are now inclined to confine themselves to declared principles—that is to run the E.O.O. on a tribal and cultural basis. They have by no means lost their fears of Ibo infiltration and Egbe will no doubt continue to have a strong anti-Ibo bias, but the new policy has mitigated the distrust of the leaders' motives previously felt by the rank and file and a fresh stirring of interest has been noticeable in the past few weeks.

9.   During the past three months, a series of efforts has been made to patch up a truce between the two main parties—N.C.N.C. and N.Y.M.—in order to present a united front on the constitutional issue. Such a reconciliation could at best be temporary, for motives and interests are too sharply opposed and personal hatreds probably run too deep for any lasting settlement to be achieved, but it is obvious that if the parties could speak from a common platform during the next year the trend of

events might be considerably altered, and there has been no lack of go-betweens and would-be mediators, most of whose efforts have been stillborn. There has, however, been one serious approach, made on the initiative of Dr. Maja and Obafemi Awolowo, the Secretary General of E.O.O., which reached the stage of pourparlers with Azikiwe, and at one stage looked as if it might come to something. The majority of the leaders on both sides, however, were totally opposed to any reconciliation—Eze in particular being alarmed at the curtailment of his personal influence which might result from it—and negotiations fell through. Judging from the severity of the attacks on Azikiwe now appearing in the 'Service' the chances of a further move towards reconciliation in the near future are remote. . . .

67   CO 583/299/2, no 7   12 Apr 1949
[Local government reform]: letter from H M Foot to A B Cohen on the need for local government reform in the North and West

I am sorry to have been some time in replying to your confidential letter of the 4th of March about the proposal to appoint a local government expert to Nigeria. We have, as you know, been in Ibadan for the past few weeks and we thought that it would be useful to take the opportunity which the Legislative Council meeting provided to discuss the matter with the Chief Commissioners.

The Governor accordingly had a full discussion in Ibadan with the Chief Commissioners and I think that the importance of pressing ahead with reform of local government in the North and the West as well as in the East is now more clearly recognised by all concerned. Apart from the discussions with the Chief Commissioners there was a debate in the Legislative Council on local government advance and a Private Member's Resolution was passed unanimously urging the necessity for urgent action to 'democratize' the existing Native Authorities in the North and West.

The Chief Commissioner of the Western Provinces announced in his speech that it is proposed to set up a special committee to consider how advance should proceed in the Western Provinces and the Chief Commissioner of the North made a speech indicating the changes which he hopes to see in the North. Indeed I think it can be said that the recognition of the need to press ahead with overhauling the Native Authority system was one of the principal points which emerged from this meeting of the Legislative Council.

Whilst we certainly agree with you on the necessity for advance in the North and the West we are doubtful, on thinking the matter over yet again, whether the best means of achieving our object will be to import an expert with solely U.K. experience. In drawing up the new legislation for the Lagos Municipality and for the Eastern reforms we certainly need U.K. advice (and we are getting it from the Local Government Panel) but we feel that at this stage at least the problem in the North and the West must be dealt with by different means. After talking to the Chief Commissioners we propose that the next step should be to select an experienced administrative officer in each Region who should be detached from other work in order to give his whole time to questions of local government advance. He would spend most of his time travelling and would be able to provide some of the co-ordination and prodding and new thinking which are necessary. Pyke-Nott has already appointed an officer for such duty in the Eastern Provinces and we hope soon to be able to make similar appointments in the West and North. We believe that that step is the best one to take at the moment and that we should hold over the proposal to bring in a U.K. expert for the time being. Perhaps the best course will be to give these regional local government officers experience, by secondments in the United Kingdom, of U.K. methods rather than bring some one out from England who could have no knowledge of the peculiarities of the Emirates of the North or the special system of Native Authorities in the West.

We certainly do not dispute the points which you bring out in your letter but after a good deal of thought we are inclined to feel that for the present we should press ahead in the way that I have mentioned rather than bring in an outside expert. The Governor has asked me to put this view to you and to say that we should very much welcome any further comment or advice which you can give us.

68   CO 537/4631, no 3   27 Apr 1949
[Political situation]: inward savingram no 893 from Sir J Macpherson to Mr Creech Jones taking stock of the current political situation

The lull in political activity following the Ibadan meeting of Legislative Council and preceding the lengthy process of constitutional review which is now to take place provides a useful opportunity to take stock of the present situation and to record developments which have taken place since I sent my saving telegram No. 435 dated the 28th of February about the political situation.[1]

2.   The Ibadan meeting of the Council went well. Savage was able to carry the Finance Committee with him in approving the budget with little or no important amendment, full support was given to legislation proposed including the extremely important marketing legislation; and the unanimous decision reached regarding the method to be adopted for review of the constitution was a most useful achievement. There was strong criticism of the Posts and Telegraphs Department for failure to provide efficient and extended services (due to desperate staff difficulties) but general appreciation of progress under the Development Plan was expressed for the first time. Throughout the proceedings there was evidence from representatives of all parts of the country of irritation and anger directed against Azikiwe particularly arising from the attacks of his newspapers on Native Authorities and traditional rulers.

3.   The N.C.N.C. convention took place in Lagos early this month. The delegates were men of little standing and the meeting was chiefly of interest for the disagreement which went on behind the scenes between Azikiwe and the most extreme of his own followers. He made appeals for discipline and has tried to persuade his supporters to postpone plans for 'positive action' until next year by which time better preparations can be made and the attack can be directed at whatever constitutional changes are then proposed. This more cautious policy has earned him a good deal of criticism (not much of which is however publicly voiced) and the Zikist Movement is now probably more inclined to disregard N.C.N.C. leadership and follow an extreme line of its own. Azikiwe himself is worried by this

[1] See 62.

restlessness amongst his followers and no doubt as a sop to them has instructed his papers to increase attacks on the Government. The proposed N.C.N.C. tour of the Provinces for which Azikiwe has shown little enthusiasm has however been postponed until later in the summer.

4.   Meanwhile there has been no very serious recrudescence of the tribal ill-feeling which threatened to have serious consequences last year although the Lagos papers still compete with one another in abusing political adversaries—and both sides are complaining that the Government does not intervene to stop their opponents.

5.   Azikiwe himself was a member of the Legislative Council Select Committee which unanimously recommended the methods to be adopted for the review of the constitution but that has not prevented his Press from criticizing the methods approved and now being put into effect. The unconvincing line of the attack is that it is no use consulting the mass of the people on such matters and that in any event the N.C.N.C. 'Freedom Charter' is the last word which need be said in the matter.

6.   Generally the political situation has somewhat improved since my report was made in February and the method decided upon for review of the constitution has taken the political initiative out of the hands of the N.C.N.C. and its extremists.

7.   There is however another aspect of the situation which I regard as potentially dangerous. When I made my last report in February I referred to the split in the Trade Union Movement and to the activities of a group of Trade Union leaders who are supporters of the N.C.N.C. or members of the Zikist Movement: they have now formed what they call the Nigerian National Federation of Labour. In particular I mentioned Eze, the paid secretary of the U.A.C. Union, and his attempts to call a strike of all U.A.C. employees. These efforts have been intensified and I think that it is probable that, seeing the circumstances unpropitious for a purely political agitation N.C.N.C. supporters propose to attempt to stir up labour trouble, starting with the U.A.C. and possibly then turning their attention to the Railway and other large employers of labour.

8.   In the U.A.C. dispute (if such it can be called when the reasons for the proposed strike are more political than industrial) the Labour Department has endeavoured to persuade both parties to resort to the proper procedure of conciliation. These efforts have been made more difficult by the fact that the U.A.C. Management has refused to deal with Eze (the Management regards itself as justified in this by Eze's unreasonable and violent attitude and by his abusive attacks on the U.A.C. in the Press) but, though I sympathize with their views on Eze, I think that they are on unsound ground in refusing to deal with whatever leaders the workers choose particularly once a dispute is declared. Negotiations are however still proceeding through the medium of the Labour Department. Eze has declared that a general U.A.C. strike will take place on the 6th of May[2] and it seems clear that the Management is prepared for the strike and determined not to give way. It is still uncertain whether Eze and his associates are strong enough to achieve a full U.A.C. strike but the present indications are that the strike will take place next month and that in many areas, particularly in Sapele and Burutu, where the largest numbers of U.A.C. employees are congregated, the Union leaders will be supported. There are

---

[2] 'It did not' was minuted in the margin at this point.

disturbing reports that the extremists intend to attempt to organise sabotage of U.A.C. buildings and equipment. Meanwhile the Labour Department is doing everything possible to proceed with the negotiations without much help from either side.

9. A further disturbing feature of the situation is that in many areas, particularly in the towns, prices and rents have continued to rise and that fact tends to play into the hands of those who wish to start labour troubles.

10. In general it can, I think, be said that our plans for advance in the political field and in the economic field have created a feeling that the Government is genuinely anxious to press forward with a progressive and constructive policy in full co-operation with the people. A comparatively small number of extremists, now more isolated from general public support, is determined to use violent and subversive methods to prevent orderly progress. They have apparently decided to attempt a first trial of strength in the labour sphere. They may not succeed by strike action in obtaining any benefits for the workers but that is not their primary intention—their main aim is to create confusion and bitterness against the large firms and against the Government.

11. Any measures which can be taken by the Government to forestall or curtail the intended U.A.C. strike and strikes of Government workers will of course be taken but, for the reasons to which I have referred, I am not optimistic that the leaders of the U.A.C. Union will be prepared to listen to reason. I shall of course keep you fully informed of developments.

69 CO 537/4727, no 3   May 1949
[Political situation]: Nigeria political summary on tensions in the Zikist movement and the increasing influence of the NYM   [Extract]

Political

1. The Budget Session of Legislative Council took place in an atmosphere of general goodwill and co-operation. The members now know each other much better than they did and many of the unofficial members, having attended together the African Conference in London last year, are now on terms of personal friendship which cuts across regional and tribal affiliations. There is ample evidence of increasingly bitter hostility amongst nearly all members against Azikiwe and impatience with the other Lagos members but apart from that the unofficial members get on well together and often decide amongst themselves on a joint line of action to be taken in the Council. The work of the Council over the past two years has certainly helped to build up a spirit of mutual respect between the representatives of the three Regions. There has also been a marked improvement in the confidence which unofficial members show in debate and most of them are now more ready to press their own views without being worried by procedural pitfalls or in any way deterred by the possibility of official disapproval. The numbers of the Council (forty four in all) are perhaps too small for good debate but there is a welcome increase in straight speaking. The Northern members though still concerned to make quite sure that their Region is not dominated by the Eastern and Western Provinces, so much more advanced from the point of view of Western education, are less inclined to

adopt an isolationist attitude and this year there were only faint echoes of Mallam Tafawa Balewa's famous 'March to the Sea' speech.[1]

2.   The dislike for Azikiwe was illustrated by the opposition from all sides to his Newspaper Bill. The main object of the Bill was the abolition of the bond which must be deposited before a new paper is launched and Dr. Azikiwe no doubt had his own interests primarily in view but personal animosity and distrust were apparent in the speech of member after member and it is doubtful whether the Bill would have been approved even if it had been completely unobjectionable in itself. The Emirs of the North and the Obas of the West are particularly embittered by the attacks on their traditional position made through the medium of Zik's Press. They naturally identify Azikiwe completely with the policy of his papers but Azikiwe himself says in private that he is only one of a Board of Directors, the other members of which are more violently inclined than himself, and that he frequently has to defer to them. In spite of this deep cleavage, Dr. Azikiwe subscribed to the unanimous and important decision reached regarding the method to be adopted for the review of the constitution. The political significance of this move by Azikiwe cannot be overlooked and subsequent events have not detracted from its importance.

3.   The N.C.N.C. Convention which followed at the beginning of April in Lagos was an anti-climax. The bands and ballyhoo of last year's Kaduna Convention were absent: the attendance was sparse—only about 150 delegates turned up, of little standing for the most part—and nothing of great importance was said or done, except for Zik's appeal to his followers for moderation and discipline, in the course of which he said:—

> 'At the present stage of the development of Nigeria and the Cameroons our national life is interwoven too much with the vagaries of human nature. Not all of our sons and daughters have the stomach for battle, and not all of them have the spunk to resist injustice. We must make allowances for the bold and for the timid, hoping that time will vindicate the correct perspective. When, therefore, the militant elements among us feel that the time of positive action has arrived they must ponder deeply that for such action to succeed, there must be first, a mobilisation of forces, second, a disciplined army, third, a well protected general staff, fourth, a line of communication and lastly a cause worth fighting and dying for'.

This did not go down at all well with the extremists and on the 6th of April the 'African Echo', which may usually be taken as speaking for the Zikist Movement; published a violently denunciatory leader including such comments as

> 'This is a disappointing and distracting declaration coming as it did from quarters most unexpected, as was evidenced by the lifting of eye-brows and the ghastly staring at one another of those national conscious citizens who congregated either to participate or to watch the proceedings of the historic event.'

and

---

[1] 24 March 1947. See introduction, p. lii.

'For our part, we wonder where Zik will get any army to mobilise when the time comes. Certainly, not those disappointed and disillusioned disciples of Zikism would again freely offer their services'.

Two days later Azikiwe in open convention accused Eze of being responsible for the article: the latter indignantly denied this and Odufuwa, the editor of the 'Echo' was sent for. Asked for his source of information, he made the embarrassing revelation that Agwuna and Oged Macaulay were the guilty parties. Naturally, this part of the proceedings was not reported in the press. For the rest, various branches of the Zikist Movement tabled resolutions counselling violence: the following extract from one by the Onitsha Branch being typical of the whole:—

'vii. *Gymnastic Exercises*
All Branch Committees shall learn:
1. Forest escapades and studies.
2. Fasting in the Campings.
3. Swimming.
4. Military Tacties.

viii *Arrests of Members*
On the pronouncement of sentences:—
(a) The Magistrate or Judge shall be dealt with
(b) The Incendiary explosive shall be laid if possible under the seat of the Judge or Magistrate and around the courts'.

This and the rest of its kind were turned down by the 'Cabinet' but Nduka Eze dissented from their decisions, not surprisingly considering that during the N.C.N.C Convention he was holding secret meetings of the Zikist Movement at which he persuaded members to swear an oath of personal allegiance to himself in support of any line of action he might decide to take.

4.   Though no open breach has yet taken place all the indications are that there is a growing rift between Zik on the one hand and the extremists led by Eze on the other and that neither of the protagonists is particularly anxious to close the gap. Eze is an ignorant and narrow would-be demagogue but he is probably the most dangerous extremist in Nigeria today and he would not be sorry to step into Azikiwe's shoes. Azikiwe, on the other hand, is growing increasingly doubtful of the value of the support of the extremists of his movement. There are even indications that he is seeking a rapprochement with the N.Y.M.—of recent weeks a number of cartoons have appeared in his papers depicting the N.C.N.C. and the N.Y.M. standing side by side to fight the common enemy of 'Imperialism' and though these cartoons have only enraged the extremists while failing to win the N.Y.M., whose leaders are still bitterly opposed to Zik, they may be regarded as a first step by Zik to educate public opinion to the idea of a centre party. That no open rift between Zik and the extremists has appeared is probably due to the doubt in Eze's mind as to whether he can afford to dispense with Azikiwe whose prestige, particularly in the Eastern Provinces, is important and to the fact that, should the Nigerian National Federation of Labour, also led by Eze, succeed in winning the support of the Trades Union movement, Azikiwe could with difficulty do without its support. In these circumstances Zik is having to tread a particularly delicate and tortuous course.

5.   Azikiwe's attitude may be influenced by the fact that the Nigerian Youth

Movement is experiencing something of a revival and its influence at any rate in Lagos and the Western Provinces is increasing: even in the North, where previously it existed virtually in name only, it is gaining some new adherents, chiefly, of course, among the Yorubas resident there, for its membership is still essentially Yoruba. The executive, greatly daring, are even planning a propaganda campaign in the East. This is not to say that its influence in the country is yet on a par with that of the N.C.N.C.—it is not; but there can be little doubt that during the past year it has developed from a shadowy debating society into a comparatively virile body, capable of formulating its views and maintaining them against the formidable opposition of the N.C.N.C., at whose expense most of its gains have been effected.

6.   The increased extent of N.Y.M. influence in Lagos may be gauged by the progress of the Lagos Conference at present discussing the revision of the Constitution. It is difficult to find a genuinely representative body for so cosmopolitan and heterogeneous a town as Lagos but it may be taken that the delegates invited form as representative a body as can reasonably be expected. The crux of the debate has been whether regionalisation should be based, as the N.Y.M. contends, on three powerful Regions or whether more numerous Regions should be created as the N.C.N.C. advocates, based on 'linguistic groups'. On this issue a vote was taken on the 13th of May, the principle of three Regions winning by 34 votes to 14. Up to this point N.Y.M. and N.C.N.C. delegates had been sitting together in apparent amity—Azikiwe and H.O. Davies sat next to each other—but the same evening a hasty N.C.N.C. 'Cabinet' meeting was held at which it was decided to stage a 'walk-out' at the next meeting of the conference. On the 20th of May, Sa'ad Zungur and L.N. Namme duly walked out. Azikiwe, wisely and typically, did not attend on that day, but he took part in the deliberations at the next meeting, held on the 27th of May, and is under fire from the extremists for having done so. (This well illustrates Zik's present dilemma of having to appear to hunt with the wolves while wishing to run with the lambs). Similar 'walk-outs' by N.C.N.C. representatives may occur at conferences in the Provinces, when it becomes apparent that the N.C.N.C. Freedom Charter is not going to win the day. . . .

70   CO 583/294/2, no 2   30 May 1949
[Revenue allocation]: inward savingram no 1175 from H M Foot to Mr Creech Jones on the need to review the allocation of revenue between the centre and the regions. *Enclosure*: memorandum by A.W.L. Savage on the allocation of revenue to the regions

Financial and Administrative Procedure under the New Constitution: Method of Allocating non-declared Revenues to Regions.

The Statement of Administrative and Financial Procedure under the new Constitution which was approved as a result of the report by Mr. (now Sir Sydney) Phillipson, copies of which were sent to you with my Despatch No.272 of the 2nd of December, 1947, provided in para. 9 for the declaration of certain revenues as 'regional' and, in para. 10, for the allocation to each Region from the revenues of Nigeria other than those 'declared regional' of amounts strictly proportionate to the contribution which such Region makes to those other revenues.[1] This allocation of revenue has proved to be one of the most contentious matters connected with the present Constitution and one which has thus far defied attempts at a satisfactory solution. In the past two years, grave practical objections to the method of allocation proposed by Sir Sydney Phillipson have become apparent and the method (which Sir Sydney explained in para. 25 of his Report results from an attempt to reconcile two conflicting principles) is not beyond objection in principle. It is certain that the framing of some more suitable financial arrangements will be one of the most difficult features of the revision of the Constitution which has recently been begun.

2.   A copy of a Memorandum recently prepared in this office which sets out the history of the allocations of revenue to the Regions and explains the problems is sent with this Savingram. This Memorandum was drafted for the information of the Finance Committee but, in the event, was not circulated. The Committee agreed that an investigation was necessary and £1,500 was provided under Head 40, Miscellaneous Subhead 74, Statistical Survey for Revenue Allocations in current Estimates. The Resolution foreshadowed in para. 18 of the Memorandum was not, therefore, necessary.

3.   In these circumstances, Sir John Macpherson directed shortly before his departure on leave that the matter should be discussed with the appropriate members of your Office by the present Financial Secretary (Mr. Savage) when he arrives in the United Kingdom. Mr. Savage expects to reach London towards the end of the third week in June and the purpose of this Savingram is to ask that he be given an early opportunity of discussing with Mr. Cohen and others the possibility of obtaining the services of an expert on federal finance, probably and preferably, from the Dominion of Canada (where problems not dissimilar from our own have been successfully solved), who could come to Nigeria for a few months this Summer and advise on the local problems.

Enclosure to 70

One of the declared objects of the Constitution which was introduced as a result of the Despatch of the 6th of December, 1944, from the Governor of Nigeria (Sir Arthur Richards, as he then was) to the Secretary of State was the devolution upon the Regional Councils of a large measure of financial responsibility. Paragraph 12 of the Despatch (Sessional Paper No. 4 of 1945) stated:—

'I propose to devolve upon the regional Councils a large measure of financial responsibility. Each would have its own regional budget, on which would be borne the cost of all Government services in the region, including the salaries of Government personnel. The only exception would be the cost within the region of services declared to be central services, such as the railway, posts and telegraphs, income tax and audit, which would continue to be carried on the Central Estimates as at present, together with the central organization of Government, the headquarters and central staff of all Departments and such charges as interest on public debt, pensions, etc. Regional revenue would consist in the first place of the share of the direct tax at present payable to the

[1] See 42.

Central Government together with any receipts from fees, licences, etc. which might be allotted to the regional budgets, and in the second place of annual block grants from central revenue'.

After the proposals in the Despatch had received the approval of the Secretary of State, it was necessary to work out in greater detail the financial and administrative procedure required to give effect to the broad principles of the new Constitution. This task was entrusted to Mr. S. Phillipson, CMG (as he then was) and at the end of 1946 he submitted the very valuable Report upon which was based the Statement of Administrative and Financial Procedure which now governs these matters.[2]

2.   The author of the Report found no great difficulty in establishing principles to govern the declaration of 'fees, licences, etc. which might be allotted to the regional budgets' but, in respect of the 'annual block grants from central revenue' he wrote (para. 24 of the Report):—

'By far the most difficult aspect of the problem of financial procedure under the new constitution is the question of the basis on which available revenues are to be allocated to the Regions for expenditure on regional purposes. In approaching this question one is confronted at the outset by two cogent but unfortunately conflicting principles which may, for convenience be called:—
(a) Principle of derivation
(b) Principle of even progress.'

The Report went on to consider these two principles and the possibility of reconciling them. The proposals finally recommended, which in due course received the Governor's approval, are thus stated in para. 10 of the Statement of Administrative and Financial Procedure:—

'(i) The interests of Nigeria as a whole must always determine the allocation of revenues and other public funds for Nigerian and Regional Expenditure.
(ii) Subject to the fundamental principle stated in sub-paragraph (i) above and also to the condition that more should not be allocated than can reasonably be expended, it will be an objective of policy to achieve, as early as may be and in any event within a period of five years, a condition of things in which it will be possible to allocate to each region for expenditure on regional services and works:—
(a) the full amount of the Government share of the tax collected under the Direct Tax Ordinance, 1940 (as subsequently amended) and all other revenues declared regional.
(b) a grant from the other revenues of Nigeria not included in (a) above or from the other public funds of Nigeria in strict proportion to the contribution which the region makes to those other revenues'.

3. Whatever the merits in principle of allocating non-declared revenues 'in strict proportion to the contribution which the region makes to those . . . revenues' (and, as will be shown later in this Memorandum, the system has grave defects in

---

[2] See 42.

principle), difficulties were immediately met with in practice. Appendix C of Mr. Phillipson's Report was devoted to the basis of allocation of revenues and he applied the formulae which he devised to a 'break-down' of the Estimates for 1946–47, that is to say, to an analysis of the Estimates for that year, prepared by the authorities severally responsible for the preparation of those Estimates, showing, in respect of revenue, the shares drawn from each region (so far as this was possible) and, in respect of expenditure, its division between Nigerian and regional services and works. It was immediately found that no reliable statistical information was available upon which to determine the proportions in which the Regions at that time contributed to Nigerian revenues not declared regional and Mr. Phillipson was careful to state that his calculation of the relative proportions was based 'on the best information at present available'.

4. The Estimates for 1947–48 were similarly 'broken down' and used as a basis for calculating the provisional allocation of revenues to the Regions for the financial year 1948–49 (the first year for which 'Regional Estimates' were to be prepared, the first year in which the financial provisions of the new Constitution were implemented). On this occasion, the work was done in much greater detail and the most intricate calculations were used in determining the basis upon which each of the major Sub-heads of Revenue should properly be deemed to be derived from the respective Regions. The absence of reliable statistics and the fact that the trade of the country is not organized upon the same geographical basis as the new constitutional arrangements were great handicaps and although the results achieved were felt to be the best possible in the circumstances, the Government was far from satisfied that the method it was compelled to adopt were satisfactory having regard to the great political and financial issues involved. The task would have been one of great complexity and administrative difficulty in a country where advanced statistics were readily available but in Nigeria, where there is not even any reliable estimate of total population or of distribution of that population the job could only be done by the use of broad assumptions and approximations. It should be recorded, however, that the percentages determined by this means were not substantially different from those arrived at by Mr. Phillipson by the use of different methods.

5. The provisional allocations of revenue for 1948–49, which were made in July 1947, had to be adjusted (as had been foreseen in the Report) because the cost of the then existing services and works in the Eastern Region was more than that Region would have received under the approved principles of allocation and it had been accepted that the introduction of the new Constitution could not be made an occasion for a sudden and drastic curtailment of expenditure on Regional services and works in a particular Region when that expenditure had been incurred or planned according to pressing needs. It is unfortunate that the Memorandum on these provisional allocations described the allocations determined by the approved means as 'ideal allocations' and went on to speak of adjustments of these 'ideal allocations'. The term was intended to signify the allocations made according to approved procedure: but these were not in themselves 'ideal' in any absolute sense— they were admittedly the result of an attempt to reconcile the two conflicting principles referred to in para. 2 above. Experience has shown that the approved method of allocating is far from 'ideal', indeed, it seems likely to offend against the very obvious principle declared by Lord Lugard in connection with the amalgamation of Northern and Southern Nigeria (at a time when, in the words of the Amalgamation

Report, the material prosperity of the South had increased 'with astonishing rapidity' whereas the North 'largely dependent on the annual grant of the imperial Government was barely able to balance its budget with the most parsimonious economy') that the revenue of the country should be so disposed 'as to benefit the country as a whole without creating jealousy and friction'.

6.   According to the procedure approved in the 'Statement of Administrative and Financial Procedure under the New Constitution', the provisional allocations of revenue made in July 1947 should have been completely revised in November or December of that year by a recalculation not only of the amount of revenue available for allocation, but also of the proportions in which, according to contributions to the newly-calculated non-declared revenues, the three Regions should share that amount. In theory, the whole process should be repeated in (say) July 1949, when the correct figures of actual revenue for 1948–49 are known. But, in July 1949, the provisional allocations of revenue for 1950–51 must be made: and they, again, would have to be twice recalculated, first in the following November and again in the following July. It has been proved in practice that these recalculations are beyond the administrative capacity of the country in its present state of development and with the present lack of reliable statistical information.

7.   The lack of accurate statistics was thought to be the chief imperfection in the approved system and it was for this reason that the Standing Committee on Finance of the Legislative Council was invited to approve in August 1948, financial provision so that Nigeria might obtain the services, for a short period, of a well-qualified statistical expert or an expert on federal systems of finance from overseas who could, with Mr. Phillipson, carry out a statistical survey and then make recommendations for the future determination of revenue allocations. But subsequent events showed that our statistical inadequacies were not the chief imperfection in the approved system.

8.   When the provisional allocations of revenue for the financial year 1949–50 were to be made in July, 1948, it appeared probable, on such indications of revenue and expenditure as there were at that time, that the draft estimates of Nigeria for 1949–50 would show a deficit of between £1,500,000 and £2,000,000 to be met by additional taxation. The formulae devised by Mr. Phillipson are not appropriate where the foreseeable revenue of the country falls short of the inevitable expenditure of Nigeria and of the Regions. In these circumstances, it was considered essential to limit the regional allocations to the minimum required to provide for the maintenance of public services then current and to provide for the earned increments of serving officers. It was agreed to adopt provisionally a total allocation of £5,500,000 and it was recognized that this would make it necessary for one or more Regions to ignore the approved margin of five per cent between revenue and expenditure.

9.   At the end of November, 1948, when it became necessary to revise the allocations and to notify the Regions of the revision in time for the impending Budget meetings of the Regional Councils, there was an estimated shortfall of revenue in 1949–50 of over £1,500,000. It was not then possible to say precisely what methods could be employed to raise this additional revenue or to see clearly what the total sum raised was likely to be. Without knowing how the total revenue is to be raised, it is not possible to determine the proportions in which the Regions respectively can be estimated to contribute to the non-declared revenues and,

consequently, to calculate what their share should be in accordance with the methods of allocation now approved. It is, as was admitted in para. 30 of the Phillipson Report, an inherent difficulty in the approved system that the allocation of revenue must be made 'long before the Nigerian Government is in a position to estimate the probable revenues for the relative year or to state with any definiteness the changes in taxation, if any, which are to be made'. The author of the Report thought it reasonable to envisage a revision stage at which 'By early in December the Nigerian Government will normally be in a position to give a revised figure based on a considered estimate and on any fiscal proposals which may have taken shape in the meanwhile'. In fact, in December 1948, largely because very heavy unforeseen expenditure had just become inevitable, the Nigerian Government was not in that position. In these circumstances, there was no alternative but to revise the provisional allocations, not in accordance with the approved methods, but by maintaining the provisional figure of £5,500,000 adopted in July 'subject only to modifications arising from approved policy and to such future increases as may later be considered essential in relation to needs proved after review by His Excellency'.

10.   Between the date of the provisional allocations and the date of revision, the decision had been taken that educational grants-in-aid should be borne on Regional Estimates. As had been stated in paragraph 17 of the Memorandum on Approved Estimates for 1948–49, expenditure on such grants is essentially regional and it was only because the amounts actually payable in 1948–49 depended on the results of an inquiry into long-term policy then in prospect that it was decided to treat the 1948–49 expenditure as Nigerian. Nevertheless, the decision was not lightly taken. The pattern of educational development is such that these grants, which are (save for 'special purposes' grants) payable automatically under the new Educational Code, aggravate the position that the cost of maintaining existing services and works in one Region is more than that Region would receive under the approved methods of revenue allocation. It was the declared intention of the Government to redress this position as speedily as possible and the regionalization of educational-grants-in-aid would further frustrate that intention. But the arguments in favour of regionalization were so compelling that the decision was taken.

11.   The review given above of the working of revenue allocations so far shows that there are serious practical defects in the approved method of allocating revenue to the Regions: but further examination has shown that, as was only to be expected in a system designed to resolve the conflict between two principles, there are objections in principle as well and those objections have proved graver than was anticipated. One objection can be clearly seen if one pictures a country divided into two regions, one of which has been fully developed in the past and so enabled to make a great contribution to the non-declared revenues of the country as a whole, and the other which may be rich in natural resources but has had no development of any kind. The latter makes little or no contribution to the non-declared revenues of the country as a whole; its 'ideal' allocation of revenue under the present system is, therefore, practically nil and consequently it is without the funds which it requires to develop its resources and so increase its contribution to the country's revenues. In other words, the system has an inherent tendency to preserve inequality of development.

12.   Apart from the extreme example given in the preceding paragraph, it is not difficult to imagine circumstances in which the system would prove quite unsuited to conditions in Nigeria. If there were to be a sudden decline in the price of cocoa,

resulting in a 'slump' in that commodity such as have been not unknown in the past, the contribution made by the Western Region to the non-declared revenues of the country would dwindle so far as to make its 'ideal' allocation of revenue quite insufficient to cover the cost of existing services and works. But it would be at the time of such a 'slump' that there would be the greatest need for the maintenance of existing services and for their extension in order to provide the people with an alternative source of livelihood. Paragraph 25 of the Phillipson Report recognized that the principle of derivation was in essence 'To him that hath shall be given' but sought to minimize that objection on the ground that the contribution made by a Region to the revenues of Nigeria may be determined to a material extent by the readiness of its people to accept a high rate of direct taxation. But this argument is not valid in circumstances which render it impossible for the people to pay a high rate of direct taxation because their main source of livelihood has dwindled almost to vanishing point. As is stated in the same paragraph of the Report, a more just criticism of the principle is that its full adoption might permanently condemn backward regions to remain backward.

13.   For the purposes of allocations so far made to the Regions, the extent of a Region's contribution to the non-declared revenues of Nigeria has been in large part related to the value of the products exported from that Region. The first problem here is to determine what 'value' should be used. In practice it has been the 'port price', which is the yardstick for measuring export duties; but the main export crops of the country are now marketed under control and the 'port price' may be very much less than the price which the Marketing Board ultimately receives after allowing for freight and other charges incurred by the Board. This difference now accrues to the Board for the creation of a stabilization fund and for use in schemes for the benefit of the people who produce the crop. It is questionable whether in measuring the contribution made (say) by the Western Region to the non-declared revenues of Nigeria, the 'port price' of cocoa is a true standard by which to measure. Furthermore, the system takes no account of any benefits derived by Nigeria from a Region other than those which can be computed mathematically as part of the non-declared revenues of the country.

14.   The difficulties which the present system has presented and the dissatisfaction in the Regions with its working over the bare two years since it was introduced threaten to be a grave danger to the political and economic development of the country. Paragraph 10 of the Phillipson Report refers to the fact that before the amalgamation of Northern and Southern Nigeria, Southern Nigeria and the Colony of Lagos had to assist Northern Nigeria financially. In paragraph 5 of the Governor-General's Report on the Amalgamation (African West No. 1070 of 1919) the late Lord Lugard wrote:—

> 'Thus the anomaly was presented of a country with an aggregate revenue practically equal to its needs, but divided into two by an arbitrary line of latitude. One portion was dependent on a grant paid by the British taxpayer. . . .'

We are tending to develop a similar anomaly now: but the relative financial contributions of North and South to the common revenue are now reversed. The anomaly has recently been painfully illustrated by the need for improvements in the administrative organization of the Cameroons Province, part of a Trust Territory under United Nations trusteeship. It is clear that the United Nations will not be impressed if we claim to be unable to put into force our plans for the development of the Trust Territory because, although the country as a whole could afford them, the system under which we allocate revenue to the Regions results in the Region principally affected being unable to afford them.

15.   The most probable form of constitutional development in Nigeria is towards a federation of several semi-autonomous Regions but the present arrangements, under which the 'revenues declared regional' are so very much less than is required to cover expenditure declared regional and under which the difference must be made up from allocations of non-declared revenues, are not only unsuited to the development of such a federation but are likely to render its achievement impossible. Sir Sydney Phillipson has stated in his Report (para. 25):—

> 'It should be an objective of Nigerian and Regional fiscal action to bring about a state of things in which the contribution made by each region to the non-declared revenues of Nigeria is proportioned to the required scale of expenditure on regional purposes in that region so that the latter may correspond to the former'.

It is obvious that under the present system some years must elapse before this objective could be achieved (if it could ever be achieved under the present system) and during those vital years a Region which required financial assistance from the revenues of Nigeria disproportionate to its contribution would be regarded by the other Regions as a financial impediment to their progress. It is improbable that the other Regions would look on it as a desirable partner in a Federation if its potential value to such a Federation were obscured by its temporary inability to 'pay its way'.

16.   It is clear that we have here a constitutional and financial problem of the utmost difficulty which can perhaps be solved only by a radical alteration in our revenue system. If, as the Constitutional Despatch foreshadowed, the Regions are ultimately to have power to appropriate revenue for regional purposes, the field of taxation in which they are permitted to operate must be very different from that bounded by the present principles governing 'revenues declared regional'. No case is known elsewhere where a federation has been formed by the separation of a unified territory into several components which then join together again in a federation so that they may present a common political and economic front to the world. Federations have occurred where independent states, realizing the benefits of presenting a common political and economic front to the world, have joined together for this purpose and have voluntarily surrendered some of their state's rights to the federal organization as the price to be paid for those benefits. Nevertheless, it is sure that Nigeria could learn much from studying the financial systems which have been evolved in such countries as the Dominion of Canada, the Commonwealth of Australia, the Union of South Africa and the United States of America to serve groups of states joining in a central organization. It is therefore proposed to collect material on the subject from these countries and to obtain the services of an expert in federal finance who will, with the Financial Secretary, examine the problem and make recommendations.

17.   It was stated in Annexure I to the Constitutional Despatch that the Regions would have no separate surplus or reserve, but the recommendation in the Phillipson Report (para. 29) that the difference between actual expenditure and the revenue

which might properly have been allocated to the Region on the basis of actual revenue returns should be carried forward for or against the Region was later accepted by the Governor. It follows, however, from what has been stated earlier in this Memorandum that even when the actual revenue returns for the year 1948–49 have been received, there will not be the statistical data on which the revenue allocations already made could be adjusted in strict accordance with the principle that the 'block grants' should be in strict proportion to the Regions' contributions to non-declared revenues. It is therefore proposed that pending such further recommendations as may result from the investigation to be undertaken by the Financial Secretary with expert assistance, the unexpended portions of the Regional Revenue Allocations for the year 1948–49 will be paid to the Regions for the establishment of Regional General Revenue Balances. The allocations for the year 1948–49 included an element in respect of expenditure under Colonial Development and Welfare Schemes which is reimbursable by the Imperial Government. It is not intended that under-expenditure of this element should be credited to the Regional General Revenue Balances, since this would, in effect, be to charge to Nigerian revenues expenditure expressly declared to be reimbursable by the Imperial Government. On the other hand, it is not proposed that the Regions should forfeit any allocation made to them for expenditure under the Development and Welfare Head which they have, in the event, been unable to spend during the financial year.

18.   If the Standing Committee on Finance agrees with the recommendation that the subject of regional revenue allocations should be investigated by the Financial Secretary with the assistance of an expert in federal finance, a Resolution to this end will be submitted to the Legislative Council at the forthcoming Budget Meeting.

71   CO 537/4625, no 29   1 June 1949
[Constitutional review]: inward telegram no 1193 from H M Foot to Mr Creech Jones on the progress of consultations for the new constitution

Reference my Savingram No. 1054 of the 17th of May. Constitutional Review.

Preliminary discussions in the Provinces continue satisfactorily. We do not expect village, Divisional and Provincial meetings to deal with all the complicated and difficult constitutional points at issue, but they will in particular be able to give an indication, before representatives of the Provincial Conferences go forward to take part in the discussions in the Regional Conferences, of how each Province wishes to be represented in the Regional Houses of Assembly and how the Provincial representatives from each Province to sit in the Regional Houses should be selected. The discussions now proceeding all over the country have had a valuable effect in educating public opinion. Many people who previously took little interest in constitutional matters are making an effort to understand the present system and to think what changes might be made.

2.   In Lagos Azikiwe was taken to task by his own 'Cabinet' for agreeing to participate in the Lagos Conference and he had to concede that the two N.C.N.C. representatives should walk out at the next meeting. Azikiwe was absent from that meeting (pleading illness) and the two N.C.N.C. representatives duly walked out,

having protested about the composition of the conference and against the decision of the conference to vote on resolutions (the supporters of the N.C.N.C. had been heavily outvoted at the previous meeting). There was a good deal of public interest as to what would happen at the next meeting of the Lagos Conference which was held last week. To our surprise Azikiwe himself attended and took part in the discussions, and representatives of all the other organizations affiliated to the N.C.N.C. were also present. The only absentees were the two N.C.N.C. delegates who had walked out at the previous meeting. Some wrangling about the system of voting continued and one other delegate walked out in protest but all the other representatives continued the discussions which, as before, were reasoned and constructive. The conference will continue to sit once a week, probably for another month or more. It is perhaps, unfortunate that three representatives have withdrawn and extremist pressure may lead to other withdrawals later but it was important that a full party boycott of the conference should, if possible, be avoided and it is satisfactory that Azikiwe himself and other organisations affiliated to the N.C.N.C. have continued to take part.

3.   These events give rise to speculation about Azkiwe's future intentions. He appears to be following a very moderate line in spite of the increasing restlessness and opposition to his leadership amongst some of his own followers and he is devoting more of his time to his business and sporting activities. At present it looks as if the Zikist Movement intend to break with him and follow an extreme line of its own.

72   CO 859/131/2, no 9   8 June 1949
[Mass education]: despatch no 78 from H M Foot to Mr Creech Jones on the relationship between the constitutional review and schemes for community development

I have the honour to refer to your despatch No. 389 of the 10th of November, 1948, on the subject of mass education and to express regret that a reply has not previously been made.

2.   The fact that no earlier reply was sent does not mean that the principles which the despatch emphasize are questioned. On the contrary the call to new thinking and a new approach to the whole problem of the objects and methods of our administration is most warmly welcomed. Nor has there been any delay in discussing all the issues involved. Mr. Cohen, during his visit to Nigeria last year, was able to hear what has been and is being done by the Government and the Native Authorities and other agencies in the directions which the despatch advocated and to take part in preliminary discussions on the future policy to be followed. The whole matter was then considered at a conference of Chief Commissioners under the chairmanship of the Governor in January last, and following that conference the Chief Commissioner of the Eastern Provinces (Commander Pyke-Nott), who had attended the Cambridge Summer School, prepared at the request of the Governor a personal letter to all Residents in the Eastern Provinces, to which was attached a digest of the Summer School papers, explaining and commenting on the ideas which emerged from the Cambridge and London Conferences (the letter was sent to other Chief Commissioners as a guide to the action to be taken in their Regions). Other action

has already been taken, including an increase from £100,000 to £250,000 a year in the Vote for village reconstruction and development, these funds to be expended by Residents and District Officers in stimulating local development and enterprise without reference to higher authority. Moreover the Nigeria Local Development Board has been divided into Regional Development Boards which have a total capital amounting to £1,250,000 available for loans to Nigerian enterprises. Regional Production Development Boards have also been established and the first allocations (totalling £4,300,000) have now been made to them by the Produce Marketing Boards to finance schemes for the development of the producing industries and for the economic benefit and prosperity of the producers. The Regional Development Boards and the Production Development Boards (on both of which there are majorities of Nigerians) operate on a Regional basis and they were not set up with the specific purpose of encouraging community development, but you will appreciate how important it is from the point of view of community development that these Boards should exist with such substantial funds at their disposal and with powers to make loans and approve expenditure on industrial enterprises and agricultural development schemes. Provincial Development Committees and others engaged on working out plans for community development will be able to turn for assistance to these Boards and the fact that the Boards have statutory powers to make loans and approve expenditure will obviate the delay which would necessarily occur if application had to be made in the usual way and through normal channels for assistance from Government funds. In regard to staff too a first step has been taken in the recent appointment of Mr. Chadwick, who has done such outstanding work at Udi, as Community Development Officer for the whole of the Eastern Provinces.

3. Although wide discussion of the issues raised in your despatch has been encouraged and although the initial steps to put into effect some of the recommendations of the conferences held in England have been taken, it would be wrong to give the impression that, with so large a Service and so vast a territory, it is possible for new ideas to be quickly or equally assimilated or for immediate results on a widespread scale to be achieved. The questions at issue effect almost every major problem of administration which faces us today and, in particular, are bound up with the reform of local government to which all Administrative Officers have been and are giving so much attention. The future of community development clearly depends to a very large extent on the success which we can achieve in creating a framework of local government which can give the people of each village and each rural and urban area not only full responsibility in running their own local affairs but also the financial and administrative means to make the improvements which they need.

An almost equally important matter which must have its effect on community development is the policy of financial and administrative decentralization which we are putting into effect. The first and most important stage in carrying out that policy must be to distribute central revenue to the Regions and the problem of how that can fairly be done is one of the most difficult of the many problems which arise from the policy of greater Regional autonomy. It is obvious, however, that until the problem of allocation of central revenue to the Regions has been solved it will be impossible to effect further financial devolution to Provinces and Divisions or to reach conclusions on the question of what Government financial assistance can be given in the future to local government bodies. With regard to administrative decentralisation good progress has already been made in the regionalisation of the principal departments.

More can be done and will be done in this direction so that those engaged on work in the Divisions and Provinces who need approval from higher Departmental authority will be able to obtain decisions at Regional headquarters rather than await directions from Departmental Directors in Lagos.

The results of the main constitutional review on which we are now engaged must also have a decisive effect on community development. If, for instance, a Constitution were evolved which concentrated power at the centre the Government of a country so large as this would unavoidably be out of touch with the needs of the great bulk of the rural population, but if, as we confidently hope, power is shifted still further to the Regional legislatures and Regional Councils made up predominantly of men who come from the rural areas we can expect that the needs of community development will be much better appreciated.

I mention these major issues to illustrate how closely the policy of community development is bound up with nearly all the principal problems which we are now tackling and to emphasize the essential point that community development can never be treated as a separate and self-contained subject. The proposals discussed in your despatch do not in fact represent a new policy but rather a call to give in all our work a new emphasis to the needs of the smallest communities and to build with them on the sound foundations of self-help and communal initiative.

4.   There is one other question on which I should comment because on its solution so largely depends the pace and extent of progress in community development—it is the old question of how Administrative staff and Departmental staff in the Provinces can be partly relieved of the great and increasing burden of office work. During the war when recruitment to the Colonial Service came almost to a stop the position grew much worse and since the war there has been such an increase in the complexity and volume of Government work, and so marked a quickening in the pace of events, that the position has still further deteriorated. There has been a most welcome acceleration of Administrative recruitment since the war but we are still well below even the pre-war Administrative establishment, and now that the influx of new recruits from the Forces which followed the war has ended I gather that recruitment to the Administrative Service is likely to be once more reduced. The new appointments and the extensive reorganization which would be necessary to give the fullest effect to the policy of community development is, therefore, I am afraid, out of the question at the present time. Nothing would be gained, for instance, by withdrawing a District Officer from a large Division, leaving that Division without an Administrative Officer in order that be should take up a post as Community Development Officer at the Provincial headquarters. I myself feel that the aim which we should eventually achieve is for Administrative Officers to become members of a Provincial team working and touring from Provincial headquarters, each becoming a specialist in some branch of the Provincial work—such as local government or community development or land tenure reform—but that cannot be achieved in most areas until a more effective and efficient system of local government has been built up and the building up of that system is largely dependent at this stage on the efforts of Administrative Officers stationed in the Divisions. We are giving renewed and special attention to this problem of organisation and, on the Governor's direction, I am during his absence on leave making a series of visits to Provincial headquarters to discuss with all the Residents and all Administrative Officers in the Province together with the principal

Departmental Officers stationed in the Province what solution to this most difficult problem can be found. Some valuable suggestions have already emerged from the meetings of this kind which I have held in recent weeks and these suggestions are now under consideration with Chief Commissioners and Needs of Departments concerned. There can, however, be no easy or quick solution to the problem and for a long time to come shortage of experienced staff is bound to be the principal factor limiting advance in carrying out the policy of community development.

5.   I have replied to your despatch in very general terms at this stage indicating only some of the principal problems and difficulties which have to be faced here in carrying out the policy which was discussed so fully in England last year. The fact that it is necessary to refer to those problems and difficulties does not mean that we do not fully support that policy. We do: and I feel sure that I can speak for all members of the Nigerian Service in saying that we believe that it is our duty, while pressing on with constitutional and economic advance, to put first the interests of the great mass of the people who are villagers and farmers. We must ensure that those interests prevail by doing everything we can to arouse the rural population and village communities to a new realization of what they can achieve by communal effort and enterprise.

Copies of this despatch are being sent to the Chief Secretary, West African Council and to the Governors of the other West African Colonies.

73   CO 583/299/2, no 8   28 June 1949
[Local government reform]: despatch no 27 from H M Foot to Mr Creech Jones on the progress of local government reform

I have the honour to refer to your despatch No. 17 of the 13th of January, 1948, dealing with local government and in particular to the request in the seventh paragraph of that despatch that the question of the machinery for the review of policy on African local government should be further examined.[1] Lord Milverton, in his despatch No. 243 of the 30th of September, 1947, explained the reasons, which still hold good, why it was not intended to re-create the post of Secretary for Native Affairs in the central Nigerian Secretariat (the post created in 1920 was abolished in 1930) but in your despatch under reference you directed that further consideration should be given to the question how work connected with local government should be organized in the Regions and how it should be co-ordinated at central headquarters.

2.   In discussion of this question in previous correspondence two closely connected matters which are usually included under the heading of 'Native Affairs' have also been considered—those of land tenure and Native Court Reform and, before coming to the main question which you have asked to be further examined, it may be useful to record very briefly what has been done in those matters since Lord Milverton's despatch of the 30th of September, 1947 was written. The Lands Department has been separated from the Survey Department and completely reor-

---

[1] See BDEEP series B, vol 1, R Rathbone, ed, *Ghana*, part I, 20.

ganised under the direction of a senior Administrative Officer with Regional Assistant Commissioners stationed at the headquarters of the Western and Eastern Regions, while in the Northern Provinces there is a separate section of the Regional Secretariat, under a Senior Assistant Secretary. In regard to Native Courts your Legal Adviser visited Nigeria last year and after consultation with him an Ordinance (The Native Courts Ordinance, 1948) was enacted at the meeting of the Legislative Council held in August, 1948. That Ordinance has effect until the 1st day of October 1951, and it was intended that before then a full review of the existing Native Court system should be made. Although it may not be possible to complete the review and work out final proposals for changes before that date we have already been considering the best method of effecting the review and we hope that it will be undertaken by Judge Brooke who is specially well qualified to undertake this work by reason of his long experience in Nigeria first as an Administrative Officer and, since 1940, as a Puisne Judge. The question of the appointment of Native Court Advisers in the three Regions has also been discussed and we well recognise how strong a case exists for appointments of this kind, but we think that it may be best to await the review of the Native Court system before such appointments are made, since it would be difficult to determine the duties of such advisory or supervisory officers until the future powers and functions of Native Courts have been decided.

3.   On the general question of the organisation for dealing with local government matters both in the Regions and in the central Nigerian Secretariat, it has been made quite clear in past correspondence first that all Administrative Officers in the Regions, whether in the Provinces or in Regional Secretariats, constantly devote the greatest amount of their time and effort to local government affairs, and also that the Governor must mainly depend for advice on such matters not on any officer stationed in the central Secretariat but on the Chief Commissioners. It is for those reasons that any attempt to concentrate responsibility for dealing with or advising on 'Native Affairs' in a particular section of the Regional Secretariats or the Central Secretariat would be inappropriate in Nigeria. Indeed the conception that 'Native Affairs' is a separate subject and only one of the preoccupations of the Government is out of place in Nigeria, and would be rightly opposed by Administrative Officers here as strongly as it would be by the Nigerian public. What is required, as already suggested in previous despatches, is the strengthening of the Political Branch of the Central Secretariat and some reorganisation in regard to local government in the Regional Secretariats.

4.   In the Central Secretariat the Political Branch has already been strengthened by the addition of two Senior Assistant Secretaries, one of whom deals with all Intelligence matters in close consultation with the newly appointed Intelligence Officers in the three Regions and with the Police and Army, and the other with a number of administrative matters, so that the Principal Assistant Secretary can be freed from some of the weight of detailed work which has in the past taken up so much of his time. We also intend to create a new post in this Branch for a Senior Assistant Secretary (External Affairs) who will be responsible for dealing with such questions as liaison with non-British West African territories, communications with the Trusteeship Council regarding the Cameroons, and international conventions. Moreover it is, I am sure, most important to select an officer to take charge of the Political Branch who can expect to remain in that post for a number of years. When

these things have been done I feel confident that the Branch will be well able to perform the duties required of it.

5. Measures taken in the three Regional Secretariats will probably not follow exactly the same pattern. We have for some time past been considering how Regional Secretariats can be strengthened to give further effect to the policy of decentralisation from Lagos and in preparation for the increasing Regional autonomy sin the political sphere which we confidently expect to arise from the present constitutional review. The initial steps in regionalisation of the principal Departments, the creation of Regional Loan Development Boards and Regional Production Development Boards and the proposal, on which we are now working, for recasting the Development Plan on a Regional basis, make it necessary to strengthen the Regional Secretariats as soon as possible. In doing so we have to bear in mind the likelihood, if not certainty, that as a result of the constitutional review Regional Houses will be given wider powers, unofficial representation in those Houses will be increased, and Chief Commissioners' Executive Councils will be established on which there will be unofficial representation. All these factors make it urgently necessary to strengthen the Chief Commissioners' headquarters staff which will in future have to carry greatly increased responsibilities both in administrative work and in the Regional Legislatures. As I have said, some variation in organisation will probably be desirable in the different circumstances of the three Regions, but proposals which we have recently been considering with Chief Commissioners provide for the creation of permanent posts in each Region of a Civil Secretary, Financial Secretary and Development Secretary, and also a Legal Secretary. These Secretaries would not only be the Chief Commissioners' principal advisers and executive officers, but would also be the leading official spokesmen in the Regional Houses and the Chief Commissioners' Councils. It is proposed that the posts should not be filled, as has usually been the case in the past, by the temporary secondment of Administrative Officers from the Provinces, but by permanent appointment, the best men for the posts being selected on merit and not on seniority and the field of choice not being limited to officers serving in the Region in question (the posts might in some cases be filled by transfer from one Region to another or even exceptionally by appointment from outside Nigeria). It might be mentioned in passing that one of the principal reasons for the proposed appointment of Regional Development Secretaries is that they would normally be appointed Chairmen of the Regional Loan Development Boards and Regional Production Development Boards. It is further proposed that there should be additional headquarters officers in each Region dealing with Local Government, Community Development and Intelligence. Regional Intelligence Officers have already been appointed in all the Regions and a Regional Local Government and a Regional Community Development Officer have been appointed in the Eastern Provinces. It is not intended that these three posts in each Region should be Secretariat posts in the usual sense. The activities of the officers concerned will cover a whole Region and they should not be tied to a headquarters office. On the contrary they should be free to spend the greater part of their time travelling throughout their Region and talking with Administrative Officers in the field. Discussions with Chief Commissioners on these proposals are not yet complete, but I refer to them now in order to indicate the kind of Regional organisation which we have in mind. Chief Commissioners are themselves constantly touring and dis-

cussing local government affairs with Residents and District Officers. Frequent conferences attended by Residents and District Officers take place to consider such matters. The principal Regional Secretariat Officers are themselves by their training and experience fully familiar with local government problems. The new Regional Local Government Officers will, under the direction of the Chief Commissioners, keep under constant review changes and reforms which are going forward in local government bodies in the Region, they will be able to give Administrative Officers in one Province information about changes being made in others, by direct discussion they will explain to all Administrative Officers in the field the over-all policy of the Government in regard to local government in the Region and they will, of course, keep Chief Commissioners fully informed of developments in different parts of the Region. These Regional Local Government Officers would also visit other Regions and keep in touch with changes there taking place in the field of local government in order to be able to pass on the experience so gained to Administrative Officers in their own Regions. I hope that they will also be able to gain wider experience from time to time by visiting other territories and by studying local government in the United Kingdom when they are on leave. It will also be useful if they can keep close personal contact with the Principal Assistant Secretary in charge of the Political Branch of the Central Secretariat (often by personal visits and demi-official letters rather than by official correspondence) in much the same way as the Regional Intelligence Officers already communicate with the Central Secretariat Officer who deals with Intelligence matters in Lagos.

6. There is one other aspect of the organisation for dealing with local government affairs in the Regions which should be mentioned. Shortage of Administrative staff makes it difficult to expect any rapid progress but there will, I believe, be an increasing tendency in the future for Administrative Officers to be concentrated in a Provincial team rather than to remain scattered in Divisional Stations. In the more backward areas this change must be a slow one but as and when it becomes possible with local government advance to attach more Administrative Officers to Provincial Headquarters it will also be possible for some of them, freed from the multitudinous duties of a Divisional Officer, to specialise in local government affairs. To take one example, an Administrative Officer in the Calabar Province was recently released from other duties in order to deal with local government matters throughout the Province and the work which he has done has well justified the experiment.

7. These then are the principal measures taken or to be taken to improve the organisation for reviewing and implementing local government policy:—

(a) The strengthening of the Political Branch of the Central Secretariat by the appointment, under the Principal Assistant Secretary in charge of the Branch, of three Senior Assistant Secretaries to relieve him of work connected with Intelligence, Administration and External Affairs.

(b) The strengthening of Regional Secretariats by the permanent appointment of a team of Secretaries and also by the appointment of Regional Local Government Officers.

(c) The appointment of Provincial Local Government Officers as staff shortages and the prior claims of the Divisions allow.

74   CO 537/4727, no 4   July 1949
[Political situation]: Nigeria political summary on continuing
tensions in the Zikist movement   [Extract]

Political situation

(a) *Lagos politics*

Azikiwe has found himself increasingly bombarded and chivvied by the Zikist
Movement and the rank and file of the N.C.N.C. with accusations of inactivity and
demands for more dynamic leadership, and an indication of the pressure to which he
is being constantly subjected is given in a letter containing the latest political news
which Tony Enahoro sent to his fellow seditionists who are still in prison:—

> 'OGBUEFI (Azikiwe) was to have left this morning (30/5/49) to open branches
> of the Continental at Aba, Onitsha and possibly Kano, but he told me
> yesterday that he could not travel today in view of 'certain developments'.
> What are these 'developments' Gentlemen? OGBUEFI has a crisis on his
> hands. The crisis began at the Convention when Zikist Movement threatened
> to walk out if the proposed N.C.N.C. tour did not come off by April end. A
> delegate from the Provinces said that he was mandated to ask O what part he
> played in the sedition crisis and why he was not in prison. O said he was
> prepared to lay down his all for the country, but not if the army was
> irresponsible and undisciplined. Tonight, EZE and ZUNGUR are to try and
> force him to reshuffle the 'Cabinet' and fix the date for the commencement of
> the tour. Otherwise the Cabinet will resign en bloc, or he must resign. Some
> branches of the Zikist Movement have asked O to step down at once or to
> proceed with positive action. Delegates of the N.C.N.C. have walked out of the
> Lagos Conference in protest against the subtle attempt to steam-roll them
> into accepting Government-sponsored, N.Y.M.—supported views. In spite of
> this, however, O remains a member of the Conference and still attends its
> meetings. He has been severely criticised for this and tonight the Cabinet will
> ask him where he stands. Either he quits the Conference or he quits the
> Presidency of the N.C.N.C.'

2.   Zik finally set out on his travels on the 6th of June. There is no reason to
suppose that he fled for the sole purpose of escaping from his critics for he had been
talking for some time of visiting the Provinces to open branches of his Continental
Bank at Onitsha, Jos and Aba and to attend the first Assembly of the Ibo State Union
at the latter place.[1] Nevertheless, he was no doubt relieved to escape from them for a
while and from the embarrassing position he had been put into by the N.C.N.C. walk-
out from the Lagos Conference on the revision of the Constitution (Possum No. 30
para 6). The tour was primarily for the purposes of business and Zik confined himself
to that for most of the time but at the Assembly of the Ibo State Union he let himself
go in no uncertain terms, delivering a most provocative speech deliberately
calculated to arouse feelings of Ibo nationalism. 'The God of Africa,' he said, 'has

---

[1] The Ibo State Union had been inaugurated in December 1948 in Aba out of the existing Ibo Federal
Union.

specially created the Ibo nation to lead the children of Africa from the bondage of the ages'. Never had they been conquered in war or been the victims of a Carthagenian treaty. 'Instead, there is record to show that the martial prowess of the Ibo nation, at all stages of human history, had enabled them not only to conquer others but also to adapt themselves to the role of preserver of all that is best and noble in African culture and tradition'. Having filled his audience up with this entirely unfounded claim to historical greatness, he proceeded to demonstrate that living in a country blessed beyond all others for its potential wealth they had an equal claim to economic greatness; and yet, in spite of all, by the studied design of Government and in breach of the treaties that govern Anglo-Ibo relations, the Ibo nation was humiliated and kept backward and he illustrated this subtle policy of discrimination and persecution with a wealth of detail ranging from an alleged 'unholy crusade' against the Ibos in the London press to the lack of fire brigades in the remoter villages. But now the time had come, he said, for the world to know that 'the Ibo giant is waking from its stupor and is asserting its inalienable rights in the scheme of things in this great country of Nigeria and the Cameroons', and in dismissing the delegates he exhorted them to 'make it clear to our folks in the villages and towns of Ibo-land that as a nation with a glorious tradition and historic past, the Ibo nation demands from the protecting power freedom from persecution, freedom from ostracization, freedom from victimization and freedom from discrimination.'

3. The immediate result of this peroration was a decision by the Assembly to charge His Majesty's Government before the Permanent Court of International Justice at the Hague with a wilful disregard of the 'Anglo-Ibo treaties' (which, incidentally do not exist) and Jaja Wachuku and other legal luminaries are now busy drawing up the indictment. Elsewhere, the speech was received with a certain amount of dismay, especially by sober and responsible Ibo opinion which feared that it would once again raise the 'Ibo domination' scare and lead to a fresh outbreak of anti-Ibo feeling, but on the whole, it caused much less reaction than might have been expected, probably because the Yoruba leaders too, had the wisdom to ignore it in their press and, behind the scenes, to damp down any indignation it may have caused. Possibly Zik, with whom more moderate Ibo opinion has remonstrated, realised he was tactless: in any event, he has not since reverted to the theme.

4. It is clear that, with the exception of this one lapse, Zik's whole strategy of late has been to play for time. His purpose is not at present clear but it may be for one, or several, of the following reasons:

Zik often says that he is tired of politics and is looking for a suitable opportunity to get out of them and devote himself to his business. It is unlikely that he really wants to give up politics, but he may want a breathing space to pull his business together.

He may be genuinely apprehensive of the courses the Zikists and other extremists are urging him to follow and is, for the moment, passively resisting them. At the same time, Government is largely setting the pace in Constitutional and economic developments. As a result of these factors, events have moved beyond his control and, Micawber-like, he is waiting to see what might turn up and enable him to recover the iniative.

It may be that he realises he has had his hey-day in Lagos and the West and is most unlikely ever to obtain an unchallenged position in the North and is consequently preparing to consolidate his position in the East where, as leader of the Ibos (or a large section of them) he would be an authoritative and established political force. His Aba speech may have been the first move in this direction.

Finally, it may simply be that he is unwilling to compromise himself by adopting any particular course until he sees what the revised Constitution might have to offer him.

At the moment, one guess is as good as another.

5. If there is any doubt about where Zik is going there is none about the direction in which the Zikist Movement is heading. It is from this body that the most stident [sic] demands for more dynamic leadership come. Not getting it, they are drifting more and more to the extreme left wing and there is every indication that they will drift so far as to separate themselves completely from the *comparatively* moderate school of thought at present represented by the N.C.N.C. A manifesto which they have recently prepared shows that they are becoming increasingly subject to Communist influence. It is clear from this document that those who prepared it have not only read a considerable amount of Communist propaganda but must also have made some study of Communist organization and methods and it is in fact known that they have recently received considerable stocks of communist literature. An occasional voice has been raised to suggest that the Movement should openly declare itself to be a Communist party but the suggestion has not so far been seriously pursued. It is very doubtful whether any of the members with the possible exception of one or two individuals, consider themselves to be Communists, and it would not be of any very great significance if they chose to label themselves as such for there is nobody in the Movement capable of organizing a proper Communist party or with sufficient intelligence fully to understand and pursue that party's aims. The danger is that the Movement seems well on the way to turning itself into an instrument ready to the hand of Communists elsewhere.

6. The N.C.N.C., with Zik away, did nothing very much but discuss arrangements for a march on Government House to protest against the manner in which the Lagos Constitution revision conference was being conducted and to express disapproval at the imprisonment of the seditionists. The arrangements, however, never got beyond the talking stage, it being felt by many that there should be no demonstration until Zik came back so that the opportunity could be taken of forcing his hand by making him lead it. The matter was discussed at a stormy public meeting early in July. None of the 'Cabinet' members of any prominence attended with the result that the critics had the field to themselves and made good use of the opportunity to voice their dissatisfaction with the 'Cabinet's' inactivity. To pacify them, Zik promised a cabinet reshuffle—which has not yet taken place—but he followed it with an announcement that it had been decided to move the N.C.N.C. headquarters to the Provinces. It has not yet been definitely stated whether the new headquarters will be at Aba or at Jos but it seems to be generally accepted that it will be at the latter place, especially as, to assuage Eastern pride, Zik has promised Aba a sort of local cabinet to run the party's affairs in that part of the country. The move to the provinces is undoubtedly an attempt to escape from the disruptive influences at present at work in Lagos and the choice probably fell on Jos rather than Aba because Zik still commands a sizeable and firm body of support in the East while the Plateau, with its minesfield labour and a population restive over the use of their land for mining purposes, seems at the moment to offer the most fruitful field for missionary endeavour.

7.   The N.Y.M. has not been very active of late, either, most of their time having been taken up with domestic affairs arising from the rivalry between Bode Thomas and H.O. Davies who was suspected, possibly rightly, of having been flirting with Zik. For the moment, the matter has died down for Davies has declared that pressure of business is too great to permit him to take any further part in Constitutional revision discussions and Bode Thomas accordingly had the satisfaction of being selected a member of final drafting committee. The party's main fire was being reserved for an attack on Government over the prosecution of Rotimi Williams for embezzling his clients' funds. The acquittal of Williams, however, damped their powder so they made the best of a bad job by changing the occasion into one of rejoicing that their General Secretary had faced his ordeal unflinchingly and come out of it with his integrity unscathed and his reputation enhanced—despite the severe strictures passed by the trial judge on his professional conduct. The Party has now decided that if it is to make any progress it must be more critical of the Government and a series of attacks on Administrative Officers which have recently appeared in the pages of the 'Service' suggests that they are beginning to put this policy into operation. . . .

75   CO 852/982/5, no 16   18 July 1949
[Oil exploration]: letter from C J Pleass to L H Gorsuch on the granting of an oil exploration licence to Shell Overseas Exploration Company

We are sending by this mail a despatch enclosing a copy of an Oil Exploration Licence which has been granted over part of the Southern Provinces and the Cameroons to the Shell Overseas Exploration Company and the D'Arcy Exploration Company jointly. For reasons which are explained in the despatch and which I need not go into here the licence had to be executed in a hurry and there was not time to send The Secretary of State a preliminary draft. It is largely based on a previous one granted to the same Companies but it contains one or two important differences. Clause 15 of the licence differs from the corresponding clause in the licence already approved by the Secretary of State. The difference occurs in paragraph (a) of that clause which used to require that in such circumstances two of the Directors and the Resident Manager shall be British subjects while the new clause 15(a) requires that the Chairman, the Managing Director (if any) and the majority of the Directors be British subjects; this is in accordance with the section of the Ordinance. The other difference is a new clause in which reference is made to the grant of an Oil Prospecting Licence (which has already been applied for) and of an Oil Mining Lease. That brings me to the point of this letter.
   The clause in question (Clause 22), reads as follows:—

   'On or before the expiration of this Licence or any renewal thereof the Licencee observing and performing the terms and conditions herein contained shall have a right (subject to the provision prescribed in any written law or regulations then in force for granting Oil Prospecting Licences) to an Oil Prospecting Licence or Licences in respect of so much of the said lands as the Licensee may select; provided that the grant of any such

> Oil Prospecting Licence shall not entitle the Licensee to the grant of a lease for mineral oils save in accordance with such terms and conditions whether in respect of the composition of the body or company to which such lease may be granted or otherwise whatsoever, as the Governor may determine at the time of the grant of such prospecting licence.'

We inserted this provision so as to make it quite clear at the outset that, in the event of oil being discovered in workable quantities, the Governor might insist on having a say in the composition of any company which might be formed to exploit it and that any Mining Lease would be granted on our terms and not those of the Shell D'Arcy interests. At a meeting attended by the local representatives, copies of the record of which are enclosed, His Excellency expanded this point and made it clear that no Mining Lease would be granted except on such terms as would ensure a share in the profits accruing to this Government. The Shell people accepted this but on the instructions of their London office, said that they must know the terms on which a Mining Lease will be granted at the time the Prospecting Licence is issued. Hence the last two lines of the clause I have quoted.

In consultation with the Shell Company a draft Prospecting Licence is being prepared which will include provision for the sinking of a deep borehole, but we cannot, of course, complete it for submission to the Secretary of State until the terms of the Mining Lease are decided, and it is here that we should be glad of your help. The Shell Company are anxious for technical reasons connected with weather conditions to start preparing for their boring operations as soon as possible, and we are just as anxious for our own reasons that if there is any oil it shall be discovered with the minimum of delay.

Here I must digress for a moment in order to give you a picture of the general situation.

The area for which the Shell D'Arcy parties want the Prospecting Licence, and more particularly the place they have selected for their borehole, are situated in an extremely densely populated part of Ibo country, the inhabitants of which are fanatically attached to their land and are intensely hostile to anything which savours to their naturally suspicious minds of an attempt to tamper with it. In addition they can count on the support of politicians of the Zikist persuasion in general and Azikiwe in particular, who is always ready to take up the cudgels in his newspapers on behalf of any cause, regardless of its merits, out of which he thinks political capital can be made. The Exploration Parties have already met with considerable opposition, including sabotage of equipment and, on one or two occasions, physical violence, but it is certain that the future holds in store even fiercer opposition probably incited by politicians and backed by sections of the Press.

It is, however, of the greatest importance that Nigeria's mineral resources be speedily developed and that new sources of revenue be discovered, particularly in the Eastern Region, the economy of which as you know is at present based almost exclusively, and quite inadequately, on the oil palm. For these reasons we feel that exploration and prospecting for oil should not be held up, and we are especially anxious that Shell D'Arcy should be enabled to sink their deep bore with the minimum of delay.

To achieve these objects we are convinced that a major effort must be made to demonstrate to the people of Nigeria in general and particularly of the Eastern

Region and of the parts of the Owerri Province concerned that the discovery and exploitation of oil would conduce immeasurably to national and local interests, and we are anxious that as a first step in an attempt to achieve this purpose a public statement should be made at the earliest possible moment. Such a public statement would have to make abundantly clear our determination jealously to safeguard national and local interests: it should also if possible give an indication of how we propose to ensure this and make it clear that decisions on these points must be made before a Prospecting Licence is issued.

As to how it is proposed to ensure that Nigeria is to be assured of a proper share in the benefits to be derived from oil production we are inclined to favour some form of profit-sharing, but apart from this we have no preconceived ideas and we should naturally welcome advice from the Colonial Office on the subject.

I am coming on leave by air on July 27th and His Excellency has minuted as follows:—

> 'the Development Secretary who is fully familiar with the local position, will be in London early next month, and that we hope that early discussions may be undertaken with him.'

76　CO 583/299/2, no 12　　　　　　　　　　12 Sept 1949
[Local government reform]: inward savingram no 2108 from Sir J Macpherson to Mr Creech Jones on the progress of reform in the Eastern provinces

Your Secret Savingram No. 1 of the 11th of January. Local Government in the Eastern Provinces.

2. The Eastern Provinces' proposals have been widely discussed at all levels, with attention directed to those sections of the population particularly interested, and unofficial Members of the Eastern House of Assembly visited all provincial headquarters to obtain the views of the public, and the administrative staff.[1] As the result of all these discussions, a Memorandum on Policy regarding Local Government was prepared in the Eastern Regional Secretariat and adopted by the Eastern House of Assembly on the 16th of July. Ten copies of the Memorandum, together with six copies of a memorandum for official use also prepared by the Eastern Regional Secretariat, are now enclosed.[2]

3. The programme to which we hope to adhere provides for the Local Government Bill being laid before the Eastern House in December or February, and before the Legislative Council in March. The policy Memorandum as finally adopted by the Eastern House differs in several respects from the first draft which we saw only at the end of June, when it was not possible to examine it in detail before it came before the Eastern House in July. We made several major alterations, which were duly adopted, and although the final text of the Memorandum still requires detailed examination here (more particularly as regards rating—paragraph 8 below), I think

---

[1] See 50.　　　　　　　　　　　　　　　　　　　　　　　[2] Not printed.

it should be furnished to you at this stage for your information and for examination by the Local Government Advisory Panel, although it cannot be taken as a formally accepted statement of policy by this Government. The drafting of legislation has already been taken in hand at Enugu, and to save as much time as possible I intend to send the first draft to you with Messrs. Briggs (counsel responsible for drafting) and Beaumont (Eastern Provinces administrative officer responsible for all liaison work in local discussion and compilation of views). These two officers will probably leave for London early in October and I suggest that the Panel consider the two Memoranda as early as possible, in order to discuss their main features, as well as major points in the legislation with Briggs and Beaumont on their arrival. Meanwhile, of course, further examination of the proposals will proceed here.

4.   The proposals, as contained in the Memoranda, will be found to differ substantially from those contained in the Report of the Eastern House Select Committee, already considered by the Panel in October 1948. The main variations are the abandonment of the idea of a Local Government Board and of a unified Local Government service, the absence of the administrative officer as a nominated member or chairman of councils, and a new conception of each class of local body having direct dealings with the Regional Authority, without any form of subordination to any local body of another class.

5.   It will be seen from the Memorandum compiled for official use that public discussions in the Eastern Provinces revealed considerable local opposition to the idea of a Local Government Board, and your Advisory Panel had already expressed doubts as regards the likely development of such a Board. Some members of the Panel were also opposed to the idea of a unified Local Government service, and the view is now taken here that it will make for the more realistic development of local government if each local body employs and controls its own staff. The only measure of outside control contemplated by the present proposals is that the appointment and dismissal of a Council officer in receipt of emoluments of £400 per annum and upwards shall be subject to the approval of the Regional Authority.

6.   The new conception of the various local bodies each having mutually exclusive functions is also in general accord with the advice of your Panel, which advocated that each council have a measure of independent authority in purely local matters, in order to spread more widely the realisation that self-government in local affairs is in force. For the same general reason it has been decided to keep the local District Officer outside the Councils as a guide and friendly adviser, rather than to introduce an element of seeming derogation from their independence by appointing him to chairmanship.

7.   Further consideration is being given here to the question of councils' functions in respect of education, having regard to Government's general education policy (paragraphs 42(5) and 45 (31) of the Policy Memorandum); of the land acquisition powers to be permitted to councils (paragraphs 94–97); and of the exaction of communal services by local councils (paragraph 29). It has been agreed, with regard to the proposals in paragraphs 42 (22) and 45 (33) (that Councils can establish a rural constabulary) that extension of the police arrangements should normally be by way of recruitment to the Nigeria Police. The whole question of the relationship of the Nigeria Police to other Police forces such as Native Administration Police is under examination but in the meanwhile it is intended that Councils may be authorised to set aside funds to finance the policing of their areas.

8.   In particular, the important question of rating, covered in paragraphs 65–86 of the policy Memorandum, has been reconsidered here, and certain modifications agreed upon. I shall shortly send a further supplementary memorandum bringing this part of the proposals up to date.

9.   There is, however, one major point to which you will no doubt wish to give immediate consideration. Certain special powers, set out in paragraph 100 of the Policy Memorandum, are proposed for reservation to the Regional Authority to ensure efficient local administration and to safeguard Government dues. The exact identity and composition of the Regional Authority (at present, of course, the Chief Commissioner) can not be known until review of the constitution has been completed, but the recommendations of the Eastern Regional Conference have already been received on this point, and are to the effect that in the Eastern Region policy shall be initiated and executive decisions taken by a Regional Council consisting of the Chief Commissioner with four or five official members and nine or ten unofficial members. Should Councils of this kind eventually be established the possibility could arise of the non-official majority of the Regional executive declining to take, in respect of a local body, the action which might seem necessary in the interests of good administration. I am therefore disposed to consider the reservation of certain powers to the Governor, to provide an ultimate safeguard for use in the last resort.

10.   I shall, of course, address you further on points arising out of these Memoranda, but I would appreciate an early expression of your own views and of those of the Panel, and an indication of whether the Panel could meet again on some date about the 10th October for discussion with Briggs and Beaumont.

11.   I should have preferred to postpone addressing you on this subject until all outstanding points had been fully considered here and a draft Bill had been prepared but it has become a matter of special urgency to push ahead with the reforms which have now been under public discussion for more than a year. In spite of irresponsible attacks from extremists the unofficial members of the Eastern House of Assembly have given their keen support to the reforms proposed and have themselves toured through the Eastern Provinces to explain the proposals and to combat destructive criticism. It is not too much to say that sound progress in the Eastern Provinces will, to a large extent, depend on whether the proposed reforms, with the main purposes of which I, like the Chief Commissioner, am in whole-hearted agreement, can be put into effect without undue delay. The Eastern Provinces officers concerned are working enthusiastically to put the proposals into shape (we are fortunate to have officers like Briggs and Beaumont engaged on this task) and I should regard it as little short of a political disaster if delay in consideration of the Bill in Lagos or London were to make it impossible to secure its enactment in 1950. If that were to happen the forces of reason and constructive reform which have scored a number of notable victories in the volatile East during the past year against considerable odds (not least in the constitutional review) would suffer a severe set-back and the forces of confusion and disorder would gain corresponding encouragement.

12.   It is because of the urgency of the matter that I have suggested that Briggs and Beaumont should visit London next month and I trust that you will forgive any faults in the necessarily hurried presentation of our preliminary proposals and assist us to put the reforms into effect with an absolute minimum of delay.

77   CO 537/4625, no 51   2 Oct 1949

[Constitutional review]: inward savingram no 2307 from Sir J
Macpherson to Mr Creech Jones on the progress of the constitutional
review

Your savingram No.86 of the 26th of July. Constitutional Review.

I had intended to make another report on the progress of the constitutional review
before the Regional Conferences met but the Eastern Regional Conference took place
in July whereas the Northern and Western Regional Conferences did not meet until
early in September, and I thought it best to wait until I was in a position to report on
the results of all the Regional Conferences.

2.   I now forward for your information the following documents:—[1]

(a) The recommendations of the Regional Conferences (including the Lagos and
Colony Conference) (Enclosures I, II, III, IV),

(b) A digest of Regional Conference proposals (Enclosure V),

(c) The minutes of the Eastern Regional Conference and a synopsis of the Eastern
Regional Review (Enclosure VI),

(d) A report on the Eastern Regional Conference (Enclosure VII),

(e) A report on the Lagos and Colony Conference (Enclosure VIII),

(f) Provincial Conference resolutions from the Northern Provinces (Enclosure
IX),

(g) A Report on the Northern Regional Conference (Enclosure X),

(h) A Report on the Western Regional Conference (Enclosure XI),

3.   As you know the next stage is for the Drafting Committee to prepare a
statement of recommendations based on the views of the Regional Conferences. The
Drafting Committee is composed of three representatives of each Regional
Conferences, one representative of the Colony Conference and one representative of
the Lagos Conference sitting with the Chief Secretary, the Attorney General and the
Financial Secretary. The Drafting Committee hopes to meet on the 10th of October
and to complete its work in November.

4.   The General Conference will, we hope, meet in January next. It is to be
composed of 53 members, all unofficials, and is to sit under the Chairmanship of Sir
Gerard Howe.

5.   I do not suggest that it is necessary for the voluminous papers which I attach
to be closely studied in the Colonial Office since it is for the Drafting Committee to
prepare a single document (an unenviable task!) based on the Regional proposals for
consideration by the General Conference, but I wish to invite your attention to
certain points of special interest which have so far emerged from the review.

6.   In the first place I am convinced that in spite of considerable diversities of
view which are apparent in the recommendations which have been drawn up in the
Provincial and Regional Conferences the system of review unanimously approved by
the Legislative Council in March last has been fully justified. It would be impossible
to overestimate the value in terms of political education of the discussions which

---

[1] Enclosures not printed.

have taken place and a rapid glance through the Provincial recommendations from the North (Enclosure IX) gives ample indication, for instance, of the thoughtful examination of constitutional problems which has taken place in all parts of the country.

7.   The second main result which has been achieved is the general support for a federal system of Government based on three Regions (there seems moreover to be wide agreement that Lagos and the Colony should in future be grouped with the Western Provinces). This is a result of first importance in view of the reactionary N.C.N.C. campaign, which was bound to make a strong appeal in many areas, for the establishment of a much larger number of states based on 'linguistic groups'.

8.   The third major subject on which general agreement has been reached is that there should be a larger measure of Regional autonomy, with Regional legislatures exercising legislative and financial powers and Regional Executive Councils.

9.   As to the Regional Conferences themselves I consider that the Eastern Conference showed the keenest appreciation of the questions at issue and the skill and responsibility shown by the unofficial members of the Eastern House in persuading a number of extremists to subscribe with them to constructive proposals were most remarkable.

The Lagos Conferences suffered from an early attempt on the part of a few N.C.N.C. supporters to wreck the proceedings by walking out but the Conference completed its work and since the main complaint of the N.C.N.C. was that voting took place on resolutions (a procedure which was subsequently adopted by all other Conferences) the N.C.N.C. has certainly not gained any prestige from its disruptive tactics.

The Northern Conference has shown a much more restrained and conservative approach than the conferences elsewhere and, as was to be expected, has laid great emphasis on the need to allot to the North representation and finance proportionate to its majority population. The Northern Conference is moreover firmly opposed to any Ministerial system at the centre. These strong views will make it particularly difficult to reach any agreed compromise on many major questions but it was not to be expected that the North would subscribe to other views, and it is satisfactory that the North, like other Regions, will welcome increased Regional autonomy.

The most surprising outcome of the Regional Conferences is the recommendations of the Western Conference which are the most extreme and also the most ill-considered. Unlike other Regions there was not a great deal of public interest in the West in the Regional review and a few people of extreme views and little experience were able to push through recommendations which certainly do not represent the opinions of the predominantly conservative Yorubas. But although the Western recommendations are not representative they will make the work of the Drafting Committee much more difficult (the Western members of the Committee, unlike nearly all the other members of the Committee, are mostly of poor calibre).

10.   The programme to which we hope to be able to adhere is for the General Conference to meet in January, and for its conclusions to be debated in the Regional Houses in February, a full debate then taking place in the Legislative Council in March. It may be desirable when that debate takes place to make a statement of the official view on some of the main questions at issue and in the meantime I shall keep you fully informed of developments in the Drafting Committee and the General Conference.

78   CO 583/299/2, no 27   25 Oct 1949

[Local government reform]: outward savingram no 113 from Mr
Creech Jones to H M Foot approving the proposals for reform in the
Eastern provinces

My secret telegram No. 1458.

Eastern Provinces Local Government

I have read with considerable interest the draft Local Government Ordinance and the
Memorandum for official use prepared by the Eastern Provinces' Secretariat as an
introduction to local government in the Eastern Provinces. I have been impressed by
the great care which has been taken to devise legislation which will provide for the
efficient and widespread functioning of local government organisations in the
Eastern Provinces and I should like to take this opportunity of congratulating all
those who have been concerned in the preparation of those documents. I have been
particularly grateful for the opportunity afforded by the presence of Mr. Briggs and
Mr. Beaumont in London for the discussion of the many problems raised by your
proposals both with the Local Government Panel and my advisers.

2.   In considering your proposals I have been very conscious of the peculiar difficulties which it is necessary to meet in the Eastern Provinces and I accept without hesitation the view that it is desirable that any system introduced should be as flexible as
possible. There are, however, certain other considerations which I have had very much
in mind and to which I would wish to direct your attention. I consider it important
that any local government organisations which may be created should possess an
assured status together with rights and privileges of which they may not be divested
without good and apparent cause. As you will see from my detailed observations in the
following paragraphs I would like to suggest that certain provisions in the draft
Ordinance might be altered in order to ensure that local government organisations
possess a greater measure of assured status than is provided for. I have also had in
mind the fact that work in local government is likely to provide the initial training
ground for many of the future political leaders of Nigeria. It therefore seems to me to
be important that such organisations should provide the greatest possible scope for
the training of such people and that as far as practicable such organisations should be
autonomous, taking decisions in the knowledge that such decisions will not be set
aside by higher authority except by constitutional and public procedures that are manifestly just. I also attach importance to measures which effectively demonstrate that
power is not concentrated either within the Region at a central point or within Nigeria
in the Central Government. It would, in my view, be an unfortunate development if
the only worthwhile political life centered round the seat of power in a Region or in
Lagos and I am therefore anxious that there should be as many opportunities as possible for public spirited citizens no matter where they live to devote their time and
labour to the service of the community in the sure and certain knowledge that their
services will be accepted and properly used and that they may expect to enjoy the exercise of power, albeit limited in an acceptable and fair manner, in the sphere which they
have chosen for their public services. I am quite sure that you will agree with these
general principles, to which the Bill is designed to give effect.

3.   I now turn to certain detailed observations which I would wish to make on your
proposals and in this connection I enclose copies of the minutes of the Local

Government Panel, with whose conclusions and recommendations I am in agreement.[1]

4.   The constitution and functions of the Regional Authority have formed the subject of detailed discussion with Mr. Briggs and Mr. Beaumont who will already have reported to you the views expressed in the Colonial Office, I consider that it would be desirable, that the definition of Regional Authority, which I understand you now propose shall be included in a separate section, should include the Chief Commissioner because it seems proper that at this stage he should be closely associated with and responsible for the development of local government within the Region. Turning to the question of the functions and powers of the Regional Authority, I am not entirely convinced that it is reasonable to vest in the Authority the powers provided in Sections 6, 9 and 11 of the draft ordinance without at the same time providing for forms of public consultation in advance of the exercise of such powers. I appreciate that it may not be possible or desirable to specify forms for every kind of enquiry which it may be necessary to hold, but I trust that it may be possible to devise satisfactory forms for the major types of enquiry which can be foreseen. In making this suggestion I am moved by my desire to ensure that as far as practicable Councils shall not be removed or changed without public process.

5.   The grant of a more assured status to a Council would seem to imply at the same time the imposition of mandatory functions. I consider that in principle it would be desirable that no Council should be constituted which could not perform a minimum number of functions, with provision that the Regional Authority may excuse a Council, where this is necessary, from performing some of these minimal functions. I appreciate that it may not be easy to translate this suggestion into practice at this stage. Nevertheless, I shall be grateful if you will give it your consideration, as the prestige of Councils must depend on the work which they perform and it might be a mistake too create Councils of a similar type which did not perform similar functions. In any case, I am sure you will agree that it is desirable and necessary to provide that certain functions should be mandatory.

6.   I should note that in discussion with Mr. Briggs and Mr. Beaumont it has been agreed that the provisions of Section 15 should be amended to avoid any difficulties which might arise by reason of membership of Co-operative Societies by the Councils. Your officers are also considering what additional provisions for disqualification are necessary, such as membership of the Police Force and Armed Services, membership of prescribed organisations and certain other categories of persons.

7.   After discussing the provisions of section 45 (b) I understand that your officers accept the view that it would be desirable to omit this provision which would appear to give members of any dissident organisation the right ostentatiously to boycott local government activity. Your officers also agreed that section 56 (d) should be omitted on the suggestion of the Local Government Panel.

8.   I should like to invite your attention to the suggestion made by the Local Government Panel that Councils should be empowered to perform any necessary work required for the abatement of nuisances and subsequently to charge the offender with the cost of such work. I should also like to mention the further point made by the Panel that Section 100 (10) did not appear to provide a Council with the power of compelling the carrying out of maintenance work on buildings.

---

[1] Not printed.

9. I have given careful consideration to the recommendation of the Local Government Panel that the submission of estimates by a Council should only occur when required by the Regional Authority. The memorandum entitled 'An Introduction to local government in the Eastern Provinces of Nigeria' refers in paragraph 31 to the need for caution by the Regional Authority in handling the estimates of local government councils, but has explained in paragraph 30 why the submission of estimates by Councils is considered necessary at this stage. I do not expect that you will feel able to accept the Panel's proposal in full, but I suggest that provision might be made for Councils to be excused from the requirement of submitting estimates as and when they become competent to control their own finances, so that they may have an incentive so to order their affairs as to justify a claim that the submission of estimates is not necessary. I also consider that the procedure set out in Section 135 of the Ordinance could with advantage be modified in order to provide that Councils may incur supplementary expenditure without the approval of the Regional Authority on any Head of the estimate within a limit of 10 per cent of that Head. I would further suggest that a Council should be permitted to incur supplementary expenditure within a limit of, say, 5 per cent of the total approved budget without the need to obtain the approval of the Regional Authority. In making this suggestion I have in mind the possibility that a Council may need to rebuild an essential building destroyed by fire and that it would be of little value to delay such rebuilding by the need to refer such expenditure for approval to the Regional Authority. It would also seem necessary to provide that any estimates which have not been disapproved at the beginning of the financial year shall be deemed to have been approved. It was pointed out to Messrs. Briggs and Beaumont in connection with Section 126 that it might be desirable to include receipts from the sale of land and grants from the Marketing Boards within the definition of Revenue.

10. On the question of rating I share the view expressed by the Panel that very few exemptions should be made and that it would be desirable to assist public institutions such as hospitals by making a grant from Revenue rather than by exempting them by rating.

11. I have given careful consideration to the provisions of Section 226 in the light of the correspondence ending in Mr. Foot's letter No. 52257/669 of the 8th October. I am not satisfied that the provisions of Section 226 constitute the best method of providing for the exercise of such powers, particularly as it is to be expected that Chief Commissioners will be required under the new Constitution themselves to exercise certain reserve powers, in relation to the Regional Authorities and Councils, perhaps by the power to defer action in case of disagreement with them on matters affecting good government etc. pending submission to the Central Government. I would therefore suggest that it would be preferable to provide in the Bill that the Chief Commissioner shall report to the Governor any act or omission to act or decision of the Regional Authority which in his opinion is contrary to the interests of public order, public faith or good government and that thereupon the Governor shall have power to call upon the Regional Authority to repair such act etc. I am sure that this is in fact the procedure which would be used and I think it important that this should be fully apparent in the Bill when the Legislative Council is called upon to pass it. I also think it is desirable that there should be no doubt about the position of the Chief Commissioner in such matters, in order that it may be apparent that any subsequent setting aside by the Governor of any act of the

Regional Authority can only take place on the recommendation of the Chief Commissioner. I hope that you will be prepared to accept the suggestions in this paragraph.

12.   Subject to the above comments I agree that the Bill should be proceeded with.

13.   I know that it is vary well appreciated to what a large extent the success of the new system of local government in the Eastern Provinces will depend on the availability of adequately trained local government staff. The provision of facilities for training in the Eastern Provinces themselves is, I am aware, receiving the active attention of the Chief Commissioner and yourself. Arrangements are proposed meanwhile for sending a number of persons to this country to receive training in the practice of local government. Separate correspondence is taking place with regard to these arrangements. I only mention the matter here again to emphasise the very great importance which I attach to the question of training and to the establishment of suitable training facilities locally.

79   CO 537/4628, no 6   15 Nov 1949
[Enugu shootings]: inward telegram no 1746 from Sir J Macpherson to Mr Creech Jones reporting a strike at Enugu Colliery

[One of the most serious outbreaks of disorder in Nigeria in the post-war period followed the shooting of miners by police at Enugu on 18 Nov 1949. 20 died and 31 were injured (of whom 1 subsequently died); further deaths occurred in the disorders across the Eastern provinces that ensued. The background to the shootings lay in a long history of poor labour relations at the colliery during 1949. Following the start of the strike in November, a police detachment under senior superintendent F S Philip attempted to remove explosives from the Iva Valley mine to prevent them falling into the strikers' hands. It was during this operation that the police opened fire. The shootings were followed by widespread rioting in Eastern Nigeria and the establishment of a National Emergency Committee in Lagos under Dr Akinola Maja and which included Azikiwe, Awolowo and others among its members. The commission of enquiry announced by Macpherson on 20 Nov was headed by Sir William Fitzgerald KC, former chief justice of Palestine and attorney-general of Northern Rhodesia. The other members were Mr Justice S O Quashie-Idun of the Supreme Court of the Gold Coast, Mr Justice A A Ademola of the Supreme Court of Nigeria and R W Williams, MP for Wigan and legal adviser to the National Union of Mineworkers. The commission's report was published in June 1950. See 99.]

Colliery strike

A go-slow strike started amongst coal hewers at Enugu Colliery last week which threatens to have serious effect on railway operations.

2.   The causes of the go-slow strike which started unexpectedly without warning were at first obscure, but it appears that Ojiyi,[1] leader of the union, has for months been assuring workers, particularly hewers, that large sums of back pay would be obtained for them. There is and has been no justification whatsoever for holding out such promises and feeling against Ojiyi and the union has been growing. The men still believe that back pay will be secured but many of them have now lost all confidence.

---

[1] Okwudili Ojiyi, secretary of the Colliery Workers' Union.

Ojiyi's recent behaviour has been so irresponsible and double-faced that it is useless to continue to negotiate with him as the men's representative. Failing all efforts to get the men to resume full work (the Nigerian members of newly formed Colliery Board have been most helpful) 150 hewers have been dismissed. Recruitment of new labour to take the place of these dismissed is already proceeding.

3.   Strike came at a most awkward time as far as our coal supplies are concerned as heavy groundnut railings last month had reduced reserves to a minimum. Curtailment of passenger and goods traffic must be effected at once. If output from Enugu does not improve groundnut railings will, I fear, soon have to be reduced. We are endeavouring to obtain coal to meet immediate emergency from the Gold Coast. We have already ordered 4,000 tons from South Africa but this will not arrive until next month. An additional order for 20,000 tons has now been placed with South Africa. It is impossible to guess how long the stoppage at Enugu will last but we are assuming that almost complete stoppage may continue for a week or two. I am greatly disappointed that this interruption in railway traffic which may well be serious should have been caused just when the railway had achieved greatly improved transportation of groundnuts. The intrigues of Colliers' Union and very poor output which have been worrying us for long past were however bound to lead to a showdown sooner or later and I am hopeful, that when present trouble is over, both general labour situation and standard of output at the colliery will show a marked improvement. I shall report further developments.

80   CO 537/4628, no 12   19 Nov 1949
[Enugu shootings]: inward telegram no 1782 from Sir J Macpherson to Mr Creech Jones reporting on the police shootings at Enugu Colliery

I very much regret to report that police in Enugu had to open fire yesterday afternoon (18th November) killing 4 and wounding 16. Police suffered only minor injuries.

2.   Police were engaged in moving explosives to safe store when they were attacked by a large crowd which made concerted attempt to disarm police and rush explosive store. Situation remains dangerous and disorder may spread.

3.   I shall send fuller report when details are available and shall keep you promptly informed of developments.

81   CO 577/4628, nos 18 and 25   21–22 Nov 1949
[Enugu shootings]: minutes by Mr Creech Jones on the events at Enugu

This is a tragic and serious business and most unfortunate in West Africa just now and terribly disturbing to the Governor and Colonial Secretary. I assume that Sir John has immediately announced an Enquiry. In this, can we help? What are the causes of the dispute. There have been telegrams. Was any wage claim put in and any arbitration suggested?

A.C.J.
21.11.49

What is the nature of the Commission which the Governor proposes to appoint? Is this a matter in which H.M.G. should intervene? It is a pretty bad affair—the loss of 18 lives and 31 wounded? Did the police lose their heads? We ought to get more information than the Governor gives. What is the story of the Dispute? I recall telegrams about the matter. It would be well for me to have the facts: was the Labour Commissioner attempting to arbitrate? Had the miners genuine grievances? How did this thing fester? We can't escape by pleading 'wild agitators'.

A.C.J.
22.11.49

82   CO 537/4628, no 44   26 Nov 1949
[Enugu shootings]: inward telegram no 1816 from Sir J Macpherson to Mr Creech Jones on the declaration of a state of emergency

My telegram No. 1813.
  Disturbances in Eastern Provinces.
  Chief Commissioner at Enugu reported that following rioting and looting which has occurred in Aba and Port Harcourt it is considered probable that similar disorders may break out in other centres in Eastern Provinces. He reports that extremist malcontents are moving about from place to place inciting people to riot and local newspapers are aiding them by publishing inflammatory material.
  2. Chief Commissioner accordingly recommended that Emergency Regulations should be introduced. I have signed Proclamation of state of emergency and made Regulations for detention of persons, curfew and deporting of persons.[1] I have also introduced Regulations for press censorship applicable to Eastern Provinces only.

---

[1] The state of emergency lasted until 8 Dec 1949.

83   CO 537/4628, no 51   28 Nov 1949
[Enugu shootings]: inward telegram no 1826 from Sir J Macpherson to Mr Creech Jones on the spread of disorder in the Eastern provinces

Disorders in Eastern Provinces.
  There were further disorders in Onitsha and Calabar yesterday (26th November). Rioting and some looting believed in the morning at Onitsha. Tear gas used and police also opened fire, three wounded one seriously. At Calabar to which police reinforcements were flown order was restored without resorting to tear gas or shooting. A curfew was imposed in Calabar in the evening. No other disorders yesterday. Arrests have been made in several Eastern Provinces towns in the past few

days and 5 sentences ranging from 2 years to 6 months were yesterday imposed by court in Aba.

2. At Port Harcourt all was quiet. One of the persons wounded on 25th November died making total killed at Port Harcourt 2.

3. In Lagos a large public meeting was planned by trade union leaders which might well have led to violence. When I saw a number of Lagos leaders in the morning to explain the reason for taking emergency powers I advised them to use their influence to prevent this meeting for which no licence under the Police Ordinance had been applied for. The Commissioner of the Colony later saw trade union leaders and in result the meeting was cancelled. It is encouraging that leaders decided to adopt this course at a critical time.

4. The situation in Enugu is most disturbing although there has been no disorder there since 18th November. The miners having been persuaded to go back on their agreement to resume full work at midnight on 23rd November are being encouraged by malcontents, including leaders sent from Lagos, to continue go-slow strike and to put in fresh demands. I am concerned about safety in the mine which is still under control of miners without European overmen who are responsible for safety. The mine should be closed but this could only be achieved when maximum force of police is available and at present considerable proportion of available police forces in Eastern Provinces is distributed amongst other Eastern towns to prevent further rioting and looting. It may be that appointment of Commission will help to end deadlock but as Ogiyi's [sic: Ojiyi] influence has now been revived and miners are being backed in extreme demands by outside politicians, I can see little prospect of early settlement and there is serious danger of further clashes between miners and police if attempt to close the mine is made. If the mine is not closed there may be an accident in the mine for which the Government will be blamed.

5. I am hopeful that rioting and looting in Eastern Provinces which has followed Enugu disorders will not be much prolonged. There has been little reaction so far in Western Provinces or in the Northern Provinces. There was and is danger of public meetings in Lagos leading to violence but cancellation of yesterday's meeting was important and encouraging. I am now chiefly concerned about extremely awkward and dangerous position at Enugu. Government authorities in Enugu yesterday saw the Lagos leaders who have gone there and explained the whole position in cordial meeting but Chief Commissioner does not believe that they sincerely wish to end the trouble, and re-emergence of Ogiyi [sic: Ojiyi] is disquieting.

84   CO 537/4631, no 11   [Nov 1949]

[Enugu shootings]: note by N H Smith[1] on the deterioration of affairs in the Eastern provinces. *Minutes* by Mr Creech Jones, A B Cohen, L H Gorsuch and Sir C Jeffries

It may help towards obtaining a clear picture of the situation at Enugu and in Eastern Nigeria if I reiterate certain information which I gave, partly orally and

---

[1] Norman Smith, CO Economic Liaison Officer for West Africa, 1948–1950.

partly in my report, on my return from Nigeria in April of this year. There was, even then, an atmosphere of tension—and a feeling of apprehension among the European inhabitants that the growing aggressiveness of the Africans in that area would sooner or later break out, on some pretext or other, into actual violence.

At the time of my visit to Enugu (February 1949) European members of the Railways Administration, the Coal Mines, the Public Works Department and the Police were gravely concerned about the growing aggressiveness of the Africans and the licence allowed them by higher authority to pursue a policy of vilification of the British and to indulge in strikes and go slow methods which, in the opinion of many, were quite unjustified. It was felt that unless appropriate action was taken the situation would continue to deteriorate. Other Europeans—missionaries and people engaged in commercial pursuits—were concerned with the lack of public security in the Enugu area. Successful raids were being made on the mines and property stolen; the occupants of a Mission were locked in a room while the place was looted and other buildings set on fire. There were many cases of insubordination in the Railways and Public Works Departments while abusive words written on coaches, private cars and premises were commonplace. Strikes and go-slow methods were either in progress or threatened. Members of private mining organisations had difficulty in carrying out prospecting operations because of interference by the native population. One responsible member of the European community went so far as to say that there was no longer any security of life or property in the Enugu area. I quote these instances as indicative of the state of affairs in Enugu during the early part of this year.

On my return to Lagos from Enugu I mentioned these matters to the Governor and others. I expressed the concern felt by members of the European community but it was the opinion of the Governor and others in Lagos that I was exaggerating the situation and the Governor went so far as to show me a letter from the Chief Commissioner who had just completed a tour of the Eastern Region where he was apparently well received as one of the passages in his letter ran 'if this is African democracy, give me more of it'. I could only inform the Governor that I had formed rather a different impression.

Telegram No. 1806 of 24th November, 1949 from Nigeria states 'communication with Enugu in emergency must nearly all be by telegram'. In paragraph 6 of my report above referred to I drew attention to the distressing state of communications in Nigeria and made particular reference to Emugu where a new £40,000 apparatus to connect Enugu and Lagos had been lying, unused, since 1947. With the exception of Ibadan, there is no telephonic communication between any Regional Headquarters and Lagos, and telegraphic communication is most inefficient. It was found simpler to send inland telegrams by West African Airways—when functioning.

In Sokoto province, Gusau is a trouble-centre. Sokoto is provincial Headquarters; but it is difficult and often impossible to establish communication between the two places owing to the inadequacy of the telegraph system. As for moving re-inforcements from Sokoto to Gusau, it would be fortunate if they got through in the wet season as the road is incapable of bearing heavy traffic at that time of year. Among other likely trouble-centres are Jos, and Buea in the Cameroons. There is an increasing amount of political agitation in Jos, fostered mainly by Ebos; and there is unrest among the African employees of the Cameroons Development Corporation stirred up, I am informed, largely by Ebo traders. (I am commenting separately on the Cameroons Development Corporation papers).

Minutes on 84

I am surprised to read Mr. Norman Smith's report of 30th November 1949 (copy attached) on the deterioration of affairs at Enugu in February of this year. It is a complaint about lack of respect for authority, of disorder and insecurity which is bound to come to light in the Enquiry and which cannot escape public attention. If things are deteriorating over the Eastern provinces what is being done to correct it? Are newspapers and agitators urging subversive action and treachery, lawlessness and violence going scott free? We cannot let a situation like this drift—particularly in regard to the press.

                                                               A.C.J.
                                                               12.12.49

As neither Mr. Gorsuch nor I had the opportunity of commenting on Mr. Smith's note about the situation at Enugu before it went to Ministers, I wonder if I may venture to comment on it now.

The suggestion in the note as I read it is that 'higher authority' in Nigeria ought for some time to have adopted a firmer attitude towards Africans. That is not a point on which I feel that we can comment in detail at the present time while the Commission of Enquiry is sitting. But it is worth noting from what he says that Mr. Smith's view was not shared either by the Governor or the Chief Commissioner (Commander Pyke-Nott). They are, of course, the people responsible for political and other relations with Africans in the area and this is the first time that I have heard it suggested that the Nigerian Government either at the centre or in the Eastern Region has been pursuing a wrong policy in this respect.

The facts that the Ibos are aggressive, that there has been much violent and often unjustified criticism of Government and Government officers in the press and elsewhere and that there is hooliganism among Africans of certain types are, of course, well known both to the Nigerian Government and ourselves.[2] There are two methods of dealing with this situation. One is the policy pursued by the present Governor of Nigeria and his senior officers, with the full support of the Colonial Office. It involves establishing friendly relations with Africans and calling responsible Africans into consultation; in a word, trying to improve relations between Africans and Europeans to the maximum possible extent. Of course it involves firmness on the part of Government where this is necessary and, as I have said, I have not heard it suggested before that the Nigerian Government has been lacking in firmness. Obviously this policy cannot succeed except gradually and no-one can expect that in a place like the Eastern Region hooliganism and other violent forms of opposition to Government will not be found. But Sir J. Macpherson's policy does, as far as I know, hold out the best hope at the present time of securing an improvement in the relations between Government and the people.

---

[2] Jeffries added in the margin, 'No less true of the British!'

The alternative policy is one of clamping down, meeting aggressiveness with aggressiveness and imposing censorship on the press in normal times (this is what Lord Milverton wanted to do when he was Governor, but the Secretary of State would not agree). It is this kind of policy which I understand from Mr. Smith's note that those he has been talking to in the Eastern Provinces have been advocating. It does not surprise me that a number of the more junior officers at Enugu have been talking in this way. We know, of course, that in his policy of conciliation Sir J. Macpherson has his critics, even in the Government service. It is, of course, a fairly common phenomenon for subordinate European staff in West Africa to criticise the Government for not being firm enough. Personally I believe such criticisms to be unjustified and it is a significant fact that after the initial Enugu incident there have only been two fatal casualties in the riots, although these were widespread and serious. One cannot express an opinion in advance of the Commission's findings, but this does suggest a degree of control over the situation by the Government which in the circumstances is, I think, rather remarkable.

I do not think that I need comment on the other part of the note except to say that the moving of reinforcements from Sokoto to Gusau is hardly likely to be necessary, since the reinforcements, if they had to be moved, would come from the other direction (i.e. Kaduna and Zaria). There is, of course, a railway as far as Gusau.

Mr. Gorsuch and I were not aware that this note had been written until it reached us with the Secretary of State's comments. It was not submitted through the West African Department, nor were either Mr. Gorsuch or I sent a copy of it at the time it was written. I have discussed with Sir H. Poynton the question of procedure involved. My own view is that it ought to be laid down that where liaison officers make notes on matters primarily the concern of the geographical departments involved, they should either submit them through the department or, if this is not possible, send a copy to the head of the department simultaneously.[3]

A.B.C.
15.12.49

Mr. Cohen
I have spoken with you about the Secretary of State's minute below.

The answer to the questions asked is that the Governor has kept us fully informed of the dangerous elements in the political situation in Nigeria as a whole, and of the policy he is adopting in respect of them. In February of this year he stated—'I am convinced that the dangerous tendencies to which I have referred cannot be checked by repressive action alone', and that it was his 'constant aim to try to win and keep the initiative by showing a readiness to make substantial advances in co-operation with all who are willing to put forward or discuss progressive and constructive proposals'. This view was fully accepted at the time.

Nevertheless the Government of Nigeria took proceedings for sedition against a number of people at the end of 1948, and sentences ranging from 2½ years' imprisonment to fines of £25 were imposed.

As regards the press, in a draft reply to a letter on the subject addressed to the Secretary of State by Lord Vansittart, I set out a few days ago the constructive side of

---

[3] Jeffries added in the margin, 'I entirely agree.'

the policy which is being pursued; i.e. the establishment of close personal relations between P.R.Os. and editors in the territories so as to enable the former to influence the papers towards a more responsible standard, and the training of young African journalists in this country so that they may absorb traditions as well as technique.

L.H.G.

15.12.49

I agree with Mr. Cohen. It is absolutely essential (and this goes for Sarawak[4] too) that we should not allow these unfortunate incidents to deflect us from our policy.

C.J.J.

16.12.49

---

[4] Sarawak was brought under direct colonial rule at the end of the Second World War, British planners arguing that this would lead to progressive social and economic development. 'White Raja' rule under the Brooke family was ended. The assumption of direct rule provoked a bitter reaction among the minority Malay population. Anthony Brooke, nephew of the last Raja (Charles Vyner Brooke) was banned from Sarawak by the governor, Sir Charles Arden-Clarke, and became the focus for Malay opposition. Arden-Clarke transferred to the Gold Coast in Aug 1949. His successor, Duncan Stewart, was assassinated in Sarawak in Dec 1949. The editor is grateful to Professor A J Stockwell for this background.

85 CO 537/4625, no 62   3 Dec 1949
[Constitutional review]: letter from H M Foot to A B Cohen on the report of the Constitutional Drafting Committee. *Enclosure* [Extract]

[The Constitutional Drafting Committee was set up to examine the recommendations made by various regional conferences as part of the review of the 1947 constitution that Macpherson had inaugurated. The committee, which had an unofficial majority, was chaired by Foot and included Abubakar Tafawa Balewa, the Sardauna of Sokoto, Bode Thomas, Rev I O Ransome-Kuti, C D Onyeama and E N Ogbuna among its members. Its report was drafted for discussion at the General Conference on the constitution held in Ibadan in January 1950.]

The Governor has asked me to send you the enclosed five copies of the Report of the Constitutional Drafting Committee. We are sending out copies of the Report to members of the General Conference at once and we hope that they will meet our request to keep it confidential until the General Conference meets in Ibadan on the 9th of January. We have to send the Report to all fifty-three members and leakage before the Conference meets is more than possible, but we must clearly give them a chance to study it before the Conference takes place.

Before the recent disorders started the Governor had in mind sending me to London some time this month for a few days in order to tell you how the work of the Drafting Committee went, and also to explain the principal difficulties which we see ahead—the chief of which is the possibility of a serious split between the North and the South. I am afraid, however, that as things are at the moment I cannot get away, though possibly I might be able to make a short visit to London some time next month.

We had a tremendous job to get the Drafting Committee to agree on a single statement of recommendations for consideration by the General Conference and I am afraid that there are still a number of major differences between the North and the South which remain unsettled, but we feel that the report of the Drafting Committee is at least a step in the direction of attaining some compromise.

. . .

B.—*General structure of the constitution*

5. All Regional Conferences recommended that our constitutional advance should be based on a federal system and we have given to the issues arising from this recommendation the greatest amount of our time and thought. We are all agreed that unity will not be achieved by attempting to concentrate all power at the centre but rather by further decentralisation of authority to the Regions, coupled with sound systems of local government.

6. It is not our function to examine questions of local government but we should, in passing, record our view that the problems of local government are certainly no less important and no less urgent than those of Regional or National government. We recognise the vital contribution which existing local government bodies make and we believe that their development and reform must be matters for each Region to decide for itself as matters of importance and urgency. Indeed, we think that one of the principal advantages of the increased Regional autonomy which is now proposed will be that the Regions will be encouraged and enabled to decide for themselves how the need for improved local government is to be met.

7. It is also unnecessary for us to state the case for increased Regional autonomy since the principle has been so whole-heartedly welcomed by the Regional Conferences. Already under the present constitution, in accordance with which the legislative functions of Regional Legislatures are purely advisory, the need for greater Regional autonomy has become increasingly apparent, and the striking fact is that in the realms of legislation, finance and initiation of policy members of Regional Houses have, in practice, shown themselves anxious and able to assume and exercise responsibilities beyond the limits of the functions with which the present constitution invests them. We have no doubt at all that the process already given constitutional sanction, and fully justified by experience, of devolution of authority from the centre to the Regions should be carried much further so that a federal system of government can be developed.

8. While recognising this fundamental need we have been impressed by the difficulty of evolving a federal system by devolution of authority from the centre. Indeed the problem which confronts us is unique. The federal governments of the United States of America, Canada and Australia, for instance, have been built on the basis of separate states surrendering to a federal government some of their powers for the benefit of all. The reverse process on which we are engaged—that of the creation of a federal government by devolution—is a political experiment for which, as far as we know, there is no precedent which can guide us and we are very conscious of the dangers inherent in such an experiment.

9. We are all most anxious that in our determination to grant real autonomy to the Regions we should do nothing to endanger the unity of Nigeria or to render the government of Nigeria as a whole weak or ineffective. It is for that reason that the proposals which we have made, while giving to Regional Legislatures and Regional Executives a far greater measure of responsibility and field of authority than has been

allotted to the Regions in the past, provide adequate safeguards to preserve central authority in questions where the overall interest of the country must be predominant. We propose that the Regional Executives and Regional Legislatures should, within the boundaries of the Regions, have power to decide policy and carry out that policy by legislation and executive action over a wide range of vital subjects. That is an advance of the highest importance in the policy of granting greater Regional autonomy. At the same time we propose that the Central Legislature should have power to review Regional legislation and to refer it back or even to reject it if the Central Legislature considers that the Regional legislation offends against the general interests of Nigeria as a whole. In the sphere of policy covering these Regional subjects we consider that the right aim should be for the Regional Executives to carry out the administration of the country within their own Regions but the authority of the Regional Executives must be subject to any general direction on policy given by the Central Executive on the ground that an overall interest of Nigeria is involved.

10.   It will be seen that we have not attempted to define too closely the functions of Regional Legislatures and Executives in relation to the functions of the Central Legislature and Executive since close definition of the respective powers of the Centre and the Regions would, we believe, lead to differences and disputes, and in the process of decentralisation in which we are engaged there is much which must inevitably be left to adjustment in the light of practical experience. The Central Legislature and Executive must retain both residual and overall powers, but since the Central Legislature and Executive will themselves be made up of representatives of the Regional Legislatures and since the policy of greater Regional autonomy is so widely accepted we do not fear that there will be any desire at the Centre unnecessarily to interfere with purely Regional legislation or administration.

C. *Regional divisions*

11.   All the Regional Conferences recommended that the three-Region system should be retained. At the same time it is recognised that in certain areas, particularly, for example, in that part of the Cameroons Trusteeship Territory which lies in the Eastern Provinces, there has been a feeling amongst the people concerned that in the past they have had inadequate representation in the Regional and National Legislatures. We believe that the proposals for a large increase in the number of elected members in the Regional Legislatures and the Central Legislature should help to dispel anxiety on this score by providing better representation for all areas and, as far as the part of the Cameroons under United Kingdom Trusteeship which lies in the Eastern Provinces is concerned, specific provision has been made in our recommendations to ensure that area is adequately represented both in the Eastern Legislature and Executive and in the Central Legislature and Executive.

12.   There are two important questions affecting Regional grouping to which we have given special attention.

The first is the position of Lagos and the Colony, and we support the recommendation of the Western Provinces Regional Conference and the Lagos and Colony Conference that both Lagos and the Colony should in future be grouped with the Western Provinces for legislative and administrative purposes. We feel that the retention of the present system under which Lagos and the Colony are directly represented in the Central Legislature could not be justified in a new system based on increased Regional autonomy and we believe that the arrangement recommended whereby representatives of the Western Provinces, Lagos and the Colony will sit together in a single Regional Legislature will best conform with the main constitutional structure now proposed.

We have also considered the question of whether there should be any variation of the existing boundaries of the Regions. There appears to us to be no case at all for any variation except possibly in limited areas in the Benin Province and the Kabba and Ilorin Provinces, and we do not feel that as a Drafting Committee we can express any opinion on the arguments for or against a change in those limited areas. The Northern representatives are opposed to any variation of the boundary between the Northern Region and the Western Region on the ground that variation of Regional boundaries should be a matter for administrative decision by Government rather than for the Drafting Committee and General Conference, whereas the Western Representatives consider that this is a question rightly dealt with by the Drafting Committee and that some variation of the boundaries between the Western Region and the Northern and Eastern Regions is justified. Most of us think that there should be an impartial investigation to be undertaken as soon as possible. We are also of the strong opinion that once the investigation has been completed decisions should be taken which must be accepted as final, as we consider that it would be entirely contrary to the interests of the inhabitants of the areas concerned if uncertainty about boundaries were to be perpetuated. . . .

86   CO 583/299/2, no 36   6 Dec 1949

[Local government reform]: inward savingram no 2886 from Sir J Macpherson to Mr Creech Jones on the progress of local government reform in the Eastern provinces

Your secret Savingram No. 113 of the 25th of October. Eastern Provinces Local Government.[1]

2.   I am very greatly obliged for the attention which has been given to the draft Local Government Bill by your advisers and by the Advisory Panel, and it has been recast in several respects as the result of the comments made in your Savingram and in the enclosures thereto. As you remark, the Bill had been designed to give full effect to local government as a training ground for participation in national politics, and the changes now made have been by way of laying greater emphasis on this intention.

3.   As regards major alterations, the term Regional Authority has been re-defined so as to cover both the Chief Commissioner in an individual capacity (as in the present constitutional arrangement), and the Chief Commissioner in association with such body of persons as may be determined by the Governor, (so as to provide for the possible emergence of a Regional Executive Council). The powers of this Authority have been recast to the extent that the Instrument constituting a council shall be amended only after the wishes of the inhabitants and the views of the council

---

[1] See 78.

have been consulted, and statutory enquiries are to be held prior to any alteration of boundaries or dissolution of a council for failure to hold meetings or to conform to statutory obligations. The enquiries contemplated by the original clause 11 will be held by direction of the Regional Authority, and additional clauses have been added to prescribe procedure.

4. The question of imposition of mandatory functions, proposed in paragraph 5 of your Savingram has been reconsidered, and certain public health functions have now been made mandatory, whilst provision has been made for the Regional Authority declaring all or some of the functions allocated under Instrument to be mandatory in the case of County and Local Councils.

5. The important question of intervention by the Governor has also been reconsidered, and the relevant clause in the revised Bill redrafted so as to conform with the suggestion in paragraph 11 of your Savingram. I agree that it is most important that the position of the Chief Commissioner should be made plain and his prestige safeguarded.

6. Certain amendments have been made in clauses 15, 45(b) and 100 in the light of your comments, and clause 56(d) has been omitted.

7. The financial provisions of the Bill have also been reviewed, more particularly with regard to the submission of estimates. I appreciate the necessity of encouraging Councils to order their affairs in such a way as not to require prior official sanction, but, as you know, the present local government experiment contemplates elected bodies operating each over a very much wider territory and with very much greater financial resources and responsibilities than the Eastern Provinces have hitherto seen. It may well be that one or two such bodies will at once prove themselves fully competent to manage their affairs in all respects, but to make statutory provisions for excusing certain Councils from submitting estimates while retaining that control in respect of others would, I feel, open the way to much discriminatory argument and the maintenance of constant pressure on Government in individual cases. I would prefer, therefore, to retain the present insistence on submission of estimates, and consider relaxation, as a general statutory measure, after we have gained some practical knowledge of the working of these experimental bodies.

8. At the same time I agree that there could be modification of the original draft provisions to allow of incurring supplementary expenditure without approval under any particular Head of the Estimates up to a limit of ten per cent of the original allotment under that Head, and up to five per cent of the total approved expenditure for emergent purposes. The Bill has been redrafted accordingly.

9. The rating provisions now confine exemption from rating only to buildings provided for public worship, cemeteries and burial grounds.

10. The Bill is now about to be published and will be introduced in the Eastern House of Assembly in February. Thanks to the careful sounding and education of public opinion when its general principles were being considered and to the care taken to meet progressive views to the greatest extent compatible with sound administration, I have every belief that it will prove acceptable and workable, and provide valuable experience to the Eastern Regional politicians of the future. I trust also that its introduction and enactment may in some measure assuage the bitterness and bewilderment engendered by the unhappy events of the last few weeks.

11.   It has not been overlooked, however, that the successful working of this projected Ordinance will very largely depend on the training of an adequate local government staff, and arrangements are now being made to send a number of officers and officials to the United Kingdom for instruction. I would take this opportunity of acknowledging the very valuable assistance which you are extending in this respect.

87   CO 537/4625, no 69   20 Dec 1949
[Constitutional review]: letter from A B Cohen to Sir J Macpherson on the Constitutional Drafting Committee's report

I have already written to Foot to thank him for his secret and personal letter of the 3rd December enclosing five copies of the Report of the Constitutional Drafting Committee.[1] We have since been considering what the best time would be for the discussion between the Colonial Office and the official side of the Nigerian Government which will no doubt have to take place before the Legislative Council meeting in March. I was very glad to hear from Foot's letter that you had been proposing to send him home for this discussion and that it might be possible for him to come in January. Our view now is that it would be best for him to come after the General Conference, i.e. when you know what has been recommended and have been able to form some view on the major points at issue. Any time towards the end of January or early in February would be suitable, if the General Conference has in fact ended by then. We appreciate that this might be a difficult time for Foot to get away, since the report of the Enugu Commission of Enquiry will presumably then have been made or be about to be made and Foot will no doubt be wanted in Lagos for urgent consideration of its recommendations. We feel that we must leave the timing to you in relation to local needs, but I thought that I had better let you know what we felt to be the most suitable arrangement for discussion here. I have consulted the Secretary of State and he agrees with what is said above.

    We realise, of course, that until the General Conference has made its recommendations it would be premature for us to express any official views on the proposals. Nevertheless we have felt that we owed it to you to let you know now whether we had any comments on the report of the Drafting Committee. We have all been considering it very carefully and the comments which we wish to make at this stage are contained in the attached memorandum.[2] A number of the comments are on points of detail but we have dealt with five more important points, the respective legislative powers of the centre and the regions, the relations between the central and regional Executives, the method of appointing Ministers, the composition of the Nigerian Legislature and the system of election.

    I want to make it clear straight away that the comments in this memorandum, are *not* sent to you with a view to influencing the discussions in the General Conference, which we appreciate is designed for the purpose of formulating an agreed unofficial view if possible. They are sent to you to give you and your official advisers some idea of the more important points which we think that the Secretary of state will want to

---

[1] See 85.   [2] Not printed.

raise in any discussions in London after the General Conference. It may be useful to you to have a chance of considering these points before Foot or whoever you send comes to London.

We appreciate that the General Conference may well produce recommendations which are different from those in the Drafting Committee's Report in a number of important respects. We realise the wide differences which still persist between the North and the South on certain important points and we have admired the skill with which the Drafting Committee has been brought somewhere near agreement on these points.

You will see that in the main our comments relate to federal relations between the centre and the regions. This is obviously a most difficult subject and requires a great deal of study of comparative federal constitutions. It would be quite wrong for us at this stage to attempt any final or even considered views. We have therefore cast our memorandum in the form of a series of questions. What we want to do is to raise a number of points for subsequent discussion here. Perhaps those who have been in the heat of the fray in these discussions in Nigeria may tend to feel that we have been a little theoretical and general. That is to a large extent inevitable and it is, I suppose, our function to try to bring to bear such general experience as we have of constitution-making on the particular problems of Nigeria.

I hope that you will not feel that we are being inconsistent in relation to the composition of the Legislative Council itself. You will remember that in the notes which I sent you with my secret and personal letter of the 4th March[3] I said in relation to the Legislative Council that I doubted whether it would be either politically safe or satisfactory in practice to cut out the Houses of Assembly as electoral colleges. In the enclosed memorandum we raise the question whether the elected membership of the Legislative Council should be entirely drawn from the regional Houses. We do not of course in any sense suggest that the regional Houses should be left out; indeed that would be quite impossible. But we have been wondering whether you can really get away with a Council entirely drawn from the regions without any more directly elected membership at all. I am not, of course, suggesting the extension of the direct franchise à la Lagos. We have been wondering, however, whether there ought to be some membership drawn from the provincial or divisional level direct to the Legislative Council in addition to the substantial number of members who must obviously be drawn from the regional Councils.

May I finish up this letter by saying what a really valuable document we think the Drafting Committee's Report is? With such a wide conflict of views between the North and the South it is really remarkable to have got such a large measure of agreement. We realise that it is going to be a very difficult job bringing the North and the South completely together; we feel that a most excellent start has been made.

We do not, of course, want you to comment in detail on the memorandum but merely to take it as an indication of some of the points we shall wish to raise with Foot or whoever else you send to London.

I have shown this letter to the Secretary of State, who was entirely agreeable that we should let you have the views contained in the enclosed memorandum. He does not himself want to be committed in detail to any comments on the Drafting Committee's Report at this stage.

---

[3] See 63.

88   CO 537/4625, no 80   9 Jan 1950
[Constitutional review]: CO note on two meetings held to discuss the
reform of the Nigerian constitution[1]

The meeting was called in order to discuss with Mr. Foot the present state of the
consultations in Nigeria about the reform of the present Nigerian constitution.
   The following points were made in discussion:—

I. *Procedure*

(a) It was expected that the Nigerian Government would have to make some
statement of their views on the proposals for the new constitution at the meeting
of the Legislative Council in March. Mr. Foot had already discussed with Mr.
Cohen the form which this statement might take and it was thought that it would
be sufficient for it to mention only the points on which the official view agreed
with the views accepted by the Legislative Council. It was expected that Mr. Foot
would be able to avoid controversial points, particularly as he would bear in mind
what had been said to him in London. The statement would simply give the views
of the Nigerian Government and would not purport in any way to convey any
decision on proposals put forward. It might be necessary to clear the wording of
any statement with the Secretary of State, but this was a matter which could be
left for subsequent decision.
(b) The time schedule for consultations in Nigeria might appear to be rigid but it
must be borne in mind that the discussions about the future constitution of the
Territory had now been going on for a period of about eighteen months.
(c) It should also be borne in mind that the General Conference was not bound in
any way by the conclusions reached by the Drafting Committee and that there was
a strong possibility in Mr. Foot's view that the General Conference might be
unable to agree on these conclusions. Mr. Foot emphasised the difficulty of
reaching agreement on the proportion of seats in the central Legislature to be
allocated to each region, the possibility that the Northern Region might be
unwilling to accept central Ministers and the possibility that those members of the
General Conference who supported the National Emergency Committee might
take the opportunity to walk out of the Conferences at an appropriate moment.
(d) It would admittedly be difficult for H.M.G. to modify substantially the
proposals which would eventually come from the Legislative Council. Mr. Foot did
not, however, expect that any of these proposals would be objectionable to H.M.G.
in the light of the discussions he had had in London. He considered that the
changes which the Colonial Office appeared to contemplate were not likely to
cause difficulty in Nigeria. It was pointed out that a certain measure of opposition,
particularly in the House of Lords, was likely on the grounds that H.M.G. were
concentrating on constitution-making to the detriment of economic development.
(e) It was expected that when the General Conference had reported the Regional
Houses would debate its recommendations in February and the Legislative
Council would debate its recommendations in March. The Governor would then

---

[1] These meetings were chaired by Creech Jones and involved Foot and senior CO officials.

transmit the agreed views of the Legislative Council to the Secretary of State early in April and both Mr. Foot and Sir G. Howe[2] would be on leave in the U.K. at that time and ready to assist in discussions. Mr. Foot mentioned the possibility that if the Northern members disagreed with the recommendations of the General Conference they might ask to be allowed to send a deputation to the Secretary of State.

II. *Object of London discussions*

(f) Although it was not possible at this stage to indicate what recommendations the General Conference were likely to make, it was necessary for the Nigerian Government to be aware of the main lines of thought of the Secretary of State in order that they should avoid as far as possible any fundamental divergence of view between the recommendations likely to emerge in Nigeria and the known views of the Secretary of State. There was no doubt that all concerned were agreed on the need to advance on the road towards a federal system in Nigeria.

III. *Major constitutional problems*

(g) The proposed structure of the Nigerian constitution outlined in the Report of the Drafting Committee implied an overlapping of the powers of regional Legislatures and the central Legislature which was remarkable, if not unique. The Nigerian Government considered that it was necessary at this interim stage of constitutional development not to be too rigid but to feel their way towards a system which might be defined with more exactitude after five or ten years, when experience had been gained of the manner in which the Nigerians themselves wished to order their affairs. Mr. Foot claimed that experience under the present constitution had shown that Regional Houses were in fact exercising what amounted to legislative power. This process had perhaps not gone very far. The S of S suggested that there might be same danger in this at a time when experience throughout the world showed the need for larger administrative units.

(h) Although it might be thought that regionalisation under the proposed new constitution was going too far, Mr. Foot pointed out that there were very strong safeguards proposed in the Report of the Drafting Committee. The Secretary of State stressed the importance of inculcating a sense of unity and of preserving a strong central power.

(i) Mr. Foot explained that the transition from a unitary bureaucracy to a working democracy necessarily meant regional autonomy because that was the only way in which the regions would agree to co-operate. Nevertheless there must be a proper reconciliation of power at the centre and in the regions and it was important in the Secretary of State's view that the centre should never wish to take back any powers granted to the regions. The overlapping of powers might well cause confusion and there was a need to keep power at the centre in order to ensure that regional Governments performed their functions effectively. It was entirely appreciated that a measure of regional devolution was inevitable and the successful working of the new constitution must in any event rely on the good sense of those working it.

---

[2] Sir G Howe, attorney-general of Nigeria, 1946–1950.

(j) The new constitution would of course include the ordinary provision making it impossible for a private member to move any Bill creating a charge on public revenue without the consent of Government.

(k) Mr. Foot stressed the importance of the expert enquiry into the division of revenue which would probably be undertaken by Sir S. Phillipson together with outside experts in consultation with a committee representing the three regions.

(l) Although much would depend upon the numbers of representatives of each region in the central Legislature, it seemed important that the rejection by the central Legislature of regional legislation should depend on a simple majority and not on a two-thirds majority.

(m) Although there were arguments against Ministers in the central Legislature, it seemed clear that without them the central Legislature would become a second-rate show.

(n) Mr. Foot explained the arguments in favour of the election of Ministers by the regional blocks in the central Legislature. Each block would elect four members to serve on the Council of State. He considered that a system of election would relieve the Governor of the extremely difficult and thankless task of selecting Ministers in the Legislature, adding that it would be clear that any useless Minister was a Minister because of the Legislature and not by choice of the Governor. Against these arguments it was pointed out that it would be a great mistake to have useless Ministers, particularly at a time when the ministerial system was on trial. It would be difficult for Ministers to be responsible to the Governor whilst tied to a regional block which had elected them. If Ministers were selected by the Governor, it was more likely that they would have a sense of unity and work as a team in the Council of State.

(o) Mr. Foot explained that he did not expect the Council of State to meet more frequently than four or five times a year and that Ministers would only be empowered to carry out the decisions of the Council of State. It was pointed out that if the Council of State were to develop into an effective instrument of government, it would undoubtedly need to meet more frequently and that Ministers would of necessity wish to supervise the day-to-day administration of the departments for which they were responsible. As, however, the General Conference might well reach conclusions different from those of the Drafting Committee on the question of Ministers, it would be preferable not to carry the discussions further at this stage but to await the outcome of the General Conference.

(p) The Secretary of State expressed his concern that any electoral system should be genuinely representative. Mr. Foot said that when the proposals for a new constitution came from Nigeria they would be accompanied by the proposals of the three electoral commissions which it was proposed to set up to recommend the electoral system which should be followed in each region.

(q) The system of electing members of the central Legislature by the members of the Regional Houses was open to criticism on the grounds that the more extreme political elements might thereby be completely excluded from the central Legislature. Mr. Foot pointed out that this criticism had not been made in Nigeria in the course of the constitutional discussions and that the Nigerian Government agreed that there should be in the central Legislature two members from each Province in the Territory. It was pointed out that this system of election had been a feature of other federal constitutions but that elsewhere in the world as far as was known no central federal Legislature had ever been completely composed of elected representatives of subordinate houses. Much depended upon how representative the members of the Regional Houses would be under the proposals to be made by the electoral commissions.

(r) No recomendation had yet been made in Nigeria for nominated members of the central Legislature. There was no objection to the nomination of members with wide experience who would be of value in a Legislature. It was possible that the present nominated members of the Legislative Council might be able to persuade the General Conference to recommend that there should be a small number of nominated members in the new constitution. It was not however, necessary to give further consideration to this point unless either the General Conference made such a recommendation or the business firms concerned made an approach on the matter. They had made such an approach concerning the Gold Coast, but of course in the Gold Coast they had had no opportunity of participating in any of the constitutional discussions.

89   CO 537/5807, no 12   31 Jan 1950
[Constitutional review]: letter from A B Cohen to Sir J Macpherson reporting on a meeting with Dr Azikiwe

Gorsuch is writing to Foot about the reports we have had about Zik's activities in the United States. This letter is to record very briefly the main points in an hour's talk I had with him last Friday. I had heard that he wanted to see me so I rang him up and invited him to come along, which he did.

Most of the talk was about the constitution. He had had reports from his people about the proceedings at Ibadan. The main points which he raised were:—

(1) The attitude of the North. He was inclined to be bitter about this and said that a separation from the North might well be necessary. At one stage he even went so far as to say that he would be in favour of not giving the North facilities for the transit of their exports, etc. without making them pay through the nose. If their attitude was as intransigent as the reports suggested the South could be equally firm. I said that the view of the Colonial Office, and as far as I knew of H.M.G., was that it would be an unmitigated disaster if Nigeria broke into two parts. It seemed to us quite essential to prevent this and I knew that everything possible had been done by the Nigerian Government, both in the Drafting Committee and otherwise, to bring Northern and other representatives together and to avoid a split. Zik then said that personally he agreed with the view that I had expressed that it would be a disaster if Nigeria broke into two parts. But for tactical reasons the South would have to take a tough line with the North.

(2) Zik expressed great disappointment at the decision of the General Conference that the central Legislature should consist primarily of regional delegates. He said that the intention of the N.C.N.C. had been to try to work the new constitution which emerged from the present discussions, even if they regarded parts of it as unsatisfactory. They had hoped that they would be in a position to put up candidates so as to secure representation on the various bodies. In view of the reported decision

of the General Conference he was doubtful whether it would be easy for them to do this. I expressed fairly strong disagreement and said that as I understood the position much depended on the results of the Regional Committees on the electoral system in each region. I gathered that both the East and the West at any rate were aiming at a system of election at the divisional level and I could not myself see any reason why a particular party should not put up candidates through this machinery. If they got a sufficient number of members in regional Houses, they would no doubt also get members on the Legislature. Zik admitted the force of this and we did not pursue the matter. (I did not mention the decision of the General Conference about Lagos, since I was not sure exactly what had happened. But if, as I understand, Lagos is to have the right to send members direct to the Legislative Council, this further weakens Zik's argument).

During this part of our talk Zik suggested that the Nigerian Government were glad to have isolated the N.C.N.C. in the constitutional discussions. I emphatically denied this and said that I was quite sure that this was not the attitude of the Nigerian Government at all. They had been anxious throughout that the discussions on the constitution should be fully representative and it was their aim that the new constitution should be equally representative.

At the end of our talk Zik referred to the trouble over his admission to the Gold Coast. He said that he had no criminal record either in the Gold Coast or in Nigeria; that the action of the Gold Coast Government suggested that he was regarded as an undesirable person; and that it would have been perfectly possible for the Gold Coast Government to let him carry out his original arrangements for transit, at the same time asking him not to make any political speeches. He referred to the Human Rights Convention and said that he was being pressed to declare his attitude on his return to Nigeria and that this incident might affect his actions. He said that he thought that the Gold Coast Government ought to apologise to him.

In replying to all this I could not of course refer to the Secretary of State's attitude in the matter as expressed in the telegram which he sent to the Gold Coast. I said that I was quite sure that the Gold Coast Government was aware that he had no criminal record and had not been deported. The fact that they had felt obliged to oppose his entry into the Gold Coast was not because they regarded him as an undesirable person, but because they were gravely anxious about the political situation in the Gold Coast and feared that a speech from a prominent political leader from outside the Gold Coast at that particular stage might add to the already rising tension. With regard to his point about the Human Rights Convention I said that every Government had the duty to take measures for the maintenance of public order and that the action to be taken in this respect must be decided upon according to the judgment of the Government concerned. As he knew, the Secretary of State was very sorry that this incident had occurred. I felt that had the Gold Coast Government had more notice it would have been possible to arrive by telegram at some arrangement quite satisfactory to all concerned. The difficulty had been due to the very short time available before Zik's proposed departure for the Gold Coast. I referred to the fact that the Gold Coast Government had been prepared to allow him to pass through Accra; he said that he had not felt able to agree to a night flight in a one-engined plane. I put him right about the number of engines of Doves and he then said that as a member of the Legislative Council he had felt doubtful about putting the Nigerian Government to this expense. I finished up by saying that I was sure he realised that this particular incident, which had arisen suddenly, did not in any sense imply any alteration in the attitude of H.M.G. or the Nigerian Government towards him. He said that he perfectly realised this.

I did not of course refer to his suggestion about an apology from the Gold Coast Government. He thanked me for what I had said; but I was not sure that he was entirely satisfied by it.

He did not say much to me about his visit to the United States. He mentioned his talk with some State Department officials which is referred to in Gorsuch's letter to Foot. He said that he had made it very clear to them that there was a great deal of suspicion in Nigeria about outside investment. He got the impression that they were not entirely clear how the Fourth Point worked (this does not surprise me at all). He himself had, I gathered, not formed the impression that Nigeria was likely to be able to take much advantage of it.

90   CO 537/5786, no 7   2 Feb 1950
[Constitutional review]: inward savingram no 34 from Sir J Macpherson to Mr Creech Jones on the results of the General Constitutional Conference at Ibadan

[The process of constitutional consultation initiated by Macpherson in 1948 reached a conclusion at the general conference held in Ibadan in Jan 1950 to consider the report of the constitutional drafting committee. The conference had 53 members, of whom all but three were Nigerian, and included the unofficial members of the Legislative Council as well as delegates elected by the regional constitutional conferences. The Ibadan conference was characterised by considerable differences over the issue of the size of regional representation in the proposed House of Representatives; the Northern delegates insisted on parity of representation with the Eastern and Western Regions combined, that there should be no change in the boundary between the North and West and that finance should be allocated on a *per capita* basis. Although the conference largely accepted the recommendations of the drafting committee, these issues were not fully resolved. The conference issued a report, *Report of the General Conference on the Review of the Constitution, Ibadan, Nigeria, 1950* (Lagos, 1950), though four minority reports on issues such as adult suffrage, franchise rights of southerners living in the North, the position of Lagos and the number of regions were also issued.]

My telegram 123 of 27th January.

2.   The General Constitutional Conference completed its session at Ibadan on January 28th, and the outlook is now more promising than when I made my previous report. The Northern delegates had been on the point of leaving the Conference after the session of January 25th, but were induced to appear on the 26th, and agreed to remain to complete the work of the Conference provided it were clearly specified in the record that they had abstained from voting on the crucial issue of Regional representation in the Central Legislature and that should their claim for 50% of seats in the House of Representatives not be conceded they must be considered to disassociate themselves from the other proceedings of the Conference.

3.   The Conference then continued consideration of other items, in the discussion of which the Northern delegates participated to the full. At the close of the Conference it was a Northern delegate, the Sardauna of Sokoto, who proposed the vote of thanks to the Chairman, and in his speech he stressed the point that the deadlock reached with regard to the Central Legislature was not impossible of

solution. He went on to hope that the results of the Conference would lead Nigeria to achieve national unity, and he made it plain that he was speaking on behalf of all Northern delegates.

4.   Copies of the recommendations made by the Conference will be sent to you as soon as possible, but I might mention here the main points on which the Conference's recommendations vary from the suggestions of the Drafting Committee. These are:—

(a) the Municipality of Lagos should not form a part of any Region, although the Colony districts should be incorporated in the Western Provinces:

(b) commercial interests should be given three nominated representatives in the Central Legislature:

(c) if expert inquiry finds that any Region has been inequitably treated in the past in respect of financial allocation from the Centre, that Region should be given a block grant from Central funds by way of compensation.

5.   The decision in respect of Lagos was carried mainly by the votes of the Northern and Eastern delegates, who also voted down a suggestion that Lagos should have representation in the Central Executive. There is likely to be much opposition to these decisions in Lagos, the Colony districts and the Western Provinces, and a minority report has been prepared on the subject by certain delegates, although it has not yet been received. The decision to give representation to commercial interests was well received at the Conference and was, in discussion, a much less controversial issue than the subject of Lagos. The recommendation for a block grant in respect of finance, should any past inequity be proved, was intended by the Eastern and Western Regions as a concession to the North.

6.   The question of the Reserve Powers of the Governor was raised and the Conference has made a definite recommendation that these powers should for the present be left untouched.

7.   The Conference's recommendations are now being circulated for consideration by Regional Houses, which meet at varying dates during the next two weeks. The recommendations should prove generally acceptable in the Eastern Region, but in the Western House much attention will no doubt be concentrated on the subject of Lagos. It is not possible to anticipate the course of discussion in the Northern Houses, but there is no reason to suppose that at this stage they will adopt an attitude markedly different from that adopted by the Northern representatives at the Conference and I do not think that any attempt to find a new basis for compromise regarding Regional representation in the Central Legislature can be attempted before the Regional Houses meet.

8.   In general I think that it can be said that the constitutional review culminating in the General Conference has put forward proposals for constitutional reform which are basically sound. The review had indicated the full agreement which exists on the need for greater Regional autonomy and for association of representative Nigerians with the executive. It was most unfortunate, particularly from the point of view of the effect on the public, that the General Conference failed to find a solution of the problem of Regional representation in the Central Legislature and although I trust that some way out of the impasse on this issue can be found, the publicity given to the disagreement on this matter and on the question of the status of Lagos has tended to overshadow the very satisfactory agreement reached on so many other vital matters.

9. I should add that Sir Gerard Howe did most admirable work as Chairman of the Conference: indeed had it not been for his tact and skill the Conference might well have broken down altogether.

91 CO 537/5804, no 1   4–8 Feb 1950
[Local government reform]: minutes by R J Vile[1] and L H Gorsuch on a savingram from Sir J Macpherson concerning colonial officers

I do not think we can be entirely satisfied with the report at 1. We have been trying for some time to obtain from Nigeria some indication of what the basic causes of the unrest in the Western Provinces have been and in 1. we have no answer to this question. From what I can gather, there has been a considerable amount of dissatisfaction among the Administrative Officers in the Western Provinces who appear mostly to have felt that the Nigerian Government were attempting to rush them in the reform of local government in the Western Provinces. I believe that it was necessary for the Governor to address a meeting of all residents in the Western Provinces in order to convince them that their grounds for dissatisfaction were not valid ones. As I understand it and I speak here with a considerable amount of reserve, residents have not only disliked the pressure put on them to undertake reforms but they also resented what seemed to them the extremely weak handling by the Central Government of libellous attacks on individual officers including the Chief Commissioner. The result of this situation seems to have been that it is impossible for the Nigerian Secretariat to press the Chief Commissioner any further in the direction of the reform of local government.

In these circumstances the basic argument on 1. seems to be that the difficulties in Ijebu-Remo have been solved and that this solution gives reason to hope that the difficult problems of the Western Provinces in local government can be resolved in a spirit of co-operation and good will. I am sure that we must accept the advice of the men on the spot that this is possible and that policy must be formed accordingly. In these circumstances I doubt very much whether there is any point in referring again to our desire to know what the basic causes of unrest are. I would therefore propose that we reply to 1. by thanking the Governor for his full account of the situation by expressing pleasure at the way in which the Yoruba leaders took the initiative in the solution of this difficult problem, and by reiterating the belief that constitutional progress in the region and at the centre must depend on an efficient representative and local system of local government, adding that the Secretary of State would wish to have as soon as convenient a general account of the situation, together with the considered view of the Governor on the policy which should be followed as soon as the Governor is able to do so.

                                                                    R.J.V.
                                                                    4.2.50

I took the opportunity of discussing with Mr. Abell recently the position in the Western Provinces generally (he was, as you know, Resident of Oyo). He said that in dealing with the unrest in the Western Provinces the administration were not faced

---

[1] R J Vile, principal CO, 1947; assistant secretary, 1963.

merely with reactionary Obas on the one hand and the progressive younger generation on the other which wished to have a greater share in the direction of affairs. There was another ingredient; i.e. that while quite a number of people might wish the basis of local government to be broadened, only a very few wished to get rid of the Oba altogether. Apart from his position as Native Authority, the Oba had a traditional and almost spiritual place in Yoruba society, and it would be quite wrong to suppose that any significant part of the people wanted to see this destroyed. The administration had, therefore, to go very delicately and to decide very carefully in each case whether or not they would support the Oba and if so how far; it might well be that the Oba should be persuaded to broaden the basis of his local government, as the Oni of Ife had already done, and even to give up some of the practices in which he indulged, as the Alake of Abeokuta had failed to do; but it was not for the administration to incur the odium of having turned the Oba out altogether except for some very good reason.

There is undoubtedly a feeling amongst the Western Province officers that Lagos does not fully understand their difficulties and is inclined to press them to go too fast. I think, therefore, that it would be preferable in view of the tone of the Governor's report at 1. to confine our answer to A of Mr. Vile's minute and not to include B.[1]

L.H.G.
8.2.50

---

[1] A and B referred to the lengthy sentence with which Vile concluded the seconded paragraph of his minute. A referred to the sentence as far as 'solution of this difficult problem'. B referred to the remainder of the sentence.

92   CO 583/314/2, no 5   7 Feb 1950
[Cameroons Visiting Mission]: letter from Sir A Burns to A N Galsworthy on the report of the UNO Visiting Mission to the Cameroons

[In late 1946 the UNO general assembly met to consider the transfer of the former League of Nations mandates in Cameroons, Togoland and Tanganyika as trusteeship territories to Britain and (in the former two cases) France. The trusteeship agreement with Britain for the Cameroons was approved by the general assembly on 14 Dec 1946. Thereafter the Trusteeship Council continued to monitor British administration in the territory and the first of what were to be several UNO Visiting Missions visited the Cameroons in Nov 1949. The key issue to be considered on this occasion, at least as far as the British government was concerned, was whether the Cameroons should continue to be administered as part of Nigeria; hitherto the Southern Cameroons had been administered as part of the Eastern provinces with, under the Richards constitution, seats in the Eastern Assembly and, from 1948, the appointment of a commissioner for the Cameroons, responsible to Enugu; the Northern Cameroons were similarly administered as part of the Northern provinces. See 96. Sir Alan Burns, previously governor of the Gold Coast, 1941–1947, and acting governor of Nigeria, 1942, was the permanent UK representative on the UNO Trusteeship Council, 1947–1956.]

I read hurriedly through the report of the Visiting Mission on the Cameroons last night. Incidentally, my lack of faith was unjustified and the report was delivered to me a day earlier than promised and I now have little doubt that we will get the remaining reports by Thursday.

My first impression is that the report is a very good one and quite satisfactory from our point of view. It shows an entirely different approach from that on Tanganyika last year and I think this is partly due to the different personnel of the Secretariat as well as of the Mission, and partly to our violent reactions to the Tanganyika report.

I invite your attention to the very generous references to the freedom of speech allowed in the Cameroons at pages 6 and 57 of the report and also to the general blessing of the Development Corporation at page 7 and the realisation at page 10 of the impertinence of the criticisms of the Fon of Bikom's matrimonial extravagances.

They point out, at page 52, that the division of the Cameroons between the French and the British adversely affects the interests of the inhabitants and the 'nationality' of the Cameroons. What they of course overlook is the fact that any boundaries in Africa e.g., as between Cameroons and Nigeria, would have exactly the same effect.

The main criticism of the administration is naturally enough, in view of what has happened before, 'the administrative union' between the Cameroons and Nigeria. The Mission realises the difficulties but is stimulated to attack the union by the demands of the people in the south. It is, however, to those who do not realise the comparative size and population of the two territories, a tempting idea that Southern Cameroons should be set up as a completely separate organisation similar to the various groups of provinces in Nigeria and without attaching the Cameroons in any way to the Eastern Provinces. On the whole I think we have come very well even out of this difficult problem.

The other serious criticism is the tax paid to the Nigerian Government by the Cameroons Development Corporation, but on this again I think they have been very reasonable.

No doubt the Nigerian Government will have a lot to say in its comments on the report but I feel personally that the Mission has gone out of its way to be as friendly and as helpful to us as possible and I hope that the tone of our reply will be similarly forthcoming.

You will observe that the Mexican Minority Report has disappeared without any detrimental compromise in the report itself. I have had many talks with Khalidy, Greig and Wieschoff and I think they have responded to my suggestions in as satisfactory a way as we could have hoped. I now await with some anxiety their report on the Ewe problem and the other territories.

93   CO 537/5786, no 9   Feb 1950
[Constitutional review]: letter from H M Foot to A B Cohen on the next stage of the constitutional review. Minute by R J Vile

We have sent you copies of the resolutions of the General Constitutional Conference and in a day or two we shall forward a descriptive note about the Conference written by A.A. Williams who was joint-secretary of the Conference. Following a meeting of Chief Commissioners a few days ago the Governor has now asked me to tell you how we think the next stages in the constitutional review may go.

As far as local reactions to the General Conference were concerned popular interest has centred in the controversies about Regional representation in the central legislature and about the future constitutional status of the Colony including Lagos township. It is a pity that these two issues are getting most of the limelight and are detracting interest from the main constitutional structure proposed which is much what we hoped would emerge. Indeed, the General Conference has improved in several respects on the Drafting Committee's recommendations. It was most helpful to get a well-backed recommendation for commercial representation in the central legislature. It was also a good thing that the Conference came down in favour of giving Western Obas places on the Western Executive Council and in the central legislature. It would clearly be unsound to have Northern Chiefs in the Northern Executive Council and in the central legislature and to deny such opportunities to Western Obas, but we had been unable to convince the Western representatives of this in the Drafting Committee. Another useful change was to leave over for later decision the actual method of election to Regional Houses rather than to appoint Commissions on this matter and to require the Commissions to make hurried recommendations (as the Drafting Committee had proposed). It was also an improvement to provide that rejection of Regional legislature should be achieved by a straight majority in the central legislature instead of a two-thirds majority. On the whole we feel that in spite of the great anxieties still ahead we have emerged so far from the constitutional review with a set of recommendations more in line with what we wanted than even the most optimistic would have dared to hope a year ago.

The next stage is for the Regional Houses to consider the General Conference's proposals and all we can hope for from that stage is that eventual compromises on the remaining issues in dispute are not made less possible by hardening of Regional differences. We propose that select committees of the Regional Houses should be set up to consider the General Conference's recommendations and that these select committees should be mainly, if not wholly, composed of unofficial members probably under an official chairman. The advantage of this arrangement (if it is adopted in the Regional Houses) will be that it will enable Regional Officials to avoid making official declarations at this stage and that it will also allow most if not all the discussion in Regional Houses to be conducted calmly in private (Select Committee proceedings are, of course, not public) rather than in open debate in which Regional representatives would no doubt feel it necessary to commit themselves even more strongly than they did in the General Conference to an uncompromising stand on the questions still in dispute.

The last stage in which Nigerian representatives will be directly involved will be in Legislative Council when we meet in Enugu in March and there again we intend to propose that a Select Committee should be set up. We have in mind that the composition of this Select Committee should be much the same as that of the Select Committee set up in March last at Ibadan to make recommendations on how the constitutional review should be carried out—that is, that it should be composed of all the unofficial members together with the Chief Commissioners, the Attorney-General, the Financial Secretary and myself. We propose that this Select Committee should meet from time to time throughout the Legislative Council session, which will no doubt last for a month or more, and that we should all make a sustained effort to find acceptable compromises on the two main questions still in dispute—Regional representation in the central legislature and the constitutional status of Lagos and the Colony. (In addition there is, of course, the problem of Finance which is always with us, and it is crucial; as you know special arrangements are proposed for tackling this, though it will colour and affect all the discussions). We cannot, of course, see clearly what sort of compromise might be acceptable and there will have to be a lot of give and take but if we could emerge from the Select Committee with workable proposals commanding substantial support from all three Regional groups for solving those two vital outstanding questions we should have carried the whole review much nearer a satisfactory conclusion. What the chances of achieving this are we can't tell—they don't look very bright at present—but we shall go at it as hard as we can in the hope that in the end the desire for compromise will prevail and some sensible plan for overcoming the disagreements can be worked out.

As I say we can't in advance guess what line of compromise is most likely to succeed but the Governor has asked me to put two suggestions to you to see what you think of them.

As to Regional representation, Southern alarm is partly but not wholly due to the possibility that the North, if it did get half the seats in the central legislature, might use its power to reject Eastern or Western Regional legislation. If it were not for this fear the objection to giving the Northerners what they ask for should be much less. (If we had been building a unitary structure the North would presumably have automatically got representation on the basis of population by electoral divisions). It has therefore occurred to us that the right to refer back or reject Regional legislation might be taken altogether out of the hands of the central legislature and vested in the central executive (in which, with Northern agreement, there is to be equal representation between North, East and West). We think that there is something to be said for this in theory as well as in practice as the power of veto is normally an executive and not a legislative function. If this suggestion were adopted we think that the Southern opposition to the North having half the seats in the central legislature might diminish since there would clearly be less force in the objection to giving the North half the seats in a body which is considering 'Nigerian' matters. The Northern representatives might well accept the proposal to shift the veto to the central executive and if they were in a compromising frame of mind (no sign of it yet) they might just possibly agree to go a bit below their parity demand—possibly on the basis of something like 40:22:22 instead of 30:22:22 as proposed by the Drafting Committee and 45:33:33 as finally voted by the Southerners in the General Conference. We don't ask you (unless you wish to!) to comment on the representation figures which must remain for the time being a matter for local horse-trading but we should be most interested to know if you see any objection in principle to the right to refer back and reject Regional legislation being vested in the central executive rather than the central legislature.

On the other question—the question of the status of Lagos and the Colony—we certainly think that the General Conference proposals are unacceptable as they stand, however much there may be to be said in theory for a capital isolated from the Regions. Apart from anything else if the Conference recommendations were accepted it would be impossible for a member elected to the legislature from Lagos ever to reach the central executive.

As we judge feelings in the Colony just now the Yorubas, apart from a few self seeking individuals like Adedoyin, Nimbe and HO Davies, who are mainly concerned with their own political prospects, are overwhelmingly in favour of the Colony (including Lagos) being joined with the Western Provinces (there is a very strong feeling against splitting Lagos from the Colony Districts). And this is also the feeling of the people of the Western Provinces. In part this is due to Yoruba solidarity (hence the argument about Lagos being a Yoruba town whose fate should be decided by its own people) but the opposition of more responsible Yorubas to direct and separate Lagos representation is also coloured by anxiety not to let the Lagos representatives (whom they fear might include people such as Zik, H.O. Davies and even, conceivably, Imoudu) have things all their own way.

The sort of compromise we have in mind is that the special position of Lagos and the Colony should be recognised by continuing to treat them as one administrative unit, by guaranteeing to them a minimum number of seats in the central legislature (on the analogy of the guarantee proposed for the Cameroons) and by making a special allocation from central funds to cover the costs arising from the fact that Lagos is the capital of Nigeria; but at the same time including Lagos and the Colony in the Western Provinces. Such an arrangement would go some way to meeting the demand for special status which comes mainly from the East and from non-Yorubas in Lagos, and would also meet the Yoruba desire for amalgamation, and also, incidentally, would have the effect of satisfying Lagos politicians that their chances of return to the central legislature (thus leaving the door to the Council of Ministers open) are not adversely affected by the merger. We should be most grateful if you would let us know if something along these lines seems to you a sound compromise.

I am sorry to put such vague and, to some extent, hypothetical questions to you but at least this letter will show you how our minds are working. We are going to have a very difficult time at Enugu and it may well be that we cannot then do anything to close the gap of disagreement on the two main issues now in dispute. Any further guidance which you can give us on those two issues before we go to Enugu at the end of the month will be very welcome.

The Governor has asked me to tell you that in spite of the difficulties and dangers ahead we are more than ever glad that we undertook this review. We feel certain that if we had not started when we did, so that consultations were carried out in an atmosphere of reasonable calm, we should now, because of what is happening in the Gold Coast and elsewhere (not to mention the Enugu incident) have been improvising something in haste and under pressure and in a very different atmosphere. The political education has been most valuable and the irresponsible and voluble politicians are finding themselves up against real problems (not just a struggle between an Imperialist bureaucracy and the people) which cannot be solved by clap-trap and cheap slogans.

Minute on 93

Forty copies of the enclosure to 8 have been sent to Press Section and they will distribute them as required and as appropriate to the press. Other copies have gone to the supervisors of Colonial Service Courses and separate copies have gone to Sir T. Lloyd, Mr. Cohen and Mr. Gorsuch.

The main problem arising out of the General Conference is the refusal of the northern representatives to agree to anything less than half the representation in the Central Legislature. This has already been reported at 3 and the Governor now says at 5 that he does not think any attempt to find a new basis for compromise regarding regional representation in the Central Legislature can be attempted before the Regional Houses meet. He further considers that there is no reason to suppose that the Northern Houses will adopt an attitude markedly different from that adopted by the northern representatives at the Conference. I am sure that we must accept the Governor's advice on this matter. I am equally sure that the Nigerian authorities will take every possible opportunity to bring about a compromise between the North and the rest of the country. I should have thought that it was only necessary for northern representatives to mention a division of the territory for them to realise how unreal such a view is. I suspect that the northern attitude has been adopted more for the purpose of horse trading than as a sober contribution to political thought. It is possible indeed that the frank statement of the extreme northern position will at the outset have impressed eastern and western representatives with the very great need to keep Nigeria together and the importance of making sacrifices to this end. In this connection the proposal that any region inequitably treated in the past should be given a block grant by central funds by way of compensation, was intended as a concession to the northern point of view by the eastern and western representatives. In short, there is I think good reason to believe that the present deadlock has perhaps more hopeful implications than might at first sight have been expected. On the other hand, there is still a danger that the deadlock may continue and that in the last resort an appeal will be made to the Secretary of State to resolve the issue. It is perhaps premature at this stage to comment on this possibility but it would seem unfortunate if events developed to that extent. The successful working of the more democratic constitution proposed should preferably depend on the people working it and not on the influence of an extraneous person.

There are some differences between the recommendations of the General Conference and the statement prepared by the Drafting Committee. For example, the General Conference have recommended that Lagos should remain as an independent municipality. On this point I do not think there is any need for us to comment at this stage because there seems to be no compelling reason why we should not accept any recommendation which finally emerges from the Legislative Council no matter which way the decision finally goes. As far as nomenclature is concerned, the General Conference wish to call the Central Executive Council, the Council of Ministers instead of the Council of State. This point is not, I think, a material one.

The membership of Regional Legislatures has undergone some change in the General Conference figures. The most important change is that the official members should have no vote. This seems to me a most peculiar proposal, and I would suggest that we should ask the Governor if he can let us have some explanation of the reasons for it. The argument would seem to be that as officials are in the minority it does not matter if they have a vote or not. This seems to assume that the unofficial should have complete power, but there are bound to be cases in which unofficial opinion is divided and in which the official vote might have a considerable effect. I do not, however, think that we can reach any conclusion without more information on this point. The number of official members has been reduced from 17 to 4 in the north and is the same in the west and the east at 3 and 5 respectively. The number of unofficial members has gone up from 50 to 66 in the northern region, from 60 to 80 in the Western House of Assembly and gone from 60 to 80 in the Eastern House of Assembly. In the east it is proposed to have at least two members for each division instead of one and similarly in the west. In the north a provision that there should be at least 2 members for each province has also been included. I do not think these changes need worry us. They seem to be intelligent in that they do make representation more exact.

The functions of Regional Legislature are substantially those proposed by the Drafting Committee, except that the word 'major' now appears in the expression 'any major overall Nigerian interest'. Apart from the bad English of this phrase, the addition of the word 'major' seems designed to strengthen the Regional Legislatures as against the Central Legislature. I do not think we need worry over much about 'major' except to note the way in which the General Conference has sought further to increase the strength and authority of the Regional Legislatures.

As far as relations between Houses are concerned, it is worthy of note that the Western House of Chiefs is to have equal and concurrent powers, including those of financial appropriation, and in the north the provision that the decision of the Lieutenant-Governor in Council should prevail has been deleted. I do not think we need worry about either of these changes.

The provisions for the operation of legislation are the same as those prepared by the Drafting Committee. Our views on this have already been made clear to the Governor and I do not think there is any more to be said at the moment on that point.

On the composition of regional executives, the figures have been altered in the northern region only from 7 to 9 elected members. I do not think this is a point which need concern us. As far as functions are concerned, no change has been made except to add local courts to the list of suggested portfolios. The objection of the provision about the arrangements for the distribution of portfolios remains. The provision about the termination of appointments has been altered to make it necessary in regions where there are two Houses for the Houses to meet together to pass a vote of no confidence. This seems a sensible amendment to which I do not think we need raise any objection.

The number of representatives in the Central Legislature has been raised from 74 to 113 unofficial members and the 6 ex-officio members have been named. Three nominated members have also been suggested. There are detailed provisions to ensure that in the north one member should be selected from each province and in the east and west one member from each division with at least two members from the Trust Territory. These additions again seem to be sensible ones on which we need raise no comment.

The composition of the Central Executive remains as before and the functions have not been altered. There is a useful additional provision that no person except a Lieutenant-Governor should be at the same time a member both of the Regional Executive Council and the Council of Ministers. The objectionable provision for the distribution of portfolios remains.

In the finance section there is an additional proposal that the recommendations of the expert commission, accepted by the Committee, should take effect at the same time as the introduction of the new Constitution, and that any region unfairly treated during past years should be allowed a block grant to make up for part of what it has lost. These additional provisions do not seem to call for any comment.

A considerable amount of thought appears to have been given to the qualifications of candidates, system of election and the distribution of seats. In the north the province is to be taken as the basis of representation and in the east and west the division. The voters must be over 21 and resident for at least one year in or a native of the province or division in which he wishes to vote. In the north, however, only men may vote and in the first five years voters[1] can only be male Northern Nigerians of 25 years or over or have been resident in the region for three years. This particular provision has called forth the minority report signed by Dr. Ibiam and others which is attached to the major recommendations. The way in which these northern qualifications have been put is unfortunate but I do not think in fact they will have the bad effect which the minority report claims. The only difference between the north and the other regions is in fact that you have to reside for three years in the north before you get a vote, but you need only reside for one year in the east and west. Furthermore this provision only lasts for five years in the north. This difference of 2 years in the residential qualification does not really seem to matter enough for us to comment on it.

The recommendation about the Trust Territory is a pious expression of hope and does not say any more than we are committed to observe under the terms of the Trusteeship Agreement. The provision about common language is equally pious. The provision about the Governor's reserve powers is, however, a valuable expression of support which it is encouraging to see.

The last recommendation is that the Constitution should be reviewed as seems necessary from time to time within a period of five years. The implication is that at the end of the five years there will be an entirely new constitution. This seems to be crystal gazing with a vengeance. I am sure that as far as the drafting of the Constitution is concerned we cannot include a provision for review in accordance with this recommendation. On the other hand, it would not be politic to raise any public doubts about this provision because it is quite likely that such a review will take place and it is far better to leave this expression of opinion as it is at the moment and consider in the future what need be done in the light of the circumstances at the time. I think there is every reason to say that at the end of five years it will be the intention to review the working of the Constitution, that it would be proper for the Legislature at any time to raise the question of review but that until experience has been gained of the working of this new Constitution, it would seem to be preferable not to make any specific commitment for review during the five year period.

The minority reports are a curious collection. The first one is simply a plea for the N.C.N.C. freedom charter and need not concern us. The second one is also part of the N.C.N.C. freedom charter. I am sure everyone agrees that universal adult suffrage must be the eventual goal in Nigeria but I see no point in pressing for it at the moment when we know it would not work. It is surely preferable to leave it to the electoral commissions to work out the kind of electoral system in each region which in their view would work best. I have already commented on the third minority report which is concerned with the qualifications for voters in the north.

The last minority report concerns the status of Lagos. It is most interesting to see the very strong support both in Lagos and in the western region for doing away with direct representation in the Central Legislature. As I have said earlier in this minute, I do not think there is any need for us to comment on this point as it is clearly a

---

[1] Gorsuch added in the margin here 'candidates'.

matter which ought to be settled locally. There will no doubt be much more discussion on this point in Nigeria and I would prefer to leave it to the local people to make their own decisions as best they can.

I have minuted at some length because it does seem important to see in some detail what alterations the General Conference have made to the statement of the Drafting Committee which we have already considered in considerable detail. I have also been anxious to consider what we should say to the Governor on these recommendations. My feeling is that generally speaking it will suffice for us to write to the Governor (I would suggest a semi-official letter for Mr. Cohen's signature) saying that we have been generally impressed by the sound sense shown by the General Conference, that we have no desire at this stage to add anything to the views already expressed, but that we would like to have some explanation of the reasons which prompted the General Conference to take away from officials in the regional legislatures the right to vote. I think we should conclude by saying that we entirely share the Governor's high opinion of the way in which Sir G. Howe chaired the Conference. It is, I think, particularly gratifying that so large and in some respects amorphous body was able in so short a time to produce so workable a document. That this was so is, of course, in a considerable measure due to the very hard work put in by Mr. Foot and his colleagues in the Drafting Committee. Finally, I think we should say that we entirely appreciate the reasons why the Governor prefers to wait until the Regional Houses have met before making any attempt to find a new basis for compromise regarding regional representation, repeating our willingness to do anything to help if that is necessary.

R.J.V.
10.2.50

94   CO 537/5801   14 Feb 1950
[Zikist movement]: minute by L H Gorsuch on further arrests of Zikist leaders

> [On 8 Feb 1950 the authorities launched a series of raids on Zikist members across Nigeria. Among those arrested was Mokwugo Okoye, general secretary since the incarceration of the movement's leaders in 1949; during this period M15 had monitored correspondence between Okoye and Harry Pollitt, general secretary of the British Communist Party (CO 537/5801, minute by R E S Yeldham, 7 Dec 1949). The arrests were followed by an assassination attempt by a Zikist member on Foot on 18 Feb, see 97. In Mar Okoye was convicted of sedition and imprisoned, see 98. Shortly after, on 12 Apr, the government took the decision to ban the Zikist movement, see 100.]

Enclosures 4 to 6 show that the Nigerian Government is taking action under the sedition law against members of the Zikist movement.

This movement, with which Dr. Azikiwe is *not* associated, is the extreme left-wing party in Nigeria. Its constitution is given in encl. 1, but it has been evident for some time that its practice tends towards violence and subversion of ordered government.

Mr. Foot told me when home recently that success by the Gold Coast Government in breaking 'Positive Action' there would greatly strengthen the hands of the Nigerian Government. It may be that this action is attributable partly to the course of events subsequently in the Gold Coast.

95   CO 537/5786, no 10   23 Feb 1950

[Constitutional review]: letter (reply) from A B Cohen to H M Foot on the next stage of the constitutional review

Many thanks for your letter of —February[1] about the constitution. I am most grateful for this full statement of the position as it now is. We have not, in present circumstances, been able to show your letter to Ministers and what follows therefore represents views at the official level only. I think that it is our views at the official level that you wanted for the purpose of your discussions during the Legislative Council. There will of course have to be full discussions with the Secretary of State at a later stage, presumably when you are here in April.

2.   We think that the results of the General Conference are on the whole very satisfactory and that Howe is to be warmly congratulated. Apart from the points you mention it is particularly satisfactory that the North has endorsed the recommendations of the Drafting Committee about Ministers and has accepted regional Ministers for the North itself. Without this there would have been a tendency, I believe, for the North to fall behind under the new constitution. Although the insistence of the Northern delegates on half the seats in the central Legislature has created a difficult situation, we should have been very surprised, as no doubt you also would have been, if they had not pressed for this and we are not too despondent about reaching some compromise. We entirely agree with the view expressed in the last paragraph of your letter that the whole constitutional review has been of the utmost value.

3.   As regards the two points with which your letter particularly deals, I can say straight away that, subject to what follows, we agree generally with the compromise suggestions which you tentatively put forward.

4.   Taking the question of the central Legislature and regional legislation first, we would see no objection in principle to taking the power to refer back or reject regional legislation out of the hands of the central Legislature and vesting it in the central Executive, if a compromise over the composition of the central Legislature could be arrived at in this way. The proposal which you now make is indeed an extension of what we ourselves suggested in the memorandum enclosed with my letter to the Governor of the 20th December and subsequently, in a different form, in the talks with you. The suggestion which emerged from these, recorded in paragraph 3 on page 2 of the note which you took back with you, was, as you will remember, that, in the event of the Council of State deciding that a Bill passed by a regional legislature was in conflict with an overall Nigerian interest, a joint committee would be set up, consisting of members of the regional legislature on the one hand and of the central Legislature and Council of State on the other. In the event of agreement being reached in this committee the amended Bill would be referred back to the regional legislature and would not come to the central Legislature at all. It would only come to the central Legislature in the event of a disagreement in the joint committee, in which case it might be rejected there by a simple majority.

5.   You now propose to cut out the central Legislature altogether and in effect what you are doing is establishing a procedure under which the Governor-in-Council

---

[1] See 93.

(i.e. the Council of Ministers) would have the right to consider every Bill passed by a regional legislature and to decide whether it conflicted with an overall Nigerian interest or not. The constitutional principle would presumably be that the Governor-in-Council would be deciding whether the Bill in the form passed by the regional legislature should be presented to the Lieutenant Governor for the Royal assent. If the Governor-in-Council (the Council of Ministers) came to the conclusion that there was something objectionable in the Bill from the overall Nigerian point of view, the procedure under your proposal would, we assume, be that a joint committee representative of the regional legislature and the Council of Ministers would be set up. The Ministers without Portfolio and the Ministers for regional subjects might well be drawn upon, with the Attorney General, for this purpose. If this joint committee reached agreement, the amended Bill would go back to the regional legislature for approval in its new form. If the joint committee failed to reach agreement, the Council of Ministers would have to decide whether the Bill should be presented to the Lieutenant Governor for assent. Incidentally, it is necessary to bear in mind that at some stage, either before or after reference to the Council of Ministers, there would have to be an opportunity for the Lieutenant Governor to consider whether there is any objection to giving assent to the Bill, quite apart from any overall Nigerian interest.

6.   I agree that from some points of view the procedure you now propose is more logical than that previously proposed. In particular it leads on more smoothly to the ultimate objective, which we have agreed must be aimed at in future amendments of the constitution, after the one now taking place, under which the central and regional legislatures would each have their own exclusive spheres of operation (there might also be a concurrent sphere) and the central Legislature would not be concerned directly with legislation within the exclusive regional sphere. I suppose that it is possible that you may have difficulty in securing sufficiently wide agreement to cut the central Legislature altogether out of regional legislation; but if you could do so, the procedure would certainly be simpler.

7.   What you are suggesting in effect is that the East and the West should be persuaded to agree to the North having the same representation on the Legislature as the East and the West put together, or something near it, in return for the North agreeing that the central Legislature should not be concerned with regional legislation. As I have said, we see no objection to the compromise proposal you suggest. But from the point of view of a bargain surely the North would be a rather substantial gainer in the compromise, since I should imagine that they themselves would not be sorry to see the central Legislature cut out in this way, and we gather that you do not think they would object to your procedure on the ground that they would be in a minority in the Council of Ministers, where there would in any case be six officials. We are inclined therefore to think that something else ought also to be added to the bargain to make it more palatable to Eastern and Western opinion. We suggest that the North should also, if possible be persuaded to agree to drop their insistance that a candidate for election to the Northern Regional House should be a 'Northern Nigerian' (IXD of the Report). We are not at all clear what the term 'Northern Nigerian' actually means. Taken literally it might well include southerners born in the North; from the Eastern minority report, however, we assume that it is intended to exclude them and to apply only to persons of Northern Nigerian descent. While we are fully aware of the historical and other reasons which have led the North

to insist on this provision, we think that it is objectionable in principle and hard to defend; and we are doubtful whether it is in the long term interests even of the North to insist on it. It would be an excellent thing, we feel, if, as part of the compromise about representation on the central Legislature, the North could be induced to drop this and perhaps also—although this is less important—reduce the period of residence required to one year, as for the other regions, instead of three. We do not of course suggest that you should try to induce the North to drop the limitation of voters and candidates in the North to males.

8. As regards the numbers in the central Legislature I agree that these for the time being must, as you say, remain a matter for local horse trading. I should, however, like to say that I believe that there are very good grounds for having enough seats in the central Legislature to enable every division in the East and West to be represented by one member on the central Legislature, as is proposed by the General Conference in VA (a) (iv). One of the criticisms which I have heard made of the system of a double electoral college (at the divisional or provincial level *and* the regional level) is that under it there would be no guarantee that all areas of the country would in fact be represented on the central Legislature. Zik has said this to me on more than one occasion and no doubt it is a criticism which would be made freely by the N.C.N.C. when pressing for direct election to the central Legislature, cutting out the Regional Houses. If it is laid down in the constitution that every division in the East and West is to have at least one member, then, although you would not completely satisfy those who want direct election, you would at any rate have a strong argument against them. Incidentally, if each division in the West and East is to have at least one member on the Central Legislature, ought not each province in the North to have at least two rather than one? This would, I imagine, be easily possible if the numbers available are 40 or 45, even allowing for the representation of the House of Chiefs. In any case I feel that the rather larger numbers suggested by the General Conference would have a considerable advantage in that they would allow each division in the East and West to have at least one member on the Central Legislature.

9. Turning now to the question of Lagos, we agree generally with what you propose. We feel strongly that if Lagos is to be treated as part of the Western Region for purposes of the constitution, special arrangements must be made on the general lines which you propose to ensure that it has adequate representation both on the regional and central Legislatures. This seems to us necessary for three reasons—because Lagos is the capital, on historical grounds (because there are at present three Lagos members) and on political grounds (because otherwise there will always be strong criticism from the Lagos politicians). We assume that, if Lagos were to be treated as part of the Western Region, as the Drafting Committee proposed, the Municipality area would be regarded as equivalent to a division. Under this arrangement Lagos would get at least two members on the regional legislature and at least one member on the central Legislature. We doubt whether this is enough and we are inclined to think that, in settling the minimum number of seats, as you propose on page 7 of your letter, you would have to provide for at least two seats on the central Legislature for the Lagos Municipality—and possibly three—with a correspondingly increased minimum for the regional legislature. Another important point seems to us to be that the Lagos Municipality should have separate representation from the Colony divisions both on the regional and central Legislatures. That is, I understand, what is intended. If this were not done, I take it that the Yorubas would be getting matters altogether too much

their own way. There is one final point about Lagos which may not directly affect the constitution. You say that it should continue to be treated as one administrative unit with the Colony. We see no objection to that; but, if it is to be in the Western Region, does this mean that the Commissioner for the Colony (or whoever was in charge of this administrative region) would have to report to Government through the Lieutenant Governor at Ibadan? This would seem to us a pretty clumsy arrangement and we hope that it could be avoided.

10.   We have considered, as no doubt you also have, whether it would be desirable to hold suggested compromises on the two major questions discussed above in reserve for the Secretary of State to bring forward if agreement cannot be reached by the members of the Legislative Council. There is evidently some risk that if the compromises you suggest are put forward in the proposed Select Committee of the Legislative Council and not accepted, it may be difficult to find further compromises which would serve as a basis for securing an agreement. On the other hand it seems to us so desirable to secure agreement in Nigeria itself on all the main points before the proposals come to the Secretary of State that we believe that the balance of advantage lies very definitely in favour of the procedure which you suggest, namely to try to secure compromises on the two points of difference while the Legislative Council is meeting. In other words we agree with the procedure which you suggest.

11.   The fact that there will be six official members on the proposed Select Committee might be regarded as raising a difficulty since, in the discussions which you will have, it may be slightly difficult for you to take the necessary initiative to secure compromises without committing the Nigerian Government to a particular point of view. Obviously in these major constitutional questions the Nigerian Government can hardly have a separate point of view from H.M. Government, and it might hence be felt that the suggested procedure would at any rate indirectly implicate H.M. Government prematurely. We have come to the conclusion that this difficulty need not be a real one, provided that in the Select Committee the objective is finally to crystallise the unofficial view, the purpose of having official members thus being to help the Africans to reach agreement on the points where there is still a difference of view. We imagine that this is in fact what you intend. I am sure that you will agree that Government—and by that I mean H.M. Government and the Nigerian Government—must be left quite free to consider whatever comes out of the Legislative Council.

12.   There are one or two other points in the Report of the General Conference on which I should like to comment. I do not intend to go over the whole ground, in particular where comments have been made in the memorandum enclosed with my letter of the 20th December and in our discussions here.[2] So do not regard these comments as exclusive.

13.   My first comment relates to the position of the Trust Territory. The conclusions of the General Conference seem to us satisfactory in this respect. The Southern Cameroons will have at least two members for each division on the Eastern Regional House and at least one member for each division on the central Legislature. Incidentally VA (a) (v) in the report seems to us to have no effect, having regard to VA (a) (iv). If each division of the Southern Cameroons is to have at least one member on the central Legislature, the whole of the area will have a good deal more than two,

---

[2] See 87.

We should in fact regard two as inadequate out of a total representation of 33 for the Eastern Region. It is also satisfactory that under IX A (i) each section of the Trust Territory in the Northern Region is to have at least one seat on the Northern House of Assembly. Would it be possible to provide in any way a minimum representation on the central Legislature to cover these areas? It is satisfactory also that the Southern Cameroons is to have one representative on the central Executive; obviously the same arrangement is not possible for the Northern Cameroons.

14. You will no doubt now have seen the report of the Visiting Mission on the British Cameroons. It seems to us generally to be a satisfactory and objective document and one is encouraged to consider how far we can go to meet the points made in it about the position of the Cameroons in relation to Nigeria. No doubt the point which follows will be discussed with Gibbons. I imagine that the Nigerian Government will wish to stand firm in arguing that the Southern Cameroons ought not to be separated from the Eastern Region, because if it were it would cease to be financially viable. But I wonder whether it might not be wise to agree in connection with the new constitution that there should be a special council for the Southern Cameroons, which would be responsible for advising inter alia on the expenditure of monies made available for general development in the area by the Cameroons Development Corporation. This is something very like what the Visiting Mission has itself recommended and it seems to us that it might go a long way to meet the aspirations of those who are pressing for separate status for the Trust Territory within Nigeria. I am not suggesting that such a council should be given any functions in relation to the constitution (e.g. as an electoral college). What I am suggesting is that the intention to set up such a council, if this were agreed to, should be announced at the appropriate stage in the constitutional discussions. Whether the council should be provided for in the constitution or not would be a matter for consideration. The idea is a tentative one and would require further consideration here if you thought that there was anything in it.

15. As regards III B of the recommendations, we are not at all clear why the General Conference has recommended that officials on the Regional Houses should have no right to vote. This seems to us to be wrong in principle. As we understand it the officials on the Regional Houses would, in the East and West and also, in the main, in the North be the official members of the regional Executive Councils. It seems to us an essential part of the scheme that they should be treated in all respects as being on all fours with the regional Ministers. In other words they, like the Ministers with portfolio, would have certain departments under their charge and as members of the regional Executive they should in our view have the vote in the Regional Houses just as Ministers will have it. This may not be a point of major practical importance; it does seem to be a point of principle on which a modification of the General Conference's recommendation would be desirable.

16. I need not say anything here about the arrangements for the appointment of regional and central Ministers or the distribution of portfolios. These were discussed fully when you were here and you know our views, which are in any case recorded in the papers which you took back with you.

17. As regards V A (b) it is very satisfactory, as you say, that the General Conference has agreed to recommend a small number of members to be appointed by the Governor for their general qualifications. We shall have to consider at a later stage whether three is enough and take into account what is proposed for the Gold

Coast, where the Coussey Committee recommended two members to represent commerce and mining and the Governor has recently agreed to the Secretary of State's suggestion of six, not all of whom would be drawn from the commercial and mining community. I think that we shall want to suggest that these members are not appointed to represent interests not otherwise adequately represented, because it is our policy to avoid the representation of *interests* in this way. We shall want the members simply to be appointed for their general competence. This, however, is a point of drafting.

18.   As regards section IX of the recommendations I agree with you that they represent an improvement over the proposals of the Drafting Committee. I was glad to see the recommendation in F of this section that the primary election in each region would be direct. It will be interesting to see how the details of this arrangement will be worked out in each region and I am sure that this is a point on which the Secretary of State will be interested when the time comes, as the method adopted is bound to have such an important effect both on the working and the acceptability of the new constitution.

19.   As regards section XIII about the review of the constitution, the General Conference seem to have gone a bit astray. Do they really mean to recommend that the constitution should be subject to review *within* the first five-year period? We should have hoped that there would be no review at any rate for five years.

20.   There are two other points which I merely mention now in preparation for the discussions which we shall be having when you come on leave. We shall want to discuss then the question of the working of the Council of Ministers under the new constitution (paragraph (o) on page 5 of the record of your meeting with the Secretary of State on the 9th January)[3] and the question of the administrative reorganisation which the further devolution will make necessary (pages 4 and 5 of the note of the discussions with you at the official level from the 3rd–5th January).

21.   May I finish up by apologising for this exceedingly long letter?

---

[1] See 88.

96   CO 583/314/2, no 25A   9 Mar 1950

[Cameroons Visiting Mission]: observations of the Administering Authority on the report to the Trusteeship Council on the Cameroons under British administration by the Visiting Mission to Trust Territories in West Africa made by the Representative of the UK on the Trusteeship Council   [Extract]

. . . (b) *Integration of the Trust Territory with Nigeria*[1]
The Administering Authority welcomes the Mission's balanced statement of this problem, to which it has little to add. The Mission's Report shows clearly that close integration is inevitable in the Trust Territory administered as part of the Northern Provinces. Regarding the Cameroons and Bamenda Provinces of the Southern Cameroons, the views of the Administering Authority are expressed in paragraphs 22–25 of the observations on document T/PET.4/16 which read as follows:—

---

[1] See 92.

'The claim made in the Memorandum is for the constitution of the Cameroons and Bamenda Provinces as a separate Region of Nigeria, instead of forming as at present two Provinces of the Eastern Region and the operative sentence would appear to be:

> 'If all the Cameroons as one man are opposed to the present Administrative system which derogates us into an appendage to a Region in the Colony and Protectorate of Nigeria, it is because of the absence of direct representation to the Legislative Council of Nigeria, through this faulty system'.

It is impossible to offer final comments on this argument until the results of the review of the constitution now taking place in Nigeria, with Trust Territory representatives participating, are known and have been considered. It may, however, be said that the early stages of the discussions have revealed a strong body of opinion in favour of guaranteeing Cameroons representation in the Central Legislature, on the assumption that the new pattern of the Nigerian Constitution will be that of a federal state with a central and three regional legislatures. Should this view prevail the only practically cogent reason for the desire on the part of the petitioners for separate regional status would have been met.

23. A grave drawback to creating a separate region composed of the Cameroons and Bamenda Provinces, even if this were practicable, would be that it would introduce a sharp distinction between the methods of political development to be followed by the Southern and Northern parts of the Trust Territory respectively, for a glance at the map and the slightest knowledge of their social structure clearly indicate that the portions of Trust Territory in the Northern Provinces cannot be administered except as integral parts of three of those Provinces. In fact, provided that their political identity and power of self-expression can be safeguarded by other means, it is difficult to see what advantages the inhabitants of the Southern Cameroons would derive from becoming a separate region. The disadvantages are obvious. If they were to have technical services in any way comparable in quality to those now provided for them by the regional organisation they would contract a crippling burden in the overhead costs of administration. They would lose the invaluable opportunities of political education offered by representation in the legislature of the Eastern Region: they have not themselves yet produced the men to form a separate legislature of real competence or value and the result of their retreating into isolation would inevitably mean that they would lag further and further behind in political development. At the same time there are overwhelming geographical and economic reasons, and some ethnic reasons, for their remaining in close association with the rest of the Eastern Region.

24. It remains to examine what steps have been taken to preserve the political identity of the Southern Cameroons and to provide its people with means of expression to the Administering Authority. Each of the two Provinces, is, of course, a political entity clearly distinguishable from the neighbouring Provinces of the Protectorate of Nigeria. They have both been placed under the administrative control of the Commissioner of the

Cameroons, (an office created in April 1949), who is thus able to direct their joint development. It is the practice for questions of policy to be discussed between the Commissioner and representatives of the Native Authorities and other popular representatives of the two Provinces sitting together. Whatever the forthcoming constitutional developments may be, therefore, an organisation for the expression of the will of the whole area is growing up.

25. In the exercise of his functions in administrative charge of the Cameroons and Bamenda provinces the Commissioner of the Cameroons is, of course, responsible to the Chief Commissioner of the Eastern Provinces. The Commissioner has, however, also been made responsible for dealing with questions arising from the application of the Trusteeship Agreement to the whole of the Cameroons under British Trusteeship and for ensuring the representation of the Nigerian Government at meetings of the Trusteeship Council of the United Nations. To enable him to discharge these responsibilities communications affecting the application of the Trusteeship Agreement are referred to him direct by the central government and he is authorised to communicate direct in this respect with the Chief Secretary to the Government as well as with the Chief Commissioners, concerned and, where necessary, with Heads of Departments. There is thus an assurance that matters concerning the Trusteeship obligations of the Administering Authority will not be overshadowed by the Administrative requirements of the two Regions in which the Trust Territory lies, and in all matters of moment, the most direct channel is provided for information and representations from the Trust Territory to the Governor of Nigeria and thus to the Administering Authority'.

Regarding the review of the constitution, the stage of public discussion outside the Legislature has now been completed. It is not the case that the Trust Territory was not specifically represented at the general conference which marked the final step in the procedure of consultation. The Southern Cameroons was specifically represented in that conference by Dr. E. M. L. Endeley, the President of the Cameroons National Federation. As an indication of the views of the educated classes of the Southern Cameroons the text of Dr. Endeley's speech in the general debate has been made available to the Trusteeship Council in connection with the reply to No. 6. of the written questions transmitted by members of the Council on the 1948 Report on the Cameroons under British Administration. While stressing the special status and claims of the Trust Territory Dr. Endeley expressed the degree of satisfaction with which the Cameroons people regarded the various guarantees for their representation proposed during the discussions, and eventually supported the recommendations of the Conference without adding to the number of Minority Reports submitted by certain other interests. These recommendations will shortly be published, together with a record of the proceedings of the Conference, and will be made available to the Trusteeship Council in the usual way. Meanwhile it may be of interest to summarize those of the recommendations which concern the Trust Territory. They include the following proposed safeguards for its effective representation:—

(a) *Regional Legislature* In the Eastern Region, besides normal unofficial representation, consisting of at least two members per Division, one of the five official members should come from the Southern Cameroons. In the Northern

Region at least one representative in the House of Assembly should come from each section of the Trust Territory in the Bornu and Adamawa Provinces.

(b) *Regional Executive Councils* In the Eastern Regional Executive Council, of nine unofficial members at least one should come from Trust Territory.

(c) *Central Legislature* Of thirty-three unofficial members from the Eastern Region, at least one should come from each Division in the Cameroons as well as in the rest of the Region.

(d) *Central Executive Council* Of four unofficial members from the Eastern Region, one should be from Trust Territory.

97 CO 583/302/13, no 11   18 Mar 1950
[Attack on H M Foot]: inward savingram no 87 from Sir J Macpherson to Mr Griffiths concerning the assassination attempt on H M Foot

My telegram No. 280. *Attack on Mr. H.M. Foot.*

The attack was made at 8.20 a.m. on the 18th of February. As Foot was entering the Secretariat a man, later identified as one Heelas Ugokwe (an Ibo of Abagana, Onitsha Province, aged about 24), attempted to stab him with a jack-knife, but the blow was badly aimed and the knife merely pierced Foot's coat and slightly scratched his skin. Ugokwe then escaped leaving his hat and the knife behind him. He was, however, recognised and was arrested the following day.

2.   When a boy, Ugokwe was sent to the reformatory school at Enugu for stealing. He joined the army during the war as a signaller, served in Burma and rose to the rank of Corporal Signal Instructor. He was, however, a trouble-maker and in December, 1948, after having been reduced in rank for accepting bribes, he was discharged. He then became a daily-paid employee in the Post and Telegraphs Department and was in that occupation at the time of the assault.

3.   When arrested, Ugokwe freely stated that he intended to kill Foot. He said that he was filled with hatred for Europeans after the Enugu incident—there were several newspaper cuttings relating to that incident on his person when he was arrested—that he had originally intended to assassinate the Governor but that after waiting for nine days and failing to find an opportunity he had decided to assassinate the Chief Secretary instead, especially since he considered the latter to have been instrumental in turning down the N.N.F.L.'s demand for increased wage rates and other recent wage claims. He repeated the substance of this during the preparatory examination before the Magistrate. He was committed for trial on a charge of attempted murder on the 27th of February and was tried at the Lagos Assizes on the 13th of March before Mr. Justice Rhodes, who found him guilty and sentenced him to imprisonment for life.[1]

4.   It seems probable that recent events have put Ugokwe into a morbid state of mind, but although he appears to be unbalanced, there is nothing to suggest that he is mentally deranged.

5.   As you are aware, the assassination of high Government officials has been the subject of the discussion in the inner circles of the Zikist Movement for some months and there is some reason to believe that this attack may have been an attempt to put these plans into operation. Ugokwe himself is reported to have said

---

[1] Reduced on appeal to 12 years.

(and there is a certain amount of evidence to support his statement) that arrangements were made at the Zikist Movement Convention held in Kaduna in December, 1949, to recruit twelve persons to act as assassins in various parts of the country. These had been selected and had received instructions from H.M. Okoye. He (Ugokwe) had been selected for Lagos. This aspect is being further investigated.

6.   While Ugokwe's act is probably applauded by a small circle of irresponsible extremists, it is viewed with disgust and concern by all responsible leaders whose forthright denunciation of this act and of the Zikist Movement's general tendency towards violence, undoubtedly reflects the feeling of the vast majority of the people of this country.

98   CO 537/5801, no 7   25 Mar 1950
[Zikist movement]: inward savingram no 94 from Sir J Macpherson to Mr Griffiths on the arrests of Zikist members

My telegram 172. ZIKIST MOVEMENT. H. M. Okoye, Secretary General of the Zikist Movement was arraigned before Mr. Justice Rhodes at the Lagos Assizes on the 7th March on three charges of being in possession of seditious documents. He refused to plead and after the Crown's case had been proved he was convicted and sentenced to a total of 33 months imprisonment.

2.   In the Northern Provinces, fifteen persons' houses were searched and seditious documents were found in eleven of them. These eleven persons have been prosecuted for being in possession of seditious documents. Nine persons have so far been convicted, of whom eight were sentenced to imprisonment for six months and one was fined £25. Four of these have lodged appeals. The other two trials have not yet been concluded. In the Eastern provinces, seven houses were searched and two persons in Onitsha and one in Enugu were arrested and charged for like offences. The trials of two have not yet been completed; the third was acquitted, though I am advised that in this case the Magistrate probably misdirected himself on a point of law.

3.   I attach copies of the principal documents[1] which were found during the searches and for the possession of one or more of which each of the accused was prosecuted. The document entitled 'The National Programme' was found in the house of Nzimiro, the Secretary of the Onitsha Branch of the Movement. This document was in code, the key to which was also found. It purported to be a code for the use of the 'National Command' comprising the Zikist Movement, the N.N.F.L. and the U.A.C. Amalgamated Workers Union, the three bodies with which Nduka Eze is intimately connected, but it is considered unlikely that the U.A.C. Amalgamated Union as such was aware that it was implicated in these seditious activities.

4.   These arrests and trials have excited little public interest, the feeling of most people being that the Zikists have got only themselves to blame for their present troubles. There are, however, those, especially among the Ibos, who consider that their actions were justified, though their methods were inept. Azikiwe is reported to have expressed considerable annoyance with the Movement and to have said that he was not prepared to waste the funds of the N.C.N.C. in defence of unplanned action. Within the Movement there has been considerable criticism of Okoye who is blamed for causing

---

[1] Not printed.

the trouble by composing and distributing the seditious papers without reference to the other members of the Central Executive. Among the ordinary rank and file there has been a tendency, especially in the Northern Provinces, to withdraw unobtrusively from the Movement, while in Lagos and Kano, certain members, including Smart Ebbi, have been accused (quite wrongly) of selling to the Police the information on which the searches were based, and 'purged' from the Movement despite their protests of innocence. At the moment, as might be expected, the Movement is somewhat disorganised and there is an apparent tendency on the part of those left at the head of affairs to conduct themselves with a greater regard for constitutional methods than has been their practice in recent months, but there is no reason to suppose that these prosecutions will result in the Movement's disintegration.

99   CO 537/5795, no 3   25–27 Mar 1950
[Fitzgerald Commission report]: minutes by R J Vile and L H Gorsuch on the recommendations of the Fitzgerald Commission

[The Fitzgerald Report, *Report of the Commission of Enquiry into the Disorders in the Eastern Provinces of Nigeria, 1949*, col. no. 256, (1950) was completed in Mar and published in June 1950]

The Report of the Fitzgerald Commission of Inquiry into the disorders in the Eastern Provinces of Nigeria in November 1949 is attached behind this file as an enclosure to 2. The copy for the Governor of Nigeria was despatched by special bag on the 23rd March and thirty printers proof copies will be despatched on the 25th March for use in Nigeria. Copies of the printers proofs have also been sent to Sir T. Lloyd, Mr. Gorsuch and Mr. Grossmith and a copy will be given to Mr. Cohen on his return from Lisbon.

For convenience I have prepared a summary of the conclusions and recommendations of the Commission of Inquiry and a short version of the Report. I have not prepared the short version because I consider that the report is too long to read, but for convenience at a later stage when it may be necessary for those concerned to refresh their memory quickly.

This Report is an authoritative document and the views it contains cannot in my view be set aside in any particular. It is possible legitimately to criticise certain points of detail but these do not affect in any way the main conclusions reached by the Report. We must recognise that these conclusions constitute a very severe criticism not only of the acts of individual officers but also of the general policy followed by the Nigerian Government and the Secretary of State. There are passages in the Report which will be of the utmost value to the Communists, to those members of the Trusteeship Council bitterly opposed to the U.K. and to the fellow travellers who delight in criticising British colonial policy. This Report constitutes a challenge to our policy and I would suggest that that challenge can only be met if we take bold and imaginative measures in the light of the recommendations contained in the Report. It would I am sure be fatal to allow our enemies to seize the initiative both in Nigeria and elsewhere.

Turning to the detailed recommendations made, they can be divided into those which the Governor should deal with on his own initiative and those in which a consultation with the Secretary of State is necessary. I would suggest that it is not necessary for the Secretary of State to take any part in the decisions about the errors of judgment committed by the Chief Commissioner and the officers who advise him and the Senior Superintendent of Police who gave the order to fire at Iva Valley. On the other questions raised by the Report, we must first consider the general political recommendation made by the Commission. It is indeed difficult to see what more the Governor of Nigeria could have done to impress upon the people of Nigeria the goodwill and enthusiasm he felt and the constructive policy to which he is committed. I am sure that there is no deficiency in our previous thinking about the need for Constitutional Reform and the rapid improvement of Local Government Organisation. The association of Africans with all forms of government enterprise in Nigeria has proceeded as quickly as the supply of competent Africans would allow. Nevertheless I think it behoves us to re-examine very carefully indeed the whole question in order to see what more we can do and to announce even more loudly the constructive policy to which we are committed.

The recommendations made about labour policy do not constitute a completely workable policy in themselves. We have, however, had the opportunity recently to consider with the Africa Sub-Committee of the Colonial Labour Advisory Committee the recommendations made in the Commission of Inquiry into the railway dispute earlier in 1949 and from that consideration there has emerged a large number of constructive suggestions. I would suggest that the time is ripe for us to take the suggestions made by that Sub-Committee and the suggestions made by this Commission in order to see what new departure in policy could be inaugurated.

The recommendations about the industrial relations at the Enugu colliery seem to be sound and I would suggest that even if there are some doubts about their practicability it would be far better to adopt these suggestions without delay.

Although the report of this Commission is to the Governor, there is no reason why we should not give him the benefit of our views on it at the earliest possible moment. I am sure indeed that he would welcome such an expression of our views. After discussion with Mr. Gorsuch I have prepared a draft letter for Sir T. Lloyd's signature to Sir John Macpherson which I now submit for consideration. After this letter has been issued it would then I think be appropriate to consult the labour advisers and Mr. Grossmith urgently in order to see what more detailed views we were able to put forward.

R.J.V.
25.3.50

Sir T Lloyd

The Fitzgerald Commission Report has been sent to the Governor, and is being printed here. I have also sent an advance copy to each of the three other Governors. I send the file forward direct to you because I think you would not wish Sir John Macpherson to be left to consider this extremely difficult report without some word from here, not only of our first reaction to it but also of sympathy.

The position with which the Governor will be faced on publication of the Report is briefly as follows.

The shock of events at Enugu brought the N.Y.M. (the leading Yoruba Party) and the N.C.N.C. (the predominantly Ibo Party of which Doctor Azikiwe is the head) together and led to the formation of the National Emergency Committee. Although this is an uneasy alliance it is still holding together, and the contents of the

Commission's Report may help to cement it. The tactics likely to be pursued by this body are indicated in para 17 of the Nigerian Political Summary flagged in 47272/3A/50 below. There can be little doubt that the adverse comment in the Report on the handling of the situation will set the extreme political elements barking at the heels of the officers whose conduct is criticised. The comments of the Commission on wider aspects may also be used by them as a pretext for prejudicing the discussions on further constitutional advance, which are now in a delicate stage, and for urging that something much more radical in the shape of Constitutional Reform is necessary.

In the labour field the position is likely also to be difficult. Another body which emerged from the Enugu incident is the National Labour Committee (see para 7 of the Nigeria Political Summary). The names of the leaders indicate that this body is likely to be anything but moderate in its views or inclined to be co-operative with the Government in any action it may take on the Commission's recommendations in regard to re-organisation of the Trade Union Movement and improvements in the field of industrial conciliation.

Nigerian political combinations are notoriously fickle; but it is clear that the Nigerian Government will have its work cut out to avoid a serious setback to its policy from the publication of this report. Its object must, I think, be to obtain the support of moderate and responsible opinion, but this can only be achieved by clear-cut action aimed at keeping the initiative. For this purpose it seems certain that the report when published must be accompanied by some definite and convincing statement of the Government's intention in regard to the recommendations made, and my feeling is that it would be of great help to the Nigerian Government if the document published with the report consisted not only of a despatch from the Governor setting out his comments on the report and his intentions with regard to its recommendations, but also a despatch to him from the Secretary of State accepting and endorsing the lines which he proposes to follow. To put the report out without something of this nature accompanying it would be to play into the hands of those who aim at using it to bedevil the political and industrial atmosphere in Nigeria.

As regards the officers, from the Chief Commissioner downwards, whose actions have been adversely criticised by the Commission, I feel that we should refrain from comment at the moment and leave it to the Governor to say the first word. As regards the wider field of labour organisation, industrial relations and trade unionism, which the Commission's Report covers, we should I suggest let the Governor know at once that we are anxious to let him have the benefit of the best possible advice which we can give him, and are for that purpose studying the report very carefully and will, if we think it would be of help, write to him again on this subject before we receive his comments. Perhaps I could have a short discussion with you on the lines which consideration of this part of the report in the office should take.

Enugu has for some time been a weak spot in Nigeria, and you may remember the letter which we sent on the subject at 18 on 30647/1C/48 below. It is a pity that the Colliery Board was not formed sooner; it might have helped to bring about not only the improvements in labour organisation but the change in the mentality of the management which seems to be essential if the colliery is to settle down properly.

I have enclosed an alternative draft in Sir J. Macpherson.

L.H.G.
27.3.50

100 CO 537/5807, no 24   29 Mar–6 Apr 1950

[Banning of Zikists]: inward telegram no 426 from Sir J Macpherson
to Mr Griffiths on his intention to ban the Zikist movement.
Minutes by Sir T Lloyd and Mr Griffiths

Following searches undertaken by police in houses of a number of leading members of the Zikist movement, prosecutions for sedition have taken place and convictions obtained. This has weakened the organisation, but there is evidence that it is still endeavouring to organise acts of violence.

2. I have considered the position in the Executive Council, and with the unanimous advice of the Council I have decided to declare the movement an unlawful society under section 62 of the Criminal Code. The announcement of this decision will be made early next month and the following Government statement will issue at the same time: *Begins:*—

> 'Conclusive evidence has been obtained from many parts of the country that the Zikist movement is an organisation which aims to stir up enmity and malice and to pursue seditious aims by lawlessness and violence.

> 2. The movement has a membership of only a few hundreds and its teachings and methods are condemned by the overwhelming majority of the people of Nigeria who wish to maintain law and order and to pursue economic and political progress without resort to violence.

> 3. Although the movement is small and unrepresentative its purposes and methods are dangerous to the good government of Nigeria and it is essential to make it quite clear that such purposes and methods will not be tolerated. The Governor in the Executive Council has therefore declared the movement an unlawful society under section 62 of the Criminal Code'. *Ends.*[1]

Minutes on 100

Secretary of State
No doubt you have already seen the Nigerian telegram at No. 24 among those circulated to you. The decision which the Governor there reports is, of course, within his legal powers and the matter at issue is one on which the policy always is to leave decisions to Governors unless there are quite unusual reasons for the contrary. Sir John Macpherson is acting with the unanimous advice of his Executive Council which includes Africans, and although his decision will no doubt provoke some Parliamentary Questions we must, I submit, trust his judgment.

The Governor does not require, and has not sought, you approval and no action is necessary.

                                                                T.K.L.
                                                                3.4.50

---

[1] The Zikists were banned on 13 April 1950.

I note the trend towards banning publications and organisations. Where there is evidence of incitement to disorder and violence this is clearly right. But otherwise my view (and my experience at home) is that banning defeats its own ends. I would like to discuss this general problem soon please.

J.G.
6.4.50

101 CO 537/5786, no 22   3 Apr 1950
[Constitutional review]: letter from H M Foot to A B Cohen on the Report of the Select Committee of the Legislative Council on the Constitutional Review *Enclosure*
Minute by A B Cohen

The Governor has asked me to send you these copies of the Report of the Select Committee of the Legislative Council on the Constitutional Review.

The main bone of contention was, as we expected, the question of representation in the Central Legislature. Up to the last moment we had hoped that the non-Northerners might be prepared to make the generous gesture of accepting the Northern claim to parity. In the event several of the Western and Eastern Members indicated that they were willing to see Northern representation considerably increased and the Oni of Ife suggested that the figures might be fifty from the North with thirty from the East and thirty from the West (Including Lagos). The Northerners, however, were quite unprepared to shift their ground and as the discussions went on opinion between North and South hardened. You will see that in the end the whole question of the Central Legislature was postponed for further consideration with special references to the possibility of establishing two Houses at the centre.[1]

It is a big disappointment to us that we were unable to get substantial agreement on the main outstanding question but we feel sure that you will agree that it was much better to postpone consideration of the issue of the Central Legislature rather than force the matter to a vote in which the North and the South would have been in direct opposition.

In the past when we have thought of the possibility of a bicameral system we have been inclined to rule the proposal out on the grounds that such a system would be cumbersome and expensive but we shall now think the whole matter over again.

The other recommendations made by the General Conference seem to us satisfactory as far as they go. The Lagos Members are against including Lagos in the West and will, I believe, submit a minority report to that effect. I also believe that Zik is busily engaged in preparing a monster minority report setting out his own views on the whole question of constitutional reform.

---

[1] The deadlock over northern representation in the central legislature led to plans in early 1950 to send a northern delegation to London under the title 'Northern Nigerian Petition of Rights' to lobby the secretary of state for equal representation, see inward telegram no 646 from Marshall to Cohen in CO 537/5786, no 26, 10 May 1950.

I am sending the report of the Committee at once so that you shall know without delay how things have gone here. I hope to leave Lagos for London within the week and I shall of course get in touch with you as soon as I arrive (although I shall try to spend Easter week-end with my family in Cornwall). There is now no tremendous hurry and I assume that we can have a full talk about the new situation in a week or two's time.

Enclosure to 101: Report of the Select Committee of the Legislative Council of Nigeria on the Constitutional Review

1.   The Select Committee of the Legislative Council composed of all Unofficial Members of the Council, the Chief Secretary, the three Chief Commissioners, the Acting Attorney-General, the Financial Secretary and the Commissioner of the Colony was appointed to consider the recommendations of the General Constitutional Conference held at Ibadan and the comments of the Regional Houses thereon.

2.   The Committee wishes to emphasize that it has no power to amend the recommendations of the Ibadan General Conference: its functions are merely to comment upon them.

3.   The Committee has duly considered the recommendations of the Ibadan General Conference together with the comments of the Regional Houses and, subject to the important reservations and proposals which are set out in this report, endorses the recommendations of the General Conference. In particular the Committee warmly welcomes the proposals

(a) for greatly increased Regional autonomy within a united Nigeria;
(b) for giving Nigerians a full share in the shaping of Government policy and direction of executive Government action in a Central Council of Ministers and Regional Executive Councils; and
(c) for the creation of larger and more representative Regional Legislatures with increased powers.

4.   The Committee deliberately did not deal in minor detail with the recommendations of the General Conference but rather directed its attention to questions of major importance on which divergence of view existed, in the hope that it would be able to give advice which would assist in resolving the differences. The three principal questions to which it directed its attention were the position of Lagos in the new constitution, the exercise of the function of referring back and rejection of Regional legislation and the composition of the Central Legislature.

5.   With regard to the position of Lagos two views have been put forward in earlier discussions. The first was that Lagos as the capital should be separate from any Region, with direct representation in the Central Legislature. The second suggestion was that Lagos should be included in the Western Region. The Committee came to the conclusion that in the kind of federal constitution envisaged the balance of advantage was in favour of including Lagos in the Western Region but it was also considered that the special status of the capital should be recognised by the following means:—

(a) all central services, including particularly the port and railway, should remain a central responsibility under the direction of the Central Government;

(b) all expenses arising from the special needs of Lagos as the capital should be met by a direct allocation of funds from the Central Government;

(c) the estimates of the Town Council should be submitted to the Governor in Council for approval through the Lieutenant-Governor in Council of the Western Region (bye-laws and regulations of the Town Council being however approved by the Lieutenant-Governor in Council);

(d) at least two members representing Lagos in the Western House of Assembly should be selected by that House to sit in the Central Legislature.

6.   With regard to reference back to Regional Houses or rejection of Regional legislation the Committee considers that it would be preferable to vest the power to do so in the Council of Ministers rather than the House of Representatives as previously proposed, on the ground that the exercise of such a function would be more properly exercised by the Executive than the Legislature.

7.   The Committee has thoroughly examined the different views put forward with regard to the composition of the Central Legislature. The Northern representatives adhere to their previous view that, on grounds of the relative populations of the Regions, the Northern Regional Houses should have representation in the House of Representatives equal with that of the other two Regions together. Most of the other members however held the view that, while the Northern representation might be considerably greater than that of either of the other Regions, the Northern claim to full parity could not be justified in a federal system of the kind recommended by the General Conference, in which only one Legislative Chamber at the centre was proposed. These members urged that representation on a population basis in the House of Representatives could only be justified if a bicameral system were introduced and if the stipulation included in the recommendations of the General Conference that only Northern Nigerians should be entitled to be candidates for election to the Northern House of Assembly were abandoned. With regard to the last point the Northern representatives indicated their readiness to agree to this stipulation being abandoned provided that their claims to parity in the Central Legislature were accepted.

In the discussion of the difficult problem of Regional representation in the Central Legislature it was thought that a solution might be found by following the example provided in other federal constitutions and having two Legislative Houses at the centre—the composition of the House of Representatives being based on population and the composition of an upper House being based on equality between the three Regions. This was a proposal which had not been previously considered in the Regions and it was therefore decided to recommend that the Regional representatives should be given an opportunity of discussing it in the Regional Houses before a final recommendation on the composition of the Central Legislature is made by the Legislative Council to the Governor and Secretary of State.

During the discussion on the question of the composition of the Central Legislature one other matter was raised which the Committee wishes to record. The Committee considered that if there is to be a second Legislative Chamber at the centre it would be advisable to reduce the size of the House of Representatives below that recommended by the General Conference (it was recommended by the General Conference that there should be 122 members of the House of Representatives).

8.   The Committee also makes the following recommendations:—

(1) At least one member representing Calabar in the Eastern Regional House should be selected by that House to sit in the Central Legislature.
(2) Official Members of the Regional Houses should have the right to vote.
(3) In the event of disagreement between the House of Chiefs and the House of Assembly in either the Northern or the Western Region the question on which the Houses disagree should be referred to a joint meeting composed of equal numbers of both Houses, where a majority vote should prevail.

Minute on 101

Sir T. Lloyd

During Mr. Foot's visit to London last week I discussed with him the action to be taken on the Nigerian constitution. As you will see from the enclosure to (22), the suggestion that there should be a bicameral Legislature at the centre, which is a new one, is to be put to the Regional Houses and later to the Legislative Council and we shall not know the conclusion on this until September. Mr. Foot, however, feels strongly that it would greatly assist the Nigerian Government to secure a satisfactory solution of the question of the representation of the Regions in the Legislative Council if the Secretary of State were shortly able to send the Governor a despatch for publication in which he would indicate that, subject to the successful resolution of this one outstanding issue and to the further examination of certain points of detail, H.M.G. would be prepared to accept the proposals of the Ibadan Conference as recommended by the Select Committee.

I believe that Mr. Foot is quite right in saying this and I think also that it would very likely be of considerable assistance to the Governor in the difficult situation likely to be created by the Fitzgerald Report if shortly after that the Secretary of State's acceptance of the constitutional proposals could also be published. This would in effect show that we mean business about constitutional advance and that there is to be no stalling on this issue.

If the Secretary of State is publicly to announce his acceptance of the proposals submitted, he will no doubt wish to consult his colleagues before doing so, as Mr. Creech Jones did before publishing his despatch of last October on the Gold Coast constitution. I therefore, submit for consideration the draft of a Cabinet Paper for this purpose. This sets out the main points in the new proposals and the main difficulties which have arisen in the Nigerian consultations. It also gives the reasons for making an early statement.

After the Secretary of State has had an opportunity of reading the proposals at (8) and (22) and the draft memorandum, he may wish to discuss the matter with the department. Mr. Foot would very much like to take part in such discussions even though that would involve his coming up from Cornwall. If he has to come up in connection with the Fitzgerald Report perhaps the two discussions could be combined.

I have told Mr. Foot that if the above procedure is agreed to we will prepare a draft despatch for the Secretary of State to send to the Governor and will discuss this with him towards the end of the month. We will at the same time discuss with him a number of points of detail which are not of sufficient importance to put into the despatch itself but will require to be settled between us and the Nigerian Government. I have agreed with Mr. Foot what generally ought to be put into the draft of the despatch and also the points of detail which will require discussion.

I attach opposite a very brief note dealing with some of these points.

We have not yet received the minority report on Lagos and that by Dr. Azikiwe personally which are referred to in (22). I do not think that that need delay us. I am sure that the decision on Lagos must be to accept the Select Committee's proposals, while Dr. Azikiwe's minority report, which covers roughly the same ground as the first minority report attached to the General Conference's report (enclosure to (8)), is, I think, more of a political gesture than anything else. At any rate the points in it are unacceptable. I did however telegraph separately to the Governor telling him of my discussion with Mr Foot and asking for the Minority reports. I am also informing the Ministry of Information about the proposals.

A.B.C.
18.4.50

102   CO 537/5801, no 8   Apr 1950
[Zikist movement]: CO memorandum on the Zikist movement.
Minute by R J Vile on the desirability of strong measures to deal with the Zikists

The Zikist Movement was founded in February, 1946, to act as an extreme movement within the organisation of the National Council for Nigeria and the Cameroons. It is now reported to consist of some 800–900 members but there are indications that many of these members are far from enthusiastic and that the central funds of the Movement do not amount in all to more than £20. The President-General of the Movement is Nduka Eze a young semi-illiterate Labour Leader who is also Secretary-General of the U.A.C. workers' union and a leading figure in the Nigerian National Federation of Labour and a prominent member of the Cabinet of the National Council for Nigeria and the Cameroons. The Secretary-General, another young man, was recently sentenced to 33 months imprisonment for the possession of seditious documents and other members of the Movement have also recently been imprisoned.

Although the Movement was founded ostensibly to propagate the philosophy of Dr. Azikiwe this latter has never been a member of the Movement and there is no place assigned to him in its constitution. Indeed the Movement has not been able to adopt a proposed new constitution and it is not quite clear under what constitution it at present works. Reports have, however, been received which indicate that discipline within the Movement is far from perfect and that it is from time to time rent by personal squabbles. Dr. Azikiwe has in the past clearly been suspicious of the Movement and when it attacked him for some remarks he made recently in the United States which indicated that he was willing to reach a working agreement with the United Kingdom he replied by saying that had been misinterpreted and by praising the Movement for the work that it had been doing. This is the first and only time that he has identified himself in any way with the Movement.

The philosophy of the Movement is largely nationalistic with a strong admixture of Communist Party terminology, the adoption of Marxist philosophy and a complete opposition to Colonial Government in any of its forms. The Movement is frankly revolutionary and considers that the present order of society must be destroyed in order effectively to build the new order. Although some attempt is made to pretend that such a revolution can be achieved by peaceful means, particularly by non-cooperation, there is no doubt that it is the intention of the leaders of the Movement to encourage violent revolution whenever possible. It is known that members of the Movement have accumulated stores of arms and ammunition and that plans have been made to encourage any acts of sabotage and assassination.

The Nigerian authorities have been able to keep a very close watch on the activities of the Movement. They appear to have at all times complete information about developments therein, and this has enabled them recently to secure the imprisonment of leading members of the Movement. The next step to be taken is to proscribe the Movement as an unlawful society under the provisions of the Criminal Code.

Minute on 102

I attach opposite a copy of a Note prepared for the Secretary of State and Minister of State at their request on the Zikist movement in Nigeria.

Although I have read the Memorial lecture[1] enclosed with 7 I would not suggest that anybody else should read it in its entirety. It is enough to read Appendix 2 and the programme of work 1950–51 and the National programme to see the line that is being taken. There is of course nothing new in this. Its people are determined to encourage any violent activities and I am sure that the answer to their activities does not lie merely in repressive measures however necessary and swift these may be. I am equally sure that it is only by the rapid development of a positive policy that we can so secure the support of the mass of the people that the attempts of this extreme movement will be regarded as unnecessary. I think we must face the fact frankly that extremist movements of this sort can count upon the apathetic support of the mass of the population. They do represent a feeling which is apt to lurk in the minds of many Nigerians because they appeal to that base element in human nature which is ready to respond to cries of envy, hatred and malice. Unless we can convince the mass of the people of our goodwill and secure their constant and intimate cooperation in the business of government both locally, regionally and nationally then the Zikist movement will have the opportunity to develop into the spearhead of the struggle for independence and we may well be faced with a situation similar to the one in Ireland and Palestine.

The attitude of Dr. Azikiwe reported in paragraph 4 is particularly significant. I think it sufficient to say that he would be ready to profit by any violent act of the Zikist movement and if for this reason if not for any other it is equally important tactically to outwit the movement at every stage. Nevertheless the mere winning of tactical skirmishes will not secure any worthwile result.

The conclusions which I then draw from this is that the forward policy we are pursuing in West Africa must whenever possible be accompanied by strong measures

---

[1] This refers to the 'Abdallah-Agwuna memorial lecture', 1950 (not printed)

against extremist movements of this nature. In the past year it has been difficult for the Nigerian Government to take the initiative in this way but I think we can hope that now that the constitutional proposals have been largely thrashed out the opportunity has come for a much more determined policy in respect of the Zikist movement. If this is so then we ought to be able to look forward to a period which will be far less troubled than recent history.

R.J.V.
6.4.50

103 CO 537/5795   14 Apr 1950
[Enugu shootings]: minute by A B Cohen on the CO reaction to the Fitzgerald Report

[The Fitzgerald Report was published in June 1950 and debated in the House of Commons on 12 July. The report criticised industrial relations at the colliery over several years and blamed several figures for their role in the tragedy. It criticised the management for sacking hewers at the start of the dispute and failing to use offers of conciliation that were made during it; it reproved Okwudili Ojiyi, the secretary of the Colliery Workers' Union, for encouraging workers to believe pay arrears had been withheld from them. The chief commissioner, Sir J Pyke-Nott, his advisers and the police were criticised for treating the problem as a political rather than industrial dispute; the report was critical of the chief commissioner's decision to order the removal of the explosives 'at all costs', rather than having them guarded and negotiating with the miners. Senior superintendent of police F S Philip was criticised for an error of judgement in giving the order to fire when the police detachment was not under attack; the report rejected the suggestion that the miners were armed. The report went on to make various recommendations for the overhaul of trade unions in Nigeria and the establishment of industrial conciliation machinery. Following the publication of the report the government gave exgratia payments to the families of the dead miners, while Philip was retired on medical grounds; Azikiwe's attempt to move a motion in the Legislative Council to have Philip tried for causing the deaths was defeated.]

Sir T. Lloyd

During most of the last week Mr. Gorsuch, Mr. Foot and I have been engaged in discussing the terms of the documents to be published with the Report of the Fitzgerald Commission.[1] We have discussed the labour aspect of this with Mr. Grossmith[2] and Mr. Parry[3] and the police aspect with Mr. Johnson.[4] We also had a two hours' discussion with the Secretary of State and Mr. Cook[5] on the 13th April, but neither the Secretary of State nor Mr. Cook have yet seen the drafts which we have been preparing.

First of all as to the form of the documents. You will remember that at the discussion with the Secretary of State just before Easter the provisional conclusion was reached that the best form would be a joint memorandum agreed by the Secretary of State and the Governor and this suggestion was put to Sir J. Macpherson. Mr. Foot definitely prefers a despatch from the Governor accompanied by a reply from the Secretary of State. He thinks—and in the light of discussion we agree with him—that it would be perfectly possible to avoid in these documents

---

[1] See 79 and 99.   [2] C A Grossmith, ass sec, CO, head of Social Service Dept (B).
[3] E Parry, assistant labour adviser, CO.   [4] W C Johnson, police adviser to sec of state for the colonies.
[5] T F Cook, parliamentary under-secretary of state for the colonies.

giving the impression that the initiative for the action to implement the Commission's recommendations is coming from the Secretary of State rather than the Governor and the drafts have been prepared on this basis. It is moreover necessary for the Governor to give his comments on certain of the views expressed by the Commission regarding the action leading up to the shooting. For this reason in particular Mr. Gorsuch and I now fully agree with Mr. Foot on this form of documents.

I propose to comment below on the various points in the drafts:—

(1) The action to be taken on the recommendations. The Nigerian Government fully accept in principle the recommendations for future action and we and they are in complete agreement that in the implementation of the recommendations regarding conciliation and negotiating procedure the trade unions and employers must take a full part. Mr. Foot has, however, called attention to certain difficulties about the proposal to appoint a commission of workers and employers under an independent chairman for the purpose of implementing the proposals, with which trade union and employers' representatives from this country would be associated as advisers. In the first place he thinks that the appointment of another commission even of this kind would give an impression of delay rather than of action. Recommendations not entirely dissimilar from those of the Fitzgerald Commission had already been made by the Brook Commission[6] on the railway at the end of last year; these have been referred by the Nigerian Government to the trade unions but so far the latter have not commented. Secondly it would be most difficult to secure representation of the trade unions owing to the rivalry between the Nigerian T.U.C. and the Nigerian Federation of Labour (the Zikist trade union organisation). Both organisations would contest the right of the other to be represented and it is quite possible that the procedure would break down at the start. Thirdly it would be extremely difficult to find a suitable African employer or employers to sit on such a commission, since the employers of industrial labour on a large scale are either Government organisations or the big firms. There would thus be the difficulty which the Secretary of State had wished to avoid of having the workers' side entirely African and the employers' entirely European. Fourthly, as you will remember, the Secretary of State has emphasised the importance which he attaches to taking early action at Enugu without awaiting the results of the Commission's work. Mr. Foot has pointed out the very great difficulty of quick action at Enugu owing to the fact that there is no union to deal with there at present. There is only Ojiyi, who has been condemned in the strongest terms by the Fitzgerald Commission.

In these circumstances the following alternative procedure has emerged from discussion with Mr. Foot which is, I think, generally acceptable to the Secretary of State, although he has of course formed no final conclusions. It is suggested that the Governor in his despatch should state his general acceptance of the Fitzgerald Commission's recommendations and his desire to see them implemented quickly and should add that he looks to the trade unions and employers to take a full part in their implementation. He should also invite the Secretary of State's advice and assistance as to their implementation. The Secretary of State in his reply should

---

[6] The Brook commission of 1949 examined the labour situation on Nigerian Railways following the rail strike of that year.

indicate that he is arranging to send out to Nigeria for the purpose of assisting in the implementation of the proposals two trade unionists (one from the T.U.C. and one working miner) and one official, probably of the National Coal Board. The functions of this mission would be:—

(i) to assist in implementing the recommendations of the Fitzgerald Commission on negotiating and conciliation machinery;

(ii) to assist in implementing certain recommendations made by the Brook Commission regarding the amendment of the trade union law;

(iii) to help the trade unions in respect of their own organisation—this obviously requires very careful wording.

The despatch from the Secretary of State should make it fully clear that the onus of implementing remained on employees and employers. The mission from this country would merely assist them. It is proposed that Mr. Parry should accompany the mission.

The mission would go about their work in Nigeria by gaining the confidence of the unions by personal contact and by discussion with employers, including Government departments, and with the Labour Department. If necessary they might call a conference of all concerned to reach agreement on implementation. They might even advise setting up some formal body in which they could take part; but the procedure would be kept quite flexible. In order to meet the Secretary of State's point about Enugu they would go there first with a view to assisting the workers and the Colliery Board to establish a satisfactory negotiating and conciliation procedure. Mr. Foot has explained that in his view it is likely that the Colliery Board, which is of course a free agent in the matter, will decide after the publication of the Report that it can have no further dealings with Ojiyi. This would obviously create a most delicate situation and Mr. Foot has suggested that, if the procedure described above is adopted, the Nigerian Government should advise the Colliery Board to defer any decision of this sort until after the mission has done its work at Enugu, in which case it may be unnecessary for any such decision to be considered. This appears an essential part of the plan.

It was agreed at the end of the discussion with the Secretary of State on this particular point that we should put down what had been suggested in the draft despatch for the Secretary of State so that he could consider the matter further.

(2) Past Government policy with regard to the trade unions. The Commission has criticised the Nigerian Government in paragraph 21 for not doing enough to help build up the trade union movement on proper lines. While the Nigerian Government fully accept that owing to the great difficulties the trade union movement, as the Commission say, is in a most unsatisfactory state, they feel that this criticism is unjust and, apart from that, is likely by giving a handle to extremist critics in Nigeria to hamper the work of Government on behalf of trade unionism in the future. The draft despatch from the Governor therefore gives very brief particulars of what the Government has in fact done. This does not involve, if I may use the expression, any head-on collision with the Commission's observations and I think that this passage from our point of view is quite unobjectionable.

(3) The Government's difficulties in negotiating with the colliery workers before and during the go-slow strike. The Nigerian Government feel it necessary to make the point that in the period immediately preceding and during the go-slow strike

there was no-one effective to negotiate with other than Ojiyi, who was quite irresponsible. With regard to the Commission's criticism that the notice of dismissal of 50 hewers on the 10th November and following days was a major blunder (paragraph 84 of the Report), the Nigerian Government wish to say that the decision of the Colliery Board to do this may have been at fault in timing, but they wish to add that 'it was and remains this Government's opinion that if go-slow tactics are employed and negotiations and warnings have been of no avail, there is no alternative to treating the behaviour of the workers as a breach of contract.' This is a general statement on which Mr. Grossmith has consulted the Ministry of Labour. The original wording has been somewhat modified from the form quoted above in the light of what the Ministry of Labour say and, in the light of his conversation with the Ministry of Labour, Mr. Grossmith believes that the proposition is justifiable in terms of United Kingdom practice.

(4) The Chief Commissioner's[7] actions. It is with regard to the criticisms of the Chief Commissioner in Part X of the Report (paragraphs 97–112) that the greatest difficulty arises. Sir J. Macpherson and his advisers feel strongly that the criticisms made by the Commission about the Chief Commissioner are unjust and they think it necessary that this should be stated in the despatch. After full discussion with Mr. Foot, Mr. Gorsuch and I support this view. There are three points:—

(a) The criticisms of the Chief Commissioner stem from the Commission's opinion (paragraph 105 and following) that the Chief Commissioner treated the disturbances at Enugu as a political agitation rather than an industrial dispute. The Nigerian Government do not accept the correctness of this conclusion. Mr. Foot says that there never has in his experience been a dispute in Nigeria which was more clearly an industrial dispute only and it is the view of the Nigerian Government that the distinction was clearly understood by the Chief Commissioner and other Government Officers concerned. The Chief Commissioner's intervention was due not to his belief that this dispute was political rather than industrial, but to his primary responsibility to maintain public security and the Nigerian Government wish to bring this point out clearly in their despatch. I have read through the whole of the Chief Commissioner's evidence and there is no statement in it that he regarded the dispute as political. There are (on page B. 64 of the evidence) two replies in answer to the Chairman and Mr. H.O. Davies to the effect that he regarded the dispute as having passed from an ordinary industrial dispute and that he decided that it had passed the bounds of an industrial dispute on November 16th. We do not think that this in any way invalidates the view referred to above. The meaning of these statements is in our view that issues of public security had been raised with which he was called upon to deal.

(b) The Nigerian Government wishes to state the view that the decision taken by the Chief Commissioner to remove the explosives was a sound and wise one and that it was right to send police to cover the operation—indeed, that had these precautions not been taken the authorities concerned would have been seriously at fault. This is not contrary to the conclusions of the Commission; indeed by implication they accept in paragraph 110 that the explosives should have been removed. Their criticism is that a final attempt was not made to negotiate with the strikers before removing them. The Government's comment on this is that there was nobody

---

[7] ie Sir J Pyke-Nott

effective to negotiate with and the Government wishes to point out in the despatch that there was an acutely urgent safety situation at the mine. The Mines Department had stated that they didn't immediately make a formal order to close the mine on safety grounds, since it was occupied by the strikers and the supervisory staff were not able to enter it. Attempts by the police to prevent one shift entering the mine had failed. If the Government failed to close the mine there might be an accident leading to serious loss of life. If they took action to close it there was likely to be a serious clash with the miners. It was felt necessary to remove the explosives before this happened.

(c) The Commission states in paragraph 110: 'Had the Chief Commissioner made this appreciation of the situation . . ., we feel confident he would not have given the drastic order to remove the explosives at all costs.' The statement that he gave an order to remove the explosives *at all costs* is incorrect. I am informed that there is nothing in the evidence in support of this statement; indeed the only reference which we have been able to find is contrary to it.[8] When Mr. Bracegirdle[9] was questioned on this point he said that he was not aware that any such order had been given (page 182 of the evidence). Mr. Foot has talked to the Chief Commissioner and all the officers who were present at his staff meeting and they all state that no reference to 'at all costs' was made. Indeed this is entirely contrary to the Chief Commissioner's attitude and policy. He repeatedly emphasised the necessity for moderation and for avoiding firing except in absolutely the last extremity. We are thus faced with the necessity for considering direct contradiction of a statement of fact in the Commission's Report, which is obviously a very serious step to take. Since it appears that the Commission's statement on this exceedingly important point is incorrect, there seems to be no alternative but to saying so; to do anything else would be very unfair to the Chief Commissioner, apart from being wrong in principle.

(5) The position of Superintendent Philip. The Nigerian Government do not wish to question at all the findings in Part XI of the Report or particularly in paragraph 119. The draft despatch therefore makes virtually no comment on this, but draws attention to the essential substance of paragraphs 119 and also 120, where the monstrous allegation that the shooting was prearranged is emphatically denied by the Commission.

There is also the question of the action to be taken with regard to Superintendent Philip; this clearly must be decided before the Report and comments are published. We have discussed this matter with Mr. Johnson. Mr. Foot has explained that in the view of the Nigerian Government's legal advisers the wording used in paragraph 119 must have been designed by the Commission to prevent criminal proceedings succeeding against Mr. Philip and we think also that it is designed to secure his pension rights. The Nigerian Government had assumed that in the light of the wording used there would be no case for disciplinary action against Mr. Philip. Mr. Johnson supports this view and points out in particular that it would be unfortunate if Mr. Philip were the only officer in respect of whom such action was taken. He was in no way responsible for the miscalculations about the detailed arrangements for removing the explosives; as the Report makes clear, these were the responsibility of

---

[8] Cohen added here in the margin the words, 'I do not know that any decision was quite taken in that way'.
[9] R Bracegirdle, colliery manager.

the colliery management. Mr. Johnson has recently seen Mr. Philip and describes him as obviously being in a very poor state of health. He thinks that we ought to arrange with him to be medically examined, in which case he thinks it quite likely that he would be passed unfit for further service in the tropics. Alternatively he has suggested that Mr. Philip should be transferred to another territory, which he thinks could be arranged. We were all agreed that it was essential that Mr. Philip should not return to Nigeria.

We discussed this matter with the Secretary of State and Mr. Cook. The Secretary of State has, of course, formed no final conclusions. He was, I think, inclined to accept the view that disciplinary action should not be taken against Mr. Philip and he thought that retirement on medical grounds would probably be the least unsatisfactory solution. The Secretary of State was extremely doubtful whether it would be right to send Mr. Philip to another territory. If Mr. Philip is not passed unfit, since he has only just reached the age of 44, the only ways in which he could be removed are either by the elaborate disciplinary procedure under Colonial Regulation 65 or by the signification of the pleasure of the Crown under Colonial Regulation 64. Although we have not taken legal advice here on this, we think it unlikely that in the light of the Report action under Colonial Regulation 65 would succeed. Action under Colonial Regulation 64 would be extremely drastic in the light of what the Report says; indeed it would be contrary to the view that disciplinary action should not be taken. I suggest that you may wish to discuss this difficult point with Mr. Johnson, Sir K. Roberts-Wray,[10] Mr. Gorsuch and myself before advice is submitted to the Secretary of State on it.

I am sending copies of this minute to Mr. Grossmith (for himself and Mr. Parry), Sir K. Roberts-Wray and Mr. Johnson. Clearly urgent decisions have got to be taken on a number of points if we are to get the Report out by the 1st May. The Secretary of State would like to discuss the matter again when he has been able to see the two draft despatches. Spare copies of this are available and perhaps it might be useful to let him and Mr. Cook have advance copies to look at. Mr. Cook has asked to read through the more important parts of the evidence and we have given him the papers.

---

[10] Sir K Roberts-Wray, legal adviser, CO.

104   CO 537/5795, no 46   27 Apr 1950
[Enugu shootings]: outward telegram no 526 from Mr Griffiths to Sir J Macpherson on the CO reaction to the Fitzgerald Report

I have been giving my most earnest consideration to the Fitzgerald Report and the two despatches to be published on it. I have discussed the matter at length with Foot on four occasions.

2.   The main purpose of this telegram is to tell you that after spending much time in anxious personal study of both the Report itself and what you propose to say in your draft despatch I do not feel able to dispute the main conclusions reached by the Commission in Part X of their Report.[1] I am fully aware of the strong views which

---

[1] This section of the report covered the events of 16–18 Nov 1949 and criticised the chief commissioner, Sir J Pyke-Nott and his advisers, for treating the dispute as political rather than industrial in origin.

you yourself hold on this matter and it seems to me essential before we proceed further that we should have a chance of personal discussion. I feel, therefore, that I must ask you to fly to London as soon as possible for this purpose. Meanwhile I am consulting my colleague the Attorney General on certain points and in particular on the question of 'at all costs', which I recognise is of a rather different character to the rest of the Commission's remarks in Part X.[2]

3.   I realise that it may be very inconvenient to you to come at this time when Foot is already away, but I hope you will be able to do so and would suggest that if possible you might be here by May 4th. Will you let me know whether you would like us to ask Howe over for the discussions? Foot will also be near London at that time.

4.   Foot has, I understand, sent you a copy of the revised draft of your despatch in a letter in bag No. 105 due to reach Nigeria on the 28th. In view of the difference of opinion between us about Part X of the Report, I am sure you will agree that it would be best to avoid any circulation of this draft at the present stage.[3]

5.   I should also like to say something about the recommendations of the Commission for future action. I have studied your telegram No. 107 Saving and your telegram No. 527 to Foot. I do not think that there is any substantial difference between us. We are both fully prepared to accept the recommendations in Chapters VI and XIII of the Report[4] in principle and I believe that you agree fully with my view that if the new machinery to be established is to be successful both sides of industry must take a full part in its implementation with the assistance of the Nigerian Labour Department and the experts from this country whom I am anxious to send out. I agree with your view that the most important task of these experts will be to assist in the implementing of the new arrangements, but I believe that their advice on these arrangements will also be of the utmost value to you. I have it in mind to secure the services of a really first-class man from the T.U.C., together with a working miner who is an experienced trade union representative of the industry and a third person who would, if possible be selected in consultation with the Employers Federation of the U.K. I would also propose to send Parry. I recognise that the Labour Department in the persons you mention in your telegram No. 527 already has men of experience in this field. The task of the experts to be sent out would be to assist them but not in any sense to supersede them.

6.   I agree entirely with your view that the first task must be to get relations and machinery at Enugu right and I would propose that the experts from here should proceed to Enugu first. How they would proceed thereafter with regard to the wider labour field would be a matter for them to discuss with Government.

7.   We shall be able to discuss this aspect of the matter fully when you are here.

---

[2] Section 110 of the report criticised the 'the drastic order to remove the explosives at all costs', given by Pyke-Nott.   [3] See 107.

[4] Chapters [sic, Parts] VI and XIII stressed the need for a system of industrial conciliation in Nigeria independent of government and recommended the establishment of conciliation boards and a national tribunal to consider disputes. It also recommended the creation of a ministry of labour.

105   CO 537/5786, no 23, CP (50) 94   3 May 1950
[Constitutional review]: Cabinet memorandum by Mr Griffiths on the
proposals for revision of the constitution

The review of the Nigerian constitution which has been proceeding locally for the
last year has now been completed. The procedure adopted for this review, although it
involved full consultation with representatives of the people, was somewhat different
from that adopted in the Gold Coast. In August, 1948, just after H.M.G. had
announced agreement in principle to constitutional advances in the Gold Coast, the
Governor of Nigeria, with the approval of my predecessor, proposed to his Legislative
Council that after a preliminary period for the expression of public opinion the
constitution should be reviewed during 1949. This was accepted and at the Budget
Session in March, 1949, the Council agreed to a procedure for popular consultation
which was then put in hand. Conferences of representatives of the people were held
in every province and subsequently in each of the three Regions of Nigeria and at
Lagos. These were followed by a General Conference of representatives of the whole
country in January, 1950, before which a Drafting Committee had produced concrete
recommendations on the basis of the reports of the Regional Conferences. The
Report of the General Conference was subsequently discussed by the three Regional
Houses of Assembly (and the Northern House of Chiefs) and last month by a Select
Committee of the Legislative Council itself.

2.   The Provincial, Regional and General Conferences were attended by the
unofficial members of the present Legislative Council and Regional Houses of
Assembly, together with a small number of officials. The process of consultation has
been most successful both in the political education which it has provided and in the
proposals which have emerged from it. The purpose of the consultation was to
produce agreed Nigerian views and the task of the officials was no more than to assist
the discussions. Their presence, however, helped to keep the Nigerian Government
closely in touch with the discussions. There was also close consultation between the
Nigerian Government and the Colonial Office during the later stages and the Chief
Secretary of Nigeria flew to London early in January specially for the purpose of
detailed discussions with my predecessor. The proposals which have emerged are
unanimous, except for minority reports by a few members on a strictly limited
number of points and for one remaining major difference between the North and the
rest of the country to which I will refer below. Subject to further discussion of a few
relatively minor points and to the satisfactory solution of this one major difference,
we now have a scheme of constitutional advance recommended by the
representatives of the people of Nigeria which in my view is entirely acceptable.

3.   The existing constitution provides for a Legislative Council for the whole of
Nigeria, with an unofficial majority but with substantial official representation, and
Houses of Assembly for the three Regions, also with unofficial majorities but with
substantial official membership. In addition there is a House of Chiefs in the
Northern Region. The Regional Houses so far have advisory powers only with regard
to legislation and finance, but policy has been followed by the Nigerian Government
of devolving responsibility for purely regional subjects from the centre to the
Regions. This policy has worked very successfully and some advance in the powers of
the Regional Houses is now called for. The Governor's Executive Council is purely

advisory with a substantial official majority and the three unofficial Nigerian members on it have no executive responsibility for departments of Government. There is need for greater participation by Nigerians in the executive machinery both at the centre and in the Regions.

4. The Select Committee of the Nigerian Legislative Council, in endorsing generally the recommendations of the General Conference referred to above, has in particular welcomed the proposals:—

(a) for greatly increased Regional autonomy within a united Nigeria;
(b) for giving Nigerians a full share in the shaping of Government policy and direction of executive Government action in a Central Council of Ministers and Regional Executive Councils: and
(c) for the creation of larger and more representative Regional Legislatures with increased powers.

These general principles are, I am convinced, absolutely sound.

5. The main proposals are as follows:—

(a) The existing Legislative Council should be enlarged and at the same time the numbers of officials on it should be reduced. The Nigerian members should, as the majority of them are at present, be selected by the Nigerian members of the Regional Houses from their own numbers.

(b) The Regional Houses of Assembly should be enlarged and the official membership reduced. The Nigerian members should be selected through electoral colleges the members of which would themselves be directly elected by the people. The Northern House of Chiefs should be retained and a House of Chiefs should be established in addition to the House of Assembly in the Western Region. No such institution is required in the Eastern Region, where there is no comparable system of traditional chieftainship.

(c) The Nigerian Legislature would approve the Nigerian budget and would retain full powers of legislation on all subjects. The Regional Houses would have power to legislate over a substantial field, subject to the power of the Council of Ministers to refer back such legislation and, if necessary, ultimately to reject it if they considered it to be in conflict with an overall Nigerian interest. The legislative fields of the Nigerian Legislature and of the Regional Houses would thus overlap considerably. It is recognised that eventually, as in most federal or partly federal constitutions, the centre and the Regions should have separate and distinct fields, possibly with concurrent powers over a third relatively limited field. But at the present stage, when the Regional Houses will still be finding their feet, it is felt that the central Legislature must retain unrestricted powers, while at the same time the Regional Legislatures must be given powers to legislate over a number of subjects. Experienced advice has been taken on the point in this country and as a result of this I am satisfied that the arrangement proposed is suitable.

(d) In place of the Executive Council there should be established a Council of Ministers with the Governor as President; six official members (the Chief Secretary, the Attorney General, the Financial Secretary and the Chief Commissioners of the three Regions, who would become Lieutenant Governors); and twelve Nigerian members drawn, four from each Region, from the Legislative Council. The Nigerian members would be Ministers, nine with portfolio and three without portfolio. The Council of Ministers would no longer, like the existing Executive Council, be purely advisory to the Governor. It would formulate policy and direct executive action. The Governor would have reserve powers which would apply both to the Executive Council and to the Legislature.

(e) Regional Executive Councils would be established under the Presidency of the Lieutenant Governor and with official and Nigerian members, the latter in the majority. The Nigerian members would be Regional Ministers with or without portfolio. The Regional Executive Councils would formulate policy and direct executive action within the Region, subject to general directions on policy by the Council of Ministers where the overall interests of Nigeria were involved.

6.   It has been no easy task to obtain substantial agreement between the representatives of the conservative and Moslem North and the more politically-minded Ibos and Yorubas of the Eastern and Western Provinces. Three major differences arose during the discussions; of these one has been settled, the second disposed of for the time being and only the third remains to be resolved. The three differences are:—

(a) The Northern representatives, while raising no objection to Ministers in the other Regions, were opposed to having Ministers either at the Centre or in the North itself. It is most satisfactory that they have now agreed to Ministers both at the centre and in the North.

(b) The Northern representatives claim that finance should be divided between the Regions on a per capita basis. This was a natural claim for them to make, as they are at once the richest and most populous Region and that with the least developed social services. On the other hand such an arrangement could not be introduced immediately without disrupting the financial structure of Nigeria and involving the retrenchment of essential existing services in the Eastern Region, which is the poorest. It has been agreed that no formula covering the allocation of finance can be introduced into the constitution, but that an expert and independent committee should be set up to undertake an enquiry into the division of revenue over a period of five years between the three Regions and the central Nigerian services. The proposals of this committee would be considered by representatives of the three Regions sitting in equal numbers under the chairmanship of the Financial Secretary. The independent enquiry will be conducted by Sir Sydney Phillipson, a former Financial Secretary of Nigeria, Professor J.R. Hicks, of Nuffield College, Oxford, and an expert on federal-provincial relationships who is to be appointed from Canada.

(c) The third difference between the North and the other Regions which remains to be resolved relates to the composition of the Nigerian Legislature; this is discussed in paragraphs 8 and 9 below.

7.   There has been some difference of opinion about the treatment of Lagos, the capital of the country, which with the immediately surrounding country areas has hitherto been administered separately from the Western Region, of which it forms a geographical part. On the basis of the proposals put forward by the Western and Lagos Regional Conferences it was first proposed that Lagos should be included in the Western Region; but the General Conference itself recommended by a majority that it should be administered as an independent municipality not under the

Western Region. The Select Committee of the Legislative Council has proposed by a majority that Lagos should form part of the Western Region, but with special safeguards to allow for its position as the capital. The three members of the Legislative Council representing Lagos have submitted a minority report opposing this, in spite of the fact that the representatives of Lagos at the General Conference who were not members of the Legislative Council had taken the opposite view. I propose to accept the majority view that Lagos should be included in the Western Region.

8.   The representatives of the Northern Region have throughout contended that the North, which has more than half the population of the country, should be given half the seats in the central Legislature. This would be a most unusual provision in a single chamber Legislature under a constitution which already has some federal elements in it and is likely to become more federal as the Regions develop. Moreover it is hardly surprising that the Eastern and Western representatives should be opposed to this arrangement, under which the North might well succeed in dominating the Legislature. In spite of all the efforts of the Nigerian Government, it has not so far been possible to resolve this difficulty. When the Northern representatives were out-voted on the point in the General Conference their spokesman stated that, if the point was not met, the North would press for separation from the rest of Nigeria as was the case before 1914. The Northern delegates thereupon prepared to leave the Conference, but were with difficulty persuaded by their colleagues to remain, on the understanding that their view would be recorded that, unless their point about representation was accepted, they would disassociate themselves from the other recommendations of the Conference. In the Select Committee of the Legislative Council the suggestion was made that, to meet the difficulty, a bicameral Legislature should be adopted at the centre, the composition of the House of Representatives being based on population and that of the Upper House on equality between the three Regions. This proposal is to be further considered by the existing Regional House and will come before the Legislative Council at its meeting in September.

9.   It is of the first importance to solve the difficulty about the composition of the central Legislature. The unity of Nigeria must be the first aim of policy for the country. Northern Nigeria is relatively rich in natural resources and its people have great potentialities. It is absolutely dependent on the Eastern and Western Regions for its communications with the coast, but at the same time it has much to contribute to the country as a whole not only in money and material resources, but through its traditions and its political stability. The new constitution must in my view be so drawn up as to give the maximum encouragement to the building of a united Nigeria. For this reason I am anxious to do all I can to encourage the three Regions to reach agreement on the one outstanding point and I am advised that the Governor would be much assisted in securing this result if I were to send him a despatch for publication in the near future informing him that, subject to a satisfactory settlement of this one outstanding issue and to further examination of certain points of detail, H.M.G. would be willing to accept the recommendations of the General Conference as amended by the Select Committee of the Legislative Council.

10.   I am sure that these proposals can safely be accepted. The scheme which is put forward succeeds in my view in creating the relationship between the centre and

the Regions which is best suited to the present stage of development. It provides for a more representative method of selecting members of the Regional Houses without importing a system of direct election which would not work under present Nigerian conditions. It gives Nigerians a large share of responsibility for the formation and execution of policy both at the centre and in the Regions, while leaving the ultimate responsibility for policy, and the means of exercising that responsibility if necessary, in the hands of the Governor through the reserve powers which, as explained in paragraph 5(d), he would still possess in relation both to the Executive Council and the Legislature. The scheme represents a logical development of the existing constitution, which was designed to promote regional development within a unified Nigeria. In the extent to which it would transfer power to Africans it is similar to the scheme recently approved for the Gold Coast, although it goes slightly less far than that scheme. Above all it is a scheme recommended by the representatives of the people of Nigeria after long and detailed consultation. I am assured that the great majority of the people of Nigeria would accept the scheme, although the extremists would no doubt say that it does not go far enough.

   11.   Subject to the concurrence of my colleagues, therefore I propose to send a despatch to the Governor in the terms indicated at the end of paragraph 9 above. I should propose that this despatch should be published at a date to be agreed with the Governor and I would then make an announcement in the House of Commons.

106 PREM 8/1310, CM 30(50)6   11 May 1950
'Nigerian Constitution': Cabinet conclusions on the proposals for reform of the Nigerian constitution

The Cabinet considered a memorandum by the Secretary of State for the Colonies (C.P. (50) 94)[1] out-lining the progress which had been made in reviewing the Nigerian constitution and proposing that he should send a despatch to the Governor of Nigeria indicating the Government's approval, subject to a satisfactory settlement of outstanding issues, of proposals which had been made by a General Conference of representatives of the whole country in January, 1950, and amended by a Select Committee of the Legislative Council of Nigeria.

   The Secretary of State for the Colonies said that the new constitution would give greatly increased regional autonomy, and would provide for the creation of larger and more representative regional legislatures, with increased powers. Nigerians would have a full share in shaping Government policy in a Central Council of Ministers and in Regional Executive Councils. Difficulties had arisen from the fact that the rich Northern Region, which contained a majority of the population and was predominantly Moslem in character, feared that under the new constitution its interests might be subordinated to those of the Eastern and Western Regions. Accordingly, the Northern Region had pressed for equal representation with the other two regions in the Central Legislative Council, and there had been some danger that the Colony would be disrupted on this issue. It had now been suggested that a bicameral constitution might be adopted, in which the regions would secure

---

[1] See 105.

the necessary safeguards through the manner in which the two Houses were constituted; this was under further examination and would come before the Legislative Council at its meeting in September. The Northern Region had also claimed that finance should be divided between the regions on a *per capita* basis, and arrangements had now been made for a committee to examine the financial structure under the new constitution. The Governor of Nigeria was of opinion that, unless the United Kingdom Government indicated at this stage that they were prepared to adopt the proposals on which agreement had been reached in Nigeria, the situation might deteriorate and the measure of agreement so far achieved might be lost.

In subsequent discussion, attention was drawn to the importance of ensuring that the administrative and other senior grades of the Nigerian Civil Service contained a progressively increasing proportion of Nigerians, so that, as self-government was progressively achieved, the transfer of responsibility at the administrative, as well as the political, level could be effected smoothly. The success of the transition in India had been largely due to the policy of increasing year by year the proportion of Indians in the Indian Civil Service.

Rather similar difficulties arose in the industrial field, and an effort was now being made to see whether more could not be done to influence Nigerian students who come to this country at their own expense to take up careers other than the professions of law and medicine, into which an undue proportion appeared to be entering. The Colonial Development Corporation had agreed to sponsor a number of apprenticeship schemes, with a view to securing, in Africa and elsewhere, that the middle range of supervisor could be recruited from native-born sources.

The Cabinet:—

(1) Approved the proposals in C.P. (50) 94, and authorised the Secretary of State for the Colonies to send for publication a despatch on the lines indicated in paragraph 9 of his memorandum.

(2) Invited the Secretary of State for the Colonies to submit to the Cabinet a memorandum indicating what steps were being taken to introduce an adequate proportion of native-born administrators into the higher grades of the Colonial Civil Service, particularly in African and other colonies which were progressing towards self-government.

107   CO 537/5795, no 65   18 May 1950
[Enugu shootings]: despatch no 12 from Sir J Macpherson to Mr Griffiths outlining his reaction to the Fitzgerald Report

I have the honour to refer to the Report of the Commission of Enquiry which I appointed in December last, after consultation with you, 'to enquire into and report on the recent disorders in Nigeria, with special reference to the recent labour troubles at Enugu Colliery and the events which followed'. I have studied the Report with the greatest care with my advisers here, and I wish to record my gratitude to the Commission for undertaking this arduous Enquiry and for making constructive proposals which will be of the greatest assistance to the Government of Nigeria in shaping its labour policy. The objectives which the Commission has outlined in this respect are unreservedly accepted by this Government, and I shall indicate in this despatch the steps which it is proposed to take to achieve them.

2.   Before I do so there are certain comments which I must make on the policy followed and the decisions taken by the Government prior to the events at Iva Valley on the 18th of November last year. I make these comments not only because I consider that in determining future policy it is essential to make clear the attitude which the Government adopted to the problems that arose, but because I feel obliged, after the most anxious thought, to say that I do not concur in the views and conclusions of the Commission on one important aspect concerned with the attitude and the actions of the Chief Commissioner of the Eastern Provinces. I realise to the full the seriousness of doing this and the obligation resting upon me to give a clear explanation of my reasons.

3.   First of all I must make a brief reference to the general policy of the Government in relation to Trade Unions. The Government has repeatedly made it plain that it wishes to see strong and responsible Unions built up and, in spite of many setbacks due to the causes to which the Commission refers, a great deal of practical evidence has been given of Government's determination to carry out that policy. Officers with long experience of work in United Kingdom Trade Unions have been recruited to guide and advise the Nigerian Unions; a team of Labour Officers has been recruited, some of them Nigerians, for conciliation work; where conciliation has failed arbitrators have been brought from overseas at Government expense; Whitley Councils on modern lines have been established; and recently scholarships have been granted to Nigerian Trade Union leaders to take courses with United Kingdom Trade Unions. The Trade Unions in Nigeria claim a membership of about 100,000. The Labour Department is a strong one, with a staff of thirty-seven Senior Service Officers, and one of its main tasks is to assist and guide these Unions. A major effort has been made to encourage Nigerian Trade Unions to develop satisfactorily under a Trade Union Law based on the principles of United Kingdom legislation. Progress has been made in the setting up of negotiating machinery and the work of Labour Officers in the sphere of conciliation has had a considerable measure of success. The Commission has suggested that the Government might have done more to assist the Trade Union Movement, and I do not contest this view. Indeed I have, in public speeches, referred to the need for improvement in industrial relations generally and I agree that there is room for improvement in the relations between Government and the Trade Unions. But I feel sure that if the members of the Commission had had an opportunity of making wider enquiries, and of studying the work done in Government Departments other than the Enugu Colliery, they would have found themselves able more fully to appreciate the constructive work which to the Labour Department and the Government have done in the encouragement of Trade Unions and in the field of labour relations generally. The difficulties to be overcome, some of which came to the notice of the Commission, have been and still are great and it would be over-optimistic to hope for very quick or spectacular progress, but the Government policy of encouraging the establishment of strong and responsible Unions will be pursued with increased energy and with a renewed determination to succeed. I refer later in this despatch to the kind of assistance we hope to receive from the United Kingdom in furthering this policy.

4.   Turning to the discussions and negotiations prior to the events of the 18th of November, I desire to stress two major difficulties which faced the Government. The

first concerns the use by the men of go-slow tactics. Whenever Ojiyi, the leader of the Colliery Union, wished to wring some concession from the management he would arrange for the miners to go slow, and he had little difficulty in persuading them to do so, since by this means they could at the same time bring pressure on the management, do little or no work, and continue to draw their pay. The action to be taken to deal with these tactics was considered by the Government when the men went slow in June last year (the Colliery Board had not then been established), and it was then decided that every effort should first be made in negotiation to persuade the men to resume full work; that if these efforts failed clear warning should be given that action leading to suspension or dismissal would be taken; and that finally, if those warnings were not heeded, a limited number of suspensions or dismissals should be made. Warning notices were accordingly issued in June and the consequences of disregarding them were made clear to Ojiyi, with the result that full work was promptly resumed, thus allowing matters in dispute to be discussed in the Colliery Whitley Council. When almost identical circumstances arose in November (though no trade dispute was declared) the same action was taken. The warning on this occasion, however, was disregarded and dismissals were consequently made. The go-slow in November was not an isolated act but a continuation of previous events, and the Union leader and the men were well aware from warnings previously given of the action which would be taken when go-slow tactics were employed.

The second factor which must be emphasised is the extreme difficulty of dealing with the miners themselves when negotiations with the Union had broken down. Contact with the men had always been difficult owing to Ojiyi's influence, but at this stage his lying statements to the men had further poisoned their minds against the management and had increased the hopes which they placed in him. It was felt that further negotiations with Ojiyi himself could do no good in view of the deceit which he practised on the miners in leading them to believe that arrears of pay were due to them and his double dealing with the management and the Board; but he remained the leader of the Union and his influence with the hewers was undiminished. He and representatives of the hewers promised that work would be resumed, but when this promise was not kept it is not easy to see with whom new negotiations could have been opened. There was no other organisation which could represent the miners and there was no reason to think that an appeal to the miners over the heads of their Union leader and representatives, even if it could have been made, would have any effect. It was the unanimous decision of the Colliery Board that negotiations having failed the time had come to issue warnings of dismissal as had been done in June with successful results; the warnings were followed the next day by notices of dismissal of fifty hewers. These dismissals, and those which followed on the two succeeding days, have been seriously criticised by the Commission, presumably because they were regarded as premature. On this assumption I do not wish to contest the Commission's view, but I assume also that this criticism is not to be regarded as implying disagreement with this Government's general views that if go-slow tactics are employed, and negotiations and warnings have been of no avail, there may often be no alternative to treating the action of the workers as a breach of contract.

5. I now turn to the events immediately preceding the shooting at Iva Valley, and to the point on which I find myself unable to agree with the Commission's conclusions. The Commission concludes that the Chief Commissioner and the

officers who were his immediate advisers regarded, or 'diagnosed', the miners' dispute not as an industrial dispute but as a political agitation, and the Report states as a fact that they treated the dispute as such. In this, it says, they erred. This finding may turn on what is meant by a 'political' dispute. There was, I think, no suggestion that the dispute had in its origin any intention to secure political aims. But the conclusions of the Commission, as for instance in paragraph 107, leave little doubt that it had passed beyond the realm of an ordinary industrial dispute in which the men were content to seek their ends by peaceful industrial means. My own view is that the Chief Commissioner regarded and treated the dispute as an industrial dispute until disorder occurred and a threat to public security developed; and that thereafter the steps he took were in discharge of his responsibility to maintain law and order. I arrive at this conclusion not only from a study of the record of the proceedings, but also from the communications I exchanged with him during this period, and from discussions with him, though these did not form part of the record. There is something more that does not appear in the record (I wish that it could have appeared) but which is known to me beyond any question of challenge: that is the Chief Commissioner's devotion to the people of Nigeria and the passionate sincerity of his desire and determination to help them to progress.

6. I well realise that it is not sufficient for my purpose to make general statements regarding this matter, and I therefore propose to discuss in some detail the attitude and actions of the Chief Commissioner. Whether he regarded, or diagnosed, the dispute as a political agitation in the sense of one designed to achieve political aims depends upon his attitude of mind at the time. So far as I can see from the record of the proceedings it was not put to the Chief Commissioner when he was giving evidence before the Commission that he regarded the dispute as a political matter. I have referred to the communications which we exchanged at the time which made it clear to me that he did not, and I have his assurance to this effect. On the other hand he did, as his evidence makes plain, come to regard the dispute, after disorders had occurred, as involving a threat to public security; but that does not mean that he mistook it for political agitation.

7. I now turn to the question of the Chief Commissioner's 'treatment' of the dispute. The Commission's conclusion that he treated it as a political agitation was presumably arrived at as an inference from his actions. I have discussed, in paragraph 4 above, the circumstances in which it was decided not to attempt to reopen negotiations with the Union or the workers, but to proceed with warning notices followed by dismissals. At this stage the dispute was regarded by everyone concerned as purely industrial. The decision was taken by the Colliery management and the Board, and the Chief Commissioner was not directly concerned. He accepted the decision, which was in line with Government policy (though the timing is held to have been at fault), but this acceptance in no way implies that he regarded the matter as political.

I must here refer to the unfortunate fact that the officer who was standing by to take over, from the 1st of January 1950, the duties of a new post of Senior Labour Officer, Eastern Provinces, had arrived in Enugu only on the 9th of November. He had not previously served in the Eastern Provinces and was unfamiliar with the Colliery and the miners and with the background of the dispute. He rightly offered his services to the Chief Commissioner, but when, on the 16th of November, he suggested that a further approach to the miners might be made by him through the

Union Executive, it was felt that the time when such intervention might have been effective had passed. It must be remembered that when this offer was made a week had passed since the issue of warning notices and that six days had passed since the first notices of dismissal were given. Before these notices were given the Colliery Board had done its utmost in discussions with the Union to break the deadlock and in particular the Nigerian members of the Board, who were able to speak to the men in their own language, had made the most strenuous efforts to persuade them to resume full work. It was only when those efforts had failed, and the Union leader and representatives of the miners had broken their undertaking that full work would be resumed, that the decision was taken not to pursue further negotiations with the Union. I maintain that in these circumstances the Chief Commissioner's endorsement of the Board's attitude and his decision not to accept the proposal to reopen negotiations at that stage do not establish a treatment of the dispute as a political agitation.

Similar considerations apply to the criticism by the Commission of the fact that no representative of the Labour Department took part in the staff conferences at which major decisions were taken. The series of formal conferences took place from the 16th of November onwards—one week after the decision not to pursue further negotiations—and these conferences were primarily concerned with problems of public security.

8.   In other respects the Chief Commissioner took two main decisions regarding the trouble at Enugu. The first was to concentrate strong police reserves at Enugu and the second was to have the explosives in the Colliery removed to a safe place. The decision to have available a strong force of police was taken, as I know from communications received from the Chief Commissioner at the time, for the very purpose of ensuring, as far as was humanly possible, that the threat to public security could be contained without recourse to stern measures; and his decision has in fact been described by the Commission itself, as a wise one. The decision to remove the explosives to a safe place is in my view by far the most important consideration in any assessment of the Chief Commissioner's treatment of the dispute, and I feel that it is necessary to consider at some length the reasons which led to the decision.

9.   The first disorder occurred on the 14th of November. The demonstrations by the women have been described by the Commission as somewhat outside the main current of events at the Colliery. I do not challenge this. In any event the Commission has commended the police and the Local Authority, Enugu, for the manner in which they dealt with these disturbances. But there was a vital factor in the situation to which the Report does not refer. From the 14th of November the miners had been in control of the mine, and owing to their attitude it had been decided that the supervisory staff, which is responsible for ensuring that safety precautions are taken, should not enter the mine. There was consequently an increasing danger that, if the miners remained in the mine without safety precautions being maintained, serious accidents possibly leading to loss of life would result. The Inspector of Mines gave repeated warnings that the mine was unsafe and would have to be closed, and that it would be necessary for the Mines Department, which is entirely independent of the Colliery, to issue, in exercise of its statutory authority, a formal order closing the mine. The formal order was in fact served on the Colliery management on the morning of the 18th of November. Moreover, an attempt made by the Police on the 14th of November to prevent one of the miners'

shifts from entering the mine had failed, the Police being overwhelmed and the men forcing their way through. There was, therefore, reason to expect that a clash would occur when a second attempt was made to prevent men from entering the mine in compliance with the closure order which it was known would soon be made.

10.   This situation held out the possibility, even the likelihood, of further disorder on a serious scale since some seven thousand men were involved, and it was this that made it essential for the Administration to intervene in the interests of public security. I must emphasise that the first duty of the Chief Commissioner was to preserve law and order, and it was in pursuance of this duty that he decided that the explosives must be removed to a safe place. If the explosives had fallen into wrong hands the Chief Commissioner would have been open to the most severe criticism to which there would have been no satisfactory answer. I think that the decision to move the explosives was correct, and if this is accepted, it will, I believe, be agreed that it was necessary to use police to cover the operation. The Commission has suggested the alternative of having the explosives guarded, but the presence of police guards might have been a continuing provocation to the miners. I believe that the plan for a quick removal of the explosives, covered by police protection, was sound. It was hoped that since the stores were some distance from inhabited areas it would be possible to move the explosives without opposition from the miners. Part of the operation was in fact quickly completed without the police coming into contact with the miners, and I am convinced that the removal of explosives at Iva Valley would also have been completed without difficulty or opposition had it not been for the miscalculations regarding the quantity of explosives to be moved and the means of moving them. This led to several hours' delay during which the crowd of miners collected. These miscalculations are criticized by the Commission and I see no excuse for them. Had they not occurred the whole objective would certainly have been carried out without a clash. When the report is published I intend to take the matter up in consultation with the Colliery Board. I can, however, see no grounds for inferring from the decision to remove the explosives that the Chief Commissioner treated the dispute as political. It must be stressed that the police were used for no other purpose than to ensure the quick and safe removal of the explosives, and I state categorically that there was absolutely no question of armed forces being used to break a strike. I should just add on this point that the Commission states, apparently as a matter of inference to be drawn from the evidence (although no such order was admitted), that the Chief Commissioner ordered the police to remove the explosives 'at all costs'. It is perhaps unfortunate that the point was not put to the Chief Commissioner in those terms when he gave evidence. He informs me that he certainly did not give such an order and did not contemplate that the order he did give could be so interpreted.

11.   In the light of the considerations which I have advanced I am bound to say, with a due sense of responsibility, that I consider that the Commission has been less than fair to the Chief Commissioner and his advisers on this question of how they regarded and treated the dispute. I fully appreciate the Commission's view that the situation at the Enugu Colliery was not a political agitation but an industrial dispute but, in my view, upon that a security problem was superimposed. I also fully agree with the Commission that it is of the utmost importance not to confuse industrial and political issues. In Nigeria, as the Commission recognises, it is not always easy to achieve such a separation, but in the Colliery dispute in early November the distinction was clear to the Government and to all the officers concerned.

12.   With regard to the shooting at Iva Valley I have no comments to make on the finding of fact which the Commission has recorded. The Senior Superintendent of Police on the spot gave the order to fire because he believed that the police were in imminent danger of being overwhelmed by a hostile and wildly excited crowd. The Commission has found that in doing so he made an error of judgment and did not measure up to that standard that might have been expected from one of his rank and seniority, but that he acted in all honesty. The Commission has further found that there is not a vestige of evidence to support the infamous suggestion that the shooting was pre-arranged.

The police throughout the disturbances before and after the events at Iva Valley were working in circumstances of great strain and difficulty, and I fully endorse the commendation made by the Commission of the action taken in other centres in the Eastern Provinces to carry out the primary duty of upholding law and order. Had it not been for the restraint and steadiness of the police in face of great provocation throughout these subsequent disturbances, which did become to some extent political in nature, and the tireless efforts of the Chief Commissioner and his Administrative Officers, the loss of life and damage to property must have been much greater.

13.   I turn now to the recommendations made by the Commission, and to my proposals for taking prompt action in the directions which the Commission have advocated.

In the first place I welcome the proposal that on Statutory Boards charged with the running of Government-owned industries at least one of the members should, if possible, have special experience of industrial relations. I hope, where possible, to appoint men from the Nigerian Trade Union Movement to these Boards but, as the Commission recognised, it may be some time before enough Nigerian Trade Unionists with suitable experience to take part in the direction of industrial enterprises are available. Until there are it will be necessary constantly to weigh the advantages of so utilizing the services of the small number who are suitable against the disadvantages of depriving the Trade Union Movement, temporarily at least, of the stabilizing influence of these individuals. I am interested in the Commission's suggestion that in the meantime officers of the Department of Labour with wide experience in dealing with problems of industrial relations should be selected to serve on the Boards. Here again the services of such officers would presumably be lost to their Department for the time being, and it will be necessary to consider the effect on the Department.

14.   I also welcome the emphasis which the Commission has given to the need for Joint Production Committees, and I am confident that the Colliery Board will be in agreement. This Government is fully alive to the necessity for consultation between management and men on all matters of joint interest, and the constitution of Whitley Councils with very wide terms of reference was a step in this direction. Moreover, Departmental Consultative Committees have already been set up in most Departments. I agree that an essential factor for the success of these and other measures of collaboration is the appreciation by the worker of the connection between a high level of production and his own well-being and practical benefit. In the Enugu Colliery recent efforts have been made in this direction by an attempt to create District Joint Consultative Committees. Such experiments are not always welcomed by Trade Union leaders or immediately appreciated by the men, but I agree

that persistent endeavours must be made to create the proper atmosphere of confidence and co-operation so that progress may be made along the lines which the Commission advocates. It is the intention that the Colliery Board should shortly consider proposals put forward by the Chairman for the reconstitution of the Whitley Council in the form of a Joint Industrial Committee with changes in membership, terms of reference and procedure for the speedy resolutions of differences. For my part I should welcome any assistance that you may be able to secure for us from the United Kingdom in the drawing up of these proposals and in their implementation; and I am confident that such assistance would be welcomed by the Colliery Board. I regard this matter as of special urgency.

15.   This Government also accepts in principle the proposal for Conciliation Boards and some form of National Reference Tribunal. Proposals along these lines were put forward by the Commissioner of Labour to the Brooke [sic: Brook] Commission which investigated labour conditions following strikes on the Railway last year, and the views of the Trade Unions were invited on the recommendations of the Brooke Commission. I feel, however, that a fresh start should be made in the light of the comprehensive recommendations now put forward. The first necessity is to provide machinery, or improved machinery, whereby disputes can be dealt with by round-table discussions between representatives of management and employees. When these discussions fail a conciliator may be brought in, and only when every possible effort to reach agreement by conciliation has been made should reference to an arbitrating authority take place. The Commission has emphasised the need to ensure that such an authority should be independent and impartial, and has urged that a fully independent standing tribunal should be established to which disputes could be referred when all attempts to reach a settlement by conciliation have failed. The need for some independent tribunal has been increasingly apparent in recent years. The Government has on several occasions brought out impartial arbitrators from the United Kingdom, at Government expense, to deal with disputes affecting different categories of Government employees. This procedure has disadvantages of expense and delay, and the establishment of a permanent tribunal, constituted on the lines of an Industrial Court, has very much to commend it. The tribunal or court might consist of a President with wide experience of industrial relations recruited in the United Kingdom, sitting with members drawn from a panel of residents in Nigeria. In working out and implementing proposals on these lines I shall be grateful to receive any advice and help which you can secure for us from the United Kingdom, and I very much hope that the Trade Unions in Nigeria and the employers as well will fully co-operate in the working out of a comprehensive scheme which will command general support and confidence.

16.   I have also given careful consideration to the Commission's proposal that a Ministry of Labour should be established. The suggestions which the Commission has made in this connection are in principle fully acceptable and are in line with the proposed constitutional changes now being evolved. Final decisions on the form of the new Constitution have yet to be taken, but under the proposals made by the General Constitutional Conference and supported by the Legislative Council a Ministry of Labour would be formed in the Central Government under a Minister who would be a Nigerian member of the Central Legislature. He would be advised by officers with special experience of industrial relations and expert knowledge of Trade Union practice in the United Kingdom. In the meanwhile I have decided to delegate

to the Commissioner of Labour my powers under the Trade Disputes (Arbitration and Enquiry) Ordinance to refer matters in dispute to a Board of Arbitration or to appoint a Board of Enquiry.

17.   Finally, I am glad that the Commission has endorsed the view that Statutory Boards should be established to run what may be called commercial and semi-commercial Government-owned enterprises. Over the past few years this Government has made important progress in carrying out such a policy, and the Marketing Boards, the Production Development Boards, the Cameroons Development Corporation, the West African Airways Corporation and the Enugu Colliery Board, which have already been established, are examples of the kind of organisation which the Government increasingly proposes to establish, though the Colliery Board is not yet on a statutory basis. An Ordinance establishing an Electricity Corporation has just been passed, and it in now proposed to consider whether other large quasi-commercial Departments of Government, such as the Railway, cannot better be run by Statutory Boards. The aim is that the management should be free to carry out its task and to deal with its staff and labour problems, without the centralisation and restrictions which are necessarily imposed on Government Departments. This form of organisation has advantages not only in more efficient administration but in freeing the Government from direct responsibility for dealing with industrial disputes. It has also the great advantage of providing opportunities for Nigerians to take a share in the direction of the enterprises as members of the directing Boards.

18.   Every possible step will be taken as a matter of special urgency to push forward with the action which I have described. It is of the utmost importance to Nigeria that industrial relations should be improved, and that such a tragedy as that which occurred at Iva Valley should never again mar the country's progress. The Commission has emphasised that recriminations over the past would bedevil that progress, and has directed its earnest attention to the measures necessary for achieving better labour relations in the future. The difficulties are certainly great, but I and my officers will pursue our policy in the same spirit and I trust that in doing so this Government will have the active co-operation both of Trade Unions and employers.

19.   I propose, with your approval to lay this despatch before the Legislative Council at its next meeting.

108   CO 537/5795, no 69   19 May 1950
[Enugu shootings]: letter from Mr Griffiths to Mr Attlee on the findings of the Fitzgerald Commission

I feel that before I leave for Malaya I ought to bring to your notice the Report, of which I enclose a copy, of the Commission of Enquiry into certain disorders which occurred at Enugu in Nigeria in November last.[1] The Governor of Nigeria has just visited this country for the purpose, among others, of discussing this Report with me. The outcome of this discussion is that despatches, of which also I enclose copies,

---

[1] ie the Fitzgerald report; enclosure not printed.

are to be exchanged between us.[2] The Report and a print containing the despatches are to be published on Saturday, the 10th of June, both in Nigeria and here.

You will see from paras. 5–11 of the Governor's despatch that he has felt obliged to dissent from some of the Findings of the Commission. He has there set out the reasons which he regards as weighty and compelling for his dissent.

There were two findings in para, 110 of the Report on which I found myself in considerable doubt—viz

(1) That the Chief Commissioner erred in diagnosing the dispute as a political agitation rather than as industrial in its character.
(2) That the Chief Commissioner gave an order to remove the explosives at all costs.

I had the advantage of the advice of the Attorney General on these two issues and I enclose a copy of his memorandum[3] to me.

Having given the most careful consideration to the matter I have felt compelled to accept the Governor's views on these two issues.

On certain other findings I have found myself unable to agree with the Governor's views, and these are set out in paras. 4 and 5 of my Despatch.[4] You will note that I have decided to support the Commission on:—

(1) Their criticism (at the end of para. 111 of the Report) that the Commissioner of Labour was not summoned to Enugu to attend the consultations with the Chief Commissioner, and that in his absence the Senior Labour Officer was not called into consultation.
(2) I also support the Commission's criticism that the offers of the Nwgo [sic: Ngwo] Clan Council and of Mr. Honey to intervene in an effort to settle the dispute were rejected (see paras. 99 and 100 of the Report).
(3) I also agree with the Commission (para. 110 of the Report) that the view that an offer to negotiate would be regarded as a sign of weakness was not a sound view, particularly since the alternative was the removal of the explosives as an operation conducted by Armed Police.

I fully expect that the publication of the Report and the Despatches will arouse considerable interest, both in Nigeria and this country, and may lead to acute controversy. There will certainly be demands for a Debate in the House and I think an early Debate after the House resumes on June 13th will be desirable.

In view of all these considerations I felt I should acquaint you of the position and send you copies of the Report and the Despatches.

---

[2] Not printed. See 107 and 109.   [3] Not printed.   [4] See 109.

109 CO 537/5795, no 71   22 May 1950
[Enugu shootings]: despatch no 323 from Mr Griffiths to Sir J Macpherson on the report of the Fitzgerald Commission

I have the honour to refer to your despatch No. 12 of the 18th May on the subject of the Report of the Commission of Enquiry into the recent disorders in Nigeria.[1] I have

---

[1] See 107.

conveyed to the Chairman and Members of the Commission the gratitude of the Nigerian Government to them for having undertaken this enquiry and for the care and labour which they have devoted to the proparation of their Report, and have associated myself cordially with your expression of thanks.

2.   I have given much thought to the picture presented in the Commission's Report of the introduction and development of trade unionism in Nigeria, and to the comments on that part of the Report which are made in paragraph 3 of your despatch. The Commission has fully described the difficulties with which the Nigerian Government were faced in giving effect to the declared policy of fostering trade unionism. In the face of these difficulties I think that the policy followed by the Government was basically the right one. A strong Labour Department was built up, seasoned with officers who had long practical experience of the working of trade unions in the United Kingdom. It was these officers who could give the movement in Nigeria the expert advice and guidance which it needed. I have reason to know that both you and your predecessors have been sincerely anxious to see trade unionism successfully established; I am sure that you will be at pains at all times to see that this policy is carried out with equal zeal in all Departments of the public service. I think also that you are justified in pointing out that the Nigerian Government as an employer has shown itself consistently ready in the past to submit to conciliation and arbitration of labour disputes in which it has been involved.

3.   The history of industrial relations at Enugu has been dealt with in great detail in the Commission's Report, and in your despatch you have explained the difficulties with which the Colliery Management was confronted. Careful study of these matters leads me to three conclusions. In the first place it is clear that the working of the trade union organisation and the quality of union leadership at the Colliery were seriously defective. Secondly the machinery for conciliation was unsatisfactory. Thirdly the story of relations at the Colliery illustrates only too clearly the difficulties of a position in which the Government, as a direct employer of labour, may find itself under Nigerian conditions both a party and a judge in a dispute. I shall have suggestions to make on the first two points later in this despatch against the wider background of the future organisation of industrial relationships in Nigeria: I refer specifically to my third point in paragraph 11 below.

4.   I have carefully studied what you say in paragraphs 4 to 11 of your despatch in regard to the events leading up to what occurred on the 18th November. I agree, as you do, that the dispute was an industrial one, and having considered the whole of the evidence I accept your assurance that the Chief Commissioner and the other officers concerned so regarded it, and that so far as any other considerations were present in their minds they arose from the responsibility of the Chief Commissioner to maintain public security and order. But since the dispute was an industrial one I feel bound to agree with the Commission that it is a matter for criticism that the Commissioner of Labour was not summoned to Enugu to help with his experience and advice. In his absence it was, I think, all the more regrettable that Mr. Honey, who had arrived in Enugu on the 9th November to take up the post of Senior Labour Officer, was not invited to be present at all the staff conferences and only attended on the 16th November when his suggestion that a further attempt should be made to negotiate a settlement was rejected. The Chairman of the Colliery Board and the Colliery Manager were present at the Staff Conferences and I think it would have been helpful if the Labour Department had also been represented in order to secure

more balanced advice. It is true that Mr. Honey was not familiar with the Colliery or the circumstances of the dispute. He was, however, an experienced Labour Officer and he had received a telegram from the Commissioner of Labour instructing him to make his services available.

5. I must say also that in spite of the many difficulties referred to in your despatch I think that a further effort should have been made to negotiate with the miners. I appreciate the efforts which had been made by the Board to persuade the men to resume full work and in particular I commend the part which had been played by the Nigerian members of the Board. Even if, however, there seemed little prospect of a further effort to negotiate succeeding I agree with the Commission that the attempt should nonetheless have been made. For this reason I also agree with the view expressed by the Commission in regard to the offer to intervene by the Ngwo Clan Council, and I think that the offer which Mr. Honey made on the 16th November to make another approach to the miners through the Union Executive ought to have been accepted. The Chief Commissioner decided against this proposal on the advice of the Chairman of the Colliery Board and of the Colliery Manager that an offer to negotiate at that stage would have been regarded as a sign of weakness by the men. I agree with the Commission that this view was not a sound one. I realise, as the Commission does, how easy it is to be wise after the event and I recognise the acutely difficult position in which the Chief Commissioner was placed by the circumstances which developed as the dispute went on. I am well aware of the efforts which he made throughout to preserve order and to prevent any disturbance of the peace. But since the alternative was to close the mine and remove the explosives I think that it would have been more prudent to accept the offers by the Clan Council and by Mr. Honey to make a further effort to negotiate with the miners.

6. I note what you say in regard to the actual events which followed at Iva Valley on the 18th November and which are dealt with in Part X of the Report, and in particular your disagreement with the Commission's conclusion that the Chief Commissioner had given an order that the explosives were to be removed 'at all costs'. I accept your assurance that the Chief Commissioner did not in fact give such an order and I do not think that it can safely be inferred that the order which was given was understood in this drastic sense. Nonetheless, for the reasons I have already indicated I think it was a mistake at that stage to have made the removal of the explosives an operation to be conducted by armed police. For the rest the Commission's findings are clear. There was a grave lack of foresight and planning in the arrangements which the Colliery management made for the removal of the explosives, and this added greatly to the hazard of the operation and contributed to the difficulties with which the police were eventually faced. But after making allowance for this the Commission has found that, although in all honesty, the police officer in command did make an error of judgment in resorting to extreme measures at the moment at which he did. I note that you have no comments on these findings by the Commission and I concur. On the other hand I am glad to observe the commendation which the Commission gives to the action which the Chief Commissioner took after the 18th November. The Commission has made it clear that these disturbances were political in nature, that they were admirably handled by the administrative and police officers concerned and that where the police had to open fire they acted justifiably in the discharge of their duty. I endorse fully the

commendation of the officers concerned which the Commission has made, and in my opinion it reflects, most creditably on the Nigerian Police and the Administration alike that disturbances of this gravity were brought under control with so little loss of life and without recourse to military assistance.

7.   I turn now to the parts of the Report which are of the most importance for the future—those which deal with the overhaul of the general conciliation machinery in industry in Nigeria. Let me say at once that I agree emphatically with the Commission that in so far as trade unionism in Nigeria is concerned there can be no turning back; as the Commission says, trade unionism 'must be made to work, and to work as it has worked in Britain to the advantage of the workers and the advantage of the State'. With that object in view the workers must recognise the desirability in their own interests of the overhaul of trade union organisation which the Commission holds to be necessary. At the same time the conciliation machinery in all branches and at all levels of industry must be re-examined and where necessary re-organised by agreement between employers and employed. The Commission has made in Part XIII of its Report important proposals for the organisation of conciliation machinery which will apply not only to the Colliery but to industry as well. You have accepted these proposals in principle and have asked me for advice and assistance in implementing them.

8.   It is clear to me, and I know that you take the same view, that the task of the highest urgency lies at the Enugu Colliery. The state of labour relations at Enugu at present is too serious to allow of delay while action in the wider field of labour relations in Nigeria as a whole is undertaken; the problem must be tackled at once of setting up by agreement between the Colliery Board and the miners suitable conciliation machinery at the earliest possible moment. It should not, however, be necessary for action in the wider field to await the settlement of the immediate problem at Enugu.

9.   I accordingly propose, after discussion with you, to arrange for the visit to Nigeria forthwith of a small group of experts in the field of trade union organisations and labour relations. Provided that such persons can be made available I have in mind that the party should consist of a senior official from the Headquarters of the Trade Union Congress in this country, a colliery worker who is an experienced trade union representative in that industry, an official of the National Coal Board with practical knowledge of the organisation of labour relations and a fourth member selected in consultation with the British Employers' Confederation. I propose also to attach to this party Mr. E. Parry, my Assistant Labour Adviser. The composition of this party is designed to ensure that while close and detailed attention is given to the Colliery, there should at the same time be an opportunity for a survey of industrial relations in Nigeria as a whole. The exact programme of the party will be a matter for later arrangement; it may be convenient that they should all go to Enugu in the first instance, and that the colliery worker and National Coal Board member should stay there for a considerable period in order to assist not only in the working out of suitable conciliation machinery, but also in putting it into operation, while the other two members of the party tour more widely in Nigeria. I trust that both the Colliery Board and the miners will welcome the assistance which is being offered and the opportunity of consultation in order to obtain advice on labour relations and union organisation. The Board will also no doubt wish to consult the visiting experts fully on the proposals which, as stated in paragraph 14 of your despatch, they will shortly

be considering for the reconstruction of the Whitley Council in the form of a Joint Industrial Committee.

10.   It is not my intention that these experts should be constituted as a formal Commission or that their functions should be merely to report and advise on a scheme for conciliation machinery. What is now required is action to work out in detail and put into effect the general principles recommended by the Commission in Parts VI and XIII of the Report. It is in my view essential to future success that this work should be performed by negotiation and free agreement between the two sides of industry, and the visiting experts will be asked to assist both workers and employers in this. For this purpose they will consult freely with all parties concerned on both sides of industry and in particular with the Nigerian trade unions. I very much hope that the unions will seize the opportunity of consulting with them and seeking their advice on the organisation and functioning of the unions and that the Government and public boards and corporations, as well as private employers of labour, will equally make use of their help. You will no doubt also wish to consult them on changes in trade union law and on the training of Nigerian trade union officials.

11.   I take up again at this point the third conclusion which I have drawn in paragraph 3 of this despatch from study of industrial relations at Enugu in the past. I welcome strongly your intention to set up statutory boards wherever possible to control the commercial undertakings of Government. It will obviously not be possible for the Government to divest itself entirely of the function of direct employer of labour, but I am convinced that under Nigerian conditions the reasons given in paragraph 17 of your despatch for setting up those Boards or Corporations are compelling, and that the Government must free itself to the greatest extent possible from the complications which, as the Commission has pointed out, arise when the Government itself has the direct management of industrial and commercial undertakings.

12.   The events at Enugu were a shock to Nigeria and to this country, and the publication of the Commission's Report will attract renewed attention to them. It would be most unfortunate if these tragic events had the effect of detracting from the good work which your administration has done over such a wide field or of discouraging you and your officers from carrying on that work with unabated enthusiasm. I am glad to see that the Commission pays tribute to the Government of Nigeria as progressive and liberal minded. I believe that tribute to be well deserved and I endorse it. In the field of constitutional advance and in economic development Nigeria is making notable progress under your administration with the full participation of the representatives of the people; in the field of trade unionism and labour relations a difficult stage has been reached. I am convinced that the right course is to press on with the development of trade unionism, and that attention should be devoted not to recrimination but to drawing lessons which will be of value in the future. It is with that object in view that I have made the proposals in this despatch for bringing in the best advice obtainable from this country. It is my earnest hope that all parties in Nigeria will be prepared to accept this offer; I believe that it represents an opportunity to open a new chapter in the history of industrial relations in Nigeria.

13.   I approve your proposal to lay your despatch before the Legislative Council at its next meeting, and I wish you similarly to lay this despatch before them.

110 CO 537/5795, no 76   5 June 1950

[Enugu shootings]: CO memorandum for Mr Attlee on the report of
the Fitzgerald Commission

The Commission's Report and the exchange of despatches[1] are concerned with three
major questions:—

(a) the labour policy of the Nigerian Government;
(b) events at the Colliery up to and including the shooting on the 18th November,
the disturbances which followed elsewhere, and the way in which these events
were handled;
(c) the system of industrial relations, with particular reference to the situation at
the Enugu Colliery and the need to improve union organisation and leadership
within Nigeria.

2.   In regard to labour policy the Commission reviews the history of the
introduction of trade unionism into Nigeria, and points to certain shortcomings in
the Government's approach to the problem, though in measured terms and with
appreciation of the difficulties. To members of the Trade Unions of Nigeria the
Commission speaks 'with brutal frankness', advising them strongly to overhaul their
organisations and choose more responsible leaders.

3.   It is on the handling of the situation at the Colliery between the start of the go-
slow strike in early November and the events of November 18th that major controversy may arise. The Commission has found that the Chief Commissioner of the
Eastern Provinces and his advisers erred in diagnosing and treating the dispute as a
political agitation rather than an industrial dispute; and the Report holds that the Chief
Commissioner's actions were dominated by the conclusion that the dispute had passed
from the phase of an industrial dispute into a political agitation. The wording of para
110 of the Report also suggests that the Chief Commissioner gave the order to remove
explosives from the mine 'at all costs'. The Governor, for reasons which are fully argued
in paras 5–11 of his despatch, dissents from the Commission's finding that the officers concerned regarded and treated the dispute as a political agitation. His argument,
briefly, is that the dispute was not in fact regarded as anything but industrial by the
Chief Commissioner and his officers until disorder occurred and a threat to public
security developed and that the steps which the Chief Commissioner took (including
the decision to remove the explosives from the mine which led up to the shooting incident) were taken in discharge of his responsibility to maintain law and order.

4.   The Governor also differs from the Commission on the question of fact
regarding the suggestion that the order was given to remove the explosives 'at all
costs'. The Governor points out that this is apparently an inference drawn from the
evidence, that it was not put to the Chief Commissioner and that the latter has stated
that he did not give such an order and did not contemplate that his order could be so
interpreted.

5.   The Secretary of State in his despatch has accepted the Governor's assurance
that the Chief Commissioner and the other officers concerned regarded the dispute
as an industrial one, and that so far as any other considerations were present in their

---

[1] See 107 and 109.

minds they arose from the responsibility for maintaining public security and order. The Secretary of State also accepts the assurance that no order to remove the explosives 'at all costs' was given. On these two points, therefore, the Secretary of State and the Governor agree in dissenting from the Report. The Secretary of State states, however, that:—

(a) he agrees with the Commission that it is a matter for criticism that the Commissioner of Labour was not summoned to Enugu to help;

(b) it is regrettable that the new Senior Labour Officer, who had taken up duties on the 9th November, was not called in to the staff conferences until the 16th;

(c) in spite of the many difficulties, a further effort to negotiate with the miners should have been made; in particular, as the Commission says, the offers of the Clan Council and of the Senior Labour Officer (on the 16th November) to intervene should have been accepted;

(d) it was, in the Secretary of State's view, a mistake at that stage to have made the removal of the explosives an operation to be conducted by armed police.

On the first three of these four points the Governor, while setting out his own appreciation of the situation, does not challenge the view taken by the Commission. On the fourth point the Governor's expressed opinion is that the decision to move the explosives was correct and that it was necessary to use police to cover the operation. On this letter point, therefore, there is an expressed difference of opinion between the Governor and the Secretary of State.

6.   Controversy may therefore arise on the two points on which the Governor and the Secretary of State dissent from the Report, on the question of the use of police in the removal of the explosives, and possibly on the extent to which blame is established and can be imputed to any particular officers. The Attorney General was consulted on the two main points of dissent in particular, and the wording of both despatches follows suggestions made by him. On the actual shooting there is a clear finding that the Police Officer concerned made an error of judgment, though he acted in all honesty. This is accepted both by the Governor and the Secretary of State.

7.   The remainder of the Report and despatches deals with the need for improvement in the system of industrial relations and the measures to be taken to that end. Paras 9–10 of the Secretary of State's despatch set out the assistance to be rendered from this country in the way of expert advice and help. These proposals are not likely to be controversial. The Commission's advocacy of Statutory Boards to run the Government-owned industries is also fully accepted in both despatches, and is in fact in accordance with the Nigerian Government's policy.

8.   A printed copy of the exchange of despatches is attached.

111   CO 583/310/8, no 9   17 June 1950
[Enugu shootings]: memorandum by the National Emergency Committee on the report of the Fitzgerald Commission

NEC comments and recommendations on the Fitzgerald Report

Commissioned by the General Meeting of the National Emergency Committee to study the Report of the Fitzgerald Commission in connection with the Enugu Massacre and its repercussions in Nigeria, and make recommendations, a Sub-Committee of Eight whose names are appended on this document, met at 74, King George Avenue, Yaba Estate, for three nights (June 12–14, 1950), and after a critical analysis of the findings of the Commission, submit the following as their observations and recommendations:—

Introduction

1.   In our view, the reasoning of the Fitzgerald Commission, has proceeded from certain basic assumptions which are in themselves false. These assumptions together with the attitude of the Commission which is dealt with later in this memorandum, have led to a number of untenable conclusions and astonishing, even insulting remarks which abound in the Commission's Report.

2.   In dealing with the 'Political Trends in Nigeria', for instance, it is assumed firstly that Nigerians as a whole and Nigerian nationalists in particular are politically immature; secondly that British Rule in Nigeria is progressive, liberal-minded, and beneficial to the people of this country; and thirdly that the beneficence and advantages of this Rule have been stultified by the 'subversive activities' of a vocal, extremist and minority class who always make 'extravagant political claims'.

3.   We emphatically disagree with these assumptions because, as we have said before, they are false; and we strongly condemn the erroneous conclusions and insulting remarks which flow from them.

4.   The Commission has misconstrued the background to the present political trends in Nigeria, and has failed completely to grasp the significance and the far-reaching implications of those trends.

5.   Since the advent of the British Rule, the white officials of the so-called Nigerian Government have shown marked contempt for and consistent lack of sympathy with the political, educational, and economic aspirations of the people of Nigeria. Whatever advancement has been made in any of these departments of human activities, has been due in the main to persistent agitation on the part of the people, and partly to the fact that British self-interests happen to coincide at some points with our own interests.

6.   In spite of this notorious indifference to our best interests, the British Government has dragged us into two major World Wars which were initiated without our knowledge or consent, and which were fought for the purpose of advancing British self-interests and of preserving what is often proudly described as British Freedom.

7.   During the last war our manpower and our economic resources were fully mobilised and ruthlessly regimented. Our raw materials were bought at low prices which were dictated by the British Government. Many of our boys laid down their lives in various theatres of war. Many of the blind and the maimed among the surviving ones are still with us. In short we gave our loyalty to Britain without hesitation or stinting. We did hope that the freedom which was ours as of right before we were deprived of it by the British, might be restored to us. But we had hoped in vain.

8.   The Richard's [sic] Constitution was our first reward; it was cut and dried behind our back and forced down our throat in spite of the strongest protest and resistance.

9.   Furthermore, we hold these truths to be self-evident; that all men are born free and equal as to their rights; that political freedom (that is, the right of a people to choose and reject its rulers) is the inalienable right of every nation; and that no nation has any legal or moral right to impose its rule over another. It is, therefore, unnatural and humiliating in the extreme for the people of Nigeria to be forced into a position where they have to negotiate with Britain for their freedom. It is British might and not British virtue that has compelled us to take this defensive and most humiliating position. It is clear from the foregoing that we have reached a stage in this country when the people will not tolerate a rule which is imposed upon them against their wish and without their consent. It is also clear that all we are demanding from the British Govt is our right to freedom and political self-determination. We have demanded nothing more and nothing less. In our view, therefore, the Commission is most unreasonable and unjust in considering our claim for freedom and for political self-determination as extravagant. It is equally unreasonable and unjust to regard any of our claim for educational, economic, and social advancement as extravagant.

10.   In this connection, we denounce the subtle suggestion made by the Commission to the so-called Nigerian Govt that the latter should embark on an intensive measure of 'divide and rule' in order to put an end to what the Commission wrongly describers [sic] as the 'extravagant claims' and the 'subversive activities' of the 'vocal extremists.' We know that the men of 'good hearts' referred to in paragraph 18 of the Report do not include the Nigerian Nationalists. And for the Commission to ask the Govt to mobilise these men of 'good hearts' to curb the subversive activities of those anti-Govt forces is to advise Govt in effect to declare war on the nationalists who legitimately and sincerely work for political freedom for Nigeria, and to incite one section of the community against another.

11.   In our opinion this advice is in keeping with the express view of Sir John Macpherson himself who, shortly before the Enugu tragedy, declared that he would use severe measures to suppress what he called extreme political and labour demands, even if his doing so would mean the end of British Rule in Nigeria. Both the suggestion of the Commission and the view of Sir John Macpherson, are in keeping with the imperialist scheme, which is always designed to keep the Colonial peoples in perpetual subjection by the relentless application of the 'divide and rule' policy, and of repressive measures against the nationalist class.

12.   In concluding our remarks under this head, we like to observe that the Commission carries its unfairness a little too far by anticipating the reaction of the people and trying to stifle it in advance. Says the Commission in paragraph 20: 'We emphasise at the start that recriminations over the past always bedevil political progress. If this report is to be used as a medium for such recriminations, and we realise that it affords biased or narrow individuals ample opportunity to do so, then our tasks will have been in vain.'

13.   We are neither biased nor narrow-minded, though we are an interested party. We do not intend to indulge in recriminations as such, or for their own sake. Indeed it is our earnest desire to point our fingers to those points from where the so-called Nigerian Govt has gone astray. We would be failing in our duty as leaders of our people if we didn't do so now. The incompetence, lack of foresight, and disregard for African life which led to the Enugu shooting are by no means confined to that tragedy. They are always with us, and unless we decry them at this psycholigical [sic] moment, they may rear their heads again in other places.

14.   Above all, it is easy to advise us not to cry over split [sic] milk; but we cannot refrain from nor can anyone conscientiously blame us for crying over the split [sic] blood of our fellow-countrymen who were shot in cold blood and without provocation at Enugu.

Part II

The shooting incident

15.   The Commission has found that the shooting of unarmed African Miners at Iva Valley was unjustified and unprovoked. The responsibility for this atrocity has been fixed on Mr Pyke-Nott—the Chief Commissioner Eastern Regin, [sic] and Mr Phillips [sic], the Senior Superintendent of Police. The Commission censured the Chief Commissioner for treating an industrial dispute as a political agitation, which resulted in his rejecting an offer of conciliation by a labour expert and the sending of armed force to effect the removal of explosives at Iva Valley at all costs. On this point we are in complete agreement with the Commission.

16.   Even where honesty existed, the conduct of the Chief Commissioner in regarding a purely labour dispute as a political unrest must be regarded as not only scandalous, but also as evidence of incompetence and unfitness to assume such heavy political responsibility as is placed on a person of his rank and high office. Where, however, evidence has been led as in this case to show that the shooting was pre-arranged and deliberate, the Chief Commissioner's conduct is easily understood as conforming to the common plan to break the strike of the Enugu Miners by armed force in order to teach the Nigerian Workers a lesson.

17.   The NEC cannot agree with the Commission in its findings that the shooting was not deliberate. The order to remove the explosives at all costs which the Commission found was given by the Chief Commissioner to armed Police necessarily contemplated the use of firearms and at the best can only be interpreted as a mandate to the Officer in charge of the detachment to open fire at his discretion.

18.   Besides evidence of inadequate provision which was made for the removal of the explosives at the Iva Valley, the alleged miscalculation as to the quantity of explosives the infuriation of workers by constant parade of Police, and the detailing of armed force, are all links in the chain of a concerted design to bring the miners into clash with armed Police which must necessarily result in and perhaps justify the use of firearms.

19.   After a close study of the evidence and after taking into full consideration all the surrounding circumstances, we have come to the conclusion that the shooting of the defenceless miners was to say the least deliberate.

20.   His Excellency the Governor argued in his dispatch to the Secretary of State that the Chief Commissioner treated the dispute as an industrial one until disorder occurred and a threat to public security developed. We must state at once that we do not see any reliable evidence of a threat to public security in what was an ordinary coal miners' strike. The allegation that there were political agitators encouraging the formation of terrorist parties and making efforts to acquire arms and explosives is entirely without foundation and such position only existed in the figments of the imagination of those who made such allegations.

21.   We accept unreservedly the guilt of Mr Philip as the person responsible for the shooting of the miners. Accordingly we entirely disagree with the extenuating

remarks of the Commission when it stated that Mr Philip's action was only an error of judgement; that he acted in all honesty, but only failed to measure up to the standard expected from one of his rank and seniority. We fail to see the proof of honesty in a man who, without the slightest provocation, made use of all the forces available to him to shoot down unarmed men and later made a report that shooting was necessary in self-defence of his men who were being attacked by the miners—an allegation which the Commission found to be false.

22.   Again we cannot accept the view that the use of the entire firing power of Mr Phillips [sic] was due to his lack of control over his men. It is quite clear that these men were ordered to open fire. It is inconceivable that African members of a stringently disciplined Police force as we have in Nigeria could of their own volition fire at their own brothers without being so ordered by a Senior Police Officer. There was no question of an error of judgement. The circumstances which might have led to that were never established in evidence. If it was a fact that the attitude of the miners was such that it manifestly threatened the safety of the Police, we have no doubt that African Police men present would have been available to give evidence in this connection. On the contrary, the witnesses who testified on behalf of the Police as to the incident which occurred at Iva Valley were all European Police Officers. We think that Mr Phillips [sic] is an irresponsible and callous Police Officer who ought to be thoroughly condemned for recklessly wounding and taking the lives of harmless coal miners. He should also be denounced as a co-operator in a common plan to break an industrial strike in Nigeria by the use of armed forces.

23.   As Nigerians we regard this shooting incident at Enugu as only a climax to a continuous show of power, frequently manifested by British Administrators in Nigeria as a constant reminder to African that they are completely at the mercy of their rulers who have full backing of forces.

24.   With regard to the shooting in other parts of the Eastern Region outside Enugu, we only think it necessary to draw attention to a fact which the Commission has overlooked that the only town where rioting was quelled without bloodshed was Calabar, where an African Police Officer was in charge. No doubt he was able to enter into the feelings of his country men and, with an understanding of his people, which a Britisher does not possess, he was able to avoid unnecessary loss of lives.

25.   We note here with regret that this credit was not given by the Commission to the African Officer concerned. It is deplorable that the Commission tried to attribute this singular success to other causes.

Part III

The attitude of the Commission
26.   This leads us inevitably to examine the attitude of the Commission as a whole in their treatment of the various establishments, organisations and individuals which they had cause to comment upon in the course of their work. Anyone who has carefully perused the report cannot fail to be struck by the discriminatory language employed by the Commission.

27.   The Commission lost no pains in justifying Govt establishments and British Officials wherever possible and making excuses on their behalf, while on the other hand on the least pretext a number of African controlled organisations, establishments and individuals were condemned in the most rigorous language.

28.   We have already referred to the manner in which the Commission attempted to reduce the gravity of Mr Phillips [sic] offence and his guilt in so recklessly taking the lives of the miners. Mr Pyke-Nott, the Sectary [sic] Eastern Provinces, Dr Raeburn (Chairman of the Colliery Board), Mr Bracegirdle (the Colliery Manager), the Secretary for Finance Eastern Province, the Assistant Commissioner of Police were all described by the Commission as able Officials although it will be remembered that these men formed the Chief Commissioners Council that blundered so woefully by rejecting the services of Mr Honey and the Ngwo Clan Council, and treating the industrial dispute as a political agitation.

29.   Nigerian Administrative service which has caused the loss of the lives of 21 miners was described as a fine one, and even Mr Pyke-Nott was also regarded as a competent Administrator. On the other hand African leadership both political and labour was condemned in the strongest language. Nigerian Press was described as irresponsible, and African witnesses as having concocted their evidence.

30.   It is a matter of regret that the African members of the Commission have found it necessary to associate themselves with such discriminatory language in the Report.

31.   The attitude of the Commission to African politicians and to the Press also calls for comment. The Commissioners call upon the Government to mobilize 'people of good hearts' to constructive efforts in order to 'curb the subversive activities' of 'anti-Government forces'. There is no indication of who is to be the judge of 'people of good hearts'; and since they are to be mobilized by the Government we have no doubt that they will find no difficulty whatever in discovering them. We on our part are convinced from past experiences that the type of Nigerians who alone can organize the 'vital, fearless, political party' which the Commissioners call for can never be regarded by a man like Commander Pyke-Nott as 'people of good heart'.

32.   The condemnation of almost the entire press of the country is a reflection of the attitude of the Commissioners to nationalist activities in Nigeria as nearly all newspapers in this country are attached one way or the other to nationalist organisations.

Part 4

Industrial aspect

33.   The National Emergency Committee is not primarily concerned with the industrial aspect of the Commission's Report as this is being intensively studied by the National Labour Congress and other Labour Organisations. We note with regret, however, that, except in its analysis of the events immediately leading up to the 'go slow' of November 1949, the Commissioners have been too ready to put all the blame for the deadlocks and set-backs in the Colliery upon the miners and their Secretary. It was said, for instance that the men did not fully appreciate the relationship between increased productivity and their wages and conditions. In the same breath, but later in the report the Commissioners were forced to the conclusion that they cannot suggest that 'the drop in productivity is a result either of inefficient management or *of slacking on the part of the workers*.

34.   Again the Report (vide paragraph 45) blamed the workers for the failure of the syndicate system recommended by the Long Award. 'We are satisfied' says the

Report 'that had the workers given their full co-operation the system proposed in the long award could have been put into operation without difficulty and the immediate consequences would have included an increase in productivity and higher wages for the hewers and tubmen. The system was not introduced in the teeth of resistance of the men. On the contrary the fullest discussion was entered into with the Union's representatives and the award was made only after they had expressed themselves as being in favour. . . . The difficulties which followed must be regarded by any fair-minded person as an indication of the needless bitterness and industrial dislocation which must result when Trade Union Leadership is weak and irresponsible as it was here. The workers suffered loss and hardship not (as they were wrongly advised) because the Arbitrator's proposals were unworkable but because their own leaders did not have the authority and some of them did not have the will to convince the men that there was not the slightest ground for suspicion and that the workers had everything to gain and nothing to lose by carrying out the terms of the award.

35.   But, when one reads the Report further, one will be convinced that but for the fact that the Commissioners were only too ready to put the blame on the workers, there really is hardly any ground why the miners should have any share of the blame at all. For at page 19 (paragraphs 45–48) of the Report the following passages occur 'from the attitude of the Trade Union leaders . . . on industrial basis' [sic].

Part V: Summary

36.   The NEC have appealed to the Nation to be calm and to hold itself in readiness for direction. Conscious of the implicit confidence which the most important sections of opinion in our country have in the ability of the NEC to guide the Nation aright, through collective action, we have after mature deliberation, come to the conclusion that, only the attain of SELF-GOVERNMENT FOR NIGERIA NOW could prevent a recurrence of this disgraceful episode in our national history.

37.   The evidence before the Fitzgerald Commission and the findings of that Commission have vindicated the stand of the NEC that, the shooting at Enugu was done deliberately and could have been averted but for official incompetence and ineptitude.

38.   The findings of the Commission in respect of the role of the Chief Commissioner of the Eastern Provinces and the Colliery Manager indicate that these high officials were guilty of 'a grave lack of foresight and planning' . . . and this added greatly to the hazard of the operation and contributed to the difficulties with which the Police were eventually faced.

39.   The Commission had no doubt about the culpability of Mr FS Philip, a senior Police Officer who, without provocation and justification, ordered the shooting of unarmed miners, only to perjure himself when he realised the gravity of his indiscretion. Justice and fairplay demand that an irresponsible Police officer of this type should not escape from the warm embrace of our Criminal Code.

40.   We have observed with a measure of satisfaction the recommendation for an *ex gratia* grant to the dependants of dead miners, but note with regret the omission to make any award to the injured miners. However, we feel that the amounts recommended are parsimonious, and we suggest £720, which is an equation of ten years' wages on the average of the miners concerned.

41.   Since the Commission proved conclusively that the shooting was delirate [sic] and that top-ranking officials failed to measure up to expectations which their high office demands, it would be most inequitable to saddle the tax-payers of this country with the responsibility not only of paying their salaries and perquisites but also of footing a bill which was created by the inefficient prosecution of their duty. Moreover, the so called Nigerian Government is answerable to the British Government and not to the people of Nigeria. In the circumstances, it would be unfair to expect the expenses incurred in connection with the Commission and the *ex gratia* grants to be disbursed from the Nigerian revenue.

42.   The conduct of His Excellency the Governor in seeking to defend one of his high officials does not impress us, in view of His Excellency's vicarious responsibility. On the ground that the Governor and his executives are collectively responsible for the administration of this country, we cannot but view with serious misgivings their continuance in office.

43.   We hereby register our satisfaction at the able and competent manner in which the African Police Officer discharged his duty at Calabar without resorting to the use of lethal weapons. This is evidence of a Police Officer who has not lost his touch. That there was no loss of life at Calabar is exemplary of a Police Officer who has lived up to 'that standard that might be expected from one of his rank and seniority'. In fairness to Mr RA Brown, Assistant Supt of Police, we wholeheartedly endorse the commendation of the Commission on his exemplary conduct in preventing further loss of life.

44.   We are convinced that had the people of this country actively participated in the management of Government affairs and enjoyed a greater measure of political responsibility, the sordid events at Enugu might have taken a different turn. To expect us to continue to have confidence in what has been proved to be an inefficient bureaucracy is to strain our loyalty to our conscience and to our country. We believe that SELF GOVERNMENT FOR NIGERIA NOW is both opportune and imperative.

45.   We, therefore, charge the Nation to press for the implementation of the Ten Points of our Recommendations. We urge every individual and group including the political parties, trade unions, ethnical societies, peasants and farmers' organisations, professional associations, ex-service-men's unions, students' and youth associations, at home and abroad, jointly and severally, to rally to the call of Nigeria-in-distress, by supporting these Recommendations and urging our foreign rulers to respect our feelings and grant our demands.

46.   We also call upon the Nation to regard the 4th day of July 1950, as a day of National Mourning, when nationalists shall not work, shops and offices owned by them shall not be opened for business, markets used by them shall be closed, and newspapers owned by them shall publish a 'Mourning Edition'.[1]

47.   In conclusion, we appeal to the Nation for patience and urge our people to stand by, holding themselves in readiness, and having an abiding faith and confidence in the wisdom, tact and honesty of the national leadership.

---

[1] In the event the Day of Mourning on 4 July 1950 passed off without incident. The NEC, which continued to be active after July, not least in attacking racial discrimination at the University College, Ibadan, eventually collapsed in late 1950.

Part 6

48. *Recommendations*

In view of the foregoing facts and reasons, we are compelled to make the following recommendations:—

1. That every European a on the Colliery Management connected with the shooting tragedy should be dismissed.
2. That the present personnel of the Coal Board should be removed forthwith.
3. That the Chief Commissioner of the Eastern Provinces (Commander JG Pyke-Nott) should be dismissed.
4. That Mr FS Philip, Senior Supt of Police who ordered the shooting should be dismissed, his retirement and pension rights forfeited; and a categorical statement from the Government that this step will be taken.
5. That Mr F S Philip shall be tried of murder at once in Nigerian courts.
6. That the financial award to the family of each fallen miner be £720.
7. That since the so-called Nigerian Govt is not answerable to the tax-payers of Nigeria but to the British Govt the cost of the Fitzgerald Commission, which was occasioned by the blunder of the former Govt, should be borne by the latter Government.
8. That both His Excellency Sir John Macpherson and Mr H M Foot, Chief Secretary, under whose regime this blood bath afflicted Nigerian people, should resign forthwith.
9. That since shooting occurred at Enugu, Aba, P Harcourt and Onitsha under the command of European Police Officers, whilst id [sic] did not occur at Calabar, where the Police was under the command of a Nigerian Officer we demand speedy Nigerianization of the Police Force.
10. That we have no confidence in this inefficient and *blood-stained administration*, and therefore, demand SELF-GOVERNMENT FOR NIGERIA NOW.

Signed
1 Dr Akinola Maja
2 Dr Nnamdi Azikiwe
3 Obafemi Awolowo
4 Mbonu Ojike
5 Chief Bode Thomas
6 FRA Williams
7 Marcus Osindero
8 FO Coker

112   CO 583/310/8, no 12   24 June 1950

[Enugu shootings]: inward savingram no 5 from Sir J Macpherson to Mr Griffiths giving his reaction to the memorandum by the National Emergency Committee on the report of the Fitzgerald Commission

I have now received from the National Emergency Committee a copy of their 'Comments and Recommendations on the Fitzgerald Report'.[1] An advance copy was sent to you under cover of my Secret Saving No. 3. The present copy is sent to me for my 'information and immediate implementation'.

---

[1] See 111.

2.   I do not propose to comment in detail on this document (a copy of which is attached), for it is clear that no honest attempt has been made to analyse the Report and its recommendations; the document is in effect a political pamphlet designed to bring the Government into hatred and contempt. The whole intention of the document can hardly be better described than in the words of a political extremist in a letter which has come into the possession of the Police and which goes on to discuss detailed plans for the assassination of the Chief Commissioner, Eastern Provinces. He writes:—

> 'Our newspapers are now trying to influence the public mind and when their feelings have been provoked, then we shall proceed to formulate our plans.'

3.   In accordance with this policy the Memorandum has received full publicity in the Press, most of which is controlled by members of the National Emergency Committee, and strenuous efforts are being made to whip up feelings. The success of this policy is still in doubt. In the Eastern Provinces among the large number of politically minded but generally ill-informed younger generation such propaganda is popular and dangerous. There is no reason to suppose that it has affected the views of the more sober elements as represented by the members of the Eastern House of Assembly, who realize the dishonesty and absurdity of the National Emergency Committee's demands and who are still solidly behind the Chief Commissioner.

4.   The situation in Lagos is somewhat similar, though with the difference that the younger Yorubas are less interested than their Ibo brothers and are less easily aroused. The general Yoruba view, and this applies not only to Lagos, but to the predominantly Yoruba parts of the Western Provinces, was illustrated by a discussion which the Commissioner of the Colony had with members of the Lagos Town Council. They were generally of opinion that the Report was fair and were mainly interested in the ex gratia payments to the relatives of the deceased which they regarded as adequate.

5.   As was to be expected reaction to the Report and to the National Emergency Committee's Memorandum in the North has been negligible except among the Ibo settlers in the larger towns.

6.   The problem which confronts me is to rally sober and moderate opinion which though individually sound has not yet summoned up moral courage to express an opinion. A first move has been made within the past few days. Judge Ademola called on me privately on 22nd June to say that a group in Lagos is considering action to rally the people of good heart throughout Nigeria. I have on two or three occasions received a delegation from the National Emergency Committee but it is particularly important that I should not give the impression that I regard it as a truly representative body, taking the place of the chosen representatives of the people in the Legislative Council and the Regional Houses of Assembly. My present intention is therefore to ignore the Memorandum of the National Emergency Committee but much depends on subsequent developments.

7.   It will be seen from paragraph 46 of the Memorandum that the National Emergency Committee proposes to organize a National Day of Mourning on the 4th of July (the choice of date is significant). While this move is, like the rest, purely political—the Nigerian Labour Congress, which is affiliated to the National Emergency Committee, has openly declared that the object is to protest against the Government—I am anxious not to give the National Emergency Committee the

opportunity to say that a heartless and authoritarian Government will not even let the people express their grief over the tragedy of last November. At the same time it is of the greatest importance that the National Emergency Committee should not be able to demonstrate its power to bring the Government machine to a standstill even for a day. I am considering with my advisers the line which Government should take and will inform you when I have reached a decision.

8. I do not now anticipate any major developments until the Day of Mourning but I must warn you that the Chief Commissioner, Eastern Provinces, is, at present, of opinion that there may be disturbances in the Eastern Region on that date.

113 CO 537/5786, no 41   26 June 1950
[Constitutional review]: letter from Sir J Macpherson to A B Cohen on the secretary of state's draft despatch on the new constitution. *Minutes* by A B Cohen and L H Gorsuch

In spite of urgent preoccupations I should have found time to write sooner about the Secretary of State's draft despatch on the Constitutional Review, copies of which I brought back with me (the latest letter on the subject is Gorsuch's secret letter No. 30453 of the 24th May). I am sorry.

2. During the first week in June I collected the Chief Commissioners and the Commissioner of the Colony for one of our periodical conferences, and while they were in Lagos I arranged for a full meeting of Executive Council, with all four Nigerian members present, including those from the Regions. The draft despatch was discussed at both gatherings.

3. Let me say at once that we are all extremely gratified by the prompt action taken in London to consider with so much understanding the results of the Constitutional Review to date. We are most grateful for the thought and effort given to the matter and for the action taken in securing the general blessing of the Cabinet. While I was in London I expressed the view that the publication of an encouraging despatch from the Secretary of State at some suitable date (after the first flurry over the Fitzgerald Report had simmered down and before the meetings of the Regional Houses which are now likely to be in mid-August) would be extremely valuable before the final stages of our discussions here. (This was the purpose you had in mind when you sent your secret telegram No. 480 of the 18th April). The knowledge that H.M. Government had given a general blessing to the Review so far as it had gone would give great confidence to the responsible elements in the country and particularly to the legislators, other than those who had made minority reports. It would, I hoped, prevent any re-opening of discussion on major matters on which a majority had agreed, and would help to get agreed conclusions on the remaining major issue of the composition of the Central Legislature. I also hoped that our comments on the draft despatch could be reduced to a minimum, our attention being directed mainly to the question of the timing of publication of the despatch.

4. As our discussions here went on, however, it seemed to us that certain parts of the draft despatch, notably the suggestions regarding the selection of Ministers and the additional safeguards proposed for the representation of Lagos at the Centre, would not only be controversial in themselves but might well re-open controversy on

a number of other points on which agreement has been reached, and might hinder rather than help to secure agreement on the outstanding question of the composition of the Central legislature.

5.   I had allotted a full day for a conference with Chief Commissioners and other officials on various subjects, including the draft despatch, and I had arranged for the Executive Council meeting to be held on the following day. Unfortunately, we got so immersed in other matters mainly relating to the Review on the first day (our afternoon session, at which we discussed with certain Heads of major Departments the relations between the Central Directorates and the Regional Departments, and the future of the Civil Service under advanced regionalisation, went on until 8.30 p.m.) that we had no time fully to consider the draft despatch before the Executive Council meeting. In Executive Council a great deal turned, of course, on the reactions of the Nigerian members, and we left the field very much to them in the early part of the discussion. They were very pleased about H.M. Government's reception of the proposals made to date but they were concerned about the suggestion regarding further Lagos safeguards, and, in a lesser degree, about the suggestion regarding the selection of Ministers. They felt that if any despatch from the Secretary of State were to be published at this stage it would be better if it did not include any reference to controversial matters.

6.   Most of the discussion turned on the position of Lagos, and here the views of Dr. Abayomi, who speaks with special authority regarding Yoruba opinion in Lagos and in the Western Region, and of Dr. Ibiam, who is similarly qualified in respect of Eastern (and particularly Ibo) opinion, were of particular importance. Dr. Abayomi strongly opposed the proposal that the members of the Western House of Assembly who would represent Lagos in the Central Legislature (a minimum of two) should be selected by those members of the Western House representing Lagos itself. He said that he was confident that the Western House as a whole would elect the best men to represent the West, including Lagos. He was strengthened in this view by his hope and belief that under the system of election adopted for Lagos (and this will certainly not be more restricted than the franchise granted to the new Lagos Town Council under which voters will not be required to register since there will be an electoral roll containing the names of all adults who have resided in Lagos for six months), Lagos will send to the Western House far more worthy and representative members than is the case at present. He also strongly opposed the suggestion that one of the four members of the Council of Ministers drawn from the Western Region must be appointed from the members representing Lagos. It was perhaps not surprising that Dr. Abayomi, who though a Lagosian is also a Yoruba, should hold these views, but the interesting thing is that Dr. Ibiam fully supported him. The discussion in Council was very frank, as always, and we faced up squarely to the danger that a non-Yoruba from Lagos, or a noisy politician belonging to any tribe, might be 'squeezed out' when the Western House of Assembly selected its members for the Central Legislature, but Council was unanimously of the opinion that taking the long view the additional safeguards suggested were undesirable.

7.   As regards the selection of Ministers, we argued the pros and cons in Executive Council at some length but came to no firm conclusion. As stated above, however, anxiety was expressed lest the opening of discussion on any major matter at this stage, resulting from a suggestion by the Secretary of State, might prejudice the final stages of the Review here.

8.   On the following day we had another long discussion—at the official level. This ranged over the whole field of Constitutional Review, including the composition of a Central Legislature with two Houses. As regards the draft despatch, we directed our attention mainly to the question of the effect which publication would be likely to have on the work of the concluding stages of our Constitutional Review, with particular reference to the two controversial suggestions regarding the selection of Ministers and the extra safeguards for Lagos. Before dealing with these points, I should mention one other passage in the draft which came up specifically; this was paragraph 4 dealing with the rejection or reference back of Regional legislature [sic: legislation] which appeared to conflict with a major overall Nigerian interest. We warmly welcomed the proposal that the Secretary of State should stress the need for full consultation between the Regions and the Centre so as to avoid to the maximum possible extent the introduction into Regional Legislatures of legislation which would so conflict. We felt, however, that such consultation, at whatever stage it took place, should be between the Council of Ministers and the Regional *Executive* rather than the Regional *Legislature*, and that the joint committee which would try to resolve the matter if conflicting Regional legislation were passed should be representative of the two Executives. This seems logical and it would be the Regional Executive which would—except in the case of a Private Member's Bill or Motion— have introduced the legislation. We hope, however, that prior consultation as suggested would make the need for a joint committee very remote. We assume that the consultation proposed would be a matter of constitutional practice, rather than that provision for such consultation should be written into the Instruments, but I am open to conviction on this point. Incidentally, we noted that the draft despatch follows the wording of the Enugu Select Committee in supporting that the power of rejection would lie entirely with the Council of Ministers, but it seems to us that constitutionally it should be the Governor as the representative of His Majesty who should have power to reject legislation, or at least the Governor in Council as you suggested in paragraph 5 of your letter to Foot of the 23rd February in this series.[1] If this is correct, the wording should be that the Governor would have power to refer back or reject Regional legislation on the advice of the Council of Ministers, or that this power would rest in the Governor in Council.

9.   As regards the additional safeguards for Lagos we felt confident, in our discussion at the official level, that the Executive Council advice on this point was sound, and in this we were not prompted by our distrust (shared by all responsible Nigerian opinion) of the present Lagos elected members. Lagos has a political importance beyond its size and it is right that at least two Lagos members should go forward from the Western House to the Central Legislature, but if the 'new West' is to be a Region the selection of the members to go to the Centre should be done by the entire House. (In Executive Council Mr. Obaseki raised the interesting point of what would happen if the selection were left to the Lagos members themselves and they could not agree! Another suggestion—not favoured—was that the two Lagos members with the largest number of votes should go forward. Moreover, important as Lagos is in the body politic, it was felt that its population of 230,000 (less than one per cent of the population of Nigeria) did not justify a prescriptive right to one of the four ministerial posts to be filled from the Western Region. Calabar, though with less

---

[1] See 95.

reason, would claim a similar right in the Eastern Region, and other towns, such as Port Harcourt, might follow suit. It is true that it is proposed that the Cameroons should have one of the four ministerial appointments from the Eastern Region, and this choice will be made from a very thin field, but this can be justified by the status of the Cameroons as a Trust Territory in respect of which we have special obligations, and it is fully in keeping with the spirit of the Report of the Trusteeship Council's Visiting Mission if we adhere to the proposal made by the General Conference.

10.   Our discussion on the proposed change in the method of choosing Ministers ranged wide. We all liked the proposal on its merits. In the short and medium term, it is most desirable that the Governor and the Lieutenant Governors should have a considerable say in the choice of the Nigerians who as Ministers will play a major part in the making and direction of policy: in being spokesmen on their subjects in the Legislatures: and in putting policy across around the country. And in the long term the proposal leads on naturally, as the draft despatch says, to the time when a Prime Minister will appoint his own ministerial colleagues, and will be himself solely responsible for the distribution of portfolios. Moreover the Ministers in the Chamber of Ministers should not (as I fear they will), regard themselves as Regional groups representing Regional interests, but should be a team looking at the problems of Nigeria as a whole and should feel responsible to the Legislature as a whole. We did not look for the snags but they emerged as the discussion went on.

11.   You will recall that during our talks in London Foot and Howe, from their respective experiences as Chairman of the Drafting Committee and Chairman of the General Conference, felt that your proposal would not be acceptable to our legislators. Reference was made to the possibility that the Central Legislature might 'knock down' the Governor's selections one by one until the majority got the Ministers of their own choice; the Governor would then be responsible for an unsatisfactory Minister. The same thing might happen in a Region. I do not regard this danger as great unless the new legislators thrown up under the Revised Constitution are very much worse than I expect but there is a much more important point which I mentioned to Gorsuch in London, and that is that we foresee considerable objection being taken to the proposal to submit to the vote of the whole Central Legislature the names of the Ministers from each Region. Your proposal would rightly emphasise the unity of Nigeria and the fact that the Council of Ministers would be taking part in the direction of Nigerian policy, and in any case the Minister chosen by a Region could have his appointment terminated by a two-thirds vote of all the members of the Legislature; but we felt that the Regions would not accept the proposed change, and that discussion about it would cause unhappiness. The North would suspect that the members from the Eastern and Western Regions would vote against the Northern names put forward unless or until they got as Ministers from the North representatives whom the North might regard as too lively. Similarly, the East and West might fear that Northern influence would eliminate the more progressive representatives from the South, with a view to the selection of more sedate Ministers.

12.   In any case your proposal could not be discussed without regard being had to the form and composition of the Central Legislature, which would vote on the resolution putting forward names of Members for appointment to the Council of Ministers, because the Regions would want to know what their voting strength would be. As the legislators understand the position, the composition of the Central

Legislature is the only major issue left for discussion. In considering the relative merits of a bicameral and a single chamber Legislature at the Centre there will inevitably be keen argument about the relationship of the Central Executive to a bicameral Central Legislature, and different views are likely to be expressed by the different Regions. I myself have no doubt that if there are to be two Houses (which is my present bet) the Lower House should be the dominant House, but if, as appears inevitable and incontrovertible this House will have fifty per cent Northern representation, the Eastern and Western Regions might demand that the Upper House which will reflect equality of the Regions (and which I should expect to have only revisionary or delaying powers) should have larger numbers, which would alter the original proportions at the Centre, particularly if the Houses were to meet in Joint Session, and greater powers. This is likely to be resisted by the North. If, on top of all this argument, a proposal is introduced that Members of the Council of Ministers should be chosen otherwise than by the Members of the Central Legislature from their own Regions there will be room for endless complications. The Chief Commissioner Northern Provinces, told us very bluntly that the Northern Representatives are tired of talk. They have it clearly in their minds that the only major matter left for consideration is the composition of the Central Legislature, and they want to get a quick and firm decision in that, if not by agreement in Nigeria then by a decision in London. If various other matters which they regard as settled so far as local discussion is concerned, such as the method of selecting Ministers and additional safeguards for Lagos, were now to be reopened, Thompstone very much fears that Northern opinion would harden still further and that the Northerners might even start a movement to revoke 'concessions' (as they regard them) which they have already made.

13.   We discussed various other suggestions, including one that after informal consultation and a certain amount of horse-trading amongst all the Members of the Central Legislature, an agreed list of Ministers might be drawn up for presentation to the Central Legislature, but in the end we came to the conclusion that there was a real danger that an attempt at this stage to secure agreement to a new method of selecting Ministers, as a result of a suggestion by the Secretary of State, might wreck the prospects of solving by agreement our main remaining problem. I do not entirely reject the possibility that the proposal might come up for consideration at some stage in our discussions here, otherwise than as a suggestion from the Secretary of State, though on the one hand I feel that discussion in the Regional Houses (especially in the North) would be undesirable and even dangerous and on the other hand there are objections to discussing at the Centre proposals which have not been considered at the Regional level. We realize of course that the final decision rests with His Majesty's Government but we felt that it was best that the Secretary of State should not publicly make this, or any new, suggestion at this stage. When the time comes for a final decision regarding the selection of Ministers it will be necessary to take account of the danger that the enforcement of a method not generally acceptable to the Nigerian representatives might make it impossible to get a Council of Ministers established.

14.   In the light of all this, it seems to us here that the choice lies between not publishing any despatch from the Secretary of State and publishing a despatch limited to an expression of approval of what the Secretary of State is prepared to approve, without introducing controversial matters. My own view is that for the

reasons given in paragraph 3 of this letter it is most desirable that the second course be followed. I should expect that the Secretary of State might wish in that event to make a wider reservation than is represented by the phrase 'subject to further examination of certain points of detail;' for example, he might say that he might wish to comment later on certain aspects of the review. Subject to that, it would ideally meet our points if the following changes were made:—

Paragraph 4	Rejection or reference back of Regional legislation. Make the changes suggested in paragraph 8 above.
Paragraph 8	Method of selecting Ministers. Stop at the word 'Regions' in line 11 but add 'I should not wish to be committed at this stage to approval of the method of electing Ministers.'
Paragraph 12	Additional safeguards for Lagos. Delete the last two sentences.

15.   I am sorry to suggest so considerable a modification in the character of a draft despatch which was discussed with me in London. But after anxious thought, and as a result of discussion here, I feel sure that the best chances of arriving at a satisfactory solution of our problems will be provided by the publication of a despatch which is limited at this stage to conveying a general blessing on the work of the Constitutional Review to date.

16.   I shall write separately about the representation of special interests in the Central Legislature (Gorsuch's letter of the 24th of May) and about the question of a special Council for the Southern Cameroons (paragraph 14 of your letter to Foot of the 23rd of February). And I hope that we may be able shortly to give you some indication of how the Regions are tackling the question of constituencies and elections to Regional Houses.

Minutes on 113

Mr. Gorsuch
This important letter arrived at 12.30 this morning, and I have been able to give a bit of thought to the point which it raises.

As regards paragraph 4 of the draft despatch (paragraph 8 of Sir J. Macpherson's letter) I don't think that any serious difficulty arises. If they prefer that the joint committee should be representative of the Regional Executive rather than Regional Legislature I should not myself raise any objection. But in the last sentence of paragraph 4 of the despatch it might be preferable to use phraseology, suggested below, which would leave the matter a little vague at this stage. I used the term 'Council of Ministers' because that was the term used by the Select Committee. I suggest that we should adopt the term 'Governor-in-Council' instead. I have marked in pencil on the draft at 40 the amendments which might possibly be made.

As regards paragraph 12 of the despatch I am not disposed to argue too strongly against omitting the last two sentences about additional safeguards. I put these sentences in very much for consideration and was surprised when Sir J. Macpherson and his colleagues accepted them; but accept them they did quite willingly. What I am concerned about is that the Yorubas in the Western Region are getting away with it too much. Clearly whatever is said if some of the Lagos members in the west were Yorubas and the others Ebos there would be a strong chance of the Yorubas rather than the Ebos being elected. Similarly, a Lagos member might never get to the Council of Ministers. The answer to the second point is I think that it would be up to the Lagos Members to make themselves agreeable to the rest and in that case they might be elected. Nevertheless I think that we must accept the view that these two sentences should be excluded from the despatch, at the same time telling the Governor that that does not necessarily mean that we should not want to suggest raising the point again at a later stage for consideration should some compromise appear desirable.

The real difficulty arises on paragraph 8. We have always made it clear that we attach importance to our suggestion on this point, both in discussions with Mr. Foot in January and before and since. We cannot depart from our view on this point without seriously embarrassing the Gold Coast Government and compromising on what seems to be an important principle. I am not happy about the suggestion that we should stop at line 11 simply saying that the S. of S. would not wish to be committed at this stage to the approval of the method of electing Ministers. That may arouse still more suspicions of our intentions than an actual statement of what we do intend. I therefore suggest that we should go on to the point which I have marked in the draft with some amendments and should in effect leave it that it is clearly inappropriate to consider this matter further until the composition of the Legislature has been settled, but that what should be aimed at is a system of appointment by the Governor in consultation with members of the Central Legislature from the Regional Council, and in the case of the Regional Legislatures by the Lieutenant Governor in consultation with the members of that Legislature.

As regards paragraph 3 of the despatch, I suggest a variance slightly different from that suggested by the Governor.

These are merely my suggestions for you and Sir T. Lloyd to consider. If you agree with them I suggest telegraphing them as soon as possible to Sir J. Macpherson so that the despatch in its amended form can be approved and issued, if possible by the 20th July. Like Sir John Macpherson I definitely prefer the proposal to publish an amended despatch than not to publish one at all. That would I think be a weak line to take and in any case would involve going back on something which has been approved by the Cabinet. I have written a brief note to Sir J. Macpherson, of which I enclose a copy.

A.B.C.
1.7.50

Sir T Lloyd

Please see the Governor's letter at 41, and Mr. Cohen's minute and letter at 42, on the subject of the draft despatch on the Nigerian constitutional review.

The points at issue are as follows:—

Para 4 of despatch. See para 8 of the Governor's letter. The Governor suggests two amendments: first, in lines 9 and 10 of para 4 to substitute for the words 'power of the Nigerian Council of Ministers' the words 'power of the Governor on the advice of the Council of Ministers.' I think this is correct; the power under the Constitution would be exercised by the Governor in Council and not by the Council itself. Secondly, the Governor wishes the Joint Committee, referred to in the last line but four of the para., to be representative of the Council of Ministers and the Regional *Executive* rather than the Regional *Legislature*. Here again I agree with the

Governor; it is, as he says, the Executive and not the Legislature which is responsible for the policy which caused the legislation in question to be propounded.

Para 12 of despatch. See paras 6 and 9 of the Governor's letter. The Governor's suggestion is that the last two sentences of para 12 should be omitted, on the ground that the suggestion of further safeguards for Lagos from here would have the effect of reviving controversy. I think we should accept his advice on this point.

Para 8 of despatch. See paras 7 and 10 to 13 of the Governor's letter. This is difficult. The Governor would prefer that the despatch should withhold comment entirely on the method of selection of ministers, while making it clear that judgment is reserved on this point. For the reasons given in his minute and letter, however, Mr. Cohen is anxious that something should be said at this stage to indicate the Secretary of State's preference for a system whereby the Governor or the Lieutenant-Governor has a say in the selection of ministers. As you know, the recommendation of the General Conference as regards the Central Executive was that the four members of the Council of Ministers from each region should be selected by the members of the Central Legislature from that region. In the Gold Coast it has been arranged that the names of ministers shall be proposed by the Governor to the Legislature after previous consultation and approved by vote of the Legislature; and it is possible that if a different system is adopted in Nigeria, it may be difficult to hold the position in the Gold Coast. This question involves a matter of principle as well as of tactics and I suggest that in order to save lengthy minuting you might prefer to discuss it with me.

There is one final point. The Governor suggests that if we make the amendments which he suggests we may wish to make in para 3 of the draft despatch a wider reservation than is suggested by the phrase 'subject to further examination of certain points of detail'. This is in fact the exact phrase used in the Cabinet paper (see para 9 of 33a);[2] but in view of subsequent developments I suggest that the phrase might be amended to 'subject to further examination of details in the light of that settlement'.

L.H.G.
10.7.50

---

[1] See 105.

114 CO 537/5789, no 7   30 June 1950
[Constitutional review]: letter from A B Cohen to Sir J Macpherson on a meeting between commercial firms and Mr Griffiths concerning the constitutional review

[This meeting followed concerns expressed by firms that, if a bicameral legislature was established in Nigeria, the members nominated to represent special interests might be allocated to the junior house. Concerns were also expressed concerning the implications for special interests of the establishment of regional houses of assembly. In response, RJ Vile minuted, 'It is important to retain the goodwill of the commercial firms in West Africa if only because on their activities depends the economic health of the territories. Furthermore, the special conditions which obtain in West Africa do give the firms the right to make special representations about constitutional development' (CO 537/5789, no 1, minute by Vile on a letter from ARI Mellor to Griffiths, 15 June 1950). The meeting with the secretary of state on 27 June was the result. Present were representatives of several firms including UAC, John Holt & Co., Cadbury Bros., Shell Co. of West Africa., Taylor Woodrow and the Bata Shoe Co. The delegation was led by ARI Mellor, a director of the UAC. Mellor had been present at a similar meeting with Creech Jones on 19 Dec 1949, concerning the place of representatives of special interests in the Gold Coast constitution, BDEEP series B, vol. 1, R Rathbone, ed, *Ghana*, part I, 72.]

As you know, the commercial firms had a meeting with the Secretary of State on the 27th June to make representations about constitutional reform in Nigeria, I enclose a copy of the memorandum they gave us before the meeting and a note of what happened at the meeting.[1]

You will see that the firms had a very full opportunity to explain their point of view and that the Secretary of State promised that he would transmit their views to you and that there would be a further meeting when he had your views.

Their main points may be summarised as follows:—

(a) The firms seek an assurance that commercial interests are a matter of concern to the Secretary of State.

(b) They sought advice on the best manner in which they could make representations in Nigeria in support of their views.

(c) They claimed that three nominated members in the Central Legislature were not enough and suggested that additional nominated members might be appointed without the right to vote.

(d) They urged the importance of including nominated members in Regional Houses.

(e) They asked for a non-discrimination clause in the constitution.

(f) They suggested the early appointment of an Economic Advisory Committee to the Nigerian Government.

The Secretary of State would like a fairly early expression of your views on the points raised by the firms. We have thought it easier to give you our views in a semi-official letter rather than a despatch because they are necessarily extremely tentative at this stage. I will deal with their main points one by one.

(1) *An assurance that commercial interests are a matter of concern to the Secretary of State.* This seems to us to present no difficulty. Such an assurance in general terms was given in the House of Lords by Lord Listowel last year in relation to the Gold Coast and I am sure you would agree that there could be no possible objection to the Secretary of State informing the firms at the further meeting with them that both he and you recognise that the firms have a most important part to play in the development of Nigeria and that both he and you are anxious for close co-operation with them. The Secretary of State at the meeting this week emphasised the importance of the firms identifying themselves as far as possible with the aspirations of the people of the Colonial Territory and he could, I think, appropriately repeat this.

(2) *The best manner of making representations.* In the case of the Gold Coast we told the firms that on questions of general policy relating to the constitution it was probably better that they should make their representations here. I think that the same applies to Nigeria. The head offices are all in London and on these broad questions of policy it is probably easier for the discussions to be with them when it is a question of having a meeting with the firms en bloc. Would you therefore agree to our telling the firms that we think it best to pursue the discussion here, but it may be

---

[1] Enclosures not printed.

that at a later stage local discussions would be desirable, in which case we will let them know?

(3) *Representation of the firms in the Legislature*. First of all I should tell you what has happened in the Gold Coast over this. The Coussey Committee[2] recommended that there should be two members of the Legislature selected by the Chamber of Mines and the Chamber of Commerce. The firms thought that this was not enough and asked for eight members. The Secretary of State suggested to Arden-Clarke[3] that there might be six members of general economic or other experience nominated by the Governor (of whom some would no doubt be drawn from the firms). The Governor suggested six or eight such nominated members in a speech to the Legislative Council; the suggestion was not enormously well-received in the press or, I gather, in the Legislative Council, but it was agreed to refer it to the Select Committee which was to consider elections and constituencies. This made no concrete recommendation, but did not at any rate turn down the proposal. The Gold Coast Government do not think that they are likely to get agreement locally to having six members and their latest proposal is that, in addition to the two members suggested by the Coussey Committee with the vote, the Governor should have the right to nominate six persons of general experience in economic or other questions who would be members for the whole life of the Legislative Council but would not have the vote.

I discussed this proposal with Arden-Clarke and Saloway[4] the other day. Both Arden-Clarke and I were a bit doubtful whether the firms would accept this idea and we were therefore considerably interested when Samuel[5] quite spontaneously put forward the same idea in relation to Nigeria at the meeting with the Secretary of State. He was supported by several of the others and, as we have heard nothing since, we may assume that the firms would be satisfied with such an arrangement in Nigeria if it were adopted. I have since had another talk with Arden-Clarke and we are now both inclined to think that the Gold Coast Government's proposal to which I have referred above would be the best course to adopt for the Gold Coast. I have written to Saloway, who is today returning to the Gold Coast, to inform him that we are inclined to take this view, but that Arden-Clarke will not want to reach any final conclusion until he has had a talk with Spears and Mellor either at the end of July or early in August.

Meanwhile we are considering here whether the proposal to have non-voting nominated members would create any embarrassment elsewhere either inside or outside Africa. There is, I suppose, the possible risk that elected members elsewhere, e.g. in Trinidad, might use this change in West Africa as an argument for denying all nominated members the vote. On the other hand, the proposed nominated members for the Gold Coast and Nigeria are in rather a special category, and we are inclined to doubt whether this risk is a serious one. As I say, however, we are going into the matter here and I will let you know as soon as we have done so what our view on this point is.

---

[2] The Coussey Commission was set up in 1948 to examine proposals for constitutional reform in the Gold Coast, Rathbone, part I, 62.   [3] Sir Charles Arden-Clarke, gov of the Gold Coast, 1949–1957.
[4] R H Saloway, colonial secretary, Gold Coast, 1950–1951; chief secretary and minister of defence and external affairs, 1951–1954.   [5] Frank Samuel, UAC.

Subject to anything which emerges in relation to other territories, I myself am inclined to think that Samuel's suggestion (which is in effect the same as the suggestion made by the Gold Coast Government) does represent a useful way out of the difficulty which we are in over this matter. The firms themselves recognise that it would be embarrassing to them if the relatively small number of members whom they are claiming were, through some grouping in the Legislature, put in the position of being able to influence the vote, one way or another. They would certainly want to avoid such a situation and the expedient of having non-voting members would enable them to do this, while at the same time their members would have full power of debate and discussion in committee. We should like you therefore to consider whether it would not be possible to have in addition to the thee members recommended, by the Ibadan Conference a provision empowering the Governor to nominate, say, eight persons of general experience as members of the Legislature without the vote. This would not be completely unprecedented, since you already, I think, have power to nominate extraordinary non-voting members; the only difference would be that the present extraordinary members are nominated, I believe, purely *ad hoc*, whereas the others would be, as I have said, for the whole period of the Legislature. If there were eight such additional members, they would not of course all necessarily be drawn from the firms; you quite naturally want to nominate Africans in this way. The firms were not prepared to commit themselves on the question whether some of their members would be in the Upper House if there are two Houses, but I got the very definite impression that they would press for them all to be in the Lower House.

(4) *Representation in Regional Houses*. The Secretary of State started off by discouraging them from pressing this point too strongly, but the firms' representatives argued that the Regional Houses in Nigeria would have very considerable and increasing powers and that they were deeply concerned in the business which would be transacted in these Houses. They therefore argued that they ought to have representation. It was pointed out that under the Ibadan Conference proposals there might be a means of getting some of them in in the Northern House, where there is provision for members nominated by the Assembly; but that of course there could be no undertaking that the Assembly would wish to nominate representatives of European firms. For the east and west no such provision is included. The firms suggested that their alternative proposal for members without the vote might help in this respect. Would you consider whether this would be possible? I must say that I think that there is something to be said for the firms' case and if it were possible without provoking too much controversy to provide for some nominated representatives in all three Regional Houses without the vote, then I think that the firms would be very satisfied. If you feel that this is not possible, an alternative would be that each House should have the right to co-opt on its own committees or even in the House itself expert advice from outside. The firms would no doubt regard this as less satisfactory.

(5) *Non-discrimination*. It has been agreed with Arden-Clarke that a clause based on the Ceylon constitution definitely prohibiting legislation discriminating either in favour of or against particular sections of the community on grounds of race or religion should be included. The alternative would of course be for such legislation to be reserved for His Majesty's pleasure. The disadvantage of this, however, would be that when at some stage in the future provision for reserved legislation disappears,

this provision would disappear with it. In Ceylon the prohibition of discriminatory legislation still remains now that the country has become fully self-governing. We are putting the same provision into the Gold Coast constitution in the hope that the same will in future happen there. We think that we ought to proceed in the same way in Nigeria and I very much hope that you will agree. Provision would not only rule out legislation discriminating against European firms; it would also rule out discrimination as between different sections of Nigeria. I enclose a copy of the Ceylon provision.

As regards the proposal for an Economic Advisory Committee, the Secretary of State told the firms that he was in general in favour of the closest co-ordination between them and Government, but that machinery for securing this was a matter for you to consider. In other words, we think the proposal a good one in principle, but how it should be put into effect is a matter which can only be considered in the light of local knowledge. We hope that you will be able to let us give the firms a reasonably forthcoming answer on this point.

115   CO 537/5263, no 49?   June 1950
['A survey of communism in Africa': FO Research Dept memorandum;
part two, regional survey—'British West Africa'   [Extract]

. . .

British West Africa[1]

222.   Communism, in the sense of a coherent philosophy or an organised and disciplined party, is still non-existent in British West Africa. Although certain individuals have shown characteristics associated with members of organised Communist Parties, and in some cases have even worked for a limited time with the British Communist Party, none of them, on present information, is now a Party member. The native 'liberation' movements with which they are associated are, however, more vocal and more widely dispersed than those of British East Africa, and the activities of the most extreme of them, such as the former Zikist Movement in Nigeria and the Convention People's Party in the Gold Coast, must be considered as serving the long-term interests of Communism. As in the French and Belgian territories, these movements have taken hold over communities in which the spread of education, commerce and industry has led to a breakdown of traditional tribal organisation and allegiance, and such a breakdown may be regarded as a prerequisite to the active growth of these movements. As might be expected, these communities exist, for the most part, in the thickly-populated and relatively advanced coastal area, and elsewhere in the larger towns.

223.   Although the British Communist Party officially regards its sphere of influence as confined to the United Kingdom (see Part I, para. 27), it considers West Africans to be more mature politically than other Africans and has, accordingly, taken several practical steps since the end of the war to encourage their political aspirations: it has organised special study classes on the basic principles of

---

[1] BDEEP series B, vol 1, R Rathbone, ed, *Ghana* part I, 85 includes the sections on the Gold Coast and Sierra Leone from the same document.

Communism for West Africans in the United Kingdom; the Party's West Africa Committee has invited sympathisers to attend its meetings; copies of the Committee's *Africa Newsletter*, circulated in the United Kingdom, find their way to West Africa; finally, the Committee has assisted and encouraged the activities of the West African Students' Union (W.A.S.U.) in the United Kingdom and has maintained personal contact with the West African National Secretariat (W.A.N.S.).

224. These two bodies have co-operated closely. The W.A.S.U., the older of the two, was formed in 1927 as a purely social concern for the welfare of West African students in the United Kingdom. From the start it has represented every shade of political opinion, but the tendency has been for an energetic minority of Communist sympathisers to take an altogether disproportionate part in its direction. The W.A.N.S. was founded in 1945 with its headquarters in London, and had as its first chairman and secretary B. A. Renner and Kwame Nkrumah of the Gold Coast (see para. 237). Although both these men have had contact with the British Communist Party, the W.A.N.S. was never under Communist control. There is no indication that it has been active since early in 1949, and it appears to have died a natural death.

225. A further body which, by supporting the forces opposed to colonial rule, can be considered as furthering the long-term aims of Communism, is the African League. It seeks to combine the interests of both East and West Africa, and has adopted a strong racial character by the total exclusion of non-Africans from its membership. Its organ *African Arrow* is essentially 'nationalist' and not Communist in tone, and there is evidence that the British Communist Party regards its strongly racial character with suspicion.([30])

226. The Soviet organs in Moscow have occasionally referred with admiration to the 'national liberation' movements in Nigeria and the Gold Coast, and Communist propaganda reaches the chief towns of British West Africa, but the Soviet Union is not represented in this area, and commercial contacts are almost non-existent. The Bata Shoe Company and its subsidiary firm, Czechoslovak-Nigerian Export and Import Company, do, however, form a medium of contact between British West Africa and Czechoslovakia. These Companies have sent some Africans to their works at Zlín in Czechoslovakia for technical training skilfully combined with political indoctrination, while Czech Communist agents from Zlín have paid reciprocal visits to Nigeria. It is possible that Bata may become a main channel for the dissemination of Communism in British West Africa, but so far its political activities have been on a small scale. There are now several Nigerians studying at universities in Prague, while the bodies in Nigeria and the Gold Coast with W.F.T.U., W.F.D.Y. and W.I.D.F. connexions provide a means of contact between British West Africa and Communist-controlled organisations in Paris.

Nigeria
227. The chief 'liberation' organisation, the National Council of Nigeria and the Cameroons (N.C.N.C.), which stands for the overthrow of British colonial rule and the creation of independent Nigeria, cannot be described as Communist in any sense. Its founder-president, Dr. Nnamdi Benjamin Azikiwe, has stated categorically that he

([30]) The latest information indicates, however, that the British Communist Party is attempting to penetrate and capture the African League. In February, 1950 it appears that the League sought affiliation with the 'Rassemblement Démocratique Africain.'

is not a Communist; but he has had talks with Palme Dutt and other British Communists and has visited the Czech Embassy in London. According to his own statement, he would be prepared to co-operate on a purely reciprocal basis with any person or group in sympathy with his aims, but would never allow himself to become a tool in other hands. The British Communist Party is critical of Azikiwe and suspicious of his purely nationalist aspirations. No evidence was found of Communist inspiration behind the rioting at the Government coal mines at Enugu in November, 1949.

228.   Until recently there was an extremist splinter group of the N.C.N.C., the Zikist Movement, headed by Nduka Eze, which claimed to be working for the establishment of a United States of West Africa. Although Eze has Communist sympathies, the movement accepted Communist technique and some of its members studied Communist literature, there was never any indication of Communist inspiration behind it. Its enrolled membership was about 800 or 900. In February, 1950, the houses of some of the principal members of the Movement in Lagos and the provinces were searched by the police, and material considered *prima facie* as seditious was found in several of them, including that of the Secretary-General, H. M. Okoye, who was arrested, convicted of sedition and sentenced to 33 months' imprisonment. On 13th April the Zikist Movement was declared an illegal organisation. About a month later, however, Mr. Jaja Wachuku, a leading Zikist figure, founded the 'New Africa' party at a meeting presided over by Azikiwe. Although Wachuku declared that the party would not use violence, there is little doubt that it will constitute the Zikist Movement in another form.

229.   The former Nigerian Trade Union Congress, at one time affiliated to the W.F.T.U., had a secretary-general, A. A. Adio-Moses, and a president, T. A. Bankole, who were in touch with the British Communist Party in 1945–46. Early in 1949, the Ibo faction within the T.U.C. broke away and formed the Nigerian National Federation of Labour (N.N.F.L.), led by Nduke Eze (see para. 228), whose expressed aim was to undermine the T.U.C., which he regarded as being too constitutional in its approach to be of any use for political purposes. By the end of 1949 the N.N.F.L. was firmly established, and would have achieved a dominant position but for the refusal of the influential Railway Workers' Union to join forces. In February, 1950, it began to publish its own newspaper, *Labour Champion*. This organ is pro-Communist in tone and is fed to some extent by Communist propaganda received from abroad. Furthermore, the N.N.F.L. had contacts with the British Communist Party (and the *Daily Worker*) and with the W.F.T.U., the W.F.D.Y. and the Council on African Affairs in New York.([31]) The latest development is that the N.N.F.L. and the Nigerian T.U.C. have joined forces to form the Nigerian Labour Congress with the *Labour Champion* as its organ. In mid-June, 1950, the new body claimed a membership of 60 unions.

230.   Of the two youth movements in Nigeria, the Youth Congress of Nigeria and the Cameroons and the Nigerian Youth Movement, the former, formed in 1947, has close associations with both the N.C.N.C. and the former Zikist Movement. It is affiliated to the W.F.D.Y. and some of its members correspond with Communist

---

([31]) In January, 1950, the International Bureau of the Free German Youth (F.O.J.) offered the N.N.F.L. five university places, ten in secondary schools and ten in recuperative centres of the German Democratic Republic.

youth organisations in Europe. The Congress was represented at the Budapest World Festival of Youth (see Part I, para. 23) of August, 1949, by Bankole Akpata, who has been studying in Prague since 1948. (As far as is known, there are at least three other Nigerian students at universities in Prague.) The second body, the Nigerian Youth Movement, is a Yoruba organisation—in contrast to the Ibo Youth Congress—and is not thought to have Communist leanings. In February, 1950, it was reported that the Nigerian Youth Movement and the N.C.N.C. had formed a temporary alliance to flight for self-government under the name of S.G.N. (Self-government Now). It seems doubtful, however, whether the Ibo and Yoruba elements represented by these two organisations will ever fuse sufficiently to form a permanent alliance.

231.   There is one further Nigerian body with Communist connexions—the Egbu Women's Association, which is affiliated to the Women's International Democratic Federation (W.I.D.F.). Its leader, Mrs. Ransome Kuti, a teacher, is, however, the only member of the Association known to hold Communist views.

232.   Dr. Azikiwe runs a press in Lagos, which produces a number of newspapers, the most important of which is the *West African Pilot*. During the past two years, these papers have shown a markedly increased tendency to use news items and articles favourable to the Soviet Union in support of their campaign against 'imperialism.' Articles from *Tass*, the *Soviet Monitor* and the *Telepress Agency* have become increasingly common, while there has also been a number of articles attributable to no particular source but bearing the hallmarks of Cominform inspiration.

233.   The circulation of foreign Communist literature is still not great, but has been increasing over the past year. Copies of the R.D.A. organ *Réveil* (see para. 215) have been seen in Lagos, while publications such as *Africa Newsletter*, produced by the Africa Committee of the British Communist Party, *Soviet Weekly, Tep*, the Czech organ of the Bata Shoe Company, and the *Guardian* from South Africa have been distributed in some of the larger towns, as well as other pamphlets and text-books produced by the British and South African Communist Parties. There is, however, no evidence of any Communist literature having been translated into the vernacular.

234.   During the past year a noticeable trend has been the increased liaison between the Nigerian nationalist extremists and the Communist-directed 'Rassemblement Démocratique African' (R.D.A.) in French West Africa.([32]) Certain members of the R.D.A. branch at Porto Novo in Dahomey appear to have visited Lagos during the summer of 1949 and to have attempted to form a R.D.A. branch there. Mention must also be made of the visit of the three French Communist deputies, General Plagny, Admiral Moullec and M. Jacques Mitterand, to Lagos in October, 1949, accompanied by Theodore Hazoume of the R.D.A. Dahomey branch (see para. 218). On their part, the leaders of the N.C.N.C. are believed to have expressed a desire to establish regular contact with the R.D.A. branches at Porto Novo, Cotonou and elsewhere. It has been reported that while Azikiwe was in Paris in February, 1950, he met R.D.A. leaders and discussed with them the formation of a *bloc* 'composed of all the political organisations in Africa.'

([32]) Gabriel d'Arboussier, Secretary-General of the R.D.A., has contributed several articles to the *Labour Champion* (see para. 229) in the past six months.

116   CO 537/5787, no 52   15 July 1950

[Constitutional review]: despatch no 464A from Mr Griffiths to Sir J Macpherson on the proposals for constitutional revision

I have now been able to study the Reports of the General Conference at Ibadan and of the Select Committee of the Legislative Council on the review of the Nigerian constitution and to discuss these with you.[1] I note that general agreement has been reached, subject to certain minority reports, on all questions except one and that this one major question, the composition of the Nigerian Legislature, is being referred back for further examination by the Regional Legislatures and the Legislative Council. I believe that it may be helpful if, without commenting on this one point of difference, I inform you of the views of His Majesty's Government on the remaining recommendations.

2.   First of all I wish to pay tribute, on behalf of His Majesty's Government, to the success of the constitutional review. Conference of Nigerian representatives have been held in the Provinces, following in many cases discussions at the divisional level; there have been further Conferences in the three Regions and for Lagos and the Colony; finally a General Conference representative of all parts of the country met at Ibadan in January and its recommendations have been considered by the Regional Legislatures and the Nigerian Legislative Council. In the view of His Majesty's Government the recommendations which have emerged are of the utmost value. I have been particularly impressed by the wide measure of agreement reached. All who have taken part in the constitutional review are to be congratulated on their contributions and Nigeria is to be congratulated on the results; these have amply justified the initiative which you took in 1948 in proposing that such a review should be undertaken and the decision of the Legislative Council to accept your proposal.

3.   The Select Committee of the Legislative Council has warmly welcomed the proposals of the General Conference:—

(a) for greatly increased regional autonomy within a united Nigeria;

(b) for giving Nigerians a full share in the shaping of Government policy and direction of executive Government action in a Central Council of Ministers and Regional Executive Councils; and

(c) for the creation of larger and more representative Regional Legislatures with increased powers.

I am in full agreement with these proposals and the main purpose of this despatch is to inform you that, provided that a satisfactory settlement can be arrived at on the composition of the Nigerian Legislature and subject to further examination of details when the constitutional review is completed in Nigeria, His Majesty's Government will be willing to accept the recommendations of the General Conference with the variations suggested by the Select Committee of the Legislative Council in its Report dated April 1st, 1950. In the following paragraphs I propose to comment on some of the main recommendations; I shall not comment on points of detail.

4.   The proposal to give increased powers to the Regional Legislatures represents a logical development from the present constitution which established these

---

[1] See 90 and 101.

Legislatures and in my view is fully justified by the successful working of the existing Regional Legislatures. I welcome the recommendation that the Regional Legislatures should be given power under the constitution to approve or reject the annual budgets of the Regions and to legislate over a substantial range of subjects of particular interest to the Regions, subject to the power of the Governor on the advice of the Nigerian Council of Ministers to refer back or if necessary to reject legislation which appears to that Council to conflict with a major overall Nigerian interest. I believe it to be right that this latter power should rest with the Central Executive rather than with the Central Legislature as was originally proposed; the procedure for exercising it will need to be carefully worked out. I hope that arrangements may be made for consultation between the Regions and the centre so as to avoid to the maximum possible extent the introduction of legislation into Regional Legislatures which would conflict with an overall Nigerian interest. If, however, on any occasion legislation is passed by a Regional Legislature which is considered by the Nigerian Council of Ministers to be in conflict with such an interest, then I would suggest that a joint committee representative of the Council of Ministers and the Regional Executive concerned should be established with a view to agreeing amendments to the legislation which would make it acceptable to both parties.

5.   I note the recommendation that the Nigerian Legislature at the centre should continue to have full power to make laws for the peace, order and good government of Nigeria, without any restriction. It follows that there will be a substantial overlap between the legislative functions of the Central and Regional Legislatures. I believe that at the present stage, while the Regional Legislatures are still gaining experience, this arrangement will be found the most appropriate; but at some stage in the future, as Nigeria develops further towards a federal state, it may well be necessary, as it has been in other countries, to establish separate and distinct fields of legislation for the centre and the Regions, with a reduction in the range of subjects over which they have concurrent powers.

6.   One of the most important features of the proposals is the recommendation that Regional Executive Councils should be established under the Presidency of the Lieutenant-Governors of the Regions, and consisting of official members and Nigerian Ministers drawn from the Regional Legislatures, the latter being in a majority in each case. The proposal that the Chief Commissioners should in future be called Lieutenant-Governors appropriately symbolises the increased powers to be given to the Regions. I fully agree also that, with these increased regional powers, Nigerian members should take a full part, with their official colleagues and under the leadership of the Lieutenant-Governors, in the formulation of policy and the direction of executive action in the Regions, subject to the general direction of policy by the Nigerian Council of Ministers in matters affecting overall Nigerian interests.

7.   I have made it clear how much importance I attach to the principle of greater regional autonomy. One of the great advantages of encouraging the Regions to develop each along its own characteristic lines will be that by that very process the unity of Nigeria will be strengthened. I wish to make it clear beyond all doubt that His Majesty's Government attaches the very greatest importance to building up a unified Nigeria on the basis of the three component Regions. The three Regions depend closely on each other and will continue to do so, and any tendency to break up Nigeria into separate parts would in the view of His Majesty's Government be contrary to the interests of the peoples of all three Regions and of Nigeria as a whole.

I therefore warmly welcome the recommendations for a strong Central Legislature and Executive for Nigeria. Final recommendations for the composition of the Legislature remain to be made. As regards the Executive, the important proposal is made that a Nigerian Council of Ministers should be established under the Presidency of the Governor with six ex officio members and twelve Nigerian Ministers, four from each Region, drawn from the Central Legislature. It is proposed that the Council of Ministers should formulate policy and direct executive action for Nigeria. I fully accept this proposal, as I am convinced that it is essential at the centre as in the Regions that Nigerians drawn from the Legislature should take a full part, along with their official colleagues and under the leadership of the Governor, in the shaping of general Government policy and the directing of executive action.

8.   The proposal is made by the General Conference that the Ministers at the centre and in the Regions should be elected by the respective Legislatures and that the arrangements for the distribution of portfolios among these Ministers should be settled at the centre by the Governor in Council (i.e. the Council of Ministers) and in the Regions by the Lieutenant-Governor in Council (i.e. the Regional Executive Council). I entirely agree with the principle that, at this stage of constitutional development, the Legislatures should have a voice in the appointment of Nigerian members to the Executive at the centre and in the Regions; but the method of appointing Ministers and of distributing portfolios is clearly a matter on which final decisions cannot be taken until the composition of the Nigerian Legislature has been settled. You will, however, be aware that in this country and in many other countries in the Commonwealth and elsewhere where there is an established party system, the Prime Minister appoints his own Ministerial colleagues and is himself solely responsible for the distribution of portfolios. I have no doubt that, when the stage of fully responsible government is reached, the same arrangement will be adopted in Nigeria. There would in my view be advantages in establishing, on the creation of a ministerial system in Nigeria, a procedure for appointment of Ministers which will lead on smoothly to the adoption of this arrangement when the time is ripe. As, at the stage now under discussion, the Governor will preside over the Council of Ministers and the Lieutenant-Governors over the Regional Executive Councils, I suggest that the aim should be to arrive at a procedure under which members of the Council of Ministers are selected in consultation between the Governor and the members of the Nigerian Legislature representing each region, and members of the Regional Executive Council are selected in consultation between the Lieutenant-Governor and the members of the Regional Legislature.

9.   I agree with the recommendation of the General Conference that the appointment of a Minister, but not of course of an ex officio member, should be terminated in the event of a vote of no confidence in him being passed by a two-thirds majority of the Legislature concerned. It will, I am sure, be agreed that this power should not be lightly exercised, and for that reason I suggest that the majority should not be two-thirds of the members present but two-thirds of all the members of the Legislature in question. I suggest also that individual members of the Council of Ministers or of the Regional Executive Councils should be under an obligation to carry out and support in the Legislature, the policy and decisions of the Council. A member of a Council who felt himself unable to carry out this obligation should resign and, in case he refused to do so, it should be provided in the constitution that the Governor or Lieutenant-Governor should be empowered in these circumstances

to terminate his appointment, with the agreement of the majority of the Council of Ministers or the Regional Executive Council.

10.   Great importance clearly attaches to the arrangements for the election of members of the Central and Regional Legislatures and I have noted with much interest the recommendations of the General Conference on this matter. I make no comment on the arrangements for the election of members of the Central Legislature, since a final recommendation on its composition remains to be made. As regards the Regional Houses of Assembly, it is proposed that the members should be elected by a system of indirect election through provincial electoral colleges in the Northern Region and divisional electoral colleges in the Eastern and Western Regions; that the primary elections in each Region should be direct; and that the detailed arrangements should be worked out in each Region and examined by the House of Assembly of that Region. I do not wish to prejudge this examination, but I would point out that the representative character of the Regional Houses of Assembly and, if they are to select the members of the Central Legislature, of that Legislature itself, will depend ultimately on the primary elections in the Provinces and Divisions. It is in my view most important that the arrangements for these primary elections should ensure that the members elected to the Provincial and Divisional electoral colleges should be genuinely representative of all the peoples of the areas concerned; that the elections should be free and fair; and that the form of election should be properly adopted to the circumstances of each area. For this last reason I welcome the proposal that the arrangements should in the first instance be worked out in the Regions themselves; I shall await the results with much interest.

11.   During the course of the constitutional review different opinions have been expressed as to the future of Lagos. The joint Lagos and Colony Conferences and the Western Regional Conference proposed that both Lagos and the rural districts of the Colony should be included in the Western Region for legislative and administrative purposes. The General Conference at Ibadan by a majority agreed as far as the rural districts of the Colony were concerned, but recommended that the independent municipality of Lagos, as capital of Nigeria, should be kept outside the Western Region. A minority report signed by seven representatives of the Western Region, three representatives of Lagos and one of the Colony, but not by the representatives of Lagos and the Colony on the Legislative Council, contested this recommendation and argued that Lagos should be included in the Western Region. The majority of the Select Committee of the Legislative Council came to the conclusion that Lagos should be included in the Western Region, subject to certain important safeguards. The representatives of Lagos and the Colony on the Legislative Council, however, submitted a minority report supporting the majority of the General Conference.

12.   I recognise that there is much to be said in support of both views; but I have come to the conclusion that the view of the majority of the Select Committee of the Legislative Council which clearly has the support of a substantial body of opinion but not of all opinion in Lagos itself, should be accepted. If it were not accepted, Lagos would have to [sic: be] separated for legislative and administrative purposes from the rural districts of the Colony, which are unanimously recommended for inclusion in the Western Region; and I understand that there are felt by many to be strong ties between Lagos and the rest of the Colony, which have been administered together for so long. Although I believe that Lagos should be included in the Western Region, I am sure that its position as capital city must be safeguarded and I therefore welcome

the proposals of the majority of the Select Committee that all central services in Lagos, including particularly the port and railway, should remain a central responsibility under the direction of the central Government; that all expenses arising from the special needs of Lagos as the capital should be met by the allocation of funds from the central Government; that the annual estimates of the Town Council should be submitted not only to the Regional Executive Council of the Western Region but also to the Nigerian Council of Ministers; and that at least two members representing Lagos in the Western House of Assembly should be selected by that House to sit in the Central Legislature.

13.   The allocation of finance between the three Regions and central Nigerian services naturally assumed much importance during the constitutional review. I welcome the proposal of the General Conference that an expert and independent committee should be set up to undertake an enquiry into the division of revenue over a period of five years between the three Regions and the central Nigerian services; that the proposals of this committee should be considered by representatives of the three Regions sitting in equal numbers, with a representative of Lagos, under the chairmanship of the Financial Secretary; and that recommendations should be submitted to the Governor and by him to the Secretary of State to take effect at the same time as the introduction of the new constitution. The Committee has already been appointed and has started work.

14.   There is one other matter directly arising from the proposed changes in the constitution to which I should like to refer. The grant of increased powers to the Regional Legislatures and the setting up of Regional Executive Councils will, I believe, if the new arrangements are to work statisfactorily, involve a further strengthening of the administrative machinery in the Regions and a re-examination of the relations between the central directorates of the technical departments at Lagos and elsewhere and the regional branches of those departments. With the appointment of Regional Ministers for certain subjects, further administrative devolution of responsibility to the Regions will, I think, be found necessary and it may well be found desirable also to raise the status of the Regional Deputy Directors of certain departments to that of Regional Directors. The Central Directors would then cease to be directly responsible for the purely regional activities of these departments; their function would be to advise the Governor and the Council of Ministers on general policy and to provide the regional directorates with technical advice and assistance not available to them in other ways. I have no doubt that these matters are receiving your careful attention.

15.   I have already dealt with the minority reports on the position of Lagos. As regards the other minority reports, I have studied them closely, but I do not think that it would be justifiable to set aside the recommendations of the large majority of the General Conference. On the proposal that Nigeria should be divided not into three Regions but into a considerably larger number of units based on ethnic grouping, I would point out that the three Regional Conferences, the Conference for Lagos and the Colony and the General Conference all either explicitly or implicitly recommended that Nigeria should consist of three Regions, although the Western Regional Conference would have preferred that they should be called States. If the alternative proposal for a larger number of smaller units were adopted, not only would the financial and administrative relations between the central and the component parts be made much more difficult, but those component parts would

themselves be weakened, whereas it seems clear to me from studying the results of the constitutional review that it is the desire of the great majority to strengthen the Regions and to give them more legislative and executive power. On the minority reports regarding the system of election. I would point out that while the Eastern Regional Conference and the Lagos-Colony Conference suggested leaving the method of election to the decision of the regions themselves, both the Northern and the Western Regional Conferences, as well as the General Conference, recommended indirect election to the Regional Houses of Assembly through electoral colleges at the Provincial or Divisional level. I see no reason to depart from the recommendations of the General Conference and I do not wish to add to what I have said in paragraph 10 of this despatch, except to point out that from the point of view of those who are in favour of direct election, the proposal that the primary elections in each region should be direct represents an important advance.

16.   I have one final point to make. When the existing constitution was introduced in 1947 it was stated that it would be subject to general review after a period of nine years and that certain features of it would be subject to review after three and six years. Its operation was so successful that you decided, with my predecessor's approval, to propose a general revision in the third year of its operation and this proposal, as I have already stated, was accepted by the Legislative Council. The reforms which have been recommended as a result of that review are, I believe, both sound and necessary and they certainly represent a logical development from the existing constitution. I do not myself think it wise to fix definite timetables for constitutional advance, whether these take the form of laying down that a particular change will be made after a given period of years or of stating that no review will take place until a given period has elapsed. Constitutional advance must in my opinion depend on the political development of the country concerned. At the same time too frequent constitutional changes are to be avoided; if changes are made too often they are bound to have an unsettling effect on the political and economic life of a country. For that reason, although I would not be in favour of fixing any stated period within which review will be ruled out, I would nevertheless urge that, when the new constitutional arrangements have been introduced, they should be allowed to operate for a reasonable period before further changes are considered.

17.   I shall await with the greatest interest the final recommendations to be submitted on the subject of the composition of the Nigerian Legislature.

117   CO 537/5787, no 64   17 Sept 1950

[Constitutional review]: inward telegram no 1374 from Sir J Macpherson to Mr Griffiths on the recommendations of the Select Committee of the Legislative Council concerning the composition of the central legislature

Constitutional Review.

During meeting of Legislative Council which ended 16th September, a Select Committee to which all Unofficial Members and 7 officials were appointed made the following recommendations:—

(i) In the present circumstances, it will be preferable to have one House rather than two in the Central Legislature.

(ii) In view of respective population of the regions, representation of Northern Region in Central Legislature should be equal to the representation of the other two regions together.

(iii) There should be 148 members in the Central Legislature.

(iv) For the present, the Governor should continue to preside.

(v) Six members should be appointed by the Governor to represent the interests which in his opinion are not otherwise adequately represented.

2.   A minority report presented by three Lagos members[1] favoured two Houses, and reiterated objections to representation of special interests.

3.   When report of Select Committee was debated in full Council of 16th September report was adopted without division, only the three Lagos members opposing.

4.   The Western members did not vote in Select Committee since they did not feel free to vary the recommendations of the Western House in favour of two Houses but they did not oppose the adoption of the Select Committee report and are, I believe, well prepared to accept the majority.

5.   During debate in the Council of 16th September, Eastern members spoke strongly in favour of mutual confidence between regions, and Balewa and Yahaya Ilorin on behalf of the North warmly supported the need for co-operation in a United Nigeria.

6.   I regard this outcome as extremely satisfactory. Fears of separatism on the part of the North are ended and the atmosphere of enthusiastic co-operation between regions in which debate finished is a very good augury for the future Constitution.

---

[1] The three Lagos members were Adedoyin, Azikiwe and Olorun-Nimbe.

118 CO 537/5787, no 69   22 Sept 1950

[Constitutional review]: letter from H M Foot to A B Cohen on discussions with chief commissioners concerning the constitutional revision

You will have seen our telegram[1] reporting the result of the Legislative Council Select Committee on the composition of the Central legislature and I am sure that you will agree that the main result achieved was as satisfactory as it could be. Since the Legislative Council dispersed on Saturday last there has been a good deal of mischievous comment in the more extreme local press which is still talking about Northern domination, but in spite of that I believe that there is an overwhelming majority of public opinion in favour of the decisions reached by the Legislative Council, coupled with a sense of great relief that the miserable prospect of increasing antagonism between North and South has been avoided.

The purpose of this letter is not to discuss the main decisions on the question of the composition of the Central Legislature but to bring you up-to-date on

---

[1] See 117.

discussions which we have had over recent weeks with Chief Commissioners and subsequently at an informal meeting of Unofficial Members of the Legislative Council. On the Governor's direction I wrote a series of letters to Chief Commissioners early this month setting out certain preliminary ideas about some of the main outstanding questions to be decided in connection with the constitutional advance and we had a long discussion with Chief Commissioners on those questions on the day preceding the Legislative Council meeting. Later last week I had an informal discussion on a number of points with Unofficial Members.

We shall of course reply in detail to the points raised in your letter of the 5th of September and the legal memorandum to which that letter refers but it will take some time to consider the many points there raised and I thought that we should let you know in advance how discussion on a number of important questions has been going.

I should also mention that on the Governor's direction I am replying separately to your letter which dealt with the requests put forward by the commercial delegation which saw the Secretary of State in London.[2] It will be sufficient as far as those requests are concerned to say now that we were very pleased to get the decision of the Select Committee to increase the representation of special interests in the Central Legislature from three to six. Rogers put this forward in Select Committee and as usual he played his cards very well. I should add that in the informal discussion which I had with Unofficial Members (which took place before the Select Committee on the composition of the Central Legislature sat) I raised the question whether there might be representation of special interests in Regional Legislatures. Although I did not attempt to bring the discussion to a final conclusion it was apparent that the Northern members were not opposed to this idea and that some of the members from other Regions are also likely to agree to it. The fact that we obtained agreement on increasing the special interests' representation in the Central Legislature and that we have made some progress towards getting agreement that there should be similar representation in the Regional Houses will be helpful to you when a further meeting with the commercial delegation takes place in London.

One of the principal matters which we have discussed at considerable length with Chief Commissioners is the time table for bringing the new constitution into effect. We first of all had in mind that the draft Instruments might be referred to the Legislative Council in March next year and that they should then be put in final form, taking into account any changes which the Legislative Council might wish to suggest. We now think however that it is unnecessary to put the draft Instruments to the Legislative Council and indeed that it is undesirable to do so since it would give members an opportunity of raising again all the questions which have already been disposed of by the Ibadan Conference and subsequent consideration in Select Committee and the Council. Instead we think we should aim at getting the Instruments into final shape as quickly as possible in the hope that they can be promulgated shortly after the Budget meeting of the Legislative Council in March, 1951. There is however quite a number of important points on which you and we may want to vary the recommendations of the Ibadan Conference and the Legislative Council and in addition there are some important questions to be settled before the Instruments are drawn up which have not been considered either at Ibadan or by the

---

[2] See 114.

Legislative Council. Our idea is that when these points have been sorted out the Secretary of State might address a despatch to the Governor, first of all welcoming the recommendations of the Legislative Council on the composition of the Central Legislature and then going on to make suggestions and ask the Governor's advice on a list of outstanding points. This arrangement would leave us free either to call a special meeting of the Legislative Council later this year to consider these outstanding points or possibly to call in Unofficial Members of the Legislative Council to consider the points in an informal meeting. The sort of points we have in mind which might be dealt with in this way are the method of appointment of ministers and distribution of portfolios and the question whether Central legislation must be first taken in Regional Legislatures. If this procedure is agreed we should hope that the despatch from the Secretary of State could reach us within say a couple of months from now.

We also considered with Chief Commissioners when we could hope to get the new Legislative bodies established and our first aim was to have a shake-down meeting of the new Regional Houses and of the new House of Representatives towards the end of 1951. That would enable the Houses to settle questions of procedure at a preliminary meeting before undertaking the big task of dealing with the 1952/53 Budget. The Acting Chief Commissioner Western Provinces was inclined to urge some postponement and suggested that the existing Legislative bodies should deal with the Budget for 1952/53, the elections for the new Legislatures taking place in the summer of 1952. His point was that it is necessary to give a great deal of time to making preparations for the new elections and he fears that if we rush things we shall not get the best representation. Most of us however felt strongly that we cannot delay things for yet another year and that we must do everything possible to get the Instruments ready for promulgation early next year (not later than April or May) and then proceed with the elections (which will take several months) as soon as possible thereafter. We felt that if there were further delay we should be playing into the hands of those who wish to sabotage orderly constitutional progress.

I shall now turn to a number of separate points:—

Ministers' salaries

The discussion which we have had on this matter has not unnaturally excited a good deal of interest, particularly among the Unofficial Members of the Legislative Council. During my informal talk with them I told them the rates of salary payable in such places as Ceylon, Jamaica, Trinidad and the Sudan and also told them that the Gold Coast had in mind a rate as high as £2,500 a year. A good deal of the discussion turned on the question of whether ministers should be permitted to retain private sources of income and the prevailing opinion amongst Unofficial Members is that they should not, and that salaries should be fixed at a sufficiently high rate to compensate ministers for losing their private income. We think that there can reasonably be a distinction between the salaries of ministers at the Centre and ministers in the Regions and we also think that ministers without portfolios might be paid less than the others. No decision of any kind on the rates has been reached. On the official side I think that we feel that about £1,500 for Central ministers and about £1,000 for Regional ministers might be about right but we may have to go higher than that, particularly if private sources of income are ruled out.

One good point about giving up private sources of income which was mentioned is that ministers who come from outside Lagos will usually have to abandon their occupations by reason of the distance of Lagos from their homes and it would clearly be unfair to put any ministers who come from Lagos at an advantage in this respect.

Allowances for members of legislatures
As you know our present system is to pay a fairly high daily allowance (£5.5.0d a day) to members of Legislatures for days on which they are absent from their homes on duties connected with their work in the Legislatures. This arrangement is not altogether satisfactory—it is suggested that it tends to prolong meetings of the Legislatures! We think that when the new constitutional arrangements are introduced we might switch to a system of paying a yearly salary. In view of the size of the new Legislatures we hope that it will be possible to keep these salaries low—a figure of £200 a year for members of Regional Houses was suggested with an additional £200 a year for those who also serve in the Central Legislature.

Distribution of subjects amongst central ministers
We do not see much difficulty in the distribution of subjects amongst Regional ministers but distribution amongst Central ministers is not very easy. Our present suggestions are as follows:—

(i) Minister of Labour | Labour
(ii) Minister of Fuel & Power | Mines
| Colliery
| Electricity
| Hydro-electric projects
| Survey
| Geological survey
| Irrigation
(iii) Minister for Transport | Railway
| Marine
| Civil Aviation
| Road Transport
| Meteorology
(iv) Minister for Industries & Commerce | Industries
| Commerce
| Marketing & Exports
(v) Minister for Posts & Telegraphs | Posts & Telegraphs
| Public Relations
| Broadcasting
| Printing
| Statistics
(vi) Minister for Public Works | Public Works.

As for the three central ministers to deal in the House of Representatives and the Council of Ministers with regional subjects we suggest:—

(i) Minister for Agricultural Development	Agriculture Forestry Fisheries Animal Husbandry
(ii) Minister for Social Services	Education Health Welfare
(iii) Minister for General Purposes	Town & Country Planning Land Co-operation Local Government Local Industries Community Development Water Supplies

Functions of ministers

You will remember that the proposed functions of the Council of Ministers and Regional Executive Councils were defined by the Ibadan Conference as being to formulate policy and to direct executive action (the Council of Ministers in overall Nigerian matters and in relation to Central Departments and the Regional Executive Councils in Regional matters).

The functions of ministers (both Central and Regional) were defined as follows:—

(a) initiation of discussion of policy in the Council

(b) introducing into the House and answering therein all business affecting his subject or subjects

(c) ensuring in co-operation with the executive Head of the Department concerned that the decisions of the Council, as they affect his subject, are carried out. (This function does not, of course, apply to Central Ministers dealing with mainly Regional subjects).

The most important point of all, in our opinion, is that decisions of policy are to be taken not by individual ministers but by the Councils. It follows from this that the main duty of ministers is to take part in discussion and decision on policy in the Councils and since all decisions on all matters (except those too trivial to refer to the Councils) must be taken in the Councils a very heavy volume of work will fall on the Councils. As far as the Council of Ministers is concerned I expect that meetings will have to take place at least once a week for most of the year and I imagine that frequent meetings of Regional Executive Councils will also be necessary.

In view of the importance of the Councils and their work it seems quite clear to us that the work of Secretariats (both Central and Regional) will mainly be to serve the Councils. Since Secretariat files should not normally be circulated to Ministers, it will be necessary for Secretariats to prepare explanatory notes for prior distribution to members of the Councils on almost every subject to be discussed and decided by the Councils. That alone will throw a considerable new strain on Secretariats. In addition it must, I think, be made quite clear from the start that decisions of the Councils must be communicated by Secretariats to Departments and not by

Ministers to Departments. It follows from that that the work of Secretariats will not be reduced but increased and that makes it essential to ensure that our existing Secretariat machinery should not be weakened just at the time that this increased strain is certain to come. Moreover it must be remembered that Secretaries at the Centre and in the Regions will have to spend much more of their time in future sitting in the Councils and in the Legislatures. Our conclusion from this is that we should avoid any major reorganisation in the Secretariat system we know at this time.

You will see that our proposals for an embryo ministerial system differ a great deal from what is proposed in the Gold Coast (our proposals are much nearer the Jamaican model) and that in consequence we do not intend to split our Secretariats either at the Centre or in the Regions in the way that the Gold Coast proposes. We have in mind that each minister should, where possible, have an office in the Department with which he is associated and that he should have a Secretary of about D.O. seniority to obtain for him material which he requires from the Secretariat and the Department in question. In addition he will of course have frequent meetings with the head of the Department and occasional meetings with the Chief or Civil Secretary.

The main purposes which we have in mind are that we must avoid making the ministers feel that they are full fledged ministers on the English model at this stage and that we must keep existing Secretariats free to take the additional strain which we know is coming.

We realise that there is a number of arguments for division of the Secretariats on the lines which the Gold Coast proposes but the essential point which we wish to emphasize is that in Nigeria decisions of policy are to be taken not by individual ministers but by the Councils. In our view that necessitates the continuation of undivided Secretariats both at the Centre and in the Regions.

Service reorganisation

It is generally agreed here that all unestablished staff and daily paid employees serving Regional Authorities should become the sole responsibility of Regional Authorities.

Secondly it seems to us that each Regional Executive Council should be free to draw up a scheme for a Regional Junior Service. We have considered whether we should attempt to create Regional Junior Services in the next few months so that they would be in operation before the constitutional changes are brought into effect. This would be a big undertaking at a time when we have so much else to do—and it seems to us that in any event it would be wrong to do the job by administrative decision now. The decisions should really be taken by the Lieutenant Governors-in-Council. There are all sorts of complicated and important questions to be decided regarding recruitment, salary scales, discipline and pensions—to mention only a few—and it is, we think, for the Lieutenant Governors-in-Council under the new regime to take such decisions.

We also have in mind that some of the Regions may not wish to tackle this job early on and will be content to carry on for some time under the existing arrangements whereby Junior staff from a Central Service is posted to the Regions. We should raise no objection if the present system is continued in one or more of the Regions for as long as they wish.

If and when a scheme for a Regional Junior Service is drawn up in any Region the Government would be prepared to allow members of the existing staff serving Regional authorities to transfer to the new Regional Service if they wish to do so. It would however be some time before new recruitment and transfer could fully meet Regional needs and in the meantime it could no doubt be arranged for secondment from the Central Service to the Regional Service. One great advantage of tackling the problem in this way would be that no existing member of the Central Service would be able to claim that he had been forced to give up his rights as a member of the Nigerian Service. There are of course all sorts of subsidiary problems which will have to be considered (e.g. pension schemes and staff negotiating machinery) but the general proposition that Lieutenant Governors-in-Council should be free to prepare schemes for Regional Services, with the present Nigerian Service continuing as at present in the meantime, seems to us sound and workable.

Senior officers (and Junior officers too) who are posted to the Regions for service under the Regional authorities would of course be fully responsible to those Regional authorities and the only interference from the Centre would be in respect of transfer from Region to Region which would be arranged in consultation with the Regional authorities concerned.

As far as the Senior Service is concerned we take the view that there should however be no attempt to split it into four (three for the Regions and one for the Centre) and we believe that any such division would be contrary to the general Nigerian interest.

The only other main question concerning Government staff which I need mention now is the proposal to establish a Public Service Commission to advise the Governor on recruitment, training, promotion and discipline of all Government staff, Senior and Junior, except in respect of holders of superscale posts and members of Unified Services. You will remember that the Ibadan Conference proposed that matters of discipline should be dealt with by a Privy Council but at present our view is that it will be preferable to establish a Public Service Commission, and I believe that is your view too. We are examining various models and will put up our proposals about a Public Service Commission separately. The Commission would of course deal only with centrally employed staff and if Regional Junior Services are established in the future it will be for consideration whether similar Commissions should be established in the Regions.

Selection of ministers and allocation of portfolios
I raised this matter at the informal discussion with Unofficial Members and pointed out that in the Secretary of State's despatch he had suggested that members of the Executive should be selected in consultation between the Governor or the Lieutenant Governors and members of the Legislatures concerned. We did not attempt to reach a final conclusion but several members agreed that it was necessary to give very careful consideration to the Secretary of State's views.

I am sorry to seem obstinate about this but personally the more I think the matter over the more I remain of the opinion that the system proposed by the Ibadan Conference whereby ministers would be elected by the Legislatures would be the best. An additional argument which emerged from the discussion with Unofficial Members is that the Secretary of State's proposed system envisages the development of a party system. It may well be that parties grow up in the different Regions but I find it very difficult to picture the emergence of national parties which could cut across Regional divisions. Indeed it may be that we shall never have in Nigeria a state of affairs where two or more parties cover the whole country. It therefore seems to me that the arguments used in respect of the Gold Coast constitution do not apply to Nigeria where we propose to work a unique federal system. You will no doubt wish to discuss this matter further with the Governor.

Central bills in regional houses

Another matter raised in the informal discussion with Unofficial Members was the question of whether it is necessary in the new arrangements for Central legislation to be discussed first of all in Regional Houses. Some of the members thought that it would be necessary to maintain this practice so that members of the Central Legislature should know the feelings of their fellow members in Regional Houses before expressing their views at the Centre. One compromise proposal which was put forward during the discussion was that Central bills should merely be laid on the Table of Regional Houses for debate there only in the event of a member making a specific motion. We did not attempt to reach a final conclusion but I myself think that if and when the point is again put to Unofficial Members they will most of them be anxious to retain the present system in spite of the delays which it causes.

Reorganisation of departments

We have for some time past been hard at it working out in detail how Departments are to be fully regionalised. Some of the main Departments can be comparatively easily divided into three Regional Departments, e.g. Education and Agriculture, whilst other Departments which are about to be constituted into Corporations or have already been so constituted will of course remain permanently central. There are other Departments, such as the Police, Survey, Public Relations and Accountant-General which will probably be regionalised to the greatest extent possible in order that each Regional administration shall have available to it technical advice on such aspects of the working of those Departments as can be appropriately administered regionally. There are a hundred and one complicated problems to be settled in this matter of departmental reorganisation. We have to decide, for instance, which specialists should be retained at the Centre on the staff of the Departmental Inspectors General on grounds that it would be uneconomical to attempt to provide a specialist on the subject in question for each Region. We also have to consider whether, for instance, big Central stores such as that of the Public Works Department should be retained at the Centre or whether Regional stores organisations should be provided. A greater difficulty is that of providing the additional housing and office accommodation which will be required in the Regions. We must, of course, make sufficient progress with this Departmental reorganisation to ensure that when the new Constitution comes into force Regional Directors of regionalised Departments can perform their obligations to Regional Executive Councils, but I anticipate that the whole process of devolution cannot be fully completed for maybe two or even three years. We have a small Committee which is consulting with each Head of Department and working out a cut and dried scheme for approval in each case as soon as possible.

Electoral system

A great deal of thought is being given in the Regions to the extremely difficult matter of the electoral system to be introduced for the new Constitution. In some ways the decision of the Legislative Council to recommend a Central Legislature of 148 members simplifies the task but there are many big snags and differing circumstances in the three Regions. The matter is being discussed with Unofficial Members of Regional Houses and we hope to call a conference here in a month or six weeks' time to try to work out final proposals.

I am afraid that even this long letter does not mention many of the important points which we still have to deal with. I hope that within the next week or two we shall be able to send you a thorough commentary on your recent letter. Meanwhile we have started working out rough draft Instruments here and AA Williams, who is helping in this, will be in England early in December carrying with him our views on points still then outstanding. He will be available for discussion in the Colonial Office until the Instruments are put into final shape.

Before then it would be of the greatest assistance if the Colonial Office draughtsman (McPetrie?) could come out here for a few weeks for discussions with us. The ideal would be for us to send him some very rough drafts in about a month's time and for him to come out at the beginning of November to discuss them, but we should be glad to see him in the second half of October if that would be more convenient to him. I am sure that discussions with him here would save a great deal of time and correspondence—and speed is now of the greatest importance.

119   CO 583/316/10, no 9   25 Sept 1950
[Islamic associations]: inward savingram no 2357 from H M Foot to Mr Griffiths on the possible arrival in Nigeria of Muslim teachers from Egypt. *Annexures*.
Minute by M Phillips

Your 1825 Saving of 26th July[1]

    1. (a) Nothing is known of the Association of Supporters of Islam.

    (b) The Muslim Congress of Nigeria is a properly constituted body of some standing amongst the Muslims of the Western Provinces of Nigeria and Lagos Colony. *Its executive personnel do not, however, as a whole command the confidence of Government. A note on the organisation is attached as Annexure A.*

    2. Assistance could be given to the Muslims of the Western Provinces and Lagos Colony through the Muslim Congress.

    3. This Government would view the arrival of such a mission with disfavour.

    4. In view of 3 above, not applicable.

    5. The main native languages and English (not Arabic)

    6. *While we would find it difficult to prohibit the entry of such missionaries we would be much happier if they did not come. Al Azhar[2] is an institute for which*

---

[1] This savingram followed an inquiry by the Egyptian ambassador in London to the FO in June 1950 about the possibility of sending Muslim teachers to Nigeria.

[2] ie Al-Azhar University, Cairo.

little good can be said from the point of view of this Government. A copy of Lord Milverton's (then Sir Arthur Richards) Secret Despatch of the 3rd of October 1947 addressed to H.M. Ambassador in Cairo is attached as Annexure B to explain why this view has been adopted. The request contained therein was referred to the Egyptian Foreign Ministry but nothing further was heard of the matter.

2.   We would naturally not wish that the passages underlined should be conveyed to the Egyptian Ambassador in their present form and the Foreign Office will no doubt use its discretion as to how our case should be presented.

3.   We very much hope that the Egyptians can be headed off. The line to take might be that the organisations to which reference is made are of no great importance and do not operate in the Northern Provinces where the majority of Nigerian Moslems live; that a visit to Nigeria at the invitation of these organisations would therefore be ill-advised; and that the language difficulty (the language in most schools attended by Moslems is Hausa and to a lesser extent Yoruba and English) makes it difficult to see how Egyptian teachers could be usefully employed in Nigerian schools.

Annexure A to 119: Note on Muslim Congress of Nigeria

The Muslim Congress of Nigeria was started about the middle of 1948 at Ijebu Ode by Mohammed Effendi El-Amin Kudaise with the object of bringing together all adherents of the Moslem faith. Beyond that they seem to have no particular aims and objects and their activities have mostly been confined to issuing pamphlets regarding the pilgrimage to Mecca. So far they have shown no interest in politics and it is probable that Kudaise started the movement for the purpose of collecting subscriptions. None of the people connected with the Congress are of any political or religious significance. The Present [sic: word missing] is Hadji Hassain Mohammed, a painter and building-contractor by trade and Imam of a small mosque at Ijebu Ode. The Vice-President is Abdul Kasim Lawal, also the Imam of a small mosque. The Assistant Secretary is Ismaila Adebule, a petty trader who deals in patent medicines. All of these are natives of Ijebu Ode. The principal man behind the movement is Kudaisi, the Secretary. After leaving school he was employed by Witt and Busch and then joined the Government service as a telegraphist in the P and T, from which he was dismissed after being sentenced to two years imprisonment for theft. In 1945 he went on the pilgrimage to Mecca. He spent 18 months in Saudi Arabia and the Sudan and founded his Congress on his return. The fact that he did so suggests that he had some contact with the Muslim Congress, which is a subversive and Communist-tainted organisation which the Egyptian Government has recently proscribed. It was probably from them that Kudaisi got the idea for his organisation and its name. He is an obvious point of contact but so far there has been no reason to suspect that he is in fact linked up with the Middle East organisation.

Annexure B to 119: despatch from Sir A Richards to HM ambassador, Cairo, 3 Oct 1947

I have the honour to refer to your despatch of the 26th of July on the subject of the University of Al Ashar's wish to send two ulema to Nigeria to give religious instruction to the Moslem population and to say that I am reluctant to accede to the request submitted by the Egyptian Minister of Foreign Affairs in this regard without further information as to the proposed Mission. As you will be aware, the political situation in Nigeria is at present most delicate, and there is danger that Government's far-reaching plans for Development of the Territory may be prejudiced, and in part disrupted, by irresposible demands for immediate political autonomy. It is, therefore, of first importance that attempts to rally the support of the constructive elements of the community for sound and progressive measures should not be impaired by extremist anti-British propaganda.

2.   As a result of a report submitted by the Lecturer in Arabic Studies at the Kano School of Higher Arabic Studies who visited Egypt in December last year it was decided that no public assistance could be given to Nigerian students to go to Al Azhar University where, so this offer stated, the prevailing atmosphere of crude nationalism was so inimical to study that many courses had only a nominal value. An extreme case quoted to him was a term reduced to ten working days only by students' strikes and disturbances of a similar nature.

3.   I am most anxious that the projected Mission should not be used as a cloak for the spread of anti-British propaganda and before giving a final decision on this subject, I should be glad to know the names of the two ulema and to receive such information as you may be able to furnish regarding them and their proposed activities, and particularly as to the areas in which it is intended these should be conducted. I should also welcome an expression of Your Excellency's views on Al Azhar University and as to the extent to which its official representatives might abuse their mission by indulging in propaganda of the type referred to.

Minute on 119

The Nigerian Government is not anxious to encourage any tendency to unite Moslems of the Northern Provinces in a way that might prejudice the unity of Nigeria as a whole. In consequence the line proposed in (9) is consistent with previous trends and I think we can endorse it as in draft now.

Mr. Bourn, Mr. Barton may like to see after issue.

M.P.
29.9.50

120   CO 537/5787, no 74   12 Oct 1950

[Constitutional review]: CO note of a meeting with Sir J Macpherson on repercussions on the Nigerian civil service, the position of the Secretariats and European interests

Repercussions on the Colonial Service in Nigeria
The following points were made in discussion:—

(a) Changes in West Africa made necessary by the advance towards self-government would clearly affect the character of the unified Colonial Service and their effect would need to be closely watched.

(b) The outcry in the Gold Coast about appointments to the posts of Secretaries to the new Ministries had brought to the fore an issue that was of concern to Nigeria also. The Secretary of State, as the recruiting agency and responsible for promotions, was vitally concerned in the issues raised by increasing Africanization of the Service. The principle of promotion on merit had to be upheld.

(c) It would probably be necessary in West Africa to dispense with the Secretary of State's control of promotions below certain superscale posts, except when the Governor specifically asked for outside recruitment (which would be either from inside the Colonial Service or without). At present posts with emoluments below £600 a year could be filled locally. This lower limit of £600 might be raised to a more appropriate level or alternatively there might be a list of posts, promotion or recruitment to which needed the Secretary of State's approval.

(d) The progress of Nigerianization was of great interest to local politicians. In accepting the Report of the Commission on the subject in 1948, the Nigerian Government had agreed to the recommendation that 'no non-Nigerian should be recruited for any Government post except when no suitable and qualified Nigerian is available' and the position of the local African had in consequence to be constantly borne in mind.

(e) There were very few Africans at present in high posts in Nigeria who could be considered for promotion to such posts as Heads or Deputy Heads of Departments. In this respect Dr. Manuwa of the Medical Department was a valuable exception.

(f) It was possible that the West African territories would become more and more self-contained for staff as progress towards self-government went on. For the present, however, outside recruitment, especially for such posts as qualified Veterinary Officers and Agricultural Officers, was likely to be needed for some time, though African recruitment of lawyers and doctors should increase. It was, however, most valuable for Nigeria to have people with experience of other territories transferred on promotion.

It was agreed that

> C.S.D. should consider changes likely to be necessary in Part I of Colonial Regulations, the relevant portion on Appointments being Section A of Chapter III.

Position of the Secretariats under the new constitution
The following points were made:—

(a) The Secretary of State had accepted the Nigerian Government's views on the position and functions of Ministers. Colonial Office misgivings were based not on political doubts so much as on doubts about the mechanics of the system. It was recognised too that the system proposed for the Gold Coast went much further than that envisaged for Nigeria.

(b) The views of the Nigerian Government had been set out in Mr. Foot's letter (see pages 8–10 of the letter, dated 22nd September).[1] The main job of the Secretariats would be to service the councils. The Ministers mainly affected by the way in which the Secretariat at the centre was organized would be those dealing with subjects purely central in character. If the proposed system was to be criticised, some alternative should be put forward.

---

[1] See 118.

(c) The official view in the office was that the Jamaican experiment had not been a successful one. The system proposed for Nigeria might encourage friction between African and European Ministers since the feeling might arise that the influence of European Ministers through the Secretariat was paramount. The Minister should feel he had a close and formal link with the Secretariat rather than one through a secretary of D.O. status, otherwise he would not feel sufficiently linked with policy in the field over which his post extended.

(d) The alternative seemed to be for the Principal Assistant Secretary in the relevant branch of the Secretariat to service the Minister direct. Much necessary advice on the difficulties of the new job would have to come from someone high up in the Secretariat rather than from within a Department. Hence it seemed wrong to retain the existing Secretariat arrangements.

(e) It was recognised that these internal arrangements were a matter for the Nigerian Government, but it was felt that the views of the Colonial Office should be made known.

It was agreed that

> the views of the office on this matter should be sent to the Chief Secretary for the consideration of the Nigerian Government.

European interests
It was pointed out that:—

(a) Special interests would quite likely be represented in each of the Regional Legislatures by three members.

(b) The Ceylon clause on non-discrimination was not suitable for Nigeria but if an appropriate one could be drafted the Nigerian Government would consider it.

(c) The Secretary of State was committed to holding further talks with the European firms in London.

It was agreed that

> approval should be sought for a meeting in the near future between Sir J Macpherson and Mr. Gorsuch on the one hand and the European firms on the other.

121   CO 537/5787, no 78   20 Oct 1950
[Constitutional review]: letter from H M Foot to A B Cohen on the selection of ministers under the new constitution

In my letter of the 14th of October I promised to write to you separately about the question of the selection of Ministers.

We well appreciate the force of the arguments for the system decided upon in the Gold Coast but it may be as well if I restate the arguments for the alternative system proposed by the Drafting Committee, unanimously approved by the Ibadan Conference and accepted by the Legislative Council. Here are the main arguments for the system of election by the Legislative bodies.

(1) The proposal for election of Ministers was strongly supported, indeed it was regarded by some of the Nigerian members as vital, when the discussions took place in the Drafting Committee.

(2) It will be a pity, when H.M.G. has accepted nearly all the main recommendations coming from Nigeria, if on this point (which will, I am sure, be regarded as important in Nigeria) disagreement is unavoidable; such disagreement would provide ammunition for those who are opposed to orderly constitutional advance.

(3) Anything which savours of nomination is disliked by Nigerian politicians: this dislike is not altogether reasonable but it is strongly felt.

(4) I can see no difficulty in changing at some future date from the elected system to a system such as that practised in the Sudan or Barbados whereby selection of Ministers is undertaken in consultation with an elected Leader of the Legislature or with the leader of the majority party: indeed I think that the first would be a natural and logical development in due course but we all agree that we don't want an elected Leader of the Legislature at this stage, nor do we see national parties emerging for a long time to come, if ever, in Nigeria.

(5) As you say, the Governor under the new constitution will of course remain ultimately responsible for the administration of the country but I am not quite sure about the analogy between the Governor or the Chief Secretary and a Prime Minister. The Prime Minister who chooses his Cabinet (without consultation with the House of Commons) by virtue of the strength of his following in the House of Commons is in a quite different position from the Governor or Chief Secretary as regards selection of ministers.

(6) We suggest that since Nigeria is to operate a constitution on a federal basis (which is quite different from that proposed in the Gold Coast) it should be possible to justify a different practice here from that which the Secretary of State has decided upon in the Gold Coast.[1]

(7) As far as Colonial precedents are concerned is it not reasonable to look not only to the Gold Coast but also to the advanced constitutional systems in operation in Jamaica and Trinidad?

(8) It is argued that the system of election would be more likely to lead to useless Ministers being appointed, but since the approval of the Legislatures is to be required the Legislatures will be in a position to insist on their nominees by turning down the Governor's or Lieutenant Governor's lists.

(9) The Governor or Lieutenant-Governor would be placed in a most embarrassing position if his list were rejected.

(10) If the original list were rejected the Governor or Lieutenant Governor would have to preside over a Council in which some, or even all, members had reached the Council in spite of the Governor's wish to have a different membership, and this would militate against the mutual confidence between the Governor and Lieutenant Governors and their Councils which is so necessary.

(11) Consultation with all unofficial members of the Legislatures before preparation of the Governor's and Lieutenant Governor's lists would be well nigh impossible when Regional Houses (including Houses of Chiefs) are to have about

---

[1] Cohen aded in the margin, 'No! I don't see this'.

112 members in the North, 130 in the West, and about 80 in the East and when in the Central Legislature there will be 68 members from the North and 34 each from the East and West.

(12) Consultation with some unofficial members and not with all might well lead to suspicion and complaint.

(13) The Legislatures are to have the power to remove members of the Councils by vote and it seems to us undesirable to allow the Legislatures to remove a Governor's nominee.

(14) There must be some Ministers who are of poor calibre and we regard that as an argument for leaving selection to the Legislatures, rather than the Governor being held responsible for their appointment.

There is a further complication arising from the semi-federal nature of our constitution. From the elected members of Regional Houses there have to be found

(a) Regional Ministers
(b) Members of the House of Representatives, and
(c) Central Ministers.

If the Lieutenant Governors were to make their pick of the best men for Regional Executive Councils those men would be ruled out from consideration as possible members of the Council of Ministers (since it is inconceivable that a man should be both a Regional and a Central Minister). We cannot picture that the Lieutenant Governor would be able to settle with the Governor which members of the Regional House should be earmarked for Regional Ministries and which for Central Ministries, since the decision on which members of Regional Houses go up to the House of Representatives is one solely for Regional Houses. The only satisfactory way in which I can see the complicated processes of selection taking place is this: Members of Regional Houses would themselves get together and decide which of their number should be elected to Regional Executive Councils. These would probably not be elected to sit in the House of Representatives at all in view of their heavy obligations in the Regions. At the same time members of Regional Houses by consultation amongst themselves would decide which of their number were best fitted to go to the Council of Ministers and these would of course be included in the Regional representatives elected to sit in the House of Representatives. We do not suggest that this practice need be laid down in the constitutional instruments (as far as they are concerned it would be sufficient to provide, as we propose, that Regional Ministers should be elected by Regional Houses and Central Ministers elected by the Regional blocs in the House of Representatives). But I can see no other way in practice whereby the decision as to who should go to Regional Executive Councils and who should be ear-marked for the Council of Ministers could be satisfactorily worked out.

In general terms the case is this. We are to work a constitution very different from that proposed for the Gold Coast. The peculiarities of our semi-federal arrangement, coupled with the fact that the Regional Houses are to elect the members of the House of Representatives and the size of the unofficial membership of the Legislatures, make it difficult or impossible to apply the Gold Coast system here. In any event we see disadvantages in Nigerian circumstances in the Governor and Lieutenant Governor preparing lists of ministers which could be rejected by the Legislatures and we see no difficulty later on in a transition from the system we propose to a system whereby Ministers would be appointed on the recommendation of elected Leaders of the Legislatures.

I am sorry to have written at such length. I was tempted to write even more to give detailed examples of the difficulties in which any system other than that we propose would, I believe, cause. I hope that what I have written will at least indicate that we have not reached our opinion without a lot of careful thought.

122   CO 537/5789, no 29   31 Oct 1950
[Constitutional review]: CO note of a meeting to discuss representations made by commercial firms on the constitutional proposals

[It had been agreed by the Legislative Council in Sept that the House of Representatives to be established under the new constitution should have six seats reserved for special interests; this was compared to the three seats in the Legislative Council allocated under the Richards constitution. However, commercial firms pushed also for representation in the new regional houses of assembly to be set up under the revised constitution, as they had had in the regional councils established by Richards. In the event it was agreed that three seats in each House of Assembly would be reserved for special interests. Present at the meeting on 31 Oct, in addition to Gorsuch, Macpherson and Vile of the CO, were A R I Mellor (UAC and Joint West Africa committee), F Samuel (UAC), Sir F Whyte (Bata Shoe Co.), H J Rawlings (John Holt & Co. Ltd.), N Edwards (Cadbury Bros. Ltd.), C Leach (Nigerian Chamber of Mines), J D Latham (Nigerian Hardwood Co. Ltd) R H Bugler (Shell Co. of West Africa Ltd.), L Olorenshaw (Taylor Woodrow Ltd.) and E Hallett (UAC).]

Mr. Gorsuch referred to the meeting which the representatives of the European interests had had with the Secretary of State on the 27th June[1] and explained that the object of the present meeting was to enable the representatives to hear from the Governor an account of developments which had taken place in Nigeria since that date and to discuss with him the points previously raised which were still outstanding. He added that the representatives would remain at liberty to ask for a further discussion with the Secretary of State if they so desired.

Sir John Macpherson referred to the recommendation recently agreed upon by the Legislative Council that there should be six members nominated by the Governor to represent interests which in his opinion were not otherwise adequately represented. He said that the total number in the proposed single Chamber Legislature, namely 148 members, was large; this latter figure had been based on the idea of divisional representation in the Southern Provinces. He said that there had been some criticism in Nigeria on the proposal to grant six seats on the ground that it might give the European officials and nominated members together a balance of power in the Central Legislature. It was, however, expected that the nominated members would observe the same practice as in the past in abstaining from voting on purely African matters. The Governor emphasised that the representatives of the special interests in addition to their knowledge and experience must also have the time to take a full part in the work of the Legislature.

On the question of representation in the Regional Houses, the Governor said that no decision had yet been reached. There had been informal talks with members of the Regional Legislatures and it would be considered by the Regional Houses at their

---

[1] See 114 and 120.

meetings in December. He himself appreciated the force of the argument that in view of the extent of the devolution to regions which was contemplated under the new Constitution, representation of the commercial interests in the Regional Houses was desirable.

Mr. Mellor said that the commercial interests while anxious to be fully co-operative over the new Constitution, wished to be sure that any representations which they might have to make were put forward at the appropriate stage and before final decisions were taken. Sir John Macpherson said that the review in Nigeria had proceeded by close collaboration at all stages between officials and unofficials and the recommendations which had been put forward had emerged from this process of collaboration. He hoped that on the matter of representation in the Regional Houses the commercial interests would notify their views to the Nigerian Government as soon as possible while the matter was still in the stage of consideration in Nigeria. He would be glad also to have personally from them any views they might have on this question of special members.

Mr. Gorsuch said that in his published despatch of the 15th July[2] the Secretary of State had announced the approval of His Majesty's Government in general terms of the recommendations which had emanated from Nigeria, subject to a satisfactory settlement of the question of the composition of the Central Legislature, and to further consideration of outstanding points of detail. An agreed recommendation on the composition of the Central Legislature had now been received from Nigeria to the effect that there should be a Single Chamber Legislature and that the representation of the Northern Region should be equal to that of the other two regions combined. Joined to this was the recommendation that there should be six representatives of special interests in the Legislature. There would probably be in the near future an announcement that H.M. Government accepted the two major recommendations regarding the composition of the Central Legislature, but this would not include any reference to the number of members for special interests recommended and if the firms wished to make further representations on this point it was now open to them to do so. As regards representation in the Regional Legislatures, no recommendation has yet been received from Nigeria and until it had been received there was no question of the Secretary of State taking any decision. When such recommendation was received it would be communicated to the representatives of the commercial interests and they would have effective opportunity of making representations to the Secretary of State if they wished before the final decision was taken.

The question was raised whether in the event of there being nominated members in the Regional Legislatures and one of those nominated members being elected by the Regional House to represent it in the Central Legislature, he would count as one of the six special representatives in the Central Legislature. No final view was expressed on this point, but it was generally considered reasonable that he should be regarded solely as a representative of the region.

After discussion the firms agreed to an expression of opinion that six members were adequate in the Central Legislature. It was understood that the Governor was at liberty to nominate persons other than Europeans to these seats but what the Governor had in mind was primarily the nomination of European business men who would be able to bring to the debate their expert knowledge of commercial and mining affairs.

[2] See 116.

The meeting then discussed the question of writing a non-discrimination clause into the Constitution. Sir John Macpherson said that he felt that the Ceylon clause was not suitable for Nigeria owing to its emphasis on religion and that the chapter in the Government of India Act 1945 was also inappropriate and too long. This was generally agreed and it was further agreed that the clause should be wide, general and short. The representatives of the firms said that they attached much importance to such a clause appearing in the Constitution and asked for the opportunity of being consulted upon it before the final decision was reached.

The question of an Economic Advisory Committee was briefly discussed. It was suggested that such a Committee might give useful support and protection to Ministers subject to outside pressures. The Governor said that he was not at present clear about the composition and functions of the Committee which the representatives of the firms had in mind and it was agreed that they should let him have their views in greater detail on these points. It was agreed that any such Committee would be outside the Constitution and that its value would lie in the opportunity which it would give to experts in economic affairs to partake in an advisory service, the benefit of whose advice would at all times be available to the Government.

Mr. Mellor on behalf of the commercial interests expressed their appreciation of the opportunity which had been given them to discuss these matters with the Governor.

123   CO 537/5787, no 85   14 Nov 1950
[Constitutional review]: letter from A B Cohen to H M Foot on the functions of ministers under the proposed new constitution

In my letter of the 10th October about the Constitution I said that we should be writing again on the subject of the functions of Ministers, as we had considerable doubt about the proposal to retain the present Central Secretariat largely in its present form. We have now had the opportunity of further discussion with the Governor on this point, and as our doubts are still not resolved I think it best that I should put them to you in some detail.

2.   Perhaps I might clear the ground at the start by saying that in the case of Central Ministers for regional subjects, and in the case of Regional Ministers, we agree that there should be no need for the system of Permanent Secretaries; and what follows in this letter applies only to the Central Ministers for central subjects. It has been agreed that the functions of a Minister are:—

(a) initiation of discussion of policy in the Council;
(b) introducing into the House and answering therein all business affecting his subject or subjects;
(c) ensuring in co-operation with the executive Head of the Department concerned that the decisions of the Council, as they affect his subject, are carried out.

On pages 8 and 9 of your secret and personal letter of the 22nd September,[1] you have emphasised that the principal function of a Minister is to participate in taking

---

[1] See 118.

decisions on policy in the Council of Ministers as a whole, rather than to fulfil ministerial functions as we understand them in this country in the direction of his department or group of departments. On this assumption you go on to explain that Secretariat files would not normally be circulated to Ministers, but that they would be briefed by the branch of the Secretariat concerned as may be necessary for carrying out their functions under (a) (b) and (c) above. You also emphasised that decisions of the Councils must be communicated to Departments by Secretariats and not by Ministers.

3.   We find it very difficult to see how this could be expected to work smoothly in practice for very long. Under the distribution of subjects which you have suggested in your letter of the 22nd September, four of the six Ministers for central subjects would be responsible for a group of departments and not, as in the case of the other two, for a single department. Each of these four would, therefore, be served not by a single officer or even branch of the Secretariat but by several officers or branches, and for purposes of co-ordination he would have a Secretary who by reason of his seniority could be in fact little more than a Private Secretary. We can see that as regards function (a) above, the Minister should normally be able, with the aid of briefing from the Secretariat and discussion with his Heads of Department, to initiate and carry on in the Council of Ministers discussion on policy matters relating to his subjects. He should also be able under function (b) to deal in the House with subjects which have previously reached Council of Ministers' level. But there are a multiplicity of matters in the day to day administration of the Government which, though important, do not reach the level of high policy which would require discussion in the Council of Ministers, and must in fact be disposed of without reference to that Council unless it is to be hopelessly clogged with work. It is in this respect that we see difficulties arising and a conflict of functions developing. Such matters are not all within the competence of the Heads of Branches of the Secretariat; they may under the present organisation need reference to the Chief Secretary or even to the Governor. Under the new dispensation to whom is this reference to be made? Is it to be to the Minister and, if necessary, through him to the Governor; or is it to be along present channels in the Secretariat to the Chief Secretary or Financial Secretary as the case may be? And if it is to be one of the latter, in what way is the Minister to be kept in touch if the matter is decided without reference to the Council of Ministers? He may well have to deal with such a subject in the House or to answer questions on it. He is not going to be in an easy position if the matter has been settled round and over him, nor is he likely to take kindly to discussing and answering questions on subjects in the discussion of which he has not participated and the decision on which has been taken without consulting him.

4.   Something of the same difficulty seems to us to arise on what I may perhaps call the downward traffic of business under function (c). The Minister will have participated in the policy decision in the Council of Ministers, but according to your plan the policy decision is communicated by the Secretariat direct to the Department concerned and not by the Minister (or apparently on his authority). It is not going to be easy for him to ensure that the policy decision is in fact being put into execution. If he neither conveys the decision himself nor has access to Secretariat files in which progress will presumably be recorded, in the absence of these records he will be in the position of having either to depend on his memory or to confine his actions under function (c) to cases in which the Secretariat thinks fit to prompt him into action.

5.   The combined effect of all these considerations seems to us to be that it is unlikely that the system of ministerial responsibility, even in the modified form which you have in mind, will run harmoniously in practice side by side with the present centralised Secretariat hierarchy; or that Ministers themselves will be content to operate under these conditions for very long. It seems to us that the restriction which you wish to impose on the activities of Ministers individually, as opposed to Ministers in Council, could be effectively maintained even after the Secretariat was reorganised into a system of Permanent Secretaries, bearing in mind that the three most important portfolios, whose functions extend over the activities of all Departments of the Government, remain in official hands. We cannot help feeling on the other hand, that the continued existence of the Central Secretariat in its present form will be irksome to Ministers from the outset, and that you will before long be forced into reorganisation with Permanent Secretaries in the case of Central Ministries for Central Subjects.

6.   I have gone into this rather fully because it is our unanimous feeling at the official level here, from Lloyd downwards, that the system which you have in mind is not likely to endure for long, and that you would be well advised to consider very carefully before final conclusions are reached whether it would not be better to reorganise the Secretariat, to provide Permanent Secretaries for the Ministers for central subjects, at the inception of the new Constitution.

124   CO 537/5787, no 88   20 Nov 1950
[Constitutional review]: letter (reply) from H M Foot to A B Cohen on the functions of ministers under the proposed new constitution

Thank you for your letter No. 30453 of the 14th of November about the functions of Ministers under our new constitution.[1] I notice that in this letter you deal only with Central Ministers and their relation with the Central Secretariat, but the same considerations apply to Regional Ministers and Regional Secretariats and I should like to get the further views of Chief Commissioners on the most important points which you raise. This I shall do, but as I am just off to the Cameroons for ten days I am making this reply to your letter at once and I shall write again when Chief Commissioners' comments come in.

I wish that we could discuss the issues which your letter raises rather than write about them for I believe that they are of fundamental importance and it is difficult to deal with them in correspondence without writing at great length. If, as I now expect, I get home in January or February next I look forward to a full discussion with you then.

I don't think that it will be irrelevant to go back to first principles. The path of Colonial constitutional advance is already well-trodden and the various stages are now fairly well accepted. First the Legislatures are made more representative, then elected rather than nominated members are admitted to Executive Councils and then gradually the elected members are given duties and powers in regard to departments or subjects in order to train them to become Ministers in the sense

---

[1] See 123.

understood in Great Britain. I believe that there will be the greatest danger, particularly in West African conditions, if an attempt is made to telescope these stages. The road to a full ministerial system must in my opinion lie through the experience in joint responsibility gained in Council. We are all confident here that good decisions can and will come from Councils with Nigerian majorities. But we definitely have not yet got enough individual Nigerians with the experience and integrity to exercise the very wide measure of administrative authority which a Minister exercises in England. I am convinced that if at one jump we try to create a system under which Nigerian Ministers exercise such responsibility we shall fail, and the results of all the good work which has been done and is being done will be brought down. The purpose must surely be to move gradually towards a full Ministerial system through a conciliar system. In the first stage the emphasis should be on the importance and power of the Councils and not on the importance and power of the individual Ministers. Never before, as far as I know, has an attempt been made in a Colonial territory to give full Ministerial powers at one jump and I am quite certain that it would lead to disaster if we attempted it here.

I believe that this view is generally acceptable to responsible Nigerian opinion. When I put the direct question to the Nigerians on the Constitutional Drafting Committee whether they wanted decisions on policy to be taken in the Councils or by individual Ministers they all unhesitatingly replied that they wanted the Councils to decide policy. I believe that the same answer would be given by any thinking group of Nigerians.

You may think that the Ministers who emerge under our new constitution will object to our system. That is a danger, but I feel sure that it can be averted. We should not of course be negative and restrictive in defining their duties: rather we should emphasize that their duties are not restricted to their subjects but that their main and overriding duty is to take part as equal members in discussion of *all* questions of policy which come before the Councils.

In thinking about these matters I have tried not to be unduly influenced by my experience in Jamaica but there, with full Colonial Office approval, we set our faces against giving Ministers wide executive responsibilities in the early stages. We took the line that they must first learn to exercise joint responsibility in the Council. If we had not done so I believe that constitutional advance would have completely broken down in Jamaica long ago—and as far as political experience is concerned the West Indies are far ahead of West Africa.

Here the functions of Ministers have been clearly defined in the recommendations of the Ibadan Conference and those recommendations have been accepted by the Secretary of State, so you may say that this discussion of general principle is unnecessary. I do think, however, that it is vital to remember what we are attempting at this stage. We are attempting to work a system whereby policy is decided in a Council of Ministers at the centre and Executive Councils in the Regions, with Central and Regional Ministers exercising functions in the Councils and Legislatures and also exercising functions in regard to the carrying out of the policy decided in the Councils. Under the agreed definition of Ministers' powers Ministers are not to make or decide policy except as members of the Councils, and their executive function is limited to ensuring that the Council's decisions or policy are carried out. That is the system we propose to carry out and the system naturally has the most direct and important bearing on Government organisation.

In considering what changes in Government organisation are necessary it is surely wise to study what has been done in other territories in which advanced constitutions are operated. We didn't alter the Secretariat organisation in Jamaica when the 1944 constitution was introduced nor, I believe, was the Secretariat organisation in the Sudan altered when they introduced their new constitution a year or two ago. The fact that we are proposing to work a conciliar system, rather than a ministerial system on the U.K. model, makes it essential, we think, that the existing Secretariats should be maintained for the present. The strain which is to be imposed on the official machine by all the changes to be made in the next few years, including particularly the huge task of region-alisation, is very great and I think that it would be the gravest mistake to reorganise the whole of our Secretariat system just when that increased strain is coming.

I think that you may over-estimate the number of decisions which will have to be taken in the Secretariats under the new system (other than on the subjects which are the responsibility of the official members of the Councils). Policy decisions will be taken in the Councils and on every-day departmental matters there need and should not be many questions which cannot be settled by a Head of the Department in consultation with his Minister. Our present Central Secretariat is made up of four main branches. The Political (and security) branch and the Finance branch must be maintained for they will have more rather than less to do in future. The Civil Service Commission will presumably become the servant of the new Public Service Commission. That leaves only the Development branch and this branch is mainly occupied not with giving day to day decisions on departmental affairs but in dealing with policy matters which will in any event have to go to the Council of Ministers. When once policy has been decided there will be no need for reference from the Departments to the Secretariat: the carrying out of the agreed policy will be a matter for the Minister and the Head of the Department.

If, as I say, the Political (and security) branch of the Secretariat and the Finance branch must in any event be maintained (the Civil Service Commission being also retained as a separate entity) you will appreciate what a great increase in headquarters staff would be required if new Ministries were to be created for all the Central Ministers. The existing Development branch could not be entirely disbanded and we should there-fore have to find most of the new under-secretaries and the staff to work under them from outside our present Secretariat. We are already alarmed at the increased costs which the new Councils and Legislatures will involve. Regionalisation of the depart-ments will also lead to increased costs (e.g. in increased housing and office accom-modation at Regional headquarters) and, although our objection to the immediate creation of new Ministries is not mainly financial, we are naturally most anxious to avoid still greater additional expenditure arising from the constitutional changes.

I also think that you may under-estimate the value of the close association which should exist between Ministers and Heads of Departments dealing with their subjects. I expect Ministers to be in the closest contact with Heads of Departments and to get most of their briefing direct from them. The Minister would get his information of progress and development in Departmental work much better from them than from Secretariat files.

As to communication of decisions of the Councils to the Departments I really don't see that there need be any objection to this being done by Secretariats. The decisions are those of the Council and delay and possibly confusion might arise if communication of these decisions to Departments were left to Ministers.

The system I advocate worked perfectly well in Jamaica. We intended to create at a second stage a system of permanent under-secretaries in the Secretariat whose subjects would correspond to those of Ministers (without setting up separate Ministries) and it may be that by now they have made some progress in that direction but I assure you from my own practical experience that we should have come to grief if we had attempted to split the Secretariat as they are doing in the Gold Coast when we introduced the 1944 Jamaica constitution.

I well appreciate that a system of official undersecretaries must be contemplated in the future but that should come at a subsequent stage and not at the stage we intend to operate at first which, as I have emphasized, is based on the responsibility of the Councils rather than individual Ministers deciding policy.

You say that a Minister under the system we propose might feel that matters were being settled 'round and over him.' I don't think that any such situation need arise. The Ministers will know that policy decisions are taken in the Councils of which they are members. They will have their work cut out to keep abreast of the many and varied subjects with which the Councils have to deal. They will be in close and constant contact with Heads of Departments dealing with their subjects. They will have to familiarise themselves with a wide range of departmental problems, and, quite apart from their duties in the Councils and the Legislatures (the Councils will meet frequently), they will have to work out plans with Heads of Departments for carrying out approved policy, tour and inspect departmental work and institutions, receive deputations and sit on various committees. I think that they will have quite as much to do as they can manage and I do not think that they would wish to spend a lot of their time working on files in a Ministry.

All my instinct and experience leads me to believe that in Government machinery as in political development we should not destroy what we know can work, but that rather we should proceed gradually, changes in Government organisation keeping pace step by step with constitutional advance. The splitting of Secretariats and setting up of separate Ministries should, I feel convinced, not be attempted now.

I have made several references to experience in Jamaica and I hope that you won't therefore think that the proposals I have made are some fad of my own. Marshall and Pleass and all the Regional representatives I have already consulted are of the same opinion as I am.

125   CO 537/5787, no 86A   24–27 Nov 1950
[Constitutional review]: minutes by A B Cohen and Sir T Lloyd on a draft letter to H M Foot concerning the selection of ministers under the new constitution

Sir T Lloyd
A letter to the Acting Governor of Nigeria is required in reply to his letter of the 20th October (78),[1] in which he puts forward the arguments as he sees them in favour of sticking to the proposal of the General Conference at Ibadan that regional and central Ministers should be elected by the respective Legislatures. Sir J Macpherson

---

[1] See 121.

has not yet taken a definite view on this matter himself. He has told us that Mr. Foot's views on this are primarily his personal views and it is clear that he (Sir J Macpherson), although he has not made up his mind, sees a great deal of force in our arguments in favour of the appointment of of Ministers by the Governor and Lieutenant Governor in consultation with members of the Legislature.

The Secretary of State has already in paragraph 8 of his published despatch of the 15th July[2] set out the case for the appointment of Ministers not by election but by consultation between the Governor and the Lieutenant Governor and the Legislatures, and has argued in favour of giving the Governor and Lieutenant Governor a definite say in this process. We had been hoping that the Nigerian Government would now work out a procedure to give effect to the Secretary of State's decision, but this has not so far been done because of the doubts expressed in Mr. Foot's letter. I do not propose in this minute to summarise the arguments against Mr. Foot's view. The two most important ones are:—

(1) Since the Governor (and Lieutenant Governors in the Regions) will be ultimately responsible for the administration, it is wrong that they should have no say in the selection of Ministers. This seems to us to be of great importance as a matter of principle.

(2) The adoption of election in Nigeria would be gravely embarrassing to the Gold Coast, where we have insisted that the Governor should have a say in the appointment of Ministers. As Sir C Arden-Clarke says in his letter of the 25th October (79), it was only after the most careful consideration that the conclusion was reached that election of Ministers by the Legislature should be ruled out.[3] There is to my mind no real force in Mr. Foot's argument in paragraph 6 of (78) that the semi-federal character of the Nigerian constitution would justify a different practice in this respect from the Gold Coast. My own view is that the time has come to make it clear to Mr. Foot that we are not prepared to accept his arguments in favour of the election of Ministers. This point is covered in paragraph 10 of Mr. Gorsuch's draft which, while not conveying an absolutely final decision, states that the Secretary of State would find it most difficult to depart from the view which he has already expressed.

I submit for approval Mr. Gorsuch's draft, which seems to me an admirable statement of our case.

A.B.C.
24.11.50

S. of S.
This draft maintains the line taken, with your approval, in para 8 of no 52.[4]

It is important to do that both on merits and because the election of ministers in Nigeria would be most embarrassing to the Gold Coast.

This draft does not convey a decision but (see para 10) presses Mr Foot to accept our view.[5]

T.K.L.
27.11.50

---

[2] See 116.
[3] For the handling of this issue in the Gold Coast, cf BDEEP series B, vol 1, R Rathbone, ed, *Ghana*, part I, 60 and 64. For the organisation of ministries in the Gold Coast, cf, *ibid*, 82.
[4] See 116.   [5] For the final version see 126.

126   CO 537/5787, no 87   28 Nov 1950

[Constitutional review]: letter from A B Cohen to H M Foot on the selection of ministers under the new constitution

We have been giving very careful consideration to the arguments set out in your letter of the 20th October on the subject of the selection of Ministers.[1] I need hardly say at the outset that we fully share your anxiety to avoid disagreement on this important subject, with the consequences which it might have, especially when, as you say, it has been found easy to achieve agreement on nearly all the main recommendations. But apart from any views which we may hold on the principle which is at stake, we have to bear in mind the warning which Arden-Clarke has given us in his letter of the 25th October, of repercussions in the Gold Coast. I must, therefore, necessarily write at some length to you.

It will help to define the issues more clearly if I say, first of all, that in the light of the arguments which you have adduced there is one change which we should like to suggest to you in the procedure for the selection of Ministers which was put forward for consideration in paragraph 7 of my letter of the 10th October.[2] We are impressed by the passage on pages 4 and 5 of your letter which deals with the task that confronts the Regional House when it has been constituted and assembles for the first time. As you say, there will have to be found from the Regional House (a) the Regional Ministers, (b) the bloc which will represent the region in the Central Legislature and (c) the four Central Ministers. It seems to us that there are strong arguments in favour of all three things being done as one process. It may well be argued that the questions who should be the Ministers in the region and who should be the Regional Ministers at the centre should be for decision not only at the same time but by the region itself. It might well be, for instance, that a man who was well suited to be a Central Minister could not undertake the task, although he might find it possible to accept a regional ministry; and subject always to the Governor's concurrence, it seems to be for the region to dispose of its available resources in the way in which it thinks best. If the Ministers for the centre are selected by an authority who is not essentially of the region, there may grow up a tendency (which will increase with the degree of devolution to the region) to keep the best men in the region, and this may apply both to Ministers and to representatives.

I should like, therefore, to modify the proposals made in my letter of the 10th October to the extent of substituting the suggestion that it should be laid down in the constitution that Regional Ministers will be selected by the Lieutenant-Governor in consultation with the Regional House, and that the four Central Ministers from the region should be selected by the Governor on the recommendation of the Lieutenant-Governor after consultation with the Regional House. The procedure would then be that there would be consultation between the Lieutenant-Governor and the Regional House in which the choice of both the Regional Ministers and the four Central Ministers would be made; the Lieutenant-Governor would then consult the Governor about the latter and obtain his concurrence; and the appointment of the four Central Ministers would then be confirmed by resolution *in the Regional House*. It seems to us on further consideration that this is a better arrangement than

---

[1] See 121.   [2] Not printed.

hiving off the bloc which is to go to the Central Legislature from the Regional House, and leaving the Governor thereafter to deal with that bloc in regard to the selection of Central Ministers.

It may be argued that if the selection of the Central Ministers were entrusted to the Regional House to this extent it might cause those Ministers to go to the centre with a feeling that they had a purely regional mandate in their pocket; and that this would militate against the feeling of unity at the centre which you are so anxious to create. There is, we feel, no doubt that in the Council of Ministers the individual Minister would feel himself under an obligation to speak for and protect his own regional interests, but this seems natural and unavoidable whatever the method may be of choosing him. On the other hand the tendency would be strongly corrected by the very nature of his work at the centre. He would have, both in the Council of Ministers and in the Legislature, to speak for and answer questions on subjects referring to all parts of Nigeria, on some of which his own region might be concerned little if at all; for instance, a Minister from the west might have to debate and answer questions on postal and telegraphic communications in the north or east, and so on. The effect of this would be to instill into Ministers a 'Nigerian' habit of thought; and indeed it is the Nigerian-wide nature of their responsibilities which provides the justification for the arrangement whereby a Central Minister whose appointment derives from the region or the regional bloc is removable by a vote of the whole Central Legislature.

I now come to the main point at issue between us, i.e. whether Ministers should be elected or whether they should be selected. Before commenting, in the light of the change in our proposals explained above, on the arguments in favour of the former course set out in your letter, I should like to restate certain principles which seem to us to be basic to the argument. However he may be chosen, a Minister, whether in the region or at the centre, must inevitably have a dual responsibility; he must be responsible to the Lieutenant-Governor or Governor so long as the latter retains the ultimate responsibility for the administration, and at the same time he is responsible to the Legislature. That being so, is it not desirable that both parties should bear a share of the responsibility for choosing him? If the Minister looks solely to his Legislature for appointment, does it not materially weaken the authority of the Governor or Lieutenant-Governor to enforce responsibility on him? Secondly, we ought to bear in mind the criteria which should govern the selection of a Minister. He should have ability and integrity; he should be able to work as a member of a team (we note how much you place the emphasis on the Minister functioning as one of a circle of counsellors rather than as the holder of a particular portfolio); and he should be likely to be acceptable both to the region and, if he is a Central Minister, to the Central House. One question which I think we must ask ourselves is whether the combination of these criteria is more likely to be achieved by a process of selection, by consultation or by the hazards of an election. May there not be men who by virtue of their qualities would command the confidence both of the Governor or the Lieutenant-Governor and of the House, but who might fail to obtain election to ministerial rank because they lacked the ephemeral quality of popular appeal? Thirdly, if a Minister has obtained his position by election, might not difficulties arise if the Governor or Lieutenant-Governor found it necessary to move for his demotion? In a case where the Minister had fallen short in his observance of the prescribed rules of conduct (which would have been laid down by the Governor) or was guilty of disloyalty in regard to collective responsibility, it would in all probability be easier to secure assent to his speedy and discreet removal if the responsibility for his original appointment had been shared and had not lain entirely on one side. On the other hand, if the Minister in question had been elected, the regional bloc might feel it incumbent on them to justify him and oppose his removal.

I now come to the detailed arguments in your letter. We appreciate the point in paragraph 3 that nomination is disliked by Nigerian politicians, but we doubt whether a system which begins with consultation and culminates in an affirmative resolution by the House could be justly regarded as coming under that description. Indeed we hope that as the system proposed gives the Regional Houses in practice a very big say in the disposition of their representatives, it will be more palatable to Nigerians as a whole and enable them to accept the constitutional provision that appointment shall be formally by the Governor or Lieutenant-Governor, as the case may be, in consultation with them. It would also have the great advantage of preserving the position vis-à-vis the Gold Coast.

You have suggested in paragraph 6 that the federal nature of the Nigerian constitution should make it possible to justify a difference in practice between Nigeria and the Gold Coast. We fully agree that considerable differences in the structure of the constitution are inevitable and that so far as variations in practice are imposed by that difference of structure they can be justified. But this appears to us to be a simple matter of principle, and we do not see how it would be possible to justify the necessity for such differing systems of appointment of Ministers.

In paragraphs 8, 9 and 10 of your letter you have referred to the difficulties and embarrassments which might arise if the names put forward by the Governor or Lieutenant-Governor were rejected. We should hope that prior consultation would as a rule avoid this possibility, though we realise that it is not always possible to be certain about it. But in any case we do not see that the Governor or Lieutenant-Governor would be in a worse position if some of his original choices had fallen by the way than if he had to deal with a Council which had been constituted by election without his having any say at all in the choice of candidates. Under the latter system it might happen, at the worst, that in the building up of mutual confidence between himself and his Council he would have to start from scratch, with Ministers many of whom he would not himself have voluntarily proposed for appointment.

As regards paragraphs 11 and 12, we realise the difficulties over consultation with bodies of the size of the Regional Houses; but whichever system of appointing Ministers may be adopted, the first business of those Houses must be to choose the regional bloc for the Central Legislature and we believe that it should not be too difficult for the Lieutenant-Governors to consult with some of the leading members of the House who would themselves take the general view. The objection raised in your paragraph 13 to allowing the Legislatures to remove a Governor's nominee is, I think, met by what I have said about nomination above; under the arrangement proposed the Legislature would share with the Governor the responsibility for the original appointment of the Minister. Similarly as regards your paragraph 14, the responsibility for having appointed Ministers of poor calibre would be shared.

We have now, I think, set out fully the arguments on either side. You will remember that in paragraph 8 of his published despatch of the 15th July,[3] the

---

[3] See 116.

Secretary of State made the suggestion that the aim should be to arrive at a procedure under which members of the Council of Ministers and of the Regional Executive Councils should be selected by a process of consultation. We have, therefore, thought it advisable to bring the subsequent correspondence to the Secretary of State's notice. He has asked me to let you know that he will reserve a final decision until you have had the opportunity of considering and replying to this letter after such consultation with your advisers as you may think necessary. At the same time he wishes you to know that he would find it most difficult to depart from the view which he has expressed in his despatch and that he is strongly reinforced in this feeling by the representation which Arden-Clarke has made. He very much hopes, therefore, that on further consideration you will find it possible to fall in with the proposal that the method of selection rather than election shall be adopted for the appointment of Ministers in Nigeria.

I have sent copies of this letter to Macpherson and to Arden-Clarke.

127   CO 537/5787, no 89   7 Dec 1950
[Constitutional review]: letter from A B Cohen to H M Foot on the functions of ministers under the proposed new constitution

Many thanks for your secret letter of the 20th November about the secretariat arrangements under the new constitution.[1] It is very good of you to have set your views out so fully and, like you, I wish that we could discuss it. I shall certainly look forward to doing so in February.

2.   I note that you are obtaining the views of Chief Commissioners and we shall look forward to hearing from you again when you have done so. But, as I said in paragraph 2 of my letter of the 14th November,[2] we are not suggesting that there should be Permanent Secretaries or Under-Secretaries in the regional secretariats. It may be useful, therefore, if I reply to your letter now.

3.   Reading through my letter again and your reply I feel that I might have set the position out as we saw it rather more clearly and that I must have given you the impression that we were basing our arguments in favour of what we suggest as much on political as on administrative grounds. There are admittedly political arguments in favour of the course we have suggested, as my letter makes clear; but our view is based primarily on administrative arguments. We of course entirely accept that the position of Ministers is to be different in Nigeria from what it is to be in the Gold Coast; that has been settled by the Secretary of State's acceptance of the recommendations of the Ibadan conference. It was not our intention to suggest that the functions of central Ministers dealing with non-regional subjects should be enlarged. We were addressing ourselves simply to the problem of providing the best administrative machinery to enable these Ministers to carry out their function, which each of them will have, of 'ensuring in co-operation with the executive head of the department concerned that the decisions of the Council as they affect his subject are carried out'.

---

[1] See 124.   [2] See 123.

4. Put very briefly, the difficulty which we see about the Nigerian Government's proposals is that, whereas on the one hand each of the nine members of the Council of Ministers responsible for non-regional subjects (i.e. including the three ex officio members) will have responsibility for his own group of subjects (although this responsibility in the case of the African Ministers will be confined to ensuring that the decisions of the Council are carried out), on the other hand when you come to the administrative level there will be certain officers in the secretariat who, although they will be dealing with the subjects with which the African Ministers are concerned, will not be part of the staffs of those Ministers. I understood from the Governor in discussion that there would in fact be officers at Principal Assistant Secretary level in the secretariat dealing with each of the groups of subjects allotted to African Ministers. To whom will these secretariat officers be responsible? They must be responsible to some member of the Council, just as the Cabinet Secretariat here is responsible to the Prime Minister. I take it that in fact they will be responsible to the Chief Secretary. If so, the position will be that while Ministers are working with departments on their own subjects, there will be Secretariat officials working on the same subjects who will be responsible not to those Ministers but to another member of the Council of Ministers, i.e. the Chief Secretary. The Cabinet Secretariat system works effectively here because the officials in it are simply concerned with the conduct of Cabinet business and not with policy. Knowing as I do the very important part which Secretariat officers at present necessarily play in advising on policy, I do not see how you can simply convert them into the equivalent of members of the Cabinet Secretariat here. If I am right in thinking that you cannot, and indeed should not at this stage, then it seems to us that, even allowing for the relatively limited functions of Ministers proposed under the new constitution, you are in danger of laying up administrative trouble, as well perhaps as political trouble, by keeping officers dealing with Ministers' subjects outside the Ministers' own organisations.

5. You suggest that we may have underestimated the value of the close association which should exist between Ministers and heads of departments dealing with their subjects. I can assure you that we have not overlooked this fact. Indeed it is just because of the obvious importance which attaches to this association that we have felt serious doubts about keeping the secretariat officers also dealing with these subjects outside rather than inside the Ministers' organisations.

6. I think that you ought to know also that as far as we are aware there is no precedent for what you are suggesting in Nigeria except in Jamaica. The system which you are proposing to adopt was not adopted in India, nor in the Sudan. The Sudan secretariat, as you know, was divided into three parts before the new constitution under the Civil Secretary, the Financial Secretary and the Legal Secretary. I am told that the new ministries set up under Sudanese Ministers are quite independent in accordance with the normal arrangements.

7. When we discussed this question with the Governor here we agreed that, since it was he and the Nigerian Government who had to work the system, it must ultimately be for him to decide what machinery should be established. He for his part, however, agreed that we ought to let you know our doubts about your proposals and that was the purpose of my letter of the 14th November. If, after you have considered the matter further in the light of your consultation with Chief Commissioners and have taken into account what I have said above, it is finally

decided to adhere to your proposals, we shall not seek to argue the matter further. I have, however, thought it right to set out the position as we see it again because, as you know, all of us at the official level who have handled the matter here believe that, if the proposed system is introduced, it will be found after a short time—and by that I do not mean a period of years but one of say a year or a year and a half—that it is in fact after all necessary to break up the secretariat and to provide Ministers with Permanent Secretaries, or Under-Secretaries or Principal Assistant Secretaries or whatever you like to call them. Our contention therefore is that it would be better to do this at the start.

8.   I am afraid you may feel that this is just another of those theories of what Milverton[3] once called 'the intellectual dreamers of Whitehall'. However that may be, I can assure you that, whatever the Nigerian Government decides to do and whether you go on with the present Secretariat system or modify it, once a decision has been taken we at this end will of course do everything we can to help make it a success.

9.   Finally may I say that I had hoped to have a talk with the Governor on this subject, but he had a bad cold on the day we had arranged for this and has now gone off to Scotland. I did, however, tell him very briefly how we felt and repeated the point I have just made, namely that we felt that it must be left to him to decide on the machinery to be established after he had considered our comments in the light of local views. I am sending him a copy of this letter.

---

[3] ie Sir Arthur Richards, cr Baron Milverton of Lagos and Clifton, 1947.

128   CO 537/6782, no 1   15 Dec 1950
[Anti-communist propaganda]: CO note of a meeting held to discuss measures to counter communist propaganda in Nigeria

Mr. Cooper[1] underlined the urgency and importance of the problem of providing material to counter Communist propaganda material which was now arriving in Nigeria in large quantities. In recognition of the need the Nigerian Government was making additional funds available to the Public Relations Office for the purchase and preparation of suitable material, but in addition assistance would be required from London.

During discussion the following points emerged:—

1.   *The appeal of communist propaganda in Nigeria*

(a) Africans are impressed by Soviet successes in world affairs.
(b) Propaganda about race equality in Russia is effective, particularly in view of the African's awareness of the racial policy of South Africa, a member of the Commonwealth.
(c) There is much value to Communist propaganda in the 'strong man' personality of Stalin.
(d) While Africans are probably not much interested in Communist ideology, they are likely to be influenced by Communist propaganda alleging that Russia will help them to gain independence.

---

[1] Public Relation Officer for the Nigerian government.

2.   *Counter-propaganda themes*. The following themes should be exploited:—

(a) Russian imperialism and aggression and enslavement of free peoples and nations.
(b) Britain's record in the creation of Sovreign [sic] States.
(c) Nigeria's future place as a sovereign [sic] state within the Western system.

3.   *'Angling' of publicity material*

(a) Anti-Communist material should not have a pro-British slant, but should interpret the world situation from an anti-Communist angle, presenting the 'Western' rather than the British point of view.
(b) Anti-Communist material should be kept separate from pro-British material. (e.g. a pamphlet opening with a denigration of Russia and leading up to praise of Britain would be suspect to Africans).

4.   *Target*. The immediate target should be the intelligentsia.

5.   *Media*

(a) Pamphlets should have priority. They need not necessarily be illustrated, but should be attractively presented and about 30 to 40 pages. They could be both distributed free to libraries and reading rooms, and sold to the public at a very low price.
(b) A book of cartoons would be useful, but caution is necessary in the use of ridicule.
(c) Mobile film vans reach an audience of about two million a year, but their impact is on a section of the population below the immediate target.
(d) Broadcasting is still in the early stages, but its influence will grow and should be well established in about two years time.

6.   *Trade Unions*

(a) Special material is wanted, particularly that published by the I.C.F.T.U.
(b) The T.U.C. has approached the Colonial Office with the suggestion that they should supply industrial notes for the Colonial press. The most effective way of ensuring publication of these notes would be for the T.U.C. to supply them direct to the press in Nigeria.
(c) An I.C.F.T.U. delegation is at present in West Africa.

7.   *British Council*. The British Council is doing invaluable work, particularly in the all-important field of race relations. Its activities are more acceptable to Africans than those of Government Departments, and every effort should be made to expand its activities.

8.   *Propaganda machinery*

(a) The Public Relations Department, Nigeria, should avoid apparent embroilment in direct anti-Communist propaganda activity since this would prejudice the success of its primary task of explaining Government to the people. It could best take action by stimulating anti-Communist propaganda through unofficial channels. (e.g. the Nigerian Bureau of Publicity has published a pamphlet on Korea for the Department. The Department is encouraging Nigerian politicians to establish a 'Freedom bookshop'.)

(b) In dealing with Communist propaganda problems in West Africa the Information Department of the Colonial Office would work through the newly appointed Adviser on Overseas Information.

(c) Anti-Communist material will have to come mainly from London. It will probably be necessary to set up an editorial unit as part of the Adviser's organisation.

(d) Consideration should be given to setting up an organisation in London on similar lines to the 'Soviet News' agency in Rosary Gardens. It might be called 'Friends of Freedom'. Its functions might include:

(i) Production of counter-material to that despatched to Africa by the 'Soviet News' Agency. In this connection steps should be taken to ascertain the contents of parcels despatched to Africa by the 'Soviet News' agency before they leave this country.

(ii) Production of a 'News-letter'

(iii) Production of other anti-Communist material e.g. an anthology from anti-Communist books such as 'The God That Failed'.

(iv) Sponsorship of lectures.

(e) In order to make fuller use of Administrative Officers, a confidential guidance on world issues should be arranged from London for adaptation locally.

(f) A commentary on current issues (on the lines of the wartime VERITAS) for publicity use should also be supplied from London.

Action points

(a) Production of a pamphlet showing up Russian imperialism, as in paragraph 4(a). *Information Department*.

(b) Consideration to be given to the organisation of a service of confidential guidances. *Information Department*.

(c) Consideration to be given to the organisation of a commentary on current issues. *Information Department*.

(d) Steps to be taken to ascertain the contents of parcels despatched from the 'Soviet News' agency. *Defence Department* (Ref. para 8.(d)(i) above).

(e) Consideration to be given to setting up an organisation on similar lines to the 'Soviet News' agency. *Information Department*

(f) The approach by the T.U.C. suggesting that they supply industrial notes to the Colonial press to be followed up. *Information Department*

(g) Arrangements to be made for the Adviser on Overseas Information to attend the meeting of the West African Council on the 22nd and 23rd January. *Information Department*

(h) A suitable communication to be sent to the West African Governments outlining the steps already taken or proposed to be taken in providing anti-Communist material. *Information Department*

129 CO 537/5790, no 8   30 Dec 1950

[Constitutional review]: letter from H M Foot to A B Cohen on the electoral system under the new constitution

Since your letter of the 23rd of November about the electoral system under the new constitution was received full discussions have taken place in the three Regional

Houses and we had a meeting here last week with Regional Secretaries to review the whole position.

I am enclosing copies of the Regional recommendations.[1] I doubt if you will wish to read them all through but a glance at them will show that there is a good deal of divergence on detail and some major differences.

Following our discussion with Regional Secretaries draft electoral regulations are being prepared and we shall send you this draft as soon as possible. You will see from that draft that we are anxious to make the regulations as simple as possible and to eliminate minor differences between the Regional recommendations, so I do not propose to go into detail now.

There are, however, one or two major questions which emerge from the Regional discussions to which I should invite attention at once.

We propose that in each Province there should be a Chief Electoral Officer (normally the Resident) with Electoral Officers (normally District Officers) and Returning Officers appointed by him. The Electoral Officers would be given wide powers to direct how the elections should be conducted and no complaint or appeal would lie to the Courts or to any authority higher than the Chief Electoral Officer. The Electoral Officers would, for instance, have power to prescribe the areas in which the primary elections should take place and the method of conducting the primary elections (this would enable variation in practice and procedure to meet local circumstances without the necessity for carrying too much detail in the electoral regulations).

The method of election in the Provincial or Divisional Electoral Colleges will, however, be defined more closely in the regulations. The Chief Electoral Officer or an Electoral Officer will preside in these Colleges where election will be by secret ballot.

The next major point is that in the North and the West there is the strongest feeling that the well-known and well-understood system of indirect election should be maintained. I well realise the theoretical objections to the indirect method (and the other objections mentioned in your letter) but I feel sure that we must accept the Regional recommendations on this. In the West there will not be more than one stage between the village elections and the Divisional Electoral College but in the North, where distances are so great and the population of some of the Provinces is so large, there will often be several stages.

The other most important point is that in the North and West there is the strongest determination that there shall be some injection of Native Authority representation and that there shall also be some means whereby persons who do not come up from the village elections are given an opportunity of being elected to the Regional Houses. The North propose to achieve these purposes by having not more than 10 per cent N.A. representation in the Provincial Electoral Colleges and by giving the Colleges freedom to elect to the Regional House anyone who is qualified to vote in the Province. The West propose to achieve the object by providing that there shall be a maximum of 50 per cent N.A. representation in the intermediate colleges (between the village elections and the Divisional Electoral Colleges) and by giving the intermediate colleges the power to elect not more than 10 per cent of the representatives to go forward to the Divisional Electoral Colleges from outside

---

[1] Not printed.

their own number. In the East when the proposal was put forward that Electoral Colleges should have the power to elect to the Regional House people who were not members of the Electoral Colleges the proposal was unanimously and firmly turned down!

It is a pity that these differing proposals look so untidy but the questions of principle are two—firstly, should there be any N.A. representation in the electing bodies and, secondly, should the electing bodies be empowered to elect other than those included in their own number. You have already said that you see no objection to the second principle. As to the first—participation of N.A. nominees—I told you that I personally do not favour it in principle but I am now fully convinced that we must give way on this to Regional opinion (which is not by any means merely conservative opinion). Many of our legislators are at present elected by the N.As. We are making a big advance away from that system but I am now persuaded that in the North and West to deny N.As any participation at all in the coming elections would be going too far at one jump (the justification for eliminating the N.As altogether in the East lies, of course, in the fact that the N.As have never played the important role in the East that they play in the North and West). Moreover if it is accepted that the N.As may participate I think that we may also agree that in the method of their participation we should be guided by the wishes strongly—indeed almost unanimously—urged by the Regional representatives.

I shall not comment further until I can send you the draft regulations which will make our purposes and proposed methods clearer. I shall them comment in detail on the points raised in your letter of the 23rd of November. The purpose of this letter is merely to send you the Regional recommendations and to let you know our reactions on the most important questions at issue.

130 CO 537/6781, no 3 23–24 Jan 1951

[Communism in West Africa]: minutes of a meeting (item 3) in Accra of West African governors held to discuss counter-measures against the spread of communism in West Africa

Coordinated drive against communism
The following general conclusions were reached:—

(i) there was now ample evidence that the Soviet Union as part of a general campaign was directing propaganda towards British territories in West Africa. This intention had been explicitly stated in the Cominform press and was confirmed by the greatly increased quantities of literature arriving in Nigeria and the Gold Coast since the beginning of December.

(ii) there was no evidence yet of a similar influx of literature into Sierra Leone and the Gambia and it appeared likely that Nigeria and the Gold Coast had been selected as targets because of the increase in recent years in nationalist feeling in those territories.

(iii) the material was being routed generally through Post Office mails both by sea and air. It was noted that there was no evidence yet of material entering in any quantities British territories over the land frontier from French West Africa.

(iv) the propaganda material, particularly the periodicals, were extremely attractively produced and it is evident that a considerable amount of money is being spent on this campaign.

(v) in all West African territories there were no Communist organizations of any significant proportions to whom such propaganda could be directed. There was however a large and increasing number of literates produced by Governments' development policy who, in the absence of other material, would provide outlets for propaganda of this kind. It was agreed that one of the first aims of policy should be to protect this newly-created reading public from such propaganda.

(vi) the meeting noted that a considerable part of the propaganda was prepared in, or despatched via, the U.K. The Governors expressed their disquiet that it should be possible for such material which was subvertive of all our aims in Africa to be prepared in and despatched from the centre of the Commonwealth without any counter-action by the authorities in the U.K. They suggested that if such counter-action were not possible, stops should at least be taken to ensure notice being given to West African Governments of the despatch and nature of consignments of communist propaganda from the U.K.

The meeting further examined in greater detail the following aspects of action against Communism:—

(a) *Counter-propaganda in West Africa (see also WAC (51)2)*
Opportunity was taken of Mr Ingrams' visit to West Africa to discuss his future plans with him.[1] The following points were made in the discussion:—

(i) the meeting understood from Mr Ingrams that while agreement had been given in principle for the provision of funds for counter-propaganda, actual expenditure was still dependent on Treasury approval of detailed plans. The Governors expressed the hope that in view of the urgency of inventing a counter-campaign there would not be undue delay in approving any schemes put forward and that, having regard to the expenditure being incurred on the Russian side funds would be made available in adequate amount. They hoped that should there be delay in reaching a final decision it might be possible to make an ad hoc beginning in the provision of counter-propaganda material.

(ii) they approved in principle of a suggestion put forward by Mr Ingrams that a system of 'panels' should be set up in the West African territories for the purpose of advising his organisation on the effectiveness in particular areas of material issuing from London and of any adaptations of the overall campaign required to suit varying local conditions and agreed separately to examine the proposal further in detail.

(iii) they emphasised the importance of counter-propaganda being 'positive' rather than 'negative' i.e. it should emphasise the advantages presented to Africa by the opportunities of constitutional advance offered by us. The aim should be to immunise the West African from a disease threatening him, not to cure him of a disease from which he was not yet suffering.

(iv) questions of terminology required careful consideration; the use of the term 'imperialism' even bracketed with the word 'Russian' was for instance inadvisable.

---

[1] W H Ingrams, adviser on overseas information, CO, from 1950.

(v) they welcomed the suggestion for the establishment of an organisation called 'the Friends of Freedom', as suggested in the note on the Colonial Office meeting of the 15th December (see Appendix II to WAC (51)2).[2] They understood that financial provision for such an organization would be separate from that already agreed upon for Mr Ingram's post and that the organization would appear to be a commercial publishing house. They also agreed that the organisation might usefully be responsible for the organization of discussion groups. Such groups would most expediently be started in the U.K. and then be spread in West Africa as members of U.K. groups returned there.

(vi) they further felt that the conclusions of the meeting of 15th December that the immediate target should be the intelligentsia required some modification. It was equally important that attention should be paid to trade unionists. The 'immediate target' should in fact cover all persons literate in English.

(vii) they considered it desirable that Governments should see pamphlet material at the draft stage. Governments would consider points which from the varying local points of view it would be useful to stress in pamphlets.

(viii) Governors also expressed the hope that any guidance material sent to them should normally be marked 'Secret' rather than 'Top Secret' as with the former grading a Governor would have discretion to decide whether, if it was useful so to do, he might consult responsible Africans on the local application of the guidance in question.

(b) *Matters arriving out of the Inter-Colony Special Branch Conference, September, 1950.*

(i) *Action in regard to communist literature*
It was noted that the Secretary of State had in his circular despatch of the 25th May 1950 expressed the view that there should be the maximum similarity of practice in regard to subversive publications, at any rate within each geographical region. It was agreed that in present circumstances in West Africa, the region within which it was desirable to aim at similarity of practice was confined to Nigeria and the Gold Coast. The Governor of the Gambia and the representative of the Governor of Sierra Leone agreed however that should a situation develop in their territories similar to that now existing in Nigeria and the Gold Coast as far as the import of subversive literature was concerned it would most probably be decided to adopt the same practice as at present obtaining in the Gold Coast.

The Governor of Nigeria recognised the desirability of Nigeria and the Gold Coast keeping in step in these matters. He further agreed that in the present state of relations with the U.S.S.R. it might well become necessary to ban all communist literature and all communist activities. The main difficulties which it was felt in Nigeria, lay in the way of adopting a selective banning of literature were:—

(1) the difficulty of finding a satisfactory test for determining whether or not individual works should be banned:
(2) the physical work involved in the examination of literature in the quantities at present being imported to see whether it should be banned or not.
(3) the risk that the adoption of such a policy by Government would antagonise independent African opinion and so weaken Government's own position.

[2] See 128.

The Governor of the Gold Coast described present practice in that country. He suggested that in the present conditions in which all were agreed that the U.S.S.R. was attempting to subvert established authority in British territories in West Africa for its own ends, there was a case for banning all material emanating from known Communist sources. It was not however the policy in the Gold Coast to ban works on Communism (e.g. those of Lenin) which could be regarded as academic textbooks. On the other hand, all past and future issues of a periodical which had once been banned were similarly excluded and these two factors operated to reduce the physical task of examining intercepted material. As regards the necessity of keeping independent African opinion on the side of Government he emphasized that under the Gold Coast legislation the power to prohibit the importation of publication was exercised by the Governor-in-Council ie by a body which contained three African members and was under the new Constitution to contain a much higher proportion of Africans. He added that there had in fact been little or no public agitation in the Gold Coast against the use at present being made of these powers.

The Governor of Nigeria undertook to consider the question further on his return to Nigeria and to inform the other Governors of his final decision. [Action: Governor of Nigeria.]

(ii) *Declaration of prohibited immigrants*
The meeting agreed:—
(1) that it would not be practicable to adopt as a policy that whenever one West African Government declared an individual to be a prohibited immigrant, the other Governments should automatically follow suit but
(2) that each Government should continue to inform the others whenever it declared any individual to be prohibited immigrant.

131   CO 583/307/1   2 Feb 1951
[Constitutional review]: minute by A B Cohen on the electoral system under the proposed new constitution

Sir T Lloyd
The West African Department, Mr. McPetrie and I have been having discussions this week with Sir H. Foot, Mr. Williams of the Nigerian Secretariat and Mr. de Winton, a Crown Counsel in Nigeria who is dealing with the drafting of the instruments, about the Nigerian constitution.[1] These discussions have gone very well. We were able to settle provisionally a number of points of detail and substance and to go through certain parts of the draft which had been prepared. Mr. McPetrie is going to Nigeria later in the month and will be taking part there in discussions with the Governor, the Chief Commissioners and the legal officers concerned with the instruments. As a result of these discussions I hope that all the outstanding points of principle will be settled and that the instruments can be completed in time to bring them into force before the end of June. I may mention here that the Nigerian Government have now

---

[1] J McPetrie, senior legal assistant, CO. See 116.

accepted our view about the method of appointment of Ministers.[2] This will be done, as we have proposed, by consultation between the Lieutenant Governor and the members of the Regional Houses at the regional level.

There are certain points in relation to the electoral system which we think should at this stage be brought to the attention of the Secretary of State and I think that the Secretary of State will wish to discuss them with Sir H. Foot and the department. I have provisionally arranged 3.30 p.m. on Thursday, February 8th, when Sir H. Foot will again be in London. The recent correspondence on this subject is registered at Nos. 2, 6, 8, 9 on 1950 file, and 1 on this file.

The main points are as follows:—

(1) *Method of legislating for the elections*

The normal procedure is for a general enabling clause to be contained in the constitution and for the actual arrangements for election to be laid down by local Ordinance. This procedure has been followed in the Gold Coast. There are, however, strong reasons against adopting this procedure in Nigeria arising from the fact that the new constitution will be semi-federal. In the view of the Nigerian Government it would be objectionable to give the power to settle the electoral procedure to the Central Legislature. After lengthy negotiations the North's claim to have half the elected seats in the Central Legislature has been conceded and Sir H. Foot informs us that there will be the strongest objections in these circumstances on the part of the East and West to allowing the electoral procedure to be settled by the Legislative Council, since this would in effect place the Northern members in the position of being able to exercise an almost decisive influence over the arrangements. On the other hand it would clearly be inappropriate to leave it to each Regional House to settle the electoral arrangements, seeing that the vast majority of the members of the Central Legislature are themselves elected by the Regional Houses.

In the circumstances the Nigerian proposal is that the electoral arrangements should be laid down by the Governor in Council in regulations issued under the constitution. This fits in well with the conception of the Governor in Council (Council of Ministers) as not only the chief instrument of policy but also as a sort of arbitral body between the three Regions. The Governor in Council is going to perform a similar function in relation to regional legislation, that of deciding whether it overrides an overall Nigerian interest and should not therefore be assented to. The Council of Ministers will consist of the Governor as President, six official members (the Chief Secretary, the Legal Secretary, the Financial Secretary and the three Lieutenant Governors) and twelve Nigerian members, four drawn from the members representing each Region in the Central Legislature. It is thus a body which is fully representative of Nigeria. Another point is that the arrangements for elections have in fact been prepared after lengthy discussion by Select Committees of the Regional Houses, so that they are in fact in accordance with the wishes of the people.

In the circumstances I feel sure that we can accept the Nigerian Government's recommendation that the arrangements for elections should be prescribed in this way. Mr. McPetrie quite agrees. It is proposed, as in the Gold Coast, to have a brief interim Order in Council in advance of the main instruments under which

---

[2] Sir T Lloyd minuted 'Good' in the margin here.

regulations for electoral preparations may be made at as early a date as possible. This will allow the arrangements for the elections to go forward quickly. It is hoped that this Order in Council may be made during April.

(2) *Methods of conducting elections*

The General Conference at Ibadan proposed that the elections to the Regional Houses should be indirect through electoral colleges at the divisional level in the East and West and at the provincial level in the North. It recommended also that the primary elections in each Region should be direct. In commenting on these recommendations in his published despatch of the 15th July, the Secretary of State wrote as follows:—

> 'Great importance clearly attaches to the arrangements for the election of members of the Central and Regional Legislatures and I have noted with much interest the recommendations of the General Conference on this matter. I make no comment on the arrangements for the election of members of the Central Legislature, since a final recommendation on its composition remains to be made. As regards the Regional Houses of Assembly, it is proposed that the members should be elected by a system of indirect election through provincial electoral colleges in the Northern Region and divisional electoral colleges in the Eastern and Western Regions; that the primary elections in each Region should be direct; and that the detailed arrangements should be worked out in each Region and examined by the House of Assembly of that Region. I do not wish to prejudge this examination, but I would point out that the representative character of the Regional Houses of Assembly and, if they are to select the members of the Central Legislature, of that Legislature itself, will depend ultimately on the primary elections in the Provinces and Divisions. It is in my view most important that the arrangements for these primary elections should ensure that the members elected to the Provincial and Divisional electoral colleges should be genuinely representative of all the peoples of the areas concerned; that the elections should be free and fair; and that the form of election should be properly adapted to the circumstances of each area. For this last reason I welcome the proposal that the arrangements should in the first instance be worked out in the Regions themselves; I shall await the results with much interest.'

In dealing with the minority reports the Secretary of State wrote in paragraph 15 of his despatch as follows:—

> 'On the minority reports regarding the system of election, I would point out that while the Eastern Regional Conference and the Lagos Colony Conference suggested leaving the method of election to the decision of the regions themselves, both the Northern and the Western Regional Conferences, as well as the General Conference, recommended indirect election to the Regional Houses of Assembly through electoral colleges at the Provincial or Divisional level. I see no reason to depart from the recommendations of the General Conference and I do not wish to add to what I have said in paragraph 10 of this despatch, except to point out that from the point of view of those who are in favour of direct election, the proposal that the primary elections in each region should be direct represents an important advance.'

The three Select Committees of the Regional Houses in the North, East and West have now submitted virtually unanimous reports (enclosures to No. 8). The Eastern report has adhered very closely to the recommendations of the Ibadan Conference and no point arises on that. Elections will be through electoral colleges at the divisional level and there will only be one tier of colleges in this Region. In the North and the West, however, the recommendations of the Select Committees have departed in certain respects from the recommendations of the General Conference.

(3) *Electoral Colleges in the North and West*

In the West it is proposed that there should be two levels of electoral colleges, the divisional electoral colleges and the district or intermediate electoral colleges below them. In the North it is proposed that in addition to the provincial electoral colleges there should be three lower levels, Emirate Native Authority or divisional colleges, district colleges and village area colleges. It was, I think, inevitable that, in view of the relatively primitive nature of most of the Northern Provinces and of the great size of the Provinces and populations concerned, there should be at any rate one extra level of electoral college in the North. In my letter of the 23rd November at No. 6 (page 3) I expressed the hope that we should be able to avoid an extra level of electoral college in the West and that, if an extra level was found necessary in the North, there would not be more than one. This hope has not been realised; but, in the light of what Sir H. Foot says in his letter at No. 8[3] and what he has since told us, I feel sure that we cannot reasonably oppose the unanimous wish of the Nigerian representatives in the West and the North. I therefore recommend that we should accept this particular recommendation.

(4) *Native Authority representatives*

Both we and the central Nigerian Government would have preferred to avoid special Native Authority representation in the process of election. There will be no such special representation in the East, where indeed Native Authorities are very weak. In the North, however, it is proposed—and this represents a very strongly held view—that on the provincial (that is the final) electoral colleges there should be representatives chosen by the Native Authorities and their Council up to a maximum of 10% of the members of the colleges. This seems to me a very moderate proportion of the total and I think that we can certainly accept this recommendation.

For the West, however, the position is less easy. The West propose that up to a maximum of 50% of the district (or intermediate) electoral colleges should be chosen by the Native Authorities. Our view is that this proportion is altogether excessive. There is to be a House of Chiefs, for the first time, in the West with concurrent powers with the lower Regional House. This House will consist of a certain number of Obas or Chiefs ex officio and in other areas a representative chosen by the Native Authorities. It seems to us inappropriate that in addition to this House of Chiefs the Native Authorities should have a 50% representation in the district or intermediate electoral colleges. We fully recognise that this represents the unanimous recommendation of the Western Select Committee and that it is no doubt supported by the strong popular regard in the Western Provinces for Chiefs and Native Authorities. We recognise also that the Native Authorities are themselves becoming increasingly representative of the whole community and not only

---

[3] See 129.

the traditional elements. None the less we think that, if this arrangement is accepted, it is not going to be at all easy to defend against the strong criticism of the political elements, who will describe it as undemocratic. Lagos is to be included in the Western Provinces, with the support of its Yoruba inhabitants but not entirely to the satisfaction of the others, including the politically-minded Ibos who live there. It seems to us that this heavy representation of Native Authorities in the electoral process for the lower House may increase the risk of a rift in the Regional Legislature between the traditional and more modern elements. Sir H. Foot tells us that there is already criticism of having an extra level of electoral college and of having any representation of Native Authorities at all. Our view is that it would be much better to limit this representation on the district electoral colleges to, say, 25%.

Sir H. Foot entirely supports our view in substance. He shares our objection to the arrangement proposed by the Western Regional House. But he feels very strongly— and this represents the view of the Nigerian Government generally—that it would be a great mistake for the Secretary of State to refuse to accept this recommendation, which is unanimous. He thinks in particular that this would be a great slap in the face for the Native Authorities, who are already under pressure from the more politically-minded elements of the people; there is certainly a great deal of force in this point. Sir H. Foot thinks that it would be perfectly proper for the Secretary of State to express his doubts about this arrangement in a published despatch, but he thinks it important that the Secretary of State should none the less accept it as having been recommended by the representatives of the people.

It is clear that because of this difference of opinion between ourselves and Sir H. Foot—it is the only one—the Secretary of State will want to discuss the matter with us.

(5) *Representation of minorities*

There is a danger, at any rate in theory, that in certain areas minorities might not be adequately represented. This is particularly so in the North, where the Province will be the unit for the final elections to the Regional House. The Northern Select Committee has specifically rejected the proposal that each tribal area or Emirate should be given a proportion of the seats on the Regional House for the Province (para. 16 of first enclosure to No. 8). Thus, in theory at any rate, it might come about that in the Kano or Sokoto Province all the members elected represented the Kano or Sokoto Emirates. The pagans in many areas might go unrepresented, while in all parts of the country stronger minority groups might not get adequate representation. To some extent this is inevitable under any system. Moreover the pagans have virtually nobody who could take any useful part in the proceedings of the Regional Houses. After discussion with Sir H. Foot we all agree that the proper course is for the Secretary of State to say in a despatch which will be published that he has noted this problem and that he trusts that those concerned can be relied upon to give fair representation to the minority groups in their selections. He would go on to say that, if this does not happen at the first election, it will clearly be necessary to consider before the second election whether some specific arrangement should be made for the representation of minorities. I feel sure that this is the right way to deal with this particular point rather than to attempt to lay down specific arrangements for the representation of minorities.

(6) *Lagos*

The present arrangements for election at Lagos will continue and there will be a direct election from the Municipality to the Western Regional House, the only modification being that the election would be to that House rather than as at present to the Central Legislature.

(7) *Electoral procedure*

In view of the vast size of Nigeria and its backwardness, it is clearly not possible for the first elections to lay down detailed procedure on the U.K. model. We have always taken the view that elections must be conducted by methods suitable to the area concerned and any other arrangement would indeed be impracticable. It is a great step forward to have elections at all and I am sure that we must support the Nigerian Government in their view that in most parts of the country a simple and flexible procedure for elections will be necessary. In some areas—probably in most of the Eastern Provinces—registration will be adopted, the tax certificates being used. The same will apply to some towns elsewhere. But generally in the North and East the village elections on the first occasion will be by more rough and ready methods under the supervision of the electoral officers (who will normally be administrative or other Government officers, but not always so). It will be for the Chief Electoral Officer of each Province to decide whether an area should be a registration area or not.

Inevitably the electoral officers will have to be given wide discretion. I am sure that this is the only way of conducting the elections successfully. The original Nigerian proposal was that electoral petitions should be barred from courts, but Sir H. Foot has agreed provisionally to a suggestion by Sir K. Roberts-Wray that this should only apply to elections up to the level of the final electoral college. In other words, if this is adopted, the courts will be able to deal with petitions against proceedings in the final electoral college, but not of course in so far as these relate to complaints against earlier parts of the proceedings. I think that this is a good modification; but I am sure that it would create a hopeless mass of litigation if petitions to the courts were allowed in respect of the lower levels of electoral colleges.

Sir H Foot has suggested that the Secretary of State might say in the despatch on the electoral arrangements that, while he recognises the necessity for relatively simple methods on the first occasion, he hopes that it may be possible to work out more precise methods by the time that the next general election is held.

These are the points for discussion. The Secretary of State may like to start the talk by asking Sir H. Foot to describe the procedure generally.

I am sending copies of this minute to Sir H. Foot, Mr. Gorsuch and Mr. McPetrie.[4]

---

[4] Sir T Lloyd minuted at the end, 'I should like to take part in this discussion.'

132   CO 537/6782, no 19   6 Feb 1951
[Communism in Nigeria]: CO note on alleged communist payments to trade unions in Nigeria

The general intention of the World Federation of Trade Unions (WFTU) to infiltrate into and otherwise use trade unions in the Colonies needs no elaboration. In July

1949, this Federation decided to set up Regional Liaison Bureau, who are to be responsible for assisting trade union organization in their regions to carry out WFTU decisions, for conducting propaganda, and for establishing contacts not only with affiliated centres but also with other trade union organizations which do not belong to the WFTU. They are required to report every three months to the Secretary-General of the WFTU. The bureau which directly concerns African Colonial territories was to be one of the subjects of discussion at the proposed Pan-African Trade Unions Congress, originally called for October 1950 at Duala (and concerning the present position, see (2) on this file.)

This file shows:—

(a) Nigeria reports that the local manager of the 'Daily Times' had obtained reliable information from local trade union sources that £2,000 had been paid over by a foreign Communist organization to the United Africa Company's Union and lodged in the Continental Bank at Lagos. It was also said that £200 of this £2,000 had been paid to the Nigeria Labour Congress which is affiliated to the WFTU.

The 'Daily Times' story was published on the 18th January and was also published on that date in the London 'Daily Mirror'.

(b) Section 5 of the Nigeria Exchange Control Ordinance prevents the making of any payment to or for the credit of a person resident in the scheduled territories by order or on behalf of a person resident outside except with permission of the Financial Secretary, this permission has in fact been given in 'blanket form'. Moreover, the Ordinance gives the Financial Secretary powers to require information only for the purpose of securing compliance with the Ordinance.

(c) It was suggested to Nigeria that consideration should be given as to whether any action can or should be taken to prevent payments as this coming into the hands of the recipients in West Africa; and Nigeria has replied that under existing law such subventions, provided they are made in sterling are legal transactions, and new ad hoc legislation would appear to be impracticable unless or until Communist activities as a whole are proscribed in British West Africa.[1]

---

[1] The original of this document has been retained by the FCO under section 3 (4) of the Public Records Act, 1958. Sections have been blanked out. They appear under (a) after 'the WFTU' and under (b) where a section is missing before 'section 5' begins. This document was followed by efforts by the CO to see if legislation could be drawn up to oblige banks in Nigeria to reveal information on payments from communist sources. Such legislation, it was decided, would have been impossible to draft.

133 CO 537/6782, no 23   8 Feb 1951
[Constitutional review]: CO note on a meeting held with Sir H Foot to discuss communist activity in Nigeria

General

Mr. Cohen said that he wanted to be sure enough was being done at this end to counter Communist propaganda and to encourage an understanding of the positive side of British policy. It appeared that Communism was more of a problem in Nigeria than anywhere else in Africa, partly due to the difficult labour situation. It also seemed that the percentage of Nigerian students in this country who were Communists was higher than that for students from any other colonial territory.

Sir H. Foot said that the Conference of the West African Governors had had this problem on its agenda. On the negative side, the Governor was reconsidering the question of banning individual books and he thought it was probable that proposals on this point would be coming from Nigeria shortly. Positively, he felt not enough had been done either here or in Nigeria in the past. The average administrative officer was not a good publicity man. However the advent of Mr. Chalmers as Head of the Broadcasting Service had been most welcome and the development of broadcasting should be a great help to government publicity. The Gaskiya Corporation had done valuable work and the Marketing Boards had recently recruited a man called Hennessy for publicity work; he would work under the P.R.O. but his salary would be met from Marketing Board funds.

Sir H. Foot said that it would be most helpful to Nigeria if Mr. Carstairs[1] could visit them for a short while to see things for himself and give a fillip to the work already being done. This visit could best take place when Mr. Cooper, the P.R.O., returned from leave. Mr. Cohen said he thought such a visit was essential. Mr. Carstairs agreed it would be most valuable. He would need to wait for the return of Mr. Ingrams from his tour of West Africa (mid-March) but would hope to go out to spend some six weeks in West Africa before the Conference of Information Officers in June.[2] It was agreed to pursue this question with Mr. Thomas.[3]

Sir H. Foot said he was sure the right policy was being followed in Nigeria, but it was not being put over with sufficient force to the people. As far as communism was concerned, the counter-measures now being discussed were being conceived in good time. The security authorities and the police were liable to take an exaggerated view of the extent of communist activities. The communists in Nigeria were having a rough time and the recent revelations about the money Eze had received had led even the West African Pilot to come out with an attack on communist influence.

Literature

Sir H. Foot felt that while the Nigerian Government could do a lot to publicise the positive side of their achievements the counter-propaganda work could best be done from London. In any case it would be difficult to persuade the Nigerian Finance Committee to find the money for such a move. There was an insatiable demand for reading matter in Nigeria as the C.M.S. travelling bookshops had found. Cheap subsidized pamphlets with plenty of facts addressed to farmers, trade unionists and so forth, should go down well. These pamphlets besides describing the evils of communism could also eulogise the British political system, local government, etc. It would be helpful if an organisation could be built up which would give local vendors in Nigeria a rake-off for literature sold. It would also be valuable to keep in close touch with the American P.R.Os in Lagos. Sir H. Foot mentioned in passing that Mr. W. Aitken M.P.,[4] who was connected with the Express newspapers, had recently visited West Africa and had been most enthusiastic about e.g. press

[1] C Y Carstairs, ass sec, CO, director of information service from 1950.
[2] See 130.   [3] A R Thomas, ass sec, CO, establishment officer.
[4] W T Aitken, Conservative MP for Bury St Edmunds, 1950–1964; nephew of Lord Beaverbrook.

developments in the Gold Coast; Mr. Aitken proposed to speak about the West African Press in the Commons when opportunity offered.

Mr. Carstairs emphasised the importance of keeping a separate organisation for the anti-communist work and not for example mixing up the British Council with it. He said that work had already started on the preparation of pamphlets. He agreed with Mr. Cohen that not too much time should be spent on swopping drafts back and forth with Nigeria but that there should be a periodical review to see how the pamphlets were being received in West Africa. 100,000 copies of part of the Prime Minister's speech against communism at Forest Hill had gone out to Nigeria. A list of bad points of presentation, which should be avoided, was being drawn up. It seemed likely that material on the relation of communism with Islam and with rural life would be valuable. More writers were needed to make presentable a mass of rather indigestible material which already existed. Mr. Cohen said that Vernon Bartlett might be able to assist.

On the question of the money, which Eze had recently received from communist sources in Europe,[5] Mr. Cohen said that the Colonial Office would take the problem up with the Treasury to see if anything could be done.

Students

Mr. Cohen said that the extent of communism among students in this country was often exaggerated. The British Council was doing most valuable work and Government-sponsored students were well catered for. The core of the matter lay in the development of individual friendships between colonial students and the peoples of this country. Mr. Carstairs said a lot was being done socially by way of tea parties etc. But the communists were able to attract those who loved to talk politics. He thought it ought to be possible to stage political discussions through existing hostels and societies to meet this need. Sir H. Foot observed that care would have to be taken in such discussions to see that extremist groups did not dominate the proceedings.

Mr. Cohen felt that there was room for at least five hostels in London on the lines of that at Hans Crescent, and the Nigerian and Gold Coast Governments ought to be able to help on the financial side. Sir H. Foot said that the view of the Nigerian Finance Committee was that too much money was already being spent on students in view of the general financial position and it would be most difficult to persuade the Committee to contribute any more. He thought some of the new C. D. & W. money might be used.

---

[5] This refers to the concern which was expressed within the CO at payments from Eastern Europe that were said to have reached a number of Nigerian organisations and individuals, and particularly £2,000 which was reported to have been transferred in early 1951 from Czech sources to Nigerian trade unions with which Nduka Eze was connected (CO 537/6781). See 132.

134 CO 583/307/1, no 7   16 Feb 1951

[Constitutional review]: letter from L H Gorsuch to Sir J Macpherson on the electoral system under the proposed new constitution

In my letter of the 7th February in which I gave you an account of the discussions we had with Foot I promised that I would write again after Foot had seen the Secretary of State about the proposed electoral arrangements in Nigeria.

I enclose a copy of the minute[1] which I wrote when submitting these questions to the Secretary of State, as I think this will give you the fullest possible account of the questions which arose. The Secretary of State saw no objection to the method of legislating for the elections which is proposed in Nigeria, as he fully appreciated the reasons why Regulations made by the Governor in Council were the only practical method in the circumstances. The Secretary of State is also ready to accept the proposals for the methods of conducting elections in the north and the west through an electoral pyramid; there are disadvantages in a system of several electoral stages, but on the other hand it is the expressed wish of the Regional Houses that the elections should be conducted in that way.

There is, however, one recommendation which the Secretary of State would find it most difficult to accept; that is, the proposal that in the Western Region there should be up to 50% of Native Authority representation in the intermediate electoral college. He raises no objection in principle to Native Authority representation in the electoral system, and is ready to accept the recommendation made in the North; but the proportion proposed in the West seems to him excessive. Foot explained that the Native Authorities in the West represented an extremely important element in the life of the community and one in which ordinary people took very great pride. He referred to the policy of broadening the basis of representation in Native Authorities, which has had a considerable amount of success in the West, and drew attention to the danger that refusal by the Secretary of State to accept a recommendation which had been worked out after considerable discussion would have a damaging effect on the prestige of Native Authorities, which would be particularly unfortunate in the light of the policy of progressive democratization of those authorities. He made the point that in the existing Constitution the Native Authorities alone constitute the equivalent of an electoral college and that it is in any case a considerable advance to reduce their position by 50%.

The Secretary of State's objection to the proposal lies in the degree of control over the composition of the Lower House which it might give to the Native Authorities. They will clearly play a large part in the choice of members of the Western House of Chiefs. An injection of 50% Native Authority representation into the intermediate electoral college for the other House might well mean that, by securing the support of a fraction of the other representatives in the college, the Native Authorities would in fact dominate the proceedings of the college and secure a clear majority of Native Authority representation in the final college. We discussed with the Secretary of State the possibility of avoiding this by laying it down that Native Authority representation in the final college should be limited to 50% also; but the objection to such a proposal is that a maximum tends to become in practice the figure which is always worked to, and a vested interest might thus be created in favour of the Native Authorities which would set up an obstacle to further amendment of the Constitution in future in a more democratic direction.

The Secretary of State feels that agreement to a 50% representation for the Native Authorities, whether at an intermediate stage or at both intermediate and final stages, might well evoke criticism in this country to which it would be difficult for him to find an effective answer. If, as seems possible (though you will be the best

[1] Not printed.

judge of this), criticism arises in Nigeria from the nontraditional elements on the ground that the scales are being too heavily weighted in favour of the traditional authorities, there is little doubt that such criticism would be taken up in this country.

In these circumstances the Secretary of State would like you to consider as an alternative that there should be up to 25% Native Authority representation in the final electoral college. Foot thought that this, as a new proposal, might be easier for Western opinion to accept than up to 25% of the intermediate colleges. The Secretary of State thinks that this arrangement could be justified on the grounds of the importance of the Native Authorities in the West and the fact that they contain a very high proportion of the people who are most suited to be members of the legislatures. This proportion would not, however, give them a dominant voice in the electoral procedure or be likely to evoke the criticism that so much weight was being given to them as to render the elections undemocratic. Unless you have strong reasons for not wishing to do so, the Secretary of State would like you to put this alternative proposal to the people concerned in the Western Region in such way as you think fit, explaining the difficulties which he sees in the present proposal and making it clear that he is anxious that a share in the electoral procedure, which adequately recognises their status and interests, shall be secured for the Native Authorities by mutual agreement.

On the other points I need only say that the Secretary of State accepts the arrangements which have been made as adequate at this stage to cater for the representation of minorities, but he will wish in his published despatch to draw attention to this problem. Similarly he will wish to draw attention to the desirability of working out more precise electoral methods by the time of the holding of the next General Election. We shall, of course, be consulting you at a later stage about the wording to be used in such a despatch.

135   CO 583/307/1, no 8   27 Feb 1951
[Constitutional review]: letter (reply) from Sir J Macpherson to L H Gorsuch on the electoral system under the proposed new constitution

This is a reply, ad interim, to your Secret letter of the 16th of February (reference No.30453/14) about our electoral arrangements.[1] A full reply will be sent after I have had discussions (about the West) with Hoskyns-Abrahall who will be here in a day or two.

I am very glad that the Secretary of State generally approves the electoral arrangements which, as Cohen pointed out in his minute of which a copy was enclosed with your letter, are in accordance with the wishes of the people.

As regards the Western Region, I note that the Secretary of State feels that a 50% representation for the Native Authorities, whether in the intermediate or final Electoral Colleges, or in both, might evoke criticism in the United Kingdom which he would find it difficult to answer. I shall discuss with Hoskyns-Abrahall and my other Advisers what we can do about this. But I am quite certain (and this is the main pur-

---

[1] See 134.

pose of this letter) that it would be exceedingly dangerous to mention it to any Africans from the Western Region until after I know what the reactions are to the statement I propose to make in my opening address to Legislative Council on the 1st of March about inter-Regional boundaries. Foot told you about this difficult and explosive subject. The Members of the Western House of Assembly, the Obas, and the educated commoners like Awolowo all feel very hotly about this, and I shall be enormously relieved if they accept my statement which makes the matter one of personal confidence in me. I know that if I were to tell Members of the Western House of Assembly now, while they are still steamed up about the Inter-Regional Boundary, that the Secretary of State found it impossible to accept the electoral arrangements they have proposed then I should have the gravest apprehensions about the attitude of the Western Members in the forthcoming Legislative Council. They feel that intransigence paid dividends to the North and they might well be disposed to stick to their threat (made at the last House of Assembly meeting) to refuse to work out electoral arrangements (or even to have anything to do with the revised Constitution) unless they received a satisfactory answer to their claims on Ilorin Province.

I may say that I do not hold any special brief for the Western arrangements regarding the 50% Native Authority representation. But I have always taken the line that these electoral arrangements were, within limits, matters for Regional decision, and the 50% was a compromise. I have been told that the Egbe Owo Oduduwa, who include in their ranks most of the progressive people like Awolowo, agreed to this compromise provided that pressure was exerted regarding Regional boundaries. Certainly there has been no criticism of the arrangements either in the 'National' or in the Regional Press.

We propose, at next week's meeting of Legislative Council, to lay on the table the reports of all three Regions on electoral procedure. This will at least give any Member an opportunity to raise the question.

If we get over the Regional Boundary question successfully, I shall discuss with Hoskyns-Abrahall the question of whether, and if so how, we can put to the West the Secretary of State's alternative proposal for representation of up to 25% Native Authority representation in the final Electoral College.

I shall report developments.

136   CO 583/307/1, no 10   30 Mar 1951
[Constitutional review]: letter from Sir J Macpherson to A B Cohen on the electoral arrangements for the Western provinces and on the formation of the Action Group. *Minutes* by M Phillips, R J Vile and L H Gorsuch.

[The debate about the electoral arrangements for the Western region was finally resolved with the CO decision, conveyed in an outward telegram, no 491, to Sir J Macpherson on 24 Apr 1951, in CO 583/307/1, no 13, to accept his proposals as outlined in this letter.]

This is a follow-up of my letter to Gorsuch of the 27th of February[1] about electoral arrangements in the Western Provinces.

---

[1] See 135.

We got through Legislative Council without any outburst from the West in open Council on the subject of the Inter-Regional boundary, but feelings ran pretty high. After my statement on the opening day—when I took the very unusual course of making the matter a question of personal confidence in myself—Sir Kofo Abayomi[2] told me that the West were saying that I 'had done a big Yoruba on them', meaning that by adroit action I had placed them in a difficult position. This seemed promising, but later the Oni of Ife[3] asked to see me. He feels as strongly as anyone about the boundary and though he understands the reasons for my attitude, he had been unable to convince the Egbe Omo Oduduwa and he urged me to tackle the boundary question now. I refused to give ground but I gave him some additional ammunition to use in argument with the Egbe people, and I also offered to receive a delegation from them, at his request, if he judged this to be desirable. He failed to persuade them to accept the position as determined by my statement and I then, with Hoskyns-Abrahall, had a session with three representatives of the Egbe Omo Oduduwa (Awolowo, Oyedeiran, Headmaster of the Methodist Boys School and a very nice person, and Bode Thomas) introduced by the Oni. We had a very frank discussion but again I refused to budge, pointing out that any move to enquire into the claims of Yorubas in Ilorin Province to be taken with the West would immediately lead to clamour for boundary adjustments by others—e.g. the Kabba-Yagba and the Ogori in Kabba Province, and the claim of the 'Western Ibos' in Benin Province to go East. (References to these claims and others had been made in speeches in Legislative Council a day or two before by Azikiwe and Nyong Essien). The next thing would be a resuscitation of the demand for a 'Central Region', and encouragement would be given to the demand, inspired by the Missions, to split the North into two Regions. If we got involved in all these we might as well give up hope of getting the new Constitution introduced within two years or more, or perhaps ever in anything like its present form. I believe that in their hearts they saw the force of my arguments but they would not admit this, saying only that they would report back to their organisation.

That was nearly three weeks ago and I have heard no more from them. I don't believe that the Yorubas have the sustained strength of character to 'walk out' on the new Constitution over this (after all the new Constitution as it has emerged is very much what the Egbe Omo Oduduwa and the Yoruba Movement wanted) but there is no disguising the fact that the Yorubas do feel very strongly on the boundary question; that they are suspicious of Government's attitude to the North; and that anything which they would regard as a rebuff to the Yorubas might cause them to stick their toes in. Much depends on their reactions to the recommendations of the Hicks Commission on Revenue Allocation.[4] It is a very good report but Hicks, in carrying out an academic exercise in a very realistic way, could not refrain from

---

[2] Sir Kofoworola Abayomi, physician and politician; founding member of the Lagos Youth Movement; president of the NYM, 1938; member of the Legislative Council, 1938–1940; chairman of University Teaching Hospital, Ibadan, 1951.

[3] Oba Adesoji Tadeniawo Aderemi I, Ooni of Ife, senior traditional ruler among the Yoruba; member of the Legislative Council from 1947; member of the House of Representatives from 1951; minister without portfolio, 1951–1955; appointed first Nigerian Governor of the Western Region, 1960.

[4] This refers to the Hicks-Phillipson Commission, established in 1950 to examine the allocation of revenue between regions; J R Hicks and S Phillipson, *Report of the Fiscal Commission on Revenue Allocation* (Lagos, 1951).

'showing his working', with the result that there are parts of the Report which can be used by each Region—and especially the North and West—to complain bitterly. We are living *very dangerously* until we know whether we can 'sell' the Report to the Regions.

It is about time that I came to the subject of this letter! After the first excitement about my statement on the boundary had simmered down, Hoskyns-Abrahall had discussions with Unofficial Members of the Western House of Assembly, who were in Lagos for Legislative Council, about Native Authority representation in the electoral colleges in the West. They gave consideration to your suggestion that instead of this being up to 50% in the intermediate electoral college it should be up to 25% in the final electoral college, but they reaffirmed their view in favour of the original arrangement. They pointed out that this recommendation was the result of long and careful deliberation and was agreed to in the Western House of Assembly by a majority of 17 to 1—all Unofficial Members—and they stated that any change now would not be acceptable.

It seems to me that there are two aspects of this matter which require consideration. The first is whether we accept the view that the arrangement, on its merits, is sufficiently 'democratic'. The second is whether, even if this is answered in the affirmative, it may lead to criticism by the non-traditional elements in this country which would be taken up in the United Kingdom and embarrass the Secretary of State.

On the first point I am bound to say that if the West wants it like that it does not shock me. And although I appreciate the danger, to which reference was made in Gorsuch's letter No. 30453/14 of the 16th of February,[5] that a maximum tends in practice to become the fixed figure, Hoskyns-Abrahall assures me that in some areas the proportion prescribed will be much less than 50%. I discussed the matter briefly the other day with the Resident of one of the more progressive Western Provinces and he told me that the 50% arrangement was just what his people wanted. The taxpayers will be brought together to choose one man to go to the intermediate college and the Native Authority will also choose one. These two will go forward to the intermediate college and from there it is entirely open. We have as yet no Nigerian political party with organizing powers comparable with those of the C.P.P. in the Gold Coast. Within the past week, however, the left-wing elements of the Egbe Omo Oduduwa, which sets out to be cultural rather than political, have announced the formation of an 'Action Group', led by Awolowo, which is frankly political, and have announced their intention of sweeping the field in the Western Region elections.[6] Their manifesto, of which I enclose a copy,[7] is moderately worded, and the development is probably not unhealthy. But even if they remain reasonably responsible there will be a temptation to send young speakers into the villages to stand on soap-boxes and promise a new heaven upon earth. Where Native Authorities are progressive and are carrying out their functions with confidence and to the satisfaction of the people, the soap-box orators will, I think, fail. But in the more backward areas the simple villagers *may* be carried away and may make a choice of representatives which they will later bitterly regret. In these circumstances, a good

---

[5] See 134.

[6] The Action Group, which first began meeting in 1950, was formally launched at Owo in April 1951.

[7] Not printed.

leavening of sound persons from the Native Authorities, who have learned to take responsibility by performing public services, will, I suggest, be no bad thing.

I turn now to the second point: the probable reactions. I cannot, of course, promise that there will be no criticism, even at this late stage, from non-traditional elements. But I said, in my letter of 27th February, that there had been no criticism of the Western Electoral arrangements, either in the 'national' or in the Regional press. That is still the position. Azikiwe had put down questions for answer in Legislative Council earlier this month, about the electoral arrangements in all three Regions. We had, as I indicated in my earlier letter, laid on the table the reports from all the Regions on electoral procedure, but supplementaries were not asked and no motion was made on the subject. Moreover, Hoskyns-Abrahall tells me that Awolowo, in conversation with Shankland, Secretary Western Provinces, said that the Egbe Omo Oduduwa were quite happy about the electoral arrangements. And you will note that the manifesto of the Action Group, though it aims at Self-Government now and makes a passing reference to 'a change in the present electoral system', does not criticize the Western electoral arrangements within the framework of the revised Constitution and proposes to run candidates. My guess is that there will be no criticism of these arrangements in advance of the elections.

I should like to have discussed the whole question frankly with Awolowo but this would not be appropriate. The 25% suggestion has been put to Western Unofficial Members of the Legislative Council and they do not favour it. It is now a matter for the Secretary of State's decision whether he will refuse to accept the 50% arrangement. The only other matter on which the Secretary of State is taking a strong line is the question of the method of selecting Ministers, and this is by agreement with the Nigerian Government though not after consultation with Legislative Council. I am obliged to say that in my view it would look somewhat out of proportion if a strong line were taken on a matter which is after all very much one for Regional, not even Nigerian, decision.

Minutes on 136

It was agreed in discussions with the Secretary of State in February that we should go back to the Governor on the proposal to have 50% Native Authority representation in the intermediate electoral colleges of the Western Region under the new constitution, and it was suggested to the Governor as an alternative that there should be 25% N. A. representation in the final electoral colleges. We now have at (10) Sir John Macpherson's views on this alternative.

The Governor discussed the alternative proposals with the Chief Commissioner, Western Provinces, and with unofficial members from the West at the recent Budget session of Legislative Council, and it is clear from (10) that they stick to their original recommendations.

The arguments in favour of the original proposal now seem to be these:—

(a) Public opinion in the West is very agitated over the problem of regional boundaries. The Governor has stated he does not propose to do anything about this until *after* the inauguration of the new constitution, and has made it an issue of personal confidence in himself. There may also be difficulties with the West over the Revenue Allocation Commission's Report, now under consideration. To administer a 'further rebuff to the Yorubas' by seeking to change a recommendation, approved by the unofficials of the Western House by 17–1, might lead to trouble.

(b) N.A. representation will provide a 'good leavening of sound persons . . . who have learned to take responsibility by performing public services' against the irresponsible elements, that may secure the favour of backward voters unused to soapbox oratory.

(c) Non-traditional elements in Lagos and the West have not as yet shewn any signs of revolt against the proposed electoral system; in fact Awolowo and the Yoruba 'Action Group', which would seem to be the sort of organisation catering for such critics, is preparing to fight the elections in the West under the system proposed, without apparently making an issue of that system.

(d) Above all the decision on this question is a decision of primary concern to the West. The proposals that have emerged are themselves the result of reconciling conflicting views and it would be therefore unwise to upset them.

Whatever we may think about these arguments as a whole (and (b) above is not very convincing, to say the least) my feeling is that it is clear that 50% representation for N.A.s in intermediate electoral colleges is what the representatives of the Western Region want and it will now be exceedingly difficult to reject. I think we shall have to accept the point but draw attention in the published despatch which is to issue to our misgivings expressed in (7). I do not think at that time there is likely to be any sustained campaign against the electoral structure.

M.P.
4.4.51

We have consistently tried, in the consideration of the Nigerian constitutional proposals, to accept wherever possible proposals to which Nigerian public opinion was committed. In this particular question we were concerned lest the arrangement proposed was designed primarily to strengthen the hands of the traditional element, and to give Native Authorities a predominating voice in the elections.

The facts that Dr. Awolowo, who is the reverse of a 'traditional element' (he has indeed frequently been a successful trouble-maker), accepts the present proposals, and that, in the light of the S. of S's suggestion, there is the unanimous view that the original proposals are preferable, suggest that the arrangements proposed by the Western House are fair and acceptable. In these circumstances I suggest that we can only accept those recommendations.

The Governor does not say in his letter what views he would have if the S of S wished to express any misgivings in his published despatch. It would, I suggest, be best to confine any remarks in that despatch to a statement on the lines of X of Mr. Cohen's minute of 2/2.[8]

There is a certain amount of urgency about this matter, as the Governor will wish shortly to issue the Electoral Regulations.

R.J.V.
6.4.51

---

[8] See 131.

Mr. Cohen
I am inclined to advise, in view of (10), that we should accept the Nigerian view on the 50% arrangement. You may wish to discuss.

L.H.G.
11.4.51

137   CO 537/7166, no 20   15 Apr 1951
[Constitutional review]: despatch no 147A from Mr Griffiths to Sir J Macpherson on the CO's decisions concerning the composition of the central legislature and the selection of ministers

In paragraph 8 of my Despatch No. 464A of the 15th July, 1950[1] on the proposals for constitutional reform in Nigeria, I referred to the recommendations made by the General Conference at Ibadan that the Ministers at the centre and in the regions should be elected by the respective legislatures, and that the arrangements for the distribution of portfolios among these Ministers should be settled at the centre by the Governor-in-Council and in the regions by the Lieutenant-Governor-in-Council. I said that these were matters on which final decisions could not be taken until the composition of the Nigerian legislature had been settled; but I went on to suggest that the aim should be to arrive at a procedure under which members of the Council of Ministers are selected in consultation between the Governor and the members of the Nigerian legislature representing each region, and members of the Regional Executive Council in consultation between the Lieutenant-Governor and members of the Regional legislature.

2.   The composition of the Nigerian legislature has now been settled, and much thought has been devoted to the methods to be adopted for the selection of Ministers and the allocation of portfolios. After careful consideration His Majesty's Government has thought it advisable to decide these two issues in a manner different from the recommendations of the General Conference. I propose to set out in this despatch the reasons which have led His Majesty's Government to these decisions.

3.   I should like in the first place to state certain principles by which, given the form which the new Nigerian Constitution is to take, it seems to me that the choice of Ministers should be governed. A Minister, whether in the region or at the centre, must inevitably have a dual responsibility; he must be responsible to the Lieutenant-Governor or Governor on whom rests the ultimate responsibility for the administration and at the same time he is responsible to the legislature. This being so, it seems to me desirable that both parties should bear a share of the responsibility for choosing him. Secondly, in deciding on the method of choice of a Minister it is necessary to bear in mind the qualities which it is desired to obtain in him. He should have ability and integrity; he should be able to work with each and all of his colleagues as a member of that particular team; and in the present circumstances in Nigeria he should be acceptable to the region from which he derives. It is the view of His Majesty's Government that this combination of qualities is more likely to be

---

[1] See 116.

obtained by a process in which selection by consultation takes some part than by election alone.

4.   As was stated in paragraph 8 of my Despatch No. 464A, His Majesty's Government are anxious that, from the outset, a procedure for appointment of Ministers should be adopted which will lead on smoothly to the stages of further evolution towards self-government. With this in mind, and after careful weighing the considerations in the preceding paragraph of this despatch, they have come to the conclusion that the system of appointment laid down in the Constitution shall provide for selection by a process combining the elements of consultation and approval by the Legislature rather than by election. The procedure for which the new Constitution will provide is that Regional Ministers will be appointed by the Lieutenant-Governor after consultation with members of the Regional House, and that the four Central Ministers from the region will be appointed by the Governor on the recommendation of the Lieutenant-Governor after consultation with members of the Regional House. In both cases formal appointment will be made only in pursuance of a resolution of the Regional House concerned.

5.   It will be seen that this procedure varies in one respect from the suggestion made in paragraph 8 of my despatch No. 464A, in which the proposal was that members of the Council of Ministers should be selected in consultation between the Governor and the members of the Nigerian legislature representing each region. A Regional House, when it has been constituted and assembles for the first time, will have to find the Regional Ministers and also the members who will represent the region in the Central Legislature. The third step which will then be necessary will be to find four Central Ministers from the region. There are strong arguments, as I believe you agree, for taking all these three steps as part of one process. Immediately the composition of a Regional House is known, it will be necessary to decide with full regard to the principles set out in the third paragraph of this despatch, which of those members who are best fitted to be Ministers should devote the major part of their time to regional business and which to the business of central government. It might well be that if a decision were taken as regards Regional Ministers alone, some of the most suitable aspirants as Central Ministers might no longer be available for selection. The procedure will accordingly be that, at the same time as the members to represent the Region in the Central Legislature are being elected, there will be consultation between the Lieutenant-Governor and the members of the Regional Legislature in which choice of both the Regional Ministers and the four Central Ministers will be agreed upon; the Lieutenant-Governor will then consult the Governor about the latter and will obtain his concurrence: and the Regional House will then be asked to confirm the appointment of the four Central Ministers by resolution in the same way as it will confirm the appointment of the Regional Ministers.

6.   I have considered whether Central Ministers selected in this way by consultation with the Regional House might be disposed to feel that their responsibility lay towards the Region alone rather than towards the centre and whether this would not militate against the feeling of unity at the centre which is so necessary. I feel, however, that any such tendency would be quickly corrected by the nature of a Minister's work at the centre. He will have to deal with questions of a Nigerian-wide nature, and also, on occasion, with questions with which his own Region might not be directly concerned. The effect of this would be to instil into him

a Nigerian habit of thought; and indeed it is the Nigerian-wide nature of ministerial responsibility at the centre which provides the justification for the arrangement whereby a Minister whose appointment derives from the region is removable by a vote of the whole Central Legislature. In short, by appointment he derives from the Region; but once appointed his responsibility is to Nigeria.

7.   I feel confident that the members of the General Conference and all others who have taken part in framing the new Constitution for Nigeria will realise that if in this one respect His Majesty's Government have not accepted the recommendations which were evolved in Nigeria, it is because His Majesty's Government are anxious, as I have said, to see a system adopted from the outset which will evolve naturally into the more advanced form of self-government which lies in the future.

8.   I shall be glad if you will cause this despatch to be published.

138   CO 537/7166, no 8   15 May 1951
[Constitutional review]: letter from Sir J Macpherson to A B Cohen on the differences between the new constitution and the proposals made at the Ibadan conference. *Annexure*

Now that the drafting of the Constitution Instruments is nearing an end—thanks in great measure to the devoted labours of McPetrie—and the main Order-in-Council is shortly to appear, we have been wondering whether publication of these documents should not be accompanied by publication of an official expression of views on your side or ours, or both. It is, I suggest, somewhat remarkable that although the idea of revision of the Constitution was taken up nearly three years ago and a succession of conferences has considered every aspect of it since, there have been so far only three formal communications-our despatch No. 11 of the 24th March, 1949, on the procedure suggested for the process of revision,[1] our further despatch No. 16 of the 27th April, 1949, on the length of time this would take, and the Secretary of State's despatch No. 464A of the 15th of July, 1950, conveying H.M.G.'s views on the General Conference proposals, and sent at our suggestion.[2] There has, of course, been much demi-official correspondence and a great many personal discussions have taken place, but I think the absence of official interchange of views may be taken as a measure of the degree of confidence that has prevailed between the Colonial Office on the one side and ourselves on the other.

None the less I feel we are coming to a stage where something more must be officially said for public consumption. I anticipate that when the Instruments are published a great deal of attention will be directed on them to see how far they really implement the recommendations of the General Conference, as modified by Legislative Council at its two meetings last year and whether there are any striking differences. A certain amount of modification of those recommendations in detail has, of course, been inevitable, and there has had to be some introduction of new matter to fill in the gap left by the General Conference—which after all was only concerned with very broad outlines. But there has also been at least one very substantial divergence in the matter of choosing Ministers.

---

[1] See 65.   [2] See 116.

We thought here that it would be a good idea to prepare a statement showing the various divergences and additions. The material might come in useful if an exchange of despatches were to be decided on, and in any event it attempts to summarise the general differences between the Instruments and the publicly agreed proposals here. I enclose six copies of this statement, drawn up as a memorandum. It deals with the executive and legislative organs proposed for the Constitution, and with certain matters of legislative procedure, but says nothing about the Public Service Commission, safeguards for the Civil Service, or finance. We take it that on the first two of these points the Secretary of State will send us a despatch similar to his despatch No. 492 of the 19th December, 1950, to the Gold Coast, and finance will probably have to be separately treated after we have made up our minds on the Revenue Allocation Report.

So far as divergences from the General Conference proposals are concerned, by far the most important is the change in the method of selecting Ministers. We have readily adopted the Secretary of State's view on this subject but we have not had consultations here, although I have informed my Executive Council of the proposed change. You will remember that the General Conference was quite clear on wanting election in preference to selection after consultation, and in the circumstances we feel that the system approved would best be introduced by a despatch from the Secretary of State explaining the reasons for the change, in pursuance of the argument in paragraph 8 of his despatch of the 15th July last year. Such a despatch could be published at the same time as the Instruments; and as this particular matter is bound to have attention focussed on it here we should very much like, if it can be so arranged, to see it in draft first.

It is for consideration whether there should not be another exchange of despatches, covering a wider field and including the other matters mentioned in the attached paper. There may be other points to which the Secretary of State would wish to refer in some detail, such as the electoral arrangements. I should, of course, be very ready to convert the memorandum attached into a formal despatch, with recommendations, and the Secretary of State might be prepared to approve the recommendations and then to go on to make any points thought desirable. But I feel sure that any despatches of this nature intended for publication should be dated later than the Colonial Office despatch on the selection of Ministers.

I should be very grateful for your views on this.

Annexure to 138: Memorandum on certain features of the constitutional arrangements

I. *Preliminary*

It has been sought to frame the revised Constitution of Nigeria mainly on the basis of recommendations made by a series of representative conferences. The extent to which these were found acceptable by His Majesty's Government, subject to further examination of detail, has been indicated by the Secretary of State in his Despatch No. 464A of the 15th of July, 1950. The recommendations were themselves based on the proposals of a series of village and local meetings invited to express their general views on the broad outlines of constitutional change, and for the purpose of drafting the various Instruments a substantial degree of elaboration, co-ordination and detailed modification of the recommendations has inevitably been found necessary. In particular, the General (and final) Conference failed to reach agreement on the major issue of composition of the Central Legislature, and the subsequent re-consideration of this matter by Regional Houses and Legislative Council involved divergence to some extent from other proposals for which general agreement had been obtained.

2.   The Instruments also incorporate one major departure in principle from the General Conference proposals, occasioned by the necessity of bringing the practice to be prescribed into line with the correct constitutional position.

3.   The main variations between the contents of the Instruments and the Conference recommendations relate to:—

    (a) the executive arrangements, with reference to:—
        (i) the method of selection of Ministers (this is the major matter mentioned in para.2 above);
        (ii) the extent of the executive authority of the Central Government;
        (iii) the number of Regional ministers;
        (iv) the provisions for terminating Ministerial appointments;
    (b) the composition of the Legislatures, specifically with reference to:—
        (i) the size of the Central and Regional Houses and basis of representation therein;
        (ii) the representation of special interests;
        (iii) the choice of Presiding Officers;
        (iv) the electoral arrangements.
    (c) procedure in respect of legislation, with regard to:—
        (i) the power of the two Houses in a bicameral Legislature;
        (ii) the disallowance of Regional Legislation;
        (iii) the Regional consideration of Central legislation.

The variations or modifications in question are set out in that order.

II. *Executive arrangements*

4.   *Selection of ministers.* The development of this issue constitutes the outstanding divergence from the General Conference recommendations. The Conference proposed that the twelve non-official Central Ministers should comprise four Ministers from each Region, and that each such group of four Ministers should be elected by the members from the Region concerned in the House of Representatives. Regional Ministers were to be elected by members of Regional Houses. These recommendations were made after a strong majority vote had been recorded in favour of the election of Ministers as against any system of selection by the Governor or Lieutenant-Governors, whether with or without consultation with the Legislatures.

5.   In paragraph 8 of his Despatch of the 15th of July the Secretary of State expressed his desire that a system of selection be established which could develop in due course into the appointment by a Prime Minister of his own Ministerial colleagues, and suggested the desirability of procedure under which members of the Central and Regional Executives would be selected by the Governor or Lieutenant-Governors in consultation with the Legislature concerned.

6.   It was subsequently further pointed out by the Colonial Office that:—

(a) A Minister will be responsible not only to the Legislature, but also to the Governor or Lieutenant-Governor, who retains ultimate responsibility for the administration of his charge. Accordingly the Governor or Lieutenant-Governor must have a voice in his selection;

(b) it is impracticable to leave to the hazard of popular election the choice of men for office requiring ability, integrity and tact;

(c) should a Minister be guilty of disloyalty or breach of the prescribed rules of conduct the Governor or Lieutenant-Governor would find embarrassment in removing him if he owed his position to popular vote;

(d) Ministerial talent should be used to the best advantage whether in the Regions or at the Centre.

The Colonial Office therefore proposed the alternative procedure of selection of Regional Ministers by the Lieutenant-Governors in consultation with the Regional Legislature, and of each group of Central Ministers by the Governor after consultation between the Lieutenant-Governor and the Regional Legislature concerned. In both cases approval of the Regional Legislature by resolution would be sought to the appointment.

7.   These proposals are in conformity with the Secretary of State's view, but contain a modification of his original suggestion in view of Regional Houses having to find from amongst their number not only Regional Ministers but also members of the House of Representatives and potential Central Ministers—a process of selection which might well be carried out at one stage as far as possible.

8.   It has been agreed that the Colonial Office view should be accepted but it has not been possible to arrange for further consultation on any appreciable scale of representative opinion on the point. Having regard to this circumstance and to the clear recommendation made by the General Conference (by 34 votes to 9) in favour of a system of pure election, it is thought desirable that the decision should be shown to be one made by the Secretary of State and that it might be so expressed in a Despatch to be published.

9.   *Executive authority of the central government.* In paragraph 7 of his Despatch the Secretary of State indicated the importance he placed on preserving and strengthening the unity of Nigeria, and the welcome which he gave to recommendations for a strong Central Legislature and Executive. It therefore seems necessary that the over-all and over-riding authority of the Central Government should be clearly expressed in the Constitutional Instruments, and that the authority of Regional Executives should be clearly defined in such a manner that, while in no way seeking to derogate from the degree of autonomous evolution proposed for the Regions, the subordination of these Regional Executives should be placed beyond doubt. The necessity of such definition, important as it is in principle, is further reinforced in respect of detail by the re-organisation of various major Departments to conform with the Regions' new status. In some cases Regional Departments will be required to perform agency functions for the Central Government, and it is important that the Central Government should be able to ensure that its requirements and instructions are duly observed. There should, therefore, be some elaboration of the recommendation of the General Conference that a Regional Executive Council should formulate policy and direct executive action subject to any general instruction on the grounds that the major overall Government of Nigeria is

involved. It is considered that the Governor, on the advice of his Council, should be able, from time to time, to give to the Lieutenant-Governors of a Region special directions with respect to the exercise of the executive authority of the Region for the purpose of ensuring good government in Nigeria. Such directions would normally relate to the subject listed in the General Conference recommendations as appropriate for Regional legislative jurisdiction, but could also include other instructions which it may be necessary for the Head of the Government of Nigeria to issue from time to time.

10. *Number of regional ministers.* The number of Ministers in the Central Executive was closely defined by the General Conference and in view of the necessity of giving each Region equal representation in the Council of Ministers there is no occasion to vary this recommendation. In respect, however, of Regional Executives, the General Conference proposed that there should be five official members and nine Ministers in the Northern and Eastern Regions, and three official members and nine Ministers in the Western Region. The position in respect of the Western Region has, of course, altered, by reason of the subsequent recommendation of Legislative Council that Lagos and the Colony should be included, for administrative and legislative purposes, within the Western Region, and it would therefore seem appropriate that the maximum number of official members of the Western Regional Council should be five, in line with the figure for the other two Regions. The number of Ministers to be found from amongst members of Regional Houses was not prescribed by the General Conference with any regard to the volume of work which might fall to these Ministers or to the division of subjects which might appear practicable. Examination of these points has shown that it may not be necessary, at the outset of the Constitution at least, to have so many as nine Ministers selected in each Region from the Regional Houses, and it now proposed that in the Northern and Western Regions the minimum number of such Ministers should be six and the maximum number nine, and that in the Eastern Region the minimum number seven and the maximum number nine. The actual number of Ministers selected would vary in each Region according to the volume and nature of work. A higher minimum figure has been proposed for the East in order to provide for one Minister from the Trust Territory of the Cameroons, as recommended by the General Conference. In view of the responsibility resting on the Governor and Lieutenant-Governor, the distribution of portfolios amongst the Ministers should be at their discretion.

11. *Termination of appointment of ministers.* It was proposed by the General Conference that the appointment of Ministers at the Centre and in the Regions should be terminated in the event of an adverse vote by the Legislature, specified as a two-thirds majority of members present of the House of Representatives at the Centre, and a two-thirds majority of a joint meeting of the House of Chiefs and House of Assembly in the Northern and Western Regions, or a two-thirds majority of the members present in the House of Assembly in the Eastern Region. It is proposed to vary this recommendation in so far as the Northern and Western Regions are concerned in order to prevent the possibility of the numerically stronger House imposing its opinion on the other House, and it is now recommended that a Regional Minister in the Northern or Western Region should be removed in the event of an adverse vote of two-thirds of the members of the House from which he was selected.

12. These various provisions do not, however, cover the contingency of a Minister refusing to abide by the policy decided by his colleagues in the Council of

Ministers or in the Regional Executive Council and refusing to resign, and yet against whom an adverse vote from the Legislature cannot be obtained. In order to deal with such cases the Governor or Lieutenant-Governor should have the power to terminate the appointment of a Minister, and such a provision is proposed for the Constitutional Instruments.

III. *Legislatures*

13.   *Composition of House of Representatives.* This constituted the main question upon which the General Conference could not agree in January, 1950. As the result of further discussion it was eventually possible to reach a settlement in Legislative Council in September of that year, when it was proposed that the House of Representatives should consist of six official members, six members representing special interests and one hundred and thirty six elected members, of whom half would represent the Northern Region, and the other half the other two Regions in equal proportions. The large size of this Legislature—substantially larger than that proposed by any Regional Conference or by the General Conference—was a concession by the Northern unofficial members of Legislative Council in response to the agreement by the other two Regions that the North was entitled to representation at the Centre equal to that of the Eastern and Western Regions together. Such agreement was given explicitly by the Eastern unofficial members, and was considered to be implicit in the Western members' attitude of refraining from pressing the objections previously voiced in the Western House of Assembly.

14.   *Basis of representation at centre.* The membership proposed for the House of Representatives was also founded on the desire to give adequate representation, so far as possible on a divisional basis, to all parts of the Territory. (The original figure for the calculation was in fact the thirty four divisions of the Eastern Region). The Western Region is still in favour of divisional representation, and intends proceeding on this basis. Each of the other two Regions, however, recommends a separate system.

15.   (a) *North.* In the North it had always been the intention that representation at the Centre should be on a provincial basis, and the General Conference had recommended that in respect of the Northern Region at least one member should be selected to represent each Province, and that the number of members, from amongst the total Northern membership, to be selected by the House of Chiefs, together with the method of their selection, should be determined by the two Northern Houses in joint session. A Select Committee of the two Northern Houses subsequently proposed that each Province should be represented at the Centre by at least one member from the House of Chiefs and one from the House of Assembly, and the balance of the Northern members should be elected with regard to individual qualifications, special local interests, and the principle of proportional representation in that order. The Order-in-Council has now been drafted to provide the minimum provincial representation recommended—the representatives being elected by a Joint Council of the two Northern Houses sitting together.

16.   (b) *East.* The Eastern House of Assembly has pointed out the inequities which could arise in that Region from a divisional basis of representation at the Centre, in view of the disparity—in some cases the marked disparity—in the size and

population of various divisions. (The range in population is as much as from 28,000 in Ikom to 547,000 in Owerri, and Calabar Province, with seven divisions, has only two-thirds of the population of the Owerri Province with five divisions). The recommendation in respect of the Eastern Region now is that minimum representation of each Province of the Region at the Centre be specified, and the balance of members for the House of Representatives be elected by the Eastern House without further restriction, so that the Eastern House will be able to reconcile the claims of population with the desirable objective of electing the most suitable individuals.

17. *Composition of regional houses.* Whilst settlement of the composition of the House of Representatives has not called for any re-consideration of the size of Houses in the Eastern or Western Regions, the Select Committee of the two Northern Houses has recommended that there should be a marked increase in the members of the two Northern Houses under the new Constitution. It is now proposed that the Northern House of Chiefs should contain fifty chiefs and the Northern House of Assembly ninety elected members in addition to certain official members in each House. This increase has been recommended partly in order to provide a wider field of selection for the increased number of representatives to be sent to the Central Legislature, and partly in order to make a substantial body of men already engaged in public affairs available for the numerous statutory Boards and Committees presently in existence or about to be created as the result of constitutional change.

18. *Special interests.* A request was made by certain commercial interests in the United Kingdom for the accord of special representation to such interests in Regional Legislatures as well as in the House of Representatives. This proposal has not been put formally to the existing Regional Houses, but informal consultation indicates that such representation in Regional Houses of Assembly would be acceptable. In the North the three members contemplated for such interests would be included amongst the ten members already provided primarily for securing the representation of minority communities. It had originally been proposed by the General Conference that these ten members in the Northern House of Assembly would be elected to the House by the members who had already found their way there by the ordinary electoral process. It is considered, however, that in respect of all the Regional Houses, including the Northern, it will be necessary for all these special members to be selected by the Lieutenant-Governor in his discretion, but after such informal consultation as may be possible and desirable.

19. *Presiding officers of houses.* In respect of both the House of Representatives and the Regional Houses, the General Conference proposed that each House decide its own method of selecting its own Presiding Officer. It seems necessary to depart from this recommendation both at the Centre and in the Regions.

20. (a) *House of Representatives.* In September 1950 Legislative Council proposed, as an integral part of its recommendations for the Central Legislature, that the Governor should preside. This recommendation has its origin in the Northern opposition to any provision which would lead to the appointment or election as Presiding Officer of a Southern politician who could rule an Emir out of order or fail to maintain dignity and impartiality in the conduct of business. The other Regions have accepted the Northern point of view. It is thought to be wholly inappropriate

that the Governor, as Head of the Executive in a Constitution designed to evolve towards self-government through responsible Ministers, should continue to preside over a Legislature, but to permit the House of Representatives to choose its own Presiding Officer would not meet the situation, as such a provision would re-awaken Northern suspicion and, if a member of the House itself were chosen, would alter the carefully adjusted basis of representation between the North and South. The best solution is thought to be a provision appointing the Governor as Presiding Officer but authorising him, with the consent of the Secretary of State, to appoint a President. Such a provision would enable the Governor, when the probable Northern reactions appear favourable, to appoint a person such as a suitable retired Judge or Law Officer (preferably African) from outside the ranks of the House, and withdraw himself from its deliberations. When the House of Representatives first meets, however, the Governor will have to preside.

21.   (b) *Regional houses*. With regard to Regional Houses, the recommendation of the General Conference was at variance with the recommendation of Regional Conferences, and on so purely Regional a matter these recommendations might be re-examined. In the North it had been proposed that the Chief Commissioner (i.e. Lieutenant-Governor) and a Senior Resident should preside over the House of Chiefs and House of Assembly respectively. It is suggested that the Lieutenant-Governor should preside over the House of Chiefs and that he appoint a President of the House of Assembly, who in the first instance would probably be a Resident. The Western Regional Conference proposed that the State Governor (i.e. Lieutenant-Governor) should preside over the House of Assembly and that the House of Chiefs should select a president from amongst its own members. It would be inappropriate that the Lieutenant-Governor should preside over the 'Lower' House and it is suggested that the Lieutenant-Governor should preside over the Western House of Chiefs, and appoint a person to be President of the House of Assembly. The Eastern Regional Conference proposed that the Chief Commissioner (i.e. Lieutenant-Governor) preside over the Regional House. This recommendation might be followed, and the Lieutenant-Governor be empowered to appoint a Vice-President from within the membership of the House to preside in his absence.

22.   *Electoral arrangements*. Details of the electoral arrangements for electing members of the Regional Legislatures are being fully worked out, on the basis of the Reports of the Select Committees of the various Regional Houses laid on the table of Legislative Council in March this year. (Copies have been supplied to the Colonial Office). In view of the disparity in size, communications and administrative structure of the various Regions it has, of course, not been possible to arrange such details with any degree of uniformity. It is contemplated that in the Eastern Region village meetings will elect representatives to divisional electoral meetings, which will then, in turn, elect representatives to the Regional House. The pattern will be somewhat similar in the Western Region, except that in certain areas there will usually be another intermediate stage between the original electoral level and the electoral college. In the Northern Region it is intended that there will be some two or three tiers between the original electoral meetings and the provincial electoral colleges. The Northern Region are now prepared to agree to a uniform age of at least 21 years in respect of candidates to Regional Houses, although still retaining insistence on candidates being male Nigerians who have resided for three years in the Region. It is proposed that the arrangements finally approved be given effect by means of

Regulations issued by the Governor under the authority of the Imperial Order-in-Council.

IV. *Procedure in legislation*

23. *Powers of houses in bicameral legislature.* As regards the powers of the two Houses in the bicameral Regional Legislatures of the North and West, the General Conference recommended concurrent and equal powers for each House, with disagreement between the two Houses in either Region resolved by a majority vote of the two Houses in joint session. Whilst ordinary legislation can no doubt be appropriately introduced for the first time before either House of a bicameral Legislature, it would be in accord with modern democratic theory and practice for money Bills to be introduced in the first instance before the lower, or more directly representative, of the two Houses. An elaboration is therefore proposed on the lines of the Ibadan Conference proposals, with the variation, in so far as a deadlock between two Houses is concerned, that in such an event each of the two Houses should select an equal number of representatives to sit in joint session, and decide the point of difference by majority vote. This emendation of the General Conference proposal would prevent the numerically stronger House imposing its wishes on the other.

24. *Disallowance of regional legislation.* Legislation emerging from Regional Legislatures is then, as proposed by Legislative Council in April, 1950, to be referred to the Governor-in-Council and would, in the light of the General Conference proposals, be examined to see whether it was in conflict with any major overall Nigerian interests or with any convention or agreement binding on Nigeria, or with the fiscal policy of Nigeria. In view of the considerations indicated in paragraph 9 of this Memorandum it should be the function also of the Governor-in-Council to determine whether the Regional legislation relates to a matter in respect of which the Region can properly make laws, whether any expenditure authorised is on subjects specified in the Regional financial field, and whether it is consistent with any executive directions given to the Region by the Governor-in-Council. Should the legislation offend all or any of these stipulations, and the offending provisions not be curable by mere amendment, it is suggested that the legislation be disallowed; should the point in issue be curable by amendment without invalidating the whole of the legislation, it is suggested that the legislation be referred again to the Regional Houses involved, for consideration only of the amendments proposed by the Governor-in-Council.

25. *Central legislation in regional houses.* As regards Central legislation, the General Conference proposed continuance of the present system whereby Central legislation is debated first in Regional Houses which are mainly advisory bodies. The position in the new Constitution will, of course, be materially altered by reason of the Regional Houses acquiring legislative powers and a defined field of jurisdiction, and as, in addition, the Central Legislature will be composed almost exclusively of members elected from Regional Houses, there should be no great necessity for Regional Houses to debate Central measures as well as their own Regional measures. It is proposed, therefore, that whilst Central Bills will be laid on the table of Regional Houses, no debate should take place on them unless a definite motion is made to that effect.

139   CO 583/307/1, no 22   **15 May 1951**
[Constitutional review]: despatch (reply) no 17A from Sir J
Macpherson to Mr Griffiths on the composition of the central and
regional legislatures and on the selection of ministers in the new
constitution

In your despatch No. 464A of the 15th of July, 1950,[1] on the review of the
Constitution of Nigeria you conveyed to me the views of His Majesty's Government
on the major recommendations of the General Conference held at Ibadan in 1950
and the variations proposed by the Select Committee of Legislative Council in April
of that year. The readiness of His Majesty's Government to accept the constitutional
proposals generally was much appreciated in Nigeria and contributed greatly towards
a settlement of the main issues which were then outstanding. In your despatch No.
147A of the 15th of April, 1951,[2] you have conveyed to me the decision reached by
H.M. Government on the method of selecting members of the Council of Ministers
and of the Regional Executive Councils.

2.   Foremost among the questions outstanding at the date of the earlier despatch
was the composition of the new Central Legislature. This matter was brought to a
definite conclusion last September, when Legislative Council recommended that the
new Central Legislature should consist of 148 members, of whom 68 would represent
the Northern Region, 34 the Eastern Region, and 34 the Western Region. The
Western Region members would include at least two representatives of the municipal
area of Lagos and the Eastern Region members would include one representative of
Calabar. The Eastern members would also include at least four from the Trust
Territory of the Cameroons by reason of the basis of representation to which I refer
later in this Despatch. The other twelve members of the Legislature would be 6
official members (the Chief Secretary, the three Lieutenant-Governors, the Attorney-
General, and the Financial Secretary) and 6 members appointed by the Governor to
represent interests and communities which, in his opinion, were not otherwise
adequately represented.

3.   The increased size of this Legislature, which is substantially larger than that
proposed by any of the Regional Conferences or by the General Conference, was
designed to give adequate representation to all parts of Nigeria and of each Region. It
was at the same time thought necessary to increase the number of members to be
appointed to represent special interests because it was considered that the figure of
three previously proposed would be inadequate in this enlarged Legislature to
represent the interests now being brought into existence by the rapid economic
development of Nigeria.

4.   It is a matter of much satisfaction that the composition of the Central
Legislature has now been settled in a manner acceptable to all Regions and that you
were able to announce in the House of Commons last November that H.M.
Government has accepted the arrangements made.

5.   The consideration of this issue involved the re-examination to some extent of
recommendations already put forward by the General Conference, and as these

---

[1] See 116.   [2] See 137.

recommendations were themselves based on the proposals of a series of popular meetings at different levels invited not to prepare a detailed constitutional scheme, but to express general views on the broad outlines of constitutional change, a substantial degree of elaboration of the details has inevitably been necessary for the purpose of drawing up the Constitutional Instruments. I propose to indicate in this Despatch the main elaborations of detail which have appeared necessary.

6. In the matter of the composition of Regional Legislatures it has been recommended by a Select Committee of the two Houses of the Northern Regional Council that there should be a marked increase in the members of the two Northern Houses under the new Constitution. It is now proposed that the Northern House of Chiefs should contain 50 Chiefs and the Northern House of Assembly 90 elected members in addition to certain official members in each House. This increase has been recommended mainly in order to provide a wider field of selection for the increased number of representatives to be sent to the Central Legislature, but partly also in order that there may be a sufficient number of members available for the numerous Boards and Committees at present in existence or likely to be created.

7. Provision had already been made in the proposals for the Northern House of Assembly that, in addition to the elected members, there should be ten other members selected to represent interests and communities not otherwise adequately represented, and it is now proposed that not less than three of these should be persons intimately acquainted with the economic affairs of the Region and similarly that three members should be appointed to the Western and Eastern Houses of Assembly to represent special interests. This proposal to the Regional Houses has not been put formally, but it is understood that it will be generally acceptable. The special members of Regional Legislatures will be selected by the Lieutenant-Governors concerned, after appropriate consultation, and to this extent there will be a departure from the proposal of the General Conference that the ten special members of the North should be selected by the other members of the Northern House of Assembly.

8. The increase in the size of the new Central Legislature now proposed has led also to re-consideration of the method of election of its members. The General Conference at Ibadan proposed that representatives of the Eastern and Western Regions should be elected in such a way as to give representation at the Centre to each division of those two Regions. This proposal continues to be favoured by the Western Region, but the Eastern House of Assembly has pointed out the inequities which could arise in that Region from a divisional basis of election, in view of the disparity—in several instances a marked disparity—in the size and population of divisions. The recommendation in respect of the Eastern Region now is that the members of the House of Representatives to be elected by the Eastern House shall include not less than two members from each of the seven Provinces. In electing the balance of members the Eastern House will be able to take into consideration the distribution of population as well as the need to elect the most suitable people. In the North it has always been the intention that representation should be on a Provincial basis and the General Conference recommended that there the number of members to be elected by the House of Chiefs and the method of their election should be determined by the Houses of the Northern Regional Council in joint session. It has now been proposed by a Select Committee of the two Northern Houses that each of the twelve Provinces should be represented by at least one Chief and

one member of the House of Assembly, and that, subject to this proviso, the 68 members required for the Central Legislature should be elected by a Joint Council consisting of an equal number of representatives from each of the two Northern Houses.

9.   Copies of the Reports by the Select Committees of the various Regional Houses on the arrangements for electing members to the Regional Legislatures—a matter in which you have expressed much interest—have already been forwarded to you and have received your general approval. In view of the disparity in size, communications and administrative structure of the various Regions it has not, of course, been possible to arrange the details of electoral procedure with complete uniformity. But the method will everywhere be popular election through electoral colleges, except in Lagos, where election will be direct as at present. In the Eastern Region the representatives elected by the people at the primary elections will form divisional electoral colleges, which will themselves elect representatives to the Regional Houses. The procedure will be similar in the Western Region, except that in many areas there will be another intermediate stage between the primary elections and the divisional electoral colleges. In the Northern Region, with its greater distances, it will be necessary to have two or three tiers between the primary elections and the provincial electoral colleges. The Select Committees of the Regional Houses for the Northern and Western Regions have recommended that Native Authorities should participate in the electoral arrangements for those Regions at the appropriate level and this recommendation has general support in the two Regions. It is a reflection of the importance of Native Authorities in the life of the Northern and Western Regions and the arrangement will ensure that in these Regions the Native Authorities can make available for service in the Regional Legislatures men of experience and ability who might not otherwise be eligible for election. I wish to pay tribute to the care with which the Select Committees of the Regional Houses have worked out their recommendations for electoral arrangements. I am satisfied that in the terms of paragraph 10 of your despatch of the 15th July, 1950 these arrangements will ensure that the members elected will be genuinely representative of all the people of the areas concerned; that the elections will be free and fair; and that the form of election will be properly adapted to the circumstances of each area.

10.   It has been found necessary to re-consider the question of presiding officers for the various legislatures. It was recommended by Legislative Council in September 1950 that the Governor should preside over the House of Representatives. I appreciate the reason for this recommendation, but as progress is made towards a system of responsible government, it would be inappropriate for the Governor, as head of the Executive, to continue to preside over that House. I accordingly recommend that provision be made for the Governor to appoint for the House of Representatives a permanent President who, I suggest, should not be a member of the House. Until such a President is appointed the Governor himself would continue to preside over meetings of the House.

11.   The recommendation of the General Conference that each Regional House should decide its own method of selecting its Presiding Officer was at variance with the recommendations of the Regional Conferences and it seems reasonable to re-examine those recommendations. In the North it had been proposed that the Lieutenant-Governor and a Senior Resident should preside over the House of Chiefs

and House of Assembly respectively. I recommend that the Lieutenant-Governor should preside over the House of Chiefs and that it be for him to appoint the president of the House of Assembly. The Western Regional Conference proposed that the Lieutenant-Governor should preside over the House of Assembly and that the House of Chiefs should select a president from amongst its own members. Here, too, I recommend that the Lieutenant-Governor should preside over the House of Chiefs and that it should be for him to appoint the president of the House of Assembly. The Eastern Regional Conference proposed that the Lieutenant-Governor should preside over the Regional House. This recommendation should, in my view, be followed, and I also consider that the Lieutenant-Governor should be empowered to appoint a Vice-President from among the members of the House to preside in his absence.

12.   I now turn to deal with the executive authority at the Centre and in the Regions. In your despatch of the 15th July, 1950, you emphasised the importance which you attached to the principle of regional autonomy, but at the same time you stated in very clear terms the importance which you attached to preserving and strengthening the unity of Nigeria and you welcomed the recommendations of the General Conference for a strong Central Legislature and Executive. I consider it a matter of the highest importance that the overall and over-riding authority of the Central Government should be clearly expressed in the Constitutional Instruments, and that the authority of Regional Executives should be clearly defined in such a manner that, while there is no derogation from the degree of autonomy proposed for them, their subordination on matters of general policy to the Central Executive is placed beyond all question. There should therefore in my view be some elaboration in the Constitutional Instruments of the recommendation of the General Conference that the Regional Administrations should formulate policy and direct executive action subject to any general instructions issued on the grounds that the major overall interest of Nigeria is involved. The Central Government must be in a position, when necessary, to give to the Regional Administrations special directions with respect to the exercise of the executive authority of the Regions for the purpose of ensuring good government in Nigeria. It is implicit in the conception of the overall authority of the Central Government that this power to give directions should relate to the subjects listed in the General Conference recommendations as appropriate for Regional legislative jurisdiction, as well as to the wide range of other subjects in which it will be necessary for the Central Government to safeguard from time to time the overall Nigerian interest.

13.   In your despatch of the 15th of July 1950 you drew attention to the need to evolve a system whereby the selection of members of the Council of Ministers would be made in consultation between the Governor and the members of the Nigerian Legislature representing each Region, and the selection of members of the Regional Executive Councils would be made in consultation between the Lieutenant-Governors and members of the Regional legislatures. I have had the opportunity of personal discussion with you on this question and have now received your despatch No. 147A of the 15th of April, 1951, setting out the considerations which have led His Majesty's Government to decide on a process of selection so designed as to be capable of leading, in due course, to a system of selection similar to that obtaining in the United Kingdom and other Commonwealth countries. You have also pointed out the advantages of carrying out selection of Central Ministers at the same time as selection of Regional Ministers. The arguments which you have advanced in this

matter seem to me, if I may say so with respect, wholly conclusive, and although, in one respect, the arrangements involve a variation of the general conference proposal, they remain in keeping with the sentiments inherent in it. I am accordingly satisfied that there will be general agreement with, and acceptance of, the decision which His Majesty's Government have reached.

14.   In dealing with the composition of the Regional Executives the General Conference proposed that there should be five official members and nine Ministers in the Northern and Eastern Regions and three official members and nine Ministers in the Western Region. The position in respect of the Western Region has of course altered by reason of the subsequent recommendation of Legislative Council that Lagos and the Colony should be included, for administrative and legislative purposes, within this Regions, and it is clearly desirable that the Western Executive should be as large as those proposed for the other Regions. I recommend accordingly that the maximum number of official members of the Western Regional Council should be five as for the other two Regions. The number of Ministers to be found from among members of Regional Houses was not prescribed by the General Conference with any regard to the volume of work which might fall to these Ministers nor to the division of subjects which might prove practicable. Examination of these points has shown that it may not be necessary, at least at first, to have as many as nine Ministers selected in each Region from the Regional Houses, and it is now proposed that in the Northern and Western Regions the minimum number of Ministers should be six and the maximum number nine, and that in the Eastern Region the minimum number should be seven and the maximum number nine. A higher minimum figure has been proposed for the East in order to provide for one Minister from the Trust Territory of the Cameroons, as recommended by the General Conference. The actual number of Ministers selected would vary in each Region according to the volume and nature of work. The distribution of portfolios among Ministers at the Centre and in the Regions should be at the discretion of the Governor and the Lieutenant-Governor respectively.

15.   It was proposed by the General Conference that the appointment of Ministers at the Centre and in the Regions should be terminated in the event of an adverse vote by the Legislature. Such a vote was to be carried by a two-thirds majority of members present of the House of Representatives at the Centre; a two-thirds majority of a joint meeting of the House of Chiefs and House of Assembly in the Northern and Western Regions; or a two-thirds majority of the members present in the House of Assembly in the Eastern Region. To avoid the possibility, in so far as the Northern and Western Regions are concerned, of the numerically stronger House imposing its opinion on the other House, it is now recommended that a Regional Minister in the Northern or Western Region should be removed in the event of an adverse vote of two-thirds of all the members of the House from which he was selected. In the Eastern Region the vote required would be of all the members of the House of Assembly.

16.   Even with these provisions, however, it would still be possible for the case to arise of a Minister who refused to abide by the policy decided by his colleagues in the Council of Ministers or in the Regional Executive Council and at the same time refuse to resign. In order to deal with such a case the Governor or Lieutenant-Governor should have the power to terminate the appointment of a Minister, and I recommend that such provision be made in the Constitutional Instruments.

17.   I come now to the question of legislative procedure, more particularly in

respect of Regional legislation. Regions are being given the right to legislate on a specified range of subjects, but the Central Legislature can legislate on all subjects, including those specified for Regions. It becomes necessary, therefore, to determine whether the Central or Regional law should prevail in the case of conflict. I suggest that the simplest arrangement is for Central legislation existing at the time of the inauguration of the new Constitution to prevail until such time as Regional legislation is enacted and replaces it wholly or in part. Occasion may subsequently arise—but in all probability only very seldom—when the Centre has to take legislative action on the same aspect of the Regional subject: the Regional law existing at the time would then become inoperative to the extent indicated in the Central legislation. I do not anticipate any serious conflict of legislation in this matter.

18.   The General Conference recommended concurrent and equal powers for each House in the bicameral Regional Legislatures of the North and West, any disagreement between the two Houses in either Region being resolved by a majority vote of the two Houses in joint session. While ordinary legislation can no doubt be appropriately introduced for the first time before either House of a bicameral Legislature, it would be in accordance with modern democratic theory and practice for money Bills to be introduced in the first instance before the more directly representative of the two Houses, that is to say the House of Assembly, and I recommend an elaboration of the Ibadan Conference proposals on these lines. I would further vary the proposals, in so far as a deadlock between two Houses may arise, by recommending that in such an event each of the two Houses should select an equal number of representatives to sit in joint session to decide the point of difference by majority vote. This amendment of the General Conference proposal would prevent the numerically stronger House from imposing its wishes on the other.

19.   Under the proposal of the Legislative Council in April, 1950, legislation passed by Regional Legislatures is to be referred to the Governor in Council for examination, in the light of the General Conference proposals, to determine whether it is in conflict with any major overall Nigerian interest, with any convention or agreement binding on Nigeria or with the fiscal policy of Nigeria. In view of the considerations which I have put forward in paragraph 12 of this Despatch, I recommend that it should also be the function of the Governor in Council to determine whether the Regional legislation relates to a matter in respect of which the Region can properly make laws, whether any expenditure authorised is on subjects specified in the Regional financial field, and whether it is inconsistent with any executive directions given to the Region by the Central Executive. Should the legislation offend any of these stipulations, and the offending provisions not be curable simply by amendment, then the legislation must be disallowed; should the point in issue be curable by amendment without invalidating the whole of the legislation, amendments would be suggested by the Governor-in-Council for adoption by the Regional House concerned, no doubt after close consultation between the Central and Regional Governments.

20.   The General Conference proposed continuance of the present system whereby Central legislation is debated first in Regional Houses. The position in the new Constitution will of course be materially altered in that the Regional Houses will no longer be merely advisory but will have their own legislative powers over a defined

field. Since moreover the Central Legislature will be composed almost entirely of members elected from Regional Houses, there should be no necessity in the normal course for Regional Houses to debate Central, as well as their own Regional, bills. I propose, therefore, that while Central Bills will be laid on the table of Regional Houses, no debate should take place on them unless on a definite motion to that effect.

21.   The recommendations made in this Despatch have already been discussed with yourself or your advisers and I trust that you will find yourself able to give formal consent to their incorporation in the Constitutional Instruments. I have not covered in this despatch questions of financial allocation or procedure, arising out of the Report of the Revenue Allocation Commission, or matters relating to the Civil Service, as these will more appropriately be the subject of separate communications.

22.   Finally I would refer to the strong indication in paragraph 16 of your Despatch of the 15th of July 1950 of your view that the new constitutional changes should be allowed to operate for a reasonable period before further changes are considered. With this view I fully concur. The changes now to be introduced are the result of a long series of meetings and conferences representative of all shades of opinion and interests in this Territory. The broad measure of general agreement reached is, I consider, evidence in itself of the timely nature of these reforms, which are in many features the logical development of the political system inaugurated in 1946. It indicates also the widespread desire by men of goodwill to give those called upon to operate the changes—that greatly increased number of Nigerians who henceforth, both at the Centre and through the devolution of responsibility to the regions, will bear a full share in the shaping of Government policy and the direction of executive action—a clear and uninterrupted opportunity to prove that their capacity is in keeping with the trust placed in them. By reason of the magnitude of the issues involved, and because of the vital importance for the Nigeria of tomorrow of ordered political, economic and social development today, these men will carry a heavy burden, particularly in the unsettled world conditions in which they begin their task. But I would record my conviction that, with goodwill and a general readiness to work in the interests of Nigeria as a whole, they will not fail, and that this new political advance will be proved by them to have been fully justified.

140 CO 537/7166, no 8						25–28 May 1951
[Constitutional review]: minutes by R J Vile and L H Gorsuch on the remaining issues requiring decision for the proposed new constitution

In submitting, as I now do opposite, the first draft of the despatch to be published about the constitutional Instruments to give effect to the proposals for a new Constitution in Nigeria, it is I think desirable first of all to give some account of the course of events which have led up to the present situation where we hope that the Constitution Order in Council will be promulgated in June.[1]

---

[1] The Nigeria (Constitution) Order in Council, 1951, establishing the new constitution, was promulgated on 29 June 1951.

It was in 1948 that Sir J. Macpherson first suggested that the existing Nigerian Constitution should be reviewed. The procedure adopted for the review involved nation-wide consultation and it culminated in a General Conference held at Ibadan in January 1950. The recommendations made by this General Conference are for easy reference attached loosely opposite, and they left unsolved at that time one major question, the composition of the Central Legislature. This question was again considered by a Select Committee of Legislative Council in April 1950 which after considering various possibilities remitted further consideration of the matter to Regional Houses. At the same time the Select Committee reached a number of important decisions about the recommendations of the General Conference, notably that Lagos should be included in the Western Region, that the Central Executive should have the power of referring back or rejecting regional Legislation and that disagreements between the two House of Regional Legislatures in the North and West should be referred to a joint meeting composed of equal numbers of both Houses. In May the major questions raised by the recommendations of the General Conference were referred to the Cabinet which approved the line of policy taken by the Secretary of State in his published despatch of the 15th July 1950, of copy of which, together with a copy of the Select Committee report, is also attached loosely opposite. In this despatch the Secretary of State said that His Majesty's Government accepted the recommendations made subject to the further examination of details when the constitutional review is completed, together with variations suggested by the Select Committee of April.

The next important step occurred in September when Legislative Council met again and adopted a report of its Select Committee that there should be one House in the Central Legislature, that in that House Northern representation should be equal to that of the other two regions together, that there should be 148 members in that House, that the Governor should continue to preside and that there should be six special members. In November 1950 the Secretary of State informed the House of Commons that he accepted the recommendations of the Select Committee of September. Since that date no public announcements have been made about the views of His Majesty's Government and the time has been taken in the consideration of the drafts of the constitutional Instruments. We have now reached the point where the major part of the final draft has been sent to Nigeria for their comments and with the exception of a small number of outstanding points agreement has been reached with the Nigerian Government on all major questions of principle. The only major point of difference which has arisen is not really one of constitutional principle but concerns the question whether there should be provision for detailed financial procedure in the Order in Council. The situation here is that it would not be possible to provide any detail for financial procedure if the Order is to be promulgated in June, and although we have not yet heard from Nigeria we can, I think, assume that they will not wish to hold up the Order in Council on this score.

There is, I think, no need to argue the case for a published statement by His Majesty's Government on the Nigerian Constitution as it is to be promulgated in the Order in Council. The previous despatch was printed in Nigeria and copies were made available to the press in the United Kingdom, but it was not printed in the United Kingdom. This despatch is, I suggest, of far greater importance and therefore it seems necessary that it should be printed and published in the United Kingdom. I would also suggest that it should be published in the Colonial series and not as a command paper. The date of publication should, I suggest, be the date on which the Order in Council is laid before Parliament. This does not leave us much time and the Governor has asked if he may have the opportunity of commenting on the terms of the despatch.

The purpose of the despatch, I suggest, is to explain the fundamental purpose of the constitutional change, to explain the points on which His Majesty's Government have not found it possible to accept certain of the recommendations made and to refer to two questions which, although not included in the Order in Council, are nevertheless highly relevant to it, those of revenue allocation and the electoral arrangements. Before I go on to mention the points in more detail, it is, I think, necessary to consider whether the Cabinet requires to be consulted again. In 1950 the Cabinet approved the general line of policy which the Secretary of State proposed to follow and the present action proposed is completely consistent with the policy which has been approved. Nevertheless the promulgation of this constitution is a matter of such importance that I suggest it is necessary for the Secretary of State to circulate to the Cabinet a paper for information showing what it is that he now proposes to do.

The important matters to which reference needs to be made in the despatch have also been considered by the Nigerian Government, and we have from them a memorandum enclosed with Sir J. Macpherson's letter which arrived during the consideration of the nature of the published despatch. The draft contains an account of the reasons why some recommendations on these matters have not been accepted and I only propose here to indicate the ways in which different views have been arrived at.

(a) *Composition of central legislature*
The General Conference made no recommendation on this point and the recommendation made by the Select Committee of September 1950 has been followed.

(b) *Review of regional legislation*
The recommendations of the General Conference (III F) have not been followed but instead the recommendation at para 6 of the April Select Committee report has been followed. The opportunity has been taken to add a further function in respect of regional legislation to the Central Council of Ministers, i.e. to decide whether regional legislation is within the powers of a Regional Legislature. The alternative was to leave this matter to the courts to decide and it was felt that this would not be satisfactory in Nigerian circumstances.

(c) *Executive authority*
The recommendations of the General Conference (IV B 1) left in considerable doubt the ability of the Nigerian Government to enforce its will on regional administrations. In view of the need to ensure that the unity of Nigeria is not damaged and in order to take account of the ultimate responsibility of the Governor for the administration of the territory as well as to provide for the ability of the Central Government to get services performed on its behalf by regional administrations properly executed, provision is being made in the constitutional Instruments to ensure that the Central Executive can give directions to Regional Executives on any matter. The relevant section in the draft Order in Council occurs in Chapter V at Section 114.

(d) *Selection of ministers and allocation of portfolios*

Considerable discussion has taken place with the Nigerian Government about the recommendations made by the General Conference which were that unofficial members of the Central Council of Ministers and Regional Executive Councils should be elected and that the Councils themselves should decide the allocation of portfolios. Following the letter sent at (81) on the 1950 papers, the Governor said that he was willing to accept the Colonial Office view. He has informed his Executive Council but the decision is not known to anyone else in Nigeria. The relevant sections of the draft are Sections 121, 123, 124, 125, 142, 143, 144, 145, 146, 147, 148, and 149. These sections give effect to the proposals in the letter at (81) on the 1950 papers. In the memorandum sent by Sir J. Macpherson at para 8, the suggestion is made that this decision should be shown to be one made by the Secretary of State and that it should be so expressed in the published despatch. I think we can accept this suggestion which clearly reflects the course of the discussion and I have attempted in the draft opposite to meet the suggestion made.

(e) *Special members*

In the case of the Central Legislature we are following the recommendation made by the Select Committee of September. In the case of the Northern Region, we are following the recommendation made by the General Conference. In the case of the Western Region, the proposal incorporated in the constitutional Instruments has been discussed by the Chief Commissioner with members of the Regional House and accepted by them. In the case of the Eastern Region, the Chief Commissioner engaged in informal discussions and has reported that the proposal is acceptable. No public announcement has been made in Nigeria of this decision.

(f) *Presiding officers*

Although the General Conference recommended that each House should choose its own Presiding Officer, it has not been considered in the discussions which have taken place since November that this would be desirable or practicable. In the memorandum furnished by Nigeria in paras 19 to 21 are set out the reasons why it is preferable in these instances to follow the recommendations made by Regional Conferences rather than recommendations of the General Conference.

I do not think it necessary to comment on the question of revenue allocation. The Governor has said that he hopes to let the Secretary of State have his final recommendations in two months and that it would be possible for the Order in Council on revenue allocation to be promulgated in October. Separate consideration is being given to its despatch. On the question of electoral arrangements, we have already suggested separately to Sir J. Macpherson at (15) on 30453/14 the line which might be taken in the published despatch and I have drafted on this basis.

I should finally say that the draft now submitted has been carefully checked by Mr. McPetrie, to whom I am grateful for a number of valuable suggestions.

R.J.V.
25.5.51

Sir T. Lloyd

Work on the Nigerian Constitutional Instruments is now approaching completion. The final drafts are in course of agreement with Nigeria and will shortly go for printing, and the Instruments will be presented to a meeting of the Privy Council which it is hoped will be towards the end of June. The Nigerian Government are anxious that fairly detailed financial provisions shall be made by Order-in-Council, but these will in any case be dependent upon the decisions finally taken on the report of the Revenue Allocation Commission which is at present under consideration in Nigeria. There must, therefore, be in any case a separate financial Order-in-Council, over which there is no immediate urgency.

The following questions now require decision and action:—

(1) Is any further reference to the Cabinet or to the Prime Minister required? A copy of the Cabinet paper of May 1950 will be found at 33A on the 1950 file and the Cabinet conclusions are at 34. As the general policy of constitutional reform was approved at that date further reference to the Cabinet may be unnecessary, but I am not sure whether the Secretary of State will wish to send a short note to the Prime Minister.

(2) Consultation with the Ministry of Defence. A very full letter was sent to the Ministry at 22E on the 1950 file in April 1950 and at 23A the Ministry replied agreeing that defence interests will be satisfactorily safeguarded under the new arrangements. I do not think, therefore, that any further reference to them is necessary.

(3) Information to Commonwealth Relations Office, other Colonial Governments, Foreign Office and our representatives in the U.S.A. There is a copy opposite of a background Intel which was issued in April of this year. I think that, concurrently with the promulgation of the new Instruments, we should arrange for the issue of a further document of this kind in which the main features of the new Constitution will be summarised.

(4) Exchange of further despatches between the Governor and the Secretary of State for publication. In this connection please see the Governor's letter at 8 opposite. As he suggests in para 3 of that letter, we shall have to issue in due course a despatch from the Secretary of State on the lines of the Gold Coast despatch No. 492 on the subject of the Public Service Commission and safeguards for the Public Service. The financial side will have to be the subject of a separate despatch also in conjunction with the financial Order-in-Council. There will presumably also have to be a despatch on ministerial responsibility on the lines of the Gold Coast despatch on that subject. It remains to consider what published despatches should accompany the issue of the new Instruments. The Governor seems to contemplate in 8 that there should be three such despatches:-

(a) a despatch from the Secretary of State setting out his reasons for the decision in regard to the selection of Ministers;
(b) a despatch from the Governor to the Secretary of State incorporating the material in the memorandum forwarded with 8;
(c) a despatch from the Secretary of State in reply giving his approval of the various changes and developments covered by this memorandum and commenting generally on the Constitution.

You will see that before 8 arrived Mr. Vile, in collaboration with Mr. McPetrie, had been working on a draft despatch to the Governor to be published simultaneously with the new Instruments. While this draft will provide valuable material, my feeling is that it would be better for several reasons that all the modifications and developments, which have occurred in the working out of the Constitution since the

Secretary of State's published despatch No. 464A of July 1950 (loose copy opposite)[2] and which have emanated from discussions in Nigeria, should be dealt with in a reporting despatch from the Governor. The despatch from the Secretary of State in reply would give his formal approval to these modifications and developments, would add comments in amplification of No. 464A where necessary (e.g. electoral arrangements) and would deal with the broader aspects of high policy which are involved in the new Constitution. It is indeed possible that we could work into these two despatches references and explanations on the subject of selection of Ministers which would avoid the necessity of having a separate despatch on this subject while, at the same time, making it clear, as the Governor wishes us to do, that the decision on this particular point has been that of the Secretary of State.

I think it would save time and further minuting if I could discuss these points with you, and if you agree I will bring Mr. Vile and Mr. McPetrie.

L.H.G.
28.5.51

---

[2] See 116

141   CO 583/307/1, no 16   28 May 1951
[Constitutional review]: letter from Sir J Macpherson to L H Gorsuch on electoral arrangements under the proposed new constitution

This is in reply to your secret letter No. 30453/14/51 of the 11th of May in which was discussed the question whether the Secretary of State in a despatch on the revised Constitution, for publication, should say anything about the electoral arrangements in general and about the Western Provinces' arrangement in particular.

I know that I need not defend, to the Secretary of State or any of you in London, the system of indirect election by means of primary elections and Divisional and Provincial electoral meetings. The Secretary of State has accepted the arrangements as suitable for Nigeria at this stage in her development. I know, too, that from a distance (e.g. in less informed quarters in Parliament) they may look rather 'bush' and not fully in line with Western ideas about the *mechanics* of democratic elections, and that as we become more mature politically we shall probably want to conform more closely to these Western ideas. (Even so, I take leave to doubt whether our thousands of stout-hearted warlike pagans, who don't wear clothes but usually carry a couple of spears, will be ready for the ballot box, and direct elections, even in five years time. Despite all our efforts to fit them for the impact of civilization—for good or ill—there are areas, such as Gwoza where I was last month, which our self-styled political leaders could not visit without a District Officer and an escort; otherwise they would almost certainly be bumped off, and perhaps eaten!)

My anxiety is that I feel that it is not easy for the Secretary of State to make a pronouncement about adopting better—or 'more precise'—arrangements in five years' time without appearing to criticize, if only by implication, our proposed arrangements, and, by a natural extension, our entire Constitution. This would play into the hands of the wreckers and confusionists.

The proposed arrangements are, as you know, favoured by the overwhelming majority of thinking Nigerians (many, of course, think that the pace is dangerously fast) and go as far as informed opinion would be prepared to let us go. Moreover, in spite of occasional references to the desirability of direct election by universal adult suffrage and to the 'bogus' nature of the new Constitution, the older political 'parties', and several new mushroom growths, are all campaigning vigorously already on the basis of the approved electoral arrangements, with a view to capturing seats at every stage.

I sincerely believe that these arrangements will give a truer representation than anything more sophisticated. And the issue is wide open. My guess is that the 'professional' politicians and their so-called political parties will have considerable success, particularly in the larger centres of population. And I am quite certain that it is better to have some of the more extreme elements inside the structure, where they will learn by having to take responsibility, rather than that they should all be outside throwing bricks at it. But though we have statesmen in the Regions (and I hope for Nigeria's sake that they will be successful at the polls) our self-styled political leaders have shown few signs of honesty or sincere desire to serve their country. A pronouncement by the Secretary of State which implied that the new Constitution was not progressive enough would be a splendid plank for their election campaign. And if they came to power they would be likely to use that argument to press immediately for further changes in the Constitution. I don't want to start discussions now about our *next* Constitution! We want to make this one work and to be able to devote all our energies to more profitable pursuits than Constitution-making!

So far as the Western and Northern Regions are concerned the electoral arrangements are a good deal more progressive than was recommended in the respective Regional Conferences. For example, it was originally proposed by the Western Regional Conference that

> 'the Electoral Colleges shall be organized by the Local (Native) Authorities but the Electoral Colleges may include non-members of the Local (Native) Authority Council as well as members'.

Now, as you know, there will be free primary elections in the West as elsewhere, and though provision is being made for an injection of up to 50% of Native Administration representation at the intermediate stage between primary elections and the Divisional Electoral Meeting or College, I understand that in many areas the proportion will not be anything like so much as 50%.

The North, too, has moved quite a long way. As a measure of their advance I need only remark that some months ago the Chief Commissioner, and others, were wondering how to ensure that the Native Administrations were not totally unrepresented in the House of Assembly! Originally the North proposed to exclude all Southerners from taking any part in the elections in that Region. Now, although they still insist upon three years' residence as a qualification *for election to the House of Assembly* the voting qualifications, restricted to males, are the same for all, and the same as in the other Regions.

In the light of all that I have written I most earnestly hope that the Secretary of State, in discussing our electoral arrangements, will emphasize that they have been worked out by the Regions themselves and are suited to our needs and circumstances; and that he will refrain, as far as he feels able to do so, from appearing to reflect adversely upon them by anticipating future changes. In short, it is the final sentence of your penultimate paragraph which bothers me.

P.S. I am still very worried about the North-West boundary question. Recently it has been squeezed out of the press by the polemics of party politics—with the elections in view—but the Egbe Omo Oduduwa have so far refused to give an undertaking not to prejudice the issue by fomenting the Yoruba elements in Ilorin Province, and the activities in Ilorin of their emissaries are making the Emir very angry and causing much trouble for the Administration. Moreover, the N.C.N.C. have started on a series of tours throughout the country and everywhere they are playing upon any quarrels or alleged grievances. We are keeping our fingers crossed!

142   CO 537/7166, no 17   27 June 1951
[Constitutional review]: letter from Mr Griffiths to Mr Attlee on the progress of the constitutional review

Prime Minister

Nigerian constitution
You will recall that in May, 1950, I circulated to the Cabinet a memorandum on the Nigerian Constitution (C.P. (50) 94),[1] in which I explained the main proposals for the reform of the Constitution which had emerged from the nation-wide discussion at all levels from the village upwards. The Cabinet approved those proposals, which can best be summarised as providing for:

(i) greatly increased Regional autonomy within a United Nigeria;
(ii) giving Nigerians a full share in the shaping of Government policy and in the direction of executive Government action in a Central Council of Ministers and Regional Executive Councils; and
(iii) the creation of larger and more representative Regional Legislatures with increased powers.

Now that the draft constitutional instruments which give effect to these proposals are about to be laid before His Majesty in Council on the 29th June, I think that you may wish to have an account of subsequent developments.

2.   When the Cabinet approved the proposals which I put forward in May, 1950, there still remained to be settled the question of Regional representation in the Central Legislature. Agreement on this point was reached in Nigeria in September, 1950, the Northern Region, which has more than half the population, securing half the seats in that Legislature, and I informed the House of Commons in November, 1950, that I had accepted this arrangement.

3.   Suitable publicity will be given to the promulgation of the constitution instruments and there will be published an exchange of despatches between the Governor and myself to explain the more important aspects of the new Constitution. The Governor and his Officers have worked extremely hard to ensure that the new

---
[1] See 105.

Constitution should be inaugurated without delay. You will recall that the review of the Constitution began in 1948 on the initiative of the Governor and its successful conclusion has owed much to his ability and to the soundness of the policy of ever-increasing participation by Nigerians in the affairs of Government.

4.   The future timetable of events will now be as follows. Elections will begin in July. They will take the form of indirect elections through a system of electoral colleges in which the primary elections will be direct. In some parts of Nigeria it may take as long as five months to complete the elections. The new Regional Legislatures will meet for the first time in December and the new Central Legislature in January, 1952.

5.   Finally, in order to complete the constitutional instruments, a further Order-in-Council will be required in October to make provision for the division of revenue between Central and Regional Governments, following the principles recommended in the report of an expert Commission which have been generally accepted in Nigeria.[2]

---

[2] Attlee briefly acknowledged this letter, at no 38, on 28 June, '. . . I am glad to have this report of satisfactory progress'.

143   CO 537/7167B   28 June 1951
[Constitutional review]: letter from A B Cohen to A R I Mellor on the representation of special interests in the new constitution

[This letter followed the meetings of representatives of business firms with the secretary of state in June 1950 and with CO officials in Oct 1950 about the place for special interests in the new constitution. See 114 and 122.]

When you called to see me on the 21st June we discussed the questions of special members in the Central and Regional Legislatures under the new Nigerian Constitution, and of the form in which it was intended to ensure that the principle of non-discrimination was provided for in the constitutional instruments. I promised to confirm in writing what I said to you on these two matters.

The constitutional instruments will provide for the appointment of three special members in the Eastern and Western Houses of Assembly to represent special interests. In the Northern House of Assembly provision will be made for the appointment of ten nominated members to represent special interests, of whom three will be appointed to represent commercial interests—although this will not be stated in the instruments. These special members in Regional Legislatures and the six special members who are to form part of the Central Legislature will be nominated 'to represent interests not otherwise adequately represented'. As I told you at our meeting, and as the Governor has already made clear in discussion with you and Gorsuch explained in his letter of the 28th February, it does not necessarily follow from this that all fifteen members—i.e. six at the centre and three in each of the regions—will be expatriate commercial employees. The Nigerian Government expect that most, if not all, of the fifteen will be representatives of commerce, but they do not regard themselves as bound in any way to fill all fifteen seats with expatriates.

On the question of the non-discrimination clause we have in the light of the Gold

Coast provision considered very carefully whether such a clause could be included in the Nigeria (Constitution) Order in Council. The matter has been fully considered in Lagos by the Nigerian Government with the assistance of the Colonial Office legal draftsman and has subsequently been considered by the Colonial Office here. The difficulty lies in the differential land legislation in Nigeria designed to protect tribal rights. It is essential as a matter of policy to maintain this legislation and it may be necessary to amend it. A general prohibition of discriminatory legislation in the Nigeria Order in Council will not therefore be possible. The Gold Coast Government when they had this point to consider did not think that it would lead to comparable difficulty there. We have considered the possibility in Nigeria that we might draw up a clause which would specifically exempt certain classes of legislation from the general prohibition on discriminatory legislation, but we are advised that such a clause would not necessarily confine discrimination to the present field and would not therefore be effective. In these circumstances we have not felt able to pursue that particular suggestion.

Another consideration of considerable importance which I mentioned to you at our meeting is the fact that under the new Nigerian Constitution the Governor will retain his reserve powers precisely in their present form. In these circumstances, and in the light of the difficulties to which I have referred in the preceding paragraph, we have been led to the conclusion that it is preferable to include the clause about non-discrimination in the Royal Instructions to the Governor. We are satisfied, as I think you will be, that the protection which will be given by the obligation placed upon the Governor to reserve for His Majesty's pleasure before bringing into operation all legislation which in his opinion imposes disabilities or restrictions on one racial community to which other communities are not subject, will fully suffice to safeguard the position. Equally we see no reason to suppose that at any future stage of constitutional development in Nigeria it will not be possible, should this be considered desirable, to ensure that provision to make discriminatory legislation completely ultra vires is included in any future constitutional instruments.

The arguments which I have mentioned in this letter are intended to be confidential, but you said that you would wish to circulate this letter to the members of your Committee and of course we should have no objection to your doing so.

144   CO 583/307/1, no 23   30 June 1951
[Constitutional review]: despatch no 270 from Mr Griffiths to Sir J Macpherson expressing congratulations on the completion of the constitutional review

I have the honour to acknowledge the receipt of your despatch No. 17A of the 15th May[1] dealing with the new constitution of Nigeria. As you say in paragraph 21 of this despatch, the recommendations made in it have already formed the subject of discussion between the Nigerian Government and the Colonial Office. The drafting of the constitutional instruments has been a task of particular complexity, and has necessarily taken much time and thought. It was, indeed, for the purpose of

[1] See 139.

shortening as much as possible the time which the work of drafting would take that one of my Legal Advisors visited Nigeria in February for full discussion of the draft constitutional instruments with yourself and your advisers. I am in agreement with all that you say in your despatch and your recommendations have been incorporated in the constitutional instruments, which have now been promulgated.

2.   His Majesty's Government and the people of this country have watched with great interest and sympathy the progress of the constitutional review in Nigeria. I wish to take this opportunity of endorsing what you say in paragraph 22 of your despatch and expressing the confidence of His Majesty's Government in the ability of the peoples of Nigeria to work the constitution and to make it a living instrument for the political progress of the country. The constitution is designed to give a greatly increased measure of responsibility to Nigerians for the conduct of their own affairs and, while granting increased autonomy to the three Regions, to build up a strong and united Nigeria. It has been a matter of great satisfaction to me that the proposals for the new constitution have been worked out so fully and with such a great measure of agreement within Nigeria itself and that His Majesty's Government have been able broadly to accept them. In sending you the warmest wishes of His Majesty's Government for the success of the new constitution I should like to express my appreciation to you for the initiative you took in 1948 in suggesting that the time had come for a review of the constitution and my conviction that the policy of bringing Nigerians into greater participation in the control of their own affairs will continue with even greater success in the future.

145   CO 554/403, no 1   22 Aug 1951
[Nigerianisation]: inward savingram no 2594 from Sir J Macpherson to Mr Griffiths outlining the number of Nigerians employed in the senior service

Your Saving No. 1828 of 21st July. Nigerianization of the Senior Service.
   Present position is as follows:—

(i)	(a)	Direct appointments to Senior Service since August, 1948	81
	(b)	Promotions to Senior Service since August, 1948	303
	(c)	African officers in the Senior Service in August, 1948	172
	(d)	African Senior Service Staff in the Railways in August, 1948	36
	(e)	Regrading of 9 A.M.OO and 2 A.V.OO	11
		Total African Senior Service officers now serving	603
		Subtract 4 officers in the Colliery, one casualty and 1 reversion to Junior Service	6
		Net total	597 [1]
(ii)		Total approved Establishment for Senior Service excluding Colliery and Electricity Corporations but including Railway and posts under Development Plan	4600

---

[1] M Phillips noted in an accompanying minute dated 3 Sept 1951 that Nigerians comprised 16 per cent of the senior service.

(iii) Total actual strength of Senior Service	3730
(iv) Normal annual wastage from retirement, invaliding etc (corrected figure)	207
(v) Awards made under the Nigerianization Report:—	
(a) Scholarships	283
(b) Training Courses	115
Total	398

2. The total under paragraph 1(v) above includes a number of partial awards. There are in fact 3 or 4 full awards still to be made out of the total of 385 recommended by the Nigerianization Commission.

3. I regret that it is impossible to give any realistic estimate of the future rate of Nigerianization. So far, Nigerianization has proceeded at the rate of approximately 140 per year. This rate may be increased in 2 or 3 years' time when Government Scholars become available in larger numbers. But many Scholars will be returning to or entering the employment of Voluntary agencies; moreover, it is impossible to assume that the Senior Service will be Nigerianized at an even rate. Nigerianization naturally proceeds very such faster in some Departments than in others.

146 CO 554/235, no 2   Sept 1951
[Northern Nigeria]: informal notes by B E Sharwood-Smith on the present political situation in the Northern Nigerian emirates

Note: No reference is made herein to the highly important and potentially explosive situation in the non-Moslem areas of Adamawa and nearby territories but the same principles as are outlined herein are, appropriately applied, relevant.

(a) *Present political trends* in the North are not, in any degree, the result of popular demand neither are the people as a whole, in any sense ready, still less anxious, for a more responsible part in the management of their affairs. Regrettably 'Freedom from interference' and continued 'Freedom from responsibility' are still a cherished aspiration on the one hand and a cherished heritage on the other as far as the mass of the population is concerned. Political awakening has yet to come and it is our responsibility to see that the awakeners are persons of integrity and experience and not self-seeking charlatans.

(b) All that we have so far got in the North is a class movement, with in certain areas in particular a definite racial bias (Habi v Fulani). This class movement has two wings. On the one hand there are the more experienced N.A. officials. The Senior African staff of Gaskiya[1] and leading members of the Northern Peoples Congress. On the other hand there is the Northern Elements Progressive Union which draws its recruits from the younger and more irresponsible members of the literate and semi-literate classes. A high proportion of Chiefs and leading personalities in the Emirates are prepared to co-operate with the moderate progressives. N.E.P.U. on the other hand and all its works is anathema to them.

---

[1] *Gaskiya Ta Fi Kwabo* ('Truth is worth more than a penny') was a Hausa language newspaper published by the Gaskiya Corporation, a government-owned printing and publishing body.

(c) It has been stressed that so far neither the N.P.C. or N.E.P.U. have any popular backing but it must be equally stressed that, should the administration (Regional and N.A.) fail to maintain the confidence of the people as a whole and fail to educate them to the true facts of the current situation, there is little doubt that the carpet-bagging demagogue will quickly step in and, by making statements that cannot be substantiated and promises that cannot be fulfilled, swing popular opinion in the direction of a revolt against the existing regime. Such a denouement can be only too easy for a practised agitator working on an emotional and unenlightened peasantry, already unduly exploited by a corrupt officialdom. Should there be a period of social or economic distress due to famine or disease there could well be trouble, for the northern agitator has come to stay and he is learning the classic techniques of his trade and acquiring financial support from outside the Region.

(d) To take the other side of the picture. At the present time 90% of the population unsubjected so far to outside influences, is completely loyal, sometimes blindly loyal, to its Chiefs. Therefore, to stampede or over-persuade these to concede, too precipitately, authority which they still feel deeply it is their moral and religious duty to retain would result in the antagonising of the great mass of the population for the sake of the fickle favour of the vocal few. Decentralisation and delegation must come as rapidly as possible but only in terms of the ability of a modernised machine to take the strain. It would be the height of political unwisdom to forfeit the confidence of the Chiefs in our good faith. We must carry with us the progressive emirs and they will carry with them in their turn the more reactionary of their number.

(e) It is most important to realise that the recent report of the J.S.C. on Native Authorities, Councils etc. constitutes in fact a very considerable advance both in terms of what the Chiefs as a body could be expected to concede, and equally important, what the people as a whole are ready from the point of view of political and administrative advancement to accept.

The Chiefs, especially the more enlightened ones, are not so much jealously clinging to privileges; they honestly feel that they will be betraying their peoples' true interests if they hand over too much authority too soon to small sections of the community whose motives, they, in certain cases mistrust and whose lack of experience is patent to all. As regards high appointments, as matters stand, with very few exceptions the best people available are, in my experience, appointed to all posts of responsibility and, as far as possible, the wishes of the local population are taken into consideration in local administrative appointments and public opinion in the case of central posts.

The substitution of a method of 'direct election' for one of 'selection after consultation' would in the case of important member posts soon play havoc with the administration. The public would, at the present stage of its political development, naturally elect the type of man who would worry it least with reforms and innovations and a state of stagnation would follow.

(f) I was continually finding myself perturbed during the recent Cambridge Conference by the insistence on *'pattern'* which characterised the 'academics' combined with a failure or refusal, to realise the necessity for studying the problem of *personnel*. Delegation there must be, but the personnel must first be found and trained and for some time onward supervised. A complex of Councils and Committees is of no value whatsoever until the manning problem is solved. On the supervisory side the administrative staff is already more than fully occupied, to the exclusion of other important work, on duties connected mainly with the new Constitution. Do let us get that in working order first. We can then try to use for local Government all suitable human material that has been brought forward whether the individuals in question have secured election to the Legislatures or not. In the meantime the process of educating public opinion at all levels for its responsibilities can go ahead in readiness for wide-spread operations in the field of Local Government in 1952.

(g) Over and above this process I fully endorse the proposal that a suitable full-time officer should be appointed to further the recommendations of the J.S.C. when finally approved, provided that the eye of the administrative staff is not taken off the constitutional ball for a further number of months and provided further that attention is concentrated on pilot schemes rather than on a general overhaul.

(h) (i) To return to the question of the future of the two main political movements in the North, the N.P.C. and the *N.E.P.U.* Regrettably the N.P.C. has lost a lot of ground in recent months owing, partly, to the fact that its leaders and principal adherents are busy men for whom politics can only be a part-time occupation, and partly to the lack of a sufficiently positive and sufficiently publicised policy. The N.E.P.U. leaders on the other hand, (vide the Kano 'Comet') are without other employment, without inhibitions, without loyalties and without scruples. The policy and tactics of the movement appeal to the imagination of the young N.A. employee class, which needs, very naturally, some outlet for its emotions and aspirations, and also to the younger elements of the mixed trading classes in Kano, in particular, who resent the status of social inferiority imposed on them by the Fulani ruling families and their supporters. Some youthful members of this same class, incidentally, are also adherents of N.E.P.U. probably from a mixed sense of adventure and hopes of a short cut to personal advancement and gain in political channels.

(ii) It is very important that note should be taken of certain sinister aspects of N.E.P.U., the idealisation and hero-worship of the leader, the distortion of local history in the movement's interests, the arrogation of the right to intervene directly in the administration of the area and finally, the creation of badged, if not yet uniformed gangs of young cyclist 'storm troopers'. This technique is only too familiar to us in Europe and any tendency to view it with tolerance or to sublimate it in this instance because it has its roots in colonial soil should be strongly resisted.

(iii) N.E.P.U.'s main weakness is its shameless assumption of omniscience, the arrogant attitude of its youthful members to parents, elders and to all in established authority and, more than anything, its mercenary and unhallowed alliance with the infidel N.C.N.C. This last step taken to ensure publicity space in the Zik Press and funds for future campaigning has made the movement and its members to all orthodox Moslems and to all who fear ultimately its domination of the country.

(iv) N.E.P.U.'s main strength, on the other hand, in the political field derives from its press campaign against corruption in the N.A. service. There is no rival organ to point out that this corruption is universal and that, so far from being confined to senior officials and District Heads, it is most rampant among the very classes from which N.E.P.U. draws its most vocal members. The roots, in point of fact, are deepest in Government service, in the Railway administration and in the Department of Post and Telegraphs where it is so closely organised that all efforts on the part of the Police and the Departments concerned have so far failed to make any impression upon it.

(i) To turn to the future. There can be no progress without stability, neither can we hope for stability until the responsible progressive elements in all communities get together and produce a policy sufficiently positive to fire the imagination of the young and sufficiently realistic to enlist the support of the present ruling classes who after all, with all their defects, know their complex job well and know too that their principal detractors are, for the most part, ignorant even of its simplest elements.

(ii) In common with the Government machine itself at the lower levels the prevalence of corruption and the exploitation by officialdom of the individual is the most vulnerable aspect of the present N.A. system. This weakness can and must be brought within bounds if the system is to justify itself in the eyes of the people and in the eyes of the outside world. Because it is endemic and universal, it cannot be eradicated. It can, however, be controlled.

(iii) A step has already been made successfully in this direction in Kano, for instance, where the trouble is far more prevalent than again for instance, in Sokoto. Less successful attempts have been made to induce the leading trading and governing families to sink their differences and that stability is essential to both and a union of power, experience and wealth is the best way to achieve that stability.

(iv) It is probable that the Fulani feel that the coming elections will result in a body of moderates manning the new House of Assembly, and that they have nothing to fear. They do not yet see, for the most part, that unless they take action, the radicalism that has won the day in the Wogi area of Kano in the face of the apathy of the orthodox, will soon cross the city walls and spread thence to the main centres in the Districts.

(v) The main hope for the future is an N.P.C. revival backed by the more progressive Chiefs and supported by the more responsible of those who now adhere to N.E.P.U. because there is no attractive alternative. The Editor of 'Gaskiya', with whom I had a long discussion in July, is one of those who is aware of this fact. He possesses more competence than most to bring it about given support and advice.

Footnote

The foregoing notes were originally jotted down for the personal information of Mr. Hudson.[2] They were not intended for a wider circulation. Since seeing them for the first time in typescript I have made four or five minor amendments. In retrospect the notes *seem* to advocate the use of the brake, the steering apparatus and the accelerator in that precise order i.e. the adoption of a somewhat over-cautious policy. Such was not at all the intention. Subject to attention being paid to the major hazards detailed, all three 'aids' should be used in the order and to the degree most appropriate. The use of the brake permits acceleration over short stretches and skilful steering at speed enables obstacles to be bye-passed before they actually obstruct!

---

[2] R S Hudson, head of the African Studies Branch, CO, 1949–1961.

Finally, I discern an intolerant attitude towards the present leaders of *N.E.P.U.* This is *freely* admitted. An intimate knowledge of the activities and the personalities of the individuals concerned leaves no room for any other outlook in anyone who cares for freedom, decency and true progress. One can respect the honest though misguided zealot and feel sympathy for the less irresponsible enthusiasms of African studentdom. N.E.P.U. leaders are of different metal.

147   CO 554/235, no 4   5 Nov 1951
[Local government reform]: CO minutes of a meeting with Sir J Macpherson to discus local government reform in Northern Nigeria

The meeting was held at the Governor's suggestion in order that he might have the opportunity of informing the Colonial Office pending the despatch of an official communication, of the line of approach taken by the Nigerian Government to the proposed reform of Local Government in the North.[1] To this effect, he outlined certain points communicated to him by the Chief Secretary.

The Governor prefixed his remarks by speaking highly of Mr. Sharwood-Smith's skill and services in preserving unity among the Emirs at a time when new ideas might easily have caused a split between them.

The following points were then considered:—

(a) *Status of the emirs under the new proposals*
The grievance of the bulk of Northern peoples have continually to be borne in mind as a background to the problem of reform or 'development'. The Emir has always appeared to them as chief in his own right, so that acceptance of the concept of Chief-in-Council might prove difficult. Nevertheless, it was essential that this relationship should evolve; the development of a Chief-*and*-Council was dangerous and strongly to be resisted. Far from exercising control over his council the Emir must be bound by it.

The meeting fully endorsed the necessity of fostering this relationship.

(b) *Necessity of internal evolution*
Agreement was also expressed on the necessity of making any reform spring from the ruling classes themselves; it should on no account be imposed upon them. For this reason the proposal for an outside Commission of Enquiry should be resisted. The new structure must evolve, from within. It was at the same time stressed that, in order to avoid an upheaval with force at a later date, fostered by undesirable parties, constitutional development and the elimination of corruption must be speedy.

(c) *Appointment of a commissioner for local government*
It was agreed that it was essential to install such an officer in the North to provide the required driving force toward reform, rather than leave encouragement and acceleration to be a duty performed by the Residents. In this connection, the name of

---

[1] This followed the Maddocks and Pott report into local government in the Northern region, which was completed in Dec 1950 and considered by a Joint Select Committee of the Northern Regional Council the following year.

Mr. Farley-Smith[2] was put forward, it being felt that he is a man highly suited for this important task. His attitude to the proposed reforms should be ascertained.

As a further step, the Governor announced his intention of stressing to the Residents of the Northern Provinces at a forthcoming meeting the extreme urgency of the matter.

---

[2] T Farley Smith, senior district officer, 1946; administrative officer, 1947; staff grade, 1949.

148   CO 554/286, no 16   13 Nov 1951
[Revenue allocation]: memorandum by R J Vile on the Nigeria (Revenue Allocation) Order in Council, 1951. *Minutes* by A B Cohen and Sir T Lloyd

The 1946 constitution for Nigeria set up Regional Councils which apart from advising on draft bills for enactment by the Nigerian Legislative Council also exercised certain financial powers concerning the spending of money allocated to the Regions by the Nigerian Government. The situation was then that the Regions had a modicum of responsibility and financial power but in practice they often were subject in all respects to the power of the Central Government of Nigeria. No revenues were assigned to them by law and they had no powers of legislation.

When the 1946 constitution was reviewed in Nigeria a major feature of the recommendations for a new constitution was the grant of certain powers of legislation to the Regions together with executive responsibility for a number of Departments. These proposals were accepted by H.M.G. in the U.K., and the Nigerian (Constitution) Order in Council, 1951, divides Nigeria into three Regions and constitutes for each Region a Regional Legislature with power to legislate on a prescribed list of subjects, notably agriculture, health, social welfare, education, public works, local government and the borrowing of money. Regional Legislatures may also spend money on a number of additional things including Administration, the Nigerian Police and Public Relations. The effect of these changes will be that the Northern Region is likely to have to meet an expenditure of £4½ millions in the forthcoming financial year, the Western Region an expenditure of £4¼ millions and the Eastern Region an expenditure of £3¾ millions. These sums are greater in aggregate by some £4¼ millions than the expenditure incurred by all three Regions two years ago.

In order to achieve a satisfactory settlement of the problems which would undoubtedly arise in considering the method of allocating revenue to the three Regions an Expert Commission of Enquiry investigated the matter in 1950 (the members were Mr. J. R. Hicks of Nuffield College and Sir S. Phillipson, Nigerian Special Commissioner, assisted by Mrs. Hicks). This Commission reported early in 1951 and its recommendations were considered by a committee, presided over by the Nigerian Financial Secretary, consisting of five members drawn from each Region (the Committee of Sixteen).

The Commission recognised that the ideal solution would be to give to Regions revenues of their own which would suffice to meet their needs. The only revenues immediately available for this purpose were those already given to the Regions under the existing system and a sales tax on motor spirit which the Regions could impose to replace the present customs duty. These revenues were insufficient and the Commission had therefore to consider what other revenues could be properly given by the Nigerian Government to the Regions. They recommended that one half of the tobacco tax should be given to the Regions in accordance with Regional consumption of tobacco (the principle of derivation), that an amount (the capitation grant), which should be the same in each Region in any one financial year, should be paid for every adult male taxpayer in the Region (the principle of needs), and that grants to cover expenditure on grants-in-aid to educational Voluntary Agencies and to cover expenditure on the Nigeria Police should be paid to the Regions (the principle of national interest). The Commission also recommended that a grant equal to 50% of the expenditure on Native Administration Police should be paid to Regions.

The Committee of Sixteen accepted these recommendations except that they proposed by a majority that 100% of the tobacco tax should be allocated to Regions. The figures now available for the probable yield on tobacco tax show that this proposal would give one Region, the West, almost all the money it needs to meet its expenditure without any capitation grant, but the two other Regions would require substantial capitation grants to enable them to meet their expenditure and this would give the West a very large surplus indeed. Because of the cost to the Nigerian Government of adopting this proposal (some £2¼ millions) the Acting Governor of Nigeria has recommended that the share of tobacco tax allocated to the Regions should be 50% (as recommended by Hicks-Phillipson). The Acting Governor has also recommended an elaboration of the Commission's proposal that Regional expenditure on the Nigeria Police should be met by a grant from central revenues. Apart from some other minor adjustments of the Commission's recommendations which are required for administrative purposes the Acting Governor recommends that the Commission's proposals be accepted. The proposals have been examined in the Colonial Office and discussed with the Governor.

The Commission also proposed that there should be paid to the Northern Region a grant not exceeding £2 millions, on the grounds that the Northern Region had received less from central revenues in the past than the other Regions. The Committee of Sixteen recommended that this sum should be increased to £3 millions but the Acting Governor has been unable to accept this variation because there is no case to support it and the Nigerian Government cannot afford to deplete its reserves.

It is now proposed to embody the recommendations, made by the Commission and supported by the Acting Governor, in a Nigeria (Revenue Allocation) Order in Council which is to be laid before the Privy Council at its meeting on the 4th December. This Order will provide that Regions shall derive revenue from matters in respect of which Regional Legislatures are competent to make laws. It will also provide that one half of the tobacco duties shall be allocated to the three Regions in proportion to Regional consumption, that all the customs duty on motor spirit shall be similarly allocated until it has been replaced by a sales tax, that a capitation grant shall be paid to the Regions from Nigerian revenues, and that an education grant, a police grant and 50% of the cost of the Native Authority police forces shall also be paid from Nigerian revenues to the Regions.

At the time of the promulgation of the Order in Council it is intended to publish the exchange of the despatches between the Acting Governor and the Secretary of State. Drafts of these despatches are attached to this memorandum. The concurrence of the Acting Governor has not yet been received in these drafts.

Minutes on 148

Sir T. Lloyd
Mr. Vile's memorandum gives the background of this matter.

The allocation of revenue as between the three Regions of Nigeria and the Central Nigerian Government has been one of the most difficult matters to handle in connection with the new constitution. The North, which generally speaking has less developed services than the other Regions, is labouring under a sense of grievance on the ground that whereas a very large part of the economic strength of Nigeria comes from the North and the North has more than half the population, they have not had a fair share of expenditure. In order to deal with the matter the Commission referred to by Mr. Vile was set up and made what in my view was a really brilliant Report, ingeniously producing what is a practical solution in terms of the division of money, and succeeding in basing this on certain justifiable principles. The Nigerian Committee of 16 which considered the Report accepted it generally, but the North and the West did a pretty disgraceful piece of horse trading, under which the North was to get a £3 million capital grant instead of £2 million, as recommended by the Hicks-Phillipson Commission, and all Regions to get 100% of the tobacco duties, instead of 50% as recommended by the Hicks-Phillipson Commission—this latter change would have particularly favoured the West.

Since the Commission reported and the Committee of 16 sat it has become evident that, as a result of the changed plans by the tobacco industry, there is going to be an enormous increase in revenue from tobacco duties. This makes any question of the Regions getting 100% of the tobacco duty quite absurd, since this would throw out the balance between the Regions and the Centre recommended by the Hicks-Phillipson Commission, while, apart from that, the finances of the Central Nigerian Government would be gravely impaired. The Nigerian Government have, therefore, after very anxious thought, recommended that the Hicks-Phillipson Commission should be accepted. We have discussed the matter at length with Sir John Macpherson and Mr. Gray, the officer on the financial side of the Nigerian Government who has been most closely concerned with this problem. We have come to the conclusion that the Nigerian recommendation is the right one.

We are now in the final stages of completing the Order in Council designed to give effect to these arrangements. It will come before the Privy Council on the 4th December. When it is published it is to be accompanied by an exchange of despatches. The draft of the Nigerian despatch has been discussed here with the Governor and Mr. Grey and we have suggested a number of amendments to it. We have sent these together with the draft of the brief reply from the Secretary of State to the Acting Governor for his comments and Sir John Macpherson himself also has copies. It is unlikely that any substantial comments will be made. We therefore submit the drafts for the approval of Ministers.

A.B.C.
14.11.51

Minister of State
Mr. Vile's very useful memorandum at No. 16, when read with Mr. Cohen's minute overleaf, will I think give you all the information that you need for a study of the two drafts (flagged A and B) now submitted below the memorandum.

Draft B is a revise of a draft (No. 1 on the file) prepared in Nigeria and submitted by the Acting Governor. The revision has been carried out in consultation with Sir John Macpherson and one of his senior Finance Officers (Mr. Grey) now in this country. I have sent Mr. Vile a note on two points of detail arising on draft B. There is no point in this draft to which I need draw special attention.

Draft A, which has been prepared here, is of a reply to the Acting Governor's despatch. Beyond accepting the local proposals it says very little, but as a matter of form it has been referred to the Acting Governor for concurrence.

Finally, there is still under preparation the draft of an Order in Council giving effect to all these proposals. That Order is expected to come before the Privy Council on the 4th of December. The Secretary of State will, of course, still be in Malaya then and arrangements should be made, if you agree, for you to attend the Council since it is customary for one of our Ministers to be present whenever the Council has before it a Colonial Order of any importance.

Nearer the time the Department would let you have a brief note about the Order in Council in case H.M. should ask questions as he sometimes does.[1]

T.K.L.
14.11.51

---

[1] Mr Lennox-Boyd noted (19 Nov): 'I agree with both drafts and I will go to the Privy Council on Dec 4th.'

149 CO 554/286, no 36   Nov 1951

[Revenue allocation]: CO note for Mr Lennox-Boyd concerning the Nigeria (Revenue Allocation) Order in Council, 1951

The Nigeria (Constitution) Order in Council 1951 divides Nigeria into three Regions. In each Region a Regional legislature will have power to legislate on a prescribed list of subjects including agriculture, health, social welfare, education, public works and local government, and the power to spend money on these subjects as well as on additional matters including Administration, Police and Public Relations.

In the past all revenues in Nigeria have belonged to the Nigerian Government. The purpose of the Nigeria (Revenue Allocation) order is to assign revenues to Regions. The revenues so assigned are:—

(a) All revenues derived from matters in respect of which Regional legislatures can make laws

(b) A sales tax on motor spirit: such a tax cannot be introduced at once and meanwhile all the customs duty on motor spirit is assigned to the Regions.

(c) One half of the tobacco tax.

(d) A capitation grant paid from Nigerian revenues which is calculated on the number of taxpayers in each Region multiplied by a capitation rate which is the same for all Regions.

(e) Grants from Nigerian revenues to cover expenditure on grants-in-aid to educational voluntary agencies.

(f) Grants from Nigerian revenues to meet expenditure on the Nigerian Police.

(g) Grants from Nigerian revenues equal to 50% of the expenditure on Native Administration Police.

The revenues derived from these sources will be sufficient to permit Regions to finance the services for which they are responsible. Because of the unequal development of Regions the West will be better off than the North and the North better off than the East in the immediate future but this state of affairs is not likely to continue for long.

The Order also provides for payment of a £2 millions capital grant to the Northern Region as recompense for past failure to spend in the North as such public revenue per head of population as has been spent in the other Regions.

150   CO 554/290, no 3   19 Dec 1951
[Elections to Houses of Assembly]: inward telegram no 1749 from Sir J Macpherson to T B Williamson on the outcome of the regional elections

[Elections to the regional Houses of Assembly under the new constitution were held between July and Dec 1951. These elections took place under an electoral college system involving several stages. In the East, the NCNC won 65 of the 84 seats, in the West the AG won 44 of the 80 seats contested but this number was increased by defections from the 30 or so NCNC seats thereafter. In the North, all NEPU candidates were defeated and the NPC, still a very inchoate organisation, won an overwhelming majority, though a number of representatives of middle belt parties were also returned. The issue to face the administration once the elections were completed was the selection of members to represent the Houses of Assembly in the House of Representatives; increasingly parties took a 'winner takes all' view of this. In Dec Chief Bode Thomas,[1] on behalf of the AG, sent a telegram to the Labour Party in Britain, complaining at delays in the calling of the first meeting of the Western House of Assembly and the failure to consult the majority leaders in the Houses of Assembly over the choice of ministers; the Labour Party forwarded this telegram to the CO who requested information from Macpherson. This episode culminated in Jan 1952 in the AG's successful manoeuvre to prevent Azikiwe, who had won one of the five Lagos seats in the Western House of Assembly, from being nominated to one of the two Lagos seats in the House of Representatives. By agreement, three of the Lagos members (all of whom belonged to the NCNC) were to refuse to stand in order to allow Azikiwe a clear run for the House of Representatives; in the event, and to allegations of bribery and corruption, Ibiyinka Olorun-Nimbe and Adeleke Adedoyin refused to do so and Azikiwe failed to be elected by the AG-dominated House; Azikiwe was thus sidelined as leader of the opposition in the West.]

Begins. You will, of course, have realised that background to all this is war between Action Group and N.C.N.C.

2.   Main business of first meeting of Regional Legislature will be:—

(a) Election of Members of House of Representatives, and
(b) Consultation about choice of Regional and Central Ministers. Meeting will be briefly suspended so that Lieutenant-Governor can fly to Lagos 14th January for
(c) consultation with me about the choice of Ministers (this has not been made public yet). They will then return
(d) to obtain formal resolution from the Regional House on the choice made.

It is not essential that meetings should open simultaneously but no one Legislature can proceed beyond stages (a) and (b) until all are ready for (c). I invite reference to paragraph 5 of S. of S's despatch No. 147 A.[2] You will appreciate that it

---

[1] Chief Bode Thomas, *Balogun* of Oyo; founding member and deputy leader of the AG; Federal Minister of Transport, 1952–1953.   [2] See 137.

would be unsatisfactory and dangerous for one Region to be four weeks ahead of the others with stage (b) completed, but in enforced idleness. If there is a long interval, between (b) and (d) the greatest difficulty is to be expected in getting (d) through (see second sentence of paragraph 5 below).

3.   First meeting of Western House was tentatively fixed by the Chief Commissioner for 10th December on the understanding that he would go to stage (a) only, but date was not officially published. Eastern Region, at the same time, proposed to open for business up to stage (a) only on 17th December. When it became apparent that North could not open meeting before the first week in January and stage (c) could not, therefore, be reached until the middle of January, Western meeting was fixed for 7th January. Eastern Region have similarly postponed until the 5th January.

4.   As regards consultation with Action Group leaders, Chief Commissioner was in difficult position until elections in Lagos and Benin had been completed and while the party affiliations remain subject of Press controversy.[3] In spite of N.C.N.C. claim to the contrary, it now appears that Action Group adherents form the majority in Western House of Assembly and Shankland had private consultation with Action Group leaders last week. They are meeting Chief Commissioner tomorrow at his invitation. This has not been made public. Intention of Constitution (ommission ?was that) Regional Legislature as a whole, not majority parties where they exist, should have voice in the selection of Ministers. See section 128 of Order in Council, paragraph 8 of S. of S. despatch No. 464 A of 15th July 1950,[4] and paragraph 5 of S. of S. despatch No. 147 A. Action Group, however, is determined completely to dominate the Western Legislature and the Executive Council and so far as possible to exclude others from the House of Representatives. In particular, such is their hatred and jealousy of Azikiwe that they mean by hook or by crook to prevent him coming to the House of Representatives. I believe their strategy in this matter misguided, but I doubt if they will change and present view of Chief Commissioner West is that he must play along with them (much as the Governor of the Gold Coast does with C.P.P) if the machine is to work at all. Fortunately they want what we want and are conscious of the need of our help, though they will not say so publicly.

5.   Situation is very fluid but should be clearer after talks tomorrow. Fulminations of Action Group were provoked by fear that N.C.N.C. would use period of postponement to wean away supporters. They should not be taken too seriously. It is a young organisation and realises it is at disadvantage in the struggle with N.C.N.C., being unknown overseas. You may get more telegrams of similar nature. *Ends.*

---

[3] The Western elections were completed in Sept, but the elections for Lagos and Benin did not take place until Nov and Dec respectively.   [4] See 116.

151   CO 554/290, no 9   31 Dec 1951
[Constitutional review]: inward telegram no 199 from Sir J
Macpherson to Mr Lyttelton on a meeting with leaders of the Action
Group concerning the new constitution

My telegram No. 1790—Action Group.
Chief Secretary and I received Action Group leaders on 28th December. Main (who will be acting L-G Western Region from 22nd January when Hoskyns-Abrahall leaves

on retirement until return of Marshall) was present, also Shankland, Acting Civil Secretary, Western Region. Awolowo brought with him Bode Thomas and Maja.[1]

2.   The meeting lasted 2½ hours. There was some pretty plain speaking—on both sides—but the atmosphere was quite good. Agreed communique (their draft) said, in part, that 'A number of subjects arising as a result of the introduction of the new Constitution were considered. The discussions took place in a frank and cordial atmosphere and to the satisfaction of all those present.'

3.   Although there was a large measure of agreement, they are still electioneering and playing politics—rather naively. They make special point that they must prove to their people that Nigerian Constitution is not inferior to that of the Gold Coast; thus justifying decision to co-operate. At this meeting I did not feel we could risk a break with them by turning down flat their less desirable demands, but I think I may have persuaded them to go slow on most of them, at least until there has been consultation with other Regions. The matters in question are as follows:—

(a) Salaries of Ministers. They want salaries of Ministers, with portfolios, to be raised to £2,500 and to be the same in the Regions as at the Centre. I said that salaries of Central Ministers must be fixed first—after discussion in Council of Ministers. They agreed but will probably promise their Regional Ministers that Western Region Budget meeting in February will raise salaries well above amounts already tentatively fixed.

(b) They want Parliamentary Under-Secretaries to relieve Ministers and enable them to tour. I am afraid that this is a case of copying Gold Coast and of finding 'Jobs for the Boys'. I told them that I had an open mind on the question, but I was not convinced that the amount of work justified these appointments. Why not wait and see? I was afraid that they might hinder rather than help close co-operation between Ministers and Heads of Departments in the initial stages at least, and I didn't like one Region starting this on its own. It was agreed that the other Regions should be told of this idea and that their views should be sought.

(c) Leader of Government Business. This, to my mind, is the most dangerous and undesirable of all the demands of the Action Group and I intend to do all in my power to kill it. It is another instance of copying the Gold Coast. They argued that Lieutenant-Governor would constantly want to consult the Leader of the majority party before raising a question in Executive Council and that leader ought to have status. I countered by saying that in my view Gold Coast had gone wrong on this. In any case, our Constitution, as agreed by General Conference, provided that ex officio members (who for a long time will be all expatriate) should be part of the very fabric of the Constitutional Structure. Party politics had come sooner than expected, but it would be wrong and dangerous to pretend that we had party Prime Minister anywhere, by whatever bogus title he was called. I am not sure how far I shook them on this, but they know that I am resolutely opposed to it and they also know that there can be no question of a similar thing at the Centre, at least until such time as there are Nigerian parties. I do not think they will press the issue pending consultation with Ministers from other Regions. And Awolowo assured me with a broad smile that they would not 'walk out' on this.

---

[1] Dr Akinola Maja, medical practitioner and politician; president of NYM, 1944–1951; chairman of National Emergency Council, 1949–1950, president of *Egbe Omo Oduduwa* from 1953. Known as 'Father of the AG'.

(d) President, Western House of Assembly. You will have seen the record of discussion of this matter at meeting which L-G Western Region had with Action Group on 18th December. At our meeting here leaders agreed that qualifications required were competence and impartiality and that the person must be recognised to be impartial. They get the point that if anyone were appointed against whom any colourable accusation of bias could be levelled, their position would be seriously weakened. They still feel they are 'committed' to accepting only a Nigerian as President of the Western House, and suggested that the duties of President be carried out by an African Judge. The Chief Justice understandably does not like the idea of a Judge being seconded, still less doubling the duties, as he fears that his value as a Judge would be impaired. Action Group suggested Jibowa who has since told Chief Justice that he agrees with Chief Justice's objections in principle, and furthermore would not wish to accept the job himself if it were offered him. I am still urgently exploring other possibilities if only to tide us over first formal meeting next week. Thereafter Action Group might feel confident enough to make no protest about appointment of acceptable expatiate. In any case, I do not believe they will go to the limit of obstruction on this.

4.   I did my utmost to convince Awolowo of our sincere desire to co-operate, but I also told him that they must respond. Once we get started, he cannot work together with us and at the same time continue his tirades of abuse in the Press.

152   CO 967/173   8 Jan 1952

[Gold Coast and Nigeria]: letter from Sir J Macpherson to Sir T Lloyd on the impact of Gold Coast policy on Nigeria

[The first meeting of the new Legislative Council in the Gold Coast with Nkrumah as leader of government business, took place in February 1951. Nkrumah's determination to press for further constitutional change, and Arden-Clarke's willingness to accommodate him, clearly posed difficulties for Macpherson's hopes that Nigerian political leaders and officials would be given a breathing space to adjust to operating the 1951 constitution. On 18 December 1951 Awolowo and other AG leaders met the chief commissioner of the Western region explicitly to stress their determination to obtain as much power for political leaders in Nigeria as their counter-parts had obtained in the Gold Coast. The immediate pressure facing Macpherson when he wrote this letter was that the first meeting of the Nigerian Council of Ministers was due to be held on 26 January and the House of Representatives shortly after. (See 155). Subsequently in February 1952 Macpherson visited London for discussions with Lyttelton concerning the implications of the appointment of Nkrumah, in March, as prime minister of the Gold Coast.]

Arden-Clarke is probably discussing the future of the Gold Coast with you as I write.[1] He told me about his visit and suggested that I might go out to the airport as he passed through here yesterday. I was very glad to do this, and I took with me Benson and Scrivenor[2] because I thought that we should be concerting together plans to ensure (with the help of His Majesty's Government, including financial help if necessary) that, in spite of the withdrawal from the Gold Coast Legislature of the

---

[1] Arden-Clarke met with Lloyd at the CO on 9 Jan 1952. See BDEEP series B, vol 1, R Rathbone, ed, *Ghana*, part I, 112.

[2] T V Scrivenor, civil service commissioner, Nigeria, 1947–1953.

Motion on Lidbury, expatriation pay, or some equivalent inducement, would continue to be paid to our chaps in the Gold Coast and in Nigeria.[3] (We had been following events in the Gold Coast with intense interest, and I called my people together for a 'war talk' as soon as I heard of the rough passage that expatriation pay received in the Gold Coast Legislature).

When we met at the airport the discussion was on a totally different basis from what I had expected. Had I not been in so critical a position at the moment—with Ministers to be chosen, in the Regions and at the Centre, within the next ten days—I should have jumped into the aircraft with Arden-Clarke, trusting that the Secretary of State would approve, *ex post facto*, my leaving my charge! Arden-Clarke told me what he proposed to ask H.M.G. to agree to—i.e. (a) that the existing situation in the Gold Coast should be recognized to the extent of calling Nkrumah Prime Minister (whatever the restrictions on his 'portfolio' in the matter of defence, external relations, etc.); (b) that the logical next step would be the disappearance of the *ex-officio* Members of the Gold Coast Executive (possibly retaining an Attorney General in the back-ground and employing expatriate Financial and Economic Advisers); and (c) a threat to liquidate all District Officers over a period of five years. As regards timing, I understood Arden-Clarke to say that he hoped that the announcement about changing Nkrumah's title to Prime Minister might be made at the end of this month.

Let me say at once that I have always fully realised the gravity of the task that was given to Arden-Clarke, and that I have watched with admiration the way in which he has kept going what I have referred to as his 'continuing miracle'. I have feared for some time that Nkrumah would feel that he had to do something dramatic to maintain his position, and I have feared that this would take the form of demanding the elimination of the *ex-officio* Ministers. But I confess that when Arden-Clarke told me that *he* was pressing for agreement to changes of this nature the shock was very great, because I was bound to think of the effects here which would, I fear, be catastrophic, despite our brave hopes. What made the shock worse was the news that discussions had taken place with Nkrumah in London many months ago, and that the former Secretary of State had agreed that it would be necessary to allow Nkrumah to win further political advance along some such lines as these.[4] With great restraint, I made no comment to Arden-Clarke (we talk the same language and I greatly admire him) but I am bound to say that I consider that the failure to tell us about these conversations is very hard to understand—having regard to the great and ever-increasing repercussions here from events in the Gold Coast.

As I say, I realise very clearly the critical situation in the Gold Coast. All I ask is that in considering what action may be necessary there to save the Gold Coast for the Empire you in London will not fail to realise that the result may be to pose the same question for Nigeria. We are in a much stronger position than the Gold Coast, because of our size and diversity. But let no one think that we are safe. The Regional Houses are meeting now, as I write, and decisions are being made about the representation in the Central Legislature, and about the Ministers who will be

---

[3] *Report of the Commission on the Civil Service of the Gold Coast, 1950–1951* (chairman, Sir D Lidbury) Accra, 1951. See Rathbone, part I, 99.
[4] Griffiths met Nkrumah in London in June 1951 to discuss proposals for further constitutional change in the Gold Coast. See Rathbone, part I, 103.

acceptable. I shall know the position more clearly in a week's time, but already it seems fairly clear that I shall have a sedate Northern Region (for a time; Thompstone himself thinks it is *too* safe); an Eastern Region dominated by the N.C.N.C.; and a Western Region dominated by a thrustful Action Group which, as you know, is modelling itself on the CPP. Difficult as that team would be to drive in 'Nigerian' harness, I was not pessimistic about the outcome. Both political parties had decided to try out the new Constitution, and responsibility has a sobering effect. But if the concessions proposed by Arden-Clarke are given to the Gold Coast I shall have the gloomiest forebodings about the future here. It is virtually certain that the Action Group in the West and the N.C.N.C. in the East will get together and demand immediate changes in the Constitution along Gold Coast lines, or will vie with each other in the extravagance of their demands. The North as at present represented will not be stampeded (thank God for their 50 per cent representation) but I foresee a sharp cleavage between North and South, and the collapse of our hopes and plans for a strong and united Nigeria.

Against this setting, the question of expatriation pay and the continued employment of expatriate officers—not least District Officers—appears to be of almost secondary importance. So far from being reasonably confident that we can make the new Constitution work, thus enabling us to hold the position in Nigeria until the politicians have learned, or been compelled by healthy public opinion, to work on reasonable, co-operative, albeit progressive lines, the whole constitutional position that we have build up so carefully is likely to be thrown into the melting pot.

I believe that five-sixths of the people of Nigeria would be desolated by the idea that District Officers might be withdrawn, but those five-sixths are incoherent and inarticulate and would be unlikely to be able to make their views heard against the extremely vocal one-sixth (or even less) who would inevitably clamour to follow the Gold Coast's lead. So far from being able to fend off, in the interests of the moderate politicians and thinking men of Nigeria and the vast silent rural population, any suggestion for a Leader of Government Business, we should be faced immediately, in the South at least, with a clamour for Prime Ministers and, in due course, for the exclusion of Official Members. We have a very large number of expatriate officers in Nigeria, the great majority of whom at the present moment, despite financial anxieties, too much work—especially paper work—and slight anxiety about the future, have not lost their 'vocation', are on their toes, intensely interested in our developments, political and other, and cheerfully looking forward to working out their careers here. The effect on them of Arden-Clarke's programme can be well imagined, even if it were still possible to offer them reasonable conditions of service.

But the main thing is that our new Constitution has still every chance of ensuring that the co-operation between British and local people in local government, at the official level, and at the Ministerial level, will be developed and maintained for many years to come: up to the time in fact when the then Governor of Nigeria would be in a position to report to the Secretary of State that public opinion throughout Nigeria was so overwhelmingly pro good government and pro British ideals, institutions and practices, that he could quite safely advocate complete self-government; and that Nigerians themselves would either be able to fill all the important posts remaining in expatriate hands or, more likely, would themselves wish to retain Britishers there. If Arden-Clarke's programme is adopted that becomes a pipe-dream, and we may well join the number of those Colonies who have had to fight a rearguard action doomed to defeat.

I gathered from Arden-Clarke that his object was to win time for the emergence of a moderate political party which could form a reasonable opposition to the CPP as at present constituted. Quite frankly, if there is any pipe-dreaming about, the thought that two or three years in the Gold Coast would be sufficient to achieve this seems the dreamiest I have ever heard of.

This is a hard letter for you to receive at this time—just as it is a hard letter to write. I have tried not to be parochial but to look at Empire interests as a whole. And the dilemma is a painful one. All that I ask is that in weighing up the Gold Coast situation full thought will be given to the effects here.

I shall write you separately about our plans for a salary revision, including expatriation pay, and about the sort of arguments we might use with our politicians (Himsworth will be in London in a few days and can tell you how our minds are working). We must go on with these plans because I refuse to give up hope, but a slide in the Gold Coast will stack the dice against us in an almost impossible way.

153 CO 554/260, no 9D   18 Jan 1952
[Gold Coast and Nigeria]: letter from Sir J Macpherson to Sir T Lloyd on the impact of developments in the Gold Coast on the prospects for the 1951 constitution

Your secret and personal telegram No. 80 of the 16th of January was handed to me at 11 p.m. that evening when we were in the midst of a large party for the Pakistani delegation. (Earlier in the day I had completed my 'Cabinet-making' and the three Lieutenant-Governors had flown back to put the names to the Regional Legislative Houses).

Benson and I went out to the Airport early on the 17th and had an hour's talk with Arden-Clarke. It was—as always—friendly and understanding.

Nationalism, once it is in the saddle, rides hard. I know, too, that once a country is set on the road towards responsible Government it is very difficult to hold the position at a transitional stage. In giving you my assessment of our position and prospects I am very conscious of the fact that I am doing this before (but less than ten days before) I meet my Council of Ministers for the first time,[1] and that in telling you of my high hopes (before I learned last week about impending events in the Gold Coast) for the success of our planned advance I may be indulging in some pipe-dreams myself.

We have by a process lasting almost three years deliberately given this country a Constitution that is in advance of its true capacity, and in doing this I have been seriously criticized not only by many of my stout-hearted British Officers, but by a great many truly patriotic Nigerians. These honest people, who know only Nigeria, had not fully realised, when I started, what was happening in other parts of the world. We couldn't put a ring fence round Nigeria, and we had to take the initiative, and not wait to be overtaken by events, because of what was happening, and is continuing to

---

[1] See 155.

happen, in the Gold Coast, the Sudan, Libya, etc. etc. We had to assess the situation, calculate the risks and make a brave cool plan. Then we had to go at it with everything we had.

We are now bringing into force—before the end of this month—a Constitution which is not what the extremists want but is that chosen by the people, accordingly to their varying degree of understanding. And we think that if we can get a straight run at it for even six months we can make a success of it, establishing mutual confidence between Ministers, Chiefs, Commoners, and British officials, who are all part of the very fabric. There are dangers, of course, but there has been a great increase in political consciousness, by reason of the wide discussions that have taken place, at all levels and all over the country, in the course of the review of the Constitution; and there is much less danger than before that the decent simple peasants will be taken for a ride by a small group of extremists with a lust for personal power. And those who thought I was going dangerously fast now see what I was getting at: they appreciate the checks and balances and safeguards that exist: and they begin to think that the thing will work.

I know more than I did when I wrote on the 8th January about the complexion of the Regional and Central Legislatures and policy-making Councils.[2] The North, though still worried lest they be carried along at a break-neck pace by political Southerners, whose way of life they do not admire, have wisely made concessions to constructive critics of the Emirate system, and they have chosen for me at the Centre their best men among the young men. In the East, although there has been a swing away to the N.C.N.C. band wagon from the few old stalwarts who were returned to the House of Assembly, the majority party gives hopes of being reasonably responsible. At least they have excluded from consideration for Ministerial posts the wildest and least worthy of their number. The Action Group in the West are riding high and will push us hard but they want to make the Constitution a success.

These are the reasons which give us hope that with all the dangers we may make a success of the Constitution. Responsibility is very sobering and we shall be bringing the new Ministers hard up against tough problems. But if we were now to be faced with a clamour for further political advance, as the extremists, who have at present lost much of their power, would wish, then the whole fabric might fall apart.

You may well ask why if I feel reasonably confident about the situation I should get so worried about so small a thing as changing Nkrumah's title from Leader of Government Business to Prime Minister, especially as Arden-Clarke says that this merely recognizes a state of affairs which already exists. (This is on the assumption that Arden-Clarke can resist for a significant period of time the abolition of the Official Ministries, and that the process of removing up to 52 British Administrative Officers from the Gold Coast, to other territories, will remain only a threat).

The answer lies in the following considerations.

The Action Group in the West feel that to justify their willingness to co-operate in making the Constitution a success they must be able to prove to their people that it is not inferior to the Gold Coast Constitution. (Awolowo has said this to me in terms). That is why they were pressing for a Leader of Government Business in the Western House of Assembly, and were making the other demands referred to in

---

[2] See 152.

recent correspondence. If Nkrumah is made Prime Minister (just as our House of Representatives is meeting for the first time) I do not believe that Awolowo could refrain from making a similar demand, at least for the West. Note that the Action Group have just squeezed Azikiwe out of the House of Representatives and that he is planning a fierce counter-attack. If they failed to clamour for concessions similar to those granted to Nkrumah (despite their shorter experience) they would play into the hands of the enemy.

Although I have hopes that the N.C.N.C. in the Eastern Region will not be too irresponsible, they could not let the Action Group in the West show themselves more hot for advance than the N.C.N.C. in the East. I don't see how they could help either joining with the West in their demands, or, more likely, outbidding them.

All this would get us off to a hopeless start. But that is not all. If Nigeria were small and homogeneous one might, conceivably, in spite of the danger to the decent folk, to traditional authority and to the country as a whole, give in to demands for further concessions such as those proposed for the Gold Coast. But we are neither small nor homogeneous. And our North, unlike the Northern Territories of the Gold Coast, is strong and conscious of its strength and of its power (arising not least from the fact that it has more than half the population of the country). The North nearly broke away during the review of the Constitution, but are at present reasonably satisfied. (To show that even now they want reassurance, I enclose a copy of a letter from the Sultan of Sokoto to the Lieutenant-Governor, Northern Region. I am working on this now and will be addressing you on the subject very shortly).[3] If a clamour for further concessions is raised by the South I believe that the North would seriously consider withdrawing from the whole set-up.

You suggest that when the West and East demand innovations similar to those given to the Gold Coast I should tell the Party leaders that I understand the basis of their demands but that they first must give proof 'as the Gold Coast have done' of their capacity for high Ministerial Office. Quite frankly that horse won't run. Any assertion that the Gold Coast have given such proof, if it could be made, would be challenged by the Action Group, who would claim, with some justification, that in spite of their inexperience they have as much ability as, and much more sense of responsibility than, the C.P.P. In any case they, and the East, would not think in terms of any period of probation that would give our Constitution a chance, or keep the North in.

I think you will see why any question of a joint statement by Arden-Clarke and myself is out of the question, much as we should like to help in this way. This letter is not a plea that concessions (already apparently promised) should not be given to the Gold Coast. It is not for me to judge what is right and practicable for the Gold Coast. (I tried to show in my letter of the 8th January that I understood the Gold Coast situation very clearly). You know me well enough to be certain that whatever happens we shall plug on and will not look for an alibi if our work for Nigeria is brought to ruin. I have given you the best assessment I can. And, as I promised Arden-Clarke, I have given it as dispassionately and undramatically as possible. I wish I were giving the assessment after three months of working with my new Ministers, because by that time, if we are not knocked off our stride by extraneous influences, I

---

[3] Not printed.

shall be able to predict with fair confidence what effect extraneous circumstances will have on Nigerian leaders (all new men), with whom we shall then be on terms of mutual confidence. I forgot to ask Arden-Clarke what was the special virtue in announcing the first concession at the end of this month, but I assume it is because the Budget Meeting starts then. The timing couldn't be worse for us because our House of Representatives meets for the first time on 29th January. Given six months I think we *might* 'wear' the effects of concessions in the Gold Coast. Given three months I could give you my assessment with full confidence in its reliability.

154   CO 554/260, no 9G   24 Jan 1952
[Gold Coast and Nigeria]: outward telegram no 1 from Sir T Lloyd to Sir J Macpherson replying to Macpherson's concerns about the impact of developments in the Gold Coast on Nigeria

Personal for Macpherson from Lloyd. *Begins.*

I have shown to Secretary of State your letters of 18th and 19th January in reply to our telegram No. 80.[1] I have also shown him Arden-Clarke's letter of 18th January to me which emphasizes that if the changes he has proposed for the immediate future are not (repeat not) made, the repercussions in the Gold Coast may reasonably be expected to have a more serious effect on the success of the Nigerian experiment than the comparatively modest suggestions he has put forward.

2.   Immediate point is that the Secretary of State is concerned, when putting Arden-Clarke's suggestions to the Cabinet, to give them some indication of probable repercussions in Nigeria and how they might be handled. He has it in mind to say that the Gold Coast changes are likely to evoke early demands for creation of posts of Prime Minister in West and East Regions of Nigeria and that in order to retain initiative he proposes to authorize you, when the Gold Coast changes are announced, to offer to have Nigerian constitution amended so as to provide for posts of Leader of Government Business in West and East, and in North if North want it. Leaders of Government Business would rank in precedence in Regional Executive Councils immediately after Civil Secretaries, but in other respects position of ex officio members would not (repeat not) be affected.

3.   In suggesting this course we have not (repeat not) overlooked your savingram No. 199 dated 31st December, 1951,[2] particularly paragraph 3 (c), but in the light of your subsequent letters to me we think you may agree that it would be wise to anticipate, on lines proposed above, the clamour for further advance which you foresee. By offering this advance we should hope it would be possible to hold position for a further twelve months or so and then to consider, in light of experience gained, whether further step to provide for Prime Ministers would or would not be justified. We also hope it would be possible for you successfully to resist, for a very much longer period, any attempt to undermine the position of the ex officio members.

4.   We appreciate that you had good reasons for taking the line which you did with the Action Group leaders on the 28th December[3] and only justification we can think of for offering early amendment of Nigerian constitution would be that political par-

---

[1] See 153. Letter of 19 Jan not printed.   [2] See 151.   [3] See 151.

ties with majorities in each region had emerged as a result of elections, a state of affairs not (repeat not) expected when constitution was worked out. We would not (repeat not) offer Leader of Government Business post in Council of Ministers on ground that no one party had majority in House of Representatives or in Council.

5.   Secretary of State hopes you will regard this line of approach as feasible and prudent. He welcomes your suggestion that you should fly home on short visit about 3rd February. He fully realises how difficult this will be for you but feels sure that it is very desirable and is most grateful to you for proposing it. From Arden-Clarke's point of view it is important that matter should be put to Cabinet within next two or three weeks at latest so that amendments to Gold Coast constitution can be made at Privy Council meeting expected at end February or early March.[4]

6.   I am repeating this telegram to Arden-Clarke. If you and he have not exchanged copies of your letters to me of 18th January I hope you will do so. *Ends.*

---

[4] See BDEEP series B, vol. 1, R Rathbone, ed, *Ghana*, part I, 115.

155   CO 1039/1   26 Jan 1952
[Council of Ministers]: conclusions of the first meeting of the Council of Ministers   [Extract]

1. *Oaths*
The Oath of Allegiance and the Ministerial Oath were taken by all Members of the Council.

2. *Introductory Remarks by the President*[1]
His Excellency said that the procedure in the Council was to be informal and that he hoped Members would speak from their chairs. His Excellency welcomed the Members of the Council and said that he was looking forward to working together with them. It was his confident hope that their deliberations would be friendly, frank and fruitful. He assured the Ministers of his wholehearted co-operation and that of his officers. Speaking from his heart he said that he felt no clash of loyalty between being British and thinking 'Nigerian'. His aim and that of the expatriate officers was so to help the country to progress, soundly and harmoniously, that when the time came the Nigerian people, of their own volition, would decide to stay within the British Commonwealth and Empire. He was convinced that this was good both for Britain and for Nigeria.

His Excellency said that the most notable characteristic of the country apart from the Africans' quick response to friendship and the fact that we all laugh at the same kind of jokes, was its diversity. He referred not only to the diversity of race, religion, language, vegetation and climate but to the differences in stages of development. We had doctors, lawyers, judges, professional and business men and an Inspector-General of Medical Services. We had traditional authorities. We had a decent simple village folk, artizans and craftsmen. We also had people living a primitive life as it might have been several hundred years ago. But it was all African diversity. We had no white settlement problem and no Indian problem. The destiny of the country was therefore

---

[1] ie Sir J Macpherson

quite clear and certain. There remained this question of the pace of advancement. His Excellency felt that the pace would be decided by responsible Nigerians and British people together. If we have a united country and responsible elements were predominant the pace could be quicker. It would, however, be a betrayal of trust if power got into the hands of irresponsible people who might exploit the silent rural population. Our aim should be construction and not confusion, we must let the country get into the hands of selfish people with a lust for power. The ability was there and experience would come quickly. British officers were all out to help.

His Excellency said that he had studied the Richards Constitution before he knew that he would ever return to Nigeria and from his previous experience in this country, short as it was, he thought how right it was, particularly as it brought in the North on terms acceptable to them. He thought two criticisms of that Constitution had some validity:—

(i) it was formed without open consultation, though this would have been difficult at the time it was introduced, and
(ii) it might shut out educated and progressive people who wished to play their part in the affairs of the country.

On coming to this country he had at first thought that it would be best to spend several years in the development and improvement of local government, before further advance in the superstructure. This had not been possible because of the legitimate aspirations of the people for further advance and because of the pressure of events in other countries. He had therefore decided to put it to the people themselves to talk the whole matter over and the discussions at all levels resulted in the recommendations on which the Constitution is based. Apart from the Constitutional framework itself which was by and large what the people asked for the discussions at all levels had greatly increased the political consciousness of the people. This would help them to resist confusionists.

His Excellency was convinced that Regional autonomy was right. This leads to efficiency and enables the Regions, in a large measure to control their own affairs; but this must be within a strong and united Nigeria and we had to be careful to resist any tendency for the centrifugal force to increase to the point where a Region might contemplate breaking away. Should there be a clash of interests, we must approach it with honest minds and respect for the other man's point of view. We must work for the good of Nigeria. If we succeeded we should be able to give a fine example to this strifeworn world of how to progress without strife or violence. This would be a very great work not only for our own people but as a contribution to the world . . .

156 CO 554/598, no 3   19 Mar 1952
[Political parties]: CO note on the political beliefs of the three principal parties in Nigeria

(1) *Action Group*
The Action Group campaigned during the elections on an appeal to Yoruba solidarity against the threat of Ibo domination (in the form of the N.C.N.C.) and used the slogans:—

'Freedom from British Rule,
Freedom from Ignorance,
Freedom from Disease, and
Freedom from Want.'

Its programme, set out in several policy papers, is generally moderate and contains many sound proposals for improvement.

The Action Group accepts the new constitution as a valuable step towards the control of policy by Nigerians, and thus towards eventual self-government. It regards the European official as a victim of divided loyalties, who serves Nigeria only in so far as his interests co-incide with those of Empire, and who has a lack of incentive to build up at the required speed the prosperity and living standards of Nigeria. Nigerianisation of the Civil Service is thus an aim of prime importance, which, given the will, could be achieved within five years. It is, however, recognised that expatriates will be required, especially in specialist tasks, for some time to come, and efficiency is not to be sacrificed for the sake of principle. Expatriation allowances should be abolished and entry into the Civil Service should be by competitive examination alone, with a road to the top for all who merit it.

The Action Group wishes to reform local government in the West (Awolowo is now the Regional Minister) in order to reduce the influence of the Chief and Elders in favour of elected representatives, and thereby to create a strong and efficient local administration which would be free from corruption.[1] Self-government at this level should be conceded at once, and the people left free to determine the form of local government they wish to adopt, provided that it is democratic and retains as its core the well-established institution of Kingship, though enlightened Kingship.

In other spheres, Action Group advocates in general a programme of expansion. It wants a considerable increase in educational facilities in the West, covering free compulsory education between the ages or 5 and 13, the establishment of secondary and technical schools, an extension of adult and rural education and teacher training. It requires the immediate improvement of communications, and postal and telegraphic services. It believes a well-balanced agriculture to be essential, and accuses the Agricultural Department of victimising the peasant through the Marketing Boards, which, though commendable in principle, do not at present employ the profits satisfactorily and are held to be unrepresentative of large sections of those primarily concerned with production. Health services should be developed, be free for all workers, and more Nigerian doctors should be trained. Private practice by Government Medical Officers should be terminated. A Nigerian Mineral Corporation should be established to take over all private companies, syndicates and operators, and would then control the production of all minerals; it is hoped that this would stimulate production and broaden the base of Nigeria's economy, which is at present too dependent upon agriculture.

(2) *National Council for Nigeria and the Cameroons*
Alone of the three major parties, the N.C.N.C. has not to date published any official party programme or policy papers, so that its aims have to be deduced from the sometimes conflicting and usually opportunist speeches of its leaders.

---

[1] See 159.

The party's watchword has been 'self-government for a United Nigeria by 1956'; it is the most nationalist of the three parties. It takes the view that British rule must go, that only a unified Nigeria would be strong enough to accomplish this, and therefore that the new constitution is a retrograde step in that it does not establish a central unified government. It is strongly opposed to the Action Group.

Dr. Azikiwe, the N.C.N.C. President, has made frequent attacks upon the terms of the new constitution. He said in 1951 that N.C.N.C. would not co-operate in working it nor would its members accept ministerial office. This attitude, however, has been rejected by the N.C.N.C. in the East, where it has had to incorporate more moderate elements in order to secure a majority in the Regional House. A.C. Nwapa, the Deputy Leader of the party, has characterised reports that the N.C.N.C. would boycott the legislature as 'nonsense', and Azikiwe himself has now conceded that the party will co-operate in the working of the constitution, but will encourage its revision at an early date. Azikiwe is in fact behaving as a model leader of the opposition in the Western House of Assembly.

At the Party Conference held at Kano in August 1951, the N.C.N.C. while agreeing not to publish its political programme, re-affirmed its intention to campaign for self-government by 1956 and emphasised the need to resist the infiltration of communism. In addition, speeches reported in the press have declared in general terms that the N.C.N.C. if returned to power, would–

(i) provide for the education of every Nigerian child, and
(ii) provide improved health facilities, including hospitals, clinics, etc.

The lack of any coherent N.C.N.C. policy derives from its previous lack of organisation and the domination of it by Dr. Azikiwe. It now has to work out a policy, and will probably take much the same line as the Action Group in detail, while seeking every means to oppose it on principle.

(3) *Northern People's Congress*
The N.P.C., formerly a body dedicated to cultural ends, represents moderate Northern opinion which viewed the action of the Northern Elements' Progressive Union in aligning itself with the N.C.N.C. as betraying the special interests of the North. It was therefore formed into a political party in order to contest the N.E.P.U. at the elections.

The N.P.C. has declared its aims as being:—

(i) to preserve Regional autonomy within a United Nigeria;
(ii) to undertake local government reform in the North within a progressive Emirate system.
(iii) to ensure that the voice of the people is heard in all the councils of the North i.e. through elected representation.
(iv) to retain the traditional system of the appointment of Emirs, but with a wider representation on the Electoral Committee.
(v) to improve the standards of education throughout the North, while retaining the Regional cultural influence.
(vi) to eliminate bribery and corruption in every sphere of Northern life.
(vii) to achieve eventual self-government for Nigeria with Dominion status within the British Commonwealth.
(viii) to preserve one North, one people, irrespective of religion, tribe or rank.

The N.P.C. will oppose anything which would in its view imperil Islam or damage the interests of the Northern Region, but provided no attempt is made to encroach upon these interests it is likely to support many Southern proposals for reform and progress. The party has declared that, as long as Action Group keeps to its present professed policy the N.P.C. will co-operate; in general, it can be said to stand for a cautious advance towards reform and self-government, and knows that the hard facts of life in the North make it impossible to dispense with British guidance as quickly as might be possible in the East and West.[2]

---

[2] This document was largely prepared by T R Godden (assistant principal, CO) and R J Vile.

157   CO 554/313, no 1   19 June 1952

[Deadlock over ministerial powers]: inward savingram no 2440 from Sir J Macpherson to Mr Lyttelton on the Action Group's criticisms of the constitution. *Annexes*
Minute **by T B Williamson**

[The establishment of regional governments in early 1952 soon revealed the determination of the AG and NCNC both to push their powers under the 1951 constitution to the utmost and to show that the constitution was ultimately unworkable and would need further review. It was in response to the situation outlined in this document that the CO first realised the legal problem with the 1951 constitution, that one regional House of Assembly could not be dissolved without all of them being so, an issue that was to have important consequences for the handling of the Eastern region crisis of 1953. See 171.]

During the past ten days we have been having what almost amounted to a Constitutional crisis with the Western Ministers (including the Central Ministers from the West). The position has been very fluid and this made it difficult to report sooner, though I should, of course, have done so at once if a walk-out had at any time appeared imminent. Chief Secretary, Lieutenant-Governor Western Region and I have spent hours in discussions, day after day.

2.   To give a full picture I think it best to send you the following attachments:–

(a) Memorandum by the Western Ministers submitted on 9th June.
(b) Note of discussion which took place on 10th June with all Western Ministers, including the four Central Ministers from the West. I was assisted by the Lieutenant-Governor Western Region, Chief Secretary and Attorney-General. This note explains how the meeting came about, and deals with the discussion on Constitutional aspects of the Western memorandum. It does not record the discussion regarding relations between Ministers and officials. The Ministers have *some* grounds for complaint because there undoubtedly have been (not only in the Western Region) cases of tactlessness and clumsy treatment of Ministers at Headquarters and when touring but most of the allegations were without substantial foundation and were due to hypersensitivity, suspicion or inflated ego. The crux of the matter was their declared intention not to cooperate with the Civil Secretary. (They are jealous of his position and accused him of arrogating too much power to himself.) This was a direct challenge which had to be dealt with.

(c) Note by Lieutenant-Governor Western Region of a talk he had with Awolowo on 12th June.

(d) Copy of a letter of 18th June from me to Lieutenant-Governor Western Region, recording talks I had with Abayomi and Awolowo (separately) on 14th June.

3.   I am still too close to these events to attempt a confident assessment of the situation, but I do not believe that the Western Ministers have any desire to wreck the Constitution. They have made grandiose promises and are beginning to be worried about their inability to implement them. And they get badly 'needled' by N.C.N.C. attacks and criticisms. They have the substance of power but are desperately anxious to show to the public that this power is exercised by them and they resent it when unimportant Gazette notices etc. are signed by officials. I shall report developments but at this stage I am satisfied that it was the part of wisdom to continue to be patient. There is a chance that relations may greatly improve.

Memorandum presented to His Excellency The Governor by Mr. Obafemi Awolowo, leader of the Action Group at a meeting held by His Excellency The Governor with central and regional ministers of the Western Region on Tuesday 10th June, 1952

In August, 1948, His Excellency the Governor announced his willingness and readiness to have the old Constitution, generally known as the Richard's [sic] Constitution, reviewed. Shortly after this decision and upon the recommendations of a Select Committee of the Legislative Council discussions concerning the nature of changes desired took place all over the country in what were commonly known as constitutional conferences which started from the divisional level and culminated in the Ibadan General Conference. At this Conference the views of the country as a whole were expressed and agreement reached on practically all points except the question of the composition of the Central Legislature and the position of Lagos. These two points were later resolved at the LEGCO meetings one held at Enugu and the other in Lagos.

2.   The Secretary of State, in his despatch to the Governor dated the 15th of July 1950,[1] dealing with the review of the Constitution of Nigeria, at a time when the only outstanding issue not yet resolved was the question of the composition of the Central Legislature, stated as follows:–

> 'Subject to further examination of details when constitutional review is completed in Nigeria His Majesty's Government is willing to accept the recommendation of the General Conference with the variations suggested by the Select Committee of the Legislative Council in its report dated the 1st of April 1950.'

This statement which constituted an assurance given by the Secretary of State was accepted in good faith in Nigeria and the Country believed that it was going to have a constitution as proposed by the Ibadan Conference with the amendments of the Select Committee of the Legislative Council.

---

[1] See 116.

3.   At the 1951 Budget Session of the Legislative Council the Governor announced his hope that the constitutional instrument would be signed by the middle of that year and that the election would start soon thereafter.

4.   It was the assurance given by the Secretary of State that the proposals of the Ibadan Conference were acceptable and the warning about the early elections given by the Governor that inspired the very lively electioneering campaigns that soon followed. As the constitutional instruments have not been published by that time there was no doubt that the campaigns then going on throughout the country and the public interest which they stimulated centered round a constitution which was proposed by the Ibadan Conference.

5.   It is interesting to note that the Nigeria Constitution (Order in Council 1951) was only published early in July, the month when the elections started. The instructions under the Royal signed manual were made and published in November of the same year, and the Nigeria (Revenue Allocation) Order in Council 1951 was made and published in December 1951. In the last two cases the publications were after the elections were concluded in the Western Region.

6.   When, however, these constitutional instruments were published it became clear that there had been a wide departure from the proposals which were made at Ibadan and which, as has been stated by the Secretary of State, was acceptable to the British Government. The reasons for some of the variations were explained in the despatch from the Governor to the Secretary of State which was published along with the Order in Council. There remained, however, a number of other very important amendments to the Ibadan constitutional proposals which were embodied in the New Constitution and to which there was no reference in any of the published despatches. Important among these are the following:—

(1) Power given to the Governor or the Lieutenant-Governor to exercise certain powers, not being power to veto, without obligation to consult the Council of Ministers or the Regional Executive Committee as the case may be.

(2) Restrictions with regard to bills and motions affecting the public service.

(3) Disqualification of persons from being elected as members of the House of Assembly on grounds of previous conviction for sedition and other offences not mentioned in the Ibadan Conference proposals.

7.   These three points warrant the following observations:—

(1) It was the intention of the Ibadan Conference to constitute the Regional Executive Committee the policy making body without any restrictions other than the Lieutenant-Governor's power of veto and his reserved powers. As the Constitution stands now, however, the Lieutenant-Governor need not consult or take the advice of the Executive Committee on a number of very important subjects that affect the general welfare and progress of the people of the Region. This, no doubt, weakens considerably the position of the Ministers and the Regional Executive Committee and makes it very difficult, if not impossible in certain cases, for the party in power to carry out the policy upon which it was elected.

(2) It was surprising and disconcerting to find in the Constitution restrictions with regard to bills and motions affecting the public service. The effect of these restrictions is that it is no more possible or lawful without the consent of the

Governor to debate the conditions of service, the salary or allowances and pensions or gratuities of any public officer. In order to appreciate the changes made it is necessary to note that under the old law there was no such restriction and the Legislative Council had unrestricted rights to deal with any of these matters. This change in the Constitution has occasioned surprise and has been resented because no-one thought that the New Constitution tion has been designed to take away any of the old and established authorities of the Nigerian Legislature.

(3) The disqualification of persons from being elected as members of the House of Assembly on grounds of previous conviction for sedition is, to say the least, unfair and certainly does not derive its authority from any proposals of the Ibadan Conference. When it is considered that nationalists all over the world are in the main generally liable for conviction for sedition it can easily be said that this was designed to exclude the nationalists of this country from participation in the Government of their country.

8. These changes were undoubtedly made without any consultation with the people of this country and they constitute by themselves additional powers being given to officials and the curtailment of the powers which the people had expected to exercise under their own proposals as made at the General Conference and which in fact they had the right to exercise under the Old Constitution. In view of the arguments already advanced it is needless to say that the changes in the Constitution are by themselves unacceptable.

9. Judging from the spirit which accompanied the review of the Constitution both on the part of His Excellency the Governor on one side and the people on the other, it was felt that no useful purpose would be served by challenging the Constitution in the middle of the elections as it was believed that in any case the spirit of the Ibadan constitutional proposals would always be preserved and will prevail. It is now, however, five months since the operative chapters of the Constitution have been put into operation and it is necessary to examine how the Constitution has been functioning and the attitude of the country towards the new set up.

10. From the onset it became clear that the interpretations given to the constitutional provisions by the officials on the one hand and by the majority of the Ministers on the other are completely at variance. The officials appeared to believe that the Constitution has effected no great changes in the general running of Government business and are generally most reluctant to yield ground for the Ministers. The Secretariat was retained as the office serving the Council of Ministers, the only body whose authority officials were willing to recognise. They were of the opinion that Ministers had no individual responsibilities and consequently no executive power. This conviction and attitude of the official are clearly discernible from the attitude towards the Ministers. Administrative procedure were issued and circulated to all Heads of Departments before they were discussed and approved by the Council of Ministers. When, however, the Council of Ministers altered the procedure at one of its very first meetings and thereby challenged the conception of the officials as to the effect of the constitution, it was noteworthy that the changes made by the Council were never circulated, nor communicated, to Heads of Departments and the Ministers had to raise the point four months later when they saw no change in the administrative machinery of the Government.

11. It is under this atmosphere of non-cooperation that Ministers have been called upon to work the Constitution. The Action Group Ministers in the Western Region and a good number of Ministers in the Council of Ministers have resisted, and continue to resist, the non-cooperative attitude and the disloyal conduct of the officials. A considerable portion of the time and energy of Ministers is now being spent to assert their rights under the Constitution and to ensure that workable administrative machinery, in keeping with the new set up and which will ensure efficiency, is provided.

12. So far, neither the changes in the Ibadan proposals which the constitutional instruments revealed, nor the attitude or conduct of the officials have been brought to the attention of the public. This is because it is the intention of the Action Group as a Party to give the Constitution a fair trial and because further we believe that the Governor would be willing to do all that is possible to ensure that the spirit of the Ibadan proposals guided the operation of the Constitution and that he would be ready and willing also to ensure that his officials displayed the proper attitude to the Constitution and are willing to cooperate fully with the Ministers and be loyal to the Government.

13. After five months of trial, however, it became clear that it is the letter and not the spirit of the Constitution that the officials intend to make their guide although, as has been stated, this Constitution varies considerably in very many vital aspects from that which was proposed and was given the blessing of the country at Ibadan. It also became evident that a good number of officials are not willing to be loyal to the new Government as now constituted. There have been instances of disloyalty, conspicuous among which are the following:—

(a) Mr. Robinson, the Resident, Ijebu Province, having been intimated of the desire of the Government to introduce local government reforms, convened a meeting of all the Obas and Chiefs of Ijebu Division and made all efforts to persuade them to reject the proposals which the Government of the Western Region was bringing and even went to the extent of setting up a Committee of Chiefs to resist the local Government reforms.

(b) On the same subject, a Mr. Henry, D.O. at Kukuruku held meetings with the Native Authorities in his Division and tried to convince them that the proposals for reforms initiated by the Minister for Local Government are not to their best interests and that his own proposals (which he had contained in a pamphlet) were to be preferred to that of the Minister (and that petitions were to be forwarded to the Government to that effect).[2]

14. In the Western Region, the Civil Secretary has allocated to himself supervisory powers over the Ministers and Heads of Departments have consequently felt themselves more closely connected with the Civil Secretary than with their Ministers. He has made it difficult for the Regional Heads of Departments to appreciate their responsibilities to their respective Ministers and has gone to the extent of writing confidential reports on the activities of Ministers which he circulated among Residents who, no doubt, are subordinate civil servants to

---

[2] A marginal note against (b) here reads, 'deleted at the request of the author at the Meeting on the 10th. June. (intld.) O.A.'

Ministers. The attitude and conduct of this officer has been a source of constant annoyance and depression for Western Regional Ministers who have now come to the definite conclusion that they can no longer accept him as their colleague in the Western Regional Executive Council.

15.   Having given the fullest consideration to the events of the past five months and the manner in which this Constitution has been working Ministers of the Western Region, both Central and Regional, have found it necessary to set out a number of points which it is believed ought to be clearly settled and accepted by all concerned in the working of this Constitution. They are as follows:—

(a) That a Minister must be regarded as Minister of the Governor or the Lieutenant-Governor as the case may be, and as such he is sworn principal adviser on questions of policy for the Executive as a whole is collectively responsible.

(b) That a Minister is the agent of the Council of Ministers in the Department which comes within his portfolio and for which he is responsible to the Governor and answerable to the Council of Ministers and that as such all communications from the Executive to the Department must be made through him or separate ministerial organisation serving his portfolio.

(c) That Heads of Departments should not be separately and privately consulted by the Governor or Lieutenant-Governor on a point which is included in the portfolio of a Minister.

(d) That power for action in all legislation should not be given to a Head of Department, but to the Minister acting under the direction of the Regional Executive or the Council of Ministers as the case may be.

(e) That Lieutenant-Governors should consult Ministers and take their advice in respect of all powers vested in him excepting the power to veto.

(f) That proper separate Ministerial organisation should be established to serve the portfolio of each Minister.

(g) That confidential reports on Ministers' activities should cease.

16.   Ministers of the Western Region, both Central and Regional, are convinced that the points raised above are in keeping with the spirit of the Constitution and form the basis of the political advance made under it. They hope that His Excellency will find the points and the principles involved acceptable and would certainly share the view that they are not in conflict with the spirit of the Constitution, and that His Excellency would accordingly issue instructions and directions to give effect to them.

17.   The people of this country have been very enthusiastic about the New Constitution, which they believe is the embodiment of the proposals promulgated at Ibadan. They are proud of their Ministers and genuinely want to give the Constitution a fair trial. It is their belief that everyone of the points set out are within the accepted principles underlying the constitutional changes. However, rumours which have been in circulation relating to the defects and imperfectness of the Constitution are making people restless and uneasy in mind. If, therefore, it is eventually discovered that any of the points are unacceptable to His Excellency the responsibilities of the Ministers are clear. They have the duty to inform the country of the true constitutional position and of the conditions under which they serve.

18.   There are three other main points to which the attention of His Excellency the Governor is hereby directed:—

(1) The first of these points deals with the question of Regional autonomy. During the discussions at the Ibadan General Conference it was generally agreed that each Region would have complete autonomy in respect of a number of subjects and that the authority of the Region in respect of these matters would only be questioned where the overall interests of Nigeria is involved. The Secretary of State dealing with that point in his despatch of the 15th day of July 1950 to His Excellency the Governor stated as follows:—

> 'I note the recommendation that the Nigerian Legislature at the centre should continue to have full power to make laws for the peace, order and good government of Nigeria, without any restriction. It follows that there will be a substantial overlap between the legislative functions of the Central and Regional Legislatures. I believe that at the present stage, while the Regional Legislatures are still gaining experience, this arrangement will be found the most appropriate; but at some stage in the future, as Nigeria develops further towards a federal state, it may well be necessary, as it has been in other countries, to establish separate and distinct fields of legislation for the centre and the Regions, with a reduction in the range of subjects over which they have concurrent powers.' The Western Region believe that the time has now come when separate and distinct fields of legislation at the centre and the Regions should be established with a reduction in the range of subjects over which they have concurrent powers.

(2) There is no doubt that in the Western Region a party system of government has been established and has come to stay. Consequently it becomes necessary that in this Region a new arrangement be made whereby recognition will be given to this system of government. It is abundantly clear from the despatches of the Secretary of State dealing with the Nigerian Constitution that it was expected that changes would become necessary when this stage has been reached. The Western Region therefore asks for a change in the Constitution which will give effect to the party system of government.

(3) A Minister under the present set up has dual responsibilities. In the first place he has to take charge of his portfolio and concern himself with initiating policy and ensuring that the policy laid down by the Council of Ministers is given effect in the departments. In the second place he has to take active part in the formulation of policy with regard to every single aspect of Government activities in the country. Besides this he accepts invitations for various public engagements and interviews and has to undertake a tour of the country from time to time. In doing this and fulfilling his other functions the Minister is naturally over-taxed. This makes it absolutely necessary for the introduction of the office of Parliamentary Under-Secretary attached to each portfolio. The Regional and Central Ministers of the Western Region consider that the creation of this office is of supreme importance and is absolutely necessary to ensure efficient running of the Government machinery relating to the portfolio of each Minister.

Note regarding representations made to His Excellency the Governor by the western regional ministers, and central ministers from the Western Region on certain constitutional issues

On the 6th June Chief Bode Thomas approached His Excellency and stated that the Western Ministers, including the Central Ministers from the Western Region, wished to see him very urgently because 'things were not going well'. He asked that the interview should take place on the following day. After consultation with the Lieutenant-Governor, Western Region, it was agreed that the Ministers should first submit a written note on the matters to be raised at a meeting and that an interview, at which His Honour would, of course, be present, should be sought for a suitable day in the following week.

On the 8th June, Chief Bode Thomas informed His Excellency that all the Western Ministers were in Lagos—having cancelled their several tours (no doubt at great inconvenience not only to themselves but to the people in the places they had arranged to visit) and were very anxious to have the interview at the earliest possible moment. By agreement with His Honour it was decided to fix the interview for the 10th June, and an undertaking was given that the promised paper would be presented not later than the 9th June.

After noon on the 9th June His Excellency received a memorandum of which a copy is attached. His Excellency had understood that the interview was sought to raise matters that were peculiarly 'Western', but perusal of the memorandum showed that it challenged various aspects of the Constitution itself—affecting all Regions and the Centre. His Excellency decided not to cancel the interview, since the Ministers had all assembled in Lagos, but when the meeting took place on the 10th June he at once made it clear to the Ministers that he could not possibly give immediate answers to the requests in the memorandum. Apart from the fact that the memorandum had been received less than twenty-four hours before, it would not have been proper for him to give answers, certainly not to Ministers from a single Region. The other Regions were involved: the Centre was involved: and in certain circumstances, Her Majesty in Council would be involved. This was readily accepted by the Western Ministers, and the discussion on the 10th June was limited to amplification by them of the contents of the memorandum, to explanation of certain points by His Excellency, and to a general exchange of views. In particular, the Governor dealt with allegations, which he challenged, that the Constitutional Instruments involved 'a wide departure' from the conclusions of the General Constitutional Conference, other than the variations explained in the exchange of despatches between himself and the Secretary of State which were published with the Constitution Order in Council.

The following notes deal with the more important matters discussed, affecting the constitution.

I. *The Royal Instructions to the Governor, Clause 4(2)(a)(iii)*
The Royal Instructions to the Lieutenant-Governors, Clause 2(2)(a)(iv)
(Exception from obligation on the Governor and the Lieutenant-Governors to consult Council of Ministers and Executive Councils respectively in the exercise, otherwise than in the formulation of policy, of power conferred upon them by any existing law (i.e. any enactment in force in Nigeria on 24th January, 1952) other than a power expressed to be exercisable by the Governor in Council or the Lieutenant-Governor in Council, respectively.)

His Excellency explained that this exception stemmed from the fact that under the new Constitution Order in Council 'the Governor' meant the Governor in Council. 'Existing legislation' (all Central of course) gave power sometimes to the Governor and sometimes to the Governor in Council. The distinction was deliberate and was fully understood by the legislators who passed those laws. The inclusion of this exception in the Royal Instructions was done:—

(a) to save the Council of Ministers from being cluttered up with routine matters, not unimportant, but largely administrative; and

(b) because some of the powers conferred upon the Governor by existing legislation would, if we were legislating afresh, be made exercisable by the Governor acting in his discretion.

In the few cases that have arisen at the Centre, His Excellency's practice had been to discuss the matter in the Council of Ministers so that the decision, which legally was his alone, was taken with the knowledge of and in the light of the views of Ministers. And, of course, where policy was involved (and it was possible to have statutory powers which involved the formulation of policy) the Governor was bound to consult the Council of Ministers and to follow their advice, subject always to his reserve powers.

So far as the Lieutenant-Governors are concerned, there was of course no 'existing legislation'* which conferred power upon the Lieutenant-Governor (or Chief Commissioner) in Council, but the same considerations applied, i.e. that some of the powers conferred upon the Lieutenant-Governor by existing legislation would, if we were legislating afresh, be expressed as being exercisable by the Lieutenant-Governor in his discretion. The Governor said that he would like to have time to examine the general issue more closely in the light of the representations in the memorandum, and proposed to invite the Law Officers to make an examination of the existing legislation with a view to general clarification.

During the discussion, it emerged that the significance of these provisions in the Royal Instructions was realised by the Western Ministers only recently, when His Honour consulted them regarding certain appointments to be made to the Western Regional Production Development Board, at the same time pointing out to them that, by reason of the relevant clause of the Royal Instructions, he was not bound to accept their advice. This particular matter was complicated by the circumstance that Mr. Awolowo, at the March meeting of the House of Representatives, had withdrawn two motions recommending changes in the relevant legislation about Production Development Boards so as to restore the position which existed prior to the amending legislation of August, 1951; and that he had taken this action because he understood that in practice the Lieutenant-Governors would consult their Executive Councils and would accept their advice. After further discussion regarding the practice followed by the Governor in these matters His Honour undertook, in this particular matter of the Regional Production Development Board, to consult Executive Council. The Western Ministers said they would be open to persuasion in the course of this consultation, and on that basis His Honour agreed to accept their advice.

II. The second matter raised under the head of variations from the Ibadan Conference was the restriction with regard to bills or motions affecting the public

---

* It has since been pointed out that by the Adaptation of Laws Ordinance, 1951, a number of powers in existing Ordinance which had been vested in the Governor in Council have been transferred to Lieutenant-Governors in Council.

service. The Governor stated that the relevant provision in the Constitution Order in Council (Section 85) was a mark of political advance. Such provisions were normal when political advance, such as had recently been accorded to Nigeria, took place. The purpose was, of course, to keep the service out of politics. Moreover, the Secretary of State had an obligation towards those officers that he selects for the Colonial Service, and the Governor had a very clear obligation to the whole Service—both expatriate and African—not to deliver them over to politicians, however good. His Excellency stated that he could hold out no hope whatever of any change being made in this provision.

III.   The third point under 'variations' related to the provision for disqualification for election as a member of a House of Assembly (Section 42 of the Constitution Order in Council and the second Schedule thereto) on grounds of conviction for sedition within the five years immediately preceding the date of election. The Governor recalled that the General Conference at Ibadan agreed that the existing disqualifications should be accepted, and also agreed to a proposal, made by Mr. Onyeama and seconded by Chief Bode Thomas, that, in addition, a person convicted of any crime involving fraud, dishonesty, bribery and corruption, or of treason, and sentenced to imprisonment for a term exceeding six months, should be disqualified for the first five years of the new Constitution. When the constitutional lawyers came to the drafting of the necessary provision they found that the only convenient and appropriate solution was to specify chapters of the Criminal Code Ordinance, and one other Ordinance. (cp. second schedule to the Constitution Order in Council.) They included in the second schedule Chapters, VI, VIA and VII which relate to treason, treachery, sedition and like offences. His Excellency said that he personally saw no objection, but virtue, in this provision. He pointed out that sedition included the promotion of ill-will and hostility between different classes of the population of Nigeria and attempts to overthrow the Government. The representations of the Western Ministers would be referred to other Regions for their views, and would be considered by the Council of Ministers.

IV. In the course of the meeting the Western Ministers said that they had come to the conclusion that the appointment of Parliamentary Under-Secretaries was necessary for the proper conduct of business. The Governor observed that, whether or not this would involve an amendment to the Constitutional Instruments, reference to the other Regions was necessary.

V. A further request made during the discussion was that the Financial Secretary should be removed from the Executive Council and his place taken by a Nigerian Minister of Finance, although the Financial Secretary would continue to work as the Head of a Department. The reason advanced for this change was that only a Nigerian Minister, who was subject to removal from office by the electorate, would be sufficiently imaginative and daring in the search for new revenue to implement his Party's programme. His Excellency stated that although the suggestion would be referred to the other Regions, he personally would resist it with all the force at his command. He pointed out that at every stage of the constitutional review it had been agreed that the Chief or Civil Secretary, the Attorney General or Legal Secretary, and the Financial Secretary would, as ex-officio members, be an integral part of the structure. Any challenge to this was a challenge to the whole fabric of the Constitution.

VI.   With regard to the view expressed in the memorandum that the time had now come when there should be a clear definition between the legislative powers of the House of Representatives on the one hand and the Regional Houses on the other, His Excellency stated that in his view there had been totally inadequate experience to justify any change at this stage.

VII.   With regard to the request for change in the constitution to 'give effect to the party system of Government', His Excellency requested the Western Ministers to put forward in writing a more precise explanation. He guessed that they were thinking in terms of a Prime Minister or a Leader of Government Business and it was indicated that the guess was correct. The Western Ministers agreed to prepare a paper for reference to the other Regions, and to the Council of Ministers.

VIII.   Certain matters raised in the memorandum, and orally at the meeting, referred to administrative and procedural matters not involving a challenge to the Constitutional Instruments. The Governor pointed out that these matters were already receiving the consideration of the Council of Ministers and a record of the discussion that took place is irrelevant to the present note. This also applies to discussion regarding co-operation and courteous exchanges between Ministers and officials.

His Excellency undertook to transmit copies of the memorandum of the Western Ministers, with a brief record of the discussion relating to Constitutional matters, to the other Regions prior to consideration by the Council of Ministers.

Note by H F Marshall of a discussion with Mr. Awolowo on the 12th of June, 1952

I started off by remarking that until last week I had believed that Mr. Awolowo and myself were following the same road and that it was going to be possible for us to go along together, but the events of the last few days had put serious doubts in my mind as to the possibility of continued co-operation. Attacks on myself did not worry me in the least, my conscience was entirely clear and in any event I was not particularly enamoured of high office. I had accepted my present appointment with considerable doubt and it was my firm intention when the time came to leave it, to retire. In the meanwhile I should continue to do what I conceived to be my duty.

2.   Attacks on my Officers were an entirely different matter, particularly when they were made behind my back. (Mr. Awolowo expressed astonishment). I would recapitulate the events of the last few days. Last Friday we had a somewhat stormy meeting of Executive Council, at which I thought that Mr. Awolowo had lost his temper (Mr. Awolowo agreed). At that meeting I heard for the first time accusations made against certain un-named Administrative Officers. The next I heard was that Western Ministers, both Central and Regional, had asked for an interview with H.E. After consulting me H.E. had agreed to grant an interview on the understanding that the matters for discussion should be first put down in writing and submitted to himself and to myself. On this understanding a meeting had been convened for Tuesday. In practice I never got the memorandum and only saw H.E's copy an hour

before the meeting. At the meeting accusations were made against a number of Officers in the Western Region. This was the first I had ever heard of such accusations. I asked Mr. Awolowo what he and his fellow Ministers thought I was here for. If they had complaints or worse, surely the person to come to was myself before going to the Governor. If I could not, or would not resolve the complaints there might be a case for an approach to the Governor, but there was certainly no case for an approach behind my back. I asked Mr. Awolowo to explain.

3.   Mr. Awolowo said that when he returned from the Benin Province it had been his intention to bring to my notice his complaints about Mr. Henry, about the use of Detectives, and other matters, but after consulting his colleagues he had decided to collect further facts which it was intended should be presented to me in the form of a petition. There had been delay in preparing the petition and before it was finally prepared the Action Group had come to the conclusion that I was leading an opposition and that an approach to me would have been useless. He stated that the memorandum presented to H.E. had only reached him at 11.30 p.m. on Monday night and that he had been unable to contact me then as he was leaving immediately for Lagos.

4.   I replied that when I took up office I had stressed the importance of removing suspicion. I thought that it was entirely wrong for the Action Group, if they had complaint, to wait to collect further facts. I admitted that it was one thing to speak about removing suspicion, and that I fully realised that it was much more difficult to remove suspicion from one's mind. The safest way was to remove the cause for suspicion and I pointed out that the best way to do this was to make an immediate approach so that the complaints, if justified, could be put right and similar complaints in the future could be stopped. Mr. Awolowo expressed full agreement with my view and regret for what had happened.

5.   I told Mr. Awolowo that I had been in on the new Constitution since its birth and had always been a strong advocate of revision. It was inconceivable that it should now be my intention to break the machine which I had had a small part in making. Before I took up my appointment I had come to the conclusion that two major tasks lay ahead of me. One was to get on a beam with the Action Group Ministers, and the other was to ensure that the Service, not only worked the Constitution, but put their heart into working it. I realised that the second of these tasks might be the more difficult. I admitted that there were a number of Officers in the Western Region who did not yet know, or appreciate, what had happened, and who had no enthusiasm for recent changes. It was my job as I saw it to inspire such enthusiasm, but it was not going to be easy, and under certain circumstances it might become impossible.

6.   I said that I was particularly distressed at the attack which had been made on Mr. Shankland[3] and at the attitude which the Western Ministers said that they proposed to adopt. Putting personalities aside, by adopting an attitude of non-co-operation, the Action Group were raising a constitutional issue which, to my mind, was of far greater consequence than any of the other issues which they had raised. It was implicit in the Constitution that there should be Officials in the Central and Regional Councils, and that these Officials should be appointed by the Governor. If Ministers, by refusing to co-operate, thought that they were going to be able to

---

[3] TM Shankland, civil secretary Western Region, 1951; deputy governor, Western Region, 1954.

dictate to Government the persons who should be the Official Members of the Regional Executive Council, they were raising a constitutional issue on which it would be quite impossible for Government to give way.

7. I then turned to the specific complaints which have been made against Mr. Shankland and stated that I did not consider that they were worth a row of beans. I realised that there had been difficulty and possibly muddle over the question of Ministers' houses and Ministers' offices, but I had thought that all that was past history. The other three complaints referred to cases in which Mr. Shankland was alleged to have consulted Mr. Awolowo about persons to be appointed to various Boards and Committees and had then taken no action. The three cases in question were the Committee to allocate American Cars, the Public Service Board, and the Nomination of a Candidate to go to the United Kingdom. The last of these had been disposed of at the meeting in Lagos. With regard to the Public Service Board, I took full responsibility, the file had been lying on my side table for some weeks awaiting an opportunity to discuss with Mr. Awolowo, but whenever we had been in the Station together there had been more important matters for discussion and I had never raised this particular one, which I regarded as unimportant. I said that if embarrassment had been caused to Mr. Awolowo or others because action had not been taken, Mr. Awolowo was at least partly to blame. I should have thought that it was clear that such consultations were confidential and that the potential candidates should not be told that their appointment was being considered until the appointments had been approved by the approving authority, whether the approving authority was the Executive Council, the Governor or the Lieutenant-Governor. I regarded Mr. Shankland as a very able, capable officer and I was quite sure that the Governor would not remove him at the request of any political party. I certainly would resist any such move. If the Ministers refused to co-operate and the machine broke down, the blame would be entirely at the door of the Ministers.

8. Mr. Awolowo, in reply, said that the Ministers had always felt that Mr. Shankland was unsympathetic and cited the instance of the houses and offices for Ministers. He said that the Ministers fully conceded the right of the Civil Secretary to speak on any subject in Executive Council and that they would give him a fair hearing. He agreed that with matters of routine it might be necessary for Ministers to consult Mr. Shankland, but he thought that on important matters of policy it would be better for Ministers to approach the Lieutenant-Governor direct. I said that I understood that Mr. Awolowo was having an interview with H.E. on this subject on Saturday and that I was not prepared to take the matter further at this stage, but I hoped that Mr. Awolowo fully realised my views.

This part of the discussion then closed and both Mr. Awolowo and myself agreed that the air had been to some extent cleared.

Letter from Sir J Macpherson to H F Marshall, 18 June 1952

This is to confirm, and amplify, the brief report I gave you by telephone on the afternoon of the 14th June regarding the interview which Goble and I had with Awolowo that morning.

I was glad to have before the interview your letter of the 12th June, with the record of your conversation with Awolowo earlier that day. I fully endorse all that you said to him, and I was glad to hear that the air had been cleared to some extent. It was on that basis that you and I agreed that it was unnecessary for you to travel to Lagos again, to be present at my talk with him.

As I told you I had had a private talk with Abayomi on 11th June, the day following our meeting with the Western Ministers. He was very glad to help, and later had a long talk with Akintola. He had a session with Awolowo early on 14th June and came round to tell me about it—just before I saw Awolowo.

He told me that in excusing his 'interference' he had reminded Awolowo of two Youruba sayings. One was that if an elder saw a woman in a market with her baby on her back, and noticed that the baby's head was falling back, the elder could not refrain from drawing the woman's attention to this and putting the matter right. The second saying was that if you gave a good cloth to a mad person, you should not be surprised to find it in tatters! He told Awolowo that the Constitution must not fail by reason of any actions of the Western Region and said that while I would do everything possible to ensure harmony Awolowo should not think that I would hesitate to use my reserve powers. He also referred to the relations of confidence which existed between him and me and explained that I had consulted him.

Awolowo had told Abayomi about his talk with you and had said that he agreed with you *in toto*. He had then gone over much of the old ground about non-co-operation, advice being spurned and being treated as schoolboys, etc. Abayomi then told him that he had committed a serious *faux pas*. Why had he not taken his complaint to you? Surely the right thing to do was to hear the other side before rushing to the newspapers. Awolowo had admitted his fault and in the course of conversation conceded that 80% of the expatriate officers were doing their best to make the Constitution work.

With diffidence and respect Abayomi put forward the suggestion that there should be a frank talk between you and Tom Shankland and Awolowo.

Abayomi then left and Awolowo came in (there was no secrecy about Abayomi's involvement in the business). I considered it very desirable that Goble should be present, I told Awolowo that my purpose in asking him to come and see me was not to discuss the constitutional issues raised at my meeting with the Western Ministers. On those [sic: these] action would proceed to consult the Regions and the Centre (and London if necessary); decisions would be taken and the Western Ministers could then determine what their line of action was to be. What I wanted to discuss was their attitude to Shankland, which was immediate and vital, and their relations with expatriate officers in general. At the end of our long meeting on Tuesday they stated that while it was not within their power or competence to interfere in the posting of officers, and while they would treat Shankland with courtesy as an individual, they would refuse to have official dealings with him. Beyond remarking that this opened up a broad vista of co-operation and teamwork in the Western Region, I restrained myself at that late hour and in so big a meeting from saying what was in my mind. But, of course, a quite intolerable situation would arise if they attempted to carry out this intention. (Earlier in the meeting I had, of course, stated that I would not be dictated to in the matter of posting officers).

I told Awolowo flatly that I would not move Shankland from his present post. Quite apart from the injustice to Shankland if I did, any value that I might have to Nigeria would be finished. The trust of the Service would be shattered; wholesale resignations would follow; and there would be a complete breakdown in the running of the country. It was equally impossible that there should be no official contacts between Ministers and the Civil Secretary. This would be a challenge to the Constitution and would mean a complete showdown.

At this stage I broadened the discussion to deal with relations between the Action Group and expatriate officers as a whole, notably the Administration, and I started by recounting my interest in, and assessment of, Awolowo during the past years. I had read his book [Path to Nigerian Freedom] before coming to Nigeria, but it was a long time before I met him. I had easy contacts with members of the late Legislative Council and Executive Council, but it had been much more difficult to have contacts, other than social contacts, with unofficial Nigerians with no Legislative or official status. I recalled that when the Legislative Council had its Budget meeting at Ibadan in March, 1949, my wife and I gave the usual series of parties, when staying at Government Lodge. For receptions the lists of guests were prepared in Ibadan for my approval. On scrutinising them I noticed that Awolowo's name was not amongst them, and on enquiring the reason for this, was told by Hoskyns-Abrahall that Awolowo never accepted invitations to Government Lodge. During my period of residence there, Government Lodge was, in effect, Government House, but after reflection I had decided not to create difficulties between myself and the Chief Commissioner by adding Awolowo's name. I hoped that there would be other opportunities for us to meet.

Later I had spoken to Abayomi, who had given Awolowo a good chit, saying that he was open to reason. Abayomi offered to invite Awolowo to come and see me, but I had thought it best to let a meeting happen naturally. At one time (two or three years ago) I had been disturbed at the apparent failure of officials in the West to get on a beam with Awolowo. I spoke to Pyke-Nott about the matter and he told me a story of how he had invited Awolowo to dinner, soon after his return from the United Kingdom, and had received a stiff little note saying that when he was in the United Kingdom it was war-time and people were too busy with the war to dress up. As a result he had no dinner jacket. Pyke-Nott had replied that he had invited Awolowo to dinner, not his dinner jacket, and in the end he had accepted the invitation and an enjoyable evening followed. The fact remained that very few officers had been able to get on friendly terms with him. Then I read a signed article by Awolowo—sometime in 1949. So far as I could recollect, the article said that when his book was published it got a good press in the United Kingdom. He was not surprised at that because the United Kingdom press was a responsible body. When he returned to Nigeria, however, and Europeans began inviting him to dinner and cocktail parties he 'saw the trap': He had refused all the invitations except four. I assumed that Awolowo thought that their motive was to quote some of the nice things he said about Britain in his book and then to use him as a stalking horse. (Mr. Awolowo murmured confirmation of this). This proved to me that any criticisms I might have had of my officers were unfounded. It was obvious that Awolowo was hyper-sensitive and had a complex about Europeans, particularly Administrative officers. I had wondered whether something had happened to hurt him and to lead him to have this grudge. (I have known it happen before in other non-European people). I did not despair, however, as I thought that with political advance opportunities would occur for Awolowo to take his part in Nigerian affairs and that he would then recognise our good faith.

When the Constitution started several of the officers in the West had spoken with admiration of Awolowo's hard work and genuine desire to help the people; but they also referred to his quick temper and prickliness. I myself was conscious that my contacts with him had been all too few apart from a few official meetings when I received delegations of which he was a member. On several occasions he had found it impossible to accept invitations to Government House. I deplored this but had not 'pulled my rank' on him, but had arranged that in future no invitation would be sent to him unless he had indicated his intention of accepting it. During the meeting of the House of Representatives in March I had suggested that he and I ought to have a talk from time to time and he had agreed. I was sorry that this had not yet been managed. Both of us were hard pressed and he lived more than a 100 miles from Lagos.

I then came to the major issue of the Action Group's attitude towards expatriates and towards making the Constitution work. I did not claim that the faults were all on one side. There were some officers, especially in the Provinces and Districts, who did not yet fully understand the true purpose of the constitutional advance and who were not enthusiastic about the recent changes. These officers had given long years of faithful work to the people of the country, with whom their relations had been completely friendly. Then had come the strain of a challenge to existing conditions, not always made with courtesy or fairness.

Awolowo must realise that these officers, and I was talking particularly about Administrative officers, were sincerely devoted to the people amongst whom they worked and genuinely feared that they would be exploited by politicians. If Awolowo reflected on the kind of politics we had had in Nigeria in the past few years he would realise that their fears were not unjustified. I spoke, too, about the vilification and the abuse which such officers had suffered from the press and otherwise. How could he expect them not to be affected by this. They knew they were doing a good job for the people. The villagers did not know much about the British connection or about the Constitution. They did know that they had nearby a District Officer or an Assistant District Officer, who would see fair play, and stop rackets, and the Administrative officers were working hard and unselfishly to develop local government and to improve the conditions of the people. They were no longer autocratic, their help was coming from behind.

I went on to say that Awolowo must face the fact that under the New Constitution officials (with politicians and natural rulers) are part of the very fabric of the Constitution and you couldn't make people co-operate by abusing them. You could, however, enlist their help by a genuine approach. His Honour had already started the process to bring full understanding of the position to all his officers.

My fear was that the politicians in Nigeria, notably the Ministers, would give public expression to their belief that expatriate officers would be necessary for a long time to come if there were not to be a complete breakdown of Government, a year too late. By that time many of the best of the expatriate officers would have resigned and those that remained would have lost their faith and sense of mission.

I then spoke about the Council of Ministers. In spite of the inherent difficulties due to the fact that they represented different Regions, they had stayed together as a team. Why was that? In part it was because all of us recognised the heavy responsibility upon the Council for maintaining the unity of Nigeria. But in part also it was because I, as President, had not been content merely to be impartial and helpful and friendly. I had gone far beyond what anyone could reasonably expect in being patient, particularly with the Western Ministers. I recognised their abilities and good qualities; I liked than personally; and I believed that we were good friends. It was their duty to put forward forcibly the Western point of view, and they did so. No-one queried that (though I often wished that Awolowo himself was in the Council of Ministers so that he could hear the weight of opinion round the table). But I was bound to say that it seemed to me that the main energies of the Western Region had been directed, not towards the solution of the problem before us in the best interest of Nigeria, but in a constant challenge to the position of ex-officio members, and to efforts to change the mechanics of the Constitution so as to build up their own prestige. I said that after a meeting of the Council of Ministers I was always completely exhausted by the effort of keeping the proceedings friendly and of giving full rein to all views, even if they were not directed towards getting the best solution of the problem before us. And there had been instances, by at least one Central Minister from the West, of boorishness and bad temper and grave discourtesy towards me.

These difficult relations between Ministers and officials did not happen in the other Regions. There the Ministers and officials were working together in harmony. Why was it that there was this clash in the West? It could not be said that the expatriates in the West are different from those in other parts of the country. His Honour would do all that he could to ensure a full understanding of the purpose of the Constitution amongst the officials there, but it took two sides to achieve co-operation. The task before us was tremendous and we could not achieve success in an atmosphere of suspicion and mistrust. What was the future to be—war or peace between the officials and the Action Group.

Mr. Awolowo said that he was grateful to me for arranging this interview and appreciated what I had said. On a personal note, he confirmed in large measure my assessment regarding his attitude to expatriate officers. Before he went to the United Kingdom he had on many occasions tried to make constructive suggestions to Administrative officers but he had always been slapped down. They would listen only to the people who said the things they wanted to hear, and had no patience with educated progressive-minded Africans. He had come to the conclusion that all British officers were bad.

He then went to the United Kingdom to take a law degree, so that he could be independent and speak his mind. It had not been so in business, though perhaps the failure in that field was due to his own faults. In England he had had very friendly relations with British people, and had made good contacts. He had then decided that the British people were really good and were sincere in their intentions towards their colonies, even if they were often rather ignorant about them.

He came back to Nigeria at the end of 1946 but found that there was no change in the general attitude of expatriate officers. Nevertheless, from the date of his return right up until 1948 he had not given expression to any critical views, because he had a carry-over of feelings of friendship from his stay in the United Kingdom. As time went on, however, he was made to feel that the Yorubas were not liked, although they were loyal and law-abiding. The Government constantly gave in to noisy clamour of agitators. What purpose was there in being good?

Awolowo then gave me the full assurance that they wanted to make the Constitution work effectively. They had no other design at all. (I interjected a remark that I had no such suspicion; my quarrel was with their attitude towards expatriates). As regards expatriates, Awolowo stated that he fully realises that for many years to come the country would need them. Even more would be required. Even if independence came they would still need expatriates, and he referred to the position in India in that respect now. He did ask, however, that the expatriates should be chosen very carefully. They must be so good that there would be no grounds for criticism.

I referred to the fact that there was full employment in the United Kingdom, and said that there were no long queues of people wanting to come to Nigeria. Nevertheless, the great majority of expatriates recruited genuinely had their heart in their work. As regards criticism, it was not enough merely to stop mass attacks in the press on expatriates as a class. When individuals were pilloried in the press, all were hurt, not least the best ones.

As regards the Council of Ministers, Awolowo explained that he had decided to stay in the West because the Action Group had made too many promises and unless a sufficient number of these were implemented they would not survive the next election! As regards the Western Ministers at the Centre, he asked whether I could not take them more into my confidence. I explained that I had to be very careful not to appear to be playing one group off against another. Moreover, the Western Ministers were so sensitive that I had been apprehensive about the effect of straight talking to them. Awolowo had suggested that I might from time to time have private conversations with a group of three, one from each Region. I agreed. I also said that now that I had had a frank talk with him I should find it easier to do some straight talking with the Central Ministers from the West.

So far as the relations between the Western Ministers and the ex-officio members in the Western Executive Council were concerned, I was passing the whole business back to Ibadan. I said that I would suggest to His Honour that he and Shankland and Awolowo might have a frank talk, following the talk which His Honour had had with Awolowo—which had cleared the air. I would watch the press carefully to see whether attacks on expatriates ceased. And I would hope to hear good reports from the West of a new spirit of co-operation and trust between the Ministers and the officials.

Awolowo thanked me and said that he would look into the matter of the press. To prove that he had no wholesale grudge against expatriates he instanced the very cordial relations which existed between himself and his 'Head of Department'— Ronnie Brown—and between their wives, and he gave me to understand that he and his people would make a genuine effort to establish good relations all round.

I am afraid this is a long rambling letter but I thought it best to give you a fairly full account. I think that it has been worth while being patient and understanding. Over to you and the best of luck.

Minute on 157

Mr. Godden has done a good précis of the main points in (1); but really all the correspondence needs to be read, especially Sir J. Macpherson's letter of the 18th June to Mr. Marshall. I have sidelined some of the more remarkable parts of this.

Both the Governor's and Lieutenant Governor's handling of the Western Ministers and particularly of Awolowo, can only evoke our admiration. (Incidentally we can feel much more confident about the high level administration in Nigeria now that the three new Lieutenant Governors are all in post.)

I had a long talk with Mr. Benson about all these matters last week. He expressed a hunch that, unless the Action Group mended their ways very considerably in the immediate future, they would over-reach themselves and become so unpopular in Nigeria and particularly with their 'fringe' supporters that they might lose their majority in the Western Region and have to go out of office. In that event it might only be possible to form a new Government in the West after further elections. But he (Mr. Benson) had only recently discovered that there was no provision in the Constitution Order for elections in any one region independently of the other two. He said that he and the Governor, and the other senior officials, were absolutely clear that generally speaking not a comma should be changed in the present Constitution Order because once any changes were made there would be immediate pressure for more and more changes. But the problem of elections in an individual region was awkward. I said I would look into the point about elections under the constitution as soon as possible (I have now sent a minute to Mr. McPetrie); but that while we were sure Nigeria was right in being determined to resist at this early stage any changes in the Order, I was not sure whether amendments might not be justifiable, and indeed necessary, if they were required simply to prevent a breakdown in the working of the constitution itself. Mr. Benson was inclined to agree with me on this.

If it were decided that constitutional amendments were necessary to permit of the holding of elections in one region, it might be necessary to act at fairly short notice. It is for this reason that I have already broached the question with Mr. McPetrie, and I will report the outcome.

I think the reply to (1) should be in warm and congratulatory terms, and I have amended the draft accordingly.

T.B.W.
4.7.52

158 CO 554/313, no 3   11 July 1952
[Deadlock over ministerial powers]: inward savingram no 2725 from Sir J Macpherson to Mr Lyttelton on the outcome of debates at the Council of Ministers on the Action Group's criticisms of the constitution. *Minute* by TB Williamson

My Secret Saving No. 2440 of 19th June.
Representations by Western Ministers on Constitutional Issues.

The memorandum of the 9th of June[1] by the Western Ministers was discussed at a meeting of the Council of Ministers on the 4th of July, after the subject had been considered by the Executive Councils of the Northern and Eastern Regions. Eastern Regional Ministers regarded the issues involved as being of such importance as to warrant consultation with the Central Ministers from the East, and Messrs Njoku and Arikpo flew to Enugu for discussions prior to the meeting of the Eastern Regional Executive Council. Central Ministers from the North were also carefully briefed with the views of the Northern Regional Executive Council before the meeting on the 4th

---

[1] See 157.

of July. Copies of memoranda by the Northern and Eastern Executive Councils dealing with the Western Ministers' representations are attached.[2]

2. At the meeting on the 4th July I decided, on tactical grounds, to discuss Ministerial Organization as a separate item before dealing with the Western Ministers' Memorandum. This subject was touched on in that Memorandum but the Council of Ministers had been considering the problem independently for some time, and the Western views on this issue were shared to some extent by Ministers from other Regions. The situation, as you know, was that Ministers generally were not happy about their ministerial organisations or 'Ministries', in so far as there was lack of definition regarding the precise relationship between Ministers and Heads of Departments, and also the means of discharging their responsibility under section 162 (b) of the Nigeria (Constitution) Order in Council, 1951, of 'ensuring, in association with the appropriate public officer, that effect is given to decisions taken by the Governor in Council of Ministers relating to such matter.'

3. Western Ministers had pressed, in a committee of the Council, for an interpretation of the present Constitution which would charge Ministers with responsibility for Departments rather than for the matters or subjects detailed in the Third Schedule to the Order in Council. They were in fact asking for full ministerial status similar to that of Ministers in the United Kingdom.

4. The Northern and Eastern Ministers, while agreeing that some changes in the organisation of Ministers' offices are desirable, were firmly of the view that such change should be carried out within the framework of the present Constitution and that no amendment of the Order in Council should be sought to furnish Ministers with more extensive powers than those provided at present by the Order in Council.

5. This subject was dealt with without any serious conflict of view giving rise to undue acerbity, and it was possible to reach a satisfactory understanding on the relationship which should exist between a Minister and a Head of Department and also on the extent to which a Department can be regarded as 'forming part of' a Ministry. It should now be possible to examine the practical possibilities of giving effect to the desire of Ministers for separate Ministerial Secretariats with a fairly clear conception of the nature of the organisation contemplated. The problem of finding the necessary staff for such a reorganisation is the outstanding difficulty, but I believe that Ministers appreciate the problem.

6. As soon as the Council turned its attention to the Memorandum by the Western Ministers, it became apparent that the West had no support from either of the other two Regions, and the discussion did not get beyond item II at page 3 of the Note which formed the second enclosure to my saving under reference.

7. The discussion on item I of the note (provisions of Royal Instructions regarding exercise of powers by the Governor and Lieutenant-Governors under 'existing legislation') was amicable and useful. The explanation given at the meeting with Western Ministers on the 10th June (as recorded in the note) had clarified the position, and the Lieutenant-Governors and I were prepared to consult our Councils, and accept their advice, in cases in which, if we were legislating afresh, our powers would not, in our opinion, be made discretionary. The Law Officers had produced a tremendous list of discretionary powers under existing legislation, and it was quite clear that a great many of these were concerned with functions which were quasi-

[2] Not printed.

judicial, or administrative, or concerned with the public service. And a host of other matters would, if discretionary powers were removed, result in bogging down the work of the Council of Ministers and the Executive Councils with business which, even if not strictly so unimportant as to come within Clause 5 (1) (b) and Clause 3 (1) (b) of the two sets of Royal Instructions, would not merit such treatment. The list of powers under existing legislation will now be scrutinized by the Lieutenant-Governors and myself, with a view to designating those which will continue to be discretionary. I judge that you will not be surprised that we should have given ground in this matter, having regard to the terms of your telegram No. 737 of the 16th June 1951. Meantime, existing practice is generally acceptable to Ministers both at the Centre and in the Regions.

8.   When the Council turned to item II of the note forming the second enclosure to my saving under reference (restrictions imposed by Section 85 of the Constitution Order in Council regarding bills and motions affecting the public service) it was at once made abundantly clear that the Western Ministers had no support from the other Regions on this point, and, indeed, that the Northern and Eastern Ministers proposed to take a firm stand against *any* proposal which would entail a change in the Constitution at this stage.

9.   After one or two somewhat stormy exchanges between Western and Eastern Ministers, which I did not check too soon, it was agreed that no useful purpose would be served by pursuing any further the other matters raised in the memorandum put forward by the Western Ministers, and the meeting was brought to a close.

10.   It is still too early to say how the Action Group will react to this sharp defeat. It is too much to hope for that they will retract anything but I believe that it has been a shock to them to find that their present methods do not command the respect or support of the rest of the country, and there may be, for a time at least, a serious attempt to get on with the working of the Constitution in its present form, with fewer attacks on the existence of officials who, as I constantly point out, are part of the very fabric of the Constitution.

11.   I believe that the Western Ministers would like to see changes made in the Constitution to meet their own particular wishes (Prime Minister for the West etc.) but that they would be strongly opposed to any major changes in the general structure. They may now realise that any change in the Constitution Order in Council would open the flood gates and play into the hands of those who oppose Regionalization, Electoral colleges etc. Opinion in the Northern Region is overwhelmingly in favour of leaving the Constitution untouched. I believe that the Eastern Ministers, both Central and Regional, are sincere in their desire to maintain the unity of Nigeria under a strong Federal Constitution. In part, however, they were moved by dislike of the Action Group. And they cannot ignore the facts that they belong to the N.C.N.C.—nominally at least—and that the Lagos end of the party (including Azikiwe, Ojike, Balogun etc. not to mention the West African Pilot), probably supported by a not inconsiderable section of the Members of the Eastern House of Assembly, has declared its opposition to Regionalization and to Electoral Colleges. With luck and good guidance we should be able to keep the Constitution as it is for a considerable period but the possibility of an explosion (e.g. on the separation of Lagos from the West or the North-West inter Regional Boundary) cannot be discounted. For the time being we can be well satisfied with the outcome of this recent flurry.

Minute on 158

Mr. Gorell Barnes
The Governor's savingram at (3) neatly summarises the outcome of the trouble with the Action Group, about which you are already informed more fully from other papers.

The North's reaction was just what one would have expected, and the East's strikes me as very sensible.

It is very difficult to summarise the position briefly, but in a nutshell it comes to this. The West's clamour for immediate changes in the constitution has found no support in the North or East, and the Council of Ministers (including the Western representatives for this purpose) have agreed to persevere with the constitution in its present form. Amongst other things, the West's proposal for Regional Prime Ministers has been rejected. (Personally I was always rather doubtful whether Awolowo would press this particular idea very hard at this stage: it struck me that anyway he might not wish to see a *Central* Prime Minister so long as he himself was not a Central Minister and not therefore in the running for the Central post. But whether he really had ambitions that way or whether he is now thinking in terms of a separate Western Nigeria—see below—remains to be seen.)

Further consideration will now be given, in the Council's Sub-Committee on Ministerial Organisation, to the practicability of establishing 'Ministries'. It has been agreed, the Attorney-General concurring, that 'Ministries' can be established under the present Constitution Order for the purpose of assisting Ministers to carry out their functions and responsibilities as defined in Section 162 of the Order. Their relations with Heads of Departments have also been satisfactorily clarified and, for the purposes of Section 162 (b), it has been agreed that a Minister may give instructions to a Head of Department to ensure that decisions of the Council of Ministers are carried out. It has also been agreed that Departments shall come within the framework of Ministries (as of course they do in the Gold Coast) though naturally they need not be housed under the same roof.

The compromise reached on the way the Governor and Lieutenant Governors shall carry out Clause 5(1) (b) and Clause 3(1)(b) of their respective Royal Instructions is sensible, and shows that agreement on these matters is possible where there is goodwill and commonsense on all sides.

The conclusion of the matter will be found in paragraphs 10 and 11 of (3). The danger that looms ahead, as Mr. Himsworth mentioned to me last week, is that if the West— meaning in this context the Action Group—remain fundamentally dissatisfied, their thoughts may turn more and more to secession. We can only watch—and pray....

T.B.W.
21.7.52

159 CO 554/241, no 7   14 July 1952
[Western Region local government reform]: inward telegram no 951 from Sir J Macpherson to Mr Lyttelton on the Western Region local government bill

[This telegram followed the tabling of a parliamentary question by R W Sorensen, MP for Leyton, concerning the local government bill introduced into the Western Region House of Assembly by Awolowo earlier that month. The bill followed the Eastern Region local government ordinance of 1950 and was in some part modelled on it. It proposed empowering the regional government to establish local authorities and introduced the elective principle for choosing councillors; the lieutenant-governor's powers—and ultimately those of DOs—over local government were correspondingly curtailed. The CO was unhappy with this and feared that the bill, both in itself and in the way it had been introduced to the House of Assembly, undermined the constitutional division of powers between the centre, understood as the British authorities, and Nigerian ministers in the regions. The significance of this episode was that it showed the determination of the AG leadership in the Western Region to utilise to the full the powers given them by the 1951 constitution. The amended Western Region local government law received royal assent in February 1953. It was followed in 1954 by legislation to systematise succession to chieftaincies.]

Your telegram No. 895.

Parliamentary Question: Local Government Proposals, Western Region.

I am sorry you should have been placed in embarrassing position through lack of official information from me. I should have passed on to you informally such information as was available to me, and I apologise for failure to do so sooner. I had not contemplated possibility of U.K. Parliament being interested at this stage.

2. Blunt fact is that the matter has not yet been formally referred to Central Government. I did not see the Bill until it appeared in the Gazette of 26th June. After stumping the Region on the subject, Awolowo, with party majority in the Western Executive Council, recently forced the bill through that body against strong advice of Lieutenant Governor and Official Members that there had been inadequate consultations and consideration of the proposals. Meeting was stormy, and Lieutenant Governor warned his Ministers that they were running serious risk by rushing matters. Bill will be introduced at meeting of Western House of Assembly which starts on 14th July.

3. We have not yet worked out satisfactory arrangements to govern relations between Council of Ministers and Regional Executive Councils in connection with Regional Legislation and other matters. Subject is down for discussion in Council of Ministers, but we have been too busy with other explosive subjects. I am advised, however, that action taken by Western Government is legally and constitutionally in order.

4. Under Sections 96 and 98 of the Constitution Order in Council, I could, on the advice of the Council of Ministers, object to the bill when it is sent to me. I shall (gp. emitted ? consult) you before assenting but, if the Bill goes through both houses in the West, I do not expect to have strong grounds for objecting. There is broad agreement on provisions of the Bill which, to considerable degree, implements reform of native administration already carried out. It is also based in considerable measure on Eastern Local Government Ordinance.[1]

5. Intention is that Local Government Inspectors should be drawn from serving Administrative Officers (though, if provisions of the bill are not changed, I foresee some battle when Ministers try to be selective). I do not like the proposal that Lieutenant Governor in Council as Regional Authority should control staff. This aspect will receive very careful consideration when the law comes to the centre.

6. As regards reply to parliamentary question, Marshall agrees that précis of Ibadan Note of 11th June, which I have not yet seen, would provide satisfactory

---

[1] The Eastern Region local government ordinance 1950.

exposition of proposals. For the rest, you may wish to say that the Bill for Western Region Local Government Laws, 1952 has not yet been considered by Nigeria Government (possibly expressing surprise at this fact) or by you, and that you are not in a position to comment on the merits of the proposals at this stage.

160 CO 554/414, no 2   12 August 1952
[Nigerianisation]: letter from Sir S Phillipson to J B Williams on the establishment of a commission to review the progress of Nigerianisation

You are probably aware that Mr. S.O. Adebo of the Nigerian Secretariat and myself have been entrusted by the Council of Ministers with the task of conducting an expert review of the policy of Nigerianization of the Civil Service in Nigeria and the machinery for its implementation. Our recommendations are to be made to the Council of Ministers.[1]

The subject of Nigerianization was, as you know, fully considered by a large and representative Commission under the chairmanship of Foot in 1948.[2] The Report of that Commission which was submitted to the Governor on the 10th August in that year formulated the policy which has since been followed with good results. It may therefore seem odd that the subject should call for review rather less than four years later and indeed, subject to the special problem mentioned in the next paragraph, no question arises or could in normal circumstances arise regarding the basic policy of appointing Nigerians to posts in the Senior Service 'as fast as suitable candidates with the necessary qualifications come forward' and of surveying the Nigerian field of recruitment before going to the non-Nigerian field. It is not, however, a matter for surprise that following the recent constitutional changes those on whom power has now so largely devolved should seek to satisfy themselves that the declared policy is being carried out with resolution and energy and that there are no deficiencies in the machinery which hinder the full and effective execution of that policy. Rightly or wrongly, the belief prevails in Nigerian circles that under the present arrangements oversea candidates have in certain instances been appointed to Senior Service posts who are less fitted to hold such posts than some of the Nigerian candidates who were found unsuitable by the Nigerianization process. Theoretically this does seem to be possible because the process of oversea recruitment is so entirely separate from the process established under the recommendations of the Foot Commission for first giving consideration to Nigerian candidates; whether it has actually happened or not

[1] S O Adebo, lawyer and civil servant; administrative officer, 1942; called to the Bar, 1948; assistant financial secretary, 1954; administrative officer, 1955; permanent secretary, Western Region Ministry of Finance, 1957. S Phillipson and SO Adebo, *The Nigerianization of the Civil Service, a Review of Policy and Machinery* (Lagos, 1954), was submitted in April 1953 but not published until after the resumed Lagos conference of January 1954. Its recommendations were thus overtaken by events and it was left to the regional and Federal governments to evolve new policies for furthering Nigerianisation.
[2] *Report of the Commission appointed by His Excellency the Governor of Nigeria to make Recommendations about the Recruitment and Training of Nigerians for Senior Posts in the Government Service of Nigeria* (Lagos, 1948).

is of course another matter. Anyway it will be the duty of Adebo and myself to make organisational recommendations designed to safeguard against this possibility.

Another and a very important problem arises from the attitude of influential Northern Nigerian opinion to Nigerianization in its application to the North. Those who at present speak for the North are strongly opposed to a policy which would, as they see it, mean the 'southernization' of the North. They prefer to retain oversea staff until such time as their own people can take over. Since the North is more backward in Western education than the other two regions, the process of Nigerianization there on this basis will be much slower than in the South. It is, I think, very largely because this difficult question has arisen that the reviewing body has been asked to review policy as well as machinery.

The foregoing paragraphs do no more than sketch in the background of a complicated subject on which much could be written. The purpose of this letter is not, however, to discuss these issues but to let you know that Adebo and myself will be in the United Kingdom from about the 22nd September for ten days to a fortnight in order to pursue our enquiry at the London end (I will actually be arriving in London on the 10th September but the earlier part of my visit will be devoted to Marketing Board and other matters). Naturally we will wish to have full discussions with you, the officials of the Colonial Service Division and others able to give us information and advice.[3] I hope to be able before beginning enquiries in London to let you have a memorandum of the points of particular interest to us. Meanwhile it will perhaps suffice to say that we want to obtain the clearest possible idea of the system of recruitment and appointment operated by the Colonial Office and the Crown Agents in relation to the *desiderata* of our problem. We would also like to obtain the broad facts relating to the methods adopted by H.M. Government in the United Kingdom for recruitment to the higher Civil Service and for the safeguarding the whole process of appointment to the Public Service against extraneous and improper influence.

It would help us greatly if you would advise us regarding the programme of discussions which we should follow. We want to make good use of our time. The United Kingdom end is scarcely less important than the Nigerian end—or so our initial approach seems to suggest.

I think that it would be a good thing if we were to give Nigerian students in the United Kingdom an opportunity to submit memoranda and, if called upon, to give evidence,[4] but before I take active steps to arrange this through the Nigeria Office I would like to know whether you or Keith have any views or advice to offer as to procedure to be adopted, organisations and bodies to be seen and what not.

---

[3] See 164.   [4] Sir Charles Jeffries noted in the margin, 'I should not encourage this.'

161 CO 554/309, no 1   13 August 1952
[Regional boundaries]: letter from Sir J Macpherson to W L Gorell Barnes on political problems concerning the position of Lagos and the boundary between the Western and Northern Regions

[Regional boundaries were to become a major issue of controversy under the Federal constitutions established in Nigeria after 1951. Under the 1951 constitutional arrangements

Lagos had been made part of the Western Region. This had been welcomed by the AG and opposed by the NCNC which had hitherto dominated Lagos politics. Thereafter the NCNC continued to press for the separation of Lagos from the Western Region. Behind this lay the struggle for political power in Lagos between the NCNC, inheritors of the older Macaulay-ite tradition in the city, and the AG (see 163). A further problem came with the boundary between the Northern and Western Regions. By accepting the pre-1914 boundary between Northern and Southern Nigeria, the 1951 constitution left large numbers of Yorubas, particularly those living in Ilorin emirate, in the Northern region and this was to be a recurring issue of controversy during the remaining years of British rule.]

You know that I have long been anxious about the effect that either or both of two very explosive subjects might have on the new Constitution, and our whole set-up; the subjects, of course, are the position of Lagos and the Western claim for the revision of the inter-regional boundary between the West and the North. In the past few weeks regional feelings have become very highly charged, and we are living dangerously. I wish that I could make more time to keep you more fully and frequently posted in all this, but the pressure is fantastic and the situation changes from day to day. This letter will be hurried and possibly not very connected but it will be followed up by more factual communications.

You have all the facts about the boundary dispute—correspondence ending with your Saving No. 1760 of 8th June. I have no doubt at all that the right decision, as I told the Secretary of State when he was here, is 'no change.' My present intention, and I should welcome approval of my proposed course of action, is to make the decision public in a Gazette Extraordinary two or three days before the adjournment of the House of Representatives at the end of the meeting which starts on the 14th. The best guess I can make is that publication would take place about the 25th, 26th, or 27th August. Developments regarding the quarrel about Lagos may lead to a change in this programme but a decision cannot be much longer deferred; the arguments which led to this proposed date for publication are as follows:—

(a) The decision must be announced before I go on leave, which I hope to do on 16th September;

(b) It would not do if I flew off from Nigeria almost immediately after the announcement of my decision!

(c) I don't want to publish the decision before the House of Representatives meets because it would greatly add to the general explosive atmosphere (the Western Ministers have uttered dark threats about the 'wrong' decision wrecking the Constitution);

(d) It would not look well to make the announcement immediately after the Members of the House of Representatives had dispersed;

(e) Ten days' notice is required of a Motion and if the announcement is made within a few days of the adjournment on completion of business before the Council there will not be time for notice of a Motion to be given before the adjournment. (There is always the possibility, of course, that a Member may ask for leave to move the adjournment for the purpose of discussing a matter of urgent public importance. However, we must risk that).

All this depends on whether I can make time to write my 'grounds of judgment' and get the Gazette printed on schedule. We shall be sending you a separate letter telling you how regional views are developing on this subject, but I can say right here and now that the campaign by the Action Group and the papers which support it has had the effect of creating a united and determined Northern opposition to any change in the boundary. Even the dissident N.E.P.U. sides with the Northern Peoples Congress and the Northern Houses of Assembly in this matter and if the N.C.N.C. takes its usual line it will support its N.E.P.U. allies—and majority opinion in the North—in this matter. The cumulative effect of (a) the rejection by the North and East of the Action Group proposals for amending the Constitution Order in Council, (b) the rejection of the Western claims for a revision of the boundary, and (c) of Northern and Eastern support for Mbadiwe's Motion (referred to below) to excise Lagos from the West might well result in the Action Group Ministers denouncing the Constitution and refusing to co-operate in running it. I have very much in mind the threat to law and order in the Western Region which might result from any such decision.

It is the Lagos problem, however, which makes this informatory letter particularly urgent. At our Budget meeting in March one of the Members from the East, Mbadiwe, gave notice of a motion for the separation of Lagos from the Western Region. All of us in the Council of Ministers realised the implications of this; if the motion were carried we should inevitably be committed to making significant changes in the Constitution Order-in-Council and the whole Constitution would be in the melting pot. Eventually, the Central Ministers from the East persuaded Mbadiwe to withdraw his motion.

In recent weeks, the anger of the North and East against the actions and attitude of the West, as dictated by Awolowo and his Party, has been steadily rising. You know the full story of the Western Ministers' memorandum, and about the rejection by the North and East of the Action Group proposals for amending the Constitution Order-in-Council. The Ministers of the North and East—both Central and Regional—rejected those proposals because they were determined to preserve the unity of the country and to keep the present Constitution going. They are also influenced to some extent by their annoyance with the Action Group. What particularly riled the East was that they were made to look as if they were resisting progressive changes, whereas certain aspects of the Constitution are not fully to the liking of the N.C.N.C.; but they have refrained from suggesting changes because they realise that once we tamper in any way with the Constitution Order-in-Council we can scarcely avoid being committed to a further constitutional review.

At a meeting of the Council of Ministers on 1st August we discussed what Government's attitude would be to a number of motions, for the forthcoming meeting of the House of Representatives, of which notice had been given. When we came to Mbadiwe's motion, the storm burst, and the Ministers from the North and East told the Western Ministers exactly what they thought of them and their Party. The gravamen of the charge was that whereas all the other Members of the Council of Ministers were applying their minds to the problems before them with the sole desire of furthering the interests of a unified Nigeria, the Western Ministers were playing party politics. I enclose an extract from the conclusions of the meeting; they might have read much more stormily![1]

I have been at pains to make it abundantly clear that if the Constitution breaks on this issue it will not be an argument between Britain and Nigeria but petty squabbles between Nigerians themselves. Many sympathetic and friendly well-wishers in the

[1] Not printed.

United Kingdom and other countries will be gravely disappointed; and enemies greatly encouraged. I made the point that a break-up at this time would be particularly tragic coming as it would just after the successful visit of Nwapa to the United Kingdom which demonstrated most clearly the degree of confidence imposed by H.M.G. and the British people in this young Nigerian Government.

I cannot at present prophesy what the outcome of all this will be. The Central Ministers from the North brought word, after the recent meetings of the Northern Legislative Houses, that Mbadiwe's motion would have strong support and that most of the Northern Members of the House of Representatives would vote for it. They are not very seriously concerned with the merits of the case and are moved mainly by disgust of the actions and attitude of the Action Group, but they also have at the back of their minds the fear which was expressed at the General Conference on the Constitution, held at Ibadan in 1950, that a Northern 'corridor to the sea' is essential and that Western control of Lagos and its port is a threat to the lifeline of the North. Sharwood Smith was here for a couple of nights before sailing on leave on 5th August, and I got him to have a very frank talk with the three Central Ministers from the North. They now fully realise the consequences if the motion is passed, namely that it would mean extensive changes in the Constitution Order in Council (and the Revenue Allocation Order in Council). And we couldn't avoid all the other controversial issues coming up (Prime Minister, abolition of Electoral Colleges etc.). I think they now hope to restrain the Northern floor members, by persuading them that while they may criticize the West they should not vote for the motion, if it is debated.

The East are of course much more heavily involved because the quarrel between the N.C.N.C. and the Action Group centres largely on the position of Lagos, not least because the merging of the Colony with the West stopped Azikiwe from getting to the House of Representatives. The Yorubas, led by Awolowo, have long felt that Lagos, which they regard as a Yoruba town, has been plagued by noisy irresponsible politicians and hooligans from the East. The new Constitution enabled them to reduce to negligible proportions the influence of these people in the Central Legislature; notwithstanding the N.C.N.C. victory in the primary elections; then Awolowo turned his attention to the Lagos Town Council, where the N.C.N.C. and its allies hold 18 seats out of 24. Awolowo was dissuaded from dissolving the Town Council, on the grounds that the best course was to let the electorate deal with the situation. The projected Commission of Enquiry into the working of the Council should greatly assist in 'educating the electorate.' Without waiting for the result of the Commission of Enquiry, however, and without any consultation with people in Lagos, Awolowo has announced far-reaching proposals for the reform of the Council, including the abolition of the appointment of a Mayor, making Oba Adele the 'ceremonial' President and adding White Cap Chiefs, who would not have to be elected. No bill has yet been presented to the Western House of Assembly, but a bill has been passed postponing the elections (of one-third of the 24 members of the Town Council) which would normally have taken place in October. (This bill has not yet been to the Council of Ministers). In effect, Awolowo wants to give Lagos a Local Government body more or less on the general Western pattern. The N.C.N.C. is screaming about this retrograde proposal to replace a modern Town Council which has a wholly elected membership based on adult suffrage, and an elected Mayor, with an old-fashioned substitute. (They are only slightly abashed by the fact that they made similar proposals a few years ago before the present Oba, who is a solid supporter of the Action Group, was appointed).

One further point about the Action Group position on Lagos. They claim that Lagos is a Yoruba town and must remain so, but assert that they are not interested in its role as capital of Nigeria. So far as they are concerned, they suggest that a new capital be established somewhere else.

So much for the general pattern—or confusion! I don't yet see the solution, but I am not sitting back waiting upon events. One suggestion is that the motion should be disallowed because, in its present form, it assumes that the House can change the Constitution. But notice of a motion in similar terms was admitted in March (later withdrawn); and the mover could be advised to change the form of the motion in such a way as to make it admissible. I feel that it would be very unwise to rule it out on a technicality, unless, by a miracle, there was tacit agreement to that course in all quarters.

I see no hope of Mbadiwe being prevailed upon again to withdraw his motion, unless there has been a truce of some kind. And that is really the best hope of surmounting the crisis. The first gesture or concession ought to come from the West, followed by a generous response from the other side. Awolowo is not the sort of person to do this, but in spite of the highly-charged atmosphere I do not despair of the Central Ministers getting together and working out some compromise which they can urge upon the Members from their Regions. The Central Ministers are quite good friends and there is a clear realization in the Council of the need to keep the Ship of State on an even keel. The only jarring note is when the Western Ministers keep 'looking over their shoulders' at the Boss (Awolowo) and do not open their minds to compromise. There have been recently some tentative gropings towards a burying of the hatchet by the main antagonistic parties. And Pant the Indian Commissioner from East Africa, who, as you know, recently spent two weeks in Nigeria, did a very good job, even if he is a little 'smooth.' He met the Ministers, both in the Regions and at the Centre, and in all his conversations, and speeches, he stressed the value and importance of belonging to the British Commonwealth (he said this in a broadcast), and spoke about the dangers of communalism, and the need to resist communism by capturing the imagination of the people. My people were very greatly impressed.

I have told the Central Ministers that it is primarily their responsibility to find a solution, but I am having talks with them individually and in groups; and they know I am ready to help, at any time of the day or night, to bring people together. I am also discreetly enlisting the support of individual responsible Nigerians outside the Council.

If we break on this it will be tragic, because none of the Regions, and least of all the Council of Ministers, wants any change in the main structure of the Constitution now or in the near future. If it breaks we shall have to set about putting the pieces together again, but it will be a serious set-back, and I doubt if we could continue to have a single country.

We can arrange the business of the House so that this particular piece of dynamite doesn't get taken before the 20th of August, or a little later. Much will depend on what we can do after the Members assemble in Lagos about the 12th or 13th—night-time confabs in smoke-filled hotel bedrooms etc. in the American style. I shall try to let you know about developments.

P.S. I dictated this several days ago. All the Lieutenant-Governors are now here and we are searching for a solution. One possibility is that Government should put in a prior motion reaffirming the status quo of Lagos in the Constitution but expressing the conviction that before any Regional legislation is passed by the West affecting the position of Lagos there should be some prior consultation. The West who regularly claim that following their defeat any measure which involves amendment to the Constitution should be agreed by all, may regard this as an unbearable defeat.

162 CO 554/676, no 10A 　　　　　　　　　　　　　　6 Sept 1952

[Deadlock over ministerial powers]: inward savingram no 3641 from Sir J Macpherson to Mr Lyttelton on the AG attacks on the constitution and on regional boundaries

Sequel to the representations by Action Group Ministers on Constitutional Issues.

In my secret savingram No. 2440 of the 19th of June[1] I gave an account of the attacks launched by the Action Group on certain provisions of the 1951 Constitution which, in their view, prevented the establishment of effective Ministerial control over both Regional and Central affairs. Later, in my savingram No. 2725 of the 11th of July[2] I informed you of the hostile attitude of the Northern and Eastern Executive Councils and of the Council of Ministers to the Western proposals. Sufficient time has now elapsed to enable me to make a more confident assessment of the reaction of the West to the rejection of these demands to which they were so deeply committed, but which they had wisely, and fortunately for them, not publicised.

2. On the 9th of July, shortly after the Council of Ministers reached its decision to reject the Western proposals for constitutional reform, Awolowo, the leader of the Action Group, addressed a mass meeting of his supporters in Lagos in remarkably conciliatory terms. The Action Group, he said, accepted the 1951 Constitution although fully conscious of its defects. No Constitution was perfect and the Action Group believed that as time went on the defects in the Nigerian Constitution would come to light and would be removed, He had in mind three major matters which required adjustment and they were (a) the removal of control of the Civil Service from the hands of the Governor, (b) the failure of Government to establish effective Ministerial control over Departments and (c) the retention by the Governor and Lieutenant-Governors of powers vested in them by legislation enacted prior to the setting up of the 1951 Constitution. These pronouncements were not, as might have been expected, followed by a press campaign nor were they seriously pursued in the Western House of Assembly which met shortly afterwards, on the 14th of July. Awolowo's parting shot on the subject was delivered at that meeting where 'amidst great cheers' he relegated constitutional changes to a conveniently distant future and declared that the Action Group was 'irrevocably committed' to the attainment of self-government within five years. The rejection of the Action Groups's proposals was also followed by a very marked improvement in the relationship between the Western Regional Ministers and the official Members of the Western Regional Executive

---

[1] See 157.

[2] See 158.

Council, based on a much more realistic view, on the part of the Action Group, of the inter-dependence of the Regions in a united Nigeria.

3.   This more conciliatory attitude can be attributed partly to the salutary impact of Eastern and Northern opinion on the Party and partly to the evident willingness of the Council of Ministers to examine proposals for Ministerial reorganisation and for further delegation of powers, at present in the hands of Lieutenant-Governors, to Lieutenant-Governors in Council. The discussion of the Western Region Local Government Bill at the July meeting of the House of Assembly and the attacks of the N.C.N.C. on the measure aroused widespread Regional interest and enabled the Party gradually to cease reference, without undue loss of face, not only to its constitutional claims but also to another issue on which it was no less deeply committed—namely, the revision of the boundary between the North and the West, in favour of the West.

4.   Interest in the constitutional issues raised by the Party receded still further (for the present) as the date fixed for the meeting of the House of Representatives approached and it became clear that the N.C.N.C., as distinct from the Eastern Ministers and the Central Ministers for the East, intended to resume its campaign for the severance of Lagos from the Western Region and to move a motion to that effect in the House of Representatives, I have briefly described the reaction of my Ministers to this proposal in communications ending with my telegrams Nos. 1196 and 1197 of the 19th of August. For the purpose of this savingram the importance of the N.C.N.C.'s move was that for the first time for some months the Action Group found itself on the defensive and strongly resisting a proposed change in the Constitution. When, therefore, the President of the House ruled the N.C.N.C. Motion out of order and the Government reaffirmed the special position of Lagos in the Constitution and announced its intention of seeking expert advice on the financial and administrative arrangements in other capitals to assist it in dealing with the problem of Lagos within the framework of the Constitution, the decision was applauded by the Action Group members. The West came out of the business well in that they have extricated themselves without too much loss of face from the constitutional impasse into which they had rushed. At the same time they can be said to have aligned themselves, for the time being at least, with majority opinion against early changes in the Constitution.

5.   The cessation by the Action Group of the press campaign for revision of the inter-Regional boundary (referred to in paragraph 3 above) and its 'victory' in the status of Lagos issue appeared to offer a suitable opportunity of announcing my decision in regard to the last of the major constitutional issues on which the West had taken a stand. As I informed you, in correspondence ending with my savingram No. 3537 of the 30th of August, I therefore decided to announce my decision in regard to the boundary on the 3rd of September.[3] It is not yet possible to be sure that the Action Group will reconcile itself to this further blow to its aspirations but there are signs that their experiences of the last two months, described above, and their desire to retain Northern support on the status of Lagos issue will induce the party to accept the decision, for the present at least. Up to this date (5th September) there has been no Press reaction. Significantly, neither the Zik press nor the Action Group papers have so far made a single Editorial comment.

---

[3] Macpherson announced on 3 September that the boundary between the Northern and Western Regions would remain unchanged and that Lagos would remain part of the Western Region.

163 CO 554/309, no 9
15 Sept 1952

[Position of Lagos]: inward savingram no 3776 from Sir J Macpherson to Mr Lyttelton on the constitutional position of Lagos [Extract]

Motion to separate Lagos from the Western Region

In correspondence ending with my secret telegram No. 1197 of 19th August I informed you of the serious threat to the stability of the present Constitution which resulted from the determination of N.C.N.C. Members of the House of Representatives (as distinct from Eastern Regional Ministers and Central Ministers from the East) to press a Motion in the following terms:—

'Be it resolved that, in the interest of national unity and fraternal fellowship among the Regions of Nigeria, Lagos be separated from the Western Region and henceforth remain independent of any and all the Regions of Nigeria.'

The purpose of this communication is to recount the measures taken to deal with the situation and to give some background information.

2. You are aware, of course, that the position of Lagos has been a bone of contention between the main political parties in the South (N.C.N.C. and Action Group) ever since the review of the Constitution was undertaken, and I need not recapitulate the history of this matter, the settlement of which is set out in paragraphs 11 and 12 of your predecessor's Despatch No. 464A of the 15th July, 1950[1], published with the Constitution Order in Council. The Lagos electorate has on several occasions' demonstrated that it is preponderantly N.C.N.C. in outlook or, more accurately, that it favours Azikiwe and his associates, rather than Awolowo and the Action Group, but the Action Group secured a very substantial majority in the Western Region elections (with the signal exception of those held in Lagos) under the new Constitution; and its leaders, who held the view that the Yoruba town of Lagos has been plagued for years by noisy and irresponsible elements from the Eastern Region, lost no time in giving proof of their intention of correcting that situation. Their efforts have been directed to gaining[2] [. . .] power politics, and the N.C.N.C. party, and elected members from the East generally, have not failed to understand what was intended.

3. During the Budget meeting in March, notice of a motion for the separation of Lagos from the Western Region was given by Mbadiwe, a floor member from the East. As President, I allowed it to go on the Order Book, because I did not consider that I had power to do otherwise, though I should probably have asked the Member to change the wording so that it would do no more than ask the House to express an opinion on the subject matter of the motion. When, however, the Council of Ministers considered the matter in March, all the Ministers appreciated that acceptance of the motion would inevitably lead to vital changes being made to the Constitution. They resolved to oppose the motion if it were moved, but, since even a debate on the subject would lead to unsettlement, the Council decided that the Central Ministers from the East should endeavour to persuade Mbadiwe to withdraw his notice of motion. In this they were successful, but the Member had, of course, the right to ask for it to be restored to the Order Book.

4. It is not difficult to understand why the request was made for the notice of motion to be restored for the August meeting. Not only had the Action Group pressed

---

[1] See 116. [2] The text in the original is broken at this point and approximately six words are missing.

on with their intentions to gain party control of Lagos but they had upset both the Northern and Eastern Regions by their unilateral demand for the revision of the Constitution to give them greatly extended powers in their Region. (I refer to correspondence ending with my saving telegram No. 3641 of the 6th September).[3] The Eastern Ministers, both Regional and Central, were opposed to any change in the Constitution at this stage but the N.C.N.C. as a party (which must be distinguished from Eastern Ministers) has never disguised the fact that there are certain aspects of the Constitution that do not meet with their wishes (particularly the system of electoral colleges and the merging of Lagos with the Western Region), and the Eastern Ministers were angry because by their opposition to the Constitutional changes proposed by the Western Ministers they were made to look unprogressive. The Northern Ministers, both Regional and Central, were no less angry with the Western Ministers because of their aggressiveness and overweening pride.

5.   When last month the Council of Ministers again came to consider its attitude towards the motion of which Mbadiwe had given fresh notice, the Ministers, in their hearts, were no less anxious than before to keep the Constitution intact. It was made clear, however, by the Central Ministers from the North that the motion, if debated, would get considerable support from the Northern Members of the House. Although the reasons were not stated, it was obvious that this was in part due to irritation with the Action Group Ministers, and to a desire to teach them a lesson. Not only was this argument likely to override, amongst the less thoughtful Members, the desire to keep the Constitution intact; there was the further thought that the West might wish to secede, and if that were to happen, the North would wish the port of Lagos to be independent of the Western Region. I do not believe that the Eastern Ministers, whether Regional or Central, were in favour of the motion being brought forward (the tail of N.C.N.C. floor Members is liable to wag the Eastern Ministerial dog) but they, too, suspected, wrongly as I think, that the Western Region had it in mind to secede, and were less ready than in March to resist the motion, or to attempt to persuade Mbadiwe to withdraw it. The Central Ministers from the West argued, with justification, that as their proposals for changes in the Constitution had been rejected by the other Regions on the grounds that it was not desired to make any changes at present, the same considerations should lead the Council of Ministers resolutely to oppose the motion.

6.   I kept postponing the issue in Council of Ministers while I had consultations with individual Ministers, groups of Ministers, Lieutenant-Governors, and private individuals upon whom I could rely. One suggestion that I favoured was the earlier introduction of a Government motion which would assert the Government's view that no changes should be made in the Constitution at this stage, would reaffirm the special status of Lagos; and would go on to record the conviction of the Government that it would be within the spirit of the Constitution that no legislation affecting Lagos should be introduced into the Western House of Assembly until after prior consultation between the Lieutenant Governor in Council and the Governor in Council. This, while saving the main stand of the Action Group, would have clipped their wings to a considerable extent.

7.   Before the Council of Ministers had decided what its attitude would be to the motion, if debated, the Gordian knot was cut by Mr. E.A. Fellowes, as President of the House of Representatives. Entirely on his own iniative, he decided that the motion

---

[3] See 162.

was out of order, that is 'disorderly', and was not debatable in the House. The statement which he eventually made in the House in answer to a Private Notice question from the mover, was as follows:—

> 'Paragraph 5 of the Constitution Order in Council, 1951 says that Nigeria shall be divided into three Regions. Within those Regions it is competent for the Governor to alter the boundaries, and so forth, as set out in the Order in Council. But the Motion which I was considering said that Lagos should be taken out of all three Regions and made into an entity of its own. It seemed to me, therefore, beyond doubt that such a Motion validated would require an amendment of the Order in Council. But if you look at Paragraph 12 of that same Order in Council, Honourable Members will see that the power to amend the Order in Council is expressly reserved not to any Authority in Nigeria, but to the Sovereign in Council. It therefore seemed to me that the Motion must be out of order.'

Mr. Fellowes had no doubt about the correctness of his action, and he has assured me that he did not have also at the back of his mind the thought that he was helping us out of a very serious political 'jam'. Be that as it may, he has a very good knowledge of the Nigerian political set-up and I can never be sufficiently grateful to him for his help.

8.   Mr. Fellowes communicated his decision to Mbadiwe, and to the Government, on the 16th August, and on the two following days the Council of Ministers met to consider the situation. The outcome was a unanimous decision to seek expert advice on the financial and administrative arrangements made in other capitals, particularly federal capitals, and to consider this advice 'within the framework of the Constitution'. The decision to seek such expert advice was not a device to gain time; it was genuinely felt that if we had some principles, and rules of practice, to guide us, the difficult problems connected with Lagos could be approached otherwise than with passion and prejudice. (For example, non-Western Ministers pointed out that the country as a whole might wish to spend large sums of money on making Lagos a worthy capital; it should not be left to the Western Region to decide such questions, or to meet the bill alone). The real argument in Council turned, surprisingly, on the question whether or not the Government should make a statement in the House regarding its position. For reasons which were not easy to fathom neither the Western nor the Northern Ministers favoured any statement by the Government. I always try to avoid a situation in which the ex-officio Members and the Ministers from a single Region carry the day. In this case, the situation was eased by my suggestion that the Council should first decide on the terms of a statement, if it were decided that one should be made. After this had been achieved the Council decided by a majority (Officials and East) that a statement should be made.

9.   This was done by the Chief Secretary immediately after the President had given his grounds for ruling Mbadiwe's motion out of order. It was in the following terms:—

> 'Under the Constitution Lagos has a dual function. It has been merged with the Western Region and it is the capital and principal port of Nigeria. The dual function gives rise to difficult problems relating to finance and administration and these have for some time been exercising the minds of the Council of Ministers. The Council have, therefore, decided to seek expert opinion on the financial and admiistrative arrangements in other capitals, especially in federal countries and will give consideration to such opinion within the framework of the Constutition.'

10.   I was not, of course, present in the House at the time, but I was informed that the statement was warmly received by both the Western and Eastern Members, and with silent relief by the Northern Members. The Western Members were obviously pleased by the statement that the problems of Lagos would be considered 'within the framework of the Constitution', while the Eastern Members applauded the reference to the dual function of Lagos and the announcement that expert advice would be sought.

11.   Both the Action Group and the N.C.N.C. later hailed the Government state-ment as a 'victory'. The intentions of the Action Group in the matter of achieving power in Lagos remains to be seen, and I am now not without hope that they will consult the Council of Ministers before introducing legislation in the Western House of Assembly affecting the Lagos Town Council. Although they were justified in arguing that the Government should be no less brisk about turning down an Eastern suggestion which would have involved changes in the Constitution than it had been in rejecting their own earlier proposals, they came out of this crisis rather better than they deserved. I was the less sorry about this because I was about to publish my decision on the Regional boundary between the North and the West. Two heavy knocks in quick succession might have caused the Action Group Ministers, both Regional and Central, to resign and to refuse to co-operate in working the Constitution. The Western Central Ministers have assured me that they do not want to break away. They went on to say, however, that the peoples of this country were never united until the British united them. Once this welding and unifying force has begun to release its hold 'the future is for deci-sion'. They fully recognise the great advantages from staying united with the other Regions, but 'if the sacrifice demanded of them were too great, they might have to be content with something less than the ideal'. I do not take this very seriously but the Action Group Ministers are afflicted with a persecution mania, claiming that it was Western money which built up the country but that the other Regions show no grat-itude for their sacrifice.

12.   It appears that the N.C.N.C. (whatever that is at present) consider that their aims in respect of Lagos are possible of achievement within the terms of the Government statement and intend to pursue those aims after expert advice has been obtained. It can be said that the difficult situation created by the motion has been overcome for the present but the N.C.N.C., though committed to a policy of giving the Constitution a 'fair trial', will not readily abandon their determination to alter the status of Lagos. Much will depend upon what happens to the N.C.N.C., to which the Eastern Ministers both Central and Regional, ostensibly belong. These Ministers are not, in my opinion, likely to continue indefinitely to pay lip service to the Party as operated by such people as Kola Balogun and Mbonu Ojike. (Where Azikiwe stands at present is uncertain). But responsible Ministers like Njoku and Arikpo have at present little influence outside their own Divisions (by the people of which they were 'drafted' into politics). Nwapa carries more weight with the public of the East, but all three of them, and the Eastern Regional Ministers, who are of like mind with him, will have to be careful about breaking away from the N.C.N.C. if the voters continue to back the noisy and irresponsible members of the Party. The Central Ministers from the West could help a great deal by recognising the difficult position in which their Eastern colleagues on the Council are placed, and I have been urging them to do this. The North is watchful, and, I quote, more neutral between East and West than formerly . . .

164 CO 554/404, no 5A   2 Oct 1952

[Nigerianisation]: CO note of a meeting with Sir S Phillipson and Mr Adebo to discuss recruitment for the Colonial Service in Nigeria

Sir Sidney Phillipson explained that, notwithstanding the policy of Nigerianisation of the Civil Service in Nigeria which had been adopted in accordance with the recommendations of the Foot Commission, local public opinion had recently indicated some dissatisfaction in regard to the recruitment of expatriate officers, and it had been alleged that cases had occurred where persons recruited in the United Kingdom for certain posts had appeared to be no better qualified for these posts than local candidates who had been turned down by the Nigeria Civil Service Commission. It had therefore been decided by the Council of Ministers that a Commission should be appointed to conduct an expert review of the policy of Nigerianisation of the Civil Service and the machinery for its implementation, and to make recommendations.

2. A general discussion followed in which the following points were made.

(1) Where set qualifications for a particular post could be laid down a uniform standard of selection would not be difficult; and where this was not already done, it might help in the case of Nigeria to lay down specific qualifications. On the other hand, too rigid insistence on exact qualifications might deprive Nigeria of good men.

(2) In the matter of general suitability, on grounds of character and background, it must be recognised that just as those responsible for selection in the United Kingdom would not claim to be able to judge the suitability of Nigerians, so those responsible for selection in Nigeria would not be in a position to assess the full suitability of United Kingdom candidates.

(3) Criticism in Nigeria had arisen not so much in respect of administrative officers but of departmental officers. It was stated, for instance, that accountants and customs officers had been sent out from the United Kingdom with no better qualifications than Nigerians who had already had long practical experience. It was however pointed out that in filling the lower ranks of the senior service it was not only a matter of finding people capable of doing the work of those ranks. Regard must be paid to the need to create a field from which officers could be selected for posts of the highest responsibility. Men who were promoted to the senior service late in their careers were at a disadvantage in this respect and it was therefore necessary to bring in some younger men by direct recruitment to a cadet class.

3. *Sir Sidney Phillipson* went on to explain that it was their present intention to recommend the establishment of a Public Service Commission in Nigeria and it would be necessary to satisfy this Commission that a uniform standard of selection was maintained.

It was suggested that it might assist if there was closer liaison with the Nigeria Office in London.[1] A possible arrangement would be for a representative of the Public Service Commission to be attached permanently to that Office, so that he would be available for consultation. When sending indents for recruits to the Colonial Office or to the Crown Agents Nigeria might then ask that in the case of such-and-such vacancies (i.e. vacancies for which there might be possible local candidates to be

---

[1] The Nigeria Office was opened in London in March 1950.

considered in competition with outside recruits), this representative should be consulted before a final selection was made.

It was made clear that, once a vacancy had been definitely remitted to the Secretary of State to select a candidate, there could be no question of his selection being subject to review or confirmation by the Public Service Commission.

4. A further point raised was the relationship of the Nigeria Civil Service to the unified Colonial services. *Mr. Adebo* felt that a unified service prejudiced the chances of Nigerians being appointed to senior posts. *Sir Charles Jeffries* said that in large Colonies the unifed service tended to create vacancies for senior posts by the transfer of officers on promotion to smaller Colonies, and he felt that on balance Nigeria would lose if it cut loose from the unifed service, especially in respect of the smaller Departments. *Mr. Adebo* said that in the case of the Colonial Audit Service it was understood that experience in more than one Colony was essential to promotion and that this automatically prejudiced the chances of Nigerians for promotion, as Nigerians were not members of the unified service and they could not be transferred to other Colonies. It was explained that the Colonial Audit Service was a special case, and it was suggested that Sir Sidney Phillipson and Mr. Adebo should discuss this point with the Director-General of Colonial Audit.

5. Mention was made of the position of Nigerian overseas students. *Sir Sidney Phillipson* said that it was their intention to recommend the establishment of a Register of overseas students so that the Nigerian Public Service Commission could take them into account when considering vacancies in Nigeria. This Register would cover students in the United States, Canada and other places overseas as well as in the United Kingdom. Clearly, the machinery for maintaining the Register would have to be closely linked with arrangements now under consideration for bringing the responsibility for supervising students under the Nigerian Commissioner's Office in London, leaving the placing of students in Universities in the hands of the Director of Colonial Scholars, at least for the time being. He considered that while the representative of the Public Service Commission in London, who would be closely associated with the work for students, might be changed periodically, the officer in charge of the executive work in connection with students should be permanent.

6. *Mr. Adebo* felt that it would be desirable to recruit more officers on short term contract, in order that they could be replaced in due course by the large number of Nigerian students now under training. He said the Crown Agents agreed that certain classes of appointment could be filled on contracts. *Mr. Whittle*[2] advised against this for appointments filled by the Colonial Office, as it would seriously handicap recruitment. The Sudan and the Gold Coast were already experiencing difficulty in this respect through eliminating or restricting the opportunities for pensionable employment for overseas officers. *Sir Charles Jeffries* felt that with the large expansion of the Civil Service in Nigeria it should not be difficult to absorb all Nigerians who were properly qualified for appointments.

7. Finally, *Sir Sidney Phillipson* referred to the possibility in future years of political opinion in Nigeria desiring to see the number of expatriate officers reduced more rapidly. No doubt ordinary wastage would help to solve this problem; and it must be remembered that if a material reduction in expatriate officers took place too quickly,

---

[2] R A Whittle, service in Uganda; principal, CO, 1939; ass sec (temporary), 1944; principal, 1956–1961.

there would not be enough qualified Nigerians to fill the senior posts. It had been suggested that Nigerians should be appointed as understudies to senior officers or that special compensation should be given to expatriate officers who were superseded by Nigerians. *Sir Charles Jeffries* said the Secretary of State clearly could not undertake to recruit expatriate officers if there was any possibility of unfair discrimination against them in the matter of promotion. *Captain Newbolt*[3] added that for so long as Nigeria wanted expatriate officers it was very important that they should be received in a spirit of welcome. *Sir Sidney Phillipson* expressed the hope that a spirit of partnership in the non-political sense would be built up between Nigerian and expatriate officers until the time came when Nigerians could stand entirely on their own feet.

---

[3] Capt A F Newbolt, assistant private secretary to the secretary of state, 1919–1930; principal, 1930; ass sec 1944; visited West Africa for the CO, 1946.

165   CO 554/312, no 8   21 Nov 1952
[Ministerial titles]: inward telegram no 1815 from A E T Benson to Mr Gorell Barnes on the impact of Sierra Leone policy on Nigeria

Following for Gorell Barnes.
Your secret and personal telegram No. 105.
Sierra Leone Ministers.
Frankly, this worries me. We have great difficulties here as a result of calling people who have only conciliar responsibility 'Ministers' instead of 'Members'. But, apart from this, I fear the immediate reaction here to calling officials in Sierra Leone 'Ministers' would be suggestion (which could be contradicted to the few who will listen but not the many who will not) that Sierra Leone had a more advanced constitution than Nigeria.

2.   Besides this, agitation might begin here for a parallel move, the intention being then to claim that the three official ministers, or some of them should be replaced by Nigerians, whilst officials became Permanent Under Secretaries. Compare with the Gold Coast.

3.   Notwithstanding the establishment here of separate ministers, intention is that ex-officio members will retain present titles, both at the centre and in the regions, and these members have executive duties and powers derived directly from the Governor and Lieutenant Governors. Clear and consistent effort is evident here, particularly on the part of the Western ministers at the centre to achieve for ministers individual executive responsibility. This effort reveals itself in numerous different ways and, inevitably, creation of separate ministries (repeat ministries) will be used as a spring-board for stronger attacks. Already we are countering demands to substitute in power of conferring ordinances 'the Minister' for 'the Governor'. Latest suggestion is to substitute 'Council of Ministers' for 'Governor in Council'. Strongest opposition is always expressed to powers conferred e.g. on the Financial Secretary, and from now on it will, I think, be almost impossible to confer any powers on the Chief Secretary by ordinance or regulation. If ex-officio members were called ministers the (? position) in this respect would be untenable.

4.   For these reasons, I should hope not to have to resist additional pressure which change of titles in Sierra Leone would inevitably put on us.

166   CO 554/241   21 Nov 1952

[Western region local government reform]: minute by E O Mercer on a possible threat to the powers of the central government and the danger of secession by the Western Region

Mr. Williamson

Mr. Oxley[1] and Mr. Hudson have now commented on Mr. Benson's reply (48) to our (46), (47) has not been commented upon by Nigeria.

It is clear that Mr. Benson is seriously disturbed lest objections by the Secretary of State, of which the Acting Governor's Legal Advisers are not convinced of the justification, should provoke a political crisis . . .

Mr. Oxley maintains his view that parts of the Bill[2] are *ultra vires* and still considers that assent should be withheld on that ground. He has discussed the matter with Mr. McPetrie, but will be very happy if, after Mr. Williamson and Mr. Gorell Barnes have considered his views, the papers are referred to Sir K. Roberts-Wray for final legal opinion.

The main political considerations seem to me to be two, and contradictory:—

(i) if the Lieutenant-Governor has to withhold his assent, the likelihood of an immediate first-class crisis provoked by Mr. Awolowo and other Western Ministers in the Region and at the Centre,

(ii) if assent is given, the fact that a dangerous concession will have been made to the power of Regional Governments, with the effect of seriously weakening the power of the Centre. One step will in fact have been taken towards making it a rubber stamp.

Apart from the question of assent, it seems to me that, if Sir K. Roberts-Wray upholds Mr. Oxley's opinion, we must not fail to make Central Ministers aware of the dangers to themselves implicit in the Bill, which contains within it not a little of what we know to be the Action Group's and Western Region's ideas for greater regional autonomy, possibly with the latent idea of facilitating a later secession. On the question of assent itself, it seems to me that if Mr. Oxley's view is upheld assent must be withheld.

In the circumstances I have not drafted a reply to (46) until you and others have seen these papers.

---

[1] H L M Oxley, assistant legal adviser, CRO.   [2] See 159.

167   CO 554/241   27 Nov–1 Dec 1952

[Western Region local government reform]: minutes by W L Gorell Barnes and Sir T Lloyd on the CO reaction to the Western Region local government bill

Sir K. Roberts-Wray
Sir T. Lloyd
You have not yet seen the Western Region Local Government Bill, of which a copy is behind (15) and which looks like landing us into a constitutional crisis in Nigeria.

[2.] We first heard of this Bill when Mr. Sorensen asked a question in the House about it (see exchange of telegrams with Sir J. Macpherson at (6) and (7)); and you will see from (7) that although the Bill was about to be introduced into the Western House of Assembly on the day on which he telegraphed, it had not then been referred to the Central Government.[1] In the letter at (8) I expressed, in the mildest possible way, the hope that we should have an opportunity of looking at the Bill with the help of our Local Government Advisory Panel; and in (14) the Governor's deputy said that he would wish to have the Secretary of State's comments and those of the Advisory Panel on the Bill which had by then passed through both Houses of the Regional Legislature before he assented to it (not actually the correct phrase—see below). Copies of the Bill finally reached us on the 25th September under cover of the savingram at (15) which asked only for the comments of the Secretary of State's Local Government Advisory Panel. The Department then arranged for the Bill to be examined as rapidly as possible both by that Panel and by the Legal Department.

[3.] At this point I should digress to summarise briefly the procedure laid down in the Nigerian Constitution for the consideration of Regional Bills. Section 96(1) lays down that, when a Bill has been passed by both Legislative Houses of a Region, the Lieutenant-Governor shall send it to the Governor (that is, in this context, the Governor in Council—see Section 146(2)) who may object to the Bill on any one of three grounds, of which one is that it relates to any matter with respect to which the Legislature of the Region has no power to make laws. Sub-Section(3) of the same section states that the validity of any objection which is taken to a Bill under this section shall not be called in question in any court. If the Governor does not object to the Bill it is presented to the Lieutenant-Governor for assent. If the Governor objects to the Bill and decides that the ground for his objection cannot be eventually removed by amendment of the Bill, then the Bill lapses. If the Governor objects and decides that the ground for the objection can be removed by amendment of the Bill, the Legislative Houses of the Region are informed, via the Lieutenant-Governor, of the required amendments and, if those amendments are duly and properly made, the Bill is presented to the Lieutenant-Governor for assent. When a Bill is presented to the Lieutenant-Governor for assent, he, acting in his discretion, but subject to any instructions addressed to him through a Secretary of State, can either assent, refuse to assent or reserve the Bill for the signification of Her Majesty's pleasure (Section 101(1)). Finally, under Section 102(1), any law to which the Lieutenant-Governor has given his assent may be disallowed by Her Majesty through a Secretary of State.

[4.] To revert now to the main story, the Western Ministers in the Council of Ministers, no doubt fearing the consequences if the Bill has not become law by the time of Mr. Awolowo's return from his grand tour on the 6th December, began to become restive at the end of October (see letter and telegram from Mr. Benson at (43) and (45)). (They were apparently informed (though not with much justification) that the Secretary of State had insisted on being consulted at this stage). Having worked fast, we had by this time got the comments both of the Local Government Advisory Panel and of the Legal Department; and at this point I would refer you to the comments of the Advisory Panel at (42) and of the Legal Department in Mr. Oxley's minute of the 21st October. After I had considered these comments in consultation with all concerned, it became clear that there was considerable doubt about the wisdom of some of the provisions about the position of local authorities in regard to the maintenance of law and order, about the functions which it was proposed to entrust to local authorities in regard to matters of customary law, and about the proposed arrangements for the control of local authorities' staffs. More serious, it was the view of the

---

[1] See 159.

Legal Department that several provisions of the Bill were *ultra vires* the Regional Legislature. These points are discussed in the exchange of telegrams at (46) and (48), in Mr. Oxley's minute of the 21st November with which should be read paragraphs 4–10 of the superseded draft flagged X below, and in Mr. Hudson's minute of the 20th November. After discussing the matter further with all those concerned, I have come to the conclusion that the right course is for the Secretary of State to send a formal despatch to the Acting-Governor on the lines of draft A opposite, and for this despatch to go out to Nigeria under cover of a personal letter from myself to Mr. Benson on the lines of draft B opposite. Meanwhile I would propose, subject to approval, to telegraph to Mr. Benson on the lines of draft C opposite.

[5.]   I hope these drafts are self-explanatory. The only point on which I myself feel any real doubt at all is the point at which the Secretary of State would intervene, if he had to intervene formally under the terms of the Constitution. The relevant passage in the draft despatch at A is based on the assumption that he would intervene by instructing the Lieutenant-Governor not to assent to the Bill. By the passage at Y in his minute of the 21st November Mr. Oxley implies that the Secretary of State could intervene by instructing the Governor in the exercise of his powers under Section 96(2) of the Constitution; but I cannot myself see how this is possible having regard to the fact that 'Governor' in this context means 'Governor in Council'.

[6.]   Whilst I myself have no wish to question the advice tendered by the Legal Department on any count but this, the action which we are bound to take on this advice may cause a constitutional crisis in Nigeria (though personally I am hopeful that, as our objections are, at any rate in the main, constitutional objections and not policy objections, it may not do so). I therefore think it right to submit the papers through Sir K. Roberts-Wray so that he can confirm the validity of this advice.

[7.]   Whilst I have consulted those concerned individually on nearly all the points of particular interest to them during the course of thinking out the drafts submitted opposite, there has not actually been time to circulate those drafts for comments. I am accordingly now sending copies of this minute and of the three drafts to Mr. Williamson, Mr. Oxley and Mr. Hudson. If Mr. Oxley has any comments he will no doubt send them direct to Sir K. Roberts-Wray. If Mr. Williamson or Mr. Hudson have any comments, I should be grateful if they would let me have them as soon as possible.

W.L.G.B.
27.11.52

Secretary of State

I must trouble you with this because there is a possibility (though not in my view a serious risk) of a clash of interest between the Western Region of Nigeria and the Central Government; that clash might (though this again I regard as unlikely) lead on to a constitutional crisis for which the Western Region Ministers would blame us rather than Lagos.

The issue is whether the Western Region Local Government Bill can be allowed to reach the Statute Book in its present form or whether (and this is the course we strongly advise), either many clauses in it must be deleted or the Central Legislature must pass a law bringing within the competence of the Western Regional Legislature matters with which those clauses deal.

You need not, I suggest, read more than the third, fourth and fifth paragraphs of

Mr. Gorell Barnes' minute of the 27th of November and paragraphs 1–3 and paragraphs 14–15 of the draft despatch.

I hope that you will also have time to look at the draft telegram (marked C) and the draft semi-official letter (marked B). As stated in the latter we cannot afford to let this slide if only because to do that would be to defeat the intentions, and the letter, of the constitution in the matter of the division of powers between the Centre and the three Regions.

This is urgent in that if the Council of Ministers is to intervene, as we are suggesting, they must do so by the 13th of December (see No. 49) and that gives us very little time within which to get the despatch out to Nigeria to amend it if necessary to meet local views (see the penultimate paragraph of Draft B) and to circulate the despatch and other documents to the Council of Ministers for their consideration next week.

May we proceed as in these three drafts?[2]

T.K.L.
1.12.52

---

[2] Lyttelton minuted 'Yes'.

168 CO 554/662, no 2   28 Nov 1952
[Press attacks]: circular by L H Goble[1] to all civil secretaries on the Nigerian government's response to press attacks. *Appendix* B

Certain Government Officers may, in moments of depression, wonder why in given cases either no overt action, or what may appear to them to be only half-hearted action, is taken about the deliberate misrepresentation of Government policy and attempts to discredit the servants of Government which are a feature of certain sections of the Press to-day. The purpose of this Circular is to tell officers what action is possible and what is not possible, and to describe some of the difficulties there are in dealing with Press Attacks of the kind made in Nigeria to-day.

2.   Press attacks are of two kinds: first, those on Government policy generally; and, second, those on the character and/or behaviour of individual officers. The procedure in relation to the first may be summed up briefly as follows. If the matter appears primia facie to be seditious, it is referred immediately it comes to notice to the Law Officers; thereafter:—

(a) in certain cases a prosecution is instituted;

(b) in certain cases a Press Release directly correcting the misrepresentations is issued;

(c) in certain cases misstatements are corrected by indirect means.

Failing all these

(d) in certain cases no further action is taken. These different lines of action are dealt with in the following paragraphs.

3.   *Sedition.* For the past eighteen months a system has been in operation whereby the whole of the Nigerian Press is examined by the Central and Regional Security Officers and all prima facie seditious matter is, through certain channels, brought to the notice of the Attorney-General, together with any political

---

[1] L H Goble, administrative secretary, Nigerian government, 1952..

considerations which the Administration sees fit to bring to his notice. The decision whether to prosecute or not is, however, solely a matter for the Attorney-General. The considerations which he must take into account in making his decision were discussed in a speech which Sir Hartley Shawcross made in Parliament on the 29th of January, 1951, and a copy of the relevant parts of this speech are attached to this circular as Appendix 'A'[1] to enable officers to appreciate these considerations. The Attorney-General has usually given his fiat for a prosecution if he is satisfied both that the matter in question is in fact seditious and that there is a reasonable prospect of a conviction, followed by a substantial penalty. The latter point is important, for the public interest suffers if there is an acquittal or a conviction followed by a fine of only a few pounds. Technically seditious matter appears frequently in the local press but much of it does not warrant prosecution. It is of interest to note that since the beginning of 1950 there have been 10 prosecutions of newspapers for sedition or similar offences involving 6 different newspapers. All the prosecutions have been successful, one editor has gone to prison (for four months) and a total of £1,930 has been exacted in fines. Newspapers fear these prosecutions and a successful one usually has a sobering effect which may last for several months.

4. *Press releases.* In certain circumstances, but only in certain circumstances, a press release may be of value. This is particularly so when it is important that the general public should know the true facts in full. As against this the fact that the release is accurate and true is unfortunately often outweighed by the fact that editors are growing steadily cleverer in counteracting its effect. They preface the release with 'Officialdom states' and conclude it with an editorial note designed to confirm readers of the paper in their acceptance of the original misrepresentation. Sometimes it is, of course, not only useless but positively dangerous to follow up the editorial note with a further correction: to enter into a wrangling match of this nature is to play into the editor's hands. Moreover, to ensure publication these press releases have to be paid for at advertisement rates, and there is no point in financing the operations of such newspapers. The question of time is also particularly important. It may be that a newspaper misrepresents an incident that has occurred in a distant province in the North: if a report on the facts is called for by this office it may take several weeks before a reply can be received, and a press release at that late date may merely result in giving renewed and wider publicity to a matter which may have been forgotten or never noticed. (Individual officers can help to prevent such delays by informing the Secretariat concerned of the true state of affairs without loss of time).

5. It will be seen that the publication of a press release must depend on the particular circumstances of each case; and because of the disadvantages inherent in this procedure it must frequently happen that the right course is to eschew it, and to go for indirect press releases.

6. *Indirect releases.* It is often more effective to counteract a misrepresentation by indirect means than by an outright contradiction. For example, there may be a release to all newspapers on a matter in which an account of the true state of affairs in a particular case is inserted without reference to the particular newspaper's misrepresentation. Then again there are letters to the paper by private individuals. There is no need to go into details but a close examination of the Press by the understanding eye will reveal how much is achieved by these oblique methods. Cases

---

[1] Appendices A and C not printed.

have occurred not infrequently when the offending newspaper itself finds published in its columns an article or a letter which directly contradicts its own offending article of a day or two previously.

7. *'Masterly inactivity.'* Suffice it to say that if all the above lines of action have been considered and discarded for one decisive reason or another this is the only course open. But beyond this there is the consideration that to correct every trifling error in the Press will not increase the public's confidence in, or affection for, the Government—it merely gives it the reputation of having a thin skin and a bad conscience. Action can be taken only on the more serious cases: minor matters are better, at present, ignored when account is paid to the fact that, apart from the 'Daily Times' no Nigerian newspaper has a circulation of more than some 18,000 copies, a certain number of which are taken on Government subscription.

8. Such is the position as it is at present. It all hangs ultimately on whether legal process is the appropriate remedy in a given case or not. The question may naturally be asked 'Why not change the law?' The answer is that that possibility has been very carefully considered continuously over the past few years but the conclusion still is that, for the present at any rate, new restrictive press legislation would be more likely to worsen the situation than to mend it. Local editors will not lack skilled advice from outside this country on how to turn it upon its originators. Some of the major disadvantages of Press Legislation are set out in the extract from a Colonial Office paper which is attached. (Appendix B).

9. *Attacks on individual officers.* These may be simply seditious attacks on Government in another form, and if they are, then the considerations outlined in the preceding paragraphs will apply. But where the attack is not seditious, but libellous, the procedure is entirely different. The law of libel is singularly difficult and complicated and no attempt can be made to summarise it here. It is necessary in the first place to distinguish mere vulgar abuse from statements which amount, in law, to defamatory allegations. In the first case it is useless to take legal action as it would almost certainly fail. Government fully realises how upsetting such attacks can be and how difficult it is to bear them with equanimity; but no action can usefully be taken. In the second case, if the allegations are unfounded, the officer libelled may in the circumstances set out in Appendix C, be sure of Government's support, both moral and material.

10. Appendix C is a note on legal proceedings arising out of the defamation of Government officers. It will be appreciated that the note deals with official *assistance* to Government officers, and not with the right of Government officers to institute civil proceedings at their own expense which, subject to the provisions of General Order 49, is exactly the same as that of any other individual in Nigeria.

11. It is emphasised that in the case of a libellous attack on a Government officer the initiative rests and must continue to rest with the aggrieved officer. If the facts are presented by him to the Law Officers, the Law Officers will examine them and will, provided that the conditions set out in Appendix C are fulfilled, recommend that His Excellency should authorise the officer to take legal proceedings and to receive legal aid. If, therefore, an officer considers that he has been libelled in the course of his duty he should put up his case giving the full facts, with the least possible delay through the Civil Secretary or Chief Secretary who, if the circumstances warrant it, will forward it to the Law Officers.

Appendix B to 168: Extract from memorandum attached to a letter from Mr Creech Jones to Sir J Macpherson, 24 February 1949

The press in the African colonies

Press Legislation

35. The methods mentioned above may not be all immediately practical. Nevertheless they represent, in howsoever small a degree they may be applied, a definite advance over any form of restrictive legislation.

36. Such legislation may be inevitable, for the time being, and may be effective in a country where the Press is very primitive. It is, however, not in accord with the spirit of the times. It is entirely non-constructive and can never result in the establishment of a responsible press, even though it may more or less effectively curb the activities of an irresponsible one.

37. Apart from hostile reaction in foreign countries, it is almost invariably greeted by adverse press comment in the United Kingdom: and serves to foster, among the millions of people in the United Kingdom who have no idea of the Colonial background, ideas of reaction and repression.

38. It can only be effective too, in inverse ratio to the acumen of the editors at which it is aimed.

It is not difficult for an editor, not only to evade restrictive press laws, but to make their operation ridiculous.

39. Even the 'right of rejoinder' is a two-edged weapon. Legislative powers to enforce publication of a correction to an untrue statement may be effective for a time. But in a Colony with a well developed press, there is a real danger that an intelligently malicious editor may publish, with the correction, another equally untrue and perhaps quite fantastic statement which he will be ordered to contradict the next day; thus reducing the whole business to absurdity.

40. There is also the danger that if one untrue statement is compulsorily corrected, the remainder of the paper, which may contain many half truths or perversions of the truth, will be given a sort of hall-mark as *not* having been denied by the Government.

41. In this connection (while it may be thought necessary in some cases to maintain the 'right of correction') consideration might be given to enlisting the co-operation of independent but knowledgeable and authoritative persons (for example, pensioners, or well-disposed legislative councillors) to write quickly letters of correction.

It is recognised however, that this course may present difficulty and will be in some cases ineffective.

42. It will often be found more efficacious not to try and chase a mis-statement by a denial: but to grasp the opportunity, which some fresh piece of news may give, to re-state the whole matter in its correct form by means of a press conference or communique.

169 CO 1039/2, no 72 3 Dec 1952

[Powers of central ministers]: conclusions of a meeting of the Council of Ministers [Extract]

[From the start of the operation of the 1951 constitution, ministers pressed to be allowed to issue instructions to heads of departments; the governor however, saw ministers primarily as advisers whose job was simply to formulate policies within a conciliar system. This raised broader issues of the relationship between ministers and officials and the degree of power allowed to ministers under the constitution. This came to ahead, as this extract shows, during a debate over the Commonwealth Economic Conference and Nigeria's membership of the sterling area, with Bode Thomas's surprise at learning that secret correspondence passed between the governor and the secretary of state which was not made available to ministers.]

1. *Commonwealth Economic Conference*

The *Minister of Transport*[1] said that he found it most embarrassing to be asked to advise on this subject at such short notice and he was not satisfied that it was in the interests of the country to be part of the sterling area. He did not consider Nigeria had been fairly treated by being asked to advise on this subject without more warning, particularly when the plans for the Conference had been laid some time in advance. He wanted it put on record that since the last meeting of the Council when he had learned that some correspondence passed between the Secretary of State and the Governor which was not automatically seen by Ministers he had been seriously considering his position and felt that he would have no alternative but to resign. He was most disappointed in the way the Council of Ministers was expected to work both in this regard and in the way decisions could be asked for at such short notice. He found himself in some difficulty in continuing to support this Government if this were the way it was to be treated.

The *President*[2] drew the Minister's attention to the fact that at any time during the eleven months in which this Council had been in existence he and every other member of the Council had been at liberty to put forward a paper on the subject of the sterling area if he wished the Council to decide to leave the sterling area. The position with regard to the subject before the Council was that Nigeria was today within the sterling bloc, and, being a member, its views had been requested. He himself regretted as much as anyone the shortness of notice and the Secretary of State had expressed his regret that the time was so short, but had pointed out that Her Majesty's Government was not in a position to decide whether or not to include the proposal on the Agenda of the Conference until it had been fully prepared by the official experts . . .

7. *Governor in Council and Council of Ministers*

Previous reference: CM(52)65th Meeting, Conclusion 4(1) (i).

The Council had before them a memorandum by the Acting Attorney-General, CM(52)469.

The *Minister of Transport* said that it was now clear that there was a difference between the Governor in Council and the council of Ministers, and that it was now also clear to him that the Governor had a special position which was different from that which he held as President of the Council: the Governor might on specific occasion act by virtue of his special powers and not on the advice of the Council. He also felt that, from the information the Council had received that the Governor undertook personal correspondence with the Secretary of State, the Governor might act on instructions from the Secretary of State without taking or against the advice of the Council without informing the Council.

In continuance of the quotation of Clause 5(2)(a) from Royal Instructions, the Acting Attorney-General read extracts from clause 4 of the Royal Instructions, which set out when the Governor must consult with the Council of Ministers and when the

---

[1] ie Bode Thomas.   [2] ie A E T Benson.

Governor must act in accordance with the advice of the Council, and quotations from clause 5(1)—when the Council need not be consulted. The Acting Attorney-General also referred to the Letters Patent 1951.

The Minister expressed the view that the change in the Constitution should be reflected by reference in new legislation to the Council of Ministers in place of the Governor in Council.

The *President* said that it had always been known that under the Constitution there were certain powers reserved to the Governor. The Governor's reserved powers had never been used since the new Constitution had been introduced and it was in his personal view, inconceivable that the Governor would use these powers and go against the advice of the Council without giving to the Council his reasons. He could not commit Sir John MacPherson on this point, but he would make this discussion known to him.

He could not understand any feeling of suspicion which one or two members of the Council had voiced on the question of the Governor's own correspondence with the Secretary of State. It was quite clear that under the present Constitution any instructions which might be sent to the Governor from the Secretary of State could only take effect contrary to the advice of the Council in a case on which the Governor used his reserved powers. The Governor was bound to consult the Council on all matters save those quoted by the Attorney-General from the Constitutional Instruments.

A brief discussion followed on the question whether the legislature could remove the reserved powers from the Governor by writing in legislation the expression 'Council of Ministers' instead of 'Governor in Council' and it was suggested that as the Council from time to time was prepared to give up rights by giving duties under certain Ordinances to the Governor at his discretion, so the Governor might on other occasions give up his reserved powers by giving duties to the Council of Ministers instead of the Governor in Council.

On this point the view was put forward that if the Council decided to put into legislation the terms 'Council of Ministers' instead of 'Governor in Council', it might oblige the Governor to use his reserved powers in relation to that very decision itself. This would place him in a difficult position. If he did not use his reserved powers when the matter was before the Council, he might have to use them later, after the Ordinance had been passed by the legislature, when the Bill came before him for assent in Her Majesty's name.

The Council:—

Agreed that the discussion had been useful and agreed to leave the matter for the time being.

170 CO 554/241, no 50   4 Dec 1952
[Western Region local government reform]: despatch no 3529 from Mr Lyttelton to AET Benson proposing amendments to the Western Region local government bill

I have the honour to inform you that I have now completed my examination of the Western Region Local Government Bill, of which you were good enough to send me 20 copies in your confidential telegram No. 3876 Saving of the 23rd September.

2.   I warmly welcome the purpose of this measure which, as I understand it, is to provide the legislative framework within which a modern system of local government

can be developed within the Western Region as rapidly as circumstances permit. (I understand that similar developments are already being pressed forward in the Eastern Region under the legislation which was enacted by the Nigerian Legislature under the old Constitution.) I have also been much impressed by the care and thought which has clearly been devoted to the preparation of the Bill. It is therefore with the very greatest regret that I have reached the conclusion that the Bill as at present drafted raises important legal difficulties. I am sure, however, that it will be in the best interests of all concerned if I bring these difficulties to your notice and to that of your Government without further delay.

3.   The legislative powers of a Regional Legislature which are conferred by Section 91 of the Constitution are to make laws for the peace, order and good government of the Region with respect to any matters specified in the Third Schedule to the Constitution and to any matter declared by a Central law to be within the competence of a Regional Legislature. The Central Legislature is thus able to confer on a Regional Legislature any part of its own legislative power and, therefore, to enable a Regional Legislature to make laws for the peace, order and good government of the Region with respect to matters other than matters specified in the Third Schedule to the Constitution. But, so far as I am aware, the Central Legislature has not yet done so.

4.   This being so, I am advised that certain provisions of the present Bill are, or in some cases may be, *ultra vires* the Regional Legislature. My Legal Advisers have called attention to the provisions in the following list, which may not, however, be complete:—

(1) the prevention of crime (clause 58 and, consequentially, clause 161, clause 57 is much less questionable since it is, in the main, restricted in its operation to the limits of the Councils functions).

(2) the declaration and modification of local customary law (except as respects customary land tenures) (clause 60);

(3) the carrying and possession of weapons (clause 71(47));

(4) the migration of persons from or to the area of a council (clause 71(48));

(5) child betrothals (clause 71(74));

(6) native marriages, including dowry and divorce (clause 71(84));

(7) all matters for the peace, good order and welfare of persons within the area of a council (clause 71(86));

(8) Bye-laws (clause 77); subsection (1) so far as it enables bye-laws to be made under Central law and subsection (2) so far as it goes beyond the purpose of items 9 to 16 in the Third Schedule to the Constitution;

(9) title to land (clause 185(5));

(10) legal proceedings against a council, particularly as respects proceedings outside the Region (clauses 206 to 209 and possibly other provisions in Part VIII).

5.   It is reasonably clear that these matters do not fall within any item in the Third Schedule to the constitution unless they come within item 20. It may be argued that a Regional Legislature could, by virtue of item 22, give to native courts jurisdiction in some of the matters specifically referred to above: but I am advised that it is very doubtful how far that is the case and that, in any event, this question does not really arise, since those provisions are not related to the jurisdiction of native courts. The matters stated in item 20 are 'local government including the constitution and powers (including the power to levy rates) of native authorities,

township authorities, and other local authorities established for the purpose of local or village administration'. I am advised that under item 20 a Regional Legislature may confer on a local authority

(a) powers relating to any matter mentioned in the Third Schedule itself (including matters declared by a Central law to be within the competence of the Regional Legislature), and
(b) such additional powers as are necessary to enable the local authority properly to discharge its functions.

6.   None of the matters listed in the preceding paragraph appear to fall under either of these headings and the question arises whether any other powers may be vested in a local authority under item 20. On this question my Legal Advisers are of the following opinion:

(1) The answer to this question is in the affirmative, if only because, there being express limitation in most of the items after item 22 in the Schedule to matters mentioned in the Schedule, a court would be unlikely to hold that a similar limitation upon the scope of item 20 is to be implied.
(2) It is hardly necessary to state, however, that there must be some limitation, for if power on any subject whatever could be conferred upon a local authority under item 20, the restriction under the constitution upon the legislative field of a Region would be largely nullified. For this reason, there seems little, if any, doubt that the provision mentioned in sub-paragraph (7) of the above list, which would appear to cover any matter whatever, would be *ultra vires*.
(3) Further guidance may be obtained from other items in the Schedule. Thus, the express mention of customary land tenures in item 11 and the registration of marriages in item 21 would appear by clear implication to exclude the provisions regarding customary law betrothals and marriages referred to in sub-paragraphs (2), (5) and (6) in the list; and the definition in items 9 to 16 of the Schedule of subjects relating to land casts serious doubt on the validity of provisions regarding to land referred to in sub-paragraphs (8) and (9) of the list.
(4) Beyond this, the answer to the problem depends upon whether the subject concerned is one which may properly be regarded as coming within the expression 'local government'. It is difficult to draw a line between matters which satisfy this test and those which do not, but it is suggested that it is relevant to consider, first, whether the exercise of the power in question may affect the interests of authorities, persons or property outside the area of the local council and, secondly, whether the subject is one which has customarily been treated as a matter within the functions of native or other local government authorities. In illustration of this suggestion, my Legal Advisers refer to subjects specified in the definition in clause 2 of the Bill of 'local government purposes' most, if not all, of which would appear to satisfy the test, subject in some cases, such as paragraph (a), to certain limitations. They are of opinion that there is considerable doubt whether provision regarding migration of persons (sub-paragraph (4) above) is valid, since it may affect persons outside the local council's area. Moreover, the question of movement of persons from place to place within Nigeria seems to be a matter of direct concern to the Central Government, especially where movement from one Region to another may be involved. With regard to sub-paragraph (8) so far as it relates to subsection (1) of clause 77, a Central law may deal with any subject, and

it seems clearly *ultra vires* for a Regional law to confer power to make bye-laws for the purposes of a Central law which vests functions in a council in matters not within the competence of the Regional Legislature. Any such power should be conferred by Central law. The remaining sub-paragraphs, namely (1) and (3), would appear to depend largely upon whether the subjects in question have in the past been treated in Nigeria as matters of local government, a question upon which your Legal Advisers are, of course, in a better position than mine to advise.

7.   In most respects these legal difficulties could, of course, be overcome by Central legislation, passed under section 92 of the constitution before the provisions in question are enacted, declaring these matters to be within the competence of the Regional Legislature; but in the case of clause 71(86) of the Bill, there are special considerations. The purport of this paragraph, when read with clause 77 of the Bill, is to enable a council to be given a power to make bye-laws which is virtually unlimited as to its field. It follows that, in order to bring the matters covered by the clause within the competence of a Regional Legislature, the Central Legislature would have to pass an enactment conferring upon that Regional Legislature powers which were similarly unlimited. It may well be argued that it would not be within the letter of the Constitution Order in Council for the Central Legislature to confer such powers upon a Regional Legislature, on the ground that the words 'any matter' in section 92 imply that the Central Legislature is to consider each subject individually and cannot properly make a declaration embracing every matter. Even if it is thought that this argument would be unsound, such a step is one which the Council of Ministers would no doubt wish to ponder most carefully before proposing. If they decided against it and it were still desired to confer these powers upon local authorities in the Western Region, they could, of course, be conferred by a Central Act (as they have been in the East).

8.   There is an additional point concerning Clause 71 (84) of the Bill. In view of the words, 'including ... divorce' which appear in this paragraph, I am advised that, so long as this paragraph stands part of the Bill, the Bill will come within paragraph 7(1) (a) of the Royal Instructions to the Lieutenant-Governor dated 27th November, 1951, and that accordingly the Lieutenant-Governor would be obliged to obtain Her Majesty's instructions before assenting to the Bill. As will be seen from paragraph 12 of this despatch, I have some doubts about the wisdom of entrusting the local authorities, at any rate in the early stage of their development, with the power to regulate and control such matters as native divorce. But, provided it is made clear that the paragraph applies only to *native* divorce I should not on this account alone consider that the Lieutenant-Governor should be instructed to withhold assent from the Bill.

9.   I now turn to the substance of the individual provisions of the Bill. I have already sent you under cover of my telegram No. 332 Saving of the 6th November the comments of the Local Government Advisory Panel. I hope that these comments will be found helpful and will be taken into account in the implementation of the Bill; and that such of the changes which they recommend as may be acceptable will be incorporated in the measure at the first suitable opportunity.

10.   There are only one or two points of substance on which I would wish to offer comment. These are dealt with in the immediately following paragraphs.

11.   I invite your attention to the comments of my Local Government Advisory Panel on Clauses 57(1) and 160 of the Bill. The Native Authority police have hitherto come under the traditional native authorities who, as part of the system of indirect

rule, were traditionally responsible for maintaining law and order. This responsibility was recognised and confirmed in the Native Authority Ordinances. The effect of the measure at present under consideration will be that in Western Nigeria, as in many other parts of Africa, many of the functions hitherto carried out by native authorities will in future be carried out by local authorities with a majority of elected members. But the field of activity of these new bodies will not be the same as those of the traditional authorities: they will have some functions which the traditional authorities did not have and which in the past, if they have been performed at all, have been performed by the Central Government on the other hand, not all the functions performed by the traditional authorities can suitably be performed by authorities composed mainly of elected members. In this connection it appears to me that the functions to be allotted to local authorities in respect of the maintenance of law and order and the employment of police require very careful consideration. Whilst I welcome the wide powers of control given to the Regional Commissioner of Police by the present Bill, there seems to me to be some possibility, under the terms of the Bill as at present drafted, that the local police might become the agents of local authorities with elected majorities, instead of remaining guardians of the Queen's peace. For example, the fact that under Clause 160 as at present drafted members of the force will be required to obey all lawful orders of councils whose functions are to include those in Clause 57(1) and may include those in Clause 71 (46) might give rise to the danger that a council, on the pretext of preventing breaches of the peace, might give directions to the police for political reasons rather than for the maintenance of the Queen's peace. The whole problem of the part to be played by local authorities in the maintenance of law and order and of the relationship of those authorities with the local and national police is one of considerable complexity, about which I hope to address you further in due course. Meanwhile I suggest, for consideration, that the above considerations should be borne in mind in the implementation of the Bill and that, as soon as a suitable opportunity presents itself, the words 'the council and' should be deleted from Clause 160 of the Bill. I would also suggest that, at the first suitable occasion, Clause 162 should be amended so as to have effect only within the area of the council's authority since there seems to be a danger under the present wording of members of local forces seeking to exercise their powers outside that area.

12.   In their comment on Section 60 of the Bill my Local Government Advisory Panel raised the question whether it is appropriate that local councils consisting mainly of elected members should become the bodies to make declarations and modifications of native customary law. The same question suggests itself in regard to such questions as child betrothals (Clause 71 (74)) and native marriages, including dowry and divorce (Clause 71 (84)). This is a question on which there may be many views and on which I should certainly not wish to be dogmatic. I cannot help wondering, however, whether these are matters which are more suitably dealt with either by legislatures or by traditional authorities.

13.   Finally, I wish to refer briefly to those provisions in Part IX of the Bill which are concerned with the appointment of local authorities staff and with arrangements for maintaining discipline amongst such staff and for regulating their conditions of service, promotion, etc. It is always a matter of some difficulty to devise arrangements which, whilst leaving adequate authority to the local government bodies themselves, provide sufficient insurance against undue political influence being brought to bear on staff matters either from within those bodies or from

outside. I feel sure that all concerned with operating this part of the Bill will be fully conscious of the undesirability of local government staff being subjected to undue political influence and that, if it is found that this point is not adequately safeguarded by the present provisions, the desirability of amending them will be considered. I therefore confine myself to drawing attention to the importance of this matter.

14. I should be glad if you would bring the contents of this despatch to the attention of the Council of Ministers when they have this Bill under consideration. The points to which I have drawn attention in paragraphs 9 to 13 above seem to me to be of some importance; but I have not, on these points, thought it necessary or proper for me to do more than to put forward suggestions which, if they are acceptable, will, I hope, be either taken into account in the implementation of the Bill or borne in mind when an opportunity arises to amend it. The points which I have raised in paragraphs 2 to 8 above are, however, of a different kind; and as at present advised, I do not see how the Bill can properly be allowed to reach the statute book unless and until most, and perhaps all, of the provisions listed in paragraph 4 above have been deleted or the Central Legislature has passed a law bringing the matters with which they deal within the competence of the Regional Legislature; and, as is pointed out in paragraph 7 above, there is substantial doubt whether such a law of the Central Legislature would be valid so far as clause 71(86) is concerned. I am advised that it is also open to question whether a law relating to a subject brought within the competence of a Regional Legislature under section 92 of the constitution would be valid if the Bill had been passed by that Legislature before the date of the enactment of the Central law, even if it is assented to after that date.

15. I greatly hope that it will prove possible to overcome these difficulties without undue delay so that the constructive work of setting up a modern system of local government in the Western Region of Nigeria can go forward; and I suggest for consideration that the Bill should now proceed with the provisions which would or might be invalid deleted, and that an amending Bill should be introduced if and when a Central law has been enacted under section 92.

171   CO 554/599, no 9   22 Dec 1952
[Eastern Region crisis]: inward telegram no 1974 from Sir J Macpherson to Mr Lyttelton reporting the NCNC's expulsion of three central ministers

[This telegram, reporting the start of the Eastern Region crisis that continued for most of 1953, refers to the opening shots in the struggle between those members of the NCNC willing to operate the constitution as far as possible, and those determined to show it was unworkable. The ensuing split in the NCNC raised numerous issues and not least that of party control over central ministers.]

You will have seen reports of expulsion of Nwapa, Njoku and Arikpo, Central Ministers, from the N.C.N.C. Party. This was attempted by Zik at the Annual N.C.N.C. Convention held at Port Harcourt in September, but failed when the Convention, which was well attended, decided to support the Constitution. Further Convention thereupon called by Zik at Jos for the 10th December, fortuitously attended by only three members of the Eastern House of Assembly and one Eastern Minister without Portfolio, Awgu. Remaining delegates mainly Zikist, including number of Lagos

Yorubas. Jos Convention decided not to work the Constitution and to expel the three persons named.

2.   On the 20th December, meeting at Enugu attended by the three persons named, all Regional Members except (possibly, though this is not yet clear) Awgu and one other, and many leading members of the Eastern House passed vote of solidarity with, and confidence in, the three persons named.

3.   Appreciation follows by air mail earliest possible. In the meantime, view commonly expressed is that this time Zik has over-reached himself.

172   CO 554/744, no 9   15 Jan 1953
[Islam in Nigeria]: Nigerian government note on Muslim religious, social and political movements in Nigeria   **[Extract]**

. . . 9.   It will be clear from the preceeding paragraphs that Moslem movements cannot be considered solely in their Northern Regional or Western Regional setting, or in their Nigerian setting. The unity of Islam and the equality of all true believers in it are ideas which tend to transcend national frontiers and, as communications improve, Nigerian Moslems appear to be responding more and more strongly to the international currents of thought which affect Islam today.

10.   One of the first signs that the conservative Moslems in the Northern Region were becoming aware of political currents in the outside world was observed in 1948 when prayers were said in Northern mosques for the success of the Arab struggle against the Jews. Nigerian Moslems form by far the largest block of Moslems south of the Sahara and the attention which Moslems from outside the area have recently paid to them is a recognition not only of this fact but of the fact that Nigerian Moslems themselves are becoming increasingly aware of their own importance as a group. The visit of the Algerian Tijani, Sidi ben Omar in 1950 marked a great increase of intercourse between the Tijanis of Morocco, French West Africa and Nigeria. Egypt has also been showing very considerable interest in the affairs of Nigerian Moslems. Most of the approaches from this direction have been made in the name of Al Azhar University in Cairo. As early as 1948 the University was in correspondence with the Society for Promoting Moslem Knowledge, a Yoruba organisation with Ahmadiyya leanings, based on Lagos, and the suggestion was made that students might be sent to Cairo for Islamic education. Nothing came of this move. In 1950 the Egyptian Ambassador in London informed the Foreign Office that a Lagos body known as the 'Supporters of Islam' (which, as far as is known, does not exist) and the so-called Muslim Congress of Nigeria at Ijebu-Ode in the Western Region had asked for ulemas (professors) to be sent to Nigeria to teach in Islamic schools.[1] In 1951 Al Azhar, with the backing of the then King Farouk, made a further effort to impress itself upon Nigeria and offered scholarships on a large scale apparently to both the Muslim Congress and the S.P.M.K. The Northern Moslem Congress, a Northern Region organisation closely connected with the political body known as the Northern Elements Progressive Union, was also apparently interested in these scholarships, but interest died down when Government made it known that University degrees obtained at Al Azhar could not be accepted as a qualification for employment in

---

[1] See 119.

Government service. But while the main Egyptian effort was directed towards the Yorubas of the Western Region, moderate Moslems in the Northern Region also showed interest and the Committee appointed to administer the Northern Self-Help Development Fund provisionally allocated £6,000 to finance the education of students in Islamic studies and did for sometime cast its eyes towards Al Azhar University. A Dr. M. El. Fahham, one of the ulemas of the University, toured Nigeria in 1951 ostensibly to examine the study of arabic education, but probably with the real purpose of co-ordinating arrangements for the award of scholarships.

11.   There have been indications in recent years that Moslem affairs within Nigeria are tending to assume a stronger political bias than formerly. In 1948 antagonism to Christian missionary penetration in the North first began to be openly voiced by a small minority in the Northern Regional House of Assembly. It has always been the aim of the Government of Nigeria to discourage religious intolerance and so far the policy has been pursued with success, but there are many indications that the intransigence of the reactionary elements among Moslems in the Northern Region is growing and is affecting local politics. The political dislikes of Northern Moslems are not confined to missionaries, however. Early in 1949 Moslems of all persuasions in the North made it clear that they took the strongest objection to the publication in the 'West African Pilot' of a series of public lectures by a supporter of the N.C.N.C. on the subject of 'Christ, Mohammed and Zik', which contained an intemperate attack on Islam and, in particular, on the character of the Prophet. Some of the Northern Moslem distrust for the political party known as the 'Northern Elements Progressive Union' can be traced to the fact that many of its aims are identical with those of the N.C.N.C. and that members of the N.E.P.U. who are also members of the Northern Moslem Congress have had contacts on a number of occasions with the Ahmadiyya-tainted Muslim Congress of Nigeria at Ijebu-Ode.

12.   Northern Moslem solidarity was still further strengthened about the middle of 1950 when pagan and Christianised groups in the 'Middle Belt' of the Northern Region, formed a Middle Zone League and began to make demands for the creation of a fourth region in which they could run their own affairs and be free from politi-cal domination by the Moslems of the North. Northern Moslems have taken this threat seriously and have done everything in their power to meet the legitimate demands of the peoples of the Middle Belt and to keep them within the Northern Regional fold.

13.   A further sign of the growing importance of Moslem opinion in Nigeria was the ready acceptance by the House of Representatives in August, 1952 of a Motion praying Government to meet Moslem wishes for a two day holiday on the occasion of each of the public holidays of Id el Kabir and Id el Fitr. Both the N.C.N.C. and the Action Group show awareness of these developments and in recent months their news-papers have shown themselves anxious to sympathise with the aspirations of Moslems.

14.   It would be quite untrue to say, however, that their [sic] exists in Nigeria today any political movement which can speak for a majority of the Moslems in Nigeria. The Moslems in the Northern Region are by far the most coherent group but political movements even in the North cannot be said to be inspired mainly by Islam. In the West and in Lagos Islam can only be said to have had a very minor effect on politics although there are, as Monsieur Mangin pointed out in his Report on Moslem movements in Nigeria, signs that the new generation of Yoruba Moslems now being educated in Moslem schools for the first time is likely to strengthen the solidarity of

Moslem opinion in the Western Region and to be much less tolerant than the present generation of educated Yoruba Moslems brought up in Mission schools.[2]

15.   It is probable that the views expressed in these paragraphs would confirm French Administrators trained by Professor Montagne and his colleagues at the School for Higher Moslem Studies in Paris in their belief that British West African Governments are insufficiently alive to the potential dangers of Moslem political and religious movements. They believe that the twin policies of assimilation and centralisation of power, which are so firmly written into the Chapter of the Constitution of the Fourth Republic dealing with the Overseas Territories, can only be realised by strangling the political aspirations of the rival centralising movement—Islam—which enjoins upon its adherents, as a sacred duty, its own religious, social and political unity. These views are clearly reflected in the instructions issued by the Ministry of Overseas France to the High Commissioner in French West Africa in September, 1950:—

> '. . . Our Islamic policy shall aim at preserving friendly but watchful relations with traditional Islam in view of the imminent dangers to the French cause arising from the spread in West and Central Africa of Islamic forms which are inspired by political programmes and anti-French ideas rather than by mystical ideas and confessional disciplines.'

French observers of Nigerian Moslem policy, including Monsieur Mangin, tend to assume that the conflict between these rival centripetal forces, which exists in French West Africa, exists in Nigeria. Monsieur Mangin does indeed note the 'very pro-Moslem feelings of the British . . .' but wrongly ascribes these feelings to 'the need to depend on the only stable political and social source of power able to implement Indirect Rule', namely the Emirs. In common with other French observers he tends to overlook the fact that our policy of determined non-intervention in matters of religion, so long as tolerance is shown, has proved itself a strong stabilising factor and gives little scope to religious extremists whose most potent asset would be intervention by European unbelievers. Nor does he give thought to the possibility that such subversive Moslem movements as may exist are far more likely to wither or be smothered by local Moslem opinion in the non-interventionist climate of thought which obtains in Nigeria.

---

[2] Louis Mangin, chef du bureau des affairs musulmanes, Afrique Occidentale Française. Mangin visited Nigeria early in 1952 for a report he was writing on Islam in West Africa.

173   CO 554/235, no 34   22 Jan 1953
[Local government]: Nigerian government report on the progress of local government reform in the Northern Region   [Extract]

Introduction
In August, 1950, the Northern Regional House of Assembly accepted the motion of M. Abubakar Tafawa Balewa calling for a commission of enquiry into the state of local government in the Northern Provinces of Nigeria. As a result, the Maddocks-Pott Report was prepared, giving a factual summary of the Native Administrations as they

stood in November, 1950.[1] The Report was then considered in July and August, 1951, by a Joint Select Committee of the Northern Regional Council.

2.   The recommendations of this Committee (which are given in the Appendix) are of great importance.[2] They have the combined approval and support of both Chiefs and members of the House of Assembly. They represent the considered opinion of all the most responsible leaders, traditional and elected, of the Region, and a Committee is now proposing a re-draft of the Native Authority Ordinance to ensure that its principles are embodied in the law. On these principles are based the policy for the next period of development of local government in the Region. They provide for a general pattern and it now rests with each Native Authority to implement the principles. The effectiveness must be dependent, if developments are to be genuine, upon the personnel available to staff and properly [sic] carry out the business of the newly created or re-organised local bodies. This will take time, but the art of government lies in the timing of each stage of development and no pre-arranged timetable can be laid down. The Native Authorities have shown—with one or two exceptions—that they are conscious of the dangers of remaining stationary or reactionary. The danger of impetuous advance, creating the form without the substance, is also recognised. As good bricks require straw, so do genuine local government bodies require a minimum of trained staff and literate members.

3.   The object of this present report is to summarise what progress has been made since the Maddocks-Pott report, up to mid-1952—a period of just over 18 months. It is proposed to give first a general view of the more important developments, followed by a summary of progress of each of the main types of administrative bodies, This is supplemented by a number of Appendices giving detailed notes of the more interesting council systems that are now being evolved, and an analysis of expenditure of District Council Funds from one Province to show what practical results are being achieved.

Part I

4.   Reviewing the state of Local Government in all its various stages after a period of eighteen months, there is no doubt that generally there has been considerable, if uneven, growth. Eighteen months is not a long period and to be able to present startling results would indicate a period of revolution instead of a process of evolution. Reports, however, from most areas show that in one level or another of the Local Government structure there has been solid progress. This development has been most noticeable in the higher levels in the establishment of Native Authority Advisory (Outer) Councils and in District and Urban Councils, but not so much at the village level. This is not surprising; education has hardly, if at all, touched the villages, and they remain the home of custom and tradition with little or no money to spend and few demands for change. It is at the centre of the district and in the urban areas that the urge of the people to be associated in public affairs is beginning to be felt, and it is here that there is enough money to produce results to make regular attendance at meetings worth-while. The Native Authorities, recognising this urge, have co-operated in meeting its needs.

5.   The administrations in the Northern Provinces may be, generally speaking,

---

[1] See 147. The report by K P Maddocks and D A Pott, *Report on Local Government in the Northern Provinces of Nigeria* (Kaduna, 1951) was completed in Dec 1950.   [2] Appendices not printed.

divided into two categories, the first, in which there are the highly-populated Emirates with financially sound and over-centralised Native Administrations, which require to delegate authority and functions; the second, in which are found the small units, some highly centralised in themselves but poor financially, independent and parochial in outlook and which require to federate and combine their meagre resources in order to be able to provide for common and essential services. In the one a degree of authority should be devolved to lower units; in the other surrendered to superior units.

6.   In the first category lie the 'classical' Emirates of the North. Here the Native Authorities have, with few exceptions, accepted the paradox that devolution of executive power and authority will, by satisfying modern local aspirations, self-expression and initiative result in the strengthening and not the weakening of their own authority. They have continued in increasing numbers to create district and urban councils, giving them greater financial and executive power in accordance with their cash and competence.

7.   Again, accepting a second principle of government, by no means easy for them, that the more the public is permitted openly to discuss and criticise administration, the stronger and more popular will be their position, they have established Advisory (Outer) Councils. These Councils contain members representative of the widest range possible of responsible public opinion, and usually have an elected majority. Leading traders, farmers, artisans; members sent up from District or Village Councils; representatives of 'minority tribes'; sophisticated members of the House of Assembly—all are to be found in these Advisory Councils, and they are at liberty to discuss all matters that affect their community. N.A. policy has thus been brought to the public forum, and local government need no longer be regarded as an esoteric art, the exclusive right of the aristocracy. It is now an occupation in which many who have the desire and the public support are now taking part, particularly in the Urban and District Councils. A comparison of the original with the most recent minutes of most councils where there has been adequate administrative supervision will prove this; so also the growing interest of the people in elections, particularly in the urban areas.

8.   Finally, perhaps the most significant evidence of progress is found in the motion of the Sultan of Sokoto, passed unanimously by the House of Chiefs in 1952, recommending that, in order to recognise the position of a chief as laid down by Moslem Law, the status of 'Sole Native Authority' be replaced by 'Native Authority in Council'. The House of Chiefs later assented to a bill originating in the House of Assembly, defining the functions of a Native Authority in Council. (See Appendix B). This legislation is a refutation of considerable force of the charge that has often been levelled against the Native Authorities of this Region that they enjoyed a position of absolute power in name and in law.

9.   The last eighteen months have, therefore, given proof in action and in outlook that the chiefs of the highly-centralised administrations are prepared to adapt themselves and their status to the changing conditions that are transforming a feudal society into a democracy.

10.   In the second category mentioned above lie most of the Middle Belt administrations—governing societies of a very mixed and heterogeneous nature. Here, as the following sections of this report will show, a variety of administrative systems have been, or are in the process of being created, in order to build up fragmentary societies into groups, federations or associations bringing with this

loose form of unity the political and financial strength that is necessary to meet the demands and requirements of the modern individual.

11.   In Ilorin the creation of groups and group area councils sending their own representatives to be members of the Native Authority 'Outer' Council has proved successful in uniting the intensely independent clans to the stronger central body of a Yoruba Emirate. In Kabba, five small independent Native Authorities and one Subordinate N.A. have agreed in principle to federate, and only the creation of a suitable form of federation is now lacking. In Plateau Province, the independent pagan tribes of Jos Division have held an inaugural meeting of an Advisory Council, and in Pankshin Division the primitive pagan chiefs have met quarterly for the past two years at a 'Conference of Chiefs' and are growing accustomed to discussing matters of common interest. In Numan Division of Adamawa Province, there were, two years ago, a variety of Native Authorities— a Chief in Council, a Council and three Chiefs. These have since merged into one Native Authority, a Council of Thirteen, covering the whole Division, the former authorities becoming Subordinate Native Authorities to the new Native Authority.

12.   In Benue, the need for some organisation to provide for common services beyond the resources of the individual authorities is leading to consideration of ways and means, possibly in the form of Joint Committees, and in Idoma there has been a strengthening of the Intermediate Council and the Native Authority Council in order to try to meet executive as well as judicial responsibilities. In Makurdi, an ingenious method of election described in detail in the Appendix E has been devised in order to satisfy both tribal loyalties and ward interests in an urban area of mixed peoples.

13. In Niger and Zaria, Provincial Councils have been evolved to meet the need for provincial discussion and agreement on matters of common interest. At present these bodies have no statutory recognition but it is probable that this will come in due course and with it, possible [sic: possibly], certain limited executive functions and authority. An interesting feature in the Niger organisation is that the political constituency is related to the administrative unit and there is an unbroken chain of representation from the lowest village council right up to the top provincial council, thence the provincial representatives go on to the Regional and Central Legislative bodies.

14. Thus one finds that during the past eighteen months, in every province, in one level or another, from bottom to top of the local government structure, the administrative units have been and are being consistantly subjected to criticism, enquiry, revision or complete reorganisation, with the guiding principle running through that the public be provided with the opportunity of associating themselves with their own government as soon as they become willing and competent to do so. . . .

174   CO 554/241, no 55   22 Jan 1953
[Western Region local government reform]: despatch no 195 from Sir J Macpherson to Mr Lyttelton reporting objections expressed by ministers on the handling of the Western Region local government bill

[The issue of the Western Region local government bill was considered at a meeting of the Council of Ministers on 16 Dec 1952. At this meeting L H Goble, the acting chief secretary and acting president of the council, reported that the secretary of state had declared the bill *ultra vires*; in response ministers, believing that the Council should have had the opportunity to examine the bill before the CO, 'expressed strong resentment at the manner in which this matter had been handled . . . the view was expressed that the action of the secretary of state indicated lack of confidence in the Council ... members felt therefore that the secretary of state should ... not do anything which might give the impression that the effective power in this country still lay with him' (CO 1039/2, no 74, conclusions of a meeting of the Council of Ministers). This despatch was the result.]

I have the honour to refer to your despatch No. 3529 of the 4th of December[1] in which you informed me of the legal difficulties raised by the Western Region Local Government Bill, and to inform you that the Bill was considered in the Council of Ministers on the 16th of December.

2.   The Council advised that for the reasons set out in your despatch I should object to the Bill under section 96(2)(a) of the Nigeria (Constitution) Order-in-Council. It agreed however that the grounds for objection to the Bill could conveniently be removed by amendment of the Bill in the following manner:

Clause 15	In paragraph (c) *for* 'Nigeria' *substitute* 'the Region'.
Clause 60	In sub-clauses (1) and (2) *for* 'any subject' *substitute* 'land tenure'.
	In sub-clause (3) *for* the subject to which it relates' substitute 'land tenure' wherever the phrase occurs.
Clause 71	*Delete* paragraphs (48), (74), (84) and (86).
Clause 77	In sub-clause (1) *delete* 'or Ordinance.
	Delete sub-clause (2).
Clause 161	*Delete*', or to exercise the powers of an authorised officer within the meaning of the Protectorate Laws (Enforcement) Ordinance, or both' and 'Cap. 180.' in the marginal note.
Clause 174	*Delete* sub-clause (1)
Clause 185	*Delete* sub-clause (5).
Clauses 206 to 209 inclusive	*Delete*

I have therefore informed the Lieutenant-Governor, Western Region, in accordance with section 99(1) of the Order in Council, that I object to the Bill on the grounds that it relates to matters in respect of which the Western Regional Legislature has no power to make laws; and I have sent him a statement of the required amendments.

3.   The Council would be prepared to see restored to the Bill all of the provisions now to be deleted with the exception of Clause 71(86). An Ordinance to delegate, under section 96 of the Nigeria (Constitution) Order in Council, such legislative powers as would enable these provisions to be replaced is now under preparation with a view to its introduction at the March meeting of the House of Representatives.

4.   Before agreeing upon this action members of the Council expressed strong resentment at the manner in which this Bill had been handled and requested me to inform you of their feelings in the matter. They felt that the position of the Council had been prejudiced by the fact that, while the Constitution Order-in-Council lays it down that a Bill shall come from the Region to the Council of Ministers, advice had been received from you before the matter had been considered by the Council, which in fact fettered the Council's freedom. However excellent and welcome such advice, the Council, when it came to consider the Bill, found itself with no opportunity to express its own opinion but felt compelled merely to endorse the advice received.

[1] See 170.

This, the Ministers felt, indicated lack of confidence in the Council of Ministers, and was likely to place Ministers in a difficult position politically.

5.   The procedure with regard to assent, or refusal to assent, to Regional Bills and disallowance of Regional Laws is laid down in sections 95–102 of the Nigeria (Constitution) Order-in-Council, 1951. Under this procedure a Regional Bill which has been passed by both the Legislative Houses of a Region is sent to the Governor, who, after consulting with the Council of Ministers, may object to it for any of the reasons set out in section 96(2) of the Order-in-Council. If he does not object to it the Lieutenant-Governor may, subject to any instruction addressed to him under Her Majesty's Sign Manual and Signet or through a Secretary of State, declare that he assents, or refuses to assent, thereto, or that he reserves the Bill for the signification of Her Majesty's pleasure thereto. Finally, even though a Lieutenant-Governor has given his assent to it, a law may be disallowed by Her Majesty through a Secretary of State. There is no specific provision in the Constitution Order-in-Council in accordance with which instructions would be given by the Secretary of State before the Bill had been considered by the Governor and returned to the Lieutenant-Governor.

6.   As I have said, members of the Council of Ministers felt that, in the absence of any such specific provision in the Constitution Order-in-Council, intervention of the Secretary of State at a stage before the Council had formally considered the Western Region's Bill the inference could only be that they were not free to take their own decision in the matter and were not yet regarded as capable of doing so. A logical conclusion of such procedure would be that all Regional legislation should be sent in draft to the Colonial Office for examination by the Secretary of State's advisers before it was put before the Regional Legislatures, and this, naturally, could only detract most seriously from the authority and responsibility given to those legislatures.

7.   I have informed the Council that the sole purpose which dictated the procedure adopted on this occasion was to ensure that a sound and valuable law, free from legal blemishes, and capable of immediate implementation, should come into force with the least possible delay. I have also explained that your intervention in the matter resulted from a question put to you in the House of Commons. When I agreed that the comments of your Local Government Advisory Panel would be valuable I should, perhaps, have foreseen the situation that later arose, and I desire to express regret that I did not do so. Notwithstanding this, Ministers feel that they were placed in a difficult position and would welcome your formal assurance that your advice was in no way indicative of a lack of confidence in the capacity and sense of responsibility of the Council of Ministers.

175   CO 554/599, no 25   31 Jan 1953

[Eastern Region crisis]: inward telegram no 137 from AET Benson to Mr Lyttelton on the resignation of Eastern Region ministers

[The crisis in the Eastern Region that developed during 1953 had its origins in the determination of Azikiwe to assert party discipline over those members of the NCNC who held ministerial posts in the central Council of Ministers and in the Eastern Region government. This was complicated by the fact that Azikiwe, although representing Lagos in the Western House of Assembly, had failed to gain one of the Lagos seats in the House of Representatives and thus held no central or eastern legislative seat (see 150). The expulsion of three central ministers (Arikpo, Njoku and Nwapa) from the party in December 1952 (see 171) because of their unwillingness to accept party instructions to refuse to co-operate with the workings of the Council of Ministers, was followed by

Azikiwe's determination to assert party authority over the Eastern regional ministers through a re-shuffle of portfolios. The result was the submission of the resignations of all nine Eastern Region ministers on 29 Jan 1953. At the last moment however six of the nine, led by Professor Eyo Ita, withdrew their resignations. The six were subsequently expelled from the NCNC and party control over the members of the House of Assembly was reflected in the passing of a vote of no-confidence in the Eastern government and the refusal to pass the budget; the budget eventually had to be passed by use of the lieutenant-governor's reserved powers. Thereafter obstructionist tactics by NCNC members of the House were designed to make government unworkable in the Eastern Region. The six so-called 'sit-tight' regional ministers, together with the three expelled central ministers, formed the National Independence Party with Eyo Ita as President. Underlying this crisis were deeper tensions within the NCNC over Azikiwe's determination to assert his leadership as well as difficulties between Efik members such as Eyo Ita, and the party more broadly.]

My telegram No. 134.

Situation East.

Facts are as follows:—

At about midnight 29th January all nine Regional Ministers wrote letters of resignation and handed them to Dr. Azikiwe and Mr. K. O. Mbadiwe. At 07.00 30th January six Ministers called on the Lieutenant Governor and withdrew resignation (which Lieutenant Governor had not received). At 08.00 Azikiwe and Mbadiwe arrived and presented nine resignations and were informed that six had been withdrawn.

2. House met with everyone in normal place. Speech from the Throne delivered and the Financial Secretary then introduced the budget. House adjourned midday with no reference to these events.

3. In the afternoon Lieutenant Governor sent for the remaining three Ministers Okpara, Muna and Awgu (who alone out of total had been promised new Ministries by Azikiwe) and asked whether their resignations stood. Muna withdrew his resignation; the other two apparently let theirs stand.[1]

4. Latest move reported this morning is that letter signed by 45 members of the Eastern House has been sent to Lieutenant Governor stating that

(a) all Ministers have resigned

(b) he must recognise the new Ministers

(c) if he does not, vote of no confidence will be passed on Ministers in the House and every Bill presented, particularly the Appropriation Bill, will be opposed.

5. I will keep you informed.

---

[1] Solomon T Muna, Cameroonian politician; minister without portfolio, Eastern Region government; later member of the KNC and then KNDP; vice-president of Cameroun, 1970. Generally, Cameroonian leaders supported Ita in this crisis.

176 CO 554/318   18–20 Feb 1953

[Eastern Region crisis]: minutes by E O Mercer, T B Williamson, Sir T Lloyd and Mr Hopkinson on provision for carrying on the administration of government in the Eastern Region

Mr. Williamson

As a result of discussion today between Mr. Peck, Mr. Rushford, Mr. Godden and myself, the draft telegram opposite was agreed as the immediate reply to (6) on the question of how provision should be made for carrying on the administration of a Region in the event of the Legislature or Executive Council ceasing to function. As you will note, the Emergency Powers Order in Council, 1939, is regarded as fully adequate for this purpose; fortunately the 1952 amendment to it provides that a proclamation under the Order may be made so as to apply only to a specified part of the territory, in other words, it may apply to one Region only.

On the question of whether it is necessary to declare an emergency in terms when making a proclamation under the Emergency Powers Order in Council, Mr. Peck is of the opinion that there is in fact no need to do so, although the fact that the Order in Council is being used leads to a sufficiently clear deduction that a state of emergency does in fact exist. The form previously used in Nigeria is at A on 14327/21/48. A precedent which could be followed would be that of the Malta Emergency Provisions No. 2 Order in Council, 1951, in which the particular reason for the current emergency was stated, but neither Mr. Peck nor I feel that this point need be mentioned in our telegraphic reply to Nigeria.

The use of the Emergency Powers Order in Council in circumstances in which there was no violence has already been considered in connection with other territories, in particular Malta. In this connection you may wish to see the minutes on MED 333/8/02.

The Emergency Powers Order in Council, 1939, would of course provide only for the first stage in any constitutional crisis such as is envisaged. For subsequent stages further courses will have to be considered, among them the proposal in (6) for an amendment to the Constitution, to provide for the separate dissolution of a Regional Legislature. These are not of the first urgency, since the Emergency Powers Order in Council provides for the immediate carrying on of government, but it is clear that this latter is no more than a temporary expedient. Mr. Rushford has drawn up a brief note (7) which is opposite, of the successive problems that might present themselves, together with the possible remedies that would have to be considered. These envisage the need to dissolve a Regional House which is no longer working and consider the possibility that a newly elected House might also refuse to co-operate, thus repeating the situation before the dissolution. Whereas the first stage of this situation might be dealt with by an *ad hoc* Order in Council or by an amendment to the Constitution such as (6) proposes, if the second stage were reached there would appear to be no long-term alternative but an overhaul of the Constitution.

It is further necessary to consider the measures needed to deal with the effect of a Regional situation such as has just been described, on the Central Legislature and the Council of Ministers. It might in fact be possible for the Central Legislature and Council of Ministers to carry on, as it were, with only two of its three constituents in operation if only one Region were affected, although this would be politically undesirable except as a short term measure. There is already provision in the constitution for dissolution of the Central House and with it of the various Regional Houses, and if no Regional solution could be found it would appear to be necessary in the long run to dissolve the Central House and hold a general election throughout the country. The alternative would be nothing less, so far as one can see, than a general revision of the Constitution.

Although it is important to foresee all contingencies and, it seems to me that we should discuss these further with Nigeria, it is only the stage of the dissolution of a Regional House that (6) asks to be considered, apart from measures to continue administration. Legal Dept will examine the draft amendment to the Constitution further. You will note that (6) suggests merely that it should be prepared for submission to HM in Council, and not actually submitted until the emergency arises. To my mind we would certainly wish to avoid amending the Constitution until it is essential, but we may find, even if all steps are taken short of submission, that the draft does not really fit the situation that has arisen and that some delay therefore arises. The Emergency Powers O. in C. should cover this.

E.O.M.
18.2.53

Sir T. Lloyd (through Mr. Peck)
I mentioned (6) to you briefly yesterday.
 There are two points

(a) the question of powers to provide for separate elections in the individual Regions of Nigeria; and
(b) the question of powers to enable a Lieutenant-Governor to carry on the administration of his Region if it is impossible to secure a quorum in the Executive Council or Legislature because of a boycott.

We need more time to consider (a), but can reply at once on (b). I should like to do so by telegram because, although we have not heard of any further trouble in the Eastern Region for the last week, the Governor might have to act at short notice.

 The Legal Advisers and my Department are satisfied (after some study of the precedents, including the recent correspondence with Malta at (2)(4) & (5), on MED 333/8/02) that the Emergency Powers Order in Council, as amended, gives the Governor all he needs. Our advice is set out in the draft telegram submitted herewith, which Mr. Peck, Mr. Rushford and I dictated together this morning. I think this is self-explanatory.

 I am passing this through Mr. Peck so that he may take a final look at it on its way up.

T.B.W.
19.2.53

Minister of State
In the absence of the Secretary of State I am troubling you with this file since the action which we are recommending ought, in my view, to have Ministerial approval.

 In paragraph 2 of No. 6 the Governor of Nigeria asked for advice about the means for carrying on the administration of the Eastern Region of that territory if Ministers and members of the Regional Legislature boycotted the Executive Council and the Legislature in such numbers as to make it impossible to secure a quorum. The Governor was advised that the use of the Emergency Powers Order in Council for this purpose would be inappropriate and suggested an amendment of the Nigerian Constitution Order in Council on the lines of a section in the Government of India Act.

 The opinion of the Secretary of State's Legal Advisers is that the Emergency Powers Order in Council could properly be used and would be more appropriate (as well as speedier) than special legislation. I agree with that view and my reason for submitting the file is that this would, so far as I can recall, be the first occasion of the use of the Order in Council for any other than 'emergency' i.e. disturbance purposes. It has been used on five occasions since the war (the places and dates of their use are mentioned at X in Mr. Bunce's minute of 22/8/52 on MED. 333/8/02) but each time there was disturbance or other threat to peace and good government. We did contemplate the use of the Order in Council in other circumstances in Malta—see paragraph 5 of No. 5 on the same file—but the need for that has not so far arisen.

If Ministers and members in the Eastern Region of Nigeria deliberately bring about a break-down of government in that area they cannot reasonably complain if Government acts quickly under whatever emergency powers are most readily available, and I submit therefore that we should proceed as in this draft.

Paragraph 7 of Nigerian telegram No. 218 of yesterday, now attached to but not yet registered on this file, explains the urgency.

T.K.L.
19.2.53

This seems to me all right, but on the face of it I should think we ought also to be aiming at new elections.

H.L.D.H.
20.2.53

177   CO 554/260, no 16   27 Feb 1953

[Ministerial powers]: inward telegram no 250 from Sir J Macpherson to Mr Lyttelton on the need to concede further powers to central ministers. *Minute* by TB Williamson

[Macpherson's determination to preserve a conciliar system for the Council of Ministers eventually gave way in the face of pressure for a ministerial system modelled on the Gold Coast. In early 1953 the Council began to be modified with the creation of the first four ministries on the Gold Coast model.]

You are aware from correspondence and personal experience of the pressure which has been exercised by Central Ministers, or some of them, ever since the Constitution came into force, to stretch the interpretation of Section 162 of the Nigeria Constitution Order in Council so as to permit establishment of Ministries and to allow Ministers to control departments. Section in question was, of course, inserted on the recommendation of the General Conference on Constitutional Reform because, at that time, Regions did not relish the thought of Central Ministers from one region exercising authority in other Regions.

2. I have given the widest possible interpretation to that Section. We are establishing separate Ministries and I concede the right of Ministers to give orders to Heads of Departments in order to ensure implementation of decisions of the Council of Ministers. Ministers have expressed appreciation of this attitude and I thought we had succeeded in satisfying their aspirations. I have now, however, been presented with unanimous request from all Central Ministers with portfolios that they should be given the same powers as Ministers in the Gold Coast. They realise that this can be done only by amendment of the Constitution Order in Council and they press for this. They claim to be supported by Regional Ministers from all three Regions and I believe this claim to be well founded. (When I was in Kaduna last month Northern Region Ministers spoke strongly in favour of this change).

3. I am convinced that we must concede this request in spite of my objection to making any change in the Order in Council (other than provision for separate dissolution of Regional Houses). If we continue to resist, the whole atmosphere will be poisoned and I badly need the continued support of the Central Ministers, who are as good as we can expect to get at this stage and better than any substitutes that

might take their places. I am not without hope that concession on this point will greatly improve relations in general.

4.   I had hoped to approach this change gradually, but my hand was forced yesterday when the Council considered the terms of my speech on the opening of the new session of the House of Representatives on 3rd March. Notice of a motion has been received from floor members for the grant of normal powers to Ministers. Ministers, rightly as I think, pressed for a Government motion instead and urged reference to this in the opening speech. They fully appreciate the importance of carrying you and Her Majesty's Government with us in this change and regret appearance of stampeding you.

5.   I have agreed to say in opening speech on 3rd March, after reference to the origin of Section 162, that the Council of Ministers has had the question of the powers and functions of Ministers under review for some time, in the light of the practical working of the Constitution, and that proposals for far-reaching changes are being considered, the results of which will be brought before the House of Representatives. There will be many complications to work out, including relations between Central Ministers who deal with regional subjects and Regional Ministers. I earnestly trust you will not feel I have improperly committed you. Ministers assure me that they want only this change and no other in the Order in Council and, in particular, that they have no desire to change the provisions relating to control of the Civil Service. The blunt fact is that if we were now framing the Constitution we should have no sufficient grounds for imposing limitations contained in Section 162 regarding ministerial responsibility for implementing policy of the Council of Ministers.

6.   It would greatly relieve my anxiety if you felt able to send a signal before 3rd March expressing understanding of the situation.

Minute on 507

Sir T. Lloyd

In his telegram No. 250 at (16) Sir J. Macpherson makes it clear that he thinks it essential for the Nigeria constitution to be amended so as to give Nigerian Ministers the same powers as Gold Coast Ministers have. Briefly, the position is as follows.

Under the Gold Coast constitution the Governor may charge any Representative Minister with the responsibility for any Department or subject. Ministers' powers in the Gold Coast are not dissimilar from those of Ministers in the U.K. They are in charge of their Departments and, except when they think it necessary to take a matter to Cabinet, they can take policy decisions on their own responsibility and give directions to their Departments that they shall be carried out. The doctrine of collective Cabinet responsibility of course applies, and if a decision which a Gold Coast Minister has taken on his individual responsibility is challenged or criticised publicly, he can rely on the public support of all his Cabinet colleagues. (At least this is how the system is supposed to work and I think it is fair to say that on the whole this is how it does work).

The position in Nigeria is different. There is a long and complicated history behind it—not all of which is clear from our files—but in short it comes to this. Neither at the Centre nor in the Regions have Nigerian Ministers (apart from the ex-officio Members, who incidentally are not called Ministers) responsibility for Departments. They are charged with responsibility for 'matters' and they cannot take any policy decisions on their own. Everything has to go to the Council of Ministers (or Regional Executive Council). Moreover when the Council has taken a decision, the Minister's responsibility is confined to 'ensuring, in association with the appropriate public officer, that effect is given to decisions taken by the Governor in the Council of Ministers relating to such matter'. Hence the wording of section 162 of the Constitution Order, which is as follows:—

'162. In this Part "responsibility" for any matter means general responsibility for—

(a) submitting to the Council of Ministers questions relating to such matter;
(b) ensuring, in association with the appropriate public officer, that effect is given to decisions taken by the Governor in the Council of Ministers relating to such matter; and
(c) conducting in the House of Representatives government business relating to such matter.'

As Sir J. Macpherson indicates in paragraph 1 of (16), the fundamental reason for this 'conciliar' system was because the Regions, and particularly the North, objected at the Ibadan General Conference in 1950 to powers being given to a Central Minister responsible for Regional subjects in pursuance of which he could decide policy affecting a Region other than his own. Under the system decided upon and enshrined in the present constitution, there is the safeguard that policy can only be decided by Ministers from all three Regions sitting in Council, and in addition there is the further safeguard provided by the fact that there are six ex-officio members in Council plus the Governor as President.

We have felt for some time in my Department (a) that the conciliar system was so cumbersome and threw so heavy a burden of work on the Council of Ministers that in due course it would have to be modified; and more particularly (b) that it was unreasonable to expect Nigerian Ministers to be content for much longer with section 162 (b) of the Constitution Order. The Governor had hoped, by stretching section 162 (b) to the utmost, that he had satisfied his Ministers aspirations. But it is clear that he has failed to do so, and they are all now unanimous—significantly enough including those from the North—in pressing to be given normal Ministerial responsibility for their Departments.

I am quite sure, for my part, that the balance of advantage lies now in making the change Sir J. Macpherson wants, even at the cost of amending the Nigeria constitution in certain important respects. Accordingly, after discussion with Dr. Mercer, I submit the attached draft telegram in reply to (16). Sir J. Macpherson has asked for a reply to reach him by Monday night.

It will be noted that in this draft reply it is proposed to say that we assume that no question of creating offices of Prime Minister will arise at this stage. I think this assumption is correct because paragraph 5 of (16) says that Ministers have assured Sir John that the only change they want is that they shall be given the same powers as Gold Coast Ministers. There would therefore appear to be no suggestion of any alteration in the precedence of Ministers in relation to the ex-officio Members. But we had better put the point specifically.

I should mention one complication. It relates to Sierra Leone. The Secretary of State has, within the last fortnight, accepted a recommendation from the retiring Governor that a Ministerial system shall be introduced in Sierra Leone on the existing Nigerian pattern. The despatches exchanged have now been published and the drafts to amend the Sierra Leone constitutional instruments are in pretty well their final stage, ready for submission to H.M. in Council (we hope) on the 11th March. We expect to hear from the Acting Governor of Sierra Leone within a few days that the draft amending instruments are acceptable to him. (They are being taken back to Freetown by the Attorney-General this weekend.) I have, however, throught it right to inform Mr. Macdonald of this latest development in Nigeria, telling him what the Governor's view is and of the terms in which he will be speaking on the 3rd March. I have added of course that I cannot anticipate the decision which will be taken on Sir John's telegram but that in any event we assume that there can be no question of proceeding otherwise than in accordance with the recommendations submitted by Sir G. Beresford-Stooke and approved by the Secretary of State.

I am sending a copy of this minute and of the draft telegram direct to Mr. Peck.

T.B.W.
28.2.53

178   CO 554/599, no 48   27 Feb 1953
[Eastern Region crisis]: inward telegram no 251 from Sir J Macpherson to Mr Lyttelton on the continuation of government in the Eastern Region   [Extract]

[The problem for the government in dealing with the Eastern crisis was their inability to dissolve the Eastern House of Assembly without dissolving all the regional houses (see 176). It was clear that in order to get round this the 1951 constitution would have to be amended, though this raised the danger of opening up the constitution for more radical changes (see 195). In the event the Eastern Region House of Assembly was dissolved on 6 May (see 199).]

Your telegram No. 213.

Parliamentary Question.

Little, save amplification, to add to my telegram No. 242.

2.   Government continues in the East because the Executive Council remains properly constituted. Legislature inoperative because of unconstitutional tactics adopted by the N.C.N.C. Party caucus attempting to set up puppet government answerable only to the N.C.N.C. Executive outside the Legislature. But Reserve Powers enable essential legislation to be enacted by the Lieutenant Governor. These are not (repeat not) emergency powers.

3.   Copy of the Legal Secretary's statement of 18th February leaves by bag No. 28. Following are the main points:—

(a) Lieutenant Governor's actions throughout legally and constitutionally correct.

(b) Six Regional Ministers had not resigned.

(c) Executive Council still properly instructed.

(d) Lieutenant Governor can revoke the appointment of a Minister only in two ways: either after adverse secret ballot, or because of failure to carry out the policy or decisions of the Executive Council (Section 130).

(e) Therefore no power to revoke the appointments.

(f) Further no power to dissolve the House save by the Governor's dissolution of all the Houses at once.

4.   Statement followed, to the surprise of everyone, by Eyo Ita saying that he might initiate approach to the Secretary of State to amend the constitution to permit separate dissolutions . . .

179   CO 554/260, no 17   2 Mar 1953
[Ministerial powers]: outward telegram no 22 (reply) from Mr
Lyttelton to Sir J Macpherson agreeing to proposals to concede
further powers to central ministers

Your telegram No. 250.[1]

I have watched with admiration your efforts over past year to keep your conciliar system (including section 162 (b) of Constitution Order) intact, but, as you may recall from our talks in Lagos last year, I felt then that pressure for something more like Gold Coast pattern might become irresistable. I agree therefore, subject to my following paragraph, that you should make your statement on 3rd March, and I shall be prepared at appropriate stage on receipt of formal recommendation from you to advise Her Majesty in Council to amend Nigeria constitution to give Nigerian Ministers powers similar to those of Ministers in Gold Coast.

2.   I am, however, much concerned about use of words 'far-reaching changes' in your paragraph 5. The changes in question are not (repeat not) far-reaching, and to use the term would be impolitic as well as misleading. I must therefore ask you to do your utmost, even at this late hour, to get agreement to substitute for 'far-reaching changes' words such as 'changes affecting their powers and functions.'

3.   I note that all Central Ministers with portfolios support this change, and that they have no desire to change provisions relating to control of Public Service. I hope recommendation, when made, will also have unanimous support of all Regional Ministers from all three Regions. I assume conciliar system would be abandoned in Regions as well as at the Centre, but that there is no question of creating offices of Prime Minister either at Centre or in Regions. Do you, however, intend that ex officio Members shall be styled Ministers?

4.   Please do not (repeat not) commit me publicly on this at this stage, and I should be grateful if you will not (repeat not) disclose that you have consulted me.

5.   Grateful to know what procedure and timetable you have in mind for proposed changes, and particularly at what stage you expect to make formal recommendation to me. As you know, amendments to constitutional instruments take time.

6.   Grateful if you would also keep other West African Governors informed. I have already warned Macdonald.[2]

---

[1] See 177.   [2] A R Macdonald, Colonial Secretary, Sierra Leone.

180   CO 554/400, no 1   13 Mar 1953
[Nigerianisation]: memorandum by M G Smith on the Africanisation
policy of the West African governments

Africanisation has been the policy of the Governments of the Gold Coast and Nigeria for many years—in the case of the Gold Coast it was first enunciated in 1925 during the Governorship of Sir Gordon Guggisberg. But lip service to this policy has not involved, except in very recent years, any pressure to implement it and in the Gold Coast, for instance, although it is now 28 years since the policy saw the light of day there is still no African head of any Department. The inaction, if not the policy, of H.M.G. is therefore partly to blame for the present difficulties which the pressure for accelerated Africanisation in West Africa is bringing. There is, however, another major reason for these difficulties in that technical and social advances since the war have so increased the demand for a larger Public Service performing tasks of much greater variety that whether or not Africanisation had been pressed before the war it would still have been necessary to bring in many more overseas officers in the technical fields.

2. It is common ground that the maintenance of the efficiency and self-confidence of the Public Services in the West African territories is a *sine qua non* of the success of H.M.G.'s constitutional experiments there, as the territories contain no substantial uncorrupt middle-class and no other reservoir of talent and experience to protect the common people from exploitation by the very inexperienced and not necessarily high-minded politicians they have voted into power. The political struggle in West Africa is largely over and only the question of the timing of further political advance remains. But the question of the preservation of the standards and integrity of the Public Services is not yet resolved and should perhaps now become the major concern of our policy.

3. On the political front, H.M.G. early recognised that self-government as the expression of the new nationalist feeling was fast becoming the African goal and that to win African good-will we must make strides towards granting this big enough to involve an element of risk for us and big enough to convince the Africans that we were handing over power out of conscious good-will and not grudgingly because of internal pressure in the territories. On the political front in West Africa this policy has been largely successful and as a result all the talk there now is of retaining the Commonwealth link when independence is gained. But if we cannot protect the position of the Public Services these new countries may either enter the Commonwealth—or be rejected by it—not as self-respecting nations but as African slums.

4. If we are to tackle this question effectively we must start as we did on the political issue with frank and not reluctant recognition that rapid Africanisation is now a pressing, perhaps the most pressing, local objective, and we must therefore seek to further it and to make it clear that we do further it by positive acts of policy and not merely stand by in passive acquiescence while Africanisation of an unbalanced sort is brought about by purely local devices. Only thus can we hope (if at all) to win enough African good-will over our attitude to Africanisation to give us a chance of being allowed to guide its progress.

5. It seems to me that to achieve this we may have, though the Governors, to argue out again in both Nigeria and the Gold Coast the basis and objectives of Africanisation and to try to get Ministers to accept a series of propositions on the following lines:—

(a) It is fully recognised by both H.M.G. and the local governments that ultimate complete Africanisation of the Public Service is a proper and inevitable corollary of the constitutional changes that are taking place.

(b) At present political advance, which as a deliberate transfer of power can be achieved quickly, has outstripped the rate of Africanisation of the Public Service which depends on the attainment by many individuals of knowledge and experience which can be gained only over a comparatively long period of time; and urgent steps must be taken to bring the two into line.

(c) The rate of Africanisation and the rate of political advance can be brought into line by one of three methods:—

(i) political advance can be retarded.

(ii) standards of service can be so lowered that the efficiency and integrity of the Government machine is seriously impaired.

(iii) some lowering of the efficiency of the Service may be accepted while all available steps are taken to speed up recruitment to this lower standard.[1]

The difference between (ii) and (iii) above is one of timing—in (iii) you agree to take longer over the job. But (i) is presumably unacceptable locally and (ii) we should strongly urge to be indefensible on every ground. We must therefore get (iii) to be the agreed objective so that further discussion is on how far standards can safely be lowered and on the timing of the programme.

(d) Any lowering of standards would come at a most inconvenient time. Because of recent great technological advances, because of the pressure of local demand for increased education and other social services and for economic development, and because political advance itself increases the complexity of, and the strains on, the Government machine, the current need is for a larger and more efficient Public Service. The public which elected the new West African Governments is therefore entitled to have put squarely to it what insistence on over-hasty Africanisation would mean: far from consolidating political advance it would at best seriously retard the promising economic and social progress made since the war, and discourage needed further investment of overseas capital, and at worst it might lead to a voluntary mass exodus of existing overseas officers which would largely paralyse the machinery of Government. A Minister without a Ministry is decorative rather than useful.

(e) In urging therefore that Africanisation should not be pressed at a rate and in a manner seriously prejudicial to the interests of serving overseas officers, H.M.G. is not concerned merely to protect the interests of these officers—that perhaps could be achieved through an adequate compensation scheme—but with guarding against a mass exodus that would stultify H.M.G's. own policy of promoting the orderly development of self-governing institutions in West Africa.

(f) There is a further consideration. Public Service standards can be lowered by a stroke of the pen. They can be raised only with great difficulty over a long period, for public servants of poor quality, accepted when standards are lowered, cannot be ejected when it is sought to raise the standards. But the West African Governments have not merely internal but external aims: they are looking to the day when self-government shall have reached the point of international recognition and they can seek their own place among the nations and perhaps as full members of the

---

[1] Williamson minuted on this (14 Mar): 'I do not agree that we should, publicly anyway, accept any lowering of standards. The traditionally high standards of the British Civil Service, whether in the U.K. or in its overseas territories, are something which, like the integrity of the Service, we ought to fight to maintain. . . . I would say that present standards in some overseas territories (including the Gold Coast) are low enough already. Furthermore, once there were any lowering of efficiency, it would be impracticable to draw the line: under pressure of opinion and events we should constantly be pushed lower and lower'. See also, BDEEP series A, vol 3, D Goldsworthy, ed, *The Conservative Government and the End of Empire 1951–1957* part II, 245 & 246.

Commonwealth family. They will find great difficulty in achieving these aims, and in particular in being accepted as equal partners in the Commonwealth, if the efficiency of their governmental machinery is sufficiently impaired to make them potentially economic and defence liabilities and generally below the standards expected of members. A low standard of government would also do little good to the general cause of African nationalism. The ultimate independence of the Gold Coast and Nigeria is not in question. What is in question in the eyes of the world is the social, political and economic levels at which these territories are capable of sustaining their independence.

(g) The West African Governments should also appreciate another implication of drastic Africanisation. Part of the emotional demand for Africanisation is based on a natural desire to prove Africans to be at least as efficient and responsible as Europeans. But this claim, as it is often pressed, goes much further than a claim of equality and approaches a point of absurdity. No European would claim that an inexperienced European junior officer, however distinguished his academic career, could in a year or two accumulate the experience and judgment required of the holder of a very senior post in the Public Service. Yet it is on the belief in the fitness of Africans for promotion as rapid as this that part at least of the case for accelerated Africanisation rests.

(h) With so much at stake H.M.G. do not therefore consider it unreasonable to counsel a certain restraint in pressing Africanisation programmes to a point that may cause chaos in the Public Service, and suggest that if the issues involved are fairly put to the public this counsel will be accepted. But H.M.G. are anxious to do all they can actively to promote rapid Africanisation and point out that their bona fides in this respect cannot be questioned as they have already taken the major steps necessary to ensure ultimate Africanisation by promoting the great projects for University and Technical Colleges as well as by awarding many scholarships to the major seats of learning in the U.K.

(i) H.M.G. are therefore prepared to co-operate to the full in any measures that will speed up Africanisation while substantially protecting the standards of the Service. It is recognised that some lowering of standards is called for just as some political risks had to be taken to launch the new constitution. This might involve the following measures:—

(i) H.M.G. attach the highest importance to the practical training of the Africans in the Service and are prepared to assist this both with money and with experienced personnel from the U.K.[2]

(ii) H.M.G. are considering means of creating a U.K. fund for the payment of pensions into which Colonial Governments could make annual payments that would rid them of further pension liability in respect of officers for whom the payments were made.[3]

(iii) H.M.G. are prepared to discuss means of funding the present pension liabilities of the West African Governments.

(iv) H.M.G. are prepared to discuss suitable compensation terms for officers whose services can be dispensed with as suitable African replacements become

---

[2] Williamson added here 'A programme will need working out'.
[3] Williamson added here 'Sir J Macpherson's idea: but he suggested confining to future recruits'.

available. (This might reassure serving officers that their interests will be protected when the time comes and reassure local governments that they can dispense with serving officers without a major row with H.M.G.)

(v) Further pensionable recruitment should be undertaken only in exceptional circumstances or where, as perhaps in the case of Northern Nigeria, it continues to be the expressed wish of the territory or region concerned.

(vi) H.M.G. undertake wherever possible to offer transfers to other Colonial territories to officers whose services are no longer required in West Africa. (The possibilities of these transfers must vary greatly from time to time and between one Service and another.)

(vii) H.M.G. suggest that to avoid friction on both sides and to provide for the careful and efficient management of the Africanisation programme, a permanent body at working level should be set up in each of the territories concerned within the present machinery of Public Service Commission and Establishment Section. There should be both African and European members on this body and the Public Service unions should either be represented on it or have easy and direct access to it. This body should initially review and then keep under review the state of and prospects for the Africanisation of each Department of Government. These reviews might bring to light a variety of circumstances:—

(a) It might appear that the prospects of complete Africanisation of a particular Department within say five years were firm enough for it to be possible to ask the Secretary of State if he could seek within that period to transfer all remaining European officers in the Department.

(b) On the other hand, the prospects of Africanisation might appear so remote that an assurance, couched in suitably guarded terms, might be given to the overseas officers concerned that their services would be required for the foreseeable future.

(c) There might appear a positive reluctance of Africans to enter particular vocations which, in the interests of Africanisation, would have to be overcome by some special inducement or form of direction.

6. The preceding suggestions for tackling the present difficulties over Africanisation are obviously extremely tentative; some of them would involve H.M.G. in considerable expenditure; others of them are by no means new or are already, to some extent, being implemented. But the essence of the matter cannot I think be challenged: the Africanisation issue has now become so important that we can no longer stand aside and leave it to be tackled by piecemeal local arrangements nor can we hope to avoid or defer its unpleasant implications without facing it in detail with the African Ministers. For example, the argument previously used, that to discuss compensation terms openly would encourage African Ministers to dispense earlier than they would otherwise have done with overseas officers, no longer has validity as they are already considering, with more enthusiasm than judgment, how to do this. Our only chance to achieve a rational settlement of these important issues is that, possessing as we do in both Nigeria and the Gold Coast very distinguished Governors who still command great personal influence and prestige in their territories, we should arm them with every argument we can think of and every proof of H.M.G's. good-will that we can muster to enable them to discuss the issues with their Ministers with complete frankness and with a view to reaching understandings that

will take account both of West African aspirations and H.M.G's. own objectives, and that can be put for approval before public opinion in West Africa.

181   CO 554/366, no 19   16 Mar 1953
[Marketing boards]: note by E Sabben-Clare on the politicisation of the Regional Production Development Boards

[Concern within the CO about the politicisation of marketing boards was prompted by the AG's changes to the membership of the Western Regional Production Development Board in July 1952, action that prompted reports of growing political influence over the Board during the latter months of the year and led to this note by Sabben-Clare, administrative officer, Nigerian government. T R Godden minuted on this note on 27 Mar: 'The attitude of the Action Group members of the Western Board to its civil service members and officers and to 'interference' from the centre is well in accord with the party line, and so far at least, does not seem to have produced any major blunders. Potentially the most disturbing situation seems to me to exist in the east, where at least two members of the Board are leading lights of the Azikiwe faction, and where their faction may well secure further power. In such an event it is very doubtful if any successful restraining influence could be exercised on a reconstituted Board by the Chairman or the General Manager' (CO 554/366).]

1. *Composition*
The present membership of the Boards is given in the attached schedule.[1]

2.   An examination of this Schedule will show that on all the Boards there is a large proportion of members of the Regional Houses and that those members are drawn from the predominant political groups in each Region. These facts are shown in summary form in the tables below:—

Northern Board—Members 12
Members in Northern House of Chiefs	4 x
Members of Board in Northern House of Assembly	3 x
Members in Central House of Representatives	5 x

x All supporters of the N.P.C.

Western Board—Members 15
Members of Board's Executive Committee	5 ∅
Members of Board in Western House of Chiefs	1 ∅
Members of Board in Western House of Assembly	4 ∅
Members of Board in Central House of Representatives	0

∅ All supporters of the Action Group.

Eastern House of Assembly—Members 10
Members of Board in Eastern House of Assembly	7 ✗
Members of Board in Central House of Representatives	3 ✗

✗ All supporters of the N.C.N.C.

(These figures exclude the Chairman. In the North he is the Financial and Development Secretary and, as such, a member of the House of Chiefs and of the House of Assembly. In the West and East he is the Development Secretary and, as such, a Member of the House of Assembly.)

---
[1] Not printed.

3. *Selection*

Sections 4, 5 and 6 of the Regional Production Development Boards Ordinance (No. 27 of 1951) prescribe that the majority of the members of the Boards shall be appointed by the Lieutenant-Governors. Constitutionally, such appointments are in the Lieutenant-Governor's discretion, but it is now the practice for Lieutenant-Governors to consult their Councils before such appointments are made. This practice started in consequence of an administrative instruction resulting from an agreed decision of the Central Government in 1952.

4.   Party politics probably enter less into appointments on the Northern Board than elsewhere. The Acting Chairman of the Northern Board wrote recently on the subject in part as follows:—

> 'Our Board members are drawn from the same class of Northern Nigerian as provides us with our Ministers, and party politics, to date, have not affected the selection and appointment of members—In the Northern Region no political significance is attached to membership of the operations of the Board. Only a week ago the Executive Council of the Northern Region agreed with my proposal to advise His Honour to approve the nomination of a man of Eastern origin with businesses in Makurdi and Enugu, to membership of the Northern Region Development (Loans) Board. He was the best nomination (from the Middle Belt) for the appointment and no significance was attached to his tribe, creed or political views.'

It will be noted that in spite of this the members of the Northern Board in the Regional Houses belong to the N.P.C. and it is doubtful whether a leading politician of the opposition, the N.E.P.U., would have a chance of becoming a member.

5.   However that may be, the position in the West is quite clear. The chances of a proclaimed opponent of the Action Group being chosen for the Board are at present nil. In the East this would have been true until recently for opponents of the N.C.N.C. Since the split in the party during recent months, it is impossible to forecast what sort of member would have a chance of selection, but it will almost certainly remain true in the East that the group which ultimately wins the present struggle for power will see to it that political opponents are not chosen for the Board. This would be in line with past developments in the East referred to in the following paragraph. Indeed, it has been rumoured that membership of the Board has lately been held out as a reward for present support of one group or the other.

6.   In the East all but one member of the Board who were unofficial members of the Eastern House of Assembly at the time when the Boards were set up in 1949 lost their seats in the elections for the present House in 1951. The Executive Council was consulted regarding the new appointments and apart from one independent (Mr. Prince Abbi), all the new selections were N.C.N.C. members. These members included Mr. K.O. Mbadiwe and Dr. Orizu who have been prominent in the recent attempt to wrest power from the present group of Ministers in the East.

7. *Operation and Administration*

Northern Board. On all Boards there is a certain amount of control exercised by British officials owing to the fact that the Development Secretary of each Region is the Chairman. (It so happens at the moment that there is no substantive holder of the post of Development Secretary in any of the Regions.) As one would expect, the influence of British officials is most marked in the operations of the Northern Board. Not only is the Financial and Development Secretary Chairman, but the Deputy Development Secretary has recently been appointed 'Agent'. The Agent's task is, under the Chairman's supervision, 'to control the routine administration of the Board and to ensure that the work of the Board is duly co-ordinated with that of Government'. It is not clear how his duties will dovetail with those of officers of the Board such as the Director of Operations (Administrative), the Director of Operations (Technical) and the Secretary, but the arrangement at any rate shows willingness on the part of the Board to accept assistance and guidance.

8.   *Western Board*. The picture in the West is very different, and the Action Group members who are in the majority are impatient of any official control. They have set up an Executive Committee, which is in fact a Board within a Board; it meets three times a month and insists on practically every administrative detail being referred to it by the Chairman; its decisions are referred when necessary to the full Board, which nearly always endorses them. The Committee consists of five Action Group supporters and the Chairman.

9.   Moreover, the Western Board has decided to appoint a General Manager who would 'relieve the Chairman of much routine administrative duties leaving the latter with, apart from presiding at meetings, general direction and policy in collaboration with the rest of the Board's members'. The Board's reason for this decision is that it must 'resist the temptation to adopt a civil service approach to its problems' and that since it 'has taken or is on the point of taking far-reaching policy decisions on industrial projects likely to involve commitments of hundreds and thousands of pounds of public money . . . it is simple prudence that the Board should take a bold business approach'. The General Manager should be responsible for 'forward planning, investigation and execution of the Board's industrial and agricultural projects', and should be 'Chief adviser on general policy'. No ceiling has been put on the salary for the post but the holder will in any event be paid not less than £5,000 a year. In spite of this a suitable candidate has not so far been found.

10.   One reason for this may be the irresponsible criticism of expatriate staff indulged in by the Action Group from time to time. A recent example of this is given in a memo- randum put to the Board by Mr. A.O. Rewane, an Action Group supporter and Manager of a Lagos night-club, on the appointment of a permanent Secretary to the Board. Mr. J.C. Gunton, an Administrative Officer, had been acting as Secretary on secondment for some time, but had refused an offer to transfer from the Administration to the Board's service. It was admitted by all on the Board that Mr. Gunton had given excel- lent service and it was noted that he was willing to continue working for the Board on secondment. Mr. Rewane, quite legitimately, pressed in spite of this for the appoint- ment of a permanent Secretary. He did so in a memorandum of which the following two extracts are typical:—

'The Board's business has developed to the stage when, if it is to succeed, it must be run on pure business lines, with which civil servants are deplorably unacquainted. For example, it is gratifying that in the Accounts Section, where there is no seconded officer with a civil service mentality to clog the wheels, the work has been of a highly satisfactory standard. . . .'

and

> 'The point here is that while employees with professional qualifications have a professional reputation to maintain and therefore lay out special efforts to acquit themselves creditably, civil servants on secondment, unless similarly qualified, have no such qualms and are more concerned with their position vis-à-vis General Orders, Colonial Regulations and Financial Instructions'.

These are not exceptional specimens of Mr. Rewane's style, and the influence of this gentleman on the Board unfortunately seems considerable.

11. *Eastern Board.* The Eastern Board, like the West, decided to recruit a General Manager, and recently appointed Mr. Robson to this post on a non-pensionable salary of £3,500 a year. The appointment was made as a result of advertisement and politics played no part in the selection. While the Eastern Board are as determined as the West not to be kept in official leading strings, there has certainly not been in their memoranda the same acrimonious note as is found in Mr. Rewane's efforts mentioned above.

12. *Functions*

The published reports of the operations of the Boards are available in the Colonial Office, and what is wanted here, presumably, is a note on the extent to which those functions are influenced by political considerations. In the North the answer is probably nil. The Board is occupying itself mainly with useful schemes for the improvement of Northern agriculture, such as the provision of machinery for the Sokoto Mechanised Rice Scheme and the protection of the livestock industry by financing the campaign against the cattle tsetse, *Glossina morsitans*.

13. The West and East, on the other hand, naturally pay attention to the vocal demand in those Regions for industrialisation, sometimes going ahead on their own with schemes which overlap or might have been better undertaken by others. The Western Board for example, have tentative plans for cement and paper manufacture and for the establishment of a spinning and weaving mill, all of which could with advantage have been co-ordinated with the Central Government's own plans for these industries. The Minister of Commerce and Industries has made tentative suggestions to the Regions, with the approval of the Council of Ministers, on the setting up of a Ministerial Committee for Economic Co-ordination, with which the Chairman of the Board would be associated, but so far nothing has come of it. The two main difficulties are likely to be, first the determination of each Regional Government and Regional Board to make its own decisions, without interference from Lagos, and secondly, even if agreement to the formation of a Committee is secured, managing to arrange meetings at a time which will be convenient for all those concerned. As the Chief Secretary to the West African Inter-Territorial Secretariat is well aware, it is most difficult to obtain a quorum even at important meetings, because of the many calls Ministers and senior officials already have on their time.

14. An interesting example of the influence of political considerations and nationalism on the economic policy of the Boards recently occurred in the West over the banking of the Board's deposits. Until recently these deposits have been placed in the Bank of British West Africa. The Western Board decided, however, to remove £500,000 and place it on deposit in the National Bank of Nigeria for two years at an

interest rate of 2% a year. This interest rate is that payable by the Bank of British West Africa for money placed on deposit at twentyone days' notice. In spite of the disadvantageous terms offered by the National Bank, the Board was determined to move the money for political considerations, and was at one time in such haste to do so that there was a risk of incurring further losses through insufficient notice being given for the transfer. There has been no such development as yet in the Eastern Region, but it is common talk that if the N.C.N.C. is successful in its struggle for power in the East the funds of the Eastern Regional Production Development Board will be placed in the African Continental Bank. There are good grounds for believing that a somewhat imperfect distinction is maintained by those responsible for that Bank between the judicious commercial investment of funds deposited with it and the application of those funds to the Party's political purposes.

15.   Political considerations are also likely to influence the future scope of all the Boards' activities. As the Colonial Office is aware, these Boards were originally set up for strictly limited purposes which were defined in the Regional Production Development Boards Ordinance (No. 27 of 1951). A Board might only use its money for schemes which were of direct benefit either to the producers of the crops with which the appropriate Produce Marketing Board was concerned, or of benefit to the area in which such crops were produced. Any attempts to widen the scope of these activities have so far been resisted on the ground that they would be unfair to the producers of those crops, who would be indirectly subsidising economic activities for the benefit of the rest of the population.

16.   On the other hand, many members of the Boards and many members of the Regional and Central Houses now hold the view that they and they alone are the representatives of the producers and can say how the producers would like their money to be spent. In line with this, the Eastern Regional Executive Council have recently had a Bill prepared to give the Eastern Regional Board powers to undertake schemes for the economic development of the Region as a whole. Professor Eyo Ita, speaking in the Central House of Representatives on March 11th, appeared to regard the Boards as much the most appropriate agency for Government economic development; what role in such development he considers should be left to the Regional Governments is not clear. The Minister for Commerce and Industries had hoped to discuss this Bill with the Lieutenant-Governor and others in the East during the recent session of the Regional House, but this was not possible owing to the political crisis. No further progress has been made with the Bill at present, and it certainly will not come forward at this present meeting of the House of Representatives. It has the support at present of the Lieutenant-Governor, Eastern Region, and a number of senior officials, who consider that if it is not passed the Eastern Regional Government—and other Regional Governments—may well turn as an alternative to a demand for large grants from Marketing Boards funds to finance both social and economic development. It is known that Mr. Awolowo is is pressing Sir Sydney Phillipson to sponsor a grant to the Western Region of £4 million by the Cocoa Marketing Board.

17.   To sum up, since each of the Boards is composed largely of men in politics, the economic policies of those Boards are naturally influenced by the political beliefs of members. These political beliefs are probably most sharply defined in the West, and consequently that Board has shown the Action Group's typical keen desire for industrialisation, coupled with its suspicion of foreign capital and expatriate staff. It

was typical of the Board that it eventually obtained the services of Messrs. Ethelburga Agencies to run the two new rubber factories which are being established in the West on a Managing Agency basis, and did not try to induce this firm to put money of its own into the venture. However, it would be fair to say that even in the West the general pattern of the Boards' activities is not moulded by doctrinaire beliefs. There are plenty of activities undertaken by that Board, as by the others, which are plain, straightforward and useful schemes for economic development. The most marked characteristic of the Boards is not the influence of politics on their policy but their independence and vigour. All three Boards are more than ready to make their own decisions and to go ahead with plans that they think economically desirable, regardless of what the Central Government and sometimes even what the Regional Government may have to say. As has been mentioned above, this tendency naturally leads to difficulties over co-ordination, but on the whole it is a good tendency and one that the Central Government is determined not to check by imposing a stifling control which would have nothing to recommend it but administrative convenience. It is known that the Action Group are concerned to see that the Western Regional Production Development Board makes a success of its work—although the Group's views of the methods by which success is most likely to be achieved are not always such as to command official confidence. It is known also that the Action Group are concerned to see that no cause is given by members of the Board for allegations of impropriety and certain members of the Board have recently been called to task because of their behaviour—but again, the Group's views of what is or is not impropriety are very much their own and would not extend to disowning Mr. Rewane's literary style.

182   CO 554/254, no 20   16 Mar 1953

[Gold Coast and Nigeria]: inward telegram no 337 from Sir J Macpherson to Sir T Lloyd on the impact on Nigeria of developments in the Gold Coast

[During late 1952 and early 1953, the pace of constitutional change in the Gold Coast increased. On 5 Mar 1953, Sir T Lloyd wrote to Macpherson outlining the likely changes that would occur; these included the abolition of *ex-officio* ministers to create an all-African Cabinet, the creation of a second chamber to include chiefs and representatives of special interests, with limited delaying powers and extensive electoral reform to include direct elections and universal adult suffrage. Further, it was likely there would be a White Paper outlining the new Gold Coast constitution in June 1953, followed by elections to a new, all African, assembly in mid-1954. Lloyd further intimated that this might be followed by the Gold Coast applying for membership of the Commonwealth with the right to attend Prime Ministers' conferences on terms of full equality. See BDEEP series B, vol 1, R Rathbone, ed, *Ghana*, part II, 123.]

Following for Lloyd.

Your secret and personal letter of 5th March.

Proposals for Gold Coast amount to almost complete self Government in 1954, and they will be openly debated in Gold Coast in June this year.

2.   You ask for my assessment of the effect on Nigeria and invite me to agree that resistance to these demands, involving major collision between Her Majesty's

Government and the Gold Coast, almost certainly resulting in the use of sanctions, would have greater damage on our position in Nigeria than acquiescence.

3. I infer from your letter that you have been re-reading correspondence beginning with my letter to you of 8th January, 1952,[1] as a result of which I visited London in February. Value of that visit was seriously affected by the fact that the Secretary of State had already been committed by his predecessor.

4. Lieutenant Governors are here for House of Representatives and their views and mine, and those of my Senior Official Advisers, are unanimous. I doubt whether I can get those views across adequately otherwise than by personal visit, but short answer is that I am unable to agree with the proposition in paragraph 2 above, and believe choice with which Her Majesty's Government is faced is between being prepared to use sanctions against the Gold Coast now, and being forced to use sanctions against part or parts of Nigeria slightly later.

5. I stand by everything in my letters of 8th January and 20th May, 1952. We have held the country together and much good work has been done. Had it not been for the constant comparison with the Gold Coast, situation would have been very encouraging. Southern politicians would not have felt compelled to press for advance and would have allowed time for the main inter-regional jealousies to be overcome. But the Gold Coast political advance, actual and bogus, has been a persistent canker. Southern political parties regard it as 'national disgrace' that Nigeria should be constitutionally more backward than the Gold Coast, and therefore outbid each other with demands for constitutional advance, which they know in their hearts is premature. North rightly wants to give full trial to constitution which has been in operation for little over a year. Northern opinion has advanced very fast, but recent events, described in the next paragraph, have revived their fear of being stampeded by the South.

6. You will recall the demands of the Western Ministers last June.[2] There has been constant pressure for the powers of Ministers to be the same as the Gold Coast. In the past two weeks, notices of motions by Southern Members for debate during the current meeting of House of Representatives include such subjects as self Government in 1956: change of constitution to be made by House of Representatives, subject to ratification by Her Majesty in Council: Select Committee to suggest changes in the constitution: Nigerian President for House of Representatives, etc. And in speeches, Southern Members have advocated replacement of Chief Secretary, Financial Secretary and Attorney General by Nigerian Ministers, also removal of Lt. Governors from the Council of Ministers and regionalisation of the police. Effect of these notices and speeches has already been to harden the Northern attitude to such extent that we may have a serious showdown in the Council of Ministers before Easter.

7. No one would pin the label of reactionary on me or my senior advisers. All of us believe in, and have faithfully followed, declared policy of Her Majesty's Government to permit constitutional advance as quickly as is consonant with reasonable measure of good Government in the interests of the people. Our objective is to keep united Nigeria in the Commonwealth of its own volition. This is good for Britain and good for Nigeria. We are prepared to take risks, and my answer to your

---

[1] See 152.   2 See 157.

question would be different if Nigeria were homogeneous and closely knitted. But it is not. It is held together solely by the influence of British officials.

8.   Effect of conceding the Gold Coast demands must be greatly to strengthen insistent demand by Southern politicians for sweeping constitutional changes. They would utterly reject any suggestion by Her Majesty's Government that similar concessions were premature for them, but such concessions would be totally unacceptable to the North, and acceptance of such demands by Her Majesty's Government would lead to categorical demand by the North for separation. Nor would disintegration stop there. South would not be united. In the East there would be irresistible demand for complete separation of the Cameroons from Nigeria, with all the resulting local and international complications, and within the Eastern and Western Regions, splits would almost certainly occur on ethnic lines. If Nigeria splits it will not be into two or three parts but into many fragments. If concessions are granted to the Gold Coast now, it is my carefully considered opinion that, within very short time, it will be necessary either to use sanctions against the North (there are 17 million of them and they would rightly regard themselves as betrayed by us) to compel them to accept Southern proposal or to resist to the utmost Southern proposal which, once similar proposals have been accepted in the Gold Coast, would itself require the use of sanctions.

9.   If the Gold Coast demands are resisted and sanction of force has to be applied, there will be sharp reaction amongst the Southern politicians, local press and subversive elements. But firm stand by Her Majesty's Government in refusing to acquiesce over hasty political advance in the Gold Coast would be welcomed by considerable majority of the people in Nigeria, and I should not expect security situation to arise which would cause serious embarrassment to Her Majesty's Government. Alternative is the disintegration of Nigeria. Even without further constitutional advance in the Gold Coast, we are going to have difficult time as a result of present clamour by Southern politicians for sweeping changes, especially as the demands will be rejected mainly, if not entirely, by the North and official votes in Council of Ministers and the House of Representatives. Extremists will be encouraged, but rejection will bring great relief to considerable body of local opinion.

10.   In this telegram I have referred only to the Nigerian situation and have not presumed to comment on the Gold Coast problems. I am not unmindful of the very difficult problems which the Secretary of State and Her Majesty's Government have to face in other parts of Africa and in regard to colonialism as a whole but, if the Gold Coast demands are conceded, I greatly fear Her Majesty's Government will be faced very shortly with a still more difficult problem in Nigeria.

11.   I am very ready to fly to London for discussion but, as I have said, situation in the Council of Ministers on constitutional issues is likely to be tense, at least for the next two weeks, and I believe it would be most dangerous for me to leave Nigeria before Easter. I trust, therefore, that the Secretary of State will not find it vitally necessary to take the Gold Coast proposals to the Cabinet before the Easter recess. If he must, you will, I think, agree that in spite of everything, there would be no alternative but for me to fly to London before the recess.[3]

---

[3] Macpherson attended meetings with Arden-Clarke at the CO on 15 Apr. See 190.

183   CO 554/318, no 19   21 Mar 1953

[Amendment of the constitution]: outward savingram no 31 from Mr Lyttelton to Sir J Macpherson on proposed amendments to the constitution

Your Savingram No. 521 dated 3rd March, 1953.

1951 Constitution: Measures for Continuing Regional Administration.

I have noted that you consider that, *for the present*, it is politically preferable not to seek an amendment of the Nigeria (Constitution) Order in Council 1951 on the lines of Section 45 of the Government of India Act, 1935. I had previously assumed that in proposing this amendment you had in mind the situation that was then arising in the Eastern Region but I now note that it was the possibility of boycott in the Western Region that led you to seek my views on the possibility of this amendment to the constitution. But whether the situation is of the Western or of the Eastern Region, my advisers remain of the opinion that the powers conferred by the Emergency Powers Order in Council, 1939, need not be regarded as applicable only to extreme situations involving violence and public disorder but are appropriate for just such a situation as you envisaged, thus appearing to make unnecessary any amendment of the Constitution Order in Council on the lines of the Section of the Government of India Act, 1935, to which you refer. This was the tenor of my Secret and personal telegram No. 13 of the 20th February, in which (see paragraph 4) I expressed the view that it would be politically preferable to make use, should the need arise, of existing powers rather than to introduce an amendment to the Constitution itself of such a radical nature. The words 'for the present' in paragraph 2 of your savingram No. 521 appear to indicate that you might still, in certain circumstances, wish to propose an amendment to the Constitution itself; and so that I may be quite clear as to your views on this matter, I should be grateful for your further comments in the light of the foregoing. I have noted your paragraph 3.

2.   On the second proposed amendment to the Nigeria (Constitution) Order in Council, 1951, to provide for the separate dissolution of Regional Houses and for which a draft, together with a legal note, accompanied your Priority Savingram No. 344 of the 6th February, I am, as my personal telegram No. 14 informed you, prepared (subject as mentioned below) on receipt of a recommendation from you to advise Her Majesty in Council to amend the Order in Council so as to provide for the separate dissolution of a Regional Legislature and for the holding of separate elections in a Region. My legal advisers have now examined the draft amending legislation submitted with your savingram No. 344. Enclosed herewith is a revised draft for the amending Order together with a Note by my legal advisers.[1]

3.   With regard to the proposal in paragraph 5 of your savingram No. 521, I have given further consideration to this in consultation with my advisers and now, notwithstanding my telegram No. 265 of 7th March, have doubts about its advisability. It seems to me that, constitutionally, the power to dissolve is, more perhaps than any other, one in the exercise of which a Governor should be formally bound to seek and accept the advice of his Executive Council (*subject, of course, to*

---

[1] Not printed. See 195.

the exercise of his reserved executive power, to which you have referred). The argument put forward in the fourth sentence of paragraph 5 of your savingram No. 521, viz. that the electorate at large is not familiar with the provisions of the constitutional instruments, could, it seems, be applied for or against almost any proposal for their amendment.

4. Moreover if this provision is to be made in respect of the power of Lieutenant Governors to dissolve, will it not be necessary, logically, to make a similar amendment in the case of the Governor's power to dissolve? And would not this be open to considerable criticism?

5. In any case, if the power to dissolve is to be discretionary, so also should be the power to prorogue. The practice in this country is normally to prorogue first, and then to dissolve.

6. I should be glad to have as soon as possible your further views on these points. It would be convenient if these could be included in your general comments on the revised draft amending Order, which is so drafted at present as *not* to confer discretionary powers on the Lieutenant-Governor.

7. While you will, I am sure, agree that it is important that we should between us achieve an agreed draft for the Nigeria (Constitution) (Amendment) Order in Council at an early date, I would not propose to take steps to submit the draft Order to Her Majesty in Council unless and until I receive your formal confirmation that you wish this to be done. I should be grateful if you would confirm that this is in accordance with your wishes.

8. You will, I have no doubt be considering what amendments if any, will be required in Regulations made under Sections 63 and 75 of the Constitution Order to provide for the holding of separate elections.

9. It would be convenient if you could reply separately to the two matters dealt with in this communication, namely (a) provision for the use of emergency powers and (b) draft amendment of the constitution to enable a Lieutenant-Governor to dissolve the Legislature of his Region.

184 CO 554/260, no 28   24 Mar 1953

[Self-government motion]: inward savingram no 676 from Sir J Macpherson to Mr Lyttelton on a debate in the Council of Ministers on the AG motion for self-government in 1956. *Minute* by T B Williamson

[One of the most bitter episodes of North-South tension in these years followed the AG motion for self-government by 1956 (the year the 1951 constitution was due to expire), put down in the House of Representatives for 31 Mar 1953 by Anthony Enahoro. This motion was discussed by the Council of Ministers on 18 Mar. For Northern leaders the prospect of self-government by 1956 raised fears of an independent Nigeria dominated by southern politicians; the Sardauna of Sokoto therefore moved an amendment to replace '1956' with 'as soon as practicable'. Macpherson, faced with a deeply divided Council, and attempting to maintain a conciliar system, argued that ministers should abstain from speaking or voting in the House debate. On the 27 Mar the Council agreed on this line, with the four Northern ministers joining with six officials to outvote four Western ministers and Dr Endeley, the Cameroon minister; the three remaining Eastern ministers abstained. This prompted the resignation of one Western minister, the Ooni of Ife, before the motion on self-government was considered. See 192. The debate in the House of Representatives was a heated affair, culminating in uproar following a slighting reference by Awolowo to Shehu Uthman dan Fodio (1754–1817), leader of the Muslim *jihad* that had established the Sokoto Caliphate and ancestor of the Sardauna. The AG and NCNC members walked out and the House adjourned. The remaining three Western ministers, Thomas, Akintola and Prest, immediately tendered their resignations. Both on arriving and leaving the House the Northern representatives were heckled and abused by the Lagos crowd; further abuse occurred during their train journey north and yet more subsequently appeared in the press. These tensions were to contribute to the tragedy of the Kano riots of May. See 203.]

My Telegram No. 383, Crisis in Council of Ministers.

At a meeting of the Council on 13th March one item was to discuss the line to be taken on an Action Group Motion praying me to appoint a suitable Nigerian as President of the House of Representatives. In this connection, see your secret and personal Despatch NO. 27 of 3rd April, 1952. Discussion was acrimonious. Western Ministers, Bode Thomas and Akintola, harangued the Council on their right to express in the House their own personal views, regardless of their position as members of the Council of Ministers, and pressed for permission for a free vote in the House of Representatives with officials abstaining. Northern Ministers, particularly Mohammadu Ribadu, said hard bitter words against the Western Ministers. Eastern Ministers and Prest helped official members to calm the atmosphere and eventually a decision was taken, by a large majority, that the Government should leave the debate to floor members and should neither speak nor vote. Bode Thomas had made it plain that this was merely a preliminary canter and that the real difficulty would arise on other Action Group motions, particularly that for self-government in 1956. Motion about President was not reached on Private Members' day on 17th March.

2.   On 18th March Council considered the line to be taken on the Action Group motion by Mr. Enahoro that self-government in 1956 should be accepted as a primary political objective. Northern amendment, of which notice had been given by Sardauna of Sokoto, would delete 'in 1956' and insert 'as early as practicable'. I enclose the relevant extract from the Conclusions of the meeting, from which you will see how sharp was the division of opinion, though tempers were controlled.[1] The North at first pressed strongly for affirmative vote for the amendment but when Bode Thomas and Akintola for the West, with some support from the East, pressed for freedom for Ministers to speak and vote as they liked, in House of Representatives, officials abstaining, Northern Ministers were very ready to accept the challenge. Eastern Ministers have sympathy for the motion (self-government in 1956 must be a plank in the programmes of all Southern political parties including new party in process of formation by responsible elements in Eastern Region) but they recognise the danger to the unity of Nigeria and would welcome any compromise short of political suicide. Oni of Ife, Nwapa and Prest were sound and conciliatory and two last were in favour of all Members of Council refraining from speaking or voting in House of Representatives. I made it clear that officials would play full part in this issue and when tempers showed signs of rising deferred further discussion until 20th March.

3.   I enclose the relevant extract from Council proceedings on 20th March. After one and a half hours: discussion Bode Thomas 'blew up' and made a completely uncontrolled scene. He was prevented from flinging out of the meeting only by a firm and decisive order from the Oni of Ife—Spiritual Head of the Yorubas. Nwapa in

---

[1] Enclosures not printed. The precise words of the motion were 'as soon as practicable'.

statesman like words stated the case for complete abstention by the Government in the cause of unity. At one stage I hoped to get fairly large majority for this course but the air had to be cleared and hard words were said. Northern Ministers were cool, hard and determined. They said that for fourteen months they had gone to the limit in trying to work with Western Ministers as friends and brothers in the interests of Nigerian unity, but they had been deceived. They knew the pace at which they wished to travel but they did not wish to retard the progress of any other Region. Let separation take place now peacefully and not, as they were bound to fear, at the last minute before Britain's departure as in India and Pakistan. Division later would be accompanied by chaos and bloodshed. Western Ministers' reply to this was by all means let us split now rather than that we should be kept in bondage by slow-moving North. Eastern Ministers believe in unity of Nigeria but are very conscious of effect on their position if they fail to appear as eager nationalists as others.

4.   Northern Ministers firmly rejected Western argument that the dispute was not between the Regions but between H.M.G. and Nigeria. In reply to the argument that the matter did not properly come within purview of Council of Ministers, it was pointed out firmly that matter under discussion would affect good government of the country not in 1956 but now. Council had clear responsibility for welfare and good government of the country and was the body upon which the unity of country rested. It could not evade that responsibility and must at all costs remain united in the eyes of the public.

5.   As reported in my telegram under reference, no decision was reached on 20th March and no solution that will keep Council of Ministers together is yet in sight. Most desirable development would be shift in the attitude of the Action Group. I do not say they do not believe in self-government in 1956 but I feel sure that the real reason for introducing this motion is not, as the North believes, in order to bulldoze the North into acceptance of Southern pace of political advance, but to outbid Azikiwe and the N.C.N.C. We have reason to believe that opinion in the Action Group is not unanimous about the introduction of this motion and that some members of the Party realise that is is likely to defeat the object which it purports to seek, that is, self-government for Nigeria as a whole in 1956. Nevertheless, Party discipline is strong and all members are likely to vote as ordered. Even if the Action Group were prepared to throw overboard Bode Thomas (who is a strong protagonist of the motion and probably inspired it) and Enahoro (who is the only influential party member in the mid-west Provinces of the Western Region which are susceptible to N.C.N.C. blandishments) I do not see how they could withdraw the motion without loss of face. (Their political ineptitude constantly gets them committed to ill-conceived courses of action from which it is impossible to extricate themselves.) But a full realisation of the consequences of pressing the matter hard (including the boost that a threatened break-up of the country would give to the N.C.N.C. which has always argued that Regionalisation would create three Nigerias) may result in Action Group speeches in the House being less immoderate than they had planned.

6.   Though situation is fluid, it appears probable that Council of Ministers will decide to move dilatory motion or its equivalent immediately question is proposed in House of Representatives. Bode Thomas almost certainly, and Akintola probably, will defy this decision, or any decision other than full support of the motion, and will make fiery political speeches in the House. They will then have to be dismissed under Section 152 (2) of the Constitution Order in Council. This might lead to a boycott by

the Action Group but fear of a dissolution and fresh elections in which N.C.N.C. might have considerable success is likely to restrain them.

7.   Whatever may be the result of this Cabinet crisis and the debate on the motion, it is quite clear that the views of the Northern Central Ministers on this issue reflect the views of the Northern Regional Ministers and the overwhelming majority of the Northern Members. The harm already done to the unity of Nigeria is very great indeed. Even if somehow we scramble through the immediate crisis the Northerners are determined, after this meeting of the House of Representatives is over, to undertake a complete re-assessment of the position of the North—probably at an extraordinary joint meeting of both Northern Houses. The North is our sheet anchor and has constantly supported Government. If they felt betrayed they might look for help in achieving independence to Egypt or Pakistan or other Moslem countries. All possible steps will be taken to ensure that both North and West realise full implications of separation and to bring home to them that future lies in continued association (possibly in some modified form) with the rest of Nigeria.

8.   As I pointed out in my Telegram No. 337, further advance in the Gold Coast must simultaneously increase the fears of the North and compel southern politicians to press with greater conviction for sweeping changes here.[2] If the unity of Nigeria is to remain our objective a very firm stand by H.M.G. will be necessary in the near future. The strength of the measures necessary in Southern Nigeria to make such a stand successful will depend largely on H.M.G.'s action in the Gold Coast. The use of sanctions to compel Northern Nigeria to remain tied to a South which was granted concessions is out of the question.

Minute on 184

Sir T. Lloyd

I think you may wish to let Ministers see Sir J. Macpherson's savingram, and enclosures, at (28), which explains what happened in the Nigerian Council of Ministers when they discussed an Action Group motion due to be debated in the House of Representatives that self-government in 1956 should be accepted as a primary political objective.

It will be seen from this communication that a sharp cleavage arose in the Council, and that the whole problem of the unity of Nigeria was called in question. Sir John's assessment, in paragraph 7, is that 'the harm already done to the unity of Nigeria is very great indeed'.

The position actually reached is set out in paragraph 6, which makes it clear that the Governor may, in certain circumstances, have to dismiss two Western (Central) Ministers, Bode Thomas and Akintola, from office. If he takes this action under Section 152(2) of the constitution it will be because he considers that they have 'failed to carry out the policy, or any decision, of the Council'.

I think the Secretary of State and Minister of State may wish to know in advance of this possible eventuality, as well as of the general position. Furthermore, the Secretary of State is seeing, on the 1st April, Mr. Griffiths and the other members of

---

[2] See 182.

the Labour Party delegation which visited West Africa in January, to hear their impressions; and as it is probable that Mr. Griffiths may repeat to the Secretary of State what he said to Sir J. Macpherson in Lagos, namely that H.M.G. ought to regain the initiative in handling constitutional problems in Nigeria, the Secretary of State will doubtless wish to be brought right up-to-date.

For convenience of reference I have placed, at (29), a copy of the note which I sent to you yesterday which outlines the history of constitutional developments in the Gold Coast with particular reference to repercussions in Nigeria.

It is becoming increasingly clear to me that if the unity of Nigeria is to be preserved, and Nigeria as a whole kept within the Commonwealth, a fairly radical overhaul of the present Nigerian constitution will have to be undertaken soon. I do not feel ready to put forward any definite proposals at the moment because we all need more time to think. But I feel sure, if I may say so, that the advice which Mr. Gorell Barnes gave to Sir John Macpherson last autumn (please see minutes of 28th October on this file), and of which you reminded Sir John in your letter at (27), that the Southern Regions might have to be given a greater degree of autonomy than the North, opens up one important line of advance. In addition the Secretary of State has already agreed in principle (see (17)) to amend the constitution so as to give Nigerian Ministers individual responsibility for Departments. I believe we may also have to do something to solve the burning problem of the position of Lagos as part of the Western Region. There may be other matters requiring revision also.

I cannot help feeling that Sir John's real difficulty is not so much what has been happening, and what is likely to happen in the Gold Coast, as that he has been trying to work an almost unworkable constitution. There has been almost continuous friction for months about the position of Lagos, the limitations on the functions of Ministers, and the powers of the Centre in relation to regional legislation. I believe it is matters of this kind rather than developments in the Gold Coast which have led to the present crisis in the Council of Ministers and elsewhere in Nigeria.

I suggest a reply to (28) might be sent as in draft herewith.

T.B.W.
27.3.53

185 CO 554/277, no 1   27 Mar 1953
[Amendment of the constitution]: minute by I B Watt on changes to the constitution

[It was clear even before the self-government debate in the House of Representatives at the end of March that the CO was considering changes to the constitution. On 25 Mar 1953 Sir T Lloyd wrote to Macpherson, accepting that the changes in the Gold Coast (see 182) would make constitutional change in Nigeria inevitable and suggesting that 'part of the solution to this will eventually have to be found along the line of giving, in due time, the southern regions a greater degree of autonomy than the north' (CO 554/260, no 27, Lloyd to Macpherson, 25 Mar 1953). Watt's minute, reproduced here, shows how far thinking had progressed along these lines.]

Mr. Williamson
Your minute of 21st March. I have seen the telegrams from Sir John Macpherson (No. 337 and No. 676 Saving) and have tried to sort out the constitutional issues which would be prominent in efforts to solve a largely political crisis.

2.   I have seen the West African Department files to which you refer, and have discussed with Mr. Huijsman and Mr. Godden with great profit to myself.

3.   In this minute I shall try to identify rather than solve the main constitutional problems which, I think, must be overcome if the present difficulties are to be surmounted, and a more sure basis laid for Nigeria's future.

4.   The crisis comes mainly from the dissatisfaction felt by influential politicians in the West and East regions with the Central Government, which they consider concedes too much to the position of the Northern region; this dissatisfaction is already serious enough to threaten the unity of the Colony, and will intensify if and when there is a constitutional change in the Gold Coast. The Governor, I think, realises that, if a United Nigeria is to be preserved for the future, it may be necessary, at this stage, to permit the three regions to develop at different constitutional speeds. Our main problem therefore is how to change the present constitution so as to permit this, and at the same time retain sufficient unifying force through the Central Government to ensure that it is a united Nigeria which will ultimately achieve nationhood.

5.   Some sort of federal arrangement seems thus to be required, but the circumstances in Nigeria are different from those in which federations are usually created. These result as a rule from a number of countries or provinces recognising that they have sufficient common interests to make it worth their while sacrificing some parts of their individual identities and surrendering some of their powers of self-government to a Central government. In Nigeria unhappily it appears to be necessary to bring about a federal arrangement by a Central Government which already exists, devolving some of its authority to provinces which want more, not less, identity and self-government. Some Ministers have apparently been talking in Council about India and Pakistan, and the political situation in Nigeria today almost suggests that the difference between the discordant regions might more logically be handled as the India/Pakistan split was handled, rather than by a federal treatment which posits a desire to go forward together. However, the policy of the Governor, and of H.M.G., will, I assume, be to arrest the tendency to split, and do what is practicable to ensure the eventual unity of the Colony.

6.   With all diffidence, I suggest that we consider amending the Constitution to provide for something on the following lines:—

(a) A federal form of government consisting of the Central Government and the three Regional Governments.

(b) The Regional Governments is the West and the East could be given, as and when appropriate in each of them, universal adult suffrage, and an all-elected Ministerial system; the North could continue to work through electoral colleges and retain greater official influence in its Executive.

(c) There would be exclusive and concurrent lists of subjects upon which the Central Government alone, and the Central and Regional Governments, respectively, could legislate; on all other matters the Regional Governments would alone have power to legislate. The subjects on the exclusive list would be few in number, notably external relations, defence, Colony economic policy, the Public Service, customs etc. (i.e. those at present handled main by the Chief Secretary and Financial Secretary's Offices). The list of subjects on which Regional Governments are at present empowered to make laws would be expanded in consequence and they would take over much more of the work at present being done by the Central Ministries, which latter would be much reduced in size and scope, and some of which would be abolished.

(d) The Central Legislature would be constituted largely as it is at present, and likewise the Central Executive. There would be more Ministers without Portfolio, but the equal representation of Regions in the Council of Ministers would remain. The composition of the Central Executive, and the relations between the Governor and the Central Executive would have to be as 'advanced' constitutionally, as those in the most 'advanced' of the regions.

(e) It would be necessary to provide the Supreme Court with authority for constitutional interpretation, i.e. to settle disputes about the extent of Central and Regional authority. To the extent that the political differences between the Regions took the form of bickerings about constitutional interpretation, some part of their settlement would thus be transferred to the Courts from the Governor and the Secretary of State.

(f) The present Article 96 of the Constitution which gives the Central Government power to disapprove Regional legislation would, surely, have to go; but the Lieutenant-Governors and the Governor would retain their powers of certification and their discretion in vetoing or reserving Bills.

(g) Members and Ministers in the Central Government would be drawn, as at present, from Members of Regional Legislatures. Most true federations forbid this, but it seems essential to preserve the conception of a united country, and to retain for the Central Government the services of the leading political figures. They would also be 'exposed' (if I may use the word) to the advice and persuasiveness of the Governor, and, through him, of the Secretary of State.

7.   It would be essential, I think, to preserve to the Central Government as much as possible of control of economic and financial policy and administration; this might be the easier because of the disproportionately high contribution which the Northern region makes to the total Colonial revenue. It is only as a united Colony that Nigeria's economic future, on which her political happiness depends, can be properly fulfilled.

8.   I hope that these notes may at least help to clarify for these concerned some of the main points. I am ready to discuss whenever you wish.

9.   I am sending copies of this minute to Mr. Gorell-Barnes, Mr. Peck, Dr. Mercer, Mr. Huijsman and Mr. Godden.

186 CO 554/241, no 63   30 Mar 1953
[Western Region local government bill]: despatch no 667 from Mr Lyttelton to Sir J Macpherson replying to criticisms of his intervention over the Western Region local government bill

I have the honour to refer to your Secret despatch No. 195 of the 22nd January[1] in which you informed me of the conclusions reached by the Council of Ministers on the 16th December last concerning the Western Region Local Government Bill.

---

[1] See 174.

2.   I have noted the action which has been taken, and which it is proposed to take, with respect to the Bill, as recorded in the second and third paragraphs of your despatch.

3.   It is with surprise and regret that I have learned of the strong resentment expressed by the Council of Ministers at my having placed them in possession of my views on the Bill before they had considered it. I should be glad if you would assure the Council that, my object was to help them in furthering the passage into law with the least possible delay and difficulty of an obviously important measure.

4.   My first knowledge of the Bill came, as you have said, from a Question which I was called upon to answer in the House of Commons, and this led me to suggest that I might be given an opportunity of seeing the Bill and of seeking the advice on it of my Advisory Panel on Local Government, whose comments I felt sure from experience would be of value to the Western Regional and Nigerian Governments. When I had received copies of the Bill I also took the opportunity to obtain the comments of my legal advisers who expressed the view that it was beyond the competence of the Regional legislature to enact certain of the provisions included in the Bill. I thought that the Council of Ministers would undoubtedly wish to know of this opinion and I therefore asked Mr. Benson in my despatch of the 14th December to convey to the Council the advice I had received. Although the terms of the Nigerian Constitution impose no obligation upon me to do this, I find it hard to believe that the Council of Ministers would have wished me deliberately to withhold from them advice of such an important nature. Had I not asked that the advice be so conveyed, one of two things would have happened. Either your advisers would have drawn attention to the defects in the Bill in which case the result would have been the same; or else they would not have done so in which case the action to remedy the position, which the Nigerian Government have already set in train, would not have been initiated till later, with consequent loss of time.

5.   A spirit of friendly collaboration has characterised the relationships of myself and my predecessors with the Governments of territories which have achieved advanced constitutions, and it was in this spirit that I acted as I did. I offer no apology for my action and I do not understand the conclusion drawn by Ministers, referred to in paragraph 6 of your despatch, that my intervention in this case at a stage before the Council had formally considered the Western Region's Bill means that all Regional legislation should be sent to me in draft. I have never suggested or contemplated this, and I would point to the amount of Regional legislation which has come into existence since the inauguration of the new constitution, very little of which I have seen before its final stages, and to the fact that in no case has a Lieutenant-Governor been instructed to withhold assent from a Bill nor has any law been disallowed. The difficulties which I foresaw arising over the present important measure seemed to me to justify my asking Mr. Benson to acquaint Ministers with them in order that the Council might deliberate the matter with a full knowledge of their existence. I readily assure Ministers that my advice was not indicative of a lack of confidence in the capacity and sense of responsibility of the Council.

6.   I should like to take this opportunity to refer to an important aspect of the working of advanced Colonial constitutions. The instruments establishing such constitutions normally include provision for the intervention at successive stages in the passage of legislation of the various constitutional authorities. There are thus

stages at which submission to higher authority is constitutionally obligatory. I cannot emphasize too strongly, however, my conviction of the value of, and need for, early consultation between all those who will eventually have constitutional *locus standi* in a legislative, or indeed an executive, act. Experience shows that such consultation, carried out in a spirit of friendliness and mutual trust, often serves to clear up misunderstandings and reconcile differences of opinion or, better still, to prevent their arising—and nearly always results in agreement being reached. Nor need it in any way blur the respective responsibilities of the various authorities concerned; for, should agreement not be reached, it is always open for one authority then to take the matter to the point when another has to decide whether or not to exercise his constitutional powers of intervention.

7.   The objections which have been raised by Ministers against my decision to offer my advice when I did in the present instance, and hence against the principle, which I hold to be of fundamental importance, that there should be early and informal consultation whenever there is occasion for it, can only have arisen, it seems to me, from some misunderstanding of our respective roles under the present constitution of Nigeria. That constitution was not intended to set up a series of entities each in opposition and concerned to widen their jurisdiction at the expense of the other. On the contrary it was intended to provide a constitutional framework within which the Regional Governments, the Central Government, and Her Majesty's Government in the United Kingdom could work together in the best interests of Nigeria and its peoples. This being so the Secretary of State has, as I see it, not merely the right but the clear duty to offer his advice at any stage if, by so doing he considers that he can in any way assist the progress of Nigeria and the Nigerian people. It is in this conviction that I myself have acted, and would wish to continue to act. It is my hope that Nigerian Ministers, both Central and Regional, will in a similar spirit, recognise the value of early, full and free consultation between Central and Regional Governments on matters which may affect more than one Region or the interests of Nigeria as a whole or in which more than one of the four Governments are constitutionally concerned.

187   CO 554/260, no 34   1 Apr 1953

[Self-government motion]: inward telegram no 1 from Sir J Macpherson to Mr Lyttelton reporting on the debate in the House of Representatives on the motion for self-government in 1956

My savingram No. 383.

Crisis in the Council of Ministers.[1]

On 27th March, the Council of Ministers decided by a majority to abstain from speaking or voting on Action Group motion for self government in 1956. Four Western ministers and Endeley dissented, and favoured free speaking and voting. Remaining three Eastern ministers were neutral and did not vote.

---

[1] See 184.

2.   Motion was put down for debate Tuesday, 31st March. At 9.30 a.m. that day the Oni of Ife told me that, having failed to persuade Action Group leaders to see reason, he was under compulsion not to abide by the Council's decision. He would not speak but would vote. This would leave me no option but to revoke his appointment and to avoid this, he felt bound to resign office before the motion was debated. He tendered written resignation dated 30th March.

3.   Debate on motion began at 10.30 a.m. After amendment moved by Sardauna of Sokoto and duly seconded Oni, in a brief speech, stated his intense worry during the past day and inability to stand aloof from the people of his Region on this matter. Hence his resignation. Northern member then moved dilatory motion.[2] Awolowo, clearly taken by surprise, made intemperate and rash speech attacking the British violently and Northerners by association with them. Reference to historic Fulani leader, Othman Dan Fodio caused, at one point, extreme tension. He ended by announcing that the West would walk out of the House, but members were recalled by order from the Oni.

4.   Mbadiwe then spoke for the N.C.N.C. group with the same ending, upon which all N.C.N.C. and Action Group members (including ministers, Oni and Alake) left the House.

5.   There followed an excellent and forceful speech by Jaja Wachuku on behalf of the new National Independence party supporting, in the interests of unity of Nigeria, dilatory motion; condemning the original motion (with whose sense, however, he and his party agreed) as ill timed, inept and mischievous; and castigating those who had walked out, both as irresponsible and as would be dictators.

6.   All remaining members of the Government and a few members of the National Independence party still in Lagos, and all Northerners sat tight except Endeley who 'went out to ascertain why members had walked out' but returned later in the day to his seat on the Government bench.

7.   Dilatory motion duly carried with no dissentient, and the House went on to public business before the sitting suspended at 1 p.m.

8.   At 2.30 p.m. I received letters of resignation signed by ? Ezee [Bode] Thomas, Akintola and Prest. Grounds therein were disagreement with the Council's decision on the self government motion, but by that time this was nonsensical as the course of the debate had not, in the outcome, called for implementation of the Council of Ministers' decision.

9.   Action Group members arrived at the House before 3 p.m. in the expectation of hearing ex ministers make personal explanations, but learnt from the President that no opportunity could arise in the midst of public business without taking seats. House completed business and rose at 5.30 p.m.

10.   I am sending a factual message to the House today, and I expect non factual personal explanations to be given by three ex ministers, which are likely to have strong anti official note, and improperly disclose details of voting within the Council of Ministers.

11.   These resignations are much to be preferred to the necessity, previously envisaged, of dismissals.

---

[2] i.e. a motion to adjourn, moved by Malam Ibrahim Imam.

188   CO 554/260, no 40   2 Apr 1953

[Self-government motion]: inward savingram no 774 from Sir J
Macpherson to Mr Lyttelton on the resignation of Western ministers
over the motion for selfgovernment in 1956. *Annex*
Minute by T B Williamson

[One consequence of the fall-out from the self-government debate was, at least in the
short term, a political alliance between the AG and the NCNC. Another came with press
threats of violence that drew on the situation in Kenya, and followed Akintola's raising of
the possibility of a Mau Mau-type rising in Nigeria in the House of Representatives in
March. On 16 Apr the *Daily Service*, an AG paper, editorialised under the heading 'Mau
Mau or no Mau Mau?': 'If constitutional methods fail to bring us self-government we
reserve the right to adopt other methods . . . The Mau Mau, with all its terror, with all its
horror, may still be the way out of Nigeria's bondage. If constitutional methods are
allowed to succeed, and if imperialist agents like Sir John Macpherson and his charming,
well-dressed, but politically egregious Benson would allow the peaceful attainment of
self-government by or before 1956, then there would be no soil in which Mau Mau or any
other form of extreme methods can germinate'.]

My telegram No. Pers. 1—*Constitutional crisis*.[1]

I enclose copies of correspondence exchanged with three Western Ministers with
Portfolio, regarding their resignation and the personal statements they proposed to
make to the House of Representatives.[2]

2.   After Prayers in House on 1st April, the President read out a message from me
regarding the resignations. I enclose a copy.

3.   At a later stage Bode Thomas and Akintola made personal statements. Prest
pleaded sickness and was not present but Bode Thomas said he was speaking for
him. Copies of the two speeches are enclosed. You will see that the speakers
totally disregarded the conditions on which they received permission to refer to
proceedings of Council of Ministers, and, in particular, that Bode Thomas disclosed how Members had voted and purported to describe the proceedings in the
Council, including my own attitude and my conduct of the proceedings. Comment
on the immoderate tone of the speeches is superfluous and it is unnecessary for
me to tell you that the mischievous allegation that ex-officio members had consistently voted with the Northern Ministers against those from the West and the
East, is totally untrue. I recall no previous case, nor does any remaining Minister
or Member of the Council of Ministers, in which this has happened, and even in
this latest case three Eastern Members were neutral, because they knew that
Western Ministers were divulging information about Council proceedings. The
Attorney General was in the course of making an investigation into this when the
Ministers resigned.

4.   After the personal statements had been made, Action Group and N.C.N.C.
Members walked out of the House. The President then permitted Njoku, Minister of
Mines and Power, to make a short statement from the Government Bench. He spoke
well. Arikpo, Minister of Lands, Survey & Local Development, who was in charge of
Government business then moved the adjournment of the House *sine die*, and in the
course of doing so managed to touch on the resignations and the attitude of the

---

[1] See 187.   [2] Enclosures not printed.

Council of Ministers in a responsible manner. On the Motion for adjournment *sine die*, Jaja Wachuku made another sound but sad speech opposing, on the grounds that the untruths heard in the personal statements that morning should not go uncontradicted. Two Northern Members then spoke, including the Sardauna of Sokoto. His final remark was that the mistake of 1914 had now come to light (a reference to amalgamation of Northern and Southern Nigeria).

5.   I was much concerned by the fact that the misrepresentations and untrue allegations of the two former Ministers had to go virtually unchallenged in the House. In particular, the three Central Ministers from the East are in a very difficult position because their courage in taking an unpopular line in an attempt to preserve the unity of Council of Ministers and of Nigeria has laid them open to further abuse and allegations of being Imperialist tools. Accordingly, I gave a short broadcast over the Nigerian Broadcasting Service last evening. I enclose a copy.

6.   Azikiwe publicly embraced Awolowo outside House of Representatives after the walk-out by Action Group and N.C.N.C. Members on 31st March, and there is a talk of N.C.N.C. and Action Group link-up. Many of the political leaders in this country are unpredictable and it is unwise to be categorical on this. There may be a joining together against us (British officials) but neither party will be sincere and it does not seem possible that any such alliance could last. You may be interested in the attached record of my conversation with the Oni of Ife and the Alake of Abeokuta when the former came to tender his resignation on 31st March. I saw the Oni again today when he came to take leave of me before returning to Ife. He told me that he was going to 'get busy' in calling the Western Obas together. On the subject of a deal between the N.C.N.C. and Action Group he said that it would be in Yoruba character if the Action Group met N.C.N.C. with an intention to deceive. But they were enemies and could never be reconciled.

7.   Responsible Yorubas in Lagos are greatly distressed and anxious and a number of them have come to see me to express their views and sympathetic anxiety. They fear, rightly, that the Action Group leaders in their present emotional state may speak or act in such a way that they can never retract. (At the risk of overburdening this communication, I enclose a copy of Awolowo's speech on 31st March).

8.   Members of House of Representatives have dispersed. The Lieutenant-Governor, Northern Region will have discussions with Northern Central and Regional Ministers at Kaduna on 4th April. He will have a difficult task to persuade them to think in terms other than of separation but he is full of faith and hope and works and will guide Northern thinking wisely and sympathetically.

9.   It is too soon to attempt a full assessment of the situation or to suggest what action or changes may be necessary. We are however thinking hard and I shall keep you informed of developments.

Annex to 188: Note by HE of interview with the Oni of Ife and the Alake of Abeokuta on 31 March 1953

The two Obas arrived at 9.30 a.m., in a state of considerable agitation and anxiety, and asked to see me, about 'the trouble in the West'.

2.   They said that they had convened a meeting, in the Alake's house in Lagos, after the House of Representatives rose at 9 p.m. on 30th March. In addition to the

two Obas, there were fourteen Action Group Ministers and Members, including Mr. Awolowo, Chief Bode Thomas and Mr. Akintola. The meeting went on till after midnight but the two Obas got nowhere with the politicians, though they had spoken to them in 'harsh tones' about their misguided attitude over the motion regarding Self-Government in 1956. They had come to me because they didn't know what to do.

3. I expressed understanding of their position but I gave them a strong pep-talk on the survival of Chiefs. One danger to the system was that the Chiefs should fail to move with the times. No less a danger was it continually to surrender to extremist political party leaders. If they did this, not only would they let down their simple peasant subjects, but the whole institution of Chieftaincy would be gradually shorn of power and influence and would not survive except in a ceremonial sense. I instanced the case of the Gold Coast Chiefs and the C.P.P.

4. The Oni said that the Action Group politicians were determined to destroy Azikiwe. If they failed to pursue this Self-Government motion with the utmost vigour it would mean death for the Action Group and the triumph of 'that evil man Azikiwe'. The Obas had criticised the Action Group severely for not consulting them in advance. The politicians had apologised and had agreed not to fail in this again. The Obas were determined to reassert their authority. After the meeting of the House of Representatives finished it was their intention to call all the Obas together for a secret conclave to decide upon their attitude. They would then meet the Action Group leaders and get the position clarified. Certainly the Obas must have representatives at all future meetings of the Parliamentary Committee.

5. I said that such action, desirable as it was, might come too late. Irreparable damage might be done during the debate on Self-Government, particularly in the splitting of the Council of Ministers. I had long thought that the Obas had been unwise not to assert their authority sooner. The Oni, supported by the Alake, explained that their reason for helping to establish the Action Group, and for supporting them, was to save the Western Region from Azikiwe. The old stalwarts of the Youth Movement had been nationalists too. They got rid of Azikiwe from the Youth Movement but they had failed to defeat or destroy him. The younger nationalist politicians of the West had undertaken to drive Azikiwe out of the West, and for that reason the Obas had supported them. They did not love them—they too were 'enemies'—but they were 'the lesser of two evils'.

6. I asked why the Obas, and particularly the Oni, could not make a stand now, rather than later. Each surrender gravely weakened their position. The Oni replied that if they gave evidence of disunity in the West the Consequences would be very serious, though he was aware that this was not the last mischief the Action Group would do. I then asked him point-blank what he intended to do when the motion was debated. Surely he would abide by the decision of the Council of Ministers to abstain from speaking or voting. The Oni said that he would not speak in the debate but that he would be obliged to vote—to preserve the unity of the West. I then felt bound to be cruel to him and said that he would be letting down his people. He would not be acting according to his conscience and he was putting a political party before Nigeria. That was not all. I should be obliged to revoke his appointment as a Central Minister, on the grounds that he had failed in his duty to abide by a decision of the Council of Ministers. That a great Oba should so act would be a shock to opinion within and outside Nigeria. . . .

Minute on 188

Mr. Gorell Barnes
Please see Mr. Huijsman's minute of the 8th April.

You have already seen Sir J. Macpherson's letter of the 1st April, and you will now wish to see his savingram No. 774 of the 2nd April temporarily registered at (40). You may also wish to let higher authority see this savingram, and perhaps the marked portions of the enclosures. (As we shall need these papers on Tuesday of next week I am sending them forward in red.)

It is clear that the discussions with the Governors next week will be concerned with constitutional problems in Nigeria as well as the Gold Coast; as to which I have already sent forward a memorandum. We shall have the opportunity for a preliminary talk with Sir J. Macpherson on Tuesday the 14th April, as the 'tripartite' talks are not due to begin until 10.30 a.m. on Wednesday 15th, when Sir C. Arden-Clarke will also be here.

I only wish to make one comment at this stage about the recent happenings in Nigeria. Undoubtedly Sir J. Macpherson was faced with an acutely difficult position, and one hesitates to offer any criticism. But I cannot help feeling that he put too much of a strain on the Action Group Ministers in subjecting them to a decision that they should neither speak nor vote on the motion about self-government by 1956. I believe his wiser course might have been to have left all his Ministers free at least to vote on the motion in accordance with the dictates of their individual consciences. Had he done so the motion would almost certainly have been defeated, and he would not have been faced with the resignation of all his four Western Ministers. It looks very much, on our present information, as though he has 'boxed' himself; and it is difficult to see how he is going to get any Western Ministers back into the Council of Ministers. He will probably have to reappoint the four who have resigned.

I have written to Sir C. Arden-Clarke as herewith, so as to continue to keep him in touch. With Sir T. Lloyd's agreement I have sent him a copy of Sir J. Macpherson's letter of the 1st April, less the first and last paragraphs.)

T.B.W.
9.4.53

189 CO 554/260, no 73   7 Apr 1953
[Self-government motion]: letter from B E Sharwood-Smith to T B Williamson on an examination of possible options for the future of the Northern Region. *Annex*

I have got my Governor's agreement to my writing to you (a copy will go to Lagos) about certain aspects of recent developments in this country. Substantially, what has occurred is that the Northern Members of the Central Legislature, resentful of, and disgusted at, the manoeuvres, manners and methods of the Southern political leaders and their followers, have found themselves mentally back where their representatives were at the opening of the Ibadan Conference, with their worst fears realised. They are now in effect demanding a complete reassessment of the position with a view, in their present frame of mind, to asking for separation with some form of association at the Centre to protect their interests. This can be taken as the worst possible alternative of all, and we hope to improve on it appreciably as time passes.

2.   We ourselves are being as objective as possible, and are in the process of assessing the situation from all angles with a view to presenting the Northern Ministers with as reasoned a picture as possible of the factual background of the situation in which they are now liable to find themselves. It will probably help if I attach extracts from a directive issued by me as soon as the storm broke to my people in Kaduna. My Governor has seen it and approved. I would be grateful if means could be found for F.D.K. Williams,[1] who is mentioned in paragraph 4(e) of the attachment, to be assisted in the appropriate quarters in his enquiries. He will be instructed to call at the C.O. and present himself to you as soon as convenient to him after his arrival on leave, which will be towards the end of this month. It may be that he will find that there are other sources of information that he could profitably explore— examples are certain aspects of the Persian story and also the picture, past and present, in Iraq (paragraph 4 (g) of the attachment).

3.   I would be most grateful for any assistance that you can contrive in these matters. I feel that I must think not only of the present, but also of the near and middle distance in terms of developments to come.[2]

Annex to 189: Extracts from directive from lieutenant-governor, Northern Region, Nigeria, to Northern Secretariat

2.   ... We must hope that this Northern feeling will moderate and do our best to cause it to moderate, but I greatly fear that continuous fanning from without, and what might be called the natural course of events, will result in, at best, only a moderate abatement ....

3.   We have already discussed the question of certain 'exercises' which we should carry out to enable us to assess the position as correctly as possible in the light of:—

(i)   the factual background in Nigeria
(ii) the experience of other countries.

4.   These 'exercises' should be:—

(a) A 'green light exercise' designed to determine how the Northern Region could most effectively, in terms of Nigeria, and satisfactorily, in terms of its own aspirations, combine with the other two Regions on lines following those operative under the present Constitution, subject to a modified form of association at the Centre.

(b) A 'red light exercise' designed to illustrate the effect on the Northern Region of separatism, even on an agreed and friendly basis, from the other two Regions. The 'exercise' should cover in summarised form all the disadvantages, political, economic and social. It should also cover ways and means, if any, of overcoming or ameliorating the position, presumably again by an appropriate form of association at the Centre. It should emphasise to what extent the 3 Regions of Nigeria are inter-

---

[1] F D K Williams, administrative officer, Nigeria, 1941.

[2] In his reply to this letter Williamson wrote: 'We firmly believe that unity is in the best interests of all regions of Nigeria, but we recognise that the only solution for present difficulties, and probably the only hope eventually of achieving and preserving that unity, lies in some modified and looser form of association at the Centre ...' (CO 554/236, no 46A, Williamson to Sharwood-Smith, 18 Apr 1953.)

dependent, particularly in terms of internal trade, communications and the manning of the Civil Service.

(c) A 'red light exercise' designed to illustrate the major implications, in terms of Nigeria as a whole, of the achievement of self-government. I am thinking particularly of

(i) external relationships
(ii) external representation
(iii) the effect on capital investment
(iv) the effect on the Civil Service
(v) the effect as regards defence in terms of land, sea and air; and finally
(vi) any other major implications.

I am aware that 'exercise' (a), the first draft of which has been completed, covers in some degree a certain amount of what I have detailed above, but it will be impossible at this stage to avoid this, my idea being that eventually, when we have completed our series of 'exercises', we then proceed to co-ordinate a complete assessment. The next exercise will be:—

(d) as a 'red light exercise', a study in summarised form of Liberia since its attainment of sovereignty; with particular relation to the manner in which it has faced its problems in terms of what should be expected of a modern sovereign state.

(e) the next exercise, also 'red light', should be a study of events in Burma since it achieved independence and the effect of that event on the life of its people, politically, economically and socially.

These two could be carried out by an officer on leave (Mr. F.D.K. Williams), assuming assistance and advice from the appropriate Ministries in the U.K.

(f) The next, an 'amber light exercise', should be a paper on Egypt under Cromer, the object being to consider the future of the Administration in the Northern Region. The functions of Cromer's British Administrative Officers, the modification of these functions, and the subsequent withdrawal of these officers should provide a very interesting parallel. This can be conducted by Mr. Greatbatch.

(g) Finally, there should be an 'amber light exercise' on the administration of Iraq, firstly under the British, and secondly since the achievement of independence . . .

6. *The 'exercises' to which I refer in my fourth paragraph must be as objective as possible. We must avoid partiality and we must avoid being over-affected emotionally by nature of our close association with the Northern leaders and Northern Peoples.* We all know that a closely integrated and united Nigeria is the optimum; failing that, we must get the best possible alternative. Three independent Nigerias, inimical to each other and in danger of further sub-division, are what at all cost we must avoid.

190 CO 554/260, no 76A   15 Apr 1953
[Amendment of the constitution]: CO note on a meeting with Sir J Macpherson and Sir C Arden-Clarke to discuss constitutional problems in Nigeria and the Gold Coast   [Extract]

[Following the proposals for constitutional change on the Gold Coast that had emerged in early 1953 (see 182) and the crisis over the Enahoro motion in the House of

Representatives (see 184), Macpherson and Marshall visited London for discussions with
Lyttelton and Arden-Clarke. Two meetings were held on 15 Apr, the first chaired by Sir T
Lloyd and the second, reproduced here, by Lyttelton, Discussion of the Gold Coast is not
included; this can be found in BDEEP series B, vol 1, R Rathbone, ed, *Ghana* part II, 128.]

Review of the political situation in Nigeria

Sir John Macpherson, reviewing the political situation in Nigeria, said that it was not
good but that a month or so must elapse before it could be seen how matters really
stood.

2.   In the East the National Independence Party (N.I.P.) might now be able to
establish a majority in the Eastern House of Assembly although they had Dr.
Azikiwe's publicity machine and Press against them. The N.I.P. were optimistic and
inclined to favour an early reassembly of the House while the tide ran in their favour.
The N.C.N.C. were not keen on a dissolution and election, not only because they
knew it was a gamble whether they would secure a majority but because they did not
wish to face election expenses, especially in the extremely shaky state of the
Continental Bank which Dr. Azikiwe had raided—quite improperly—to the extent of
nearly £100,000 to bolster up the N.C.N.C. The first step would be for the present
House to reassemble but the Lieutenant-Governor took the view that this step need
not be hurried. By use of the Lieutenant-Governor's reserved powers the Regional
Appropriation Bill had been passed and there was no essential legislation
outstanding. It was therefore possible that the House might not be recalled until
after the Coronation. It was desirable to give time for a knowledge of the situation to
percolate down to the villages where Ibo shrewdness might set opinion in favour of
the N.I.P. Already the declaration of neutrality as between the N.I.P. and N.C.N.C. of
all but one of the Cameroons bloc was a heartening sign and might even mean that
the N.I.P. would obtain Cameroons support in continuing the work of the House. If,
however, there proved to have been no significant change in the mood of the House
and Government business was still held up, then the Lieutenant-Governor would
have the alternatives either of inviting the less extreme N.C.N.C. members to form a
Government or; under the Constitution (Amendment) Order in Council which would
have then become law, to order a dissolution and fresh elections.

3.   The attitude of the *North* over recent events was hard, cold, and implacable.
They had been angered by the consistent bad manners and political tricks of the
Southerners, and resented extremely the accusation that they were under the
thumbs of the British. They took the view that they had for 14 months tried hard to
collaborate with the South, but having met only with abuse they would prefer to
withdraw. Without a marked change of mood it was unlikely that it would be possible
to persuade the Northern members to attend another session of the House of
Representatives, anyway as at present constituted. The two Northern Houses were to
meet in succession in May and between the meetings there would be a joint meeting
of members of both Houses, but with no officials present, at which they would assess
their position. The North were clearly thinking of separation from the southern
Regions, but the Lieutenant-Governor would try to persuade them not to take any
drastic steps for the present.

4.   In the *West* the House of Assembly was due to meet on the 4th May. The first
step to be taken would be to attempt to fill the vacancies created by the resignations
of the four Western members of the Council of Ministers. The Joint Council of the
Region was likely either to refuse any proposals from the Governor or to agree only

to put forward the four Ministers who had resigned. (A telegram received in the course of the meeting from the Olowo of Owo, Secretary of the Western House of Chiefs, indicated that the latter course was the one that would be adopted.) The Lieutenant-Governor intended to refuse to submit the names of two anyway of the ex-Ministers, namely Chief Bode Thomas and Mr. Akintola, not merely because of their bad faith in divulging the voting in the Council of Ministers over the issue of self-government in 1956, but because of their almost certain responsibility for leakages of information about the proceedings of the Council of Ministers over a period. Although the exercise of attempting to replace the Western Ministers might well prove to be a sterile one, it would have to be undertaken. The first steps might be taken before the Western Houses reassembled but there would be advantage in the procedure as a whole (which would involve the submission and resubmission of various alternative names) not being undertaken at any great speed.

5.   In reply to a question from the Secretary of State, *Sir John Macpherson* said that the Eastern and Northern members of the Council of Ministers had been against his coming home for consultations at this juncture, as they felt that much capital would be made out of it by the Action Group and the N.C.N.C. who would claim that this showed that the Council of Ministers was worried and anxious and unsure of its position. He had told them that his intention was to bring the Secretary of State up to date on the latest developments and not to determine future plans. He added that the people of the Northern Region had throughout been loyal, trustworthy and reasonable, although they were now beginning to wonder whether they might be let down by Her Majesty's Government. He felt it was unthinkable they should be so let down; on every count, including that of numbers, the North had claims to consideration.

Course of action to be followed

6.   Agreeing with Sir John Macpherson's concluding sentiments, the *Secretary of State* said that in his view the constitution would certainly have to be radically recast. He would revert later to the imperfections in the present constitution and to the changes likely to be necessary. His immediate concern was to settle what dilatory tactics could be adopted which would give a chance for a more tranquil atmosphere to develop.

7.   Considerable discussion then took place in which the following points were made:—

(a) The present constitutional set up corresponded neither with present feelings nor with the facts. Radical constitutional revision, such as the Secretary of State proposed and which took account of facts as they were, would be received with relief in many quarters.

(b) The changes to be envisaged should include a looser form of association at the Centre, which nevertheless safeguarded the interests of all three Regions, and greater 'autonomy' in legislation for the Regions themselves, possibly over a wider range of subjects than at present. The creation of separate Ministries and the appointment of some (African) Parliamentary Under-Secretaries in the Regions might also be agreed to. All Regions could be given the same degree of additional 'autonomy', as regards the creation of separate Ministeries etc., there would be no objection to some differences between Regions, though no changes agreed for one Region would be refused to either of the other two, if they wanted them.

(c) A conference on the lines of the General (Ibadan) Conference of 1950 was no longer possible and proposals for the best means of working out the constitutional changes might have to come from the Secretary of State, even at the risk of ultimate failure to secure general agreement on a new constitution being laid at the door of Her Majesty's Government.

(d) Nigerian co-operation in any discussions must be sought and there was reason to hope that at any rate the North and the N.I.P. would agree to participate. The West would be more difficult; Mr. Awolowo took the view that Her Majesty's Government ought to push the North into the speedier advance which the West advocated.

(e) In due course a predominantly Nigerian conference or commission should if possible be arranged in which all three Regions would be represented. The chairman would probably have to come from outside Nigeria in any case, and all or part of the proceedings might have to be held in London under the chairmanship of the Secretary of State.

(f) No public announcement should be made of a decision to overhaul the constitution for the time being; certainly not until after the meetings of both Northern Houses in May.

(g) The Minister of State, during his forthcoming visit to Nigeria to preside over the conference about the Royal West African Frontier Force, should take the opportunity to have private discussions with representatives of all three Regions, beginning with the North if the timetable permitted.[1] In such discussions the Minister of State would have to be guided by the situation as he found it, but his primary object should be to obtain the views of the Regions informally rather than to state a policy. He could, however, say privately that Her Majesty's Government considered the constitution would without prejudicing the unity of Nigeria, have to be revised, and he could refer to the possibility of changes as outlined in (b) above.

(h) In such discussions the North might especially be assured, as from the Secretary of State, that progress would not be made over their heads, and that they would be fully consulted when the constitution was looked at afresh. To press them too hard at this stage to agree to remain within a united Nigeria might cause them to react violently against the idea.

(i) The West did not fully appreciate the seriousness of the attitude of the North and the impetuosity and lack of political sense of its leader, despite his other merits, would make it necessary to handle the West with the greatest care. It was important that nothing should be done to alienate them further.

(j) Sir J. Macpherson emphasized that our aim had been and still was to bring a united Nigeria to political maturity and that any changes either at the Centre or in the Regions should be such as would further the achievement of that aim.

(k) There should be no suggestion of any weakening of the Governor's powers.

(l) The preservation of a united Nigeria was regarded as of particular importance in the comparatively poor Eastern Region and both the N.C.N.C. and the N.I.P. supported it. Any suggestion of an intention to modify the powers of the Central Government in such a way as to undermine that unity would render more difficult the task of the N.I.P. in establishing itself against the N.C.N.C.

---

[1] See 193 and 194.

(m) Enquiries from Parliament and from the Press should not in the meantime be answered by any definite statements of policy. It should be explained that the Governor had reported to the Secretary of State in London and that the Minister of State in his forthcoming visit to Nigeria would have the opportunity to learn the views of representatives of all Regions; the problems however were complex and would call for patient, unhurried and understanding consideration; no further statement should be expected for some time . . . .

191 CO 554/260, no 62   15 Apr 1953
[Amendment of the constitution]: conclusions of a meeting held at the CO under the chairmanship of Mr Lyttelton to discuss the need radically to revise the constitution

It is agreed that the Nigeria constitution will have to be radically revised. But no *public* statement to this effect should be made for the time being; certainly not before the views of the North are known following the meetings of both Northern Houses in May.

2.   When the time comes, proposals for a revised constitution should, if possible, be framed by a predominantly Nigerian commission or conference representative of all three Regions. Outside help would be needed and probably a chairman from outside Nigeria and circumstances might arise in which the proceedings or part of them could preferably take place in London under the Chairmanship of the Secretary of State. Every effort must accordingly be made to dissuade the leaders from the different Regions from committing themselves to public statements which would make it impossible for them to sit down together later on. But this may well prove impossible; in which case the initiative may have to come from outside.

3.   In his *private* discussions with Nigerian and Regional Ministers the Minister of State will be guided largely by the situation as he finds it and his main objective will be to listen rather than to speak.[1] It is important that, when meeting the Northern Ministers, he should not at this stage press them so hard to agree to remain within a united Nigeria that they react violently against the idea. At the same time it is important that, in his talks with representatives of the East, he should not over-emphasize the necessity for a much looser association at the Centre, as the East ('good' and 'bad' alike) favour a unitary constitution.

4.   Accordingly the Minister of State's basic line, in *private* discussion, should be that H.M.G. consider that the constitution will have to be revised; and that, whilst they still believe that unity is in the best interests of all Regions of Nigeria, they recognise that the only solution of the present difficulties, and indeed the only hope of eventually achieving that unity, lies in some modified and looser form of association at the Centre at this stage.

5.   Elaboration on this basic theme would be along the following lines:—

(a) The Regional Governments could be given greater 'autonomy' in legislation, i.e. be less subject to 'interference' from the Centre and also possibly deal with

---

[1] Hopkinson travelled to Nigeria on 17 Apr to attend the West African Forces conference in Lagos. During his visit he met leaders from each region. See 193 and 194.

more subjects; but they would all be given the same degree of additional 'autonomy'.

(b) Other changes in the Regions such as the creation of separate Ministries and the appointment of some (African) Parliamentary Under-Secretaries would be by no means ruled out. In this respect there would be no objection to some differences between Regions, though no changes agreed for one Region would be refused to either of the other two, if they wanted them.

(c) It is inherent in the idea of a looser form of association that the interests of all three Regions must be fully safeguarded by the arrangements to be made at the Centre.

6. In dealing with enquiries from the Press etc., both the Governor and the Colonial Office will for the time being take the following line. The Governor has reported in London to the Secretary of State on the present position in Nigeria. The problems are complex and call for patient, unhurried and understanding consideration. The Minister of State for Colonial Affairs, during his forthcoming visit to Nigeria to preside at the conference about the financing of the Royal West African Frontier Force, will have the opportunity of hearing at first hand the views of representatives of all three Regions. It is unlikely, because of the complexity of the problems involved, that any further statement can be made for some time.

192   CO 554/262, no 221   15 Apr 1953
[Political situation]: Nigerian government notes of a discussion with heads of department on the current political situation

Mr. Benson said that he had asked Heads of Departments to come together in order that he might tell them something about the current political situation and the events leading up to it, and might make an attempt to answer any questions which they might raise. Had His Excellency been in Lagos it was, of course, a thing which he would wish to do himself.

2. Some of those present might have a very fair picture of what had been happening and would have the proper background in that picture: others might know less, either about the immediately past events or about the fuller background which led up to those events. All present were officials, and if they were to carry out their various duties properly as officials they must have a certain part at least of the facts behind the present crisis. All were bound by the Official Secrets Act and what he was going to say was committed to their secrecy. They would only be permitted to pass on any of it to their juniors if, in their considered judgment, it was both desirable and necessary that those juniors should have the information in order to enable them also to discharge their official functions properly.

3. Mr. Benson said that if anyone thought that the present political crisis had arisen within the last four or five weeks only, he was under grievous error. This crisis had been brewing ever since the beginning of 1952, and its origins went back even before that to the time when the new Constitution was being drafted. They should bear in mind certain facts about that time, and firstly that it was only with the greatest difficulty that the North had been persuaded to come in under this Constitution at all. They had only agreed to do so on the understanding that they

should have a 50% representation in the House of Representatives, an arrangement to which the West had strongly objected at the time, but which the East had eventually persuaded them to accept. The East, more than any other part of the country, had desired a united Nigeria and had shown themselves prepared to make considerable compromises and even sacrifices in order to secure it.

4.   They would remember also that at election time the Awolowo-Zik battle was at its height. Awolowo and the Action Group had come to power in the West really on one platform only; and that was that they would break down the power of Zik in the West and no doubt, by implication, gradually in the East also: but the Westerners' horizon had seldom been outside the boundaries of the Western Region.

5.   Heads of Departments would also remember that at the time when the Constitution was being framed and elections were taking place, there were two other strong pressure points tending to divide Nigeria: firstly, the Ilorin boundary question—a fight between the North and the West; and, secondly, the position of Lagos—a fight between the East and the West, with the North also much interested because of the North's need for an outlet to the sea. At that time, as he had said, the Awolowo-Zik battle was raging and the Eastern point of view was represented by Zik, himself a detribalized Easterner and the strong supporter of the party within Lagos which was both anti-Action Group and desired to keep Lagos out of the West. This party controlled the vast majority of the seats on the Lagos Town Council.

6.   The North had done a little horse trading over these two issues. They had said 'Hands off Ilorin and we will support you in your demand that Lagos goes into the West.'

7.   The North kept its bargain and so the position of Lagos was determined. The West, on the other hand, right from the beginning of 1952, directly they had got what they wanted over Lagos, allowed the attack on Ilorin to develop all over again. During the first four or five months of 1952, time and again Northern Ministers had expressed to him (Mr. Benson) their disgust and rage at this breach of faith.

8.   Ministers took office at the end of January, 1952, and even before that, but after the Action Group had won its elections in the West, Awolowo and other Western leaders came to see His Excellency and demanded things which were not in the Constitution. They demanded a Nigerian President of the Western House; they demanded Parliamentary Under-Secretaries; and they demanded a Leader of Government Business. Right from that date the Westerners had never ceased their demands either for amending the Constitution, or for whittling down its carefully drawn provisions which ensured in the interests of all (and in complete accord with the recommendations of the Ibadan Conference and the previous Regional Conferences) that officials were part of the fabric. Western Central Ministers, and in particular Bode-Thomas, raised such an issue almost every week from February, 1952, onwards. His method was to take a small unimportant item on the agenda (e.g. to appoint a member of some Board or other) and to demand that before such appointment were made the whole question of constitutional principle and practice should be settled (e.g. that the Governor's power of appointment should pass either to a Minister or to a Regional Executive Council). He was continually also trying to get powers away from the Centre to the Regions.

9.   So much for general background. Mr. Benson now wanted to go through the history of the months almost month by month, high-lighting certain near-crises, which had only been solved by the greatest patience on the part of the Governor, and

after the greatest forbearance by Northern and Eastern Ministers. Eastern Ministers in particular had continually had themselves thrust into a most awkward predicament: any opposition they might show to Bode-Thomas' wilder flights made them appear less progressive nationalists than the Action Group.

10.   Right at the beginning of February, 1952, as part of the manoeuvres to stop Zik from becoming a Member of the House of Representatives, Awolowo proposed to dissolve the Lagos Town Council. It would be remembered that Lagos had to elect five Members to the Western House, of which two must come forward to the Centre. Lagos elected five N.C.N.C. candidates by overwhelming majorities. Zik then arranged that three of those should refuse to accept nomination to the Centre, so that he and one other would be sure, even in face of the Action Group majority in the West, of coming forward. Bribes passed rapidly on all sides and in the end the Action Group bribed Adedoyin to accept nomination to the Centre. So Zik was kept out. Zik countered by getting the Lagos Town Council to offer Adedoyin the job of Town Clerk, involving his resignation from the Centre: whereupon the Western Regional Executive Council proposed, within their proper powers, to wind up the Lagos Town Council and put in an Action Group-nominated Committee of Management. Ineptly they also at the same time proposed to ask the Governor to appoint a Commission of Inquiry into the allegations of corruption in the Lagos Town Council.

11. Now 90% of the object in all this was to keep Zik down: the other 10% a policy of 'Now we can show that under the Constitution we control Lagos'. There was immediate fierce reaction from the East, including, of course, Eastern Central Ministers; and the North's reaction was annoyance with themselves. They had horse traded with the West 'Lagos to be part of the West' in exchange for 'Hands off Ilorin', and had never expected the West to show their iron hand in Lagos so blatantly and so early.

12.   The Acting Lieutenant-Governor, West, was in constant telephone consultation with us here; and, by making it plain that in the last resort he would use his reserve powers, managed to hold the fort against this attempt by the Action Group to achieve what could be argued was a quite proper objective for a blatantly improper motive. They finally accepted a Commission of Inquiry into the affairs of the Lagos Town Council.

13.   That, a week after Ministers had taken office, is a fair indication of the type of policy to be pursued by the West consistently throughout the next fourteen months. The matter, of course, came up in the Council of Ministers and Bode-Thomas, Akintola and Prest all argued that Lagos was a matter for the West alone and that the Centre had nothing to do with it, and that there must be no interference from the Centre in the affairs of the Regions. North and East, on the other hand, stressed that as Lagos was both the capital and the chief port of Nigeria the Centre was very much concerned; and that action about Lagos should not be taken by the Western Region without prior consultation with the Centre. It was then North and East versus the West.

14.   The whole of February was taken up with preparation for the Budget Meeting of the House of Representatives, which was to open on about the 2nd March. The Council of Ministers was persuaded generally to accept the Budget, necessarily already prepared by the officials, and they had no real difficulty in doing this, save over one thing: and that was 'Personal Emoluments'. Personal Emoluments led the Westerners immediately into a strong attack on expatriates, and the whole question

of Nigerianisation was hammered at by them, with the Easterners also showing sharp concern over the matter. The reaction of the North was sharp and instantaneous: they said that Nigerianisation meant Southernisation and they would bitterly oppose any increase in the number of Nigerians holding Senior Service posts in the North. Here again, within a couple of weeks of the coming into force of the Constitution, a vital pressure point comes to light. The North, who probably have a much better realisation (because of their long generations of administrative experience) than have either the East or the West, of what is involved in such phrases as 'self-government', understand that the Civil Service of a country wields an enormous amount of power. At that time virtually no Northerners held Senior Civil Service posts. (To-day only thirty do so out of 700 Nigerians holding such posts). Their great, lasting and increasing fear was and is that Southerners would get control of all these posts; and their long and bitter experience has shown them that when a Southerner holds such a post all the Junior Civil Servants under him also rapidly become Southerners.

15.   This problem was solved by the inclusion in the Governor's Speech from the Throne of an announcement to appoint the Phillipson-Adebo Commission on Nigerianisation. But the Northerners' bitter fear remained and, indeed, during the meeting of the House of Representatives a very strong Northern deputation met the Chief Secretary to oppose even the posting of two Southerners to the North as Administrative Assistants in Departments.

16.   When the House of Representatives opened, Awolowo, extraordinarily enough, was the first speaker on the second reading of the Appropriation Bill and he promptly alienated a great deal of Northern sympathy. From then on the Western Members of the House (even the Central Ministers from the West) were much more often out of the House than in it, a fact which caused extreme offence to the North who, with most N.C.N.C. members, were regularly in attendance. During that meeting also, Awolowo ineptly showed his mistaken belief that he had only to lift his finger and see the North follow him more or less blindly in opposition to the East. The Action Group violently opposed the Lead-Zinc Bill and the Pioneer Industries Bill. When Divisions were taken on these unanimously agreed Government measures, Western Central Ministers were conspicuously absent from the House.

17.   In June, Njoku circulated a paper to the Council of Ministers drawing attention to the fact that it had previously decided unanimously to be bound by the principle of collective responsibility, and to abide by, and show open support for, any decision of the Council (the Notes on Administrative Procedure and the Code of Conduct for Ministers, both accepted by the Council, with no dissentient voice, both laid down this principle; and also, by the way, the important rule that no Minister should take part in journalism). Njoku went on to draw attention to the fact that at the March meeting certain Ministers had not always voted for the Government; sometimes they had absented themselves from the House; or—on at least one occasion had 'unfortunately been too late to get into the lobbies before the doors were closed'. Njoku asked the Council to decide that every Minister must be in his place when a Government motion was being discussed and must go through the lobbies in any Division. It is significant that this was put forward by an Eastern Minister.

18.   Going back to April. In that month Bode-Thomas and Akintola started a strong demand for separate Ministries. At first all Northern Ministers were opposed to it and so [sic: was] Nwapa. Gradually Nwapa and Ribadu were persuaded, and the other

Eastern Ministers were also for it. But Abubakar remained constant in strong opposition, fearing that such a change would inevitably be followed by further changes. It was with the greatest difficulty that official members of the Council persuaded him to remove his strong opposition even to the establishment of a committee to consider the matter. The committee began its work and the Law Officers decided that such an administrative arrangement could be made without a change in the Constitution; and at the end of May, when the Secretary of State was in Nigeria, he was approached by Ministers everywhere on the subject and readily agreed to the suggestion for separate Ministries. The Committee then had to continue its monumental task of finding both the staff and the accommodation required.

19.   And so to June, when the Action Group made a very strong concerted demand for further constitutional advance. They demanded:—

(a) that power for action in all legislation should not be given to a Head of Department or other official, but to the Minister concerned;
(b) that Lieutenant-Governors and the Governor should take the advice of Ministers in respect of all powers (subject to reserve powers);
(c) that separate and distinct fields of legislation should be established for the Centre and the Regions;
(d) that there should be a change in the Constitution to give effect to the party system of government;
(e) that there should be Parliamentary Under-Secretaries;
(f) removal of restrictions with regard to Bills and Motions affecting the Public Service;
(g) removal of disqualification of persons from election on grounds of previous conviction for sedition and other offences.

20.   All these would have involved changes in the Constitution and both the East and the North were solidly opposed to any such change. There were meetings of the Council of Ministers to consider the demands; and in the end the demands were rejected on the grounds that neither the East nor the North wanted any change in the Constitution. Both East and North, and particularly the North, again felt embittered with the Action Group and all its actions.

21.   Meanwhile, there remained the Ilorin question, stimulated by provocative speeches, and actions in Ilorin by Yorubas, particularly Lagosians from that part of the world. On the 4th September His Excellency announced his decision on the Ilorin boundary question and this was met by a silence from the West lasting about six weeks—a reaction most surprising to the North. At this time Zik was starting his come-back campaign in the East and he was building it mainly on an anti-Action Group platform—the same platform as he had used to bring the independent Easterners on to the band wagon at election time. Eastern Central Ministers sought interviews with His Excellency and said that if only the West would give one sign that they were genuinely interested in Nigerian unity they could defeat Zik's manoeuvres. His Excellency drew attention to this reaction of silence over the Ilorin question as such a positive sign but, frankly, it was the only positive sign he could give other than strongly expressed faith in the Action Group's ultimate good intentions.

22.   Throughout the whole of this period Bode-Thomas had continued to behave atrociously in the Council of Ministers meetings. Whenever he found himself in a

minority he lost his temper and gradually directed his attack on to the Governor sitting as President of the Council. On every occasion His Excellency had shown incredible patience, to a degree which exasperated the Northerners, but was generally understood by the Easterners. It might, however, be of interest at this stage to tell of a conversation which he (Mr. Benson) had had with Nwapa after Nwapa's return from the United Kingdom. Nwapa had said 'I could never understand why the Governor was so incredibly patient with all the rudeness and the ignorant blustering of Bode Thomas, until one day at five minutes to seven in the morning I tuned in to the B.B.C. while I was shaving. I listened to 'Five Minutes with God', or some such broadcast, and the speaker said 'Patience is a great virtue and we continually say that. But no man is ever patient with the patience of God. God's patience is a thing which men cannot understand, and until we understand God's motives for his patience we never shall understand it'. Only at that moment did I understand Sir John's patience with Bode Thomas.' The point of the whole thing was this—that nothing was holding Nigeria together except the Council of Ministers. So long as the Council of Ministers presented a united face before the country, so long could the three Regions be held, in the face of all the points of pressure—Lagos, Nigerianisation, Constitutional Advance, etc. etc.—together.

23.   In October Awolowo went to India and during this period, while he was away, there were considerable signs of two things:—

(a) of Ministers at the Centre getting closer and closer together;

(b) of manoeuvres by Awolowo's rivals in the West to increase their power at Awolowo's own personal expense.

24.   As regards (a); Ministers at the Centre were regularly holding private meetings of their own immediately before Council meetings to decide what line they would take on the subjects on the agenda. When they came into Council meetings it was obvious that decisions had already been taken amongst themselves at these preliminary discussions, leaving the officials with nothing to say. This was good provided that in taking their decisions they had the full facts of the problem before them, and we were fortunate in that not many controversial items appeared on the agenda. There were, however, as throughout the past fifteen months there had always been, the appalling inter-Regional jealousies and pressure points. One example was the important decision which had to be taken as regards Revenue Allocation—Capitation Rate for the forthcoming year, coupled with the very heavy shortfall in tobacco revenue. It was an appalling problem, over which the Acting Governor and the Lieutenant-Governors and all their official advisers had spent five hours in conclave the evening before, discussing how on earth the separate Regions could be brought to accept the right decision—a grant from the Centre for one year to make up the shortfall. In the event the Council of Ministers disposed of the item— and reached the right conclusion—in seven minutes, that conclusion being announced on behalf of the Ministers by the Oni of Ife, who was put up as spokesman. On the other hand, there was the question whether Nwapa should or should not accept the Secretary of State's invitation to attend the Commonwealth Prime Ministers' Conference in London at the end of November. The decision of the Council was that he should, Akintola and Bode Thomas strongly opposing. The arguments they adduced within Council were repeated again in the Daily Service in a succession of five articles strongly attacking Nwapa and the Government on five

successive days. All the Northern and the Eastern Ministers knew that Akintola had written them; and all, of course, were fully aware that they had all agreed that no Minister should 'indulge in journalism, save on matters of literary or scientific interest.'

25.   At the beginning of November the Ilorin boundary question came up again: there were inflammatory speeches and articles, culminating in the Oke-Odde riots, in the course of which an attack was made on the local Native Court while it was in session and a Court Messenger beaten to death. These riots were organised by Oke-Odde 'sons abroad' in Lagos, but it was most difficult to convince the North that the Action Group was not behind it. Or, if not the Action Group, at least the Egbe Omu Oduduwa, with which of course the Action Group is most closely allied. Once more, the Eastern Ministers came to see the Acting Governor and expressed their alarm and their fears that if this was how the Action Group behaved they, the Easterners, had no chance of defeating the Zikists in the East.

26.   There followed the Jos Convention, organised by Zik, with a decision 'in the interests of Nigeria' not to work the Constitution. And hard on its heels Awolowo's return from India and the Benin Action Group Convention, which decreed a policy of non-fraternisation with the Governor. The Northerners were watching the increase of Zik's influence in the East and they were appalled at the Action Group's attempts to outbid him.

27.   And then at the end of January and early February the Eastern crisis, with Zik supporters showing complete irresponsibility and relying on intimidation and corruption, of which everyone knew; the North again appalled that the steady elements in the East could not command even a simple majority. Nevertheless at this time, because of a common hatred for Zik and everything he stood for, the Council of Ministers was more united than ever before. Eastern Central Ministers, it is true, had shown signs of wavering, and the Northerners were very worried about that: but when they finally came out firm in support of the Regional Ministers and severed all connection with the old firm of Zik, Northern and Western and Eastern members of the Council were solid together. The 'good East' also was very glad of the West's tacit support, but had the greatest difficulty in preventing it from being shown too openly (which would, of course, have put Zik right back into the anti-Western position in which in 1951 he was able to sway all the elected independents to join his band).

28.   It was strange to think back to the weeks immediately preceding the House of Representatives' meeting and consider the astonishing degree of unity which then existed amongst the Ministers. In spite of Abubakar's grave misgivings earlier over separate Ministries he and the other Northern Ministers-with-portfolio had all signed a document with Eastern and Western Ministers-with-portfolio demanding that Ministers should be given control of Departments. They made it plain that they meant the same control as Ministers in the Gold Coast have.

29.   The Government prepared to go into the House of Representatives in March, 1953, with such a feeling of unity in the Council as never before. They were solidly united: for example on the whole of the Budget in the early days Eastern, Western, and Northern Ministers made it clear in speeches that this was their Budget, and that they accepted full responsibility for it.

30.   A number of Motions had been put down by Private Members, and continued to be put down during the first days of the meeting. It was soon apparent that eight or ten of them were Action Group Party Motions, all in the name of Enahoro. The

first four days of the meeting were spent in debating His Excellency's speech from the Throne and appalling damage to unity was done by Action Group members, including Awolowo, in those four days. They demanded in turn the removal from the Council of Ministers of the Financial Secretary, the Attorney-General, the Lieutenant-Governors and 'the dividing up of the Chief Secretary's portfolio amongst Ministers.' There were strong attacks of expatriates—this time not on their pay but on their presence. At each such demand and attack the Northerners grew steadily angrier and more obstinate.

31. As was said at the beginning, if anyone thought that the Motion for self-government in 1956 was the sole cause of the crisis he was in error. Apart from the attacks on expatriates and the demands for further constitutional advance there were four Motions which led up to the crisis:—

(a) that a Nigerian should be President of the House;
(b) that special scholarships should be awarded to train Nigerians for the Nigerian Foreign Service;
(c) that there should be self-government in 1956; and (believe it or not)
(d) that a decency Bill should be introduced to prohibit nudity in Nigeria.

32. Without any exaggeration this last, which came before the House first, exercised a very great effect. When considered in the Council of Ministers there was complete unanimity of view that the Motion must be opposed by Government. In the House Awolowo quite unexpectedly got up to support it. The North reacted most strongly against what appeared to them to be a danger of Southern interference with the administration of the pagan tribes in the North. Chief Bode Thomas and Akintola ratted on the Government's decision and asked for an emergency meeting of the Council to reconsider Government's attitude to the Motion. This request was vigorously opposed both by the North and the East. Eventually Jaja Wachuku introduced a dilatory Motion adjourning the debate, but the damage had been done.

33. Both Northern and Eastern Ministers (and again particularly the North) were disgusted and angered at seeing Western Ministers 'rat' on a decision which they had fully supported in Council, simply because the Leader of the Action Group had taken a different line in the House. Note also, incidentally, that the Mover of the Motion was Mr. Okwu, an N.C.N.C. Member, and it was, so far as can be remembered, the first occasion on which there had not been an automatic opposition from the Action Group to anything which the N.C.N.C. proposed.

34. The next motion taken in the House was one asking for special Scholarships for the Nigerian Foreign Service, and this was one of the Action Group Motions in the name of Enahoro. Once more the decision in Council had been taken unanimously: efforts were to be made to explain the futility of such a scheme to the mover, upon which it was hoped that he would withdraw his motion; if he did not do so the Government was to oppose the motion. Note again that this was a unanimous decision of the Council.

35. Once again the Action Group Leaders went all out in support of the motion in the House, and again they were joined by N.C.N.C. members, though not unanimously. The North were angered once more by the constant reference to the need of a Nigerian Foreign Service in 1956. Quite apart from the clear explanation of the impracticability of the motion which had been given to the House, all Northern

members were solid, and Government had declared its stand. A division, therefore was unavoidable.

36. Bode Thomas and Akintola sat in their seats and Njoku and Abubakar persuaded them to rise in their places en route for the division lobby. Awolowo rushed round and told them in the hearing of these Ministers and of the Chief Secretary, that they were not to vote. The Chief Secretary attempted to reason with Awolowo, but he was in a berserk state and reiterated his orders to Bode Thomas and Akintola, who obeyed them.

37. The next motion was that for the appointment of a Nigerian President of the House. This had also been discussed in the Council of Ministers early in March, and it had been a stormy meeting at which Ribadu, particularly, showed intense anger with Bode Thomas and Akintola. A little background to this problem is necessary:

38. Early in 1952 the North had sought from the Secretary of State a secret guarantee that the Governor was always to be President of the House; and failed to get it. They had, however, got an assurance that the President of the House would always be someone, acceptable to them. Their fear, of course, was that there would be a Southerner as President. Prest and the Oni of Ife, and all other members of the Council save Bode Thomas and Akintola were for complete abstention; and in the face of Ribadu's strong feelings and intense anger on the matter Bode Thomas contented himself with saying; 'All right, but this is only a curtain raiser. The really important motion will have to be discussed later.' (He was, of course, referring to the 1956 motion). Note, however, that he did not ask for his dissent to be recorded, and there was therefore, an unopposed clear decision of the Council for abstention. (In the event the motion never came before the House).

39. At the time when the self-government motion came first before the Council of Ministers the split in its ranks was, therefore, wide. Ministers were even refusing to meet informally outside the Council. The Northern amendment to substitute 'as soon as practicable' for 'in 1956' had been tabled, and at the first of three grim and difficult meetings on the subject Njoku said that if the question to amend it to read 'as soon as practicable' were put first, he would certainly support the amendment. This, of course, could not happen: because the question had to be put in two parts— firstly, 'to leave out the words in 1956' and only secondly 'to insert other words.' On this, all Eastern Ministers and Prest spoke strongly for complete abstention, as in the case of the motion on the President of the House. Akintola on the other hand said it was a matter for Her Majesty's Government in the United Kingdom, and not for the Council of Ministers; that Ministers should speak as they wished; and that officials should remain silent. The Northern Ministers declared that they were going vigorously to oppose the motion, and emphasised the view that if officials abstained they would be shirking their duty: officials must vote against the motion. There was, therefore, at this stage a complete deadlock between Bode Thomas and Akintola on the one hand and the Northern Ministers on the other; with Prest the Eastern Ministers, and the officials all opting for complete abstention. The Oni of Ife was not present. The Governor deferred the meeting in the hope of softening the Northern attitude, and he further hoped that the Westerners would see the red light and persuade their party either to drop the motion altogether, or agree that it should be argued out on the floor of the House without involving the Council of Ministers.

40. At the next meeting no progress had been made with Bode Thomas and Akintola, but the Northerners announced their readiness to accept complete

abstention. This meeting was marked by two things; the cold, self-possessed, statements made by all Northern Ministers in turn, in quiet, cool voices; and a complete loss of temper by Bode Thomas.

41.   The Northerners spoke as follows:—

'For the last fifteen months we have gone far beyond any reasonable limit in trying to make this Constitution work and co-operate with these people in the South. We have had no difference with the Eastern Ministers which we have not been able to resolve by compromise, but we can never work with these people from the West. Now they have gone far beyond any limit which anyone could regard as reasonable. You have spoken at length, Sir, about the unity of Nigeria, and I tell you that is impossible of achievement. You and your officials are the only people who have faith in that idea, or work for it, save that some people from the East also believe in it. The West do not want it, and we certainly do not want it. You have faith in it because you believe that it is the best thing for Nigeria. It has nothing to do with the interest of Britain. Both your faith and your works are in vain. We saw what happened in India— rivers of blood flowed; and we saw what happened in Burma where blood is still flowing; and our great fear is that you will do what you did in these places and run out on us. Our prayer to you is this: Divide us now, and stay while you divide us, and for sometime thereafter. We can shake hands now and go our separate ways, and perhaps our children's children will want to come together again. But if you go out now at short notice the blood which flowed in India will be nothing to the blood which will flow here.'

42.   At this meeting Nwapa made a strong, statesman-like plea for total abstention and was warmly supported by Prest and the Oni of Ife. Had it been possible to take a vote then the voting would have been sixteen to two for complete abstention. But, unfortunately, Bode Thomas became completely uncontrolled in the face of the cold Northern speeches. He accused the Governor of plotting to thwart the West and to delay self-government, and of bringing every kind of pernicious influence to bear on the North. It is difficult to remember precisely what he said, and precisely what insults he hurled at the Governor and other Members of the Council; because he was completely out of control: He jumped up out of his chair, seized his papers and said he was not going to stay. On his way to the door he saw the Governor's eye fixed coldly on him and said, 'I have your permission to leave?' The Governor said, 'I would prefer you to stay, Minister.' He said, 'I won't stay,' and started to walk out, upon which the Oni of Ife shouted to him twice in Yoruba, and, after a long silence, he resumed his seat. When the question of a vote was raised all members said they were in no fit state to vote, Njoku saying, 'We cannot even sit in our seats. How can we vote?' Council proceeded to other business and for ten minutes Bode Thomas sat in his chair mouthing—quite audibly to those sitting within 10 feet of him—such phrases as 'Bloody British', and 'Bring your soldiers and shoot us down'. At the end of ten minutes he sought, and was granted, permission to leave. Then Council continued on other business for another hour.

43.   That evening there was a christening party given by a Yoruba in Lagos. When Prest and other Ministers got there they were told by other guests precisely what had happened in Council, and what every member had said. Bode Thomas had preceded

them. Members of the House attacked Prest on the stand he had taken, as they did also the Eastern Ministers, one of whom was also present.

44.   When the matter was reopened in Council at the next meeting in four or five days time, Nwapa said that he found himself utterly unable to make any contribution to the discussion in Council at all, because proceedings were not secret, and anything he said in Council made his position politically, outside the Council, untenable. Other Eastern Ministers and Prest were similarly affected, and the Oni had clearly been 'got at'. In this event a vote was taken on Government's attitude in the House of Representatives, and the Northerners and officials tabled ten votes for complete abstention; Bode Thomas and Akintola made it absolutely plain that, whatever the decision of Council, they intended to speak for the Motion; the four Western Ministers and Endeley voted for free speech, and the three Eastern Ministers with Portfolio refused to vote or utter.

45.   It may be as well to note here that Bode Thomas's subsequent statement in the House of Representatives, 'that continually the officials and the North voted together to down the other members of the Council,' was a complete lie. On only two occasions in its life had the Council seen officials voting solidly with the members of one Region against either the opposition or the neutrality of Ministers from the other two Regions. This was one occasion. The other occasion was in August, 1952, when the Council of Ministers had decided unanimously that expert advice should be sought on the position of Lagos as part of the West on the one hand, and as the capital and principal port of Nigeria on the other. Having decided that such assistance would be sought, the Council considered whether a public statement should be made to that effect. The officials and the Easterners then voted together *for* a statement, against the West and the North. Never before had officials and Northerners voted solidly together.

46.   During the few days that remained before the motion for self-government actually came up in the House, most strenuous efforts were made by the Oni of Ife, the Emir of Katsina, Chief Arthur Prest and the Lieutenant-Governors, West, North and East to avert the disaster. Again, the depth of Northern feeling on the matter can be evidenced by the fact that all efforts to get the Northern leaders to meet the Western leaders, or even the Northern Central Ministers to meet the Western Central Ministers, failed. The Westerners were arrogant and blustered whenever they were approached, and the Northerners were cold and determined. Nevertheless, Chief Arthur Prest came, on one occasion, near to saving the day, and very near it on another. He wrote a memorandum for Awolowo and the party showing how dangerous it was (because only Zik could profit) to induce a crisis. Prest's own story was that Akintola was persuaded and Prest went to bed happy that night. Next morning Awolowo sent for him and told him that he had misrepresented to him opinion in the Council of Ministers, and that Bode Thomas had now given him a more correct version. He intended, therefore, to go ahead with the motion. On the next occasion Prest went one better by persuading Akintola to come along with him and say that Prest's memorandum represented the truth. An additional page was added to it which Prest hoped to get Akintola to sign, but although Akintola agreed with it he was unwilling to sign it. Nevertheless, at a party executive meeting Akintola did state that Prest's version, both of events and of feelings, was the true one. The matter was argued for an hour and a half and at one stage Prest said that he had won; but once again flights of oratory by Bode Thomas carried the party leaders

and the majority opinion was to go ahead with the motion. It was of interest that Prest stated that Enahoro was supporting him at this meeting, and that the day was lost once more simply because of the loss of face which the Action Group would incur by its withdrawal: Zik, was bound to make capital out of that loss of face.

47.　Meantime the House was going through the business of Committee of Supply. Mr. Benson said he did not intend to recount the events when the motion came before the House, save to draw attention to the fact that there were some ten motions down on the Order Paper that day, with the self-government motion last but one. There were also a large number of questions. When the House opened all the questions but two were withdrawn and all the motions were similarly withdrawn, so that the 1956 motion was immediately before the House, and by 10.30 Enahoro had finished his speech moving it. At 9.15 that morning the Oni of Ife had tendered his resignation to His Excellency, stating that he had no other course before him; the Action Group party had compelled him to promise them that he would vote in favour of the motion though he had no intention of speaking on it. When His Excellency enquired what he meant by 'compel' he made it clear that he feared intimidation and gangs of hooligans in Ife, and that he could not for long retain his Stool save by the support of the Action Group. He asked whether, if he defied the decision of the Council of Ministers and voted for the motion, His Excellency would have to revoke his appointment as a Minister, and His Excellency told him that that would necessarily follow. He then said that the only course he could follow therefore was to resign before the motion came up in the House, because if he voted for the motion—as he would have to—he should not be a Minister at the time when he defied the Council's decision. The Oni's course of conduct (as distinct from his lack of judgment and guts) was therefore entirely correct; whilst, as the Governor's broadcast had shown, the other Western Ministers had resigned after the motion had been disposed of, and in circumstances in which the turn of events had made it entirely unnecessary for them to resign at all. Mr. Benson also drew attention to the fact that it must have been sheer obstinacy which, in these circumstances, led the Action Group leaders to walk out of the House and the Action Group Ministers to resign. Mr. Fellowes had since said, and every Member of the House who had followed events in the East knew well, that the range of debate on a dilatory motion was to all intents and purposes coextensive with the range of debate on a substantive motion. Certainly the whole question of self-government in 1956 could have been discussed on the dilatory motion, and Mr. Enahoro himself could have had another go on the subject.

48.　In conclusion the Governor's Deputy said he was quite certain that everyone present and, indeed, every officer in Nigeria was now saying 'Well, what does Government intend to do about the matter?' There was no answer to that question at the present moment. The Council of Ministers was carrying on with its work; it was properly constituted and the remaining Ministers from the East and the North were determined to show just that fact. His Excellency in pursuance of an arrangement he had made as far back as the beginning of March, had flown to the United Kingdom where he was discussing the whole situation with the Secretary of State and Colonial Office officials. The Northern Members of the House and all their political leaders had lost no time in shaking the dust of Lagos off their feet: they had vowed that they would never come back to Lagos; and the Northern Central Ministers had returned under clear instructions that they were to continue their work as Ministers with two objects in view:—

(a) to show Her Majesty's Government in the United Kingdom that the North would do nothing to alienate Her Majesty's Government in the United Kingdom's sympathies; and

(b) to watch the situation from the point of view of the North.

In such circumstances time was absolutely essential to allow tempers to cool and objective thinking to begin once more. Pending His Excellency's return there was nothing to be done beyond making every effort to spread the truth of the events leading up to the crisis; and it was with this in view that he had taken the earliest possible opportunity to get Heads of Departments together, who, through their junior officers, represented virtually the only sure means of disseminating truth in this country at the present time.

49.   Mr. Benson said that for the last fifteen months it was well known that all the proceedings of the Council were being distorted to Western political leaders by Bode Thomas and Akintola, but it had perhaps not been fully realised until the last few weeks to what an enormous extent these misrepresentations had spread amongst Yoruba leaders and leading personalities generally. It was his sincere opinion now that such lies as that about the North and the Officials always downing the West and the East had been generally believed—in the West anyway; that belief was practically ineradicable. The first great problem then before Government was how to get as much as possible of these distortions corrected.

50.   Mr. Benson was asked a number of questions and in reply to them made the following points:—

He agreed that it was most important that as much publicity as possible should be given to the work that was still being done by remaining Members of the Council. Ministers should be encouraged to broadcast, but these broadcasts must not be politics.

It seemed unlikely that the Action Group would stage a boycott in the West. They would carry on. It was indeed true that action taken to get the truth over to the people might induce them to stage such a boycott, but this was, in his opinion, much the less of two evils. He felt that great risks would have to be taken in order to get the truth across to the people. One thing in particular was of great importance; it would be disastrous if the opinion grew up that 'self-government was a thing not to be discussed. In his view self-government ought to be discussed ad nauseem by debating societies, by village councils, by Native Authority meetings and by every kind of meeting which could be called for the purpose. District Officers ought to encourage such discussions, though they would have to be extremely careful, particularly in the West, to present themselves rather in the guise of chairmen at debating societies, and it would be intensely valuable if they could ensure that Members of the Legislatures took part in those discussions; the object, of course, would be to get across to the people what was meant by self-government: it was extremely doubtful if Awolowo himself knew precisely what he meant by it; he certainly had no appreciation of its full implications. Mr. Benson cited Awolowo's repeated assertions that there were more British in India today than there had been ever before. What Awolowo failed to realise was that those British were not in Government posts. Awolowo wanted to have British in key Government posts and have self-government at the same time.

The true victor in the whole business was, as had of course been foreseen from the beginning, Zik. The Action Group's position had not been strengthened by the crisis.

They might have consolidated some small elements of gangster opinion in Lagos and Ibadan, but the N.C.N.C. was certainly stronger in the West than it had been before; they had worried a large number of Yoruba businessmen and, unless within the next few weeks they could break the power of the Obas finally, they had put themselves into a difficult position there. They would not feel in difficulty vis-a-vis the Obas unless there were a dissolution of the Western House.

The Zik Awolowo alliance might last a few weeks but the pressure points were too great and it could never be a true alliance. Eastern Central Ministers thought Zik would now be torn as between West and East and they might be right, but if Zik was as astute as he usually had shown himself he had nothing now to prevent him from concentrating first on the East.

Immediately after the explosion he had believed that both the North and the West could be brought back to an August meeting of the House of Representatives. He now thought it most improbable that the North could be so persuaded.

Chief Arthur Prest's illness on the 31st March had, of course, been a diplomatic illness. Mr. Benson had had, at Prest's request, a long session with him a few days before, at which he had blown off all the steam and fury in the world about Bode Thomas and Akintola. But Prest had only one interest in view and that was to come back as a Central Minister. He was instructed firstly 'by fear of a knife in his back,' and secondly by his lack of money. He was compelled therefore to make the kind of statements in the press that he had been making and to declare his solidarity with the Action Group.

It was as yet too early to give any ideas of what form a future association at the Centre might take. At that moment the whole problem was to dissuade the North from committing economic suicide and severing all their connections with the other Regions. Heads of Departments must also realise that within the next few months we should be faced not merely with a North and South split, but with other separatist movements; the most glaring example was, of course, the Cameroons. If the N.I.P. won in the East, then there seemed to him to be a chance of holding the position as regards the Cameroons: if the Zikists won, there would immediately be the strongest demand for separation of the Cameroons from the rest of Nigeria.

51.   Finally, Mr. Benson asked Heads of Departments to be most circumspect in what they passed on to their junior officers. The rule must be that they should only pass on as much as it was necessary to pass on to ensure that those junior officers should have sufficient information to enable them properly to discharge their duties to Britain and Nigeria. They must, therefore, be in a position to contradict gross and apparent misstatements of fact; at the same time they must not have, obviously, the details of the proceedings in the Council of Ministers, which he had thought it proper to give to Heads of Departments.

193   CO 554/260 no 71   24 Apr 1953
[Political situation]: inward savingram no 950 from Mr Hopkinson to Mr Lyttelton on meetings with Nigerian political leaders

My Telegram No. 575.
    Following Personal from Minister of State. *Begins*.
    The following is a fuller summary of subject matter of telegram under reference.

On 22nd April in presence of Governor I had private discussion on Constitutional Crisis with two Northern Central Ministers, Abubakar Tafawa Balewa and Shettima Kashim.[1] Mohammadu Ribadu was unable to be present.

2. The two Northern Ministers were clearly deeply disturbed by events and their views, though expounded with great calm and dignity, were charged with emotion. Abubakar, who acted as spokesman, stressed the long-standing differences between North and South. Even before the 1947 Constitution the South regarded the North as backward and ignorant and as offering blind obedience to anybody in authority whether black or white. He said that in the North over 90% of officials of all grades were Southerners. They brought their wives and families and other villagers with them to fill local jobs as messengers, labourers, etc. For the North Nigerianisation meant Southernisation. For this reason the North preferred British officers wherever possible, until they had enough trained officials of their own, since they would in due course return to United Kingdom and not impede Northern development. But because of their preference for British officers South accused North of being British stooges.

3. North had long been fearful in its relations with other Regions but had nevertheless tried to work with them. In face of the trickery and insults which they had experienced, however, they could see little purpose in continuing to attempt to work together.

4. The North would have preferred to gain more experience under the 1947 Constitution before attempting a revision. But South were insistent on change. Under the new Constitution the North asked for 50% of seats in Central Legislature. East agreed for sake of Nigerian unity. At a meeting at Enugu West agreed to 50% for North, provided Lagos became part of West. Abubakar not present at this meeting and much regretted acceptance by his Northern colleagues of West's conditions. Eventually, West got Lagos but North obtained 50% of seats only in face of strong Western protest that North was preventing West from achieving its national aspirations.

5. Under new Constitution Northern Central Ministers' strong regional feelings were increased by provocation by South but Governor insisted on all working together. Without Governor's insistence on unity Northern Ministers would not have stuck it.

6. Informal meetings of Central Ministers were started to iron out regional differences but Western Ministers used these meetings to commit Northern Ministers on matters before they were discussed in Council. Northern Ministers would not agree to this and they were accused of frustrating political progress of Nigeria. It became clear that Western Ministers were disclosing confidential Council discussions. British officials were accused of dividing Regions on such issues as North/West boundary revenue allocation and status of Lagos. But fact was that unity maintained only through British insistence.

7. In latest crisis North had tried to help in reestablishing good relations between the Regions by holding discussions with Action Group representatives at Kaduna. These discussions were continued at Ibadan. At that time crisis in East developed and Action Group said that the North and West must come together. Later

---

[1] Shettima Kashim Ibrahim, minister of social services, 1952–1955.

if responsible elements came to power in the East that Region could be brought in. But at the same time an attempt was made by the Action Group and N.P.C. to get the North to agree to a hurried Press Release on a coalition between the West and the North. The North said that they did not oppose self-government for Western and Eastern Nigeria but did oppose it for Nigeria as a whole. Because of this the South accused the North (quite erroneously) of opposing self-government on British instructions. In Lagos unruly bands of hooligans were organised to jeer at Northern Members of the House of Representatives (including Emirs) at end of last meeting of the House. It was clear to Abubakar that the South despised the North and were doing all they could not only to attack them in the South but to foster movements in the North aimed at over-throwing the present Northern leaders. In his view no good could come to the North from co-operation with the South.

8.   I told Abubakar that I fully understood and greatly sympathised with the view he had expressed. The Governor had given the picture in broad outline to you during his recent visit to London and the Governor had your full support. It was clear that the present Constitution would not work. H.M.G. hoped that it would be possible to keep a united Nigeria. But big changes would have to be made. In our view this would mean giving far greater powers to the Regions. All this would need very careful working out and would take time. We would favour wide powers of self-government in the Regions but we should want something kept in the Centre. When revision came each Region would have right to go as fast or as slow as agreed for other Regions. We proposed to wait to see the results of regional deliberations during next few weeks or month and hoped that meanwhile nothing would be said to prejudice eventual consideration of problem by H.M.G. who in this matter were working in best interests of the North.

9.   The two Northern Ministers thanked me for what I had told them and said they were grateful for the opportunity given to them of expressing their views

10.   On 23rd April I had private informal meeting with A.C. Nwapa, O. Arikpo and E. Njoku at their request, to hear their views. They spoke quite freely and frankly and their general attitude was most friendly. They said that in their view Awolowo had not planned this crisis but he had been manoeuvred into his present position out of fear of Bode Thomas. In the Council of Ministers the Western Ministers had consistently taken a regional line even when it conflicted with their party line, e.g. over the proposed Cement Industry. They were not moved by the national interest if regional interests were not also served. Sometimes Western Ministers had agreed to proposals made in Council of Ministers but had gone back on them after talking outside the Council to Awolowo whose aim was to build up the Western Region at the expense of central unity.

11.   In the Eastern Central Ministers' view, it had been a great mistake to allow Lagos to be part of the West. It gave the West great strength and fostered their regional nationalism. They thought in terms of the Gold Coast for the Western Region. It gave them the feeling that they were ripe for self-government and were only held back from this goal by being tied to the other Regions.

12.   In discussing possible ways of meeting the present situation, I threw a fly over them as to the desirability of some looser form of association. But the three Ministers reacted strongly against this idea. They said that regional autonomy was just what the West wanted, and were in fact quite prepared to contemplate complete separation. In the Eastern view Nigerian unity was all important and that meant

maintaining a strong Centre. Without strength at the Centre there would be no Nigeria. They did not think that the West should be allowed to break up the unity of the country. In their opinion if Lagos were taken away from the West and made a separate Federal Capital and if the West were then told firmly that regional autonomy could not be permitted to prejudice national unity the West would give way. The Eastern Ministers also thought that if the West wished to put back the same four Ministers at the Centre there should be no harm in that since it would show that they were willing to take part in working the Constitution and it would show the foolishness of their action in precipitating a crisis. I pointed out that two of them had blotted their copybooks badly and that, above all, it would not do to give any appearance of weakness. On this they agreed. As for the North, they realised that they felt sore and hurt but they thought that they had not been permanently estranged. In their opinion some Northerners' views on this subject were over-gloomy. On this point, however, I said I would of course have an opportunity myself to hear the views of other Northerners during my forthcoming visit to Kaduna.

13.   With regard to the present tie-up between Azikiwe and Awolowo, the Eastern Ministers thought that it could not possibly last. Azikiwe, although irresponsible and self-seeking, was really interested in preserving Nigerian unity and on this there was a fundamental cleavage between him and Awolowo.

14.   I hear that Awolowo and Azikiwe are having a meeting to decide, among other things, whether they should ask for a joint interview with me. If they do I shall see them. I shall, of course, in any case see Awolowo in Ibadan.[2]

---

[2] See 194.

194   CO 554/260, no 79   29 Apr 1953
[Political situation]: inward savingram no 8 from Mr Hopkinson to Mr Lyttelton on a meeting with AG leaders   **[Extract]**

[Following his meetings with Northern and Eastern leaders, Hopkinson met Awolowo and the Executive Committee of the AG in Ibadan on 26 Apr. At this meeting Awolowo put forward various proposals to amend the constitution, including the appointment of a prime minister at the centre.]

. . . In replying, I dealt with number of detailed points he had made, and, in particular, I referred to the danger of breaking up Nigerian unity through forcing a breakdown in the constitution. It seemed to me very foolish for a man to set fire to a house he was in, especially if it was his own. Awolowo had likened relations between the Western and Northern regions to a man with a stone tied to his leg who, if he wished to walk, could only cut off the stone. I suggested that a better analogy was a man with a broken leg who needed time for a bone to set, and it would be foolish to amputate the leg merely to gain time. Awolowo and his colleagues took the point.

I said that Her Majesty's Government recognised that drastic revision of the constitution was needed and that changes to be made should be in the direction of greater regional autonomy. I personally saw no objection to appointment of Parliamentary Under-Secretaries in regions, but there were clearly difficulties about doing so at the centre. Aim of greater regional autonomy seemed to me to be incompatible with his proposals for build up of Central Government. Awolowo appeared to appreciate the force of this.

I reserved my comments on the other points, but promised that they would be carefully studied by Her Majesty's Government. I emphasised that Her Majesty's Government wanted Nigeria to progress towards self government within the Commonwealth. I had no feelings about date of 1956 or any other date. We had immediate political situation to deal with and changes required in the constitution would take time to work out. In answer to a question by Awolowo I said that time needed would be months, not weeks, but I thought would be less than a year, I also assured him that there would be full consultation. Meanwhile it was essential that Action Group should not say or do anything to alienate other regions.

I met Awolowo, Awokoya[1] and Enahoro in the afternoon to agree communique for the press. Afterwards I took Awolowo aside and asked him what ideas he had for the solution of the present crisis. At the morning session Bode Thomas had given defence of his resignation and subsequent behaviour, which I had rejected. I realised that for the Action Group it was a question of face. The Governor could hardly be expected to accept the same four names. Awolowo had no suggestions to make, but I urged him strongly to consider the problem in the interests of a wider settlement. His attitude at the end of the morning meeting and in the afternoon was most friendly.

Full report of the discussion follows by air bag. *Ends.*

---

[1] Stephen Oluwole Awokoya, Western Region minister of education, 1952–1956.

195   CO 554/318, no 25   Apr 1953
[Eastern Region crisis]: CO note for Mr Lyttelton on the Nigeria (Constitution) (Amendment) Order in Council 1953

[The Nigeria (Constitution) (Amendment) Order in Council 1953 to allow for the dissolution of regional houses on the advice of regional executives was laid before Parliament on 1 May 1953.]

Section 118 of the Nigeria (Constitution) Order in Council, 1951, provides that the Lieutenant-Governor of a Region may prorogue the Legislative Houses of such Region or either of them, and, further that the Legislative Houses of every Region shall be deemed to be dissolved upon a dissolution of the (central) House of Representatives. There is in the Order no provision to enable a Regional Legislative House to be dissolved except on a dissolution of the House of Representatives.

Recent developments, in the Eastern Region of Nigeria in particular, have made it clear that circumstances are liable to arise in which it may be politically desirable for a particular Regional House to be dissolved, although no reason for a simultaneous dissolution of the Houses in the other Regions or of the House of Representatives may exist.

The particular circumstances in the Eastern Region, referred to in the last paragraph, are that the National Executive Committee of the main political party of that Region (the National Council for Nigeria and the Cameroons), has attempted to force members of the Regional Executive Council to resign in order that the leader of the party, who is not himself a member of the Eastern legislature, might reallocate portfolios to members more ready to follow the party line. This the majority of those Members have declined to do, despite a motion of 'no confidence' in them adopted by a majority in the Eastern Regional House. Although the continuation of these Ministers in office is fully justified by the provisions of the existing constitution, the business of the House has been interrupted and if the present uneasy situation continues when the House in due course reassembles, it will be politically desirable that the Lieutenant-Governor should be in a position to dissolve the House and arrange for new elections.

The turn of political events in the Western Region makes it not unlikely that it may also become desirable to dissolve the Houses of that Region.

The amending Order now submitted for the approval of Her Majesty in Council provides for the separate dissolution of Regional Legislative Houses, for the continuation of the Region's representation in the (central) House of Representatives and Council of Ministers pending the election of new regional representatives, and for certain other consequential amendments.

196 CO 554/236, no 51   1 May 1953
[Political situation]: letter from B E Sharwood-Smith to T B Williamson on relations between the Northern Region and Southern political leaders

Firstly, we are delighted to hear that you are hoping to pay us another visit; we shall look forward to seeing you.

Secondly, thank you very much for your letter of 18th April, and for your undertaking to help FDK Williams. Now for my 'system of coloured lights'.[1] What I meant to convey was that a 'green light' exercise would be designed to illustrate the safest and best course to pursue, a 'red light' exercise would illustrate either what not to do in terms of historical evidence elsewhere, or what might be done provided the manifold dangers are fully realised, and, finally, an 'amber light' exercise would be one which offered material from which useful lessons could be learnt, provided one looked before leaping. I am sorry that I puzzled you. My intention was, in terms of my own Secretariat, to make it clear that these exercises were to be undertaken with differing objects in view. In other words, the exercise on the effect on the Northern Region of separatism should not be undertaken with a view to showing how separatism could be effected, but rather to show how extremely dangerous an operation it would be.

To turn to the other matter you mention. My Governor has already attempted at considerable length to persuade Awolowo that he has got the Northern picture wrong, but without any success. My personal view is that you must bring yourself regretfully to realise that Awolowo and his ilk, and Azikwe and his for that matter, are just not interested in reforms in the Northern Region. In fact, to put it quite bluntly, they would regard it as 'so much bad news,' because the North becomes the stronger thereby. Awolowo's plan, which he proclaims for all to hear, is to destroy

---

[1] See 189.

Northern unity by encouraging any extremist group he can find and exploiting any grievances he can uncover. His present line, loudly published, is to persuade the world that what he terms 'the Sardauna Group' is a mere 'handful of invaders', to use his own expression, which is dominating the masses of the country. When the appeal to the Region for a mandate is complete, you will learn how much there is in that particular myth!

In terms of the progress of Nigeria, or I might even say the survival of Nigeria, Messrs. A & Z. are principally what Messrs. A. & Z. say and do in public gatherings, and what they write in their lamentable daily publications; i.e. their effect on the public is what is relevant. They are hag-ridden by their 'egos', and it is highly dangerous to sublimate them in any sense.

Finally, there is another matter. It has been fashionable in Nigeria and at home for so many years to refer to the reactionary outlook and the corrupt practices pertaining in the Northern Administrations. It has been, on the other hand, unfashionable to refer to the probably far worse state of corruption existing in the other Regions despite the almost daily admissions to this effect made both in the Local Press and by Eastern and Western Members of the Legislatures. Such exposures, for instance, as the Storey Report pass almost without comment. Were such a Report written about Kano, for instance, one feels that the Heavens would shake! I do not wish for one moment to pretend that we are better that we are. We, at least, are getting on with the cleansing process where it is most necessary. It is not inapt to remember that when the Elections took place in 1951, there were no accusations of corruption in the North, whereas in the East and West the stench rose to High Heaven.

197   CO 554/236, no 47   3 May 1953
[Northern Region]: letter from Sir J Macpherson to T B Williamson on the changing political situation in the Northern Region. *Enclosure*: letter from B E Sharwood-Smith to the Emir of Kano, Feb 1953

In my letter of the 5th of March (G. 103/54) about recent developments in the North, I mentioned that Sharwood-Smith's next target was Kano. You will be interested to hear that he has again been successful in obtaining important changes.

The Emir of Kano's Council consisted until recently of his eldest son, the Ciroma; his younger brother, the Galadima; the aged and nearly blind Madaki; the equally aged and conservative Wali, (who died a few months ago); and the Sarkin Shanu, who alone had a secondary-school education and progressive ideas. In practice the Council had very little influence and the Emir depended almost entirely on the Ciroma.[1]

I now enclose copies of a letter which Sharwood-Smith wrote to the Emir of Kano before his visit and of the informal note of his subsequent discussions with the Emir,[2] which will give you a good idea of the changes that have now been made. The

---

[1] Alhajji Abdullahi Bayero, Emir of Kano, 1926–1953, died in Dec 1953. He was succeeded by his son, Muhammad Sanusi.

[2] Informal note not printed.

most interesting development is the inclusion for the first time of a member of the Hausa commercial community. Alhassan dan Tata is an old man and he may not take a very active part in the Council's deliberations, but the mere fact that he has been accepted is in itself a big step forward and I have every hope that it may soon lead to the inclusion of others who are not members of the ruling Fulani families.

When Sharwood-Smith forwarded the letter and informal note to us he remarked on the astonishing change in outlook that had taken place in the North in recent months. This, he considers, is fundamentally due to a growing realisation of the implication of events and to innate commonsense in political matters. The Region is waking up very rapidly.

Enclosure to 197

After greetings, I write to you concerning the matter of your Council, which, as you are aware, has caused me grave concern dating from the time when I was Resident, Kano. Under the pressure to which the traditional system of Government in the North is now being subjected, it is quite impossible for there to be either a feeling of confidence and stability or hope of real progress for Kano if your Council consists, as it does now, to all intents and purposes, of the Ciroma and little else. I am fully aware of the Ciroma's administrative ability and of his experience and industry, but the fact must be faced that in Kano there is a powerful and mounting opposition to the state of things as they are, and the only way to counter that opposition is by broadening and strengthening your Council. To leave matters as they are, I am convinced, will only lead to disaster, and, may be before very long, to the disappearance of your House from the high position that it now holds. Believe me, I write as a friend who has known Kano for many years dating from 1924; I also write as a friend possessing the very deepest respect for your personal integrity, deep knowledge, and sense of justice. Unhappily the time has passed when one man alone, unaided by others of wisdom, experience and authority could control the affairs of Kano. I must, therefore, urge you to take heed of the advice that I and your Resident have so often given, and that is to introduce fresh blood into your Council, so that it may be strong, independent and, most important of all, trusted and respected by the people of Kano.

Firstly, with regard to the post of Wali; I cannot under any circumstances accept the recommendation which has been made. All my information is to the effect that the present Alkali does not carry the respect or the confidence of the people. Neither am I prepared to press any recommendation on behalf of the administration; such things must come from within and not from without.

Secondly, with regard to the rest of your Council; I have a very [sic: great?] respect for Sarkin Shanu's ability and character, but he is heavily over-burdened and unsupported. Equally, I agree that the Galadima can offer valuable advice on district matters, but the Madaki has long passed his period of usefulness, and the time has come when he should be retired. M. Bello is a Minister and his counsel is by that nature to all intents and purposes lost to you except upon rare occasions. His duties are, I know, being carried out by Alhaji Usuman Gwarzo, who is well-educated, but who does not carry much weight of his own. I must earnestly urge you to adopt the following courses:—

(a) Firstly to recommend as a successor to the Wali a man whom I can be assured has the respect and confidence of the people, both as a jurist and as a man.

(b) Secondly, honourably to retire the Madaki and to recommend a successor of authority and experience whom the people of Kano will respect.

(c) Thirdly, to consider two further appointments:—

  (i) One member of traditional standing, possibly drawn from the District Heads, with modern education, to be in charge of certain of the services now the responsibility of the Sarkin Shanu, whose burden should be reduced.

  (ii) Another from amongst the commercial community.

As you are aware, it is from the more radical elements of this extremely wealthy, powerful and sophisticated community that N.E.P.U. and the forces of disorder gain their adherents. I am convinced, as I have often told you personally, that this community has long felt itself under-privileged, both in terms of its share in the administration of affairs and of its status, social and political, vis-a-vis the ruling caste of Kano. Provided you choose the right man, you have much to gain and nothing to lose by securing an alliance with this large and very influential section of the Kano community. Should you and all you represent become further estranged from them, the result could be disastrous. I ask you to consider very carefully what I have written in this letter and to let me know what your conclusions are. I must emphasise that what is to be done must come from within and not from without. Failing a solution, I do not intend to impose any solution of my own; I should rather feel myself compelled to ask you to seek advice on a broader front than is at present available to you.

198 CO 554/261, no 92A   5 May 1953
[Amendment of the constitution]: CO note of a meeting with Mr Lyttelton on the need to reform the constitution

The Secretary of State assured the Minister of State that the House would be sympathetic to delay in making a statement on the situation in Nigeria before the end of May. He felt that the present policy should be to wait until after the Northern House of Assembly had met before making any statement to the House of Commons. When such a statement was made he felt that the line should be to state that there would have to be less Central responsibility in Nigeria and more devolution to the Regions. In his opinion there should be some retracing of our steps; if too much were done at the present moment it might result in a disintegration of Nigeria. Short of adopting the suggestion of a non-political High Commission he felt that the list of subjects should be revised in order to place more responsibility on the Regional authorities.

Mr. Gorell Barnes felt that the nub was going to be the North's view that there should be no further politics at the Centre. He felt that the only way of getting over this would be by 'buying' the North since the latter were afraid of domination by Southern Civil Servants. He put forward the suggestion that this might be done by putting the whole of a future slice of C.D. and W. Funds into the North. This suggestion was not practicable now, in the opinion of those present. It was felt, however, that this possibility should be kept in mind.

The Minister of State pointed out that what had been discussed in Nigeria between himself and the political leaders would probably soon leak out and that an early statement would be desirable. There was some discussion on the machinery for achieving a revision of the Constitution and it was agreed that early thinking was required in the Colonial Office. It was agreed that a start should be made with revising the list of subjects to be dealt with respectively by the Centre and the Regions, with a view to seeing whether any further subjects might be devolved to the Regions.

199   CO 554/318, no 38   6 May 1953

[Eastern region crisis]: inward telegram no 11 from Sir J Macpherson to Mr Lyttelton on the dissolution of the Eastern House of Assembly

[The dissolution of the Eastern House of Assembly reported in this document effectively marked a triumph for Azikiwe, who now resigned from the Western House of Assembly to stand for election in the East. In the subsequent Eastern Region elections held in Sept-Dec 1953, the NCNC won 72 of the 97 seats and the NIP of Eyo Ita only nine. Three seats were won by the UNP and the 13 Cameroon seats by the KNC.]

My telegram Personal No. 5.

Eastern House of Assembly opened yesterday and first Government business was motion to reappoint Muna as a Regional Minister.[1] Motion lost by 45 votes to 32, official and special members not, of course, voting. Ballot was secret, but it is believed that four out of thirteen Cameroons members voted with N.C.N.C.

2.   Government motion then introduced declaring united front with other regions for self government in 1956 and proposing the establishment of a committee to consult and negotiate with other regions for the achievement of this objective. N.C.N.C. took the line that they had already made the position clear and no further indication to the country on this question necessary. They (? could omitted) win self government without the aid of N.I.P. Thereupon N.C.N.C. proposed dilatory motion, which was carried. Note in (corrupt group ?passing) the anomaly that N.C.N.C. members walked out of the Central House because dilatory motion had been moved on the same subject by Northern members.

3.   At subsequent meeting of the Executive Council the Lieutenant Governor was advised unanimously to dissolve the Eastern House, and he will do so this morning. Indications yesterday were that dissolution was expected and desired by both parties.

4.   Above represents victory for Azikiwe and follows inevitably, like Greek tragedy, recent activities by his arch enemies the Action Group.

5.   General assessment of the present position follows earliest possible by bag. In the meantime, you will appreciate that this result in the East can only harden Northern determination not to compromise with the South. Eastern elections likely to take between three and four months. Estimate of attitude likely to be adopted by the N.C.N.C. towards loosening of association at the centre also follows. Your telegram Personal No. 54 refers.

---

[1] See 175.

200   CO 968/401, no 110   7 May 1953

[Future of RWAFF]: minutes by J N A Armitage-Smith[1] and R J Vile on the decisions of the West African Forces Conference

[The West African Forces Conference which involved representatives from all four West African colonies and the UK, was chaired by Hopkinson in Lagos between 20–25 Apr. The major issues intended to be considered included the size of the West African military and how its costs should be met, though much of the discussion in fact came to centre on demands from the Gold Coast and Nigeria for greater control over their land forces.]

Copies are now available of the Report of the West African Forces Conference which was held at Lagos at the end of April. I have sent one copy to Lt. Col. Russell-Edmunds of the Treasury (who was present at the Conference); and I attach at the back of the file three loose copies,[2] of which I suggest Mr. Gorell-Barnes, Mr. Williamson and Mr. Vile might care to take one each.

2.   The main purpose of the Conference was to review the arrangements agreed at the 1949 Conference for financing the West African Forces; but in the event a very much wider field than this was covered, as the report shows. The chief interest of the Nigerian and Gold Coast delegations, in fact, was not financial; it was rather a determination to obtain a greater degree of control over their land forces than they felt they had at present. This issue dominated the first three days of the Conference, and explains the considerable length which has been given to the subject in the report (see paragraphs 3 to 8).

3.   The financial settlement which was eventually reached was satisfactory to all the four West African Governments, though as I shall show later there is a tiresome little legacy of the Conference which we shall have to settle with the War Office.

4.   One of the chief merits of the Conference was the 'full and frank' discussion that took place on subjects like African Officers' pay, pension codes, training of African Officers etc., which were not technically on the Conference's agenda. Apart from the fact that a number of loose ends were thus tied up, there is no doubt that both the West African delegates and those from the U.K. found great mutual benefit in exchanging points of view on these subjects in a way which might not have been possible had the Conference been held in the U.K.

5.   The report speaks for itself, but I should perhaps draw attention to the following points in it:—

(1) I have already mentioned the comparatively large part of the report which is devoted to the question of control of the local forces: see paragraphs 3 to 8. Some difficulty was experienced in drafting these paragraphs, and the result is rather long-winded; but the West African Ministers agreed to the form of words, and I doubt whether anything much shorter would have been acceptable. It will be noticed that the aim of these paragraphs is to make it appear as if this report was the start of a new era in the history of the four territorial forces making up the Royal West African Frontier Force. In fact much of these paragraphs is a re-statement of the present position. In paragraph 6 however there is a recommendation that the West African Governments should invite the Army Council to appoint a General Officer Commanding in Chief, a proposal which was

---

[1] J N A Armitage-Smith, principal CO, 1948; ass sec 1960.   [2] Not printed.

accepted without demur by the War Office representatives; and, more important, in paragraph 7 there is the recommendation that an Army Advisory Council for West Africa should be established: the idea is that this Council should meet at least once a year to hear a report by the G.O.C. in C. of the existing state of the four territorial forces, and to discuss West African Army matters in general; and that by this means the West African Governments would feel that they were really 'in' on the running of their Armies.

On this question of Armies, paragraph 4(a) recommends that each Government should consider enacting legislation to provide for the integration of its Regiment and supporting troops into a single military organisation known as, e.g. the Nigerian Army, Nigerian Defence Force or any other suitable title. This question of title proved impossible to decide at the Conference, and it was thought that it was a matter which might well be further discussed in the Army Advisory Council.

From the U.K. point of view perhaps the most satisfactory achievement in this section of the report is the full retention of the concept and functions of H.Q. West Africa Command. Before the Conference opened we had understood that this concept would be attacked on the ground that it was an organisation imposed upon West Africa from outside and interfered with the growing tendency in the minds of West African Ministers towards controlling their own individual territorial forces. The War Office representatives, however, were able to satisfy West African delegates that H.Q. West Africa Command was in fact carrying out a whole number of very valuable and essential co-ordinating functions which individual West African Governments were in no position yet to replace.

(2) Paragraphs 30 to 36 deal with the financial settlement. As will be seen from paragraph 35, the total contributions offered by the four West African Governments together amounted to £2,476,500. This was a little less than the U.K. delegation were hoping for, but I am quite satisfied that it represents the maximum which the territories can afford or can persuade their Legislatures to accept. Indeed, the difficulty experienced by the Nigerian and Gold Coast delegates in raising their figure is shown by their refusal to include in their contribution the comparatively trifling cost of training African Officers.

The report is mercifully silent on the negotiations that took place about the U.K. share of the cost. The West African delegates pointed out that they were not interested in the distinction which the U.K. had to draw between the War Office and the Colonial Services Votes, and consequently it was agreed that the total money to be found from these two Votes should be shown as a single U.K. contribution of £3,023,500. But behind this figure there lies a somewhat troubled story. As paragraph 32 states, the services which the War Office agreed to accept as a proper charge to the War Office Vote amounted to £785,000. Mr. Gardner began by stating that figure as his offer, and later, under some pressure, he increased his offer by £100,000. Before the Conference opened however he told the rest of the U.K. delegation that he had £1 million set aside in his Vote for West African forces, and stated that if pressed he would bid up to that limit. In the event however he did not do so, even though it should have been clear to him that the West African Governments had honestly reached their financial limit. In the difficult situation created it became necessary for me to show that, although the Colonial Services Vote was a residual Vote in this context, we were very willing to play a generous part in the settlement, and I said that the Colonial Services Vote would bear

£1,938,500. This had the effect of leaving the final £200,000 of the U.K. share unaccounted for; and as Mr. Gardner declined to offer the further £115,000 which he had been authorised by his superiors to do, I felt unable to make any further concession on the Colonial Services Vote. There is in my opinion no doubt that we should press Mr. Gardner very hard indeed to accept £115,000 out of this remaining £200,000; and in order to avoid tiresome correspondence Mr. Gorell-Barnes has, I believe, agreed to invite Mr. Gardner to a meeting. Mr. Gardner has now returned from West Africa, and I will arrange the meeting at Mr. Gorell-Barnes' convenience.

(3) I need not comment in detail on the question of works services, beyond saying that the Gold Coast Government's contribution towards their cost is decidedly generous, and the Nigerian Government's by no means unsatisfactory. The questions of African Officers' pay, pensions, etc., will be dealt with on the individual files.

(4) On the question of printing the report, I understood from Mr. Benson before I came away that the Nigerian Government could handle that perfectly well. I have told the War Office about this, and am awaiting their views. I do not think that it is necessary for the report to be printed in this country.

I know that the West African Governments are extremely keen that the report shall be approved by all the five participating Governments at the earliest moment. I am sure that the Minister of State will agree that this is a fair statement of the West African Governments' views and that he will be willing to submit the report to the Secretary of State as soon as possible.

J.N.A.A-S
7.5.53

The major impression which has been left on me by the report of the West African Forces Conference is that it has been extremely valuable in getting the West African Governments as they are now constituted to understand the functions of the Army, and to support the measures which are necessary in order to ensure that there is no gulf between the Army on the one hand and Governments and public opinion on the other. Although it was not, as far as I could tell, the intention that the Conference should primarily fulfil this function, I am sure that we can only welcome very much indeed the full discussion which took place, and the recommendations under paragraphs 3 to 8.

2.   I think it is also safe to say that the educational effect of the Conference was not confined to the West African Governments but also extended to the War Office representatives. If this is the case then we should have less difficulty in the future in persuading the War Office to take an understanding attitude towards military problems in West Africa. The report contemplates further discussions in London on a number of questions of particular difficulty, and I think we shall have to be careful to ensure that the general atmosphere of understanding which now exists is not dispelled in the later discussions.

3.   Mr. Williamson may wish to comment further on the way in which the Nigerian delegation appears to have been the only one in step from time to time. I know the difficulties in West Africa in getting the Governments to agree on a common attitude, and if no more progress can be made in this matter then we shall have to accept the difficulties. I cannot however escape the impression that the

Nigerian delegation were being unduly pernickety, and I wonder if this stickiness on matters of relative detail does not derive much more from officials than from Ministers.

4.   Mr. Bourdillon will wish to comment on paragraph 5(2) of Mr. Armitage-Smith's minute above. When we have the proposed meeting with Mr. Gardner we might at the same time, if Mr. Gorell-Barnes agrees, invite the Treasury to be present so that even if we fail there and then to reach agreement with the War Office on the allocation of the U.K. share between their Vote and ours we can nevertheless agree with Treasury concurrence that the settlement of this question need not delay the notification of H.M.G.'s approval of the report.

R.J.V.
7.5.53

201   CO 554/261, no 98   9 May 1953
[Political situation]: inward savingram no 1109 from Sir J Macpherson to Mr Lyttelton on the need for a statement on the revision of the constitution. *Enclosure*: An assessment of the political situation in Nigeria on 9 May 1953

At our talks in London on 15th April[1] it was decided that no pronouncement should be made regarding the revision of the Constitution—so as to loosen association at the Centre and to grant much greater autonomy to the Regions—until after the Minister of State's visit and until after the meetings to be held during May, of the Legislative Houses of all three Regions.

It only remains for the Northern meetings to take place—they begin on the 18th of May and should finish about the 25th—but recent developments point to the absolute necessity for a statement to be made immediately thereafter, preferably within a matter of days. I refer particularly to the victory of the N.C.N.C. in the Eastern House of Assembly on the 5th of May, followed by the dissolution of that House and an announcement by the majority of the Cameroons Members, led by Dr. Endeley, that because of their insistent demand for separate Regional status they will take no part in the Elections in the Eastern Region. It is also vitally important that Her Majesty's Government should not leave the Northern leaders in doubt about their determination to fulfil their obligations to the seventeen million people of Northern Nigeria.

Events in Nigeria at this time move fast and the situation can change from day to day, but I feel strongly that we should be giving attention now to the kind of statement that might be made by you on behalf of H.M.G.

To assist the consideration of this proposal I have had an assessment made of the political situation as on 9th May, 1953, and I enclose a copy of this.

In the light of this assessment, which is made before the Northern Legislatures meet and which may be altered by developments in the next week or two, the kind of statement that I have in mind might be built up on the following framework:—

---

[1] See 190.

Experience over the past fifteen months has shown that it is not possible in present circumstances for the three Regions of Nigeria to work together effectively in a federation so closely knit as that for which the present Constitution provides; H.M.G. in the U.K., while greatly regretting this, are not prepared to compel any Region, against its will, to continue in such close association; H.M.G. therefore envisage that the Constitution must be redrawn to provide for greater Regional autonomy and for the removal of powers of intervention by the Centre in matters which can, without detriment to other Regions, be placed entirely within Regional competence, while at the same time ensuring that the essential economic and defence requirements of all Regions are secured. In order to ensure these vital requirements of all Regions there will continue to be a need for a Central organisation, and the form which that Central organisation should take, and the powers which must be reserved to it, will now be the subject of urgent consideration. In this work H.M.G. in the U.K. would wish to work in association with the leaders of the people in all three Regions, and the first requirement, therefore, is to decide how this work can best proceed. To this end H.M.G. will invite representatives from each Region to visit London for discussions in the Colonial Office and with the Secretary of State for the Colonies. It is H.M.G.'s intention to carry through the projected reform of the Constitution in the shortest time possible, but in a territory of such a size, with so large a population, with so many different groupings, and with so many shades of public opinion, the work will inevitably take time. While that work is carried out Nigeria will continue to be governed under its existing Constitutional Instruments (which include the Letters Patent and the Royal Instructions to the Governor and the Lieutenant-Governors) and it will be necessary for the leaders in all three Regions to ensure that the Central Government is so composed that it is enabled to carry out its caretaker task. That task will be impossible if those composing the Central Council of Ministers are persons who cannot work together; it is the clear duty, therefore, of the Regions to ensure that the Ministers sent forward by the Regional Houses to the Centre are people who will prove determined and able to work harmoniously with the representatives of the other Regions; and any failure by those responsible to recognise this essential requirement could only result in the use by the Governor of his reserved powers to ensure that, during the necessary interim period, the good government of Nigeria in the interest of all its people is maintained.

It will be apparent that if a statement on the above lines is to achieve its object—to put us into the position where, for at least a year, the territory can be administered peacefully and effectively whilst the reform of the Constitution is carried out—a considerable degree of firmness will have to be shown. Firmness must be shown to the North, who must continue to play their part in both the executive and the legislature at the Centre; this will go far more against the grain for them than is generally recognised. Firmness must be shown to the East; if N.I.P. wins, to persuade them that they must, in the interests of the East, accept a loosening at the Centre in order to avoid the disappearance of the Centre; and if the N.C.N.C. win, to persuade them of the same truth, and that they must send to the Centre people with whom the

Ministers from the other Regions will be prepared to work. And finally, but most immediately, great firmness must be shown to the West on this same last point; and furthermore, on the point that power, for this interim period, will lie where the present Constitution places it, and in the last resort with the Lieutenant-Governor and the Governor.

I have not had an opportunity to consult the Lieutenant-Governors on this proposal but they are visiting Lagos on 13th May and I shall let you have their views immediately thereafter.

My reason for suggesting that Nigerian leaders should be invited to go to London to discuss how the revision should be carried out is that it seems to me that if the first talks take place in London—where the participants will be away from the tense, emotional, quarrelsome atmosphere of Nigeria at this time—and if the discussion at this first stage is restricted to the mechanics of the projected review, there may be a reasonable chance that action towards the revision of the Constitution, with its truly formidable problems, can start calmly. It was contemplated, at our talks on the 15th of April, that part of the discussion on the revision of the Constitution should take place in London.

I shall be most grateful if you can let me have, as soon as possible, your first reactions to these proposals. There will be difficult problems to decide regarding representation of Regions and political parties, and these have been aggravated by the recent declaration by a part of the Southern Cameroons bloc. I shall send my views on this aspect after consulting the Lieutenant-Governors.

I shall also keep you constantly informed of further developments as they occur.

Enclosure to 201

Political differences between Northern political leaders on the one hand and Southern political leaders (excluding the Eastern 'National Independence Party') on the other, the original causes of which were deep-seated, and which had been hardening over many months, flared into an open breach on the 31st of March. The spark which fired the magazine (but it was no more than this) was the Action Group motion of Self Government in 1956.[2]

2. Northern political leaders returned to the North with two objects in view:—

(a) to check their firm belief that they had the North solidly behind them; and
(b) if they found that they had solid support, to stand on it and demand separation of Northern Nigeria from the rest of Nigeria. (N.E.P.U. is not a negligible force despite the discreditable nature of its present leaders, but although it will continue to attack the Native Authority systems and gain support by uncovering cases of oppression and injustice, it does not follow that its members are solidly with Southern political parties. There are signs that N.E.P.U. may split on the North versus South issue).

Both political leaders and Emirs stated categorically at the time that they would never attend a further meeting of the House of Representatives. Northern Central Ministers followed the other Northerners up to Kaduna two days later. When they

---

[2] See 184.

returned to Lagos on the 7th April they came with clear instructions that they were to continue to do their work as Central Ministers; but only on the clear understanding that there must be time for the drastic revision of the Constitution which they had in mind, and that during that time the North must do nothing to prejudice the North's position vis-a-vis Britain. There was full and openly-expressed realisation of the North's dependence on Britain—

(a) to maintain peace; and

(b) to ensure that the North were permitted to advance politically at the rate at which the North wished to go; and were not compelled to accept further political advance at a time when it meant Southern domination.

3. The Lieutenant-Governor's plan, in the face of this cold, implacable determination, was to convince the Northern political leaders and Emirs by cold, implacable facts and objective reasoning (at which the Northerners, when their tempers are cool, excel) that it would be economic suicide for the North to sever, or seriously weaken, their links with the rest of Nigeria. In the face of their then spirit it was essential for the Lieutenant-Governor and his officers to show a complete understanding of their point of view in order that they might keep with them in their journey through the wilderness and lead them back, gently and firmly, to safety. For this the Lieutenant-Governor and his officers also needed time, and this was provided by the decision that a joint meeting of the Northern Houses of Assembly and Chiefs should not take place until 18th May. The Lieutenant-Governor has hitherto been successful beyond expectation,

(a) in dissuading Northern political leaders from making pronouncements which they might later wish to retract. (The Sardauna of Sokoto's broadcast early in April and subsequent press releases did nothing more than explain to the North, and to the country at large, the united stand Northern Members of the House of Representatives had taken, and the reasons which led them to take that stand. Not once has anything been said which could adversely affect the National Independence Party in the East. There has been no attack on Azikiwe or the N.C.N.C. There has, indeed, been no personal attack on any Southern political leader save in so far as an objective account of happenings during the meeting of the House of Representatives involved criticism of the actions of Action Group leaders. The emphasis throughout has been on the North's unwillingness to be hurried along at a pace which the people of the North would not agree to their leaders adopting);

(b) in persuading the Northern political leaders that, for the vital needs of the Northern Region, there must be some form of association with the other Regions at the Centre. Their ideas on this particular question are still necessarily vague. In their meeting with the Minister of State at Kaduna they showed that they are thinking of something on the lines of a High Commission like the East Africa High Commission, but more limited in its scope. They have not excluded the idea of some form of small Central Legislature and Executive to run essentially Central organisations; but their hope is to arrange that those organisations and institutions can, for the most part, be run by statutory corporations or self-contained and self-financing departments; and their ideas on the composition of any Central Executive and Legislature are that they should consist largely of

British officers and, for the rest, of specially selected and nominated Regional representatives. On one thing they are, and will continue to be, adamant: British control of defence, including Police.

4.   The Action Group representatives remained in, or kept visiting, Lagos for the first week or ten days in April. Their newspapers and all their public utterances were completely uninhibited, the main theme being condemnation of the Northern political leaders as a reactionary minority ('the Sardauna group') working as tools of the British, with two objects in view:—

(i) to keep down the alleged mass of popular opinion in the North which would otherwise revolt against the Native Authority system and declare itself at one with the Action Group;

(ii) to prevent the South from advancing politically at its proper and justified speed to Self Government. The British and the Northern political leaders were working hand-in-glove with these objects in view.*

5.   When Action Group leaders returned to their Region they made it clear that they intended firmly and vigorously to continue their Governmental work in the Western Region. They realised that it is more than ever important for them to maintain party solidarity. They know:—

(a) that some of their policies are unpopular with the people—notably the sharply increased capitation tax;

(b) that the non Yorubas of the 'Mid-West' resent the Yoruba domination of the party;

(c) that the Obas, though they have allied themselves with the Party, secretly fear and resent its power and the consequent weakening of their own status and influence.

Additional dangers are the spectre (which they themselves have brought to life) of a triumphant Azikiwe; and personal rivalries within the party which might lead to a struggle for personal power.

In the face of these difficulties and dangers Awolowo has set himself rigidly to enforce a strong party 'discipline', and the existence of these difficulties and dangers has enabled him to do this successfully. The party has felt compelled to refuse overtures from the Centre (an invitation to send a Regional Minister to join the Nigerian delegation at the Forces Conference was refused), and to insist that only the four Ministers who resigned should fill the vacancies in the Council of Ministers.

6.   The Action Group's meeting with the Minister of State on the 26th April[3] showed a readiness, indeed a desire, to weaken the bonds tying the Regions to the

---

* Note here the conflict between two basic fears:

(a) the intense, real, and *openly-expressed* fear on the part of the North that further political advance now would mean (because Southerners hold so many key Civil Service and Commercial positions in the North) complete Southern domination of the North; and

(b) the intense, real, but *concealed* fear on the part of the West that delay in further political progress, when the North is catching up so fast, would mean domination of the West's six million people by the North's seventeen million.

[3] See 194.

Centre, but always in order to bring more power to the political leaders in the Region and to weaken the power of political leaders at the Centre. The quite impracticable suggestion for a Prime Minister at the Centre and for an Upper House with equal representation of all three Regions betokened either lip service to the idea of a united Nigeria, or (once again) a complete misassessment of the strength of the North and the solidity of Northern opinion. Most significant, because it has been most consistent, is the demand that control of policy in regard to the Civil Service should be removed from the Governor and given to the Legislature. Any Public Service Commission which the Action Group would be likely to accept would have to have a number of Action Group nominees on it.

7.   Eastern representatives left Lagos very early in April. They were divided as between N.C.N.C. and N.I.P., and they left Lagos to resume their own 'domestic' battle in the Eastern Region. Azikiwe, the only leader to emerge enormously strengthened from happenings in the House of Representatives (on which he could exercise no decisive influence until after the event), was astute enough, as was to be expected, to permit his vital interests in the West to appear to be abandoned. (Appear, because at any time in Lagos, his main stronghold, Azikiwe can come back and with every chance of defeating the Action Group, if only for the reason that every Action Group political manoeuvre has been dictated by the wish to 'out-Zik Zik'—an impossible task). In his resumed battle in the East he has had the whole local press working for him: Action Group papers have taken off his shoulders much of the task of shooting down the N.I.P.; his own 'Pilot' could avoid any attack on the Action Group and concentrate on the glorification of Zik and his N.C.N.C. party; and the 'Daily Times', (interested under its present editor only in maintaining its circulation by making its articles more sensational than those in the 'Service' or 'Pilot') could be relied upon to help confusionism in its battle against objective thinking.

8.   Azikiwe was content, therefore, to have one major campaign rally at Port Harcourt, the constituency of Nwapa, against whom a new phrase 'Nwapaism' had been coined to denote 'Eagerness to obey the dictates of imperialism in order to enjoy the spoils of office'. N.I.P. calculations as regards Azikiwe's strategy were at fault; and on the 5th May the N.C.N.C. proved in the Eastern House that they could command forty-five votes against thirty-two (which figure did not include Official or Special Members who hold eight seats between them) on a motion to reinstate, as a Regional Minister, Muna, a Cameroonian. Dissolution of the Eastern House on the advice of the Executive Council has followed.

9.   The Minister of State's meeting on the 28th April with National Independence Party Ministers in the East showed, firstly, emphasis on a united Nigeria. It is the East throughout who have been the protagonists for this conception. The difference between the N.C.N.C. Party and the National Independence Party is that the latter look at the problem objectively and are content to come to Self Government, *within a united Nigeria*, at the time when they think the North can be persuaded to accept it. Their estimate of the time needed is, of course, much lower than the North's present estimate, but they have grounds for their assessment. They point to the pace at which the North has come along during the past fifteen months, and the readiness of Northern Ministers to be persuaded and to compromise. What they do not appreciate (partly because they are unwilling to see it) is the strength of feeling in the North over the fact that the overwhelming majority of the Africans who hold posts in the Public Service in the North (both Senior and Junior Service) are

Southerners. (cp. footnote page 574, (a).) Unless this situation is changed there will be no scope for Northerners when, after late start with Western education, they become qualified. The Northern leaders say that it will take them many years to convince the mass of the population of the Region that Northern Ministers and officials can be trusted—as the British Administrative Officer is to be trusted—to secure for the common man his essential rights. They are therefore determined to have a separate Regional Public Service, and to fill the posts with as many Northerners as possible—and, failing them, with overseas officers. Until they can provide the men themselves they will not permit either the number or the power of the British officials to be diminished in any way.

10. The N.I.P. demand (compare the Action Group demand) for the disappearance of ex-officio members of the Council of Ministers and Executive Councils arises because it has arisen in the Gold Coast, and is regarded as the next step towards Self Government. There is also (contrast the North) the almost complete lack in the South generally of the administrative experience which would show the impracticability in the interest of good government of such a step at the present time.

11. The demand for universal adult suffrage, which has consistently been one of the key demands of the N.C.N.C., comes from the National Independence Party leaders for a different reason: the impossibility which the N.C.N.C. would find under an adult suffrage system of carrying out the same degree of bribery and intimidation as the electoral college system permits.

12. Opinion in the East as between N.C.N.C. and N.I.P. is thus less divided than might be expected. It is probable, however, that whichever party is returned to power will find great difficulty in agreeing to any reorganisation at the Centre which might either

(a) adversely affect the East financially; or
(b) circumscribe Eastern lebensraum: (by far the greater number of Civil Servants and tradesmen from the South in the North are Ibos, and there is great pressure of population on the land in the East).

13. The foregoing assessment does not mention the problem of the Trust Territory of the Cameroons, which is of particular relevance to the situation in the Northern and Eastern Regions, but which, of course, affects the general constitutional issue, and H.M.G.'s position as the Administering Power. In para. 8 of Nigeria Secret Telegram No. 337 of the 16th March[4] it was stated that if Nigeria split it would not be into two parts but into a number of warring segments; and it was prophesied that there would be an irresistible demand for complete separation of the Cameroons from Nigeria—'with all the resulting local and international complications'.

It appears that the first announced threat of disintegration has come from the Cameroons, or a part of it. Following the N.C.N.C. victory in the Eastern House of Assembly, and the subsequent dissolution of that House,[5] the major section of the Cameroons bloc of members (eight out of thirteen, led by Dr. Endeley) has declared that they will take no part in the elections because they are determined to have

[4] See 182.
[5] See 199.

separate Regional status. If the N.C.N.C. put forward candidates in the Cameroons and elections can be held Dr. Endeley's bloc may change their minds, but this development, and its repercussions in the Northern Region (by which a part of the Trust Territory is administered) and in the United Nations, make a review of the Constitution all the more necessary and greatly increase the urgency of a pronouncement being made by H.M.G. at the earliest possible moment following the meetings of the Northern Legislative Houses, which are likely to end about the 25th of May. The knowledge that the Constitution is to be re-examined may make the Endeley bloc more ready to take part in the Eastern elections.

14.   In making this assessment of the position at this date it must be emphasised not only that the Northern Legislative Houses have not yet met but that at this time of tension and emotion any estimate can be upset by any turn of events. There is, however, one hard incontrovertible fact, and that is that Azikiwe's victory in the East will cause the North to be more determined than ever to have the greatest possible degree of cleavage with the South. (Until Awolowo and the other Action Group leaders began to play Azikiwe's game the North regarded Azikiwe as the incarnation of everything they dislike and fear in the South). To this extent the good work that has been done by the Lieutenant-Governor and his officers has suffered a sharp set-back. The N.I.P. whose representatives Northern leaders respect and with whom they have declared their ability to work, represented for the North the only possible political link with the South. Whatever may be our assessment of N.I.P. chances in the Eastern elections which cannot be completed in less than three or four months! time, the assessment made by Northern political leaders and Emirs today will certainly be that the conclusion is foregone: the N.C.N.C. will win by their normal methods of bribery and intimidation. Even if the Cameroons situation could be temporarily straightened out, the Northern leaders would not be content to await the outcome of the Eastern elections. They are impatient now. As soon as they have had their meetings they will expect a pronouncement by H.M.G. in the U.K. both that there will be a loosening at the Centre, and that H.M.G. in the United Kingdom will remain in a position of control in Nigeria adequate to secure essential Northern interests for as long as the Northern leaders wish to remain under British protection. Unless they can be reassured that such a pronouncement will be made in the very near future, the great difficulty now will be to persuade the North not to withdraw their Northern Central Ministers from the Centre. Such a withdrawal would take place immediately if there were the slightest sign by the Governor or by H.M.G. in the United Kingdom that it was prepared to meet any Action Group demand which affected the Centre and not the Western Region alone. And any suggestion that either Bode Thomas or Akintola might return as Central Ministers would immediately induce such a withdrawal.

15.   The position in the West is that the Action Group have committed themselves, apparently irrevocably, to a demand for Self Government in 1956 *for a united Nigeria*. Awolowo has stressed that he means Self Government for a united Nigeria, and that the British must compel the North to accept it. Nevertheless, continually over the past fourteen months, and particularly over the last eight weeks, Action Group politicians have stated that, if needs must, they would go for complete Regional autonomy with separation from both North and East. It is probable that the Action Group will decline to accept any loosening arrangement which did not leave them with complete authority over the forces of law and order in the West. Inevitably

any loosening which takes place will be condemned by the Action Group as due solely to imperialist manoeuvres: if the British cannot keep the West in bondage the British will at least, with the help of their stooges, keep the North in a state of slavery, in order that Britain may have groundnuts, tin and columbite. Note here that any influence which the Obas exercised two months ago has now—at least temporarily—disappeared; and nothing can revive that influence while the Action Group remain undisturbed in power in the Western Region. Note also, however, that the Obas would, if there were a dissolution in the West, exercise a certain influence at the village election level.

16.   The Action Group are also publicly committed to accepting no alternatives as Central Ministers to the four resigned Ministers.

17.   It is difficult to estimate how long the uneasy alliance between the Action Group and the N.C.N.C. will last. Already it has lasted longer than most people expected and on the 6th May it survived a difficult test when the Bill to reform the Lagos Town Council was passed—the N.C.N.C. opposition contenting itself with a statement that the Ordinance would be repealed when they came to power. Much depends upon whether Azikiwe decides to stand for election in the East or to remain in the Western House. There is a difference of opinion in the Party on this issue, and no decision has yet been taken. It appears inconceivable that the alliance could continue once the position of Lagos under any re-drawn Constitution comes under discussion.

18.   The Eastern Region specialises in producing the unexpected, and it is not by any means beyond doubt that in the Elections in the East Azikiwe will secure an outright victory for the old guard of the N.C.N.C., and other similar noisy and extreme candidates. The N.C.N.C. has, however, a party organisation and it has its Press. N.I.P. is greatly handicapped in the fight, and the Government newspaper (a weekly) and a Government-controlled broadcasting service cannot fight political campaigns. It is therefore likely that the party machine, unscrupulous as it is in employing intimidation and corruption, will win.

19.   The best assessment that can be made at present of the attitude of the various political parties towards a review of the Constitution with the objective of loosening the association at the Centre and giving much greater autonomy to the Regions might, with considerable reservations, be summarised as follows:—

N.P.C. regard the review as essential and, at the best, want the association at the Centre to be reduced to the absolute minimum.

The *Action Group* will be in favour of the review, with the intention of securing complete power in the West. They know that association at the Centre must be loosened and that there can be no advance at the Centre, but they will not openly admit this, and will charge H.M.G. (and the North) with responsibility both for retarding the political advance of a united Nigeria and for dividing Nigeria. They refuse to recognise the true situation in the North and will try to foment such disruptive forces as they can find in that Region.

N.I.P. will know in their hearts that the review is necessary but they will not admit this, partly because they truly desire to maintain a united Nigeria, both on visionary grounds and because financially the Eastern Region is least able to look after itself; and partly because any such admission would be political sui-cide for them in the face of the consistent N.C.N.C. plank of 'one Nigeria'. They want to co-operate with the North but deceive themselves in underestimating the strength of Northern feeling against the South as a whole.

N.C.N.C. claim to be a nation-wide party and have always been in favour of a united Nigeria—preferably in the form of a unitary State, though they might give the colour of a federation by creating eight or more provinces (or 'States') based on ethnic grouping. They intend to achieve power first in the East, and later in the West, and to wreck the present Constitution or anything that resembled it. Like the Action Group they hope to disrupt the North and would be quite undeterred by the thought that a period of chaos would result. Their approach to a review would be destructive, not constructive.

N.E.P.U. will continue to attack the Emirate system but the majority of the Party will be in sympathy with the stand of the N.P.C. against domination by the South. It is possible that the Party may split on this issue.

202   CAB 129/61, C (53) 154   13 May 1953

'Constitutional developments in the Gold Coast and Nigeria': Cabinet memorandum by Mr Lyttelton   [Extract]

[This memorandum, which was considered at the Cabinet meeting of 27 May, was prompted by proposals for further constitutional advance in the Gold Coast. These included the abolition of ex-officio ministers and an increase in the membership of the Legislative Assembly which would thereafter consist only of members directly elected by universal adult suffrage; elections for the new Legislative Assembly were envisaged for 1954. The creation of such an all-African Cabinet was, of course, a prime demand of political leaders in Nigeria. See BDEEP series B, vol 1, R Rathbone, ed, *Ghana*, part II, 131. In the Cabinet discussion, Lyttelton pointed out that the collapse of the 1951 constitution 'provided an opportunity of according a larger measure of autonomy to the 14 million Moslem inhabitants of the Northern provinces who were more favourably disposed to this country than the Southern Nigerians'. (CO 554/261, no 137, extract from Cabinet conclusions, 27 May 1953.]

. . . Nigeria

13.   I have taken into account the possible repercussions of these developments on West Africa, particularly in Nigeria, and have consulted the Governor of Nigeria about them. At one time he was apprehensive lest they should quicken still further the demand for political advance in the Southern Regions and thus lead to divisions, and strife, between the South and the conservative North. But as my colleagues will be aware, the latent discord between the three Regions has already been brought to the surface by recent events in Nigeria and in particular by the debate on 31st March in the House of Representatives on a private member's motion about the attainment of self-government in 1956.

14.   As I informed the House of Commons on 22nd April, the situation in Nigeria is complicated and will require further patient and careful study. But I am clear that the present cumbersome constitution will have to be radically revised and that the best hope of preserving the unity of the territory will lie in seeking to reach agreement on some modified and looser form of association at the Centre. The Governor agrees that this would probably have to be coupled with some measure of political advance—for example, the widening of the responsibilities and functions of

Ministers—but that the arrangements at the Centre would have to be such as to satisfy the North that their interests were effectively safeguarded.

15.   A further constitutional advance in the Gold Coast will not make a difficult situation in Nigeria any easier. But by and large Nigeria's future will, I think, be settled by events in Nigeria; and in any case I see no alternative but to proceed in the Gold Coast on the lines I have described which, as the Governor has advised me, represent the minimum concessions if we are to secure peaceful and ordered progress by successive stages.

Conclusion
16.   My colleagues will wish to take note of the position now reached in both territories. When the final proposals of the Gold Coast Government are received later this year I will consult them again. I may need to consult them before long about Nigeria.

203   CO 554/428, no 3   17 May 1953
[Kano riots]: inward telegram no SX 1176 from HQ West Africa Command to Mr Lyttelton reporting the outbreak of serious disturbances in Kano

[The Kano riots which began on 16 May and lasted for four days, saw the most serious inter-ethnic fighting in Northern Nigeria since the start of British rule. The immediate spark came from the decision of the AG to hold a rally in Kano on 16 May to be addressed by Akintola as part of a northern tour designed to attack 'reactionary elements' and 'the dutiful allies of British Imperialism',[1] but underlying this were longer term resentments between northerners and southerners living in the cities and towns of the North, resentments further provoked by the self-government debate in the House of Representatives on 31 Mar and its aftermath (see 184). Although the AG rally was cancelled at the last moment by the authorities, rioting between the inhabitants of Fagge, the old caravan quarter of Kano, and southerners living in the *Sabon Gari* ('strangers town') broke out during the afternoon of 16 May. The riots rapidly became straightforward clashes between Hausa and Igbo, which were exacerbated on the one hand by complaints that most of the NPF contingents in Kano consisted of southerners and on the other by suspicions that the Kano NA had prompted the rioting. Troops and extra police were brought in by the authorities, though the former were not deployed, and Macpherson broadcast an appeal for calm. A State of Emergency throughout the Northern Region was declared on 18 May (and not rescinded until mid-July) and it was only on 20 May that order was fully restored. The official figures reported 36 dead and 241 injured but other estimates speak of up to 50 killed. 61 people were sentenced on charges arising from the riots. *Report on the Kano Disturbances, 16th–19th May 1953* (Kaduna, 1953).]

Political demonstrations by North Nigerians against Southern politicians led to serious disturbances Kano, North Nigeria, afternoon 16th May. Rioting began again morning 17th May. Situation reported as deteriorating. Regional Government has requested military assistance. Detachment 100 of Nigeria Regiment en route from Kaduna, e.t.a Kano 17.00 hours, with two further companies following. Full sitrep will follow.

---
[1] Cited in G O Olusanya, *The second world war and politics in Nigeria 1939–53* (Lagos, 1973) p 157.

204   CO 554/261, no 104   17 May 1953

[Political situation]: inward telegram no 700 from Sir J Macpherson
to Mr Hopkinson on the need for an immediate statement on the
revision of the constitution

Your telegram Personal No. 56.
    Following for Minister of State.
    Begins.
    Constitutional Position.
    I am dismayed to realise that the House of Commons will be in recess from 22nd
May until 9th June. I fully appreciate the desirability of statement by the Secretary of
State being made in the House but sands are running out here and although advance
announcement in the Lords on 20th May should help to cool things down I cannot
(repeat cannot) give assurance that the position can be held until 10th June. This was
my considered view even before the flare up in Kano today, which is being separately
reported.
    2.   Savingram follows with account of the latest that there is. Main points are as
follows:—

(a) *opinion generally, including responsible opinion, is increasingly critical of
this Government's failure to take action or even utter.*
(b) East. Central Ministers from East are very disheartened and threaten to resign
from the Council of Ministers. They say if they resign Central Ministers from the
North will follow suit, but this is not certain. They strongly press for
postponement of the elections in Eastern Region pending statement by Her
Majesty's Government and the revision of the Constitution. Alternatively, and
preferably, they press for dissolution of the House of Representatives involving
fresh elections in all three Regions. Dates for election in the East will become
immediate issue in the Council of Ministers. Lieutenant Governor of East wants
announcement made on 1st June, elections to start 1st July. Regulation must be
approved by me in Council and Eastern members will vote against. Upon the
attitude of the Northern members will depend whether the majority of the Council
approves the programme leading to the resignation of the Eastern Ministers or
disapproves leaving me the difficult choice between postponing the elections
(which would lead to eruption of N.C.N.C.) or using reserve powers to enforce the
election programme which would probably lead to the resignation of all the
remaining Ministers. My present intention is to stall on the election dates at least
until statement has been made by the Secretary of State. I am doing all I can to
hearten the Eastern Ministers and to retain them on the Council.
(c) West. Civil Secretary had long private conversation with Awolowo on 14th
May. Latter stated that dissolution of the House of Representatives would be
regarded by Action Group as abrogating the present Constitution. Demand of his
party for immediate self government would, at once, become operative and they
would make election issue of this. He favoured major adjustments to the present
Constitution, more or less on the lines indicated to you. This should be carried out
with the least possible delay at round table conference of representatives of all
Regions (4 members from each) to be held outside Nigeria under strong impartial

chairman. He also objected that return of 4 ex-Ministers could not be delayed indefinitely. Party had set dead-line and if the demands had not been met by then action already planned would be set in train. He refused to disclose date of the dead-line (I am trying to discover this) or evoke plan (probably civil disobedience and the encouragement of strikes on the railway).

(d) North. Meetings of the Legislature start, as you know, on 15th October. Meantime provocative action of the Action Group in sending delegation led by (?Akintola) to Kano has touched off magazine there—separately reported. Azikiwe similarly plans provocative action and encouragement of dissident elements in the North by arranging meeting of N.C.N.C. Executive at Kaduna on 19th May. He has been advised not to go to Kaduna.

205   CO 554/428, no 24   21 May 1953
[Kano riots]: inward savingram no 1192 from Sir J Macpherson to Mr Lyttelton giving details of the disturbances in Kano

Disturbances in Kano
It is now possible to give a fuller report on the disturbances in Kano which broke out on the 16th of May, though some time must necessarily elapse before detailed information is available.

2.   As you are aware, deep resentment was caused throughout the North by the treatment afforded to the Northern Members of the House of Representatives during the Budget Meeting in March and this resentment was exacerbated by the subsequent Press campaign in the Action Group and N.C.N.C. papers.[1] In the light of this, nothing could have been more ill-advised or politically inept than for the Action Group to stage a rally in Kano and for the N.C.N.C. to call a meeting of its Executive Committee at the very time when all the Northern Chiefs and political leaders were due to assemble there to discuss major political issues and especially the relationship between the North and the South.

3.   Shortly after a visit by the Sardauna to Kano in the middle of last week, the local branch of the N.P.C. decided to stage a demonstration on the 15th of May against the proposed visit of Akintola and other Action Group leaders on the following day. It also decided to ask all Kano Native Authority employees of Northern origin to stay away from work on the 16th of May to demonstrate their solidarity in objecting to the Action Group meeting. It is understood that Malam Wada, a Member of the House of Representatives and a senior Native Authority official, visited the N.A. Public Works Department on May 15th and made an ill-advised and inflammatory speech to the employees. The N.P.C. protest meeting and procession, which is stated to have been about 2,000 strong, were nevertheless orderly and free from incident. There is no doubt, however, that the activities of the N.P.C. led to a heightening of tension and increased resentment against the Southern population. Southern members of the population, on their part, were clearly preparing for trouble and an increase in the sale of matchets—the traditional weapon of the Ibo—was reported.

[1] See 184.

4.   On the morning of the 16th of May the general tension throughout the city and suburban areas was such that the authorities decided that the permit for the Action Group meeting, which had already been issued, must be withdrawn. All possible steps were taken to calm popular feeling.

5.   Rioting broke out during the afternoon. It is not known exactly how the rioting started, but it is reported that at about 3.15 p.m. gangs of hooligans armed with matchets gathered in several areas and that some stone-throwing occurred between rival mobs. The Police intervened and made a small number of arrests but owing to the widely dispersed nature of these incidents, they were unable to restore order. Throughout the afternoon and evening raids by groups of hooligans from the predominantly Northern suburb of Fagge were followed by retaliatory attacks by groups of Ibos from the predominantly Southern suburb, known as the Sabon Gari. It appears that as soon as these disturbances began nearly all Yorubas kept well away from the troubled areas, and that the fighting was almost entirely between Hausas and Ibos. It had in fact, ceased to be political or in any way related to membership of the Action Group or the N.P.C. and had developed along tribal lines. Casualties by evening totalled two killed and fifteen injured and admitted to hospital. Three Native Authority Police were also slightly injured.

6.   All was quiet during the night but early next morning mobs gathered again and a major clash between the inhabitants of Fagge and the Sabon Gari would have occurred but for the action of the Police who struggled all day with a reasonable degree of success to keep the opposing forces apart. They were reinforced early in the morning by 100 additional Nigeria Police from Kaduna and during the day, another 100 Police and two Companies of Infantry were flown to Kano in transport aircraft sent from Lagos. A Battery was also sent up by road in an infantry capacity. Despite the reinforcements, which arrived piecemeal during the day, it was impossible to prevent isolated encounters and it was later found that several of the Hausa corpses had been emasculated. The situation became a little quieter during the night but on the morning of Monday, 18th May, the situation again became extremely ugly, both sides having reached a state of hysteria. Only with the greatest difficulty was a major battle prevented and some looting by Northern rioters took place both in the Sabon Gari market, in African shops on the edge of the commercial area and at one or two places within the city walls. Further atrocities took place during the morning; at least nine persons being soaked in petrol and burnt.

7.   During the day barbed wire was flown up from Kaduna and by nightfall a barbed wire obstruction had been erected by the military between Fagge and the Sabon Gari. By afternoon the fever began to work itself out and it became possible for Southerners living in the Fagge area to be evacuated to the Sabon Gari and for Northerners in the Sabon Gari to be evacuated to Fagge. A number of Southerners living inside the City walls were also moved into the Sabon Gari.

8.   By Tuesday morning the position had greatly improved and it seems unlikely that there will be any further incidents in this area. Casualty figures to date are 46 dead and 205 treated or admitted to hospital. Full details of the tribal composition is not yet available but it is understood that there were no recorded Yoruba fatalities and that only seven Yorubas are in hospital. Of the rest, the proportion between Northerners and Easterners is roughly 60:40% and the majority of the Northern casualties are people of no fixed occupation. It should perhaps be pointed out that while the rioters of Northern extraction were armed largely with cudgels, spears,

swords and bows and arrows, the Southerners had a number of Dane guns and shotguns as well as matchets.

9. There has throughout been no evidence of any anti-European feeling amongst the Northern population but some racial feeling was shown by the Southerners. Only one actual attack has been reported, however, and that was on the car of a Medical Officer who was taking injured Northerners to hospital. The Medical Officer fortunately escaped injury.

10. The behaviour of the Sabon Gari leaders, once they could effect some measure of control over the rioters has been excellent, as too has been the attitude of the Native Authority officials.

11. The Lieutenant-Governor has commented on the courage and discipline of the Police and also on the complete disregard of personal danger shown by both Administrative and Police Officers, together with members of the Council of the Emir of Kano who penetrated into danger areas at a time when the mob was uncontrollable. He also praised the gallantry of four European unarmed Special Constables who attempted to rescue a Southerner from murder and subsequent incineration without any regard for their personal safety.

12. I will keep you fully informed of further developments.

206 CO 554/261, no 122   21 May 1953
[Constitutional revision]: outward telegram no 608 from Mr Lyttelton to Sir J Macpherson giving the text of his statement to the House of Commons on the decision to revise the constitution

I made following statement in the House of Commons today. *Begins*.

Recent events have shown that it is not possible for the three Regions of Nigeria to work together effectively in a federation so closely knit as that provided by the present Constitution. Her Majesty's Government in the United Kingdom, while regretting this, consider that the Constitution will have to be redrawn to provide for greater Regional autonomy and for the removal of powers of intervention by the Centre in matters which can, without detriment to other Regions, be placed entirely within Regional competence. It is at the same time necessary to ensure that the common economic and defence requirements of all Regions are secured. In order to ensure these vital requirements of all Regions and at the same time to preserve the common interests of all the peoples of Nigeria there will of course be a continuing need for a central organisation. The form which that central organisation should take, and the powers which must be reserved to it, will require careful study. In the work of redrawing the Constitution Her Majesty's Government in the United Kingdom would wish to co-operate as closely as possible with the leaders of the people in all three Regions. The first requirement is to decide how this work can best be carried out. To this end Her Majesty's Government will invite representatives from each Region to visit London for discussions with the Secretary of State. It is Her Majesty's Government's intention to carry through the projected reform of the Constitution in the shortest time possible, but in a territory of such a size, with so large a population, and with so many different groupings and many shades of public opinion, the work will inevitably take time. While that work is carried out Nigeria will continue to be governed under its existing Constitutional Instruments, and it will be necessary for the Central Government to be so composed that it can carry out its task in the meanwhile. It is the clear duty of all the Regions to assist the Governor by ensuring that the persons composing the central Government are able and determined to work together during this interim period. It is equally the clear duty of Her Majesty's Government to ensure that in all circumstances government in Nigeria is effectively carried on in the interests of all the peoples of the country. *Ends.*

2. Various supplementaries were asked as to whether statement had been discussed with Nigerian Ministers. Text of these will follow as soon as Hansard is available.

207 CO 554/261, no 127   21 May 1953
[Political situation]: inward telegram no 741 from L H Goble to W L Gorell Barnes on a motion in the Northern House of Assembly demanding greater regional autonomy

[In the aftermath of the 31 March self-government debate in the House of Representatives (see 184), separatist sentiment grew stronger among Northern political leaders. The day after order had been restored following the Kano riots, the Northern Region House of Assembly debated the motion (the so-called 'Eight-points Motion') outlined in this document; the motion was carried without any dissenting vote and was passed by the Northern Region House of Chiefs on the same day. In effect the motion called for regional autonomy in all but the most limited spheres; there would in effect be no central government for Nigeria and only a restricted central agency. In a earlier debate on the same day rejecting self-government in 1956—also passed unanimously—Malam Yahaya Gusau stated 'the offices of the government in the North are filled by non-Northerners. . . . Is it not madness for the North to ask for self-government at a time when the majority of the junior service in the North are filled entirely by non-Northerners' (CO 554/262, no 218, inward savingram no 1430 from Macpherson to Lyttelton). The House of Assembly was still in session when news of Lyttelton's statement to the House of Commons (see 206) reached it.]

Following for Gorell Barnes from Goble.
Begins.
It is understood motion in following terms will be introduced House of Assembly tomorrow.
Begins.
Be it resolved that this House prays that a message be sent to the Government of the United Kingdom requesting them to advise Her Majesty to amend the Constitutional Instruments at present in force and to make provision for a new constitutional arrangement for Nigeria on the following principles:—

First, Each region shall have complete legislative and executive autonomy with respect to all matters except the following:—
1 Defence
2 External Affairs
3 Customs
4 West African Research Institutions.
Second, There shall be no central legislative body and no central executive or policy making body for the whole of Nigeria.
Third, There shall be a central agency for all regions which will be responsible for

the matters mentioned in paragraph first, 1 to 4 and any other matters delegated to it by a region.

Fourth, The central agency shall be at a neutral place, preferably Lagos.

Fifth, The composition powers and responsibility of the central agency shall be defined by the Order in Council establishing the new constitutional arrangements. The agency shall be a non political body

Sixth, The services of the railway, air services, ports, electricity and coal mining shall be organised on an inter-Regional basis and shall be administered by public corporations. Such public corporations shall be independent bodies governed solely by the statutes under which they are created. The boards of such corporations shall be composed of experts with a minority representation of the Regional Governments.

Seventh, All revenues shall be levied and collected by the Regional Governments except customs revenue. Customs duties shall be collected at the port of discharge by the central agency and paid to each Region. The administration of the customs shall be so organised as to ensure that goods consigned to each Region are separately cleared and charged to duty.

Eighth, Each Region shall have a separate public service.

BE IT FURTHER RESOLVED that should general support be accorded to these proposals they be forthwith communicated to the Government of the United Kingdom requesting that Her Majesty be advised to amend the constitutional instruments accordingly. *Ends*

208 CO 554/261, no 163c   22 May–3 June 1953
[Constitutional revision]: minutes by N B J Huijsman[1] and I B Watt outlining principles for a revised constitution

Mr. Williamson

Attached are two copies of my first thoughts on a Child's Guide to the New Constitution for your perusal and criticism.[2] I am sorry that recent events have made it impossible to submit it to you before, and that they have in the event also not left me enough time to do some more thorough thinking on the financial suggestions. You may wish to have a discussion with me, in which case you will know where I can be reached before June the 3rd. In the meantime I am circulating copies of this minute and its enclosure to Mr. Bourdillon, Mr. Peck and Mr. Watt for their comments, as I have not had the opportunity of more than casual discussion of this very intricate and difficult question with those others in the Office who will be concerned with it.

2.   I should explain that the note attached is in effect an attempted synthesis of the views on a revised constitution which have flowed into W.A.D., plus some additional thoughts of my own. Looking over it again I now feel:—

(a) that we must resist any attempt to create more Regions. I now feel that any acceptance of the demand for a separate Cameroons Region might lead to violent

---

[1] NBJ Huijsman, principal CO, 1949; ass sec, 1962.   [2] Not printed.

Southern agitation for a Middle Belt Region and possibly to a reopening of the Western Region frontier dispute;

(b) that we must put an end to the present form of conciliar government and instead leave the *Governor* free within limits to select a Council which will cooperate. I am more than ever convinced that much of the failure of the Council of Ministers is due to the fact that the individual Ministers are in effect the creatures of the Regional Governments.[2] The attempt to give the Central Ministers an independent existence and source of authority is at the back of my suggestions for the future form of political existence. Mr. Watt may wish to criticise my suggestions.

(c) that the creation of a statutory Revenue Fund is a possible way out of the political difficulties created by Nigeria's peculiar financial set-up, and that we should seek to preserve flexibility in the allocation of revenue by using C.D. & W. funds as our instrument rather than by complicating the revenue allocation machine in Nigeria. The net result may well be greater financial rigidity, plus slower development in the East and the North. I see no easy way round this difficulty but no doubt Finance Department will have better sight than I!

(d) the problem of the judiciary requires more consideration. Mr. Awolowo wants to control Native Authority Courts; I think the reasons are obvious, but I don't know if he wants to extend his 'regionalisation of the judiciary' to the Supreme Court. We should ask for Legal Department advice.

I hope that the obvious weakness of my note will not make it completely useless as a start for our thinking on the subject. More work went into it than appears on the surface!

N.B.J.H.
22.5.53

Mr. Williamson
May I offer a very limited number of comments on Mr. Huijsman's paper.

2.   If we divide Nigeria into four, i.e. a Centre and three Regions, with each of the latter allowed to develop at its own pace, we are producing a system rather like those in the Central African and West Indies Federations.

3.   However in Central Africa and the West Indies it is agreed that *only* as an entity will or can the component territories get Dominion status. To that extent the leading politicians will take an active part in the Central Governments in each Federation.[3] The emphasis in each of these Federations will be for a gradual increase in the authority and legislative scope of these Central Governments. There is not likely to be pressure for advance of the component territories, individually, to Dominion status.

4.   In Nigeria pressure for Dominion status for the Regions individually appears a distinct possibility, especially if the leading politicians, (confronted as they would be with the choice between office either in the Centre or in the Regions, if Mr. Huijsman's proposal were adopted) decided to concentrate on holding office in the Regional Ministries.

---

[2] Huijsman added in the margin at this point 'This applies with particular force to the West'.
[3] This did not prove to be the case in the West Indies where the leading politicians concentrated their efforts on their own local governments.

5.   We contemplate I take it that no Regional Government in Nigeria, however complete a control of internal affairs it may achieve, shall, if at all feasible, be allowed to obtain a degree of control of external affairs and defence which would enable it as a Regional Government to claim Dominion status. Therefore should we not try, in the forthcoming negotiations with Nigeria, to get agreement all round that control of external affairs and defence by Nigerian Ministers, responsible to an all-elective Nigerian Legislature, will not be conceded except to a Central Government in which all Regions will agree, at the time when such control is conceded, to participate?

6.   I agree with Mr. Huijsman that a good deal of the present frustration is probably due to the fact that Central Ministers have been the creatures of Regional Governments, but I am not sure that his proposal to make activity in Central and Regional politics mutually exclusive is well adopted to political conditions in the country. For one thing are there enough capable bodies to serve four political organisations, leaving enough educated and responsible Africans over to take some part in filling more high posts in the Public Services? In any case surely we must recognise that any influential Nigerian politician will for the time being retain his regional prejudices and draw his political strength from his regional backing. I therefore suggest for consideration that for, say the first five years of a revised constitution we adopt the West Indies Federation model and allow people to be members of Regional and of Central legislatures and executives. We should however make the choice of Central Ministers depend only upon the approval of the Central Assembly. In the political circumstances of Nigeria, we should have to give the Governor some discretionary power over the choice of Ministers, in order to ensure that some members of the executive would represent regional rather than purely party opinion. Therefore we could not approve a method of choice of a Ministry as advanced as that now working in Jamaica where, once a Chief Minister is approved by the House of Representatives the other Ministers are appointed on his nomination. I suggest that something like the present arrangement in the Gold Coast would be more suitable for Nigeria, with a slight but I think significant modification. Thus the Governor, in his discretion should submit to the House of Representatives, for approval, the name of the person whom he proposes for appointment to his Chief Minister; then after consultation with that Chief Minister, but still acting in his discretion, the Governor shall appoint the other members of the Executive Council.

7.   I don't like Mr. Huijsman's proposal that a two-thirds majority vote should be required to revoke the appointment of an individual Minister, Such a system has been one of the main curses of the old Jamaica constitution as it did allow certain individual Ministers who were in complete disagreement with their colleagues to be retained. Unless and until a two-thirds majority could be secured it meant that the Opposition could, if it wished, keep a Minister in Office even if he had forfeited the confidence of his fellow Ministers. It would be better in Nigeria to provide simply, as in the Gold Coast, that when the Chief Minister goes out all the elected members of Executive Council do the same.

8.   These are tentative and provisional thoughts which I put forward very much for discussion only. I am sending copies to Mr. Huijsman, Mr. Peck and Mr. Bourdillon, and keeping spares for others who will be coming to Mr. Gorell-Barnes' meeting on Thursday.

I.W.
3.6.53

209   CO 554/261, no 144   25 May 1953
[Political situation]: letter from L H Goble to E O Mercer on the
potential for disturbance in Nigeria   [Extract]

... There is, indeed, never a dull moment in Nigeria these days. In the words of the
Prime Minister in another connection, there are 'complex, changing uncertain and
unpredictable situations' with which the Governor is ceaselessly confronted. Not
only is there never a dull moment, but there are insufficient moments.

Today it looks as if we might get by without serious inter-tribal disturbances in
the immediate future, though tension is very high, especially in places in the
North where there are large Southern elements. Nigeria at the moment seems to
be a very unstable compound and a detonation wave of very little force could
touch off a most calamitous explosion. The trouble is that there is scarcely a single political party which has not an adequate supply of detonators, and whose irresponsible leaders would be astounded at the violence of the explosion that they
touch off . . . .

210   CO 554/261, no 139   29 May 1953
[Constitutional revision]: inward telegram no 776 (reply) from Sir J
Macpherson to Mr Lyttelton on Nigerian reaction to the
announcement of talks in London

Your telegram No. 608.[1]

Nigeria Constitution.

Local press comments generally favour the idea of London talks but there is clear
misunderstanding of the purpose of this preliminary meeting, which will discuss the
machinery for consultation only.[2]

So far no cumulative policy has emerged in N.C.N.C. and Action Group papers,
although there have been joint meetings of leaders of both parties. N.C.N.C. papers
purport to read into your statement victory over present constitution. Action
Group/N.C.N.C. axis has been strengthened in this way. It holds together because of
the desire to gang against the North and for anti-Imperialist motives.

---

[1] See 206.

[2] The original intention of the CO was that the London talks would discuss the mechanics of how to set
about amending the constitution (see 208). This had been explicitly set out by Gorell Barnes in a letter to
Macpherson dated 27 May 1953 (CO 554/261, no 135); the CO hope was that the constitution itself would
be drawn up by a panel of three or four British experts and then put to a conference in Nigeria for
discussion. Macpherson had endorsed this approach on 29 May (CO 554/261, no 141). Nigerian political
leaders however, were determined that any talks in London should be substantive and should discuss the
actual changes to be made in the constitution. As a consequence on 1 June both Awolowo and Azikiwe
refused their invitations to London; a further contributing factor, particularly for Azikwe, was the
invitation to the NIP to attend. This threat to boycott the talks was followed by a meeting in Lagos between
Macpherson, Awolowo, Azikiwe and the Sardauna of Sokoto on 19 June and led to a reconsideration by the
CO of its plans for the London conference (see 212).

Nothing yet said publicly to prevent acceptance of the invitation by principal leaders, but there is tendency to suggest conditions for acceptance. Great danger is that axis will commit itself to conditions from which impossible to retract.

Apart from the press, reliable but most secret information is that meeting of N.C.N.C. leaders on 22nd May agreed that party would oppose any form of government with 'a loose federation'. Before the London meeting, party would summon 'Constituent Assembly' to draw up mandate and draft constitution for presentation in London as the only form of government acceptable. Any other proposals would be opposed by N.C.N.C. representative.

Similar report on Action Group meeting of 22nd May is that party leaders considered looser federation would be advantageous to the West and in accord with their proposals to the Minister of State. Party favour fuller Regional autonomy. Danger of clash with N.C.N.C. on this issue discussed.

Most secret and reliable source states that at joint meeting of the two parties on 23rd May agreement reached as follows:—

(a) N.P.C. programme unacceptable except as regards establishment of corporations.

(b) They will oppose the present 50% representation of the North at the centre.

(c) Constitution should be federal and bilateral [sic? bicameral] at the centre.

(d) Break away by any territorial region from the centre should be opposed.

(e) Central legislature (sic) should not be 'a loose one'. Power of intervention should be retained in matters of common interest.

(f) Proposed London talks welcome and invitation will be accepted provided (1) Azikiwe included; (2) North not given 50% representation but all regions have equal representation, and (3) 'no stooge invited'.

(g) Present constitution should be amended as opposed to new one being redrafted.

(h) Representatives should remain in London until amendments drawn up and signed by all concerned, and published.

In my view, major misconception about scope of talks (see paragraph 6(h) above) must be corrected quickly. I realize that removing this misconception might stop the axis accepting invitation on the grounds that no need to consider mechanics: obviously redraft must be done by Nigerians (presumably in 'constituent assembly'). On the other hand, North, N.I.P., and Cameroons will be encouraged to accept by appreciation of joint scope of talks. On balance, rejection of invitation by the axis, in my view, much less damaging than discovery of misconception only in London, with consequent walk-out and accusation of Imperialist trick. This conception about function and composition of constituent assembly is also dangerous. I propose, therefore, to have broadcast made analysing and explaining your statement with contents of first two sentences of paragraph 2 of my immediately following telegram. I will bear your supplementary answers carefully in mind. Lt. Governors similarly being asked to explain to political leaders. My immediately following telegram suggests form in which invitation should be couched.

211   CO 554/430, no 3   3 June 1953
[Coronation day riots]: inward telegram no 802 from Sir J
Macpherson to Mr Lyttelton reporting the Coronation day
disturbances in Lagos

My immediately preceding telegram.

2.   About 30 supporters followed persons named[1] to prison, were then reinforced
to about 150 by band of hooligans and together proceeded to the race course where
they doubled up and down behind crowd singing freedom song. Crowd took no notice
and mob dispersed while ceremony of Trooping the Colour was starting. There were
no incidents during ceremony. Mob re-formed in three or four groups after leaving
race course, stoned buildings in commercial area of Marina and near Carter Bridge
and Government and commercial buildings in Broad Street, breaking windows. No
cases of entry have been reported. Coronation decorations were torn down or broken
in certain areas. Victoria Street and War Memorial receiving particular attention.

3.   Care returning to homes after Cathedral state service were stoned and about
10 cases of minor injuries, including both Europeans and Africans, and one Army
driver were treated in hospital.

4. In afternoon band of youths dressed as cowboys[2] visited prison and were
dispersed peacefully, but a mob of hooligans who followed them had to be dispersed
forcibly by police.

5. On same afternoon a public meeting of Convention Peoples Party was convened
without permit and was dispersed by police who arrested five leaders of the party,
including Adewole Thompson and Dele Bakare.

6. Total number of arrests made by police to date eleven, although police were
handicapped by tip and run methods of hooligan gangs which, in no case, numbered
more than 60 to 70. They successfully prevented them from interfering with the
Coronation celebrations which were attended by happy crowds of thousands of
Africans (attendance at afternoon ceremony over twenty thousand) many of whom
have expressed disgust at the activities of the hooligans. See my immediately
following telegram for paragraph 7.

---

[1] 2 June 1953, Coronation day, was chosen by the youth movements of the AG and NCNC and the Lagos
branch of NEPU as a day of mourning for those killed in the Kano riots. Permits for a meeting however,
were refused by the authorities and, following a refusal by the leaders of the three organisations to alter
their plans, seven were arrested and brought before magistrates to be bound over to keep the peace.
Awolowo and Azikiwe attended court in their support. Following their refusal to enter into recognisance
to keep the peace, the seven were committed to prison for three days.
[2] The curious trend for NCNC supporters to appear in cowboy dress in this period is remarked on by B E
Sharwood-Smith, *Recollections of British administration . . . but always as friends* (London, 1969) p 272.

212   CO 554/261, no 164   3 June 1953
[Constitutional revision]: outward telegram no 65 from W L Gorell
Barnes to Sir J Macpherson agreeing to substantive talks in London

Following for Macpherson from Gorell Barnes. *Begins*. London conference on
constitution.

To-day's London 'Times' reports that Azikiwe and Awolowo have rejected invitation on the grounds that (1) they object to the manner in which the selection of representatives has been made and suggest that this was 'deliberately and arbitrarily done to include friends of His Excellency the Governor, who by their recent acts have forfeited such little following as they ever had in the country'; and (2) they consider that it would be a 'sheer waste of our time to go to London on such a futile mission as a mere exchange of views on the method by which the work of revision of the constitution should be undertaken'.

2.   If this report is substantially correct, you will no doubt soon be telegraphing your recommendations on action we should now take. Meanwhile it may be helpful to know Secretary of State's immediate reactions.

3.   He is not (repeat not) prepared to consider withdrawing the invitation to N.I.P. Indeed, he considers that, in the present political situation in the East, their exclusion would be wholly wrong. He will, however, be ready and willing to have a full exchange of views with the Nigerian representatives on the issues of substance which will arise in a revision of the constitution; and, if it were the general desire of the Nigerian representatives, he would, subject to your views, see no objection to the conference attempting to reach some broad conclusions on at any rate some of the principal points of substance as well as on the method by which the actual revision should be carried out. He does not, however, think that it would be possible for the complete work of revising the constitution to be carried out within the time which a conference such as it is proposed to hold in London would be able to devote to it.

4.   The Secretary of State considers, subject to your views, that in the last resort conference must be held even if Azikiwe and Awolowo still stand out. *Ends*.

213   CO 554/261, no 184   4 June 1953
[Constitutional revision]: CO note of a meeting of officials held to discuss changes to be made in the present Nigerian constitution

It was *agreed* that in discussion the meeting should discuss the Note on Constitutional Changes compiled by Mr. Huijsman, an amended version of which could serve as the first draft of a memorandum setting out the changes which Her Majesty's Government would be prepared to see made in the present Nigerian Constitution.[1] After submission to the Secretary of State, this memorandum would have to be referred to Sir J. Macpherson for his comments, it being made clear that the Secretary of State was not at that stage committed in any way. After further consideration in the light of any views expressed by the Governor, it could then serve as the brief for the Colonial Office representatives at the forthcoming London discussions.

Paragraph numbers in the succeeding minutes refer to those of Mr. Huijsman's Note.
Paragraph 5. Composition of a Federal Nigeria.
It was *agreed* to accept the conclusions of this paragraph.
Paragraph 6. Position of Lagos.
Mr. Gorell Barnes said that if there was no history to this we would probably favour a solution similar to that of Washington, D.C. The question was not, however,

---

[1] Not printed but see 208.

a 'sticking point' from our point of view, and we should preserve an open mind at this stage, remembering that we might, at some future time, be called upon to arbitrate. What our decision would then be would depend upon the circumstances arising. Both the 'Washington' and the 'Ottawa' solutions were technically feasible. It was *agreed* that paragraph 6 of the Note should be redrafted along these lines.

Paragraph 7. The Centre.

Mr. Gorell Barnes pointed out that if we accepted the recommendations in this paragraph, as we had to if the Centre is to retain its powers in respect of defence, external affairs, etc., we would be rejecting one of the major points of the North. This was recognised by the meeting. It was felt that the only way in which acceptance of both the North and the South to a central legislature could be secured would be by retaining the present North/South parity of membership in the House; equal membership of each Region would be unacceptable to the North, while if members were drawn from the Regions proportionately to their population the North would obtain a clear majority over the combined South which would be totally unacceptable to the South. We should retain the right of the Governor to address the House when he wished, so that he might continue to act as President if no Speaker could be found. *Mr. Gorell Barnes* felt it was right to remove the Lieutenant-Governors from the Central Legislative House, but that we should take the line that the Special Members should probably remain. *Mr. Huijsman* said that, judging by Awolowo's demands, we might have to give consideration to the establishment of a Second Chamber at the Centre; it was *agreed* that we should, on the whole, be against this, but that if the point became important we would be prepared to consider a Second Chamber on the lines of the House of Lords, with limited delaying and initiating powers of legislation. *Mr. Watt* suggested, and *Mr. Gorell Barnes agreed*, that the Second Chamber might be a suitable place for the Special Members to sit.

Paragraph 8. Council of Ministers.

Mr. Williamson said that it might be necessary to avoid evil connotations and to adopt a new title for the Council, e.g. the Council of State. With the increase of matters to be a Regional responsibility, however, the number of Ministers required at the Centre would be less. On the question whether the Order-in-Council should lay down the number of Ministers representing each Region (including the Cameroons), or whether in the interests of flexibility the Governor should act in his discretion but be called upon in his Instructions to take account of equal representation of Regional interests, *Mr. Peck* felt that higher authority would probably require such details to be written into the Constitutional Instruments, preferably the Royal Instructions, if we wished them to have legal force. If it were not intended to give such directions legal force they should not be in legal form; and it would seem to be more appropriate to incorporate them in an exchange of despatches. *Mr. Gorell Barnes agreed* with this view.

Mr. Peck then asked whether it was intended to retain the present provision that the Governor should consult the Lieutenant-Governors over the choice of Central Ministers. *Mr. Gorell Barnes* felt that this provision should be omitted in order to give the Governor a real initiative. Ministers should, however, be acceptable to the Central House. By the provision that an affirmative vote of two-thirds of all members of the Central House, taken in secret ballot, would be required to revoke the appointment of a Minister, Ministers would not be placed at the sole mercy of either the North or the South. *Mr. Watt* pointed out that in Jamaica the two-thirds vote provision had allowed a Minister who had lost the confidence of his colleagues to be kept in office by the Opposition in order to handicap the Government. It was *agreed* that to avoid this we should follow the Gold Coast and British Guiana precedents which provide in addition, that the Governor can take the initiative in dismissing a Minister. It was also *agreed* that the memorandum should stipulate that the Governor's existing powers to act in his discretion should remain intact, except with regard to 'existing legislation'.

Paragraph 9. It was *agreed* that the form of individual ministerial departmental responsibility recently introduced in Nigeria should continue. In respect of statutory corporations, only those operating throughout Nigeria should be a special responsibility. The wording of the penultimate sentence of this paragraph should be changed to provide that the Governor should have general reserve powers and that the portfolios of Defence, External Relations, the Federal Police and the Federal Public Service would be the responsibility of the ex-officio members of the Council. *Mr. Gorell Barnes* said that we should keep those provisions whereby the Governor alone would have adequate powers of government if the need ever arose.

Paragraph 10.

Mr. Peck confirmed that it would be possible to permit Regional advance at varying speeds by amendment of the Constitution when each occasion arose. It would suffice to provide for a general power of amendment in the new constitution, and to make it clear in covering despatches that this power would be exercisable in the Regions as well as at the Centre. With regard to the electoral provisions, it was discussed how the present regulations should be amended; it was *agreed* that, in the cause of Regional autonomy, we should allow the Lieutenant Governor of each Region to make the regulations the Region desired. *Mr. Gorell Barnes* said that we should have to make it clear whether the Lieutenant Governor should act in or out of Council; he believed that the former should be the case and that we should not try at the Conference to impose uniformity of electoral regulations between the Regions. While in principle we were in favour of moving away from the Northern (and Western) methods of a series of Electoral Colleges and injection of Native Authority representatives, we should not ourselves raise this at the Conference, as it would be fatal to give the North the impression that we were using the occasion to bring pressure upon them. If the N.I.P. or others made a demand, it might be necessary to negotiate an agreement on the question, but otherwise we should leave the matter and should exercise our influence with the Lieutenant-Governors afterwards.

Mr. Gorell Barnes said that Sections (c) and (d) of paragraph 10 were very important. It was *agreed* that, particularly in view of developments in the Gold Coast, we could not refuse the Regions all-African Cabinets if they wanted them. *Mr. Williamson* raised the question of a similar concession to the Cameroons if they achieved Regional status. In *Mr. Huijsman's* view, once we had started along the road with other Regions we could not afford to exclude the Cameroons, however nonsensical this might in practice be. It was *agreed* that on this point the memorandum should content itself with saying that if a separate Region were established for the Cameroons, the question of an all-African Cabinet there would need separate consideration. On the question of African Cabinets in the existing Regions, the memorandum should set out our arguments for supporting the proposal, namely, that in view of developments in the Gold Coast a concession on this point would be the only way to gain support for the general constitutional revision. *Mr. Gorell Barnes* said, however, that we should keep an open mind on when we would show our hand.

Mr. Watt pointed out that an upgrading of the Lieutenant Governors' title might be necessary in the Regions, with the consequential problem of what to call the present office of Governor. After some discussion of the relative merits of the terms 'Governor-General' and 'High Commissioner', the former was adjudged more suitable.

Paragraph 11

Mr. Watt asked whether this proposal would not attract all the best and most influential men to the Regions, making eventual unification of the territory more difficult. *Mr. Williamson* pointed out that the Centre would attract the Zikists, who supported a unitary Nigeria, and this in turn might force other Regions to send better men to the Centre. Further, some able men (e.g. Nwapa) might prefer to go to the Centre to avoid the worst of the hurly burly of politics in the Regions. It was *agreed* that the terms of paragraph 11 were right and inevitable.

Paragraph 12. Division of Jurisdiction.

Mr. Huijsman explained that by 'the usual provisions' regarding the re-allocation of subjects from the Centre to the Regions and vice-versa he meant that the Governor-in-Council should be able to move a subject from one list to another and that the Regions should be able to transfer subjects from regional to federal jurisdiction. It was *agreed* that while there was no harm in transferring a subject from the Regions to the Centre in this manner, any devolution from the Centre should be first approved by the Secretary of State. The memorandum should make this clear.

List of Subjects. *Mr. Williamson* said that as much as possible should be given to the Regions without antagonising the East. It was *agreed* that the memorandum should state that the lists therein were illustrative and for consideration only. On the question of the final approval of legislation, it was considered that Regional legislation should come direct to the Secretary of State for signification.

Paragraph 13 The Public Service.

Mr. Gorell Barnes said that the North would insist upon a separate Regional service. Officers from Nigeria to whom he had spoken had been of the opinion that there would have to be central terms of service, but he himself was not so sure that competition between the Regions would not be a good thing. *Mr. Williamson* said that the latter would mean that the poorest Region would be penalised by having to compete with the others; there would also be a danger of a march to the North where the expatriate officer felt himself more secure. Further, the Centre would have to pay the highest Regional rate in respect of the federal service. *Mr. Tegetmeier* said that in East Africa competition was avoided if possible; agreement was reached by conference, which, however, could not be relied upon in present Nigerian conditions. *Mr. Bourdillon*[2] felt that we were perhaps subscribing to administrative convenience by leaning towards uniform terms: he himself would like to see competition. It was *agreed*, however, that the balance of advantage lay with uniform conditions, with control of each service in the hands of the respective Lieutenant-Governor, and that it would be to our own credit politically to advocate this. We should therefore start with this idea in view and put the pros and the cons in the memorandum, but it should not be a sticking point.

Mr. Williamson said that we could expect pressure from the Western Region at least for political control of its public service; this would in turn raise the whole

---

[2] H T Bourdillon, assistant secretary, CO, 1947; assistant-under-secretary, 1954.

question of compensation for officers who wished to leave. It was *agreed* that our aim should be to secure agreement that appointment to a Regional service should be by the Lieutenant-Governor acting in his discretion, but assisted by a Public Service Commission (of which there will be one in each Region). If there should be a decision to have an all-African Cabinet in a Region then this would open the question of who would deal with public service questions in the Legislature and if there were pressure to make this the responsibility of a Nigerian Minister we should make it quite clear from the outset that this would immediately involve consideration of compensation.

Paragraphs 14–16. The Judiciary.

Mr. Peck said that he could not commit his superiors, but as the powers proposed for the Supreme Court were those of the Central African Scheme they should be acceptable. However, the provision that an appeal would lie direct to the Judicial Committee of the Privy Council, rather than through the West African Court of Appeal, might be criticised on the grounds that it would expose the Judicial Committee to too much extra work. *Mr. Gorell Barnes* and *Mr. Williamson* thought that, as only purely Nigerian constitutional matters would be involved, this would be unlikely; it was *agreed*, however, that the point should be discussed with Sir Sidney Abrahams before the memorandum was re-drafted.

Mr. Huijsman referred to the position of the native authority courts, which Awolowo wished to turn into magistrates' courts. It was *agreed* that the question whether the lower courts should be a Regional responsibility should be discussed with Sir Sidney Abrahams and that the re-drafted memorandum should pass through Sir Kenneth Roberts-Wray.

Paragraph 17. Financial Implications.

Mr. Gorell Barnes said that he thought that the use of C.D. & W. funds to make good the East's shortfall would be objectionable as the East would suffer when C.D. & W. ceased. He would have seen no need to alter the present system; the trouble was, as *Mr. Huijsman* pointed out, the West's complaint that it was being mulcted. *Mr. Bourdillon* said that the system proposed did not get away from the present objection that the Regions were dependent on the Centre; if the principle of derivation were applied and the East fall short, then the East would be dependent on the Centre and would have grounds for objection. He felt that the ideal would be to adopt the principles which had been propounded elsewhere by Sir Jeremy Raisman, namely, to work out the financial needs of the Regions and then to fix the distribution of revenue for a period of, say, five years. *Mr. Gorell Barnes* agreed that this might be politically acceptable and would give more autonomy to the Regions, therefore being superior to present arrangements. If, however, Sir J. Raisman were to be asked to go to Nigeria in the expert touring team we should give only a general indication of our views in the memorandum. We should, if possible, not take up too firm a position, but if pressed at the Conference we should suggest, after listening to views, that something along the Raisman lines might be a possible solution. It was *agreed* that Mr. Huijsman should discuss this further with Mr. Bourdillon.

It was *agreed* that Mr. Huijsman should draft a Memorandum[3] based on his Note, incorporating the points made during this meeting, and setting out the reasons for the various recommendations made at some length, for concurrence and submission to Ministers.

---

[3] See 214.

214   CO 554/262, no 200   15 June 1953

'Summary outline of proposals for a revised Nigerian federal constitution': CO memorandum by N B J Huijsman. *Minute* by W L Gorell Barnes

(Paragraph references are to attached Notes)[1]

I. *Territorial divisions*

(a) *Regions* The balance of advantage lies with discouraging the creation of more Regions, but if there should be a real and powerful demand for a separate Cameroons Region we should be prepared to discuss the proposal. (See paragraphs 4 to 7).

(b) *The federal capital.* The obvious choice for federal capital is Lagos, and it is probable that this will also be the view of the main Nigerian parties. We should keep an open mind on the question of the status of Lagos which is largely a question for Nigerians to settle but we should be prepared to arbitrate in order to prevent it endangering agreement on the new constitution. From the technical point of view both a solution which gave Lagos the position of a federal enclave inside Nigeria (following the example of Washington D.C.) or left it a Western Region municipality with certain special arrangements to meet its requirements as federal capital (following the example of Ottawa) would be feasible. (See para. 8).

II. *Political organisation of the centre and the regions*

(a) *Centre.* The new Constitution should provide for a Federal Legislature and a Federal Cabinet (See paragraph 9).

(i) *The Legislature.* The Federal Legislature should be unicameral with a directly-elected membership. The present proportion in which the Regions are represented in the Nigerian House of Representatives should be retained for the new Federal Legislature. If it should prove essential the establishment of a second chamber with limited powers of delaying and initiating legislation might be considered.

The Lieutenant Governors (or Governors) of the Regions should cease to be *ex officio* members of the Federal Legislature, but the other *ex officio* members, and probably the special members specified in the 1951 Order-in Council should remain members. (If it were agreed to establish a second chamber the special members might more appropriately sit in it). Section 68 of the 1951 Order-in Council (dealing with the presidency of the House and the Governor's right to address it) should be incorporated in the new Constitution. (See paragraphs 10 and 11.)

(ii) *The Cabinet.* There should be a Federal Cabinet with the Governor (or Governor-General) as President, three *ex-officio* members (Chief Secretary, Financial Secretary, and Attorney-General) and not more than [nine] Nigerian Ministers. The Governor should be left free to appoint the Nigerian members of the Federal Cabinet from the members of the Federal Legislature, subject to an affirmative vote of say two-thirds of the Legislature. He should however ensure appropriate representation of regional interests in the Federal Cabinet. The votes of not less than two-thirds of the strength of the Federal Legislature, cast in a secret ballot, should be required to revoke the appointment of an individual

---

[1] Not printed.

Minister or for a motion of no confidence in the Cabinet. In addition, the Governor should have the right in his discretion to propose to the Cabinet that the appointment of a Minister should be revoked and, if the Cabinet so resolve, should be required to revoke the appointment. Ministers should be given Departmental responsibility, this responsibility extending also to 'existing legislation' falling within the scope of their portfolios. The Governor should retain general reserve powers and the following portfolios should be held by the *ex officio* members of the Cabinet:—

External Affairs and Defence—Chief Secretary

Finance—Financial Secretary

Justice—Attorney-General

The Cabinet should have full executive responsibility for all subjects exclusive to the Centre and for subjects on the concurrent list on which executive power rests with the Centre and would have to exercise a coordinating responsibility in regard to all other subjects on the concurrent list, while the Federal Legislature would have the right to legislate on subjects exclusive to the Centre, or on the concurrent list. The Cabinet should operate on the principle of collective responsibility and its deliberations should be secret. (Paragraphs 12–14)

(b) *The Regions.* The existing provisions regarding the legislative and executive organisations in the Regions should be carried over into the new Constitution. Some changes may be required to be made at once in the new constitution and others, will probably be made later and at different stages in regard to the different Regions. It would probably be desirable to make it clear in published despatches that Lieutenant-Governors in Council would be free to propose amendments to the Secretary of State for submission to H.M. in Council for the purpose of introducing greater autonomy in the conduct of Regional affairs, and, so far as possible, it might be desirable to indicate in the despatches what further changes would be likely to be acceptable to the Secretary of State. To make it clear that this power of amendment would not be confined to the Centre, there should be an appropriate gloss on this provision in published despatches, making it clear that in principle Lieutenant-Governors-in-Council would be left free to propose appropriate amendments to the Secretary of State for the purpose of introducing a greater measure of self-government in the conduct of Regional affairs. (See paragraph 15).

(i) *Legislatures.* There should be bicameral Legislatures in the Northern and Western Regions and a unicameral legislature in the Eastern Region. If a Cameroons Region were established it is more than doubtful whether it would require or could afford more than a unicameral legislature. (See paragraph 16).

(ii) *Elections.* Our aim should be to leave the existing electoral provisions as they are until the new Constitution is in force and, if necessary in a particular Region in the interests of wider agreement, to secure earlier changes by negotiation or pressure through the Lieutenant-Governor of the Region concerned. (See paragraph 17.) It would be desirable for the Constitution to provide for separate elections to the Regional and Federal legislatures, and exclusive membership of the Federal and Regional Legislatures, i.e. no member of a Regional Legislature being permitted to be a member of the Federal Legislature. (See paragraph 18.) We should be prepared to accept changes in the Regional electoral regulations to allow for direct elections and single-member constituencies. The Constitution should also provide that the electoral regulations in force in a particular Region should apply to elections to the Federal as well as to the Regional Legislature. In other words we should be prepared to accept elections to both the Regional and Federal Legislatures under widely differing Regional electoral regulations. (See paragraph 19.)

(iii) *Regional Executives*, Ministerial Departmental responsibility should also be conceded to the Regions, and there would be no objection if the Lieutenant-Governors adopted the Gold Coast practice of drawing their Ministers from the majority party or coalition. We should be prepared to accept all-Nigerian Ministries in the Regions, subject to the Lieutenant-Governor retaining general reserve powers, control of the police, and control of the Public Service in association with a Public Service Commission. (See paragraphs 20 and 21.)

III. *Division of jurisdiction between the Federal and Regional governments*
The new constitution should divide legislation into three categories:—

(a) within the exclusive jurisdiction of the Centre;
(b) within the exclusive jurisdiction of the Region; and
(c) within the concurrent jurisdiction of the Centre and the Regions, with Central legislation prevailing in the event of inconsistency.

A subject exclusive to the Region should be transferable to the concurrent list or to the exclusive jurisdiction of the Federal Government by an affirmative vote of the three Regional Legislatures, if confirmed by the Federal Legislature. No subject exclusively within Federal jurisdiction should be transferred to concurrent or exclusive Regional jurisdiction without the approval of the Secretary of State on the recommendation of the Governor-in-Council. The Governor and Lieutenant-Governor should continue to reserve for Her Majesty's pleasure Bills on the subjects listed in Clause 10 of the Royal Instructions. (See paragraph 22 and Annex I.)

IV. *The Public Service*
We should, if pressed, be prepared to accept a splitting of the Nigerian public service into a federal and regional service. Control of the federal and regional public services should be exercised by the Governor and Lieutenant-Governors in association with a federal and regional public service commissions. The balance of advantage would lie with uniform conditions of service and we should take the initiative in proposing them, but should not regard acceptance as an essential requirement on our part. (See paragraphs 23 to 25.)

V. *The judiciary and interpretation of the constitution*
(a) *Judiciary.* We should not raise the question of revising the present organisation of the Nigerian judiciary, but if this becomes a live issue, we should be prepared to accept the introduction of legislation transferring responsibility for the lower courts to the Regions, and, if necessary, creating regional and appellate divisions within the Supreme Court of Nigeria. (See paragraph 26.)

(b) *Interpretation of the constitution.* We should propose that the Supreme Court of Nigeria should be vested with additional powers similar to those contained in paragraphs 124 and 125 of the Central African Federal Scheme (Cmd. 8754). (See paragraphs 27 and 28 and Annex II.)

VI. *Financial relations between the Centre and the Regions*
While not actually stipulating any financial changes, we should take such opportunities as may occur to advise an alteration along the lines of the recommendations put forward by the Fiscal Commission under the chairmanship of Sir Jeremy Raisman which recommended the percentage division of the Central revenue of the Central African federation, representing a compromise between the principle of derivation and the principle of need, to include the Central Government as well as the Regions. It also seems important that the Centre should retain the power under any future arrangement to make *ad hoc* grants-in-aid to individual Regions. (See paragraphs 30 to 34.)

Minute on 214

Sir T. Lloyd
I have had second thoughts about one feature of the proposals for a revised Nigerian Constitution which should be reaching you via Sir K. Roberts-Wray this morning.

The feature about which I now feel doubtful is the suggestion that confirmation of the Central Ministers chosen by the Governor should be by simple majority of the Central Legislature. This would, on paper, make it possible for the Northern and Official Members together to force through Ministers who were acceptable neither to the East nor to the West. I doubt very much whether the West and East can be expected to accept this; and I think, therefore, that we should either propose or be willing to accept an arrangement whereby confirmation of Central Ministers had to be by a larger proportion of the Members of the Central Legislature—say two-thirds. Under such an arrangement the North would still be able to veto Ministers they do not like but would not be able, even if supported by officials, to force through the appointment of Ministers objectionable to both the other Regions. An alternative would be to provide that officials should not vote on this matter; but that would leave the possibility of a deadlock.

If you agree with this view, which Mr. Huijsman on reflection shares, perhaps you would very kindly make a suitable amendment either in the proposals themselves or in my covering letter to Sir J. Macpherson.

W.L.G.B.
18.6.53

215 CO 554/261, no 196   17 June 1953
[Constitutional review]: CO note on recent constitutional developments in Nigeria

On the 21st May, the Secretary of State announced in the House of Commons that Her Majesty's Government had decided that the Nigerian Constitution would have to be redrawn, and that as a first step representatives of all three Regions would be invited to London to discuss with him the best way in which this work could be carried out.

2. This raised the question of what principles should guide the selection of Nigerian representatives. It was felt to be important for instance, that the Northern

Elements' Progressive Union, the only Northern opposition organisation worth noting, and which may become a force to be reckoned with in the North in future, should be represented even though the party has no members in the present Northern House of Assembly. It was also felt that the National Independence Party, formed in opposition to the National Council of Nigeria and the Cameroons in the East, and at present conducting the Government of the Region, though with a minority in the Legislature, should attend. The U.K.'s obligations under the Cameroons Trusteeship Agreement also required separate Cameroons representation. After consultation with the Governor, the following guiding principles, later published in Nigeria, were put forward by the Secretary of State:—

(i) there should not be more than 15 representatives at the Conference;
(ii) while as far as possible representations should be on a Regional basis the major political parties, together with the Cameroons under U.K. Trusteeship, should be represented;
(iii) The persons selected should, as far as possible but not necessarily exclusively, be popularly elected representatives of the people, i.e. they should have had experience of the operation of the present Constitution in a Legislature and, if possible, in Ministerial Office.

3.   Invitations were extended on this basis on the Secretary of State's behalf to the three leaders of the Action Group, the N.C.N.C. and the Northern People's Congress to nominate three representatives each, to the N.I.P. to nominate two representatives, and to one representative each of the Cameroons and the N.E.P.U. This choice can be described as of 'parties or groups which have shown command of a substantial number of votes in the legislatures or which contested the 1951 elections in their own name'. They were asked to a Conference at which there would be a full exchange of views with the object of reaching agreement on the method by which the work of re-drawing the Constitution should be undertaken, and on the interests which should be consulted in the process.

4.   The invitation has so far been accepted outright by the N.I.P. and the N.P.C., and the Cameroons are expected to follow suit. There is also an unconfirmed Press report that N.E.P.U. have accepted it. It was, however, initially refused by Mr. Awolowo and Dr. Azikiwe, leaders of the Action Group and the N.C.N.C. respectively, who objected to the inclusion of N.I.P. representatives and felt that a visit to London to discuss only the method by which the Constitution should be revised would be a waste of their time. Acting on a mandate from the Secretary of State, and with the approval of the Council of Ministers, the Governor then asked Mr. Awolowo and Dr. Azikiwe to reconsider their decision, assuring them that the full exchange of views referred to in the invitation would not be confined to method but that each representative would be able to indicate to the Secretary of State both in what respects, in his opinion, the present Constitution was unsatisfactory and in what particulars it should be redrawn. The Governor added that if there was a sufficient consensus of opinion there would be nothing to prevent conclusions being recorded as a basis for a settlement of the present constitutional difficulties. He also rebutted the objections to the inclusion of the N.I.P. in the invitations.

5.   To this, Mr. Awolowo and Dr. Azikiwe have replied expressing their willingness to attend the Conference provided:—

(i) that 15 (instead of 13) representatives are invited, composed as follows:—
From the North: 3 N.P.C., 1 N.E.P.U. opposition, and 1 Chief;
From the West: 3 Action Group, 1 N.C.N.C. opposition, and 1 Chief;
From the East: 3 N.C.N.C., 1 N.I.P., and 1 Cameroons.

(ii) that the main purpose of the Conference is to consider those defects in the Constitution which have made it unworkable, and to amend or revise it in the light of such consideration. This would exclude amendments on such a scale that the revised version could be called a new Constitution—as in effect it would be if the Northern demands for no further political organisation at the Centre were to be accepted—thereby enabling H.M.G. to argue in 1956 that longer experience of the working of the constitution was needed before self-government could be granted.

6.   The effect of the proposal in paragraph 5 (1) above would be to give the Nigerian political parties the following representation at the London talks:—

N.P.C. –	4	(3 nominees plus 1 chief)
Action Group –	4	(3 nominees plus 1 chief)
N.C.N.C. –	4	(3 Eastern, 1 Western nominee)
N.I.P.		
N.E.P.U.		1 nominee each
Cameroons		

The object behind paragraph 5 (ii) is of course to preserve the present constitution, which is due for review in 1956, the date by which the Action Group and N.C.N.C. claim full self-government for Nigeria.

7.   These proposals involve a sacrifice on the part of the N.I.P., which it is believed the party would accept. The Governor believes that the North would agree to the revised representation but that they would not agree to commit their people to any constitutional amendments until these have been approved at least by the Regional Legislature. This is directly opposed to the Action Group/N.C.N.C. attitude which insists on final decisions of substance in London. At the time of writing (the 17th June), the Governor hopes to bring about a meeting in Lagos between Awolowo, Azikiwe, the Sardauna of Sokoto (leader of the N.P.C.) and himself to try and reconcile this difference. This meeting, if it takes place, will be preparatory to the London meeting and without prejudice to the decisions which the latter may reach.

8.   The constitutional talks are complicated by a further issue. The remaining Central Ministers from the East have told the Governor that they will resign from the Council of Ministers if the Western Ministers, who resigned at the end of March, are not replaced by the 30th June. The Northern Ministers have stated that if the Eastern Ministers resign, they too will do so. They have added that they will also resign if Chief Bode Thomas and Akintola, previously Minister of Transport and Minister of Labour respectively, are included among any new Ministers. The Action Group have, however, committed themselves publicly by resolutions of both Regional Houses to submitting for re-appointment only the names of the resigned Ministers. Nevertheless, the Governor feels that an attempt must be made to avert mass resignation on the 10th June by asking the Joint Council of the Western Regional Legislature—the body responsible for approving the names of Western Central Ministers proposed by the Governor—to consider other names. If the Council

persists in nominating Chief Bode Thomas and Akintola, the ensuing deadlock may affect arrivals at the London Conference, even if prior agreement on its constitution and terms of reference had been reached.

216   CO 554/261, no 197a   17 June 1953
[Constitutional review]: minute by N B J Huijsman on an inward telegram no 878 from Sir J Macpherson to Mr Lyttelton on the revision of the constitution

Mr Watt

We spoke. The background to the Gov's tel. is that there is at present a good deal of loose talk in Nigeria about what happens in 1956, the date when the present constitution comes up for review. The general line which appears to be adopted by the local Southern politicians is somewhat as follows: 'we are prepared to consider changes in the present constitution which will make it more workable; on the other hand, this is the last time we will accept a constitution from British hands. The next constitution (ie 1956) will not be a British grant, but will be one which we shall have worked out ourselves in a constituent assembly representative of all shades of Nigerian opinion.' The Northerners hold somewhat similar views in that they maintain that any constitutional changes which may be required must be worked out by agreement and must then be submitted to popular consultation.

As pointed out by you, the question of a constituent assembly is irrelevant to the issue of full self-government, as this can only be granted by HMG under the provisions of the Foreign Jurisdiction Act. That is the formal posn; but to go further, it does raise the question of the way in which HMG can confer full self-government. You pointed out that there are two main ways of so doing in these days:—

(a) By HMG withdrawing the Governor's reserve powers and formally vesting foreign affairs and defence responsibilities in the local government (Ceylon, India, Pakistan, New Zealand); or

(b) By HMG incorporating the constitutional recommendations of a local 'national convention' or parliament in a new Act of the Imperial Parliament (Australia, South Africa)

In neither case is a constituent assembly involved, in the sense that it is a sovereign constitution-making body.

Our discussion also brought out that, judging by recent history, constituent assemblies are generally established *after* a country has gained its independence. This probably holds good for remoter periods of history as well, I think. We thought, however, that it would be sufficient to quote the recent examples of India, Pakistan, France and Italy, which in themselves also illustrate the essential function of a constituent assembly, ie that it is a sovereign body charged with drawing up a constitution, either for immediate promulgation (e.g. India) or for confirmation by a referendum (France, Italy). The later, from my recollection, tends to be Latin practice. The three all-German constitutions which have been drawn up in the past century were promulgated after adoption by the constituent assembly concerned.

The foregoing discussions may serve as a guide towards a definition of the term 'constituent assembly'.

With regard to (b) of the Governor's telegram I think that we both felt that circumstances determined the method of representation. In France (and Italy, I believe) the assembly was elected by a system of proportional representation. In India and Pakistan it endeavoured to be representative, in the absence of an established electoral procedure.

It seems to me that the above points may serve as a basis for a reply to the Governor. You kindly undertook to look at these points in greater detail. Although the Gov's query does not specify any fixed date for a reply, we did, I think, aim at getting at least a telegraphic reply to him by Friday as I have just received a cable from Nigeria indicating that the three major leaders may see him by then. It wld therefore be most desirable to have him briefed on these points. I have therefore given these pp priority.

N.B.J.H.
17.6.53

217   CO 554/262, no 207   20 June 1953
[Constitutional review]: inward telegram no 905 from Sir J Macpherson to Mr Lyttelton reporting his discussion with Nigerian political leaders on arrangements for the London conference

My telegram No. 881.

London Talks.

On my invitation the Sardauna, Awolowo and Azikiwe met me last night for frank discussion of the position reached. As regards subjects to be discussed in London, Sardauna said he had read the joint letter sent to me by Awolowo and Azikiwi [sic] and had no comment to make. In the favourable atmosphere so induced, it soon became clear that no point of major difference either as regards the object of London talks or composition of the delegation was likely to form obstacle to agreement between the leaders of majority parties. They agreed that the object of the talks in London should be to consider:—

(a) defects in present constitution;
(b) what changes are necessary;
(c) what steps are necessary to put those changes into effect.

Elaborating, Azikiwe stressed the need for ensuring that even with changes made, no further breakdown would occur and therefore political objective must be definitely ascertained. This was self government in 1956. Sardauna stated no objection to discussion of this point. Awolowo enquired whether you would agree that the subject should be discussed and I promised to put the suggestion to you for your favourable consideration in view of the fact that present political difficulties in Nigeria have arisen over this very question.

2.   As regards composition, Sardauna stated that he had no objection to proposals in the joint letter. I explained the special consideration as regards representation of the Cameroons which Her Majesty's Government in the United Kingdom must take

into account, as also the fact that the greater part of the Cameroons, both area and population, was in the North. All agreed that the Cameroons representation must be separate from regional representation. Awolowo and Azikiwe found themselves unable to agree that five places for the East should be divided as to three for N.C.N.C. and two for N.I.P. Moreover, they could not agree that these two should be divided one for N.I.P. and one for U.N.P. They considered such allocation quite disproportionate. They suggested that as in the North and West, one place should be allocated to a public figure without political affiliation, possibly a Chief, to be nominated by the majority party, i.e. N.C.N.C.

3. Discussion then turned to the question of advisers to accompany the delegates. It was suggested that difficulty over N.I.P. representation might be overcome by permitting sole N.I.P. delegate to have N.I.P. adviser with him. Azikiwe and Awolowo stated acceptable provided the following were agreed: there should be one adviser from each region and from the Cameroons paid for by the Centre and nominated by the majority party. Sardauna stated 'and this was accepted as a generous gesture' that, as regards the North, adviser to be paid for from central funds would be Northern Cameroonian. In addition, other advisers could accompany to be paid for by the regions. N.E.P.U. must be allowed adviser. In the East both N.C.N.C. and N.I.P. would have one adviser each paid for from regional funds. Sardauna had no personal objection to the proposals but had to reserve the question of N.E.P.U. agreement by Northern Executive Council. Azikiwe similarly had to reserve the question whether N.C.N.C. would guarantee not to query the Eastern Regional expenditure on the advisers' expenses for reference to N.C.N.C. Party Executive.

4. Three political leaders, subject to the above reservations, agreed that composition of the delegation should be as follows:—

West:	Three Action Group,
	One N.C.N.C.
	One Oba (to be nominated by the majority party).
North:	Three N.P.C.
	One N.E.P.U.
	One Emir (to be nominated by the majority party).
East:	One N.C.N.C.
	One N.I.P.
	One public figure, possibly a chief (to be nominated by the majority party).
Cameroons:	One, representing both North and South.

In addition, each Region and the Cameroons to take one adviser whose expenses would be met from the centre. Other advisers could be taken to be paid for from Regional funds. These should include one adviser N.I.P., one adviser N.C.N.C., one adviser N.E.P.U.

5. I undertook to report immediately to you the views so expressed, and to request you to let me have your comments upon them for communication to persons named as early as possible. I estimated that reply might possibly be received within four days.

6. All three political leaders agreed that the London meeting should begin the earliest date you can manage, but not before 15th July.

218   CO 554/262, no 216   26 June 1953

[Western ministers]: outward telegram no 75 from W L Gorell Barnes to Sir J Macpherson on the deadlock over the appointment of Western members to the Council of Ministers

[The resignation of the four Western members from the Council of Ministers at the time of the self-government debate on 31 March raised important constitutional issues (see 187). Under the 1951 constitution the Council of Ministers had to have four ministers from the Western Region. When in June the lieutenant-governor attempted to nominate four new appointees to fill the vacancies, Awolowo argued that he could only nominate on the advice of the regional government, in short the AG, and insisted that the original four ministers—Akintola, Prest, Thomas and the Ooni of Ife—be re-appointed. Deadlock ensued for several months. In the event the four were re-appointed in Sept 1953 (see CO 554/338, no 17, acting governor to Lyttelton, 10 Sept 1953).]

Following strictly personal for Governor from Gorell Barnes.

Begins. I am glad that, except for the carelessnesses for which I apologise, you liked our telegram Personal No. 73. We in turn like the way in which you propose to handle it.

2.   At the same time I think I ought to let you know that the more I think about it, the more concerned I am about the threatening crisis about the Western Members of the Central Council of Ministers. If I were quite certain that we were on the right lines, I should not worry about effect on London Conference; for I am sure we should not buy that conference at the expense of lending ourselves to anything that is wrong in the West any more than in the East. But I must confess to some rather gnawing doubts about the Western affair.

3.   My doubts arise from the following considerations:—

(a) If we are to get Nigerian politics back on to the rails, I feel we have got to have with us one of the leading Southern Nationalist figures.

(b) There is no hope of having Azikiwe genuinely with us. If therefore (a) is correct, we must win over Awolowo, and this means that we must rescue him from the arms of Azikiwe into which his own political impetuosity has driven him.

(c) Awolwo has committed himself in public so deeply to the return to the Centre of the former Western Ministers that, if we make no concession at all, it seems that we are bound to drive him further into Azikiwe's web.

(d) We know that the other Central Ministers will resign if the deadlock is not resolved very soon (paragraph 9 of your telegram No. 822). Then Awolowo will no doubt seek to place the whole blame on you and to make out that, whatever you may say, they would not have resigned if the former Western Ministers had been re-appointed. Nor, I imagine, can we be quite certain, in spite of paragraph 9 of your telegram No. 877, that he will not be able to find some way of supporting this statement (see in this connection paragraph 12 of the Minister of State's secret and personal savingram No. 950 of 24th April[1] about early attitude of N.I.P. Ministers), or that one or more of existing Central Ministers will not let you down on this point sooner or later. This would all be fine material for Azikiwe.

4.   As I understand it the reasons for which you and at any rate Northern Central Ministers have hitherto felt—and we have agreed—that Bode Thomas and Akintola

---

[1] See 193.

cannot be taken back are firstly that they revealed proceedings of Council of Ministers without your permission, and secondly that, after their resignation, they used irresponsible language which amounted almost, if not quite, to encouragement to violence and showed them to be unsuitable to be Ministers.

5.   Whilst I naturally have not a complete picture of what happened, I have a feeling that on the latter count a distinction can be made between Bode Thomas on the one hand and, on the other, Akintola who, so far as I am aware, is the only one who made references to the possibility of a Nigerian Mau Mau. If this is so, would it be possible to make a distinction between Bode Thomas and Akintola on the ground that unpermitted revelation of proceedings of Council of Ministers, though a very grave thing for a Minister, is not perhaps unforgivable when committed in a state of excitement by a man new to Ministerial life; but that Nigeria cannot have in a Ministerial capacity a man who is prepared even to contemplate without horror the kind of primitive savagery which is Mau Mau?

6.   You may feel that this, even if it could be negotiated, would not be fair or desirable as it would bring back Bode Thomas, who was the worst nuisance in the old team, and sacrifice Akintola, who was capable of doing a good job. But I wonder whether Bode Thomas, the consistent growler, may not be preferable to the smooth and competent, but treacherous, Akintola.

7.   If you decided to try this, you might think it advisable to ask me first to make sure that it would be acceptable to higher authority here. But you are more likely to feel that I am right off the beam, in which case be assured that this telegram is the product of my own cogitations alone, and carried no other authority. *Ends.*

219   CO 554/338, no 9   29 June 1953
[Western ministers]: letter (reply) from Sir J Macpherson to W L Gorell Barnes on his reluctance to re-appoint the Western ministers

I am most grateful to you for your personal telegram No. 75 of the 26th of June,[1] in which you put to me your personal anxiety about the crisis over the Western Ministers. I have been more worried about this than anything else. I explained briefly in my telegram No. 970 the main reasons which have led me to the conclusion that your proposition about Bode Thomas is not possible. I will now set these out in rather more detail.

2.   While it is not possible to say now what the final result will be, the principal points which I have had to bear in mind are as follows:—

(a) It was not only during and after the March crisis that Bode Thomas and Akintola divulged Cabinet secrets. This had been going on for months, as had anti-Government articles in 'Service',[2] and the Council was extremely disturbed. The other Ministers knew, and we knew, that Bode and Akintola were responsible but we could not produce evidence without compromising the source of our information.

(b) The result was that other Ministers did not dare to express their real views in Council and Cabinet responsibility became meaningless.

(c) Whenever the Central Ministers drew closer together at informal meetings outside Council, harmony was disrupted by those two, particularly Bode Thomas.

---

[1] See 218.   [2] ie the *Daily Service*, the AG newspaper.

(d) If they return, and even if Ministers from the North and East could be prevailed upon to continue in office, there could be no mutual confidence.

(e) As regards the method of appointing Central Ministers and the qualities required of them, see despatches published with the Constitution Order in Council—especially paragraph 8 of C.O. Despatch 464A and paragraphs 3–7 of C.O. Despatch 147A.[3]

3.　On the face of it, there is force in Awolowo's argument that the final decision should rest with the Joint Council[4] and party in power. And constitutionally he is no doubt correct. But I cannot include either Bode Thomas or Akintola in the four names proposed to the Joint Council. Apart from losing four Northern and two Eastern Ministers (they have repeatedly affirmed this), the effect on responsible opinion would be very bad indeed. Even inside the Action Group there has been a sharp difference of opinion about insisting on having the same four Ministers back, and alternative names were proposed and agreed by Parliamentary Executive as recently as the 21st of June. Within the past 48 hours the faction headed by Bode Thomas and Akintola, which favours extreme action against Central Government (civil disobedience, strikes and possibly even assassination) has won for the time being.

4.　As you know, I hoped to let things ride at least until after the London talks. And I think the remaining Central Ministers would have agreed to this. But leaving aside their threat of resignation, and despite the danger to the London talks, Marshall and I agreed that the exercise must go on, however sterile or even dangerous. The reason is that recently Awolowo himself has been pressing Marshall on this question and the Action Group Press in the past few weeks has been attacking me and the Council of Ministers for not having any Western Ministers, the allegation being that decisions are being taken adverse to Western Region. Marshall accordingly saw Awolowo on the 21st of June and told him of his intention to summon the Joint Council for the 2nd of July and to seek my authority to nominate the Oni, Awokoya, Ighodaro and Enahoro, unless Awolowo had alternative suggestions, excluding Bode and Akintola. Awolowo erupted, but suggested further deferment of action. When, however, Marshall asked if he would give a categorical assurance that the campaign for filling the vacancies would be suspended, Awolowo bluntly refused. There was then no option but to go ahead.

5.　The Joint Council meets on the 2nd of July. Marshall is broadcasting today to explain the purpose of meeting and the considerations involved, but without mentioning personalities or disclosing the proposed names. In the unlikely event of other names being suggested in the course of proceedings, Marshall would suspend the sitting briefly and consult me by telephone.

6.　On this picture I am sure you will agree that at this stage I could not possibly suggest the insertion of Bode Thomas's name. It is possible that attempts will be made to create bad trouble (we are trying very hard to get firm information) but this must be faced. If nothing positive emerges from this exercise we can then consider the next steps. It may be best to do nothing more until after the London talks (if they

---

[3] See 116 and 137.

[4] The Western Region Joint Council was set up under the 1951 constitution and consisted of forty members elected from each of the Western House of Assembly and Western House of Chiefs.

take place) but at least we shall have shown that we want the Western Ministers and are not reluctant to take strong Nationalists. Failure to secure Western Ministers acceptable to other Central colleagues may involve the threat either to dissolve the Western House or even the House of Representatives, probably the latter.

220   CO 554/312, no 25   30 June 1953
[Ministerial powers]: despatch no 1502 from Sir J Macpherson to Mr Lyttelton on a request from the Council of Ministers for greater responsibilities over departments

[Under the 1951 constitution, the Council of Ministers was to operate under a conciliar system, with the Council acting as a policy making rather than policy executing body. Although Heads of Department were bound by the decisions of the Council, they were not subject to direction by ministers. From the start of the operation of the system, ministers pushed to be given responsibilities for departments such as were being conceded in the Gold Coast (see 177). From 1953 this was conceded stage by stage in Nigeria.]

I have the honour to inform you that on the 30th of March the House of Representatives, upon a Motion by the Minister of Mines and Power, seconded by the Chief Secretary to the Government, resolved:—

'That in the opinion of this House the time has come for Ministers to have general direction and control of, and individual responsibility for, the Departments within their portfolios, and this House prays Her Most Gracious Majesty to amend the Nigeria (Constitution) Order in Council, 1951, accordingly.'

2.   I made reference to the Government's intention in this matter in my speech at the opening of the new Session of the House of Representatives on the 3rd of March, and I quote the relevant part of my speech:—

'It will be noted that a change has been made in the form in which the Estimates are set out, in that departmental expenditure has been grouped in a way which reflects Ministerial responsibilities. My Ministers are in process of establishing separate Ministries, and this process would have been completed earlier but for difficulties, which are being surmounted, in matters of accommodation and staff.

'It is well known that policy is determined by the Council of Ministers at the Centre and by the Executive Councils in the Regions, but that in respect of the implementation of policy, the Nigeria (Constitution) Order in Council places certain limitations on the responsibility of Ministers. These limitations were in accordance with the recommendations of the Constitutional Conferences, notably the General Conference which was held at Ibadan in 1950. The delegates to the Conference were influenced, I am sure, not by lack of confidence in the calibre of the Ministerial material that would be available, but by their recognition of the special circumstances of this large and diverse country. The Council of Ministers has had the question of the functions and powers of Ministers under review for some time, in the light of practical experience of working the Constitution. Proposals for far-reaching changes are being considered and the results will be presented to you.'

3.   The decision of the Council of Ministers to introduce this Motion was taken only a day or two before the opening of the Session and the Council of Ministers was anxious that you should be aware of this development. In an exchange of informal telegrams I ascertained that you would be prepared in principle to support a request for changes in the functions and powers of Ministers if in due course a recommendation to this effect were made following the consideration of the Motion by the House of Representatives.

4.   I do not consider that it is necessary to describe at any great length the circumstances which led to this decision by the Council of Ministers. From the very start of the present Constitution there was a strong feeling, amongst some at least of the Central Ministers, that modifications were desirable to the limitations set upon the individual responsibility of Ministers by Section 162 of the Nigeria (Constitution) Order in Council, 1951. You will recall that the subject was raised in the discussion you had with the Council of Ministers during your visit to Nigeria at the end of May last year. In the latter part of 1952 it was decided that the Nigerian Secretariat should be replaced by separate offices of the Chief Secretary and the Financial Secretary and by nine separate Ministries; this decision was reported to you in a telegram from the Governor's Deputy, No. 260 of the 28th of January. The Law Officers advised that this arrangement did not conflict with the provisions of the Constitution Order in Council. Four Ministries have already been established and plans were made for the setting up of the other Ministries as quickly as staff and accommodation became available.

5.   The Ministers appreciated that in making these arrangements, and in modifying the Notes on Administrative Procedure under the new Constitution to give Ministers the right to give instructions to Heads of Departments in order to ensure the implementation of decisions of the Council of Ministers, I had stretched to the utmost the interpretation of section 162 of the Order in Council; and they were grateful. After further experience and reflection, however, they came to the conclusion that the changes that they wanted could not be effected without an amendment to the Order in Council, and, in a memorandum, dated 24th February, signed by all nine Ministers with Portfolio, they asked that the Constitution be amended to secure:—

'(i) that Ministers should have full executive authority over their Departments, short of control of the Civil Service which had already been provided for under the Constitution; and

(ii) that all executive authority in Legislation and Regulations be given to Ministers and the Council of Ministers, and not officials and the Governor-in-Council, providing, of course, that this does not prevent powers being given to the Governor acting in his discretion.'

6.   In the discussions which took place in Council on this subject, on various dates, the principal arguments adduced in support of the case for a change were as follows:—

(a) Experience had shown that the wording of the Order in Council, with its limitations on individual responsibility, gave to the Ministers powers substantially less than those which the Nigerian public thought they possessed.

(b) The fact that the Constitution provides for Ministerial responsibility for 'matters' and not for 'Departments' tended to encourage the staff of the various Departments to continue to look only to the Head of the Department, not to the Minister, as being in charge of the Department.

(c) Experience had shown that the expression 'in association with the appropriate public officer' in Section 162(b) of the Order in Council did not easily lend itself to precise interpretation, and was likely to lead to difficulties between a Minister and the Departments concerned with matters for which he had constitutional responsibility. The Ministers also felt that the imprecision of the expression made it difficult for them to answer with confidence when matters within their portfolios were raised in the House of Representatives.

(d) Powers which in other countries are conferred upon Ministries were, in Nigeria, conferred upon the Governor, the Governor-in-Council or officials; as a result, the public did not sufficiently appreciate the extent of the work carried out by Ministers.

7.   Before reaching a conclusion on this subject the Council had the advantage of having before it a Memorandum by the Attorney-General. It had earlier been suggested that the changes to be made should bring Nigeria into line with the Gold Coast in the matter of Ministerial responsibilities. The Attorney-General therefore analysed the differences between the constitutional instruments of the Gold Coast and of Nigeria, and drew attention to the fact that the federal, or Regional, structure of Government in Nigeria introduced complications which were not present in the Gold Coast. He pointed out, for example, that any changes made in Nigeria would have to take into account, in the case of Central Ministers, the differing responsibilities of those Ministers who are responsible for 'Central' matters, to which the legislative and executive powers of the Regions do not extend, and of those Ministers who are responsible for 'Regional' matters, as set out in the Third Schedule to the Constitution Order-in-Council. After very full discussion, the Council of Ministers agreed in principle that a request should be made for the amendment of the Constitution so that Ministers in Nigeria might be given fuller powers on the lines of those held by Ministers in the Gold Coast. It was also decided that a Government Motion be moved, at the then impending meeting of the House of Representatives, in the terms which I have quoted in the first paragraph of this despatch.

8.   It is proper that I should emphasise the fact that Ministers were at pains to make it clear that they had no wish for control over the Civil Service. This point was made specifically on several occasions during the discussions in Council; the Memorandum of the Attorney-General drew attention to the fact that the Constitution of the Gold Coast, as well as that of Nigeria, provided that appointment, promotion, dismissal and disciplinary control of public officers is vested in the Governor, acting in his discretion, and that there shall be a Public Service Commission to advise the Governor on such matters; and the memorandum presented by the nine Central Ministers stated (as the extract quoted in paragraph 5 above shows) that their desire was for executive authority over Departments 'short of control of the Civil Service which has already been provided for under the Constitution'.

9.   The Ministers recognise, of course, that, because of the complication of our Regional structure, effect could not be given to the prayer of the House of Representatives merely by incorporating in the Nigeria (Constitution) Order-in-Council the relevant provisions of the corresponding Gold Coas instrument. The Attorney-General has prepared a draft amending Order-in-Council which will be

considered by the Council of Ministers and will be referred to the Regions. In the meantime, and without prejudice to developments which may take place as a result of the proposal that the Constitution should be re-drawn, I seek formal confirmation of your agreement in principle to support a request for changes to be made on the lines proposed.

221   CO 554/600, no 1   30 June 1953
[Political situation]: inward telegram from Sir J Macpherson to Mr Lyttelton on AG threats of a campaign of civil disobedience

During the past weeks there have been dark hints given by Action Group leaders that they have plans for campaign of civil disobedience if they do not get their way. These hints are confirmed by Special Branch reports which indicate that plans are still very general and have not yet been worked out in effective detail.

2.   Civil disobedience campaign first threatened by Action Group in the event of Her Majesty's Government refusing grant of self government in 1956. Awolowo himself stated at Campos Square meeting on Youth Day, 28th April, that in the event of self government not being granted 'we would not consider ourselves bound by any law, regulation or decree. We would deliberately disobey and break such laws and bear the consequences'. Since then, threat of civil disobedience at earlier date has frequently been hinted. 30th June, then 31st July have been mentioned and now it is suggested that campaign may start on or after 2nd July when members of Western Joint Council meet to consider appointment of Western Ministers to the Centre. Latest information is that Action Group intend to insist on return of four resigned Ministers with no compromise.

3.   It is not considered that Action Group has sufficient general support or support in labour field to organise effective campaign of civil disobedience at this stage, but we are (omission? concerned at) possibility of hooliganism, illegal processions, and possibly demonstrations by women at Lagos and Ibadan following on stalemate over question of Western Ministers,

4.   There is no cause for alarm, but these people are unpredictable and you will not wish to be unprepared for news of incidents.

222   CO 554/262, no 232A   2–11 July 1953
[Self-government]: minutes by T B Williamson, W L Gorell Barnes and Sir T Lloyd on Williamson's visit to Nigeria

Mr. Gorell Barnes
I am dictating the following minute on my return from a fifteen day visit to Nigeria.

2.   I spent a few days in Lagos both at the beginning and at the end of my trip, and in between I visited Enugu, Kano, Katsina, Zaria, Kaduna and Ibadan. In addition to long talks with the Governor, Chief Secretary and other senior officials in Lagos, I had discussions with all three Lieutenant Governors, with several of their senior (European) advisers, with a fair selection of Nigerian Ministers, including the

Sardauna of Sokoto, Mr. Awolowo and Professor Eyo Ita (but not with Zik), with N.P.C. representatives in Kano and Zaria, and with the Emirs (and their leading councillors) in Kano, Katsina and Zaria. I was also able to visit two of the three pits at the Enugu colliery, and Dr. and Mrs. Mellanby kindly took me over the new buildings at the University College at Ibadan. The trip was a strenuous one, but no effort was spared to make it worth while, and I was received with the greatest kindness and warmest welcome wherever I went. I left with the feeling that Nigeria had been absolutely right in pressing that I should make the visit when I did, and that it was indeed high time that a member of the West African Department should acquaint himself at first hand with developments in the territory.

3.   There are a number of important matters arising from my visit which I should like to discuss with you, and others with which I intend to deal on paper, in separate notes. This note is concerned with the principal problem which I set myself to attempt to solve during the fortnight I was away; namely how the Secretary of State should be advised to deal with the demand now categorically set forth by the Action Group and N.C.N.C. that H.M.G. should concede self-government to Nigeria by 1956.

4.   The first point which I wish to make in this connection, and it is an absolutely fundamental one, relates to the (expatriate) Public Service, particularly (though not exclusively) the Administrative Grade. There is no doubt at all that the European officials, not only in the East and West but also in the North, are deeply disturbed about what the future holds for them, and their sense of insecurity is increasing. I cannot emphasize too strongly my view (which I am sure is shared by the Governor and his principal official advisers) that unless, within the next few months, H.M.G. enunciates clearly the policy which it intends to follow as regards the future government of Nigeria, a situation is almost certain to arise in which there will no longer be a Public Service of sufficient quality and strength left in Nigeria to implement any policy that may later be devised. In fine, H.M.G. have got to 'come clean'—and clear—now.

5.   The second preliminary point which I want to make is that, if I may say so with respect, I am sure that the Secretary of State was absolutely right when he informed his Cabinet colleagues that the pattern of constitutional advance in the Gold Coast was not necessarily applicable in Nigeria. Compared with the tribal diversities in Nigeria, not only as between the Regions but within the Regions (for example the substantially non-Ibo minorities in the East), the Gold Coast is a relatively homogeneous unit. Moreover, I think there is no doubt—though Nigerian political leaders would never admit this—that broadly speaking the Gold Coast is a much more sophisticated and 'advanced' territory than the conglomeration of ethnic groups which are comprised within Nigeria. All this is, of course, very obvious; but it is sometimes overlooked.

6.   Coming now to the crux of the problem, namely what the Secretary of State should say to Awolowo and Zik when they ask whether H.M.G. is, or is not, prepared to grant Nigeria self-government by 1956, I suggest that the Secretary of State's first answer should be: 'What do you mean by Nigeria in this context? Do you mean the whole of Nigeria, or only the West and East?'. Awolowo may attempt to hedge on this, because personally (I am sure) he would be content for the West alone to be given self-government by 1956 (or indeed even a little later), but he may not wish to commit himself openly so long as he is working in alliance with Zik. Zik, on the other hand, if ever he comes to London, will be speaking in terms of a united Nigeria

and will demand self-government for the whole territory by 1956. In other words he will be out to insist that the North should be 'liberated' by that date.

7.   The Secretary of State will then presumably ask the Sardauna for his views; and we know perfectly well what his answer will be.

8.   At this point I would urge that the Secretary of State should make it clear beyond all doubt—and should go on the record to that effect—that H.M.G. have no intention whatever of bringing pressure to bear on the North to take self-government before they consider themselves ready to assume the burden. It was emphasized to me several times in Nigeria that the North (who, we should do well to remind ourselves, comprise roughly a quarter of the total population of the Colonial Empire) are rapidly losing faith in H.M.G's integrity and determination to defend them from pressure from without. They feel that, because they are 'gentlemen', H.M.G. feel they have an easier problem in the North than in the South and that consequently there is a marked tendency for H.M.G. to seek agreement on important matters of policy with the Southern politicians first and then to bring unfair pressure on the North to come into line even against the North's better judgment and firmly held convictions as to what is in the best interests of their people. In fact one of the Northern Ministers (Mr. Peter Achimugu) put it to me perfectly bluntly in the words: 'Is H.M.G. going to let us down?.' The next few weeks present us, in my view, with our last chance of demonstrating to the North that we are not going to let them down: and if we miss that chance I do not think it will ever recur. We had better, while we still have the opportunity, go all out to secure the loyalty and faith in us of the North, rather than to lose the North, probably for ever, in an effort to placate an unreliable South, at the behest of their anyway to some extent unrepresentative spokesmen.

9.   This point is fundamental, and I believe will be readily accepted. I will not attempt, in this note, to discuss the large question whether the Sardauna and his colleagues from the North are truly representative of the North. By and large, I believe they are; and in any event the Sardauna will make it perfectly clear that he is not prepared to commit himself to anything in London but will insist on referring everything back to the Northern people through the most representative organs of Northern opinion which exist at this time. I only wish to add in this context that I think it is important that the Secretary of State should emphasize to the Sardauna (in a private session with him) that the quite remarkable progress which has been made in the last eighteen months in democratising organs of local government in the North must be continued and carried upwards at the fastest pace which is compatible with the movement of public opinion in the North. And I believe that the best judge of how fast, or how slow, that pace should be is the Lieutenant-Governor of the North himself. He will not wish to go faster with this process than the North can 'take' (without endangering stability or the advances already achieved), but he will certainly wish to go faster tha some of his principal European advisers think necessary. I hope to dictate a separate note on this question, and would merely emphasize here that unless progress continues the North may run the risk of playing into the hands of ill-disposed and misinformed people not only in Southern Nigeria but also possibly in London.

10.   The Secretary of State will then be left with the question whether H.M.G. is prepared to give the Southern Regions (I exclude the Cameroons, which is a separate problem) self-government in 1956, as distinct from the North. Here there seem to me to be three alternative courses, viz:—

(a) One answer could be a plain 'No', on the ground (which I believe to be well-founded) that neither the East nor the West will be ready for self-government in three years' time; and that to concede it could only result in something not far short of chaos in administration. If this answer were given, we should certainly have to face the strong probability of civil disobedience and violence in both Regions. I have every reason to believe that the authorities in Nigeria could cope with this situation effectively, and without calling for assistance from outside Nigeria. The police and military (including reinforcements from the North) would have to be used on a considerable scale, but if vigorous and prompt action were taken the situation could no doubt be fairly quickly contained. I discussed this matter with both the Chief Secretary, the Lieutenant-Governors in the East and West, and with the Civil Secretary and Commissioner of Police in the East. The specific question which I put in the East was whether, for example, if Zik himself had to be arrested and detained, there would be a danger of a general and prolonged state of dissatisfaction and indeed violence in that Region; and whether the police could be relied upon. Sir C. Pleass seemed fully confident that the situation could be handled, and the consensus of opinion was that (as mentioned above) Nigeria would not have to ask for outside assistance. Senior officials in Lagos take the view that the number of really dangerous potential trouble makers in Nigeria are 'not more than would fill one Hermes', and that if the worst came to the worst the arrest and detention of some fifty such people, together with Press censorship for not much more than a week, would see them over any threat of a real rising. The vast masses of the population, in spite of Zik's 'mystique' would soon settle back, with a sense of happy relief, to the important business of making a living under conditions of good government and stability. They agreed however that it might be necessary after any initial swoop, to arrest and detain up to perhaps an additional 2,000 or 3,000 persons for varying periods.

From one point of view this course has attractions, but I am sure that it is out of the question and I do not think any responsible official in Nigeria would wish to press it for a moment. It would be purely negative, and H.M.G. could never get away with it either in the U.K. or before world opinion.

(b) The second alternative would be a policy of 'gradualism', or step by step, which is the line being followed in the Gold Coast. The Secretary of State could say that he could give no undertaking about self-government in 1956, but that it would be necessary to proceed stage by stage. I believe, and I hold the view very strongly, that this course too must be ruled out, as an opening gambit with Awolowo and Zik. So long as it was being followed it would lead to increased friction and bitterness, with inevitably a further deleterious effect on the Public Service, and in the end (which could not be more than a few years off) H.M.G. would still be forced to concede self-government before the South was ready for it.

(c) The third alternative, and the one which I suggest the Secretary of State should be advised to adopt, is the following. He should ask the Action Group and the N.C.N.C. why they claim self-government in 1956 instead of forthwith. He should emphasize that there is no reason whatever to suppose that they will be materially readier for self-government three years hence than now; but that if they insist on pressing their demand for self-government in 1956 H.M.G. will be prepared, subject to certain conditions, to concede full Regional self-government to them now (i.e. in 1954), to see what they can make of it. The conditions would have to include:—

(i) satisfactory arrangements with the North as regards communications, railway, ports etc., and for the establishment of a central organisation to deal with these and such other matters, e.g. defence, external affairs, which would remain outside the ambit of purely Regional government. Satisfactory arrangements would also have to be made for suitably qualified people from all Regions to have right of entry to institutions such as the University College at Ibadan and the Technological College, which have been financed partly by C.D. & W. funds and partly by Central Nigerian funds;

(ii) fair and adequate arrangements to enable expatriate pensionable members of the Public Service to leave the service of the Eastern and Western Regional Governments with compensation if they felt unable to tolerate the new conditions and could not be found vacancies in the North or elsewhere in the Colonial Empire. Those who wished to remain would of course be free to do so.

The Lieutenant Governors would remain, as H.M.'s representatives, but they would be 'constitutional monarchs', ready to advise if their advice was sought, but carrying no responsibility at all for good government. The exercise of their reserved powers would be suspended, and it would have to be made abundantly clear that the responsibility for success or failure of the experiment would rest fairly and squarely with the leaders of the party elected to office.

I believe it should also be stated that if the East or West proved quite incapable of running their own affairs, and chaos ensued, it would be necessary for the clock to be put back and for Colonial government, possibly with a structure not dissimilar from that prevailing at present, to be resumed.

As I see it there are many advantages in throwing out this challenge at the London Conference. It would take the magic out of the date 1956, and would restore the initiative to H.M.G. If, as is more likely than not, the Action Group and N.C.N.C. refuse the offer, H.M.G. would be in the highly advantageous position of being able publicly to state that the majority parties in the East and West had been offered self-government now but had refused it; and H.M.G. would be in a much stronger position to adopt a policy of gradualness and to implement it at a really gradual pace with some hope of carrying it to a reasonably fruitful conclusion. It would put an end to the uncertainty and unease in the Public Service, and would provide a really clear cut issue on which General Elections in the East (and the West) could be fought. If on the other hand the challenge were accepted, and the electorate in the East and West showed that they supported the Action Group and N.C.N.C., then of course H.M.G. would have to go through with it. And if chaos ensued, as it probably would, I believe H.M.G. would be able, say eighteen months hence, to resume responsibility for the government of the South, and to do so with the goodwill of the vast majority of the people.

11.   After I had reached, in my own mind, during the course of my travels, the conclusions set out above, I discussed them first with the Chief Secretary on my return to Lagos, and then with him and Sir J. Macpherson. Mr. Goble was also present at this final discussion. I may say that both Mr. Benson and Sir J. Macpherson agreed with me in all broad essentials, except that Sir J, Macpherson

seemed doubtful whether it would in fact prove possible for H.M.G. to 'come back' if the challenge were accepted and the experiment resulted in chaos. He did not, however, completely rule out the possibility. Mr. Benson, on the other hand, seemed, I think, to feel that a come back would be practicable. But they both thought it much more probable that the challenge would be refused.

12. Sir J. Macpherson naturally said that he would wish to give further consideration to the foregoing ideas, and to consult with his Lieutenant-Governors on them as quickly as possible. He may in fact be having a meeting with two if not all three of them tomorrow, the 3rd July; after which we may expect to receive his considered views. I emphasized of course that while I might venture, if he saw no objection, to put forward the results of my thinking in a preliminary way to higher authority when I got back, what really mattered was that the Secretary of State should have his (Sir J. Macpherson's) own recommendations.

13. I should like at this point to emphasize that while I personally believe that the course suggested in paragraph 10 (c) above presents us with the least undesirable of the alternatives, I attach much more importance to paragraphs 4 and 8.

14. I will conclude by saying that if any offer of self-government in 1954 were made and rejected, it would then no doubt be H.M.G's aim to seek agreement to a new constitution modelled on Mr. Huijsman's draft, which was very well received in Lagos and for which all concerned there were most grateful. We may expect to receive the Governor's detailed comments on that draft shortly.

T.B.W.
2.7.53

Sir T. Lloyd

You should see this stimulating minute which Mr. Williamson submitted on return from his short visit to Nigeria.

I agree with everything that Mr. Williamson says in the first nine paragraphs of his minute. The statements to be made to-day and to-morrow about the Public Service in the Gold Coast are likely to have some reassuring effect in Nigeria, but not enough; and the impressions which Mr. Williamson has recorded in paragraph 4 of his minute provide yet further evidence of the need to do something on the lines of the proposals which, at the recent meeting under your chairmanship, it was decided to submit to the Secretary of State.

The reason for which I have delayed sending Mr. Williamson's minute forward to you is that I have found it necessary to think over very carefully the suggestion which he has put forward in paragraphs 10–13 of his minute that we should, so to speak, accept the challenge of the demand by Awolowo and Azikiwe for self-government by 1956 by saying that, if they persist in this demand, we shall hand them regional self-government in 1954.

Mr. Williamson is of course right in saying that this demand for self-government in 1956 will be the most difficult point with which we will have to deal at the conference, if it takes place. As Mr. Williamson himself points out, we should clearly not make up our minds on the line to be taken in response to this demand until we have the views of the Governor. Subject to that, I have, after very careful thought, come to the conclusion that I must advise caution. Mr. Williamson's proposal is daring and has its attractions. But I see various dangers and disadvantages. Thus:—

(a) I do not myself believe that either Awolowo or Azikiwe would reject the challenge. Awolowo might at any rate want to do so, but I am pretty confident that, rightly or wrongly, he would not feel that it was politically possible for him to do so.

(b) It seems to me most important that the Secretary of State should, during the conference, do everything he can to bring it home to Awolowo firstly that the philosophy which he appears to have swallowed, during his visit to India, that chaos with self-government is better than order and progress with dependence is dangerous nonsense; and secondly that self-government is not earned by abusive attacks on the Queen's representative and veiled threats of violence or passive lawlessness, but rather by patient and careful work in building up a machine which can sustain self-government. The Secretary of State is hardly likely to be successful in doing this if, wholly irrespective of the readiness of the Eastern and Western Regions in Nigeria for self-government, he is prepared to offer self-government as, so to speak, a tactical move in negotiations. We must surely maintain the position that, whilst doing all we can to bring Colonial territories forward to self-government, we have some responsibility for satisfying ourselves that self-government, when it comes, has some chance of being reasonably good government.

(c) An offer of self-government now in response to irresponsible clamour for self-government in 1956 by the leaders of the Western and Eastern Regions would, I suggest, have a very bad effect in the Gold Coast where, in spite of the fact that he came to power on a cry of 'self-government now', Nkrumah has been persuaded to proceed in an orderly fashion stage by stage, and without demanding that dates be fixed in advance for each stage.

(d) Mr. Williamson suggests that an offer of self-government in 1954 would provide a clear-cut issue on which general elections could be fought in the East and West. I doubt very much whether it would turn out this way; for I do not believe that any party in either of the Regions of Southern Nigeria would have the courage to fight an election on a programme of which the main feature was a proposal to reject such an offer by H.M.G.

(e) I share Sir J. Macpherson's doubts whether it would prove possible for H.M.G. to 'come back' if the challenge were accepted and the experiment resulted in chaos. This would of course be possible if in some way we reserved the power to do so; but if we did that then we should not really be granting self-government but retaining the Lieut.-Governor's reserve powers, at any rate in a restricted way. If, however, no reserve powers are retained, it would be only too easy for the galaxy of talent which is only too ready to try to make trouble for us in Africa to brand us as aggressors and to say that the excuse of rescuing the Region in question from chaos was no more valid than the similar excuse used by Italy when she attacked Abyssinia. What this really boils down to, I think, is that, if the offer were made at all, it would have to be made subject to some reservation as regards internal security.

Subject to further consideration when we have the Governor's own views, my present feeling is that the correct response for the Secretary of State to make to a demand for regional self-government in 1956 in the East and West is to say that, whilst it remains the policy of H.M.G. to bring Colonial territories forward towards self-government as rapidly as circumstances justify, and whilst he does not think that, in matters which concern individual Regions only, the pace of advance towards self-government in each Region in Nigeria need necessarily be the pace of the slowest, he is not prepared to commit himself in advance to any particular date for full internal self-government in any one Region. This does not mean that he utterly rules out 1956 or indeed any other date, though he must say that a very considerable increase in the responsibility shown by political leaders in their public utterances will be needed before he can be persuaded that the time is ripe for full self-government in any one Region. He might then go on to say what he is prepared to agree to now (on the lines of the proposals in our memorandum, if they are agreed with Lagos), but make it quite clear that he is satisfied that for the present the reserve powers and the Lieut.-Governor's control of the Public Service, etc. must remain.

If, in response to this line, Awolowo and/or Azikiwe start to organise campaigns of lawlessness or passive resistance, I am sure we shall be able to deal with the situation and shall have wide support in doing so. Actually I agree with Mr. Williamson in thinking that this line is more likely to lead to a period of some strain and friction; but I fear that that will have to be faced.

W.L.G.B.
9.7.53

Secretary of State

Mr. Williamson returned towards the end of last week from a visit of just over a fortnight to Nigeria. In the attached minute he has recorded conclusions which he then reached (and with which he believes the Governor and his principal Advisers to agree in broad essentials) about the reply to be returned to the demand which Mr. Awolowo and Dr. Azikiwe will make to you, if a conference with them is held here next month, for the grant of self-government to Nigeria by 1956.

Mr. Williamson's main conclusion (see paragraph 10 (c) of his minute) is that if after questioning by you the two Nigerian political leaders persist in their demand for self-government in 1956, you should offer on behalf of H.M.G. *regional* self-government in the West and South in 1954 on conditions which Mr. Williamson has set out in detail.

There is no need to attempt final judgment on this now. That can wait for the Governor's views on both general policy, and detailed tactics, at the conference.

My own first reaction is definitely against Mr. Williamson's proposal. The two Nigerian politicians would, I think, regard it as a psychic opening bid on a weak hand—a piece of bluff to be fully exploited to their own advantage. They would be bound as politicians to accept the challenge of such an offer and the very fact that they had 'extracted' it from H.M.G. would be the greatest help to their political and electioneering prospects in Nigeria. It would also, as Mr. Gorell Barnes has said, have a bad effect on the Gold Coast and the better tactical line in handling Awolowo and Azikiwe is, I feel, that suggested in Mr. Gorell Barnes' last two paragraphs.

This, as I have said, needs no action now and I submit, for information only, because of the complexity of the problem and the interest of the minutes.

T.K.L.
11.7.53

223   CO 554/338, no 14   4 July 1953

[Western ministers]: letter from A E T Benson to T B Williamson on AG attitudes to the reappointment of the Western ministers

Yesterday Gunning sent you copies of the Daily Times and Daily Service, as well as a copy of Hugo Marshall's broadcast (at 8 p.m. on Monday, 29th June) about the efforts we are making to get back Western Ministers to the Centre. Today I send you copies of yesterday's Tribune and of today's. You will remember that the Daily Service is largely run by Akintola, whereas the Tribune is Awolowo's own paper and takes its orders direct from its master.

I think the highlight of all this is exemplified by the second headline of the Daily Service of the 3rd July, which said: 'I am to appoint Ministers—Awo' and the passage then quoted from Awolowo's speech in the same paper as follows:—

'Speaking, therefore, in respect of the three Ministers from among the commoners in this Region, the responsibility for appointment is not, as he very wrongly held, that of the Lieutenant-Governor, but mine and mine alone, after due consultations with our noble and respected Obas.'

This, read in conjunction with the following:—

'Before I take up the next point, it is, I think, appropriate that some reference should be made to the Constitutional position as it obtains in analogous case in the United Kingdom. By the law of Constitution, it is the British Monarch that appoints all his Ministers.

But by the convention of the Constitution it is the Party in power that in actual fact makes all the appointments. Even the Prime Minister who is ostensibly appointed by the Monarch, is in reality an appointee of the majority party. For, the Monarch cannot, without serious consequences, supersede the person chosen by the Party in power as its Leader.

I have, in passing, drawn this distinction between the law and the convention of the Constitution in the United Kingdom, because the Lt. Governor in his broadcast on this subject glossed over this point, and to that extent misled his hearers. The point I would like to emphasize is that in his own homeland it is the spirit or the convention of the Constitution that prevails rather than the letters thereof.'

really gives in a nutshell the whole history of what has happened since the Constitution was brought into force. The Action Group, notably Awolowo, Bode-Thomas and Akintola, have consistently arrogated to themselves the right to stick most closely to the actual letter of the Constitution when it suits them (compare their objections to the Secretary of State's action over the Western Regional Local Government Bill), and to say that what the Constitution actually lays down is of no importance whatsoever whenever it best suits their book to say that. In other words, the sole interpreter of the Constitution is Awolowo, and when the Nigerian Constitution doesn't suit him he ferrets round until he finds something either in British usage or in Indian usage or in French usage, and I have no doubt that if he failed there he would go to Mexican usage, to justify his interpretation of the Nigerian Constitution.

That and that alone in my view is the reason why we are now in our present position. It has been the Action Group, who have deliberately caused the breakdown by adopting this attitude towards the Constitution, which is responsible: there is no failure in the Constitution itself, which would have worked if there had been the will to work it.

At the risk of making this letter too long, I would cite what the Northern Ministers were saying in an informal meeting of the Council of Ministers yesterday: invariably, since February, 1952, when the Council of Ministers took a decision which either Bode-Thomas or Akintola didn't like as regards the way the Council of Ministers should vote in the House of Representatives, they either absented themselves on that particular day from the House altogether, or failed to go with the rest of the Government through the lobby. There have been three meetings of the House of Representatives and there are three or four clear cases which can be quoted from each meeting. The number of cases where they just did not happen to be in the House at the particular time is, of course, very large. They never actually voted against the Government. All this is in very sharp contrast to all the Northern and Eastern Ministers who, on a number of occasions—in fact whenever the occasion arose—have regularly obeyed their pledge to the Council's corporate responsibility.

The Northern Ministers were saying this in connection with their repeated categoric statement yesterday that if Bode-Thomas or Akintola returned to the Council, they regretfully would immediately leave it. Endeley was there and associated himself again (after the event in the Joint Council) with this, and said that he was speaking for both Nwapa and Arikpo also. Nwapa had indeed confirmed the thing to me the evening before, but left Lagos at crack of dawn yesterday on the news that his wife had presented him with a daughter.

224 CO 554/236, no 69   10 July 1953
[Local government]: minute by T B Williamson on the reform of local government in Northern Nigeria

I want to set down, very briefly, the results of various enquiries which I made and discussions which I had during my recent visit to Nigeria about local government in the Northern Region. (This is the note promised in paragraph 9 of my minute of 2nd July on the subject of self-government by 1956.)[1]

2. *Regional* Government in the North has, for the last eighteen months, been conducted under a (largely) ministerial system, Ministers being—broadly speaking—the elected representatives of the people. This contrasts markedly with the position of the Native Authorities in the 'classical' Emirates of the North, no members of which are elected. Although, under pressure from the Lieutenant-Governor, some Native Authorities have recently become more broad based, the position still is that all members are nominated by the Emirs.

3. At lower levels, however, quite remarkable progress in the direction of more representative forms of local government has been achieved in the last eighteen months or so, following the report of the Joint Select Committee of the Northern Regional Council of the summer of 1951. The present position is summarised in the progress report produced by Mr. Pott, the present Acting Resident of Kano, which

---

[1] See 222.

has recently been published and of which African Studies Branch may have sent you a copy. Much of this progress has, I believe, been due to the initiative of the Lieutenant-Governor himself.

4.   I asked Mr. Pott (and certain other senior officials in the North) when they thought the time would come for the Emirs' Councils to become elected bodies. Mr. Pott's view, which I think is shared generally by officials in the North, is that it would be very dangerous for H.M.G. or British officials to state openly that the aim of local government reform in the North is ultimately to convert the Emirs' Councils from nominated to elected bodies. He thinks this would violently upset the Emirs at this stage, that it might well be misunderstood by the broad masses of the people, and that it might result in putting the clock back, not forward. He thinks—and I have little doubt that he is right—that in due time the Native Authorities will become elected bodies, but that the pressure should come from Nigerians themselves in the North, and not from the British—anyway openly.

5.   Various Northern Nigerians themselves expressed views to me on this subject. Mallam Abubakar Tafawa Balewa held forth to me at considerable length on the subject, and urged progress. In the course of his remarks he said, with considerable bitterness, that in his experience not a single first-class Chief in the North had ever been brought before a court of law by a British officer for malpractice, although many Chiefs had been guilty of punishable conduct. (I mentioned this to the Lieutenant-Governor, who said that while he sympathised with Mallam Abubakar Tafawa Balewa he thought that much of his bitterness arose from the fact that his experience was in Bauchi Province where the position had not been improved by a rather conservative Resident). Party members, including members of the Northern Regional House of Assembly, & of the N.P.C. in both Kano and Zaria, also urged to me that the Emirs' Councils ought to become elective bodies. My general line with them was to say that if they felt strongly on these matters they should raise them, on an appropriate occasion, in their own legislature. In the case of the Kano N.P.C. members I asked what timetable they had in mind for this reform; and was told in reply that in Kano they would not wish to make any change during the lifetime of the present Emir (an old man, as you know) who was much liked and respected.[2]

6.   One danger which we face is that the North are, anyway to some extent, vulnerable to criticism on this question from ill-informed people, both in Southern Nigeria and even in this country. Progress must continue—and as I suggested in my earlier note, I think this is a point which the Secretary of State might well put to the Governor of Nigeria, or the Lieutenant-Governor, North, during the London conference—but not at such a pace as to jeopardise the advances already made. Mr. Hudson expressed the view a year or two ago that what the North really needed was a senior officer, who knew the North and who would go round stimulating progress wherever progress appeared possible. This suggestion was put to Nigeria but was not adopted. The position has changed since then because of the appointment of the Sardauna of Sokoto as Minister of Local Government in the North, and we do not know what his own views are about the reform of the N.A. Councils themselves. An opportunity for ascertaining his views, discreetly, may present itself when the Sardauna comes for his discussion with members of the Local Government Advisory Panel on the draft Northern Local Government Bill. The proposal is that one of the

---

[2] Alhajji Abdullahi Bayero, Emir of Kano 1926–1953.

members of the panel (*not* an official of the Colonial Office) should be requested to ask the Sardauna one or two gentle questions on this matter so that his views may be ascertained, but without his knowing that the questions have been prompted by H.M.G. Mr. Hudson and Mr. Wallis are going to arrange this.

7. One further point. I believe we may be faced at any time, and possibly at very short notice, with a question by somebody like Mr. Fenner Brockway[3] or Mrs. Eirene White[4] on this subject. The former has made a number of references recently to 'the feudal, reactionary Emir-ridden North'; and I took the opportunity while I was in Nigeria of sketching out a draft answer and getting it agreed with officials in the North and in Lagos in case there were not time to seek telegraphic concurrence if and when the question were raised here. The draft answer which I prepared, which would be in reply to a question about, say, the progress of local government in the North, is as follows:

> 'Very rapid, if uneven, progress has been made in the last two years in the development of representative and elected organs of local government in Northern Nigeria, particularly at the District, Urban and Outer Council level. I am placing in the Library of the House a recent Progress Report prepared for the Northern Regional Government which shows the position in detail.'

This answer avoids explicit reference to the Emirs' Councils, but supplementary notes could point out that these Councils contain by nomination the leading representatives of the traditional and of the educated elements in the community, and that some have also recently introduced leading members of the trading community. If the Secretary of State were pressed on the question of introducing the elective principle into the N.A. Councils, he would have to say that the time was not yet ripe for this, and that to attempt to force the pace beyond what the broad mass of the people and their Chiefs are yet ready for would be to court disaster, and indeed might undo the remarkable progress that has been achieved, at other levels in so short a time. He could add that progress, if it is to be lasting, must continue to be evolutionary, not revolutionary; and he could point out that the N.A. Councils consider all subjects effecting policy submitted to them by the elected Outer or District Councils; and that a Minister of Local Government had recently been appointed.

I am sending copies of this note to Mr. Hudson, Mr. Wallis and Mr. Huijsman.

[3] Fenner Brockway, Labour MP for East Leyton, 1929–1931; Labour MP for Eton and Slough, 1950–1964; chairman of Movement for Colonial Freedom, 1954; cr Baron Brockway, 1964.
[4] Eirene White, Labour MP for East Flintshire, 1950–1970; parliamentary undersecretary CO, 1964–1966; minister of state FO, 1966–1967; minister of state for Wales, 1967–1970.

225   CO 554/262, no 250   15 July 1953
[Constitutional revision]: letter from Sir J Macpherson to W L Gorell Barnes on CO proposals for revision of the constitution. *Enclosure*: Notes on a revised Nigerian constitution

I am most grateful for the memorandum which you sent us under cover of your secret and personal letter of the 19th June. Your ideas about the main provisions of a new Constitution are very much in line with ours, and although there are, naturally, a number of points in the memorandum on which I have comments to make, I think, if I may say so, that in view of the complexity of the political situation here, your people have produced a remarkably useful foundation of what ought to be encouraged to emerge.

As Williamson will have told you, we have gone through it in detail with him here and he knows our preliminary views on all the main points. I have, therefore, thought it unnecessary to send my comments by telegraph. I have also been able to discuss the paper in general terms with the Lieutenant-Governors of the Eastern and Western Regions. I now enclose a brief statement of our views on your Notes, paragraph by paragraph. I should add that not all our comments have been agreed with the Lieutenant-Governors but I do not want to delay any further my reply to your letter.

On the question of tactics, we are very much attracted by Williamson's suggestion that a strong attempt ought to be made during the London talks—and in fact quite early in them—to take the wind out of the sails of the 'Axis' by taking the 'magic' out of the words 'self-government in 1956'. As we see it, the Secretary of State will have to be prepared at the opening of the conference to sit back and listen. He will hear from the political leaders in turn what defects they consider exist in the present Constitution which have made it unworkable; and those political leaders will find it difficult not to go on immediately to tell the Secretary of State what amendments ought to be made in it in order that it shall work satisfactorily. It is quite inevitable, we think, that at that stage Awolowo, anyway, will have to say: 'to make it work *until 1956*'; and the question of self-government in 1956 will inevitably loom large in the expositions made both by the Action Group and the N.C.N.C., and probably N.I.P. also (the last not because they want it, but because there are elections pending in the East and they must not show themselves to lag behind the N.C.N.C. or the Action Group). If then the Northerners are called upon to speak, they are going to make it absolutely clear that the first thing they want is as complete a division of the North from the rest of Nigeria as is compatible with their economic requirements. In terms of 'politics' they want a complete break. They will say at the same time that they have no wish whatsoever to retard the progress of the South, and that they are only too willing to permit the South to go its own way towards self-government at any time, provided they are not called upon to take any part in it. The Constitution must be redrawn, they will say, in such a way that '1956' has no meaning for the North whatsoever.

At this stage there is likely to be a certain deadlock, and it may be well to have a slight adjournment. It is immediately after the adjournment, we think, or at any rate when this stage has been reached, that the Secretary of State will have to make some points crystal clear; first and foremost, that H.M.G. in the U.K. will not bring any pressure whatsoever to bear on the North to accept any self-government in Nigeria which would affect the Northern Region before the North wish it to do so. (This would not, of course, have any bearing on the importance—regarded as such by the Northern leaders themselves—of hastening the development of local democratic government.) It is now, we think, that Williamson's suggestion, or at any rate something very near it, should be put into effect. The Secretary of State might say that he also would not wish that the South should be held back—if it desires and is ready for self-government—simply because the North does not want it. But if that is the situation in the South, why not self-government now? What difference between self-government in 1956 and self-government now? In any event the handover will take a certain amount of time and, if H.M.G. is going to agree to self-government in 1956, H.M.G. would have to take that decision now. For the South, therefore, either as one unit or as two, and they must make up their minds on that question, there can be no half measures other than those necessary to ensure a smooth handover in the quickest possible time. In other words, as quickly as possible the organs of government in the South would be completely Nigerian and, whether or not a Lieutenant-Governor remained, he would have no reserve powers. The Secretary of State would have to accompany this by a statement that he would require two separate guarantees: firstly, that the North's economic interests were entirely safeguarded and secondly that the interests of the Public Service were entirely safeguarded in precisely the same way as Mr. Nkrumah now proposes to safeguard them in the Gold Coast. More: if the arrangements made in the South went further than those now proposed for the Gold Coast—viz. the withdrawal of the Public Service from the Lieutenant-Governor's control (which the Secretary of State would regard as essential)—even greater safeguards than those now proposed by Mr. Nkrumah would be required.

This, we think, would lead on to a frank discussion of the pros and cons for immediate self-government for the West and East; and the position of the Cameroons also would certainly be made plain at this stage. Marshall and Pleass think that if anything in the nature of a firm offer of self-government is so made, the political leaders would have no alternative but to accept it. Their constant clamour over the past few years would make it politically impossible for them to refuse. Some of us here, however, don't take that view. We believe that the implications of such acceptance would be so devastating, both to Azikiwe and Awolowo, that they would realise that the depth of feeling against self-government amongst the farmers and the townsmen would recoil on their heads.

One thing we are all firmly agreed on: the offer must not be made as a bluff. If the offer is accepted, H.M.G. must go through with it. But H.M.G. would be going through with it in the full knowledge

(a) that anything short of this is only postponing the evil day for a few short and bitter years, during which all the opprobium which can be hurled at H.M.G. and overseas officers and which has been hurled in the past few years, will be repeated ad nauseam;

(b) that the angle of descent will be much steeper even than it has been in the Gold Coast;

(c) that, as Williamson put it, so great a degree of mal-administration, inefficiency and ineptitude will show itself within eighteen months, that comparison with the good order and progress over the Northern and Cameroons borders, as well as a comparison with the good order imposed by us up to now, will provoke a revulsion of feeling and a demand for the return of British influence.

My belief is that if this line is adopted in the conference room we shall have got rid of the phrase 'self-government in 1956' for all time, and replaced it by the phrase 'self-government as soon as practicable.' And in that atmosphere and as a result of defects which have been pointed out previously, suggestions for amendments precisely on the lines of the Colonial Office memorandum will appear to emerge from the Nigerian representatives at the conference themselves. Whether the Secretary of

State will be prepared to take the wind out of their sails in this way or not, we believe that it would be fatal to produce anything like the Colonial Office memorandum early in the conference or at any time, save as heads for discussion which have themselves emerged as such in the course of the debate.

Just in the same way it would, we think, be fatal, without bringing the leaders themselves to suggest it as the next step (and this we think could easily be done towards the end of the conference) to make the suggestion in your secret and personal letter of the 27th May of a team of experts to come out to Nigeria. Once agreement has been reached that all the questions discussed in the Colonial Office memorandum must be settled (we think it unlikely that agreement on them can be reached during this particular conference), it will be necessary to make it clear to the Nigerian delegates that the Secretary of State will require at some stage an expression of opinion on each point by the people of Nigeria: the North in any event will insist on this. Whether this expression of opinion is to be given by Regional Houses or by consultation at meetings on a lower level, there will inevitably be the need for some such team as you suggest: but at what stage they should come to Nigeria; or at what stage the conference should discuss the sending of a team of British experts to Nigeria; must, I think, depend on how the conference goes.

Enclosure to 225

(1) BASIC REQUIREMENTS (Para. 2)
We prefer the original wording of sub-paragraph (c)
Add: (d) an efficient Public Service.

(2) TERRITORIAL DIVISIONS (Paras. 4 and 7)
It is agreed that the creation of more Regions should be discouraged but unless (as is hoped) the Southern Cameroons decide to throw in their lot with the Northern Region, it will probably be impossible to avoid the creation of something in the nature of a separate Cameroons Region. But very strong resistance to the idea of an 'all-Cameroons' Region is to be expected from the Northern Region and the *Northern Cameroons*.

(3) THE FEDERAL CAPITAL (Para. 8)
This is a most contentious subject but it is so important to all three Regions that we believe it will be impossible to skate over it or to have it discussed as an issue entirely separate from the rest of the agenda. The solution most likely to be accepted is to provide for a Federal enclave covering the port area and the principal Federal offices and institutions. They might, however, agree to something more on the Ottawa model provided the West agrees to certain guarantees being written into the constitution.

(4) THE CENTRE (Para. 9)
It is agreed that there must be a Federal Legislature and a Federal Cabinet. (The North is prepared to accept some form of political authority at the Centre; what it wants is that any such authority should have an official—British official—majority).

(5) THE LEGISLATURE (Para. 10)

It is agreed that there should not be a second chamber, and we agree in principle that the Federal Legislature should be directly elected. There are, however, very great practical difficulties in the way of such direct elections, and these are seen most clearly by those with the greatest experience of Nigeria. The difficulties include the following:—

(i) the great majority of the electorate, particularly in the less sophisticated areas, would not understand the need for separate elections to the Federal and Regional Legislatures. A system of election must be basically intelligible. To superimpose yet another type of election in addition to elections to local government bodies and to Regional Houses would, at the present stage of political development, lead to confusion.

(ii) a Centre which got out of tune with the Regions would have a centrifugal effect and not a unifying effect.

(iii) the number of Nigerians who can think objectively from the point of view of Nigeria as a whole is at present negligible; direct election to the Centre would not in itself produce a body of people with Nigerian as opposed to Regional loyalties;

(iv) it would probably be impossible to find men who would be prepared to back their own judgment without consultation with the Regional legislatures; the idea that members of legislatures are essentially delegates whose duty it is to seek a mandate from those whom they represent is very deep rooted.

(v) there are not enough good candidates of the right calibre and the best men would be drawn to the Regional Legislatures.

(vi) there would be considerable practical difficulties in the formation of constituencies if the size of the Federal Legislature is to be kept small (vide paragraph (7) below).

(6) The present proportion in which Regions are represented in the House of Representatives should, if possible, be retained; the North would agree to nothing worse than this from their point of view unless there is an official majority. But difficulties will arise if a separate Cameroons Region is formed.

(7) The Federal Legislature should be kept as small as possible. The total number of members should not be more than 40, preferably less.

(8) The Lieutenant-Governors should cease to be members, but they ought to be replaced by the Civil Secretaries. (This is on the assumption that Civil Secretaries remain members of Regional Executives—see (19) below). The other ex-officio members should remain, but special members should either vanish or be reduced in numbers to two or three. (Paragraph 11).

(9) THE CABINET (Para. 12)

The greatest defect from which the present Council of Ministers suffers is that it contains none of the chief political leaders. The best way of overcoming this deficiency would be for the Parliamentary leaders of the majority parties in each Region (or the leaders of Government business in each Region) to be ex officio Ministers without portfolio in the Federal Cabinet. (They would not be required to attend frequently). In view of the proposed devolution to the Regions, there will be no need for more than three or, at the most, four Nigerian Ministers with portfolio. The Cabinet should therefore consist of three ex-officio members (Chief Secretary, Financial Secretary and Attorney-General), three representative Ministers with portfolio (or four if the Cameroons becomes a separate Region) and three (or four) 'ex-officio' Ministers without portfolio. (It may be necessary to have a Cameroons Minister, without portfolio, even if the Cameroons does not become a separate Region). The Governor should not, normally, preside though he should be the nominal president; he would thus be in a much more satisfactory position to make use of reserve powers. Note also that it might be preferable for the three officials to be 'members of the public service, nominated by the Governor, to exercise responsibility in respect of external affairs and defence, financial matters, and legal matters'. The title 'Chief Secretary' should disappear.

(10) It is agreed that the Governor should be free to appoint the Nigerian members of the Cabinet from the members of the Federal Legislature, subject to an affirmative vote of the Legislature; but it must be made crystal clear that this does not imply nomination by the Legislature. We agree that it will probably be desirable to provide for more than a single majority: 60 per cent or two-thirds.

(11) Agreed that the votes of not less than two-thirds of the strength of the Federal Legislature, cast in secret ballot, should be required to revoke the appointment of an individual Minister or for a motion of no confidence in the Cabinet. In addition to the powers proposed in the last sentence of paragraph 12, the Governor should have the *right* to dismiss any member of the Cabinet who had forfeited *his* confidence, and to dismiss the Cabinet if it receives a vote of no confidence by simple majority by secret ballot in the Federal Legislature. This is necessary to prevent a deadlock such as arose in the Eastern House of Assembly in February, when the N.C.N.C. majority was too small to secure the revocation of the appointments of the Ministers but was enough to prevent the transaction of any Government business.

(12) As regards responsibilities of Ministers, the North may have changed its mind about granting departmental responsibility to *Central* Ministers, and would be certain to oppose it if the present constitution was to remain in force without significant change. But as nearly all departments are likely to be either under Regional control or converted into statutory corporations, the question of the grant of departmental responsibility over the few departments which will still remain within the jurisdiction of the Centre is unlikely to be a source of serious contention.

(13) Para. 14
Agreed: (but we think the Federal list is too large and that a great deal of what is in the concurrent list ought to go to the Regional list).

(14) THE REGIONS (Para. 15)
No comments: save that, with respect, we do not think the phrase 'Regional autonomy' is rightly used here. It seems to us that the paragraphs following would not affect a region's autonomy.

(15) REGIONAL LEGISLATURES (Para. 16)
Agreed. If a Cameroons Region were established, special provision should be made for the inclusion of Chiefs in its Legislature. If the Cameroons join the Northern Region, some of the Chiefs would be found places in the Northern House of Chiefs.

(16) ELECTIONS (Para. 17)
It is agreed that the present electoral procedures should stand until amended by Lieutenants-Governors in Council.

(17) The proposals in paragraph 18 regarding separate elections and exclusive membership of Federal and Regional Legislatures are regarded as *desirable*, but there are great practical difficulties, cf. para. 5 above.

(18) It is agreed that we should be prepared to accept elections to both Regional and Federal Legislatures under widely differing Regional electoral regulations.

(19) REGIONAL EXECUTIVES (Para. 20)
It is agreed that ministerial Departmental responsibility should be conceded to the Regions: but we feel that this must be accompanied by a clear indication that the position of the individual departmental officer will not thereby be affected in any way.
    As regards the acceptance of all-Nigerian Cabinets in the Regions, the principle that should be insisted on is that either we retain all the present ex-officio members or none. What we should steadfastly refuse is to have (as has been proposed by Awolowo) only one ex-officio member (the Civil Secretary) who would inevitably become a 'whipping-boy'. The Lieutenant-Governor should retain his reserve powers and, by delegation from the Governor, control of the police and control of the public service.

(20) DIVISION OF JURISDICTION (Para. 22)
Agreed, but the concurrent list should be kept as small as possible. The control and organisation of Federal and Regional police presents a difficult and complicated problem, whose solution must not only depend on the arrangements worked out as regards other subjects, but will, to some extent, condition them.

(21) THE PUBLIC SERVICE (Paras. 23–26)
Agreed. We should be prepared to accept a Regionalisation of the public service, but as we have said in our covering letter, arrangements similar to those guaranteed in the Gold Coast, must be made if this is to happen. There would be, in addition, a Federal Service.

(22) THE JUDICIARY (Para. 26)
In view of the strength of Northern feeling on this matter, it will almost certainly be necessary for the Judiciary to be Regionalised.

(23) INTERPRETATION (Paras. 27–28)
If possible we should avoid giving the Courts jurisdiction over the interpretation of the Constitution and constitutional disputes. The considerations which led us to avoid this when the present Constitution was formed still apply, namely, the probability of prolonged litigation and endless delays. Interpretation should either remain a matter for the Governor or should be for the Secretary of State.

(24) FINANCE (Paras. 29–33)
The financial relations between the Federal and Regional Governments is not a subject suitable for discussion at the London conference. It is, of course, vital but the answer must be that a special investigation will be necessary.

Index of Main Subjects and Persons: Parts I–II

This is a consolidated index for both parts of the volume. It is not a comprehensive index, but a simplified index to major subjects and individuals. It gives document numbers, together with page references to the Introduction in part I, the latter being given at the beginning of the entry in lower case roman numerals. The index is designed to be used in conjunction with the summary lists of the preliminary pages to both parts of the volume. A preceding asterisk indicates inclusion in the Biographical Notes at the end of Part II. Azikiwe appears extensively throughout the volume, with around 150 entries in the documents alone. His entries in the Introduction are listed below, thereafter his appearance can be traced by use of the document summaries. Similar considerations apply to the Action Group, the National Council of Nigeria and the Cameroons and the Northern People's Congress.

The following abbreviations are used:

App – Appendix in Part II (pp 761–768)

N   – editor's link note (before main text of document)

n   – footnote

Documents are divided between the two parts of the volume as follows:

nos 1-225   Part I

nos 226-545 (+ Appendix)   Part II